To
Dadiji & Dadaji
and
Maa & Papaji

2025-26

6e

INDIAN ECONOMY

For Civil Services and Other Competitive Examinations

Nitin Singhania, IAS
M.Sc (Applied Economics), CA, CS

Sudipta Singhania
M.Com, CS

McGraw Hill Education (India) Private Limited

Published by McGraw Hill Education (India) Private Limited
Registered Office: Anjana Complex No: 5/90 A, Butt Road, St. Thomas Mount, Chennai – 600016

Indian Economy, 6e

Second reprint 2025

Print Edition:
ISBN (13): 978-93-6444-669-3
ISBN (10): 93-6444-669-0

E-Book Edition:
ISBN (13): 978-93-6444-276-3
ISBN (10): 93-6444-246-8

03 04 05 06 07 RAJ 29 28 27 26 25

Typeset at APS Compugraphics, 4G, PKT 2, Mayur Vihar Phase-III, Delhi 96 and printed and bound in India at Rajkamal Electric Press, Kundli, Haryana-131028.

Cover Designer: Anita Kanojia
Cover Image Source: Shutterstock

Visit us at: www.mheducation.co.in.
Write to us at: support.india@mheducation.com
CIN: U80302TN2010PTC111532
Toll free Number: 1800 103 5875

COUNTER THE COUNTERFEIT & BUILD A STRONG FOUNDATION FOR SUCCESS

Books are our best friends, is the adage we have grown up with. However, the pirates of piracy are continuously forging 'our best friends'. Our books and their supplementary online resources are copyrighted, and we don't lend any right-to-copy. Piracy is synonymous to stealing books.

Knowledge comes real, let's not encourage its counterfeit. Therefore, we appeal all our readers to discourage pirated books and **choose authentic ones.**

HOW TO IDENTIFY THE PIRATED BOOKS?

1 TRANSPARENCY CODE ON THE BOOK

Scan with the Transparency app XXXXXXXX

Congratulations! The book you have purchased is protected by Transparency. Transparency by Amazon is a unit-level product serialization service that verifies a unit's authenticity and enables you to view rich information about the product you purchased. Please look for the Transparency logo and code on the book back cover (Transparency barcode is a square code that can be found next to the "T" symbol). You can scan the barcode with the Transparency app to verify the book's authenticity. Simply download the Transparency app from the App Store or Google Play. Scan the barcode with the app. The app will display a green checkmark when the book has been verified as authentic.

2 COVER AND SPINE

- Look and feel (new or used book)
- Blurred images on the cover
- Hologram pasted on front
- Defective spine (wrinkles) or air pocket at its bottom
- Unclear ISBN/bar codes
- Missing/non-operational Unique Coupon Code for exclusive access to McGraw Hill Edge

3 TEXT/PRINTING/BINDING

- Uneven inking of pages
- Poor quality or blurred photographs/images/charts
- Substandard paper quality and opacity
- Misaligned pages
- Missing pages
- Inferior binding quality

You can further watch this video on How to identify a pirated book

For more information about identifying piracy, visit https://www.mheducation.co.in/piracy

To report a pirated book, send 'Hi' on WhatsApp code given on the back cover or write to us at support.india@mheducation.com.

Reported pirated books are examined to combat their piracy.

Let's fight the Pirates of Piracy and resolve to go for original!

ABOUT THE AUTHOR

Nitin Singhania is an IAS officer of 2013 batch and is currently posted as District Magistrate and Collector of Malda district. He is a graduate in Economics and postgraduate in Applied Economics from Presidency College, Kolkata, and is also a Chartered Accountant and Company Secretary. He is also the author of bestselling book *Indian Art and Culture for Civil Services and other Competitive Examinations*.

NEW TOPICS IN SIXTH EDITION

- **Chapter 1 – Basic Key Concepts:** Economic Activity, Scope of Macro Economics, Consumer Behaviour, Budget Line
- **Chapter 2 – National Income:** First Advance Estimates of National Income for 2024–25 Important facts based on the report of MOSPI
- **Chapter 3 – Economic Growth *versus* Economic Development:** Amartya Sen's Concept of Development, Global Gender Gap Report 2024, World Happiness Report 2025
- **Chapter 4 – Poverty and Inequality:** Key Finding of Multi Dimensional Poverty Index 2024
- **Chapter 5 – Unemployment and Labour Reforms (New Chapter):** Labour Reforms, Social Security Schemes for Employees, Time Use Survey 2024, Quarterly Employment Survey, Reforms in Industrial Labour Laws
- **Chapter 6 – Inflation:** Inflation Premium, Recent Efforts by Government to Control Inflation
- **Chapter 7 – Indian Tax Structure:** Capital Gains Tax, Capital Assets, Income Tax Bill 2025, EBITDA
- **Chapter 8 – Public Finance:** Types of Fiscal Policy, Cyclicality of the Fiscal Policy, Updates in the present trends in Deficits, Fiscal Neutrality, RBI Report on State Finances
- **Chapter 9 – Economic Planning in India:** Performance Evalution of NITI Aayog, Fiscal Health Index 2025, National Multidimensional Poverty Index: A Progress Review 2023
- **Chapter 10 – Money and Money Supply (New Chapter):** Characteristics of Money, Impact of Cryptocurrencies on Indian Society, Blockchain Technology
- **Chapter 11 – Banking Sector in India:** Major Acts Administered by the RBI, PRAVAAH Portal, New Umbrella Entity (NUE) Scheme
- **Chapter 12 – Financial Market:** The Securities Contracts (Regulation) Act, 1956, Dividend and its Classifications, Yield to Maturity, Government Bond, Major Types of Swaps
- **Chapter 13 – Technology and Finance:** Growth of UPI in India, Global FinTech Fest, Internet in India Report 2024, Third Global Hackathon, 2024
- **Chapter 14 – Co-operative Sector in India:** Evolution of Cooperative Sectors, Convergence of PM-KUSUM at PACS level as one of the recent Govt. initiatives
- **Chapter 15 – Agriculture and Allied Sectors in India:** PM-PRANAM, 21st Livestock Census
- **Chapter 16 – Food Security and Food Management:** Food Corporation of India (FCI), High Level Committee on restructuring of FCI
- **Chapter 17 – Land Reforms in India:** Land Pooling Policy, Land Records and Titles in India
- **Chapter 18 – Irrigation in India:** Gap in Irrigation Potential and Usage, Rainfall and Irrigation System, Updates according to Economic Survey 2024–25

- **Chapter 19 – Indian Industry:** The Updated list of Navratna and Maharatna CPSEs , Latest Changes in the CSR
- **Chapter 20 – MSME Sector:** Latest Updates on Udyam Registration
- **Chapter 21 – Food Processing Industry in India:** Operation Greens – the latest component of Pradhan Mantri Kisan SAMPADA Yojana; the latest Production Linked Incentive Schemes for the Food Processing Industry
- **Chapter 22 – Service Sector:** New Strategies of India's Service Sector as per NITI Aayog, Demand Elasticity of Services in India, Latest Changes in the Tourism Sector
- **Chapter 23 – Insurance Sector of India (New Chapter):** Importance of Insurance Sector in Economy, Recent Reforms in Insurance Sector, Significance of IRDAI in Transforming the Insurance Sector, Insurance Schemes backed by the Government, Challenges and Possibilities in the Insurance Sector
- **Chapter 24 – Infrastructure:** Strengthening Multimodal and Integrated Logistics Ecosystem (SMILE), Leads Report 2024
- **Chapter 25 – Power and Energy Sector of India:** Status of Power Sector Growth & Installed Capacity
- **Chapter 26 – Health and Education:** Rural Education Statistics, Updates in the Key Challenges to Health Coverage in India, Bharat Health Initiative for Sahyog Hita & Maitri (BHISHM), 100-days Campaign and its goal
- **Chapter 27 – Balance of Payments:** Factors that affect the FDI inflows, Benefits of FDI in Developing Countries
- **Chapter 28 – India's Foreign Exchange and Foreign Trade:** Latest Updates on India's Forex Reserves
- **Chapter 29 – International Economic Institutions:** Key Points of World Development Report 2024, World Trade Report 2024, G20 Summit 2024
- **Chapter 30 – Population and Demographic Dividend:** Squandering Demographic Dividend
- **Chapter 31 – Skill Development:** Linkages between education, skill and employment, Pradhan Mantri Kaushal Kendra (PMKK), National Skills Qualifications Framework (NSQF), PM Vishwakarma
- **Chapter 32 – India's Gig Economy (New Chapter):** Emergence of Gig Economy in India, Key Features, Gig vs Platform Economy, Social implications of the gig economy as a new economic paradigm, Gig economy from the business perspective, Gig economy from workers' perspective, Potential of India's Gig Economy, Size of Gig Economy in India, Different Collar Jobs, Challenges associated with the Gig Sector, Gig economy as empowerment of women in India, Labour Code for the Gig Economy, How could the conditions of gig workers be improved
- **Chapter 33 – Care Economy and Gender Transformative Approach in India:** Rise in Female Labour Force Participation Rate (FLFPR) in India
- **Chapter 34 – Investment Models:** Rao-Manmohan Model
- **Chapter 35 – Sustainable Development and Climate Change:** Spillover Rankings, Sustainable Climate Finance, Sustainable Aviation Fuel, Recent Developments

PREFACE

I am pleased to place before the readers a thoroughly revised and updated sixth edition of the ***Indian Economy***. This new edition of the book is intended to meet the expanded needs of the readers in this subject. This revised edition equips the aspirants to successfully attempt complex and integrated questions that are asked from this section in the UPSC Civil Services and other competitive examinations.

Improvements made in this edition

1. Addition of **FOUR NEW CHAPTERS**
   a. **Money and Money Supply**
   b. **Unemployment and Labour Reforms**
   c. **Insurance Sector of India**
   d. **India's Gig Economy**
2. Important **UPDATES IN ALL THE CHAPTERS** of the book
3. Inclusion of more than **100 new topics**, on the basis of thorough analysis of the examination pattern and current affairs
4. Addition of latest updates from the Economic Survey 2024–25 in relevant chapters
5. Multi-coloured pluck-out chart at the end of the book featuring key points from Union Budget 2025–26
6. Chapter-wise previous years' questions of UPSC Civil Services Preliminary and Main examinations for practice and understanding the examination trend

At the end, I thank all the readers for the success of the previous editions and submit my gratitude to them for their constructive feedback. With each new edition, I am motivated to improve the content in such a way, that it becomes more relevant and student-friendly, keeping intact the trend of the examination. To continue with this tradition, I humbly request feedback and suggestions for this edition as well on *nitinsinghania.ca@gmail.com*.

Sincere Regards!

May 2025 **Nitin Singhania**

ACKNOWLEDGEMENTS

The beautiful journey of book writing started only after getting inspiration from Dr. Saumitra Mohan, IAS during my initial years in Indian Administrative Service.

At the outset, I thank all the aspirants and well-wishers who encouraged me to write this book on Indian Economy. It would not have been possible without their genuine suggestions.

Heartfelt acknowledgements are due to a long list of the scholars of repute whose valuable works along with various Government websites & online sources, acted as an aid in enriching my knowledge. I sincerely express my gratitude to each one of them. Moreover, the administrative exposure that I received while serving the Government of West Bengal and the Government of India, was of immense help while developing the content.

Now, coming to family, I submit deep regards to my parents for being a constant source of inspiration at all walks of my life. I fall short of words to express my humble obeisance and utmost respect for them. They, along with my wife Sudipta, siblings Nancy, Noyal, my sons Namit and Namay were so kind in allowing me time I needed to research and write. I thank them for their love and motivation.

I extend my heartfelt gratitude to Dr. Kapil Sharma (NIT, Delhi) and Dr. Gaurav Kumar Singh, IAS for their continuous support and motivation.

Also, I am particularly indebted to CA Rahul Kumar (of Diademy IAS) for being an impetus in the timely completion of book.

Special thanks are due to Shri Ankit Jalan, Shri Chandan Jha, Ms. Isita Bhattacharya, Shri Arka Adhikari, Shri Uddipan Mukherjee, Shri Souradeep Mondal, Shri Neeraj Mishra, Shri Sushil Kumar and Ms. Preeti Sharma, for their kind assistance and support.

I also offer my sincere appreciation to the learning opportunities provided by Dr.Mahesh Lalwani (Axiom IAS Institute), Vajiram & Ravi Institute, ALS, Vision IAS and Atul Photostat during my exam preparation days. It still acts as stimulus for me.

Finally, I express my sincere gratitude to Shri Lalit Singh, Shri Tanmoy Roychowdhury, Janab Tanweer Ahmad, Shri Nikhil Wadhera, Shri Atul Gupta, Ms. Anjali Nair, Ms. Mausumi Mukherjee, Mr. Krishan Kumar Verma and the entire support team of McGraw-Hill (India) for their wholehearted cooperation.

I pray to almighty for the wellbeing of all readers.

Sincere Regards!

Nitin Singhania

TREND ANALYSIS

Year-wise Marks in Civil Services Preliminary Examination

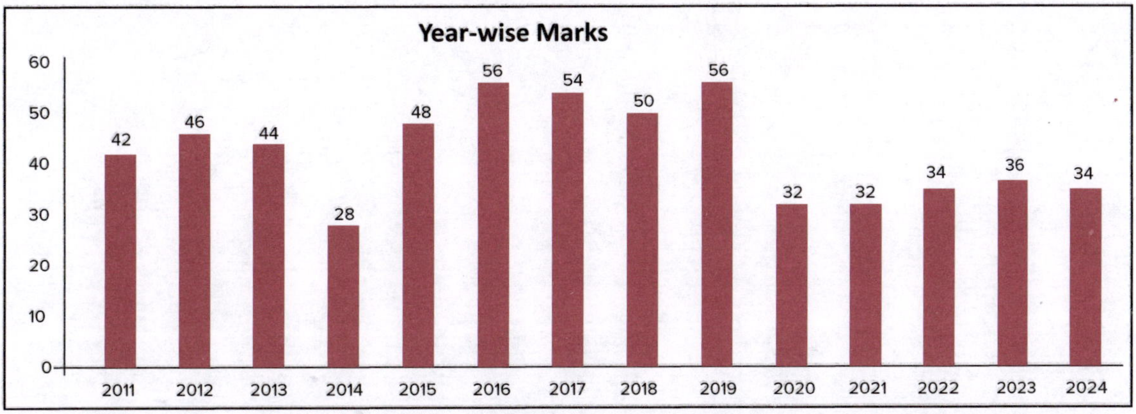

Note: In 2011, UPSC changed the pattern and syllabus of the preliminary examination. In the new scheme, Indian Economy is included in General Studies Paper-I where every question carries 2 marks each.

Year-wise Marks in Civil Services Main Examination

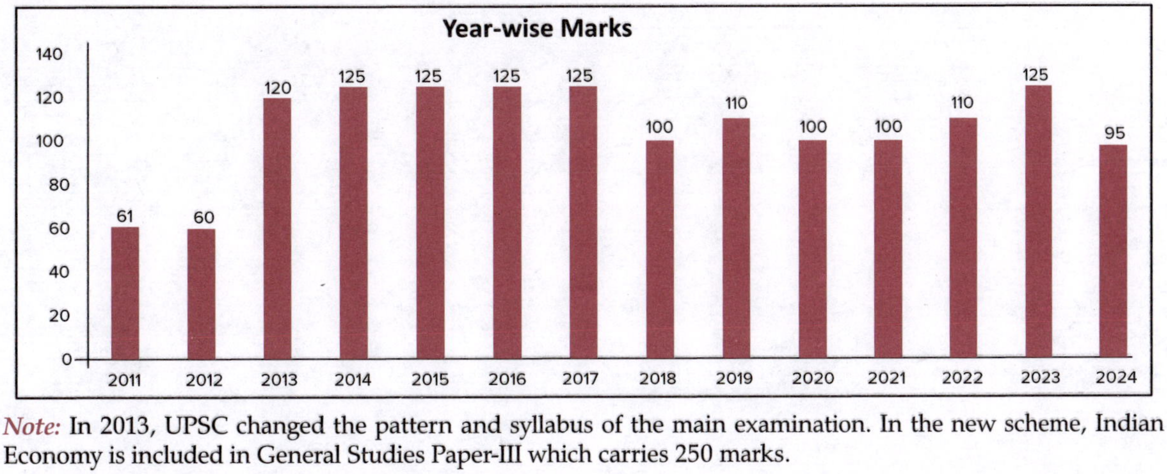

Note: In 2013, UPSC changed the pattern and syllabus of the main examination. In the new scheme, Indian Economy is included in General Studies Paper-III which carries 250 marks.

CONTENTS

5. UNEMPLOYMENT AND LABOUR REFORMS 81–100

6. INFLATION 101–120

8. PUBLIC FINANCE 150–177

9. ECONOMIC PLANNING IN INDIA 178–203

10. MONEY AND MONEY SUPPLY 204–214

11. BANKING SECTOR IN INDIA 215–281

15. AGRICULTURE AND ALLIED SECTORS IN INDIA 352–411

16. FOOD SECURITY AND FOOD MANAGEMENT 412–429

17. LAND REFORMS IN INDIA 430–449

18. IRRIGATION IN INDIA 450–469

19. INDIAN INDUSTRY 470–493

20. MSME SECTOR 494–500

21. FOOD PROCESSING INDUSTRY IN INDIA 501–515

22. SERVICE SECTOR 516–532

23. INSURANCE SECTOR IN INDIA 533–544

24. INFRASTRUCTURE 545–578

27. BALANCE OF PAYMENTS 617–636

28. INDIA'S FOREIGN EXCHANGE AND FOREIGN TRADE 637–656

29. INTERNATIONAL ECONOMIC INSTITUTIONS 657–699

31. SKILL DEVELOPMENT 718–731

32. INDIA'S GIG ECONOMY 732–741

33. CARE ECONOMY AND GENDER TRANSFORMATIVE APPROACH IN INDIA 742–751

34. INVESTMENT MODELS 752–765

35. SUSTAINABLE DEVELOPMENT AND CLIMATE CHANGE 766–784

CHAPTER

1

BASIC KEY CONCEPTS

CHAPTER OUTLINE

- Economics and Economy
- Economic Activity
- Types of Economics
- Microeconomics Vs Macroeconomics
- Types of Economy
- Central Problems of an Economy
- Positive Economics and Normative Economics
- Stock Variable and Flow Variable
- Sectors of an Economy
- Concept of Demand and Supply
- Elasticity
- Consumer Behaviour
- Opportunity Cost
- Indifference Curve
- Budget Line
- Engel Curve
- Production
- Production Function
- Production Possibility Frontier
- Isocost Line
- Isoquant Line
- Laws of Returns to Scale
- Market Structure
- Business Cycle Theory
- Dynamic Pricing
- Predatory Pricing
- Invisible Hand
- Kuznets Curve
- Paradox of Thrift
- Pareto Efficiency

ECONOMICS AND ECONOMY

Economics is a **social science** that studies how products and services are produced, distributed, and consumed. It studies how individuals, corporations, governments, and nations allocate resources to meet their demands and needs, as well as how these entities should organise and coordinate their activities to **maximise output**.

British economist Lionel Robbins, in 1935, described the discipline as **'the science of scarcity'. Adam Smith** is the founding father of modern economics.

An economy is a **huge collection of interconnected production and consumption activities** that aid in the allocation of scarce resources. The production and consumption of goods and services are utilised to meet the requirements of those living and operating within the economy, which is also known as an **economic system**.

Economy is economics at play in a certain region, viz. a country in modern parlance. For example, the Indian Economy.

Economic Activity

Economic activity refers to the **use of limited resources to satisfy unlimited human wants**.

All economic activities do not essentially generate income, i.e. all activities which generate income are economic activities, but all economic activities do not essentially generate income.

Kinds of Economic Activities

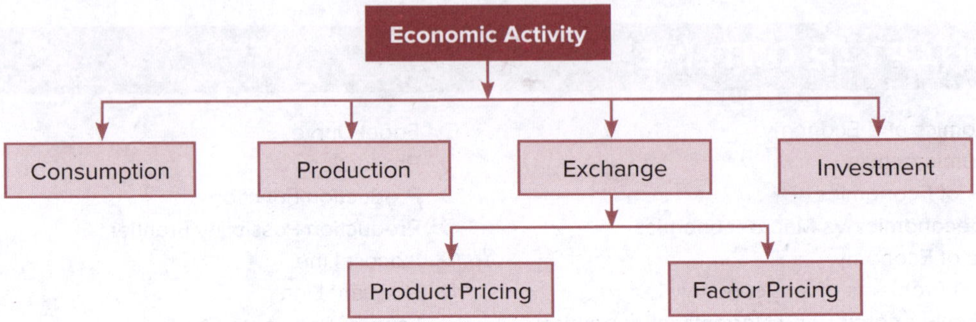

- **Consumption:** Consumption is that economic activity in which utility of goods and services is consumed for satisfying various individual and collective wants. Eating food and drinking water are examples of consumption.
- **Production:** Production is that economic activity which is associated with adding the utility or value in goods and services. Stitching the cloth after cutting it by the tailor is an example of production activity.
- **Exchange:** Exchange is that activity in which goods or a factor of production is sold or bought and this transaction is usually made in money. This activity of exchange is also called price determination. Price determination can be divided into two parts:
  - **(i) Product Pricing:** It deals with price determination of goods in various market situations like perfect competition, monopoly and imperfect competition.
  - **(ii) Factor Pricing:** It is related to the price determination of factors of production.

  In other words, it deals with price determination of land (i.e. rent), of labour (i.e. wage), of capital (i.e. interest) and of entrepreneurship (i.e. profit). Factor pricing is also known as **Distribution**.
- **Investment:** Investment is an economic activity that involves the production of capital goods used to produce goods and services in the future. Investment indirectly satisfies human wants. For example, producing machine for a tailor is an investment because it makes shirts for people and thus helps indirectly in satisfying human want.

Micro and Macro Levels of Economic Activity

The analysis of economic activities may be done both at the individual level and at the entire economy level. Eminent economist of Norway, Ragnar Frish has classified 'Economics' into two branches: (i) Micro Level, (ii) Macro Level.

At present, two methods – 'Micro Economic Analysis' and 'Macro Economic Analysis' – are used in analysing economic activities. 'Micro' and 'Macro' have been taken from the Greek words '*Micros*' and '*Macros*', respectively. Micro means 'Small' and Macro means 'Huge'.

Types of Economics

(i) **Microeconomics:** Microeconomics examines the actions and behaviour of small economic units, like demand for particular goods by an individual household. It also studies the theories emerging from production, demand, price determination and distribution.

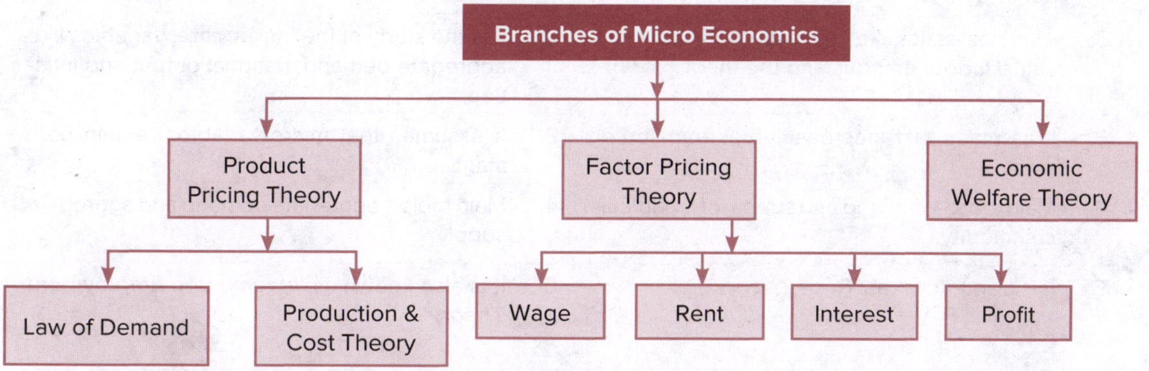

(ii) **Macroeconomics:** During the great economic depression of 1929, the output and employment levels fell radically and Macroeconomics emerged as a separate branch of Economics when **John Maynard Keynes** published his book **'The General Theory of Employment, Interest and Money'** in 1936. The new thoughts and ideas emerged to tackle the new challenges and examine the interdependence between different sectors.

In Macroeconomic study, we generally simplify the analysis of how a country's total production and the level of employment are related to different attributes (also known as 'variables') like prices, rate of interest, wage rates, profits, and so on by focusing on a single imaginary commodity and what happens to it.

Here, the economy is seen as a combination of four sectors – firms, government, households and external sector.

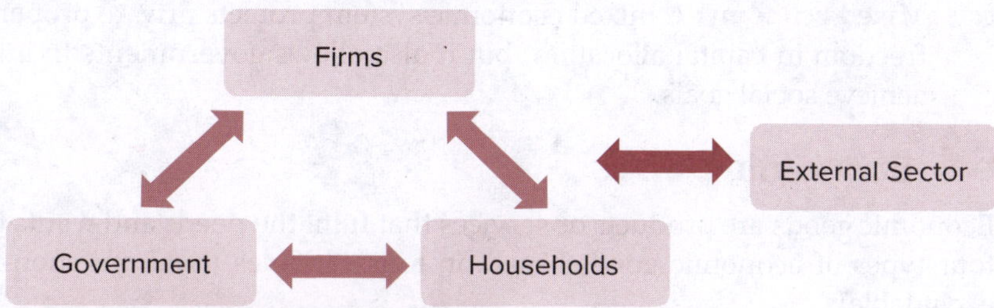

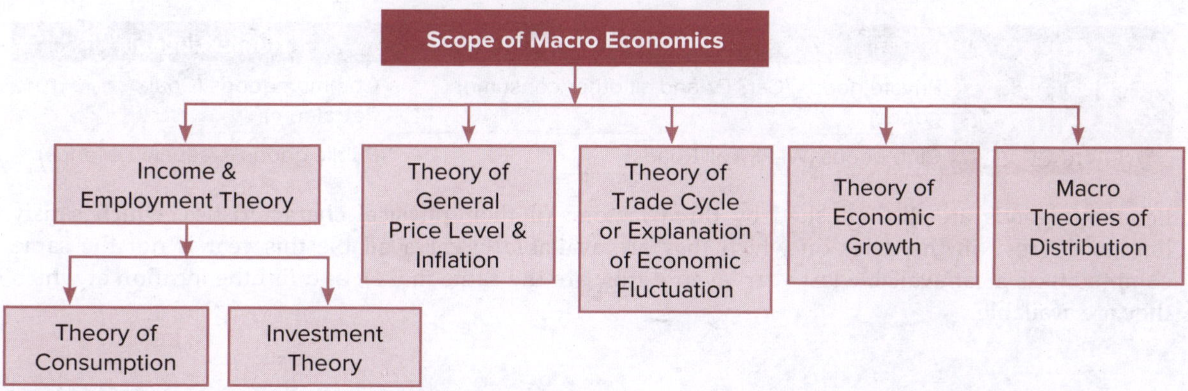

Microeconomics vs Macroeconomics

Microeconomics	Macroeconomics
1. It examines the behaviour of individual economic units or individual markets.	1. It studies the economy as a whole.
2. It studies issues like consumer behaviour, individual labour markets and the theory of firms.	2. It is the study of the **'aggregate'** variables like aggregate demand, national output and inflation.
3. It assumes that macro-variables remain constant.	3. It assumes that micro-variables remain constant.
4. Main tools – demand and supply of a particular commodity.	4. Main tools – aggregate demand and aggregate supply.
5. It is also known as ***'Price Theory'***.	5. It is also known as ***'Income and Employment Theory'***.

Types of Economy

Economy largely depends on the demand and supply of goods and services in its domain. Based on the nature of demand and supply and underlying values, economies can be divided into three major types:

a. **Market Economy:** An economic system in which unrestrained competition between privately owned enterprises determines the production and prices.

b. **Non-market Economy:** A non-market economy in which government intervention is important in allocating goods and resources and determining prices.

c. **Mixed Economy:** A mixed economic system protects private property and permits some economic freedom in capital allocation, but it also allows governments to intervene in economic activity to achieve social goals.

Economic Goods

Economic goods are products or services that fulfil the needs and wants of consumers. There are mainly four types of economic goods based on four variables (rivalrous, non-rivalrous, excludable and non-excludable).

	Excludable	Non-Excludable
Rivalrous	Private goods (Car, TV and all other consumer goods)	Common goods (Coal, Petroleum)
Non-Rivalrous	Club goods (Wi-Fi, Toll Roads)	Public goods (National Defence)

Economic goods are distinguished by three factors: (i) their physical characteristics, which satisfy human desires; (ii) the dates on which they are available (a car available this year is not the same commodity as a car available last year, even if they are the same make); and (iii) the location at which they are available.

Economic Agents

Economic units or economic agents refer to those individuals or institutions that take economic decisions. They can be consumers who decide what and how much to consume or they may be the producers of goods and services, who decide what and how much to produce. They can also be entities like the government, corporation, banks which also take different economic decisions like how much to spend, what interest rate to charge on the credits, how much should be the tax rate, etc.

Economic Models

Economic models are theoretical representations of the economic process by a set of variables and the relationship among themselves. Some of such economic models are supply-demand models and circular flow models.

BONUS KNOWLEDGE

Circular Flow of Income in an Economy

It is a model of economy which represents the concept of economic exchange in simple terms. Money and goods & services flow in the opposite direction but move in a closed circuit.

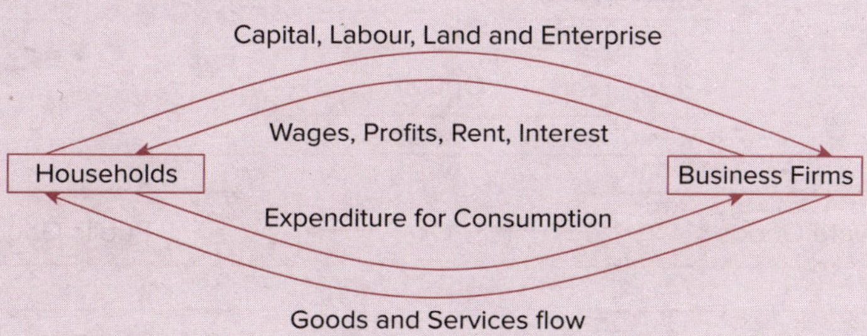

CENTRAL PROBLEMS OF AN ECONOMY

Scarcity of resources gives rise to the problem of choice in an economy and resources must be allocated properly. The allocations can be studied under three fronts:

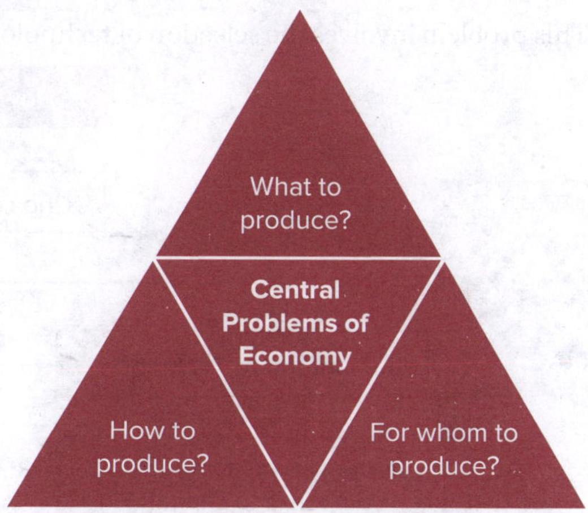

1. What to Produce and in What Quantities?

Economy must decide the **selection of goods** to produce and the **quantity** to be produced. For example – whether to produce more agricultural goods or to have more industrial products.

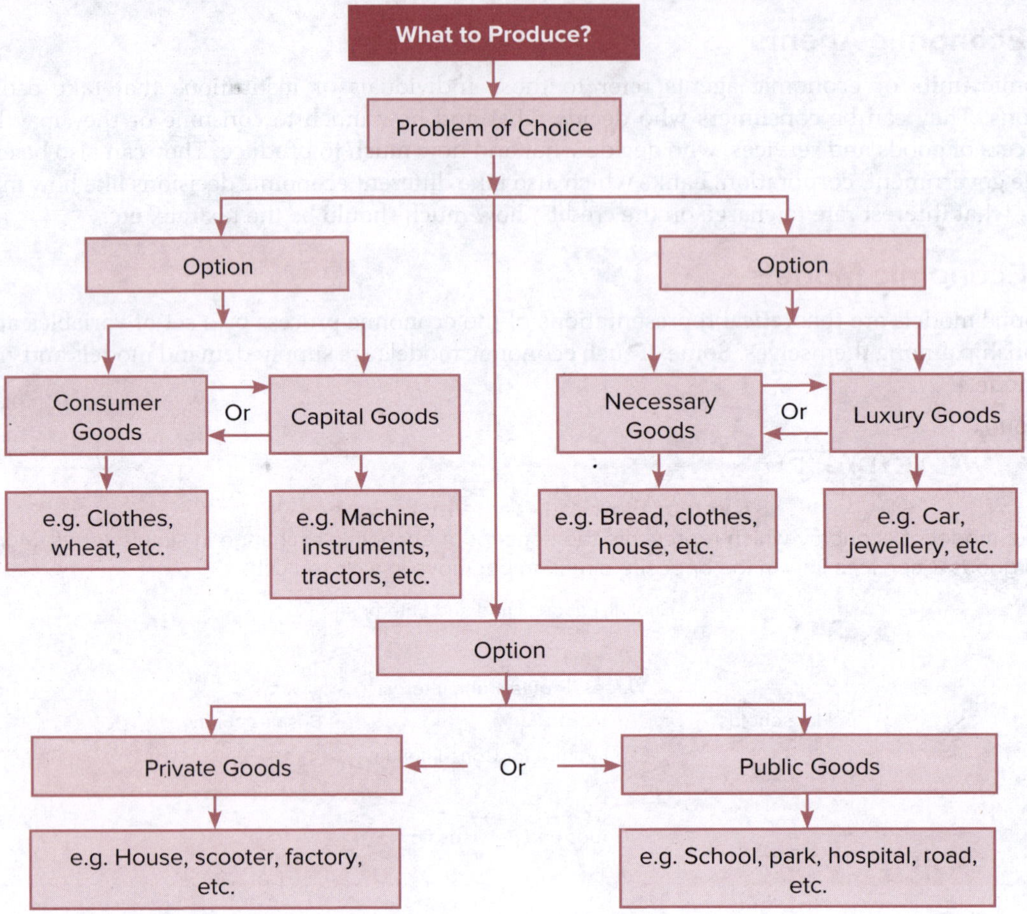

2. How to Produce?

This problem involves the selection of technology to be adopted for the production of goods and services.

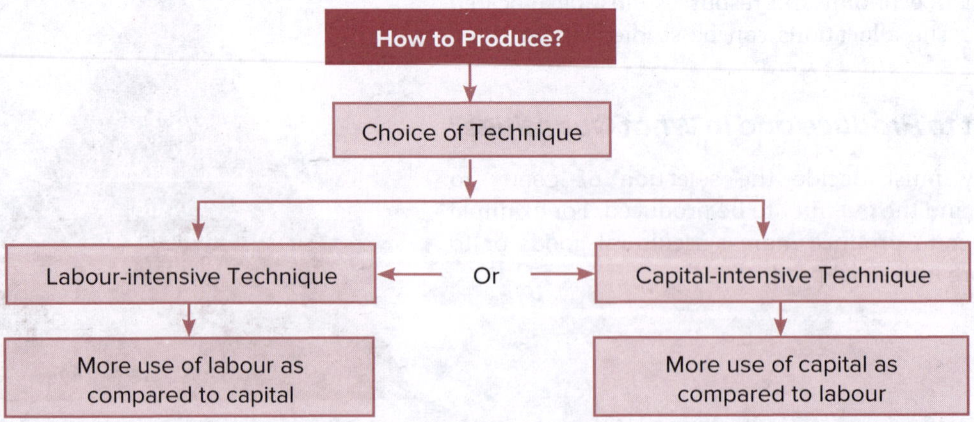

3. For Whom to Produce?

It refers to the **distribution of the produced goods and services** and selection of the consumers.

The allocation of resources and distribution of final goods and services are the basic problems of any economy.

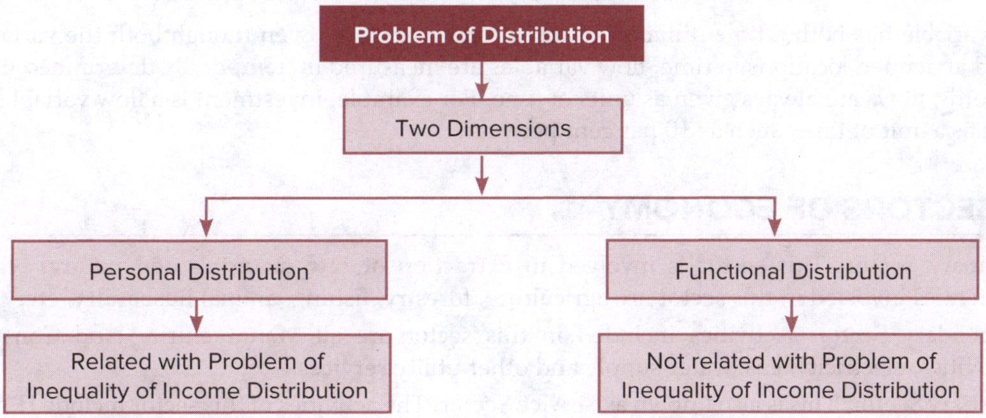

Positive Economics and Normative Economics

Positive economics deals with **how the problems are actually solved in real world** and make a real description based upon the actual data. **Professor J.B. Say, Senior** and **Robbins** have placed economics in the category of Positive Science.

Normative economics deals with the **opinion and suggestions of the economists** and the statements are derived from the ideological perspective about different solutions of the economic problems. It cannot be verified with actual data.

Economists Marshall, Pigou, Hawtrey and Keynes classified economics in the category of normative science.

Basis	Positive Economics	Normative Economics
Meaning	Positive Economics deals with what is or how the economic problems are actually solved.	Normative Economics deals with what ought to be or how the economic problems should be solved.
Verification Purpose	It can be verified by actual data. It aims to make real description of an economic activity.	It cannot be verified by actual data. It aims to determine the ideals.
Suggestive	It is based upon facts and thus not suggestive.	It is based upon individual opinion and, therefore, it is suggestive in nature.
Value Judgements Examples	1. It does not give any value judgements, i.e. it is neutral between ends. 2. Prices in the Indian economy are constantly rising. 3. There are inequalities of income in our economy. 4. In India, unemployment is growing.	1. It gives value judgements. 2. The Indian economy should take steps to control rising prices. 3. Inequalities of income in our economy should be reduced. 4. In India, unemployment should be checked.

Stock Variable and Flow Variable

In economics, we work with two sorts of variables: **Stock variables** and **Flow variables**.

Stocks are usually expressed as a point in time. For example, capital is a stock variable since it has no time dimension and merely a time reference, such as the stock of capital on January 1, 2000.

A flow variable has both a **time dimension** and a **time reference**. Even though both the variables are recorded at defined locations in time, flow variables are measured in **'temporally determined units'**. In other words, flows are always given as units of time. For example, investment is a flow variable since it is stated as a unit of time, such as 10 per cent per year.

SECTORS OF ECONOMY

1. **Primary Sector:** This sector is involved in **extraction of raw materials and natural resources**. Activities involved in this sector are agriculture, forestry, fishing, animal husbandry, etc.
2. **Secondary Sector:** Activities included in this sector are all **Manufacturing** and Construction activities, electricity, gas, water supply and other utility services.
3. **Tertiary Sector:** This is also known as **Service Sector**. The activities of this sector include IT services, transportation, tourism, storage, communication, banking, etc.
4. **Quaternary Sector:** This sector comprises **intellectual or knowledge-based** activities like consultancy, R&D, etc.
5. **Quinary Sector:** Activities in this sector involve high level decision making in government, industry, etc.

CONCEPT OF DEMAND AND SUPPLY IN ECONOMY

Demand

Demand is the quantity of goods or services that a consumer is willing and able to buy.

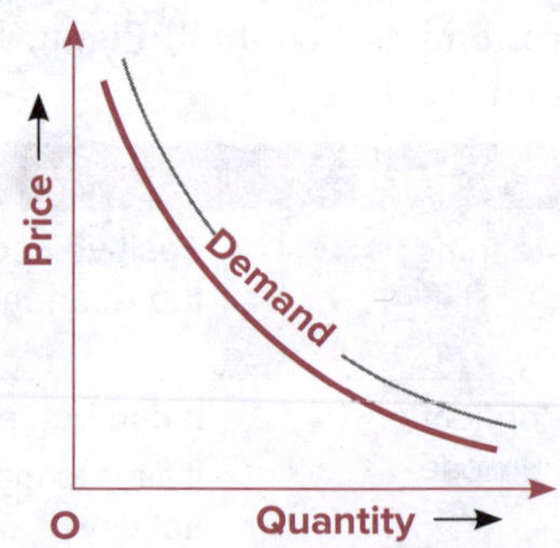

Demand Curve

Demand Function

The demand function of goods expresses the connection between the quantity demanded of a commodity and its own price, all other things being constant. It is generated from the utility function using an optimisation technique. It represents the consumer's maximising behaviour. Generally, there exists an **inverse relationship** between price and quantity demanded of goods.

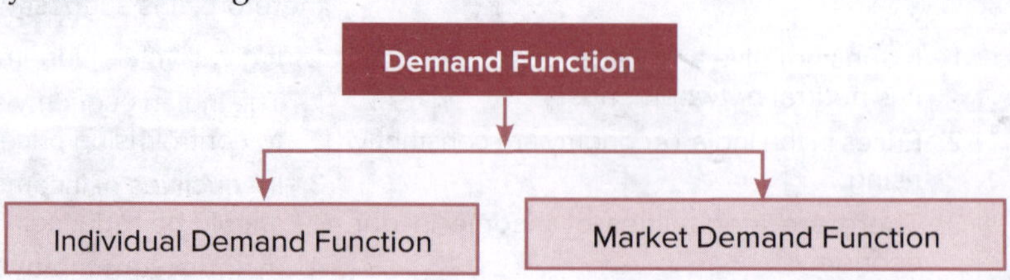

Individual Demand Function

Individual Demand Function expresses the relation between demand for goods and factors determining it for a consumer. It can be expressed through the following equation:

$$D_r = f(P_x, P_r, Y, T)$$

where P_x = Price of Goods-x,
P_r = Price of Related Goods,
Y = Monetary Income of Consumer,
T = Tastes and Preference of Consumer,
D = Demand for Goods-x

Market Demand Function

Market Demand Function expresses the relationship between market demand of any goods and various elements determining it. Two more factors have been included in Market Demand Function:

$$D_x = f(P_x, P_r, Y, T, E, P, Y_d);$$

where D_x = Demand of Goods-x,
P = Size of Population,
Y_d = Distribution of Income
P_x = Price of Goods-x,
P_r = Price of Related Goods
Y = Income of all Consumers for Goods in Market,
T = Tastes of Consumers,
E = Expectations of Consumers

Law of Demand

It states that there exists an **inverse relationship** between the price and quantity demanded for goods, assuming all other factors as remaining unchanged. Higher the prices, lower will be the demand and vice-versa. For example, when the price of onion increases, its demand falls.

However, there are few types of goods such as **Giffen goods** and **Veblen goods** (explained later) which do not obey the law of demand.

Exceptions to the Law of Demand

In a few cases, law of demand is not applicable. These conditions are called 'Exceptions' and are as follows:

(i) **Expected rise in Future Price**: In a few unexpected circumstances like natural calamities, war, etc., consumers continue to demand goods even after price increases because they expect future increase in price. In this case, Law of Demand invalidates and direct relation between demand and price of goods comes into existence.

(ii) **Prestigious Goods**: Due to false show, Law of Demand is not applicable in prestigious goods. To show prestige and social status, rich persons of the society purchase dear goods, i.e., change in price does not affect demand of prestigious goods such as diamond, jewellery, etc. In fact, rich people increase the consumption of prestigious goods when price increases because they show false prestige.

(iii) **Ignorance of Consumer**: When a consumer, due to ignorance, considers that by giving high prices, he has purchased superior and durable goods, then high price does not affect demand. On the other hand, when the price of any goods is decreased, then, due to ignorance, the consumer considers that goods as **inferior**. In this case, when price decreases, consumption also decreases and Law of Demand becomes inapplicable.

(iv) **Giffen's Paradox**: Giffen's paradox arises when one of the two goods of consumption is superior and the other is inferior. **Inferior goods** are those goods which are consumed by the consumers due to their low income level. In such a case, when the price of inferior goods decreases, then the consumer decreases the consumption of inferior goods due to their increased purchasing power. In this way, a decrease in the price of inferior goods decreases its consumption. This paradox was first observed by an English economist Robert Giffen and thereafter named after him.

Determinants of Demand

(i) Price of the commodity

(ii) Price of the other related goods

> did you KNOW?
>
> **Why does Demand Curve slope downwards?**
>
> There are many reasons for downward slope of demand curve, such as (a) Law of Diminishing Marginal Utility, (b) Other Effects, (c) Substitution Effect and (d) Change in Number of Consumers.

Other Types of Demand

1. **Joint Demand:** Joint Demand appears in the case of **complementary goods.** When two commodities are complementary to each other and cannot be used separately, they have joint demand. Bread and butter, sugar and tea, pen and ink are a few examples of joint demand. In joint demand, a change in demand of one commodity brings about a proportionate change in the demand for complementary goods.
2. **Derived Demand**: Demand for a factor of production is not a direct demand, it is an indirect or derived demand. Derived demand is a demand which arises or is derived from the demand for some other commodity or factor. Demand for labour or raw material is dependent on (or derived from) the demand of that final product in which this factor is used.
3. **Composite Demand**: When goods can be put to a variety of uses, the total market demand for such goods makes 'Composite Demand'. Electricity has composite demand because electricity can be put to several uses like domestic lighting, heating, industrial energy source, etc. When these varieties of demand are added together, we get composite demand for electricity.

ELASTICITY OF DEMAND

Elasticity indicates the tendency of increasing or decreasing elasticity, which depends on two factors—'Nature of Goods' and the 'Pressure on it'. When goods undergo greater change in response to less pressure (or force), it is said to be highly elastic and when it produces less change in response to high pressure, it is said to be less elastic. Goods which produce meagre or no change are said to be inelastic. On the basis of this concept, elasticity of demand has been explained to observe **change in demand due to change in price.**

Price Elasticity of Demand: Elasticity is the measurement of rate of change in the quantity of goods demanded in relation to the change in prices.

$$\text{Price Elasticity of Demand} = \frac{\text{Percentage change in quantity demanded}}{\text{Percentage change in price}}$$

Elastic and Inelastic Demand: If there is a change in the quantity demanded with the change in prices, it is called Elastic Demand. If the quantity of demand of goods does not change much with a change in its price, then that goods is considered Inelastic.

Zero Price Elasticity of Demand: Whatever is the change in price, there is absolutely no change in demand.

Degrees of Elasticity

- **Elastic Demand ($E > 1$):** A large change in quantity demanded in response to a price change.
- **Inelastic Demand ($0 < E < 1$):** A small change in quantity demanded in response to a price change.
- **Unitary Elastic Demand ($E = 1$):** The percentage change in quantity demanded is equal to the percentage change in price.
- **Perfectly Elastic Demand ($E = \infty$):** Any price increase leads to zero demand.
- **Perfectly Inelastic Demand ($E = 0$):** Demand remains constant regardless of price changes.

Factors affecting Elasticity of Demand

1. Nature of the Goods
2. Availability of Substitutes
3. Alternative Uses
4. Postponement of Consumption
5. Expenditure Amount
6. Income Level
7. Price Level
8. Time Period
9. Joint Demand or Complementarity of Goods
10. Nature and Habits

BONUS KNOWLEDGE

UNIQUE FACTS ABOUT PRICE ELASTICITY

1. The coefficient of price elasticity of demand is always a negative number due to inverse relationship between price and quantity demanded. So, minus sign is ignored while writing the value of elasticity.
2. The coefficient of price elasticity of demand is a pure number and is independent of price and quantity units. It does not contain 'Rupee' or 'Kilogram' , etc.)

Types of Goods

- **Substitute Goods:** If the price of the substitute goods increases, the demand for the given commodity also increases. Example – Tea and coffee.
- **Complementary Goods:** If the price of the complementary goods increases, then the demand of the given commodity decreases. Example – Tea and sugar.
- **Normal Goods:** The demand for these goods increases with the increase in income. Example – Ordinary TV.
- **Inferior Goods:** Their demand falls with the increase in income. Example – When households get richer, they consume less kerosene (negative income elasticity of demand).

- **Giffen Goods:** People consume more when the price rises. Example – If the price of potato increases, people may not be able to buy other alternatives, so they are compelled to buy more potatoes.
- **Veblen Goods:** The increase in their price encourages people to buy more because they think more expensive products are better. Example – Art and artifacts, branded clothes.

Supply

Supply is the quantity of a commodity that a firm is willing and is able to sell at a given price.

Supply Function

The supply function of goods expresses the connection between the quantity supplied of a commodity and its own price, all other things being constant.

Supply Schedule

When the quantities of a commodity sold at different prices are presented in a table, it is called supply schedule. In other words, a supply schedule is a tabular representation of the quantities a seller is willing to offer at various possible prices.

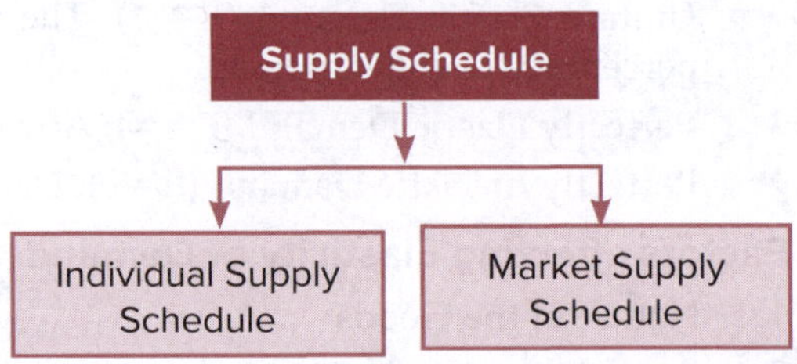

Individual Supply Schedule

Individual supply schedule refers to supply schedule of an individual firm in the market. It shows supply response of a particular firm in the market.

Individual supply schedule expresses different quantities supplied by a firm at different prices.

Market Supply Schedule

When the total quantity which all the firms (or sellers) are ready to sell at various prices in the market, it becomes market supply schedule. Thus, market supply schedule refers to supply schedule of all the firms in the market producing a particular commodity.

Law of Supply

According to the Law of Supply, keeping other factors constant, if price increases, supply of goods also increases. (If price increases, the producers want to maximise profits.)

Exceptions to Law of Supply

The law of supply states the **direct relationship** between price of commodity and its supply but in certain circumstances, this law does not operate, i.e., the direct relation between the price of a commodity and its supply is not established. Such cases are termed exceptions of the law of supply.

Certain exceptions of the law of supply are as follows:

1. The law of supply does not apply strictly to agricultural products whose supply is governed by natural factors. If, due to natural calamities, the production of wheat is less, then its supply will not increase, however high the price may move.
2. The law of supply is not operative in case of perishable goods. Sellers may be willing to sell more units of perishable goods although their price may be falling.

3. The law also fails in goods having social distinctions. Supply of goods having social distinction will remain limited even if their price may rise high.

Determinants of supply:

1. Price of Commodity,
2. Price of Substitutes,
3. Price of Production Factors,
4. Technological Level,
5. Number of Firms in the Market,
6. Goal of Firm,
7. Expected Future Prices,
8. Government Policy.

Elasticity of Supply

Like the Law of Demand, the Law of Supply is also a 'qualitative statement'. The law of supply indicates only the direction of change in quantity supplied in response to a change in price, but it does not quantify this change. This quantitative change is measured by the 'Elasticity of Supply'.

Elasticity of supply is the measurement of quantitative change in supply due to change in price. In other words, price elasticity of supply is the proportionate change in supply consequent upon proportionate change in price.

Price Elasticity of Supply

Price elasticity of supply is a measurement of the percentage change in quantity supplied of a commodity in response to some percentage change in its price.

$$\text{Price Elasticity of Supply} = \frac{\text{Percentage change in quantity supplied}}{\text{Percentage change in price}}$$

Degrees of Elasticity

- **Elastic Supply (E > 1):** A large change in quantity supplied in response to a price change.
- **Inelastic Supply (0 < E < 1):** A small change in quantity supplied in response to a price change.
- **Unitary Elastic Supply (E = 1):** The percentage change in quantity supplied is equal to the percentage change in price.
- **Perfectly Elastic Supply (E = ∞):** Any price increase leads to zero supply.
- **Perfectly Inelastic Supply (E = 0):** Supply remains constant regardless of price changes.

Equilibrium

In economics, equilibrium is a **state in which economic factors such as supply and demand are balanced** and the (equilibrium) values of economic variables do not change in the absence of outside influences. For example, in the **perfect competition,** equilibrium occurs when the quantity requested and the quantity provided are equal.

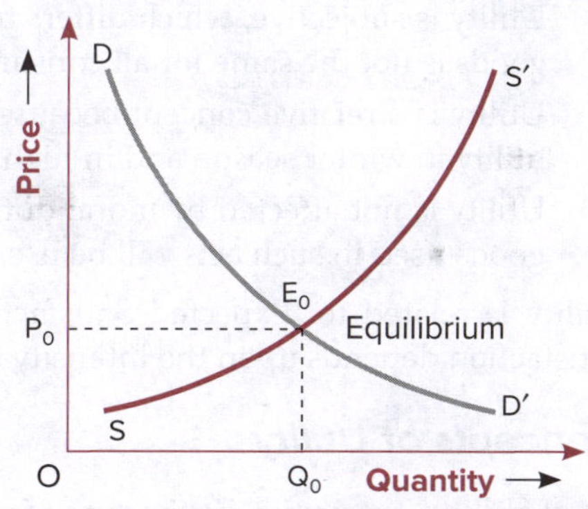

Demand and Supply

CONSUMER BEHAVIOUR

Who is a Consumer?

A consumer is an economic agent who uses goods and services for satisfaction of his/her wants. The term 'consumer' broadly includes individuals, families, and institutions. Consumer behaviour refers to a process by which a consumer decides that in what way he should plan his expenditure on different goods and services, so as to maximise utility from limited income.

What is Consumer's Equilibrium?

Consumer's equilibrium refers to the process in which a consumer chooses or selects those goods and services from which he/she can attain maximum satisfaction or utility through his/her limited income.

At the point of consumer's equilibrium, the consumer attains maximum possible satisfaction with his limited resources which is the ultimate aim of the consumer. According to Samuelson, *"The consumer is in equilibrium when he maximises his satisfaction given by his income and the market prices. "*

With unlimited wants and limited factors or resources, the aim of a consumer is to derive or obtain maximum satisfaction from his expenditure. When he attains this objective, he is said to be in equilibrium. Thus, a consumer is in equilibrium when he considers his selection as the best choice in present circumstances, and does not change his selection until present or prevalent conditions change. In other words, "A consumer is said to be in equilibrium, until he does not change his method of expenditure in prevalent conditions or present circumstances."

Utility

Utility means 'Want Satisfying Power of a Commodity' or the capacity of a commodity to satisfy a particular want of a consumer. Every commodity has some inherent want satisfying capacity.

Characteristics of Utility

1. Utility is a psychological phenomenon. It depends upon the mental status of the consumer.
2. Utility is subjective, which differs from person to person and place to place. Utility of a particular goods is not the same for all consumers.
3. Utility is a relative concept because it changes from time and place. Woollen clothes have greater utility in winter season and in high altitude areas but have no utility in summer.
4. Utility is not affected by moral duties or principles. If a person derives utility from immoral acts, goods used in such acts will be useful for that person.

Utility is related to 'Expected Satisfaction' and not 'Actual Realised Satisfaction' because expected satisfaction depends upon the intensity of consumption.

Concepts of Utility

Total Utility: Total utility is the sum of marginal utilities obtained from different units of consumption.

$$TU = S(MU)$$

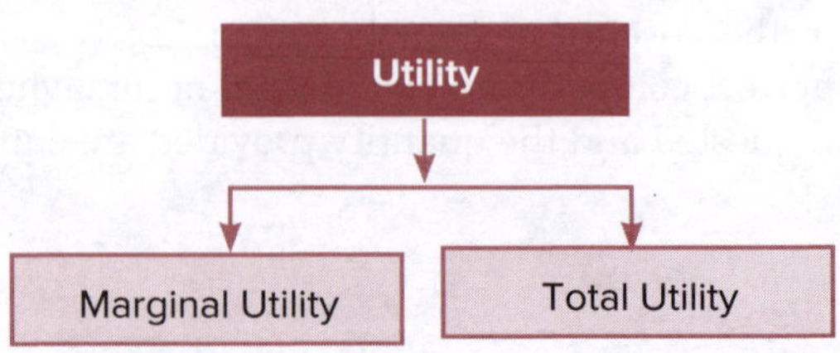

Marginal Utility: The word 'Marginal' means 'One Additional'. Additional utility derived from the consumption of one additional unit of a commodity is called 'Marginal Utility'. In other words, "Increase in total utility by consuming one additional unit of a commodity is called marginal utility. "

(i) According to **Boulding,** *"The marginal utility of any quantity of a commodity is the increase in total utility which results from a unit increase in consumption."*

(ii) According to **Samuelson**, *"The term marginal utility refers to extra utility added by one extra last unit of goods."*

If utility obtained from the consumption of 10 units is 150 utils and from 11 units, it is 160 utils, then additional utility obtained by consuming 11th unit is 160 – 150 = 10 utils. This is called Marginal Utility of 11th unit.

Relationship between Total Utility and Marginal Utility

(i) When marginal utility obtained from the consumption of goods is positive, total utility increases.

(ii) When marginal utility is zero, total utility is maximum.

(iii) When marginal utility is negative, total utility decreases.

Law of Equi-marginal Utility

'Law of Equi-marginal Utility' explains the consumer's equilibrium in utility analysis. This law is also called **Gossen's Second Law.** A consumer is rational and his aim is to obtain maximum satisfaction by distributing his income in different fields of consumption. Basis of this law is the 'Law of Substitution' according to which a consumer replaces less useful goods by more useful goods. This substitution process continues until all consumption items have equal marginal utility. A consumer attains equilibrium when he does not change his consumption.

Statement of the Law

'Law of Equi-marginal Utility' states that the consumer will distribute his money income between the various goods in such a way that the utility derived from the last rupee spent on each goods is equal. In other words, a consumer is in an equilibrium position, when marginal utility of money expenditure on each goods is the same.

According to **Lipsey,** *"The household maximising its utility will so allocate its expenditure between commodities that the last unit spent on each is equal."*

INDIFFERENCE CURVE

Indifference Curve is a graphical representation of different combinations of two goods that provide the **equal level of satisfaction and utility** to the consumer, resulting in indifference. **Hicks and Allen** presented 'Indifference Curve Analysis' as an alternative viewpoint of Marshall's 'Utility Analysis'.

Indifference curve analysis presents an 'Ordinal Viewpoint' in which the behaviour of a consumer is studied on the basis of 'Ordinal Preferences'. Ordinal approach suggests that utility cannot be measured in terms of units.

Consumers have equal preferences for diverse combinations of goods along the curve.

When family of indifferent curves representing the consumer preferences over all bundle of two goods are drawn, it is called **Indifference Map**.

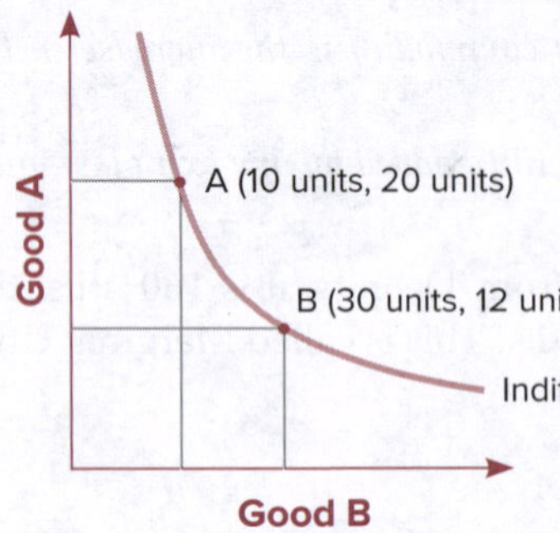

Indifference Curve

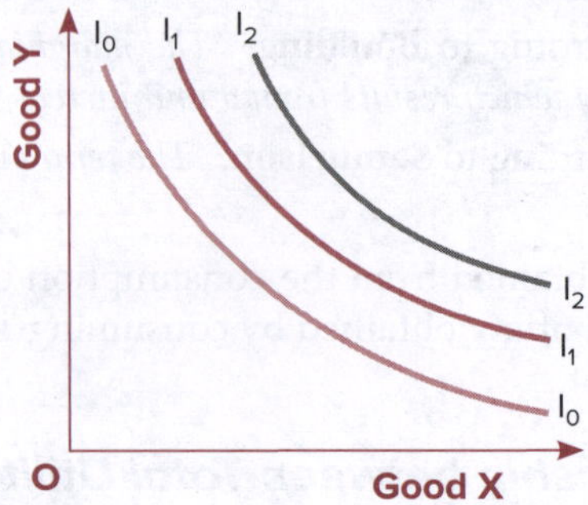

Indifference Map

The indifference curve approach is based on the following assumptions:

1. **Rationality:** The consumer is assumed to be rational. He aims at maximising his benefits from consumption, given his income and prices of the goods.
2. **Ordinality:** Utility is expected satisfaction that a consumer gets from the given market basket. In indifference curve analysis, utility is an ordinal concept. Consumers can order or rank the subjective utilities derived from the commodities.
3. **Diminishing Marginal Rate of Substitution:** Scale of preferences are ranked in terms of indifference curves. Indifference curves are **downward sloping convex** to the origin curves. The **slope of indifference curve** is called Marginal Rate of Substitution (MRS) of X for Y. MRS is defined as the amount of goods Y the consumer is willing to give up to consume an additional unit of goods X, while leaving total utility unchanged.

   An important assumption is that the MRS of X for Y, decreases with greater quantities of goods X, i.e. a consumer's willingness to give up good Y decreases with each new unit of good X he consumes. This relationship is known as **Law of Diminishing Marginal Rate of Substitution**.
4. **Weak Ordering:** The consumer shows weak ordering in his choice. It means that the consumer can be indifferent in selection between two combinations of goods, but he cannot express the superiority of one combination over the other.

Properties of Indifference Curves

(i) Indifference curves are **convex** to the origin.
(ii) The slope of the curve is called the Marginal Rate of Substitution.
(iii) Indifference curve slopes **downward**.
(iv) Higher Indifference curve indicates higher level of satisfaction.
(v) An Indifference curve never touches X- or Y-axis.
(vi) Two Indifference curves never intersect each other.
(vii) The curvature of the indifference curve shows the degree of substitute and complementary nature between two goods.

EXAM ESSENTIAL

WHY SHOULD MRS BE DIMINISHING IN INDIFFERENCE CURVE?

Marginal Rate of Substitution (MRS) is declining in indifference curve because as the consumer goes on increasing goods X, the intensity of desire of obtaining one additional unit of X starts declining and the intensity of obtaining other goods Y starts increasing. This is the reason why the consumer becomes ready to sacrifice lesser amount of goods Y for any additional unit of X. Consequently, MRS becomes diminishing. Thus,

Aa > Bb > Cc > Dd > Ee > Ff

Due to this declining nature of MRS, indifference curve becomes convex to the origin.

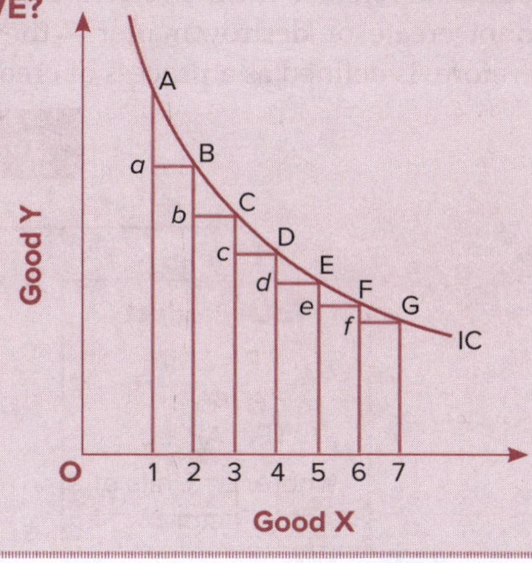

BUDGET LINE

Budget line is the graphical representation of all possible combinations of two goods which a consumer can afford to buy with all his/her available income or budget.

Budget line **slopes downwards** and it is a straight line. The **slope of the Budget line is called Price Ratio,** which is constant.

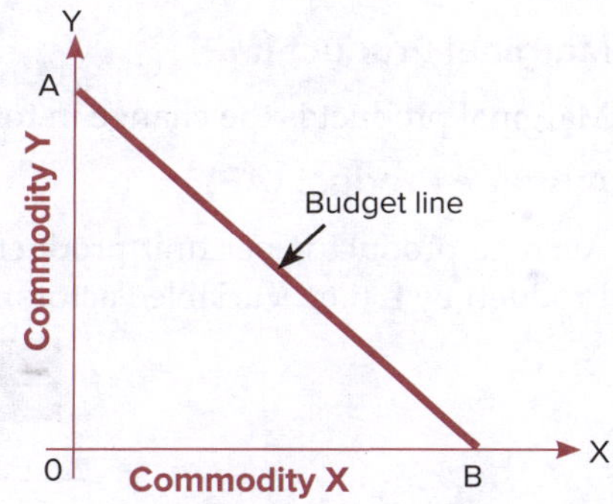

Budget Line

ENGEL CURVE

German scholar **Ernst Engel** gave the idea of Engel curve. It is defined as the locus of all the **points relating to the equilibrium** quantity of the same goods and level of money income, i.e., how much quantity of a commodity a consumer is consuming at different levels of income.

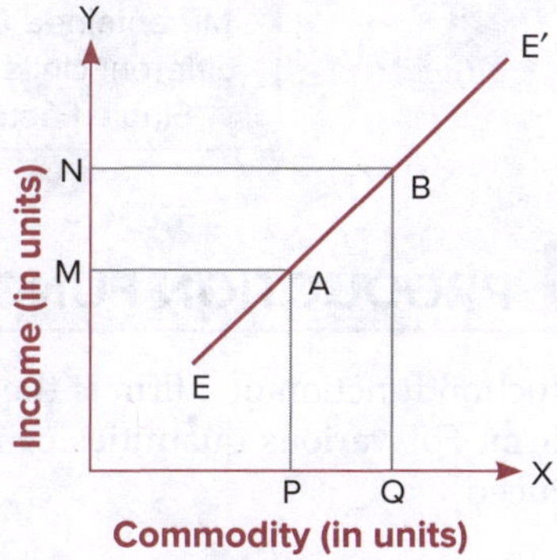

Engel Curve

PRODUCTION

Production refers to the manufacture of physical goods. However, from a scientific perspective, humans cannot create or destroy matter – they can only transform it to make it more useful. Production, therefore, is defined as a process of creating or increasing the utility of goods.

Three Concepts of Production

Total Product

$TP = \Sigma MP$

or

$TP = AP \times L$

where, L = Units of Factor

Marginal Product

$MP_n = TP_n - TP_{(n-1)}$

or

$MP = \frac{\Delta TP}{\Delta L}$

Average Product

$MP = \frac{TP}{L}$

where,

L = Units of Factor

Total Product (TP)

Total product is the total amount of goods and services produced in a given period by using various factors of production.

Marginal Product (MP)

Marginal product is the change in total product due to applying one more or less unit of variable factor.

Average Product (AP)

Average product is per unit production of the variable factor. It is obtained by dividing TP (i.e., Total Product) by L (i.e., Variable Factors). AP is also called per unit productivity.

Total Product (TP)

$TP = \Sigma MP$

or, TP is the sum of MP obtained from different Units of a Single Factor

or

$TP = AP \times L$

or, TP is equal to multiplication of Average Product (AP) and Total Units of Factor (L)

PRODUCTION FUNCTION

Production function of a firm is the relationship between the inputs used and the output produced by the firm. For various quantities of inputs used, it gives the maximum quantity of output that can be produced.

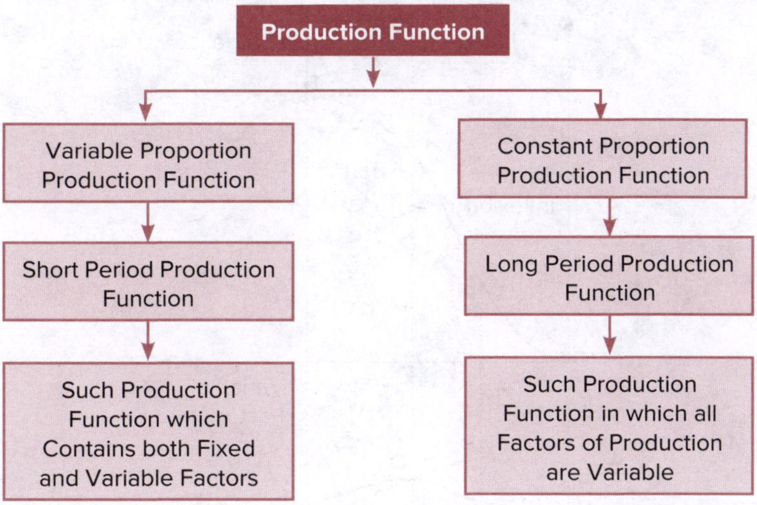

A firm pays for the inputs. This is called the **cost of production**. Once the output has been produced, the firm sells it in the market and earns **revenue**. The difference between the revenue and the cost is called the firm's **profit**.

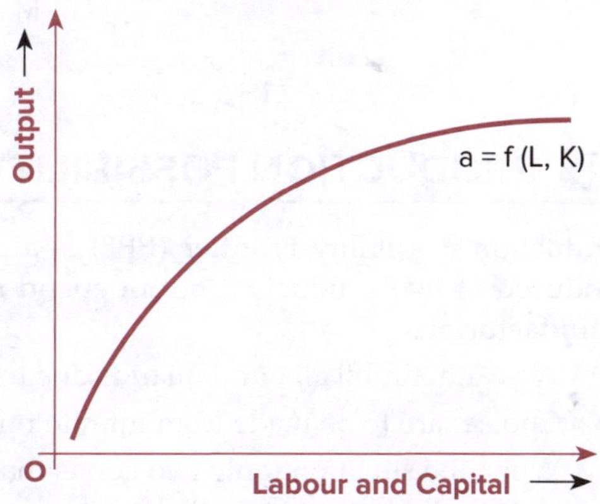

Production Function

Three Stages of Production:

	Stage	TP	MP	Phases Reference Point (Fig.)
Stage I	Increasing Returns to Factor	Starts from origin and increases at an increasing rate. TP is convex.	Increases, reaches a maximum.	From origin to point K
Stage II	Diminishing Returns to Factor	Increases at a decreasing rate till it reaches the maximum point. TP is concave.	Falls continuously till it is equal to zero.	From point K to point T
Stage III	Negative Returns to Factor	Falls continuously but is positive. TP is downward sloping.	Negative	Point T onwards

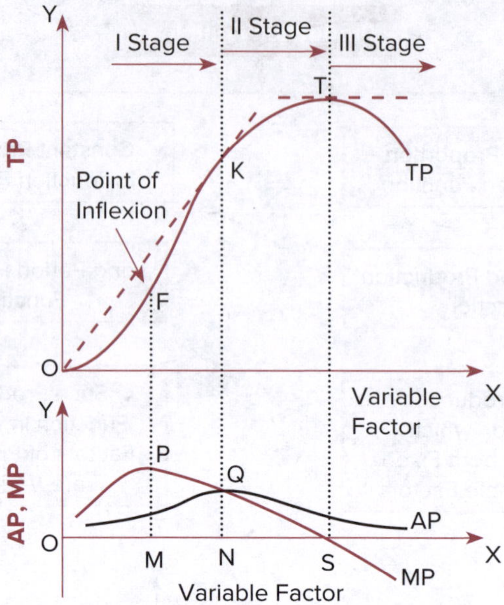

PRODUCTION POSSIBILITY FRONTIER

Production Possibility Frontier (PPF) is a curve that illustrates the possible quantities that can be produced of two products if both depend upon the same finite resources and technology for their manufacturing.

- We cannot fulfil all our demands due to scarcity of resources.
- Choices are to be made from infinite numbers of possibilities and the range of choices.
- When the situation (only two goods that can be produced with given resources and technology) is graphically represented, the graph is called **'Production Possibility Frontier (PPF)' or 'Production Possibility Curve (PPC)'.**
- PPF is based on the assumption that resources are efficiently utilised and the level of technology is constant.

Marginal Rate of Transformation (MRT): It is defined as the number of units of one goods that must be forgone to produce one unit of another goods.

Assumptions of PPF

The production possibility frontier is based on following assumptions:

(i) **Fixed and Limited Quantity of Factors of Production :** Factors of production are limited but they can be transferred from one use to the other.

(ii) **Fuller and Efficient Utilisation of the Available Resources:** All factors are fully and efficiently utilised in the economy.

(iii) **Constant and Given Technology:** Technology of production remains constant, i.e. there is no change in the technology used.

(iv) **Two Goods:** For convenience, it is assumed that only two goods or two sets of goods are being produced in the economy (e.g., wheat and clothes or capital and consumer goods).

Characteristics of PPF

(i) **PPF slopes downwards:** one goods can be produced more by reducing the production of other goods if resources are taken away.

(ii) PPF is **concave shaped** because of **increasing marginal rate of transformation.**

(iii) All points inside PPF are inefficient.

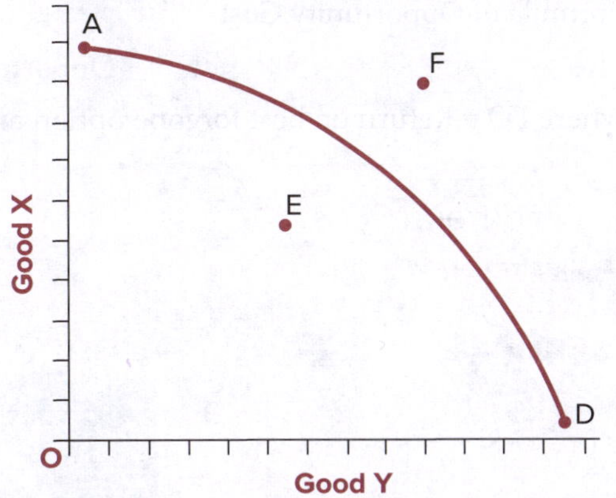

- Point E – Resources are inefficiently utilised
- Point F – Impossible
- Any point on the frontier – efficient use of the available inputs.

Production Possibility Frontier (PPF)

PPF Schedule

Possibilities	Cotton (in Units)	Corn (in Units)
A	20	0
B	18	1
C	15	2
D	12	3
E	8	4
F	4	5
G	0	6

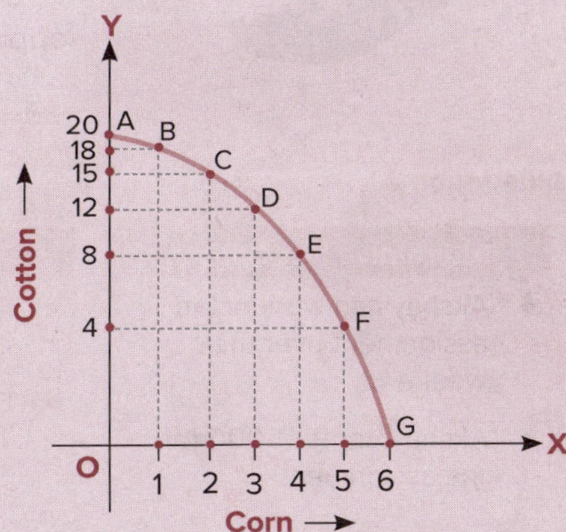

The PPF demonstrates that each economy must decide what combination of goods and services should be produced in order to attain **maximum resource efficiency**.

OPPORTUNITY COST

If more scarce resources are used to produce particular goods, less resources are available for the production of other goods, there always exists a cost of having a little more of one goods in terms of other goods. The cost of the next best alternative foregone is known as the **'Opportunity Cost'**.

Formula of Opportunity Cost

Opportunity Cost = FO – CO

where FO = Return on best forgone option and CO = Return on chosen option

OPPORTUNITY COST

Illustration 1

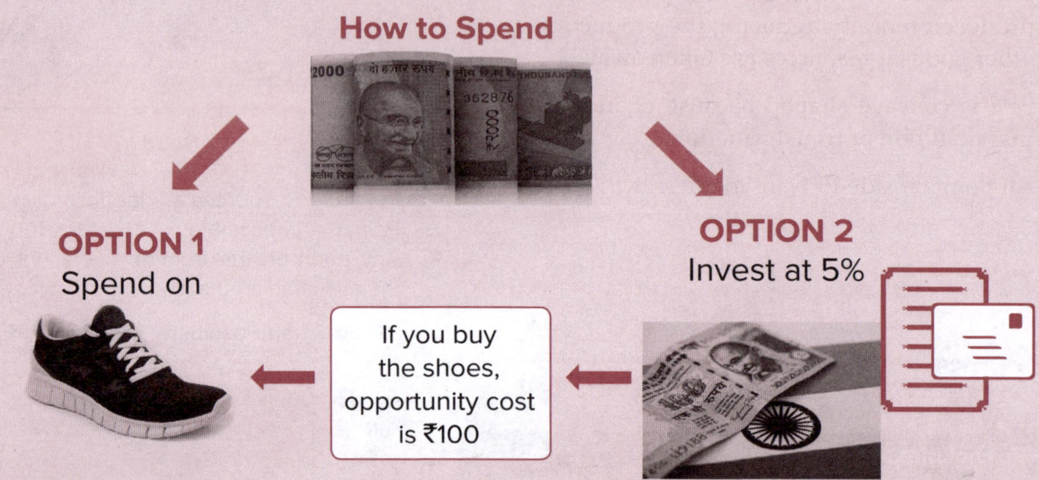

Illustration 2

Alternative Not Chosen	Alternative Chosen	Opportunity Cost
• Akshay can work on an assignment over the weekend • Akshay earns ₹5000 for the assignment	• Akshay can go to a solotrip during the weekend • Expense of the trip is ₹3000	• Opportunity cost is ₹5000 + ₹3000 = ₹8000

Marginal Opportunity Cost: The rate of sacrifice of commodity Y for additional production of commodity X, is called marginal opportunity cost.

The slope of PPF shows Marginal Opportunity Cost. The slope of production possibility curve increases (because production possibility curve is concave to the origin). Due to this, when resources are transferred from one use to other, increasing tendencies are found in marginal opportunity cost.

When does PPF take shape of a straight line?

PPF takes the shape of a straight line when marginal opportunity cost or marginal rate of transformation becomes constant. Marginal rate of transformation becomes constant when the ratio between the loss of output in goods Y and the gain of output in goods X remains constant while some resources are shifted from the production of goods Y to the production of goods X.

Shifting/Rotation of Production Possibility Frontier

Production possibility frontier never remains constant. Its situation keeps on changing because of changing nature of its assumptions.

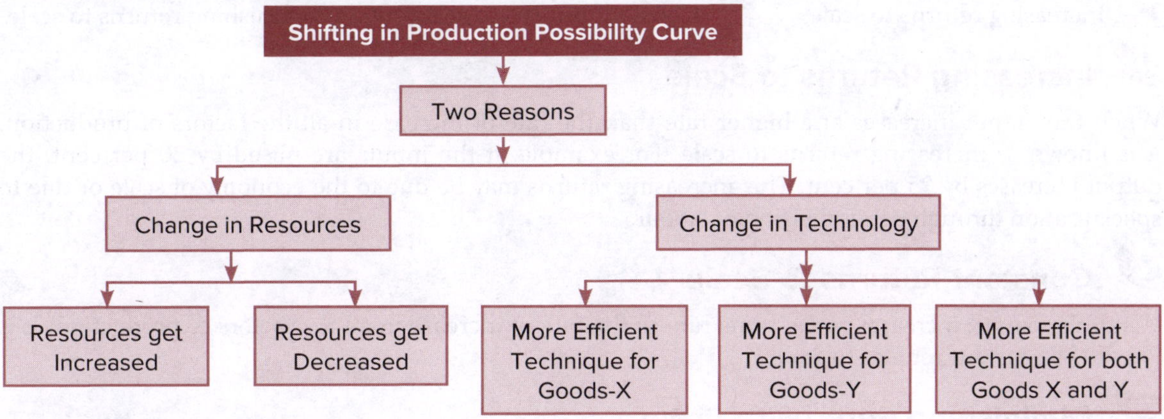

ISOCOST LINE

An isocost line represents the combination of inputs (e.g. labour and capital) which the firm can purchase with the given budget.

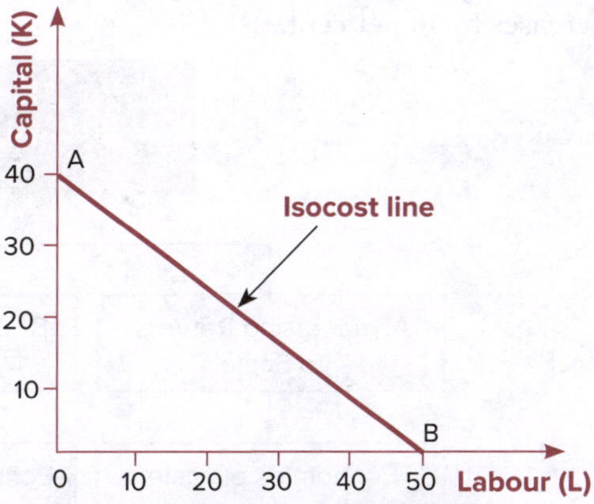

Representation of Isocost

ISOQUANT LINE

An isoquant is the locus of points at which the same quantity of output is produced while changing the quantities of two or more inputs.

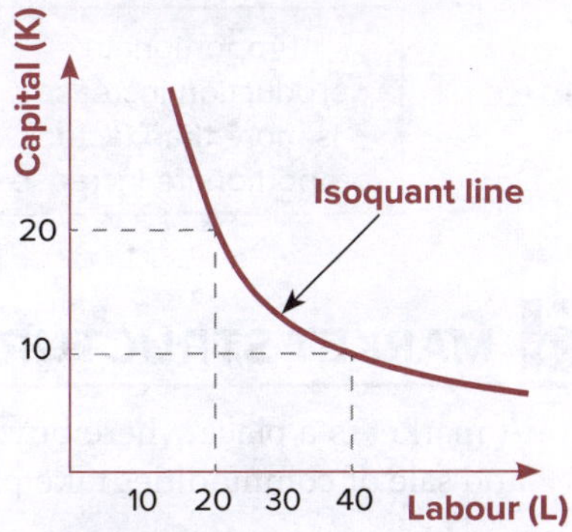

Representation of Isoquant

LAWS OF RETURNS TO SCALE

Laws of returns to scale refer to the changes in output due to change in all factors by the same proportion. Returns to scale are of the following types:

- Increasing returns to scale
- Constant returns to scale
- Diminishing returns to scale

Increasing Returns to Scale

When the output increases at a higher rate than the rate of increase in all the factors of production, it is known as increasing returns to scale. For example, if the inputs are raised by 20 per cent, the output increases by 25 per cent. This increasing returns may be due to the economy of scale or due to specialisation through better division of labour.

Constant Returns to Scale

When the output increases at the same rate as the rate of increase in all the factors of production, it is known as constant returns to scale.

Diminishing Returns to Scale

When the output increases at a lower rate than the rate of increase in all the factors of production, it is known as diminishing returns to scale. For example, if the inputs are raised by 15 per cent, the output increases by 10 per cent.

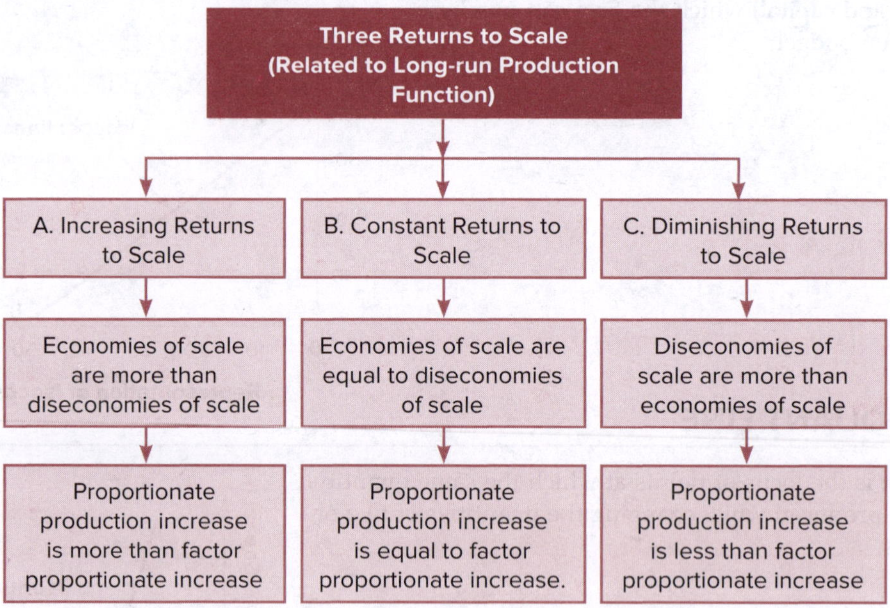

MARKET STRUCTURES

- A market is a place where buyers and sellers come to close contact with each other and purchase and sale of commodities take place.

➤ Market structure refers to how different industries are classified and differentiated based on the type of goods and services and the nature of competition for their operations.

Main determinants of the market structure are:

i. number of buyers and sellers of commodities
ii. freedom of entry and exit of firms
iii. nature of commodities
iv. knowledge
v. mobility of goods etc.

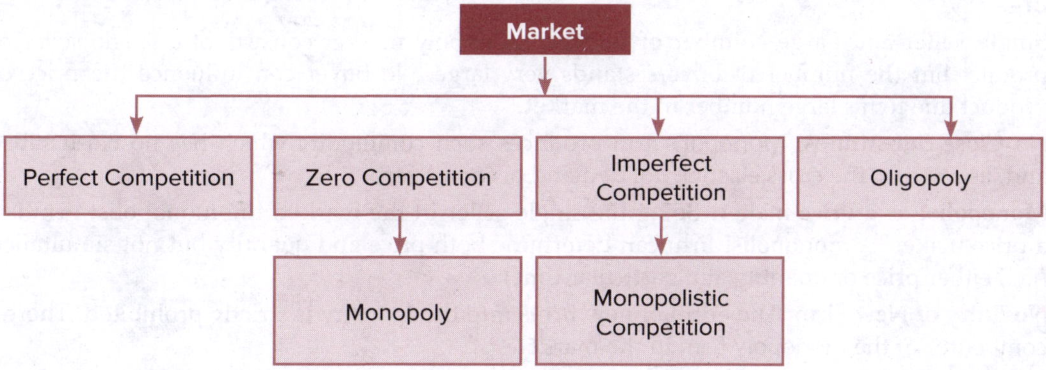

Different Types of Market Structures

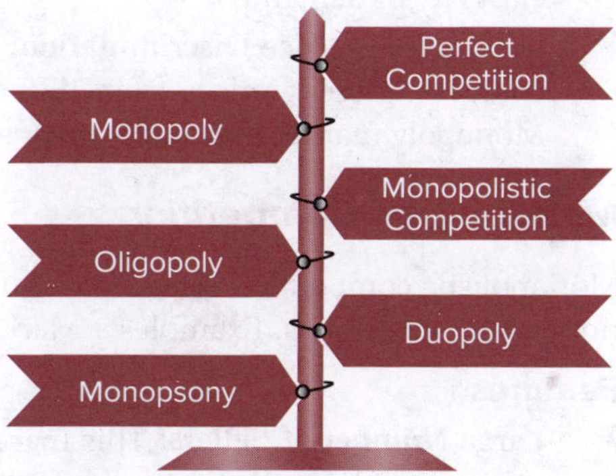

Perfect Competition

In this market situation, there exists a large number of buyers and sellers and they sell identical products at a price fixed by the market. Perfect competition never exists in reality but market for agricultural goods is the closest example of it.

Features

➤ **Large Number of Buyers and Sellers:** Perfect competitive market has a large number of buyers and sellers and hence, any buyer or seller cannot influence the market price. In other words, individual buyer or seller cannot influence the demand and supply conditions of the market.

➤ **Homogeneous Product:** The units sold in the market by all sellers are homogeneous (or identical) in nature.

➤ **Free Entry and Exit of Firms:** In perfect competition, any new firm may join the industry or any old firm may quit the industry. Hence, there is no restriction on free entry or exit of firms into/from the industry.

➤ **Perfect Knowledge of the Market:** In perfect competition, every buyer has the perfect knowledge of market conditions. None of the buyers will buy the commodity at higher price than the prevailing price in the market. Hence, only one price prevails in the market.

➤ **Perfect Mobility of Factors:** In perfect competition, the factors of production are perfectly mobile. Factors can easily be mobile from one industry to other industry (or from one firm to other firm) without any difficulty.

- **No Transportation Cost:** Transportation cost remains zero in perfect competition due to which one price prevails in the market.

Monopoly

Monopoly is a market condition where there exists a single seller selling a product and the product has no close substitutes. Indian Railways is an example of this market condition.

Features

- **Single Seller and Large Number of Buyers:** Monopoly market consists of a single seller of the product but the number of buyers stands very large. No buyer can influence the price of the product due to his large number in the market.
- **No Close Substitutes:** Monopoly firm produces such commodity which has no close substitute and, as a result, the cross elasticity of demand becomes zero.
- **Monopolist as a Price-maker:** Being the single seller in the market, the monopolist firm is itself a price-maker. A monopolist firm can determine both price and quantity but not simultaneously (i.e., either price or quantity at a particular time).
- **No Entry of New Firm**: The entry of new firms into the industry is strictly prohibited. There is no competitor of the monopoly firm in the market.
- **Demand Curve Negatively Sloped:** Monopolist demand curve is negatively sloped and marginal revenue (MR) is less than average revenue (AR). The slope of demand curve depends on the elasticity of demand.
- **Possibility of Price Discrimination:** Price discrimination refers to the situation in which the seller charges different prices from different consumers of different places for the same commodity. Monopoly market may have the possibility of price discrimination.

Monopolistic Competition

Monopolistic competition refers to a situation in which many firms sell products which are similar but not perfect substitutes. Examples – Markets of toothpaste, soap, etc.

Features

- **Large Number of Sellers:** This market contains a large number of sellers who compete with each other with close substitutes. In monopolistic competition, an individual firm has a limited share in the market.
- **Differentiated Product:** The products produced by the firms of the group are not identical but close substitutes to each other. Their products differ from one another in shape, size, packing, etc.
- **Unrestricted Entry and Exit:** Any firm may join the group and may produce another close substitutes. Unrestricted entry of firms increases the production of close substitutes.
- **Selling Costs:** Selling cost is the unique feature of monopolistic competition. Advertisement and publicity are important in this market situation. The expenses on advertisement and publicity are called 'Selling Costs'.
- **Imperfect Knowledge of the Market:** Buyers have imperfect knowledge of the market under monopolistic competition due to which they prefer particular goods in comparison with its close substitution.

- **Non-price Competition:** It is a salient feature of monopolistic competitive market. Firms provide many facilities for attracting the buyers. Such facilities include post-sale services, replacements, discount sale, gift scheme, etc.
- **Price Policy of Firm:** Like perfect competition, a monopolistic competitive firm is not price-taker but every firm in the group has its own price policy. A monopolistic competitive firm decides price and quantity of its product.

Oligopoly

Oligopoly refers to **'competition among the few'**. It is a market situation where few firms are selling identical or differentiated products. Examples – Cement, automobile markets in India.

Features

- **Few Sellers:** Under the Oligopoly market, few sellers are there, and many customers are there. Few firms dominate the market and enjoy a considerable control over the price of the product.
- **Interdependence:** The seller has to be cautious about any action taken by the competing firms. Since there are few sellers in the market, if any firm makes a change in the price, all other firms in the industry have to comply with it to stay in the competition. Thus, every firm remains cautious about the actions. Hence, there is a complete interdependence among the sellers with respect to their price output policies.
- **Advertising:** Under Oligopoly market, every firm advertises their products to reach more and more customers and increase their customer base. This advertising makes the competition more intense. Each firm spends lots of money for advertisement in order to stay in the market.
- **Competition:** As there is a huge competition, any move by one firm will have a considerable impact on its rivals. Thus, every seller keeps an eye over its rivals and be ready with the counterattack.
- **Entry and Exit Barriers:** Firms can easily exit the industry whenever they want, but have to face certain barriers to enter such as Government license, Patent, large firm's economies of scale, high capital requirement, complex technology, etc. Also, sometimes, the government regulations favour the existing large firms, thereby acting as a barrier for the new entrants.

EXAM ESSENTIAL

CARTEL THEORY OF OLIGOPOLY

A cartel is a **collection of firms that band together** to decide the prices and output. A cartel can form under the same circumstances that lead to an oligopolistic market. Cartels are more likely to form in markets with a small number of firms and a sizable market share held by each firm. In order to gain more market power, oligopoly firms join cartels, and members collaborate to decide on the quantity of output and/or price that each member will charge. The cartel members can act like monopolists by joining together.

Duopoly

A Duopoly is a special type of oligopoly market where **two firms dominate the market** and sell a product to a large number of consumers. From consumers' side, it is a competitive market where the choice of an individual consumer cannot affect the firm. For example, Pepsi and Coca-Cola control almost the entire cola beverage market in India.

Monopsony

A monopsony refers to a market that is dominated by a single buyer and the product has no close substitutes. It commonly experiences low prices from wholesalers. Example – Central Government is the only buyer in the domestic defence manufacturing sector.

BUSINESS CYCLE THEORY

Income growth in any economy is achieved by raising the amount of production, or real Gross National Product (GNP). It indicates that progress needs more growth, or higher levels of economic activity. The government of an economy seeks to keep economic activity high by implementing suitable economic policies.

However, the economy regularly fails to meet this aim. As a result, economies alternate between the highest and worst levels of economic activity, known as **boom** and **depression**, respectively. They may be classified into several stages of an economy's economic activity. There may be a variety of different economic activity conditions, including **stagnation, slowdown, recession**, and **recovery**.

Economists refer to these fluctuations between depression and boom as the business cycle or trade cycle, with recession and recovery acting as the primary intermediate stages. It is also referred to as an 'economic cycle'.

Significance of Business Cycle

Major macroeconomic indicators such as the Index of Industrial Production (IIP), income, and employment are all susceptible to the business cycle.

The business cycle is an effective instrument for analysing the economy.

It serves as the foundation for key financial choices by investors, companies, and the government.

Phases of Business Cycle

Expansion

- This stage of the business cycle is also known as the **'Economic Boom'**, which is characterised by an increase in real GDP.
- During this phase, the economy expands in all dimensions, resulting in rapid and sustained demand, as well as increased investment, output, and employment.
- The economy may also suffer structural issues such as a lack of investable capital, reduced savings, a declining standard of living, etc.

Contraction

- This phase is most often known as '**recession**'.
- During this period, overall economic activity falls, resulting in low economic production, or real GDP.
- Consumption, corporate profitability, investment, employment, retail sales, and other macroeconomic factors are all declining during this phase.

Depression

- Depression is often defined as an economy experiencing a recession for two or more consecutive quarters.
- During this phase, an economy's productivity declines drastically.
- Both GDP and GNP indicate negative growth as well as unemployment.

Recovery

- It is the stage during which the economy attempts to recover after a period of low output. A recession or depression may occur during the low-production era.
- To rebuild the economy, both the government and the central bank implement a variety of fiscal and monetary policies to improve demand, investment and output. The price mechanism is critical to the economy's revival.
- During the recovery phase, manufacturers replace certain depreciated capital goods while maintaining others.
- As a result, organisations' investment and employment levels improve. As this process gets pace, the economy returns to a state of expansion. Thus, the business cycle continues.

Business Cycle

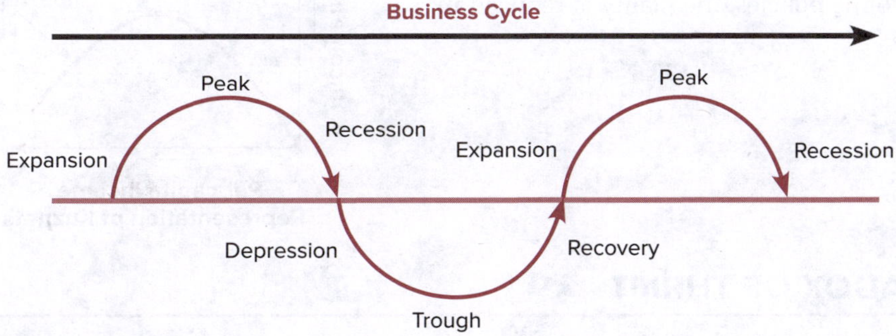

Dynamic Pricing

Dynamic pricing, also known as **surge pricing, demand pricing**, or **time-based pricing**, is a business technique in which prices are adjusted to reflect changing demand. For example, an airline will adjust seat rates based on seat type, quantity of remaining seats, and time till departure.

Predatory Pricing

Predatory pricing is a **commercial price strategy** that uses large-scale undercutting to remove competitors. This is where an industry dominant corporation with considerable market dominance will intentionally decrease the pricing of a product or service to loss-making levels in order to attract all users and form a monopoly.

INVISIBLE HAND

The concept of '**invisible hand**' was introduced by **Adam Smith** in his book *'The Theory of Moral Sentiments'* (1759) and later in *'An Inquiry into the Nature and Causes of the Wealth of Nations.'*

This is the unseen market force that maintains the equilibrium in the demand and supply of goods in a free market by the self-interested individuals with the help of mutual interdependence.

Adam Smith was a proponent of laissez-faire economic policies and tendency of free markets to regulate themselves using competition, supply and demand, and self-interest.

Laissez-faire ('leave alone' in French) is an economic theory from the 18th century which is a key part of free-market capitalism.

Adam Smith's **Four Canons of Taxation**: In his book *'The Wealth of Nations'*, Adam Smith introduced four canons of taxation. They are:

(i) Canon of equality
(ii) Canon of certainty
(iii) Canon of convenience
(iv) Canon of economy

KUZNETS CURVE

Kuznets curve shows the relationship between **inequality** and **economic growth**. The shape of the curve is **inverted U**. In the initial phase, economic growth leads to greater inequality. With the help of different economic policies, inequality is reduced in the later phase.

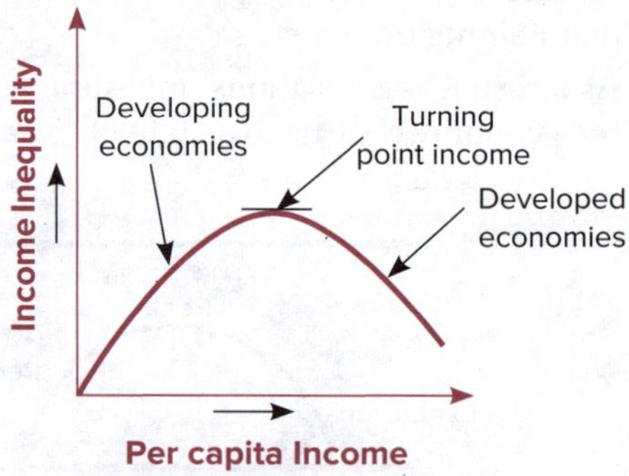

Representation of Kuznets Curve

PARADOX OF THRIFT

The concept was given by economist **John Maynard Keynes**. It states that personal savings can be detrimental to economic growth. During an economic recession, individuals try to save more, which essentially leads to a fall in aggregate demand and hence in economic growth.

BONUS KNOWLEDGE

Adam Smith (1723–1790)

Also known as **The Father of Economics** and **The Father of Capitalism**.

His works include – The Theory of Moral Sentiments (1759); Lectures on Jurisprudence (1763); An Inquiry into the Nature and Causes of the Wealth of Nations (1776).

John Maynard Keynes (1883–1946)

Also known as The **Father of Macroeconomics.**

His works include – The Economic Consequences of the Peace (1919); The End of Laissez-Faire (1926); The General Theory of Employment, Interest and Money (1936).

PARETO EFFICIENCY

Pareto efficiency is an economic situation where it is impossible to make someone better off without making others worse off. In Pareto optimum state, resources are allocated in such a way that no economic changes can make one individual better off without making others worse off.

SUMMARY

- **Market Economy** – Production and prices are determined by unrestricted competition between privately owned businesses.
- **Non-market Economy** – Government intervention is important in allocating goods and resources and determining prices.
- **Economic Activity –** Related to the use of limited resources to fulfil unlimited human wants.
- **Microeconomics** – Individual units (e.g., household demand, pricing).
- **Macroeconomics** – Entire economy (e.g., GDP, inflation, unemployment).
- **Mixed Economy** – Protects private property and allows a level of economic freedom in the use of capital, allows governments to interfere in economic activities to achieve social aims.
- **Economic Agents** – Responsible for taking economic decisions, government, banks, consumers, etc.
- **Primary Sector** – Agriculture, fishing, etc.
- **Secondary Sector** – All manufacturing and construction activities.
- **Tertiary Sector** – Also known as Service Sector, IT services transportation, tourism, banking, etc.
- **Quaternary Sector** – Intellectual or knowledge-based activities like consultancy, R&D, etc.
- **Quinary Sector** – High-level decision making in Government, University, etc.
- **Demand Function** – Shows the relationship between quantity demanded and price.
- **Law of Demand** – Inverse relationship between the price and quantity demanded for goods. Higher the prices, lower will be the demand and vice-versa.
- **Law of Supply** – If price increases, supply of goods also increases and vice-versa.
- **Opportunity Cost** – The cost of the next best alternative foregone.
- **Indifference Curve** – Graphical representation of different combinations of two goods which gives a consumer equal satisfaction.
- **Indifference Map** – Set of indifference curves showing preferences.
- **Budget Line** – Shows all affordable combinations of two goods. Straight, downward-sloping line.
- **Engel Curve** – Shows how demand for goods changes with income. Developed by **Ernst Engel**.
- **Perfect Competition** – Large number of buyers and sellers and they sell identical products at a price fixed by the market.
- **Monopoly** – A single seller selling product and the product has no close substitutes, example – Railways in India
- **Oligopoly** – refers to **'competition among the few'**. It is a market situation where few firms are selling identical or differentiated products.
- **Business Cycle Theory** – An economy goes through several phases such as stagnation, slowdown, recession, and recovery. Economists refer to these fluctuations between depressions and booms as the business cycle or trade cycle, with recession and recovery acting as the primary intermediate stages.

- **Invisible Hand** – The unseen market force that maintains the equilibrium in the demand and supply of goods in a free market.
- **Kuznets Curve** – Shows the relationship between inequality and economic growth. The shape of the curve is inverted U.
- **Paradox of Thrift** – Personal savings can be detrimental to economic growth – by John Maynard Keynes.

UPSC CSE PREVIOUS YEARS' PRELIMINARY EXAMINATION QUESTIONS

1. Consider the following statements: **[2021]**

Other things remaining unchanged, market demand for a good might increase if

1. Price of its substitute increases
2. Price of its complement increases
3. The good is an inferior good and income of the consumers increases
4. Its price falls

Which of the above statements are correct?

(a) 1 and 4 only
(b) 2, 3 and 4
(c) 1, 3 and 4
(d) 1, 2 and 3

2. If a commodity is provided free to the public by the Government, then **[2018]**

(a) the opportunity cost is zero.
(b) the opportunity cost is ignored.
(c) the opportunity cost is transferred from the consumers of the product to the tax-paying public.
(d) the opportunity cost is transferred from the consumers of the product to the Government.

☞ NO QUESTIONS ASKED
2024, 2023, 2022, 2020, 2019, 2017, 2016, 2015, 2014, 2013, 2012

ANSWER KEY

1. (a) 2. (c)

UPSC CSE PREVIOUS YEARS' MAIN EXAMINATION QUESTIONS

☞ NO QUESTIONS ASKED
2024, 2023, 2022, 2021, 2020, 2019, 2018, 2017, 2016, 2015, 2014, 2013, 2012

CHAPTER

2

NATIONAL INCOME

CHAPTER OUTLINE

- National Income
- History of National Income in India
- Important Concepts under National Income
- Measures of National Income – GDP, GNP etc.
- Real versus Nominal GDP
- Transfer Payments
- Other Variants of National Income
- Methods of Computing National Income
- Role of Measuring National Income
- Limitations in the Measurement of National Income
- First Advance Estimates of National Income for 2024–25
- Important Facts based on the Report of MoSPI
- Shapes of Economic Recovery

NATIONAL INCOME

- National Income (NI) is the **aggregate of the factor incomes** earned by the normal residents of a country in an accounting year. It is the sum total of the factor income such as wages, salaries, rent, interest, profit, etc., received by factors of production, i.e. labour, capital, land and entrepreneurship of a nation.
- In other words, NI is the sum total value of all **final** goods and services produced within its domestic boundaries or outside by the residents of a country in an accounting period (i.e. from 1 April to 31 March).
- It is measured in terms of **Gross Domestic Product (GDP)** and its variants are Net Domestic Product (NDP), Gross National Product (GNP), Net National Product (NNP), etc.
- NI aggregates are either estimated based on **Factor Costs (FCs)** or on the **Market Price (MP)**.

> **did you KNOW?** A measure of the value of aggregate amount of goods and services produced by the economy in a year is called Gross Domestic Product (GDP). Thus, GDP ≡ Sum total of Gross Value Added (GVA) of all the firms in the economy.
>
> – NCERT

EXAM ESSENTIAL

ECONOMIC PERFORMANCE INDICATORS

- **GDP growth rate** – It indicates performance of the country
- **GDP per capita** – It indicates level of economic development in comparison to other countries

HISTORY OF NATIONAL INCOME IN INDIA

Several estimates of NI were made in the British period by notable economists like Dadabhai Naoroji, William Digby, V.K.R.V. Rao and R.C. Desai.

a. **First attempt** was made by **Dadabhai Naoroji in 1868**. Annual Per Capita Income (PCI) computed by him was **₹20**.

b. **First scientific method** to compute NI was used **by Dr V.K.R.V. Rao in 1931–32**. In doing so, he divided the Indian economy into two parts:
   i. **Primary sector** which included agriculture, forest, fishing and hunting, and
   ii. **Secondary sector** which included industries, construction, transport, public services and business.

   He computed **₹62** as the PCI of India.

c. **First official attempt to compute NI** was made by **P.C. Mahalanobis** as the head of the **National Income Committee** appointed by the Government of India, which also had D.R. Gadgil and V.K. R.V. Rao as members.

   The first report of the Committee was presented in 1951, according to which the NI of India for 1948–49 was ₹8,710 crore and the PCI was **₹225**.

d. Later, the task of estimating GDP was transferred to the **Central Statistics Office (CSO)** and a fully developed NI division under CSO was created at the national level. Since 1955, the NI estimates were compiled by CSO based on the national level survey conducted by **National Sample Survey Office (NSSO)**.

   However, **in 2019**, Central Government merged the CSO and the NSSO and established **National Statistical Office (NSO)** under the Ministry of Statistics and Programme Implementation (MoSPI).

BONUS KNOWLEDGE

National Statistical Office (NSO) – It is under the Ministry of Statistics and Programme Implementation (MoSPI). It was created through the merger of the NSSO and CSO, in 2019.

National Statistical Commission (NSC) – It is an autonomous body, which was formed in 2005 under the recommendation of *Rangarajan Commission*.

Now for computation of NI, NSO divides the Indian economy into three sectors:

i. **Primary sector** ii. **Secondary sector** iii. **Tertiary sector**

EXAM ESSENTIAL

BROAD SUB-HEADS UNDER PRIMARY, SECONDARY AND TERTIARY SECTOR

(as per the Economic Survey)

Primary (or Agri and Allied) Sector includes:

1. Agriculture
2. Forestry
3. Fishing
4. Animal husbandry

Secondary (or Industry) Sector includes:

1. Mining and quarrying
2. Manufacturing
3. Electricity, gas, water supply and other utility services
4. Construction

Tertiary (or Service) Sector includes:

1. Trade, hotel, transport, storage, communication and services related to broadcasting
2. Financial, real estate and professional services
3. Public administration, defence and other services

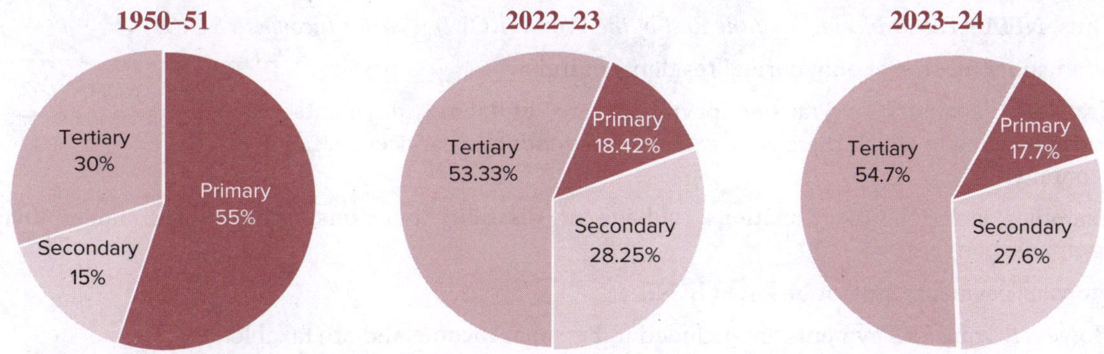

Sector-wise Contribution in the Indian GDP: A Comparison

Important Concepts under National Income

Domestic/Economic Territory It refers to the geographical territory administered by the Indian Government within which the person, goods and capital can circulate freely. Foreign embassies located in India are **not** a part of domestic/economic territory, whereas Indian embassies located abroad are a part of domestic/economic territory.

Thus, domestic/economic territory also consists of the following:

- Military establishments, consulates, embassies, etc., located in a foreign country.
- Fishing vessels, ships, aircrafts, etc., operated by the residents of a country fall under the domestic territory even if these frequent the foreign geographic or political boundaries. For example, the revenues and profits of Air India are counted within India's GDP.

Market Price (MP) MP is the price that a consumer pays for the product while purchasing it from the sellers. It is the price at which the units are sold in the economy taking into effect the indirect taxes and subsidies.

Factor Cost (FC) It refers to the cost of factors of production that is incurred by a firm when producing goods and services.

Examples of such production costs include paying the salaries and wages, cost of renting machinery and obtaining capital, interest of land and profit margins to entrepreneur. The FC **does not include**

indirect taxes like GST that are paid to the government since payment of taxes is not directly related to the production process, **but subsidies received are included in the FC** as these are direct inputs into the production.

Factor Cost = Market Price − Net Indirect Taxes

where Net Indirect Taxes = Indirect Taxes − Subsidies

Depreciation or Consumption of Fixed Capital – It refers to the loss in value of fixed assets which are in use due to wear and tear, accidental damages and obsolescence.

NDP = GDP – Depreciation

Net Factor Income from Abroad (NFIA) – Difference between factor income (rent, wages, interest and profit) earned by **normal residents** of India who are temporarily resident abroad and factor income earned by non-residents temporarily residing in India.

Thus, ***NFIA =*** *Factor Income from the Rest of the World (ROW) − Factor Income to ROW*

NI includes income of only normal residents of India.

NNP = NDP + NFIA

Transfer Payments – Transfer payments are **unilateral payments** corresponding to which there is no exchange of goods and services in the economy.

Examples include **gifts, donations, old-age or disability pensions, scholarships, unemployment compensation, etc.**

Transfer payments are not **included in** NI.

However, Transfer Payments are included in **Personal Income** and are taxable.

did you KNOW?

WHO ARE TERMED AS NORMAL RESIDENTS OF INDIA?

A person is said to be a normal resident:

i. Who ordinarily resides in India, **and**

ii. Whose centre of economic interest lies in India.

Please note:

- A person residing for **one year or more** in India is considered as ordinarily residing in India. A normal resident **may or may not be a citizen of India**.
- A person has **economic interest in India** if he carries out his economic activities like production, consumption or investment in India at a significant scale as compared to his wealth and income.

Normal Residents also include:

1. Indians working in the Indian embassies abroad (e.g. ambassadors, etc.)
2. Foreign citizens living in India for more than one year. (However, foreigners who come to India **for medical treatment or study purpose are not considered normal residents** even if they stay for more than one year.)

Normal Residents **do not** include:

1. Foreigners working in the Indian embassies abroad.
2. Foreigners working in the office of WHO, IMF, etc., located in India.
3. Ambassadors of other countries posted in India.
4. Foreign technical experts working in India for a period of less than one year.

Above are just some of the few important examples.

Capital Output Ratio

- Capital output ratio is the amount of capital needed to produce **one unit** of output.

Capital Output Ratio = Capital/Output

In other words, it reflects the relationship between the level of investment in an economy and the economic growth (increase in GDP) corresponding to this level of investment.

- For example, if ₹1,00,000 is needed to produce 100 units then Capital Output Ratio will be 1000. Similarly, if ₹50,000 is needed to produce 100 units, then it will be 500 only.
- Thus, Higher the ratio – more capital is required – less efficiency or productivity is there in the economy and vice versa.
- Thus, a **low capital-output ratio is always desired**.

Incremental Capital Output Ratio (ICOR) The ICOR indicates additional unit of capital or investment needed to produce an additional unit of output.

Types of Goods

- **Raw Material:** Goods that are primarily used as inputs in the production or manufacturing of other goods.
- **Intermediary Goods:** Those goods which have undergone processing but are again used as inputs in the production of final goods.
- **Finished/Final Goods:** Those goods which do not require further processing and are fit for final consumption by the consumer.
- **Capital Goods:** They are used in the process of production of final products. They are durable and wear out gradually. They include tools, buildings, vehicles, machinery and equipment.
- **Consumption Goods:** Goods like food and clothing, and services like recreation that are consumed when purchased by their ultimate consumers are called consumption goods or consumer goods.

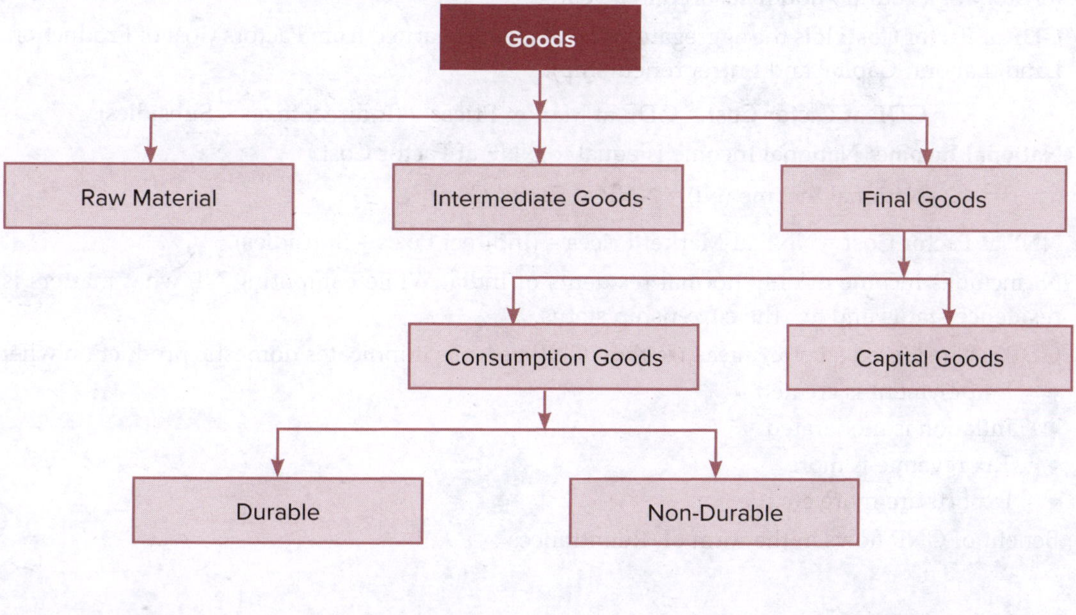

BONUS KNOWLEDGE

CAPITAL GOODS ARE NOT INTERMEDIATE GOODS. WHY?

- Capital Goods support production of other Goods, **they themselves don't get transformed**. They remain with their producers/manufacturers for the production of products/services.

Flows versus Stock

- **Flows** are defined over a period of time. For example, monthly or yearly income, output etc. Usually, Financial Year (from 1st April to 31st March) is taken as the basis for calculation.
- **Stocks** are defined at a particular point of time. For example, assets value, inventory, etc. on a particular day (say 1st January) is called stock.

Measures of National Income

- **Gross Domestic Product (GDP):** It measures the aggregate production of "final goods and services" taking place within the domestic economy during a year.
- **Gross National Product (GNP):** GNP is an estimate of total value of all the final products and services turned out in a given period by the means of production **owned by country's residents**.

  GNP = GDP + Net Factor Income from Abroad
- Thus, GDP is concerned with borders, whereas, GNP is concerned with Nationals.

  Net Domestic Product = GDP – Depreciation

  Net National Product = GNP – Depreciation
- **GDP at Market Prices** = the market value of all final goods and services produced within a domestic territory of a country and measured in a year.
- **GDP at Factor Cost:** It is the aggregate value of income earned from Factors Cost of Production (i.e. Land, Labour, Capital and Entrepreneurship).

  GDP at Factor Cost = GDP at Market Prices – (Indirect taxes – Subsidies)
- **National Income:** National Income is equal to NNP at Factor Cost.

  National Income (NI) = NNP at Factor Cost
- **NNP at Factor Cost** = NNP at Market Prices – (Indirect taxes – Subsidies)
- NI includes income of only normal residents of India. While computing NI, what matters is the **residence status** and not the citizenship status.
- GDP is considered a **better measure** than GNP because it indicates domestic production where:
  - Employment is created
  - Inflation is moderated
  - Tax revenue is more
  - Exports are more etc.
- Benefit of GNP flows in the form of 'Remittances'.

Real *versus* Nominal GDP

Real GDP is an **inflation-adjusted** measure that reflects the value of all goods and services produced by an economy in a given year (expressed in constant prices or base year* prices). Real GDP is computed using the **expenditure approach** to output.

Nominal GDP is the market value (**Current MP × Quantity produced**) of all goods and services produced in India in a financial year. This final value changes every year due to two reasons:

i. Change in actual or physical production of goods and services.
ii. Change in prices.

As the second aspect is a mere inflationary effect, the real change which impacts the investment and the employment scenario is the first one. So, this inflationary impact is discounted to compute GDP in real terms. This discounting factor is also called the **GDP deflator**.

GDP Deflator = Nominal GDP/Real GDP × 100

This GDP deflator is the **best indicator of inflation** in the economy.

Please note: *Nominal GDP is nothing but **GDP at Current Prices**, and Real GDP is GDP at Constant Prices.*

Real GDP indicates a change in output, whereas Nominal GDP may or may not. Thus, ***Real GDP is considered as a better indicator*** of economic growth as compared to Nominal GDP.

BONUS KNOWLEDGE

***Base Year** – The GDP at current prices is converted into base year prices to measure the 'real increase' in the GDP or the Real GDP. Generally, the base year is a normal year devoid of price fluctuations. The base year used at present by the Government of India is **2011–12**.

Base year is revised time to time. Recently, the Government has proposed to change the base year to 2017–18 (*but not yet done*).

EXAM ESSENTIAL

Why GDP Deflator is preferred in Real GDP computation as compared to other inflation indexes like WPI, CPI?

Since the GDP deflator covers the entire range of goods and services produced in the economy – as against the limited commodity baskets for the wholesale or consumer price indices – it is seen as a more comprehensive measure.

CPI is not preferred because:

- All goods and services produced are not consumed by the retail consumers.
- It assigns fixed proportion to the goods in the index instead of dynamic weightage based on level of consumption.
- Imported consumption goods are also counted in CPI.

WPI is not preferred because:

- Services inflation (which contributes more than 50% in GDP) is not considered here.
- WPI considers the intermediate wholesale prices, and not the final market prices.

EXAM ESSENTIAL

POTENTIAL GDP

The **Potential GDP** measures/estimates the highest level of output that an economy can sustain over a period of time at a constant inflation rate.

The **GDP Gap** depicts the difference between Potential GDP and Real GDP.

The factors that affect/determine Potential GDP can be:

- Sustainability
- Full employment (gender inequality, unemployment, underemployment)
- Technological usage
- Regulatory framework
- Steady currency

Major challenges for India in achieving Potential GDP:

- Gender inequality (for reference that gender equality boosts potential GDP by 26%).
- The issue of unemployment and under-employment.
- Use of old-age production methods to produce goods.
- Need for a user-friendly regulatory framework in terms of easy entry and exit policy for corporates.

As per recent reports, it has been predicted that the introduction of GST has boosted the potential GDP of India by 6.7 per cent. Moreover, the use of Artificial Intelligence (AI) can add to GDP as predicted by National Association of Software and Service Companies (NASSCOM).

EXAM ESSENTIAL

Eight (8) Measures or Aggregates of National Income:

1. GDP_{MP} = Gross Domestic Product at Market Price.
2. GDP_{FC} = Gross Domestic Product at Factor Cost = GDP_{MP} – Indirect taxes + Subsidies
3. NDP_{MP} = Net Domestic Product at Market Price = GDP_{MP} – Depreciation
4. NDP_{FC} = Net Domestic Product at Factor Cost = NDP_{MP} – Indirect taxes + Subsidies
5. GNP_{MP} = Gross National Product at Market Price = GDP_{MP} + NFIA
6. GNP_{FC} = Gross National Product at Factor Cost = GDP_{MP} – Indirect taxes + Subsidies + NFIA
7. NNP_{MP} = Net National Product at Market Price = GDP_{MP} – Depreciation + NFIA
8. **NNP_{FC} (or National Income)** = Net National Product at Factor Cost = GDP_{MP} – Depreciation + NFIA – Indirect taxes + Subsidies

To understand easily, please remember the below flowcharts:

Gross	Domestic	Market Price (MP)
↓	↓	↓
(–) Depreciation	(+) NFIA	(–) Indirect Taxes (+) Subsidies
↓	↓	↓
Net	National	Factor Cost (FC)

Other Variants of National Income

- **Personal Income (PI):** It is the sum of all types of factor income actually received by the households including current transfers. PI is the aggregate of earned and unearned income.

Personal Income (PI) = *National Income – Undistributed profits – Net Interest Payments made by Households - Corporate tax + Transfer payments to the households from the government and firms.*

OR

Personal Income (PI) = *National Income – Undistributed profits of corporations – Net interest payments for Social Security provisions – Wage accruals less disbursements + Transfer payments + Personal interest and dividend income.*

Difference between PI and NI

Personal Income	National Income
PI is the income received by factors of production. So, it is a concept related to the **receipt of income**.	NI is the income generated by factors of production. So, it is the concept related to the **generation of income**.
PI **includes** both factor income and transfer receipts.	Transfer receipts or payments are **not included** under NI.
Interest on national debt is **included** in PI.	Interest on national debt is **not a part** of NI.
Undistributed profit of the companies and Corporate Taxes are **not** part of PI.	Undistributed profits of the companies and Corporate Taxes are **included** in NI.

- **Personal Disposable Income (PDI):** It is the income that remains with the individuals or households **after deduction of all direct taxes** levied against their income and property by the government.

  PDI = *PI – Direct taxes – Miscellaneous fees and fines paid by the households.*

  PDI reflects the **purchasing power** of the households.

- **National Disposable Income (NDI):** NDI is the income from all sources (earned income as well as transfer payments from abroad) available to the residents of India **for their consumption expenditure or for saving** during a financial year.

  NDI = *NNP_{FC} or NI + Net indirect taxes + Net current transfers from ROW.*

Gross National Disposable Income (GNDI) measures the income available to the total economy for final consumption and gross saving.

GNDI = GNP + current transfers receivable by resident units from rest of the world – current transfers payable to non-resident units to rest of the world.

Net National Disposable Income (NNDI) is derived by deducting depreciation from GNDI.

NNDI = GNDI – Depreciation

Difference between National Disposable Income and Personal Disposable Income

National Disposable Income (NDI)	Personal Disposable Income (PDI)
It refers to the *disposable income of the country as a whole*.	It refers to the *disposable income of the individuals or households* in the country.
It is the sum total of NNP_{FC}, net indirect taxes and net of current transfers from the rest of the world.	It is the income remaining with individuals after paying direct personal taxes (income tax and property tax).

Subcategories of Aggregate Income

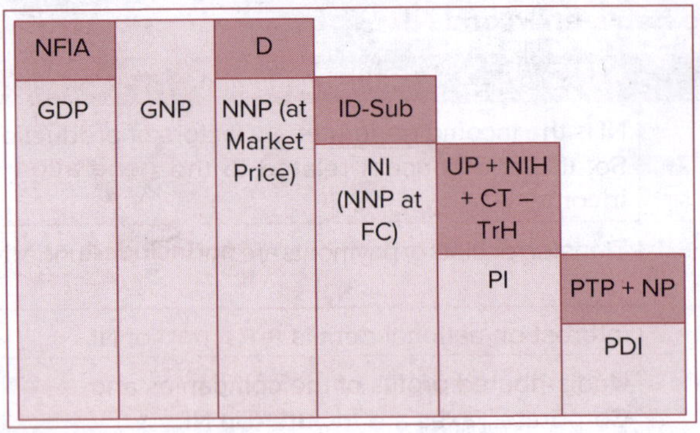

NFIA: Net Factor Income from Abroad
D: Depreciation
ID: Indirect Taxes
Sub: Subsidies
UP: Undistributed Profits
NIH: Net Interest Payments by Households
CT: Corporate Taxes
TrH: Transfers received by Households
PTP: Personal Tax Payments
NP: Non-Tax Payments
PDI: Personal Disposable Income

Source: NCERT Class XII Macroeconomics

BONUS KNOWLEDGE

VARIOUS ESTIMATES OF NATIONAL INCOME

- **Advance Estimate** (AE) – It is the first estimate of GDP/National Income released by NSO around **2 months before** the completion of the financial year. Release Date – **7 January**.
- **Provisional Estimate** (PE) – This estimate of GDP/National Income is released by NSO **2 months after** the completion of the financial year. Release Date – **31 May**. Provisional Estimate (PE) was earlier termed as **Revised Estimate** (RE).
- **First Revised Estimate** – This estimate of GDP/National Income is released by NSO **10 months after** the completion of the financial year. Release Date – **31 January**. First Revised Estimate was earlier termed as **Quick Estimate** (QE).
- **Second Revised Estimate** – This estimate of GDP/National Income is released by NSO **1 year and 10 months after** the closure of the financial year. Release Date – **31 January of the succeeding year**.
- **Third Revised Estimate** – This estimate of GDP/National Income is released by NSO **2 years and 10 months after** the closure of the financial year. Release Date – **31 January after 2 succeeding years**.

After the release of 3rd Revised Estimate of a particular financial year, data gets more or less stabilised, but there are always some additional information flowing from the States after the discussions with them of comparable estimates which is incorporated in the annual estimates at the time of subsequent revisions.

Example: As per the present schedule of NSO, the ***1st AE*** of 2024–25 was released in the evening of 7 January 2025. The ***PE*** of 2024–25 will be released on 31 May 2025. The ***1st RE*** of 2024–25 will be released on 31 January 2026. The ***2nd RE*** of 2024–25 will be released on 31 January 2027. The ***3rd RE*** of 2024–25 will be released on 31 January 2028.

Methods of Computing National Income (or GDP)

There are three different methods to estimate NI:

Methods of Computing National Income (or GDP)

- Product method (or *Value Added Method*)
- Income method (or *Distribution Method*)
- Expenditure method (or *Total Outlay Method*)

Expenditure method is the most used one due to the easy availability of data required under this method.

1. *Product Method*

- This is also called **'Output method'** or **'Value added method'**.
- This method is used to estimate national income when data are collected at the income creation stage.
- Under this method, Gross Value Added (GVA) or GDP_{MP} is computed, which is nothing but the **difference between the value of output and intermediate consumption** of all the three sectors, i.e. primary sector, secondary sector and tertiary sector.

GVA or GDP_{MP} = Value of Output of all three sectors − Intermediate consumption of all three sectors

did you KNOW? Intermediate consumption refers to intermediate goods (in the form of raw material) used in the production of a final good. While computing GVA, Intermediate consumption is subtracted **to avoid double counting**. If not subtracted, the value of that intermediate product will be counted twice in the national income (once as final good and once as intermediate good).

Following goods and services **are included** in NI under Product Method:

a. *Goods and services sold in the market to earn profit.*

b. *Goods and services not sold but supplied free of cost. For example, free lunch to schoolchildren.*

c. *Own account production of fixed capital.*

d. *Imputed rent or imputed interest.*

Imputed Rent: *When a property is owned and used by the same person, then rent is not actually paid by him to himself. That notional rent is termed as Imputed Rent and it is a part of NI. Similar is the imputed interest.*

Following activities **are not included** in NI under Product Method:

a. *Illegal activities like smuggling and gambling*

b. *Non-economic goods (water, air)*
c. *Second-hand purchase/sale of goods*
d. *Intermediate goods*
e. *Transfer payments, e.g. gifts, donation, etc.*
f. *Capital gains*

EXAM ESSENTIAL

GDP or GVA at Basic Prices:

- In 2015, it was decided by CSO (now NSO) that sector-wise estimates of Gross Value Added (GVA) or GDP will now be given at '*basic prices*' instead of '*factor cost*'.
- The basic price measures the amount retained by the producer and is, therefore, the price most relevant for the producer's decision-taking.
- The concept of GVA at Basic Prices is different from GVA at factor cost or market price.

GVA or GDP at Basic Prices = GVA at Factor Cost + Net Production Taxes

where Net Production Taxes = Production Taxes (not Product Taxes) – Production Subsidies (not Product Subsidies)

- Production Taxes and Production Subsidies are independent of the volume of Production whereas Product Taxes and Product Subsidies are paid or received based on per unit of product.
- Examples of Production Tax include Land Revenue, Stamp and Registration fees, etc., and that of Production Subsidies include subsidies to railways, input subsidies to farmers, subsidies to village and small industries, etc. While for Product Taxes, examples include GST, Custom duty, etc., and for Product Subsidies, examples include food subsidy, petroleum and fertiliser subsidies, etc.

And, **GVA at Market Price or GDP_{MP} = GDP at Basic Prices + Product Taxes – Product Subsidies**

EXAM ESSENTIAL

GVA vs GDP

(i) GVA is the value of all the goods and services produced within a country after deducting the value of intermediate goods and services. While GDP is the market value of all the final goods and services produced within the boundary of a country.

(ii) GVA gives insight of the economy from the input or supplier side. While GDP gives insight from output or consumer side.

(iii) GVA is generally calculated on a sector wise approach like, GVA for Primary Sector (Agriculture Sector), Secondary Sector (Manufacturing Sector) and Tertiary Sector (Service Sector). And these GVA of different sectors are added to give GDP of a country.

(iv) GVA is generally calculated at basic prices while GDP is calculated at market prices.

2. Income Method

- This is also known as the '*distribution method*'.
- Under this method, factor incomes under the following three major heads are added to compute NDP_{FC} (NDP at FC):

Components of NDP_{FC}

- **Compensation to Employees** (*Wages and Salaries, Employer's Contribution to Social Security Schemes*)
- **Operating Surplus** (Rent, Interest, Royalty and Profit)
- **Mixed Income of Self-employed**

i. **Compensation to Employees** – It includes wages and salaries, employer's (not employee's) contribution to social security schemes, dearness allowances, etc.

ii. **Operating Surplus** – It includes rent, profit, royalty and interest. Profit includes corporate tax, dividend and undistributed profit.

iii. **Mixed Income of Self-employed** – It refers to earnings from farming enterprises, sole proprietorships and other professions, such as medical and legal practices. In these professions, owners themselves assume the role of entrepreneurs, financiers, workers and landlords.

$$NDP_{FC} = \text{Compensation to Employees} + \text{Operating Surplus} + \text{Mixed Income of Self-Employed}$$

Items **included in NI** under Income method:

a. *Commission charged by broker on sale proceeds of even second-hand goods*

b. *The value of production for self-consumption is also included in NI*

Items **not included in NI** under Income method:

a. *Windfall gains (like lottery income)*

b. *Death duty*

c. *Transfer receipts*

d. *Income from sale of second-hand goods*

e. *Income from sale of shares, bonds and debentures*

3. Expenditure Method

- It is also called '*total outlay method*'.
- In a country, income earned is either spent on consumer goods and services or saved and invested. In this method, total national expenditure incurred in a particular year is taken into consideration to compute NI.
- Through this method, GDP_{MP} is derived at first.

$$GDP_{MP} = \text{Personal Consumption Exp (C)} + \text{Investments (I)} + \text{Government Exp (G)} + \text{Exports (X)} - \text{Imports (M)}$$

Items **to be included** in NI under expenditure method:

a. *Personal consumption expenditure of households*

b. *The gross private domestic investment, i.e. business spending on capital goods*

c. *The net foreign investment, i.e. net spending by foreign nationals, firms and governments for the country's goods and services*

d. *Government purchases of goods and services*

Items **not to be included** in NI under expenditure method:

a. *Government spending on old-age pension, scholarship, unemployment allowances, etc., is not included (these are counted in the private final consumption expenditure)*

b. *Expenditure on semi-finished goods is also not included*

c. *Expenditure on purchase of second-hand goods*

d. *Expenditure on purchase of shares, bonds and debentures*

e. *Imputed expenditures*

Thus, $\mathbf{NNP_{FC} = GDP_{MP} - Depreciation - Indirect\ Taxes + Subsidies + NFIA}$

did you KNOW?

Green GDP – In **1993**, it was first proposed by **United Nations**. It is calculated by taking into consideration the depletion of natural resources, environmental degradation and savings of resources of the environment into the national income accounts.

EXAM ESSENTIAL

PER CAPITA INCOME

It indicates the average income per person earned in a given area in a particular time period.

For a nation, Nominal PCI = NNP_{FC} at Current Prices/Total Population

Real PCI is then computed by adjusting inflation with the nominal PCI.

Year	1950–51	2024–25 (AE)
Indian Nominal Per Capita Income (at current prices)	₹7,513	₹2,00,162

Internationally, the PCI may be compared based on **Purchasing Power Parity** (PPP) method. **Purchasing Power Parity method** compares economic productivity and standards of living between countries. It compares different countries' currencies through a '**basket of goods**' approach where the prices of goods are compared. However, the task of this comparative analysis is not easy as the methods of computation of NI differ across nations and there are also exchange rate-related bottlenecks while computing PCI.

ROLE OF MEASURING NATIONAL INCOME

- Formulation of NI **quantifies the economic growth**; hence we can easily understand whether it is adequate or not for the stated objectives of the economy.
- It lets us **understand the potential** of the economy and accordingly helps to set objectives.
- NI data helps to take steps in order to **reduce inequalities** in income distribution.
- It also helps to **forecast tax revenues**.
- It **helps the corporate sector** to plan their business activities and investments.
- NI figures give us an idea of **inflationary or deflationary gaps**.
- NI figures help us compare **the standards of living of people in different countries and of people living in the same country at different times**.

LIMITATIONS IN THE MEASUREMENT OF NATIONAL INCOME

- It measures domestic economic performance only; it **does not measure the social welfare**.
- It **does not capture the non-market transactions** like the service of the homemakers, barter-based activities still done in some village haats, etc.
- It does not take into account the **negative externalities** of economic growth where there is a usual trade-off between economic growth and environmental degradation. More manufacturing activities could discharge more industrial waste, higher carbon dioxide emission, etc.
- Inclusion or exclusion of certain items in NI accounting can lead to erroneous results. **Difficulties in data collection** lead to more approximation errors.

FIRST ADVANCE ESTIMATES OF NATIONAL INCOME FOR 2024–25

- The Indian economy is predicted to grow at a solid 6.4 per cent in FY 2024–25, down from 8.2 per cent in the previous fiscal year.
- The construction sector is predicted to grow by 8.6 per cent. Furthermore, it is observed that Real GVA of Financial, Real Estate, and Professional Services sector will grow at a rate of 9.3 per cent in FY 2024–25.
- Real GVA of Agriculture and allied sectors has been estimated to grow at a rate of 3.8 per cent in FY 2024–25.
- Real GDP or GDP at Constant (2011–12) Prices in the year 2024–25 is estimated to be at a level of ₹184.88 lakh crore, as against the Provisional Estimate of GDP for the year 2023–24 of ₹173.82 lakh crore, released on 7th January, 2025.

IMPORTANT FACTS BASED ON THE REPORT OF MOSPI

First Advance Estimates of Annual GDP for FY2024–25 and its Expenditure Components (at Current Prices) (Rupees in Crore)

SL No.	Item	2022–23 (FRE)	2023–24 (PE)	2024–25 (FAE)	Percentage Change Over Previous Year	
					2023–24	2024–25
	Domestic Product					
1	GVA at Basic Prices	2,46,59,041	2,67,62,147	2,92,63,609	8.5	9.3
2	Net Taxes on Products	22,90,605	27,73,520	31,47,797	21.1	13.5
3	Gross Domestic Product (GDP)[@]	2,69,49,646	2,95,35,667	3,24,11,406	9.6	9.7
4	Net Domestic Product (NDP)	2,38,09,748	2,61,27,976	2,86,85,197	9.7	9.8
	Expenditure Components[#]					
5	Private Final Consumption Expenditure (PFCE)	1,64,22,535	1,78,22,526	2,00,29,580	8.5	12.4
6	Government Final Consumption Expenditure (GFCE)	28,83,649	30,68,970	33,30,598	6.4	8.5

SL No.	Item	2022–23 (FRE)	2023–24 (PE)	2024–25 (FAE)	Percentage Change Over Previous Year	
					2023–24	2024–25
7	Gross Fixed Capital Formation (GFCF)	82,86,979	91,07,021	97,63,363	9.9	7.2
8	Changes in Stocks (CIS)	2,77,120	2,95,198	3,19,249	6.5	8.1
9	Valuables	3,35,730	4,39,024	5,13,009	30.8	16.9
10	Exports	62,52,449	64,53,015	69,66,331	3.2	8.0
11	Imports	72,13,027	71,10,310	78,15,050	–1.4	9.9
12	Discrepancies	–2,95,789	–5,39,778	–6,95,674	–1.8	–2.1
13	GDP	2,69,49,646	2,95,35,667	3,24,11,406	9.6	9.7
	Share in GDP (%)					
14	Private Final Consumption Expenditure (PFCE)	60.9	60.3	61.8	–	–
15	Government Final Consumption Expenditure (GFCE)	10.7	10.4	10.3	–	–
16	Gross Fixed Capital Formation (GFCF)	30.7	30.8	30.1	–	–
17	Changes in Stocks (CIS)	1.0	1.0	1.0	–	–
18	Valuables	1.2	1.5	1.6	–	–
19	Exports	23.2	21.8	21.5	–	–
20	Imports	26.8	24.1	24.1	–	–
21	Discrepancies	–1.1	–1.8	–2.1	–	–
22	GDP	100.0	100.0	100.0	–	–
	National Product					
23	Gross National Income (GNI)	2,65,79,339	2,91,04,354	3,19,09,037	9.5	9.6
24	Net National Income (NNI)	2,34,39,442	2,56,96,663	2,81,82,828	9.6	9.7
25	Gross National Disposable Income (GNDI)	2,73,98,551	2,99,85,708	3,28,65,546	9.4	9.6
26	Net National Disposable Income (NNDI)	2,42,58,653	2,65,78,017	2,91,39,338	9.6	9.6
	Per Capita Income, National Product and Final Consumption					
27	Per Capita GDP (₹)	1,94,879	2,11,725	2,30,195	8.6	8.7
28	Per Capita GNI (₹)	1,92,201	2,08,633	2,26,627	8.5	8.6
29	Per Capita NNI (₹)	1,69,496	1,84,205	2,00,162	8.7	8.7
30	Per Capita GNDI (₹)	1,98,125	2,14,951	2,33,420	8.5	8.6
31	Per Capita PFCE (₹)	1,18,755	1,27,760	1,42,256	7.6	11.3

FRE: First Revised Estimates; PE: Provisional Estimates; FAE: First Advance Estimates

@GDP (Production/Income Approach) = GVA at Basic Price + Net Taxes on Products

#Following Expenditure Approach, GDP – PFCE + GFCE + GFCF + CIS + Valuable + Export – Import. Discrepancy refers to gap between GDP (Production/Income Approach) and GDP (Expenditure Approach). In case of Discrepancy percentage share in GDP is given instead of percentage changes over previous year.

SHAPES OF ECONOMIC RECOVERY

When economy goes into recession/depression due to situations like COVID-19 pandemic, then it recovers again when the situation normalises. However, this recovery can take various shapes:

- **Z-shaped recovery:** It is the most-optimistic scenario in which the economy quickly rises like a phoenix after a crash.

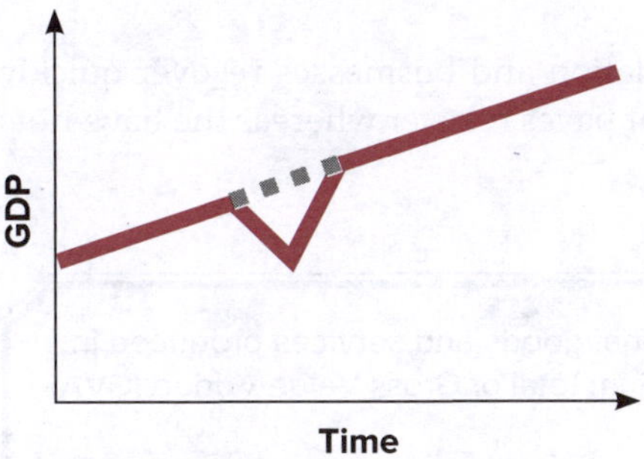

V-Shaped Recovery*

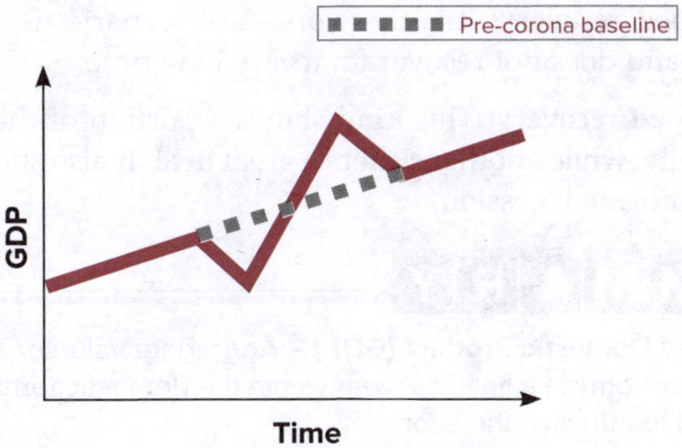

Z-Shaped Recovery*

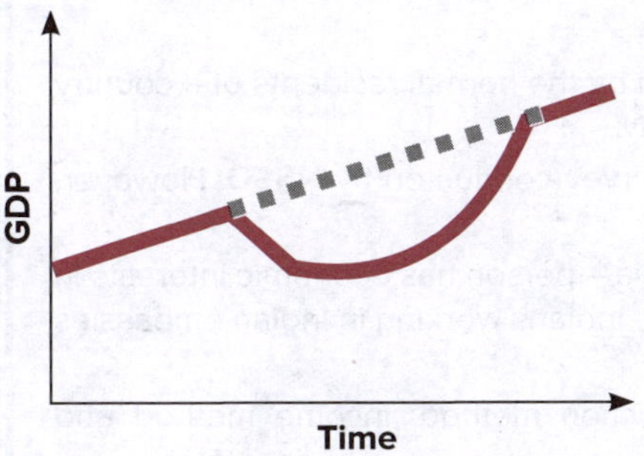

U-Shaped Recovery*

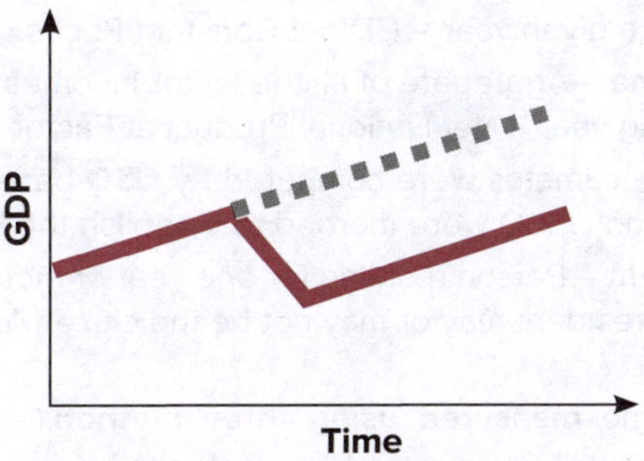

L-Shaped Recovery*

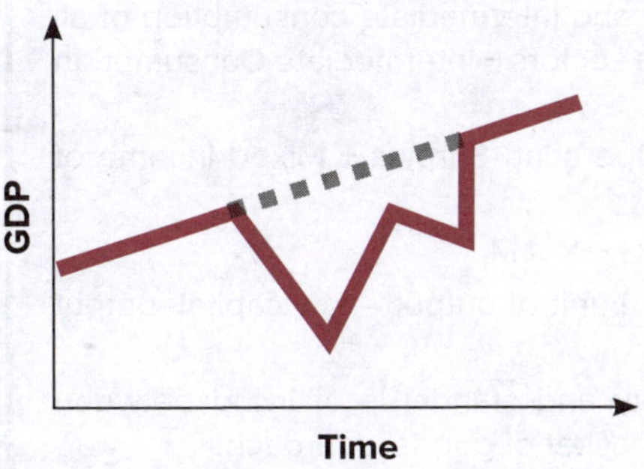

W-Shaped Recovery*

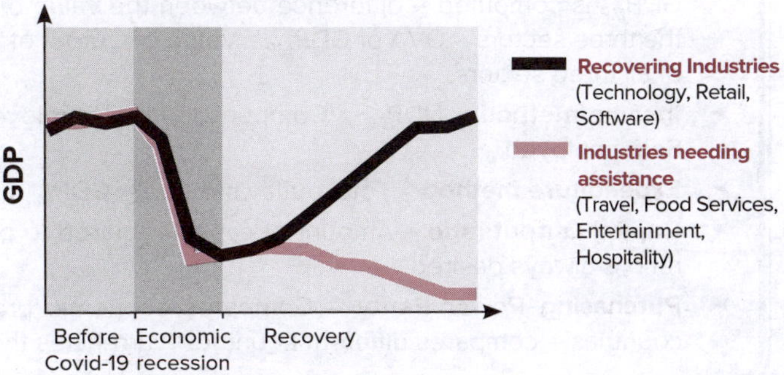

K-Shaped Recovery**

*Sources: *Hutchins Center on Fiscal and Monetary Policy, Brookings*
***US Chamber of Commerce*

- **V-shaped recovery:** In this, economy quickly recoups lost ground and gets back to the normal growth trend-line.
- **U-shaped recovery:** In this, the economy, after falling, struggles and muddles around a low growth rate for some time, before rising gradually to usual levels.
- **W-shaped recovery:** It is a dangerous scenario. Under this, growth falls and rises, but falls again before recovering yet again, thus forming a W-like chart.
- **L-shaped recovery:** It is the worst-case scenario, in which growth after falling, stagnates at low levels and does not recover for a very long time.
- **K-shaped recovery:** This kind shows a portion of the population and businesses recover quickly and fully, while another suffers a great deal. It also shows that haves recover whereas the have-nots suffer during recession.

SUMMARY

- **Gross Domestic Product (GDP)** – Aggregate value of all the final goods and services produced in an economy in a financial year within the domestic territory – Sum total of Gross Value Added (GVA) of all the firms in the economy.
- **Nominal GDP** – Market value of all goods and services in a financial year – GDP at Current Prices.
- **Real GDP** – Inflation-adjusted measure that reflects the value of all goods and services produced by an economy in a given year – GDP at Constant Prices.
- **National Income** – Aggregate of all the factor incomes earned by the normal residents of a country in an accounting year – Net National Product at Factor cost (NNP_{FC}).
- Since 1955, NI estimates were computed by **CSO** based on survey conducted by **NSSO**. However, in 2019, CSO and NSSO were merged to establish the **NSO**.
- **Normal Resident** – Person residing for one year or more in India – person has economic interests in India – normal resident may or may not be the citizen of India – Indians working in Indian embassies abroad.
- **National income measured using three methods** – Production method, Income method and Expenditure method.
- **Production method** – 'Output method' or 'Value added method' – Gross Value Added (GVA) or GDP_{MP} is computed – difference between the value of output and intermediate consumption of all the three sectors – GVA or GDP_{MP} = Value of Output of all three sectors – Intermediate Consumption of all three sectors.
- **Income method** – NDP_{FC} = Compensation to Employees + Operating Surplus + Mixed Income of Self-employed.
- **Expenditure method** – Total outlay method – $GDP_{MP} = C + I + G + X - M$.
- **Capital-Output ratio** – Amount of capital required to produce 1 unit of output – low capital–output ratio is always desired.
- **Purchasing Power Parity** – Compares economic productivity and standards of living between countries – compares different countries' currencies through 'basket of goods' approach.

UPSC CSE PREVIOUS YEARS' PRELIMINARY EXAMINATION QUESTIONS

1. With reference to the sectors of the Indian economy, consider the following pairs: **[2024]**

	Economic activity	*Sector*
1.	Storage of agricultural produce	Secondary
2.	Dairy farm	Primary
3.	Mineral exploration	Tertiary
4.	Weaving cloth	Secondary

How many of the pairs given above are correctly matched?
(a) Only one (b) Only two
(c) Only three (d) All four

2. Increase in absolute and per capita GNP do not connote a higher level of economic development, if **[2018]**
(a) industrial output fails to keep pace with agriculture output.
(b) agricultural output fails to keep pace with industrial output.
(c) poverty and unemployment increase.
(d) imports grow faster than exports.

3. Despite being a high-saving economy, capital formation may not result in significant increase in output due to **[2018]**
(a) weak administrative machinery.
(b) illiteracy.
(c) high population density.
(d) high capital–output ratio.

4. With reference to Indian economy, consider the following statements: **[2015]**
1. The rate of growth of Real GDP has steadily increased in the last decade.
2. The GDP at MP (in rupees) has steadily increased in the last decade.

Which of the statements given above is/are correct?
(a) 1 only (b) 2 only
(c) Both 1 and 2 (d) Neither 1 nor 2

5. The NI of a country for a given period is equal to the **[2013]**
(a) total value of goods and services produced by the nationals.
(b) sum of total consumption and investment expenditure.
(c) sum of PI of all individuals.
(d) money value of final goods and service produced.

6. A 'closed economy' is an economy in which **[2011]**
(a) The money supply is fully controlled.
(b) Deficit financing takes place.
(c) Only exports takes place.
(d) Neither exports nor imports take place.

7. With reference to Indian economy, consider the following statements: **[2010]**
1. The GDP has increased by four times in the last 10 years.
2. The percentage share of Public Sector in GDP has declined in the last 10 years.

Which of the statements given above is/are correct?
(a) 1 only (b) 2 only
(c) Both 1 and 2 (d) Neither 1 nor 2

☞ NO QUESTIONS ASKED
2023, 2022, 2021, 2020, 2019, 2017, 2014, 2012

ANSWER KEY

1. (b) 2. (c) 3. (d) 4. (b) 5. (d)
6. (d) 7. (b)

UPSC CSE PREVIOUS YEARS' MAIN EXAMINATION QUESTIONS

1. Explain the difference between computing methodology of India's Gross Domestic Product (GDP) before the year 2015 and after the year 2015. **[2021]**

2. Do you agree that the Indian economy has recently experienced V-shaped recovery? Give reasons in support of your answer. **[2021]**

3. Define potential GDP and explain its determinants. What are the factors that have been inhibiting India from realising its potential GDP? **[2020]**

4. What are the salient features of **'inclusive growth'**? Has India been experiencing such a growth process? Analyse and suggest measures for inclusive growth. **[2017]**

☞ NO QUESTIONS ASKED
2024, 2023, 2022, 2019, 2018, 2016, 2015, 2014, 2013, 2012

CHAPTER

3

ECONOMIC GROWTH *VERSUS* ECONOMIC DEVELOPMENT

CHAPTER OUTLINE

- Economic Growth and Economic Development
- Amartya Sen's Concept of Development
- Underdevelopment
- Inclusive Growth *versus* Economic Growth
- Major Indices of Economic Development
- Human Development Index (HDI)
- Gender Inequality Index
- Gender Development Index
- World Happiness Report
- OECD Better Life Index
- The Physical Quality of Life Index
- Sustainable Development Report
- Classification of Countries based on Economic Activities

ECONOMIC GROWTH AND ECONOMIC DEVELOPMENT

Economic Growth measures the **change in output or GDP** over a period of time. It refers to increase in the production of goods and services in an economy. It includes increase in capital goods, labour, technology and human capital.

Economic Growth Rate $= \frac{\text{Change in GDP}}{\text{Last Year's GDP}} \times 100$

On the other hand, Economic Development is a **broader concept,** and it deals with other socio-economic indicators like poverty, unemployment, gender equity, income equality, health, education, etc., **along with** the aspect of economic growth.

Thus, economic growth only signifies the quantitative changes, whereas economic development reflects both improvements in the quantity and quality of well-being in the economy. Economic growth can be measured in the **short term** and for a certain period, but economic development is a **continuous process** and is measured in the **long term.**

It is not possible to quantify economic development.

Basis	Economic Growth	Economic Development
Meaning	It takes into account **quantitative aspects only**.	It takes into account **both quantitative and qualitative aspects**.
Scope	The scope of economic growth is **narrow**.	The scope of economic development is **broader**.

Basis	Economic Growth	Economic Development
Measurement Indicators	Indicators like **GDP, GNP, Per Capita Income**, etc., are considered to measure Economic Growth.	Indicators like **HDI, GII, GDI, GNHI**, etc., are considered.
Term	It is a **short-term** process, measured in a specific time period.	It involves more a **long-term** process.
Target	Target is on the **production** of resources, like goods and services.	Target is on the **optimum distribution and utilisation** of resources.
Applicable to	It is a more relevant indicator to measure the progress in **Developed Countries**.	It is more relevant for measuring the development in **Developing Countries**.

Factors that influence Economic Development

Economic Factors

- Natural Resources
- Capital Formation
- Excess Output in Agriculture
- Structural Change
- Efficient Financial System, etc.

Non-Economic Factors

- Human Capital
- Education, Technology and Skill Development
- Effective Law and Order System
- Ethical and Social Values, etc.

Challenges/Obstacles to Economic Growth and Development

- Extensive population burden as compared to available resources.
- High dependence on agriculture.
- Less per-capita income and unequal distribution of income.
- Unavailability of adequate infrastructure facility for speedy growth and development.
- Possible menace of corruption in the developmental and growth process.
- Unsustainable use of natural resources in many instances.
- Problem of unemployment, skill mismatch and unskilled labour force.
- Distracted priorities regarding economic growth and development.

Ways to Overcome Challenges

- Improvement of infrastructure by investing more capital.
- Improvement in the systems of education through proper implementation of New Education Policy (NEP) and skill-based education.
- Strengthening the financial system by improving the banking network and addressing the issue of NPAs.
- Improving the health sector by spending more capital and better implementation of welfare schemes.
- Improving the productivity of agriculture sector by using modern technologies and by reducing disguised unemployment.

- To reduce the levels of corruption through relevant measures such as digitalising the processes involved, etc.

AMARTYA SEN'S CONCEPT OF DEVELOPMENT

Development as Freedom is a book about international development written by economist Amartya Sen in 1999. The treatise has been praised as a way forward and approach for a more humane society.

- According to Sen, "We live in a world of unprecedented opulence, of a kind that would have been hard even to imagine a century or two ago. And yet we also live in a world with remarkable deprivation, destitution and oppression." Overcoming these problems is crucial for exercise of development. The concept Development is associated with the elimination of various types of unfreedoms which present little choice and opportunity.
- Development needs doing away with major sources of unfreedoms, poverty, tyranny, poor economic opportunities, systematic social deprivation, etc.
- He has argued that, Freedom is essential to the process of development for two reasons.
  (i) "Assessment of progress has to be done primarily in terms of whether the freedoms that people have, are enhanced";
  (ii) "Achievement of development is thoroughly dependent on the free agency of people".
- **Five distinct types of freedom**, investigated in the empirical studies are:
  (i) political freedoms,
  (ii) economic facilities,
  (iii) social opportunities,
  (iv) transparency guarantees
  (v) protective security.
- Economic development has other dimensions. It is precisely linked with economic security. Economic insecurity is associated with the lack of democratic rights and liberties. The working of democracy and of political rights can assist to address economic disasters.

UNDERDEVELOPMENT

Underdevelopment or low-level development is characterised by the low level of per capita income of a country. In underdeveloped countries, the primary sector provides employment to a large extent.

There are several common features of underdeveloped countries like low GNP per capita, relatively low capital formation, high levels of unemployment and underemployment, low levels of productivity of labour, high level of poverty and income inequality, low human capital, etc.

Composite Development Index – The **Raghuram Rajan Committee** submitted its report on a new underdevelopment index called Composite Development Index, in **2013.**

The Committee suggested this index to determine (under)development of States. The index had **10 subcomponents** carrying equal weightage: (i) monthly per capita consumption expenditure, (ii) education, (iii) health, (iv) household amenities, (v) poverty rate, (vi) female literacy, (vii) per cent of SC–ST population, (viii) urbanisation rate, (ix) financial inclusion, (x) connectivity.

EXAM ESSENTIAL

INCLUSIVE GROWTH *VERSUS* ECONOMIC GROWTH

Inclusive growth reflects economic growth, the benefits of which percolate to all the sections of the society. It should **benefit everyone** regardless of their economic class, sex, caste, creed, region or religion. Thus, inclusive growth is a **better approach** than economic growth, and it should be the target of policymakers.

Salient Features of Inclusive Growth:

- Reduction of vertical as well as horizontal income inequalities in the economy
- Reduction in regional disparities
- Balanced growth of all the three sectors in the economy
- Reduction in the levels of poverty in a way that the gap between the 'haves' and 'have nots' gets reduced

The approach for economic growth should be focused on the **principle of equity**.

Inclusive growth is expected to reduce poverty faster in the sense that it has a higher elasticity of poverty reduction.

Inclusive growth must ensure access of people to basic infrastructure and basic services/capabilities such as basic health and education. This access should include not only the quantity but also the quality of these basic services.

Keeping in mind these salient features, inclusive growth may be planned either based on a **trickle-down** approach or through direct attack on poverty using targeted welfare schemes.

Challenges in achieving Inclusive Growth in India:

- According to Global Multidimensional Poverty Index 2024, India has still more than 234 million people who are poor. India has successfully halved its MPI value over the past 15 years. According to the NITI Aayog's Discussion Paper '*Multidimensional Poverty in India since 2005–06*', India has registered a notable reduction in multidimensional poverty from 29.17% in 2013–14 to 11.28% in 2022–23, i.e. a reduction of 17.89 percentage points. However, India still suffers from poverty due to reasons such as corruption, lack of education, mismatch between skill and job requirement, etc.
- Other factors include low job growth, lack of modernisation in agriculture, social backwardness, regional disparities, etc.

Inclusive Development Index (IDI) – The index measures progress of 103 countries on three pillars – growth and development; inclusion; inter-generational equity. India ranked 62nd among the 74 Emerging Economies on Inclusive Development Index (IDI-2018) **published by the World Economic Forum (WEF)**.

HUMAN DEVELOPMENT INDEX (HDI)

- The term 'human development' refers to the process of enlarging people's choices, expansion of human capabilities, freedom and human rights. According to the noted economist Mahbub ul Haq, there are **four essential pillars** of human development – **Equality**, **Sustainability**, **Productivity**, and **Empowerment**.
- The **Human Development Index (HDI)** is a summary measure of average achievement in key dimensions of human development: **a long and healthy life, being knowledgeable and having a decent standard of living.**
- HDI is a part of Human Development Report published **annually** since 1990 by the United Nations Development Programme **(UNDP).**

- The **other 4 indices** that form the part of Human Development Report are: Inequality-adjusted Human Development Index **(IHDI);** Gender Development Index **(GDI);** Gender Inequality Index **(GII)** and Multidimensional Poverty Index **(MPI).**
- HDI is used to rank countries in terms of human development by combining the measurement of 3 dimensions: Long and Healthy Life, Knowledge and Decent Standard of Living. The HDI is the geometric mean of normalised indices for each of the three dimensions.
- HDI may be used to question the country's national policy choices and asking how two countries with the same level of GNI per capita may end up with different human development outcomes.
- The index value of HDI varies between **0 and 1.**
- Countries are grouped into four categories depending on the value and ranking:
  - **very high** for HDI of 0.800 and above
  - **high** from 0.700 to 0.799
  - **medium** from 0.550 to 0.699
  - **low** below 0.550
- Details about dimensions and parameters used to compute HDI are placed below:

Dimension	Indicator within the Dimension
Long and Healthy Life	Life Expectancy at Birth
Knowledge	Expected Years of Schooling for School Entering Child
	Mean Years of Schooling for Adult Aged 25 Years
Decent Standard of Living	Gross National Income per capita (in PPP $)

- **Inequality-Adjusted Human Development Index:** Continuing since 2010, IHDI considers **inequality** as the fourth dimension. IHDI indicates percentage loss in HDI due to inequality. The IHDI considers not only the average achievements of a country on health, education and income but also how those achievements are **distributed** among its citizens by 'discounting' each dimension's average value according to its level of inequality.
- As per Human Development Report 2023–2024 (based on 2022 data), India's IHDI value in 2022 is 0.444, overall loss from HDI is 31.1 per cent (inequality in life expectance is 17.3 per cent, inequality in education 36.9% and inequality in income 37.4 per cent)
- **According to Human Development Report 2023–2024 / HDR 2023–2024 (Based on 2022 Data)**
  - **India's Rank/Position in HDI is 134th out of 193 countries** (India's rank was 132nd out of 191 countries in HDR 2021–22) but **India's HDI value is increased to 0.644** (it was 0.633 in HDR 2021–22). India is placed in Medium Human Development Category.
  - India's performance **improved in 2022 across all HDI indicators** – Life Expectancy for India rose from 67.2 to 67.7 years, GNI Per Capita increased from \$6542 to \$6951, Mean Years of Schooling increased to 6.57 and Expected Years of Schooling increased to 12.6.
  - Switzerland maintains top position (HDI value 0.967) followed by Norway (HDI value 0.966) and Iceland (HDI value 0.959). Somalia ranked last (HDI value 0.380).
  - The **Theme** of Human Development Report 2023–24 was – **'Breaking The Gridlock: Reimaging Cooperation in a Polarized World'**
  - If we look at our neighbours, Nepal is at 146th, Bhutan's rank is 125th (Medium Human Development Category), Pakistan is at 164th, Afghanistan is at 182nd (Low Human Development

Category), China's rank is 75th and Sri Lanka is at 78th position (High Human Development Category).

- **Planetary Pressures-adjusted HDI (PHDI): UNDP** introduced a new metric in 2020, to adjust the HDI value by the impact caused by each country's per-capita **carbon emissions** and its material footprint. It measures the amount of fossil fuels, metals and other resources used to make the goods and services, to account for excessive human pressures on the planet.

Gender Inequality Index (GII)

Gender Inequality Index is a new index for determination of gender disparity that was pioneered in the 2010 HDI Report by UNDP. This index is a composite evaluation which captures the loss of accomplishment, within a nation, due to gender inequality and uses three dimensions to do so:

1. Reproductive health
2. Empowerment
3. Labour market participation

According to Human Development Report 2023–2024:

- The GII value for India shows progress, **India's value 0.437** which is better than Global Average of 0.462 and South Asian Average of 0.478.
- **India's rank is 108 out of 166 countries in this report**.
- India's adolescent birth rate in 2022 is 16.3 (births per 1000 women ages 15–19), it is improved from 17.1 in 2021.
- It is also noted that India' has one of the large Gender Gaps in the Labour Force Participation Rate (% aged 15 and older) – a 47.8% difference between male: 76.1 per cent and female: 28.3 per cent.

Gender Development Index (GDI)

UNDP calculates GDI as a part of its Human Development Report. GDI is the ratio of female to male HDI values.

- GDI measures Gender Gap on three dimensions: 1. Life Expectancy at Birth, 2. Schooling Year for Adults and 3. Standard of Living (GNI Per Capita)
- According to HDR 2023–2024, India's performance is not up to the mark in eradicating Gender Gap.
- **India's GDI value in 2022 was 0.852, GDI value for males was 0.684 and for females was 0.582.**
- According to this report, Life Expectancy at Birth for males and females are 66.3 and 69.4 years respectively.
- Mean Years of Schooling is 7.6 for males and 5.5 for females. Expected Years of schooling for both females and males is 12.6. GNI Per Capita for females stood at US$2958 and for males stood at US$10696.

GLOBAL GENDER GAP REPORT AND INDEX

- This report is released by **World Economic Forum (WEF)**. This report evaluates the status of gender parity.
- It was first introduced in 2006.

- This report is calculated on the basis of four important dimensions – 1. Economic Participation and Opportunity, 2. Educational Attainment, 3. Health and Survival, 4. Political Empowerment.
- On the basis of the above four sub-indices, the Global Gender Gap Index is prepared (Score lies between 0 and 1, where 1 shows full gender parity and 0 shows complete imparity).

> **did you KNOW?**
>
> **According to Global Gender Gap Report 2024:**
> - Iceland (score – 0.935) remains the **world's most gender-equal country**, followed by Finland, Norway, and New Zealand.
> - India ranked 129 (score – 0.641) among 146 countries.
> - The **global gender gap score** in 2024 was **68.5%**, a 0.1% point improvement from 2023.

WORLD HAPPINESS REPORT

- The World Happiness Report is published **annually** by the *United Nations Sustainable Development Solutions Network.*
- The Report was first published in the year 2012.
- The said **rankings are based on polling** (based on Gallup World Poll data) which takes into account **six key variables:**
  1. *GDP per capita [in terms of Purchasing Power Parity (PPP)]*
  2. *Social support*
  3. *Healthy life expectancy at birth*
  4. *Freedom to make life choices*
  5. *Generosity*
  6. *Perceptions of corruption*

World Happiness Report 2025

- India improved its rank to **118th among 147 countries.** The country's score improved from 4.054 to 4.389 out of 10.
- Finland topped the list for the eighth consecutive year, followed closely by Denmark and Iceland. Afghanistan holds the last spot. Joining it at the bottom of the rankings are Sierra Leone and Lebanon.
- India's strength lies in high social support due to strong family structures and community bonds, its weaknesses include low perceived freedom.

> **did you KNOW?**
>
> **International Day of Happiness** is celebrated every year on **March 20** under the initiative of the United Nations, which recognises the pursuit of happiness as a fundamental human goal.
> - The theme for 2024 was *Reconnecting for Happiness: Building Resilient Communities.*
> - The theme for 2025 is *Caring and Sharing.*

Gross National Happiness (GNH) Index

Gross National Happiness is a term coined by His Majesty, the Fourth King of Bhutan, Jigme Singye Wangchuck, in the 1970s. The concept implies that sustainable development should take a holistic approach towards notions of progress and give equal importance to non-economic aspects of well-being. The **Gross National Happiness Index** is a single number index developed from 33 indicators categorised under nine domains.

The concept of GNH has often been explained by its four pillars: good governance, sustainable socio-economic development, cultural preservation and environmental conservation.

BONUS KNOWLEDGE

Delhi's Happiness Curriculum – The curriculum is one of the flagship schemes of the Delhi government in the education sector launched in 2018. The learning outcomes are spread across four categories: becoming mindful and attentive, developing critical thinking and reflection, developing social-emotional skills and developing a confident and pleasant personality.

Madhya Pradesh became the first State in India to set up **'Happiness Department'** (in 2016). The Department **(Anand Sansthan)** works as knowledge resource centre about happiness on the lines of Bhutan. Andhra Pradesh became the second State to have Happiness Department.

- **Organisation for Economic Co-operation and Development (OECD) Better Life Index:** This Index compares well-being across countries, based on 11 topics which OECD has identified as essential, in the areas of material living conditions and quality of life. The 11 topics include Housing, Income, Jobs, Community, Education, Environment, Civic Engagement, Health, Life Satisfaction, Safety and Work–Life Balance.
- **The Physical Quality of Life Index (PQLI):** It measures the quality of life or well-being of a country. The value is the average of three statistics: basic literacy rate, infant mortality and life expectancy at age one. It was developed for the Overseas Development Council in the mid-1970s by Morris David Morris.

CLASSIFICATION OF COUNTRIES BASED ON ECONOMIC ACTIVITIES

Based on Per Capita Income, World Bank has classified countries into four categories:

Category	Per Capita Income (US$)
Low income	<1,005
Low middle income	1,006–3,995
Upper middle income	3,956–12,235
High income	>12,235

- **Developed Country:** An industrialised country (or post-industrial country), more developed country, or More Economically Developed Country (MEDC) is a sovereign state that has a developed economy and advanced technological infrastructure relative to other less industrialised nations. Example is the USA.
- **Developing Country:** A relatively less industrialised nation which is based on primary activities but is thriving for new industrial development such as services (India) or mass production (China).
- **Least Developed Countries:** Least Developed Countries (LDCs) are low-income countries confronting severe structural impediments to sustainable development. They are highly vulnerable to economic and environmental shocks and have low levels of human assets. Examples include Somalia, Sudan, etc.

SUMMARY

- **Economic Growth** – Measures the change in output or GDP over a period of time.
- **Economic Development** – Deals with socio-economic indicators like poverty, unemployment, gender equity, income equality, health, education, etc., along with the aspect of economic growth.
- **Inclusive growth** – Reflects economic growth, the benefits of which percolate to all the sections of the society – better approach than economic growth, and it should be the target of policymakers.
- **Composite Development Index** – Determines (under)development of States – suggested by Raghuram Rajan Committee in 2013 – has 10 sub-components which carry equal weightage.
- **Inclusive Development Index (IDI)** – Growth and development; inclusion; inter-generational equity – published by the World Economic Forum (WEF).
- **Human Development Index (HDI)** – Summary measure of average achievement in key dimensions of human development – a long and healthy life, being knowledgeable and having a decent standard of living.
- **Planetary Pressures-adjusted HDI (PHDI)** – New metric to adjust the HDI value by the impact caused by each country's per-capita carbon emissions and its material footprint. **Global Gender Gap Index (GGGI)** – Published by World Economic Forum.
- **World Happiness Report** – Published annually by the United Nations Sustainable Development Solutions Network.
- **OECD Better Life Index** – Compares well-being across countries – based on 11 topics in the areas of material living conditions and quality of life.
- **Physical Quality of Life Index (PQLI)** – Measures the quality of life or well-being of a country – value is the average of three statistics: basic literacy rate, infant mortality and life expectancy at age one.

UPSC CSE PREVIOUS YEARS' PRELIMINARY EXAMINATION QUESTIONS

1. Consider the following statements: **[2018]**
   Human capital formation as a concept is better explained in terms of a process which enables
   1. individuals of a country to accumulate more capital.
   2. increasing the knowledge, skill levels and capacities of the people of the country.
   3. accumulation of tangible wealth.
   4. accumulation of intangible wealth.

   Which of the statements given above is/are correct?
   (a) 1 and 2 (b) 2 only
   (c) 2 and 4 only (d) 1, 3 and 4 only
2. Economic growth in country X will necessarily have to occur if **[2013]**
   (a) there is technical progress in the world economy.
   (b) there is population growth in X.
   (c) there is capital formation in X.
   (d) the volume of trade grows in the world economy.
3. Which of the following can be said to be essentially the parts of Inclusive Governance? **[2012]**
   1. Permitting the Non-Banking Financial Companies to do banking
   2. Establishing effective District Planning Committees in all the districts
   3. Increasing the government spending on public health
   4. Strengthening the Mid-day Meal Scheme

   Select the correct answer using the codes given below:
   (a) 1 and 2 only (b) 3 and 4 only
   (c) 2, 3 and 4 only (d) 1, 2, 3 and 4

NO QUESTIONS ASKED
2024, 2023, 2022, 2021, 2020, 2019, 2017, 2016, 2015, 2014

ANSWER KEY

1. (c) 2. (c) 3. (c)

UPSC CSE PREVIOUS YEARS' MAIN EXAMINATION QUESTIONS

1. Is inclusive growth possible under market economy? State the significance of financial inclusion in achieving economic growth in India. **[2022]**
2. It is argued that the strategy of inclusive growth is intended to meet the objectives of inclusiveness and sustainability together. Comment on this statement. **[2019]**
3. What are the salient features of 'inclusive growth'? Has India been experiencing such a growth process? Analyse and suggest measures for inclusive growth. **[2017]**
4. Comment on the challenges for inclusive growth which include careless and useless manpower in the Indian context. Suggest measures to be taken for facing these challenges. **[2016]**

NO QUESTIONS ASKED
2024, 2023, 2021, 2020, 2018, 2015, 2014, 2013

CHAPTER

4

POVERTY AND INEQUALITY

CHAPTER OUTLINE

- Poverty
- Causes of Poverty in India
- Absolute Poverty
- Multi-Dimensional Poverty Index
- Methods to Estimate Absolute Poverty
- Various Estimates of Poverty in India
- Pre-Independence Estimates
- Post-Independence Estimates
- BPL Census
- Amartya Sen's Capability Approach on Poverty
- Randomised Controlled Trial
- Universal Basic Income
- Inequality
- Causes of Income Inequality
- Methods to Measure Income Inequality
- Present Status of Income Inequality in India – A Global Comparison
- Impact of Income Inequality
- Measures taken by the Government to Combat Income Inequality

POVERTY

- It is a state in which a person or community lacks the financial resources and is **unable to fulfil even its basic necessities** of life.
- In India, the generally accepted definition of poverty emphasises on **minimum level of living** rather than reasonable level of living.
- Previously, the Planning Commission was the authority which published poverty estimates based on various rounds conducted by the **National Sample Survey Office** (NSSO) based on monthly per capita consumption expenditure.
- At present, the poverty estimates are compiled by the **National Statistical Office (NSO)** under the **Ministry of Statistics and Programme Implementation**.

> **did you KNOW?** 17 October is declared as the *International Day for Eradication of Poverty* by the United Nations (**since 1987**).

BONUS KNOWLEDGE

IBSA TRUST FUND AGREEMENT, 2017

India, Brazil and South Africa signed the IBSA Trust Fund Agreement that seeks **to fight poverty** in **other** developing countries. Each country contributes **USD 1 million** annually to this fund, which is managed by the UNDP Special Unit for South–South Cooperation. Since inception, India has contributed around US$ 15.1 million to IBSA Fund.

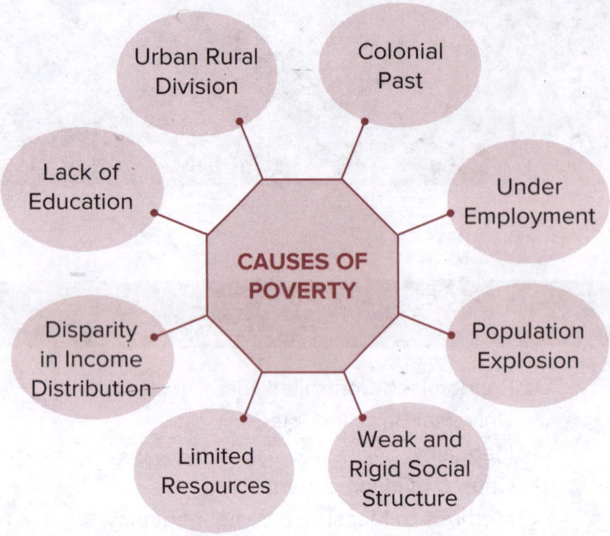

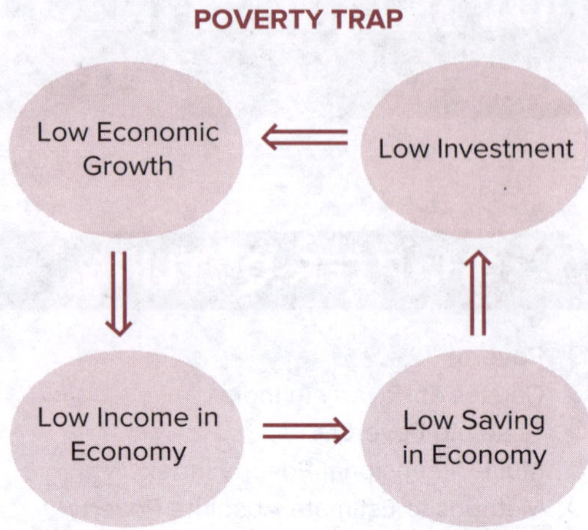

Concept of Poverty

The concept of poverty can be classified into the following four types:

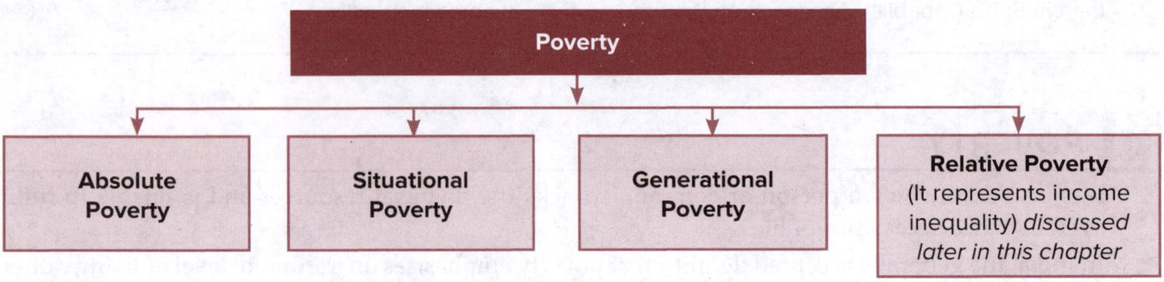

ABSOLUTE POVERTY

- It is a condition which occurs **due to deprivation from basic human needs** such as food, clothing, health, education, sanitation facilities, shelter, etc.
- It is measured through the concept of **poverty line** and refers to the actual number of people living Below Poverty Line (BPL).

Measures used to Estimate Absolute Poverty

1. Poverty Line

- It is the **required level of income to fulfil basic necessities** of life.
- It can be represented in terms of either *per capita calorie intake or per capita consumption expenditure* required to attain a minimum living condition.
- It **may vary from one country to another**. It may also vary from one state to another in India due to different price levels prevailing in the country.

Example: A poverty line may be ₹47 per capita consumption expenditure per day. Any person who is not able to spend this amount on an average for his/her personal consumption in a day is considered poor.

did you KNOW? As per the **World Bank**, the present **International Poverty Line** is **$2.15** per capita per day consumption expenditure (based on 2017 prices) and is found out by averaging the national poverty lines of the poorest 15 countries.

As per the World Bank, any person living on less than **$2.15 per day** is considered facing **extreme poverty**.

2. Head Count Ratio (HCR)/Poverty Incidence Ratio
(for measuring the incidence of poverty)

- It indicates the **percentage of people living** BPL.
- $$\text{HCR} = \frac{\text{Total no. of BPL people}}{\text{Total population}} \times 100$$
  - For example – 13.31 crore/121 crore × 100 = 11 per cent
  - This 11 per cent is nothing but the Percentage of BPL people living in a country.
- HCR indicates the *incidence of poverty* in a nation. Hence, it is also termed as **poverty incidence ratio**.

A previous World Bank report indicated that India's poverty HCR reached a maximum of 61.6 per cent in 1977. However, as per the **2022 report by the World Bank**, India's HCR had reduced to 11.9 per cent in 2021 (*based on International Poverty Line at $2.15 per day (2017 PPP)*). The driving factor behind this drastic reduction in poverty (in comparison to previous years) has been identified as **rural electrification, spending on schooling of girls**, etc. However, as per the findings of NITI Aayog's Discussion Paper: '**Multidimensional Poverty in India since 2005–06**', there is steep decline in Poverty Headcount Ratio from 29.17 per cent in 2013–14 to **11.28 per cent in 2022–23**.

3. Poverty Gap Ratio (for measuring the intensity of poverty)

- Poverty gap is the difference between the poverty line and the average actual monthly consumption expenditure of a BPL household. It **indicates average shortfall from the poverty line**.
- *In mathematical terms,*

  Poverty gap ratio = *(Poverty line in monetary terms – Average actual monthly consumption expenditure per capita of a BPL household)/poverty line*

  For example: (400 – 330)/400 = 0.175, which indicates that there is a gap of 17.5 per cent.
- Through this measure, the government can derive the **per capita amount of transfers** required to eliminate poverty. It may be done **through perfectly targeted cash transfers**.
- More the poverty gap, more are the transfers required to be done by the government to bring BPL households above the poverty line.

4. Squared Poverty Gap Index

- The **Squared Poverty Gap Index determines the degree of poverty for a given area**.
- This method **squares the poverty gap** for each individual/household.
- The shortfalls of BPL people are squared giving the very poor much more weight than those falling only a few cents short of the poverty line.

- The Squared Poverty Gap Index is more beneficial to the very poor who are further away from the poverty line because they will receive more amount as aid from the government.

EXAM ESSENTIAL

MULTI-DIMENSIONAL POVERTY INDEX (MPI)

- It is a **broader concept** which says that poverty not only depends upon the income but also includes deprivation such as poor *health, lack of education and inadequate standard of living*.
- These deprivations are measured **on the household as well as on an individual level**.
- MPI **measures 'acute' poverty** based on overlapping deprivations instead of the World Bank's measure of 'extreme' poverty that captures those living on less than $1.90 a day.
- This MPI concept was developed by **the UN Development Programme (UNDP) and OPHI (Oxford Poverty and Human Development Initiative)** and first introduced in 2010.
- MPI replaced the concept of Human Poverty Index.
- Instead of income, MPI **uses three dimensions** (having **10 indicators** to measure absolute poverty)
- Those 3 dimensions and 10 indicators under MPI are mentioned in the below table.

Dimensions of Poverty	Indicator	Condition for Treating It (Deprivation)	Weight	Related SDG Area
Education	Years of Schooling	Deprived if no family member (≥*10 years of age*) has completed 6 years of schooling	$1/6^{th}$	SDG 4 (Quality Education)
	School Attendance	Deprived if any school-aged child is not attending school up to class VIII	$1/6^{th}$	SDG 4 (Quality Education)
Health	Child Mortality	Deprived if any child of the family has died in the past 5 years	$1/6^{th}$	SDG 3 (Health and Well-Being)
	Nutrition	Deprived if any adult (*under 70 years of age*) or child is stunted	$1/6^{th}$	SDG 2 (Zero Hunger)
Standard of Living	Electricity	Deprived if no electricity	$1/18^{th}$	SDG 7 (Affordable and Clean Energy)
	Sanitation	Deprived if sanitation facility not improved as per Sustainable Development Goals (SDGs) guidelines or it is improved but shared with other households	$1/18^{th}$	SDG 6 (Clean Water and Sanitation)
	Drinking Water	Deprived if does not have safe drinking water as per SDGs guidelines or it is a 30-minute walk (*round trip*) from home	$1/18^{th}$	SDG 6 (Clean Water and Sanitation)
	Housing	Deprived if housing material is inadequate for one roof, walls and floor and/or made up of natural materials	$1/18^{th}$	SDG 11 (Sustainable Cities and Communities)
	Cooking Fuel	Deprived if cooks with dung, wood, charcoal or coal	$1/18^{th}$	SDG 7 (Affordable and Clean Energy)

Dimensions of Poverty	Indicator	Condition for Treating It (Deprivation)	Weight	Related SDG Area
	Assets	Deprived if household does not own any of these – radio, TV, telephone, computer, animal cart, bicycle, motor bike or refrigerator and does not own a car or truck	1/18th	SDG 1 (No Poverty)

Mathematically,

MPI = Percentage of people who are MPI poor (*Incidence of Poverty*) × Average intensity of MPI poverty across the poor (%)

A person is considered multi-dimensionally poor (or 'MPI poor') if he/she is **deprived in at least one–third of the weighted indicators** shown above; in other words, the cut-off for poverty is 33.33 per cent.

Key Findings of 2024 MPI Report

- Across 112 countries and 6.3 billion people, 1.1 billion people (18.3%) live in acute multidimensional poverty in 2023.
- 83.7% of poor people live in rural areas.
- Nearly two-thirds of poor people live in middle income countries.
- Large proportions of the poor people lack adequate sanitation, housing and cooking fuel.
- Majority of the countries significantly reduced poverty according to the MPI value in at least one time period.
- Countries at war have higher deprivations in every Multidimensional Poverty Index indicator.
- **India's MPI score is 0.105 with 234 million people living in multidimensional poverty** as per the 2024 report.

National Multidimensional Poverty Index (NMPI)

- **NITI Aayog has released** the NMPI based on the National Family Health Survey (NFHS-4) 2015–16.
- India's headcount ratio is **11.28 per cent** in 2022–23.
- **Uttar Pradesh** registered the largest decline in the number of poor with 5.94 crore people escaping multidimensional poverty during the last nine years, followed by Bihar at 3.77 crore, Madhya Pradesh at 2.30 crore and Rajasthan at 1.87 crore.

Methods to Estimate Absolute Poverty

EXAM ESSENTIAL

The following **three methods** are used:

(a) Uniform Reference/Recall Period (URP)

(b) Mixed Reference/Recall Period (MRP)

(c) Modified Mixed Reference/Recall Period (MMRP)

(a) URP Until 1993–94, the poverty line estimated by NSSO was based on URP. Under URP, consumption data **for ALL items** are collected for a **30-day recall period**. When URP is applied, the households are surveyed about their consumption in the last 30 days preceding the date of survey.

(b) MRP From 1999–2000 onwards, NSSO started using MRP instead of URP. MRP takes into account consumption expenditure for **five non-food items** (*clothing, footwear, durable goods, education and institutional medical expenses*) **for a 365-day** recall period, and consumption data for the remaining items are collected for a 30-day recall period.

Currently, all poverty line estimates **use the MRP method**.

(c) MMRP

- MMRP is the most recent concept out of the three.
- Under MMRP, **(a)** 365-day recall period is used for *clothing, footwear, education, institutional medical care and durable goods*, **(b)** 7-day recall period for *edible oil, egg, fish and meat, vegetables, fruits, spices, beverages, refreshments, processed food, paan, tobacco and intoxicants* and **(c)** 30-day recall period for the *remaining food items, fuel and light, miscellaneous goods and services including non-institutional medical, rents and taxes*.
- The MMRP method was used by NSSO to compute poverty for the years 2009–10 and 2010–11.
- The Rangarajan Committee in its 2014 report recommended MMRP as a more suitable method to measure poverty as compared to URP and MRP methods.
- The World Bank in 2015 also supported the idea of shifting from MRP to MMRP.

Poverty Estimates under URP vis-à-vis MRP vis-à-vis MMRP – *A Comparative Analysis*

If URP Method is Used	If MRP Method is Used	If MMRP Method is Used
Poverty estimates will be highest as compared to MRP or MMRP.	Poverty estimates will be less as compared to URP but will be more than in the case of MMRP.	Poverty estimates will be lower as compared to URP or MRP.

BONUS KNOWLEDGE

INCOME-BASED POVERTY LINE *vs.* CONSUMPTION EXPENDITURE–BASED POVERTY LINE

NSSO estimates the poverty line based on consumption expenditure to be a better measure than the income-based poverty line for reasons such as the following:

- Income is irregular for a majority of households in the informal sector, but their consumption patterns are comparatively stable.
- Use of URP, MRP or MMRP may not be feasible to compute income-based poverty line.

SITUATIONAL POVERTY

It is defined as when someone falls below the poverty line because of sudden causes like death, unemployment, natural disaster, divorce, etc. It persists until they find new sources of income or assets.

GENERATIONAL POVERTY

It is defined as staying under poverty for two or more generations consecutively. Like assets, this poverty is passed down to the next generation. This phenomenon is also termed intergenerational poverty.

VARIOUS ESTIMATES OF POVERTY IN INDIA

Pre-Independence Estimates

- The first estimate of poverty was made by **Shri Dadabhai Naoroji** in his book **Poverty and the Unbritish Rule in India**. He computed subsistence based on poverty line ranging from **₹16 to ₹35 per capita per year** at 1867–68 prices.
- He never used the word 'poverty line' **but instead used 'subsistence-based poverty line'**.
- Later in 1938, the National Planning Committee (headed by Shri J.L. Nehru) regarded an irreducible minimum income between ₹15 and ₹25 per capita per month at pre-war prices. However, **it was not tagged as poverty line of the country**.
- In 1944, the Bombay Plan suggested a poverty line of ₹75 per capita per year.

Post-Independence Estimates

Name of the Committee/Group	Data Based on	Details of Method Used	Estimates of Poverty (HCR)
B.S. Minhas's Study (in the 1950s)	1956–57	All these four committees used the same source of data for their studies, but their estimates of poverty were different due to the different methodologies adopted by them.	65%
M.S. Ahluwalia's Study (in the 1960s)	1960–61		39%
P.D. Ojha's Estimate (in the 1960s)	1960–61		44%
P.K. Bardhan's Study (in the 1960s)	1968–69		54%
V.M. Dandekar and Neel Kantha Rath Committee (*report submitted in 1971*)	1960–61	• It fixed 2,250 calories intake as the desired minimum level of nutrition (Minimum Consumption Line) per capita per day and on that basis estimated poverty by converting it into the required monetary consumption expenditure.	HCR for rural areas – 40% HCR for urban areas – 50%
Y.K. Alagh Task Force (*constituted in 1977 and submitted report in 1979*)	1973–74	• For rural areas, calorie intake of 2,400 per capita per day and 2,100 for urban areas was fixed to estimate poverty. The logic used was that rural people do more physical work than their urban counterpart. • Health and education was not taken into account to measure poverty on the assumption that government would take care of it.	–

Name of the Committee/Group	Data Based on	Details of Method Used	Estimates of Poverty (HCR)
D.T. Lakdawala Committee *(constituted in 1989 and submitted report in 1993)*	1973–74	• Used calorie intake–based per capita consumption expenditure, i.e. *2,400 for rural areas and 2,100 for urban areas.* • URP was used to collect data. • This committee recommended **state-specific poverty line**. • As per the report, poverty line to be updated using CPI (Agricultural Labour) in rural areas and CPI (Industrial Worker) in urban areas.	54.9% (All India)
Suresh Tendulkar Committee *(constituted in 2005 and submitted report in 2009)*	2004–05	• This committee did not construct a poverty line. It adopted the officially measured urban poverty line of 2004–05 based on the Lakdawala methodology and converted this poverty line from URP to **MRP** consumption. • Private expenditure on health and education was **also** taken into account. • Uniform urban poverty line basket was used for both rural and urban areas.	37.2% (All India) *(This was much more than 21.8% poverty figure computed by the 61st round of NSSO.)*

ESTIMATES AS PER THE 61st ROUND OF NSSO *vs.* TENDULKAR COMMITTEE ESTIMATES

The 61st round of NSSO (2004–05) – As per this round, poverty (HCR) was estimated to be 28.31 per cent as per URP and 21.8 per cent as per MRP. However, as per the Tendulkar Committee report, HCR was much higher, i.e., 37.2 per cent based on MRP.

The following can be inferred:

- The estimate of the **Incidence of Poverty** by the Tendulkar Committee at both 1993–94 prices and 2004–05 prices **was much more than** other official estimates.
- However, the **Extent of Poverty reduction** as found by the Tendulkar Committee was almost similar to other official estimates by the NSSO.

Name of the Committee	Data Based on	Details of Method Used	Estimate of Poverty (HCR)
Rangarajan Committee *(constituted in 2012 and submitted report in 2014)*	2011–12	• Used a method of calculating urban and rural poverty separately (*similar to the Lakdawala Committee*). • Took into account both food and non-food items of expenditure. • Used the MMRP method instead of MRP. • Poverty was based on monthly expenditure of a family of five (and not individual as in case of the Tendulkar Committee). • All three, i.e., Calorie + Protein + Fat intake values were taken into account to estimate poverty.	29.5%

EXAM ESSENTIAL

Tendulkar Committee *versus* Rangarajan Committee

Tendulkar Committee	Rangarajan Committee
Submitted Report in **2009**	Submitted Report in **2014**
Per capita monthly expenditure was used	Monthly expenditure of a **family of five** was used
Used MRP method	**Used MMRP method**
Only calorific value was used in evaluating expenditure	**Calorie + Protein + Fat** value was used to compute expenditure
Estimate of poverty derived was **37.2%** based on 2004–05 data	Estimate of poverty derived was **29.5%** based on 2011–12 data
Used the all India urban poverty line basket to derive both urban and rural poverty	Used **separate** rural and poverty line baskets

Later, the Planning Commission estimated poverty ratios for the years 2009–10 and 2011–12 by using the Tendulkar method and Rangarajan method separately. The results derived were as follows:

Methodology Applied	Poverty in 2009–10	Poverty in 2011–12	Extent of Reduction in Poverty
Applying the Tendulkar Methodology	29.8%	21.9%	7.9%
Applying the Rangarajan Methodology	38.2%	29.5%	8.7%
Thus, it can be interpreted that all-India poverty ratio derived through the Rangarajan method for both the financial years is higher than that derived through the Tendulkar method.			

BPL Census

I. BPL Census in Rural Areas

BPL Census for rural areas is conducted by the **Ministry of Rural Development (MoRD)**. The 1st BPL Census for rural areas was conducted in 1992 under the 8th Five-Year Plan. The 2nd and 3rd BPL Census for rural areas were conducted in 1997 and 2002, respectively.

Later in 2008, MoRD constituted the **N.C. Saxena Committee** to advise a suitable methodology to conduct BPL Census in rural areas. The committee in its report in 2009 recommended that:

1. The methodology of **automatic inclusion and automatic exclusion** for conducting census may be adopted.
2. The Percentage of people entitled to BPL status in India to be revised to **at least 50 per cent**.
3. There should be a **proportionate increase in state-level estimates also**.

Thus, the estimates of the N.C. Saxena Committee **varied largely with the estimates of the Planning Commission**. This difference in estimate is a bone of contention between the Planning Commission and MoRD.

As per the report of the last (i.e., 4th) BPL Census or the **1st Socio Economic and Caste Census** conducted **in 2011**, there are 24.3 crore households in India, of which 17.91 crore live in rural areas and **60 per cent** of the 17.91 crore rural households have been considered to be *deprived or poor*.

II. BPL Census in Urban Areas

In 2012, the *Ministry of Housing and Urban Poverty Alleviation* appointed the **S.R. Hashim Committee** to recommend a methodology for identification of BPL families in **urban** areas.

The committee recommended a **three-stage identification process** – (a) automatic exclusion (b) automatic inclusion and (c) Scoring Index of remaining urban families in this order.

(a) Stage 1 – Automatic Exclusion

- Households with ≥ 4 dwelling rooms to be excluded from the BPL list.
- Households with either of four-wheeler/motor cycle/AC/computer or laptop with Internet, to be excluded from the BPL list.
- Households possessing any three of the following assets to be excluded –refrigerator, telephone, washing machine or two-wheeler motor cycle.

(b) Stage 2 – Automatic Inclusion

- Households facing certain specific residential or social or occupational vulnerability to be automatically included in the BPL list.

(c) Stage 3 – Scoring Index for Remaining Households

- To be included in the list, they will be assigned scores from 0 to 12 based on various indicators.

The recommendations of the S.R. Hashim Committee are yet to be implemented.

Amartya Sen's Capability Approach on Poverty

The capability approach is a **people-focused approach**. It focuses on **enhancing people's well-being by expanding their capabilities** so that they can lead the life they value.

It does not encourage welfare programs, but advocates empowerment initiatives.

The capability approach consists of the following two elements:

1. **Freedom** to achieve well-being is of primary moral importance.
2. Well-being should be understood in terms of people's **capabilities and functioning**.

As a result, development is now seen as the process for creating an enabling atmosphere so that people can achieve valuable functioning and have the freedom to pursue what they value.

However, many have criticised the capability approach for being **individualistic and under-theorised and having information gaps**.

Sen Index of Poverty

Developed by Nobel Laureate **Prof. Amartya Sen in 1976**, it accounts for the extent and severity of poverty as well as level of inequality in a country. It is based on three elements: HCR, Poverty Gap Index and Gini Coefficient.

Mathematically,

$$S = H [I + (1 - I) G]$$

Where, S = Sen Index of Poverty; H = Head Count Ratio; I = Poverty Gap Index; G = Gini Coefficient

Randomised Controlled Trial

Economics Nobel Laureates of **2019** – *Abhijit Banerjee, Esther Duflo and Michael Kremer* – are considered to be instrumental in using Randomised Controlled Trial (RCT) to test the effectiveness of various policy interventions to alleviate poverty.

RCT is an experiment that is designed to isolate the influence that a certain intervention or variable has on an outcome or event.

For example, a researcher who wants to find the effect of employing more teachers in schools on children's learning outcomes, for instance, can conduct a Randomised Controlled Trial to find the answer.

BONUS KNOWLEDGE

BARE NECESSITIES INDEX

Economic Survey 2020–21 has introduced the concept of Bare Necessities Index and has highlighted the importance of access to bare necessities of housing, water, sanitation, electricity and clean cooking fuel, which are consumed by all the members of the household.

It is derived using **26 indicators** which are based on **5 dimensions** – water, sanitation, housing, micro-environment and other facilities.

EXAM ESSENTIAL

UNIVERSAL BASIC INCOME (UBI) – Is this single UBI scheme an alternative to all existing welfare schemes?

UBI was highlighted upon in one of the chapters in the Economic Survey 2016–17.

UBI is a concept under which there is a periodic cash payment, unconditionally delivered to everyone on an individual basis, without means test or work requirement.

Various countries are now deliberating upon the option of going for UBI by providing citizens a guaranteed amount of income, irrespective of their economic or employment status.

Thus, UBI is based on the principle that every citizen should have the right to basic income for covering their needs. In other words, UBI is based on three hallmarks:

1. Universality (targeting all population)
2. Unconditionality
3. Agency

Rationale for UBI

- It may provide freedom to an individual to spend as per his or her own choice.
- UBI may be a solution to technology-induced unemployment in developed countries.
- It may reduce inequality and increase aggregate consumer demand.
- It may promote social justice by empowering the poor to make their own economic decisions and choices.
- UBI may replace all welfare schemes (around 950 schemes running at present) which accounts for expenditure amounting to around 5.2 per cent of GDP (based on 2016–17 GDP figures).
- It may overcome leakages and wastages which occur during implementation of welfare schemes.
- Also, it will be easy to monitor one UBI instead of a huge number of welfare schemes.
- May be a solution to leakages and corruption.
- May help to tackle expected unemployment due to obsolescence of workforce as a result of rapid technological advancements.
- May improve the status of financial inclusion.

Cost of implementing UBI

As per the estimates of the Economic Survey 2016–17, UBI will involve expenditure amounting to around 4.9 per cent of the GDP, which is lower than the present expenditure of 5.2 per cent of GDP spent on all welfare schemes taken together.

Economic Survey further suggests that the per capita UBI amount will be indexed to prices and will be revised/increased periodically.

Challenges in implementing UBI

- Pre-requisite of for an **effectively functional JAM** (Jan Dhan, Aadhar and Mobile) infrastructure for implementing UBI.
- Deciding on expenditure **share of the centre and the states**.
- Stress of implementation on the banking system in the left out rural areas.
- In the present scenario, if one scheme fails to deliver, another scheme can compensate for that loss. However, in the case of UBI, there will be **no alternative for any mishandling of UBI**.
- A poor person may spend the UBI amount on **unwanted activities** like alcohol, gambling, etc. However, a 2011 pilot project in Madhya Pradesh has given results in favour of UBI.
- There are concerns raised by some critics as to whether UBI will actually replace all welfare schemes **or complement them**. If both welfare schemes and UBI are implemented parallelly, there will be a huge burden on the government exchequer.
- There are some countries like Canada, Brazil, Iran, etc. which have experimented with UBI on a pilot basis. However, **no major economy** across the globe has implemented it fully fledged until now.

Thus, there is an urgent need for a serious analysis of and discussions on UBI so that a pathway may be thought of and derived regarding its viability and implementation over a period of time.

INCOME INEQUALITY

There are several types of inequality in society like social inequality, income inequality, etc. Here, we will look into income inequality. The **gap** in income between the rich and the poor is referred to as Income Inequality. In other words, it indicates the disparity in the distribution of economic assets and income.

Causes of Income Inequality

- Concentration of assets in the private sector
- Urban bias in private investment
- High Inflation in goods and services
- More focus on capital-intensive ways of production
- Lack of skill up-gradation of mass population
- Lack of efficient health and education services in many of the rural areas of the country
- Lack of financial inclusion in many parts of rural and semi-urban parts of the country, etc.

Methods to Measure Income Inequality

The **concept of relative poverty** is used to indicate the level of income inequality of a nation. It is measured through **Gini Coefficient** in mathematical terms and **Lorenz curve** in graphical terms.

1. Gini Coefficient or Gini Index

- It was developed by the Italian statistician and sociologist **Corrado Gini in 1912**.
- It measures the **degree of income inequality in a country** by calculating the ratio of the area between the diagonal (line of perfect equality) and the Lorenz curve divided by the total area of the half square in which the curve lies.
- The value of Gini Coefficient **varies between 0 and 1**.
- 0 (zero) represents perfect equality, i.e. a situation where every resident has the same income.
- 1 (one) indicates perfect inequality; i.e. one resident earns all the income and the others have no income.
- For understanding it simply – say an **increase in value** from 0.29 to 0.36 indicates more income inequality, which is certainly **not good** for an economy.
- The higher is the Gini Coefficient, the more is the gap between rich and poor in a country, i.e. higher level of income inequality.

$$\text{Gini coefficient} = \frac{\text{Shaded area A}}{\text{Total area BCD}}$$

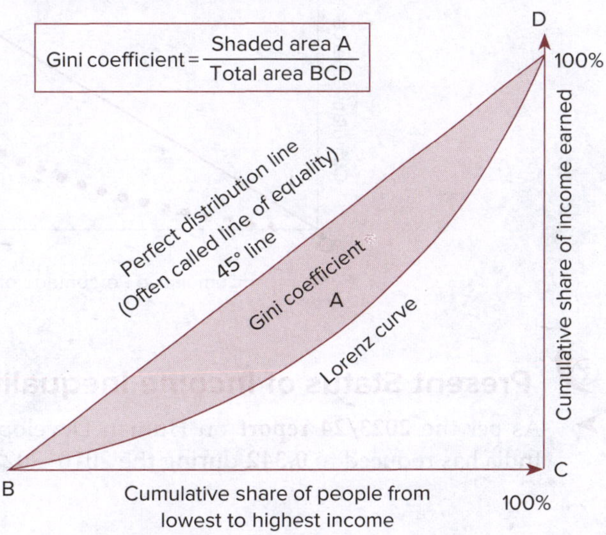

2. Lorenz Curve

- It is a curve that measures the **relationship between the Percentage of income earned and the Percentage of people** who earned that particular Percentage of income.

- It is a **graphical representation of Gini Coefficient**. In other words, Gini Coefficient can be represented graphically through the Lorenz curve.
- Cumulative population share (in %) is presented on the *X*-axis and cumulative income share (in %) is presented on the *Y*-axis.

Lorenz Curve Explained

- Perfect equality is represented by a straight 45-degree curve.
- Curve placed below the line of perfect equality represents the Lorenz curve.
- The closer is the Lorenz curve to the perfect equality line, the less is the level of income inequality and vice versa.
- 'A' indicates the shaded area.
- From the graph, Gini Coefficient = shaded area A/area of BDC.
- If A = 0, it means the Lorenz curve is actually the line of equality, and then it indicates perfect equality with Gini Coefficient = 0.

Hoover Index

It is also known as the Robin Hood index or the Schutz index. Hoover index is a measure of income inequality. It is equal to the percentage of the total population's income that would have to be redistributed to make all the incomes equal.

Higher value = more inequality

Lower value = less inequality

The 45 degree line shows the perfect equality.

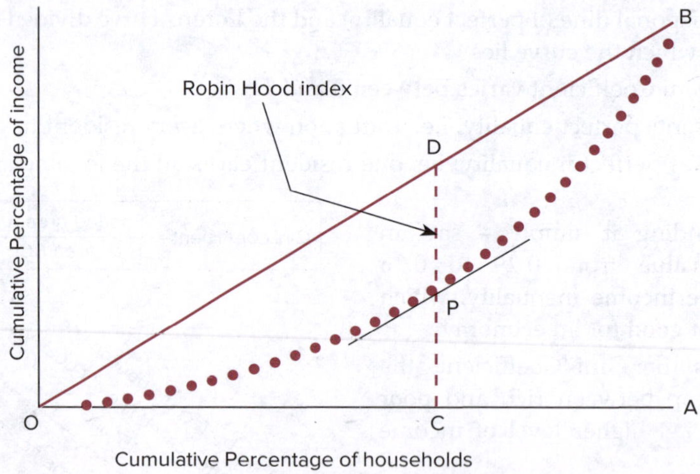

Present Status of Income Inequality in India – A Global Comparison

- As per the **2023/24 report** on Human Development by UNDP, the **Income Gini Coefficient** of India has reduced to **0.342** during the 2010–2022 period. As per the 2011 report, it was 0.368.

- In the 2023/24 report, it was mentioned that there were many developed nations whose income inequality was **much higher than that of India**. Some of them included China (0.382), the United States (0.398), Israel (0.386), Russia (0.360), etc.

INCOME AND WEALTH INEQUALITY IN INDIA, 1922–2023: The Rise of the Billionaire Raj

By World Inequality Lab

This report of World Inequality Lab has estimated that "inequality declined post-independence till the early 1980s, after which it began rising and has skyrocketed since the early 2000s". Following are some key highlights of the report:

- The **average income of India grew at 2.6% per annum** in real terms between 1960 and 2022. As per the report, this period of 62 years can be broadly divided into two halves –
  i. Real growth rate of average income was 1.6% per annum between 1960 and 1990.
  ii. Real growth rate of average income was 3.6% per annum between 1990 and 2022.
- The report also highlighted that the periods 2005–2010 and 2010–2015 saw the fastest growth rate of 4.35 and 4.9% respectively.
- The report pointed out that the **percentage of income taxpayers has increased significantly**. Till 1990s, below 1% of adults filed income tax return. After the economic reforms of 1991, this share increased to 5% and in the last decade (particularly between 2017 and 2022) this share has grown to 9%.
- Apparently, this report states that the number of individuals whose net worth exceeds USD 1 billion at market exchange rate, has increased from one in 1991 to 52 in 2011 and 162 in 2022.
- It is notable that the **wealth accumulation of top 1%** in India has increased from 13% in 1961 to 39% in 2023. Globally, **India is at the highest levels** where this small population has major share of the economy.
- The following graph shows the concentration of wealth with top 10% and 1% of the population of some major countries including India:

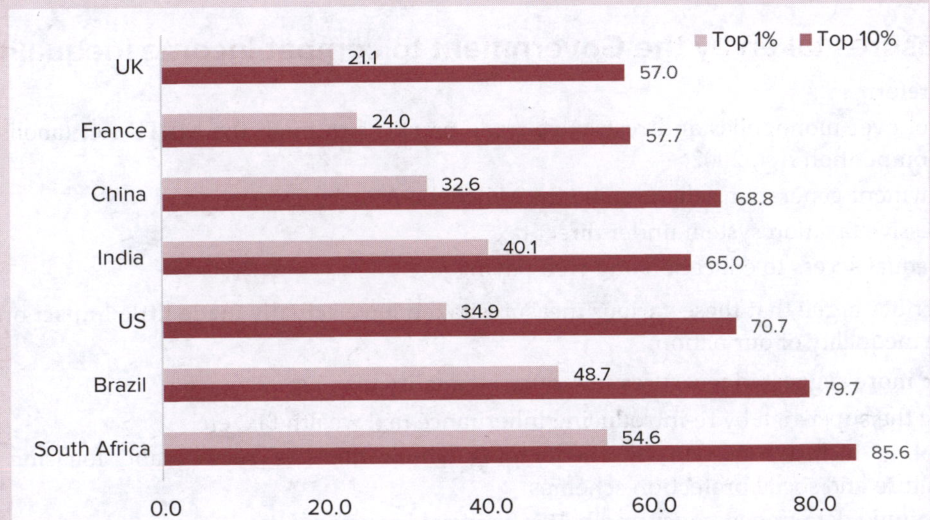

"The suggested policy solution by the report states **Implementing a super tax on Indian billionaires and multimillionaires**, along with restructuring the tax schedule to include both income and wealth, so as to finance major investments in education, health and other public infrastructure, could be effective measures," to address the issue of increasing inequalities.

WORLD INEQUALITY REPORT 2022

The report was published by the **World Inequality Lab** based in Paris. As per their report:

- The **Middle East** and **North Africa** stand as the world's **most unequal** regions (the income share of the top 10 per cent was 58 per cent).
- **Europe** stands as the **most equal** of all the regions (the income share of the top 10 per cent was 36 per cent).
- Europe, Latin America, and South & Southeast Asia experienced the greatest drops in national income in 2020 (between –6 and –7.6 per cent), while East Asia (*the epicentre of the pandemic*) was able to maintain its 2020 income at the level of 2019.
- **India** is **one of the world's most unequal** countries, with the top 10 per cent of Indians capturing 57 per cent of national income while the bottom 50 per cent gets only 13 per cent.
- Income inequality in India today is worse than it was during the British rule (*during the British rule, the top 10 per cent received approximately 50 per cent of national income, which is lower than it is today*).

Impact of Income Inequality

- Rich becomes richer, poor becomes poorer
- A continuous class conflict between the 'haves' and 'have nots'
- Political instability in the nation

Measures taken by the Government to combat Income Inequality

1. Land reforms
2. Control over monopolies and restrictive trade practices through the MRTP Act (abolished now) and Competition Act, 2002
3. Employment generation schemes like the MGNREGA
4. Progressive taxation system under direct tax
5. More equal access to education and well-paying jobs

However, critics argue that these various measures taken **have actually made little impact** on reducing the income inequality of our nation.

Thus, some more suggested measures to reduce inequality may be:

1. Taxing the super-rich by re-introducing inheritance tax, wealth tax, etc.
2. Promoting inclusive growth by encouraging labour-intensive sectors and focusing more on agriculture and social protection schemes
3. Maintaining data transparency and better financial inclusion

SUMMARY

- **Poverty** – State of lack of financial resources – person or community is unable to fulfil its basic necessities – in the Indian context, it emphasises on minimum level of living rather than reasonable level of living.
- **Relative Poverty** – Represents income inequality.
- **Absolute Poverty** – Deprivation from basic human needs such as food, clothing, health, education, sanitation facilities, shelter, etc. – measured through Poverty Line.
- **Poverty Line** – Required level of income to fulfil basic necessities – may vary from one country to another – As per the World Bank, International Poverty Line is $1.90 per capita per day.
- **Head Count Ratio (HCR)/Poverty Incidence Ratio** – Ratio between total number of BPL people and total population – indicates the incidence of poverty in a nation.
- **Poverty Gap Ratio** – Difference between poverty line and the average actual monthly consumption and expenditure of BPL households – it indicates the intensity of poverty in a nation.
- **Multidimensional Poverty Index (MPI)** – Measures 'acute' poverty based on overlapping deprivations – developed by UNDP and OPHI – uses three dimensions (education, health and standard of living).
- **Three methods used to estimate poverty** – Uniform Reference/Recall Period – Mixed Reference/ Recall Period – Modified Mixed Reference/Recall Period.
- **BPL Census in rural areas** – Conducted by Ministry of Rural Development – first such census was conducted in 1992 – latest or fourth BPL census (1st SECC) was conducted in 2011 – as per the census, 60 per cent of 17.91 crore rural households have been considered poor/deprived.
- **BPL Census in urban areas** – Under Ministry of Housing and Urban Poverty Alleviation – three-stage identification process – recommended by S.R. Hashim Committee.
- **Bare Necessities Index** – Based on five dimensions – water, sanitations, housing, micro-environment and other facilities (like electricity and clean cooking fuel).
- **Income Inequality** – Gap in income between rich and poor – measured through Gini Coefficient and Lorenz Curve.

UPSC CSE PREVIOUS YEARS' PRELIMINARY EXAMINATION QUESTIONS

1. In a given year in India, official poverty lines are higher in some States than in others because **[2019]**

(a) Poverty rates vary from State to States
(b) Price levels vary from State to States
(c) Gross state product varies from States to States
(d) Quality of public distribution varies from State to State

2. The MPI developed by the Oxford Poverty and Human Development Initiative with UNDP support covers which of the following? **[2012]**

1. Deprivation of education, health, assets and services at household level.
2. Purchasing power parity at national level.
3. Extent of budget deficit and GDP growth rate at national level.

Select the correct answer using the codes given below:

(a) 1 only (b) 2 and 3 only
(c) 1 and 3 only (d) 1, 2 and 3

☞ NO QUESTIONS ASKED
2024, 2023, 2022, 2021, 2020, 2018, 2017, 2016, 2015, 2014, 2013

ANSWER KEY

1. (b) 2. (a)

UPSC CSE PREVIOUS YEARS' MAIN EXAMINATION QUESTIONS

1. Most of the unemployment in India is structural in nature. Examine the methodology adopted to compute unemployment in the country and suggest improvements. **[2023]**
2. The nature of economic growth in India in recent times is often described as **jobless growth**. Do you agree with this view? Give arguments in favour of your answer. **[2015]**

☞ NO QUESTIONS ASKED

2024, 2022, 2021, 2020, 2019, 2018, 2017, 2016, 2014, 2013, 2012

CHAPTER

5

UNEMPLOYMENT AND LABOUR REFORMS

CHAPTER OUTLINE

- Unemployment in India
- Methods to Measure Unemployment in India
- The Jobs Gap: Measuring Labour Underutilisation beyond Unemployment
- Types of Unemployment
- Size of Workforce and Current Rate of Unemployment in India
- Important Organisations under the Ministry of Labour & Unemployment
- Various Reports/Surveys related to Labour Statistics and Unemployment
- Periodic Labour Force Survey
- Occupational Structure in India
- Beveridge Curve or UV Curve
- Casualisation and Informalisation of Workforce
- Recent Government Initiatives to Reduce Unemployment
- Labour Reforms
- Recent Reforms In Industrial Labour Laws
- Industrial Employment (Standing Orders) Central (AMENDMENT) RULES, 2018
- Two New Pension Schemes Launched In 2019 (by the Ministry of Labour & Employment)
- Social Security Schemes for Employees
- Way Forward

UNEMPLOYMENT IN INDIA

The definition of unemployment brings out the following features:

- It is not permanent in nature.
- It applies only to able-bodied persons of working age, i.e. persons of age group between 15 and 60 years and who are mentally and physically fit for work.
- Ability to work also implies willingness to work.

Therefore, an unemployed person is one who has the ability to work, willingness to work and is of working age (15–60 years) but does not get work at the current wage rate.

Reasons for Unemployment in India

- Slow economic development
- Population explosion
- Improper education system
- Mismatch between required skills and available skills
- Limited effect of government planning

> ***Underemployment*** *– When persons are employed below their education or skill level, it is termed 'underemployment'. It may be of two types – visible and invisible underemployment.*

Various Concepts under Unemployment

1. Labour Supply

- It refers to the supply of labour **(in man-days)** that workers are willing to offer at different wage rates.
- Labour supply is always related to **wage rate**.
- Supply of labour can increase or decrease **even when** the number of workers remains constant.

Normally, 1 man-day refers to 8 hours of work.

2. Labour Force

- It refers to the number of persons actually working or willing to work.
- It is not related to wage rate.
- It is measured in terms of **number of persons** (not in terms of man-days or person-days).

3. Workforce

- It refers to only those persons who are actually working.
- It **does not** take into account those who are willing to work (but not working).

A beggar, thief or gambler is not considered a worker.

EXAM ESSENTIAL

Number of persons unemployed = Labour force – Work force

Rate of Unemployment = Number of persons unemployed / Total labour force × 100

Proportion of Unemployed = Number of persons unemployed / Total Population above 15 years of age × 100

Labour Force Participation Rate (LFPR) = Labour force / Total Population above 15 years of age × 100

Work Force Participation Rate (WFPR) or Worker Population Ratio (WPR)
= Workforce / Total Population above 15 years of age × 100

Employment Intensity = Number of employed persons per lakh of Real GDP

METHODS TO MEASURE UNEMPLOYMENT IN INDIA

As recommended by the Prof. **M. L. Dantwala Committee** set up by the Planning Commission in 1960, there are **three methods** used by the NSSO (*since 1972–73*) to measure unemployment using the National Sample Survey data:

- Usual Principal Status
- Current Weekly Status
- Current Daily Status

Unemployment Trap *– Occurs when opportunity cost of going to work is higher than the income received. For example, fresh graduates.*

1. The Usual Principal Status (UPS)

- This method estimates the number of persons who are **chronically unemployed** for a major part of the reference period (i.e. 1 year) preceding the date of survey.
- This measure generally **gives the lowest estimate of unemployment**. This is because only a few people can afford to remain without work over a long period.

USUAL PRINCIPAL SUBSIDIARY STATUS (UPSS) OR USUAL STATUS (PS + SS)

- This recent approach seeks to identify workers out of those who were classified as 'unemployed' or as 'outside labour force' on the basis of majority time criteria of the UPS approach.
- UPSS is a more inclusive measure as compared to UPS.
- **If a person is engaged in any economic activity for a period of 30 days or more during the preceding 365 days**, the person is considered as employed under this approach.

2. The Current Weekly Status (CWS)

- Here, the reference period is taken as **1 week (7 days) preceding the date of survey**.
- According to this estimate, a person is termed 'employed' **even if he or she is employed only for a day during that week for at least 1 hour.**
- The percentage of unemployment **is higher** under this measure as compared to the UPS.

3. The Current Daily Status (CDS)

- The reference period here is a day preceding the date of survey.
- He/she is considered as **employed** if he/she has worked for **at least 4 hours** during that day.
- If a person has worked for more than 1 hour but less than 4 hours, he/she is considered **half-day employed.**
- A person who has **no gainful work even for 1 hour** during that day is considered **unemployed**.
- Compared to the other two methods, estimate of **unemployment is highest under CDS**.

did you KNOW? Current Daily Status or CDS is the broadest measure and is more inclusive, captures open unemployment to a great extent, takes care of seasonality, and CDS indicates the magnitude of both unemployment and underemployment.

THE JOBS GAP: MEASURING LABOUR UNDERUTILISATION BEYOND UNEMPLOYMENT

Recently, a new indicator called *jobs gap* has been introduced by **International Labour Organisation (ILO)** to measure **the intensity of labour underutilisation** as an important complement of unemployment.

Labour underutilisation can be divided into **two broad categories: underemployment and underutilisation**. The former includes employed persons, who are affected by insufficient working time and the latter include those not in employment. **Jobs gap comes under the second category**.

Jobs gap includes those people who want employment regardless of whether they are currently available or searching for a job. It can be thought of as the measure with the most relaxed definition of underutilisation on the extensive margin. Jobs gap is particularly relevant to assess the difficulties that women face in finding a job. It also highlights job creation challenges in the developing world.

The 19th International Conference of Labour Statisticians (ICLS) has recognised **three different degrees of labour market attachment for measuring labour underutilisation**.

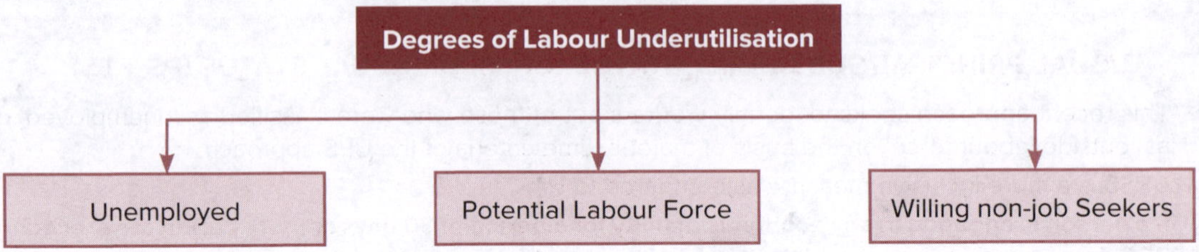

a. **Unemployed:** To be considered unemployed, a person has to satisfy the following two conditions –
   i. He/she has to be available to take up employment at a very short notice (typically a week).
   ii. He/she has been recently searching for a job.

b. **Potential Labour Force:** In order to include a person under potential labour force, the conditions can be defined as follows –
   i. Those who have recently been searching for a job but are not available to work within a short reference period.
   ii. Those who have not searched recently but are available to work within a short reference period.
   (i.e. they fail to satisfy only one of the criteria to be considered unemployed).

c. **Willing Non-Job Seekers:** It is composed of those who want employment but have not recently searched and are not available at a short notice.

In the above three categories, **the unemployed are very likely to have a higher probability of finding a job**. Willing non-job seekers will tend to be at the other end of the spectrum, with the lowest probability of finding a job. Thus, the distinction between these categories is highly relevant for economic analysis and policy making.

Though unemployment is included in the jobs gap, it is to be noted that **unemployment is the most countercyclical component of the jobs gap, with the potential labour force being sizeably less reactive to the business cycle and willing non-job seekers being essentially acyclical**.

As per International Labour Organisation Database (ILOSTAT), the trend of the jobs gap at cyclical frequencies is not only similar to unemployment, but, in fact, it is driven by it. Moreover, it is also observed that the **negative correlation** between unemployment and inflation (which is represented by Phillips Curve) also **holds true for inflation and jobs gap**.

As far as GDP per capita is concerned, it shows markedly different results for unemployment and jobs gap. ILOSTAT data suggests that different economic structures – related to economic development – influence the behaviour of those wanting a job and alter the relative importance of unemployment in overall labour underutilisation. The difference is large in the case of low income countries. Thus, analysing levels of labour underutilisation, complementing the unemployment rate with the jobs gap indicator is of critical importance in the developing world.

Moreover, the ability to job-search and the availability to take up employment at a short notice is not evenly distributed across demographic groups, or various levels of national income. For instance, usually for women, the time of one week is too short to look for a job because of their extra involvement in domestic affairs. Also, in developing countries, both the job search and availability at a short notice criteria can be highly restrictive due to informal work arrangements.

TYPES OF UNEMPLOYMENT

Unemployment can be classified into two categories – voluntary and involuntary unemployment.

I. Voluntary Unemployment

It is a situation when persons who are **able to work are not willing to work** or where jobs are available but the people are unwilling to do them. In other words, they are voluntarily unemployed, i.e. *unemployed by their own choice*. Such people are not included in labour force of the country.

II. Involuntary Unemployment

It is a situation where able-bodied people are willing to do a job but are **unemployed due to unavailability of jobs** in the economy. Hence, they are unemployed against their wishes. These people are included under different categories of unemployment.

The following are the sub-categories of involuntary unemployment:

1. Structural Unemployment

- This type is associated with the **economic structure** of the country. Economic structure implies (i) rapidly growing population and (ii) slow rate of capital formation, etc.
- When the demand for labour falls short of supply of labour due to the rapidly growing population and their immobility, the problem of unemployment appears in the economy. This type of unemployment is also caused due to **skill mismatches**.
- This type of unemployment **is long term in nature**.

2. Disguised Unemployment

- If a person **does not contribute** in the production process, or, in other words, if he or she can be removed from the work without affecting productivity adversely, the situation will be treated as disguised unemployed.
- Here, the marginal productivity of labour **(MP_L) is equal to zero**.
- It is a common phenomenon **in the agricultural sector** in a developing or less developed economy.

did you KNOW? Disguised unemployment is widespread in the agricultural sector, primarily due to limited vocational opportunities outside agriculture, the joint family system, and high population pressure. However, it is not limited to agriculture alone. Critics point out that it also exists in public sector enterprises, where many employees remain idle because the workforce often exceeds actual requirements.

3. Frictional Unemployment

- The unemployment here is generated **due to change in market conditions**. Here, some workers are temporarily out of work due to reasons such as strikes, layoffs by the company (suspension), time gap between changing/switching jobs, lock-outs, imperfect mobility of labour, etc.
- This is a common phenomenon in the **industrial sector**.

4. Cyclical Unemployment

- It occurs due to the trade cycles, especially **recessionary cycles** and the cycle of **depression**. The downswing in business activities results in unemployment.
- It is a common phenomenon in **developed countries** which are capital buyers.
- It is a **temporary** and short-term phenomenon.

5. Chronic Unemployment

- When unemployment tends to be a **long-term feature** of a country, it is called chronic unemployment.
- It is due to the vicious circle of poverty, underutilisation of resources, use of traditional techniques or technology, etc.

6. Technological Unemployment

- Due to the **introduction of new technology, machinery improvement** in method of production, labour-saving devices, etc., some workers tend to be replaced by machines.

7. Casual Unemployment

- In sectors such as construction, catering or agriculture where the labourers are employed on a day-to-day basis, there are chances of casual unemployment arising due to shortage of raw materials, fall in demand, change of ownership or short-term contracts, which are terminable at any time.

8. Seasonal Unemployment

- Persons are employed only during particular seasons in some sectors.
- For example, sectors like agriculture where labourers work for a season and are unemployed for the remaining year.

9. Vulnerable Unemployment

- It refers to the sum of **own-account workers** (self-employed individuals who do not employ others) and **contributing family workers** (unpaid family members who work in an enterprise owned by another family member), who are more likely to lack formal work arrangements and decent working conditions.

SIZE OF WORKFORCE AND CURRENT RATE OF UNEMPLOYMENT IN INDIA

As per the **last available 6th** ***Annual Employment–Unemployment Survey Report*** *(2016–17)* conducted by the *Ministry of Labour and Employment*, the rate of unemployment is as follows:

Rate of Unemployment	Rural	Urban	Total
As per the UPS method	5.2%	6.1%	5.4%

Rate of Unemployment	Male	Female	Total
As per the UPS method	4.2%	9.2%	5.4%

From the analysis of the said report, it is also observed that –

- LFPR in India is around 51.2 per cent and WFPR is 47.8 per cent.
- About 75 per cent of the workforce comprises male workers.
- 70 per cent of the workforce is found in the rural area.
- Female workforce in the rural area is nearly 30 per cent, while it is 20 per cent in the urban area.
- Unemployment in the rural area is more.
- As compared to males, unemployment is more in the case of females (more in the case of urban females).

Important Organisations under the Ministry of Labour & Unemployment

Name of Organisation	Headquarters	Details
Dattopant Thengadi National Board for Workers Education and Development (DTNBWED)	New Delhi	An autonomous body, started in 1958, functions to create an enlightened and disciplined work force and to bring behavioural changes in workforce in the organised, unorganised and rural sectors.
Directorate General Factory Advice Service and Labour Institutes (DGFASLI)	Mumbai	It was set up in 1945, with the objective of advising Central and State Governments on administration of the Factories Act and coordinating the factory inspection services in the States.
Directorate General of Mines Safety (DGMS)	Dhanbad	Regulatory agency in matters pertaining to occupational safety, health and welfare of persons employed in mines (Coal, Metalliferous and Oil-mines).
Indian Labour Archives (ILA)	Noida	Set up in 1998 for preserving and making accessible the fast-depleting documents on the working class.
Labour Bureau	Chandigarh	Labour Bureau is responsible for the collation, collection and publication of statistics on wages, earnings, productivity, absenteeism, labour turn-over, industrial relations, working and living conditions and evaluation of working of various labour enactments, etc. It is a storehouse of important economic indicators like Consumer Price Index Numbers for Industrial, Agricultural and Rural Labourers; wage rate indices, etc. The functions of Labour Bureau can be classified under three major heads: a. Labour Intelligence b. Labour Research

Name of Organisation	Headquarters	Details
		c. Monitoring and evaluation studies under the Minimum Wages Act, 1948.
V.V. Giri National Labour Institute (VVGNLI)	**Noida**	Established in 1974, it is an autonomous body involved with research, training, education, publication and consultancy on labour related issues.

VARIOUS REPORTS/SURVEYS RELATED TO LABOUR STATISTICS AND UNEMPLOYMENT

EXAM ESSENTIAL

Type of Report/ Survey	Published By	Detail
Periodic Labour Force Survey **(PLFS)**	By **NSO** under the Ministry of Statistics and Programme Implementation	Introduced in 2017. Conducted annually, to estimate the key employment and unemployment indicators.
Employment-Unemployment Survey **(EUS)**	By the **Labour Bureau**, under the Ministry of Labour and Unemployment	Continued till 2017 and thereafter replaced by PLFS. It was a comprehensive household survey that provided labour force statistics, including employment and unemployment rates.
Quarterly Employment Survey **(QES)**	By **Labour Bureau**, under the Ministry of Labour and Unemployment	The Labour Bureau conducts QES in nine select non-farm sectors, providing quarterly data on employment.
Annual Survey of Unincorporated Sector Enterprises **(ASUSE)**	By **NSSO**, under the Ministry of Statistics and Programme Implementation.	It measures various economic and operational characteristics of unincorporated non-agricultural establishments in manufacturing, trade and other services sector (excluding construction).
Payroll Reporting	By **NSO** under the Ministry of Statistics and Programme Implementation	It measures employment related statistics in the formal sector using information on the number of subscribers who have joined social security schemes: • Employees' Provident Fund (EPF) Scheme • Employees' State Insurance (ESI) Scheme • National Pension Scheme (NPS). The yearly net payroll additions to the EPFO have more than doubled from **61.1 lakh in FY19 to 131.5 lakh in FY24**, driven by new job creation and greater formalisation of employment.
Occupational Wage Survey **(OWS)**	By the **Labour Bureau**, under the Ministry of Labour and Unemployment	Occupational wage data are collected in respect of workers in selected Service Sector, Plantations, Mines and Manufacturing Industries at periodic intervals, to obtain occupation-wise data on employment, wage rates and dearness allowance for building up base year weights for updating the base of Wage Rate Index Numbers.

Type of Report/ Survey	Published By	Detail
Wage Rate Index	By the **Labour Bureau**, under the Ministry of Labour and Unemployment	Wage Rate Index Numbers depict movement of relative change experienced in the wage rates over a period of time (compiled for 37 select industries on base 2016 =100)
Other Socio-Economic Surveys	By the **Labour Bureau**, under the Ministry of Labour and Unemployment	• Survey of working and living conditions of workers belonging to Scheduled Castes and Scheduled Tribes Communities in Urban Areas. • Survey of working and living conditions of workers engaged in the unorganised sector of Industries Employment. • All India Survey on the Evaluation of Minimum Wages Act, 1948.
Annual Report based on various industrial aspects	By the **Labour Bureau**, under the Ministry of Labour and Unemployment	• Industrial disputes resulting in work stoppages • Absenteeism • Closures • Retrenchments • Lay-offs

PERIODIC LABOUR FORCE SURVEY

- **EUS** has been discontinued and the **PLFS** has been introduced in 2017.
- PLFS is **conducted annually** to generate the estimates of labour statistics indicators.
- PLFS is conducted by NSO under the Ministry of Statistics and Programme Implementation. EUS was conducted by the Ministry of Labour and Unemployment.
- The first PLFS was conducted for the period 2017–18 (July 2017 to June 2018) using **education levels** as a criterion for stratification instead of the **monthly per capita expenditure** which was used as a criterion under the EUS.
- **Use of technology** for survey by using the World Bank Computer-Assisted Personal Interviewing **(CAPI)** solution platform has been a major intervention introduced in the PLFS for the first time by the National Sample Survey. This was never done in EUS.

Periodic Labour Force Survey (PLFS) Annual Report 2023–24

The objective of PLFS is primarily two-fold:

1. To estimate the key employment and unemployment indicators (viz. Worker Population Ratio, Labour Force Participation Rate, Unemployment Rate) in the short time interval of three months for the urban areas only in the 'Current Weekly Status' (CWS).
2. To estimate employment and unemployment indicators in both 'Usual Status' (ps+ss) and CWS in both rural and urban areas annually.

Following are the key findings of the seventh Annual Report on the basis of Periodic Labour Force Survey conducted during July 2023–June 2024:

In Usual Status (ps + ss)

- In rural areas, LFPR (for age group 15 years and above) increased **from 50.7 per cent in 2017–18 to 63.7 per cent in 2023–24** while for urban areas it increased **from 47.6 per cent to 52 per cent.** LFPR for male in India increased **from 75.8 per cent in 2017–18 to 78.8 per cent in 2023–24** and the corresponding increase in LFPR for female was **from 23.3 per cent to 41.7 per cent.**
- In rural areas, Worker Population Ratio (WPR) (for age group 15 years and above) increased **from 48.1 per cent in 2017–18 to 62.1 per cent in 2023–24** while for urban areas it increased **from 43.9 per cent to 49.4 per cent**. WPR for male in India increased **from 71.2 per cent in 2017–18 to 76.3 per cent in 2023–24** and the corresponding increase in WPR for female was from **22.0 per cent to 40.3 per cent.**
- In rural areas, UR decreased (for age group 15 years and above) **from 5.3 per cent in 2017–18 to 2.5 per cent in 2023–24** while for urban areas it decreased **from 7.7 per cent to 5.1 per cent.** UR for male in India decreased **from 6.1 per cent in 2017–18 to 3.2 per cent in 2023–24** and the corresponding decrease in UR for female was **from 5.6 per cent to 3.2 per cent.**

Labour market indicators in India have improved substantially in the last few years. As per Periodic Labour Force Survey (PLFS), the unemployment rate in India has dropped significantly and labour force participation and the worker population ratio have shown considerable improvements.

Labour Force Participation Rate (LFPR), Worker Population Ratio (WPR) and Unemployment Rate (UR) in Usual Status (ps+ss) for age group 15 years and above

Year	LFPR (person)			WPR (person)			UR (person)		
	Rural	Urban	Rural + Urban	Rural	Urban	Rural + Urban	Rural	Urban	Rural + Urban
2023–24	63.7%	52.0%	60.1%	62.1%	49.4%	58.2%	2.5%	5.1%	3.2%
2022–23	60.8%	50.4%	57.9%	59.4%	47.7%	56.0%	2.4%	5.4%	3.2%
2021–22	57.5%	49.7%	55.2%	55.6%	46.6%	52.9%	3.2%	6.3%	4.1%

In Current Weekly Status (CWS)

- In rural areas, LFPR (for age group 15 years and above) increased from 48.9 per cent in 2017–18 to 58.9 per cent in 2023–24 while for urban areas it increased from 47.1 per cent to 50.8 per cent. LFPR for male in India increased from 75.1 per cent in 2017–18 to 77.5 per cent in 2023–24 and the corresponding increase in LFPR for female was from 21.1 per cent to 35.6 per cent.
- In rural areas, WPR (for age group 15 years and above) increased from 44.8 per cent in 2017–18 to 56.5 per cent in 2023–24 while for urban areas it increased from 42.6 per cent to 47.4 per cent. WPR for male in India increased from 68.6 per cent in 2017–18 to 73.8 per cent in 2023–24 and the corresponding increase in WPR for female was from 19.2 per cent to 33.8 per cent.
- In rural areas, UR (for age group 15 years and above) decreased from 8.4 per cent in 2017–18 to 4.2 per cent in 2023–24 while for urban areas it decreased from 9.5 per cent to 6.7 per cent.

UR for male in India decreased from 8.7 per cent in 2017–18 to 4.8 per cent in 2023–24 and the corresponding decrease in UR for female was from 9.0 per cent to 5.0 per cent.

Labour Force Participation Rate (LFPR), Worker Population Ratio (WPR) and Unemployment Rate (UR) in current weekly status (CWS) for age group 15 years and above

Year	LFPR (person)			WPR (person)			UR (person)		
	Rural	Urban	Rural + Urban	Rural	Urban	Rural + Urban	Rural	Urban	Rural + Urban
2023–34	58.9%	50.8%	56.4%	56.5%	47.4%	53.7%	4.2%	6.7%	4.9%
2022–23	56.7%	49.4%	54.6%	54.2%	46.0%	51.8%	4.4%	7.0%	5.1%
2021–22	53.0%	48.6%	51.7%	49.9%	44.6%	48.3%	6.0%	8.3%	6.6%

Quarterly Employment Survey (QES)

It is conducted by **Labour Bureau** with 10 or more workers in 9 major sectors, consisting 83 per cent of the total employment.

1. As per the last quarter QES of 2021–22, total employment increased to 3.2 crore in the selected sectors due to the revival of IT/BPO, health, education sectors.
2. Manufacturing sector accounted for the largest percentage of the total number of workers.
3. Regular employees constituted 86.4 per cent of the total workforce. Only 1.9 per cent are self-employed.
4. 31.8 per cent of the total workforce is female and 68.2 per cent is male.

Last Minute SNIPPETS

As per the Centre for Monitoring Indian Economy (**CMIE**), a privately owned and professionally managed company headquartered at Mumbai, unemployment rate in India is estimated around **9.2 per cent** in June 2024. It is 8.9 per cent in urban India and 9.3 per cent in rural India.

*As per International Labour Organisation's **(ILO's) World Employment and Social Outlook (WESO) Report 2025,***

- The global economy is expanding at a moderate rate. But this expansion may lose the pace which will, in turn, affect the comeback of a strong and durable labour market.
- The **global unemployment rate stood at 5% in 2024,** which is **lesser than** the corresponding value of 5.1% of unemployment rate in **2023**. Apparently, the global jobs gap and labour market participation rates have also shown improvement in 2024.

Type of Countries (in 2024)	Jobs Gap Rate	Unemployment Rate
High Income Countries	7.1% (for men)	4.5%
Low Income Countries	15.2% (for men)	5.7%

OCCUPATIONAL STRUCTURE IN INDIA

Occupational Structure (Overall) (2020–21)

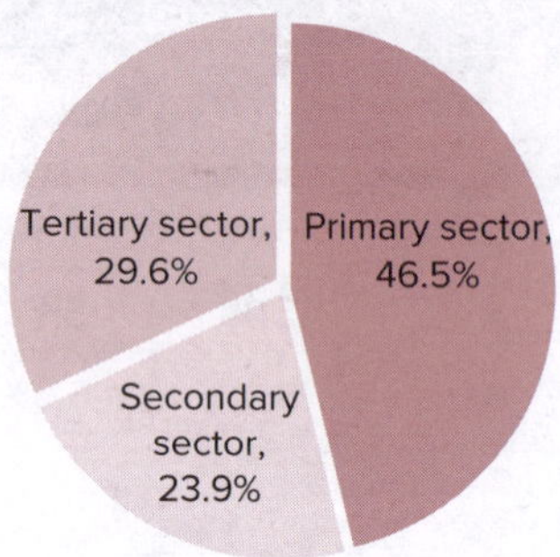

Occupational Structure among Rural Workforce (2020–21)

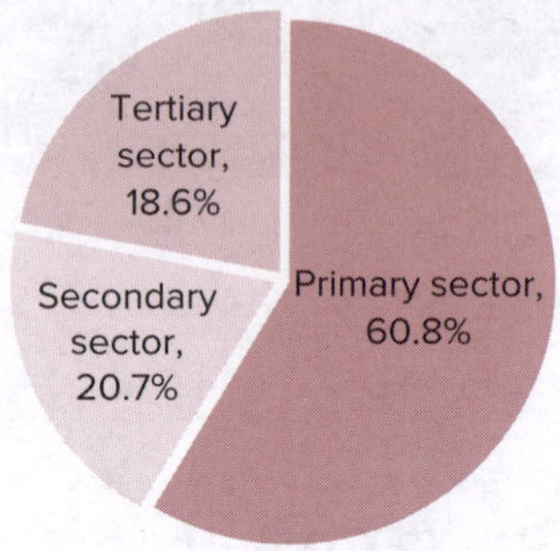

Occupational Structure among Urban Workforce (2020–21)

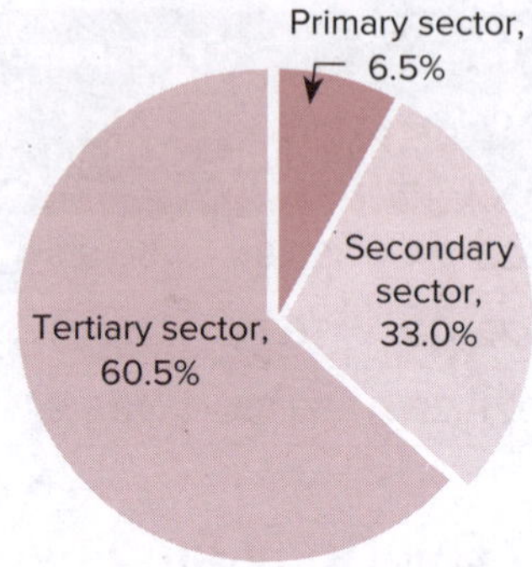

From the above graph and other analysis, it is observed that

➤ **In rural areas,** workforce is mainly engaged in the **primary sector**.

➤ **In urban areas, tertiary sector** has the largest chunk of workforce.

➤ **Overall, the primary sector** has the largest proportion of workforce employed.

Change in Occupational Structure since Independence

Occupational Structure in	Percentage of Workforce	
	In 1950–51	In 2024–25
Primary sector	72.7%	45%
Secondary sector	10%	25%
Tertiary sector	17.3%	30%

Last Minute SNIPPETS

TIME USE SURVEY, 2024

➤ The 'Time Use Survey'" (TUS) provides a framework for measuring the activities that are performed by the population and the time duration for which such activities are performed. Its primary objective is to measure the participation of men and women in paid and unpaid activities.

➤ The **National Statistical Office (NSO),** MoSPI conducts this all-India Time Use Survey. This is the **second** such All-India Survey. (first in 2019)

➤ **Key findings** of the survey include –

a. As compared to 2019, there is an increase in the average time spent per participant on employment and related activities in 2024. (by both men and women)

b. Women spend 20% of their day on Unpaid Domestic and Care Work, while men spend just 3%, indicating a stark contrast in how household responsibilities are shared.

c. More time is spent by people on leisure and media, less on socialising and self-care, in both urban and rural areas.

EXAM ESSENTIAL

JOBLESS GROWTH

It is a phenomenon where the level of GDP increases in the economy without a perceptible rise in the level of employment; i.e. **GDP growth happens to be faster than employment growth**.

Jobless growth leads to **chronic unemployment** even when there is a rise in the GDP growth rate.

It occurs due to the following possible reasons:

- **Greater use of efficient technology rather than greater use of manpower** in achieving the desired level of GDP growth.
- After the economic reform of 1991, the service sector has been the major force behind the economic growth of India. It is a less labour intensive sector as compared to the manufacturing sector. This can be empirically corroborated as India's service sector accounts for almost 54 per cent of GDP but employing only 30 per cent of workforce.
- Poor implementation of **Labour Reforms.**
- **Stagnation** in the share of manufacturing sector.
- Lack of high skill sets in Services sector such as IT and BPM, Telecommunication, etc.
- **Disguised unemployment** in agriculture accompanied by poor skill sets hindering job creation.
- **Large scale of NPAs** in infrastructure sector and MSMEs which absorbs a large number of workforce.

In India, between 1951 and 2000, while annual GDP growth rate had risen from 3.6 per cent to around 8 per cent, the growing rate of employment has tended to slide down from 1.5 per cent to just about 1 per cent, thereby resulting in jobless growth.

Employment Elasticity (*ratio of employment growth to growth in value added*) has **declined progressively** over time and across sectors.

During 1972–73 to 1983, employment elasticity was 0.52 per cent and it declined to 0.41 per cent in the next 10-year period and further to 0.29 per cent during 1993–94 to 2004–05.

During 2004–05 to 2011–12, employment elasticity came down further **to just 0.04 per cent** (almost zero).

In the agricultural sector, employment elasticity has fallen quite fast and has **even turned negative** (−0.42%) between 2004–05 and 2011–12. It was 0.46 per cent between 1972–73 and 1983.

This has occurred as we have relied more and more on labour-saving Western technology.

- Our economy has been bound to adopt labour-saving technology as the economy lacks sufficient investment capital and we have to depend on FDI.
- **FDIs coming to India** are generally linked with efficient foreign technology, and due to this, less labour is used in the process of production. As a result, we find the occurrence of better GDP growth but without sufficient growth in employment.
- As the reliance on FDI cannot be minimised in the current scenario, correction of jobless growth stands as **a great challenge** for the Indian economy.

BEVERIDGE CURVE OR UV CURVE

- It is a graphical representation of the relationship between *unemployment rate* (X-axis) and *job vacancy rate* (Y-axis).
- The curve is **hyperbolic** shaped and slopes downward.

- It is because higher rate of unemployment normally occurs with lower rate of vacancies and vice versa.
- A recessionary period is indicated by that point on curve where there is high rate of unemployment and low rate of job vacancy.

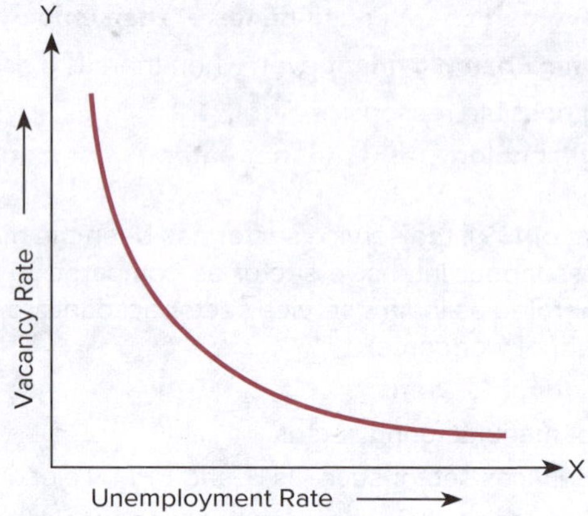

CASUALISATION AND INFORMALISATION OF WORKFORCE

The NSO data classifies the workers on the basis of employment status into three categories: **self-employed workers**; **regular wage/salaried employees** and **casual labourers**.

To understand this, let us first define the following:

- **Self-Employed** – This category consists of **employers**, **own account workers** and **unpaid family labour**. This category primarily includes those who work for themselves and do not sell their labour power to anyone else in return for wage. Own account workers work with one and more partners but have not engaged employees on a continuous basis.
- **Casual worker** versus **regular worker** – Workers are either self-employed or hired. Hired workers are further categorised as casual workers or regular workers.

Casual workers work on daily wages and are not given all social security benefits like gratuity or pension. However, they are entitled to employees' provident fund, regular working hours and even overtime payment.

Regular workers are on permanent payroll and are entitled to all social security benefits.

- **Formal worker** *versus* **informal worker** – As per the *National Commission for Enterprises in the Unorganised Sector* (NCEUS), workers working in the organised sector (which includes government departments, public enterprises and private establishments hiring 10 or more workers) are termed **formal workers**. However, workers working in the unorganised sector (i.e., enterprises hiring less than 10 workers) are called **informal workers**.

The reasons for increasing casualisation may be as follows:

- **Migration of disguised employed rural workers to urban areas** in search of non-farm employment and where they get employment mostly as casual workers due to lack of proper skills and training.

- Due to rapid growth in the real estate sector in urban areas and **MGNREGA in rural areas,** there has been an **increased employment in the construction sector**, thereby resulting in rise in casual or daily-rated workers.
- Informalisation has also led to casualisation of workforce.

The solution to it lies in **educational reforms** and **more skill development initiatives** by the government. To decrease this casualisation, **self-employment** should also be promoted by the government through facilitating opportunities of easy access to credit and supportive infrastructure.

Increasing Informalisation in India

In the current scenario, 90 per cent of workers are informal workers and only 10 per cent work in the formal sector.

Reasons for this rapid informalisation may be:

- **Transition from 'controlled economy' to 'market economy'** as a result of LPG reforms since 1991–92, and there is a strong correlation between market economy and informalisation of the workforce.
- **Lack of proper vocational skills** among the labour force at the entry level.
- Large number of **complex labour laws** and rules become an obstacle for the growth of private firms in the formal sector who, as an easy alternative, resort to use of casual/contractual workers.
- **Less-than-required focus on the MSME sector** till now, which actually offers a great potential as the formal sector.

Therefore, this growing informalisation makes the workforce more vulnerable to the uncertainties of market economy, and it is high time for preparing and undertaking a justified strategy towards reducing the same.

BONUS KNOWLEDGE

Did MGNREGA play a crucial role in reducing unemployment and whether it is to be continued or not? Elucidate

The **Mahatma Gandhi National Rural Employment Guarantee Act** (MGNREGA), launched in 2006, aims to provide 100 days of guaranteed wage employment annually to every rural household willing to do unskilled manual work, at wage rates notified by the Government of India (GoI). These rates, revised periodically, ranged from ₹171 to ₹284 as per the March 2019 notification and were further increased by ₹20 in March 2020 as part of COVID-19 relief measures. Additionally, in response to the pandemic-induced livelihood crisis, the GoI allocated an extra ₹40,000 crore to MGNREGA as part of its 2020 stimulus package.

Achievements of MGNREGA:

- **Increased Rural Employment:** The scheme significantly enhanced employment opportunities in rural areas.
- **Social Inclusion:** There has been notable participation of marginalised communities, including SCs, STs, and women, making the scheme more inclusive.
- **Financial Inclusion:** Wage payments through bank and post office accounts have promoted financial literacy and inclusion.
- **Asset Creation:** MGNREGA has facilitated the construction of durable rural assets such as ponds, check dams, concrete roads, and plantations.

Criticisms and Challenges:

- **Delayed Wage Payments:** Workers in several instances have faced delays in receiving their wages.
- **Declining Wage Component:** A decreasing share of the wage component in annual action plans has been observed in some panchayats.
- **Unemployment Allowance Issues:** There is often a reluctance to provide unemployment allowance to eligible households who did not receive work despite applying.

Despite these challenges, MGNREGA has played a transformative role by revitalising Panchayati Raj institutions and fostering a sense of entitlement and empowerment among rural populations. The United Nations Development Programme (UNDP), in its 2015 Human Development Report, recognised MGNREGA as a milestone and described it as the 'best-known' employment guarantee scheme globally for providing direct employment to the rural poor.

In conclusion, while the continuation of MGNREGA is both desirable and necessary for rural development and employment generation, there is a need to address the inefficiencies that hinder its effective implementation.

RECENT GOVERNMENT INITIATIVES TO REDUCE UNEMPLOYMENT

- **Aatmanirbhar Bharat Rojgar Yojana (ABRY)** (*as a part of the Aatmanirbhar Bharat 3.0 package*) was announced by the Government of India (GoI) to boost employment generation and to minimise socio-economic impact of COVID-19 pandemic. It is to help in the formalisation of informal employment and create new employment opportunities during and post COVID-19 pandemic.
- **Employees' Deposit Linked Insurance (EDLI)** Scheme provides assurance benefit to the eligible family members to provide financial assistance in the event of an employee's untimely death while on the job.
- The *Ministry of Social Justice and Empowerment* has developed the '**SMILE** – Support for Marginalised Individuals for Livelihood and Enterprise' scheme for the Comprehensive Rehabilitation of Beggars.
- '**PM-DAKSH**' (*Pradhan Mantri Dakshta Aur Kushalta Sampann Hitgrahi*) Portal and 'PM-DAKSH' Mobile App to make the skill development schemes accessible to some targeted groups.
- **Pradhan Mantri Kaushal Vikas Yojana (PMKVY) 4.0**, which aims to provide over 300 skill courses to India's youth in order to equip them with employable skills.
- **Prime Minister's Employment Generation Programme (PMEGP):** Launched by Ministry of Micro, Small & Medium Enterprises as a **credit-linked subsidy programme**, aimed at generating self-employment opportunities through establishment of micro-enterprises in the non-farm sector by helping traditional artisans and unemployed youth.
- **Future Skills PRIME:** Launched by Ministry of Electronics and Information Technology (MeitY) for Re-skilling/Up-skilling of IT Manpower for Employability in 10 new/emerging technologies, including Artificial Intelligence.
- **Deen Dayal Upadhyaya Grameen Kaushal Yojana:** Launched by Ministry of Rural Development for trainees belonging to SC/ST, Minority and Women category.
- **Skill Strengthening for Industrial Value Enhancement (STRIVE):** It is a World Bank assisted Central Sector Scheme which aims at improving the relevance and efficiency of skills training provided through Industrial Training Institutes (ITIs) and apprenticeships.

LABOUR REFORMS

The Constitution of India allows both Union and State governments to frame laws related to Labour which is mentioned in the **concurrent list of the Seventh Schedule**. For any industry, labour is one of the most essential constituents apart from capital. And if industries have to grow to its true potential in India, then labour reform is needed.

Labour reforms essentially envisaged taking steps to increase production, productivity, and employment opportunities in the economy in such a manner that the interests of the workers are not compromised. Such reforms include skill development, retraining, redeployment, updating knowledge base of workers and teachers, promotion of leadership qualities, etc. Labour reforms also include labour law reforms that are concerned with the trade union rights of the workers, industrial relations and job security and policies relating to wages, bonus and other incentive schemes.

RECENT REFORMS IN INDUSTRIAL LABOUR LAWS

Substantial legislative reforms were undertaken by GoI as per the recommendations of the **2nd National Commission on Labour. The four recently enacted labour codes are as follows:**

Recently Enacted Labour Codes	Details
The Code on Wages, 2019 (by subsuming 4 labour laws)	• Provisions for regulation of wages and bonuses. • Central government to fix the floor wages considering the living standards of different geographical locations. • Above floor wages, the minimum wages are determined on the basis of nature of work and skill.
The Code on Industrial Relations, 2020 (by subsuming 3 labour laws)	Provides the definition of worker, provision of seeking permission of the Government for closure, lay-off and retrenchment, prior intimation of strikes and lockouts, negotiation with trade unions, employment terms and re-skilling fund provisions.
The Code on Social Security, 2020 (by subsuming 8 labour laws)	• Provides a fund by Central government for various types of workers such as unorganised, gig, and platform workers. • Central government, State government and aggregators will contribute to the fund.
The Code on Occupational Safety, Health and Working Conditions, 2019 (by subsuming 13 labour laws)	Defines factory, enlarges the purview of the Act to contract workers, limits the working hour to 8 hours, same provisions for women. It also guarantees the rights of inter-state migrant workers.

INDUSTRIAL EMPLOYMENT (STANDING ORDERS) CENTRAL (AMENDMENT) RULES, 2018

- **Ministry of Labour and Employment** notified **fixed-term employment for all sectors** by amending the Industrial Employment (Standing Orders) Central Rules, 1946. **Previously,** fixed-term employment was there only for specific industrial sectors.
- Workman for a fixed-term employment has to be engaged on the basis of a written contract of employment for a fixed period. However, the **existing permanent workmen cannot be converted to fixed-term employment.**

- The amended rule provides for equal work hours, wages, allowances and other benefits as that of a permanent workman.
- However, **no notice of termination of employment** shall be necessary in the case of a **temporary workman.**
- These amendments have been made **to promote 'ease of doing business'** among industries.
- However, this move towards fixed-term employment for all sectors **will make it easier for companies to lay off workers.**

TWO NEW PENSION SCHEMES LAUNCHED IN 2019 (BY THE MINISTRY OF LABOUR & EMPLOYMENT)

Pradhan Mantri Shram Yogi Maan-dhan (PM-SYM)

It is a voluntary and contributory pension scheme to benefit **unorganised sector workers** (18–40 years old) whose monthly income is ₹15,000 or below. The beneficiary has to pay prescribed monthly contribution and the central government to provide equal contribution. In return, minimum monthly pension of **₹3,000** is given after 60 years of age.

National Pension Scheme for Traders, Shopkeepers and Self-Employed Persons

It is again a voluntary and contributory pension scheme for traders, shopkeepers and self-employed persons (18–40 years old) having an **annual turnover not exceeding ₹1.5 crore** and who are not a member of EPFO/ESIC/NPS/PM-SYM or an income taxpayer.

50 per cent monthly contribution is payable by the beneficiary and equal matching contribution is paid by the central government. After attaining the age of 60 years, minimum monthly pension of **₹3,000/-** is given.

SOCIAL SECURITY SCHEMES FOR EMPLOYEES

Employees' Provident Fund (EPF)

Employees' Provident Fund is a social security scheme aimed at salaried individuals run by EPFO which comes under the labour ministry.

Coverage: Organisations that employ 20 people or more need to offer EPF benefits to their employees.

It is compulsory only for those who earn up to ₹15,000 a month to contribute 12 per cent of their basic salary plus dearness allowance to EPF. The employer contributes an equal percentage (12%) to the corpus, out of which 3.67 per cent goes to the EPF and the rest 8.33 per cent goes towards employees' pension scheme (EPS). For those who earn above the threshold of ₹15,000, contribution to EPF is optional.

Employees' State Insurance (ESI)

The Employees' State Insurance is an integrated social security scheme tailored to provide socio-economic protection to the workers in the organised sector and their dependants, in contingencies, such as sickness, maternity and death or disablement due to an employment injury or occupational hazard. The wage ceiling of the same is ₹21000/- per month.

Atal Pension Yojana

Atal Pension Yojana is a voluntary and contributory pension scheme which seeks to provide guaranteed pension of ₹1000 to ₹5000 (depending upon contribution) receivable at the age of 60 years. The scheme is primarily focussed on unorganised workers, but any Indian citizen in the age-group 18 to 40 years can join through their savings bank account or post office savings bank account.

BONUS KNOWLEDGE

IMPLICATIONS OF ARTIFICIAL INTELLIGENCE (AI) IN LABOUR FORCE

- The increasing complexity of the AI models being developed today represents a paradigm shift in the equation of labour markets and technological development, showing the world that in a few years, 'intelligent machines' will be capable of performing tasks that are predominantly handled by humans today.
- The rate of progress in research and development of AI is outpacing the regulatory and ethical frameworks needed to manage its risks. Apparently, expectations point towards a trend where AI begins outperforming humans in critical decision-making processes in areas like healthcare, criminal justice, education, business and financial services among others.
- As per International Monetary Fund (IMF), AI poses risks of job displacements, notably for emerging markets and developing economies, which are not well placed to leverage the technology relative to the advanced economies. Incidentally, the International Labour Organisation (ILO) estimates that nearly 75 million jobs globally are at complete risk of automation due to AI. A prolonged labour displacement is something that a labour-surplus country like India cannot afford. Moreover, the Economic Survey 2023–24 highlighted that India would have to create an average of 78.5 lakh jobs annually in the non-farm sector by 2030 to cater to the rising workforce.
- Furthermore, India is majorly a services-driven economy, with a significant share of the I.T. workforce employed in low value-added services. Such jobs are the most susceptible to automation, as firms, in a bid to cut costs, may substitute labour for technology.
- India is also a consumption-based economy. Thus, the fall in consumption due to the displacement of its workforce is bound to have macroeconomic implications.

Responding to these uncertainties requires coordinated efforts aimed at addressing the structural issues that can intensify the impact of AI on India's labour market. The establishment of new, and upgrading existing institutions will play a pivotal role in this aspect. Social infrastructure will provide the required foundation for ensuring that the gains from technology can translate into inclusive growth.

SUMMARY

- **Unemployment** – One who has the ability to work, willingness to work and is of working age (15–60 years) but does not get work at current wage rate – measured by NSSO using three methods, viz. Usual Principal Status, Current Weekly Status and Current Daily Status.
- **Disguised Unemployment** – When a person does not contribute in the production process – marginal productivity of labour (MP_L) is zero in this case.
- **Quarterly Employment Survey (QES)** – It is conducted by Labour Bureau with 10 or more workers in 9 major sectors, consisting of 83 per cent of the total employment.
- **Beveridge Curve** – It is a graphical representation of the relationship between *unemployment rate* (X-axis) and *job vacancy rate* (Y-axis). The curve is hyperbolic shaped and slopes downward.

➤ **Reforms in Industrial Labour Laws** – Substantial legislative reforms were undertaken by the GoI as per the recommendations of the 2nd National Commission on Labour. The four recently enacted labour codes are - The Code on Wages, 2019, The Code on Industrial Relations, 2020, The Code on Social Security, 2020, The Code on Occupational Safety, Health and Working Conditions, 2019.

UPSC CSE PREVIOUS YEARS' PRELIMINARY EXAMINATION QUESTIONS

1. In India, which one of the following compiles information on industrial disputes, closures, retrenchments and lay-offs in factories employing workers? **[2022]**

(a) Central Statistics Office
(b) Department for Promotion of Industry and Internal Trade
(c) Labour Bureau
(d) National Technical Manpower Information System

2. With reference to the casual workers employed in India, consider the following statements: **[2021]**

1. All casual workers are entitled for Employees Provident Fund coverage.
2. All casual workers are entitled for regular working hours and overtime payment.
3. The government can by a notification specify that an establishment or industry shall pay wages only through its bank account.

Which of the above statements are correct?

(a) 1 and 2 only
(b) 2 and 3 only
(c) 1 and 3 only
(d) 1, 2 and 3

3. Disguised unemployment generally means **[2013]**

(a) large number of people remain unemployed
(b) alternative employment is not available
(c) marginal productivity of labour is zero
(d) productivity of workers is low

4. The MPI developed by the Oxford Poverty and Human Development Initiative with UNDP support covers which of the following? **[2012]**

1. Deprivation of education, health, assets and services at household level.
2. Purchasing power parity at national level.
3. Extent of budget deficit and GDP growth rate at national level.

Select the correct answer using the codes given below:

(a) 1 only (b) 2 and 3 only
(c) 1 and 3 only (d) 1, 2 and 3

☞ NO QUESTIONS ASKED
2024, 2023, 2020, 2019, 2018, 2017, 2016, 2015, 2014

ANSWER KEY

1. (c) 2. (d) 3. (c) 4. (a)

UPSC CSE PREVIOUS YEARS' MAIN EXAMINATION QUESTIONS

1. Most of the unemployment in India is structural in nature. Examine the methodology adopted to compute unemployment in the country and suggest improvements. **[2023]**

2. The nature of economic growth in India in recent times is often described as **jobless growth**. Do you agree with this view? Give arguments in favour of your answer. **[2015]**

☞ NO QUESTIONS ASKED
2024, 2022, 2021, 2020, 2019, 2018, 2017, 2016, 2014, 2013, 2012

CHAPTER

6

INFLATION

CHAPTER OUTLINE

- Economic Growth and Inflation
- Types of Inflation (Rate-Wise)
- Types of Inflation (Cause-Wise)
- Methods to Measure Inflation
- Wholesale Price Index
- Consumer Price Index
- GDP Deflator
- Headline Inflation
- Core Inflation
- Cause of Inflation
- Effects/Impact of Inflation
- Measures to Check Inflation
- Some Inflation-Related Concepts
- Deflation
- Disinflation
- Stagflation
- Reflation
- Skewflation
- Recent Efforts by the Government to Control Inflation
- Trends and Reports on Inflation

Inflation refers to the **rise in general price level** in the economy over a period of time. In other words, it is nothing but the rise in the average price level **of all the goods and services** in the economy.

BONUS KNOWLEDGE

Economic Growth and Inflation go hand in hand **(directly proportional)** in the short run, i.e. Economic Growth rate falls with any policy to reduce rate of inflation. On the other hand, higher growth rate can be achieved at the cost of high inflation rate in the short run.

However, in the long run, it is the price stability which matters more, by maintaining inflation at a desired rate.

The rate of inflation is measured as the rate of change in the average price of products over a period of time, and is expressed in percentage. The formula is:

Rate of inflation in this period = (Price in this period – Price in the previous period) * 100 / Price in the previous period.

Usually, the same period of the previous year is used as reference for the measurement of inflation. Ex. April 2024 may be used as the base for April 2025 period.

Moreover, inflation is **measured through a price index** (where price index is a percentage number that shows the extent to which prices have changed over a period of time and as compared to prices of a base year which is taken as the standard).

The Wholesale Price Index (WPI) was considered as the primary inflation measure in India, but from 2014, RBI adopted Consumer Price Index Combined as its key measure of inflation in India.

The percentage change in the CPI over a period of time (with respect to the base year) gives us the rate of inflation over that period.

TYPES OF INFLATION (RATE-WISE)

Depending upon the rate of growth of prices, the following are the different types of inflation:

(a) Creeping Inflation

It is the **mildest form** of inflation, also known as mild inflation or low inflation. In this case, the rate of the rise in general prices, is low and **varies between 2 per cent and 3 per cent**. If this rate or rise in price is continued, then it is considered good for the economy as producers and traders make reasonable profits which encourage them to invest more. This inflation is **manageable**.

(b) Walking/Trotting Inflation

When the rate of rising prices is more than creeping inflation (i.e. **3–10 per cent**), then it is called walking inflation. This inflation must be taken seriously as this is a **warning for the occurrence of running/galloping inflation**. If not checked, it can result in galloping inflation.

(c) Galloping Inflation

When inflation is **more than 10 per cent and up to 50 per cent**, it refers to galloping inflation. Due to this, businesses and employees' income cannot keep up with the costs and the prices. Even foreign investors avoid such unstable economies for investment. This situation is also termed as **hopping or running inflation**.

(d) Hyperinflation

It is an extreme form of inflation where the **prices rise at an alarmingly high rate** (i.e. more than 50 per cent every month). In hyperinflation, not only the price but also the pace of increase of price is alarmingly fast. Hyperinflation occurs **when there is a large increase in money supply**. In extreme situations, the **value of national currency reduces to almost zero** and paper money becomes worthless. In such a case, even to buy a loaf of bread and some vegetables, one needs to carry money in big gunny bags.

Thus, money **stops to function** as a **store of value** and as a **medium of exchange**.

> **did you KNOW?**
>
> Germany experienced hyperinflation in the 1920s, Hungary in 1946, and Zimbabwe during 2004–09.
>
> The Venezuelan economy is experiencing an alarming rate of hyperinflation. It was around 282,972.80 per cent in 2019 (*according to the data from Trading Economics*).

BONUS KNOWLEDGE

NEW CURRENCY TO TACKLE HYPERINFLATION

The **Iran Government**, in 2020, changed the national currency from Rial to **Toman**. One Toman equals 10,000 Rials. Gheran is another new denomination introduced by the Iranian Government. 100 Gheran makes 1 Toman.

In 2023, Zimbabwe launched Gold Backed Digital Currency to strengthen and stabilise its currency. The country is suffering from a significant economic challenges like hyperinflation and weakening Zimbabwean Dollar. By launching the Gold Backed Digital Currency, the country tries to address the issue of excess liquidity in the economy and to bring back confidence in its own currency.

- A Gold Backed Digital Currency is a form of currency that ties its value with Gold with a view to maintaining its value stability. (This currency can be bought or sold by using the country's currency or other foreign currencies.)

TYPES OF INFLATION (CAUSE-WISE)

(a) Demand–Pull Inflation

- It is caused by an increase in aggregate demand and consumption **due to**
  i. Increased private and Government spending,
  ii. Lower rate of savings by households,
  iii. Depreciation in local exchange rate,
  iv. Reduction in taxes,
  v. Increase in money supply and bank credit, and
  vi. Increase in exports.
- This **leads to increased disposable income** in the hands of households, thereby resulting in the **increase of the aggregate demand** with no change in aggregate supply.
- To check this inflation, the supplies need to be increased to match the increased demand, hence relieving the economy from higher level of inflation.

(b) Cost–Push Inflation

- It is also called **'supply shock inflation'**. It occurs when the general prices rise **due to growing cost of 'factors of production' of goods and services** such as land, labour and raw materials.
- For example, if wage of the labourer rises, then the unit cost of production also rises and as a result, the prices of goods and services that are manufactured get hiked. When the supply of inputs of production is reduced, it leads to increased prices or even when production of agricultural products is adversely affected due to various factors such as droughts, floods, etc.
- In 1973, as a result of **oil shock** (i.e. unexpected increase in oil prices by OPEC countries), there was a massive rise in general price level across the globe.
- Cost–Push Inflation is also caused by (i) increase in indirect taxes, (ii) increase in import prices and (iii) higher cost of capital and interest rates (iv) higher profit margins of producing firms.

(c) Structural Inflation

In this case, inflation **persists for a longer period** due to deficiencies existing in the economy, such as

- backward agricultural sector (poor productivity)
- inefficient distribution and storage facilities, and many more

These deficiencies in the economy lead to shortages, which in turn cause inflation.

It is also termed as **Bottleneck Inflation**, and the Government faces a tough time tackling this particular type of inflation. It can be handled through major structural reforms.

BONUS KNOWLEDGE

BUILT-IN INFLATION

Built-in inflation (sometimes referred to as a wage-price spiral) is a phenomenon wherein workers begin demanding higher wages to keep up with the rising cost of living. This leads to businesses increase in their prices in order to offset their rising wage costs; creating a self-reinforcing loop of wage and price hikes.

METHODS TO MEASURE INFLATION

Inflation can be measured in three different ways:

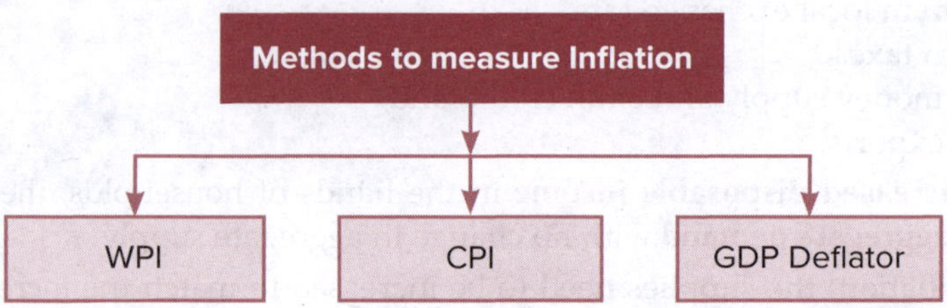

(a) Wholesale Price Index

Wholesale Price Index (WPI) measures the change in **wholesale prices on a monthly basis** (previously it was weekly basis).

WPI takes into account **697 commodities** of various types to measure inflation, but it **does not take into account services.**

WPI uses the **ex-factory prices** of these commodities to measure inflation. In other words, it takes into account prices of commodities before they reach consumers. Therefore, **indirect taxes are not included** in the prices considered for WPI computation and as a result WPI-based inflation is **less affected by any change in the fiscal policy** of the Government.

did you KNOW? WPI was first published in the year 1942 in India. Presently, **Department of Industrial Policy & Promotion (DIPP) under Ministry of Commerce & Industry** compiles and publishes WPI.

BONUS KNOWLEDGE

BASE YEAR AND BASE EFFECT

Base Year is the year on the 'basis' of which we compute price index for the purpose of calculating rate of inflation.

'Base Effect' shows the impact of different reference data which is reflected in the interpretation of comparative results. Criteria for deciding a particular Financial Year as Base Year:

- Year with less monsoon deficit
- Year with no major natural calamity, drought or famine
- That year should not have inflation at alarming rates
- Unstable years in terms of economic activity are not considered as base year
- There should not be much gap between base year chosen and current year

Current **base year used is 2011–12** = 100 as base (earlier it was 2004–05).

The commodity basket of **697 commodities** (previously 676) is classified majorly **into three categories** of components:

Products	Weights under Old Base Year 2004–05	Weights with New Base Year 2011–12	Remarks
Primary Articles (cereals, fruits, vegetables and minerals)	20.12%	22.62%	**Increased**
Fuel and Power (coal, electricity and mineral oil)	14.91%	13.15%	**Decreased**
Manufactured Products	64.97%	64.23%	**Decreased**
Total	**100%**	**100%**	

Conclusion: **Weight of primary articles has increased** under new base year of 2011–12, **whereas weights of fuel and power** and **manufactured products has decreased**.

BONUS KNOWLEDGE

WPI Food Index: To monitor food inflation more effectively, Department for Promotion of Industry and Internal Trade **(DIPP) has been publishing WPI Food Index** since 2017. It measures the rate of inflation in food items at the level of producers. Aggregate of all the food items within the list of 697 commodities under WPI is considered to compute WPI Food Index.

As per the Economic Survey 2024–25, food inflation, measured by the Consumer Food Price Index (CFPI), has increased from 7.5 per cent in FY24 to 8.4 per cent in FY25 (April–December), primarily driven by a few food items such as vegetables and pulses.

(b) Consumer Price Index

- **Consumer Price Index (CPI) measures** the change in **retail prices** on **monthly basis**. It **includes both goods and services**.
- It focuses on **homogeneous group of consumers**, i.e. consumers with the same likings in terms of commodity basket. Presently, it takes into consideration two homogeneous groups: rural households and urban households.
- It **reflects the cost of living** of the **two** concerned categories of consumers.

EXAM ESSENTIAL

Various Types of CPIs

S. No.	Index	Base Year Used	Compiled by
1	CPI – Industrial Worker, designed to measure the changes in the pricing of a given basket of products and services used by Industrial Workers throughout time.	2016	**Labour Bureau** under the Ministry of Labour and Employment, GoI
2	CPI – Agricultural Labourer, **designed** to revise minimum wages for agricultural labour in different states.	1986–87	
3	CPI – Rural Labourer	1986–87	
4	CPI Rural, CPI Urban, CPI (Rural + Urban) or CPI (combined)	2012	**National Statistics Office** (NSO) which was previously known as Central Statistics Office (CSO). The Indian Government issued an order in 2019, to merge the NSSO (National Sample Survey Office) and the CSO to form National Statistical Office (NSO).

CPI Rural, CPI Urban and CPI (Combined)

- It covers **448 items in the rural basket** and **460 items in the urban basket**.
- Base year used to compute CPI has been revised from the year 2010 = 100 to **2012** = 100
- For computing **Dearness Allowance**, CPI is used (not WPI).
- **For inflation targeting**, Reserve Bank of India (RBI) and the Central Government since 2015 uses **CPI (Combined)** (instead of WPI) for policymaking based on the report of the Urjit Patel Committee.
- **Headline Inflation** is based on **CPI (Combined)**.

EXAM ESSENTIAL

Relative weights under CPI (Combined)

Title	Weights under Old Base Year 2004–05	Weights under New Base Year 2011–12	Remarks
Food and Beverages	47.6%	45.86%	**Decreased**
Paan/Betel leaves, Tobacco and Intoxicants	2.1%	2.38%	Increased
Clothing and Footwear	4.7%	6.53%	Increased
Housing	9.8%	10.07%	Increased
Fuel and Light	9.5%	6.84%	**Decreased**
Miscellaneous	26.3%	28.32%	Increased
Total	**100%**	**100%**	

Analysis

- Housing component is **not included** under CPI Rural.
- Weight of food and beverage **is more in case of** CPI Rural (54.2 per cent) compared to CPI Urban (36.3 per cent).
- **Weight of Fuel and light has decreased** under new series of CPI with base year 2012.

BONUS KNOWLEDGE

CPI FOOD INDEX

It is released **by CSO since 2014**. It is computed on point-to-point monthly basis with same base year (2012) as used in case of CPI.

'Cereals & Products' carries the **highest weight** (34.2 per cent) in the computation of CPI Food Index. Other sub-groups considered in this computation are Milk & Milk Products, Vegetables, Oils & Fats, Egg, fish & meat, etc.

Globally, FAO Food Price Index (FFPI) released by Food & Agriculture Organization (FAO) of the United Nations reflects the monthly change in international prices of a basket of food commodities. It consists of the average of 05 commodity group indices, i.e. Cereal, vegetable oil, meat, dairy and sugar. The FAO Food Price Index (FFPI) averaged at 118.0 points in January 2024 (1.2 per cent down from its December 2023 level).

EXAM ESSENTIAL

WPI *vs* CPI

Basis	WPI	CPI (Combined)
Base year	2011–12	2012
No. of commodities	697 products	200 weighted items
Whether includes services or not?	WPI takes into account **only** goods	CPI takes into account **both** goods and services
Weight of food products	Food items have lesser weights in WPI (around 22%)	Food items have greater weight in CPI (around 46%)
Stage of production	WPI measures inflation at each stage of production.	CPI measures inflation only at final stage of production
Data collection	Centralised collection	In 1,181 villages and 310 towns
Time lag	Lower time lag, data are available relatively quicker	Greater time lag
Rate of inflation	Rate of WPI-based inflation is generally low compared to CPI-based inflation	Rate of CPI-based inflation is generally high compared to WPI-based inflation

Based on the above points, it can be said that **CPI is a better measure of inflation** as compared to WPI and is more reliable for monetary policy decisions.

Nevertheless, it is worth mentioning that WPI estimates inflation at the wholesale level or at the entry level of the economy. If the government timely intervenes, then inflation can be checked before the effect reaches the consumers.

(c) GDP Deflator

It refers to the **ratio between GDP at Current Prices and GDP at Constant Prices**.

$$\text{GDP deflator} = \frac{\text{GDP at Current Prices}}{\text{GDP at Constant Prices}}$$

If GDP deflator is 1, it implies no change in general price levels.

If GDP deflator is >1, it implies increase in general price levels.

As compared to WPI and CPI, GDP deflator is **a better measure of inflation** as it takes into account all the goods and services of the economy. But still, it is not used to frame short-term inflation targeting policy as GDP-related data are not available on monthly basis.

BONUS KNOWLEDGE

PRODUCER PRICE INDEX

- PPI measures price changes **from the perspective of producers** (whereas CPI measures price changes from consumers/buyers perspective.
- PPI measures the **average change in prices that the producer receives** for his goods/services sold in the domestic market/exports and thus **excludes the effect of indirect taxes on inflation**.
- PPI takes into account both goods and services (unlike WPI).

- There is a **bias of double/multiple counting inherent under WPI** which can be avoided by using PPI.
- GoI in 2014 appointed **B.N. Goldar Committee** to examine whether or not PPI should replace WPI and suggest a methodology.
- The Committee majorly recommended:
  1. **Shifting from WPI to PPI** on experimental basis to measure inflation.
  2. Data from **'Supply Use Tables'** to be used to compute experimental PPI.
  3. Base year for experimental PPI should be 2011–12.
  4. **Including services price** in the PPI basket.
  5. **Including major export and import items** while calculating experimental PPI.
- A number of advanced economies like USA and even some emerging economies have already switched to using PPI instead of WPI.
- IMF has also recommended the use of PPI instead of WPI for measuring inflation.

Headline Inflation

It is what consumers experience. It is a raw inflation figure reported through CPI (Combined). It includes both volatile and non-volatile categories of items. It is best understood when contrasted with Core Inflation.

Core Inflation

This measure is **computed by policymakers** to analyse inflation data, which **excludes the more volatile categories like food items and energy (fuel and power) products**. Core inflation is calculated using **CPI** by excluding the aforesaid categories of commodities **to remove the impact of temporary and short-term shocks**.

Refined Core Inflation

As per survey it has been constructed by excluding main fuel items that means petrol for vehicle, diesel for vehicle and lubricants & other fuels in vehicle, in addition to food and beverages and fuel and light from the headline core inflation.

CAUSE OF INFLATION

Inflation occurs either due to rise **in aggregate demand or fall in aggregate supply**. Thus factors/causes of inflation can be divided into two broad categories:

(a) Demand Side Factors/Causes for Inflation

- Due to rise in non-developmental Government expenditure.
- **Due to increase in deficit financing**, i.e. financing the deficits by borrowing funds from the banking system.

(b) Supply Side Factors/Causes for Inflation

- Due to **erratic agricultural** production (because of its dependence on monsoon and extreme weather events such as El Nino).

- Supply chain shock due to any conflict. (For example, Ukraine–Russia conflict)
- **Hoarding** of essential commodities by big farmers and wholesalers.
- Higher **Minimum Support Prices** (MSPs) are announced by the Government year after year.

EFFECTS/IMPACT OF INFLATION

EXAM ESSENTIAL

On lender and borrower	Inflation **benefits the borrower (debtors) as the value of the previously borrowed money reduces**, whereas it causes **loss to the lender (creditors)**.
On bond holders	As bond gives a fixed return after maturity, the bond holder **tends to lose** due to rise in rate of inflation.
On fixed income groups	Inflation very **badly affects** the **salaried and pension class** as with inflation, the purchasing power of income falls drastically without any increase in income.
On big farmers and big businesses	Big farmers and big businesses usually gain as they get better prices due to inflation, thereby earning more profits.
On exchange rate and exports	Exchange rate may depreciate due to inflation, and there is a benefit to exporters because of this. However, exports may also discourage as domestic sales are attractive due to higher prices.
On employment	In the short run, employment may increase with rise in inflation (see Phillips curve). However, it may not hold true in the long run.
On savings	Marginal Propensity to Save (MPS) decreases as most of the savings in India is done by households. On the contrary, it skews the savings pattern in favour of unproductive assets like gold.
On inequality or distribution of income	Inequality may rise in the economy due to inflation as the lower strata of society are more severely affected.
On fiscal deficit	It may rise due to rise in inflation as the Government needs to give more subsidies in order to make goods affordable to low-income groups.
On marginalised class	According to ADB, 1% food inflation leads to 0.3% increase in both infant and child mortality rates and 0.5% increase in undernourishment.

Inflation Tax

It is measured as the effect of **holding cash in an inflationary scenario**. If currency is held in an inflationary scenario, rising prices of the products will decrease the purchasing power of the currency held. As a result, it can be inferred that the currency is losing its value and not earning any interest at the same time. This depreciation is termed inflation tax.

Inflation Premium

It is the opposite phenomenon of the inflation tax for the borrowers. It is defined as the reduction of real rate of return on investment at the time of maturity. Borrowers have to return a lesser value of currency as inflation has reduced the value of the same.

EXAM ESSENTIAL

PHILLIPS CURVE

It reflects the relationship between rate of inflation and rate of unemployment.

It describes the **INVERSE relationship between the rate of inflation and the rate of unemployment** in an economy.

New Zealand–born economist A.W. Phillips first put forward this theory **in 1958**.

He observed that price stability has a trade-off against unemployment. In other words, if unemployment decreases, inflation will increase and vice versa.

But if inflation runs in an economy for a longer time, then it leads to a stagnant economy. Unemployment increases in a stagnant economy. Thus, we can safely say the phenomenon of Phillips Curve will not hold/will be invalid during Stagflation.

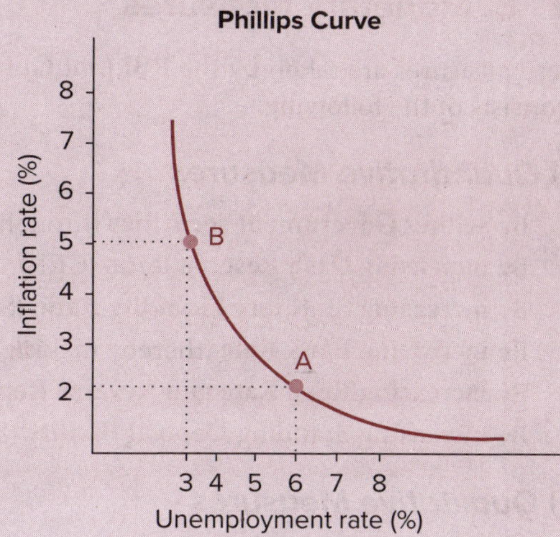

MEASURES TO CHECK INFLATION

Inflation can be controlled by different measures. Inflation is controlled to **ideal rates** (zero rate of inflation is never preferred). **For a developing country like India, desired rate of inflation is 3–4 per cent**.

It is not easy to control inflation by using a specific measure or an instrument. The prime objective of any measure to check inflation is to reduce the flow of money supply in the economy or reduce the liquidity in the market. Following are the three categories of measures:

A. Fiscal Measures

B. Monetary Measures

C. Administrative Measures

A. Fiscal Measures

The **Government** uses fiscal measures to control inflation. The two main components of fiscal policy are **Government revenue** and **Government expenditure**. Under fiscal policy, the Government (not RBI) controls inflation and in the following ways:

1. **By reducing private spending** (by enhancing taxes on private businesses), i.e. when the Government reduces private spending by increasing taxes, individuals decrease their total expenditure; and the money supply in the economy is reduced.
2. **By decreasing non-developmental Government expenditure**.
3. **By avoiding deficit financing** as far as possible.

Use of option 2 above may not be feasible all the time as the Government expenditure may be required for ongoing projects and managing strategic sectors like health, education, defence, etc.

B. Monetary Measures

These measures are taken **by the RBI (not GoI) to check inflation by controlling supply of money**, and it consists of the following:

(a) Quantitative Measures

- By **selling Government securities** through Open Market Operation (OMO)
- By **increasing Cash Reserve Ratio** (CRR)
- By **increasing Statutory Liquidity Ratio** (SLR)
- By **increasing Bank Rate** (thereby making borrowings costlier)
- By **increasing Repo Rate and Reverse Repo Rate**
- By **increasing Standing Deposit Facility** (SDF)

(b) Qualitative Measures

- Margin requirement
- Credit Rationing
- Effective implementation of counter cyclical fiscal policy and normalisation of the economy
- Moral (per)suasion, etc.

C. Administrative Measures

It includes

- Prevention of black marketing and prevention of hoarding.
- Banning export of constrained materials.
- Facilitating supply of goods and services in case of demand–pull inflation.
- Suspending future trading, etc.

EXAM ESSENTIAL

INFLATION TARGETING: A CHOICE OR A NEED

Urjit Patel Committee was appointed by RBI in 2013:

1. To revise and strengthen Monetary Policy Framework
2. To recommend an appropriate nominal anchor for the conduct of monetary policy

The Committee (in its report in 2014) recommended to focus on only one objective, i.e. INFLATION TARGETING.

Inflation Targeting – It is a central banking policy that focuses on adjusting the monetary policy to achieve a specified annual rate of inflation.

Strict Inflation Targeting – It is used when the central bank is only concerned with keeping inflation as close to a given target as possible.

Flexible Inflation Targeting – It is used when the central bank is also concerned about other things, such as interest rate, exchange rate, output and employment stability.

Why Inflation Targeting is needed in India – As per the report, it is required because:

- Real interest rates have remained negative during most of the post-global crisis period.
- External competitiveness is getting eroded due to continuous higher levels of inflation.
- Due to inflation, there has been a large import of Gold due to its increasing demand and it has resulted in widening of the Current Account Deficit.
- Continuous weakening of exchange rate has occurred due to persisting high inflation.
- Rise in inequality in the Indian economy due to increased rates of inflation.

CPI or WPI as the Nominal Anchor for Inflation Targeting

Committee recommended **to adopt CPI (Combined)** [instead of WPI (minus food & fuel)-based inflation targeting] in order to anchor Monetary Policy. The reasons were that:

- WPI ignores the effect of service sector which contributes almost 60 per cent to the overall GDP
- CPI is based on retail prices which depicts a broader picture of the effect of inflation.

Numerical Target of CPI-Based Inflation

Committee recommended inflation target of **4 per cent (± 2 per cent)**.

Based on the recommendations, **RBI in 2015 signed an agreement with Government of India**, agreeing on the following points:

- **Flexible Inflation Targeting (FIT)** as the official goal of RBI. **FIT for 2016–17 to 2020–21 was 4 per cent (± 2 per cent)**.
- Flexible Inflation target to be set by GoI once in every 5 years in consultation with RBI.
- CPI (combined) to be used as the measure of nominal anchor for policy decisions.

In its Currency and Finance (RCF) Report for 2020–21, the RBI recommended that the inflation target be retained at **4 per cent (± 2 per cent)** for the next five years.

Under the Reserve Bank of India Act, 1934, the inflation target for the period between 1 April 2021 to 31 March 2026 has been kept at the same level as for the previous 5 years.

SOME INFLATION-RELATED CONCEPTS

Deflation

It is a decrease in general price levels of goods and services throughout an economy. If there is a higher supply of goods and services but **not enough money supply** to combat the situation, deflation can occur. Deflation is mainly caused by shifts in supply and demand. Deflation is usually associated with significant **unemployment**. However, deflation increases the value of money.

When inflation becomes negative, it leads to deflation. It is invariably **associated with recession**, i.e. negative growth in the economy.

To check deflation, the following measures can be taken to increase money supply:

- Increase Government spending
- Lower bank rate and repo rates

- Print more currency
- Decrease taxes to boost demand

Disinflation

Disinflation, on the other hand, **shows the rate of change of inflation over time**. In this case, the **inflation rate is declining over time, but it remains positive**. For example, if the inflation rate in India was 5 per cent in January but decreases to 4 per cent in March, it is said to be experiencing disinflation in the first quarter of the year. Under disinflation, the rate of inflation falls and **tends towards zero but never becomes negative**.

Stagflation

Stagflation emerges when **both stagnation (i.e. zero economic growth) and inflation occur** simultaneously. It is an economic period of no growth, relatively high unemployment and rise in prices of goods and a decline in GDP. Generally, when unemployment strikes, there is a fall in spending and prices of goods. But in case of stagflation, the price of goods rises, unemployment increases and spending declines. Stagflation is **a rare phenomenon** and is bad for an economy.

For example, the US economy went into stagflation in the 1970s due to extraordinary rise in global oil prices.

Reflation

Reflation is a phenomenon when inflation returns after a spell of deflation, thereby indicating that the economic growth is back in the economy.

Skewflation

It occurs when there is **inflation in some commodities and deflation in others** such as a rising cost of living (inflation) coupled with falling asset prices, such as of housing (deflation). It is the opposite of stagflation, but is neither inflation nor deflation.

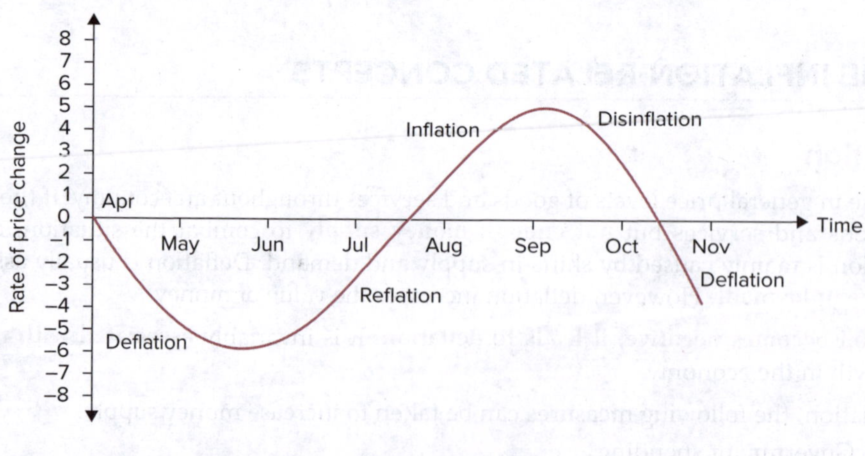

EXAM ESSENTIAL

HOUSING PRICE INDEX

It is based on property price transactions in the **10 major cities of India**. The base year used by RBI for its compilation is 2010–11. Housing Price Index is published **by RBI**.

RECENT EFFORTS BY THE GOVERNMENT TO CONTROL INFLATION

The GoI has taken several steps to control inflation (especially on food items):

1. Encouraging the State Governments to take **strict action against hoarding and black marketing** and effectively enforce the *Essential Commodities Act, 1955* and the *Prevention of Blackmarketing and Maintenance of Supplies of Essential Commodities Act, 1980* for commodities in short supply.
2. Facilitating **ease of doing business** which reduces various transactional and logistics costs for producers.
3. **Goods and Services Tax** was introduced in 2017 which reduced the cascading effect of taxes on many commodities.
4. **Banning exports of certain commodities** to boost supply in the domestic market.
5. The Government has taken several measures **to augment the supply of essential commodities**:
    - To ensure effective intervention during price rise through the use of buffer stocks, the **Government purchased pulses** from farmers/Farmer Producer Organisations (FPOs) in 2020–21 and 2021–22.
    - The target for **pulse buffer of 23 LMT** and **onion buffer of 2.08 LMT** was created by the government in 2021–22.
    - Different steps to augment domestic availability of pulses like free import duty, reduction in agriculture infrastructure and development cess, etc.
    - The Government has imposed **stock holding limits** on various commodities like edible oils and oilseeds.
6. For perishable essential commodities, the Government launched **Operation Green** [which has been expanded from Tomato, Onion, Potato (TOP) to total 41 perishables], **Kisan Rail** to enable speedy movement of perishables from production or surplus regions to consumption or deficient regions.

Last Minute SNIPPETS

In FY25 (April–December), food inflation has risen due to rise in prices of vegetables (mainly tomato and onion) and pulses. Vegetables and pulses have a weightage of 8.42% in CPI basket, but their contribution to the overall inflation is 32.3% in FY25 (April–December).

Government has taken the following steps to combat food inflation:

Cereals

- Limit on stock on wheat from 24 June 2024 to 31 March 2025.
- **Open Market Sale Scheme(OMSS*):** Wheat and rice was offloaded in the market from the central pool.

- Sale of wheat flour and rice under Bharat brand.

Pulses

- Sale of chana dal, moong dal and masoor dal under Bharat brand.
- Limit on stock on tur and desi chana from 21 June to 30 September 2024.
- Until 31 March 2025 Government has allowed duty-free import of desi Chana, Tur, Urad and Masur.
- Until 20 February 2025 Government has allowed duty-free import of yellow peas.

Vegetables

- Buffer Stock of Onion: Under Price Stabilisation Fund, a total of 4.7 lakh MT of rabi onion has been procured.
- Export duty on onion has been increased to 20 per cent since 13 September 2024.
- Sale of onion at a subsidised rate of 35 per kg from September–December 2024, and sale of onion at a subsidised rate of 65 per kg in October 2024.

TRENDS AND REPORTS ON INFLATION

RBI Launches Surveys

In 2023, RBI introduced two important surveys for Monetary Policy Insights. These two surveys provide valuable inputs for RBI's bi-monthly monetary policy.

1. **Inflation Expectations Survey of Households:** It is to gather subjective assessment of price movements based on individual consumption pattern of households across 19 major cities like Delhi, Chennai, Chandigarh, Bhopal, etc. This survey provides information on both **qualitative and quantitative responses** from households.
   - **Qualitative Responses:** It is to enquire about households' expectations regarding price changes about three months ahead and one year ahead period.
   - **Quantitative Responses:** It is for collecting data on current inflation rates, expected inflation rates in the three months and one year ahead period, respectively.
2. **The Consumer Confidence Survey:** It tries to measure the sentiments of households on various economic aspects like views on general economic condition, employment scenario, price levels, household income, household spending, etc. It has also been conducted across 19 cities like Delhi, Chennai, Chandigarh, Bhopal, etc.

Last Minute SNIPPETS

Index	January 2024	January 2025
WPI	0.27 (P)*	2.31 (P)*
CPI (Combined) or CPI-C	5.10 (P)*	4.31 (P)*

(P)* – Provisional

Source: For WPI = Office of the Economic Advisor, DPIIT, Ministry of Commerce and Industry, For CPI-C = NSO, MoSPI

The results of these surveys is going to help RBI to sharpen its monetary policy decisions by analysing the perception and expectation of households on inflation and broader economic conditions.

BONUS KNOWLEDGE

HOW IS THE CURRENT INFLATION DIFFERENT FROM THE 1970S?

Unprecedented global inflation in the current year may be like the 1970s, particularly the fallout from the oil crises in 1973 and 1979. Both crises resulted in elevated commodity prices worldwide and their effects on the prices of other goods and services. However, the environment and intensity of the crises differ in many aspects:

1. Recent oil price rises are proportionally smaller than the 1970s crisis, which had oil as the main component.
2. Commodity supply disruptions have played a smaller role in recent price increases when compared to the 1970s. The rise in commodity prices over the past year has been followed by a moderate rise in the production of many commodities (although not oil). Global commodity supply chains have now become more efficient than in the 1970s and hence, the inflationary pressure can be absorbed with more ease. However, supply disruptions could intensify over the coming years.
3. Global inflation, which has risen significantly since the start of 2021, follows several years of low inflation. In contrast to this, the 1973 crisis took place against a backdrop of several years of steadily rising world inflation.
4. The 1973 crisis followed close on the heels of the collapse of the exchange rate regime managed by Bretton Woods; as the goals and even instruments of monetary policy were poorly defined in many countries. Arguably, central banks today have much clearer and robust institutional frameworks that focus on price stability. This has prevented inflation expectations of the public from becoming unanchored despite a sharp rise in inflation in 2022.

Besides commodity market behaviour, higher energy prices may matter less today than in the past. Besides that, the sources of energy are now more diversified compared to 1970s and also there is more availability of nuclear and solar energy, which makes it less impactful. With better coordination among the global central banks and the application of unconventional monetary policy tools, inflation is managed efficiently so that its negative spillovers are limited and transitory. The energy intensity of GDP (the energy required to produce a given amount of goods and services) has fallen by around 40 per cent since the late 1970s. With the diversification of input baskets and destinations for sourcing, commodity shocks' impact has been tamed to some extent. Hence, we may expect recent commodity price rises to be less disruptive than those of the 1970s.

SUMMARY

- **Inflation** – Rise in general price level in an economy – measured on year-on-year basis.
- Economic growth is directly proportional to inflation.
- Based on growth of prices, inflation can be classified as: creeping (2–3 per cent), walking (3–10 per cent), galloping (10–50 per cent), hyperinflation (rise at an alarmingly high rate).
- Based on causes, inflation can be classified as demand–pull, cost–push and structural.
- **Demand–Pull inflation** – Caused by increased private and Government spending, lower rate of savings by households, depreciation in local exchange rate, reduction in taxes and increase in money supply and bank credit – increased disposable income – increase in the aggregate demand.
- **Cost–Push inflation** – Supply shock inflation – caused by growing cost of factors of production of goods and services, increase in indirect taxes, increase in import prices, higher cost of capital, interest rates, etc.

- **Structural inflation** – Bottleneck inflation – persists for a longer period.
- **Inflation can be measured through** – Wholesale Price Index (WPI), Consumer Price Index (CPI) and GDP Deflator.
- **WPI** – Change in wholesale price on monthly basis – measured by DIPP under Ministry of Commerce and Industry – goods included are of three categories: primary articles, fuel and power and manufactured products.
- **CPI** – Change in retail price on monthly basis – CPI for Industrial workers, Agricultural Labourer and Rural Labourer is measured by Labour Bureau – CPI Rural, Urban and Combined are measured by CSO – both goods and services are taken into account – headline inflation is based on CPI (combined) – Core inflation is measured through CPI excluding food items and fuel and energy products.
- **GDP Deflator** – Ratio of GDP at current price to GDP at constant price – GDP Deflator>1 means increase in general price levels.
- **Phillips Curve** – Rate of inflation is inversely proportional to rate of unemployment.
- **Producer Price Index** – Price changes from the perspective of producers – excludes the effect of indirect taxes on inflation.
- **Deflation** – Decrease in general price levels of goods and services throughout an economy – inflation is negative in this case.
- **Disinflation** – Inflation rate is declining over time but remains positive.

UPSC CSE PREVIOUS YEARS' PRELIMINARY EXAMINATION QUESTIONS

1. Consider the following statements: **[2023]**

   Statement-I: In the post-pandemic recent past, many Central Banks worldwide had carried out interest rate hikes.

   Statement-II: Central Banks generally assume that they have the ability to counteract the rising consumer prices via monetary policy means.

   Which one of the following is correct in respect to the above statements?

   (a) Both Statement-I and Statement-II are correct and Statement-II is the correct explanation for Statement-I.
   (b) Both Statement-I and Statement-II are correct and Statement-II is not the correct explanation for Statement-I.
   (c) Statement-I is correct but Statement-II is incorrect.
   (d) Statement-I is incorrect but Statement-II is correct.

2. Which of the following activities of the Reserve Bank of India is considered to be part of 'sterilisation'? **[2023]**

   (a) Conducting 'Open Market Operations'
   (b) Oversight of settlement and payment systems
   (c) Debt and cash management for the Central and State Governments
   (d) Regulating the functions of Non-banking Financial Institutions

3. In India, which one of the following is responsible for maintaining price stability by controlling inflation? **[2022]**

   (a) Department of Consumer Affairs
   (b) Expenditure Management Commission
   (c) Financial Stability and Development Council
   (d) Reserve Bank of India

4. With reference to the Indian economy, consider the following statements: **[2022]**

   1. If the inflation is too high, Reserve Bank of India (RBI) is likely to buy government securities.
   2. If the rupee is rapidly depreciating, RBI is likely to sell dollars in the market.

3. If interest rates in the USA or European Union were to fall, that is likely to induce RBI to buy dollars.

Which of the statements given above are correct?
(a) 1 and 2 only (b) 2 and 3 only
(c) 1 and 3 only (d) 1, 2 and 3

5. With reference to the Indian economy demand-pull inflation can be caused/increased by which of the following? **[2021]**
1. Expansionary policies
2. Fiscal stimulus
3. Inflation-indexing wages
4. Higher purchasing power
5. Rising interest rates

Select the correct answer using the code given below:
(a) 1, 2 and 4 only
(b) 3, 4 and 5 only
(c) 1, 2, 3 and 5 only
(d) 1, 2, 3, 4 and 5

6. Consider the following statements: **[2020]**
1. The weightage of food in Consumer Price Index (CPI) is higher than that in Wholesale Price Index (WPI).
2. The WPI does not capture changes in the prices of services, which CPI does.
3. Reserve Bank of India has now adopted WPI as its key measure of inflation and to decide on changing the key policy rates.

Which of the statements given above is/are correct?
(a) 1 and 2 only (b) 2 only
(c) 3 and 4 only (d) 1, 2 and 3

7. Which of the following brings out the CPI number for industrial workers? **[2015]**
(a) The RBI
(b) The Department of Economic Affairs
(c) The Labour Bureau
(d) The Department of Personnel and Training

8. With reference to inflation in India, which of the following statements is correct? **[2015]**
(a) Controlling the inflation in India is the responsibility of the GoI only.
(b) The RBI has no role in controlling the inflation.
(c) Decreased money circulation helps in controlling the inflation.
(d) Increased money circulation helps in controlling the inflation.

9. Consider the following statements: **[2013]**
1. Inflation benefits the debtors.
2. Inflation benefits the bond holders.

Which of the statements given above is/are correct?
(a) 1 only (b) 2 only
(c) Both 1 and 2 (d) Neither 1 nor 2

10. A rise in general level of prices may be caused by **[2013]**
1. An increase in the money supply.
2. A decrease in the aggregate level of output.
3. An increase in the effective demand.

Select the correct answer using the codes given below:
(a) 1 only (b) 1 and 2 only
(c) 2 and 3 only (d) 1, 2 and 3

11. Which one of the following is likely to be the most inflationary in its effect? **[2013]**
(a) Repayment of public debt
(b) Borrowing from the public to finance a budget deficit
(c) Borrowings from banks to finance a budget deficit
(d) Creating new money to finance a budget deficit

12. Economic growth is usually coupled with **[2011]**
(a) Deflation (b) Inflation
(c) Stagflation (d) Hyperinflation.

13. A rapid increase in inflation is sometimes attributed to the 'base effect'. What is base effect? **[2011]**
(a) It is the impact in drastic deficiency in supply due to failure of crops.
(b) It is the impact of the surge in demand due to rapid economic growth.
(c) It is the impact of the price levels of the previous year on the calculation of inflation rate.
(d) None of the statements given above is correct in this context.

14. India has experienced persistent and high food inflation in the recent past. What could be the reasons? **[2011]**
1. Due to a gradual switchover to the cultivation of commercial crops, the area under the cultivation of food grains has steadily decreased in the last 5 years by about 30 per cent.

2. As a consequence of increasing incomes, the consumption patterns of the people have undergone a significant change.
3. The food supply chain has structural constraints.

Which of the statements given above is/are correct?

(a) 1 and 2 only (b) 2 and 3 only
(c) 1 and 3 only (d) 1, 2 and 3

15. With reference to India, consider the following statements: **[2010]**

1. The WPI in India is available on a monthly basis only.
2. As compared to CPI for industrial workers [CPI (IW)], the WPI gives less weight to food articles.

Which of the statements given above is/are correct?

(a) 1 only (b) 2 only
(c) Both 1 and 2 (d) Neither 1 nor 2

16. Which of the following statements is an appropriate description of deflation? **[2010]**

(a) It is a sudden fall in the value of a currency against other currencies.
(b) It is a persistent recession in both the financial and real sectors of economy.
(c) It is a persistent fall in the general price level of goods and services.
(d) It is a fall in the rate of inflation over a period of time.

☞ NO QUESTIONS ASKED
2024, 2019, 2018, 2017, 2016, 2014, 2012

ANSWER KEY

1. (a)	2. (a)	3. (d)	4. (b)	5. (a)
6. (a)	7. (c)	8. (c)	9. (a)	10. (d)
11. (d)	12. (b)	13. (c)	14. (b)	15. (b)
16. (c)				

UPSC CSE PREVIOUS YEARS' MAIN EXAMINATION QUESTIONS

1. What are the causes of persistent high food inflation in India? Comment on the effectiveness of the monetary policy of the RBI to control this type of inflation. **[2024]**

2. Do you agree with the view that steady GDP growth and low inflation have left the Indian economy in good shape? Give reasons in support of your arguments. **[2019]**

☞ NO QUESTIONS ASKED
2023, 2022, 2021, 2020, 2018, 2017, 2016, 2015, 2014, 2013, 2012

CHAPTER

7

INDIAN TAX STRUCTURE

CHAPTER OUTLINE

- Three-Tier Tax structure in India
- Different types of Taxes
- Direct Tax
- Indirect Tax
- Goods and Services Tax (GST)
- Details about GST
- GST Council
- GST Network (GSTN)
- Benefits of GST
- Recent Reforms in GST
- National Anti-Profiteering Authority
- Advance Ruling
- Reverse Charge Mechanism in GST
- Revenue Neutral Rate
- Other Terms Related to Taxation
- Taxpayers' Charter
- Tax Expenditure
- Tax Administration Reform Commission (TARC)
- Central Board of Direct Taxes (CBDT)
- Central Board of Indirect Taxes & Customs (CBIC)
- Carbon Border Tax
- OECD's Two Pillar Plan
- Double Taxation Avoidance Agreement (DTAA)

INDIAN TAX STRUCTURE

Tax is legally imposed by the Government and an undenied **compulsory payment** by the individuals, households, firms or other institutional units to the Government to meet public expenditure.

Three-Tier Tax Structure in India

The tax structure in India is a three-tier structure involving government at three levels: union or central government, state government at the provincial level and the rural or urban local bodies at the local government level.

Union Taxes

- Corporate Tax
- Income Tax
- CGST/SGST
- Customs Duty

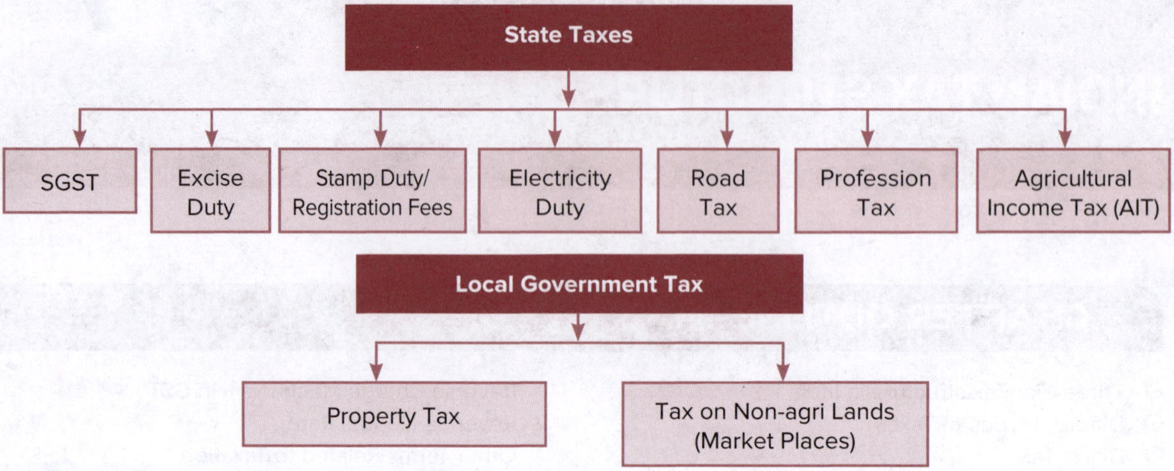

Different Types of Taxes

Taxes can be classified into several ways, depending upon their structure, nature and the way of imposition. They are as follows-

1. Proportional, Progressive, Regressive and Degressive Taxes

Type of Taxes	Features
Proportional Tax	A tax is called proportional when it deducts the same proportion from each income group. Proportional tax is also known as flat tax because it is levied at a single rate for all taxpayers, regardless of income level. Example: Sales Tax.
Progressive Tax	A tax where high-income groups pay a higher percentage of their income than the percentage paid by low-income groups. Example: Income Tax.
Regressive Tax	A tax that takes a larger percentage of income from low-income groups than from high-income groups. Example: Excise Duty.
Degressive Tax	It is a combination of proportional and progressive taxes. With degressive taxation, the tax rate rises initially in accordance with income and then stays flat or constant while income continues to rise. Example: Income Tax in some countries.

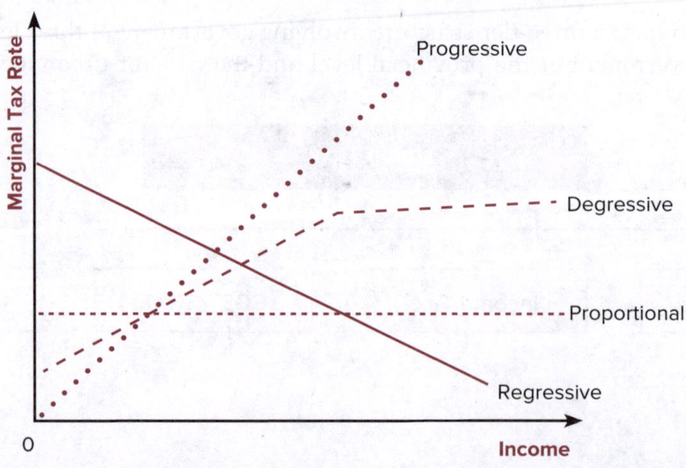

2. Direct and Indirect Tax

Direct Tax	Indirect Tax
Tax is levied on and collected from the same person	Tax is levied on one person and collected from another person
Falls on the same person	Falls on different persons
Income tax, corporate tax, property tax, etc.	GST, state excise duty, customs duty, etc.
May help in reducing inflation	May promote inflation

3. Specific Tax and Ad valorem Tax

Specific Tax	Ad Valorem Tax
Unlike ad valorem tax, when the tax is levied on a commodity on the basis of its unit, size or weight (and not on its value), it is termed specific tax. Example: Excise duty on liquor products. A specific tax is regressive in nature.	It is a tax levied as a percentage of the value of an item it is imposed on, and not on the item's quantity, size, weight, or other such factors. Example: GST, Customs Duty, etc.

DIRECT TAX

It is borne by a person on whom it is levied, i.e. the **impact** (burden) **and incidence** fall on the same person and cannot be shifted to another person. Direct taxes include income tax, corporate tax, minimum alternate tax, dividend distribution tax (*abolished in 2020*), securities transaction tax, fringe benefit tax (abolished in 2009), wealth tax (abolished in 2016), professional tax, capital gains tax, stamp duty, gift tax (abolished in 1998), estate duty (abolished in 1985), banking cash transaction tax (abolished in 2009), etc.

Different Types of Direct Taxes

Personal Income Tax

- It is governed by the Income Tax (IT) Act, 1961.
- It is levied on individuals, Hindu Undivided Family (HUF), partnership firms, etc.
- It is levied on taxable income, i.e. gross income minus standard deductions and exemptions allowed as per the IT Act.
- Various types of income covered under income tax are – salary, profits from business/profession, rent income, long-term and short-term capital gains from the sale of asset and income from other sources like interest, royalty, etc.
- Income tax is imposed on individuals as per different income slabs.

Corporate Income Tax

- It is levied on profits earned by companies.
- For taxation purpose, a company is treated as a separate entity, and thus, it must pay a separate tax different from the personal income tax of its owner.

- Companies (both public and private) which are registered in India under the Companies (Amendment) Act, 2019 are liable to pay corporate tax on their income worldwide.
- Presently, corporate tax rate is 25 per cent for domestic corporations with gross turnover up to ₹250 crore. For > ₹250 crore turnover, tax rate is 30 per cent.
- In 2019, the Central Government slashed the tax rate from 25 per cent to 15 per cent for new manufacturing companies.
- A beneficial rate of 22 per cent (plus surcharge of 10 per cent and applicable health and education cess of 4 per cent) can be availed with effect from FY 2019–20 by the companies subject to certain conditions.
- Indian corporate tax rates are now among the lowest in the world.

Minimum Alternate Tax (MAT)

- It was introduced from 1997–98. (Section 115JB of IT Act).
- It is imposed on zero tax companies at 18.5 per cent of their book profit.
- Explanation – Generally, income tax is computed as per the provisions of the IT Act. However, companies compute their book profit as per the provisions of Companies (Amendment) Act, 2019, and as IT Act allows several kinds of exemptions, depreciations and deductions from gross income or book profit, companies in many instances can show their taxable income as very less, on which the amount of tax comes out to be very low.

Therefore, for these zero taxes or very less tax companies, MAT was introduced. Now, a company must pay at least either corporate tax or MAT, whichever is higher.

Dividend Distribution Tax (DDT)

- Any domestic company declaring/distributing dividend was required to pay DDT at 15 per cent on the gross amount of dividend. It was levied under Section 115O of IT Act, 1961.
- Only domestic companies as defined under IT Act had to pay DDT.
- However, DDT has been abolished w.e.f. 1 April 2020.

Securities Transaction Tax (STT)

- It was introduced in 2004.
- It is levied at the time of purchase or sale of securities (shares, debentures, bonds, equity oriented mutual funds, etc.) listed on stock exchange.
- The intention behind levying STT is to curb the evasion of capital gains tax on profits earned by transacting in securities.
- The rate of STT varies across the types of securities. For equity shares, STT of 0.1 per cent of the transaction value is levied on both the purchaser and the seller. For equity oriented mutual funds, no STT is levied on the purchaser, but from the seller, 0.001 per cent is charged.

Banking Cash Transaction Tax (BCTT)

- It was introduced in 2005, and was levied at 0.1 per cent on cash withdrawals exceeding ₹25,000 in a day by an individual or HUF from a bank account (other than savings bank account). In case of any other person, BCTT was levied on a cash withdrawal exceeding ₹1 lakh.

- It was applicable on two types of transactions: cash withdrawal and receipt of cash on encashment of term deposits.
- However, BCTT was withdrawn in 2009.
- In 2017, the Committee of Chief Ministers on Digital Payments recommended for the reintroduction of BCTT to promote digital payments.

Fringe Benefit Tax (FBT)

- Fringe Benefit Tax (FBT) (introduced in 2005) was fundamentally a tax that an employer had to pay in lieu of the benefits that were given by him to his employees like telephone reimbursements, free or concessional tickets, etc.
- It was levied on employers at 30 per cent of the cost of benefit provided to employees.
- However, FBT was withdrawn in 2009.

Wealth Tax

- It was governed by the Wealth Tax Act, 1957.
- It was levied on the net wealth owned by an individual, an HUF or a company on the date of valuation (31 March).
- It was levied at 1 per cent of the amount of net wealth exceeding ₹30 lakh.
- Definition of wealth included – Land/building, motor cars, gold/silver jewellery, cash in hand in excess of ₹50,000, etc.
- However, wealth tax was not applicable to trusts, partnership firms, co-operative societies, political parties, etc.
- Abolished w.e.f. 1 April 2016.

Professional Tax

- It is levied and collected by the State Governments (unlike other Direct Taxes).
- It is imposed on professionals or employees who earn a salary.
- Examples of professional tax payees include practising chartered accountants, doctors, lawyers, etc.

GAFA Tax or Equalisation Levy

- It was introduced in 2016, by the Central Government, based on the recommendations of the **Akhil Ranjan** Committee.
- It was introduced as part of Finance Act, 2016, and later incorporated into the Income Tax Act. Globally, it is also known as GAFA (Google, Apple, Facebook, Amazon) Tax.
- Introduction of this levy also forms part of India's response to OECD's BEPS (Base Erosion and Profit Shifting) agenda.
- This direct tax is applicable on payment exceeding ₹1 lakh during a financial year.
- It is withheld by recipient Indian companies at the time of payment to service providers (non-resident companies) for digital service rendered.

- Non-resident service providers cannot claim tax credit against it in their home country under the Double Taxation Avoidance Agreements.
- In 2020, foreign based e-commerce companies were added in its ambit. A tax rate of 2 per cent is now levied on the amount of consideration.

Capital Gains Tax (CGT)

- Capital Gains Tax (CGT) is a tax which is levied on the **profit** a person makes from the sale of a **Capital Asset.**

Capital Asset

- A 'Capital Asset' is any kind of property kept with an assessee, excluding goods held as stock-in-trade, agricultural land, and personal effects.
- Examples of Capital Asset are – land, buildings, house property, trademarks, leasehold rights, machinery, vehicles, patents and jewellery.
- The following are **not considered Capital Assets:**
  - Stock in trade.
  - Consumable goods or raw materials kept for professional or corporate use.
  - Any movable items, with the exception of jewellery, artifacts from archaeology, sculptures, paintings, sketches, and other works of art kept for private use.
  - Agricultural Land: A municipality, Municipal Corporation, notified area committee, town committee, or cantonment board with a minimum population of 10,000 people cannot be located within 8 kilometers of the land.
  - Bonds issued under the Gold Deposit Scheme.

There are **two types of Capital Assets:**

- **Long-term capital asset** – It means a capital asset which is not a short-term capital asset.
- **Short-term capital asset** – It means any capital asset held by a person for a period of not more than:
  a. 36 months (if a capital asset is transferred before July 23, 2024) or
  b. 24 months (if a capital asset is transferred on or after July 23, 2024), immediately preceding the date of its transfer will be a short-term capital asset.

Long-Term Capital Gains (LTCG) and Indexation Benefit

- Profits from the sale of capital assets, including stocks, bonds, and real estate, are subject to capital gains tax.
- There are two types of capital gains taxation: Long-Term Capital Gains (LTCG) Tax and Short-Term Capital Gains (STCG) Tax.
- Profits from the sale of assets held for longer periods of time are subject to LTCG tax.
- The holding period varies depending on the type of asset (more than 12 months for Listed equity shares, Equity oriented Mutual funds; 24 months for Unlisted equity shares, immovable assets like House/land, etc.; and 36 months for movable assets like Gold).

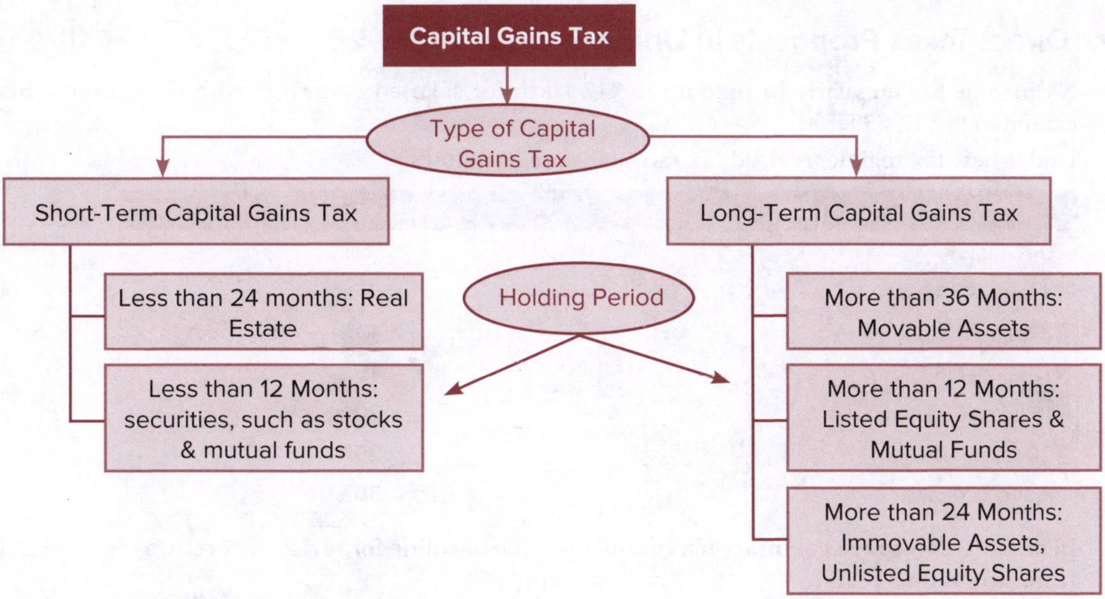

Lok Sabha cleared the Finance Bill, 2024 amending Long-Term Capital Gains (LTCG) tax provision on immovable properties.

Provisions of the Amendment Act

- Abolishment of Indexation Benefits: Indexation benefits (adjusting the purchase price of an asset for inflation while computing the capital gain) have been abolished by this amendment.
- It allows grandfathering for properties acquired before 23 July 2024.
- Grandfather Clause allows properties purchased before the cutoff date to still benefit from indexation despite the new rules for future acquisitions.
- **Choices for Taxpayers:** The amendment provides taxpayers with a choice to pay the lower tax amount:
  - Old Scheme: 20 per cent LTCG tax with indexation on properties acquired before July 23, 2024 has to be paid.
  - New Scheme: 12.5 per cent LTCG tax without indexation (reduced from the earlier 20 per cent) has to be paid.
- For properties purchased after July 23, 2024, only the new scheme applies.
- Indexation benefits apply only to gains, and they will not be applicable to any losses incurred.
- Enhanced Exemption: The limit of exemption for LTCG on listed equity, equity-oriented mutual funds, and business trust units has been increased from ₹1 lakh to ₹1.25 lakh.
- The LTCG Tax for these assets has been increased from 10 per cent to 12.5 per cent.

Direct Taxes Proposals in Union Budget 2025–26

BONUS KNOWLEDGE

- **No income tax on yearly income up to ₹12 lakh; for salaried taxpayers with deductions, this is extended to ₹12.75 lakh.**
- Under new tax regime, **revised tax rate slabs** are as follows:

Income (INR)	Tax Rate
₹0–₹4 lakh	Nil
₹4 lakh–₹8 lakh	5%
₹8 lakh–₹12 lakh	10%
₹12 lakh–₹16 lakh	15%
₹16 lakh–₹20 lakh	20%
₹20 lakh–₹24 lakh	25%
Above ₹24 lakh	30%

- **In order to encourage voluntary tax compliance, the deadline for revised tax returns was extended from two to four years.**

Income-Tax Bill, 2025

BONUS KNOWLEDGE

- In order to replace the outdated Income-tax Act of 1961 with a more straightforward and effective tax structure, the government has proposed a new bill.
- Income Tax Bill 2025 aims to simplify Income Tax Act 1961. The new bill has less chapters and words for more clarity.
- It aims to reduce litigation and increase compliance. Once it is passed, the new name will be Income Tax Act, 2025, and is expected to take effect in April 2026.

Features

- Simplified language that makes the law easier to understand.
- Reduction of fragmentation by amendment consolidation.
- For more clarity, superfluous and outdated provisions have been removed.
- Tables and formulas to be used to rationalise the structure for better reading.
- Maintaining current taxation principles, it ensures continuity, and improves usability.
- Cryptocurrencies and other virtual digital assets are now considered to be capital assets under the definition of property.
- This section clarifies the methods for issuing DRP instructions. It gives the points of determination, conclusion, and the rationale behind it.
- Section 54E of the Act, which details exemptions for capital gains on transfer of capital assets prior to April 1992 has been removed.
- The Bill introduces the concept of 'tax year', which has been defined as the 12-month period beginning April 1.

Prohibition of Benami Transactions (Amendment) Act, 2016

- The Amendment Act amended the provisions of the Prohibition of Benami Property Transactions Act, 1988, to curb the issues of black money and money laundering in the country. Person found guilty of offence of *benami* transaction by the competent court shall be punished with rigorous imprisonment of not less than one year, which may extend to seven years, and shall also be liable to fine which may extend to 25 per cent of the fair market value of the property.
- As per the amended Act, Benami transaction means:
  1. A transaction or an arrangement –
     (a) Where a property is transferred to, or is held by, a person and the consideration for such property has been provided, or paid by, another person; and
     (b) The property is held for the immediate or future benefit, direct or indirect, of the person who has provided the consideration;
  2. A transaction or an arrangement in respect of a property carried out or made in a fictitious name; or
  3. A transaction or an arrangement in respect of a property where the owner of the property is not aware of, or denies knowledge of, such ownership;
  4. A transaction or an arrangement in respect of a property where the person providing the consideration is not traceable or is fictitious;

INDIRECT TAXES

It is a tax whose impact and incidence fall on different persons. Indirect taxes are imposed on goods and commodities. Examples include Customs Duty, GST, etc.

GOODS AND SERVICES TAX (GST)

- In 2003, the **Kelkar Task Force** on indirect tax had mentioned a comprehensive Goods and Services Tax (GST), which is based on the principle of VAT (Value Added Tax). A proposal to introduce a National level Goods and Services Tax (GST) by 1 April 2010, was first made in the Budget Speech for the financial year 2006–07.
- With an objective to achieve a 'One Nation One Tax' system, Goods and Services Tax (GST) as an **indirect tax** was introduced on **1 July, 2017** on pan India basis.
- It was introduced as the Constitution **(One Hundred and First Amendment)** Act, 2017, following the passage of the **122nd Constitutional Amendment Bill**.
- Constitutional amendment provided concurrent powers to both the centre and states for levying GST (*Centre to tax sale of goods and states to tax provision of services*).
- Through this amendment, three new Articles were introduced in the Constitution:
  1. **Article 246A** – Both the Parliament and the state legislatures to have **concurrent power to make laws** related to GST. However, the Parliament to retain exclusive power to legislate in the case of inter-state trade of goods and services.
  2. **Article 269A** – In the case of inter-state trade where GST is levied and collected by the union Government, the **tax revenue proceeds to be apportioned** by the centre between the centre

and states in a manner as may be provided by the Parliament by law **on the recommendations of the GST Council**.

3. **Article 279A** – It empowers the President of India to constitute the **GST Council**. Constitution and functioning of the GST Council is also stated under this new Article.

➤ **Four separate Acts were enacted**:
1. Central GST Act, 2017
2. Integrated GST Act, 2017
3. The GST (Compensation to States) Act, 2017
4. The Union Territory GST Act, 2017

Also, the State GST (SGST) Bill was passed by each state in order to enact the State GST (SGST) Act.

The **evolution of GST** can be understood from the diagram below:

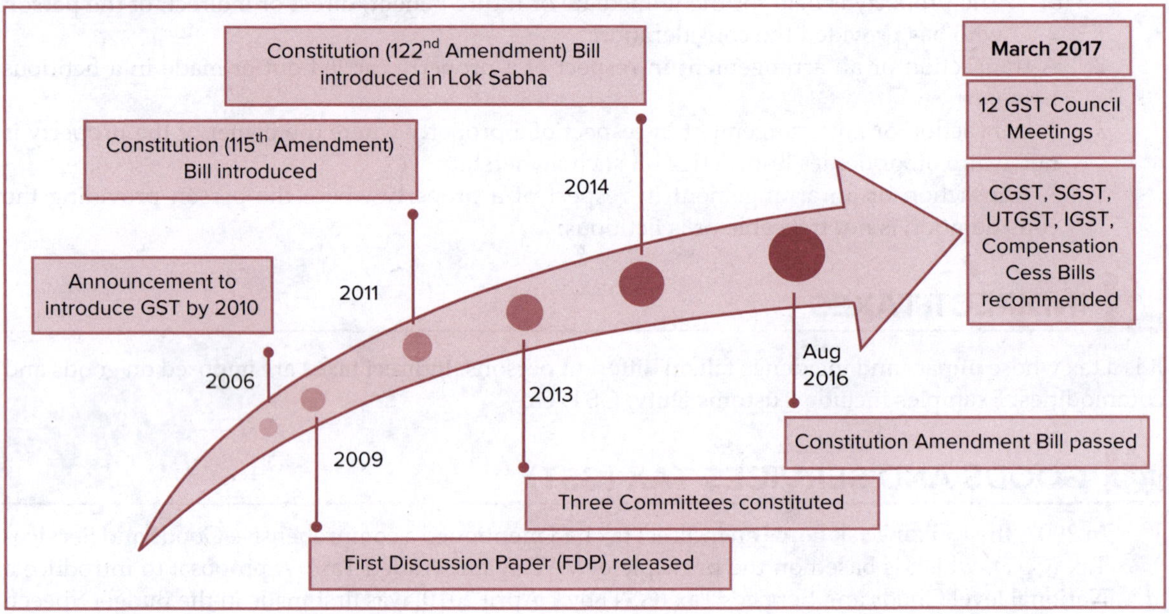

Details about GST

➤ Under GST, taxable event is **'supply'** of goods or services, and events like manufacture, sale, etc. do not matter now.

➤ GST is a **consumption-based tax**; therefore, taxes are paid to the state where the goods or services are consumed, not the state in which they were produced.

➤ The GST is governed by a GST Council whose **Chairman is the Finance Minister** of India.

➤ GST comprises four types of taxes:
1. **Integrated GST (IGST)** – It is levied in the course of **inter-state trade** of goods and services. It is levied and collected by the Central Government, but the revenue is shared between the centre and states at a fixed rate. The **import of goods or services** also attracts IGST. However, in the case of imports, Basic Customs Duty is also levied along with GST. Exports have zero-rated GST.

2. **State GST (SGST)** – It is applicable only on **intra-state (within the state) trade** of goods and services. However, CGST will also be charged on that. **For example**, for any supply of goods within West Bengal, which attracts 12 per cent GST, SGST and CGST will be 6 per cent each.
3. **Central GST (CGST)** – Like SGST, it is also applicable only on intra-state trade of goods and services.
4. **Union Territory Goods and Services Tax (UTGST):** UTGST is similar to SGST but is applicable in union territories. Unlike SGST and CGST, UTGST has a consistent rate within the union territory.

Indirect Taxes That Have Been Subsumed Under GST

Central Taxes	State Taxes
Central Excise Duty	State VAT/Sales Tax
Additional Duties of Excise	Purchase Tax
Excise Duty levied under Medicinal and Toiletries Preparation Act	Entertainment Tax (*other than those levied by local bodies*)
Additional Duties of Customs and Special Additional Duties of Customs	Luxury Tax
Service Tax	Octroi Duty and all other forms of Entry Tax
Central Surcharge and Cess relating to supply of goods and services	Taxes on lottery, betting and gambling
Central Sales Tax (*levied by Centre and collected by States*)	Mandi Tax

- Under GST, there is **no uniform tax rate**. Various goods and services are taxed at the following rates – **0 per cent**, **5 per cent**, **12 per cent**, **18 per cent** and **28 per cent**.
- There is a special rate of 0.25 per cent on rough precious and semi-precious stones and 3 per cent on gold.

Rate of GST	Illustrative List of Related Goods
0%	Jute, fresh meat, fish, chicken, eggs, butter milk, curd, natural honey, fresh fruits and vegetables, flour, besan, **bread**, prasad, **salt**, bindi, sindoor, **stamps, judicial papers, printed books, newspapers**, bangles, handloom, Sanitary napkins, Fresh Milk and Pasteurized Milk, Rice (not labelled or pre-packaged), Fresh Meat (not pre-packaged) and Eggs, Fresh Curd and Paneer (not pre-packaged), Fresh Fruits and Vegetables, Natural Honey (not branded/pre-packaged)
5%	Cashew nuts/cashew nuts in shell, insulin, numismatic coins, agarbatti and kites, fly-ash blocks, Sugar and Tea, Milk food items for babies, Indian sweets, Hearing aids, Radio/App-based Taxis, Economy-class flight and Railway tickets

Rate of GST	Illustrative List of Related Goods
12%	Exercise books and note books, pencils, sharpeners, corrective spectacles, all diagnostic kits and reagents, **Computers and, Mobile phones, Packaged Ghee, Business class flight tickets, Fruit juices or Fruit Pulp-based drinks, Preserved Fruits and Vegetables, Condensed Milk**
18%	Kajal pencil sticks, set-top box for TV, CCTV, aluminium foil, computer monitors not exceeding 17 inches, bamboo furniture, **Mineral Water (natural or artificial), Pasta, Life Insurance and Health Insurance, Cornflakes, Toothpaste, etc**
28%	Pan masala, caffeinated beverages, lottery authorised by State Governments, personal aircrafts, **Cigars and Cigarettes (tobacco-based), Passenger Cars, Portland/Slag/Aluminous Cement, Air Conditioners, Dish Washing Machines.**
3%	Imitation jewelry, coin, Articles of Precious Metal or Metal Clad with Precious Metal, Natural Pearls or Cultured Pearls (unworked or graded), Diamonds (excluding non-industrial), Precious Stones (other than diamonds), Semi-precious Stones, Silver, Gold, Waste & Scrap of Precious Metal
0.25%	Non-industrial Diamonds, Unworked Precious/Semi-precious Stones, Synthetic or Reconstructed Precious or Semi-precious Stones

- In addition, a cess of 15 per cent or other rates on top of 28 per cent GST applies on few items like aerated drinks, luxury cars, tobacco products, etc.
- Businesses with annual turnover up to ₹40 lakh are exempted from GST (This limit is ₹20 lakh for northeastern and hilly states) in the case of those dealing with goods.
- In the case of services or both goods and services, the prescribed limit is ₹20 lakh (₹10 lakh for northeastern and hilly states).

These GST rates remain uniform throughout India. However, they can be reviewed based on the recommendations of the GST Council.

did you KNOW?

Since the introduction of GST in 2017, various goods and services have been shifted from one slab to another in the last five years. The decision in this regard is made by the GST Council.

(55 meetings have been held by GST Council as on 31 January 2025. 55th GST Council meeting tookplace on 21st December, 2024, at Jaisalmer.)

Input Tax Credit

- This term is very commonly used by people nowadays. It is the tax already paid by a person and which is *available as deduction from tax* to be payable by him/her. For instance, GST is paid by a manufacturer/producer when buying raw material or services as inputs used in the production process. This tax paid by the manufacturer can be adjusted against the final payment of GST by him at the time of sale of final product. This, in a way, helps to charge GST only on the value added by that manufacturer. Suppose a shoe manufacturer procures leather as raw material for ₹100 + 5 per cent GST. This ₹5 is input tax credit. Later, when the finished leather product is sold for ₹300 + 12 per cent GST, this ₹5 input tax will be adjusted against the final GST (i.e. 12 per cent of 300 = 36) on the output to be paid by manufacturer. Thus, tax to be paid by a manufacturer to the Government at the time of sale of final product = ₹36 – input tax credit of ₹5 = ₹31.

- This input tax credit **removes the cascading effect** of tax and in a way helps to lower the price of final products.
- Input tax credit can be enjoyed at all levels, be it raw material suppliers, manufacturer, distributors or retailers.
- The **cross-utilisation** of input tax credit of CGST is allowed between goods and services. Similarly, it is allowed in the case of SGST. However, cross-utilisation of CGST and SGST is not allowed except in the case of inter-state supply of goods and services.
- Input tax credit on account of IGST to be first utilised for payment of IGST – then CGST and then for payment of SGST or UTGST.
- Input tax credit on account of CGST to be first utilised for payment of CGST and then for IGST. But it **cannot be used for adjusting against payment of SGST or UTGST**.
- Similarly, input tax credit on account of SGST/UTGST to be first utilised for payment of SGST/UTGST and then IGST **but not for payment of CGST**.
- Input tax credit is not allowed on goods and services for personal use.
- In case GST on inputs is higher than GST on output, one is **allowed to carry forward** the balance input credit or claim a refund. However, **no interest is paid** on input credit balance by the Government.

GST Council

Through the 101st Constitutional Amendment Act, **Article 279A** was inserted in the Constitution. It empowered the President of India to constitute the *GST Council*.

Constitution of GST Council

- **Chairperson** – Union Finance Minister.
- Also consists of the **Union MOS (Finance) and the Finance Ministers of all States**.
- Vice Chairperson – chosen among the Ministers of the State Governments.
- Quorum to be 50 per cent of the total members.
- Resolution requires 75 per cent majority of members present and voting.
- The voting weightage of the Central Government is 1/3rd of the total vote and for all the state government together it is 2/3.
- GST Council makes recommendations on everything related to GST, including laws, rules, rates, etc.

Compensation Mechanism of States

- Compensation to be provided for loss of revenue to States for a period of **five years**.
- It is to be based on the revenue of all taxes which had been subsumed under GST considering **2015–16** as the base year.
- Assumption of 14 per cent annual growth rate.
- Compensation to be provided through **cess** levied along with GST on few specified luxury and sin goods.

Last Minute SNIPPETS

The compensation cess has been extended till 31 March 2026 which was to end on June 30, 2022, five years after the single tax rolled out on July 1, 2017. It has been done with an objective to repay the borrowings incurred in FY 2020–21 and FY 2021–22 to compensate States for GST revenue loss.

GST Network (GSTN)

It is a **Special Purpose Vehicle** which was incorporated as a Section 25 **non-profit private limited company** with strategic control in the hands of the Government in 2013. Later, in September 2018, the ownership status changed as the GST Council approved the decision to convert GSTN into a **fully Government-owned entity** having equal shares of state and Central Government. It functions as the **technology backbone for GST in India**. The Council is entrusted with maintaining the GST portal as single user interface for the registered taxpayers which deals with taxpayer registration, return, refund, etc. as well as the IT infrastructure required for GST. Major projects rolled out by GSTN are E-Waybill, E-invoice, TINXSYS, etc.

Events not included as 'SUPPLY' – *thus do not attract GST*

1. Service by employee to employer in relation to employment.
2. Funeral, burial, crematorium services including transportation of the deceased.
3. Sale of land and building where entire consideration has been received after completion certificate is issued or after its first occupation.

Other Indirect Taxes Not replaced by GST

- **Basic Customs Duty** – It is charged on goods imported to India. It is imposed under the Customs Act, 1962. The rates of basic customs duty vary from 5 per cent to 40 per cent from product to product.
- **Surcharge on Customs Duty** – It is basically tax on tax. A social welfare surcharge of 10 per cent is levied on aggregate duties of customs on import of goods.
- **Customs Cess** – It is again tax on tax and is levied for a specific purpose. Customs cess is 3 per cent on aggregate of customs duty.
- **Motor Vehicle Tax** – It is imposed by State Government on two wheelers, cars and passenger and commercial vehicles.
- **Stamp Duty** – It is a type of tax or duty which is paid for transactions performed within the state by way of documents, where such documents are liable to be stamped as per the provisions of the State Stamp Act and Indian Stamp Act, 1899. Such documents include all agreements, bonds, powers of attorney and others. It differs from state to state. Example – When a person buys a property, he or she has to pay stamp duty along with registration fees.
- **State Excise Duty** – Excise duty is an indirect tax levied on excisable goods which are manufactured in India and are meant for home consumption. It is a **tax on manufacturing,** which is paid by the manufacturer, who passes its incidence to the customers. Majority of excise duties were levied by Central Government, and they have been subsumed into GST. However, **excise duty on liquor,** which is levied by State Governments, is **not** subsumed into GST.

  Also, **excise duty on petroleum products,** which is levied by Central Government, is **not** subsumed under GST.
- **VAT on petroleum products** – GST has replaced CENVAT, state VAT and even service tax. However, VAT on petroleum products is not subsumed under GST.
- **Anti-Dumping and Safeguard Duties** – When any product is exported by an exporter/producer into the territory of India **at less than its normal value** in its home country, the Central Government levies Anti-Dumping Duty.

Whereas *Safeguard Duty* is imposed if unexpectedly increasing imports pose a threat to domestic industries of that particular product. It can be imposed only if a sudden increase in imports has caused or threatened to cause serious injury to the domestic industry. Both the above duties are levied under **Customs Tariff Act, 1975**.

Along with the above-mentioned taxes, toll tax, entertainment tax levied by local bodies, etc. are not subsumed under GST. Also, central excise duty on crude petroleum, high-speed petrol, natural gas, aviation turbine fuel (ATF) and tobacco and tobacco products are levied separately and have not been subsumed under GST.

Benefits of GST

1. **For Businesses** – **Easy compliance** through online portal, **removal of cascading effect** of earlier indirect taxes, **removal of complexities** in handling various indirect taxes at one go, **seamless movement of trucks** through introduction of **E-Way Bill**.
2. **For Central and State Governments** – **Widening of tax base, easy handling** of a single tax regime instead of a variety of indirect taxes by the Governments, **better controls on tax leakage**, higher revenue efficiency.
3. **For Consumers** – Single tax payment instead of paying multiple taxes has ensured **more transparency** in the taxes paid by the consumers. Also, **overall tax burden is expected to reduce** due to efficiency gains and better check on leakages on the part of Government.

Critical Evaluation of GST

Even if GST comes with the above-mentioned benefits, there have been a number of criticisms by various stakeholders. They are:

- Introduction of GST in a hurry without proper implementation mechanism.
- Increased administrative and compliance burden on the part of taxpayers.
- Locking up of working capital due to slow tax refund processing.
- Lack of clarity to State Governments on discontinuation of local taxes.
- Lack of clarity to State Governments on coping mechanisms to preserve and sustain similar level of revenue collections as was existing in the pre-GST regime.

However, the GST Council is continuously taking measures and bringing in reforms to bridge the above-mentioned gaps.

Reforms in GST

1. **Rationalisation of GST rate structure** by the GST Council for a number of **goods** in terms of rate cuts, shifting from higher GST rate to lower GST rate, etc.
2. Similarly, **rationalisation of GST rate structure** for a number of **services** by shifting them from higher GST rate to lower GST rate, exemption from levy of GST in the case of certain services, etc.
3. Ease of doing business for small traders by **raising exemption limits** for GST registration from ₹20 lakh to ₹40 lakh annual turnover in case of goods (for hilly and northeastern states, exemption limit raised from ₹10 lakh to ₹20 lakh).
4. Threshold of annual turnover for **composition scheme** extended to ₹1.5 crore and ₹50 lakh for manufacturers and suppliers of goods and services, respectively.

5. **E-Invoice** has become mandatory for all the registered persons whose aggregate turnover exceeds ₹20 crores in the previous year.

E-Way Bill

- Introduced under the GST regime, an electronic way bill, or e-Way Bill, is a document required to be carried by the person in-charge of the conveyance carrying consignment of goods of value exceeding `50,000 for sale beyond 10 km.
- A single e-Way Bill is valid throughout the country for the movement of goods.
- Every registered supplier has to do prior online registration in e-Way Bill portal before starting the movement of goods.
- e-Way Bill in the form of print-out, SMS or written invoice is considered valid.
- For movement of goods either within the state or outside the state, an e-Way Bill is mandatory.
- E-Way bill, once created, will be valid for 1 day for up to 200 km of travel.

GST Appellate Tribunal

Section (109) of the Goods and Service Tax Act, 2017 (CGST Act) mandates the constitution of a GST Appellate Tribunal (GSTAT) and its Benches.

- All disputes related to GST laws at the appellate level are resolved by the GST Appellate Tribunal (GSTAT).
- The principal bench of the GSTAT to be located at New Delhi but each state can decide on the number of benches or boards they require, subject to the approval of GST council.
- The bench to consist of two judicial members and two technical members and the selection panel including a senior judicial member from the State High Court.

Inverted Duty Structure (IDS)

It refers to situation where import duties on input goods are higher than on finished goods, i.e, the GST rate paid on purchases is more than the GST rate payable on sales.

Impact

- Expensive inputs make products expensive.
- Domestic industry is affected and it is difficult to compete in the export market.
- Taxpayers who face an inverted duty structure will always have Input Tax Credit (ITC) in their GST electronic credit ledger.
- Creates working capital issues for the taxpayers as their resources are blocked in the form of Input Tax Credit (ITC) because of high input tax. IDS also leads to refund-related issues under the GST regime.

NATIONAL ANTI-PROFITEERING AUTHORITY

- It is related to **GST**.
- **The National Anti-Profiteering Authority** (NAA) comprises a chairman and four members.

- Since the introduction of GST in 2017, the Government has gradually reduced the rate of GST for a large number of goods and services by shifting them from a higher tax rate category to the lower one.
- In order to ensure that the benefit of these reduced GST or benefit in the form of input tax credit is passed on to final consumers through reduction in prices by the suppliers of goods and services, the Central Government has set up the **NAA**.
- The **action of not passing such benefits** to the recipient amounts to 'profiteering'.
- Any consumer/organisation can file a complaint at NAA for investigation. Moreover, any supplier/ trader/wholesaler/retailer not getting benefit of input tax credit may also file a complaint with NAA.
- If proved, NAA can order the defaulter to return the amount not passed on by way of commensurate reduction in prices. In case the applicant is not identifiable later, the recovered amount is deposited in a newly created *Consumer Welfare Fund*.
- Orders of NAA are appealable in High Court.

BONUS KNOWLEDGE

HSN CODE AND SAC CODE

- HSN – Harmonised System Nomenclature
- SAC – Service Accounting Code
- It is an internationally adopted system for commodity description and product nomenclature developed by the **World Customs Organisation (WCO)** in 1988.
- In the GST regime, **goods are classified under HSN** and **services under SAC**.
- The HSN Code and SAC codes are used in almost 200 countries as a basis for customs tariffs. Almost 98 per cent of all merchandise in international trade are classified under the HSN Code.
- **HSN 2022** – WCO regularly updates its database of HSN codes (every 5 years) to add new products and standardise new product categories. The latest (7th edition) set of codes has been implemented from **1 January 2022**. India, being a party to the HSN Convention, has brought necessary changes through the Finance Act, 2021, to align the coding of commodities in India with the **HSN 2022**.

Advance Ruling

Any advance tax ruling is a **written interpretation of tax laws**. It is issued by tax authorities to corporations and individuals who request for clarification of certain tax matters when the taxpayer is confused and is uncertain about certain provisions. Advance tax ruling is applied for before starting the proposed activity.

The **objective** of any advance ruling, including under GST, is to:

- attract Foreign Direct Investment (FDI) – By clarifying taxation-related rules and showing a clear picture of the future tax liability of the FDI. The clarity in the taxation system will help to attract those non-residents who do not want to get involved in messy tax disputes.
- reduce litigation and costly legal disputes.

Reverse Charge Mechanism in GST

Generally, the supplier of goods or services is liable to pay GST. However, in specified cases like imports and other notified supplies, the **liability may be cast on the recipient** under the reverse charge mechanism. Reverse Charge means the liability to pay tax is on the recipient of goods or services instead of the supplier of such goods or services in respect of the notified categories of supply.

Applicability

A. Supply from an unregistered dealer to a registered dealer
B. Services through an e-commerce operator
C. Supply of certain goods and services specified by CBEC

BONUS KNOWLEDGE

SELF-INVOICING

Self-invoicing is to be done when you have **purchased from an unregistered supplier** and such purchase of goods or services falls under Reverse Charge. This is because the supplier cannot issue a GST-compliant invoice to the receiver, and thus, the receiver becomes liable to pay taxes on their behalf. Hence, self-invoicing, in this case, becomes necessary.

Revenue Neutral Rate

- The focus under GST is to arrive at such rates which would not decrease the current revenue generation of the Central and State Governments.
- **Revenue Neutral Rate** (RNR) is a structure of different rates established to match the current revenue generation with the revenue under GST.
- RNR calculation must include the cascading effect on certain goods having no excise or sales tax implications.
- *For example* – Wheat would get costlier due to the RNR fixed for diesel being higher than the current tax rate even though wheat does not have any excise or sales tax implications.

EXAM ESSENTIAL

LAFFER CURVE

- Laffer curve, introduced by *Arthur Laffer*, represents the **relationship between tax rates and the amount of tax revenue collected** by the Government.
- The Laffer curve is **inverted U-shaped**.
- The curve explains that as the tax rate rises, there is an increase in tax revenue. However, after reaching a maximum point, the tax revenue starts decreasing with further increase in tax rate as many people start evading tax payments. Thus, with the help of Laffer curve, the **optimum tax rate** can be found so that the tax collected by the Government can be maximised.

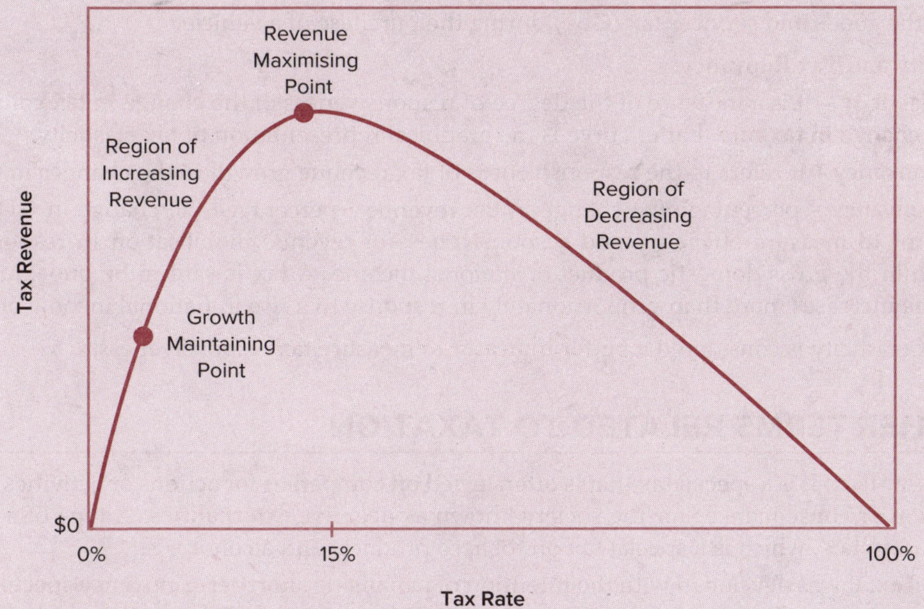

Laffer Curve

> **did you KNOW?** Circular trading is issuing of invoices in transactions among multiple companies without the actual supply of goods. This is performed by using input tax credit in the GST regime. Circular trading is a type of cyclical order that occurs when a company tries to create a flow of fake sales transactions with other parties by producing fake invoices.

Sin Goods

Sin goods are goods which are considered harmful for the society. Example: Alcohol and Tobacco, Gambling, Drugs, Fast foods, etc.

Sin Tax

It is levied on goods which adversely affect health. Such goods are considered harmful for the society which includes Alcohol, Tobacco, Fast Foods, etc.

Motor Vehicle Tax – State Level Tax

In India, motor vehicle tax, which is also known as Road tax, is imposed on the vehicle owners by respective state governments. The motor vehicle tax is usually calculated considering various factors like engine capacity of the vehicle, seating capacity, unladen weight, laden weight and cost price of vehicle, etc.

This tax has to be paid during the purchase and registration of a vehicle in a particular state. It is levied along with the goods and services tax (GST) during the purchase of a vehicle.

Tax Elasticity and Tax Buoyancy

- **Tax Elasticity** – It is a measure of the degree of responsiveness of the **change in tax collection due to the change in tax rate**. Laffer curve is the graphical representation of tax elasticity.
- **Tax Buoyancy** – It refers to the responsiveness of tax revenue growth to the changes in GDP.
- **Tax Buoyancy** = percentage (%) change in tax revenue / percentage (%) change in GDP. It is an indicator to measure efficiency and responsiveness of revenue mobilisation in response to the growth in the gross domestic product or national income. A **tax is said to be buoyant if** the tax revenue increases more than proportionately in response to a rise in national income or output.

Usually, tax elasticity is considered a **better indicator** to measure tax responsiveness.

OTHER TERMS RELATED TO TAXATION

- **Pigouvian Tax:** It is a special tax that is often levied on companies for actions or activities that cause pollution or consequences for the society known as **negative externalities**. A type of a Pigouvian tax is a 'sin tax', which is a special tax on tobacco products and alcohol.
- **Tobin Tax:** It was developed with the intention of **penalising short-term currency speculation,** and to place a **tax on all spot conversions of currency**. Revenues from this tax are intended to be used for environmental and basic human needs. The tax is named after its proponent, Nobel laureate and economist James Tobin.
- **Tax Haven:** It is a geographical area where certain **taxes are levied at a low rate or not at all**. Tax haven leads to loss of revenue for Governments, money laundering, etc. However, almost every country (in one way or the other) is a tax haven for non-nationals because it wants to attract foreign capital by offering incentives. Some examples of tax haven countries include *Andorra, the Bahamas, Belize, Bermuda, the British Virgin Islands, the Cayman Islands, the Channel Islands, the Cook Islands, the Island of Jersey, Hong Kong, the Isle of Man, Mauritius, Lichtenstein, Monaco, Panama, St. Kitts and Nevis.*
- **Transfer Pricing:** It is the price at which divisions of a company transact with each other. Transactions may include the trade of supplies or labour between departments. Transfer prices are used when individual entities of a larger multi-entity firm are treated and measured as separately run entities.
- **Tax Evasion:** It is an illegal practice where a person, an organisation or a corporation intentionally avoids paying his or her true tax liability. Those caught evading taxes are generally subject to criminal charges and substantial penalties.
- **Tax Avoidance:** An arrangement made to beat the intent of the law by taking unfair advantage of the shortcomings in the tax rules is known as tax avoidance. It refers to finding out new methods or tools to avoid the payment of taxes which are within the limits of the law. This can be done by adjusting the accounts in a manner that it will not violate any tax rules as well as the tax burden will also be minimised.
- **Tax Deducted at Source (TDS):** A person who is liable to make payment of a specified nature to any other person shall deduct tax at source and remit the same into the account of the Central Government. The deductee from whom income tax has been deducted at source would be entitled to get credit of the amount so deducted. Taxes shall be deducted at the rates specified in the

relevant provisions of the Act. In the case of payment to non-resident persons, the **withholding tax** rates specified under the *Double Taxation Avoidance Agreements* shall also be considered.

- **Withholding Tax:** It is an obligation on the payer to withhold tax at the time of making payment under a specified head such as rent, commission, salary, professional services and contract at the rates specified under the tax regime.
- **Inheritance Tax:** Inheritance tax is levied on property/asset inherited after the death of an individual. It differs from estate tax, which is levied on the total value of a deceased person's estate. It is levied in Japan, South Korea, and USA, etc.
- **Presumptive Taxation:** Often, filing complex tax returns and paying taxes are expensive and troublesome affairs for **small businesses**. To incentivise them to pay tax, tax law allows them to declare their turnover and pay taxes according to that fixed turnover. The composition scheme in the GST regime is an example of presumptive taxation where small taxpayers can pay GST **at a fixed rate of turnover**. The composition scheme can be opted by any GST taxpayer whose turnover is less than ₹1.5 crore.
- **Arm's Length Price:** It is the price at which a willing buyer and a willing **unrelated** seller would freely agree to transact or trade, so that there is no conflict of interest in the transaction. This price is used by the Government to compute and levy income tax in the case when transactions occur between related entities (say, transfer pricing). Those related entities should agree to the same terms and conditions which would have been agreed between non-related entities for comparable uncontrolled transactions so that the Government gets a fair amount of tax revenue.
- **Tax Shelter:** It is a place to legally store assets so that current or future tax liabilities are minimised. It is a tax minimisation strategy and should not be confused with the illegal practice of tax evasion. Qualified retirement accounts, certain insurance products, partnerships, municipal bonds and real estate investments are all examples of potential tax shelters.
- **Commodities Transaction Tax (CTT):** It is a tax levied on exchange-traded commodity derivatives in India on the lines of the Securities Transaction Tax or STT. CTT was introduced in the 2008–09 Budget.
- **Angel Tax:** It is the income tax payable on capital raised by unlisted companies via issue of shares where the share price is seen more than the fair market value of the shares sold. The excess realisation is treated as income and is taxed accordingly. Angel tax was introduced in the 2012 Union Budget to arrest laundering of funds. It has come to be called angel tax since it largely impacts angel investments in start-ups.
- **Grandfathering Clause:** When a new clause or policy is added to a law, certain persons may be relieved from complying with the new clause. This is called 'grandfathering'. 'Grandfathered' persons enjoy the right to avail concession because they have made their decisions under the old law.
- **EBIT:** Earnings Before Interest and Taxes (EBIT) is an organisation's total revenue before income tax assessments and interest costs are removed. EBIT is used to break down the performance valuation of an organisation's core functions excluding charge costs and capital structure expenses that affect benefit or profits.

$$\text{EBIT} = \text{NI} + \text{IE} + \text{TE}$$

where, NI = Net Income; IE = Interest Expense; TE = Tax Expense Or,

$$\text{EBIT} = \text{Sales Revenue} - \text{COGS} - \text{Operating Expenses}$$

- **EBITDA:** EBITDA, or earnings before interest, taxes, depreciation, and amortisation, is a measure of a company's total financial performance that can be used instead of net income in certain situations.
  - EBITDA is simply net income (or profits) plus interest, taxes, depreciation, and amortisation.
  - EBITDA may be used to analyse and compare profitability across organisations and sectors since it excludes the impacts of financing and capital expenditures.
  - EBITDA is a commonly used valuation measure that may be compared to enterprise value and revenue.
  - EBITDA is calculated by adding net income, interest, taxes, and depreciation.

$$EBITDA = NI + I + T + D + A$$

where, NI = Net Income; I = Interest; T = Taxes; D = Depreciation; A = Amortisation

A Good Tax System

A good tax system should meet five basic conditions: **fairness, adequacy, simplicity, transparency and administrative ease**. Although opinions about what makes a good tax system will vary, there is consensus that these five basic conditions should be maximised to the greatest extent possible.

1. **Fairness, or equity** – means that everybody should pay a fair share of taxes.
2. **Adequacy** – means that taxes must provide enough revenue to meet the basic needs of society.
3. **Simplicity** – helps taxpayers better understand the system and reduces the costs of compliance.
4. **Transparency** – means that taxpayers and leaders can easily find information about the tax system and how tax money is used.
5. **Administrative ease** – means that the tax system is not too complicated or costly for either taxpayers or tax collectors.

Taxpayers' Charter

The Taxpayers' Charter was announced during the **2020–21 Union Budget**. The aim of introducing it is to build a trust between a taxpayer and the tax administration and reduce harassment. There are taxpayers' various rights and obligations under the charter. It also specifies the tax department's commitment to providing services to the taxpayers.

Taxpayers' Rights under the Charter

- To assist taxpayers in a courteous, fair and reasonable manner
- To treat taxpayers as honest unless the department has a reason to believe otherwise
- To provide for a fair and impartial appeal procedure and review mechanism
- To provide accurate and complete information for tax compliance purposes
- To complete and decide income tax proceedings in a time-bound manner
- To ensure the collection of the correct amount of tax dues
- To ensure taxpayer's privacy
- To maintain the confidentiality of information provided by the taxpayers
- To put in place a procedure to raise complaints and grievance redressal mechanisms
- To adopt a fair and impartial approach to the resolution to tax disputes

Taxpayers' Obligations under the Charter

- To make a complete and honest disclosure of facts and information to the department
- To maintain accounting records and documents as prescribed under the income tax law
- To respond to income tax notices and information requests in a time-bound manner
- To pay their income tax dues and comply with their filing requirements within the due dates

Financial Secrecy Index

The Financial Secrecy Index ranks jurisdictions according to their secrecy and the scale of their offshore financial activities. A politically neutral ranking, it is a tool for understanding global financial secrecy, tax havens or secrecy jurisdictions, and illicit financial flows or capital flight.

The index was unveiled by the **Tax Justice Network (TJN)**. The TJN is an independent international network, launched in 2003. The **Financial Secrecy Index** is a biennial publication of the TJN which was started in 2009.

The 2022 Index was topped by USA and followed by Switzerland among 141 countries. India's rank improved from 47th as per the 2020 report to 36th as per the 2022 report.

Tax Expenditure

- Though the main objective of any taxation system is to raise revenues, the Government allows several concessions and tax rebates to the taxpayers, which also shows how the Government's actions align with their purposes and goals. The range of special taxation measures, viz. special tax rates, exemptions, deductions, rebates, deferrals and credits affect the amount of revenue collection. These measures are also known as 'tax preferences'.
- They have an impact on Government revenue (i.e. they have an opportunity cost) and also reflect the policy choices of the Government. The amount of such impact in terms of the **potential revenue foregone** by the Government is known as **'Tax expenditure'**.
- Tax preferences may be viewed as subsidy payments to preferred taxpayers and thus appear as implicit payments to promote specific sectors.
- Hence, they should be part of the expenditure items in the budget. In a democratic set-up, tax policy demands transparency along with efficiency, which calls for the explicit mentioning of such tax expenditures by the Government.
- **Tax expenditures or a Revenue Foregone Statement** was laid before the Parliament for the first time during **Union Budget 2006–07**. It was well received and also gave rise to a constructive debate on the issues concerning fiscal policy. Through this, Government envisaged **to bring transparency** in the matter of tax policy and tax expenditures.
- During Budget 2007–08, it was presented as a separate budget document titled '**Statement of Revenue Foregone**'.
- At present, it is placed as the '**Statement of Revenue Impact of Tax Incentives under the Central Tax System**', as it actually involves an analysis of revenue impact.

The elements of tax expenditures include:

1. Concessional tax rates for the **corporate sector,** viz. concessional tax rate of 22 per cent for existing domestic companies and of 15 per cent for newly incorporated domestic companies (which make fresh investment by 31 March 2023) inserted through Sections 115BAA and 115BAB of Taxation

Laws (Amendment) Act, 2019 (TLAA).

2. Tax incentive for **individual taxpayers** for investments in various savings instruments, repayment of housing loan and payment of tuition fees for children.
3. Tax exemptions to various **Charitable entities** including Government funded entities and specific exemptions to entities engaged in certain activities to fulfil social purposes.

Tax to GDP Ratio

A **tax-to-GDP ratio** is the volume of a country's tax revenue relative to the size of its economy measured by GDP. The ratio provides an idea of the country's **tax revenue potential** relative to the economy. Tax to GDP ratio is an indicator of the financial capacity of the government to finance its necessary expenditure. While a higher ratio denotes higher capacity to finance expenditure and reduced dependence on borrowings, a lower ratio indicates the hindrances for the investment in critical infrastructure by the government.

Traditionally, the tax-to-GDP ratio values are low for developing countries compared to developed countries. Although tax-to-GDP ratio is very low in India compared to 34 per cent in OECD countries, India has shown improvement in its tax-to-GDP ratio over recent years. India's tax-to-GDP ratio for Direct Tax reached a 15-year high of 6.11 per cent in 2022–23.

The tax-to-GDP ratio is expected to reach 11.7 per cent for India in FY 2024–25.

TAX ADMINISTRATION IN INDIA

Central Board of Direct Taxes (CBDT)

CBDT is the apex authority for tax administration pertaining to direct tax, viz. Income Tax in India. It is a statutory body, established as per the Central Board of Revenue Act, 1963. It is administered by the Department of Revenue, under the Ministry of Finance. Initially, the Central Board of Revenue was set up under the Central Board of Revenue Act of 1924 and was in charge of both direct and indirect taxes. In 1964, the Central Board of Revenue got split into two boards, namely,

1. Central Board of Direct Taxes (CBDT)
2. Central Board of Excise and Customs (CBEC)

CBDT is entrusted with the policy formulation related to levying and collecting Direct Taxes, supervision of the entire Income Tax Department, suggesting changes in taxation laws and structure to Government, etc.

Central Board of Indirect Taxes and Customs (CBIC)

The Central Board of Indirect Taxes and Customs (CBIC) is the authority responsible for administration of indirect taxes such as GST, central excise, customs in India. It functions under the **Department of Revenue**, Finance Ministry, Government of India.

The Central Board of Indirect Taxes and Customs (CBIC), formerly known as the Central Board of Excise and Customs (CBEC), **is subordinate to the Department of Revenue under the Ministry of Finance**. It deals with **policy formulation and implementation related to the** levy and collection of Customs duties, Central Excise duties, GST, administration of these taxes, and prevention of smuggling and narcotics. CBIC is an administrative authority. Custom Houses, Central Goods and Services Commissionerates and Central Revenues Control Laboratory are its subordinate organisations. CBIC is a statutory body **established under** the Central Boards of Revenue Act of 1963.

Tax Administration Reform Commission (TARC)

The Tax Administration Reform Commission or **TARC** was established by the GoI in 2013 to review the application of tax laws and tax policies in India, with respect to the global best practices. The mandate of the commission was to suggest measures for reforms needed in tax administration to augment its effectiveness and efficiency. It was headed by **Dr. Parthasarathi Shome** as the Chairman and submitted its report in 2014. Recommendations included changes in structure, improvement in taxpayers service, enhanced use of Information and Communication Technology, exchange of information with other agencies, Customs Capacity Building, Impact assessment, Expansion of Base, Compliance Management, Revenue Forecasting, Predictive Analysis and Research for tax Governance, etc.

Project Insight

- It is a project launched by the Union Finance Ministry in 2016 to monitor high-value transactions and **detect tax evaders** using technology with a view to curbing the circulation of black money.
- It uses data mining and big data analytics to scoop out tax evaders from social media platforms to deduce mismatches between spending pattern and income declaration.
- The linking of PAN (Permanent Account Number) with Aadhaar is a key identifier used by the IT Department to link and analyse various transactions relating to taxpayers.

Carbon Border Tax

- **European Union (EU)** has proposed a carbon tariff on imports from the countries that are not taking similarly aggressive steps to slash their own greenhouse gas emissions. The idea behind the tax is to disincentivise companies outside the European Union that are exporting to EU four carbon extensive goods, i.e. steel, cement, fertilisers and aluminium.
- The existing **Emissions Trading System** of the EU makes operating within the region expensive for certain businesses. As a result, the EU authorities fear that these businesses might prefer to relocate to countries that have more relaxed or no emission limits (resulting in **'carbon leakage'**) and thereby increasing the total emissions in the world.
- In the United States, a similar tax has been envisaged on imports from the countries that lack substantial climate policies as part of a US$ 3.5 trillion budget plan. It indicates that climate policy is increasingly becoming interwoven in trade policy.
- EU being India's third largest trading partner, this tax may **impact demand for Indian goods in EU** in future by increasing the prices of goods exported from India.

Panama and Paradise Papers

The Panama Papers refer to the 11.5 million leaked encrypted confidential documents that were the property of the Panama-based law firm Mossack Fonseca. These contain financial information dealing in shell corporations that were perhaps used for illegal purposes. Paradise Papers and Mauritius leaks are similar set of confidential documents exposing tax haven activities.

Base Erosion and Profit Shifting (BEPS)

As the tax havens are in play, companies as well as individuals are using tax havens for shifting their profits to the tax havens and enjoying the low taxes there. There are two methods.

1. **Place of management**: Most of the multinational companies such as Amazon, Facebook, and Apple shift their official territory to these tax havens and plan their tax accounting accordingly to evade the relatively high tax rates in the actual place of businesses.
2. **Shell companies**: These are bogus companies created only in paper at these tax havens to shift the profits to the tax havens to evade taxes. They even participate in round tripping of the investments and money-laundering activities.

These tax evasions not only lower the tax collections of the countries but also weaken the financial base needed for sustainable economic developments. OECD has a BEPS framework to curb this phenomenon. India participates in this effort. India also suffers from BEPS due to misuse of double taxation avoidance agreement.

OECD's TWO PILLAR PLAN

Organisation for Economic Cooperation and Development (OECD) has facilitated a global deal to ensure big companies pay a minimum tax rate of 15 per cent, known as **Global Minimum Corporate Tax Rate** and deter them from tax avoidance. The deal has been agreed by **137 countries (including India)** accounting for over 90 per cent of the global economy.

This is part of the inclusive framework on Base Erosion and Profit Shifting (BEPS) agreed upon by G20 countries and OECD (Organisation for Economic Cooperation and Development).

OCED's Two-Pillar Plan

1. **Pillar One** – Reallocation of taxing rights: It reallocates part of profits of MNCs to places where products and services are sold.
2. **Pillar Two** – Global anti-base erosion mechanism: Setting 'Global Minimum Corporation Tax Rate (GMCTR)' of 15 per cent from 2023 to large MNCs.
    - In 2016, **6 per cent equalisation levy was implemented by India which was Digital tax on non-resident digital companies** (Google, Facebook) for **online advertisement services**.
    - In 2020, **the scope of the Equalisation Levy was expanded** as part of the **Finance Act 2020**. This is commonly referred to as '**Equalisation Levy 2.0 or EL 2.0**'. The new levy is imposed as a **2 per cent Digital Service Tax on trade and services of foreign ecommerce companies** such as Amazon and Walmart-owned Flipkart and others having an annual turnover of ` 2 crores or more.

BONUS KNOWLEDGE

DIGITAL TAX

Digital tax is levied on digital services or online business activities as a direct tax.

This is part of the OECD's two-pillar plan which was agreed upon by 137 countries (including India) in 2021 to reform international taxation rules and a key part of the OECD Project in addressing the tax challenges arising from the digitalisation and globalisation of the economy.

Double Taxation Avoidance Agreement (DTAA)

In this globalised world, many multinationals are working in a cross-country scenario. In this situation, profits earned and taxed in a country must be immune to the taxation in other countries too. To achieve this, DTAA is being signed between countries to avoid double taxation. This arrangement also facilitates greater foreign investments.

Sometimes DTAA also results in some problems like, in many occasions, Indian money has been round tripped through Mauritius to evade taxes in India. It is often exploited for the money-laundering activities. DTAA has been also used for BEPS on several occasions.

Place of Effective Management (PoEM)

To curb the flight of taxes and determine the residential status of foreign companies, the Financial Act, 2015 introduced the concept of place of effective management (PoEM). If a company's place of effective management is India, it will be treated as an Indian resident and its global income will be taxable in India. The aim of PoEM is to curb shell companies.

Automatic Exchange of Information (AEOI)

AEOI is the systematic and periodic transmission of 'bulk' taxpayer information by the source country to the residence country, which is possible under most of the DTAAs and Multilateral Convention on Mutual Administrative Assistance in Tax Matters (MAC).

SUMMARY

- The **tax structure** in India is a three-tier structure involving government at three levels: union or central government, state government at the provincial level and the rural or urban local bodies at the local government level.
- **Different types of taxes** are – Progressive and Regressive, Ad valorem and Specific, Direct and Indirect Taxes.
- **Examples of Direct Taxes in India** are – Personal Income Tax, Corporate Tax, etc.
- **Goods and Services Tax (GST)** is the largest Indirect Tax in India which was introduced on **1 July 2017** with an intention to have a 'One Nation One Tax' system.
  - **Goods and Services Tax (GST)** replaced a multiple number of cascading taxes levied by the Central and State Governments.
- GST was introduced as the Constitution **(One Hundred and First Amendment)** Act, 2017, following the passage of the **122nd Constitutional Amendment Bill.**
- **Four separate Acts** were enacted, viz. – 1. Central GST Act, 2017, 2. Integrated GST Act, 2017, 3. The GST (Compensation to States) Act, 2017, and 4. The Union Territory GST Act, 2017 – The State GST (SGST) Bill was passed by each state in order to enact the State GST (SGST) Act.
- Under GST, various goods and services are taxed at the following rates – **0 per cent**, **5 per cent**, **12 per cent**, **18 per cent** and **28 per cent**.
- Article 279A provides for the **GST Council** with Union Finance Minister as its Chairperson and Union MOS (Finance) and the Finance Ministers of all States as members.

- Laffer curve, introduced by Arthur Laffer, represents the **relationship between tax rates and the amount of tax revenue collected** by the Government – Laffer curve is **inverted U-shaped**.
- A **Tax-to-GDP ratio** is the volume of a country's tax revenue relative to the size of its economy measured by GDP – It provides an idea of the country's **tax revenue potential** relative to the economy.
- **Direct Taxes** and **Indirect Taxes** in India are administered by Central Board of Direct Taxes (CBDT) and Central Board of Indirect Taxes & Customs (CBIC), respectively.

UPSC CSE PREVIOUS YEARS' PRELIMINARY EXAMINATION QUESTIONS

1. With reference to India's decision to levy an equalisation tax of 6 per cent on online advertisement services offered by non-resident entities, which of the following statements is/are correct? **[2018]**

1. It is introduced as a part of the Income Tax Act.
2. Non-resident entities that offer advertisement services in India can claim a tax credit in their home country under the 'Double Taxation Avoidance Agreements'.

Select the correct answer using the code given below:

(a) 1 only (b) 2 only
(c) Both 1 and 2 (d) Neither 1 nor 2

2. What is/are the most likely advantages of implementing 'Goods and Services Tax (GST)'? **[2017]**

1. It will replace multiple taxes collected by multiple authorities and will thus create a single market in India.
2. It will drastically reduce the 'Current Account Deficit' of India and will enable it to increase its foreign exchange reserves.
3. It will enormously increase the growth and size of economy of India and will enable it to overtake China in the near future.

Select the correct answer using the code given below:

(a) 1 only (b) 2 and 3 only
(c) 1 and 3 only (d) 1, 2 and 3

3. A decrease in tax to GDP ratio of a country indicates which of the following? **[2015]**

1. Slowing economic growth rate.
2. Less equitable distribution of national income.

Select the correct answer using the code given below:

(a) 1 only (b) 2 only
(c) Both 1 and 2 (d) Neither 1 nor 2

4. Which one of the following is not a feature of 'Value Added Tax'? **[2011]**

(a) It is multipoint destination-based system of taxation.
(b) It is levied on value addition at each stage of transaction in the production distribution chain.
(c) It is a tax on the final consumption of goods or services and must ultimately be borne by the consumer.
(d) It is basically a subject of the Central Government, and the State Governments are only a facilitator for its successful implementation.

5. In India, the tax proceeds of which one of the following as a percentage of gross tax revenue has significantly declined in the last five years? **[2010]**

(a) Service tax (b) Personal income tax
(c) Excise duty (d) Corporation tax

☞ NO QUESTIONS ASKED
2024, 2023, 2022, 2021, 2020, 2019, 2016, 2013, 2012

ANSWER KEY

1. (a) 2. (a) 3. (a) 4. (d) 5. (c)

UPSC CSE PREVIOUS YEARS' MAIN EXAMINATION QUESTIONS

1. Explain the rationale behind the Goods and Services Tax (Compensation to States) Act of 2017. How has COVID-19 impacted the GST compensation fund and created new federal tensions? **[2020]**
2. Enumerate the indirect taxes which have been subsumed in the Goods and Services Tax (GST) in India. Also, comment on the revenue implications of the GST introduced in India since July 2017. **[2019]**
3. Discuss the rationale for introducing the Goods and Service Tax (GST) in India. Bring out critically the reasons for the delay in roll-out for its regime. **[2013]**

☞ NO QUESTIONS ASKED

2024, 2023, 2022, 2021, 2018, 2017, 2016, 2015, 2014

CHAPTER

8

PUBLIC FINANCE

CHAPTER OUTLINE

- Fiscal Policy
- Objectives of Fiscal Policy
- Components of Fiscal Policy
- Revenue Receipts
- Tax Revenue
- Non-Tax Revenue
- Capital Receipts
- Public Expenditure
- Different Types of Deficits
- Budget Deficit
- Revenue Deficit
- Effective Revenue Deficit
- Fiscal Deficit
- Primary Deficit
- Monetised Deficit
- Present Trend in Deficits
- Deficit Financing
- Status of Deficit Financing in India
- Fiscal Consolidation
- Fiscal Responsibility and Budget Management Act, 2003
- Challenges Ahead towards achieving the targets of Fiscal Consolidation
- RBI Reports on State Finances
- Budget
- How is the Budget prepared by the Government?
- Procedure of Laying Budget
- Recent Budget Reforms
- Chakravyuha Challenge of the Indian Economy
- Finance Commission

Public finance is a concept that includes all the matters connected to receipts and payments/expenditure of public money. It basically deals with the financing of Government, or in simple terms budget. Let us now discuss the concept of budgetary policy or fiscal policy under public finance.

FISCAL POLICY

'Fiscal' is a Latin word, which means 'treasure of the Government'. Fiscal policy refers to that segment of national economic policy which is primarily concerned with **steering the important parameters of an economy** through changes in receipts and expenditure of the Central Government.

Objectives of Fiscal Policy

1. **To achieve higher rate of economic growth**, through the following measures:
   a. Raising the ratio of saving (s) to income (y) by controlling consumption (c)

b. Raising the rate of investment
c. Encouraging the flow of spending in productive areas

2. **Price stability** – Government uses fiscal measures, such as taxation and public expenditure, to stabilise the prices and control inflation. Government also generates employment by speeding up infrastructure development.
3. **Reduce inequality** – Inequality is one of the main features of the underdeveloped economies. If inequality is not reduced, there will be discontentment among the people that will generate instability in the economy.

The following fiscal measures may help reduce the inequalities of income and wealth in the society:

i. Progressive taxes may be imposed on rich people to curtail the unnecessary consumption expenditure.
ii. The poor section of the society should be exempted from taxes or the taxes should be levied on them at a very low rate.
iii. The luxury goods, which are generally used by the upper class, may be heavily taxed and the proceeds so collected may be diverted to more productive sectors of the economy.
iv. Public expenditure should be tailored so as to benefit the poorer sections of the society.

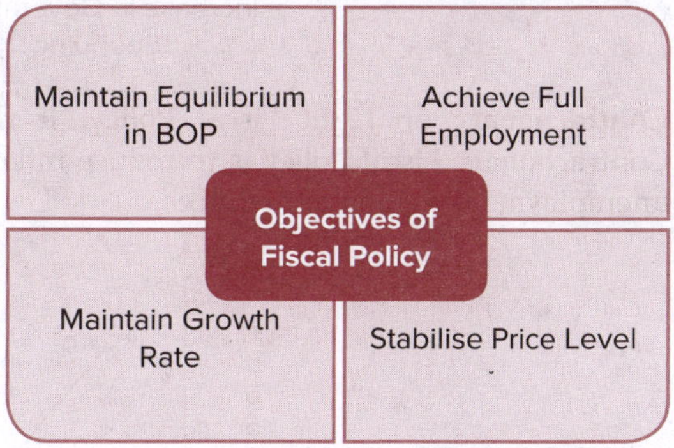

Types of Fiscal Policy

Fiscal policy can be categorised into three main areas based on the condition of the economy and the goals that governments aim to achieve.

Expansionary Fiscal Policy: Expansionary fiscal policy directly increases aggregate demand by increasing government expenditure. It reduces unemployment and also results in better GDP. It is obtained during recession to increase the level of economic activity.

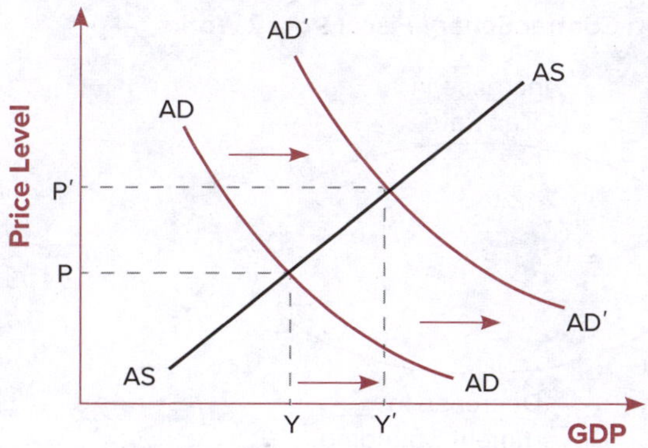

Expansionary Fiscal Policy

How an Expansionary Fiscal Policy Works

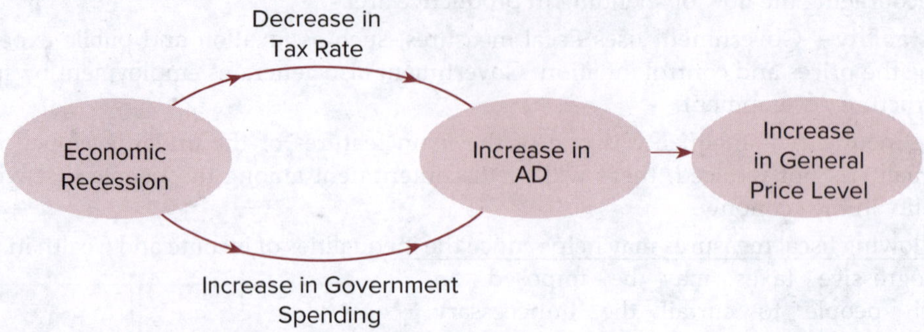

Contractionary or **Tight Fiscal Policy**: It reduces demand by lowering spending. The goal of Contractionary Fiscal Policy is to reduce inflation and control excess money supply. It might trigger unemployment as inflation reduces.

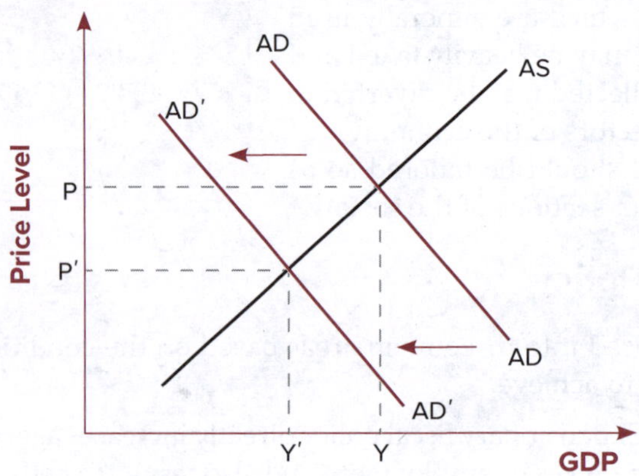

Contractionary Fiscal Policy

How a Contractionary Fiscal Policy Works

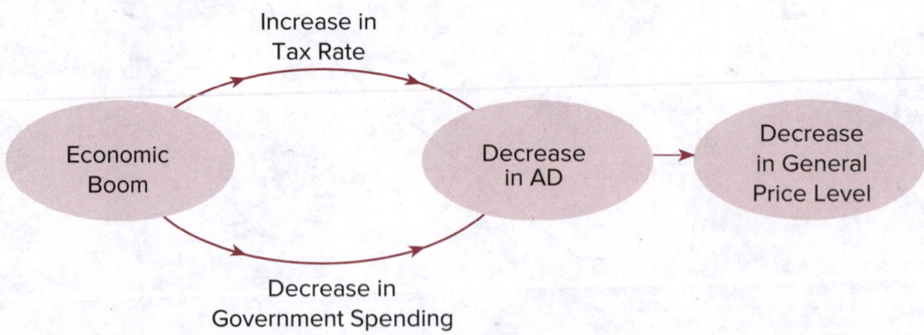

Neutral Fiscal Policy: In this policy, government's budget is designed in such a way that it neither stimulates nor restrains economic growth. It maintains the status quo in the economy. It is typically used when an economy is in equilibrium.

Cyclicality of the Fiscal Policy

A change in the direction of government spending and taxation in response to changes in the economy and fluctuations in economic growth is referred to as the cyclicality of fiscal policy.

There are mainly **two kinds of cyclical fiscal policies:**

Counter-Cyclical Fiscal Policy

It describes the measures taken by the government which is against the direction of the business cycle.

During recession, the government generally takes the help of expansionary fiscal policy. This raises government expenditure (G) and reduces taxes (T) to create a demand that leads to economic boom. This raises the purchasing power of the economy and helps in reducing the recession.

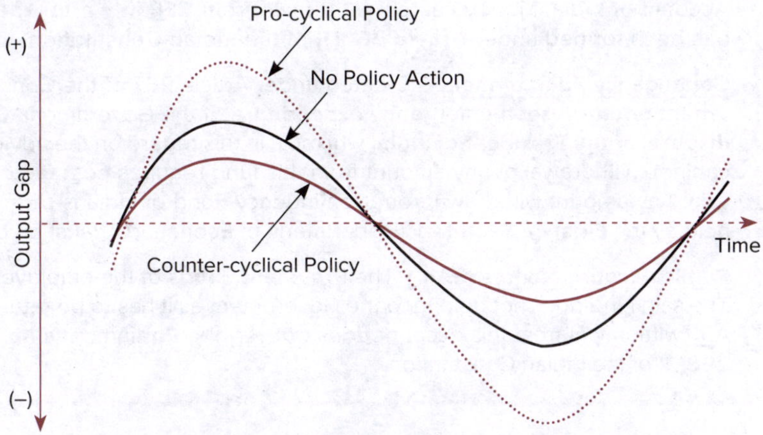

Business Cycle under Various Fiscal Policy Stance

In countries like India, greater public expenditure and job creation are paramount in economic recession. On the other hand, during economic boom, the Government must restrain itself from excessive public expenditure to prevent the crowding-out effect, which is detrimental to private investments.

During ancient and medieval times, the kings used to build monuments during famines and droughts to generate employment.

Pro-Cyclical Fiscal Policy

It highlights the measures that the government takes to support the business cycle by implementing contractionary policies during recessions and expansionary policies during booms.

A pro-cyclical fiscal policy can be harmful as it might lead to macroeconomic volatility and reduction in investment, restricting growth. The adoption of Contractionary Fiscal Policy during a recession will reduce the government expenditure (G) and increase the taxes (T). This will again reduce the purchasing power of the economy and lead to recession.

Components of Fiscal Policy

The fiscal policy comprises the following **three** aspects:

1. Government receipts, i.e. money received by the Government
2. Government expenditure, i.e. money spent by the Government
3. Public debt

In the process of using fiscal policy, a country may either run into surplus or deficit or balanced budget.

All the receipts and expenditure of the Government are credited to (goes into) and debited from (taken out from) the **Consolidated Fund of India**, **Contingency Fund of India** and **Public Account of India**.

BONUS KNOWLEDGE

Consolidated Fund of India (CFI) – CFI is a **Government of India's account** which is similar to a normal bank account. All the revenues, borrowings, receipts against loans and advances, etc. of the Government are **credited to CFI**. All Government expenditures are **paid (debited)** from this account except a few exceptional items which are dealt by the Contingency Fund of India or the Public Account of India. Money can be withdrawn from CFI **only after the approval of the Parliament**. CFI has been formed under **Article 266(1)** of the Indian Constitution.

Contingency Fund of India – Created under Article 267 of the Constitution, its purpose is **to meet any urgent or unforeseen emergency expenditure** of the Government. Contingency Fund of India is **at the disposal of the President of India,** who acts in this regard on the advice of the Prime Minister and his/her cabinet. Withdrawal of any amount from this fund requires **post facto approval** of the Parliament (unlike CFI). Any amount withdrawn from Contingency Fund of India is **returned to the fund from the CFI**. It is held by the **Finance Secretary** (Department. of Economic Affairs) on behalf of the President of India.

Public Account of India (PAI) – The **Provident Funds** of the employees and **small savings** flow into PAI. The said fund does not belong to the Government as it has to be returned to the rightful owners in future. Any withdrawal from this account **does not require Parliament's approval**. PAI is formed under **Article 266(2)** of the Indian Constitution.

The Government Receipts can be categorised into the following components:

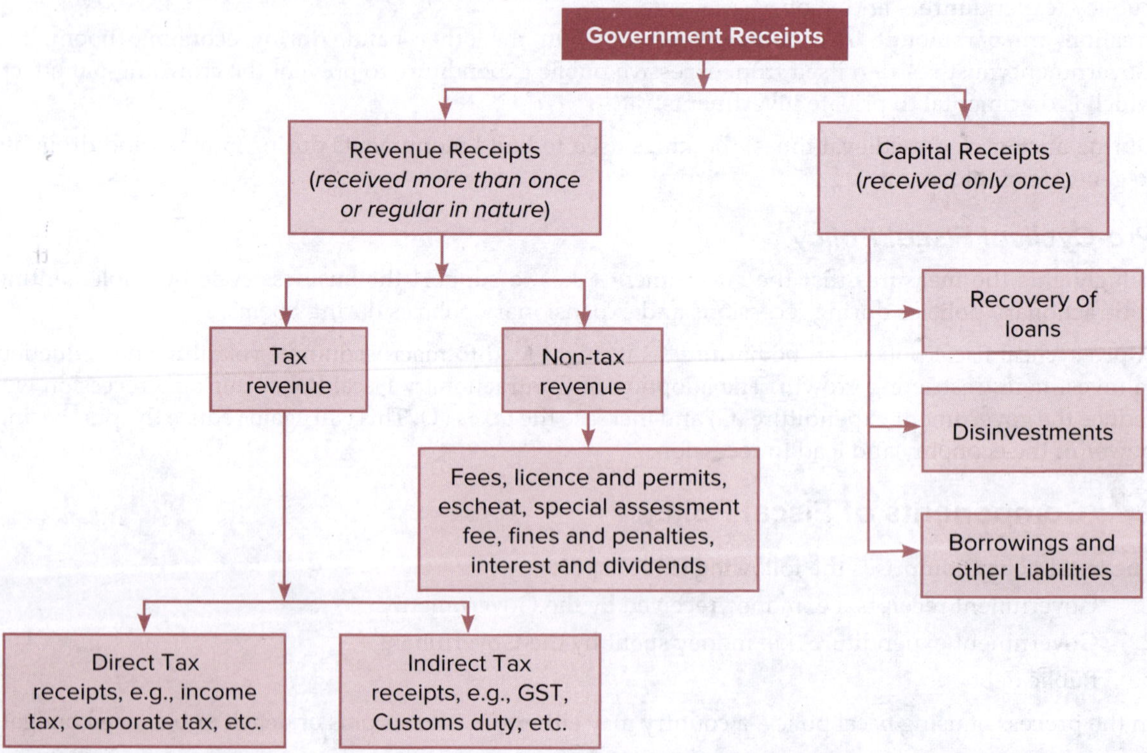

REVENUE RECEIPTS

These are the receipts which neither create any liability nor cause any reduction in the assets of the Government. They are **regular and recurring** in nature, and the Government receives them in the normal course of activities.

Revenue receipts can be of **two types**:

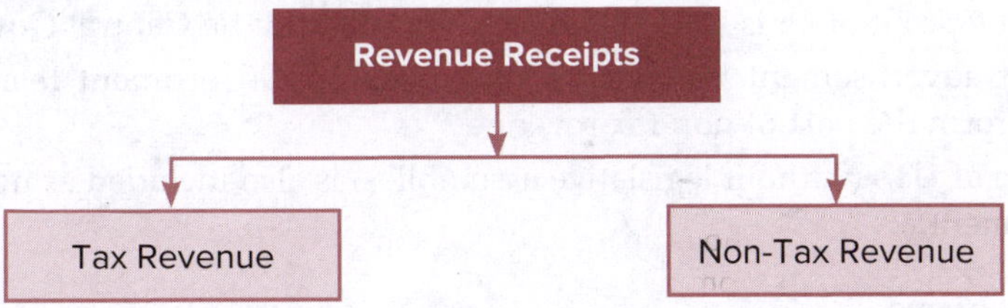

TAX REVENUE

Tax is a **compulsory payment** by the individuals, households, firms or other institutional units to the Government to meet public expenditure. It is legally imposed by the Government, and tax bearers cannot deny paying the same. Taxes in India consist of mainly two types – Direct Taxes and Indirect Taxes.

The major source of Direct Taxes is **Income Tax and Corporate Tax**, whereas the largest source of Indirect Taxes in India is Goods & Services Tax (GST).

NON-TAX REVENUE

These are revenues and resources which are received from sources other than taxes, like fines and penalties, fees, grants and gifts. Some of the non-tax receipts of the Government are:

- **Interest receipts:** The Central Government, many a time, provides loan to State Governments, UTs with legislative assemblies, Public Sector Enterprises, statutory bodies, etc. Interest paid by them to the Central Government is considered as non-tax revenue receipt and the principal amount returned is included under capital receipt.
- **Dividend and profit receipts:** In public sector enterprises, the Government has majority shareholding (51 per cent or more). The dividend and profit forms the revenue of the Central Government.
- **Grants-in-aid** or **external assistance:** Various foreign nations and international monetary institutions (*like World Bank group, UNDP, ADB, etc.*) provide grants-in-aid to the Central Government. It is included under the head non-tax revenue receipts and not under capital receipts because it need not be paid back unlike loan.
- **Fee:** It is a payment to the Government for administrative and judicial services (*not the commercial services*) rendered to people, e.g. land registration fees, passport fees, court fees, etc.
- **Licence and permit:** It is charged for allowing people to perform a given job. For instance, the driving licence. Under this, no service is provided by the Government.

- **Escheat:** It refers to that income of the Government which arises out of property that comes to it for want of legal heir. The State has the legal right over such property which has no claimant.
- **Special assessment:** It is that payment which is made by the owners of those properties whose value has appreciated due to development activities undertaken by the Government. *For example, construction of highway leads to the appreciation of the value of neighbouring properties.*
- **Fines and penalties:** Payments made by law breakers as economic punishments to the Government.
- **Profit from printing currency notes and minting coins**: For instance, if the cost of manufacturing ₹10 note is ₹2, the profit of ₹8 is shared between the RBI and the Central Government.
- Receipts against advertisement by private companies on Government television channels, FM radios, etc. also form the part of non-tax revenue.
- **Non-tax revenue of UTs** (without legislative assemblies) is also included as non-tax revenue of the Central Government.

Capital Receipts

1. Debt Creating Capital Receipts

- **Loans taken by the Central Government** from foreign Governments (external debt), public financial institutions, etc. are included under capital receipts.
- Borrowings from the market by sale of Government securities (G-Secs) through RBI also result in capital receipts.
- GoI, under **National Small Savings Fund (NSSF),** raises money from the public through small saving schemes like postal deposits, National Small Savings Certificate, Kisan Vikas Patra, etc. The NSSF is a part of Public Account of India. This NSSF is then invested in G-Secs. This amount raised by the Central Government through investment in G-Secs is nothing but capital receipts.

2. Non-Debt Creating Capital Receipts

- **Recovery of loans and advances –** The principal amount of loans which are repaid by State Governments, Public Sector Enterprises, other foreign Governments, etc. to Central Government is considered capital receipts, and it does not leave a burden of debt on the Central Government.
- **Disinvestment** of GoI shareholding in various Central Public Sector Enterprises like Air India, NTPC, ONGC, etc. is also a non-debt creating capital receipt for the Central Government.

EXAM ESSENTIAL

DISINVESTMENT

- Disinvestment means **sale or liquidation of assets** by the Government, usually in central public sector enterprises (CPSEs), state public sector enterprises (SPSEs), projects or other fixed assets. In some cases, disinvestment may be done to privatise assets. However, not all disinvestment is privatisation.
- **Major objectives of Disinvestment** in India include – reducing the fiscal burden on the exchequer, encouraging private ownership, shifting investments from non-strategic to strategic sectors, etc.
- Department of Investment and Public Asset Management **(DIPAM) under the Ministry of Finance** is the nodal agency dealing with disinvestments of Government of India. It was earlier called the Department of Disinvestment and was renamed as DIPAM in 2016.

- With DIPAM coming into play, there has been a paradigm shift in the approach **from Disinvestment to Investment Management**.
- **Disinvestment Data**

For Financial Year	Disinvestment Target	Actual sum collected through disinvestment
2022–23	₹65,000 crore	₹35,293.52 crore
2023–24	₹51,000 crore	₹30,000 crore
2024–25	₹50,000 crore	₹8,625.05 crore
2025–26	₹47,000 crore	–

Source: Union Budget 2025–26, DIPAM

- **Financial instruments used by DIPAM** to achieve the above disinvestment targets or, simply, various methods of disinvestment are as follows:
  1. **Initial Public Offers (IPOs)** – i.e. proceeds from offer of shares by an **unlisted CPSE** or the Government out of its shareholding or a combination of both to the public for subscription **for the first time.**
  2. **Follow-on Public Offers (FPOs)** – i.e. proceeds from offer of shares by a **listed CPSE** or the Government out of its shareholding or a combination of both to the public for subscription.
  3. **Offer for Sale (OFS)** – of shares by promoters through stock exchange mechanism – it is the method which allows auction of shares on the platform provided by the Stock Exchange.
  4. **Employees Offer for Sale**
  5. **Buyback of Shares**
  6. **Strategic Disinvestment** – sale of substantial portion of the Government shareholding of a CPSE of upto 50 per cent or such higher percentage as the competent authority may determine **along with the transfer of management control**. This is done after consultation with Union Ministries and the NITI Aayog.
  7. **Institutional Placement Programme (IPP)** – only institutions can participate in the offering.
  8. **Exchange Traded Funds (ETF)** – disinvestment through the ETF route allows **simultaneous sale of GoI's stake in various undertakings** across diverse sectors **through single offering**. It provides a mechanism for the GoI to monetise its shareholding in those CPSEs which form part of the ETF basket.

PUBLIC EXPENDITURE

Public expenditure refers to the **Government expenditure**. It is incurred by the central and State Governments. Public expenditure is incurred on various activities for the welfare of the people and also for the economic development. In other words, the expenditure incurred by public authorities like Central, State and Local Governments to satisfy the collective social wants of the people is known as Public Expenditure.

In developing countries, the public expenditure policy not only accelerates economic growth and promotes employment opportunities, but also plays a useful role in reducing poverty and inequalities in income distribution.

Public expenditure can be classified into two types:

Classification of Government Expenditure based on its Nature

- Revenue Expenditure (*Regular Expenses*)
  - Interest Payments
  - Major Subsidies
  - Defence Expenses
  - Grants by Centre to States
  - Salaries and Pensions to Central Government employees
  - Revenue Expenditure of UTs without legislature
  - Postal deficit of the Department of Posts of GoI
  - Revenue expenditure related to various welfare schemes, etc.
- Capital Expenditure (*One-time Expenses*)
  - Repayment of Loans
  - Extension of Fresh Loans to the States by the Central Govt.
  - Loans to Public Enterprises
  - Expense on Irrigation Projects, etc.

1. Revenue Expenditure

These are current or consumption expenditures incurred on civil administration, defence forces, public health and education, maintenance of Government machinery, etc. This expenditure is of **recurring type** which is incurred year after year. It **does not impact the asset-liability status** of the Government. Such expenditure **does not increase the long-term efficiency** of the firm, nor does it result in the acquisition of something permanent. **High-revenue expenditure indicates poverty and backwardness** of the economy.

2. Capital Expenditure

Capital expenditure results in the acquisition of a tangible or intangible asset or payment of liabilities. Thus, it **impacts the asset-liability status** of the Government. Capital expenditures are **focussed on GDP growth** and thereby incurred on building durable assets like highways, multipurpose dams, irrigation projects, buying machinery and equipment. They are **non-recurring type** of expenditures also in the form of capital investments. Such expenditures are expected to **improve the productive capacity** of the economy. However, **high capital expenditure indicates lack of private investment** in the economy.

BONUS KNOWLEDGE

Classification as Plan and Non-Plan Expenditure – *Scrapped after abolishment of Planning Commission*

- During the five-year plan period, every financial year's budget estimates were formulated in the form of plan and non-plan expenditure.

- **Plan expenditures** were those expenditures which were **detailed under five-year plans** and were taken into account in every year's general union budget in order to enhance the overall productive capacity of various sectors and improve socio-economic parameters in the economy. It included both revenue expenditure (like grant-in-aid to states, etc.) and capital expenditure (expenditure on construction of highways, hospitals, etc.).
- **Non-plan expenditures** were related to **obligatory yet routine** functioning of the Central Government such as interest payment, subsidies, defence expenditure, salaries and pension, etc.
- However, this classification has been scrapped and now the budget is classified only in terms of **revenue expenditure and capital expenditure**.

TYPES OF BUDGET (CENTRAL BUDGET OR STATE BUDGET)

- **Balanced Budget** – when budgeted receipts = budgeted expenditure. It raises moderately the level of aggregate demand in the economy and **is recommended when** economy is close to achieving full employment.
- **Deficit Budget** – when budget receipts < budget expenditure. It **is recommended when** there is a state of depression and aggregate demand needs to be increased.
- **Surplus Budget** – when budget receipts > budget expenditure. It **is recommended when** there is an inflationary gap and aggregate demand needs to be reduced.

Out of the above three, normally **deficit budget** occurs in a developing country like India.

DIFFERENT TYPES OF DEFICITS

EXAM ESSENTIAL

Different Types of Deficits

- Budget Deficit
- Revenue Deficit
- Effective Revenue Deficit
- Fiscal Deficit
- Primary Deficit
- Monetised Deficit

I. Budget Deficit (or Government Deficit)

- It refers to a situation when the total budgeted expenditure of the Government is larger than budgeted receipts.
- **Budget Deficit = Budgeted expenditure (Revenue + Capital) – Budgeted Receipts (Revenue + Capital).**
- The use of this concept *as a major policy parameter was discontinued in 1997* as it reflects the Government borrowings only from RBI.

II. Revenue Deficit

- It is the **excess of** revenue expenditure over revenue receipts.
- **Revenue Deficit** = Revenue Expenditure – Revenue Receipts.
- This revenue deficit is funded either through borrowings from the public or through disinvestment or by cutting revenue expenditure (*mainly subsidies*).

Last Minute SNIPPETS

Implications of Revenue Deficit

1. Higher revenue deficit **forces Government to cut its expenditure** on social welfare programmes, thereby impacting socio-economic development.
2. Raising money through borrowings to fund the deficit, raises liabilities and unproductive interest payments and also lowers the credit worthiness of the Government.

III. Effective Revenue Deficit

- This term was introduced in the **Union Budget 2012–13**. It is the difference between revenue deficit and grants-in-aid provided by the Central Government to States, constitutional and statutory bodies, etc. for the creation of capital assets.
- **Effective Revenue Deficit = Revenue Deficit − Grants for creation of capital assets.**
- *It signifies that amount of revenue receipts that are actually used for consumption expenditure of the Central Government.*

IV. Fiscal Deficit

- It is the difference between what the Government earns and its total expenditure.
- It indicates the total **borrowing requirements of the Government from all sources**.
- This tool is used to determine the **actual liability of the Government** at a certain point of time.
- **Fiscal Deficit = Budget Deficit (i.e., Borrowing from RBI) + Market Borrowings and liabilities**.
- **It is one of most important policy parameters** to measure the fiscal performance of the Central Government.

BONUS KNOWLEDGE

IMPLICATIONS OF FISCAL DEFICIT

- It implies greater borrowings by the Central Government. Borrowings from RBI raise the money supply in the economy, which results in rise in the general price level over a period of time. This leads to **inflationary spiral**.
- It **affects GDP growth** as a significant amount of budgeted revenue is **spent on the payment of interest** on borrowings by the Central Government, thus resulting in reduced investment. This, if not checked over a period, **leads to a vicious circle** of high fiscal deficit and low GDP growth.

- High fiscal deficit also leads to the **'crowding out effect'** as it leads to a situation when large borrowings by the Government to manage large fiscal deficit reduce the availability of funds for private investors.
- Creditworthiness or **credit rating of the Government also gets lowered** due to high fiscal deficit.

Measures to Check Fiscal Deficit

By *reducing the public expenditure* through

- Rationalisation of subsidies
- Reduction in revenue expenditure in terms of bonus, LTC, leaves encashment, etc. to Government employees
- Curtailing other avoidable revenue expenditure

By *increasing the revenue* through

- Increasing the tax base in the economy
- Checking tax evasion
- Restructuring the Public Sector Enterprises through disinvestment and utilising the received fund in strategic sectors like health and education

V. Primary Deficit

- While fiscal deficit shows borrowing requirement of the Government inclusive of interest payment on past loans, primary deficit **indicates borrowing requirement excluding interest payment**.
- This concept was introduced in the 1993–94 budget.
- The amount by which a Government's total expenditure exceeds its total revenue, excluding interest payments on its debt, is termed 'primary deficit'. In other words, it is the **difference between fiscal deficit and interest payments** by Government.
- **Primary Deficit** = Fiscal Deficit – Interest Payments by Government.
- Implication of Primary Deficit: It does not carry the load of interest payments on past loans. It simply indicates total borrowings (and not total liabilities).

VI. Monetised Deficit

- It refers to the **borrowings made by the Central Government from RBI through printing fresh currency against special securities** of the Central Government. It is resorted to when Government cannot borrow from the market to fund fiscal deficit.
- It increases the level of inflation in the economy due to increased money supply in the economy (*because of issue of fresh currency*).

***Kindly note**: All the above-mentioned deficits are **indicated as the percentage of GDP** of the economy.*

PRESENT TREND IN DEFICITS

Last Minute SNIPPETS

	FY 2021–22	FY 2022–23	FY 2023–24	FY 2024–25	FY 2025–26
Fiscal Deficit	6.9% of GDP	6.4% of GDP	5.6% of GDP	4.8% of GDP*	4.4% of GDP#
Revenue Deficit	4.7% of GDP	3.8% of GDP	2.6% of GDP	1.9% of GDP*	1.5% of GDP#
Effective Revenue Deficit	3.7% of GDP	2.6% of GDP	1.6% of GDP	1.0% of GDP*	0.3% of GDP#
Primary Deficit	3.3% of GDP	2.8% of GDP	2.0% of GDP	1.3% of GDP*	0.8% of GDP#

*Revised estimate of 2024–25; #Union Budget 2025–26

Note: Central Government largely uses instruments like G-secs, Treasury Bills, Cash Management Bills and access to the Ways and Means Advances facility from RBI, in the case of a fiscal deficit.

DEFICIT FINANCING

Deficit financing is defined as financing the budgetary deficit **through public loans and creation of new money**. Deficit financing in India means the expenditure which is in excess of current revenue and public borrowing. The Government may cover the deficit in the following ways:

1. By running down its accumulated cash reserves from RBI
2. By issuing new currency itself (also known as Monetised Deficit)
3. By borrowing from the RBI and RBI giving the loans to the Government by printing more currency notes

Objectives of Deficit Financing

1. To act as a remedy for depression
2. To grant subsidies
3. To increase aggregate demand
4. For payment of interest
5. To overcome the losses of public sector enterprises
6. For implementing anti-poverty programme

Adverse Effects of Deficit Financing

1. **Leads to inflation**: Deficit financing may lead to inflation. Due to deficit financing, money supply increases and the purchasing power of the people also increases, which increases the aggregate demand, and the prices also increase.
2. It puts an **adverse effect on saving and investment**.

3. It may lead to rise in the level of **inequality**.
4. It may create a **deficit in balance of payments** due to price rise, which may lead to exports becoming uncompetitive in the global market.
5. It may increase the cost of production.

BONUS KNOWLEDGE

IS DEFICIT FINANCING A NECESSARY EVIL?

The answer to this question depends on the composition of fiscal deficit in terms of revenue expenditure and capital expenditure.

If the deficit financing is undertaken to finance lower revenue expenditure and higher capital expenditure, it is good for the economy. It is because the borrowings in this case are routed to create capital assets in the economy, which may lead to increased production and higher GDP.

On the other hand, if the majority of deficit financing is spent to meet revenue expenditure, it could be worst for a developing economy like India. It is because only routine expenses are tackled through this huge liability in terms of borrowings and not in the creation of capital assets, which may increase productive capacity of our economy.

Status of Deficit Financing in India

India first used this tool in 1969, and since then it became a routine phenomenon till 1991 in order to tackle higher and higher fiscal deficits. The fiscal deficit, which was below 4 per cent of GDP till the 1970s, climbed above 7 per cent in the second half of the 1980s. The revenue deficit also increased considerably. Thus, India was bound to resort to deficit financing.

However, India, after 1991, gradually moved towards fiscal reforms in the form of **fiscal consolidation** to reduce its dependence on deficit financing. In this regard, the Fiscal Responsibility and Budget Management Act (FRBM Act) was enacted in 2003.

However, even after various measures undertaken, Government has not been able to bring fiscal deficit to the desired level.

FISCAL CONSOLIDATION

It is a process through which the economy's fiscal health is improved by taking measures to reduce fiscal deficit to a manageable level. Among the components of fiscal consolidation include improved revenue receipts and better aligned expenditure. The FRBM Act, 2003, along with its later amendments, is also a step in that direction. To summarise, fiscal consolidation reforms in India include the following:

1. Tax Revenue reforms in terms of introduction of GST, abolition of wealth Tax, rationalisation of tax exemptions, improving efficiency of the tax collection along with tax stability.
2. Improvement of stable capital receipts in terms of disinvestment and privatisation.
3. On the expenditure front, rationalisation of subsidies, tackling leakages though digitalisation and allocation of resources to priority and strategic sectors.

It is of great importance that reduction in fiscal deficit should not be achieved by reduction in capital expenditure. Reduction in the revenue expenditure should be targeted to achieve better results of fiscal consolidation.

FISCAL RESPONSIBILITY AND BUDGET MANAGEMENT ACT, 2003

➤ The FRBM Act was enacted to pursue a prudent fiscal policy framework through revenue-led fiscal consolidation. The major **objectives** of the Act were to reduce fiscal deficit, imbibe fiscal discipline and ensure long-run macro-economic stability. **Main highlights** of the targets undertaken in the FRBM Act, 2003 were as follows:

(a) To **reduce fiscal deficit** by 0.3 per cent per annum and reach the levels of 3 per cent FD by 2008–09.

(b) To **reduce revenue deficit** by 0.5 per cent per annum and to eliminate revenue deficit by 2008–09.

(c) **Fiscal deficit** and **revenue deficit** may exceed the targets only on the ground such as national security, calamity or any other exceptional grounds.

(d) Government not to borrow from RBI except by **Ways and Means Advances (WMAs)** to meet temporary excess of cash disbursements over cash receipts. WMA is a financial tool used by RBI to support States with funds to manage temporary mismatches in the cash flow of their receipts and payments. It has to be repaid by States within three months. The interest rate on WMA is presently the **repo rate**.

(e) Along with the budget and demands for grants, the Government to lay the following three statements before the Parliament every financial year:

i. Fiscal Policy Strategy Statement **(FPSS)**

ii. Medium-Term Fiscal Policy Statement **(MTFPS)**

iii. Macro-economic Framework Statement **(MFS)**

➤ However, the set targets **could not be achieved by the end of 2008–09**. One of the major reasons behind such failure was the 2008 international sub-prime crisis.

➤ **FRBM 2.0:** Later **in 2012, the FRBM Act was amended** with two major features:

1. To target **Effective Revenue Deficit** in place of Revenue Deficit.
   Effective Revenue Deficit = Revenue Deficit – Expenditure on creation of capital assets.
   Therefore, a target was set to reduce effective revenue deficit to 0 per cent **by 31 March 2015**.
2. Secondly, **Medium-Term Expenditure Statement** to be placed in the Parliament along with the Union Budget.

➤ Thereafter in 2016, **the N. K. Singh Committee** was constituted by the Central Government **to review the implementation of the FRBM Act**. The Committee suggested to have a rule-based fiscal policy by limiting Government debt, fiscal deficit and revenue deficits to certain levels for better fiscal consolidation in India.

Last Minute SNIPPETS

Major Recommendations of the N. K. Singh Committee

1. To enact the **Debt and Fiscal Responsibility Act** by repealing the existing FRBM Act.
2. To consider **debt as the new fiscal policy parameter** instead of fiscal deficit. In this regard, combined debt of Centre and States to be targeted.
3. To reduce overall Government debt to 60 per cent by 2022–23 with 40 per cent threshold for the centre and 20 per cent for the states altogether (*against the existing 49.4 per cent for the Central Government and 21 per cent for states at the time of giving recommendations*).
4. To **reduce the fiscal deficit** to 2.5 per cent of GDP **by 2022–23**.
5. To **reduce revenue deficit by 0.25 per cent every year** and reach 0.8 per cent by 2022–23.

6. **Escape Clause** recommended by the Committee. As per escape clause, **deviations of up to 0.5 per cent** of GDP from the stipulated fiscal deficit target may be allowed under special circumstances. Those special situations include national security concerns, natural calamities, collapse of agricultural sector, far-reaching structural reforms with unanticipated fiscal implications.
7. Borrowings from RBI to be done only under certain specific circumstances.
8. To establish an **autonomous fiscal council** for preparing multi-year fiscal forecasts and recommending changes in the fiscal strategy.

- The Central Government, in the later Union Budgets, has adopted some key recommendations of the N. K. Singh Committee. They include:
  - i. **Debt rule** which recommended Government to reduce the debt–GDP ratio to 40 per cent.
  - ii. **Fiscal glide path**, which allowed some flexibility in targeting the deficits on both sides (downwards when growth is good and upward when it is not).

Challenges Ahead towards achieving the targets of Fiscal Consolidation

1. Apprehensions of **slow growth** to have implications on revenue collection.
2. Need for improving revenue buoyancy of GST owing to **shortfall in GST collections** in the last fiscal year.
3. **High projected expenditure** in view of recently launched Ayushman Bharat and other welfare schemes.
4. Government may have to spend high on **petroleum subsidy** owing to the United States' recent sanction on oil import from Iran, thereby impacting oil prices.

EXAM ESSENTIAL

OTHER IMPORTANT TERMS RELATED TO PUBLIC FINANCE

Crowding-Out

- Excessive borrowings by the Government to manage fiscal deficit lead to shrinkage of the liquidity in the market and force interest rates to go up. This leaves **less availability of funds for the private sector**. Therefore, investment suffers and growth decelerates. If the Government spends the borrowed funds in populist schemes as a revenue expenditure, it **may lead to Crowding-out**.
- However, if the Government spends funds in capital expenditure as well, say, infrastructure projects, it may lead to **crowding-in** and can have a multiplier effect on investment, jobs, tax collections, etc.

Fiscal Cliff

A **sudden condition** of availability of less cash with the public due to **high taxes and reduced public expenditure** after a long period of tax cuts and liberal public expenditure is known as **Fiscal Cliff**. It was experienced in the United States during 2013 due to sudden downsizing of Government spending and expiry of existing tax cuts.

Fiscal Drag

- When **inflation or income growth moves taxpayers into higher tax brackets**, Government tax revenue increases without actually increasing the tax rates. The increase in tax payments by taxpayers reduces the overall consumer spending as a larger share of their income now goes into taxes, which leads to **deflationary pressure or drag** in the economy.

- **Progressive taxation**, whereby individuals automatically move into higher tax brackets because of inflation or increased income, results in fiscal drag.
- Fiscal drag can be seen as an **automatic fiscal stabiliser** as it controls a rapidly expanding high-inflation economy from overheating.

Fiscal Neutrality

Fiscal neutrality is a situation in which a tax, spending, or borrowing decision has or is intended to have no net effect on the economy. Any new spending brought about by a policy change that is fiscally neutral is expected to be fully offset by additional revenues generated. Thus, Fiscal Neutrality creates a condition where demand is neither increased nor decreased by taxation and government spending.

Off-budget Liabilities

- These liabilities arise **not because of borrowing or use of public money** by the Government.
- These are money liable to be paid by the Government to various entities as a **policy matter**.
- For example – the *Government does not allow Oil Marketing Enterprises to raise prices when the price of crude oil rises. To bear the losses by these Oil Marketing Enterprises, the Government issues interest bearing bonds.*
- These are **not considered in the calculation of deficits** in the budget even though they are borrowed expenditure.

Fiscal Slippage

- If the **actual fiscal deficit is more than what was expected,** it is called fiscal slippage.
- *For example in Budget 2018–19, the estimated fiscal deficit was 3.3 per cent* but the actual deficit at the *end of the financial year was 3.4 per cent, thereby indicating a fiscal slippage.*

Fiscal Stimulus

- Fiscal stimulus consists of **the attempts by Governments** or Government agencies to financially **stimulate an economy**.
- A fiscal stimulus is the **use of monetary or fiscal policy** changes to kickstart economic growth during a recession.
- Governments can **accomplish this by using tactics** such as lowering interest rates, increasing Government spending and quantitative easing, to name a few.

Pump Priming

The practice of **using tax cuts, interest rate reductions, and government spending** to stimulate an economy usually during a recession is known as Pump priming. The practice of injecting relatively small amounts of public funds into an economy that is struggling in an attempt to stimulate growth is known as Pump priming.

Fiscal Marksmanship

- It refers to **precision or accuracy** of forecasts, targets and estimates in, say, a budget-making exercise.
- *This term came into significance when it was used multiple times in the* **Economic Survey 2012–13**.

Fiscal Space

- Fiscal space is commonly defined as the **budgetary room** that allows a **Government to provide resources for public purposes** without undermining fiscal sustainability.
- According to the International Monetary Fund (IMF), fiscal space exists if the **Government can raise spending** or lower taxes **without endangering market access** and putting debt sustainability at risk.
- This implies that fiscal space analysis must be made keeping current and future expenditure along with revenue in mind.
- Therefore, fiscal space analysis should be done within the context of at least a **medium-term expenditure framework** that has a comprehensive perspective on the Government's expenditure priorities.

RBI Report on State Finances

The State Finances – A Study of Budgets of 2024–25 by the RBI emphasised the state governments' fiscal reduction efforts while also pointing out major obstacles such as mounting debt and growing subsidies. Important aspects highlighted were:

- **Improved Tax Revenue**: Tax buoyancy increased from 0.86 (2013–20) to 1.4 (2021–25), reflecting better tax collection efficiency.
- **Higher Capital Expenditure**: Rise from 2.4 per cent of GDP (2021–22) to a budgeted 3.1 per cent (2024–25), indicating a focus on infrastructure investment.
- **Fiscal Deficit & Debt**: The gross fiscal deficit is budgeted at 3.2 per cent of GDP (FY25), with debt-to-GDP decreasing to 28.5 per cent (2024) but still above pre-pandemic levels (25.3 per cent in 2019).
- **Increased Borrowing**: Market borrowings now account for 79 per cent of the fiscal deficit, with total borrowings rising 32.8 per cent to ₹10.07 trillion (FY24).
- **Financial Strains**:
  - **High Deficits in Some States**: Smaller states like Arunachal Pradesh and Himachal Pradesh have higher deficits, while larger states like Gujarat and Maharashtra have lower deficits.
  - **DISCOM Losses**: Electricity distribution companies' losses reached ₹6.5 lakh crore (FY23), affecting state finances.
  - **Rising Subsidies**: Loan waivers and free/subsidised services (electricity, transport, cash transfers) strain budgets, reducing funds for infrastructure.
  - **Revenue Concerns**: Declining non-tax revenue and slower SGST growth pose risks.
  - **Lack of Fiscal Transparency**: Off-budget liabilities are often underreported, hiding the true fiscal situation.

Recommendations by RBI on State Finances

- **Debt Control**: Clear, time-bound targets for debt reduction with transparent reporting.
- **Flexible Fiscal Rules**: Adoption of policies that balance financial stability with the ability to handle economic shocks.
- **Better Spending**: Focus on outcome-based, climate-sensitive budgeting and streamline Centrally-Sponsored Schemes (CSS).
- **Subsidy Optimisation**: Prevention of subsidies from overshadowing critical investments.
- **Reduced Borrowing Dependence**: Limit over-reliance on market borrowings to avoid financial risks.
- **Stronger Revenue Generation**: Improve tax collection (SGST, stamp duty) and increase non-tax revenues to reduce borrowing needs.

BONUS KNOWLEDGE

STATE'S OWN TAX REVENUE (SOTR) AND STATE'S OWN NON-TAX REVENUE (SONTR)

Revenue receipts of states comprise: (i) Own revenue, and (ii) Transfers from the central government. Own revenue of states includes revenue earned by state governments from tax and non-tax sources known as **State's Own Tax Revenue (SOTR) and State's Own Non-Tax Revenue (SONTR)**, respectively.

Central transfers include devolution of central taxes as recommended by the Finance Commission and grants-in-aid. The grants-in-aid given by the Centre to the states include grants recommended by the Finance Commission, grants for centrally-sponsored schemes and other grants such as GST compensation grants. In FY 2023–24, states on aggregate are estimated to raise 57% of their revenue receipts from own tax and non-tax sources while 43% is estimated to come from devolution of central taxes and grants from the Centre.

BUDGET

Government budgeting is a method by which governments organise, distribute, and keep controls on the use of public funds. Within a specific fiscal period, usually a year, it involves estimating government revenue (from taxes, fees, and other sources) and deciding the expenditures required to meet the policy goals of the government.

As per **Article 112** of the Indian Constitution, the yearly financial statement of Union Government for a certain fiscal year is referred to as the Union Budget. It includes a thorough breakdown of the government's estimated revenue and expenditures for a specific fiscal year, which takes place from April 1 to March 31.

Budget Division of the *Department of Economic Affairs, Ministry of Finance* is the nodal agency for the preparation of the general budget. It is based on the data provided by each Ministry.

The data in the **Union Budget of India** can be divided into the following three categories:

1. **Budget Estimates (BE)** (of receipts and expenditure) for the **coming** financial year or budget year (say BE for 2025–26).
2. **Revised Estimates (RE)** (of receipts and expenditure) for the **current** financial year (say RE for 2024–25).
3. **Provisional Actuals (PA)** (of receipts and expenditure) of the **previous** financial year (say PE for 2023–24).

Based on the above data, the **Annual Financial Statement** is prepared and placed before the Parliament.

BONUS KNOWLEDGE

IMPORTANT DETAILS OF THE UNION BUDGET

- The Union Finance Minister presents the Union Budget on February 1st of each year from the 2017–18 budget year.
- According to colonial custom, the budget was submitted in the last week of February prior to the 2017–18 budget year.
- Following the Acworth Committee's recommendations, the British separated the Railway Budget from the General Budget in 1924.
- On the recommendation of Bibek Debroy Committee, the Railway Budget was combined with the General Budget for the 2017–18 budget year.
- The Budget Division of the Department of Economic Affairs (Ministry of Finance) is the nodal institution responsible for preparing the Union Budget.
- The distinction of budget expenditure as **Plan and Non-Plan expenditure has been eliminated**. Instead, now the budget is divided into revenue and capital expenditure.

The process of government budgeting in India has four distinct phases:

- **Budget Formulation:** It is the process of creating estimates of the revenue and expenditures for the next fiscal year.
- **Budget Enactment:** This process entails the Legislature to approve the proposed budget by passing the Finance bill and Appropriations bills.
- **Budget Execution:** It involves enforcement of the provisions in the Finance Act and Appropriation Act by the government. It basically consists of collecting receipts and disbursing funds for different services that have been authorised by the legislation.
- **Legislative Review:** It describes financial audits conducted by the government on behalf of the legislature.

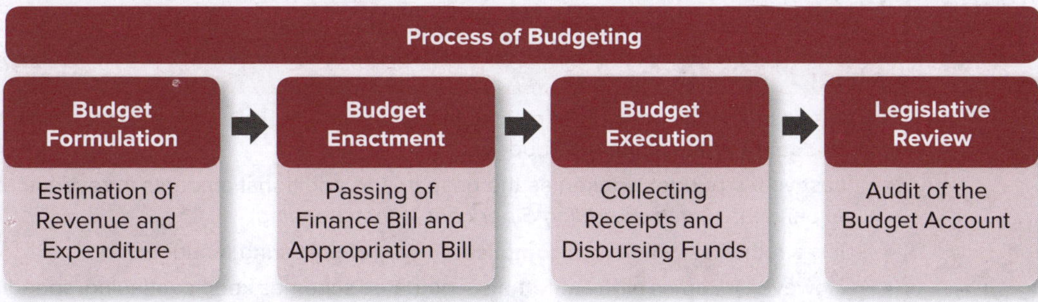

Process of Budgeting

- At first, the President's recommendation is taken for introduction and consideration of the budget in the Lok Sabha.
- The budget is then laid before the Lok Sabha along with the budget speech by the Union Finance Minister, followed by the presentation of *Finance Bill*.
- Discussion on the budget in the Lok Sabha is conducted in two stages – *first general discussion* (with no voting) and then *detailed discussion* after a period of adjournment.
- After a detailed discussion, voting for *demand for grants* takes place.
- After voting, *Appropriation Bill* is introduced and voted upon, thereby legally authorising the Central Government to spend money from the Consolidated Fund of India.
- *Appropriation Bill* and *Finance Bill* are then sent to the Rajya Sabha for discussion. Unlike Lok Sabha, Rajya Sabha does not have power to vote on demands for grants and has to return them within 14 days with or without recommendations. However, the Lok Sabha may not accept the recommendations.
- *Finance Bill* is then sent to the President of India for his assent. The President does not have the power to reject it.

BONUS KNOWLEDGE

INTERIM BUDGET

An Interim Budget is usually presented by a government during the final year of its term or when the general election is ensuing.

The presentation of an interim budget ensures that all necessary expenditures of the government can be made for the specific duration of the government in office. The full budget is presented by the new government after its formation.

Types of Budget and its Suitability in the Indian Context

Type	Details
Incremental Budgeting	• It is based on the principle of making just **small incremental changes in the existing budget** to arrive at the new budget. • Last year's budget is taken as the base to add additional amounts in revenue and expenditure (*such as adding 5 per cent in the spending*). • It is a rather **easy and less complicated way** of preparing a budget. • However, it **comes with limitations** – outdated schemes keep continuing, spending in low-priority sector continues, etc. • At present, this is, however, **followed in India**, along with some modifications.
Zero Base Budgeting	• The whole budget is prepared **from the scratch** taking **base as zero**. • **Last year's budget is not considered** in this case. • Close and critical examination of all Government schemes and programmes is done. They are discarded in next year's budget if they do not fit in after the cost-benefit analysis. • All expenses must be justified for being considered for each new period. • This technique of budgeting has yielded substantial results in countries like **New Zealand**. • However, it is still to be implemented in India in its true sense as it comes with certain **limitations**: 1. It involves a tedious and complicated time-taking exercise. 2. There are certain public services which defy cost-benefit analysis such as defence, law and order, foreign relations, etc.
Performance Budgeting	• Since 1968, Government Ministries were preparing Performance Budgets. • From 2007–08 onwards, Performance Budget has been **merged with outcome budget** due to its hardly any perceptible impact on resource allocation.

Type	Details
Outcome Budgeting	• It measures the development outcomes of all Government schemes. • It is a **means to develop linkage** between the expenditure incurred and results which follow. • Outcome is measured in terms of not only rupees but **also in terms of physical units** like tonnes of steel produced, kilowatt of energy produced, etc. • All Ministries have to prepare Outcome Budget while preparing budget details since 2005–06.
Gender Budgeting	• It indicates planning, executing, monitoring and auditing budgets **in a gender-sensitive manner** and ensuring that benefits of development **reach women as much as men**. • It is **not an accounting exercise** but is about keeping gender perspective in policy/programme formulation. • **Since 2005–06**, the Ministry of Finance issues separate note (*Statement 20*) on Gender Budgeting as a part of Expenditure Budget Document every year. • **Statement 20 comprises two parts** – 1. **Part A** reflecting women schemes with **100 per cent allocation** of funds for women. 2. **Part B** reflecting pro-women schemes with **at least 30 per cent allocation of funds** for women.

Chakravyuha Challenge of the Indian Economy

After independence, the Indian economy adopted socialism with limited entry. Since the early 1980s, the Indian economy has made a remarkable progress in increasing the entry. However, a market economy requires not just unrestricted entry of new firms, new ideas and new technologies but **also their exit** so that resources are enticed away from inefficient and unsustainable uses. In India, there has been less progress in relation to exit. Thus, the Indian economy is characterised by **'marketism' without exit**. This is called the *Chakravyuha* Challenge of the Indian economy.

FINANCE COMMISSION

- Finance Commission places its recommendations regarding allocation of taxes and other fiscal matters between Centre and States for the next five years.

Background

- Article 280 of the Indian Constitution provides for a Finance Commission as a quasi-judicial body.
- The Commission is formed by the President of India every fifth year or at a stage when he considers its necessity.
- The last time the Commission was granted a 6-year term was for the 9th Finance Commission, which was formed in 1987.

- The Commission is formed with a Chairman and four other members appointed by the President of India.
  - The members continue in office for a particular tenure decided by the President in his order.
  - They have eligibility for reappointment.

Objectives of Finance Commission

- Strengthening **cooperative federalism**
- Improving the **quality of public spending**
- Helping to **protect fiscal stability**.

Qualification of Members

- The Parliament has mentioned certain qualifications for the selection of the Chairman and members of the commission.
- The Chairman should be a person having experience in public affairs and the four other members should be selected from the following:
  - A judge of a high court or one qualified to be appointed as one.
  - A person who has specialised knowledge of finance and accounts of the government.
  - A person who has wide experience in financial matters and administration.
  - A person having special knowledge of economics.

Powers of the Finance Commission

- Based on the **Code of Civil Procedure 1908**, the **Finance Commission of India** has powers equivalent to the **powers of a Civil Court.**
- The Commission has **powers to call witnesses**, and ask for the production of a public document or record from any office or court.
  - The Finance Commission determines the formula for allocating tax revenues between the Centre and the States, taking into account variables such as tax effort, population, area, forest cover, income distance, and demographic performance.

How does the formula work?

- Taking into consideration the requirements and conditions of various states, the formula is intended to guarantee an equitable allocation of resources between the Centre and the States.
- Each state's contribution is determined by the commission using a weighted average of the various parametres.

The **income distance criterion** has been a key factor in determining how India's Finance Commissions recommend sharing tax revenues between the Centre and states. It was introduced by the **Ninth Finance Commission,** and it aims to promote **fiscal capacity equalisation** by allocating more funds to poorer states. Over time, the **weight given to this criterion has decreased**, reducing its redistributive impact. The criterion has evolved from earlier models like the **Gadgil–Mukherjee formula** and has been used in various forms up to the **Fifteenth Finance Commission**.

BONUS KNOWLEDGE

The **Gadgil-Mukherjee formula**, introduced in **1990**, was used in India to allocate central assistance to State plans. It was a revised version of the **original Gadgil formula** (used in the 4th and 5th Five-Year Plans) and was developed under **Pranab Mukherjee (the then Deputy Chairman of the Planning Commission).**

Key Criteria and the Weights used were

- **Population (1971)** – 60%
- **Per Capita Income** – 25% (20% deviation method, 5% distance method)
- **Fiscal Performance** – 7.5% (2.5% tax effort, 2% fiscal management, 3% national objective)
- **Special Problems** – 7.5%

The formula balanced equity and performance to ensure fair resource distribution among states.

Formula designed by 15th Finance Commission

The 15th Finance Commission recommended granting the states complete control over 41 per cent of the divisible pool of taxes.

By multiplying the 2011 population by the Own Tax Revenue (OTR) to Gross State Domestic Product (GSDP) ratio, the 15th Finance Commission calculated the Tax Effort.

Following factors have been taken into consideration while designing the formula.

- **Income Distance:** A weight of **45 per cent** to income distance has been assigned, reflecting the difference in per capita income between states.
- **Population:** A weight of **15 per cent** has been assigned to the population in 2011.
- **Area:** It assigned a weight of **15 per cent** to the area of the state.
- **Forest and Ecology:** It assigned a weight of **10 per cent** to forest and ecology.
- **Demographic Performance:** A weight of **12.5 per cent** has been assigned to demographic performance.
- **Tax and Fiscal Efforts:** It assigned a weight of **2.5 per cent** to tax and fiscal efforts.

BONUS KNOWLEDGE

16th FINANCE COMMISSION

Government has constituted the Sixteenth Finance Commission on 31.12.2023 with **Shri Arvind Panagariya**, former Vice-Chairman, NITI Aayog as its Chairman. It will present its recommendations by **31 October 2025**.

Other members of the Commission are:

1. **Shri. Ajay Narayan Jha,** former member, 15th Finance Commission and former Secretary, Expenditure (Full time Member)
2. **Smt. Annie George Mathew,** former Special Secretary, Expenditure (Full time Member)
3. **Dr. Niranjan Rajadhyaksha,** Executive Director, Artha Global (Full time Member)
4. **Dr. Soumya Kanti Ghosh,** Group Chief Economic Advisor, State Bank of India (Part time Member)

The Sixteenth Finance Commission has been requested to submit its report within 31 October 2025. The award period of the 16th FC recommendations will be 5 years commencing from 1 April 2026.

Financial Stability and Development Council

The Financial Stability and Development Council **(FSDC)** is an apex level regulatory body which was constituted in **2010**. This institution was envisaged for maintaining **financial sector stability** in response to the global economic slowdown in 2008. The Council is chaired by the **Union Finance Minister** and its members include the RBI Governor, Finance Secretary, Secretary of the Department of Economic Affairs, Secretary of the Department of Financial Services; Chief Economic Adviser of the Ministry of Finance and Chairmans/Heads of different financial sector regulators (SEBI, PFRDA, IRDA, etc.).

The FSDC was created as an institutional mechanism for maintaining financial stability, enhancing coordination amongst different regulatory bodies and promoting financial sector development.

The Council deals with issues relating to financial stability, financial sector development, macro prudential supervision of the economy and financial inclusion, including the functioning of large financial organisations.

Last Minute SNIPPETS

The 28th meeting of the Financial Stability and Development Council (FSDC) was held in New Delhi in February, 2024.

SUMMARY

- **Fiscal Policy** – Primarily concerned with steering the important parameters of economy – has three parts – Government Receipts, Government Expenditure, Public Debt.
- **Revenue Receipts** – Received more than once – regular in nature – no direct impact on assets and liabilities – divided into two parts – tax revenue (income tax, custom duty, etc.) and non-tax revenue (fees, fine and penalties, interest and dividends, etc.).
- **Laffer Curve** – Represents the relationship between tax rates and the amount of tax revenue collected by the Government – with the help of Laffer curve, the **optimum tax rate** can be found so that the tax collected by the Government can be maximised.
- **Capital Receipts** – Received only once – has direct impact on assets or liabilities – divided into two parts – debt creating (sale of Government Securities) and non-debt creating (Recovery of loans and advances, disinvestment, etc.).
- **Revenue Expenditure** – Regular expenses – expenditures incurred on civil administration, defence forces, public health and education, maintenance of Government machinery, etc. – does not impact the asset–liability status – high-revenue expenditure indicates poverty and backwardness of the economy.
- **Capital Expenditure** – One-time expenses – acquisition of a tangible or intangible asset or payment of liabilities – impacts asset–liability status – improves the productive capacity of the economy – high capital expenditure indicates lack of private investment in the economy.
- **Budget** – Referred as Annual Financial Statement in Indian Constitution under Article 112 – comprises estimated receipts and expenditure – reallocation of resources – has two components, namely Revenue Budget and Capital budget – can be surplus or balanced or deficit.
- **Budget Deficit** – When budgeted expenditure of the Government is larger than budgeted receipts – reflects the Government borrowings only from RBI.
- **Revenue Deficit** – Excess of revenue expenditure over revenue receipts – funded either through borrowings from the public or through disinvestment or by cutting revenue expenditure (*mainly subsidies*).

- **Effective Revenue Deficit** – Difference between revenue deficit and grants-in-aid provided for creation of capital assets – amount of revenue receipts that are actually used for consumption expenditure.
- **Fiscal Deficit** – Total borrowing requirements of the Government from all sources – actual liability of the Government – sum of budget deficit and market borrowings and liabilities.
- **Primary Deficit** – Indicates borrowing requirement excluding interest payment – difference between fiscal deficit and interest payments by Government – indicates total borrowings (and not total liabilities).
- **Fiscal Consolidation** – Process through which the economy's fiscal health is improved by taking measures to reduce fiscal deficit to a manageable level.

UPSC CSE PREVIOUS YEARS' PRELIMINARY EXAMINATION QUESTIONS

1. Which one of the following effects of creation of black money in India has been the main cause of worry to the Government of India? **[2021]**

(a) Diversion of resources to the purchase of real estate and investment in luxury housing
(b) Investment in unproductive activities and purchase of precious stones, jewellery, gold, etc.
(c) Large donations to political parties and growth of regionalism
(d) Loss of revenue to the State Exchequer due to tax evasion

2. Along with the budget, the Finance Minister also places other documents before the Parliament, which include 'The Macro Economic Framework Statement'. The aforesaid document is presented because this is mandated by **[2020]**

(a) Long-standing parliamentary convention.
(b) Article 112 and Article 110(1) of the Constitution of India.
(c) Article 113 of the Constitution of India.
(d) Provisions of the Fiscal Responsibility and Budget Management Act, 2003.

3. With reference to India's decision to levy an equalisation tax of 6 per cent on online advertisement services offered by non-resident entities, which of the following statements is/are correct? **[2018]**

1. It is introduced as a part of the Income Tax Act.
2. Non-resident entities that offer advertisement services in India can claim a tax credit in their home country under the 'Double Taxation Avoidance Agreements'.

Select the correct answer using the code given below:

(a) 1 only
(b) 2 only
(c) Both 1 and 2
(d) Neither 1 nor 2

4. Consider the following statements: **[2018]**

1. The Fiscal Responsibility and Budget Management (FRBM) Review Committee Report has recommended a debt-to-GDP ratio of 60 per cent for the general (combined) Government by 2023, comprising 40 per cent for the Central Government and 20 per cent for the State Governments.
2. The Central Government has domestic liabilities of 21 per cent of GDP as compared to that of 49 per cent of GDP of the State Governments.
3. As per the Constitution of India, it is mandatory for a state to take the Central Government's consent for raising any loan if the former owes any outstanding liabilities to the latter.

Which of the statement(s) given above is/are correct?

(a) 1 only (b) 2 and 3 only
(c) 1 and 3 only (d) 1, 2 and 3

5. With reference to the 'Prohibition of Benami Property Transactions Act, 1988 (PBPT Act)', consider the following statements: **[2017]**

1. A property transaction is not treated as a benami transaction if the owner of the property is not aware of the transaction.
2. Properties held benami are liable for confiscation by the Government.
3. The act provides for three authorities for investigations but does not provide for any appellate mechanism.

Which of the statements given above is/are correct?

(a) 1 only
(b) 2 only
(c) 1 and 3 only
(d) 2 and 3 only

6. Consider the following statements: **[2017]**

1. Tax revenue as a percentage of GDP of India has steadily increased in the last decade.
2. Fiscal deficit as a percentage of GDP of India has steadily increased in the last decade.

Which of the statements given above is/are correct?

(a) 1 only (b) 2 only
(c) Both 1 and 2 (d) Neither 1 nor 2

7. There has been a persistent deficit budget year after year. Which action/actions of the following can be taken by the Government to reduce the deficit? **[2016]**

1. Reducing revenue expenditure
2. Introducing new welfare schemes
3. Rationalising subsidies
4. Reducing import duties

Select the correct answer using the code below:

(a) 1 only (b) 2 and 3 only
(c) 1 and 3 only (d) 1, 2, 3 and 4

8. Which of the following is/are included in the capital budget of the Government of India? **[2016]**

1. Expenditure on acquisitions of assets like roads, buildings, machinery, etc.
2. Loans received from foreign Governments.
3. Loans and advances granted to the states and union territories.

Select the correct answer using the code given below:

(a) 1 only (b) 2 and 3 only
(c) 1 and 3 only (d) 1, 2 and 3

9. The term 'Base Erosion and Profit Shifting (BEPS)' is sometimes seen in the news in the context of **[2016]**

(a) mining operation by multinational companies in resource – rich but backward areas.
(b) curbing of the tax evasion by multinational companies.
(c) exploitation of genetic resources of a country by multinational companies.
(d) lack of consideration of environmental costs in the planning and implementation of developmental projects.

10. The sales tax you pay while purchasing a toothpaste is a **[2014]**

(a) tax imposed by the Central Government.
(b) tax imposed by the Central Government but collected by the State Government.
(c) tax imposed by the State Government but collected by the Central Government.
(d) tax imposed and collected by the State Government.

11. With reference to Union Budget, which of the following is/are covered under non-plan expenditure? **[2014]**

1. Defence expenditure
2. Interest payments
3. Salaries and pensions
4. Subsidies

Select the correct answer using the code given below:

(a) 1 only (b) 2 and 3 only
(c) 1, 2, 3 and 4 (d) None

12. Which of the following is/are among the noticeable features of the recommendations of the 13th Finance Commission? **[2012]**

1. A design for the goods and services package linked to adherence to the proposed design.
2. A design for the creation of lakhs of jobs in the next 10 years in consonance with India's demographic dividend.
3. Devolution of a specific share of central taxes to local bodies as grants.

Select the correct answer using the code given below:

(a) 1 only (b) 2 and 3 only
(c) 1 and 3 only (d) 1, 2 and 3

13. Consider the following actions by the Government: **[2010]**

1. Cutting the tax rates

2. Increasing the Government spending
3. Abolishing the subsidies

In the context of economic recession, which of the above actions can be considered a part of the 'fiscal stimulus' package?

(a) 1 and 2 only (b) 2 only
(c) 1 and 3 only (d) 1, 2 and 3

14. Which one of the following was not stipulated in the Fiscal Responsibility and Budget Management Act, 2003? **[2010]**

(a) Elimination of revenue deficit by the end of the fiscal year 2008–09.
(b) Non-borrowing by the Central Government from the Reserve Bank of India except under certain circumstances.
(c) Elimination of primary deficit by the end of the fiscal year 2008–09.
(d) Fixing Government guarantees in any financial year as a percentage of GDP.

☞ NO QUESTIONS ASKED
2024, 2023, 2022, 2019, 2015, 2013, 2011

ANSWER KEY

1. (d)	2. (d)	3. (a)	4. (c)	5. (b)
6. (d)	7. (c)	8. (d)	9. (b)	10. (d)
11. (c)	12. (c)	13. (a)	14. (c)	

UPSC CSE PREVIOUS YEARS' MAIN EXAMINATION QUESTIONS

1. Distinguish between Capital Budget and Revenue Budget. Explain the components of both these Budgets. **[2021]**

2. The public expenditure management is a challenge to the Government of India in the context of budget making during the post-liberalisation period. Clarify it. **[2019]**

3. What are the reasons for the introduction of **FRBM Act, 2013**? Discuss critically its salient features and effectiveness. **[2013]**

4. What is the meaning of the **tax expenditure**? Taking housing sector as an example, discuss how it influences the budgetary policies of the Government? **[2013]**

☞ NO QUESTIONS ASKED
2024, 2023, 2022, 2020, 2018, 2017, 2016, 2015, 2014

CHAPTER

9

ECONOMIC PLANNING IN INDIA

CHAPTER OUTLINE

- Types of Economic Planning
- Need for Economic Planning in India at the Time of Independence
- Evolution of Indian Economic Planning
- Strategies of Planning in India
- Planning in Pre-1991 or Pre-Reforms Phase
- Planning in Post-1991 or Post-Reforms Phase
- Five Year Plans in India
- Achievements and Criticisms of Five-Year Plans
- NITI Aayog
- Composition of NITI Aayog
- Recent Appointments to NITI Aayog
- Objectives of NITI Aayog
- Functions of NITI Aayog
- NITI Aayog's Performance Evaluation
- Key Performance Indices Published by NITI Aayog
- Planning Commission vs NITI Aayog

Economic planning refers to the allocation of resources in a comprehensive way to achieve the pre-determined objectives with optimal utilisation of the resources.

EXAM ESSENTIAL

Types of Economic Planning

Type	Details
Imperative Planning	• It is also known as Directive or Authoritative Planning or Planning by direction or command. • There is **one Central Authority** which decides all aspects of planning. • Generally practised in **socialist economies**. • Entire resources are used to the maximum to fulfil targets. • India followed this type of Planning till 7th Five Year Plan.
Indicative Planning	• Also known as inducement planning (*flexible in nature*). • **Government acts as a facilitator** and encourages private sector's role in the economy. • However, it also regulates the private sector to achieve specific targets. • Generally practised in **mixed economy**. • India followed this type of planning method from 8th Five Year Plan

Type	Details
Perspective Planning	• It is planned for a **long period** of time, usually 15–20 years (*but not one plan for the whole period*). • It is operationalised through Five Year Plans (FYPs) and Annual Plans. • In this, the planner sets a perspective plan that broadly defines the direction desired to be taken by the economy. • **NITI Aayog** has adopted this type of planning structure.
Fixed Plan	• It is fixed for 4, 5, 6 or 7 years. • Physical targets are fixed along with the total outlay.
Decentralised Plan	• Execution of the plan from the grassroots level. • Formulated by the Centre in accordance with the State authorities. • The prices of the goods are determined through market mechanism.
Rolling Plan	• Under Rolling Plan, **every year three new plans** are prepared and acted upon: 1. Plan for the current year which includes the annual budget. 2. A plan for fixed numbers of years (e.g. 3–5 years) and it is revised every year as per the requirements and changes in economic conditions of the economy. 3. A perspective plan for 10, 15, 20 years. • Thus, there is **no fixation of dates** in respect of commencement and end of the plan under rolling plan. • It was introduced **by Janata Government** led by Morarji Desai, in 1978 for the period 1978–83. However, it was abandoned in-between due to the change in Government.
Core Plan	• As per this, the planning authority requests the States to submit their projected revenue estimates. • On the basis of such estimates, planning authority determines the expenditure for the State annual plans. • This helps to prevent diversion of funds from the priority sectors to the non-planned account.

Need for Economic Planning at the Time of Independence

- Employment Generation
- Poor Economic Condition at the time of Independence
- Lack of significant Private Sector
- For Effective Mobilisation of Resources
- For balanced Economic Development
- International Influence

EXAM ESSENTIAL

EVOLUTION OF INDIAN ECONOMIC PLANNING

Plan	Feature
M. Visvesvaraya Plan (1934)	• It emphasised on **shifting from** agriculture to industrialisation and also to increase employment in industries. • It aimed to double national income within 10 years. • In his book titled **Planned Economy for India (1934)**, he set the goal of poverty eradication through growth.
FICCI Proposal (1934)	• It vouched **to end laissez-faire** and presented the opinion of capitalist class. • It also advocated for setting up National Planning Commission.
Congress Plan (1938)	• With the initiative of Subhas Chandra Bose, **National Planning Committee (1938)** was formed with J.L. Nehru as its Chairperson. • However, some documents in the form of its report were published later in 1949.
Bombay Plan (1944)	• Sponsored by top eight industrialists of Bombay. • Aimed for **agricultural restructuring** through abolition of Zamindari system, rapid industrialisation, development of essential and consumer goods and small medium and cottage industries. • Emphasised on **industrialisation** in order to reduce the hardships of the population due to inflation.
Gandhian Plan (1944)	• Drafted by Acharya Shriman Narayan Agarwal. • Emphasised on economic decentralisation and on the promotion of small-scale and cottage industries.
People's Plan (1945)	• Drafted by **M.N. Roy** for a period of 10 years. • Main priorities of the plan were agricultural development and increase in agricultural production along with maintaining an equal balance with industrialisation.
Planning Advisory Board (1946)	• Set up by the interim Government of the time. • To review plans and future projects and to provide recommendations upon them.
Economic Programme Committee (1947)	• Formed by the **All India Congress Committee** to make a plan to balance private and public partnership and urban and rural economies. • This recommended for forming the **Planning Commission**.

Plan	Feature
Sarvodaya Plan (1950)	• Drafted by Jayaprakash Narayan. • Emphasised on agriculture and small and cottage industries. • It suggested freedom from foreign technology and stressed upon land reforms. • It also recommended decentralised and participatory planning.
Planning Commission (1950)	• It was established on 15 March 1950 by a cabinet resolution. • It was established as an extra-constitutional, non-political, non-statutory advisory body. • It was charged with the responsibility of making an assessment of all the resources of the country and formulating plans for the most effective and balanced utilisation of resources. • **J N Nehru**, being the Prime Minister, was its **First Chairman**.
National Development Council (1952)	• It was set up on 6 August 1952 by an executive order. • Established as an extra-constitutional non-statutory body. • Comprised of Prime Minister, cabinet ministers, chief ministers of all states and Lt Governors of all UTs and members of planning commission. • Served as the highest decision-making body, and it also approved five-year plans. • It aimed to ensure balanced and rapid development of all parts of the country. • Last meeting of NDC was held in 2011. Now NITI Aayog's Governing Council (same composition and aim as NDC) performs the task of NDC.
NITI Aayog (2015)	• Established on 1 January 2015. • Replaced the Planning Commission. • NITI Aayog's entire gamut of activities can be divided into four main heads: 1. Policy and Programme Framework 2. Cooperative Federalism 3. Monitoring and Evaluation 4. Think Tank, and, Knowledge and Innovation Hub

STRATEGIES OF PLANNING IN INDIA

Planning in India: Pre-1991 vs. Post-1991

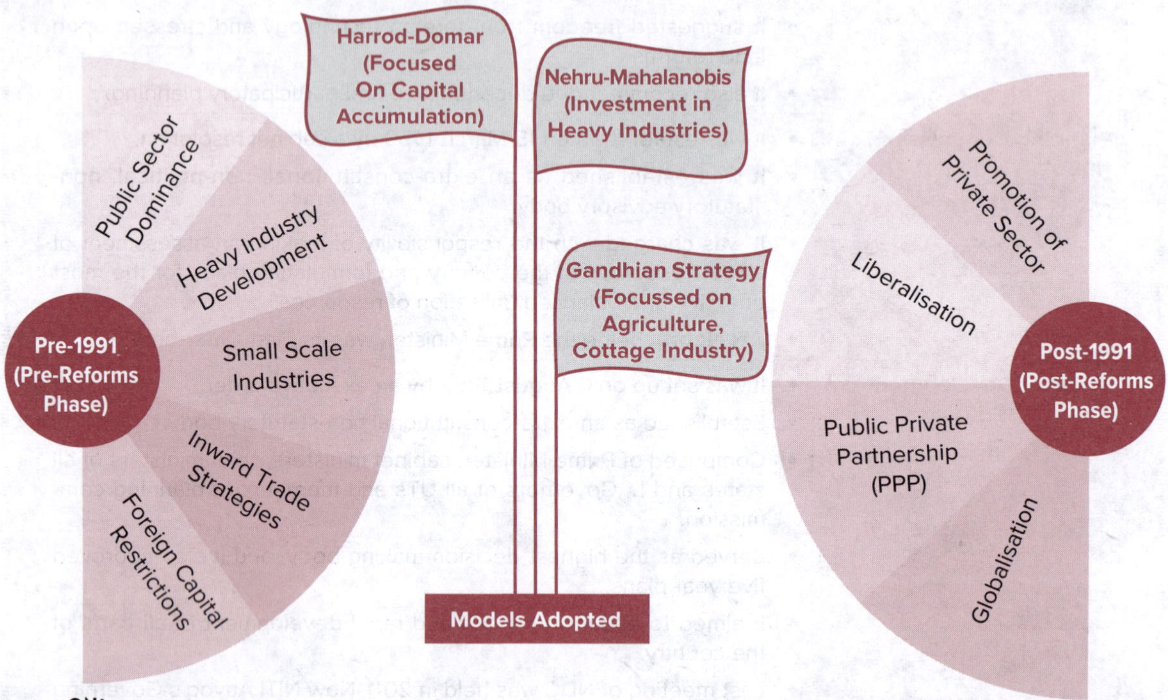

BONUS KNOWLEDGE

LPG (LIBERALISATION, PRIVATISATION AND GLOBALISATION) STRATEGY

- This was coined by Rao–Singh (P.V. Narasimha Rao and Manmohan Singh, Prime Minister and Finance Minister of India, at the time of economic reforms in 1991, respectively).
- This strategy somewhat **ended the Licence-Permit Raj**.
- It encouraged privatisation and allowed **Foreign Direct Investment (FDI)**.
- **Export Promotion policy** was adopted to boost economic growth.
- This model changed the nature of planning from centralised to **indicative planning**.

Liberalisation: It meant a policy of deregulation of different segments of the economy and reducing Government controls over industry and other sectors. Measures undertaken for liberalisation included:

- **Delicencing** most of the industries, thereby enabling entrepreneurs to enter any industry or trade. However, complete deregulation (laissez-faire) was not undertaken. There were now a few industries which required compulsory licencing.
- Liberalisation of industrial location policy.
- Restrictions on mergers, takeovers etc. were largely removed.
- Capital market was liberalised to a great extent. However, **SEBI was established in 1992** to keep an eye on regulating its functioning.

Privatisation: It meant the policy of transfer of ownership of public sector enterprises from the Government sector to the private sector. It also implied granting more autonomy to public sector enterprises in decision-making. Major steps taken for privatisation included:

- **Policy of De-reservation**, i.e. initially as per Industrial Policy resolution 1956, total number of 17 industries were reserved for the public sector. Post-1991, this number was reduced to 8. As of 2019, the number of industries reserved for the public sector stands at 2 (atomic energy and railway operations).
- From 1992 onwards, **Sick Public Sector Enterprises** were brought within the purview of Board for Industrial and Financial Reconstruction (BIFR) for their revival.
- Policy of **Miniratnas and Navratnas** was adopted to grant more **financial autonomy** to public sector enterprises.
- Policy of **Disinvestment** was adopted by selling Government equity in Public sector enterprises in the market.

Globalisation: It implies opening up of the Indian economy to world economy. Measures undertaken to channelise globalisation included:

- Import liberalisation programmes through reducing import duties and import quota.
- Opening up the economy to FDI.
- Free flow of technology to and from other countries.
- Allowing convertibility of rupee on current account of BOP in 1994.

BONUS KNOWLEDGE

PURA (PROVIDING URBAN AMENITIES IN RURAL AREAS) STRATEGY

- This was the brainchild of A.P.J. Abdul Kalam.
- This strategy focused on providing **four types of connectivity** to rural areas:
  1. Physical connectivity (roads, railways, bridges, etc.)
  2. Electric connectivity
  3. Knowledge connectivity
  4. Economic connectivity
- The objective of this strategy was to enhance the prosperity of clusters of villages in rural areas. However, PURA could not take off well to accomplish the desired objectives.
- In 2012, a revamped concept of PURA was formulated by the Ministry of Rural Development, GoI, naming it **PURA 2.0**. It emphasised on physical infrastructural development of **Census Towns** under Public–Private Partnership (PPP) mode. A town should fulfil the following three criteria to be considered a **Census Town**:
  1. Population of at least 5,000.
  2. Density of 400 persons per square km.
  3. At least 75 per cent of male population engaged in non-agricultural activities.
- In 2016, a new **Shyama Prasad Mukherji Rurban Mission (SPMRM)** was launched by the **Ministry of Rural Development** with similar objectives but with different features and perspectives as compared to PURA or PURA 2.0. SPMRM focusses on development of a **cluster of villages** that preserve and nurture the essence of rural community life with focus on equity and inclusiveness without compromising with the facilities perceived to be essentially urban in nature, **thus creating a cluster of "Rurban Villages"**.

FIVE YEAR PLANS IN INDIA

The FYPs in India were framed, executed and monitored by the Planning Commission of India. The targets and achievements of the 12 FYPs in India are briefly discussed below:

Plan	Objective
First FYP (1951–56) Target Growth: 2.1% Actual Growth: 3.6%	• Based on the **Harrod–Domar Model**. • **Community Development Programme** was launched in **1952**. • Renowned economist **K.N. Raj** was one of the main architects of this plan. • Focus was on – ◆ Agriculture, for large-scale import of foodgrains and food security ◆ Irrigation (*River Valley Projects like Bhakra Nangal, Damodar Valley, Hirakud, etc. were undertaken*) ◆ Rural development ◆ Price stability ◆ Power and transport • During this plan – ◆ **National Programme for Family Planning** was launched in 1952. ◆ **State Financial Corporation Act** was passed in 1951. ◆ **Estate duty** was introduced in 1953. ◆ **Village and Small Industry Development Committee** was set up in 1955 (Small scale industrial committee was also known as **Karve Committee**). ◆ The West Bengal Land Reforms Act was drafted in 1955 and was passed in 1956.
Second FYP (1956–61) Targeted Growth: 4.5% Actual Growth: 4.27%	• It was based on the **Nehru–Mahalanobis Strategy**. ◆ Articulated by J.L. Nehru's vision and P.C. Mahalanobis was its chief architect • Focus was on **rapid industrialisation, self-reliance** and investment in **heavy capital goods** industries. • Emphasised on import substitution and public sector to provide basic infrastructure like power, transport etc. • During this plan, prices increased by 30%, as compared to a decline of 13% during the first FYP. • During this plan – ◆ **Industrial Policy Resolution of 1956** (IPR 1956) was adopted. ◆ **Durgapur, Bhilai and Rourkela** steel plants were established in collaboration with Britain, Russia and Germany respectively. ◆ **Gift Tax Act, 1958**, was enacted. ◆ **LIC** was formed by an Act of Parliament in **1956**. ◆ **India signed P. L. 480** agreement with US. (The programme of food aid to India under Title I of the II of P. L. 480 commenced in 1954).

<table>
<tr><th>Plan</th><th>Objective</th></tr>
<tr><td>Third FYP (1961–66)

Targeted Growth: 5.6%
Actual Growth: 2.84%</td><td>At its conception, it was felt that the Indian economy had entered a take-off stage.
• Its aim was to make India a
◆ 'Self-reliant' and
◆ 'Self-generating' economy.
• Focus was on both
◆ Heavy industrialisation and
◆ Food grains production.
• Based on the experience of the first two plans, agriculture was given top priority to support the exports and industry.
• However, there was a complete failure in reaching the plan targets due to unforeseen events such as Chinese Aggression (1962), Indo-Pak War (1965) and severe drought (1965–66).
◆ India resorted to borrowing from the IMF due to severe foreign exchange crisis. The rupee was devalued for the first time in June 1966, though technically it was not during the 3rd FYP.
◆ India also faced acute food shortage and United States exported food grains to India in exchange of Indian rupee. The food aid was popularly called PL-480 as it was provided under section 480 of Public Law of US.
• During this plan –
◆ Food Corporation of India was established in 1965.
◆ Industrial Development Bank of India (IDBI) was set up under the Industrial Development Bank of India Act, 1964.
◆ Unit Trust of India (UTI) was established in 1963.
◆ Agricultural Prices Commission was set up in 1965, later it was renamed as Commission for Agricultural Costs and Prices (CAPC).
◆ National Dairy Development Board (NDDB) was established at Anand in 1965.
◆ Central Sheep and Wool Research Institute (CSWRI) was set up at Avikanagar in 1962.
◆ The Intensive Cattle Development Project (ICDP) was launched in 1964.
◆ Rural Manpower Programme was initiated in 1960.
◆ Third FYP was based on John Sandy and Sukhamoy Chakraborty's model. Third FYP was also known as Gadgil Yojana (as D.R. Gadgil was the deputy chairman of the Planning Commission).</td></tr>
<tr><td>Three Annual Plans (1966–69)</td><td>• Though draft of the 4th FYP was ready, the Annual Plan was planned and formulated for the next three years due to worsened financial conditions. This three-year period was termed as Plan Holiday by the critics.
• During these three Annual Plans, a whole new agricultural strategy was implemented, involving:
◆ Widespread distribution of High-Yielding Variety (HYV) seeds under the larger umbrella of the Green Revolution,
◆ Extensive use of fertilisers,</td></tr>
</table>

Plan	Objective
	◆ Exploitation of irrigation potential, and ◆ Focus on soil conservation. • During these three Annual Plans, the economy absorbed the shocks generated during the Third FYP.
Fourth FYP (1969–74) Targeted Growth: 5.7% Actual Growth: 3.3%	• Based on the Gadgil strategy with main focus on growth in agriculture and self-reliance in other sectors. • First two years of the Plan saw record production. The last three years, however, did not meet the target due to poor monsoon. • Bank Nationalisation, privy purse abolition to princes, results of green revolution, family planning, social justice, and Indo-Pak War were significant developments in this plan period. • Influx of Bangladeshi refugees before and after the 1971 Indo-Pak War was a major challenge. • During this plan – ◆ The **Monopolistic and Restrictive Trade Practices Act, 1969** was introduced. ◆ The **Command Area Development Programme (CADP)** was launched in 1974–75. ◆ **Drought Prone Area Program (DPAP)** was launched in 1973–74. ◆ **The concept of a buffer stock** was introduced during the 4th Five-Year Plan (1969–74). A buffer stock of 5 million tonnes of foodgrains was envisaged. ◆ The slogan ***Garibi Hatao*** was first introduced in 1971.
Fifth FYP (1974–79) Targeted Growth: 4.4% Actual Growth: 4.8%	• It was prepared by **D.D. Dhar**. • It proposed to achieve two main objectives: ◆ Poverty eradication ***(Garibi Hatao)*** and ◆ Attainment of self-reliance. • The following programmes were launched: ◆ Minimum Needs Programme to provide certain basic minimum needs and thereby improve the living standards of the people. ◆ Directed anti-poverty programme: **Twenty–point Programme** was adopted in 1975 with the objective of improving the quality of life of people, especially BPL families. • The key instruments were: ◆ Promotion of high rate of growth, ◆ Better distribution of income and ◆ Significant growth in the domestic rate of savings. As Emergency was declared in 1975, the plan was terminated and **Rolling Plan** (1978–83) was introduced by the new Janata Government in 1978. However, the Rolling Plan too got abandoned due to a change in Government in 1980. The Congress Government treated 1978–79 as part of the original 4th FYP and 1979–80 as a separate annual plan. • During this plan, **Desert Development Programme** was launched as a centrally sponsored scheme in 1977–78.

<table>
<tr><th>Plan</th><th>Objective</th></tr>
<tr><td>Sixth FYP (1980–85)

Targeted Growth: 5.2%
Actual Growth: 5.66%</td><td>• Focus was laid on
◆ Increasing national income,
◆ Modernisation of technology,
◆ Ensuring continuous decrease in poverty and unemployment.
• The plan was adopted with the slogan Garibi Hatao to alleviate poverty with more targeted approach.
• A shift was seen from industrialisation towards infrastructure.
• Some programmes focused to generate employment were:
◆ National Rural Employment Programme
◆ Integrated Rural Development Programme
◆ Village and Small Industries Development Programme
• The highest financial allocation during this Plan went to the Energy Sector.
• During this plan –
◆ NABARD was established in 1982.
◆ Export-Import Bank of India was established in 1982, under the Export-Import Bank of India Act, 1981.
◆ The Sukhamoy Chakravarty Committee was formed in December 1982 to reform the Indian Monetary System.
◆ Industrial Reconstruction Corporation of India (IRCI, set up in 1971) was converted into the Industrial Reconstruction Bank of India (IRBI) in 1984. IRBI was set up in 1985.</td></tr>
<tr><td>Seventh FYP
(1985–90)

Targeted Growth: 5%
Actual Growth: 6.1%</td><td>• Focus was laid on
◆ Rapid growth in food grain production,
◆ Increased employment opportunities and
◆ Productivity within the framework of planning.
• Long-term fiscal policy started
• A 3 years export–import policy was announced for the first time.
• The Plan was also termed as the Infrastructure Plan.
• Import Substitution strategy was given due importance and the economy began its journey towards gradual liberalisation.
• During this plan –
◆ Jawahar Rozgar Yojana was launched in 1989.
◆ Operation Blackboard was launched in 1987.
◆ National Literacy Mission was introduced in 1988.
◆ SEBI was established on 12 April 1988 as an executive body.</td></tr>
<tr><td>Annual Plans
(1990–92)</td><td>The Eighth Plan could not take off in 1990 due to the fast-changing political situation at the centre and the years 1990–91 and 1991–92 were treated as Annual Plans. The Eighth Plan was finally formulated for the period 1992–97.
Moreover, the BOP crisis in 1991 and the conditions put forward by IMF brought humongous changes in the Indian economy and led to the delay of the eighth FYP by 2 years.
During this plan –
◆ Chelliah Committee on Tax reform – appointed in 1991.
◆ National Renewal Fund (NRF) was set up in February 1992.</td></tr>
</table>

Plan	Objective
Eighth FYP (1992–97) Targeted Growth: 5.6% Actual Growth: 6.8%	• Policy of Liberalisation, Privatisation and Globalisation (LPG) was undertaken. • Structural reforms were adopted. • Plan based on the Rao–Manmohan Singh model of liberalisation. • Some of the major outcomes of the plan were: ◆ Rapid overall economic growth ◆ High rate of growth in agriculture, manufacturing and allied sectors ◆ Growth in imports and exports ◆ Improvement in trade and current account deficit • However, social spending was neglected in this plan. • During this plan – ◆ **Employment Assurance Scheme** was launched in 1993. ◆ **Swarna Jayanti Shahari Rozgar Yojana** was launched in 1997. ◆ **Rashtriya Mahila Kosh (RMK)** was established in 1993. ◆ **Midday Meal Scheme** was launched in 1995. ◆ **Indicative planning** was adopted. ◆ **Child Labour Eradication Programme** was introduced in 1994.
Ninth FYP (1997–2002) Targeted Growth: 6.5% Actual Growth: 5.35%	• It was developed in the context of four important dimensions: ◆ Quality of life ◆ Generation of productive employment ◆ Regional balance and ◆ Self-reliance • Priority was also given to agriculture and rural development. • The Ninth FYP focused on "growth with social justice and equality". • Swarnajayanti Gram Swarojgar Yojana (SGSY) launched in 1999 and Pradhan Mantri Gram Sadak Yojana (PMGSY) started in 2000. • Privatisation of public sector units was started in this plan while disinvestment began in the previous plan. • During this plan – ◆ **Antyodaya Anna Yojana** was launched in 2000. ◆ **Sarva Shiksha Abhiyan (SSA)** was launched in 2001.
Tenth FYP (2002–07) Targeted Growth: 8% Actual Growth: 7.6%	The main objectives were: • Reduction of: ◆ Poverty ratio by 5% points by the end of the plan period ◆ Gender gaps in literacy and wages by at least 50% ◆ Decadal rate of population growth between 2001 and 2011 to 16.2% ◆ Infant mortality rate to 45 per 1,000 births by 2007 and 28 per 1,000 births by 2012 ◆ Overall capital outflow ◆ Forest and tree cover to 25% by 2007 and 33% in 2012 ◆ Domestic savings, foreign investment and foreign exchange • Universal access to primary education • Providing gainful high-quality employment to the addition in labour force

Plan	Objective
	• Cleaning of all major polluted rivers by 2007 and other notified stretches by 2012 • Outcome: ◆ Severe drought in 2002–03 ◆ NREGA and National Rural Health Mission started • The **National Food for Work Programme (NFWP)** was launched in 2004. • **Bharat Nirman** programme was introduced in 2005 to develop rural infrastructure.
Eleventh FYP (2007–12) Targeted Growth: 9% Actual Growth: 8%	• Plan launched amidst emerging Global Financial Crisis (2008). • The major highlights of the plan were: ◆ To increase: ▪ Overall GDP growth from 8% to 10% ▪ Agriculture sector growth to 4% ▪ Real wage rate of unskilled workers by 20% ▪ Literacy rate for persons of age 7 years or above to 85% ▪ Sex ratio for age group 0–6 to 935 by 2011–12 and to 950 by 2016–17 ▪ Forest coverage by 5% points ▪ Energy efficiency by 20% points within 2016–17 ◆ To reduce: ▪ Dropout rates of children from elementary school from 52.2% in 2003–04 to 20% by 2011–12 ▪ Total fertility rate to 2.1% ▪ Infant mortality rate to 28 ▪ Malnutrition among children aged 0 to 3 years to half of its present level ▪ Anaemia among girls and women by 50% ◆ Ensure that at least 33% of the direct and indirect beneficiaries of all Government schemes were women and girl children ◆ Ensure all-weather road connectivity to habitations with population 1,000 and above by the end of 2009 ◆ Connect every village through telephone by 2007 and provide broadband connectivity to all villages by 2012 ◆ Attain WHO standards of air quality in all major cities by 2011–12 • The theme of the **eleventh** five year plan was – '***towards faster and more inclusive growth***'.
Twelfth FYP (2012–17) Targeted Growth: 8.2% Actual Growth: 6.9%	• The plan aimed at: ◆ Achieving growth of 4% in agriculture ◆ To reduce poverty by 10% points ◆ To achieve faster, sustainable and more inclusive growth. • The theme was '***Faster, More Inclusive and Sustainable Growth***'.
The Twelfth Plan was the last plan of the Planning Commission. In 2015, NITI Aayog was set up to replace Planning Commission **(discussed later in this chapter)**.	

Achievements and Criticisms of Five-Year Plans

Achievements

- Increase in GDP, per capita income, savings and investment
- Improvement in social indicators, viz., MMR, IMR, literacy rate, etc.
- Progress in industry and industrial growth
- India achieved self-sufficiency in almost all basic and capital goods industries and consumer goods industries
- There was a good deal of diversification in **industrial** structure
- Development of huge educational system
- Development of economic infrastructure particularly in the fields of transport, irrigation and telecommunications
- Development in the field of science and technology

Criticisms

- Failure to eliminate poverty
- Failure to eliminate income and gender inequality
- Failure to provide employment to all able persons
- Failure to implement land reforms fully
- Failure to check the growth of black money
- Failure to prevent concentration of economic power
- Quality of education outcomes was not satisfactory
- Regional imbalances were noticed in development
- Centralised nature of planning (*the plans were programme-driven rather than demand driven*)

NITI AAYOG

- **National Institution for Transforming India (NITI) Aayog** is a **non-constitutional** and **non-statutory body** which was set up on 1 January **2015**, replacing the 65-year-old Planning Commission.
- It is a policy **think tank** established to provide strategic and technical advice to the Central Government. Therefore, it is an **advisory body with no financial role**. Its **recommendations are not binding** on the Government.
- Unlike the Planning Commission, it **does not enjoy the financial power to allocate funds to States**. Now fund allocation is done by the Ministry of Finance, GoI.

Composition of NITI Aayog

1.	Chairperson	Prime Minister
2.	Governing Council	CMs (States) and Lt Governors (UTs)
3.	Regional Councils	Formed on need-basis, comprising CMs and Lt Govs of the region
4.	Members	Full-time basis
5.	Part-time Members	Max 2, rotational, from relevant institutions
6.	Ex-officio Members	Max 4 from Council of Ministers, nominated by PM
7.	Special Invitees	Experts, specialists, practitioners with domain knowledge
8.	Chief Executive Officer	Appointed by PM for fixed tenure, Secy rank
9.	Secretariat	As deemed neces-sary

- The whole staff of NITI Aayog is divided into two hubs:
  1. **Knowledge and Innovation Hub** – It has 12–14 verticals which deals with different sectors and builds NITI's think tank capabilities.
  2. **Team India Hub** – It works as an interface between Central Government and the States.
- **Offices attached to NITI Aayog:**
  1. **Development Monitoring and Evaluation office (DMEO)** – Established in 2015, as an attached office of the NITI Aayog by merging the erstwhile Programme Evaluation Organisation and the Independent Evaluation Office, it **monitors the schemes, policies and programmes** of GoI and provides research input wherever relevant.
  2. **National Institute of Labour Economics Research and Development (NILERD)** – It is in existence since 1962 (created at the time of the Planning Commission) and is a Central Autonomous Organisation. Its main task includes **research and data collection** related to various aspects of development.

Last Minute SNIPPETS

RECENT APPOINTMENTS TO NITI AAYOG

On November 2023, NITI Aayog appointed four distinguished fellows under fellowship guidelines for a period of one year. The four reputed individuals are:

- Prof. (Dr.) Anoop Singh – Member of 15th finance commission, also worked in IMF, expert in macroeconomics and management
- Dr. O. P. Agarwal – IAS of 1979, has expertise in urban transport
- Dr. Ajay Chowdhury – One of the co-founders of HCL, IT expert
- Shri V. Lakshmikumaran – Legal expert with a career spanning over 3 decades

NITI Aayog's Seven Pillars of Effective Governance

- **Pro-People**: fulfils aspirations of society as well as individuals
- **Participation**: involvement of Citizenry
- **Inclusion of All**: SC, ST, OBC, minorities, gareeb, gaon, kisaan
- **Pro-Activity**: in anticipation of and response to citizen needs
- **Empowering**: women in all aspects
- **Equality**: of opportunity for the youth
- **Transparency**: making govt visible and responsive

Objectives of NITI Aayog

- Fostering **Cooperative Federalism**, Active Involvement of States
- Formulation of plans at **Village**-level, aggregation at higher levels
- **Special Attention** to sections at risk of not benefitting adequately from economic progress
- Economic policy that incorporates **National Security Interests**
- Feedback for constant **Innovative Improvements**
- Partnerships with national and International **Think Tanks**
- Creating a **Knowledge, Innovation & Entrepreneurial** support system
- Platform for **Resolution** of inter-sectoral & inter-departmental issues
- State-of-the-art resource center for **Research** on good governance
- Focus on **Technology** upgradation and **Capacity Building**

Functions of NITI Aayog

- To act as a **think tank** and provide Central and State Governments' strategic and technical advice across the spectrum of the key elements of policy.
- Developing itself as a state-of-the-art resources centre to provide strategic policy vision for the Government and deal with contingent issues.
- To **foster cooperative federalism** through better Centre–State coordination.
- To develop mechanisms to **formulate credible plans** and **policy framework** at the village level and at higher levels of the Government.
- To monitor and evaluate the **implementation of programmes**, focus on technology upgradation and capacity building.
- To publish various socio-economic indices.

BONUS KNOWLEDGE

NATIONAL DEVELOPMENT AGENDA REPLACED THE FIVE-YEAR PLAN

Instead of preparing a Five Year Plan as done by the erstwhile Planning Commission, NITI Aayog has formulated a National Development Agenda. The National Development Agenda of NITI Aayog includes following three documents:

1. **Vision document** – a perspective plan covering a duration of 15 years (2017–18 to 2031–32). It combines national development goals and international **Sustainable Development Goals along with the plan relating to internal security, defence, etc.**
2. **Strategy Document** – a seven-year-long plan (2017–18 to 2023–24) to convert long-term vision into an implementable policy.
3. **Action Plan Document** – a three-year short-term action plan (2017–18 to 2019–20) to translate policies into action.

Performance Evalution of NITI Aayog

India's policy think tank NITI Aayog has made valuable **contributions to the development of the country in various sectors. These are discussed below:**

I. Agricultural Sector Reforms

1. **Implementation of Minimum Support Price (MSP) for Notified Crops:** It advised the Ministry of Agriculture to launch the *Pradhan Mantri Annadata Aay Sanrakshan Abhiyan* (PM-AASHA) in 2018, encompassing:
   - Price Support Scheme (PSS)
   - Price Deficiency Payment Scheme
   - Pilot on Private Procurement Stockists Scheme
2. **Model Act on Contract Farming:** Formulated to empower farmers to negotiate prices and establish contracts with buyers.
3. **Business Model for Doubling Farmers' Income:** Established a task force to promote the application of science and technology in agriculture, minimise farmers' risks, and incorporate modern business practices.

4. **Agriculture Export Policy:** Provided inputs to the Ministry of Commerce and Industry, emphasising the inclusion of a section on the global export environment and emerging demand.
5. **Gramin Agricultural Markets (GrAM):** Announced in the 2018–19 Budget to develop and upgrade 22,000 rural *haats* into GrAMs.
6. **Model Agriculture Land Leasing Act, 2016:** Recognises tenant rights and safeguards landowners' interests, accompanied by a dedicated cell for land reforms.
7. **Agriculture Marketing and Farmer-Friendly Reforms Index:** Introduced to assess the need for reforms in market access, land leasing, and forestry on private land.

II. Nutritional Sector Reforms

1. **National Nutrition Strategy:** Formulated to guide the launch of the National Nutrition Mission (POSHAN Abhiyaan) by the Ministry of Women and Child Development (MoWCD), with NITI Aayog responsible for monitoring and evaluation.
2. **National Council on India's Nutritional Challenges:** Constituted under the Chairmanship of NITI Aayog's Vice-Chairman to provide policy directions and coordinate efforts among ministries to address nutritional challenges.
3. **National Technical Board of Nutrition (NTBN):** Established under the Chairmanship of a NITI Aayog member to offer technical, evidence-based recommendations on nutrition policies for women and children.

III. Health Sector Reforms

1. **Ayushman Bharat Scheme:** Played a pivotal role in the conceptualisation and design of this health insurance scheme aimed at providing affordable healthcare to the masses.
2. **National Medical Commission Bill:** Contributed to the formulation of this bill, proposing the replacement of the Medical Council of India with the new National Medical Commission.
3. **National Commission for Homoeopathy (NCH) Bill, 2018:** Assisted in the formulation of this bill to regulate homoeopathy practices.
4. **National Commission for Indian System of Medicine Bill, 2018:** Contributed to the development of this bill to regulate traditional Indian medical systems.
5. **National Commission for Yoga and Naturopathy Bill, 2018:** Assisted in formulating this bill to regulate yoga and naturopathy practices.

IV. Educational Sector Reforms

1. **Performance-Based Graded Autonomy Framework for Universities:** Contributed to the formulation of this framework to provide greater autonomy to universities based on the performance metrics.
2. **Strengthening Accreditation Framework:** Assisted in enhancing the accreditation process, enabling additional agencies, including third-party organisations, to accredit higher education institutions.

V. Mineral Sector Reforms

1. **Draft National Mineral Policy – 2018:** Played an active role in framing this policy by constituting committees on the utilisation of fly ash and slag.

2. **Strategy for Self-Reliance in Rare Earth Minerals:** Constituted various committees to develop strategies for self-reliance in rare earth minerals and to combat restrictive trade practices.

VI. Energy Sector Reforms

1. **National Energy Policy 2018:** Initiated the drafting of this policy to address objectives such as increased energy accessibility, enhanced energy independence, greater sustainability, and higher economic growth.

VII. Transforming India's Gold Market

1. **Committee on Transforming India's Gold Market:** Constituted to recommend measures for tapping into the potential of the gold market in India, aiming to stimulate exports, economic growth, and employment.

VIII. Aspirational Districts Programme

1. **Transformation of 117 Underdeveloped Districts:** Launched a unique initiative to transform 117 districts, including 35 affected by Left-Wing Extremism, focusing on improving key social indicators and enhancing economic efficiency.

IX. Atal Innovation Mission (AIM)

1. **Fostering Innovation and Entrepreneurship:** Launched under NITI Aayog to build an innovative mindset in the country's entrepreneurship ecosystem.
2. **Atal Tinkering Labs (ATLs):** Established in schools to foster creativity and scientific temperament among students, enabling them to design and create prototypes to solve local challenges.

X. Building Inclusive and Sustainable India

1. **Ek Bharat Shrestha Bharat:** Aims to promote unity and excellence through long-term inter-State engagements via cultural exchanges and education.
2. **Sustainable Action for Transforming Human Capital (SATH):** Aims to bring transformative change by assisting states in improving their social sector indicators and providing technical support.
3. **Development Support Services to States (DSSS):** Launched to address key structural issues in project development and build institutional and organisational capacities, establishing a Centre–State partnership model and promoting Private-Public Partnerships across infrastructure sectors.
4. **State Human Development Reports:** Assisted states in preparing these reports to assess and address human development challenges.

XI. Report on India's Gig and Platform Economy

1. **Workforce Engagement:** In 2020–21, 7.7 million workers were engaged in the gig economy. They constituted 2.6 per cent of the non-agricultural workforce.

XII. Report on Carbon Capture, Utilisation, and Storage (CCUS) Policy Framework

1. **Emission Reduction Strategy:** CCUS is identified as a crucial method for reducing emissions from hard-to-abate sectors such as steel, cement, and petrochemicals.
2. **Policy Interventions:** The report outlines necessary policy measures across various sectors to facilitate the deployment of CCUS technologies.

3. **Alignment with National Targets:** The recommendations align with India's updated Nationally Determined Contributions (NDCs), aiming for 50 per cent of total installed capacity from non-fossil-based energy sources and a 45 per cent reduction in emission intensity by 2030.

XIII. Launch of the National Data and Analytics Platform (NDAP)

1. **Enhance Accessibility:** Make data accessible, interoperable, and interactive for users.
2. **Support Decision-Making:** Provide a user-friendly interface for policymakers, researchers, and the public to access and analyse data.
3. **Promote Transparency:** Foster transparency and accountability in governance by making data readily available.

Through these initiatives, NITI Aayog has played a pivotal role in steering India towards sustainable and inclusive development across various sectors.

However, there are issues associated with NITI Aayog

- NITI Aayog has less role in influencing private or public investment.
- Inequality has continued to grow in the Indian society and the effect of NITI AAYOG in combating this has not been such.
- Solutions to solve structure issues in the country are still not forthcoming.
- NITI Aayog has been transformed into a glorified recommendatory body which lacks the requisite power to bring positive change in the government's actions.
- Inadequate resources to the new think tank.

Way Forward

- Equipping the think tank with requisite powers so that it can effect change.
- Allocation of adequate resources.
- NITI AAYOG could be made legally accountable to the legislature for its inability to meet the targets. This would bring in more accountability.
- Ensure the organisation remains a non-partisan institution.

Thus, the setting up of NITI AAYOG has brought positive results. However, there is a need to effect changes in the organisation so that it can meet its objectives.

Key Performance Indices published by NITI Aayog

EXAM ESSENTIAL

Name of the Index	Details
State Health Index	• NITI Aayog, in collaboration with the *Ministry of Health and Family Welfare* (MoHFW) and with technical assistance from the World Bank, has been spearheading the Health Index initiative from 2017 to measure the annual performance of states and union territories on a variety of indicators – health outcomes, governance and processes. • The index aims to nudge states towards transformative action in the health sector and to focus the attention of the country on achieving better health outcomes.

Name of the Index	Details
	• According to the State Health Index 2021, Kerala, Tamil Nadu, and Telangana occupied first, second and third spot, respectively, for 2020–21. • Bihar is at the bottom. • Among UTs, Lakshadweep is at the top and Delhi is at the bottom. Based on incremental performance, Rajasthan, Uttarakhand, and Odisha emerged as top performers in 2020–21.
Composite Water Management Index (CWMI)	• Developed by NITI Aayog in partnership with the **Ministry of Road Transport and Highways, Shipping and Water Resources** and States/UTs. It was released for the first time in 2018. • It is a tool to assess and improve the performance of States/Union Territories in efficient management of water resources. • CWMI comprises **nine themes** (each having an attached weight) with **28 performance key indicators** covering groundwater and surface water restoration, major and medium irrigation projects, watershed development, participatory irrigation management, on-farm water use, rural and urban water supply, and policy and governance. • CWMI was first published in 2018. Thereafter, CWMI 2.0 was published in 2019. • **CWMI 2.0 was launched in 2019**, for the reference year 2017–18, as against the base year of 2016–17. While Gujarat continued to hold the first position, on an average, 80% of the States assessed on the Index over the last three years improved their water management scores, with an average improvement of +5.2 points. ◆ Several water-scarce States are the leaders in index performance. ◆ 60% of the States have improved their scores in the FY 2016–2017 as compared to FY 2015–2016.
School Education Quality Index (SEQI) (*published in 2019*)	• Developed by NITI Aayog to evaluate the performance of States and UTs in school education sector. • SEQI indicators were revised as a complete subset of *Ministry of HRD*'s Performance Grading Index (PGI). Objective is to shift the focus to educational outcomes rather than inputs and programmes. • Index consists of **30 critical indicators** that assess the delivery of quality education. • Indicators are categorised into: ◆ **Outcomes** *(Learning outcomes, access outcomes, infrastructure and facilities for outcomes, equity outcomes)* ◆ **Governance processes aiding outcomes** *(student and teacher attendance, administrative adequacy, training, accountability and transparency)* • Base year considered is 2015–16. • To facilitate like-to-like comparisons, States and UTs have been grouped as Large States, Small States and Union Territories.

<table>
<tr><th>Name of the Index</th><th>Details</th></tr>
<tr><td></td><td>
• As per the 2019 report:
◆ Among Large States – performance score ranged from 76.6% for Kerala to 36.4% for Uttar Pradesh.
◆ Among Small States – performance score ranged from 68.8% for Manipur to 24.6% for Arunachal Pradesh.
◆ Among UTs – performance score ranged from 82.9% for Chandigarh to 31.9% for Lakshadweep.
</td></tr>
<tr><td>India Innovation Index 2020</td><td>
• Developed by NITI Aayog in cooperation with Institute for Competitiveness as knowledge partner.
• The index has been developed on the lines of the Global Innovation Index (GII), to examine innovation capabilities and performance of Indian States/UTs and to design policies to drive innovation across regions..
• The Index is developed to examine innovation capabilities and performance of Indian States/UTs.
• Index is calculated as the average of the scores of its two dimensions:
1. Five Enablers (Human Capital, Investment, Knowledge Workers, Business Environment, Safety and Legal Environment)
2. Performance dimension (Knowledge Output, Knowledge Diffusion)
• India Innovation Index 2021:
◆ Karnataka, Manipur and Chandigarh have topped in their respective categories in the third edition of India Innovation Index.
◆ Karnataka has topped in the 'Major States' category. Manipur is leading the 'North East and Hill States' category and Chandigarh is the top performer in the 'Union Territories and City States' category.
◆ The number of indicators has increased from 36 (in the India Innovation Index 2020) to 66 (in the India Innovation Index 2021)
</td></tr>
<tr><td>Sustainable Development Goals (SDG) India Index 2020–21</td><td>
• It was created in partnership with the United Nations in India to track the progress of all States and UTs on the basis of 115 indicators. These 115 indicators are aligned with National Indicator Framework (NIF). NIF was developed by MoSPI.
• The SDG India Index 2020–21 was more comprehensive than previous editions, as it incorporated a broader range of targets and indicators which were more closely aligned with the NIF.
• The 115 indicators include 16 out of 17 SDGs, and a qualitative assessment on Goal 17 (cover 70 SDG targets).
• Kerala retained top rank (score 75), followed by Tamil Nadu and Himachal Pradesh (both scored 74).
</td></tr>
</table>

Name of the Index	Details
The SDG India Index 2020–21 dashboard	The SDG India Index 2020–21 is also live on online dashboard. It facilitates to identify crucial gaps related to tracking the SDGs and to develop a statistical system at the State/UT levels.
SDG Urban Index	**NITI Aayog**, under the **Indo-German Cooperation**, developed the **Sustainable Development Goals (SDGs)** Urban Index and Dashboard 2021–22. • **Total 56 urban areas have been considered for computation** on 77 SDG indicators across 46 targets of the SDG framework. • **Top Urban Areas:** Shimla (Composite Score **75.50**), Coimbatore (Composite Score **73.29**), Chandigarh (Composite Score **72.36**), Thiruvananthapuram (Composite Score **72.36**), Kochi (Composite Score **72.29**).
District Hospital Index	• NITI undertook the exercise of tracking the performance of district hospitals based on outcomes. • It has been done in collaboration with Indian Statistical Institute (ISI) and the National Accreditation Board of Hospitals, Quality Council of India. • Data validation of the health-management-information system for 707 district hospitals (97%) has been completed and the analysis of results is underway.
State Energy and Climate Index 2022 (Round 1) *(based on 2019–20 data)*	• Work was initiated in 2021 to develop the State Energy and Climate Index to compare energy accessibility, affordability and sustainability across all Indian States and Union Territories with technical assistance from the World Bank. • The index comprises **27 indicators** under **six broad categories**: (1) Access, Affordability and Reliability (2) Clean Energy Initiatives (3) Energy Efficiency (4) DISCOM's performance (5) Environment Sustainability (6) New Initiatives. As per 2022 Round 1 report – Gujarat topped, followed by Kerala and Punjab.
India Energy Dashboards (Version 2.0)	India Energy Dashboards (Version 2.0) has been launched by NITI Aayog. India Energy Dashboards (IED) is an attempt to provide single-window access to the energy data provided by Central Electricity Authority, Coal Controller's Organisation and Ministry of Petroleum and Natural Gas. **Key features:** • The IED 2.0 provides time series data from FY 2005–06 to FY 2019–20; • Enhanced data download into convenient spreadsheet formats in more intuitive way. • IED provides data at sub-yearly frequencies, API linked data from some portals maintained by the Government agencies. • UJALA, Vidyut PRAVAH and PRAAPTI, has been incorporated in the portal.

Name of the Index	Details
	• New 'Feedback and Suggestions' forum for the engagement of energy data user community.
Promoting Millets in Diets: Best Practices across States/UTs of India (2023)	• The report puts emphasis on the good and innovative practices adopted by state governments and organisations in various aspects of the millet production, processing, and consumption. • There are **nine commonly known traditional millets** produced, including Sorghum, Pearl, Finger, Foxtail, Proso, Little, Barnyard, Browntop and Kodo Millet. • Millets are highly secure crops for small farmers due to their ability to withstand climatic changes, including hot and dry conditions. • Odisha Millet Mission, launched in 2017, was the first in this regard, because it simultaneously focuses on production, processing, consumption, marketing, and inclusion of millets in government schemes. • The report serves as a guideline to revive millets in our diets. It is also hoped that it will contribute to a more sustainable and healthy food system in India.
A Green and Sustainable Growth Agenda for the Global Economy (2023)	• The report indicates a swift, just transition to renewable energy and reduced carbon emissions. • It was developed by NITI Aayog in partnership with IDRC and GDN. • NITI Aayog calls for regulation of credit rating agencies and reforms in Multilateral Development Banks to fund green growth in developing nations.
National Multidimensional Poverty Index: A Progress Review 2023	• This report is based on National Family Health Survey 2019–21 (NFHS-5). • As per the report, 13.5 crore Indians escape Multidimensional Poverty in 5 years. • Percentage of Multidimensionally poor declined from 24.85 per cent in 2015–16 to 14.96 per cent in 2019–21 (9.89 per cent decline). • Highest decline in the number of poor people was observed in Uttar Pradesh. • Top five performers are – 1. Tamil Nadu 2. Maharashtra 3. Karnataka 4. Gujarat 5. Haryana.
Fiscal Health Index 2025	• Fiscal Health Index (FHI) has been designed to assess state performance, evaluating states across key pillars of fiscal prudence. • This composite index evaluates states across five key indicators: Quality of Expenditure, Revenue Mobilisation, Fiscal Prudence, Debt Index and Debt Sustainability, which are important to analyse the state's fiscal position. • The FHI is more than just a rating tool; it offers a methodical framework for evaluating financial health using publicly available key indicators,

Planning Commission *vs* NITI Aayog

Sl. No.	Planning Commission (PC)	NITI Aayog (NA)
1	PC enjoyed the power to allocate funds to Ministries and State Governments.	NA has **no financial power** of fund allocation. It is only a **think tank**
2	It issued dictums to State Governments for its implementation.	It issues guidelines in consultation with State Governments.
3	A kind of **Top-Down approach** was followed in formulating plans.	**Bottom-up approach** is followed by NA.
4	Decisions were more centralised under PC.	Decentralisation to ensure **cooperative federalism** is one of the guiding principles of NA. States now play a more significant role in policy making.
5	PC had **eight full-time members**. No provision for part-time members.	**Four full-time members** and maximum two part-time members.
6	Had Deputy Chairperson and Member Secretary other than full-time members. Did not have the post of Vice-Chairperson and CEO.	Has the post of Vice-Chairperson. Also, there is one post of CEO (of Secretary rank in GoI) nominated by Prime Minister.
7	PC reported to National Development Council comprising of Chief Ministers and Lt. Governors.	NA has Governing Council with Chief Ministers of States and Lt. Governors of UTs as members.
8	PC used to impose policy on States.	NA has no power to impose policy. It is essentially an advisory body.

Is Economic Planning Still Relevant as a Tool for Government in Today's Perspective?

Critics opine that the initiative to determine development priorities **de facto** lies with the Finance Ministry rather than planning authorities. Therefore, the budgets, rather than the plans, determine the development priorities.

However, planning as an important function cannot be outdated. Its relevance lies in all aspects of not only individual human life but even in an effective Government functioning. Good planning may act as a development aid in following manners:

1. As a balancing instrument between commitments and outcomes.
2. As a mechanism to imbibe greater accountability into the Government to achieve whatever it has planned.
3. As a yardstick to measure implementation of strategies.
4. Lastly, planning helps to provide a shape and framework to the future strategies of the Government as per priorities. It provides assurance to public at large to implement them in future.

Thus, with NITI Aayog having replaced the Planning Commission, the role of economic planning cannot be discarded. However, it has now become more indicative, decentralised along with ensuring cooperative federalism.

SUMMARY

- **Economic planning** – Allocation of resources in a comprehensive way to achieve the predetermined objectives with optimal utilisation of resources.
- **Evolution of Indian Economic Planning**
  - 1934 – M. Visvesvaraya Plan – shifting from agriculture to industrialisation and also bincreased employment in industries
  - 1934 – FICCI Proposal – to end laissez faire
  - 1944 – Bombay Plan – agricultural restructuring through abolition of zamindari system and rapid industrialisation
  - 1944 – Gandhian Plan – drafted by Acharya Shriman Narayan Agarwal – economic decentralisation – small-scale and cottage industries
  - 1950 – Planning Commission – responsibility of making assessment of all the resources of the country
  - 2015 – NITI Aayog
- **Goals of Planning** – Growth, Modernisation, Self-Reliance and Social Justice.
- **Harrod-Domar Model** – Adopted in 1st FYP (1951–56) – emphasised on the role of capital accumulation's dual character – increases national income (demand-side role) and increases production capacity (supply-side role).
- **Nehru-Mahalanobis Model** – Adopted in 2nd FYP (1956–61) – emphasised on investment in heavy industries – in order to achieve industrialisation for rapid economic development.
- **LPG (Liberalisation, Privatisation and Globalisation) Strategy** – Adopted in 8th FYP (1992–97) – ended licence permit raj – encouraged privatisation and allowed FDI – export promotion policy was adopted.
- **PURA (Providing Urban Amenities in Rural Areas) strategy** – A.P.J. Abdul Kalam – emphasised on physical infrastructural development – of Census Towns – under PPP mode.
- **Achievements of Planning** – Significant improvement in GDP – improvement in social indicators and industrial infrastructure – Forex reserves increased substantially.
- **Failures of Planning** – Continued existence of poverty, gender inequality, unemployment, imbalance in regional development.
- **National Institution for Transforming India (NITI) Aayog** – 1 January 2015 – non-constitutional and non-statutory body – think tank – no financial role – PM as Chairperson.
- **Governing Council of NITI Aayog** – Chief Ministers of States and Lt. Governors of UTs as members – headed by PM.
- **Objectives of NITI Aayog** – Co-operative federalism, bottom-up approach for plans, special focus on vulnerable sections, national security interests, resolution of inter-sectoral and inter-departmental issues.
- **National Development Agenda** – Instead of FYP – includes three documents: 1. Vision Document; 2. Strategy Document; 3. Action Plan Document.

UPSC CSE PREVIOUS YEARS' PRELIMINARY EXAMINATION QUESTIONS

1. **Atal Innovation Mission** is setup under the **[2019]**
   (a) Department of Science and Technology
   (b) Ministry of Labour and Employment
   (c) NITI Aayog
   (d) Ministry of Skill Development and Entrepreneurship
2. Which of the following has/have occurred in India after its liberalisation of economic policies in 1991? **[2017]**
   1. Share of agriculture in GDP increased enormously.
   2. Share of India's export in World trade increased.
   3. FDI flows increased.
   4. India's foreign exchange reserves increased enormously.

   Select the correct answer using the codes given below:
   (a) 1 and 4 only (b) 2, 3 and 4 only
   (c) 2 and 3 only (d) 1, 2, 3 and 4
3. The GoI has established **NITI Aayog** to replace the **[2015]**
   (a) Human Rights Commission
   (b) Finance Commission
   (c) Law Commission
   (d) Planning Commission
4. The main objective of the Twelfth FYP is **[2014]**
   (a) Inclusive growth and poverty reduction
   (b) Inclusive and sustainable growth
   (c) Sustainable and inclusive growth to reduce unemployment
   (d) Faster, sustainable and more inclusive growth
5. In the context of India's FYP, a shift in the pattern of industrialisation with lower emphasis on heavy industries and more on infrastructure began in the **[2010]**
   (a) Fourth Plan (b) Sixth Plan
   (c) Eighth Plan (d) Tenth Plan
6. Inclusive growth as enunciated in the Eleventh FYP does not include one of the following: **[2010]**
   (a) Reduction of poverty
   (b) Extension of employment opportunities
   (c) Strengthening of capital market
   (d) Reduction of gender inequality

☞ NO QUESTIONS ASKED
2024, 2023, 2022, 2021, 2020, 2018, 2016, 2013, 2012, 2011

ANSWER KEY

1. (c) 2. (b) 3. (d) 4. (d) 5. (b) 6. (c)

UPSC CSE PREVIOUS YEARS' MAIN EXAMINATION QUESTIONS

1. How are the principles followed by the NITI Aayog different from those followed by the erstwhile Planning Commission of India? **[2018]**
2. How has globalisation led to the reduction of employment in the formal sector of the Indian economy? Is increased informalisation detrimental to the development of the country? **[2016]**
3. Examine the impact of liberalisation on companies owned by Indians. Are they competing with the MNCs satisfactorily? **[2013]**

☞ NO QUESTIONS ASKED
2024, 2023, 2022, 2021, 2020, 2019, 2017, 2015, 2014, 2012, 2011

CHAPTER

10

MONEY AND MONEY SUPPLY

CHAPTER OUTLINE

- Money
- Money Supply
- Determinants of Money Supply
- Sources of Money Supply
- Tools to Measure Money Supply
- Monetary Aggregates

MONEY

Money is anything that is legally recognised as a medium of exchange, such as paper currency and coins.

Types of Money

- Commodity Money
- Fiat Money
- Fiduciary Money
- Commercial Bank Money
- Representative Money

Functions of Money

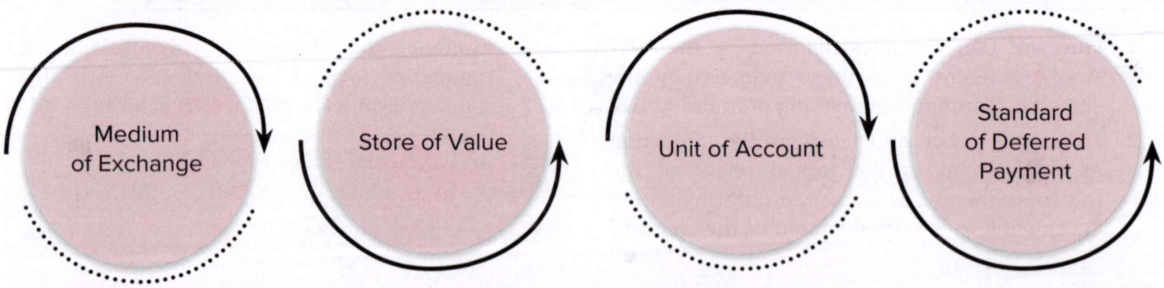

did you KNOW? The store of value function of money was not acknowledged by classical economists. Keynes emphasized this role of money.

Characteristics of Money

In modern economy, money performs a number of essential functions, which have been categorised as follows:

- **Medium of Exchange:** By facilitating the buying and selling of products and acting as a means of exchange, money eliminates the necessity for barter system, which requires two coincidences of demands. A man can sell his wheat for cash and buy rice if he wishes to exchange it for rice.
- **Store of Value:** In this instance, money is stored as a form of "asset." Money is an asset or a form of wealth because it is a claim. It is the most practical way to claim such goods and services as one wishes to buy. As a result, people prefer to keep their wealth in the form of money.
- **Unit of Account:** In order to compare prices and make accurate purchasing decisions, money enables us to express the value of goods and services in common currency.
- **Standard of Deferred Payment:** Money serves as a standard of deferred payment because it gives people and businesses a common unit of worth for future transactions, allowing them to pay later instead of immediately. By enabling the accurate estimation and planning of future payments, this function of money promotes lending and borrowing, agreements and economic growth.

Economists have identified six characteristics of money. They are as follows:

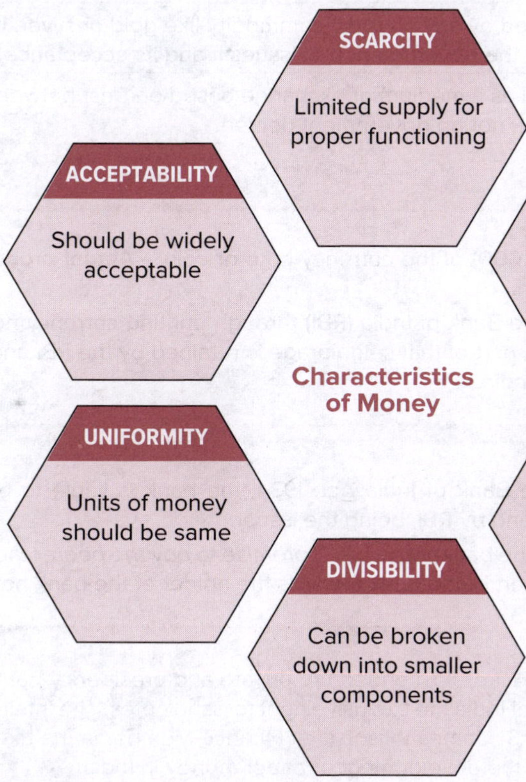

The different types of money that circulate in an economy are as follows:

Type	Definition
Actual Money	Medium of exchange for goods and services.
Metallic Money	Coins, made up from metals like gold, silver, copper, or iron.
Paper Money	Made of paper.
Full-bodied Money	A kind of money whose worth as money equals its value as a commodity. For example: a gold coin.
Representative Full-Bodied Money	A type of token money that is backed by an equivalent value of bullion (gold and silver in bulk) with the issuing authority.
Legal Tender Money	Limited Legal Tender Money (used to pay a debt up to a certain limit, beyond which a creditor can refuse it) Unlimited Legal Tender Money (can be used to pay any debt amount)
Optional Money	Non-legal tender instruments like cheques, bills of exchange, and promissory notes that are accepted for payments, but there is no legal obligation to accept them.
Standard Money	Legally recognised currency with full face value.
Token Money	Money that has a lesser intrinsic value compared to its face value.
Fiat Money	Not backed by any physical commodity like gold or silver. Its value is determined by the government that issues it and its acceptance by the public.
Fiduciary Money	Accepted as a medium of exchange based on trust between the payer and the payee, not on government decree.

BONUS KNOWLEDGE

- **Seigniorage** = **Face value** (say ₹2,000) of the currency note or coin – **Actual production cost** (say ₹3.50) of that currency note or coin.
- Seigniorage earned by the Reserve Bank of India (RBI) through printing currency notes becomes a major source of surplus or profit. A part of that seigniorage is retained by the RBI and the rest of it is transferred to the Government of India.

- As per Section 26 of the Reserve Bank of India Act, 1934, the bank is liable to pay the value of banknote. This is payable on demand by RBI, being the issuer.
- The promissory clause printed on the banknotes, i.e., *"I promise to pay the bearer the sum of Rupees ..."* denotes the obligation on the part of the bank towards the holder of the bank note.

did you KNOW?

- The Paper Currency Act of 1861 ended the private and presidency banks' note issuance by giving the Government of India the exclusive right to issue notes. The intellectual stimulation and personal dynamism of Sir James Wilson (first Finance Member in the Executive Council of the Viceroy of India) were crucial to the development of paper money in India.
- Prior to the establishment of the Reserve Bank of India on April 1st, 1935, the Indian government kept issuing currency notes. Reintroduced in August 1940 as a wartime necessity, one-rupee note was issued by the government.

MONEY SUPPLY

It is a stock concept. The **total stock of money in circulation among the public** at a particular point of time is called money supply. Supply of money does not include the stock of money held by the Government or by the banking system of the country (apart from demand deposits) because they are the suppliers or producers of money. Therefore, the stock of money held by them is not part of the stock of money held by the people.

Determinants of Money Supply

Several variables affect the money supply in an economy. They are as follows:

- **Open Market Operations by Central Banks:** Central banks regulate the money supply through open market operations, which involve buying and selling government assets.
- **Reserve Requirements:** Banks must retain a certain percentage of deposits in reserve, which affects their lending capacity.
- **Trade Cycle:** During boom, money supply increases and during recession, money supply falls.
- **Role of Commercial Banks in Lending Practices:** Commercial banks' lending practices impact the money supply by determining how much they lend to firms and people.
- **Public Preferences:** The public's propensity for retaining currency rather than putting it in interest-bearing accounts impacts the money supply.
- **New Financial Products:** The introduction of new financial instruments and innovations can alter the content and quantity of the money supply.
- **Money Velocity:** The rate at which money circulates in the economy has an impact on total economic activity.
- **Government Expenditure:** Government spending and fiscal policies have an influence on the money supply, particularly if they are financed with borrowed funds.

Sources of Money Supply

In India, both the central bank (RBI) and commercial banks contribute to the money supply. The major sources are:

1. Central Bank Sources

- The Central Bank (RBI) issues currency notes and coins, which contribute to the physical component of the money supply (M_0).
- The RBI uses monetary policy instruments to impact the money supply by modifying interest rates, conducting open market operations, and establishing reserve requirements.

2. Commercial Bank Sources

- Commercial banks produce money by lending. When banks offer loans, they essentially generate fresh deposits in the borrower's account, which expands the overall money supply.
- Banks also maintain reserves with the central bank, which influences the high-powered money component (M_0).

TOOLS TO MEASURE MONEY SUPPLY

Monetary Aggregates

Monetary aggregates measure a country's total money supply. The money supply in the economy is sometimes represented using a monetary aggregate known as 'wide money', also abbreviated M_3. There are also additional monetary aggregates. From 1977 to 1998, the RBI utilised four monetary aggregates to estimate the money supply: M_1, M_2, M_3, and M_4. However, measurement standards changed in 1998.

The current terminology is M_0, M_1, M_2, and M_3. To distinguish between new and old aggregates, RBI occasionally refers to new aggregates as NM_0, NM_1, NM_2, and NM_3.

In addition to the monetary aggregates, the Working Group recommended the compilation of three liquidity aggregates, L_1, L_2, and L_3, which include select items of financial liabilities of non-depository financial corporations such as development financial institutions and non-banking financial companies accepting public deposits, with the exception of post office savings bank.

Name	Equals
M_0 (Reserve money)	= Currency in circulation + Bankers' deposits with RBI + 'Other' deposits (Deposits of quasi-government and other financial institutions including primary dealers, Balances in the accounts of foreign Central banks and Governments, Accounts of international agencies such as the International Monetary Fund, etc.)
M_1 (Narrow money)	= Currency with the Public + Net demand deposits held by Commercial Banks
M_2	= M_1 + Savings deposits with Post Office Savings Banks
M_3 (Broad money)	= M_1 + Net time deposits with the banking system
M_4	= M_3 + Total deposits with Post Office Savings Organisations (excluding National Savings Certificate)

While the measures M_0, M_1 and M_3 are widely used in India, M_2 and M_4 are rarely used.

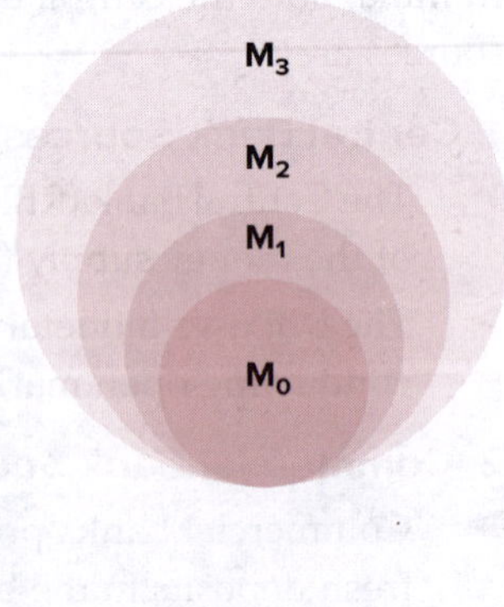

The decreasing order of liquidity of these monetary aggregates is – **$M_0 > M_1 > M_2 > M_3 > M_4$.** This decline in liquidity indicates the shifting of its feature as **'medium of exchange'** to **'store of value'.**

- **New Monetary Aggregates:** NM_0 (Monetary Base), NM_1 (Narrow Money), NM_2 and NM_3 (Broad Money)
- **Liquidity Aggregates:** L_1, L_2 and L_3

NM_0 = Currency in Circulation + Bankers' Deposits with RBI + 'Other' Deposits with RBI (Deposits of quasi-government and other financial institutions including primary dealers, Balances in the accounts of foreign Central banks and Governments, Accounts of international agencies such as the International Monetary Fund, etc.)

NM_1 = Currency with the public + Demand deposits and current deposits with the banking system + 'Other' deposits with RBI

$NM_2 = NM_1$ + Short-term time deposits of residents (including and up to the contractual maturity of 1 year)

$NM_3 = NM_2$ + Long-term time deposits of residents + Call/Term funding from financial institutions

$L_1 = NM_3$ + All deposits with Post Office Savings Banks (excluding National Savings Certificates)

$L_2 = L_1$ + Term deposits with term-lending institutions and refinancing institutions + Term borrowing by the financial institutions (FIs) + Certificates of Deposit (CD) issued by FIs

$L_3 = L_2$ + Public deposits of Non-Banking Financial Companies (NBFCs)

Note:

- Data on M_0 is published by RBI on a weekly basis, while data for M_1 and M_3 is published on a fortnightly basis.
- Data on L_1 and L_2 is published monthly, while data on L_3 is published quarterly.

EXAM ESSENTIAL

Money Multiplier – It is the ratio of Broad Money to Reserve Money. It indicates how an initial deposit leads to a greater final increase in the total money supply.

Money Multiplier = M_3/M_0 – Money multiplier may be impacted by any change in the components mentioned under M_3 or M_0.

Any step to increase M_3 improves the Money Multiplier. Examples include increase in banking habit of people, which can be achieved through better financial inclusion.

From mid-1990s to 2016–17, the money multiplier was mostly increasing. However, it has been **declining since 2017–18**. However, in 2019–20, 2020–21, 2021–22, 2022–23, money multiplier had recorded a slight decline, reflecting large deposits by banks with RBI under reverse repo.

THE VELOCITY OF MONEY

It is the average number of times money moves from one hand to another during a specific time period. It is usually measured as a ratio of GDP to a country's Total Money Supply. Thus,

Velocity of Money = GDP/Total Money Supply

GDP = Money Supply × Velocity of Money

Thus, GDP cannot be controlled through the supply of money alone.

Factors influencing the velocity of money circulation:

- **Income allocation:** People in poverty spend their money right away. So, money in the hands of the impoverished has a higher velocity.
- **Boom:** During the period of boom, the velocity of money increases.
- **EMI:** If more people utilise EMIs for purchasing things, the velocity of money increases.
- **Minimal financial inclusion:** It indicates lower velocity since the banks' intervention is minimal. People prefer to preserve more in real assets, thus money does not move hands frequently.
- **Development of a nation:** As the nation develops, there is a greater velocity of money, since individuals save less and spend more because of lifestyle and faith in government social security.

Expansion of Money Supply

The money supply can expand through a variety of mechanisms. They are as follows:

- Bank lending increases the money supply by creating deposits in borrower accounts.
- The central bank's open market operations, such as purchasing and selling government securities, can alter the money supply.
- Government spending, especially through borrowings, can increase the money supply.
- Lowering reserve requirements for commercial banks boosts lending capability and expands the money supply.
- The central bank's foreign exchange operations can have an influence on the domestic money supply.

BONUS KNOWLEDGE

The Indian currency is known as the Indian Rupee (INR), and its symbol is ₹. One Rupee is made up of 100 Paise. The ₹ symbol looks like a mix of the Devanagari letter "₹" (ra) and the English letter "R", with two horizontal lines on top.

All banknotes issued by the Reserve Bank of India (such as ₹2, ₹5, ₹10, ₹20, ₹50, ₹100, ₹200, ₹500, and ₹2000) are legal to use anywhere in India unless the government withdraws them. These notes are guaranteed by the Central Government. The ₹1 note, issued by the Government of India, is also considered legal money.

However, ₹500 and ₹1000 notes from the Mahatma Gandhi series, issued before November 8, 2016, are no longer valid and stopped being legal tender after midnight on that day.

The highest value note ever printed in India was the ₹10,000 note. It was first introduced in 1938 and later removed from use in 1946. It came back in 1954 but was again demonetised in 1978.

Things to Know about Banknotes

- Fifteen languages appear in the language panel of banknotes in addition to Hindi prominently displayed in the centre of the note and English on the reverse.
- In India, banknotes are currently printed on paper that is 100 per cent cotton based.
- Two or more banknotes with the same serial number can exist but they would either have a different Inset Letter or year of printing or signature of a different Governor of RBI.
- An Inset Letter is an alphabet printed on the Number Panel of the banknote. There can be notes without any inset letter also.
- In accordance with international best practices, non-sequential numbering was used in 2011 with a view to improving operational efficiency and cost effectiveness.
- The Star series banknotes have an additional character, viz., a *(star) in the number panel in the space between the prefix.
- All banknotes issued by RBI are backed by assets such as gold, Government Securities and Foreign Currency Assets, as defined in Section 33 of the RBI Act, 1934.

- The first banknote issued by independent India was the one rupee note issued in 1949. The same designed new banknotes were issued with the symbol of Lion Capital of Ashoka Pillar at Sarnath in the watermark window in place of the portrait of King George.
- In 1970, banknotes with the legend "*Satyameva Jayate*", i.e., 'truth alone shall prevail' were introduced for the first time.
- In October 1987, ₹500 banknote was introduced with the portrait of Mahatma Gandhi and the Ashoka Pillar watermark.

Various Types of Banknotes issued since Independence

Ashokan Pillar Banknotes: The first banknote issued by independent India was the one rupee note issued in 1949. While retaining the same design, the new banknotes were issued with the symbol of Lion Capital of Ashokan Pillar at Sarnath in the watermark window in place of the portrait of King George.

Mahatma Gandhi (MG) Series 1996: All the banknotes of this series bear the portrait of Mahatma Gandhi on the obverse (front) side, in place of symbol of Lion Capital of Ashoka Pillar, which has also been retained and shifted to the left side next to the watermark window. This means that these banknotes contain Mahatma Gandhi's watermark as well as Mahatma Gandhi's portrait.

Mahatma Gandhi series – 2005 banknotes: MG series 2005 banknotes were issued in the denomination of ₹10, ₹20, ₹50, ₹100, ₹500 and ₹1000 and contain some additional/new security features as compared to the 1996 MG series. The year of introduction of these banknotes is as: ⟶

Denomination	Month and year of Introduction
₹50 and ₹100	August 2005
₹500 and ₹1000	October 2005
₹10	April 2006
₹20	August 2006

The Legal tender of banknotes of ₹500 and ₹1000 of this series was subsequently withdrawn w.e.f. the midnight of November 8, 2016.

Mahatma Gandhi (New) Series (MGNS) – Nov. 2016

The Mahatma Gandhi (New) Series, introduced in 2016, highlights the cultural heritage and scientific achievements of the country. The banknotes in the series are more wallet friendly, being of reduced dimensions and hence expected to incur less wear and tear. For the first time, designs for banknotes have been indigenously developed on themes reflecting the diverse history, culture and ethos of the country as also its scientific achievements. The colour scheme is sharp and vivid to make the banknotes distinctive.

The first banknote from the new series was introduced on November 8, 2016 and is a new denomination, ₹2000-with the theme of Mangalyaan. Subsequently, banknotes in this series in denomination of ₹500, ₹200, ₹100, ₹50, ₹20 and ₹10 have also been introduced.

did you KNOW?

On January 1, 2020, the **MANI App** was launched to help **visually impaired people** identify the value of Indian banknotes. The app announces the denomination through audio in Hindi and English, and also supports 11 other languages, including Assamese, Bengali, Gujarati, Kannada, Malayalam, Marathi, Odia, Punjabi, Tamil, Telugu, and Urdu.

CRYPTOCURRENCIES

Cryptocurrency is a **digital money** transferred over the internet. **Cryptocurrencies** are based on the decentralised ledger-based **blockchain technology** which seeks to make the currency system decentralised, unlike the present Government-issued centralised form. Some popular cryptocurrencies are **Bitcoin, Ethereum, Litecoin,** and **Ripple.** There are certain **advantages** of cryptocurrencies like:

- Transaction costs are very low.
- Can lead to improved financial inclusion.
- Increase the safety of the financial system.
- Potentiality of a better directed monetary or fiscal policy.

However, cryptocurrencies have the **following disadvantages**:

- These are not backed by any physical assets, like gold or silver reserves.
- They are still prone to hacking, and there have been instances of theft of Bitcoins from digital wallet, making them risky.
- The anonymity in use of cryptocurrencies may actually facilitate several illegal activities like terror funding, smuggling, drugs trade, money laundering and other criminal activities.
- The extreme volatility of their prices rather makes them ideal for speculation and gambling which are not expected of a stable currency system.
- The electricity and the environmental costs involved to 'mine' the cryptocurrencies are too high.

In 2018, **RBI banned** the trading of virtual currencies or cryptocurrencies in India.

However, **in 2020**, the Supreme Court lifted the ban on cryptocurrencies which was imposed by the RBI. The SC held that the complete ban on trading was excessive.

There is **no** such Act enacted yet to regulate cryptocurrencies in India. The Finance Ministry informed in 2021 that a bill on cryptocurrency titled **'The Cryptocurrency and Regulation of Official Digital Currency Bill,** 2021' is under finalisation for consideration of the Cabinet.

did you KNOW?

Central African Republic (CAR) became the second country, after El Salvador, to accept Bitcoin as legal tender. Some universities in Switzerland, Germany, and the United States have recently accepted cryptocurrency as payment for education on their official websites.

Impact of Cryptocurrencies on Indian Society

- **Growing Interest:** Many people in India, especially the youth, are getting interested in cryptocurrencies like Bitcoin and Ethereum. Indian youth has invested hugely in cryptocurrency, a new crypto community has thus emerged.
- **New Opportunities:** Cryptocurrencies have opened new ways to earn money, invest, and even start businesses, especially in the technology and finance sectors.
- **Lack of Clear Rules and Regulations:** The RBI issued a circular preventing all banks from dealing in cryptocurrencies in 2018. This circular was declared unconstitutional by the Supreme Court in May 2020. Since cryptocurrencies are mostly unregulated, some people have lost money due to scams and fake platforms.

- **Government Action:** Government has announced to introduce a bill called Cryptocurrency and Regulation of Official Digital Currency Bill, 2021, to create a sovereign digital currency and simultaneously ban all private cryptocurrencies.
- **Access to Finance:** Crypto gives people, especially those without access to traditional banks, a new way to manage and send money. It has made it easier for entrepreneurs to reach international markets rather than strictly sticking to the national markets.
- **Still Developing:** The use of crypto in India is growing, but it needs better rules and more awareness to be safe and useful for everyone.

BONUS KNOWLEDGE

BLOCKCHAIN TECHNOLOGY

A decentralised digital ledger that tracks transactions over a network of computers is known as blockchain technology. There are several transactions in each block of the chain, and each time a new transaction takes place on the blockchain, a record of it is added to the ledger of each participant.

As technology is decentralised, there is a high level of security and transparency because no individual or entity can change or remove past transactions.

Although blockchain serves as the basis for cryptocurrencies like Bitcoin, it has other potential applications outside of the realm of virtual money.

NON-FUNGIBLE TOKEN

Non-Fungible Token (NFT) is an irreplaceable, unique cryptographic blockchain-based token, which can be used as an **evidence of ownership for digital assets** like music, photos, artwork, tweets and even memes. Unlike other currencies, Non-Fungible Tokens cannot be exchanged for an equal value and they are unbreakable into smaller values and thus **cannot** be used as a medium of commercial transactions. For example, a ten-rupee note can be exchanged with another ten rupee note, but it is not possible in case of NFT, because of its uniqueness.

An NFT **can be traded and sold on digital markets.** NFTs function like cryptographic tokens, but unlike cryptocurrencies such as Bitcoin or Ethereum, NFTs are **not mutually interchangeable,** and so are **not fungible.**

STABLE COIN

These **cryptocurrencies** are **tied to stable assets,** most often to dollar and are designed to give the same consistent value as Government-issued money in digital form for blockchain transactions, but are issued by private businesses.

SUMMARY

- **Money** – Money is anything that is legally recognised as a medium of exchange, unit of account, store of value, and standard of deferred payment.
- **Functions of Money** – Money facilitates transactions, helps to value goods, helps in saving wealth, and settling future payments.
- **Commodity Money** – Early money forms like gold or salt had intrinsic value and were used in exchange.

- **Fiat Money** – Modern paper currency has no intrinsic value but is accepted by law and government backing.
- **Fiduciary Money** – This includes instruments like cheques and drafts, accepted based on trust rather than legal tender status.
- **Commercial Bank Money** – Created through credit and loans, this type expands the money supply without printing currency.
- **Currency Issuers in India** – The Reserve Bank of India issues ₹2 and above notes; Government of India issues ₹1 notes and all coins.
- **Legal Tender** – Currency that must be accepted for payments within the country as per the law.
- **Monetary Policy** – RBI uses tools like repo rate, CRR, and SLR to control money flow and inflation.
- **Definition of Money Supply** – Refers to total stock of money (currency + deposits) available in the economy.

UPSC CSE PREVIOUS YEARS' PRELIMINARY EXAMINATION QUESTIONS

1. The money multiplier in an economy increases with which one of the following? **[2021]**

(a) Increase in the Cash Reserve Ratio in the banks.
(b) Increase in the Statutory Liquidity Ratio in the banks.
(c) Increase in the banking habit of the people.
(d) Increase in the population of the country.

2. With reference to **'Blockchain Technology'**, consider the following statements: **[2020]**

1. It is a public ledger that everyone can inspect, but which no single user controls.
2. The structure and design of blockchain is such that all the data in it are about cryptocurrency only.
3. Applications that depend on basic features of blockchain can be developed without anybody's permission.

Which of the statements given above is/are correct?

(a) 1 only
(b) 1 and 2 only
(c) 2 only
(d) 1 and 3 only

3. Supply of money remaining the same when there is increase in demand for money, there will be **[2013]**

(a) a fall in the level of prices
(b) an increase in the rate of interest
(c) a decrease in the rate of interest
(d) an increase in the level of income and employment

☞ NO QUESTIONS ASKED
2024, 2023, 2022, 2019, 2018, 2017, 2016, 2015, 2014

ANSWER KEY

1. (c) 2. (d) 3. (b)

UPSC CSE PREVIOUS YEARS' MAIN EXAMINATION QUESTIONS

☞ NO QUESTIONS ASKED
2024, 2023, 2022, 2021, 2020, 2019, 2018, 2017, 2016, 2015, 2014, 2013

CHAPTER

11

BANKING SECTOR IN INDIA

CHAPTER OUTLINE

- Banking in India
- History of Banking
- Reserve Bank of India
- Monetary Policy in India
- Quantitative Instruments of Credit Control
- Qualitative Instruments of Credit Control
- Structure of Banking System in India
- Commercial Banks
- State Bank of India
- Nationalised Banks
- Private Sector Indian Banks
- Private Sector Foreign Banks
- Regional Rural Banks
- Co-operative Banks
- The Banking Regulation (Amendment) Act, 2020
- Development Banks
- Non-Banking Financial Companies
- Primary Dealers
- Differentiated Banking
- Small Finance Banks
- Payments Banks
- Banks Board Bureau
- National Payments Corporation of India
- Banking Codes and Standards Board of India
- Advisory Board for Banking Frauds
- Indian Financial System Code
- MICR Code
- SWIFT Code
- Core Banking Solution
- Know Your Customer Norms
- Zero-Rupee Note
- Legal Entity Identifier
- Non-Performing Assets
- Asset Reconstruction Company
- Bad Bank
- Prompt Corrective Action
- Banking Stability Index/Indicator
- Basel Norms
- Systemically Important Financial Institutions
- Credit Rating of Banks in India
- Financial Inclusion
- National Strategy for Financial Inclusion (2019–24)
- National Strategy for Financial Education (2020–25)

BANKING IN INDIA

What is a Bank?

According to the Banking Companies Act of 1949, a bank is a financial entity that provides banking and other financial services to its customers. A bank is typically defined as an institution that provides basic financial services such as loan origination and deposit receipt.

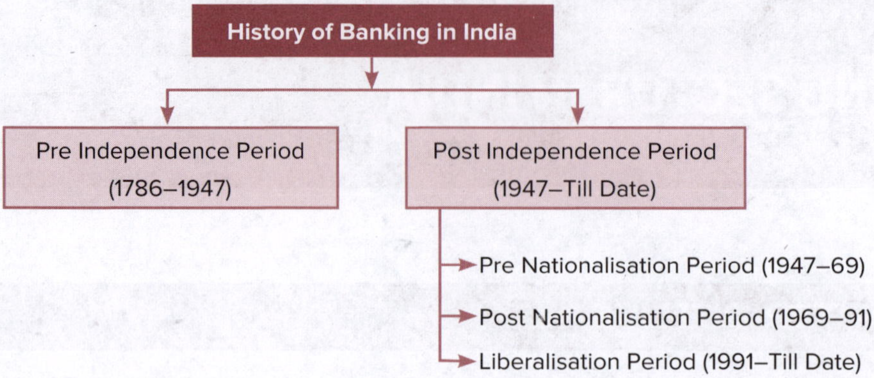

- Banking in India started in **1770** with the establishment of the **Bank of Hindustan.**
- The General Bank of India was established in 1786.
- Later, three Presidency Banks were set up:
  1. Bank of Calcutta in 1806
  2. Bank of Bombay in 1840
  3. Bank of Madras in 1843

  These banks worked as quasi-central banks for many years.
- In 1921, all these three banks were amalgamated to form the **Imperial Bank of India.** Imperial Bank of India continued functioning till 1955, after which it got renamed as **State Bank of India.**

did you KNOW?

- The Union Bank, which was established by Indian Merchants in 1865, failed within a decade.
- The Allahabad Bank was also established in 1865, which is the oldest PSB in India, serving for the last 146 years.
- The first bank completely managed by Indians was the Punjab National Bank.

- In 1922, the **Royal Commission on Indian Currency and Finance** was established under the chairmanship of **Hilton Young.** This Commission recommended the operation of money management in 1926. Based on the recommendations of this Commission, the 'Reserve Bank of India (RBI) Act' was passed in 1934 which came into effect on 1 April 1935.
- Initially (1935–37), the headquarters of RBI was located in Kolkata. Thereafter, it is situated in **Mumbai**.
- RBI continued to work as a Central Bank of:
  (i) **Burma**, till 1947 (ii) **Pakistan**, till July 1948
- Nationalisation of banks took place in **1969. Fourteen private banks were nationalised in 1969, and in 1980, six more were nationalised.**
- Post-1990s, many nationalised banks amalgamated gradually (*discussed later in the chapter*).

RESERVE BANK OF INDIA (RBI)

- The RBI was set up on the basis of the recommendations of the **Hilton Young Commission** (set up by the British Government in the 1920s).
- RBI was established in **1935** in accordance with the RBI Act, of 1934, and is India's central banking institution. It started its operations on **1 April 1935** during British rule as per the provisions of the RBI Act, 1934.

- RBI started as a shareholder's company (i.e. privately owned), but it became **nationalised in 1949** under RBI (Transfer of Public Ownership) Act, 1948, and, thereafter, is **fully owned by the Government of India (GoI).**
- The first Governor of RBI was **Sir Osborne Smith** (1935–37).
- The first Indian Governor of RBI was **C.D. Deshmukh** (1943–49).
- **Manmohan Singh** was the only Prime Minister who till now has also served as the Governor of RBI during different spans of time.
- At first, RBI's main office was located in Kolkata. But it was **moved to Mumbai** in **1937**. It has 4 Zonal Offices and about 22 Regional Offices.
- The emblem of RBI is a Tiger (earlier it was Lion) and a Palm tree.
- **First Reserve Bank note** was issued in January **1938**.
- In 1940, the silver rupee was replaced with the quaternary alloy rupee, and the one-rupee note was revived. This note had the status of a rupee coin and marked the advent of official fiat money in India.
- The RBI implemented **exchange control in India** for the first time in **1939** under the Defence of India guidelines. These limitations were also enforced in 1945 due to increased speculative activity in the banking and bullion markets.
- Security threads were initially used on rupee notes in 1944 as a security measure.
- RBI served as Pakistan's central bank till June 30, 1948. On July 1, 1949, the State Bank of Pakistan began operating as the country's central bank.
- On January 12, 1946, high-denomination bank notes of ₹500, ₹1000, and ₹10,000 were demonetised to reduce undeclared money.
- The **Preamble of RBI** describes the basic functions of RBI as: '*to regulate the issue of bank notes and keeping of reserves with a view to securing monetary stability in India and generally to operate the currency and credit system of the country to its advantage*'.
- Earlier the accounting year of RBI was from 1 July to 30 June. But from 2020–21 financial year, it has changed to 1 April to 31 March.
- RBI has **five fully owned subsidiaries**, namely:
  1. Deposit Insurance and Credit Guarantee Corporation **(DICGC)**
  2. Bharatiya Reserve Bank Note Mudran Private Limited **(BRBNMPL)**
  3. Reserve Bank Information Technology Private Limited **(ReBIT)**
  4. Indian Financial Technology and Allied Services **(IFTAS)**
  5. Reserve Bank Innovation Hub **(RBIH)**
- The affairs of the RBI are governed by a Central Board of Directors which comprises the following 21 members:
  - **Official Directors** which include:
    - Governor + not more than four Deputy Governors (for a tenure not more than 5 years)
  - **Non-Official Directors** which include:
    - 10 Directors from various fields (nominated by GoI and they hold office for 4 years).
    - 1 Director nominated by each of the 4 Local Boards of RBI.
    - 2 Government officials nominated by GoI.
- Governor and Deputy Governors of RBI are nominated by GoI, and they have tenure not more than 5 years.

- The Governor of the RBI draws his powers from the RBI Act. He shall have powers of general superintendence and direction of the affairs and the business of the RBI.

> **did you KNOW?** **Presently,** the Reserve Bank of India has **Shri Sanjay Malhotra** as the Governor (26th Governor) and **three Deputy Governors** namely, Shri T. Rabi Sankar, Shri Swaminathan J, and Shri M. Rajeshwar Rao.

Previously, the RBI had complete ownership of NHB and NABARD. However, in 2019, the government acquired the full stake in these institutions from the RBI. In the early 1990s, the Narasimham Committee suggested that the RBI, as a regulator, do not own financial firms.

Subsidiaries of RBI

Deposit Insurance and Credit Guarantee Corporation (DICGC)

- It was established in 1978 after Parliament approved the Deposit Insurance and Credit Guarantee Corporation Act of 1961, which amalgamated the Deposit Insurance Corporation (DIC) and the Credit Guarantee Corporation of India Ltd.
- It is a completely owned subsidiary of the Reserve Bank of India that offers deposit insurance.
- It covers deposit accounts up to a maximum of ₹5 lakh per bank account holder.
- If a bank account holder's deposit amount in a single bank reaches ₹5 lakh, the DICGC will pay up to ₹5 lakh, which includes interest and principal, if the bank goes bankrupt.

Bharatiya Reserve Bank Note Mudran Private Limited (BRBNMPL)

- In 1995, the Reserve Bank launched BRBNMPL as a wholly-owned subsidiary to boost bank note manufacturing in India and to bridge the country's supply and demand mismatch for bank notes. The BRBNMPL is a Public Limited Company incorporated under the Companies Act of 1956, having its registered and corporate offices in Bengaluru.
- The company operates two presses, one in Mysore, Karnataka, and the other in Salboni, West Bengal.

Reserve Bank Information Technology Private Limited (ReBIT)

- The Reserve Bank of India (RBI) established Reserve Bank Information Technology Pvt. Ltd. (ReBIT) in 2016 as a fully owned subsidiary to manage the Reserve Bank's and its regulated firms' IT requirements, including cyber security.

Indian Financial Technology and Allied Services (IFTAS)

- It is a completely owned subsidiary of the Reserve Bank of India.
- The IFTAS has taken over the Indian Financial Network (INFINITE), Structured Financial Messaging System (SFMS), and Indian Banking Community Cloud (IBCC) from the IDRBT.

Reserve Bank Innovation Hub (RBIH)

- The Reserve Bank Innovation Hub (RBIH) is a fully owned subsidiary of the Reserve Bank of India. It was established to encourage and enable an environment that fosters innovation in the financial industry. RBIH serves as a forum for all financial ecosystem players to share a common vision and develop forward-thinking innovation strategies while tackling the most critical concerns in the Indian financial sector.

Functions of RBI

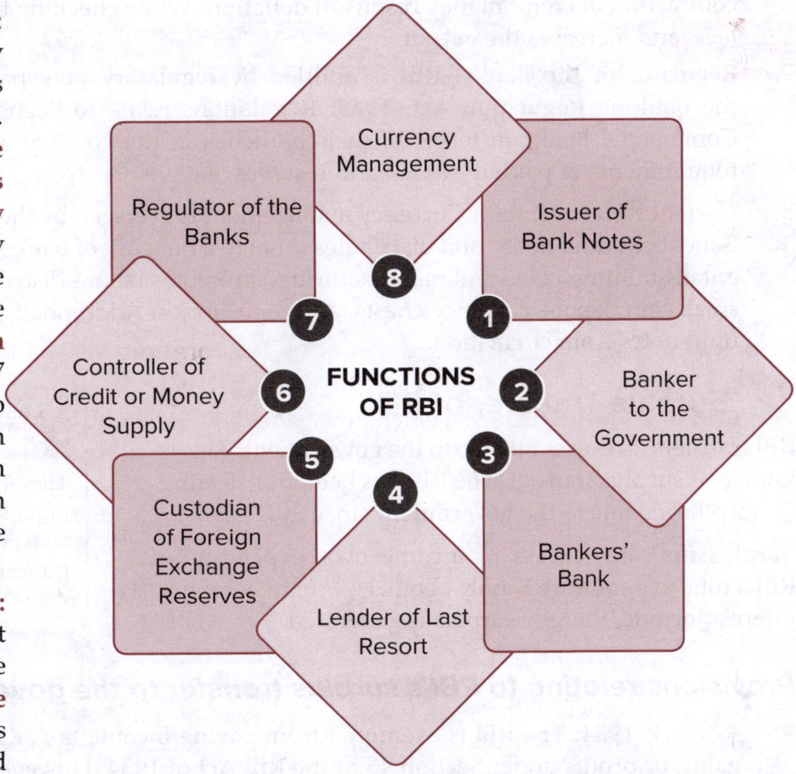

1. **Issuer of Bank Notes:** RBI enjoys the monopoly of issuing currency notes **except** for 1 rupee note. The **1 rupee note and the coins of all denominations are minted and issued by GoI** (and not RBI), but they are circulated through the RBI. The RBI adopted the **minimum reserve system** for note issue since 1957 according to which it has to maintain gold and foreign currency reserves of worth **₹200 crore**, out of which minimum of ₹115 crore should be in gold.
2. **Banker to the Government:** RBI acts as a banking agent and financial advisor to the **Central as well as the State Governments**. It manages Government accounts and treasuries. RBI provides short term loans to Central and State Governments through ways and Means Advances (WMA) for covering temporary shortfalls in their cash flow. Short term loan is provided for a maximum period of 90 days at an interest rate of the prevailing repo rate. RBI **buys and sells Government Securities (G-Secs)** on Government's behalf. It gives monetary and financial advice to the Governments.
3. **Bankers' Bank:** All the other banks in the country keep their part of cash balances with RBI as deposit to meet the liabilities in the time of crisis scheduled. Scheduled Commercial Banks keep cash balances in two ways:
    a. They keep part of cash balance with themselves, and
    b. The other part is kept with the RBI as deposits.
4. **Lender of Last Resort:** RBI is not only a banker to the banks but also a lender of last resort. That means, in times of crisis, the Scheduled Commercial Banks approach the RBI to get financial assistance. As RBI is the lender of last resort, it gives opportunity, enabling itself to exercise control over the banking system of the country.
5. **Custodian of Foreign Exchange Reserves:** RBI functions as the custodian of nation's foreign exchange reserves. In order to stabilise the rupee's external value, the RBI maintains the reserves of foreign currencies which also helps to stabilise exchange rate and promote international trade.
6. **Controller of Credit or Money Supply:** RBI controls the increase or decrease in the volume of money supply according to the monetary requirement of the nation. This is important so as to

control the inflation and deflation in the economy (by controlling the level of money supply in the market). More expansion of credit money or money supply can lead to inflation, whereas huge contraction of credit money results in deflation. While checking these, RBI stabilises general price level and increases the output.

7. **Regulator of the Banks:** RBI is entitled by regulatory powers under the **RBI Act, 1934,** and the **Banking Regulation Act, 1949.** Regulations relate to licencing of banks, expansion of the Commercial Banks in terms of their branches in the country or abroad, prescribing minimum requirements of paid-up capital and reserves, etc.

8. **Currency Management:** Currency management is overseen by the RBI, as it also forecasts demand, issues coins and notes, and distributes them to a network of banks and government treasuries. This entails minting coins and manufacturing banknotes before distributing them to a vast network of small coin depots, currency chests, and repositories. Additionally, the RBI oversees the removal of unfit notes from circulation.

Surplus Transfer of RBI

RBI transfers its excess income to the government. This is known as surplus transfer. The RBI has been transferring its surplus income to the government since 2018–19.

Surplus indicates excess of income over expenditure. RBI's total expenditure is only about $1/7^{th}$ of its total net interest income, thereby surplus is generated.

Last Minute SNIPPETS

The Reserve Bank of India approved highest-ever surplus transfer of ₹2.11 lakh crore to government for FY24. This is more than double the previous year's ₹86,416 crore.

Provisions relating to RBI's surplus transfer to the government

- **RBI Act, 1934:** The RBI is exempted from paying income tax or super tax on any of its earnings, gains, or profits under Section 48 of the RBI Act of 1934. However, after allocating funds for ADF and contingencies, it transfers its excess to the government.
- **Recommendations of different Committees:** Previously, RBI used to keep a major chunk of this surplus for its Contingency Fund (CF) and Asset Development Fund (ADF). Transfer of surplus to government increased after Malegam Committee's (2013) recommendations.

V Subrahmanyam (1997), Usha Thorat (2004), Y H Malegam (2013) and Bimal Jalan (2018) Committees were formed to decide the ideal amount of surplus transfer.

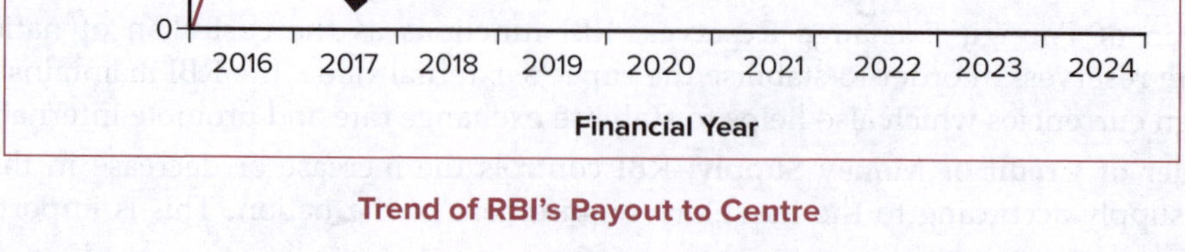

Trend of RBI's Payout to Centre

- **Economic Capital Framework (ECF):** It provides a method for figuring out how much profit sharing and risk provisions should be provided.
- **Economic capital (Currency and Gold Revaluation Account – CGRA):** It should be maintained in the range of 20.8–25.4 per cent of the balance sheet and the rest of the amount should be transferred to government.
- **CGRA** is the **unrealised gain/loss** in the value of gold and foreign exchange that RBI holds based on movements in their value which is not considered in the income account but taken as a balance-sheet item. The balances in CGRA provide a buffer against exchange rate/gold price fluctuations.

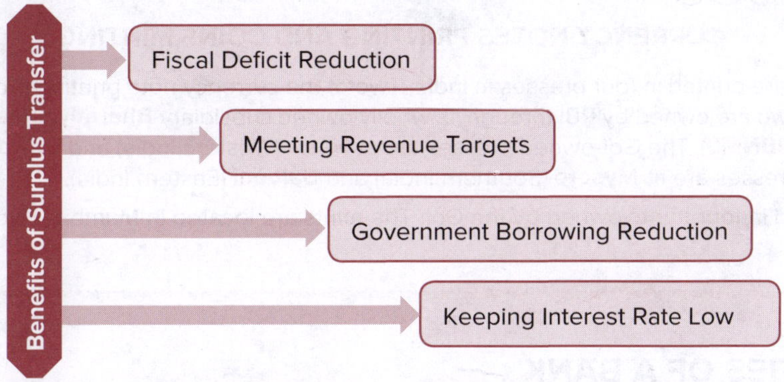

RBI's Income and Expenditure

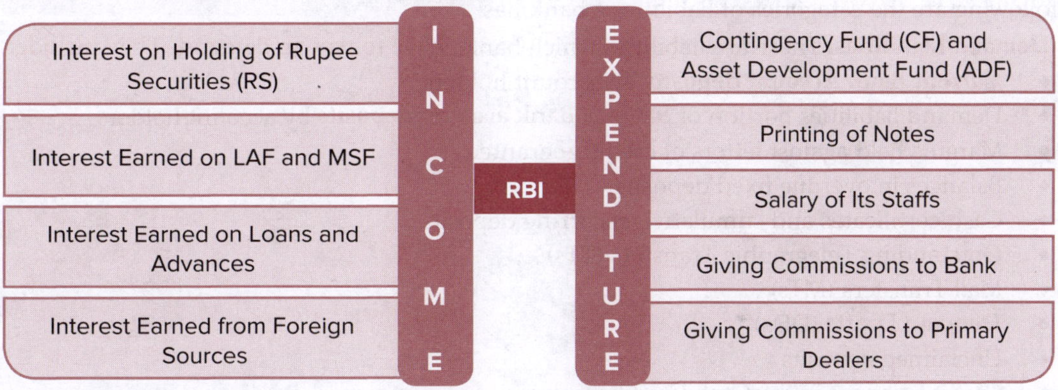

The Reserve Bank – Integrated Ombudsman Scheme, 2021

RBI integrated its three erstwhile Ombudsman Schemes viz. (i) the Banking Ombudsman Scheme, 2006, (ii) the Ombudsman Scheme for Non-Banking Financial Companies, 2018, and (iii) the Ombudsman Scheme for Digital Transactions, 2019, into one Scheme – 'The Reserve Bank – Integrated Ombudsman Scheme, 2021' **with effect from 2021. The Scheme simplifies the grievance redressal** process at RBI by enabling the customers of Regulated Entities (REs) like banks, Non-Banking Financial Companies (NBFCs), Payment System Participants (PSPs) and Credit Information Companies to register their complaints at one centralised reference point. The objective of the Scheme is to resolve the customer grievances involving 'deficiency in service' on part of REs in a speedy, cost-effective and satisfactory manner.

did you KNOW?

- As per Indian Coinage Act, 1906, Coins can be issued up to the denomination of ₹**1,000.** As per the Reserve Bank of India Act, 1934, Currency Notes can be issued up to the denomination of ₹**10,000**.
- The 1 rupee note is the only currency note which bears the signature of the **Finance Secretary** of the Government of India and not of the Governor of the Reserve Bank of India.

BONUS KNOWLEDGE

CURRENCY NOTES PRINTING AND COINS MINTING

Currency notes are printed in four presses in India. Two of the currency note printing presses are owned by the GoI and two are owned by RBI through its wholly owned subsidiary **Bharatiya Reserve Bank Note Mudran Ltd. (BRBNML)**. The GoI-owned presses are at **Nasik** (Western India) and **Dewas** (Central India). The other two presses are at **Mysore** (Southern India) and **Salboni** (Eastern India).

Coins are minted in four **mints** owned by the GoI. The mints are located in Mumbai, Hyderabad, Kolkata and Noida.

LIABILITIES OF A BANK

Deposits received by a bank are considered as liabilities to that bank as it has to pay back them in future. The following are the categories of liabilities a bank has:

1. **Demand Liabilities:** These are liabilities which banks **have to pay on demand. They include:**
   - **Current Bank Account deposits** by account holders
   - Demand liabilities portion of **Savings Bank account deposits** by account holders
   - Margins held against letters of credit/guarantees
   - Balances in overdue fixed deposits
   - Cash certificates and cumulative/recurring deposits
   - Outstanding Telegraphic Transfers (TTs)
   - Mail Transfers (MTs)
   - **Demand Drafts** (DDs)
   - Unclaimed deposits
   - Credit balances in the Cash Credit account
   - Deposits held as security for advances which are payable on demand
2. **Time Liabilities:** These are liabilities which banks have **to pay after specific time period.** They include:
   - **Fixed Deposits**
   - Cash Certificates
   - Cumulative and Recurring deposits
   - Time liabilities portion of Savings Bank deposits
   - Staff Security deposits
   - Margin held against Letters of Credit (LoC) if not payable on demand
   - Deposits held as securities for advances which are not payable on demand
   - **Gold deposits**

3. **Other Demand and Time Liabilities:** These include all those miscellaneous liabilities which are not specified under the above two types of liabilities. They include:
   - Interest accrued on deposits
   - Unpaid dividend
   - Suspense account balances showing the amount due to other banks or public
   - Participation Certificates issued to other banks
   - Cash collaterals, etc.

Total Demand and Time Liabilities **(DTL)** includes items mentioned in 1, 2 and 3 above.

Net Demand and Time Liabilities **(NDTL)** = DTL – Assets of the bank with other banks.

Assets of the bank include assets of the banks with other banks, advances by bank, investments by bank and money at call and short notice.

MONETARY POLICY IN INDIA

- It is a macro-economic policy tool used by **RBI** to influence the supply of money in the economy. As a part of Monetary Policy, the RBI uses various instruments to control the money supply or credit.
- Policy measures by RBI to increase money supply in the economy in order to promote economic growth are termed as **Monetary Easing**, and vice versa.

Monetary Policy Committee

The RBI Act, 1934, was amended in 2016 to provide a statutory and institutionalised framework for the creation of Monetary Policy Committee (MPC).

MPC was **set up in 2016** to meet the objective of Monetary Policy Framework Agreement (entered in 2015 between RBI and GoI) by entrusting RBI with the additional responsibility of **inflation targeting,** while keeping in mind the **objective of economic growth**.

As per Monetary Policy Framework Agreement, RBI is responsible **to contain annual inflation at 4 per cent (±2 per cent)** until March 2026 as per the current mandate. RBI is answerable to GoI if the inflation exceeds the range for three consecutive quarters. To target this inflation, policy interest rate (repo rate) is reviewed and changed periodically by RBI.

Before the constitution of MPC, the Governor of RBI in consultation with the Technical Advisory Committee of RBI and other experts used to fix the policy interest rate (repo rate). But from 2016, the MPC reviews and fixes the **benchmark policy rate (repo rate)** which is required to contain inflation within the specified target level.

Composition of MPC

As per the provisions of the amended RBI Act, out of the **total six members** in MPC:

- **Three members** are **from the RBI,** i.e. Governor, one Deputy Governor (who is in charge of monetary policy), and one official nominated by RBI.
- **Remaining three members** are **nominated by GoI**. These three external members hold office for 4 years and are not eligible for re-appointment. Parliamentary MPs, MLA/MLCs or public servants cannot be appointed as members of MPC by the GoI.

RBI Governor is the **ex-officio Chairperson** of MPC. The Committee **meets at least four times** in a year.

INSTRUMENTS OF CREDIT CONTROL

RBI uses various instruments as a monetary policy tool to effect the amount of money supply or the control of credit in the economy. These instruments can be divided into two categories.

- **Instruments of Credit Control**
  - Quantitative Instruments
  - Qualitative Instruments

Quantitative Instruments of Credit Control

- **Quantitative Instruments of Credit Control**
  - Bank Rate
  - Liquidity Adjustment Facility (LAF)
    - Repo Rate
    - Reverse Repo Rate
    - Marginal Standing Facility
    - Standing Deposit Facility
  - Open Market Operations (OMOs)
  - Reserve Requirements
    - Cash Reserve Ratio
    - Statutory Liquidity Ratio

1. Bank Rate

It is the rate of interest at which RBI provides **long-term loans** to Scheduled Commercial Banks (SCBs) **without** any approved securities (Treasury Bills, Cash Management Bills, Dated Securities and State Development Bills). Bank rate is fixed by RBI at **25 basis points (or 0.25 per cent) above the repo rate**.

As of 12 March 2025, bank rate stood at **6.5 per cent**.

2. Liquidity Adjustment Facility

Liquidity Adjustment Facility (LAF) is a monetary policy tool which allows banks to borrow money from RBI through repurchase agreements (repos) or to make loans to RBI through reverse repo agreements. As a result of the **Narasimhan Committee Report** on Banking Sector Reforms (1998), RBI introduced the LAF. It comprises the following four sub-instruments:

a. **Repo Rate (Re-purchase Option Rate):** It is the rate of interest at which RBI provides **short-term loans** to SCBs against approved securities. Repo rate as of 24 April 2025 stood at **6 per cent.**

Variable Repo Rate (VRR): A VRR is the rate of interest set by the Reserve Bank of India (RBI) that changes based on market conditions. RBI uses this monetary tool to manage liquidity in the banking system.

> **BONUS KNOWLEDGE**
>
> **LONG TERM REPO OPERATIONS (LTROS)**
>
> - It is a tool through which the Reserve Bank of India (RBI) provides **1 to 3 year loan** to **SCBs** at the prevailing repo rate, and accepting Government securities with matching or higher tenure as the collateral.

- Purpose of introducing LTRO by RBI is **to assure SCBs** about the availability of durable liquidity (1 to 3 years) at a reasonable cost, i.e. at repo rate. LTRO will help **bring down short-term market interest rates** charged by SCBs and will also boost investment in corporate bonds.
- Using LTRO, RBI aims to ensure that the impact of **increase in money supply** is appropriately converted in terms of **improved economic growth** of the Indian economy.

TARGETED LONG TERM REPO OPERATIONS (TLTRO)

- Targeted Long Term Repo Operations (TLTRO) used by RBI differs from LTRO in the sense that here loans provided are 'targeted', i.e. the SCBs have to deploy the funds availed under TLTRO scheme in specified securities (investment-grade corporate bonds, Commercial Paper and Non-convertible debentures) within the stipulated time frame. If the SCB does not abide, it has to pay penal interest which is quite high than the prevailing repo rate.

b. **Reverse Repo Rate**: Reverse Repo rate is the rate at which the RBI borrows funds from the Commercial Banks in the country. In other words, it is the rate at which Commercial Banks in India **park their excess funds** with RBI for a short period of time. As of 24 April 2025 reverse repo rate stood at 3.35 per cent.

c. **Marginal Standing Facility (MSF)**: This facility was introduced by RBI in 2011.

Eligibility: All the SCBs having current account with RBI can avail MSF. They can avail an **overnight short-term loan up to 2 per cent** of their Net Demand and Time Liabilities **(NDTL)** outstanding at the end of second preceding fortnight, against Government securities as collateral. This facility is in addition to loans on repo rate.

The minimum amount which can be accessed through MSF is ₹1 crore and in multiples of ₹1 crore. The rate of interest under MSF is 25 basis points (i.e. 0.25 per cent) above the repo rate. MSF rate of interest on 24 April 2025 stood at **6.25 per cent**.

d. **Standing Deposit Facility (SDF)**: RBI has introduced the Standing Deposit Facility (SDF) in 2022 as an additional tool for absorbing liquidity in the system and control inflation, without any collateral. The 2018 amended Section 17 of the RBI Act empowered the RBI to introduce the SDF. SDF is **also a financial stability tool** in addition to its role in liquidity management.

The SDF rate is **25 basis points below the policy rate** (Repo rate), and it is applicable to **overnight deposits** at this stage. It would, however, retain the flexibility to absorb liquidity of longer tenors as and when the need arises, with appropriate pricing.

The SDF has **replaced** the fixed rate reverse repo **(FRRR)** as the floor of the liquidity adjustment facility corridor. Both the standing facilities – the MSF (marginal standing facility) and the SDF are **available on all days** of the week, throughout the year.

As on 24 April 2025, SDF stood at 5.75 per cent.

Implications of LAF Deficit

- To raise funds, banks may increase the Deposit rates or introduce Special Deposit Schemes.
- Potential change in Repo rate from RBI may result in higher loan interest rates for consumers.
- Rise in money market rates may lead to increase in cost of borrowed funds. For instance, recently, there was a spike in yields on T-Bills because of tighter liquidity conditions.

3. Open Market Operations

Open Market Operations (OMOs) refer to the **buying and selling of** G-Secs in the open market (i.e. in the public) by the RBI. The RBI, by selling G-Secs, reduces the money supply by withdrawing cash balances from within the economic controls, thereby controlling inflation. Under OMO, sterilisation is a type of monetary policy objective in which a central bank aims to restrict the impact of capital inflows and outflows on the money supply. Classical sterilisation entails central banks buying and selling in open markets. It is often achieved by central bank's purchase or sale of financial assets, with the goal of offsetting the effects of foreign exchange intervention. It is a procedure that manipulates the value of one local currency compared to another.

BONUS KNOWLEDGE

OPERATION TWIST BY RBI

In **2019**, Operation Twist was done by RBI to **incentivise long-term investment** by lowering long-term interest rates.

This was done through **Open Market Operations** (OMOs) by selling short-term securities to buy long-term securities (or converting short-term securities into long-term securities).

The goal of Operation Twist is to lower the interest rate on long-term government bonds.

Operation Twist debuted in 1961 as a method to strengthen the US currency and boost capital flow into the economy.

4. Reserve Requirements

It comprises two ratios:

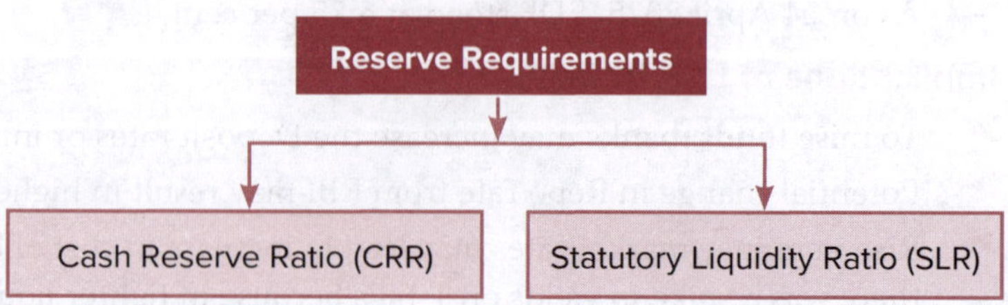

a. **Cash Reserve Ratio (CRR)**: It is the minimum percentage of a bank's **Total Demand and Time Liabilities** (DTL) (adjusted for certain exemptions) that a Scheduled Commercial Bank (SCB) is obliged to deposit with the Central Bank (RBI) in the form of cash.

RBI does not pay any interest on CRR balances maintained by SCBs with RBI.

The provisions of RBI Act do **not** prescribe any range (ceiling rate or floor rate) for fixing CRR.

To decrease money supply, the RBI increases CRR, and vice versa.

CRR is maintained on an **average basis during the fortnight**. All SCBs are required to daily maintain a minimum CRR balance of **95 per cent** of the average requirement.

> **Last Minute SNIPPETS**
>
> Initially, CRR was quite high, but it has been gradually brought down over years. The rate of CRR as of 24 April 2025 stood at 4.5 per cent of the Net DTL.

If the SCB fails to maintain CRR as fixed by RBI, then it is liable to pay penal interest at 3 per cent per annum above the bank rate, on the shortfall amount. If the shortfall continues for next succeeding day, penal interest is to be paid at Bank Rate + 5 per cent.

> **did you KNOW?**
>
> **Incremental Cash Reserve Ratio**
>
> In addition to **Cash Reserve Ratio** (CRR), the concept of Incremental CRR was introduced **by the RBI in 2016** as a purely temporary measure **to manage excess liquidity** in the economy post-demonetisation. This strategy aids the central bank in liquidity management and serves as a buffer during times of stress in the financial sector. **At present,** SCBs are **not required** to maintain any Incremental CRR.

b. **Statutory Liquidity Ratio (SLR)**: It is the percentage of Net Demand and Time Liabilities (NDTL) of SCBs that are to be kept with them only, in the form of:
   i. **Cash,** or
   ii. **Gold,** valued at a price not exceeding the current market price or
   iii. **SLR Securities** (certain dated securities or GoI Bonds, Treasury Bills, State Development Loans of the State Governments under Market Borrowing Programme and any other instrument notified by RBI).
   iv. Any combination of above three.

Note: Securities acquired by SCBs under RBI's LAF shall not be treated as SLR securities.

SLR can be seen as a mechanism used by SCBs to provide **credit to Government** through purchase of Government Securities.

Range of SLR prescribed by RBI is from **0 per cent to 40 per cent**.

To reduce inflation, RBI increases SLR, and to increase economic growth, RBI decreases SLR. (Please note: Generally, inflation and economic growth go hand in hand upto a certain level of inflation, i.e. they are directly proportional to each other in the initial stage but not in the long run.)

If the bank fails to maintain the required SLR, then it is liable to pay penal interest at 3 per cent per annum above the bank rate, on the shortfall amount. If the shortfall continues for next succeeding day, penal interest is to be paid at Bank Rate + 5 per cent.

Initially, the rate of SLR fixed by RBI was quite high (as high as 38.5 per cent of NDTL in 1991–92). However, based on recommendations of Narasimham Committee on banking sector reforms, the rate of SLR was gradually reduced.

Rate of SLR as of 24 April 2025 stood at 18 per cent of NDTL.

Marginal Cost of funds-based Lending Rate (MCLR) – It is the **minimum interest rate below which a bank cannot lend**. RBI introduced the MCLR methodology for fixing interest rates from **1 April 2016** replacing the base rate structure, which had been in place since July 2010. MCLR requires banks to charge interest rates based on marginal cost or incremental cost incurred by the banks to obtain the funds while the base rate was based on the average cost of funds.

Use of Quantitative Tools (in a nutshell)

Name of Instrument	To Reduce Inflation	To Increase Economic Growth
Cash Reserve Ratio (CRR)	Increase CRR	Decrease CRR
Statutory Liquidity Ratio (SLR)	Increase SLR	Decrease SLR
Repo Rate (RR)	Increase RR	Decrease RR
Reverse Repo Rate (RRR)	Increase RRR	Decrease RRR
Bank Rate (BR)	Increase BR	Decrease BR
Open Market Operations (OMOs)	Sell G-Secs	Buy G-Secs

EXAM ESSENTIAL

CASH RESERVE RATIO (CRR) *vs* STATUTORY LIQUIDITY RATIO (SLR)

Both the reserve requirement tools are used by the Reserve Bank of India (RBI) to regulate the supply of money in the economy. However:

- CRR is maintained by SCBs with RBI in cash, whereas SLR is maintained by SCBs themselves in the form of cash, gold and even Government-approved securities.
- SCBs are able to **earn money while maintaining SLR** in terms of Government-approved securities, whereas maintaining CRR with RBI does not earn any interest to them.
- **CRR is a short- to medium-term tool** of RBI, whereas change in **SLR has a long-term** impact on money supply.

Qualitative Instruments of Credit Control

These instruments aid or restrict the flow of credit to specific areas of the economic activity. Some of them are as follows:

- **Margin Requirements:** It refers to the part of loan amount which cannot be borrowed from bank. This is the difference between the value of securities offered for loans and the value of loans granted. To decrease money supply, the margin requirement is increased by RBI, and vice versa.
- **Rationing of Credit:** It refers to the **credit ceilings** (that can be granted by SCBs) being controlled by the RBI.
- **Moral (Per) Suasion:** RBI makes the banks adhere to the policy and directives through persuasion or pressure in order to maintain a certain level of money supply in the economy.

➤ **Consumer Credit Regulation**: RBI issues oral/written guidelines to the banks with regard to the down payments and maximum maturities of instalment credit for purchase of goods.

EXAM ESSENTIAL

POLICY STANCES OF THE RBI

The Reserve Bank of India's Monetary Policy Committee meets every two months to make crucial monetary policy decisions for the country. Monetary policy stances are mainly classified as **Dovish**, **Hawkish**, **Accommodative**, and **Neutral**.

Hawkish Monetary Policy Stance

- To keep inflation under control, the Hawkish approach advocates for **high interest** rates.
- Borrowing (taking out bank loans) will become less appealing as interest rates rise.
- Due to a lack of funds, customers would refrain from purchasing or purchasing less, as well as from obtaining credit (loans) from banks.
- This would result in **lower domestic demand** for goods and services. Because of the limited demand, prices for goods and services tend to stabilise. This would stop inflation. This forms a full circle.
- Interest rate increases might also lead the country's currency to strengthen.

Dovish Monetary Policy Stance

- This monetary policy stance includes low interest rates.
- Low interest rates would encourage people to get credit (loans) from banks and other sources.
- As demand rises, so will the prices of goods and services.
- Inflation will help to **balance economic growth**.
- Economists that advocate a Dovish Monetary Policy Stance often assume that lower interest rates will lead to an increase in employment and economic growth.
- This position may also result in the **devaluation of the country's currency**.

Accommodative Monetary Policy Stance

- This occurs when a central bank (RBI) seeks to increase the general money supply to stimulate the economy when growth is lagging. The primary goal is to boost spending.
- This is sometimes referred to as '**easy monetary policy**'.
- It accomplishes this by implementing a series of interest rate cuts, lowering the cost of borrowing.
- Accommodative money policy is used to stimulate increased expenditure by making money more affordable to borrow by decreasing short-term interest rates.

Neutral Monetary Policy Stance

- A 'neutral stance' suggests that the central bank can **either cut rate or increase rate**. This stance is typically **adopted when the policy priority is equal on both inflation and growth**.
- Taxation and government expenditure have little effect on stimulating (accelerating) or slowing economic growth.
- Economic circumstances are ideal.

Sometimes, the RBI goes a step further and mentions words like:

- **Quantitative Easing**
- **Calibrated tightening**

Quantitative Easing (QE): It is a policy under which the RBI **purchases longer-term securities from the open market** and injects money in the economy, thereby increasing the money supply to encourage lending and investment and ultimately promote economic growth. It is the last resort which is used by RBI to stimulate spending in an economy **when interest rates fail** to work.

Calibrated Tightening: It means during the current rate cycle, a cut in the repo rate is off the table. However, the **rate hike will happen in a calibrated manner**. This means the **central bank may not go for a rate increase in every policy meeting** but the overall policy stance is tilted towards a rate hike. This can happen outside the policy meetings as well if the situation warrants.

did you KNOW?

Consolidated Sinking Fund (CSF)

- Article 266(1) of the Indian Constitution contains provisions for this fund.
- **State Governments maintain a CSF with the RBI** as a buffer for repayment of their liabilities.

BONUS KNOWLEDGE

MONETARY POLICY REPORT AND FINANCIAL STABILITY REPORT

The RBI is required to publish, once in **every six months**, a Monetary Policy Report (MPR) which contains

1. an explanation of inflation dynamics in the last six months and near term inflation outlook
2. projections of inflation and growth for the period between six to eighteen months from the date of publication.

The RBI also publishes **Financial Stability Report** (FSR) **biannually** which reflects an assessment of the sub-committee of the Financial Stability and Development Council (FSDC) on the risks to financial stability.

(Before the examination, aspirants may benefit by reading the most recent MPR and FSR published by RBI.)

Major Acts Administered by the RBI

- Reserve Bank of India Act, 1934
- Public Debt Act, 1944/Government Securities Act, 2006
- Government Securities Regulations, 2007
- Banking Regulation Act, 1949
- Foreign Exchange Management Act, 1999
- Securitisation and Reconstruction of Financial Assets and Enforcement of Security Interest (SARFAESI) Act, 2002 (Chapter II)
- Credit Information Companies (Regulation) Act, 2005
- Payment and Settlement Systems Act, 2007 (as amended upto 2019)
- Factoring Regulation Act, 2011

PRAVAAH PORTAL

PRAVAAH *(Platform for Regulatory Application, VAlidation and AutHorisation)* portal is a secure and centralised web-based portal for any individual or entity to seek authorisation, license or regulatory approval on any reference made by it to the **RBI**.

STRUCTURE OF BANKING SYSTEM IN INDIA

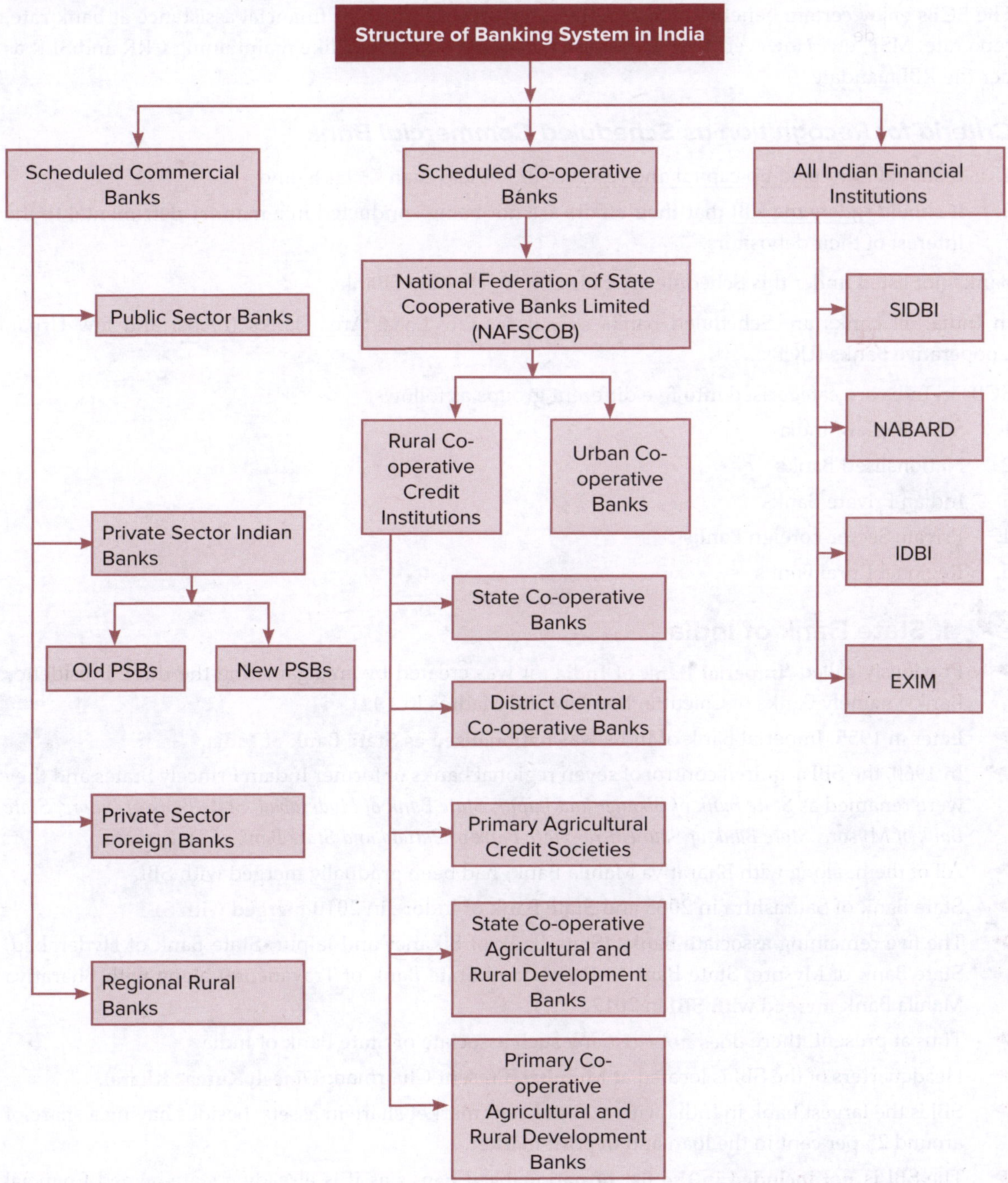

A Scheduled Commercial Bank (SCB) refers to a bank which is **listed in the Second Schedule** of the RBI Act, 1934. SCBs are **regulated** under the provisions of Banking Regulation Act, 1949.

The SCBs enjoy certain benefits such as – they can approach RBI for financial assistance at bank rate, repo rate, MSF, etc. However, they are bound by certain obligations like maintaining CRR and SLR as per the RBI mandate.

Criteria for Recognition as Scheduled Commercial Bank

1. It should have paid-up capital and reserves of not less than **₹5 lakh,** and
2. It should satisfy the RBI that their affairs are not being conducted in a manner detrimental to the interest of their depositors.

Banks not listed under this Schedule are called Non-Scheduled Banks.

In India, all banks are Scheduled banks **except for** few Local Area Banks (LABs) and few Urban Cooperative Banks (UCBs).

SCBs in India are categorised into five different groups as follows:

1. State Bank of India
2. Nationalised Banks
3. Indian Private Banks
4. Private Sector Foreign Banks
5. Regional Rural Banks

1. State Bank of India

- Previously called **'Imperial Bank of India'**, it was created by amalgamating the three Presidency Banks, namely Banks of Calcutta, Bombay and Madras in **1921**.
- Later in 1955, Imperial Bank of India was **nationalised as State Bank of India**.
- In 1960, the SBI acquired control of seven regional banks of former Indian Princely States and they were renamed as *State Bank of Bikaner and Jaipur, State Bank of Hyderabad, State Bank of Indore, State Bank of Mysore, State Bank of Saurashtra, State Bank of Patiala and State Bank of Travancore*.
- All of them, along with Bharatiya Mahila Bank, had been gradually merged with SBI.
- State Bank of Saurashtra in 2008 and State Bank of Indore in 2010 **merged with SBI**.
- The five remaining associate Banks (State Bank of Bikaner and Jaipur, State Bank of Hyderabad, State Bank of Mysore, State Bank of Patiala and State Bank of Travancore) along with Bharatiya Mahila Bank **merged with SBI** in 2017.
- Thus at present, there **does not exist** any such associate of State Bank of India.
- Headquarters of the SBI is located at **Mumbai** (Present Chairman: **Dinesh Kumar Khara**).
- SBI is the largest bank in India with a 23 per cent market share in assets, besides having a share of around 25 per cent in the loan and deposit market.
- The SBI is **not included in the list of nationalised banks** as it is already a state-owned financial institution in the country since its inception. GoI has more than 50 per cent shareholding in SBI.

2. Nationalised Banks

- Due to the banking crisis of 1913–17 and the failure of 588 banks in various parts of the country at the end of 1949, it was necessary to regulate and control Commercial Banks.
- The **Banking Companies Act** was passed in 1949, which later became **Banking Regulation Act, 1949.** It provides a legal framework for the regulation of banking system in India.
- In the year 1969, certain provisions were introduced in Banking Regulation Act, 1949, that brought social control on banks. Thereafter, **14 banks were nationalised in 1969**.
- This provision brought some restrictions on advances made by banking companies so that the bank advances were not concentrated only in large-scale industries, and to shift their priorities towards sectors like agriculture, small-scale industries and exports.
- **In 1980**, six more banks having DTL of minimum ₹200 crore were nationalised (now taking the total number of nationalised banks to 20).
- **In 1993**, New Bank of India was merged with Punjab National Bank. It happened to be the only merger between nationalised banks and that reduced the number of nationalised banks from 20 to 19.
- Reasons for Nationalisation:
  1. Concentration of economic power in few hands.
  2. Private ownership of Commercial Banks.
  3. Banks previously located mainly in urban areas, thereby neglecting the development of agricultural and rural areas as it was not the priority sector.
- Progress after Nationalisation:
  1. Expansion of the number of branches (even in rural areas).
  2. Priority sector lending increased.
  3. Level of deposit mobilisation and bank lending increased.
  4. Banks started financing schemes which promoted entrepreneurship.

AMALGAMATION OF PUBLIC SECTOR BANKS

In 2020, the Government of India accomplished the **mega amalgamation of 10 Public Sector Banks (PSBs) into four PSBs** with effect from 1 April 2020:

- Amalgamation of Oriental Bank of Commerce and United Bank of India into **Punjab National Bank**.
- Amalgamation of Syndicate Bank into **Canara Bank**.
- Amalgamation of Andhra Bank and Corporation Bank into **Union Bank of India**.
- Amalgamation of Allahabad Bank into **Indian Bank**.

Benefits of such amalgamation:

- This mega consolidation would help create banks that can **compete with global banks** effectively.
- **Greater scale and synergy** through consolidation would lead to cost benefits to these banks.
- It will also provide impetus to amalgamated banks by increasing their **ability to support larger lending** and greater financial capacity.
- Access to a **wider talent pool** and a larger database will enhance their competitive advantage.
- **Adoption of best practices** across amalgamating entities will facilitate banks in improving their cost-efficiency and risk management.

Therefore, at present, there are **following 12 PSBs (11 Nationalised Banks + SBI)**. They are:

1. Punjab National Bank (PNB)
2. Bank of Baroda
3. Bank of India
4. Central Bank of India
5. Canara Bank
6. Union Bank of India (UBI)
7. Indian Overseas Bank
8. Punjab & Sind Bank
9. Indian Bank
10. UCO Bank
11. Bank of Maharashtra
12. State Bank of India (SBI)

After this merger, the PNB stands as the second-largest PSB in India after SBI.

3. Private Sector Indian Banks

- The bank whose major share of capital is held by a private stockholder is known as a Private Sector Bank. Private Sector banks are of **two types** in India, namely:
  a. **Old Private Sector Banks**: These are banks that were not nationalised in 1969 and in 1980 due to their small size and regional focus.
  b. **New Private Sector Banks**: These are banks that came into existence after 1991 with the introduction of economic reforms and financial sector reforms. Banking Regulation Act got amended in 1993 and allowed the entry of New Private Sector Banks.
- Private banks in India are regulated by the RBI under the Banking Regulation Act, 1949, with guidelines covering aspects such as capital requirements, ownership, governance, and operations.

Examples of Indian Private Banks include HDFC Bank, Axis Bank, ICICI Bank, Bandhan Bank, Yes Bank, etc.

4. Private Sector Foreign Banks

Foreign banks seeking to operate in India must apply to the RBI, providing detailed information about their shareholders' financial position, and other relevant details.

Those operating in India, including private foreign banks, are regulated by the RBI and must comply with the same regulations as domestic banks, with some exceptions. Additionally, they are encouraged to operate through Wholly-Owned Subsidiaries (WOS).

Foreign banks can set up its Wholly-Owned Subsidiary (**WOS**) and also convert existing branches of foreign banks into WOS. The rules for it, as prescribed by RBI, are given hereunder:

Eligibility of parent bank for WOS

1. Foreign banks are subject to adequate prudential supervision in their home country. In considering the standard of supervision exercised by the home country regulator, the RBI will have regard to the Basel standards.
2. The setting up of a WOS in India should have the **approval of the home country regulator**.
3. Other factors (but not limited to) that will be taken into account by RBI are given below:
   i. Economic and political relations between India and the country of incorporation of the foreign bank
   ii. **Financial soundness** of the foreign bank
   iii. **Ownership pattern** of the foreign bank

iv. International and home country ranking of the foreign bank
v. **Rating of the foreign bank** by international rating agencies
vi. **International presence** of the foreign bank

Capital Requirement

The **minimum start-up capital requirement** for a WOS would be **₹3 billion** and the WOS shall be required to maintain a capital adequacy ratio of 10 per cent or as may be prescribed from time to time on a continuous basis, from the commencement of its operations.

The parent foreign bank will continue to hold **100 per cent equity in the Indian subsidiary** for a minimum prescribed period of operation.

Corporate Governance

The composition of the Board of Directors of WOS of a Foreign Bank should meet the following requirements:

- **Not less than 50 per cent** of the Directors should be **Indian nationals** residing in India.
- **Not less than 50 per cent** of the Directors should be **non-executive directors**.
- A minimum of one-third of the directors should be totally independent of the management of the subsidiary in India, its parent or associates.
- The directors shall conform to the **'Fit and Proper'** criteria as laid down in RBI's extant guidelines dated June 25, 2004.

Accounting, Prudential Norms and other requirements

i. The WOS will be subject to the licensing requirements and conditions, **broadly consistent with those for new private sector banks**.
ii. The WOS will be treated on par with the existing branches of foreign banks for branch expansion. The Reserve Bank may also prescribe market access and national treatment limitation consistent with WTO as also other appropriate limitations to the operations of WOS, consistent with international practices and the country's requirements.
iii. The banking subsidiary will be governed by the provisions of the **Companies Act, 2013, Banking Regulation Act, 1949, Reserve Bank of India Act, 1934,** other relevant statutes and the directives, prudential regulations and other guidelines/instructions issued by RBI.

Examples of Private Sector Foreign Banks include CitiBank, HSBC, Deutsche Bank, American Express, etc.

5. Regional Rural Banks

- As the purpose of nationalisation of banks was not that much served, in **1975,** the concept of Regional Rural Bank (RRB) was introduced. Examples of RRB include Paschim Banga Gramin Bank, Andhra Pragathi Grameena Bank, etc.
- The RRBs were established under the provisions of an Ordinance passed in 1975 and the RRBs Act, 1976, to provide sufficient banking and credit facility for **agriculture and other rural sectors**. RRBs were set up on the recommendations of the **M. Narasimham Working Group**.
- At present, each RRB is owned by three entities: **Central Government, Concerned State Government and the Sponsor Bank** in the proportion of **50:15:35**, respectively.

- RRBs are **SCBs**.
- There **may be one or more RRBs in a particular State**.
- RRBs mobilise deposits primarily from rural/semi-urban areas and provide loans and advances mostly to small and marginal farmers, agricultural labourers, rural artisans and other segments of the priority sector.
- The sources of funds of RRBs comprise owned funds, deposits, borrowings from NABARD, Sponsor Banks and other sources, including SIDBI and National Housing Bank.
- The RRBs are **supervised by NABARD and have to follow the regulatory norms prescribed by RBI**.

> **did you KNOW?** **As of 24 April 2025**, there are 43 RRBs in India.

CO-OPERATIVE BANKS

- Co-operative Banks in India are incorporated and registered under the States' Co-operative Societies Act (passed by States). The Co-operative Banks are also **regulated** through the following Acts of Central Government:
    1. **Banking Regulations Act, 1949**
    2. **Banking Laws (Co-operative Societies) Act, 1955**
- Co-operative Banks are involved in all kinds of activities, namely production, marketing, distribution, possessing, servicing and banking in India.
- They function with the rule of **'one member one vote'** and on **'no profit no loss'** basis. Hence, they do not pursue the goal of profit maximisation.
- **Customers are the owners** of the Co-operative Banks.
- Co-operative Banks mainly focus on **agricultural and rural sector lending**.
- For providing short-term credit, Co-operative Banks in India exist in three tiers:
    1. State Co-operative Banks (at the State level)
    2. District Co-operative Central Banks (at the District level)
    3. Primary Agricultural Credit Societies (PACS) (at the village level)

  Co-operative Banks dealing with long-term credit are:
    - Land Development Banks (LDBs), and
    - Co-operative and Rural Development Banks (CARDBs)
- Co-operative Banks are the first Government-sponsored, Government-supported and Government-subsidised financial agency in India.

BONUS KNOWLEDGE

In **2020**, the Government of India has approved to bring regulation of Co-operative Banks **under the Reserve Bank of India (RBI)** by bringing amendments in Banking Regulation Act, 1949. Before this, they were under the dual control of RBI and State Governments (through Registrar of Co-operative Societies).

This amendment was done in the wake of the recent Punjab and Maharashtra Co-operative (PMC) Bank crisis.

The amendments will also **apply to all Urban Co-operative Banks (Primary Co-operative Banks) and Multi-State Co-operative Banks**. Urban Cooperative Banks were brought under the purview of the Banking Regulation Act, 1949 through an Amendment **in 1966.**

As per the changes:

- Co-operative Banks should be **audited according to RBI's norms.**
- **RBI can supersede** the board, in consultation with the State Government, if any Co-operative Bank is under stress.
- Appointment of CEOs of Co-operative Banks will also require permission from RBI.

Revised Regulatory Framework for Urban Co-operative Banks (UCBs)

In 2021, the RBI had constituted an Expert Committee on Urban Co-operative Banks under the chairmanship of **Shri N. S. Vishwanathan**, former Deputy Governor, RBI, to scrutinise the issues related to UCBs, to suggest measures for faster resolution and to provide a medium-term road map to strengthen this sector.

Following are the major recommendations of the committee:

i. The committee has recommended to replace the current two-tiered framework with **four-tiered regulatory framework** to strengthen the financial soundness of the existing UCBs.

TIER IV	UCBs with deposits more than ₹10,000 crore.
TIER III	UCBs with deposits more than ₹1,000 crore and less than equal to ₹10,000 crore.
TIER II	UCBs with deposits more than ₹100 crore and less than equal to ₹1,000 crore.
TIER I	UCBs having deposits up to ₹100 crore.

ii. To strengthen the financial soundness of the existing UCBs, a minimum net worth of ₹2 crore has been stipulated for Tier I UCBs operating in single district and that for other UCBs of all tiers, it is ₹5 crore. If any of the UCBs does not meet the requirement, then a glide path of five years shall be provided to facilitate a smooth transition to revised norms.

iii. The minimum Capital to Risk Weighted Assets Ratio (CRAR) is to be retained at 9 per cent for Tier I UCBs under current capital adequacy framework based on Basel I norms. On the other hand, CRAR for the rest of the UCBs to be revised at 12 per cent to strengthen their capital structure.

iv. To introduce automatic route for branch expansion to UCBs, they have to fulfil the revised criteria of Financially Sound and Well Managed (FSWM), which are as follows:

a. Net NPA should not be more than 3 per cent.
b. No default in the maintenance of CRR/SLR during the preceding financial year.
c. Sound internal control system with at least two professional directors on the Board.
d. Core Banking Solution (CBS) fully implemented.

v. The Committee has also made certain recommendations regarding Umbrella Organisation for UCB Sector which will be examined once the entity is fully operational.

The Banking Regulation (Amendment) Act, 2020

The existing 1949 Act was amended **in 2020,** to expand RBI's regulatory control over Co-operative Banks in terms of management, capital, audit and liquidation, so as to provide for better management and proper regulation of Co-operative Banks.

This was done to ensure that the affairs of the Co-operative Banks are conducted in a manner that protects the interests of the depositors, increases professionalism, enables better access to capital, improves the governance and ensures sound banking through the RBI.

The Amended Act **does not apply** to certain categories of co-operative societies/banks namely:

(i) Primary Agricultural Credit Societies (PACS) and

(ii) Co-operative Societies whose principal business is long-term financing for agricultural development.

In short, only certain categories of Co-operative Banks have been brought under the RBI supervision process, same as that applicable to Scheduled Commercial Banks (SCBs).

Such a move to bring Urban Co-operative Banks (UCBs) under the supervision of the RBI comes after several instances of fraud and serious financial irregularities [major scam/crisis at the Punjab and Maharashtra Co-operative (PMC) in 2019].

DEVELOPMENT BANKS

They provide long-term finance and support to the sectors of the Indian economy, which possess higher risks and cannot have access to adequate loans from Commercial Banks.

Major Development Banks in India include:

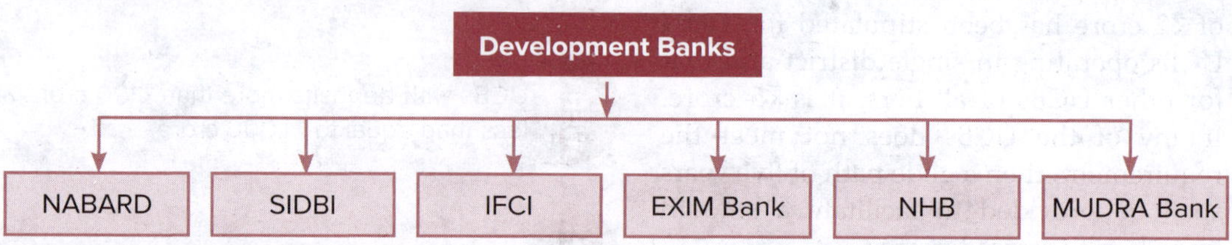

National Bank for Agriculture and Rural Development

National Bank for Agriculture and Rural Development (NABARD) is the apex development bank, **headquartered at Mumbai**, with branches all over India.

NABARD was established on the recommendations of **B. Sivaraman Committee** on **12 July 1982** to implement the *National Bank for Agriculture and Rural Development Act, 1981.* It **replaced the Agricultural Credit Department (ACD)** and **Rural Planning and Credit Cell (RPCC)** of RBI, and also **Agricultural Refinance and Development Corporation (ARDC)**.

The Bank has been entrusted with matters concerning policy, planning and operations in the field of credit for agriculture and other economic activities in the rural areas of India.

The authorised capital of NABARD has been raised to **₹30,000 crore** in 2018.

NABARD is the main agency for implementing **Rural Infrastructure Development Fund (RIDF)** scheme. NABARD discharges its duty by undertaking the **following roles**:

1. Serves as an **apex financing agency** for the institutions providing investment and production credit for promoting the various developmental activities **in rural areas**.
2. NABARD **refinances the financial institutions** which finance the rural sector.
3. NABARD **supervises** the **RRBs**.

NABARD's refinance facility is available to State Co-operative Agriculture and Rural Development Banks (SCARDBs), State Co-operative Banks (SCBs), RRBs, Commercial Banks and other financial institutions approved by RBI.

In 2019, RBI sold its stake in NABARD to GoI. Thus, **now NABARD is fully owned by GoI**.

Small Industries Development Bank of India

Small Industries Development Bank of India (SIDBI) was set up in **1990**, as an independent financial institution aimed to aid the growth and development of **Micro, Small and Medium scale Enterprises (MSMEs)** in India.

It was incorporated initially as a **wholly owned subsidiary of Industrial Development Bank of India (IDBI)**. Currently, the **ownership is held by GoI** and many other **GoI-owned/controlled institutions**.

Beginning as a **refinancing agency to banks** and State-level financial institutions for their credit to small industries, it has expanded its activities including direct credit to the SMEs. SIDBI is **headquartered in Lucknow**.

To promote and develop the MSME sector, SIDBI adopts a **'Credit+' approach** under which, besides credit, it supports enterprise development, skill upgradation, marketing cluster development, technology modernisation, etc., through its promotional and developmental support to MSMEs.

Industrial Finance Corporation of India

Industrial Finance Corporation of India (IFCI) Ltd. was set up in **1948** as **Industrial Finance Corporation of India** (a Statutory Corporation), through **'The Industrial Finance Corporation of India Act, 1948'** to provide medium- **and long-term finance to industry**.

IFCI became a Public Limited Company in 1993 by being registered under the Companies Act, 1956. IFCI is also a Systemically Important Non-Deposit–taking Non-Banking Finance Company **(NBFC-ND-SI)** registered with the RBI. The primary business of IFCI is to provide **medium- to long-term financial assistance** to the **manufacturing**, **services** and **infrastructure** sectors. Through its subsidiaries and associate organisations, IFCI has diversified into a range of other businesses, including broking, venture capital, financial advisory, depository services, factoring, etc.

Export–Import Bank

Export–Import Bank (EXIM Bank) was set up in **1982** to take over the operations of international finance wing of the IDBI and to provide financial assistance to exporters and importers. The EXIM Bank is **wholly owned by the Central Government**.

Functions of EXIM Bank include the following:

1. It provides direct **financial assistance to exporters** of plant, machinery and related services in the form of medium-term credit.

2. It **rediscounts the export bills** for a period not exceeding 90 days against short-term export bills discounted by Commercial Banks.
3. It gives overseas **buyers credit to foreign importers** for import of Indian capital goods and related services.
4. It facilitates in developing and **financing export-oriented industries**.

National Housing Bank

- National Housing Bank (NHB) was set up as a statutory organisation, in **1988**, under the National Housing Bank Act, 1987. It is under the jurisdiction of **Ministry of Finance**, Government of India.
- NHB is an **apex financial institution for housing**.
- NHB has been established with an objective to operate as a principal agency **to promote housing finance institutions** both at local and regional levels and to provide financial and other support incidental to such institutions and for matters connected therewith.
- NHB registers, regulates and supervises **Housing Finance Companies (HFCs)**, keeps surveillance through on-site and offsite mechanisms and co-ordinates with other regulators.
- **Headquarters of NHB** are located in **Delhi**.
- **NHB is regulated by RBI.**
- After RBI sold its stake in NHB in 2019, the NHB is **now 100 per cent owned by GoI**. It was done based on the recommendations of the Narasimham panel, which stated that RBI should not own entities that are regulated by it.

MUDRA Bank

Micro Units Development and Refinance Agency Bank (MUDRA Bank) was set up in **2015** by the GoI to provide **loans at low rates to Micro Finance Institutions (MFIs) and non-banking financial institutions** which then provide credit to MSMEs. The MUDRA Bank was set up under the Pradhan Mantri MUDRA Yojana scheme.

Persons eligible to borrow from MUDRA Bank include: small manufacturing units, service sector units, shopkeepers, fruits/vegetable vendors, truck operators, food-service units, repair shops, machine operators, small industries, artisans, food processors and others, in rural and urban areas.

Its products of loan have been named 'Shishu', 'Kishore' and 'Tarun' to signify the stage of growth of the beneficiary micro units/entrepreneurs.

- **Shishu**: Covering loans up to ₹50,000
- **Kishore**: Covering loans above ₹50,000 and up to ₹5 lakh
- **Tarun**: Covering loans above ₹5 lakh and up to ₹10 lakh

The MUDRA Bank are largely responsible for:

- Establishing regulatory parameters for micro/small enterprise funding businesses.
- Registration of MFI Entities.
- Regulation of MFI Entities.
- Accreditation and grading of MFI entities.
- Establishing appropriate financing processes to avoid debt and provide effective client protection principles and means of recovery.

- Creation of a standardised set of covenants controlling last-mile financing to micro/small businesses.
- Promoting appropriate technological solutions for the final mile.
- Developing and implementing a Credit Guarantee system to provide guarantees for loans provided to micro firms.
- Developing an effective Last Mile Credit Delivery infrastructure for micro companies under the Pradhan Mantri Mudra Yojana.

Local Area Banks

Introduced in 1996, **Local Area Banks** (LABs) are small private banks which provide financial intermediation services in a limited area of operation (primarily in rural and semi-urban areas, comprising **three contiguous districts**). The objective of setting up LABs was to enable mobilisation of rural savings and to make them available for investments in the local areas. RBI guidelines for LABs include the following:

a. LABs should have a minimum capital of ₹5 crore.
b. Promoter of LAB may comprise private individuals, corporate entities, trusts and societies with a minimum capital contribution of ₹2 crore.
c. Area of operation is limited to a maximum of three geographically contiguous districts.
d. Should have priority sector lending targets at 40 per cent of the Net Bank Credit (NBC).

In 2014, the RBI permitted LABs to be converted into Small Finance Banks *(explained below)* subject to meeting prescribed eligibility criteria.

Examples of LAB includes Coastal Local Area Bank Limited, Capital Local Area Bank Limited, etc.

Neobanks

The term 'Neobank' refers to '**fintech firms**' that solely have a **digital presence** and have no physical locations. They **provide banking services** such as savings accounts, instant loans, credit cards, mutual funds and fixed deposits. They accomplish it by forming partnerships with banks that are licensed by the RBI. Example: Fampay, Mahila Money, RazorpayX, Fi Money, Jupiter, Niyo, etc.

Neobanks typically obtain investment adviser licences for items such as wealth management. They usually form alliances with the SFBs or small SCBs. They are increasingly making inroads into the Indian market.

Neobank vs. Traditional bank: While traditional banks struggle to modernise their legacy-based infrastructure, neobanks use new digital platforms to evaluate client data and make data-driven choices.

Neobanks vs. Digital banks: A digital bank and a neobank are not the same. While digital banks are frequently the online-only arm of a larger participant in the banking sector, neobanks are entirely digital and operate independently of traditional banks.

Benefits

- They are typically mobile-first, relying on technology to cut expenses and provide a user-friendly experience.
- Neobanks have partnered with small banks to offer greater interest rates on savings accounts.
- They help to analyse and track the spending.

Issues

Complex IT legacy, inadequate data architecture, higher cost management, organisational resistance, lacking advanced technology.

NON-BANKING FINANCIAL COMPANIES

- Non-Banking Financial Company (NBFC) is a company which is engaged in the business of loans and advances, acquisition and selling of shares, bonds, debentures, or leasing, insurance, chit-fund, etc. It is a **very broad concept** and has many variations.
- In 2016, the Government allowed 100 per cent FDI in 'other financial services' carried out by NBFCs.
- NBFC's **financial assets should constitute more than 50 per cent of the total assets** and **income from financial assets should constitute more than 50 per cent of the gross income**.
- NBFCs **cannot accept demand deposits** from the public. However, debentures and bonds are not demand liabilities; therefore, it can be used by NBFCs to raise funds.
- **Not all NBFCs** are regulated by RBI. For example, the Venture Capital Fund/Merchant Banking companies/Stock broking companies are regulated by SEBI, Insurance Companies by IRDA, etc.

NBFCs Regulated by RBI

Structure of NBFIs under the RBI Regulation
(as of 28 February 2024)

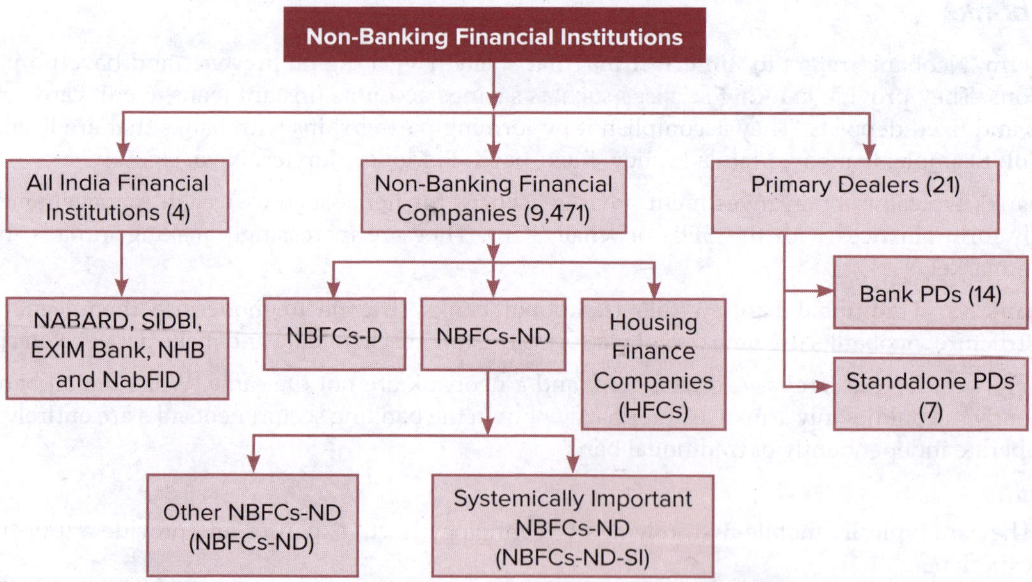

Notes: 1. Data are provisional D – Deposit taking; ND – Non-deposit taking

2. Figures in parentheses indicate the number of institutions.

Source: RBI.

Out of the above flow chart, details of **some major types of NBFCs regulated by RBI** are as follows:

Type of NBFC	Activity involved
NBFC-Investment and Credit Company **(NBFC-ICC)**	• Initially, types of NBFCs included Asset Finance Company (AFC), Investment Company (IC) and Loan Company (LC). **In 2019**, above three categories of NBFCs have been merged into a new category NBFC – Investment and Credit Company (NBFC-ICC). It has been done to harmonise the rules and regulations and provide greater operational flexibility to the NBFCs. • It deals with the business of lending and investment.
NBFC-Infrastructure Finance Company **(NBFC-IFC)**	• It is a non-deposit–accepting loan company which finances for infrastructure projects. It has to comply with all the following criteria: ◆ A minimum of 75% of the total assets of an IFC-NBFC should be deployed in infrastructure loans. ◆ The company should have minimum net worth of ₹300 crore. ◆ The CRAR of the company should be at 15% with Tier I capital at 10%. ◆ The minimum credit rating of the company should be at 'A' or equivalent of CRISIL, FITCH, CARE, ICRA, BRICKWORK or equivalent rating by any other accrediting rating agencies.
NBFC-Systematically Important Core Investment Company **(CIC-ND-SI)**	• It deals with investment in equity shares, preference shares, debts or loans of group companies. It has to satisfy all the following conditions: ◆ It holds more than 90% of its total assets in the form of investment in equity shares, preference shares, debt or loans in group companies. ◆ Its investment in equity shares of the group companies constitutes not less than 60% of its total assets. ◆ It does not trade in its investments in shares, debt or loans in group companies except through block sale for the purpose of dilution or disinvestment. ◆ Its asset size is ₹100 crore or above. ◆ It accepts public funds.
Infrastructure Debt Fund-NBFC **(IDF-NBFC)**	• It is an institution to facilitate the flow of long-term debt into infrastructure projects. It raises resources through issue of Rupee or Dollar denominated bonds of minimum 5-year maturity. Only Infrastructure Finance Companies (IFC) can sponsor IDF-NBFCs.
NBFC-Micro Finance Institution **(NBFC-MFI)**	• It is a non-deposit–taking NBFC engaged in micro-finance lending. It was introduced after the recommendations of Malegam Committee.
NBFC-Factor	• It is a non-deposit–taking NBFC engaged in the business of factoring. • **Factoring** is an arrangement where an individual or entity can sell/transfer its accounts receivable or debtor to another financing company for a discount. Instruments generally used are Bills of exchange, Promissory notes, etc. • **Factoring** can help companies **improve their short-term cash needs** by selling their receivables in return for an injection of cash from the factoring company.

Type of NBFC	Activity involved
Mortgage Guarantee Company **(MGC)**	• MGC are NBFCs for which at least 90% of the business turnover is from mortgage guarantee business or at least 90% of the gross income is from mortgage guarantee business and net owned fund is ₹100 crore.
Housing Finance Company **(HFC)**	• HFCs are specialised lending NBFCs for housing finance in India. Examples include LIC Housing Finance, PNB Housing Finance, Housing Development Finance Corporation (HDFC), etc. • The sources of funds for HFCs are debentures, bank borrowings, public deposits, External Commercial Borrowings (ECBs), commercial papers and even refinance support by NHB. • HFCs were initially regulated by National Housing Bank. But, recently it has been decided that HFCs **will be regulated by RBI**. It is because in the recent years, there has been a deceleration in credit growth and muted profitability of HFCs.

EXAM ESSENTIAL

DIFFERENCE BETWEEN BANKS AND NBFCs

- Unlike Banks, NBFCs **cannot accept** demand deposits.
- Unlike Banks, NBFCs **do not form part** of the payment and settlement system and **cannot issue cheques** drawn on itself.
- **Deposit Insurance Facility is not available** to investors/depositors of NBFCs.
- NBFCs are **not required to maintain Reserve Ratios** prescribed by RBI (CRR, SLR, etc.).
- Banks are regulated under Banking Regulation Act, 1949 whereas NBFCs are regulated under Companies Act ,1956 or The Companies (Amendment) Act, 2019.
- Foreign investment allowed is upto 74 per cent for private sector Banks but this limit for NBFCs is up to 100 per cent.

NBFCs and Liquidity Crisis

RBI's prudential norms over the years have been **to discourage creation and growth of deposit-taking by NBFC (also called NBFC-D) and encouraging the entry of non-deposit-taking NBFCs (also called NBFC-ND)**. This has been done to protect the depositor's capital (often general public) because deposits of NBFCs-D are not covered by the DICGC and it may result in total loss of deposit.

This has led to increase in wholesale funding (loans from Banks, Debt Mutual Funds, Debentures, Commercial Paper) as the funding sources of the NBFCs, rather than deposits. Financial institutions and NBFCs prefer short-term financing sources because of its lower cost and easy availability and liquidity.

However, dependence on frequent short-term funding causes an Asset Liability Management (ALM) problem and **makes NBFCs vulnerable to increase in costs of short-term funding** because they have to constantly repay their short-term loans and seek fresh loans.

Liquid Debt Mutual Funds is a primary source of short-term funds to the NBFC sector. Thus, the NBFC sector is deeply connected with the Liquid Debt Mutual Fund (LDMF) sector making mutual funds prone to transmission of systemic risk from the NBFC sector. Shocks in the NBFC sector may lead to large-scale redemptions by investors in the LDMF sector at low prices. To overcome, policy changes have been made by the Government in recent past.

Recent Major Policy Changes by Government in the NBFC Sector

To maintain stability of the larger financial system and boost confidence, RBI and the Government has taken the following major measures in the recent past:

- Amendments in the RBI Act, 1934, to confer powers on the RBI to improve governance of NBFCs, to protect depositors'/creditors' interest and ensure financial stability of the sector.
- Amendment in relevant rules to reduce the cost of raising funds for NBFCs and HFCs and deepening of the corporate bond market.
- NBFC-Investment and Credit Company (NBFC-ICC) was created by merging Asset Finance Companies, Loan Companies and Investment Companies. This was **done to reduce complexities** arising from multiple categories and for greater flexibility in their operations.
- An independent Chief Risk Officer (CRO) to be appointed for large NBFCs (with asset size more than ₹5,000 crore) for identification, measurement and mitigation of risks.
- Ombudsman Scheme for NBFCs-D extended to NBFCs-ND (with an asset size of ₹100 crore or above) for resolving grievances.

Last Minute SNIPPETS

Recently, RBI has proposed new regulations for the NBFCs that include:

(a) Making of **four layer regulatory framework** which comprises of a Base layer, a Middle layer, an Upper layer and a Top layer. There will be a progressive increase in the intensity of regulation with the increasing layer.

(b) There will be a **change of classification for NPAs**. RBI has proposed changing of period from 180 days to 90 days overdue for classification of NPAs for Base layer NBFCs.

Scale-Based Regulation for NBFCs

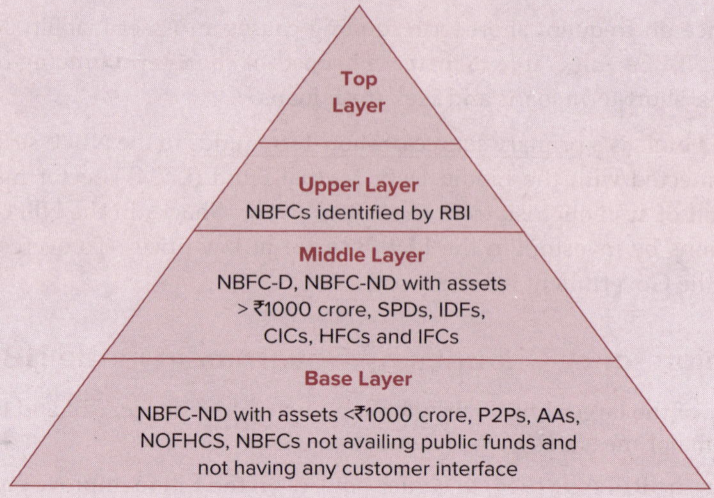

Notes:

1. NBFCs-D. CICs, NBFC-IFCs and HFCs will be included in the middle or the upper layer.
2. The remaining NBFCs, viz., NBFC-ICC, NBFC-MFI, NBFC-Factors and NBFC-MGC could lie in any of the layers, depending on the parameters of SBR.
3. Government-owned NBFCs shall be placed in the Base Layer or Middle Layer, as the case may be.

Source: RBI.

BONUS KNOWLEDGE

SHADOW BANKING

Economist **Paul McCulley** coined the phrase 'Shadow Bank' in 2007, at the Kansas City Federal Reserve Bank's annual financial conference in Jackson Hole, Wyoming.

Shadow Banking comprises a set of markets and institutions that **operate partially (or fully) outside the traditional commercial banking** and are either lightly regulated or unregulated. Simply, it is **not illegal**; it is **just not strictly monitored** as Commercial Banks are monitored by the RBI. **Examples include** Housing Finance Companies (HFCs), Retail-NBFCs and Liquid Debt Mutual Funds (LDMFs).

Shadow Banks do not have direct access to central bank liquidity. The shadow banking system is highly leveraged with **risky and illiquid assets**, whereas its liabilities are disposed to 'bank run'.

Please Note: ***Bank Run*** *occurs when many clients withdraw their money from a bank because they believe the bank may become insolvent or cease to function in near future.*

PRIMARY DEALERS

- The concept of Primary Dealer (PD) was introduced **by RBI** in **1995**.
- PDs deal with the market of **G-Secs** of both the Central and State Governments.
- They play active role in both primary market and secondary market of G-Secs.

➤ **Major Functions of PD** include:
- Providing **underwriting services** in G-Secs.
- Providing **broking services** in G-Secs.
- Offer firm **buy-sell/bid ask quotes for Treasury Bills** and **Dated securities.**

DIFFERENTIATED BANKING

EXAM ESSENTIAL

➤ The concept of differentiated banking was introduced by RBI, based on the recommendations of **Nachiket Mor Committee** in 2013.

➤ Differentiated Banks are banks which **cater or serve a specific segment** of customers unlike other normal universal banks (who offer all financial products).

➤ The differentiation may be based on capital requirement, scope of activities or areas of operations.

➤ This differentiated banking concept was introduced in order to offer **specialised services** or **unique products** designed to very much suit that particular sector.

➤ The Differentiated Banks **offer limited range of services/products** as compared to universal banks.

➤ Therefore, the following two types of Differentiated Banks were launched:

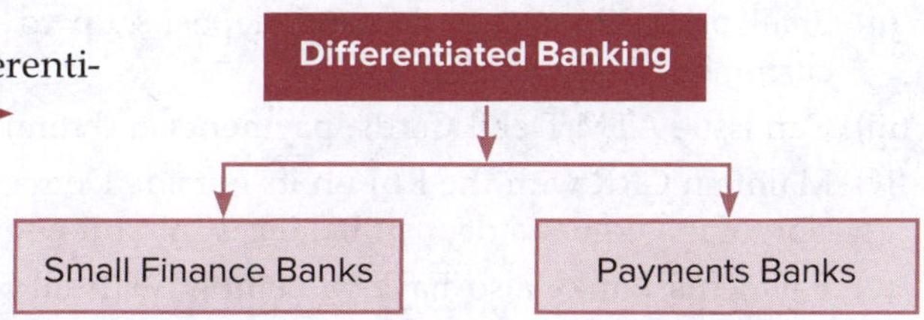

Small Finance Banks

➤ Small Finance Banks (SFBs) are **SCBs** that lend to small business units, small and marginal farmers, micro and small industries, unorganised sector entities, etc.

➤ They are **private financial institutions** established as a **Public Limited Company** under the Companies (Amendment) Act, 2019. They are licenced under the Banking Regulation Act, 1949, and are **governed by the RBI Act, 1934**.

➤ They can be promoted by individuals, corporate, trusts or by societies. Existing **NBFCs,** Micro Finance Institutions **(MFIs)** and Local Area Banks **(LABs)** can also opt for conversion into SFB.

➤ In 2019, RBI started the **'On Tap Facility'** under which RBI can accept applications and grant licence for SFBs throughout the year.

➤ Following are the guidelines related to **SFBs**:

(i) Eligible promoters of SFBs could be **resident** individuals/professionals with **10 years** of banking and finance experience, including companies controlled by them.

(ii) They shall primarily undertake basic banking activities of acceptance of deposits and lending to unserved and underserved sections.

(iii) The minimum paid-up equity capital for SFBs shall be **₹100 crore**.

(iv) All prudential norms and regulations of RBI as applicable to existing Commercial Banks, including requirement of maintenance of CRR and SLR shall apply.

(v) Their 75 per cent of loan is to be for priority sector lending, and

(vi) Atleast 50 per cent of loans and advances should be upto ₹25 lakh.

Examples of SFB include Capital Small Finance Bank (first SFB and it started in 2016), Ujjivan Small Finance Bank, etc.

Payments Banks

- A payments bank is similar to any other bank; however, it operates on a smaller scale and without any credit risk.
- It was founded on the recommendations of the **Nachiket Mor Committee**.
- Its objective is to promote financial inclusion by providing banking and financial services to the unbanked and underbanked, as well as assisting migratory workers, low-income households, small businesses, and so on.
- It is registered as a **public limited company** under the Companies Act of 2013 and licenced by Section 22 of the Banking Regulation Act of 1949.
- It is overseen by many pieces of law, including the Banking Regulation Act of 1949, the RBI Act of 1934, and the Foreign Exchange Management Act of 1999, among others.

The guidelines for **Payments Banks** provide the following:

(i) Eligible promoters can be **non-bank Prepaid Payment Instrument (PPI) issuers** and other entities like mobile telephone companies, etc.

(ii) Shall primarily accept demand deposits up to **maximum balance of ₹2,00,000** per individual customer.

(iii) Can issue ATM/Debit Cards, payments and remittance services.

(iv) Maintain CRR with the RBI on its outside Demand and Time Liabilities and invest **at least 75 per cent of its 'demand deposit balances' in SLR eligible G-Secs/Treasury Bills**.

(v) Payments Banks also have to comply with all regulatory and supervisory frameworks that are applicable to Commercial Banks.

(vi) Payments Banks are unable to provide loans or credit cards.

(vii) It does not take time deposits or NRI deposits.

(viii) It cannot establish subsidiaries to conduct non-banking financial activity.

At present, many Payment Banks are operating in India. They are – Airtel Payments Bank, India Post Payments Bank, Fino, NSDL Payments Bank and Jio Payments Bank..

Small Finance Banks *vs* Payments Banks

Small Finance Banks	Payments Banks
Can accept all types of deposits like a Commercial Bank (Current Account, Savings Account, Fixed Deposit, Recurring Deposit, etc.).	Take deposit only on Current Account, Savings Account and cannot accept Fixed Deposits (FD). They also can-not issue Credit Card but can issue a Debit Card.
They can give out depositor's money as loans to other customers, but have small area of operation.	They cannot give depositor's money as loans. They can invest depositor's money in Government Securities (G-Secs) only.
Focus: Deposits and loans.	**Focus**: Payment/remittances only, including cross-border remittances.
Conditions: 75% of the loans is to be for Priority Sector Lending.	**Conditions:** Maximum balance per customer: ₹2 lakh. Minimum leverage ratio to be 3%, i.e. liabilities should not exceed 33 times of its net worth.

EXAM ESSENTIAL

INDIA POST PAYMENTS BANK

India Post Payments Bank **(IPPB)** is a public limited company set up in **2017,** under the **Department of Posts** with 100 per cent GoI equity. IPPB **offers demand deposits** such as Savings and Current Accounts up to a balance of **₹2 lakh**. It is a type of **Payments Bank**.

Digital Payment Security Controls

RBI (Digital Payment Security Controls) Directions, 2021 has been published to secure digital payments architecture of India. It is directed towards setting up a robust governance structure and implementation of **common minimum standards** for digital payment security controls.

These Directions are **applicable for** the Scheduled Commercial Banks, Small Finance Banks, Payments Banks, credit-card issuing NBFCs, third party payment applications, payment operators and gateways.

The Directions include **components such as** *multi-tier application architecture, database and presentation layer, fraud risk management, real time or near-real time reconciliation framework, customer protection, card payment security controls, etc.*

OTHER ORGANISATIONS RELATED TO BANKING SECTOR

EXAM ESSENTIAL

Banks Board Bureau

- Based on the recommendations of **P.J. Nayak Committee,** Banks Board Bureau (BBB) was set up in **2016** as an autonomous recommendatory body to improve the governance of **Public Sector Banks (PSBs)**.
- BBB was also one of the seven aspects of the **Indradhanush plan** of Government which deals with **revival of PSBs.**
- The main function of BBB is to **recommend the name of Head of PSBs** and financial institutions. Moreover, it also advices **on ways of raising funds** and dealing with the **issue of stressed assets.** Besides, BBB is also a link between the Government and the Public Sector Banks.
- BBB comprises a **Chairman** and **six members** (out of which three are ex-officio). The present chairman of BBB is **Bhanu Pratap Sharma**.
- BBB is headquartered in **Mumbai.**

Financial Services Institutions Bureau (FSIB)

- Recently, the Appointments Committee of the Cabinet (ACC) has approved the government resolution to establish **Financial Services Institutions Bureau (FSIB)** in place of Banks Board Bureau (BBB).
- It is set up to recommend persons for the appointments of directors and non-executive chairpersons on the boards of financial services institutions which include public sector banks, public sector

insurers and financial institutions. It is to work under the Department of Financial Services, Ministry of Finance.

- FSIB shall promote excellence in corporate governance in public sector financial institutions.
- FSIB is envisaged to provide advice on the desired management structure at the board level for financial services institutions.
- FSIB is aimed at building a databank containing the data related to the performances of financial services institutions.

Composition of FSIB

i. **Chairperson** is to be nominated by Central Government who shall be:
   a. a retired official from the banking sector or a regulatory institution, or
   b. a business person of repute with sufficient knowledge of the financial sector, or
   c. a person with at least 25 years of experience in public administration with experience in banking and financial sector.

ii. **Ex officio members:** Secretary in charge of DFS, Department of Public Enterprises, Chairperson of the Insurance Regulatory and Development Authority of India (IRDAI) and the Deputy Governor of RBI.

iii. 3 persons with subject matter knowledge relating to PSBs and FIs and 3 persons with subject matter knowledge relating to PSIs (to be nominated by the Central Government) as part time members.

National Payments Corporation of India (NPCI)

- National Payments Corporation of India (NPCI) is an umbrella organisation to operate **retail payments and settlement systems** in India.
- It is an **initiative of RBI and Indian Banks' Association (IBA)** under the provisions of the Payment and Settlement Systems Act, 2007, for creating a robust Payment and Settlement Infrastructure in India. It was formed as a 'Not for Profit' company under Section 25 of the Companies Act 1956.
- The headquarters of NPCI is located in **Mumbai. Dilip Asbe** is the current MD and CEO of NPCI.
- NPCI may run several payment systems, including the National Financial Switch (NFS), Immediate Payment System (IMPS), Aadhaar-Enabled Payments System (AEPS), and National Automated Clearing House (NACH).
- **Let us discuss some of the major products/services launched and provided by NPCI:**
   i. ***Unified Payments Interface (UPI)***: It is a payment system developed by NPCI which allows **money transfer between any two bank accounts** by using a smartphone. It allows a customer to pay directly from a bank account to different merchants, both online and offline, without the hassle of typing credit card details, Indian Financial System Code (IFSC) or net banking/ wallet passwords. It is **regulated by RBI** and is built over IMPS (Immediate Payment Service).
   ii. ***RuPay Card***: It is the Indian version of the card network which was started by **NPCI** in **2012**. RuPay primarily provides **debit cards**. Apart from this, RuPay also issues 'Kisan Credit Cards' for farmers. These cards are accepted only domestically.
   iii. ****99# Service***: **NPCI** launched *99# service which works on Unstructured Supplementary Service Data (USSD) channel. This service was launched envisioning the potential of Mobile Banking and the need for immediate low-value remittances which will help in financial deepening and inclusion of underbanked society in the mainstream banking services.

iv. ***BHIM App***: It is an app developed by the NPCI based on UPI and is used for digital payments. It does not 'hold' money like other digital wallets like, Amazon Pay or MobiKwik. Money can be sent to non-UPI linked accounts using IFSC and account number.

v. ***Bharat Bill Payment System (BBPS)***: BBPS is an integrated bill payment system which offers interoperable bill payment service to customers online as well as through a network of agents on the ground. The system provides multiple payment modes and instant confirmation of payment.

vi. ***National Automated Clearing House (NACH)***: NACH has been launched for banks, financial institutions, corporates and the Government as a web-based solution to facilitate interbank, high volume, electronic transactions which are repetitive and periodic in nature. It consolidates the multiple ECS systems running across India and provides a framework for the harmonisation of standards and practices.

vii. ***USSD Services***: NPCI established **Unstructured Supplementary Service Date** (USSD) to allow individuals to conduct banking transactions without the need for the internet or cellphones.

viii. ***National Financial Switch (NFS)***: It is an ATM network having 37 members and connecting about 50,000 ATMs.

BONUS KNOWLEDGE

NEW UMBRELLA ENTITIES (NUES)

- The RBI proposed a "New Umbrella Entity" (NUE) scheme in 2019 to establish entities that could compete with the National Payments Corporation of India (NPCI), but the process was paused in 2021 due to a lack of innovative proposals.
- The RBI envisioned NUEs as non-profit entities that would set up, manage, and operate new payment systems, including ATMs, white-label PoS, Aadhaar-based payments, and remittance services.
- The RBI aimed to foster competition in the digital payments landscape and encourage innovation by allowing new entities to enter the market.
- In 2020, the RBI invited applications for NUE licenses, but the process was paused in 2021 due to a lack of innovative proposals.

Banking Codes and Standards Board of India

- As per the recommendations of the *Committee on Procedures and Performance Audit of Public Services* under the Chairmanship of Shri S.S. Tarapore, Banking Codes and Standards Board of India (BCSBI) was set up in 2006. The **independent banking industry watchdog** is based in **Mumbai**. It functions as an independent and autonomous body and is registered as a society under the Societies Registration Act, 1860.
- Initially, the membership of BCSBI was open to SCBs but has now been extended to include RRBs and select Urban Co-operative Banks (UCBs).
- BCSBI is envisaged to ensure that the common person, as a consumer of financial services from the banking industry, is in no way at disadvantageous position and gets what he/she has been promised.

Advisory Board for Banking Frauds

- In 2019, the Central Vigilance Commission **(CVC)** in consultation with RBI has reconstituted the Advisory Board on Bank, Commercial and Financial Frauds (ABBCFF) into Advisory Board for Banking Frauds (ABBF).
- It conducts the **first-level examination of all large fraud cases** before recommendations are made to the investigative agencies.

CHEQUE AND ITS TYPES

A cheque is a sort of negotiable instrument signed by the drawer that instructs the bank to pay a certain amount of money to a certain individual. In simple words, a cheque is an order to a bank to pay a stated sum from the drawer's account, written on a specially printed form. Cheque is used to make safe and convenient payment. It is less risky and the danger of loss is minimised.

Number of Parties engaged in a Cheque

There are three people engaged in a cheque. They are:

- **Drawer or Maker** – The client or account holder who issues the check is known as the '**drawer**' or '**rf**'.
- **Drawee** – The bank from which the cheque is drawn. Remember that cheques are usually drawn on a certain banker.
- **Payee** – This is the individual identified on the cheque who receives payment for the amount specified on the cheque. In some circumstances (where the drawer writes a self-cheque), the drawer and the payee may be the same person.

Two other people are also involved in the process:

- **Endorser:** When a party, or payee, transfers his or her right to receive payment to another party, he or she is referred to as an endorser.
- **Endorsee:** The party to whom the right is transferred is referred to as an endorsee.

Some of the crucial informations about a cheque are:

- A cheque is an **unconditional order**
- A cheque is usually drawn on a certain bank
- A cheque is always payable upon demand
- Signature on the exchequer is required and should only be done by the creator
- The amount is always a set amount of money from one's account
- This monetary sum is to be paid to the individual named in the document, the order, or the bearer

Bearer Cheque – Bearer cheque refers to a cheque that is **payable to whoever presents the cheque**, rather than to a designated payee.

Order Cheque – This sort of cheque cannot be endorsed; thus, only the payee whose name appears on the cheque is eligible to receive cash for that amount. The drawer must strike the 'OR BEARER' mark as specified on the cheque so that the cheque can only be cashed by the payee.

Uncrossed/Open Cheque – When a cheque is not crossed, it is known as an 'open cheque' or an 'uncrossed cheque'. The payment of such a cheque can be obtained at the counter of the bank.

Crossed Cheque – Crossing of cheque means drawing **two parallel lines** on the face of the cheque. A crossed cheque cannot be encashed at the cash counter of a bank but it can **only be credited to the payee's account**.

Cheque Truncation – Truncation is the process of **stopping the flow of the physical cheque** by the presenting bank en-route to the paying bank branch. **In its place, an electronic image of the cheque is transmitted** to the paying branch through the clearing house, along with relevant information. Cheque truncation therefore, obviates the need to move the physical instruments across bank branches, thereby eliminating the associated cost for movement of the physical cheque and reducing the time for the entire activity of cheque processing.

Antedated Cheque – If a cheque bears a date earlier than the date on which it is presented to the bank, it is called as 'antedated cheque'. Such a cheque is **valid up to 3 months** from the date of the cheque.

Post-Dated Cheque – If a cheque bears a date which is yet to come (future date), then it is known as post-dated cheque. A post-dated cheque cannot be honoured earlier than the date on the cheque.

Self Cheque – If the drawer wants cash for himself, she/he can put 'SELF' instead of the payee's name on the cheque and have it encashed at the bank where she/he has an account.

Stale Cheque – If a cheque is **presented for payment after 3 months** from the date of the cheque, it is called as stale cheque. A stale cheque is not honoured by the bank.

Traveller's Cheque – As the name implies, a traveller's cheque can be used while going overseas where Indian currency is not accepted. If a person is going overseas, she/he can carry a traveller's cheque and encash it in foreign nations.

Mutilated Cheque – A mutilated cheque is one that has been ripped when it arrives at the bank. If the cheque is **ripped into two or more parts**, with the required information shredded, the bank will refuse and deem the cheque void until the drawer certifies its validity. If the cheque is torn at the edges but all of the relevant data is still intact, the bank may process it further.

Blank Cheque – A blank cheque is one that simply bears the drawer's signature and leaves all other areas blank.

Penalty for dishonouring a cheque – If found guilty of dishonouring a cheque, the defaulter may face a monetary penalty equal to twice the amount of the cheque, imprisonment for up to two years, or both. The bank may also suspend the chequebook and account for repeated offences on bounced cheques.

Demand Draft (DD) – It is a kind of pre-paid negotiable instrument that is used to direct payments from one bank to another bank, or one of its own branches, to pay a certain sum to the specified person.

NEGOTIABLE INSTRUMENTS

A Negotiable Instrument is a promissory note, bill of exchange or cheque payable either to order or to bearer. Negotiable Instrument Act, 1881, defines promissory notes, bills of exchange, cheques, drawer, holder, etc. It specifies penalties for bouncing of cheques and other violations with respect to such negotiable instruments.

PREPAID PAYMENT INSTRUMENTS

These are instruments that facilitate purchase of goods and services, including financial services, remittances, funds transfers, etc., against the value stored in/on such instruments. PPI issuers are companies incorporated and registered in India. A company can issue and operate PPIs after receiving authorisation from RBI. PPIs can be issued as smart cards, magnetic stripe cards, online wallets, internet accounts, etc.

BONUS KNOWLEDGE

HUNDI

Hundi is a financial instrument (Bill of Exchange) evolved on the Indian sub-continent during medieval period. It was used in trade and credit transactions. Hundis have **no legal status** and are not subject to the Negotiable Instruments Act of 1881 because they are part of the informal system.

OTHER KEY TERMS RELATED TO BANKING SECTOR

Debit Card

It is a plastic payment card that is used instead of cash when making purchases.

The different types of Debit Card in India depend upon the type of payment platform linked to the card. They include **Visa Card, Maestro Card, RuPay Card, MasterCard,** etc.

Credit Card

A Credit Card is a plastic card issued by banks to enable the cardholder to pay a merchant for goods and services based on the cardholder's promise to the card issuer to pay them for the amounts so paid plus other agreed charges. **Central Bank of India** was the first public sector bank to introduce Credit Card in India.

Prepaid Card

A Prepaid Card works like a gift card – you top it up with money and you can only spend up to that amount. It is **often used by travellers** to carry holiday money, and by individuals without a traditional bank account such as kids, teens and people with poor credit ratings.

Smart Card

It contains an electronic chip which is used to store cash. No identification, signature or payment authorisation is required for using this card. The exact amount of purchase is deducted from the smart card during payment and is collected by smart card reading machines.

Automated Teller Machine

Automated Teller Machine (ATM) is a computerised machine that provides the customers of banks the facility of accessing their account for dispensing cash and to carry out other financial and non-financial transactions without the need to actually visit their bank branch. A particular Bank's ATM card can be used at any ATM/WLA in the country. Recently, RBI has **also allowed cardless withdrawals** at ATMs.

Types of ATM includes the following:

1. ***Onsite ATM:*** This type of ATM is situated either within the branch premises or in very close proximity of the branch.
2. ***Offsite ATM:*** It is not situated within the branch premises and is located at other places, such as malls, airports, petrol pumps, etc.
3. ***Worksite ATM:*** It is located within the premises of an organisation and is generally meant only for the employees of the organisation.
4. ***White Label ATMs (WLAs):*** ATMs set up, owned and operated **by non-banks** are called WLAs. Non-bank ATM operators are authorised by the RBI under the Payment and Settlement Systems Act, 2007. The purpose to allow non-bank entities to set up WLAs is to increase the geographical spread of ATMs.
5. ***Brown Label ATMs:*** Brown label ATMs are those ATMs where hardware and the lease of the ATM is owned by a service provider, but cash management and connectivity to banking networks is provided by a sponsor bank whose brand is used on the ATM.
6. ***Green Label ATM:*** The ATM is available for agricultural transactions.
7. ***Orange Label ATM:*** Available for share transactions.
8. ***Yellow Label ATM:*** Set up for E-commerce.
9. ***Pink label ATM:*** These ATMs are guarded by guards who guarantee that only women use them. The main goal of such ATMs is to alleviate the problem of women waiting in long lines at ATMs.
10. ***Biometric ATM:*** These ATMs employ client security features such as fingerprint scanners and eye scanners to access bank account information and undertake transactions.

Point-of-Sale Machine

A Point-of-Sale (PoS) terminal is a computerised replacement for a cash register which can process Credit and Debit Cards. A customer needs to enter the card PIN to complete the transaction using PoS terminal.

Merchant Discount Rate

Merchant Discount Rate (MDR) is the **fee paid by a merchant to a bank** for accepting payment from their customers via digital means. The MDR is expressed in percentage of the transaction amount. Rate of MDR is fixed and revised by RBI time to time. From 1 January 2020, **no MDR charge** lies on transactions made through **RuPay and BHIM UPI platforms.**

Indian Financial System Code

The concept of Indian Financial System Code (IFSC) was developed by the RBI. It is an **11-digit alpha-numeric code** that **uniquely identifies a bank branch** participating in any RBI-regulated funds transfer system. The IFSC helps to transfer money using National Electronic Funds Transfer (NEFT), Real-Time Gross Settlement (RTGS) and Centralised Funds Management System (CFMS) method.

The 11 characters in IFSC are as follows:

- First four characters represent the entity
- Fifth position has been defaulted with a 0 (zero) for future use
- Last six characters denote the bank branch identity, e.g. ICIC0000438

MICR Code

An MICR (Magnetic Ink Character Recognition) code is a **nine-digit code** that **uniquely identifies a bank and a branch** participating in an Electronic Clearing System (ECS). The first three digit of the code represents the city code, the middle three represents the bank code and the last three represents the branch code. The MICR number is written at the bottom of the cheque.

SWIFT Code

It is a unique identification code **for both financial and non-financial institutions** approved by the International Organisation for Standardisation. SWIFT Standards, a division of the Society for Worldwide Interbank Financial Telecommunication (SWIFT), handles the registration of these codes. SWIFT codes are used **when transferring money between banks,** particularly for international wire transfers, and also for the exchange of other messages between banks.

Core Banking Solution

Under Core Banking Solution (CBS), Core stands for 'Centralised Online Real-time Exchange'. CBS is a network of branches which enables account holders to operate their accounts and avail banking services **from any branch of the Bank on CBS network, regardless of where he maintains his account.** The customer is no more the customer of a Bank's Branch. He becomes the overall Bank's Customer.

BONUS KNOWLEDGE

E-KUBER

It is the Core Banking Solution **(CBS) platform of RBI** which is used by RBI **to conduct auctioning of G-Secs**. Commercial Banks, Scheduled UCBs, Primary Dealers, Insurance Companies and Provident Funds who maintain Current Account and Securities Accounts with RBI are the members of E-Kuber and can take part in auction.

Know Your Customer Norms

KYC means **'Know Your Customer'.** It is a process through which banks obtain information about the identity and address of the customers.

This process helps to ensure that banks' services are not misused. The KYC procedure is to be completed by the banks at the time of opening accounts. Banks are also required to periodically update their customers' KYC details. *e-KYC or Electronic KYC* is possible only for those who have **Aadhaar numbers.**

One can still open a bank account known as 'Small Account' by submitting his/her recent photograph and putting the signature or thumb impression in the presence of the bank official. However, **'Small Accounts'** have certain limitations, such as:

- Balance in such accounts at any point of time **should not exceed ₹50,000.**
- **Total credits** in 1 year **should not exceed ₹1,00,000.**
- **Total withdrawal** and transfers **in a month should not exceed ₹10,000.**
- Foreign remittances **cannot** be credited to such accounts.

Zero-Rupee Note

Zero-rupee notes are distributed by the NGO **'5th Pillar'.** It is a banknote imitation issued to raise awareness about bribery and systematic political corruption.

Legal Entity Identifier

The Legal Entity Identifier (LEI) is a 20-character, **alpha-numeric code** based on the ISO 17442 standard developed by the International Organisation for Standardisation (ISO). It is a unique global reference number that connects to key reference information for clear and unique identification of legal entities participating in financial transactions.

LEI is accredited by the **Global Legal Entity Identifier Foundation (GLEIF).** It is recognised by the RBI. RBI is the issuer of LEI under the **Payment and Settlement Systems Act, 2007.**

Digital Lending

It is an **automated lending process,** majorly by use of seamless digital technologies in customer acquisition, credit assessment, loan approval, disbursement, recovery and associated customer service. There are several digital lending models across the globe like Online Lender, P2P Lender, Mobile Money Lender, Market Platforms, etc.

NON-PERFORMING ASSETS

At banks, loans made to customers are listed as assets. A Non-Performing Asset (NPA) is that asset of a bank **which is not producing any income,** i.e. a loan or lease that is not meeting its stated principal and interest payments. As per RBI, a loan/advance on which interest or principal amount is **pending for 90 days or more** is considered NPA. **RBI's biannual Financial Stability Report** (FSR) highlights achievements in Non-Performing Assets (NPA). It is based on the assessment of **Sub-Committee of Financial Stability and Development Council (FSDC).**

Categories of NPA include:

1. **Sub-standard assets:** When the NPAs have aged ≤ **12 months.**
2. **Doubtful assets:** When the NPAs have aged **> 12 months.**
3. **Loss assets:** When the bank or its auditors have identified the **loss,** but it has not been written off.

Note: Stressed assets = NPAs + Restructured loans + Written-off assets.

Impact of NPAs

- It leads to **scarcity of funds** in the Indian securities market as banks become unwilling to give loans.
- The shareholders of the banks will lose a lot of money as banks themselves will find it **tough to survive** in the market.
- It leads to a crisis of confidence in the market. The **interest rates shoot up** which directly impact the investors who wish to take loans for setting up industrial projects.
- Low offtake of funds from the security market **hurts the overall demand** in the Indian economy.

- Ultimately, high NPAs lead to **lower economic growth rates** and **higher inflation** because of the higher cost of capital. This trend may continue in a vicious circle and deepen the crisis.

Reasons for Rising NPAs

- Falling debt servicing ability of Indian firms.
- Lack of due diligence and background checks by Public Sector Banks (PSBs) before giving loans and incorrect classification of assets by them.
- Delay in projects implementation.
- Review of decisions by Vigilance Committee prevents strong decision-making.
- Banks do not have a large buffer set aside for absorption of losses.

In tackling NPAs, the following measures were taken by the Government in the past:

Measure	Outcome
5/25 Scheme - 2014 Flexible refinancing and repayment option for long-term infrastructure projects to the existing ones where the total exposure of lenders is more than ₹500 crore.	Refinancing was done at a higher rate of interest so that banks could preserve the Net Present Value (NPV) of the loan amount. There were few disclosures of the accounts getting refinanced under the scheme, and it was perceived that this was a tool deployed by banks to cover NPAs.
Strategic Debt Restructuring (SDR) - 2015 Banks who have given loans to a corporate borrower gets the right to convert the complete or part of their loans into equity shares in the loan taken company.	It was observed that difficulties in finding buyers and disagreement over valuations were challenges in implementation.
Asset Quality Review - 2015 To classify stressed assets and undertaking provisioning for them so as to secure the future of the banks and further early identification of the assets and prevent them from becoming stressed by taking appropriate action.	Helpful in increasing transparency, but provides no solution.
Scheme for Sustainable Structuring of Stressed Assets (S4A) - 2016 Optional framework which involves the determination of sustainable debt level for a stressed borrower and bifurcation of the outstanding debt into sustainable debt and equity/quasi-equity instruments which are expected to provide upside to the lenders when the borrower turns around.	Banks were unwilling to grant write-downs as there were no incentives to do so, and write-downs of large debtors could quickly exhaust banks' capital cushions.
Insolvency and Bankruptcy Code - 2016 An all-in-one solution for insolvency.	It aims to safeguard small investors.

In spite of the above measures taken, reduction in NPA could not be achieved. Thus, some more effective measures were undertaken in the form of **4R strategy,** which included the following:

1. **Recognition** of NPAs transparently
2. **Resolution** and recovery of value from stressed accounts
3. **Recapitalising** PSBs
4. **Reforms** in PSBs and wider financial ecosystem for a responsible and clean system

Provisioning for NPA

- Provisioning norms, a part of RBI's prudential regulation, is one of the several mechanisms to tackle the NPA or bad assets problem in the banking sector.
- Under provisioning, banks have to set aside or provide funds to a prescribed percentage of their bad assets.
- **Provisioning Coverage Ratio (PCR)** is essentially the ratio of provisioning to gross NPAs and indicates the extent of funds a bank has kept aside to cover loan losses.
- Thus, PCR is the percentage of bad assets that the bank has to provide for (keep money) from their own funds.

Gross NPA

- Gross NPA (GNPA) is the total amount that have been defaulted by the borrowers within the provided period.
- GNPA does not amount to the actual loss of the organisation because the provision for unpaid debts has not been deducted.
- GNPA leads to a bad effect on the company's goodwill and lowers its equity value.

Net NPA

- Net NPA (NNPA) is the amount that results after deducting provision for unpaid debts from GNPA.
- NNPA amounts to the actual loss of the organisation because the provision for unpaid loans has already been deducted.
- This leads to low profitability and liquidity in the company's cash reserves.

EXAM ESSENTIAL

PRUDENTIAL FRAMEWORK BY RBI FOR RESOLUTION OF STRESSED ASSETS

In 2019, RBI issued **'Prudential Framework for Resolution of Stressed Assets'** after the Supreme Court, in April 2019, had struck down the then existing guidelines issued by the RBI in February 2018 because it was too stringent and harsh.

This prudential framework is a set of **guidelines to banks for early resolution of stressed assets in a transparent and time-bound manner.**

The **fundamental principles** underlying this regulatory approach for resolution of stressed assets are as follows:

1. Early recognition and reporting of default in respect of large borrowers.
2. Complete discretion to lenders with regard to design and implementation of resolution plans.
3. Harmonised framework for resolution of stressed assets. It **suspends all the earlier resolution schemes like S4A, SDR, 5/25, etc.**
4. Disincentives in the form of additional provisioning for delay in implementation of resolution plan or insolvency proceedings.
5. Withdrawal of asset classification dispensations on restructuring. Future upgrades to be contingent on satisfactory performance.
6. Definition of **'financial difficulty'** to be aligned with the guidelines issued by the Basel Committee on Banking Supervision (BCBS).
7. Signing of **Inter-Creditor Agreement** (ICA) by all lenders to be compulsory, which will ensure a majority decision-making criteria.

Asset Reconstruction Company

An Asset Reconstruction Company (ARC) is a specialised financial institution that buys the NPAs or bad assets from banks and financial institutions so that the latter can clean up their balance sheets. **Narasimham Committee (1998)** recommended setting up an ARC specifically for purchasing NPAs from banks and financial institutions.

- Subsequently, the **SARFAESI Act, 2002,** created the legal framework for establishing multiple private ARCs.

GoI has proposed to set up **ARC** by state-owned and private sector banks, without any equity contribution from the Government to eliminate the need of high level of provisioning by public sector banks of their stressed assets. This will serve the purpose of Bad Bank in India which was on the Government agenda for quite some time for reducing the burden of non-performing assets and to improve the health of the country's banking sector.

BONUS KNOWLEDGE

NATIONAL ASSET RECONSTRUCTION CO. LTD. (NARCL)

To clean up the bad loans from the bank books, recently the RBI has given the Asset Reconstruction Company (ARC) License to NARCL.

A **minimum NOF** (Net Owned Fund) of **₹100 crore** is to be maintained by the ARCs and a **capital adequacy ratio of 15 per cent** of its risk weighted assets, is also to be maintained.

Four banks namely SBI, PNB, ICICI and IDBI in 2002 had set up the Asset Reconstruction Company (India) Ltd or ARCIL, the first ARC of India.

Bad Bank

- A Bad Bank is a **bank set up to buy the bad loans stressed assets** of a financial institution. The banks sell their NPAs to bad bank at market price. By transferring such assets to the bad bank, the original institution clears its balance sheet – although it is still forced to take write-downs.

- The concept of 'bad bank' was first mooted in India by the then Chief Economic Adviser Arvind Subramanian **in 2017.**
- A bad bank is termed so simply because it **houses bad loans,** or in financial parlance, Non-Performing Assets (NPAs). It is basically **a Public Sector Asset Rehabilitation Agency that would take on public sector banks' chronic bad loans and focus on their resolution and the extraction of any residual value from the underlying asset.**

BONUS KNOWLEDGE

SARFAESI ACT, 2002

The Securitisation and Reconstruction of Financial Assets and Enforcement of Security Interest Act, 2002, or also as SARFAESI Act, is a legislation that allows banks and other financial organisations to recover bad loans effectively. The act enables the banks and financial institutions to tackle the problem of Non-Performing Assets (NPAs) through different procedures.

The SARFAESI Act allows financial institutions to 'seize and desist'. They send a notification to the delinquent borrower requesting that he return the amount within 60 days. If the debtor does not cooperate, the bank can take one of the following three steps:

1. Take control of the loan security.
2. Sell, lease, or assign the right to the security.
3. Manage the asset itself or delegate responsibility for it.

The Act also authorises the formation of Asset Reconstruction Companies (ARCs) to buy assets from banks and other financial institutions. The **RBI regulates ARCs.**

Prompt Corrective Action

- Prompt Corrective Action (PCA) is a norm prescribed by RBI under which **banks with weak financial position are put under scrutiny by the RBI.**
- It was introduced in **2002,** and was revised in **2017** by the **RBI.** It is a framework for structured early intervention and resolution.
- The PCA framework **considers banks as risky if** they fall below certain norms/criteria based on **three parameters – capital ratio, asset quality and profitability.**
- **Importance of PCA is as follows:**
  - Identification of concerns at an earlier stage to prevent a bigger crisis later on.
  - It helps RBI in monitoring key financial performance indicators of banks and accordingly devising corrective measures to improve the financials of a bank.
  - To prevent any bank failures and systemic crisis.
- Banks put under PCA have to follow **'Mandatory Action Plan'** prescribed by RBI. RBI can also prescribe 'Discretionary Action Plan' depending on the bank's needs and situation. Mandatory actions are essentially:
  - Restriction on dividend distribution/remittance of profits
  - Requirement on promoters/owners/parents to bring in more capital
  - Restrictions on branch expansion
  - Higher provisioning requirement
  - Restrictions on management compensation

did you KNOW? With effect from April 1, 2025, the RBI will be replacing the previous Supervisory Action Framework (SAF) for Primary Urban Co-operative Banks (UCBs) with the Prompt Corrective Action (PCA) framework, which aims to improve UCB financial health and provide prompt supervisory intervention. It will be applied to all UCBs in tier 2, tier 3, and tier 4 categories, with the exception of those under All Inclusive Directions (AID).

Banking Stability Index/Indicator

- The RBI defines Banking Stability Index (BSI) as 'the expected number of banks that could become distressed given that at least one bank has become distressed'.
- It is an asset quality indicator for banks.
- Higher BSI indicates that more banks are expected to become distressed if one bank in the system is distressed.

BASEL NORMS

These norms are prescribed by the **Bank for International Settlements** (BIS) as a set of global standards which prescribe for assets to minimum capital requirements for Commercial Banks, Foreign Banks or even RRBs.

Basel is a city in **Switzerland,** which is also the **headquarters** of **BIS.** The BIS, established in **1930,** is the world's oldest international financial organisation.

In total, BIS is owned by 62 Central Banks representing countries from all over the world and covers approximately 95 per cent of the world's GDP.

Till now, **three Basel Norms** have been released by BIS:

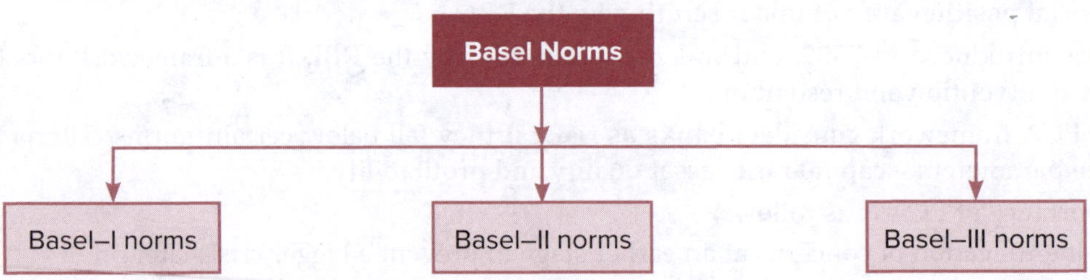

Basel-I Norms

- In 1988, the Basel Committee on Banking Supervision (BCBS) introduced capital measurement system called Basel Capital Accord, also known as Basel-I.
- It focussed only on **credit risk.**
- It prescribed minimum capital requirement at **8 per cent** of the Risk Weighted Assets (RWA) for banks.
- India adopted Basel-I norms in the year **1999.** Under Basel-I, the RBI issued guidelines to maintain a CRAR (Capital to Risk Assets Ratio) or CAR (Capital Adequacy Ratio) of 9 per cent by every **SCB.**

EXAM ESSENTIAL

CRAR

It is defined as the proportion of bank's total risk-weighted assets that are held in the form of shareholders equity and certain other defined class of capital.

Mathematically, **CAR or CRAR = (Tier-I + Tier-II capital)/Total risk-weighted assets.**

Where:

- **Tier-I Capital** also called the **Core Capital** is the core measure of a bank's financial strength from a regulator's point of view. It is composed of core capital and consists of mainly share capital and disclosed reserves. It is the highest quality capital because it is fully available to cover losses. Tier 1 capital is more in the form of equities.
- **Tier-II Capital** also called the **Capital on Call** consists of Subordinate Debt, Revaluation Reserve, General loan-loss reserves, and Hybrid (debt/equity) capital instruments.
- Most of the Tier 2 capital is in the form of debts and reserves etc.

The debt absorption capacity of Tier-II capital is less than Tier-I capital.

Basel-II Norms

- BCBS published the Basel-II norms in **2004.**
- Basel-II was considered to be the refined and reformed version of Basel-I. It took a three-pillared approach:
  1. **Minimum capital requirement** of 8 per cent of risk assets: concerned with three types of risks – operational risk, market risk and capital risk.
  2. **Supervisory review:** focuses on bank's internal processes and systems.
  3. **Market discipline:** under it, the banks were needed to develop and use better risk management techniques in monitoring and managing all the three types of risks.

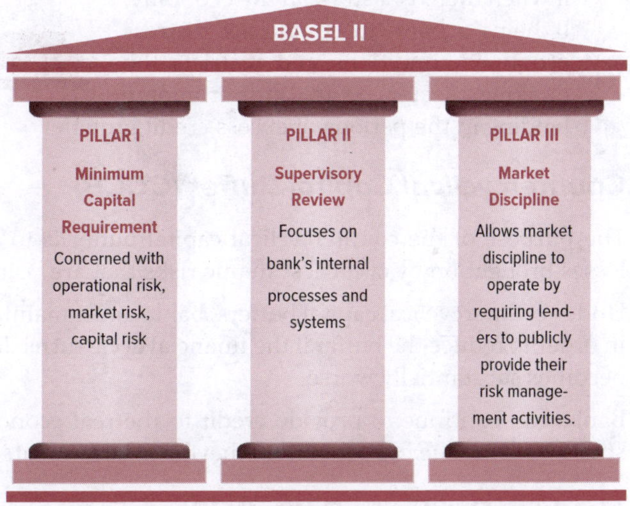

- Implementation of Basel-II norms was done in India by RBI following a gradual approach.
- As per RBI, all **SCBs** were bound to comply with Basel-II norms.

Basel-III Norms

- It became operational from 1 January **2013** in a phased manner.
- Banks are required to increase and maintain the Tier I capital ratio of 4.5 per cent.
- Banks are required to maintain capital conservation buffer of 2.5 per cent.

- Also, counter cyclical buffer to be maintained in the range of 0–2.5 per cent to prevent excess credit growth in the banking sector.
- Total **CRAR** proposed to be maintained is **9.5 per cent.**
- As per RBI, Basel-III norms have to be complied **by all commercial banks (both scheduled and non-scheduled).**
- RBI directed for a phased manner implementation of Basel-III guidelines by commercial banks.

The RBI issued master circular on 1 April 2022 regarding Basel III capital regulations.

- Basel-III Framework also introduced liquidity standards in the form of **Liquidity Coverage Ratio (LCR).**
- The framework of **Countercyclical Capital Buffer (CCCB)** was also introduced (as an extension of capital conservation buffer). CCCB is a mandatory capital that is required to be set aside by the banks during boom when loans are growing rapidly and use it when there is distress in the economy. It helps a bank to counteract distress economic conditions and restricts the banking sector from indiscriminate lending in the periods of excess credit growth.

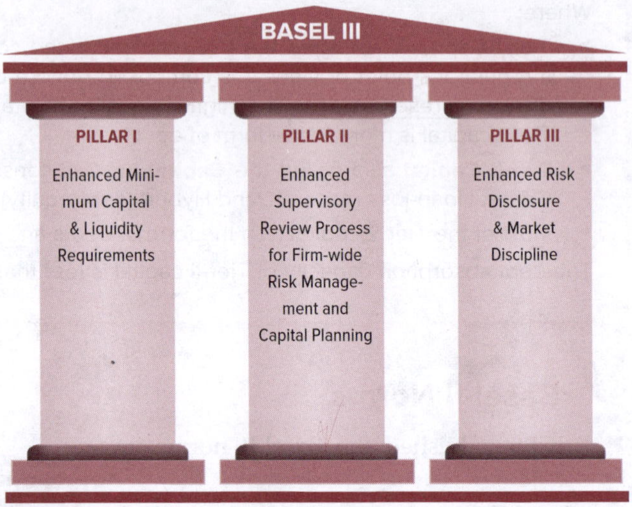

Countercyclical Capital Buffer (CCCB)

The purpose of the countercyclical capital buffer is to safeguard the banking industry from potential losses brought on by cyclical systemic risks that are rising in the economy.

Under countercyclical capital buffers, banks must maintain capital during periods of fast loan expansion in order to reduce the buffer if the financial cycle turns down or the economic and financial environment becomes substantially worse.

Banks can continue to provide credit to the real economy and cover potential losses during times of stress by using the capital buffers they have accumulated during the financial cycle's boom phase.

Liquidity Coverage Ratio (LCR)

Liquidity Coverage Ratio is a requirement under **Basel-III norms,** whereby banks are required to hold an amount of **High-Quality Liquid Assets** (HQLAs) that is sufficient to fund cash outflows for 30 days.

In other words, LCR refers to the amount of HQLAs maintained by financial institutions as a proportion of Total Net Cash Flow Amount in order to ensure their ability to meet short-term financial obligations and disruptions.

Assets are considered to be high-quality liquid assets if they can be easily and immediately converted into cash at little or no loss of value. The liquidity of an asset depends on the underlying stress scenario, the volume to be monetised and the timeframe considered.

Following assets can be included in the stock of liquid assets without any limit:

i. Cash including cash reserves in excess of the required CRR
ii. Government Securities in excess of the minimum SLR requirement
iii. Within the mandatory SLR requirement, Government Securities to the extent allowed by RBI under Marginal Standing Facility (MSF)
iv. Marketable securities issued or guaranteed by foreign sovereigns satisfying some conditions

Mathematically, **LCR of a bank** = $\frac{\textbf{High-Quality Liquid Assets}}{\textbf{Total Net Cash Flows}}$

Further, as per Banking Regulation Act, 1949, the Banks in India are required to hold liquid assets to maintain SLR. In view of the fact that liquid assets under SLR and HQLAs under LCR are largely the same, RBI allowed banks to use a progressively increasing proportion of the SLR securities for being considered as HQLAs for LCR so that the need to maintain liquid assets for both the requirements is optimised.

Entire SLR-eligible assets held by banks have been permitted by RBI to be considered as HQLAs for meeting the LCR requirement.

As per initial RBI directive, Banks are required **to maintain LCR of 100 per cent** with effect from 1 January 2019.

SYSTEMICALLY IMPORTANT FINANCIAL INSTITUTION

A **Systemically Important Financial Institution** (SIFI) is a bank, insurance company or other financial institution whose failure might trigger a financial crisis. They are colloquially referred to as **'too big to fail'**. Certain large banks are recognised by several authorities as systemically important financial institutions, depending on the scale and the degree of influence they hold in global and domestic financial markets.

G-SIBs: Since 2011, the **Financial Stability Board** has started publishing a list of Global Systemically Important Banks **(G-SIBs).** They are identified by Basel Committee on banking supervision.

D-SIBs: Domestic Systemically Important Banks **(D-SIBs)** in India are recognised by RBI under its framework issued in 2014. **D-SIB means that the bank is too big to fail.** Banks whose assets **exceed 2 per cent of GDP** are considered as D-SIBs. SBI, ICICI Bank and HDFC Bank have been identified as **D-SIBs** by the RBI.

CREDIT RATING OF BANKS IN INDIA

As per the recommendations of **Padmanabhan Committee,** the Banks in India may be rated on a five-point scale from A to E, based on international **CAMELS Rating Model.**

Consequently, RBI evolved a model for credit rating of banks based on **CAMELS.** The following **six components** are weighed on a scale of 1 to 100 and contain several parameters with individual weightage:

1. **C**apital Adequacy Ratio
2. **A**sset quality
3. **M**anagement effectiveness
4. **E**arning
5. **L**iquidity
6. **S**ystems and controls

Important Committees related to Banking Reforms

Name of the Committee	To Recommend on
Nachiket Mor Committee, 2013	Comprehensive financial services for small businesses and low-income households
Justice M.B. Shah Committee, 2014	Investigating **Black Money**
P.J. Nayak Committee, 2014	Governance of Boards of Public Sector Banks
Jasbir Singh Committee, 2015	Differential premium system for banks
Deepak Mohanty Committee, 2015	Medium-term path of financial inclusion
L.P. Parthasarathi Committee, 2015	Urban Co-operative Banks Committee on data standardisation
Shankar Acharya Committee, 2016	Feasibility of a **new Financial Year**
Bimal Jalan Committee, 2018	Economic Capital Framework of RBI
Suresh Mathur Committee, 2018	Reviewing the regulatory framework of **Micro-insurance**
Harsh Vardhan Committee, 2019	Development of Housing Finance Securitisation Market
Usha Thorat Committee, 2019	RBI's Task Force on Offshore Rupee Markets
Surjit Bhalla Committee, 2019	High-Level Advisory Group for issue of **Elephant Bonds** (EB) to recover $500 billion Black Money. People declaring undisclosed income will be bound to invest 50% of that income in EB which is a 25-year sovereign Bond to fund long-term infrastructure projects
V.G. Kannan Committee, 2019	ATM Interchange Fee Structure
Tapan Ray Committee, 2019	Strengthening the supervisory framework of **Core Investment Companies** (CICs)
T.N. Manoharan Committee, 2019	Improving secondary market for Corporate Loans
Nandan Nilekhani Committee, 2019	Deepening of Digital Payments
P.K. Mohanty Committee, 2020	To review the present ownership guidelines and corporate structure of Indian Private Sector Banks
Deepak Pathak Committee, 2020	To study the use of QR Codes to process contactless transactions

Financial Stability and Development Council (FSDC)

- The Financial Stability and Development Council (FSDC) was established in **2010** as an apex level forum with the goals of institutionalising and strengthening the system for preserving financial stability, improving inter-regulatory cooperation, and encouraging the growth of the financial sector. It is not a statutory body.
- The **Finance Minister** serves as the **Chairman of FSDC.**

Its members comprise RBI Governor, financial sector regulators (RBI, SEBI, PFRDA, and IRDAI), Finance Secretary and/or Secretary, Department of Economic Affairs, Secretary, Department of Financial Services, and Chief Economic Adviser.

- **Responsibilities of FSDC include** - Financial Stability; Financial Sector Development; Inter-Regulatory Coordination; Financial Literacy; Financial Inclusion; Macro prudential supervision of the economy including the functioning of large financial conglomerates; Coordinating India's international interface with financial sector bodies like the Financial Action Task Force (FATF), Financial Stability Board (FSB), etc.
- No funds are separately allocated to FSDC for undertaking its activities.

FINANCIAL INCLUSION

Committee on Financial Inclusion (2008) defined Financial Inclusion as 'the process of ensuring access to financial services, timely and adequate credit for vulnerable groups such as weaker sections and low-income groups at an affordable cost'.

Basket of basic formal financial products and services generally includes savings, remittances, credit, Government-supported insurance and pension products.

United Nation's Sustainable Development Goals (SDGs) of 2030 view financial inclusion as a key enabler for achieving sustainable development for at least seven of its goals.

Achieving **Universal Financial Access** by 2020 (UFA 2020) has been one of the key developmental agenda of the **World Bank** too.

Benefits of Financial Inclusion

1. Culture of savings and financial safety is promoted through financial inclusion.
2. It has multiplier effect on the economy.
3. It helps in poverty alleviation.
4. It gives access to cheaper and formal credit sources.
5. It boosts jobs and self-employment.
6. It helps in achieving gender equality and women's economic empowerment.

India's Efforts for Financial Inclusion

Successive Indian Governments have taken a lot of initiatives since 1950s to encourage financial inclusion.

In 1956, the nationalisation of life insurance companies was done. The general insurance companies were nationalised in 1972. Nationalisation of banks was done in 1969 and 1980 to give impetus to financial inclusion.

As another measure to promote financial inclusion, **Lead Bank Scheme** was introduced in **1969** by assigning lead roles to individual banks (both in public sector and private sector) for a particular district. A bank having a relatively large network of branches in the rural areas of the given district are generally entrusted with the Lead Bank responsibility for that district. Accordingly, all the districts in the country have been allotted one Lead Bank each. The Lead Bank acts as a leader among all banks present in the district and co-ordinates their efforts to increase the flow of credit to priority sectors such as agriculture, small-scale industries, etc. in that district. The Lead Bank scheme is based on **Service Area Approach (SAA)** which was introduced in 1989, and is applicable on all SCBs and RRBs. The SAA was revised by RBI after its review in 2004. As per the revised SAA, while the SCBs and RRBs are free to lend in any rural and semi-urban area, the borrowers have the choice of approaching any bank branch for their credit requirements. **Lead Bank for every district is decided by RBI**. At present, **SBI** acts as a Lead Bank in the maximum number of districts in India.

Another scheme of **Banking Ombudsman** was introduced in **1995**, to receive and consider the complaints of the bank customers relating to deficiency in banking services. The Banking Ombudsman is appointed by RBI. This scheme is applicable to all Commercial Banks, Regional Rural Banks and Scheduled Primary Co-operative Banks having business in India. Any person (including NRI) having bank account in India may file a complaint with the Banking Ombudsman. No fee is charged for providing such grievance redressal services. However, the order passed by the Banking Ombudsman is not binding on the parties and they can file an appeal before appellate authority. The Banking Ombudsman scheme **continues** even today.

Recent Major Initiatives to improve Financial Inclusion

1. **Pradhan Mantri Jan Dhan Yojana** (PMJDY): Launched in 2014, it is a national mission for Financial Inclusion. It seeks to provide access to basic financial services through banks. Over 34 crore accounts have been opened under PMJDY.
2. **Pradhan Mantri Suraksha Bima Yojana** (PMSBY): It provides a renewable 1-year accidental death cum disability cover of ₹2 lakh to all subscribing bank account holders (in the age group of **18–70 years**) at a minimal premium of **₹12 per annum per subscriber**.
3. **Pradhan Mantri Jeevan Jyoti Bima Yojana** (PMJJBY): It provides 1-year term life insurance of ₹2 lakh to bank account holders (in the age group of **18–50 years**) for a premium of **₹330 per annum per subscriber**.
4. **Atal Pension Yojana** (APY): Under APY, a subscriber (in the age group of 18–40 years) will receive fixed monthly pension in the range of ₹1,000 to ₹5,000 after completing 60 years of age depending on the contributions made by the subscriber.
5. **Pradhan Mantri MUDRA Yojana** (PMMY): It was launched in 2015 to finance self-employment and small business enterprises, whereby the lending institutions provide finances to micro-entrepreneurs up to ₹10 lakh.
6. **For MSMEs**: **'National Mission for Capacity Building of Bankers for financing MSME Sector' (NAMCABS)** was launched for training of Bankers with credit-related issues of the MSME sector. Also, **Interest Subvention Scheme** has been launched for MSMEs to reduce cost of borrowings.
7. **For Agriculture**: Under Priority Sector Lending (PSL), domestic SCBs have to lend a certain percentage of their net credit to agriculture sector. Banks also extend collateral free loans to small and marginal farmers up to ₹1.6 lakh.

   Kisan Credit Card Scheme (KCC), introduced in 1998, is a tool for providing cash credit facility to the tenant farmers, oral lessees and share croppers. Recently, KCC facility has been extended also for animal husbandry and fisheries.
8. **Small Finance Banks** (SFBs) and **Payments Banks** were given licences in 2015. It was done to promote small savings accounts, remittance services and credit facility for migrant labours, small and marginal farmers, micro and small industries and unorganised sector entities.
9. **India Post Payments Bank** (IPPB) was launched in 2018. There are over 1.55 lakh Post Offices, and more than 3 lakh postmen and Grameen Dak Sewaks that are deepening financial inclusion.

10. 'Aadhaar' Card with biometric and Unique Identification numbers (UID) has helped in eliminating duplication and has helped in implementing Direct Benefit Transfers (DBTs) to bank accounts of beneficiaries. Along with Jan Dhan Accounts and mobile numbers, **JAM Trinity** (Jan Dhan, Aadhaar, Mobile) has been instrumental in driving financial inclusion.

11. **Mahila Samman Saving Certificate (MSSC)** is a new small savings scheme designed exclusively for female investors that was unveiled in Union Budget 2023–24 to encourage women to invest.

    Accounts created via this system is single-holder account that may be opened at the Post Office or at any registered bank. Any woman can create a Mahila Samman account, either for herself or for a little girl.

    A three-month gap must be maintained between the existing account and the establishment of another account. The minimum investment is ₹1000, while the maximum investment allowed under the scheme is ₹2 lakh. Interest rate is 7.5 per cent annually. After two years from the date of opening, the depositor will receive the qualifying balance.

Priority Sector Lending

RBI mandates banks to lend a certain portion of their funds to **specified vulnerable sectors of the economy**, which otherwise may not be attractive for banks from the profitability point of view.

All Scheduled Commercial Banks and Foreign Private Banks (with a sizeable presence in India) are mandated to set aside **40 per cent** of their **Adjusted Net Bank Credit (ANBC)** for lending to these sectors.

Regional Rural Banks, Co-operative Banks and Small Finance Banks have to allocate **75 per cent** of ANBC for PSL.

Priority Sector included the following categories:

a. Agriculture
b. Micro, Small and Medium Enterprises (MSMEs)
c. Export Credit
d. Education
e. Housing
f. Social Infrastructure
g. Renewable Energy
h. Others

In 2020, RBI assigned PSL status also to India's **Startup sector**.

Priority Sector Lending Certificates (PSLCs): Priority Sector Lending Certificates (PSLCs) are a mechanism to enable banks to achieve the priority sector lending target and sub-targets by purchase of these instruments in the event of shortfall. This also incentivises banks with surplus PSL as it allows them to sell their excess achievement over targets thereby enhancing lending to the categories under priority sector.

Existing Challenges for Achieving Financial Inclusion

1. Number of access points is less in some areas such as North Eastern Region, Left Wing Extremism–affected districts, Himalayan region and the identified aspirational districts.
2. Telecom connectivity, availability and affordability of smartphones also act as hindrance.
3. Illiteracy, fear of scams and risk averseness also prevent adoption of new technologies.

4. Ensuring viability and sustainability of business of the financial services provider in this space is equally challenging.

National Strategy for Financial Inclusion (2019–24)

RBI announced the National Strategy for Financial Inclusion (2019–24).

It identifies financial inclusion as a key driver of economic growth and poverty alleviation over the world. It aims to strengthen the broader ecosystem for promoting various modes of digital financial services.

It has been prepared by **Financial Inclusion Advisory Committee** (FIAC) of the RBI.

RBI has identified **six major strategic objectives** for financial inclusion:

Strategic Pillars of National Strategy for Financial Inclusion

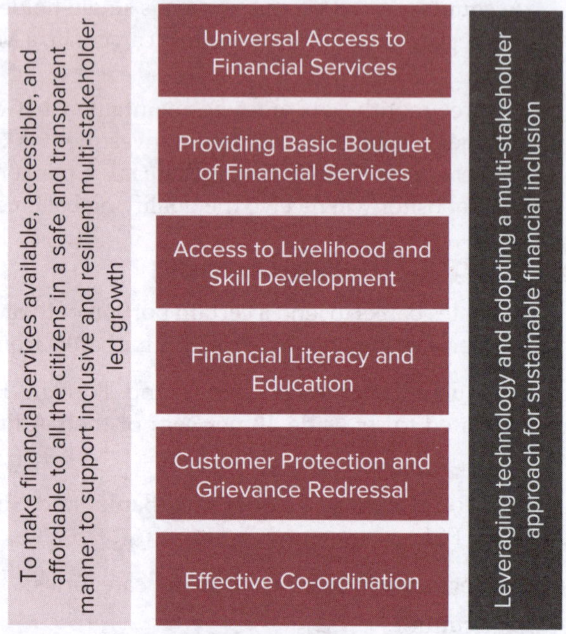

Source: Reserve Bank of India, 'Strategic Pillars of National Strategy for Financial Inclusion'. www.rbidocs.rbi.org.in.

In detail, these six strategic objectives are as follows:

1. **Universal access to financial services:**
   - Every village to have access to a formal financial service provider within a reasonable distance of 5 km radius.
   - It includes increasing outreach of banking outlets and also using innovations in Fin-Tech sector for increasing access.
2. **Providing basic bouquet of financial services:**
   - It includes a Basic Savings Bank Account, credit facilities, a micro life and non-life insurance product, a pension product and an investment product.
   - **Customised financial products** should be made.
   - In the Union Budget 2022–23, it was announced to set up a **National Financial Information Registry** (Public Credit Registry* – under a new name).

EXAM ESSENTIAL

***PUBLIC CREDIT REGISTRY**

It is a digital platform created by **RBI** to capture and store financial information of **borrowers** in India. Information on both existing and new borrowers will be stored in PCR. Lack of credit information gap will be filled by PCR. The RBI formed a High Level Task Force (Chair: Mr. Y. M. Deosthalee) to explore the scope of setting up a Public Credit Registry in India.

3. **Access to livelihood and skill development:**
    - New entrants should be informed about livelihood programmes such as National Rural Livelihoods Mission (NRLM), National Urban Livelihoods Mission (NULM) and Pradhan Mantri Kaushal Vikas Yojana (PMKVY).
4. **Financial literacy and education:**
    - Process Literacy along with Concept Literacy empowers the customers to understand about the products and also how to use them.
    - RBI, NABARD, NRLM resource persons, NGOs, Panchayats, SHGs, Farmers' Clubs, etc., should encourage financial literacy at the grassroots levels.
    - Development of financial literacy modules through National Centre for Financial Education (NCFE) to be undertaken to provide information to segments such as children, young adults, women, new workers/entrepreneurs, senior citizens, etc.
    - Expanding the reach of Centre for Financial Literacy (CFL) at block level in the country.
5. **Customer protection and grievance redressal:**
    - Internal Grievance Redressal Mechanism should be strengthened. Development of Common Toll-Free Helpline, customer grievance portal/mobile app to be ensured.
6. **Effective coordination:**
    - Ensuring continuous coordination between the key stakeholders, namely GoI, State Governments, the Regulators, financial service providers, Telecom Service Regulators and Skills Training Institutes.

National Strategy for Financial Education (2020–25)

In 2020, RBI released the NSFE which is to be implemented over next five years. The multi-stakeholder-led approach is aimed at creating a financially aware and empowered India.

It is the second NSFE *(first one was released in 2013).*

Basic objective of NFSE 2020–25 is **to manage the risk at various stages of life** through relevant and suitable insurance cover besides planning for old age and retirement through coverage of suitable pension products.

It has been prepared by the National Centre for Financial Education (NCFE) in consultation with the **RBI, SEBI, IRDAI, PFRDA** and other relevant stakeholders.

Key recommendations under NSFE are as follows:

a. To adopt a **'5 C' – Content, Capacity, Community, Communication and Collaboration** – approach to achieve the financial well-being of all Indians.

b. To develop a Financial Literacy content for school children, teachers, young adults, women, new entrants at workplace/entrepreneurs (MSMEs), senior citizens, persons with disabilities, illiterate people, etc.

c. To integrate the financial education content in the school curriculum, various professional and vocational courses and BEd/MEd programmes.

d. To develop a Code of Conduct for financial education providers.

e. To adopt a robust **'Monitoring and Evaluation Framework'** to assess the progress made under the strategy.

Significance: The strategy seeks to develop credit discipline and encourage availing of credit from formal financial institutions as per requirement. It wants to improve usage of digital financial services in a safe and secure manner.

EXAM ESSENTIAL

TWIN BALANCE SHEET PROBLEM

A balance sheet is a financial statement that displays an organisation's assets, liabilities, and equity holdings at any one time.

The twin balance sheet problem in India deals with the balance sheets of Indian companies and Indian Banks.

In a situation where banks are severely stressed and corporates are so overleveraged that they are unable to repay their loans, this is known as a twin balance sheet problem.

ACCOUNT AGGREGATOR

An Account Aggregator (AA) is a type of **RBI regulated entity** that **helps an individual to securely and digitally access and share information from one financial institution they have an account with, to any other regulated financial institution** in the AA network. Data cannot be shared without the consent of the individual. The individual's bank just needs to join the Account Aggregator network. Eight banks have already been part of this network; Four are already sharing data based on consent (Axis, ICICI, HDFC, and IndusInd Banks) and the other four are also working on the same lines (State Bank of India, Kotak Mahindra Bank, IDFC First Bank, and Federal Bank). Registering with an AA is **fully voluntary for consumers**.

For kind reference that Aadhaar eKYC and CKYC only allow sharing of four 'identity' data fields for KYC purposes (e.g. name, address, gender, etc.). Similarly, the credit bureau data shows only loan history and/or a credit score. The Account Aggregator network allows sharing of transaction data or bank statements from savings/deposit/current accounts.

SUMMARY

- **Reserve Bank of India** – Established in 1935 on the recommendations of Hilton Young Commission – Banker to the Government – Issuer of notes and coins (except ₹1) – Banker's Bank – custodian of Foreign Exchange Reserves – controller of credit or money supply.
- **Monetary Policy** – Macro-economic policy tool – used by RBI to influence the supply of money – quantitative instruments and qualitative instruments are used under it.
- **Quantitative Instruments** – Bank Rate (RBI provides long-term loans to SCBs without any approved securities) – Repo Rate (rate of interest at which RBI provides short-term loans to SCBs against approved securities) – Reverse Repo Rate (the rate at which SCBs deposit funds with RBI) – Open Market Operations (buying and selling of G-Secs in the open market) – Cash Reserve Ratio (minimum percentage of a bank's Total Demand and Time Liabilities that an SCB is obliged to deposit with RBI in the form of cash) – Statutory Liquidity Ratio (percentage of Net Demand and Time Liabilities of SCBs that are to be kept with them in the form of cash, gold or SLR securities)
- **Scheduled Commercial Bank (SCB)** – Listed in the Second Schedule of the RBI Act, 1934 – regulated under the provisions of Banking Regulation Act, 1949 – paid-up capital and reserves of not less than ₹5 lakh – types are: public sector banks, private sector Indian Banks, private sector foreign banks and regional rural banks.

- **Regional Rural Banks** – Set up on the recommendations of M. Narasimham Working Group – stakeholders are Central Government, Concerned State Government and the Sponsor Bank in the proportion of 50:15:35, respectively – supervised by NABARD.
- **Co-operative Banks** – Regulated through Banking Regulations Act, 1949 and Banking Laws (Co-operative Societies) Act, 1955 – functions with the rule of 'one member one vote' and on 'no profit no loss' basis.
- **Development Banks** – Provide long-term finance and support to the sectors of the Indian economy which possess higher risks and cannot have access to adequate loans from Commercial Banks – examples are NABARD, SIDBI, EXIM Bank, etc.
- **Non-Banking Financial Company (NBFC)** – Engaged in the business of loans and advances, acquisition and selling of shares, bonds, debentures, leasing, insurance, chit fund, etc. – cannot accept demand deposits – do not form part of the payment and settlement system and cannot issue cheques drawn on itself – not required to maintain reserve requirements.
- **Non-Performing Asset (NPA)** – An asset which is not producing any income – loan on which interest or principal amount is pending for 90 days or more.
- **Basel Norms** – Prescribed by Bank for International Settlements – set of global standards which prescribe for assets to minimum capital requirements for banking sector – three Basel Norms prescribed till date – Basel I, Basel II and Basel III Norms.
- **Financial Inclusion** – Process of ensuring access to financial service – timely and adequate credit for vulnerable groups such as weaker sections and low-income groups.

UPSC CSE PREVIOUS YEARS' PRELIMINARY EXAMINATION QUESTIONS

1. Consider the following statements: **[2024]**

1. In India, Non-Banking Financial Companies can access the Liquidity Adjustment Facility window of the Reserve Bank of India.
2. In India, Foreign Institutional Investors can hold the Government Securities (G-Secs).
3. In India, Stock Exchanges can offer separate trading platforms for debts.

Which of the statements given above is/are correct?

(a) 1 and 2 only (b) 3 only
(c) 1, 2 and 3 (d) 2 and 3 only

2. With reference to the rule/rules imposed by the Reserve Bank of India while treating foreign banks, consider the following statements: **[2024]**

1. There is no minimum capital requirement for wholly owned banking subsidiaries in India.
2. For wholly owned banking subsidiaries in India, at least 50% of the board members should be Indian nationals.

Which of the statements given above is/are correct?

(a) 1 only (b) 2 only
(c) Both 1 and 2 (d) Neither 1 nor 2

3. Consider the following statements: **[2023]**

Statement-I: In the post-pandemic recent past, many Central Banks worldwide had carried out interest rate hikes.

Statement-II: Central Banks generally assume that they have the ability to counteract the rising consumer prices via monetary policy means.

Which one of the following is correct in respect of the above statements?

(a) Both Statement-I and Statement-II are correct and Statement-II is the correct explanation for Statement-I.
(b) Both Statement-I and Statement-II are correct and Statement-II is not the correct explanation for Statement-I.
(c) Statement-I is correct but Statement-II is incorrect.

(d) Statement-I is incorrect but Statement-II is correct.

4. Which one of the following activities of the Reserve Bank of India is considered to be part of 'sterilisation'? **[2023]**

(a) Conducting 'Open Market Operations'
(b) Oversight of settlement and payment systems
(c) Debt and cash management for the Central and State Governments
(d) Regulating the functions of Nonbanking Financial Institutions

5. With reference to Central Bank digital currencies, consider the following statements: **[2023]**

1. It is possible to make payments in a digital currency without using US dollar or SWIFT system.
2. A digital currency can be distributed with a condition programmed into it such as a timeframe for spending it.

Which of the statements given above is/are correct?

(a) 1 only (b) 2 only
(c) Both 1 and 2 (d) Neither 1 nor 2

6. Consider the following statements: **[2023]**

1. The Self-Help Group (SHG) programme was originally initiated by the State Bank of India by providing microcredit to the financially deprived.
2. In an SHG, all members of a group take responsibility for a loan that an individual member takes.
3. The Regional Rural Banks and Scheduled Commercial Banks support SHGs.

How many of the above statements are correct?

(a) Only one (b) Only two
(c) All three (d) None

7. With reference to the 'Banks Board Bureau (BBB), which of the following statements are correct? **[2022]**

1. The Governor of RBI is the Chairman of BBB.
2. BBB recommends for the selection of heads for Public Sector Banks.
3. BBB helps the Public Sector Banks in developing strategies and capital raising plans.

Select the correct answer using the code given below:

(a) 1 and 2 only (b) 2 and 3 only
(c) 1 and 3 only (d) 1, 2 and 3

8. With reference to Non-Fungible Tokens (NFTs), consider the following statements: **[2022]**

1. They enable the digital representation of physical assets.
2. They are unique cryptographic tokens that exist on a blockchain.
3. They can be traded or exchanged at equivalency and therefore can be used as a medium of commercial transactions.

Which of the statements given above are correct?

(a) 1 and 2 only (b) 2 and 3 only
(c) 1 and 3 only (d) 1, 2 and 3

9. Consider the following statements: **[2021]**

1. The Governor of the RBI is appointed by the Central Government.
2. Certain provisions in the Constitution of India give the Central Government the right to issue directions to the RBI in the public interest.
3. The Governor of the RBI draws his power from the RBI Act.

Which of the above statements are correct?

(a) 1 and 2 only (b) 2 and 3 only
(c) 1 and 3 only (d) 1, 2 and 3

10. The money multiplier in an economy increases with which one of the following? **[2021]**

(a) Increase in the Cash Reserve Ratio in the banks.
(b) Increase in the Statutory Liquidity Ratio in the banks.
(c) Increase in the banking habit of the people.
(d) Increase in the population of the country.

11. In India, the Central Bank's function as the 'lender of last resort' usually refers to which of the following? **[2021]**

1. Lending to trade and industry bodies when they fail to borrow from other sources
2. Providing liquidity to the banks having a temporary crisis
3. Lending to Governments to finance budgetary deficits

Select the correct answer using the code given below:

(a) 1 and 2 (b) 2 only
(c) 2 and 3 (d) 3 only

12. With reference to Urban Cooperative Banks in India, consider the following statements: **[2021]**

1. They are supervised and regulated by local boards set up by the State Governments.

2. They can issue equity shares and preference shares.
3. They were brought under the purview of the Banking Regulation Act, 1949 through an Amendment in 1966.

Which of the statements given above is/are correct?
(a) 1 only (b) 2 and 3 only
(c) 1 and 3 only (d) 1, 2 and 3

13. With reference to **'Blockchain Technology'** consider the following statements: **[2020]**
1. It is a public ledger that everyone can inspect, but which no single user controls.
2. The structure and design of blockchain is such that all the data in it are about cryptocurrency only.
3. Applications that depend on basic features of blockchain can be developed without anybody's permission.

Which of the statements given above is/are correct?
(a) 1 only (b) 1 and 2 only
(c) 2 only (d) 1 and 3 only

14. If you withdraw ₹1,00,000 in cash from your Demand Deposit Account at your bank, the immediate effect on **aggregate money supply** in the economy will be: **[2020]**
(a) to reduce it by ₹1,00,000
(b) to increase it by ₹1,00,000
(c) to increase it by more than ₹1,00,000
(d) to leave it unchanged

15. If the RBI decides to adopt an **expansionist monetary policy**, which of the following would it not do? **[2020]**
1. Cut and optimise the Statutory Liquidity Ratio
2. Increase the Marginal Standing Facility Rate
3. Cut the Bank Rate and Repo Rate

Select the correct answer using the code given below:
(a) 1 and 2 only (b) 2 only
(c) 1 and 3 only (d) 1, 2 and 3

16. Consider the following statements: **[2020]**
1. In terms of short-term credit delivery to the agriculture sector, **District Central Co-operative Banks (DCCBs)** deliver more credit in comparison to Scheduled Commercial Banks and Regional Rural Banks.
2. One of the most important functions of DCCBs is to provide funds to the Primary Agricultural Credit Societies.

Which of the statements given above is/are correct?
(a) 1 only (b) 2 only
(c) Both 1 and 2 (d) Neither 1 nor 2

17. What is the importance of the term **'Interest Coverage Ratio'** of a firm in India? **[2020]**
1. It helps in understanding the present risk of a firm that a bank is going to give a loan to.
2. It helps in evaluating the emerging risk of a firm that a bank is going to give a loan to.
3. The higher a borrowing firm's level of Interest Coverage Ratio, the worse is its ability to service its debt.

Select the correct answer using the code given below:
(a) 1 and 2 only (b) 2 only
(c) 1 and 3 only (d) 1, 2 and 3

18. Which of the following phrases defines the nature of the **'Hundi'** generally referred to in the sources of the post-Harsha period? **[2020]**
(a) An advisory issued by the king to his subordinates
(b) A diary to be maintained for daily accounts
(c) A bill of exchange
(d) An order from the feudal lord to his subordinates

19. Which of the following is not included in the **assets of a Commercial Bank** in India? **[2019]**
(a) Advances
(b) Deposits
(c) Investments
(d) Money at call and short notice

20. What was the purpose of **Inter-Creditor Agreement** signed by Indian Banks and Financial Institutions recently? **[2019]**
(a) To lessen the Government of India's perennial burden of fiscal deficit and current account deficit.
(b) To support the infrastructure projects of Central and State Governments.
(c) To act as independent regulator in case of applications for loans of ₹50 crore or more.
(d) To aim at faster resolution of stressed assets of ₹50 crore or more which are under consortium lending.

21. The Chairman of Public Sector Banks is selected by the: **[2019]**
(a) Banks Board Bureau
(b) Reserve Bank of India
(c) Union Ministry of Finance
(d) Management of concerned bank

22. Which one of the following is not the most likely measure the Government/RBI takes to stop the slide of Indian rupee? **[2019]**
(a) Curbing imports of non-essential goods and promoting exports
(b) Encouraging Indian borrowers to issue rupee-denominated Masala Bonds
(c) Easing conditions relating to External Commercial Borrowings
(d) Following an expansionary monetary policy

23. Consider the following statements: **[2019]**
The Reserve Bank of India's recent directives relating to 'Storage of Payment System Data', popularly known as **data diktat**, command the payment system providers that:
1. They shall ensure that entire data relating to payment systems operated by them are stored in a system only in India.
2. They shall endure that the systems are owned and operated by Public Sector Enterprises.
3. They shall submit the consolidated system audit report to the Comptroller and Auditor General of India by the end of the calendar year.

Which of the statements given above is/are correct?
(a) 1 only (b) 1 and 2 only
(c) 3 only (d) 1, 2 and 3

24. The money multiplier in an economy increases with which one of the following? **[2019]**
(a) Increase in the Cash Reserve Ratio
(b) Increase in the banking habit of population
(c) Increase in the statutory liquidity ratio
(d) Increase in the population of the country

25. The Service Area Approach was implemented under the purview of **[2019]**
(a) Integrated Rural Development Approach
(b) Lead Bank Scheme
(c) Mahatma Gandhi National Rural Employment Guarantee Scheme
(d) National Skill Development Mission

26. Which one of the following best describes the term **'Merchant Discount Rate'** sometimes seen in news? **[2018]**
(a) The incentive given by a bank to a merchant for accepting payments through debit cards pertaining to that bank.
(b) The amount paid back by banks to their customers when they use debit cards for financial transactions for purchasing goods or services.
(c) The charge to a merchant by a bank for accepting payments from his customers through the bank's debit cards.
(d) The incentive given by the Government to merchants for promoting digital payments by their customers through point-of-sale (PoS) machines and debit cards.

27. Consider the following statements: **[2018]**
1. **Capital Adequacy Ratio** (CAR) is the amount that banks have to maintain in the form of their own funds to offset any loss that banks incur if the account holders fail to repay dues.
2. CAR is decided by each individual bank.

Which of the statements given above is/are correct?
(a) 1 only
(b) 2 only
(c) Both 1 and 2 only
(d) Neither 1 nor 2

28. Which one of the following statements correctly describes the meaning of legal tender money? **[2018]**
(a) The money which is tendered in courts of law to defray the fee of legal cases.
(b) The money which a creditor is under compulsion to accept in settlement of his claims.
(c) The bank money in the form of cheques, drafts, bills of exchange, etc.
(d) The metallic money in circulation in a country.

29. Consider the following statements: **[2018]**
1. The Reserve Bank of India manages and services the Government of India Securities but not any state Government securities.
2. Treasury Bills are issued by the Government of India and there are no Treasury Bills issued by the State Governments.

3. Treasury Bills offers are issued at a discount from the par value.

Which of the statements given above is/are correct?

(a) 1 and 2 only (b) 3 only
(c) 2 and 3 only (d) 1, 2 and 3

30. With reference to the governance of public sector banking in India, consider the following statements: **[2018]**

1. Capital infusion into Public Sector Banks by the Government of India has steadily increased in the last decade.
2. To put the public sector banks in order, the merger of associate banks with the parent State Bank of India has been affected.

Which of the statement given above is/are correct?

(a) 1 only (b) 2 only
(c) Both 1 and 2 (d) Neither 1 nor 2

31. Which of the following statements is/are correct regarding the **Monetary Policy Committee** (MPC)? **[2017]**

1. It decides the RBI's benchmark interest rate.
2. It is a 12-member body including the Governor of RBI and is reconstituted every year.
3. It functions under the Chairmanship of the Union Finance Minister.

Select the correct answer using the code given below:

(a) 1 only (b) 1 and 2 only
(c) 3 only (d) 2 and 3 only

32. Which of the following statements best describes the term 'Scheme for Sustainable Structuring of Stressed Assets **(S4A)**' recently seen in the news? **[2017]**

(a) It is a procedure for considering ecological costs of developmental schemes formulated by the Government.
(b) It is a scheme of RBI for reworking the financial structure of big corporate entities facing genuine difficulties.
(c) It is a disinvestment plan of the Government regarding Central Public Sector Undertakings.
(d) It is an important provision in 'The Insolvency and Bankruptcy Code' recently implemented by the Government.

33. What is the purpose of setting up of **Small Finance Banks** (SFBs) in India? **[2017]**

1. To supply credit to small business units
2. To supply credit to small and marginal farmers
3. To encourage young entrepreneurs to set up businesses particularly in rural areas

Select the correct answer using the code given below:

(a) 1 and 2 only (b) 2 and 3 only
(c) 1 and 3 only (d) 1, 2 and 3

34. Consider the following statements: **[2017]**

1. National Payments Corporation of India (NPCI) helps in promoting the financial inclusion in the country.
2. NPCI has launched Rupay, a card payment scheme.

Which of the statements given above is/are correct?

(a) 1 only (b) 2 only
(c) Both 1 and 2 (d) Neither 1 nor 2

35. Which of the following is a most likely consequence of implementing the 'Unified Payments Interface (UPI)'? **[2017]**

(a) Mobile wallets will not be necessary for online payments.
(b) Digital currency will totally replace the physical currency in about two decades.
(c) FDI inflows will drastically increase.
(d) Direct transfer of subsidies to poor people will become very effective.

36. The establishment of **'Payments Banks'** is being allowed in India to promote financial inclusion. Which of the following statements is/are correct in this context? **[2016]**

1. Mobile telephone companies and supermarket chains that are owned and controlled by residents are eligible to be promoters of Payments Banks.
2. Payments Banks can issue both credit cards and debit cards.
3. Payments banks cannot undertake lending activities.

Select the correct answer using the code given below:

(a) 1 and 2 only (b) 1 and 3 only
(c) 2 only (d) 1, 2 and 3

37. The term **'Core Banking Solution'** is sometimes seen in the news. Which of the following statements best describes/describe this term? **[2016]**

1. It is networking of a bank's branches which enable customers to operate their accounts from any branch of the bank on its network regardless of where they open their accounts.
2. It is an effort to increase RBI's control over commercial banks through computerisation.
3. It is a detailed procedure by which a bank with huge non-performing assets is taken over by another bank.

Select the correct answer using the code given below:

(a) 1 and 2 only (b) 2 and 3 only
(c) 1 and 3 only (d) 1, 2 and 3

38. Pradhan Mantri MUDRA Yojana is aimed at **[2016]**

(a) bringing the small entrepreneurs into formal financial system
(b) providing loans to poor farmers for cultivating particular crops
(c) providing pensions to old and destitute persons
(d) funding the voluntary organisations involved in the promotion of skill development and employment generation

39. **'Basel-III Accord'** or simply 'Basel-III' often seen in the news seeks to **[2015]**

(a) develop national strategies for the conservation and sustainable use of biological diversity
(b) improve banking sector's ability to deal with financial and economic stress and improve risk management
(c) reduce the greenhouse gas emissions but place a heavier burden on developed countries
(d) transfer technology from developed countries to poor countries to enable them to replace the use of chlorofluorocarbons in refrigeration with harmless chemicals

40. When the Reserve Bank of India reduced the **Statutory Liquidity Ratio** by 50 basis points, which of the following is likely to happen? **[2015]**

(a) India's GDP growth rate increases drastically.
(b) Foreign Institutional Investors may bring more capital into our country.
(c) Scheduled Commercial Banks may cut their lending rates.
(d) It may drastically reduce the liquidity to the banking system.

41. With reference to Indian economy, consider the following: **[2015]**

1. Bank Rate
2. Open Market Operations
3. Public Debt
4. Public Revenue

Which of the above is/are component/ components of Monetary Policy?

(a) 1 only (b) 2, 3 and 4
(c) 1 and 2 (d) 1, 3 and 4

42. What is/are the facility/facilities the beneficiaries can get from the services of **Business Correspondent** (Bank Saathi) in branchless areas? **[2014]**

1. It enables the beneficiaries to draw their subsidies and social security benefits in their villages.
2. It enables the beneficiaries in the rural areas to make deposits and withdrawals.

Select the correct answer using the code given below:

(a) 1 only (b) 2 only
(c) Both 1 and 2 (d) Neither 1 nor 2

43. The terms **'Marginal Standing Facility Rate'** and **'Net Demand and Time Liabilities'** sometimes appearing in news are used in relation to **[2014]**

(a) banking operations
(b) communication networking
(c) military strategies
(d) supply and demand of agricultural products

44. Consider the following liquid assets: **[2013]**

1. Demand deposits with the banks
2. Time deposits with the banks
3. Saving deposits with the banks
4. Currency

The correct sequence of these assets in the decreasing order of liquidity is

(a) 1-4-3-2 (b) 4-3-2-1
(c) 2-3-1-4 (d) 4-1-3-2

45. In the context of Indian economy, 'Open Market Operations' refers to **[2013]**

(a) borrowing by scheduled banks from the RBI

(b) lending by commercial banks to industry and trade
(c) purchase and sale of Government Securities by the RBI
(d) none of the above

46. Priority Sector Lending by banks in India constitutes the lending to **[2013]**
(a) Agriculture
(b) Micro and Small enterprises
(c) Weaker Sections
(d) All of the above

47. Supply of money remaining the same when there is increase in demand for money, there will be **[2013]**
(a) a fall in the level of prices
(b) an increase in the rate of interest
(c) a decrease in the rate of interest
(d) an increase in the level of income and employment

48. Which of the following grant/grants direct credit assistance to rural households? **[2013]**
1. Regional Rural Banks
2. National Bank for Agriculture and Rural Development
3. Land Development Banks

Select the correct answer using the codes given below:
(a) 1 and 2 only (b) 2 only
(c) 1 and 3 only (d) 1, 2 and 3

49. The Reserve Bank of India regulates the commercial banks in matters of **[2013]**
1. liquidity of assets
2. branch expansion
3. merger of banks
4. winding up of banks

Select the correct answer using the codes given below:
(a) 1 and 4 only
(b) 2, 3 and 4 only
(c) 1, 2 and 3 only
(d) 1, 2, 3 and 4

50. An increase in the Bank Rate generally indicates that the **[2013]**
(a) Market rate of interest is likely to fall
(b) Central Bank is no longer making loans to commercial banks
(c) Central Bank is following an easy money policy
(d) Central Bank is following a tight money policy

51. The Reserve Bank of India (RBI) acts as a **banker's bank**. This would imply which of the following? **[2012]**
1. Other banks retain their deposits with the RBI
2. The RBI lends funds to the commercial banks in times of need
3. The RBI advises the commercial banks on monetary matters

Select the correct answer using the codes given below:
(a) 2 and 3 only (b) 1 and 2 only
(c) 1 and 3 only (d) 1, 2 and 3

52. Which of the following measures would result in an increase in the money supply in the economy? **[2012]**
1. Purchase of Government securities from the public by the Central Bank
2. Deposit of currency in commercial banks by the public
3. Borrowing by the Government from the Central Bank
4. Sale of Government Securities to the public by the Central Bank

Select the correct answer using the codes given below:
(a) 1 only (b) 2 and 4 only
(c) 1 and 3 only (d) 2, 3 and 4

53. The basic idea of **Lead Bank Scheme** is that **[2012]**
(a) big banks should try to open offices in each district
(b) there should be stiff competition among the various nationalised banks
(c) individual banks should adopt particular district for intensive development
(d) all the banks should make intensive efforts to mobilise deposits

54. The lowering of bank rate by the Reserve Bank of India leads to **[2011]**
(a) more liquidity in the market
(b) less liquidity in the market
(c) no change in the liquidity in the market
(d) mobilisation of more deposits by commercial banks

55. In India, which of the following has the highest share in the disbursement of credit to agriculture and allied activities? **[2011]**
(a) Commercial Banks
(b) Co-operative banks
(c) Regional Rural banks
(d) Micro Finance Institutions

56. With reference to the institution of **Banking Ombudsman** in India, which one of the statements is not correct? **[2010]**
(a) The Banking Ombudsman is appointed by the Reserve Bank of India.
(b) The Banking Ombudsman can consider complaints from Non-Resident Indians having accounts in India.
(c) The orders passed by the Banking Ombudsman are final and binding on the parties concerned.
(d) The service provided by the Banking Ombudsman is free of any fee.

57. With reference to the India, consider the following: **[2010]**
1. Nationalisation of Banks
2. Formation of Regional Rural Banks
3. Adoption of villages by Bank Branches

Which of the above can be considered as steps taken to achieve the 'financial inclusion' in India?
(a) 1 and 2 only (b) 2 and 3 only
(c) 3 only (d) 1, 2 and 3

58. Consider the following statements: **[2010]**
The functions of commercial banks in India include
1. purchase and sale of shares and securities on behalf of customers
2. acting as executors and trustees of wills

Which of the statements given above is/are correct?
(a) 1 only
(b) 2 only
(c) Both 1 and 2
(d) Neither 1 nor 2

59. In India, the interest rate on savings account in all the nationalised commercial banks is fixed by **[2010]**
(a) Union Ministry of Finance
(b) Union Finance Commission
(c) Indian Banks' Association
(d) None of the above

60. Which of the following terms indicates a mechanism used by commercial banks for providing credit to the Government? **[2010]**
(a) Cash Credit Ratio
(b) Debt Service Obligation
(c) Liquidity Adjustment Facility
(d) Statutory Liquidity Ratio

61. With the reference of the Non-Banking Financial Companies (NBFCs) in India, consider the following statements: **[2010]**
1. They cannot engage in the acquisition of Securities issued by the Government
2. They cannot accept demand deposits like Saving Account

Which of the statements given above is/are correct?
(a) 1 only
(b) 2 only
(c) Both 1 and 2
(d) Neither 1 nor 2

62. When the Reserve Bank of India announces an increase of the Cash Reserve Ratio, what does it mean? **[2010]**
(a) The Commercial Banks will have less money to lend.
(b) The Reserve Bank of India will have less money to lend.
(c) The Union Government will have less money to lend.
(d) The Commercial Banks will have more money to lend.

ANSWER KEY

1. (c)	2. (b)	3. (a)	4. (a)	5. (c)
6. (b)	7. (b)	8. (a)	9. (c)	10. (c)
11. (b)	12. (b)	13. (d)	14. (d)	15. (b)
16. (b)	17. (a)	18. (c)	19. (b)	20. (d)
21. (a)	22. (d)	23. (a)	24. (b)	25. (b)
26. (c)	27. (a)	28. (b)	29. (c)	30. (b)
31. (a)	32. (b)	33. (a)	34. (c)	35. (a)
36. (b)	37. (a)	38. (a)	39. (b)	40. (c)
41. (c)	42. (c)	43. (a)	44. (d)	45. (c)
46. (d)	47. (b)	48. (c)	49. (d)	50. (d)
51. (a)	52. (c)	53. (c)	54. (a)	55. (a)
56. (c)	57. (d)	58. (c)	59. (d)	60. (d)
61. (b)	62. (a)			

UPSC CSE PREVIOUS YEARS' MAIN EXAMINATION QUESTIONS

1. **Pradhan Mantri Jan Dhan Yojana (PMJDY)** is necessary for bringing unbanked to the institutional finance fold. Do you agree with this for financial inclusion of the poorer section of the Indian society? Give arguments to justify your opinion. **[2016]**

☞ NO QUESTIONS ASKED
2024, 2023, 2022, 2021, 2020, 2019, 2018, 2017, 2015, 2014, 2013

CHAPTER

12

FINANCIAL MARKET

CHAPTER OUTLINE

- Financial Market
- Money Market
- Terms relating to Money Market
- Common Money Market Instruments
- Capital Market
- Primary Market vs Secondary Market
- Financial Instruments in Capital Market
- Shares
- Debentures
- Bonds
- Some Major Bonds in India
- Sovereign Gold Bond Scheme
- Mutual Funds
- Derivatives
- Real Estate Investment Trust (REIT)
- Exchange Traded Fund (ETF)
- The Securities Contracts (Regulation) Act, 1956
- SEBI
- Functions of SEBI
- SEBI and Capital Market Reforms
- Securities Appellate Tribunal
- Stock Exchange
- Bombay Stock Exchange
- National Stock Exchange
- International Financial Services Centres Authority (IFSCA)
- Spot Exchanges
- Harnessing Digital Technologies in Central Banks: Opportunities and Challenges
- Indian Energy Exchange
- Indian Gas Exchange
- Foreign Account Tax Compliance Act
- Credit Rating Agencies

FINANCIAL MARKET

A Financial Market is a place or system where buyers and sellers trade financial instruments like **bonds, equities, stocks, various international currencies and derivatives**. Financial markets facilitate the trade between those who need capital with those who have capital to invest. It is basically of two types: **Capital Market** and **Money Market**.

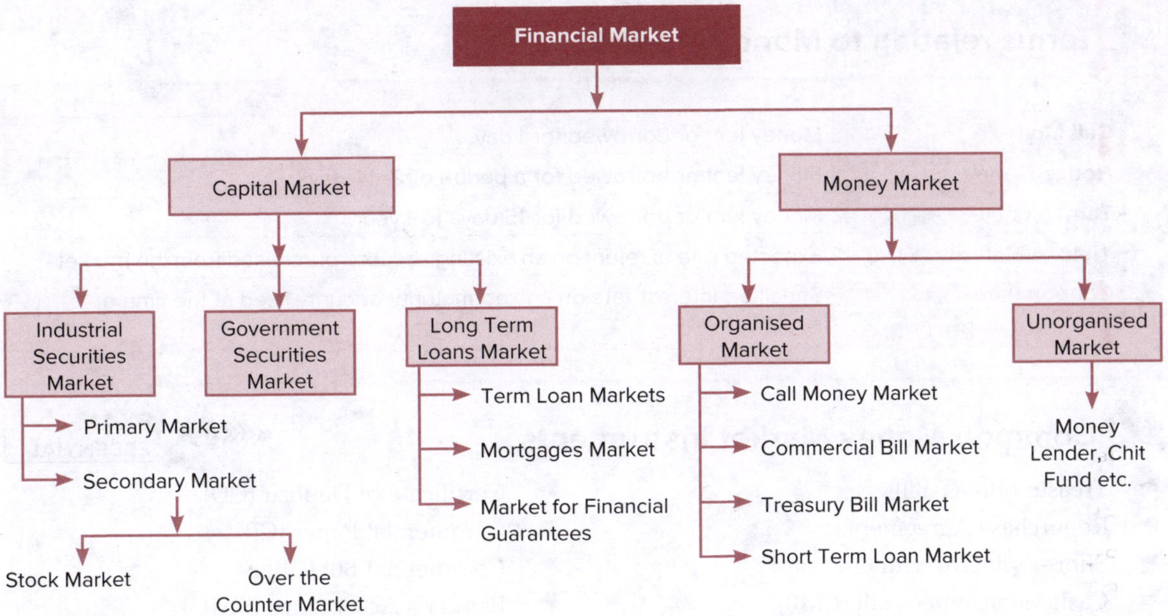

Functions of Financial Market

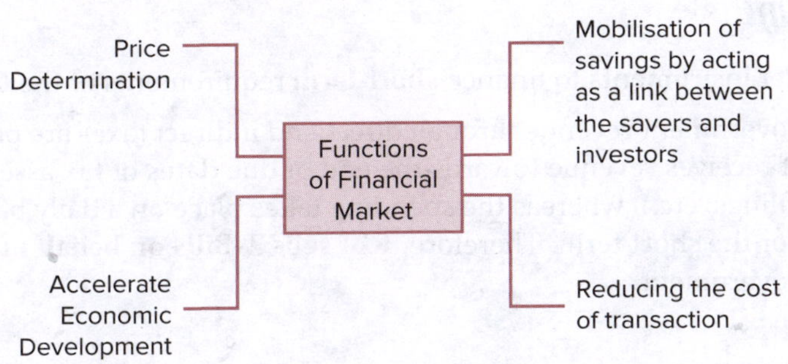

MONEY MARKET

- A money market is a place where short-term loans and financial assets **(maturity up to 1 year)** are bought and sold. **Participants** in the organised money market are RBI, banks, Non-Banking Financial Companies (NBFCs), mutual funds, insurance companies, Financial Institutions (FIs), insurance companies, etc.
- There is **no fixed place** to buy and sell these securities and the transactions can take place online.
- India also has an unorganised money market since ancient times, which includes local moneylenders, chit funds, etc. They are unregulated by the Government.

Terms relating to Money Market

Call Money	Money lent or borrowed for 1 day.
Notice Money	Money lent or borrowed for a period of 2–14 days.
Term Money	Money lent or borrowed for 15 days to 1 year.
Yield to Maturity (YTM)	Expected rate of return on an existing security purchased from the market.
Coupon Rate	Specified interest rate on a fixed maturity security fixed at the time of issue.

Common Money Market Instruments

EXAM ESSENTIAL

- Treasury Bill (T-Bill)
- Repurchase Agreements
- Short-term Government Bond
- Cash Management Bill (CMB)
- Ways and Means Advances (WMAs)
- Certificate of Deposit (CD)
- Commercial Paper (CP)
- Commercial Bill (CB)
- Banker's Acceptance (BA)
- Money Market Mutual Fund (MMMF)

Treasury Bill (T-Bill)

These are money market instruments to finance **short-term** requirements of the Government of India.

Generally, receipt of Government revenue through direct and indirect taxes are periodical and seasonal in nature. Government receives revenue towards the end of due dates of tax assessment (GST returns, quarterly advance tax filings, etc.), whereas the spending takes place on a daily basis, for which there is requirement of funds for the short term. Therefore, **RBI sells T-Bills on behalf of Central Government** as it is banker to the Government.

Features of T-Bills

- These are discounted securities, i.e., they are **issued at discount** and redeemed at par or at face value. For example, T-Bills can be issued at ₹97 with ₹100 as par value or face value; ₹3 difference will be interest income of the lender.
- These bills are considered **risk free.** They are highly liquid.
- These bills are issued by the Central Government and the bills are **sold by RBI** on behalf of the Government. State Government **does not** issue the T-Bills.
- **Buyers of T-Bills** include RBI itself, Commercial Banks, NBFCs, LIC, UTI (Unit Trust of India) and GIC (General Insurance Company). Individuals, trusts, and institutions can buy T-bills. They can be bought through–
  a. **Retail Direct Scheme Account:** Setting up an account with the RBI to purchase T-bills.
  b. **Stock exchange:** Buying T-bills through the stock exchange.
  c. **Authorised brokers:** Buying T-bills through authorised brokers.
- There are four types of active/auctioned T-Bills depending upon their tenure:
  - 14-day T-Bill

- 91-day T-Bill
- 182-day T-Bill
- 364-day T-Bill

- Banks can keep T-Bills as a part of SLR requirements and they also give T-Bills to RBI to receive loan under Repo.
- T-Bills are available for a minimum amount of ₹25,000 or in multiples of ₹25,000.

BONUS KNOWLEDGE

YIELD RATE ON TREASURY BILLS

The percentage of yield generated from a treasury bill can be calculated by using the following formula –

$$Y = (100 - P)/P \times 365/D \times 100$$

where Y = Return per cent

P = Discounted price at which a security is purchased

D = Tenure of the bill

Example: If the RBI issues a 91-day treasury bill at a discounted value of ₹96 and the face value of the bill is ₹100, then the yield on such G-Secs can be calculated as follows –

$$\text{Yield} = (100 - 96)/96 \times 365/91 \times 100 = 16.71\%$$

Repurchase Agreements

- Repurchase agreements, often known as repos, are short-term lending arrangements in which a bank sells securities to an investor, typically government bonds or other debt instruments with stable values and then buys them back a short while later at a slightly higher price.
- There are two types of repos – **Overnight repo** (mature the following day) and **Term repo** (mature at a future date). Repos that do not have a maturity date are referred to as Open Repo and are subject to termination at any moment by any party.

Short-Term Government Bond

- Government debt securities with a short maturity period, usually a few months to a few years, are known as short-term government bonds. As the government itself is issuing these bonds with its complete faith and credit, they are regarded as low-risk investments.

Cash Management Bill (CMB)

- CMB was introduced in 2010.
- It is a short-term security sold by RBI on behalf of Government of India to raise money for temporary needs of the Central Government.
- It is **similar to T-Bills,** but the **tenure is less than 91 days.**
- It is **issued at discount** to the face value through auctions as in the case of the T-Bills, to meet the short-term cash flow mismatches of the Government.
- CMB investments are also accepted by banks as qualified government securities investments for SLR purposes under Section 24 of the Banking Regulation Act of 1949.

Ways and Means Advances (WMAs)

- WMAs was introduced as per an agreement between RBI and Government of India. WMAs are temporary loans/overdrafts by RBI to Government (**both Central and States**) under Section 17(5) of RBI Act, 1934. WMAs replaced the adhoc T-Bills system.
- The objective of WMAs is **to bridge the time interval of mismatch** between Government expenditure and receipts. These are not a source of finance. If the government avails immediate cash from the RBI under WMA, the amount should be returned within 90 days.
- If the WMA repayment surpasses 90 days, it is treated as an overdraft.
- Ways and Means Advances can be classified as either normal or special.
- The state's government securities are used as collateral for a special WMA, or special drawing facility.
- The state receives normal WMA once the SDF limit has been reached.
- For normal WMA, the rate of interest applicable for funding from RBI is the repo rate and overdrafts are given at a rate of repo plus 2 per cent.

Certificate of Deposit (CD)

- Certificates of Deposit (CDs) are issued by Scheduled Commercial Banks (SCBs) (excluding Regional Rural Banks and Local Area Banks) and selected Financial Institutions (FIs) that have been permitted by RBI to raise short-term funds. It is used by banks to meet its own short-term funds requirement.
- Minimum amount of a CD should be ₹1 lakh, and in multiples of ₹1 lakh thereafter.
- The maturity period of CDs issued by SCBs is more than **7 days and less than 1 year.** The FIs can issue CDs for a period not less than 1 year and not exceeding 3 years from the date of issue. Withdrawal of CD before the due date results in a penalty.
- CDs can be issued to individuals, corporations, companies (including banks and Primary Dealers), trusts, funds, associations, etc. Non-Resident Indians (NRIs) may also subscribe to CDs, but only on non-repatriable basis.
- CDs are **issued at a discount** on face value. Deposits can be done by individuals, corporates, mutual fund companies, insurance companies, etc.
- CDs are freely transferable.
- It is taxable under the Income Tax Act.
- Banks/FIs cannot grant loans against CDs. Furthermore, they cannot buy-back their own CDs before maturity.

Commercial Paper (CP)

- Commercial paper (CP) introduced during 1990, is a short-term money market instrument issued as an unsecured promissory note and is privately placed.
- Companies, Primary Dealers (PDs) and FIs permitted by RBI, can issue CPs to meet their short-term funds requirement. A corporate would be eligible to issue CP provided it complies to certain financial conditions.
- Maturity is **minimum 7 days and maximum up to 1 year** and amount is minimum **₹5 lakh or multiples thereof.** It is necessary for the issuers to get their credit rating done.

- CP can be bought by individuals, banking companies, other corporate bodies registered or incorporated in India and unincorporated bodies, Non-Resident Indians (NRIs) and Foreign Institutional Investors (FIIs).

Note:

The formula for estimating discounted price of a commercial paper:

Price = Face Value/ [1 + yield × (no. of days to maturity/365)]

Yield = (Face value – Price)/ (price × no. of days to maturity) × 365 × 100

Commercial Bill (CB)

- Bills are **negotiable instruments** drawn by the seller or buyer of goods for the value of goods delivered. These are called **trade bills.**
- The trade bills become CBs **when they are accepted by Commercial Banks.** The maximum allowed period is 90 days.
- These bills are discounted by the Commercial Banks first and then it is further re-discounted by RBI.
- It is **not popular in India** and the market for CBs is under-developed in India.

Bankers Acceptance (BA)

A time draft that has been drawn on and approved by a bank is known as a Bankers Acceptance (BA). The draft is an instruction from the drawer to the bank to pay a certain amount of money to a designated individual or to the draft bearer on a certain date. It is not an obligation of a bank prior to acceptance.

Money Market Mutual Funds (MMMFs)

A Money Market Mutual Fund invests in debt securities with short maturities and little credit risk. MMMFs are among the least volatile forms of investing. A money market mutual fund's income might be taxable or tax-exempt, depending on the securities in which it invests.

Money Market Reforms

On the recommendations of the **Sukhamoy Chakravarty Committee** (1985), **Vaghul Committee** (1987) and the **Narasimham Committee** (1991):

- Interest Rate was deregulated.
- Electronic transactions were promoted to impart more transparency.
- Money Market Mutual Funds (MMMFs) allowed to sell units to corporates and individuals.
- Discount and Finance House of India (DFHI) was set up jointly by the RBI, Public Sector Banks and Financial Institutions.
- Liquidity Adjustment Facility (LAF) introduced. LAF adjusts liquidity in the market through absorption and or injection of financial resources by the RBI.
- Development of new market instruments like Market Stabilisation Scheme (MSS), etc.

CAPITAL MARKET

In a broader context, it is a place where savings and capital from investors are channelised to those companies or entities that require money for their business or operations.

Businesses require capital or finance to fund their growth. For example, purchase of new land, building or machinery, hiring of new employees, development of new products, etc. And generally, no business can grow only through its own financial resources. It has to look out for newer and outside source of funding. Such businesses can tap capital markets for their funding requirements.

Individuals and entities having **surplus funds** or **savings** look for avenues to invest for capital gains and income in Capital markets. Thus, capital markets serve the purpose of **channelising savings** and surplus funds into **investments.**

Even the Government, for meeting its development goals, likes creating new infrastructure and capital formation, participates in capital market by raising funds from individuals and financial institutions through Government Bonds or **Dated Government Securities.**

Capital Markets include both debt (**bond, debentures,** etc.) and equity (**shares**). Generally, the period of investment in Capital Markets is more than 1 year, as it caters to long-term needs of the borrower.

The Capital Market can be of two types:

1. **Primary Markets** are those where fresh capital or funds are raised, generally, for the first time, such as through Initial Public Offer (IPO), Follow-on Public Offer (FPO), etc. It is also called **new issue market.** Individuals (called retail investors), financial institutions, mutual funds and insurance companies can subscribe to new issue of a company. Prior permission from Securities and Exchange Board of India (SEBI) is required for IPOs.
2. **Secondary Markets** are where existing securities of companies are traded through stock exchanges like Bombay Stock Exchange (BSE) and National Stock Exchange (NSE). Here, publicly traded companies can raise additional funds. It is suitable for investors who are looking to invest in well-established companies. Investors need a **demat account** with a depository like Central Depositories Services Limited (**CDSL**) or National Securities Depository Limited (**NSDL**) and a trading account with a stock broker to purchase/sell securities.

Secondary markets are very important and are **regulated by SEBI.** They are places where **constant buying and selling of securities** take place.

PRIMARY MARKET *VS* SECONDARY MARKET

Primary Market	Secondary Market
New market securities are sold.	Only existing shares are traded.
Only buying of securities takes place.	Both buying and selling of securities take place.
The price of securities is decided by the management of the company with due compliance with SEBI's requirement.	The price of the securities is determined by the demand and supply of the market.
There is no fixed geographical location for new issue market.	They are located at specified places, e.g., NSE is situated in Mumbai.
Major intermediaries in primary market are merchant banks, underwriters, debenture trustees, portfolio managers etc.	Major intermediaries in secondary market are brokers, jobbers etc.

FINANCIAL INSTRUMENTS IN CAPITAL MARKET

EXAM ESSENTIAL

Shares

- The capital of a company is divided into shares. Each share forms a unit of ownership of the company and is offered for sale so as to raise capital for the company.
- The shareholders receive dividends (not interest) as return from the company
- They also enjoy/suffer capital gains/losses at the time of sale of shares.
- Shares can broadly be divided into two categories:
  1. **Equity shares**
  2. **Preference shares**
- **Equity shares** give their holders the power to **share the earnings/profits** in the company as well as a vote in the AGMs of the company. Such a shareholder has to share the profits and also bear the losses incurred by the company.
- **Equity shareholders** are regarded as the **real owners** of the company.
- On the other hand, **Preference Shares** earn their holders only dividends, which are fixed, giving **no voting rights.** Preference share has sub-types such as:
  (a) Cumulative Preference Shares – Preference Shares whose dividend (if not paid in a particular year by company due to loss) gets accumulated and is paid in the year of profit.
  (b) Non-cumulative Preference Shares – Preference Shares whose dividend does not get accumulated if not paid by the company due to losses incurred in that year.

BONUS KNOWLEDGE

WHAT IS A DIVIDEND?

A dividend, which comes from the company's net profit, is a benefit that publicly listed companies give to their shareholders. These rewards are often provided from the remaining portion of earnings after necessary expenses are covered. Following are the types of dividends:

- **Special Dividend:** It is paid on common stock. In certain situations, it is often issued when a company has made significant profits over a number of years.
- **Preferred Dividend:** Preferred stock owners get this type of dividend, which typically accrues a fixed amount and is paid on a quarterly basis. Additionally, shares that function more like bonds get this type of dividend.
- **Interim Dividend:** Before the final full-year accounts are prepared, firms declare interim dividends.
- **Final Dividend:** A final dividend is declared after the accounts for the year are prepared.

Debentures

These are the **debt instruments with a fixed rate of interest** issued by a company and are not backed by any specific security. It can be for medium or long term and is fully repayable on the maturity date. Many investors prefer debentures because it offers higher rate of interest than fixed deposits (FDs).

Interest rates also depend upon the credit rating given by the Credit Rating Agencies (CRAs) such as CARE, ICRA, etc. A lower rated debenture will carry a higher rate of interest because the risk involved is considered high.

Features of Debentures

- It is for medium to long-term tenure.
- The company is liable to pay the debenture holders a specified amount with interest. Although debentures form part of a company's capital structure, it is not considered as share/equity capital.
- Debentures are generally transferable.
- The holder **does not get any right to vote** in the company's general meetings unlike equity shareholders.
- The interest paid on debentures is a charge against profits of the company and it reduces the gross profit.

Common types of Debentures include

- Convertible Debentures – which can be converted into shares;
- Non-Convertible Debentures (NCDs) – which cannot be converted into shares;
- Redeemable Debentures – which are redeemed by the issuer after maturity;
- Irredeemable Debentures – which are not redeemed by the issuer.

Bonds

- A bond is a **debt instrument** through which Government, Government agencies or large corporations borrow funds for a defined period of time at a floating or fixed interest rate.
- Government uses bonds as a means to raise funds to meet its expenditure requirements which are generally capital in nature. Bodies like National Highways Authority of India (NHAI) issue bonds frequently to fund the creation of infrastructure.
- Bonds are also similar to debentures but the term 'bond' is generally used when such security is issued by Government or Governmental body like municipalities. However, in India, bonds and debentures are often used interchangeably.

The Bond Yield

- In simple words, the yield of a bond is **the effective return that it earns. Yield fluctuates according to numerous factors including global markets and the economy.**
- Every bond has a face value and a coupon payment (interest to be paid **on face value**).
- For example, if someone buys a bond of face value ₹100 and gets coupon interest of ₹10 for a year, then his yield is 10 per cent (10*100/100).
- However, the bonds **can be purchased in the market at a value which is lower or higher than the face value, this is called actual purchase price of bond.**
- Now, the important question is that what are the factors which affect the actual price of bond to fall or rise.
- Imagine a situation, where the interest rate in the broader economy is different from the initial coupon payment promised by a bond. For example, interest rate on savings is only 4 per cent, whereas, the bond is giving 5 per cent interest rate. Then, more and more people will go to buy

the bond. This will increase the price of the bond. Opposite to it, if interest rate on savings is 6 per cent, then fewer people will go to buy the bond thus, fall in its price.

- Other factors which can affect the actual price of the bond and the bond yield, in a similar manner, are:
  a. Inflation.
  b. Open Market Operations by RBI – sell or purchase of bonds.
  c. Fiscal policy of the Government.
  d. Position of domestic economy as well as global economy – investors will look for safer economies.
  e. Yield from competitive instruments like bonds in USA.

BONUS KNOWLEDGE

YIELD TO MATURITY (YTM)

Yield to maturity is the total return one would expect to receive if the security is being held until maturity. Yield to maturity is essentially the discount rate at which the present value of future payments (investment income and return of principal) equals the price of the security.

YIELD CURVE

It is the graphical relationship between yield and maturity among bonds of different maturities and the same credit quality. This curve shows the term structure of interest rates. It also enables investors to compare debt securities with different maturities and coupons.

Some Major Bonds in India

Government Bond

A government bond is a debt instrument that is issued **by the Central and State Governments** of India. It is issued when the issuing authority (Central or State governments) face a liquidity crisis and fund requirement is necessary for the purpose of infrastructural development.

This type of bond is a contract between the issuer and the investor, in which the issuer guarantees interest earnings on the face value of bonds held by investors along with repayment of the principal value within a stipulated time period.

Zero Coupon Bond

A regular bond (coupon bond) pays interest to bondholders over the life of the bond and repays the principal at the time of maturity. But a zero-coupon bond does not pay interest. The face value of the bond is received by the bondholders after it reaches maturity.

Corporate Bond

A corporate bond is a type of bond that a company issues to raise money for a number of purposes, including ongoing operations, mergers and acquisitions, or business expansion. It is a long-term debt instrument that certifies that a business has taken out a certain loan and agrees to pay it back over time under predetermined conditions.

Tax-Free Bond

Public enterprises issue fixed-income securities. These are referred to as tax-free bonds. They provide investors the potential for **yearly pre-fixed interest returns** and are a relatively safe investment option. Furthermore, the interest earned is tax-free, allowing investors to boost their savings. As with other bonds, the principal amount is due upon maturity.

These bonds typically have maturities ranging from **10 to 20 years,** with lower interest rates than other fixed-income investment choices. As a result, they are regarded as a safe investment option, ideal for investors seeking a dependable, long-term investment with tax benefits.

Inflation Indexed Bond

Inflation Indexed Bond (IIB) provides a constant return **irrespective of the level of inflation** and protects the investor against macroeconomic risks.

Initially, IIBs were issued in the name of Capital Indexed Bonds (CIBs) during 1997. The CIBs provided inflation protection only to principal and not to interest payment. However, IIBs provide inflation protection to both principal and interest payments.

IIBs are G-Secs and are issued as part of the Government market borrowing programme. They are eligible for maintaining Statutory Liquidity Ratio (SLR) by banks. Government can cut down the coupon rates on its borrowing by way of IIBs.

Capital Gain Bond

Capital Gain Bonds, also known as **54EC Bonds**, are bonds issued by NHAI, REC, and PFC in accordance with Section 54EC of the Income Tax Act. 54EC Bonds are an excellent alternative for investors who anticipate long-term financial gains from the sale of a property. These bonds help one get tax breaks worth up to ₹50 lakh every year.

Negative Yield Bond

A negative yield bond is when an investor **receives less money at the bond's maturity** than the original purchase price of the bond.

They are **issued by the Central Banks** during times of stress and uncertainty, as investors look to protect their capital from significant erosion.

During COVID-19 pandemic, Negative Yield Bonds were in high demand in European and many other countries.

Municipal Bond

Municipal bonds, also known as **'Munis'**, are fixed-income instruments or debt securities issued by the government or semi-government institutions to fund civic projects. The interest earned on these bonds is tax-free, provided the buyer adheres to the guidelines set by the municipal corporation.

There are two main types of municipal bonds: General Obligation Bonds and Revenue Bonds. General Obligation Bonds are used to improve civic amenities such as water supply, sanitation, and garbage disposal, while Revenue Bonds are issued for specific projects like constructing toll roads or bridges. Municipal bonds have been present in the Indian market since 1997. The Bangalore Municipal Corporation was the first urban local body to

> **did you KNOW?** In 2017, the Pune Municipal Corporation (PMC) became the first local body in the country to issue these in nearly 15 years, raising ₹200 crore for the Smart City project.

issue municipal bonds, while the Ahmedabad Municipal Corporation made history in 1998 by being the first to offer them to the public.

- Indore became the first city to list municipal bonds on the National Stock Exchange (NSE) **in 2018.**
- SEBI circulated detailed guidelines for Urban Local Bodies (ULBs) in 2015 to raise funds by issuing municipal bonds.
- **Eligibility for issue:**
  - The municipality must not have a negative net worth in each of the three previous years.
  - The issuer (municipal corporations) should get the bonds rated by credit rating agencies.
  - There should be no default in any kind of loan in the past one year and it must maintain full collateral/asset cover to repay the principal amount.
  - For revenue bond, the revenue generated from the project should be kept in a separate escrow account and financial institutions would monitor their accounts regularly.
- **Present status:**
  - As per the new rules, municipal bonds will now be offered not only to financial institutions but also to the public, which will be listed on stock exchanges.

Last Minute SNIPPETS

- As of 2024, the share of municipal bonds in India's total debt market was estimated to be around 0.06%.
- As of 2024, Karnataka and Gujarat are the leading states for issuing municipal bond.

Sovereign Gold Bond

- Sovereign Gold Bond (SGB) is a substitute for holding physical gold. The bonds are **issued by RBI** on behalf of the Central Government and are **denominated in gold.**
- The Government issues such bonds in tranches **at a fixed price** that investors can buy through banks, post offices and also in the secondary markets through the stock exchange platform.
- SGB has a **fixed tenure of 8 years,** though early redemption is allowed after the fifth year from issuance.
- Since the bonds are **listed on exchange,** these can be transferred to other investors as well.
- The bonds are priced in rupees based on the simple average of closing price of gold of **999 purity,** published by the India Bullion and Jewellers Association for the last three business days of the week preceding the subscription period.
- At the time of redemption, cash equivalent to the number of units multiplied by the then prevailing price would be credited to the bank account of the investor.
- Those who apply online for the latest tranche are eligible for a discount of ₹50 per gram.
- Everyone **except Non-Resident Indians (NRIs)** can invest.
- Investment in these bonds can be made through cash (up to ₹20,000), cheque or demand draft.
- The bonds are issued in **denominations of 1 gm** and in multiples thereof.
- Maximum investment in a year is capped at **4 kg** for individuals. Minimum permissible investment is 1 gram of gold.
- The **RBI fixes the price** of the bond.

- **Benefits of buying SGB:**
  - These bonds are backed by a sovereign guarantee and can also be held in demat form.
  - They are priced as per the underlying spot gold prices.
  - Hence, investors who want to invest in gold can buy the bonds without worrying about safekeeping of physical gold along with locker charges, making charges or purity issues.
  - These bonds offer an interest at 2.5 per cent per annum on the principal investment amount.
  - While the interest on bond is taxable, the capital gain at the time of redemption is exempt from tax.
  - The expense of buying or selling SGB is very nominal compared to the physical gold.
  - These bonds can also be used as collateral for availing loans from banks and NBFCs.
- **Risk in investing in SGB** – Capital loss is a risk since the bond prices would reflect any change in gold prices. If gold prices fall, the principal investment would fall proportionately.

EXAM ESSENTIAL

SOVEREIGN GREEN BOND

According to the World Bank, a green bond is a debt security issued to raise funds **for environmental or climate-related activities.** Governments issue sovereign green bonds to raise funds for such programmes.

India just issued its first sovereign green bonds. The Green Bonds are expected to not only support India's energy transformation efforts, but also provide funding for green infrastructure and renewable energy projects. The first-ever Green Bond was issued by the World Bank in 2008.

The Indian Government stated that the green bonds will be utilised for green initiatives that -

- encourage energy efficiency.
- reduce carbon emissions and greenhouse gases.
- promote climate resilience and adaptation.
- improve natural ecosystems and biodiversity, particularly using the concepts of Sustainable Development Goals.

SOVEREIGN BLUE BOND

It is a financial instrument designed to support sustainable marine and fisheries projects. The Republic of **Seychelles** launched the world's first sovereign blue bond to support sustainable marine and fisheries projects in 2018. The World Bank supported Seychelles in reaching out to investors and advised how to structure the use of proceeds from the bond. In 2023, **Indonesia** issued a first-of-its-kind Blue Bond in the Japanese debt capital market.

CONVERTIBLE BONDS

Convertible Bonds have features of both debt and equity. These debt instruments can be converted into equity shares at a future date. They can be converted into predetermined amount of company's equity. Convertible bonds pay a lower rate of interest because there is an option to exchange the bond for equity.

BONUS KNOWLEDGE

MASALA BOND

Before the introduction of Masala Bonds, companies and financial institutions borrowed through issuing bonds in the overseas markets such as the US, the UK, Singapore, etc., in foreign currencies because of the easy availability of funds and at lower interest rates. This exposed the Indian borrowers to foreign currency exchange risks. Depreciation in Rupee led to increase in their cost of capital.

For example, XYZ Ltd. borrowed \$1 million in 2021 when \$1 was equal to ₹70. Total borrowing was **₹7** crore. Now, let's say in 2022, \$1 has become ₹75 due to depreciation of Rupee. XYZ Ltd. wants to repay its loan in 2022. It would now have to pay \$1 million as per the current foreign exchange rate, i.e. \$1 = ₹75. This amounts to ₹7.5 crore, thus causing a net loss of ₹50 lakh due to Rupee devaluation. This caused the need to introduce rupee-denominated bonds instead of dollar denomination.

Thus, **Masala Bonds are the rupee-denominated bonds** which **can be issued by the entities** such as Governmental bodies, NBFCs and eligible corporates **to raise money from overseas markets.** In Masala Bonds, the foreign currency **exchange rate risks are borne by the international lenders** and not the Indian borrowers.

The **first Masala Bond** was issued by International Finance Corporation (**IFC**) in 2014 to raise

₹1,000 crore to fund infrastructure projects in India. The word 'Masala' was used by IFC (arm of World Bank group) to symbolise culture of India for specifically distinguishing Indian rupee- denominated bonds from other bonds. Similarly, **'Dim Sum Bonds'** are used for bonds issued in Hong Kong, denominated in Chinese Renminbi and **Komodo Bonds** for Indonesia.

Issue of Masala Bonds creates demand for Rupee and thus helps in preventing depreciation of currency. Masala Bonds **cannot be used for** investing in capital markets, purchasing land, etc.

Maturity	Minimum maturity period is 3 years. ➤ Up to \$50 million per financial year – 3-year maturity. ➤ Above \$50 million per financial year – 5-year maturity.
Who can issue?	Any corporate, Real Estate Investment Trusts (REITs) and Infrastructure Investment Trusts (InvITs). Indian banks can also issue these bonds in the form of: ➤ **Perpetual Debt Instruments** (PDIs) qualifying for inclusion as Additional Tier 1 capital and **Debt Capital Instruments** qualifying for inclusion as Tier 2 capital, and ➤ For financing infrastructure and affordable housing.
Where can these bonds be issued?	The rupee-denominated bonds can only be issued in a country and can only be subscribed by a resident of a country which: ➤ Is a member of Financial Action Task Force (FATF) or whose Securities market regulator (SEBI in our case) is a member of International Organisation of Securities Commission. ➤ Has Multilateral Memorandum of Understanding or is a signatory to Bilateral Memorandum of Understanding with SEBI for information sharing arrangements.

The Concept of Government Securities (G-Secs)

- The RBI has introduced the **'RBI Retail Direct'** system, which allows small retail investors to invest in Government Securities (G-Secs) by creating gilt accounts with the Central Bank.
- Some **features of G-Secs and Gilt Accounts:**
  - A G-Sec is a tradable instrument issued by the Central Government or the State Government.
  - It acknowledges the Government's debt obligation.
- G-Secs are mainly of 2 types:
  - **Short Term** with maturity of less than one year (like Treasury Bills).
  - **Long Term** with maturity of more than one year (like Government Bonds).
- G-Secs are **issued through auctions conducted by RBI**. Auctions are conducted on the electronic platform called the **E-Kuber**, the Core Banking Solution (CBS) platform of RBI. Commercial banks, scheduled UCBs, Primary Dealers, insurance companies and provident funds, who maintain funds account (current account) and securities accounts [Subsidiary General Ledger (SGL) account] with RBI, are members of this electronic platform.
- These are called **risk-free gilt-edged instruments.**
- An account formed and maintained by an entity or a person permitted by the RBI for the purpose of holding Government securities, is referred as a **'Gilt Account'.**
- The Foreign Exchange Management Act, 1999, governs the operations/maintenance of Gilt Account in the case of a 'Person living outside India'.

Mutual Funds

A mutual fund is a financial instrument in which money is collected from many investors to form a pool of money which is then invested in financial assets like stocks, Government and PSU bonds, corporate bonds, etc., **by professional managers** for income and capital increment.

Each investor owns 'units', which represents a portion of the holdings in the fund. The income or dividends generated from this pool of money are distributed among the investors after deducting the management expenses of the fund managers.

How a Mutual Fund Works?

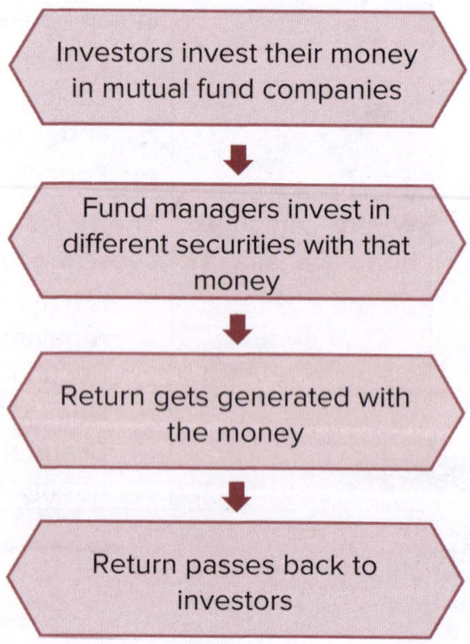

'Net Asset Value' or NAV **represents the current market value of the mutual fund.**

There are **various types of mutual funds** such as:

1. **Equity funds:** These funds or schemes invest their entire money in the shares/equities of companies listed in the stock exchanges. There are varieties in equity depending on the market capitalisation of the company like multi-cap, large cap, mid cap and small cap, micro cap funds.
2. **Debt or fixed income funds:** These funds invest in fixed income instruments such as bonds issued by the Central Government, State Governments, PSUs, corporates, NBFCs, etc.
3. **Hybrid or balanced funds:** These schemes/funds invest in more than one type of asset class. It is invested in equity as

well as debt. (e.g. 65 per cent in equities and 35 per cent in debt). Some hybrid fund may invest in gold as well.

4. **Equity-Linked Savings Scheme (ELSS):** It is a unique fund specific to India that invests in equities. Investment in ELSS in a financial year allows an individual to claim a deduction up to ₹1.5 lakh from total income under Section 80C of the Income Tax Act, 1961. It is a tax- saving instrument brought to promote savings and investment in equities.

Advantages of Mutual Funds

1. Mutual funds are **managed by professionals.** Also, the investor doesn't have to engage in research and keep himself abreast of the developments.
2. Low cost is involved and even small investment may be done.
3. It **offers diversification** which lowers the risk associated with investments.
4. Large varieties of mutual funds are available which can be **chosen as per needs and requirements** of the investor.
5. **Liquidity is high** as the mutual funds can be sold easily.

Derivatives

- A derivative is a financial instrument whose value is **derived from one or more underlying assets or securities.** The underlying assets could be shares, bonds, indexes, currencies or commodities like gold, silver, sugar, coffee, etc.
- The derivative itself is a contract between two or more parties based upon the asset or assets.
- Its value is determined by fluctuations in the underlying asset.
- Derivatives protect from the future price fluctuations and uncertainties. It is commonly used by importers/exporters, farmers and dealers in agricultural commodities.
- It leads to hedging of risk and is an established risk management practice.
- **SEBI** regulates the derivatives market in India.
- Derivatives can either be traded Over-The-Counter (OTC) or at an exchange. OTC derivatives constitute the greater proportion of derivatives in existence and are unregulated, whereas derivatives traded at exchanges are standardised.
- OTC derivatives generally have greater risk for the counterparty than standardised derivatives.
- Some common forms of derivatives are:

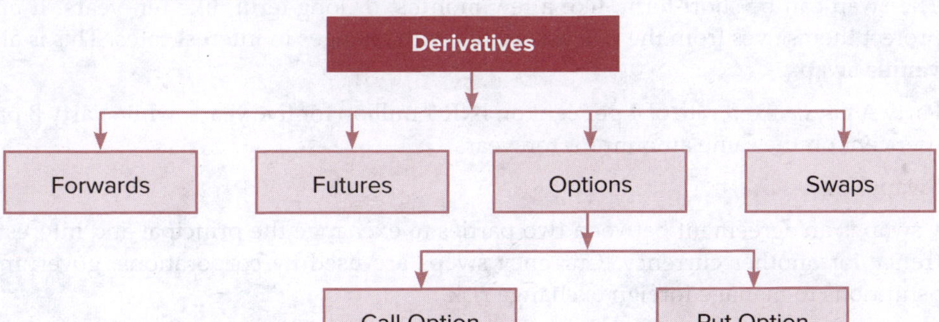

Forwards

It is an agreement or contract between two parties **to buy or sell a particular asset at a certain price and date.** They are **unregulated** and are **traded OTC.** They can be customised as per the needs of the parties involved.

Futures

It is similar to Forwards but these are **regulated** and **traded on the stock exchanges** and the parties are under an **obligation** to perform the contract.

In other words, it is a **standard contract** between two parties to buy or sell a particular asset at an agreed price and a certain date.

Options

It is a contract where the buyer has a right to buy/sell the underlying asset at a certain price (called as **strike price**) during a certain period of time. There is **no obligation on the buyer** to perform the contract.

Options are also **traded on the stock exchanges.** Types of options include:

- **Call option:** It gives a right to the buyer to **'buy'** the underlying asset at a certain price and time. It is purchased when the prices are **expected to rise**.
- **Put Option:** It gives a right to the buyer to **'sell'** the underlying asset at a certain price and time. It is purchased when there is **pessimism** about the price of the asset.

Swaps

Swaps are derivatives which are **used to manage risks** of various kinds. These are generally used to manage **interest rate risk** and **currency risk.**

It is a contract between two parties for exchange of **pre-agreed cash flows** of two different financial instruments. The cash flows are usually determined using the **notional principal amount** (loan or bond).

Major Types of Swaps

Interest Rate Swaps

This is the most common type of swap contract in which the fixed interest rate is swapped for a floating interest rate. Throughout the term of the contract, these interest payments are made at predetermined intervals. The swap can be short-term, like a few months, or long-term, like ten years. It enables the parties to protect themselves from the risk associated with changes in interest rates. This is also known as a **plain vanilla swap.**

Example: Party A pays a fixed rate of 4 per cent on INR 1 million for five years, while Party B pays a fixed rate of 3.5 per cent on the same amount for ten years.

Currency Swaps

A currency swap is an agreement between two parties to exchange the principal and interest of a loan in one currency for another currency. Currency swaps are used by corporations, governments, and financial institutions to manage foreign exchange risk.

This principal is in different currencies. This helps a lot of firms acquire quick loans in local currency and avoid paying foreign exchange taxes. These agreements are also made by governments to control fluctuations in the exchange rate.

Credit-default swaps

This kind of swap functions similarly to insurance for a lender against the borrower's default risk. In this case, if the borrower is unable to repay, a third party promises to pay the lender both the principal and interest. It makes it easier for the borrower to obtain loan and it lowers the risk that the lender takes. However, the swap agreement only becomes operative in the event of the borrower's default.

Debt-equity swaps

In this swap, debt can be converted into equity or vice versa. It is a technique used to reorganise the capital of a company. Companies frequently take this action when they are unable to pay their dues on the debt taken. By switching to equity, they can accelerate the repayment.

BONUS KNOWLEDGE

Open interest: It is the total number of outstanding derivative contracts that are yet to be resolved. The contract is considered open from the time it is initiated by the buyer and the seller until it is closed by the counter-party.

REAL ESTATE INVESTMENT TRUST (REIT)

Its functioning is similar to that of a mutual fund, where a trust or Asset Management Company (AMC) pools a sum of money from investors **to invest in physical real estate assets.** The rent accrued is distributed to the unit holders (investors). Any appreciation in value of assets is reflected in the NAVs of the Real Estate Investment Trust (REIT). Recently, Embassy Group and Blackstone launched the first REIT of India.

REITs can be publicly traded on major exchanges, publicly registered but non-listed, or private. The two main types of REITs are: **Equity REITs** and **Mortgage REITs**.

BONUS KNOWLEDGE

INFRASTRUCTURE INVESTMENT TRUST (INVIT)

It is similar to REIT and the mutual funds, but the investment goes towards **infrastructure projects.** It helps in infrastructure funding and diversification of investment avenues for investors.

Exchange Traded Fund (ETF)

EXAM ESSENTIAL

- ETF is similar to Mutual Fund as it also involves a basket of securities **except that ETFs are bought and sold throughout the day on stock exchanges while mutual funds are bought and sold based on their price at day's end.**
- ETF share price fluctuates throughout the day.
- An ETF **may contain all type of investments** such as stocks, bonds, currencies, debts, futures contracts, and/or commodities such as gold bars.
- ETFs offer low expense ratio and less broker commissions as compared to individually buying stocks.
- **Examples** of ETFs include Bond ETFs, Industry ETFs, Commodity ETFs, Currency ETFs, Gold ETFs, etc.

- **Government of India has issued two main ETFs – CPSE ETF and Bharat-22 ETF.** CPSE-ETF comprises shares of 10 Central Public Sector Enterprises, namely NTPC Ltd., Power Grid Corporation of India Ltd., Oil and Natural Gas Corporation Ltd., Coal India Ltd., Bharat Electronics Ltd., NHPC Ltd., Oil India Ltd., SJVN Ltd., NBCC (India) Ltd., Cochin Shipyard Ltd. Bharat-22 ETF covers shares of 16 CPSEs, 3 Public Sector Banks and 3 Private Sector Companies.
- India's first international Debt ETF has been launched by IDFC mutual fund – 'US Treasury Bond 0–1 year Fund of Fund'.

Mutual Fund (MF)	Exchange Traded Fund (ETF)
MFs can be purchased only at the end of each trading day based on a calculated price.	ETFs can be traded like stocks throughout the day on stock exchanges.
MFs typically come with a higher minimum investment requirement than ETFs.	Investment requirement is less in case of ETF as compared to MFs.
MFs are actively managed. Thus, higher fees and higher expense ratios are involved.	ETFs are passively managed.

BONUS KNOWLEDGE

GOLD ETF *vs.* SOVEREIGN GOLD BOND

Total returns on investment through gold ETFs is lower than actual return on gold [*Actual return (per gram) is assumed as = Price of gold per gram on trading exchange on date of sale – Cost of purchase of that gram of gold] whereas it is higher than actual return on gold in case of Sovereign Gold Bonds (due to the interest paid on the bond during holding period).

Unlike Sovereign Gold Bonds, Gold ETFs can't be used as collateral for loan.

Depository Receipt

A **Depository Receipt (DR)** is a negotiable certificate issued by a bank. It enables investors to own equity in foreign nations and reflects shares of a foreign firm that are traded on a local stock exchange. They have an alternative to trading on a global market. Originally, a depository receipt was a physical document that allowed investors the ability to buy shares of foreign stocks. In the Indian context, Depository Receipt may be of three types: ADR, GDR, IDR.

ADR, GDR, and IDR

- **American Depository Receipt (ADR)**
  - Issued by the US Depository Bank
  - Denominated and traded in US Dollars (US$)
  - Listed and traded on American Stock Exchange
- **Global Depository Receipt (GDR)**
  - Negotiable all over the world
  - Denominated in any freely convertible currency, but mostly in dollars (USD) or euros (EUR)
  - Listed and traded on multiple international stock exchanges
- **Indian Depository Receipt (IDR)**
  - Issued by domestic depositories registered with SEBI
  - Denominated and traded in Indian Rupees (INR)
  - Listed and traded on Indian Stock Exchanges

Sovereign Wealth Fund

- A **Sovereign Wealth Fund (SWF)** is primarily owned by the National Government **or an entity that is commonly established from** balance of payments surpluses or official foreign currency operations or the proceeds of privatisations, etc.
- These funds generally invest in financial instruments such as bonds, stocks, gold and real estates.
- **An SWF's primary objective is to generate good returns over a long-term duration** rather than providing liquidity.
- Singapore's Government Investment Corporation (GIC) is known to be the first SWF.
- **Santiago Principles are laid down which dictates that an SWF must compulsorily invest for good returns and has a transparent structure.** However, these rules apply only to those countries that volunteer to follow.
- The National Investment and Infrastructure Fund (NIIF) is **India's first Sovereign Wealth Fund (SWF).**

ESG Fund

- ESG (Environment, Social and Governance) investing is used synonymously with sustainable investing or socially responsible investing.
- While selecting a stock for investment, the ESG fund shortlists companies that score high on **environment, social responsibility and corporate governance,** and then looks into financial factors.
- As ESG funds have started gaining momentum in India, fund managers say that companies will be forced to follow better governance, ethical practices, environment-friendly measures and social responsibility.
- Industry insiders say that **tobacco companies** and **companies in the coal business** may find it tough to make the cut; so will **companies that generate hazardous waste** and do not manage them properly.
- Some ESG mutual funds available to the investor in India are – Aditya Birla Sun Life ESG Fund, Axis ESG Fund, SBI Magnum Equity ESG Fund, etc.

Difference between Money Market and Capital Market

Basis	Money Market	Capital Market
Duration	It deals with short-term funds (having maturity of 1 year or less).	It deals with long-term funds (having maturity of more than 1 year).
Nature of Funds	Funds are raised for short-term needs like working capital requirement or cash flow mismatches.	Funds are raised for long-term commitments and needs.
Instruments	T-Bills, Commercial Papers, Certificates of Deposit, etc.	Equity shares, preference shares, debentures, bonds, etc.
Amount of Instrument	Each single instrument is generally of large amount.	Each single instrument is generally of small amount.
Related Institutions	RBI, Commercial Banks, NBFCs, primary dealers, bill brokers, etc.	Stock exchanges, Commercial Banks, NBFCs, insurance, pension funds, individuals, merchant banks, underwriters, etc.

Basis	Money Market	Capital Market
Risk	Lesser risk due to lesser maturity.	Default risk or market risk is higher.
Transactions	Transactions are done over phone and there is no formal place.	Transactions are held at a formal place, e.g., stock market.
Broker	Transactions take place without the help of broker.	Transactions are done with the help of a broker.
Basic Role	Liquidity adjustment between borrowers and lenders.	Employment of capital for long-term needs, investment and productive employment.
Relation with Central Bank	Closely linked with central bank of the country which is RBI in our case.	Indirect influence of RBI and it is through the liquidity in the money market.
Market Regulator	**RBI**	**SEBI**

THE SECURITIES CONTRACTS (REGULATION) ACT, 1956

SCRA was passed on the recommendation of the **Gorwala Committee**. It governs securities contracts and the stock market. It was enacted to safeguard investors and stop unwanted securities transactions.

Objectives of the SCRA

- To ensure fair and ethical trading practices
- To protect the interests of investors
- To encourage the steady expansion of the securities market
- To stop unwanted securities exchanges
- To regulate the operations of Indian stock exchange

SEBI

EXAM ESSENTIAL

- SEBI was established on **12 April 1988** and given statutory powers on **30 January 1992 through the** SEBI Act, 1992.
- The basic function of SEBI is **to regulate the securities market** in India and to **protect** the interests of investors.
- **Controller of Capital Issues** (CCI) was the predecessor to SEBI which used to regulate the capital markets in India prior to SEBI.
- In 2015, **Forward Markets Commission** (FMC) was merged with SEBI. SEBI is now responsible for regulation of even **commodity derivatives** market.
- SEBI is governed by a board which is headed by a Chairman. There are eight other members (two from Ministry of Finance, one from RBI, five other members of which at least three are whole-time members).
- Tuhin Kanta Pandey took charge as the chairman of SEBI from March 1, 2025.

BONUS KNOWLEDGE

FORWARD MARKETS COMMISSION (FMC)

It was set up under the Forward Contracts (Regulation) Act, 1952. FMC **was** the chief regulator of commodity futures market. It has been **merged with SEBI in 2015** and now SEBI is the regulator for commodity futures market.

The major Commodity Exchanges in India are:

- Multi-Commodity Exchange of India Limited (MCX), Mumbai.
- National Commodity and Derivatives Exchange Limited (NCDEX), Mumbai.
- National Multi-Commodity Exchange of India Limited (NMCE), Ahmedabad.

Functions of SEBI

- SEBI is entrusted with regulation of **stock exchanges** and their efficient functioning.
- SEBI is responsible for regulation of **Mutual Fund** industry in India.
- SEBI performs the task of registration and regulation of **market participants** like brokers and sub-brokers, underwriters, FIIs, advisors, merchant bankers.
- SEBI strives to prevent **malpractices** in the financial services sector prohibiting fraudulent and **unfair trade practices** relating to securities markets such as insider trading and manipulation of stock prices.
- SEBI is also responsible for managing the **Investor Protection Fund** and using it for greater awareness.

SEBI and Capital Market Reforms

- SEBI came up with **'Issue of Capital and Disclosure Requirements Regulations, 2018'** (ICDR Regulations, 2018) which updates many SEBI regulations with the Companies Act, 2013 and new developments in financial sector.
- SEBI now keeps a tab on utilisation of funds by a company raised through an IPO **above ₹100 crore.** Earlier, SEBI was monitoring only if funds raised were above ₹500 crore. It was done to ensure proper utilisation of funds by companies and protect investors.
- A **single trading licence** and platform for trading in both commodities and shares has been introduced. It was earlier separate. For example, NSE and BSE can now provide services for commodity trading.
- **Separation of Chairperson and CEO** role to ensure better corporate governance. However, according to SEBI, the separation of positions of chairperson and MD/CEO of the company is voluntary.
- Strengthening the role of **Independent Directors** and making them more responsible rather than being a mute spectator.
- Improved disclosure of related party transactions.
- Easier norms for SMEs' IPO and listing on stock exchanges.
- Easier KYC for Foreign Portfolio Investors (FPIs) to promote foreign investment.
- Streamlining IPO process and making it easier for retail investors.

Securities Appellate Tribunal

- Securities Appellate Tribunal (SAT) is a **tribunal set up under the SEBI Act, 1992** and has power to hear and dispose appeals against the orders passed by SEBI, Pension Fund Regulatory and Development Authority (PFRDA) and Insurance Regulatory and Development Authority (IRDA).
- SAT comprises of one presiding officer and two members. They act as judges and deal with the appeals.
- Any person aggrieved by decision of the SAT **can approach the Supreme Court** directly through appeal.

Sweat Equity Rules: SEBI (Share Based Employee Benefits and Sweat Equity) Regulations, 2021

- These regulations are created after merging the following regulations:
  - SEBI (Share Based Employee Benefits) Regulations, 2014; and
  - SEBI (Issue of Sweat Equity) Regulations, 2002.
- The new regulations have **widened the scope of employees** who can be offered stock options and made other significant modifications that will benefit both employees and corporations that issue these options.
- **Sweat Equity Share:**
  - It is a **non-monetary contribution** that the individual or founders of a company make towards the company.
  - Sweat equity is **commonly used** by cash-strapped start-ups and business owners to fund their companies.
  - It is **issued for the purpose of** providing know-how or making available intellectual property rights or value additions.
  - The **maximum yearly limit** of sweat equity share that can be issued by a listed company has been prescribed at **15 per cent** of the existing paid-up equity share capital within the overall limit.
  - The yearly limit for businesses listed on the Innovators Growth Platform (IGP) will be 15 per cent and the overall ceiling will be 50 per cent of the paid-up capital.
  - It will be in effect for **10 years,** beginning on the day of company's incorporation.
- The new rules will be applicable only to the listed companies, as these have been framed by SEBI, which only regulates the listed companies.
- For unlisted companies, any change needed, will have to be brought into the Companies Act, 2013.

STOCK EXCHANGE

Stock exchange is a **platform** where buyers and sellers trade securities such as shares, bonds, derivatives, etc. Such trade takes place through an electronic means. Price of a security is affected by the demand and supply of the security. It may be noted that such security for being traded **must be 'listed'** in that stock exchange.

After an IPO, a company can get listed on the stock exchange, but they have to meet the listing requirements of the stock exchange which seek to prevent fraudulent practices and prohibit insider trading. Stock exchanges are important for mobilising savings and capital, raising funds for corporates and promoting economic growth. India now follows **T+1** (trading plus one day) settlement cycle. Presently, India's leading stock exchanges are the two:

Indian Stock Exchanges
- Bombay Stock Exchange
- National Stock Exchange

- **Bombay Stock Exchange:** It is the **oldest stock exchange in Asia** and is also known as Stock Exchange of Mumbai, established in **1875,** which, at that time, was called Native Share and Stock Brokers Association. Trading is done in equity, currencies, debt instruments, derivatives and mutual funds. BSE also established **India INX,** India's first international stock exchange in GIFT City, Ahmedabad.

  SENSEX is the popular index of BSE. SENSEX is a free float market capitalisation weighted stock market index of 30 well-established companies listed in BSE. The base year of SENSEX is 1978–79 with a base value of 100. The list of these 30 blue-chip companies is revised time to time.

- **National Stock Exchange:** It was set up in **1992** and was India's first fully automated electronic exchange with a nationwide presence. It is also India's first dematerialised (non-paper) stock exchange. NSE is **the largest exchange in the country** in terms of trading volumes. Headquarters of NSE is located in **Mumbai.**

> **Last Minute SNIPPETS**
>
> **SENSEX = Total weighted market capitalisation of 30 blue-chip companies/Index divisor.**
>
> At the market closing of 24 April 2025, SENSEX stood at 79,801.43.

> **Last Minute SNIPPETS**
>
> The index of NSE is **NIFTY,** which is based on the value of the equity shares of **50 well-established/stable companies.**
>
> At the market closing of 24 April 2025, NIFTY stood at 24,246.70.

NSE allows for new listings, IPOs, debt issuances and Indian Depository Receipts (IDRs) by overseas companies raising capital in India. NSE provides a trading platform for all types of securities – equity and debt, corporate, Government and derivatives.

IMPORTANT TERMS RELATED TO STOCK MARKET

Stock Depository	A depository is an organisation or institution where something is submitted for storage or safekeeping. A stock depository is an institution that holds shares and other securities for the depositors. It enables transfer of securities from holder to another person (mainly in demat form), making the process of securities transfer safer and faster. It eliminates the risk of physical handling of security certificates. Thus, they are like banks for security transactions.
	In India, there are **two depositories** – **NSDL** (National Securities Depository Limited) and **CDSL** (Central Depositories Services Limited) which came into existence as a result of the Depository Act of 1996. A depository operates through its agents called Depository Participants (DPs). They are **regulated by SEBI** and facilitate securities trade by maintaining demat account of traders and providing other trading services.

Demat Account	A demat (dematerialised) account is an account that helps investors hold securities in electronic form, eliminating the need for physical certificates. In India, demat accounts are kept by NSDL and CDSL. It enables e-settlement of securities transactions.
Market Order	A market order is a request by an investor to a broker to buy or sell stock, bonds, or other assets at the best possible price in the current financial market.
Limit Order	A limit order allows an investor to specify a maximum acceptable buy price or a minimum acceptable sell price when making an order. The order will only be completed if the asset reaches the specified price.
Bull Market	A bull market refers to a condition when the stock markets/security prices are **rising or expected to rise**. There is optimism among the investors, and they are interested in buying securities in the hope of making profits in the future, thus fuelling demand. On the other hand, the supply is limited as security holders are not willing to sell. Increase in demand is coupled with a decrease in supply, driving up share prices. A bull market is generally associated with a growing economy and strong corporate performance.
Bear Market	A bear market is a condition when stock prices are **on the decline** and stocks are **not expected to do well** in the near future. There is a tendency among the investors to sell their stakes to minimise their losses, while there is a shortage of buyers willing to buy securities. This creates a condition of increase in supply and decrease in demand, resulting in fall in security prices. A bear market is generally associated with a downturn in the economy and weak corporate performance.
Leverage	Leverage in the stock market refers to borrowing money to invest in more shares than one is financially capable of purchasing with the sole purpose of increasing earnings. Leverage is the amplification of a relatively modest investing force into a proportionally larger return.
NASDAQ	NASDAQ (National Association of Securities Dealers Automated Quotations) is the world's first electronic exchange based in **New York**. It is global stock exchange that includes the world's leading technology companies like Microsoft, Google, Apple, etc. The NASDAQ composite is an index of around 3000 stocks listed on the NASDAQ stock exchange.
Blue Chip	Blue chip generally refers to a stock/company that is a market leader in the segment and has strong financial and growth credentials. They are considered to be good investment options and have a stable and reliable growth record. For example, TCS, Reliance Industries, HDFC Bank.
One-sided Market	It refers to rare occasions in which a market has only potential buyers and sellers, but neither is present at the same time. This is a situation in which the market is only moving in one direction. In such cases, market makers will merely quote the bid or ask prices.
Market Capitalisation	The current market value per share times the number of outstanding shares of a publicly traded company gives the market capitalisation (market cap) of the company. It is an indicator of the investor's opinion of the company's net worth. Market capitalisation is generally taken to be the unit of measurement of size for a company. Market size is a good indicator of the characteristics that an investor is looking for while making an investment. It also helps investors diversify their portfolio as per different market sizes.

Large Cap **Mid Cap** **Small Cap**	Based on their market capitalisation, stocks are divided into large cap, mid cap and small cap: **Large Cap** – Companies having a market capitalisation of **more than ₹20,000 crore** are termed as large cap. They are well-established companies and investing in such companies is considered to be low-risk investment. As these are large companies, they disclose their annual statements to the public regularly. For example, TCS, Airtel. **Mid Cap** – Companies with a market capitalisation of **₹5,000 crore to 20,000 crore** fall in the bracket of mid cap companies. They are considered to be riskier than investment in large cap stocks but generally have the potential to give higher returns in the 3- to 5-year horizon. Investors are interested in such stocks in the hope that they are good ventures that will turn into large cap. For example, Bata, Apollo Hospitals, TVS Motor, etc. **Small Cap** – Companies having a market capitalisation of **less than ₹5,000 crore** are termed as small cap. They are either start-ups or companies that are still in their development stage. They are considered to be the **high-risk–high-returns** investments. However, as they are smaller companies, generally not much investor information is available. For example, Andhra Bank, Bombay Dyeing, etc.
Initial Public Offerings (IPOs)	These are a type of issue in which an unlisted company generates capital by issuing new securities and makes it available for purchase by the general public. A company that does not have its shares listed on a public stock exchange is termed unlisted. A company that has any of its securities offered through an offer document listed on an established stock exchange is referred to as a listed company.
Follow-on Public Offer (FPO)	A public company issuing more shares following its Initial Public Offering (IPO) is known as a Follow-on Public Offer (FPO). Therefore, FPOs indicate that companies that are already listed on exchanges are offering more shares to the general public.
Diversification	Diversification is a risk-reduction technique that involves distributing assets over many asset classes, industries, or locations. By diversifying their portfolio, investors want to reduce the influence of any single stock's performance on their whole portfolio.
Book Building	It is a process used by companies for raising capital through public offerings, both Initial Public Offers (IPOs) and Follow-on Public Offers (FPOs), to aid price and demand discovery.
Beta	Beta is a notion that measures a stock's predicted movement in relation to the wider market. Stocks with betas greater than one, are more volatile than their index counterparts, while stocks with smaller betas are less volatile. Beta allows investors to determine how much risk they are willing to take. If they expect higher returns, they may be prepared to invest in equities with high betas. However, they should be warned that these equities are more likely to lose value. If investors want more stability, they may want to invest in equities with low beta values.
Alpha	Alpha is the extra return of a stock or investment beyond the return expected by its beta. It displays the stock's performance in comparison to the market while taking into account the amount of risk assessed by beta. Positive alpha denotes superior performance, whereas negative alpha indicates worse performance.
Round Tripping	Round-tripping refers to a series of transactions involving the movement of money between countries, culminating in a return to the country of origin. For example, an Indian corporation establishes a subsidiary outside the country, and the revenues are used to invest back in India.

Insider Trading	Trading in a publicly available stock based on information that is not publicly available and that affects investment decisions is called insider trading. This generally happens when key employees have access to strategic information and use such information to gain in the stock market. It puts a regular investor at a disadvantage and results in **unfair trading**. **SEBI discourages** illegal insider trading and aims to promote a fair and transparent exchange mechanism.
Buyback of Shares	A buyback occurs when a company **repurchases its own shares** in the market. This results in the reduction of a total number of shares of the company that are traded publicly, increasing the earnings per share and the value of the share. Thus, a buyback generally has a **positive effect on the market value** of the share. A buyback also gives confidence to the investors that the company has sufficient cash and liquidity to handle a crisis situation.
Short Selling	Short selling is an investing or trading technique that bets on the decrease of a stock or other security's price. It is a complex method that should be used by experienced traders and investors.
Pyramiding	It is a way of leveraging a raised margin to grow position size by using unrealised gains from a rise in the value of current holdings of the same securities.
Primary Dealers	A primary dealer is a financial institution that has the license to trade securities with a national Government. In India, they are registered entities with the RBI and they are approved to purchase and sell Government securities. The Primary Dealer system was introduced by the RBI in 1995.
Discount and Finance House of India (DFHI)	It was set up in 1988 under the Companies Act, 1956. The institution was incorporated to provide liquidity and bring stability in financial markets. DFHI deals with T-Bill, Government securities, Certificate of deposit, commercial papers, call money notice money, term money etc. DFHI is a Primary Dealer and is a subsidiary of SBI.
Active Return	Active return is the extra return achieved by the portfolio as compared to the benchmark, index, or market as a whole. Active returns are additional returns that occur outside the scope of the portfolio's exposure to risks and returns to the investment benchmark, index, or market. They are the result of the portfolio's strength and the portfolio manager's active management decisions, i.e. the deliberate decision to underweight or overweight the assets.
Absolute Return	Absolute return is simply the rate of return on an investment over a certain time period. It essentially calculates the gain and loss made as a proportion of the initial investment over a given time period.
Application Supported by Blocked Amount (ASBA)	It is an application by an investor to block the application money in the bank account, for subscribing to an issue. Investors fill in the designated IPO application form and submit it to any Self-Certified Syndicate Bank (SCSB) through any of its branches. **Self Certified Syndicate Bank** is recognised as a bank capable of providing ASBA services to its customers. The ASBA facility was **initiated by SEBI** for retail investors in 2008, then it was extended to corporate investors and high-net-worth individuals (HNIs).
Capital Asset Pricing Model (CAPM)	The Capital Asset Pricing Model (CAPM) is a frequently used financial model that ties a stock's predicted return to its beta and risk-free rate. It offers a framework for calculating the optimal return on investment based on its risk profile.

Initial Coin Offering (ICO)	It is an unregulated means of raising fund for project using **cryptocurrencie** (Bitcoin, Ethereum, Litecoin, Z-cash, etc). Start-up firms dealing in block chain technology and virtual currencies use ICO. There is **no regulator** for this kind of crowd funding in India.
Merchant Bank	It is a financial institution which **provides assistance and advice to companies** in raising capital (debt or equity). They help companies to come out with IPOs. It doesn't provide these services to the general public. During IPOs, they **may also undertake guarantee** to raise sums of money if there is any shortfall from retail investors.
Volatility	Volatility is a statistical measure of the spread of returns for a particular securities or market index. In most circumstances, more volatility indicates riskier security. Volatility is frequently assessed using the standard deviation or variance of returns from the same securities or market index.
Anchor Investor	The concept of Anchor Investor (or cornerstone investor) was launched by SEBI in **2009**. They are institutional investors who are invited to subscribe for shares ahead of the IPO to jazz up the popularity of the issue and boost confidence of potential IPO investors. They are required to take shares at a fixed price to improve confidence of other investors and also increase the demand of the shares. Each Anchor investor is to invest at least ₹10 crore in the issue. The share allotment is done to them one day before an IPO opens. One-third of the anchor investor portion shall be reserved for domestic mutual funds.
Open-High-Low-Close-Chart	An open-high-low-close chart (OHLC) is a type of chart that is commonly used in technical analysis to show price movements of a financial instrument over time. Each vertical line on the chart represents the price range (the highest and lowest prices) across a single unit of time, such as a day or an hour.
Venture Capitalist (VC)	They are entities that give capital **funding to a newly formed company or start-ups** with huge long-term potential. VCs pool money from different investors and companies and then invest on their behalf in start-ups. Generally, lending to such **high-risk projects** is avoided by banks and traditional sources of funding. Venture capitalists give capital and often managerial expertise to provide a boost in scaling up the business. Venture capitalists are then **rewarded with higher valuations** of their equity shares in successful start-ups. Such funds are used for scaling up the operations and meet the expected potential. **Softbank, Naspers, Accel partners and Sequoia Capital** are some of the VCs in India.
Arbitrage	Arbitrage is the simultaneous buying and selling of the identical assets in separate marketplaces in order to have profit from the immediate price differences between them. Arbitrage guarantees that slight price variations between the identical assets in multiple markets are minimised, resulting in consistent pricing across exchanges.
Angel Investor	An angel investor (also known as informal investor or seed investor) is an individual who **provides capital for business start-ups**, usually in exchange for convertible debt or ownership equity. Angel investors usually give support to start-ups at the initial moments when most investors are not prepared to back them. They **invest in high-risk, high-reward start-ups** but typically use their own funds (unlike VCs). They are generally High Net-Worth Individuals (HNIs) who also act as mentors. Angel investors **are first or very early investors**, generally even before VCs. They have greater risks than VCs; however, the quantum of investment is lower than that of VC firms which have a bigger pool of money.

Intraday Trading	Intraday trading is the purchase and sale of stock exchange-listed securities on the same day. The major goal of using this strategy is to generate capital gains on acquired assets while also minimising risks by investing money over a lengthy period of time.
P2P Lending	Peer-to-peer lending is an emerging area in financial services. It deals with **unsecured loan** that can be taken by individuals and businessmen **on the online platform**. It enables individuals to **obtain loans directly** from other individuals, cutting out the financial institution as the middleman. The lending website connects borrowers directly to the investors. The website sets the rates and terms for the transaction. However, the **interest rates are generally high** and therefore personal loans offered by banks are cheaper. Some of the famous platforms in India are **Faircent** and **LendBox**. RBI has recently approved norms for P2P lending in India. P2P platforms **have to register themselves as NBFC-P2P** and meet certain criteria and norms. The loan amount is presently **restricted to ₹10 lakh** for borrowers and lenders and one transaction shouldn't exceed ₹50,000. The RBI norms are strict to prevent any systemic risk and hence it is yet to take-off in India, whereas in China it has been successful.
Market Index	A market index, such as the S&P 500 or Dow Jones Industrial Average, is a collection of equities chosen to reflect the performance of a certain market or industry. It is used as a benchmark to compare the performance of specific stocks or investments.
Risk-free Rate	The risk-free rate is the hypothetical return on an investment that has no risk. It is often based on government bonds or other low-risk securities. In finance, the risk-free rate serves as a standard for comparing the returns of various assets.
Business Incubator	It is a company that helps new and start-up companies to develop by providing services such as management training or office space.
The Negotiated Dealing System-Order Matching (NDS-OM) System	**Negotiated Dealing System-Order Matching System (NDS-OM)** is an electronic, screen based, anonymous, order driven trading system **for dealing in Government Securities**. The **RBI owns NDS-OM** and the Clearing Corporation of India Limited **(CCIL) maintains NDS-OM**. The platform is an addition to the existing facility of Over-The-Counter (OTC) or phone market in Government Securities. The NDS-OM brings transparency in secondary market transactions in Government Securities. Members can place bids (buy orders) and offers (sell orders) directly on the NDS-OM screen. Recently, the RBI launched '**RBI Retail Direct Scheme**' through NDS-OM. It is **aimed at enhancing the access to Government securities market for retail investors**.
Square Off	Squaring off is a trading strategy that day traders employ to profit from market volatility. The trader purchases a lot of stocks in one firm and sells them on the same day at a higher price, resulting in a profit. Or vice versa.
Unicorn	'Unicorns' are such enterprises valued at more than $1 billion. Whereas, 'Minicorns' are startups, with a valuation over $1 million and 'Soonicorns' are startups funded by the angel investors or venture capitalists, while Decacorns have the valuation above $10 billion. According to the Hurun Report, by adding 33 'unicorns' in a single year in 2021, India has displaced the U.K. to be third in the list of countries that are home to most number of Unicorns. U.S.A. occupies first place with 661 unicorns, followed by China with 312 unicorns, whereas India has 114 unicorns (as of March 2024).
Systematic Risk	Systematic risk refers to the risk that exists in the entire market or a specific market sector. It is not diversifiable and impacts a wide variety of equities and investments. Beta captures the systematic risk that cannot be removed by diversification.

Unsystematic Risk	Unsystematic risk, also known as particular risk or idiosyncratic risk, is the risk associated with a single firm or investment. It may be decreased by diversification because it is particular to individual stocks rather than the whole market.
IPO Grey Market	An IPO grey market is an **unofficial market** where IPO shares or applications are bought and sold before they become available for trading on the stock market. It is also termed as a parallel market or an over-the-counter market. Since, it is unofficial, inevitably, there are **no regulations** that govern it.
Third Market	Trading of exchange-listed assets on the Over-The-Counter (OTC) market is known as the third market. These trades offer buyers liquidity and anonymity by enabling institutional investors to trade blocks of securities directly rather than trading through an exchange.
Fourth Market	When securities are traded directly between institutions on a private, over-the-counter (OTC) computer network instead of trading through an established exchange, this is referred to as the fourth market.

Social Stock Exchange (SSE)

The concept of SSE was first introduced in the Union Budget 2019–20. Recently, SEBI has introduced a new framework for SSEs in order to provide additional avenues to **Social Enterprises** (non-loss, non-dividend-paying companies established to address social problems) for raising funds.

In the new framework, BSE and NSE have got SEBI's nod for SSEs. This will allow the investors to purchase shares in SSEs which have been vetted by an official Exchange.

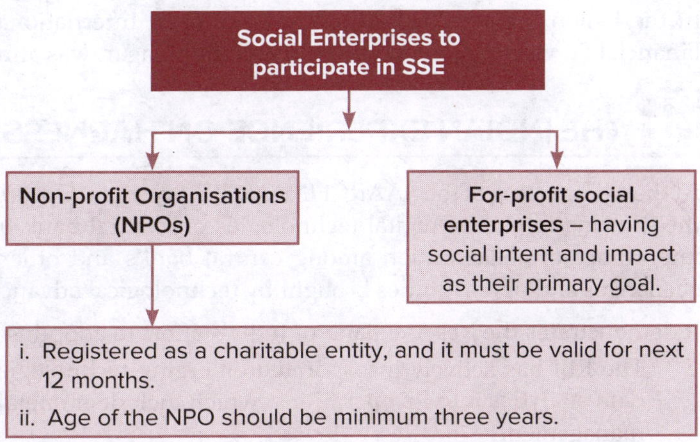

Examples of SSE: Social Stock Exchange (UK) Social Venture Connexion (Canada) and Impact Investment Exchange (Singapore).

International Financial Services Centres Authority (IFSCA)

- The International Financial Services Centres Authority (IFSCA) is a statutory authority **established in 2020** under the International Financial Services Centres Authority Act, 2019.
- Its HQ is situated at GIFT City, **Gandhinagar** in Gujarat.
- It is a **unified authority to regulate all financial services** in International Financial Services Centres (IFSCs) in the country. Prior to the establishment of IFSCA, the domestic financial regulators, namely, RBI, SEBI, PFRDA and IRDAI, regulated the business in IFSC.

- The **main function of IFSCA is to regulate financial products** such as securities, deposits or contracts of insurance, financial services and financial institutions which have been previously approved by any appropriate regulator in an IFSC.

Spot Exchanges

In a spot market, financial instruments and commodities are traded for immediate delivery. In India, Spot Exchange is an electronic trading platform, here purchase and sale of specific commodities, agricultural products, metals, bullion, etc., take place. In spot exchanges, price is determined by wider cross-section of people from across the country, so price determination is more efficient. They are of various types:

- **National Commodity & Derivatives Exchange Limited (NCDEX) e-Markets Limited** – It is the leading National Spot Exchange in India. It was incorporated in 2006. NeML is a wholly owned subsidiary of NCDEX (majority owned by LIC, NABARD, IFFCO, PNB, Canara Bank, NSE). NCDEX is India's largest agricultural commodity exchange with more than 90 per cent market share. Its headquarters is located in Mumbai.
- **National Spot Exchange Limited (NSEL)**
- **Indian Bullion Spot Exchange Limited** – It is a non-Government company established in 2008. It is a public unlisted company and is majorly in Mining & Quarrying business.

In the Union Budget 2020–21, setting up of an International Bullion Exchange at the International Financial Services Centre in GIFT City, Gandhinagar, was announced.

THE INDIAN EXPERIENCE ON HARNESSING DIGITAL TECHNOLOGIES

At the 44th meeting of the SAARCFINANCE Governors' Group in Marrakesh in 2023, the RBI recognised the growing impact of digital technologies on central bank operations worldwide. It emphasised the importance of collaboration among central banks and other stakeholders to effectively address the challenges and opportunities brought by technological advancements.

It demonstrates the Reserve Bank of India's effort to adopting new technology across many functions–

- The RBI has actively incorporated emerging technologies like as **AI, machine learning, and big data analytics into its operations,** which include monetary policy formulation, research, and data management.
- The regulatory **sandbox and hackathons** have been developed to encourage innovation in the financial sector. These initiatives resulted in practical solutions for retail payments, cross-border transactions, MSME loans, and fraud protection.
- The RBI's achievements in payment and settlement systems, particularly the **Unified Payment Interface (UPI),** have received international attention. Further advancements, such as offline payments, phone-based transactions, and conversational payments, illustrate India's dedication to financial technology innovation.
- RBI is creating digital infrastructure such as cloud services and lightweight portable payment solutions in order to address capacity limits and reduce risks linked with geopolitical and climate-related issues.

SAARC central banks vary significantly in their usage and embrace of modern technology. Hence, Central banks should learn from each other's experiences and emphasis should be given on the collaboration and knowledge exchange for successfully navigating the challenges of developing the digital technology.

BONUS KNOWLEDGE

FINANCIAL ACTION TASK FORCE (FATF)

- Global money laundering is a big challenge as it funds international organised crimes such as drug trade, human trafficking, illegal weapon trade and terrorism.
- Financial Action Task Force (FATF) was initially created **by G-7** (USA, UK, Canada, France, Germany, Italy and Japan) in **1989** to check **global money laundering and terror funding** and to maintain the integrity of the international financial system. It is located in OECD headquarters in **Paris.**
- **FATF currently has 40 members:** 38 countries and 2 Regional organisations (European Commission and Gulf Cooperation Council)
- India became observer of FATF in 2006. Subsequently, **India became its member in 2010.**
- **Functions of FATF:** This inter-Governmental body sets international standards, called **FATF Recommendations,** and persuades other countries around the world to bring legislative and administrative changes necessary to adopt and adhere to FATF standards, rules and procedures.
- Countries which are un-cooperative with other jurisdictions in efforts against money laundering are placed under a list called **FATF Blacklist** or it is also called 'Non- Cooperative Countries or Territories' (NCCTs). The FATF Blacklist is also called **'Call for Action'.** FATF updates the Blacklist regularly.
- **FATF Grey List** i.e., **Jurisdictions under Increased Monitoring** recognises nations who are actively working with the FATF to solve key gaps in their regimes to tackle money laundering, terrorist funding, and proliferation finance.

Foreign Account Tax Compliance Act

Foreign Account Tax Compliance Act (FATCA) is the United States Tax regulation brought in by the US Government to prevent the offshore tax evasion by US nationals. Inter-Government Agreement was signed **in 2015,** between India and the US to implement FATCA declarations in India.

The primary goal of FATCA is **to obtain information about income and financial assets about US nationals** from countries other than the US. All Indians holding financial assets like NPS, mutual funds, bank accounts, etc. had to give a declaration that they are not under the US's tax jurisdiction.

Credit Rating Agencies

A Credit Rating Agency (CRA) **analyses and evaluates an individual's or a company's financial position and creditworthiness** in order to find the credit risk associated with the entity or individual. Credit rating helps in better decision-making of the lenders and investors.

CRA ratings are very important for issue of bonds, debentures, commercial papers, Government debt, etc. A good rating helps in securing lower interest rate as the underlying risk is assumed to be low. The ratings are changed continually, depending on the changing financial position and prospects of the company or Government. For example, rise in fiscal deficit would lead to lowering or downgrading in ratings.

Credit ratings are very important when entities are looking to borrow from international markets. Various factors are considered while assigning a rating or score such as present and past financial statements, borrowing history, repayment ability, etc.

SEBI is responsible for regulation of CRAs in India. CRAs were criticised during the 2008 global financial crisis for not evaluating properly the risks associated with sub-prime lending and derivatives issued by the banks of the US.

Recently, in the wake of IL&FS, DHFL and Yes Bank defaults, the role of CRAs has again been criticised. These failed financial institutions had secured positive ratings in contrast to their true financial position. It was argued that CRAs didn't evaluate and assess these NBFCs diligently. And these CRAs were too late to downgrade the ratings of these entities.

Recently, SEBI has devised the standardised symbols and their definitions for issuer rating or corporate credit rating. According to new guidelines, **the CRA's first name should be used a prefix** for rating symbols (like AAA, AA, A, BBB, etc.)

The **major CRAs in India are:**

1. CRISIL Ltd
2. India Ratings & Research Pvt Ltd
3. CARE
4. ICRA
5. Brickwork Ratings (BWR)

The **major global CRAs,** which also give the sovereign ratings, are:

1. Fitch
2. Moody's
3. S&P (Standard and Poor)

SUMMARY

- **Financial Market** – Comprises Money Market and Capital Market.
- **Money Market** – Highly liquid – short-term financial assets with maturity up to 1 year are traded.
- **Treasury Bills** – Money market instrument to finance short-term requirements of the Government issued at discount and redeemed at par – RBI sells T-Bills on behalf of the Central Government – are of four types namely, 14-day T-Bill, 91-day T-Bill, 182-day T-Bill and 364-day T-Bill – Buyers of T-Bills include RBI itself, Commercial Banks, NBFCs, LIC, UTI and GIC.
- **Cash Management Bill** – Short-term security sold by RBI on behalf of the Government – to raise money for temporary needs of the Central Government – tenure is less than 91 days.
- **Capital Market** – Period of investment in Capital Markets is more than 1 year, as it caters to long-term needs of the borrower – are of two types – Primary Market and Secondary Market.
- **Primary Market** – Fresh capital or funds are raised such as through IPO, FPO – also called new issue market.
- **Secondary Market** – Existing securities of companies are traded through stock exchanges like Bombay Stock Exchange (BSE) and National Stock Exchange (NSE) – need a demat account – regulated by SEBI.
- **Shares** – A unit of ownership of the company – offered for sale so as to raise capital for the company – dividend is paid by company on shares.
- **Debentures** – Debt instruments with a fixed rate of interest – generally unsecured – generally offers higher rate of interest than FDs.
- **Mutual Fund** – Money is collected from many investors to form a pool of money which is then invested in financial assets like stocks, Government and PSU bonds, corporate bonds, etc. – managed by professionals.

- **Municipal Bond** – Fixed income instrument, i.e. debt securities issued by the Government or semi-Government institutions which need funding for civic projects – two types of municipal bonds – General Obligation Bonds and Revenue Bonds.
- **Masala Bond** – Rupee-denominated bond – can be issued by Governmental bodies, NBFCs and eligible corporates to raise money from overseas markets – first Masala Bond was issued by International Finance Corporation (IFC) in 2014.
- **Zero Coupon Bond** – Does not pay interest – face value of the bond is received by the bondholders after it reaches maturity.
- **Sovereign Gold Bond Scheme** – Substitute for holding physical gold – bonds are issued by RBI on behalf of the Central Government and are denominated in gold – everyone except NRIs can invest – RBI fixes the price of the bond.
- **Sovereign Blue Bond** – Republic of Seychelles has launched the world's first sovereign blue bond to support sustainable marine and fisheries projects.
- **Real Estate Investment Trust** – Similar to mutual fund – a trust or Asset Management Company pools sum of money from investors to invest in physical real estate assets.
- **SEBI** – Securities and Exchange Board of India – established on 12 April 1988 and given statutory powers on 30 January 1992 – to regulate the securities market in India and to protect the interests of investors.
- **Angel Investors** – Invest in high-risk, high-reward start-ups – use their own funds – are generally high-net-worth individuals (HNIs).
- **Anchor Investors** – Institutional investors that are invited to subscribe for shares ahead of the IPO to jazz up the popularity of the issue.

UPSC CSE PREVIOUS YEARS' PRELIMINARY EXAMINATION QUESTIONS

1. In India, which of the following can trade in Corporate Bonds and Government Securities? **[2024]**

1. Insurance Companies
2. Pension Funds
3. Retail Investors

Select the correct answer using the code given below:

(a) 1 and 2 only (b) 2 and 3 only
(c) 1 and 3 only (d) 1, 2 and 3

2. Consider the following: **[2024]**

1. Exchange-Traded Funds (ETF)
2. Motor vehicles
3. Currency swap

Which of the above is/are considered financial instruments?

(a) 1 only (b) 2 and 3 only
(c) 1, 2 and 3 (d) 1 and 3 only

3. With reference to the Indian economy, "Collateral Borrowing and Lending Obligations" are the instruments of: **[2024]**

(a) Bond market
(b) Forex market
(c) Money market
(d) Stock market

4. In the context of finance, the term 'beta' refers to **[2023]**

(a) the process of simultaneous buying and selling of an asset from different platforms.
(b) an investment strategy of a portfolio manager to balance risk versus reward.
(c) a type of systemic risk that arises where perfect hedging is not possible.
(d) a numeric value that measures the fluctuations of a stock to changes in the overall stock market.

5. Consider the following markets: [2023]
   1. Government Bond Market
   2. Call Money Market
   3. Treasury Bill Market
   4. Stock Market

   How many of the above are included in capital markets?

   (a) Only one (b) Only two
   (c) Only three (d) All four

6. With reference to the Indian economy, what are the advantages of 'Inflation-Indexed Bonds (IIBs)'? [2022]
   1. Government can reduce the coupon rates on its borrowing by way of IIBs.
   2. IIBs provide protection to the investors from uncertainty regarding inflation.
   3. The interest received as well as capital gains on IIBs are not taxable.

   Which of the statements given above are correct?

   (a) 1 and 2 only (b) 2 and 3 only
   (c) 1 and 3 only (d) 1, 2 and 3

7. With reference to Convertible Bonds, consider the following statements: [2022]
   1. As there is an option to exchange the bond for equity, Convertible Bonds pay a lower rate of interest.
   2. The option to convert to equity affords the bondholder a degree of indexation to rising consumer prices.

   Which of the statements given above is/are correct?

   (a) 1 only (b) 2 only
   (c) Both 1 and 2 (d) Neither 1 nor 2

8. Consider the following statements: [2022]
   1. In India, credit rating agencies are regulated by Reserve Bank of India.
   2. The rating agency popularly known as ICRA is a public limited company.
   3. Brickwork Ratings is an Indian credit rating agency.

   Which of the statements given above are correct?

   (a) 1 and 2 only (b) 2 and 3 only
   (c) 1 and 3 only (d) 1, 2 and 3

9. With reference to India, consider the following statements: [2021]
   1. Retail investors through Demat Account can invest in 'Treasury Bills' and 'Government of India Debt Bonds' in primary market.
   2. The Negotiated Dealing System-Order Matching is a Government Securities trading platform of the Reserve Bank of India.
   3. The Central Depository Services Ltd. is jointly promoted by the Reserve Bank of India and the Bombay Stock Exchange.

   Which of the statements given above is/are correct?

   (a) 1 only (b) 1 and 2
   (c) 3 only (d) 2 and 3

10. Indian Government Bond Yields are influenced by which of the following: [2021]
    1. Actions of the United States Federal Reserve.
    2. Actions of the Reserve Bank of India.
    3. Inflation and short-term interest rates.

    Select the correct answer from the codes given below:

    (a) 1 and 2 only (b) 2 only
    (c) 3 only (d) 1, 2 and 3

11. In the context of the Indian economy, non-financial debt includes which of the following? [2020]
    1. Housing loans owed by households
    2. Amounts outstanding on credit cards
    3. Treasury bills

    Select the correct answer using the code given below:

    (a) 1 only (b) 1 and 2 only
    (c) 3 only (d) 1, 2 and 3

12. With reference to the Indian economy, consider the following statements: [2020]
    1. 'Commercial Paper' is a short-term unsecured promissory note.
    2. 'Certificate of Deposit' is a long-term instrument issued by the Reserve Bank of India to a corporation.
    3. 'Call Money' is a short-term finance used for interbank transactions.
    4. 'Zero-Coupon Bonds' are the interest bearing short-term bonds issued by the Scheduled Commercial Banks to corporations.

    Which of the statements given above is/are correct?

    (a) 1 and 2 only (b) 4 only
    (c) 1 and 3 only (d) 2, 3 and 4 only

13. Which of the following is issued by registered foreign portfolio investors to overseas investors

who want to be part of the Indian stock market without registering themselves directly? **[2019]**
(a) Certificate of Deposit
(b) Commercial Paper
(c) Promissory Note
(d) Participatory Note

14. With reference to **'IFC Masala Bonds'** sometimes seen in the news, which of the statements given below is/are correct? **[2016]**
1. The International Finance Corporation which offers these bonds is an arm of the World Bank.
2. They are the rupee-denominated bonds and are a source of debt financing for the public and a private sector.

Select the correct answer using the codes given below:
(a) 1 only (b) 2 only
(c) Both 1 and 2 (d) Neither 1 nor 2

15. What is/are the purpose/purposes of Government's **'Sovereign Gold Bond Scheme'** and **'Gold Monetisation Scheme'**? **[2016]**
1. To bring the idle gold lying with Indian households into the economy.
2. To promote FDI in the gold and jewellery sector.
3. To reduce Indian's dependence on gold imports.

Select the correct answer using the code given below.
(a) 1 only (b) 2 and 3 only
(c) 1 and 3 only (d) 1, 2 and 3

16. What does **venture capital** mean? **[2014]**
(a) A short-term capital provided to industries
(b) A long-term start-up capital provided to new entrepreneurs
(c) Funds provided to industries at times of incurring losses
(d) Funds provided for replacement and renovation of industries

17. Under which of the following circumstances may **'capital gains arise'**? **[2012]**
1. When there is an increase in the sales of a product.
2. When there is a natural increase in the value of the property owned.
3. When you purchase a painting and there is a growth in its value due to increase in its popularity.

Select the correct answer using the codes given below:
(a) 1 only (b) 2 and 3 only
(c) 2 only (d) 1, 2 and 3

☞ NO QUESTIONS ASKED
2018, 2017, 2015, 2013

ANSWER KEY

1. (d)	2. (d)	3. (c)	4. (d)	5. (b)
6. (a)	7. (c)	8. (b)	9. (b)	10. (d)
11. (d)	12. (c)	13. (d)	14. (c)	15. (c)
16. (b)	17. (b)			

UPSC CSE PREVIOUS YEARS' MAIN EXAMINATION QUESTIONS

☞ NO QUESTIONS ASKED
2024, 2023, 2022, 2021, 2020, 2019, 2018, 2017, 2016, 2015, 2014, 2013

CHAPTER

13

TECHNOLOGY AND FINANCE

CHAPTER OUTLINE

- What is FinTech
- Evolution of FinTech in India
- FinTech – Indian Scenario at Present
- Different types of Technology related to Finance
- Factors of Growth for FinTech in India
- Government Initiatives for Boosting FinTech in India
- Challenges of FinTech in India

Words like Cryptocurrency, Bitcoin, Blockchain, etc., have become very familiar due to their frequent usage in various media over the last few years. The recurrent use of these terms in relation to the world of finance indicates the extensive use of technology in finance and economy.

With the rise of digitisation in the economy, a plethora of technology-based applications are entering market at regular intervals.

In 2025, it is expected that Nine Digital technology areas will emerge as fastest-growing and highest-impacting and will together contribute to one third of the total targeted US$ 1 trillion.

Last Minute SNIPPETS

According to NASSCOM, technology-based products and services will generate value of worth half of the global GDP of US$ 100 trillion by 2025.

Among these, **three are foundational technologies**, viz. **Cloud Computing**, **Big Data Analytics** and **Cyber Security**. Other six are identified as **advanced technologies** which are **Artificial Intelligence (AI)**, **Internet of Things (IoT)**, **3D Printing**, **Robotics**, **Blockchain** and **Immersive Media**.

WHAT IS FINTECH

FinTech (Financial Technology) is a catch-all term referring to software, mobile applications, and other technologies created to improve and automate traditional forms of finance for businesses and consumers alike. FinTech can include everything from straightforward mobile payment apps to complex blockchain networks housing encrypted transactions.

The Financial Stability Board (FSB) defines **FinTech** as 'technology-enabled innovation in financial services that could result in new business models, applications, processes or products with an associated material effect on the provision of financial services.'

The term '**FinTech company**' describes any business that uses information technology to modify, enhance, or automate financial services for businesses or consumers. Some examples include mobile banking, peer-to-peer payment services, automated portfolio managers or trading platforms.

It can also be applied to the development and trading of **cryptocurrencies** (e.g., Bitcoin, Dogecoin, Ethereum).

Note: The Financial Stability Board (FSB) is headquartered in **Basel, Switzerland** and funded by Bank for International Settlements (BIS). It was established in **2009** as the successor to the Financial Stability Forum, with a broadened mandate to promote financial stability in G20 Member economies and to coordinate the work of national financial authorities at the international level.

Cryptocurrency

- A cryptocurrency is a **digital or virtual asset** designed to work as a medium of exchange that uses **cryptography** for security.
- It is a decentralised currency, meaning it is **not controlled by any government or institution** in contrast to centralised digital currency and central banking systems.

did you KNOW? Cryptography is the practice of concealing messages or data through the use of coded algorithms or techniques, ensuring that only authorized parties can access or understand the information

- It is based on strong cryptographic algorithms to secure transaction records, to control the creation of additional coins, and to verify the transfer of coin ownership. It typically does not exist in physical form (like Fiat money) and is typically not issued by a central authority.
- A cryptocurrency is a form of digital asset based on a network that is distributed across a large number of computers. This decentralised structure allows them to exist outside the control of governments and central authorities.
- Some examples of cryptocurrencies include **Bitcoin, Ethereum, Litecoin, XRP**, etc.

BONUS KNOWLEDGE

BLOCKCHAIN TECHNOLOGY

- Central to the appeal and functionality of Bitcoin and other cryptocurrencies is **blockchain technology**. A blockchain is a **distributed ledger** that duplicates and distributes transactions across the network of computers participating in the blockchain.
- A blockchain is essentially a **set of connected blocks of information on an online ledger**. Each block contains a set of transactions that have been independently verified by each validator on a network.
- Every new block generated must be verified by each node before being confirmed, making it almost impossible to forge transaction histories. The contents of the online ledger must be agreed upon by a network of individual nodes, or computers that maintain the ledger.
- Blockchain technology can serve multiple industries, supply chains, and processes such as online voting and crowdfunding.

SOFTWARE TECHNOLOGY PARKS OF INDIA (STPI)

- It is the premier S&T organisation under the Ministry of Electronics and Information Technology (MeitY). It promotes software exports, including emerging technologies like IoT, Blockchain, AI, etc.
- STPI was set up in **1991**.
- STPI has set up a '**state-of-the-art incubation facility**' **at its Gurugram** campus to promote entrepreneurship in Blockchain Technology in 2023.

Bali FinTech Agenda

- The Bali FinTech Agenda is a globally accepted set of 12 policy elements established to help member countries harness the benefits and opportunities of rapid advances in financial technology (FinTech), while at the same time also managing the risks that arise. **International Monetary Fund (IMF)** and the **World Bank** launched the Bali FinTech Agenda **in 2018**.
- The agenda proposes a framework of high-level issues that countries should consider in their own domestic policy discussions and aims to guide in their own work and dialogue with national authorities.
- It provides a **framework to support the Sustainable Development Goals**, particularly in low-income countries, where access to financial services is low.

BONUS KNOWLEDGE

THE FUTURE OF GLOBAL FINTECH

It is a research initiative, jointly initiated by the World Economic Forum and the Cambridge Centre for Alternative Finance (CCAF). The project intends to explore the future of global FinTech, public and private sector needs, robust data and empirical evidence, and facilitate evidence-based regulation on FinTech.

Evolution of FinTech in India

Indian FinTech has evolved at a breakneck speed in the past decade. The Indian economy has been transformed from being a fully cash dependent economy to a partly digital economy by the implementation of digital services. As we march ahead into the tech decade (**Techade**), inclusive technologies, innovation ecosystem and progressive policies show the way to India's FinTech revolution for the world.

BONUS KNOWLEDGE

TECHADE 2020

Technology innovation in the last decade (2010–19) was breathtakingly fast as business got intertwined with technology like never before. A key indicator of this trend was the growth of the Indian technology industry, which added over US$100 billion in revenues, and over 2 million tech jobs in the decade.

The ongoing decade of 2020s is the **Techade** or **'Tech-Decade'**, where technology will create endless possibilities for a fulfilling and happy world. It is to be kept in mind that the technology enabled disruption in the next decade promises to be even faster and sufficient safeguards need to be built to tackle that.

Timeline of Different Payment Systems in India

EXAM ESSENTIAL

- **RTGS** or **Real Time Gross Settlement** was implemented in 2004. It is operated by the RBI and it enables inter-bank electronic cash remittance. It is used for high value transactions.

- **NEFT** or **National Electronic Funds Transfer** was introduced in 2005 for smaller value transactions. It is maintained by the RBI for electronic fund transfers between bank accounts.
- **IMPS** or **Immediate Payments Service** is an electronic fund transfer system, which was launched in 2010. It was started to provide 24×7 fund transfer facility.
- **AePS (Aadhaar Enabled Payment System)** was launched in 2010, to ensure financial inclusion in rural areas.
- **Aadhaar Payment Bridge System** has made recurring bulk payments of government subsidies and benefits easier to implement.
- **CTS (Cheque Truncation System)** was launched in 2011, to enable faster clearance of cheques.
- **NACH (National Automated Clearing House)** was launched in 2012. It is a web-based platform for inter-bank electronic transactions that are repetitive and of high volumes.
- **RuPay** is a global card payment network launched by the NPCI in 2012.
- **BBPS (Bharat Bill Payment System)** commenced in 2014.
- **BHIM or Bharat Interface for Money** is a mobile wallet app developed by NPCI based on the UPI. It was launched in 2016.
- **BharatQR Code** is an integrated payment system launched in **2016**. It is a QR Code-based digital payment mechanism developed by NPCI, VISA, MasterCard and American Express. Its interoperability feature means that merchants need to display only one QR code for customers to make payments (as opposed to separate QR codes specific to different payment networks).

Digital Payment in India – The UPI Story

EXAM ESSENTIAL

- One of the major objectives of Digital India is to achieve '**Faceless, Paperless, Cashless**' status. The promotion of digital payments has been accorded the highest priority by the Government of India to provide the facility of seamless digital payment to all citizens of India in a convenient, easy, affordable, quick and secured manner.
- Digital Payments transactions have been consistently increasing over the last few years, as a part of the Government of India's strategy to digitise the financial sector and economy.
- **Unified Payments Interface (UPI)** has been termed a revolutionary product in the payment ecosystem. Launched in 2016, it has emerged as one of the most popular tools in the country for carrying out digital transactions.

Last Minute SNIPPETS

As on **December 2024**, the **value of transactions** conducted through UPI stands at **₹23,24,699.91 crore**, as compared to December 2020, when it was **₹4,16,176.21** crore and **December 2016**, when it was **₹707.93 crore**. (PIB)

Growth of UPI In India

	Dec, 2016	Dec, 2020	Dec, 2024
Number of Live Banks	35	207	641
Number of Transactions	1.99 million	2,234.16 million	16,730.01 million
Value of Transactions (in ₹ Crores)	₹707.93 crore	₹4,16,176.21 crore	₹23,24,699.91 crore

Source: PIB

- **Bharat Interface for Money-Unified Payments Interface (BHIM-UPI)** is an instant payment system developed by the **National Payments Corporation of India (NPCI)**. It powers multiple bank accounts into a single mobile application, merging several banking features, seamless fund routing and merchant payments under one umbrella.
- The Unified Payment Interface is a **real-time payment system**. It is designed to enable peer-to-peer inter-bank transfers through a single two-click factor authentication process. The interface is regulated by the **Reserve Bank of India (RBI)**.
- UPI has given a boost to small businesses and street vendors as it enables **fast and secure bank-to-bank transactions** even for considerably small amounts. It's also the ready-to-go solution for quick money transfers for migrant workers.

India has signed Memorandum of Understandings (MoUs) with 13 countries that want to adopt the Unified Payments Interface (UPI) for digital payments.

did you KNOW?

UPI currently constitutes well over 40 per cent of all digital transactions taking place in India. Transactions through UPI interface have touched an unprecedented high since its inception to present date.

UPI is available for live transaction in 7 countries as on January, 2025, which are UAE, Singapore, Bhutan, Nepal, Sri Lanka, France, and Mauritius.

BONUS KNOWLEDGE

NATIONAL PAYMENTS CORPORATION OF INDIA (NPCI)

NPCI is an initiative of RBI and Indian Banks' Association (IBA) under the provisions of the Payment and Settlement Systems Act, 2007, for creating a robust payment and settlement infrastructure in India. It was established with its headquarters in **Mumbai in 2008**. It is the umbrella organisation for operating retail payments and settlement systems in India.

Following systems are operated by NPCI –

- RuPay (Indigenously developed Payment System)
- IMPS (Immediate Payment Service)
- NACH (National Automated Clearing House)
- ABPS (Aadhaar Payment Bridge System)
- NFS (National Financial Switch)
- Bharat Bill Payment System, etc.

FINTECH – INDIAN SCENARIO AT PRESENT

- India has emerged as one of the largest digital markets in the world. **FinTech adoption rate of India is 87 per cent** against the global average of 64 per cent.
- As per the **Internet in India Report 2024** by the Internet and Mobile Association of India **(IAMAI)**
- Rural India, with 488 million users, accounts for 55 per cent of the total internet population.
- This surge is driven by users accessing content in Indian languages, including Tamil, Telugu, and Malayalam; with 98 per cent users in rural India and 57 per cent users in urban India accessing contents in regional languages.

Last Minute SNIPPETS

- India's internet user base is expected to exceed 900 million by 2025, propelled by increased usage of Indic languages in digital content
- Active internet users in India have reached 886 million in 2024, showing a 8% YoY growth rate

- With 47 per cent of internet users being women, the **digital gender gap** is narrowing down.
- India now hosts the **3rd largest ecosystem for startups globally** after USA and China; 59,593 startups have been recognised by DPIIT across 57 unique industries, of which 3085 startups are operating in Fintech Sector.
- India is among the world's fastest growing FinTech market, with approximately 7,000 FinTech startups. Indian FinTech industry's market size was US$ 31 billion in 2021 and is approximately US$ 110 billion in 2024, which is expected to reach around US$ 420 billion by 2029, reflecting a cumulative annual growth rate of 31 per cent.
- According to the **'State of the FinTech Union 2023' report**, Indian FinTech industry could produce US$190 billion revenue by FY2030.
- The total digital payment transactions increased from ₹2,071 crore in FY 2017–18 to ₹18,737 crore in FY 2023–24 at Compounded Annual Growth Rate (CAGR) of 44 per cent.
- There has been an exponential growth of technological enablers in India. Telecom penetration, availability of internet services, adoption of technology in facilitating access to credit, more efficient payment systems and deepening of financial inclusion have made significant progress and are continuing to progress further.

DIFFERENT TYPES OF TECHNOLOGY RELATED TO FINANCE

With the expansion of application of technology in the field of finance and economics, a plethora of business models have come into existence in FinTech industry. This has led to different categories of FinTech applications as illustrated below.

PayTech – Digital Payments

- FinTech companies have introduced innovations in the traditional payments ecosystem to leverage their technological capabilities and customer centricity. PayTechs are offering integrated solutions for both consumers and merchants to meet the demand of seamless payments with growing digital economy.
- **Digital wallets** are financial applications that allow consumers to store funds, make transactions, and track payment histories on devices like phones and tablets. One can store all financial information in a digital wallet, even ID cards in case of some apps.
- **Digital wallets** may be included in a bank's mobile app or payment apps like PayPal. Digital wallets essentially eliminate the need to carry a physical wallet by storing the consumer's payment information securely and compactly. **Examples** – Amazon Pay, Paytm, MobiKwik, Yono by SBI, ICICI pockets.
- **Mobile wallets** are apps for storing financial information and other documents such as credit cards, bank information, and even driver's licenses.
- At present, the technologies used by mobile devices and digital wallets are:
  - **QR codes**: Quick Response codes are matrix bar codes that store information. One can use the device's camera and the wallet's scanning system to initiate payment.
  - **Near Field Communication (NFC)**: NFC is a technology that allows two smart devices to connect and transfer information using electromagnetic signals. It requires two devices to be within about 4 centimetre from each other to connect.

- **Magnetic Secure Transmission (MST)**: The same technology used by magnetic card readers that read credit/debit card when users swipe it through a slot on a point of sale. The phone generates one encrypted field that the point of sale can read.
- **Prepaid Payment Instruments (PPIs)**: PPIs facilitate purchase of goods and services against the value stored on such instruments. Value stored on them is paid by the holder using a medium (cash, debit card, credit card, etc). These are generally issued in the form of smart cards, mobile wallets, paper vouchers, internet accounts/wallets.
  PPIs come with a pre-loaded value and in some cases a pre-defined purpose of payment. They facilitate the purchase of goods and services as well as inter-personal remittance transactions. PPIs are licensed and regulated by the Reserve Bank of India. There are three types of PPIs– closed system PPIs, semi-closed system PPIs and open system PPIs. **Examples** - A brand-specific gift card like Amazon gift card is a closed system PPI.
- **Unified Payment Instrument (UPI)**: *(Discussed earlier)*
- **Blockchain and Cryptocurrency**: With the availability of smart contracts, Proof-of-Work, Peer-to-Peer transactions, blockchain-powered trading platforms, decentralised ledgers, and immutable records, FinTech and Blockchain are good examples of how FinTech is affecting the growth of financial services.
- **Central Bank Digital Currency**: *(Discussed in a later section)*
- **Payment Gateways**: It is a technology implemented by merchants where consumer-facing interfaces are used to collect payment information.

In physical stores, payment gateways consist of the **Point of Sale (POS)** terminals used to accept credit card information by card or by smartphone. In online stores, payment gateways are the checkout portals used to enter credit card information or credentials for services. **Examples** - BillDesk, PayU, RazorPay, CCAvenue.

LendTech – Alternative Lending

- To provide customers with financing options through more accurate and quicker procedures. Technologies like Artificial Intelligence and Machine Learning algorithms are employed to process and validate identify credentials and make it easier to forecast income expectations, evaluate the borrower's track record, appraise collateral value, and foresee changes.
- **Peer to Peer Lending** – also known as 'social lending' or 'crowd lending.' These platforms enable individuals to obtain loans directly from other individuals without going through the banks. **Examples** of P2P Lending platforms – The Money Club, Finzy, Lendbox, Cred, **IndiaP2P**, **Faircent**.
- **Buy Now Pay Later (BNPL)**: It is a type of short-term financing that allows consumers to make purchases and pay for them over time, usually with low interest rates.
- BNPL apps usually don't charge interest or fees, and they have a fixed repayment schedule. **Examples** – Zest Money, Amazon Pay Later, LazyPay.

did you KNOW?

Crowdfunding Crowdfunding is the use of small amounts of capital from a large number of individuals to finance a new business venture. **Crowdfunding** makes use of the easy accessibility of vast networks of people through social media and crowdfunding websites to bring investors and entrepreneurs together. Crowdfunding sites generate revenue from a percentage of the funds raised. Examples – Indiegogo, Catapooolt, Fueladream, Fundabale, Ketto, Impactguru.

Banking – BankTech

EXAM ESSENTIAL

- BankTech is the use of digitised platforms to provide banking solutions and products to consumers. BankTech has several advantages over traditional banking methods, including improved user experience, lower costs, and less operational friction.
- **Open Banking** – It is also known as 'open bank data'. Open banking is a banking practice that provides third-party financial service providers open access to consumer banking, transaction, and other financial data from banks and non-bank financial institutions through the use of **application programming interfaces (APIs)**. Open banking allows the networking of accounts and data across institutions for use by consumers, financial institutions, and third-party service providers.
- **NeoBanks**: These are FinTech firms that offer apps, software and other technologies to streamline mobile and online banking. A neobank is a digital bank that does not have any branches and provides financial services online.

These FinTechs generally specialise in specific financial products and provide digital and mobile-first services like payments, debit cards, money transfers, lending, and more. In the U.S., these FinTechs are more commonly referred to as **neobanks** to describe FinTech-based financial providers that were challenging traditional banks. They are also known as **challenger bank** in the U.K.

> **did you KNOW?** In India, neobanks don't have a bank license of their own because the **Reserve Bank of India (RBI) doesn't allow banks to be 100 per cent digital yet.** Instead, they work in partnerships with traditional banks to provide bank-licensed services.
>
> **Examples** – Jupiter (partnered with Federal bank), FI Money, Niyo, Razor-payX, Open Money, etc.

Personal Finance – WealthTech

- Generating wealth for investors using technology to manage data sets, conduct analysis, and ensuring a positive investor experience.
- WealthTech businesses offer **B2B business solutions** for banks, investment firms, and wealth management businesses, and solutions under **B2C business model**, where they offer services directly to end users.
- **Roboadvisory:** Online wealth management services from robo-advisors that provide automated investment advice based on advanced portfolio management algorithms.
- **Enhancing financial literacy** for young, first-time investors by helping them choose their preferred platforms and investment vehicles.
- Investment tools to assist investors in achieving their financial goals and diversifying their investment portfolios based on their risk and return profiles.
- **Examples** – Zerodha, Groww, Upstox, Kuvera, Cube Wealth

Insurance – InsurTech

- Allowing companies to explore avenues like offering ultra-customised policies like **Micro Insurance**, social insurance, and using new streams of data for dynamic premium pricing according to observed behaviour.
- Used to process claims more effectively, evaluate risk, process contracts, or underwrite policies.

- Insurance web aggregators' platforms.
- On-demand insurance for micro-event and the adoption of the peer-to-peer model to both create customised group coverage and incentivise positive choices through group rebates.
- **Examples** – PolicyBazaar, Acko, Digit Insurance

Regulatory – RegTech

- It is a sub-category of FinTech that uses cutting-edge technology that may support the delivery of regulatory obligations more efficiently and effectively than existing capabilities.
- Regulatory Sandbox based on good data governance model which can help innovators to increase efficiency, manage risks within the regulatory framework; Identity management and control for fraud detection; Risk management; RegTech applications focused on KYC (Know Your Customer) and AML (Anti-Money Laundering) compliance.
- **Examples** – Finchat, Kyo Lab, Enforcd.

DIFFERENCE BETWEEN DIGITAL WALLETS AND MOBILE WALLETS

'**Digital wallet**' is often used interchangeably with 'mobile wallet' or 'mobile payments'. Though implemented differently, both are used to store payment information. Digital wallets are mostly used for online transactions and may not necessarily be used on mobile devices. Mobile wallets are used by people who would rather not carry a physical wallet when making in-store purchases. For this reason, these wallets need to be used on mobile and easy-to-carry platforms.

BONUS KNOWLEDGE

TYPES OF DIGITAL WALLET

Digital wallets belong to three different types, viz. **Closed, Semi Closed** and **Open.**

Closed Wallet: These are digital wallets that are created by companies that deal with products or services, and allow users to transact only with the issuer of the wallet or other users of the same wallet. **Examples** – Ola Money, Amazon Pay.

Semi-Closed Wallets: These are digital wallets that allow users to make transactions at listed merchants and stores by making both online and offline payments. The merchants must sign an onboarding agreement with the issuer of the wallet to accept payments from these wallets. **Examples** – PhonePe, MobiKwik, Oxigen.

Open Wallets: These are digital wallets that can only be issued by banks or institutions partnered with another major bank. These wallets allow users to make the same transactions as semi-closed wallets, but also offer the additional feature of being able to withdraw money from ATMs. **Examples** – YONO by SBI, ICICI Pockets, YesPay.

FACTORS OF GROWTH FOR FINTECH IN INDIA

The factors responsible for rapid growth in FinTech sector in India are as follows:

- **Embracing advanced Technologies**: The rapid growth of FinTech is mainly propelled by new technologies that have revolutionised the ways in which financial products and services are created, provided and managed. It has enabled creation of entirely new products like prepaid payment instruments, Non Fungible Tokens (NFTs), cryptocurrencies, etc.

- The combination of JAM Trinity (Jan Dhan accounts, Aadhaar, and mobile technology) has facilitated the evolution and growth of digital transactions in India.
- **Conducive Regulatory Framework**: Sincere and unrelenting efforts of Government have ensured proper regulatory environment and infrastructure development for new FinTech firms. RBI has been constantly monitoring the FinTech space since long and issued guidelines and frameworks for this sector from time to time.
- **Changes in Behaviour Pattern of Young Population**: Rise of young tech-savvy population has created the scope for innovative financial services like money transfers, investment, neobanks, etc.
- **Economy Post-demonetisation and Covid pandemic**: While demonetisation initiated the shift away from a paper based, cash-based economy towards digital, cashless economy, the lockdown during pandemic years 2020 and 2021 and social distancing norms fuelled the innovation and digitalisation across the financial sector.
- **Financial Inclusion and Rising Digital Literacy**: Schemes like Pradhan Mantri Jan Dhan Yojana, Digital India Programme, PM Gramin Digital Saksharata Abhiyaan (PMDISHA), etc., have helped in raising financial literacy on a broad scale and expanding the consumer base of FinTech applications.
- **Socio-economic Culture of Entrepreneurship**: The rise of new enterprises in the FinTech sector, especially in digital payments, lending and wealth segments, trading platforms, etc. is a consequence of India's startup and innovation ecosystem built through initiatives like Startup India, Atal innovation Mission, Production-Linked Incentive (PLI) Scheme, **Industrial Information System (IIS)**, **PM Gatishakti**, NITI Aayog FinTech Hackathon, etc.
- Developments in digital identity infrastructure under the umbrella of IndiaStack.
- Unserved consumer base in Tier II and III cities in India may play a key role in the growth of FinTech in the future. Customised FinTech solutions like buy now pay later, customised microinsurance, etc., have immense scope in catering to the financial needs of unbanked or under-banked population, especially burgeoning middle-class and their growing purchasing power. Embracing digital transactions post lockdown has opened up the scope for further intrusion of FinTech in this segment of economy.

GOVERNMENT INITIATIVES FOR BOOSTING FINTECH IN INDIA

The infrastructure for this large-scale implementation of digital economy has been built over the years by several government initiatives, which have resulted in a FinTech ecosystem in India on the basis of which FinTech Revolution seems achievable today.

1. The **Steering Committee on Fintech Related Issues** was constituted with the objective of making Fintech related regulations more flexible and to enhance entrepreneurship. The Committee headed by **Chairman Subhash Chandra Garg**, submitted its report in 2019.
    - The Committee proposed a comprehensive legal framework for consumer protection in FinTech and digital services.
    - Adoption of **Regulation Technology (or RegTech)** by all financial sector regulators.
    - Institutional framework of **Supervisory Technology (or SupTech)**.

The Committee highlighted the positive impact of FinTech innovations on the Agriculture sector and MSMEs like credit registry for farmers to be developed by NABARD, greater use of FinTech, Core Banking Solutions (CBS), etc.

2. **India Stack**: India Stack is a set of APIs that allows governments, businesses, startups, and developers to utilise a unique digital Infrastructure to solve India's hard problems towards presence-less, paperless, and cashless service delivery. The development of India Stack has been the foundation of the robust FinTech ecosystem in India.

   India Stack is the name used to describe a collection of disparate technology products and frameworks. The components of this collection are owned and maintained by different agencies:
   - **Aadhaar** products such as e-auth and e-KYC are owned by the Unique ID Authority of India.
   - **eSign** is a technology specification which is maintained by the Ministry of Communications and Information Technology.
   - **Digilocker** is owned by the Ministry of Electronics and Information Technology.
   - **UPI** is owned by the National Payments Corporation of India.
   - **The Account Aggregator Framework** is regulated by RBI and its technology standards are owned by Reserve Bank Information Technology Private Limited (ReBIT).

3. **Central Bank Digital Currency**: The idea of India's own Central Bank Digital Currency (CBDC) was announced in the Union Budget 2022–23. This was followed by a concept note on Central Bank Digital Currency (CBDC) published by RBI in 2022.

BONUS KNOWLEDGE

DIGITAL RUPEE (e₹)

- Also known as Central Bank Digital Currency (CBDC), it is the digital currency launched by RBI. RBI has launched pilots of CBDC in both Wholesale and Retail segments. The pilot in wholesale segment, known as the **Digital Rupee-Wholesale (e₹-W)**, was launched on 1 November 2022, with use case being limited to the settlement of secondary market transactions in government securities. Use of (e₹-W) is expected to make the inter-bank market more efficient. Settlement in central bank money would reduce transaction costs by pre-empting the need for settlement guarantee infrastructure or for collateral to mitigate settlement risk.
- The pilot in retail segment, known as **digital Rupee-Retail (e₹-R),** was launched on 1 December 2022, within a closed user group (CUG) comprising participating customers and merchants. The **e₹-R** pilot currently covers the five cities of Mumbai, New Delhi, Bengaluru, Bhubaneswar, and Chandigarh.
- The CBDC pilot launched by the RBI in retail segment has components based on **blockchain technology**.

Features of Digital Rupee (e₹)

- The **e₹-R** is in the form of a digital token that represents **legal tender**.
- It is being issued in the **same denominations as the paper currency and coins**. It is pegged to the value of the country's fiat currency.
- It is being distributed **through financial intermediaries**, i.e., the banks.
- Users will be able to transact with **e₹-R** through a digital wallet offered by the participating banks.
- Transactions can be both Person to Person (**P2P**) and Person to Merchant (**P2M**).
- The **e₹-R** offers features of physical cash like trust, safety, and settlement finality.

> ➤ CBDC is a fungible legal tender which means it can be converted to other forms of money, like deposits with banks. Although the CBDC will not earn any interest like cash.
>
> ➤ Central Bank Digital Currency (**CBDC**) is issued by RBI on behalf of Government of India, and it is a liability of the RBI.
>
> ➤ A separate **e₹ wallet** has been conceived in the pilot considering that **e₹** forms part of the **currency system** while other digital wallets form part of **the payments system.** Users will be able to transact with **e₹-R** through a digital wallet offered by the participating banks and stored on mobile phones/devices.

4. **Regulatory Sandbox** by RBI, IRDA, and SEBI
   - The **Regulatory Sandbox (RS)** framework by RBI, was released in 2019, with a view to fostering innovation. After launching initial four theme-based cohorts on retail payments, cross-border payments, MSME lending and prevention of financial frauds, a theme neutral **fifth cohort** was announced in 2022 which paves the way to increase the footprint of innovation in the FinTech space.
   - A **regulatory sandbox** is a framework set up by a regulator that allows FinTech startups and other innovators to conduct live experiments in a controlled environment under a regulator's supervision. This is live testing of new products or services on a pilot basis.
   - The RS framework has been updated in 2024 which requires sandbox entities to ensure compliance with the provisions of *The Digital Personal Data Protection Act, 2023*.
   - RBI announced a **standard operating procedure (SOP)** for **interoperable regulatory sandbox** to regulate newer FinTech products and services falling in the ambit of more than one regulator. The move is aimed at developing a clear jurisdiction where there are overlapping areas involving multiple regulators, including the RBI, Securities and Exchange Board of India (SEBI), Insurance Regulatory and Development Authority (IRDAI), Pension Fund Regulatory and Development Authority (PFRDA).

   The success stories emanating from Regulatory Sandbox initiative include, among others, the 'Framework for facilitating Small Value Digital Payments in Offline Mode' and the UPI123Pay, a payment system developed by NPCI that allows users to make digital transactions without an internet connection.

5. **Account Aggregator Network:** It is a **financial data-sharing system** that could revolutionise investing and credit, giving millions of consumers greater access and control over their financial records and expanding the potential pool of customers for lenders and FinTech companies.

   An **Account Aggregator (AA)** is a type of RBI regulated entity (with an NBFC-AA license) that helps an individual securely and digitally access and share information from one financial institution they have an account with to any other regulated financial institution in the AA network. **Data cannot be shared without the consent of the individual**.

   This is the first step towards bringing open banking in India and empowering millions of customers to digitally access and share their financial data across institutions in a secure and efficient manner.

   As of 2022, 94 Financial Institutions have onboarded on Account Aggregator (AA) platform as Financial Information User (FIU). Among these entities, 73 are regulated by Reserve Bank of India (RBI), 10 entities are regulated by Securities and Exchange Board of India (SEBI), 9 regulated by Insurance Regulatory and Development Authority of India (IRDAI)and 2 are Pension Fund Regulatory and Development Authority (PFRDA)regulated entities.

6. RBI announced the '**Framework for facilitating Small Value Digital Payments in Offline Mode**' in 2022. RBI has also launched new UPI services for feature phones called **UPI123Pay** for non-internet users to make digital payments, and a 24×7 helpline for digital payments called '**Digisaathi**'. This is aimed at enhancing digital financial inclusion by enabling over 40 crore feature phone users to access the benefits of UPI in a safe and secured manner.
7. RBI introduced **UPI Lite in 2022** to speed up and simplify low-value UPI payments. **UPI Lite is an on-device wallet** function which allows real-time small-value payments up to ₹200 without entering a UPI PIN.
8. RBI has set up the **Reserve Bank Innovation Hub (RBIH)** as a subsidiary in **Bengaluru**.
9. A new **FinTech Department** has been created in the **RBI** from 2022 to give focused attention to this evolving and dynamic sector.
10. **National Electronic Toll Collection (NETC) system:** It enables the customer to make electronic payments at NETC-enabled toll plazas on the highway without stopping at the toll, using **FASTag** based Radio Frequency Identification (RFID) technology.
11. A central repository, known as **Central KYC,** has been developed for reducing the hassle of undergoing multiple KYCs for different financial institutions. This allows the KYC process of consumers to be conducted only once unless there are any changes in consumer details.
12. **Joint Working Groups on FinTech:** India has formed bilateral joint working groups with several other countries to promote FinTech solutions for businesses and other sectors. Two such examples are:
    i. **The UK-India FinTech JWG** – To facilitate faster and cheaper flow of remittances between two countries. The countries are also exploring options to improve connectivity between India's UPI system and UK's payment system.
    ii. The **Singapore-India FinTech JWG** – For collaboration in the areas of API development, regulatory sandbox, integration of payment networks, security in payments and digital cash flow and e-KYC.
13. The **International Financial Services Centres Authority (IFSCA)** has issued a detailed '**Framework for FinTech Entity in the IFSCs**' with an objective to give boost to the establishment of a worldclass **FinTech Hub at GIFT** City, Gujarat comparable with other International Financial Centres (IFCs). Under this framework, authorisation certificates were granted to five FinTech firms. By promoting and nurturing innovation-oriented entities, IFSCA intends to create a thriving FinTech ecosystem in GIFT-IFSC.
14. **Digital Banking Units (DBUs)**: 75 DBUs have been launched in 75 districts of the country to commemorate the 75 years of independence of our country. The DBUs are being set up with an objective to ensure benefits of **digital banking** reach every nook and corner of the country. 11 Public Sector Banks, 12 Private Sector Banks and one Small Finance Bank are participating in the endeavour. As on February 2023, **84 DBUs are operational across the country.**
15. **Fincluvation**: India Post Payments Bank (IPPB), a 100 per cent government owned entity under the Department of Posts (DoP), announced the launch of **Fincluvation – a joint initiative to collaborate with FinTech Startup community** to co-create and innovate solutions for financial inclusion. **Fincluvation is aimed to**be a permanent platform of IPPB to co-create inclusive financial solutions with participating startups.

16. **FinTech Open month** was organised by NITI Ayog as a first-of-its-kind initiative bringing together regulators, FinTech professionals and enthusiasts, industry leaders, the startup community, and developers on a common platform to collaborate, exchange ideas, and innovate. NITI Aayog, in association with PhonePe, hosted the first-ever **open-to-all Hackathon event** for ideating and coming up with the most creative solutions for the FinTech space. The Hackathon provided an opportunity for innovators, digital creators and developers from all over India to think, ideate and code. The participants had to use open government data platform.
17. Technology infrastructure initiatives in several other sectors may help innovative FinTech solutions to grow using the infrastructure. For example, **TReDS** platform for facilitating the financing/ discounting of trade receivables of Micro, Small and Medium Enterprises (MSMEs) through multiple financiers, may pave the way for FinTech solutions in Trade financing.
18. RBI has launched Unified Lending Interface (ULI) and urged NBFCs to onboard on the ULI platform, conducting regular interactions with FinTech ecosystem and also working on video-based KYC projects in their regulatory sandbox framework.

Last Minute SNIPPETS

The Reserve Bank of India (RBI) organised the global hackathon **HaRBInger** in 2021 to improve retail payments. In 2024, the third edition of **HaRBInger**, focused on using technology to prevent financial fraud. Its main themes were 'Zero Financial Frauds' and 'Being Divyang Friendly.'

CHALLENGES AND RISKS OF FINTECH SECTOR IN INDIA

FinTech has the potential to fundamentally reshape the financial services and financial inclusion landscape in India. But, there are some challenges and potential risks in the adoption of FinTech in large scale in India:

- Regulating developing and upcoming FinTech technologies is a challenge. An example of this is the **regulation** of cryptocurrencies.
- Rising illegal lending apps and crypto lending, unregulated entities engaged into lending and unreported products like 'Buy Now Pay Later (BNPL) are concerns for governments which poses serious issues in the absence of any regulatory framework in the digital lending market.
- The wide range of FinTech products make it challenging to create a single, all-encompassing strategy to govern them specially when FinTech solutions come under the overlapping jurisdiction of different regulators like SEBI, RBI, etc.
- **Cyber security threats** and **data privacy needs** are a major concern for safeguarding the financial data accessed and held by FinTechs generated by the users. **Movement of data** from one company to another without the consent of the individual user is a governance challenge.
- **Cyber frauds** in the case of digital transactions are very frequent now-a-days. This is a potential deterrent for common public to embrace new FinTech solutions in their everyday financial needs. Proper cyber security measures need to be imbibed to boost the confidence of users.

- Risk of proliferation of **money laundering activities, financing of terrorism** and other criminal activities using the anonymity of the FinTech platforms and cross-border nature of the technological firms.
- Regulation of large technological companies related to cyber security and risk management is a big challenge due to the change of the nation state boundaries and respective laws of the countries.
- Skewed development of technology and venture capital ecosystems, shortage of skilled tech/ finance entrepreneurs, small markets, limited revenue potential are some of the major challenges. Cash dominance in transactions, informal credit and savings and lack of digital literacy are also matters of concern for expanding FinTech in the unbanked population of the country.
- Development of RegTech and SupTech sectors for ensuring regulatory compliance and proper supervision is one imperative.

BONUS KNOWLEDGE

REGTECH AND SUPTECH

In the context of potential risks and their mitigation, **RegTech** and **SupTech** have an important role.

- **RegTech** or **Regulatory Technology** helps a regulator use technology solutions to ensure that companies are complying with the norms.
- **SupTech** or **Supervisory Technology** is the use of technology by regulatory authorities themselves to monitor and ensure regulatory compliance by regulated entities.
- Both the technologies aim at improving efficiency using automation, introducing new capabilities and streamlining workflows.
- In India, the Reserve Bank of India has been using SupTech for data collection and analysis. The examples are Import Data Processing and Monitoring System (**IDPMS**), Export Data Processing and Monitoring System (**EDPMS**) and Central Repository of Information on Large Credits (**CRILC**), among others.
- The risk-based supervision of banks is extensively data-driven and is an example of SupTech.
- The future of RegTech and SupTech technologies lies in big data analytics, artificial intelligence, machine learning, cloud computing, geographic information system (GIS) mapping, data transfer protocols, biometrics, etc.

Last Minute SNIPPETS

GLOBAL FINTECH FEST (GFF)

The Global Fintech Fest (GFF) 2024 was held in Mumbai, jointly organised by the Payments Council of India, the National Payments Corporation of India, and the Fintech Convergence Council. The event highlighted India's advancements in the FinTech sector and served as a platform to bring together key industry stakeholders. It emphasised that the trinity of Jan Dhan, Aadhaar and Mobile have broken down the mentality of 'Cash is King' and made way for approximately half of the digital transactions in the world taking place in India.

SUMMARY

- **FinTech** – Referring to software, mobile applications, and other technologies created to improve and automate traditional forms of finance for businesses and consumers alike.
- **Cryptocurrency** – Digital or virtual asset designed to work as a medium of exchange that uses cryptography for security. For example: Bitcoin, Ethereum, Litecoin, XRP, etc.
- **Blockchain Technology** – Set of connected blocks of information on an online ledger which is central to the appeal and functionality of Bitcoin and other cryptocurrencies.
- **National Payments Corporation of India (NPCI)** – An initiative of RBI and Indian Banks' Association (IBA) under the provisions of the Payment and Settlement Systems Act, 2007, for creating a robust Payment and Settlement Infrastructure in India.
- **Digital Wallets** – Financial applications that allow consumers to store funds, make transactions, and track payment histories on devices like phones and tablets.
- **QR codes** – Quick Response codes are matrix bar codes that store information.
- **Digital Rupee** – The digital form of currency notes issued by RBI in order to settle secondary market transactions in government securities.
- **Supervisory Technology** – Use of technology by regulatory authorities themselves to monitor and ensure regulatory compliance by regulated entities.

UPSC CSE PREVIOUS YEARS' PRELIMINARY EXAMINATION QUESTIONS

1. Consider the following statements in respect of the digital rupee: **[2024]**

1. It is a sovereign currency issued by the RBI in alignment with its monetary policy.
2. It appears as a liability on the RBI's balance sheet.
3. It is insured against inflation by its very design.
4. It is freely convertible against commercial bank money and cash.

Which of the statements given above are correct?

(a) 1 and 2 only (b) 1 and 3 only
(c) 2 and 4 only (d) 1, 2 and 4

2. With reference to Central Bank digital currencies, consider the following statements: **[2023]**

1. It is possible to make payments in a digital currency without using US dollar or SWIFT system.
2. A digital currency can be distributed with condition programmed into it such as a time-frame for spending it.

Which of the statements given above is/are correct?

(a) 1 only (b) 2 only
(c) Both 1 and 2 (d) Neither 1 nor 2

3. With reference to '**Blockchain Technology**', consider the following statements: **[2020]**

1. It is a public ledger that everyone can inspect, but which no single user controls.
2. The structure and design of blockchain is such that all the data in it are about cryptocurrency only.
3. Applications that depend on basic features of blockchain can be developed without anybody's permission.

Which of the statements given above is/are correct?

(a) 1 only (b) 1 and 2 only
(c) 2 only (d) 1 and 3 only

4. The Reserve Bank of India's recent directives relating to 'Storage of Payment System Data', popularly known as data diktat, command the payment system providers that: **[2019]**

1. They shall ensure that entire data relating to payment systems operated by them are stored in a system only in India.
2. They shall ensure that the systems are owned and operated by public sector enterprises.

3. They shall submit the consolidated system audit report to the comptroller and Auditor General of India by the end of the calendar year.

Which of the statements given above is/are correct?

(a) 1 only (b) 1 and 2 only
(c) 3 only (d) 1, 2 and 3 only

5. With reference to digital payments, consider the following statements: **[2018]**

1. BHIM app allows the user to transfer money to anyone with a UPI-enabled bank account.
2. While a chip-pin debit card has four factors of authentication, BHIM app has only two factors of authentication.

Which of the statements given above is/are correct?

(a) 1 only (b) 2 only
(c) Both 1 and 2 (d) Neither 1 nor 2

NO QUESTIONS ASKED
2022, 2021, 2017, 2016, 2015, 2014, 2013

ANSWER KEY

1. (d) 2. (c) 3. (d) 4. (a) 5. (a)

UPSC CSE PREVIOUS YEARS' MAIN EXAMINATION QUESTIONS

1. What is the status of digitalisation in the Indian economy? Examine the problems faced in this regard and suggest improvements. **[2023]**

NO QUESTIONS ASKED
2024, 2022, 2021, 2020, 2019, 2018, 2017, 2016, 2015, 2014, 2013

CHAPTER

14

CO-OPERATIVE SECTOR IN INDIA

CHAPTER OUTLINE

- What is a Co-operative?
- Evolution of Cooperative Sector in India
- Constitutional Provisions and Laws relating to Co-operatives in India
- Functioning of Co-operatives
- Significance of Co-operatives in Indian Economy
- Different Types of Co-operatives
- National Co-operatives
- Women's Participation in Co-operatives
- Challenges in Co-operative Sector
- Recent Initiatives by the Government
- Institutions related to Co-operatives in India
- International Cooperative Alliance

The idea of cooperation has existed since the inception of human civilisation. Co-operatives are an almost universal form of organisation today found in practically all countries and used by people in many ways. They are formed to secure low-cost credit, to purchase supplies and equipment for farming and household needs, to market products, and even to secure many services, like electric power, irrigation, health, and insurance. Co-operatives can be beneficial for people in many ways in their everyday life.

WHAT IS A CO-OPERATIVE

A co-operative has been defined by the **International Co-operative Alliance (ICA)** as 'an autonomous association of persons united voluntarily to meet their common economic, social, and cultural needs and aspirations through a jointly-owned and democratically-controlled enterprise.'

- The concept of co-operation dates long back to the early days of human civilisation. In primitive societies, co-operation was an integral part of life and was found in cultural, religious and social aspects.
- The modern concept of co-operation is the outcome of the Industrial Revolution in Europe, especially in Great Britain.
- The Industrial Revolution resulted in the development of two classes in society, namely, the capitalist class and the working class. During this time, **Robert Owen** (1771–1859), a British Industrialist and Philanthropist, envisaged a new philosophy which ultimately led to the birth of co-operative movement. **Robert Owen** is called the **pioneer of the co-operative movement**.
- Another definition of co-operative society has been given by Lambert which states that 'a co-operative society is an enterprise, formed and directed by an association of users, applying within itself the rules of democracy and directly intended to serve both its own members and community as a whole.'

- The **International Labour Organisation** (**ILO**) states that a 'Co-operative society is an association of persons, varying in number, who are grappling with the same economic difficulties and who, voluntarily, associate on a basis of equal rights and obligations, endeavour to solve those difficulties mainly by conducting at their own risk an undertaking to which they have transferred one or more of such of their economic functions as correspond to their common needs, and by utilising this undertaking in joint co-operation for their common material and moral benefits.'

EVOLUTION OF CO-OPERATIVE SECTOR IN INDIA

- **1889** – **Anyonya Sahakari Mandali** [India's First co-operative arrangement]
- **1904** – **Co-Operative Credit Societies Act** [Arranged for institutional credit to farmers]
  Kan Jivaram [First urban co operative credit society]
- **1912** – **Cooperative Societies Act** [Provides non credit services to the members]
- **1914** – **Maclagen Committee on Cooperation** [Recommended a strong three tier structure of credit cooperatives]
- **1925** – **Bombay Co Operatives Societies Act** [Introduced the principle of one man one vote]
- **1942** – **Multi Unit Cooperative Societies Act** [Removes duplicity of provisions of different acts]
- **1945** – **Co-operative Planning Committee (1945)** – The Co-operative Planning Committee, under the chairmanship of Shri R.G. Saraiya, was set up in 1945. The Committee found co-operative societies to be the most suitable medium for democratisation of economic planning.

BONUS KNOWLEDGE

In 1946, inspired by Sardar Vallabh Bhai Patel and led by Shri Morarji Desai and Shri Tribhuvan Das Patel, the milk producers of Khera District of Gujarat went on a fifteen-day strike refusing to supply milk and forced the Bombay Government against the monopoly procurement rights given to Polson, a private dairy company. As a result of this, the Khera District Co-operative Milk Producers Milk Union, known as **Amul**, was established on 14 December 1946.

Post-Independence

- The Government of India, immediately after independence, recognised co-operatives as the third economic sector, realising the significant role of co-operatives in the development of national economy. They were entrusted with the responsibility of taking care of the needs and aspirations of rural India, with special emphasis on uplifting the small and marginal farmers as well as weaker sections of the society.

- The need of co-operatives has been recognised in successive Five-Year-Plans (FYP) to ensure holistic community development in various aspects.
- In 1963, the **National Co-operative Development Corporation (NCDC)** was established as a statutory corporation by an Act of Parliament. The establishment of the NCDC gave a great boost to the growth of co-operative marketing and processing societies.
- Multi State Co-operative Act of 1984, 2002 and amendments of 2023 have been passed.
- At present, **India has the largest network of co-operatives** in the world.

CONSTITUTIONAL PROVISIONS AND LAWS RELATING TO CO-OPERATIVES IN INDIA

- **97th Constitution (Amendment) Act, 2011** granted constitutional status to the Co-operative Societies and the following provisions have been made.
  (a) Insertion of **Part IXB** of the Constitution, which contains provisions for incorporation, regulation and winding up of co-operative societies and for democratic functioning of co-operative societies (Articles 243-ZH to 243-ZT). It was inserted by the Constitution (Ninety-seventh Amendment) Act, 2011.
  (b) **As a Fundamental Right: Right to form co-operative societies** was included as a Fundamental Right by insertion of the words '**co-operative societies**' in **Article 19(1)(c)** in Part III of the Constitution. The Article states that – *All citizens shall have the right to form associations or unions [or co-operative societies].*
  (c) **As part of DPSP: Article 43B** was inserted in Part IV of the Constitution as Directive Principle of State Policy for promotion of co-operative societies.
- Co-operative Societies come under the **State List as per the 7th Schedule of the constitution** (Entry 32 of List II).

Related Laws

Co-operative laws are framed for organisation and registration of co-operatives following co-operative principles while preserving co-operative character. These laws provide for the appointment of Registrar and sub-ordinate officers and entrusts the powers and functions under the statute to respective authorities.

Some of the important Acts of pre-independence time are as follows:

1. **The Co-operative Credit Societies Act, 1904** – It was modelled largely on the English Friendly Societies Act, 1896. It followed Nicholson's recommendation for the creation of village banks and the operation of the Act was restricted to agricultural credit only.
2. **All India Co-operative Societies Act, 1912** – This Act recognised the necessity of organising large societies for proper supervision of credit and enabled the establishment of co-operatives of non-credit activities.
3. In 1919, the implementation of **Montagu-Chelmsford reforms** transferred cooperation as a subject to the Provincial (State) governments. Accordingly, provincial governments enacted their own Co-operative Societies Acts during 1925–32. The Bombay Provincial Government was the first to pass its own Act, 'Bombay Provincial Co-operative Societies Act' in 1925.
4. **Multi-Unit Co-operative Societies Act, 1942** – The central government passed this Act in 1942 to remove duplicity of provisions of different Acts. This act provided for the regulation of affairs of

such society by the provisions of co-operative societies Act of the state where the principal business of the society is located.

Some of the important co-operative laws of post-independence India are as follows:

1. **National Co-operative Development Corporation (NCDC) Act, 1962** – This was enacted to establish National Co-operative Development Corporation as a statutory organisation.
2. **Multi State Co-operative Societies Act, 1984** – This Act replaced the Multi-Unit Co-operative Societies Act, 1942. The objective of the Act was to avoid different multi-unit co-operatives being governed by different state co-operative laws in the country.
3. **Multi State Co-operative Societies Act, 2002** – This Act replaced the Multi-State Co-operative Societies Act of 1984. The 2002 Act provided for the special provision for registration and functions of Federal Co-operative Societies.

BONUS KNOWLEDGE

MULTI STATE CO-OPERATIVE SOCIETIES

Though Co-operative societies are mentioned as state subject in the constitution, many co-operative societies have been established whose operation areas are spread across more than one state with members from all participating states. Such co-operative societies are called multi-state co-operative societies.

These societies allow membership from multiple states, and they are thus registered under the Multi State Co-operative Societies Act, 2002. Their board of directors usually has representation from all states of operation.

Administrative and financial control of these multi-state co-operative societies lies with the central registrar, as the operation is not confined to any single state.

4. **Multi State Co-operative Societies (Amendment) Act, 2023** – Some of the most important objectives of this amendment Act are as follows:
   - To establish the Co-operative Election Authority to conduct and supervise elections to the boards of multi-state co-operative societies by amending the Multi-State Co-operative Societies Act, 2002.
   - Requirement of government permission before the redemption of shareholding of a multi-state co-operative society.
   - Setting up of Co-operative Rehabilitation, Reconstruction and Development Fund for the revival of sick multi-state co-operative societies. The Fund will be financed through contributions by profitable multi-state co-operative societies.
   - Provision for state co-operative societies to merge into an existing multi-state co-operative society, subject to the respective state laws.

MINISTRY OF COOPERATION

In 2021, a dedicated ministry in Government of India was created for the realisation of vision **'Cooperation to Prosperity' (Sahakar-se-Samriddhi)**. The Ministry of Cooperation has been created by transferring the existing entries related to cooperation and co-operative in the business of the erstwhile Ministry of

Agriculture, Cooperation and Farmers Welfare vide Cabinet Secretariat's Gazette Notification dated 6 July, 2021.

The Ministry is headed by the Hon'ble Minister for Cooperation, and is assisted by the Hon'ble Minister of State for Cooperation.

The Responsibilities of the Ministry include:

- To provide a separate administrative, legal and policy framework for strengthening the co-operative movement in country.
- To deepen co-operatives as a true people-based movement reaching up to the grassroots and develop a co-operative based economic model where each member works with a spirit of responsibility.
- Streamlining processes for 'Ease of doing business' for co-operatives and enabling development of Multi-State Co-operative Societies.
- Strengthening and bringing transparency, modernisation, computerisation, creating competitive co-operatives, working constantly to meet the challenge of accessibility to development for every underprivileged in rural areas and on connecting every village with co-operatives, making every village prosperous with the mantra of '**Sahakar se Samriddhi**'.

Panch Pran (5 vows) of Amrit Kaal

The Ministry of Cooperation is guided by the Panch Pran (5 vows) of Amrit Kaal. These 5 vows are: →

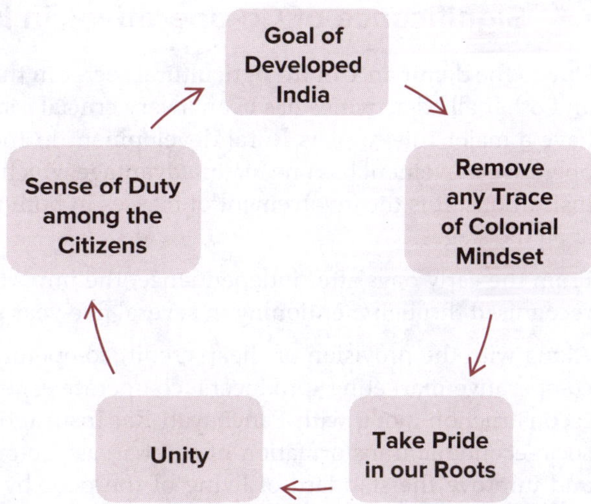

The Co-operatives Principles

The vision of Co-operative in India is based on the 7 universally accepted Co-operative Principles, which are mentioned below:

1. Open and Voluntary Membership
2. Democratic Member Control
3. Members' Economic Participation
4. Autonomy and Independence
5. Education, Training, and Information
6. Cooperation among Co-operatives
7. Concern for Community

Functioning of Co-operatives

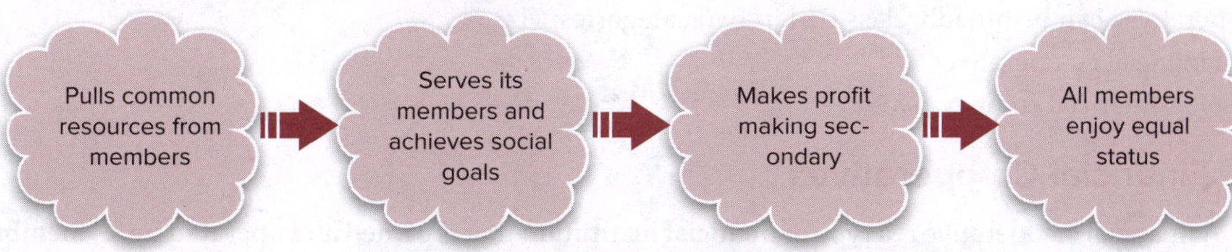

There are differences between co-operatives and other businesses in relation to three main groups of people responsible for bringing them into existence and keeping them in operation.

The three groups are:

A. The persons who own them (the shareholders, the investors),

B. The persons who control them (the effective decision-makers) and

C. The persons who use them (the customers).

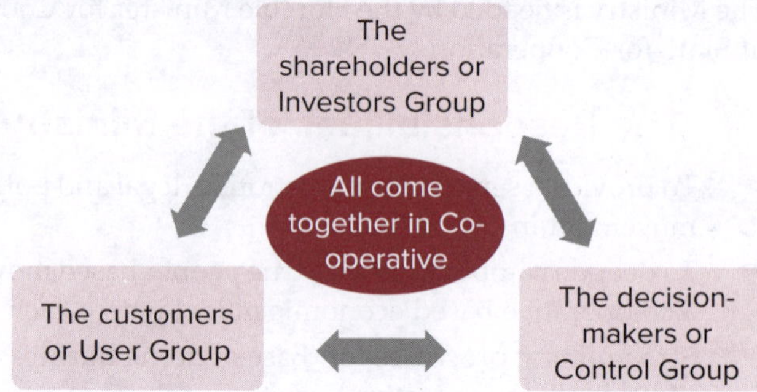

In traditional businesses, especially large enterprises and multinational corporations, these three are separate and distinct groups. In small private business, the situation is generally much better because of the close connection between shareholders (investors) and control group. In a small retail business, the first two components are often identical. But still, the users, the customers, are a separate group.

In a co-operative, all three come together to form a **unity**; those who own, those who control, and those who use are one entity.

Significance of Co-operatives in Indian Economy

Due to the dominance of the agricultural sector in the Indian economy since long, credit for agricultural and other allied activities has been a very crucial issue. In the areas of agricultural credit, co-operatives have a major role to play. Rural development in India is very much dependent on co-operatives. Co-operative movement has one major advantage which makes its position unique among all other financial institutions. It is the involvement of masses in both their decision-making and implementation process at all the stages.

From the early days after independence, the importance of co-operatives in Indian economy has been recognised through mentioning in several five-year plans.

Along with the provision of cheap credit, co-operatives have been expanded in several new areas like co-operative marketing, producers' co-operatives, etc. Co-operatives have emerged as a pillar of rural reconstruction along with Panchayati Raj Institutions in India. Both are envisaged as instruments of socio-economic transformation of rural areas. Co-operatives have great potential to reduce inequality and improve the standard of living of the poor by bringing marginalised sections within the fold of formal economy.

DIFFERENT TYPES OF CO-OPERATIVES

Co-operatives can be broadly classified in two categories, viz.

I. Financial co-operatives

II. Non-financial co-operatives

Financial Co-operatives

- A financial co-operative is a type of **financial institution** that is **owned and operated by its members**. The goal of a financial co-operative is to act on behalf of a unified group to offer traditional banking services. These co-operatives are focused on the financial wellness of their members instead of maximising profits like traditional banks, while offering quality service along with competitive rate.

- In India, the lack of institutional lending of agricultural credit led to the formation of credit co-operatives dating back to the year 1894 when this new system of rural finance was introduced in India.
- Over the years, this system introduced the system of co-operative banking in India. The structure of Co-operative Banking in India is as follows:

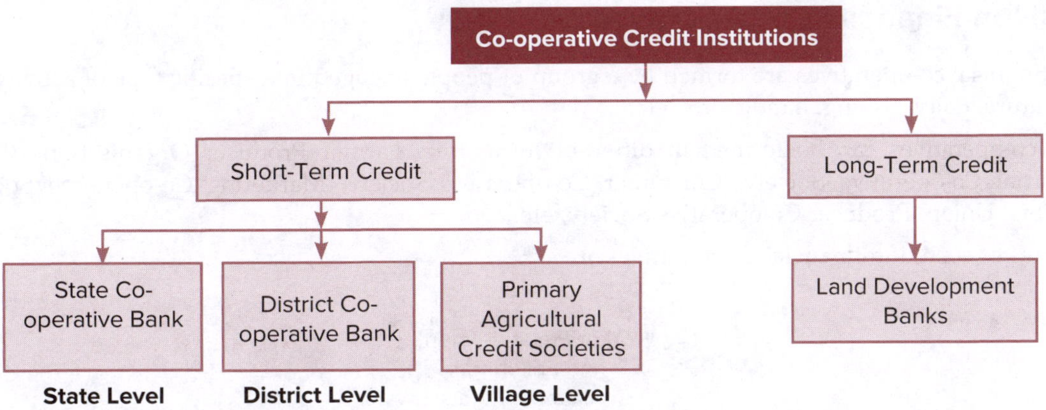

Co-operative credit institutions in India can be broadly classified into two categories:

(i) **Agricultural credit institutions** (ii) **Non-agricultural credit institutions**

Agricultural Credit Institutions

- Agricultural credit institutions can be categorised into two types – viz. short-term agricultural credit institutions and long-term agricultural credit institutions.
- The short-term agricultural credit institutions are meant to cater to the short-term financial needs of people related to agricultural sector. These institutions have a three-tier federal structure –
  (a) At the state level, the state co-operative bank exists in each state;
  (b) At the district level, there are district central co-operative banks;
  (c) At the village level, the units are primary agricultural credit societies.

Last Minute SNIPPETS

As per the National Co-operative Database, as on March, 2025, the data on co-operative societies are as follows:

Type of Institution	Count
Primary Level Co-operative Societies	825397
State Federation	231
National Federation	19
Multistate Co-operative	1734
State Co-operative Banks	32
District Co-operative Banks	338
Primary Co-operative Agriculture and Rural Development Banks (PCARDB)	526
State Co-operative Agriculture and Rural Development Banks (SCARDB)	14

Source: National Co-operative Database, Ministry of Cooperation, GoI

➤ The need for long-term credit in agricultural sector is usually covered by the **Land development banks.**

Financial co-operatives have played a crucial role in the financial inclusion of rural and marginalised people of India. In the developing nations, co-operative banking is the most suitable to bring the inclusion of traditionally neglected segments, e.g. women borrowers in the mainstream economy.

These institutions are pivotal for rural uplift and overall development of the economy by people's participation.

Non-Financial Co-operatives

Non-financial co-operatives are formed by a group of people engaged in a specific type of activity like agriculture, dairy, fishing, handicrafts, etc.

Such co-operatives can be formed in different forms, viz. Farmer Producer Organisations (FPO), Industrial Co-operative Society, Consumer Co-operative Society, Marketing Co-operative Society, Workers' Union, Producer Co-operative Society, etc.

Features of such non-financial co-operatives are:

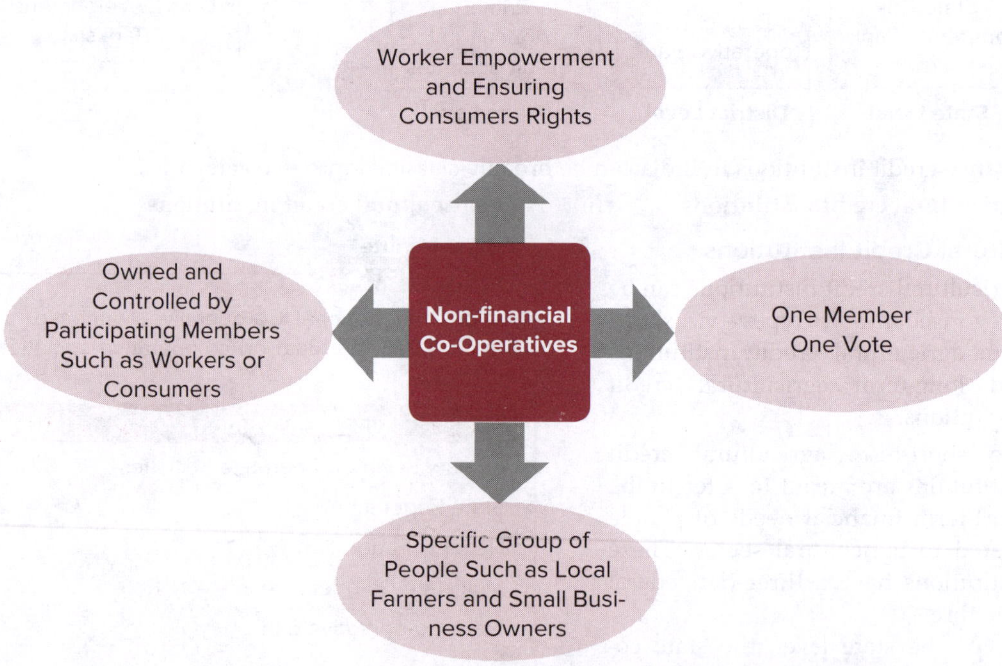

In India, co-operatives have been formed successfully in various sectors such as retail, banking, housing, marketing, agriculture, manufacturing, purchasing, and employment among others. Some of the most notable co-operatives in India are:

1. **Amul** (Anand Milk Union Limited) owned by co-operative society named Gujarat Milk Marketing Federation based in Anand, Gujarat – Largest Dairy co-operative in India
2. Shree Mahila Griha Udyog (**Lijjat Papad**) – An Indian women's worker co-operative involved in manufacturing of various fast-moving consumer goods.

3. Indian Farmers Fertiliser Co-operative (**IFFCO**)
4. National Agricultural Co-operative Marketing Federation (**NAFED**)
5. **Karnataka Milk Federation** (second largest milk co-operative in India)
6. **Indian Coffee House**
7. **Krishak Bharati Co-operative Limited (KRIBHCO)**, a central government co-operative under the ownership of Ministry of Cooperation, Government of India is a manufacturer of fertilisers.

Three co-operatives of India, namely **Amul, IFFCO, and KRIBHCO** are included in the list of 300 largest co-operative societies of the world.

did you KNOW?

THE AMUL STORY

Amul Or Anand Milk Union Limited is owned by co-operative society named Gujarat Milk Marketing Federation based in Anand, Gujarat. Presently it is controlled by 3.6 million milk producers. Amul was formed as a part of a co-operative movement against the monopoly of Polson Dairy in Anand, Gujarat, the company which procured milk from local farmers of Kaira (now Kheda) District at very low rates and sold it to the then Bombay government as part of Bombay Milk Scheme. Everyone was satisfied with the system except the milk producers. They were compelled to sell the milk at low prices due to the perishable nature of the milk. To change the situation the milk producers obtained support from Sardar Vallabhbhai Patel and refused to sell the milk to contractors. The farmers called a 'milk strike' which lasted for 15 days jeopardising the Bombay Milk Scheme. Finally, the British government accepted the demand of farmers to form a co-operative and the **Kaira District Co-operative Milk Producers' Union Limited** was found in Anand, in 1946.

Its objective was to provide proper marketing facilities for the milk producers of the district. The co-operative union began pasteurizing milk on their own in June 1948, with farmers of just two village co-operative societies producing about 250 liters a day. The brand name Amul was envisaged in 1955.

Under the leadership of **Dr. Verghese Kurien**, this co-operative spearheaded the **White Revolution** of India in 1970s. The Gujarat Co-operative Milk Marketing Federation Ltd., an apex marketing body of the district co-operatives, was established in 1973 to expand the market and to avoid competing amongst the district co-operatives themselves. **National Dairy Development Board** was founded in **1965** with an objective to replicate the Amul model throughout the country under the chairmanship of Dr. Kurien.

From this humble beginning, Amul has come a long way to become a household name synonymous with its tagline – *the taste of India*.

The Amul has not only propelled India to be largest milk manufacturer in the world, but has established itself as the most successful co-operative in the history of co-operative in India.

NATIONAL CO-OPERATIVES

'National Co-operative Society' means a multi state co-operative society specified in the Second Schedule of the **Multi State Co-operative Societies Act, 2002**.

The National Co-operative Societies have the responsibility of providing specialised training, education, undertake research and develop market information system, logo brand promotion, quality control and technology upgradation besides evolving code of conduct, viability norms for its members and ensuring the compliance of co-operatives principles by them.

As of March 2025, the list contains 19 National co-operative societies which are as follows:

Sl No.	Name of National Co-operative
1.	National Federation of Fishermen's Co-operative Limited, New Delhi
2.	National Federation of State Co-operative Bank Limited, Mumbai
3.	National Federation of Co-operative Sugar Factories Limited, New Delhi
4.	National Co-operative Dairy Federation of India Limited, Anand, Gujarat
5.	National Co-operative Consumer's Federation of India Limited, New Delhi
6.	National Federation of Labour Co-operative Limited, New Delhi
7.	National Co-operative Housing Federation Limited, New Delhi
8.	National Federation of Urban Co-operative Banks and Credit Societies Limited, New Delhi
9.	Tribal Co-operative Marketing Development Federation of India Limited, New Delhi (TRIFED)
10.	National Agriculture Co-operative Marketing Federation of India Limited, New Delhi
11.	National Co-operative Union of India Limited, New Delhi
12.	Krishak Bharati Co-operative Limited, New Delhi
13.	Indian Farmer's Fertiliser Co-operative Limited, New Delhi
14.	National Co-operative Organics Limited, Anand, Gujarat
15.	Bhartiya Beej Sahakari Samiti Limited, New Delhi
16.	National Co-operative Exports Limited, New Delhi
17.	National Co-operative Land Development Banks Federation Limited, Mumbai
18.	All India Handloom Fabrics Marketing Co-operative Society Limited, New Delhi
19.	All India Federation of Co-operative Spinning Mills Limited, Mumbai

After a long gap of 36 years since the formation of TRIFED in 1987, three new National Co-operative Societies have been formed under the MSCS Act, 2002 for Exports, Organic produces, and Seed related activities, respectively. These societies have been registered under MSCS Act, 2002.

Last Minute SNIPPETS

Among these 19 National Federations, **Indian Fertiliser Co-operative Limited (IFFCO)**, headquartered in New Delhi, is the largest, having turnover of ₹39,330 crore in the Financial Year 2023–2024.

These Three new National Level Multi-State Societies are as follows:

1. **New National Multi-State Co-operative Seed Society for certified seeds**: This is a new apex multi-state co-operative seed society under the MSCS Act, 2002, namely Bharatiya Beej Sahakari Samiti Limited (BBSSL) which will act as an umbrella organisation for quality seed cultivation, production and distribution under a single brand. Wheat, mustard, and pulses (gram, pea) breeder seeds have been planted across 1,750 acres. The operations will be expanded to cultivate foundation/ certified seeds for groundnut, paddy, maize, and millet.
2. **New National Multi-State Co-operative Organic Society for organic farming**: This is a new apex multi-state co-operative organic society, namely National Co-operative Organics Limited (NCOL). It is an umbrella organisation to produce, distribute and market certified and authentic organic products. Six organic products have been launched by NCOL under '**Bharat Organics**' brand.
3. **New National Multi-State Co-operative Export Society for promoting exports**: This is a new apex multi-state co-operative export society under the MSCS Act, 2002, namely National Co-operative

Export Limited (NCEL). It is an umbrella organisation to give thrust to exports from co-operative sector. As on February 2024, NCEL has got permission to export 23.9 LMT rice to 20 countries and 50,000 MT sugar to 2 countries.

EXAM ESSENTIAL

PRIMARY AGRICULTURAL CREDIT SOCIETIES

Primary Agricultural Credit Societies (PACS) are the grassroot level wings of the three-tier short-term co-operative credit structure. PACS, a village-level institution, are formed to deal directly with the rural borrowers for agricultural needs, provide them loans and collect repayments of the credit provided and also perform distribution and marketing functions.

The functions of PACS include –

i. creating practice of savings among the farmers,

ii. accepting deposits from them,

iii. providing agricultural loans to the persons in need, and

iv. collecting repayments for the loans.

PACS act as the link between the rural borrowers at the village level on one hand and the higher agencies, viz. District Central co-operative bank, state co-operative bank, on the other.

Organisational Structure of PACS

A PACS usually consists of the General Body of PACS (responsible for management of affairs);

Management Committee (elected general body entrusted to work following the society's rules);

Chairman, Vice-Chairman, and Secretary and other Office Staff to carry out the daily office work.

Significance of Primary Agriculture Credit Society

- A PACS is the ground level building block of the century-old co-operative credit system of India.
- The key role in giving access to credit, inputs, market and value addition to the people of rural agricultural communities.
- Major role of integrating the warehouse with the supply chain of agro-products in the rural markets or large warehouses maintained by the private sector.

Strengthening of PACS through Computerisation

- At present, it is imperative to enhance the capacity, efficiency, and effectiveness of the Primary Agriculture Credit Societies (PACS) beyond their functions of credit institutions. Through this process, PACS will be strengthened to provide several other non-banking services to the people of rural agricultural communities along with credit and financial services.
- **Total 63,000 functional PACS are being linked with NABARD on a single National Software Network**. Computerisation plays a crucial role in strengthening Primary Agricultural Credit Societies (PACS) by enhancing their efficiency, transparency, and overall effectiveness in delivering financial services to members. This will strengthen PACS by modernising their operations, improving service delivery, reducing operational costs, and promoting financial inclusion.

WOMEN'S PARTICIPATION IN CO-OPERATIVES

Co-operatives are ideal institutions to formalise more women participation in economic activities.

Women have played a significant role in the success of many co-operative movements like **AMUL** (Anand Milk Union Limited) and Shree Mahila Griha Udyog (**Lijjat Papad**). Around 45,000 women were associated with Lijjat's co-operative movement while Amul co-operatives have engaged 36 lakh families, especially women farmers.

These women co-operatives have successfully transformed the lives of rural women. Examples of other successful Women Co-operatives are:

- Women's Industrial Co-operative Society Limited
- Self Employed Women's Association (SEWA) Co-operatives
- Swashrayi Mahila SEWA Bank
- Mahila Sewa Lok Swasthya Co-operative
- Mulkanoor Women's Co-operative Dairy (MWCD)
- Sangini Child-Care Workers Co-operative
- Abodana Mahila Kapad Chapkam Utpadak SEWA Sahakari Mandali Limited
- Bhramaramba Mahila Co-operative Banking Society, etc.

These co-operatives have contributed to the holistic empowerment of women in society.

Promoting more village level co-operatives can mainstream women participation towards empowerment and socio-economic development. Rural women are primarily engaged in agriculture and allied activities. Therefore, co-operatives need to take up gender-responsive initiatives, viz. parity in payment, promoting local products of rural women's co-operatives among others.

Co-operatives generate a significant source of employment and support the formalisation of informal employment through collective voice, economies of scale and extension of social protection. India has a significant female workforce that can be mainstreamed to enhance their contribution in transforming society at large.

CHALLENGES IN CO-OPERATIVE SECTOR

The co-operative sector in India has emerged as a powerful instrument for promoting inclusive growth and equitable development while serving social justice. However, despite its potential, there are several challenges in harnessing the full benefits of the co-operative sector to ensure equitable distribution of resources and opportunities.

- **Growing bad debts and non-performing assets** in credit co-operatives have distorted their financial shape. The reasons for their losses include increased number of wilful defaulters, poor loan recovery, waiver practices of governments, ineffective credit administration and monitoring, inflated profits reported in the books, growth in fraud and money theft, etc.
- Failures in non-credit co-operatives due to inability to draw customers due to lack of effective advertising, **unsuccessful marketing strategies**, inability to expand market, etc.
- Issues of governance of co-operatives due to **lack of transparency and accountability**. Participation of limited members and **concentration of power within a few members** violate the principles of co-operative operation.
- Lack of coordination between multiple co-operatives.
- **Political interference** faced by co-operatives like the sugar co-operatives in Maharashtra.
- Less demand of goods produced by co-operatives due to **lack of better branding** of such goods.
- Lack of awareness among people about the co-operative movement, its rules and regulations.
- **Lack of professional training and skills** among employees of the co-operatives.

RECENT INITIATIVES BY THE GOVERNMENT

Government has planned or launched a slew of initiatives to overcome the challenges related to functioning of co-operatives in the country. The initiatives are aimed at incorporating modern technology and best practices in this sector and to enable the co-operative sector to bolster the economy.

- **Model Bye-Laws for PACS** have been prepared and circulated to all the States/UTs to make them **multipurpose, multidimensional and transparent entities**. This will enable PACS to undertake more than 25 business activities, improve governance, transparency and accountability in their operations.
- Government is aiming to set up new **multi-purpose PACS** or **primary dairy/fisheries co-operatives** covering **every Panchayat/village in the next five years**, with the support of National Bank for Agriculture and Rural Development (NABARD), National Dairy Development Board (NDDB), National Fisheries Development Board (NFDB), National Corporative Development Corporation (NCDC) and other National level Federations. As of 2023, the process for registering 9,961 new PACS/Dairy/Fishery co-operative societies in 24 States/UTs is in various stages.
- **World's Largest Decentralised Grain Storage Plan in Co-operative sector**: This has been launched with the plan to create Grain Storage capacity of **700 lakh tonnes** over the next 5 years, with an investment with ` 1.25 lakh crore. As part of this project, warehouses, primary processing units and other agri-infrastructure for grain storage will be created at PACS level, converging various central government schemes together. This will reduce wastage of food grains and transportation costs, enable farmers to realise better prices for their produce and meet various agricultural needs at the PACS level itself. 27 States/ UTs and National level Co-operative Federations such as National Co-operative Consumers Federation (NCCF) and National Agricultural Co-operative Marketing Federation of India Ltd. (NAFED), have identified more than 2,000 PACS for creation of storage capacity under the Pilot Project.
- To strengthen Primary Agricultural Credit Societies (PACS), the project for **Computerisation** of 63,000 functional PACS with a total financial outlay of ` 2,516 crore has been approved by the Government of India, which entails bringing all the functional PACS onto an ERP based national software, linking them with NABARD through State Cooperative Banks (StCBs) and District Cooperative Banks (DCCBs)
- **New National Co-operative Database**: A comprehensive database of co-operatives in India has been prepared with the support of State Governments to facilitate the policy making process and streamline the implementation of schemes related to co-operatives across the nation.
- **PACS as Common Service Centres**: PACS has been enabled to provide more than 300 e-services such as banking, insurance, Aadhaar enrolment/ updation, health services, issue of PAN card and booking of IRCTC/Bus/Air ticket, etc. through collaboration between Ministry of Cooperation, MeitY, NABARD and CSC e-Governance Services India.

> **Last Minute SNIPPETS**
>
> Already more than such 30,000 PACS have started providing CSC services to rural citizens which will also augment the income of these PACS. (as on February 2025)

- Government is promoting PACS to operate **Pradhan Mantri Kisan Samriddhi Kendras** (PMKSK) for ensuring easy accessibility of fertiliser and related services to farmers in the country.

- **Convergence of PM-KUSUM at PACS level**: Farmers who are associated with PACS can adopt solar agricultural water pumps and install photovoltaic modules in their farms.
- Government is promoting PACS to operate **PM Bharatiya Jan Aushadhi Kendra** which provide access to generic medicines for rural citizens along with generating additional income source for the PACS.
- 1,100 **new Farmer Producer Organisations (FPOs)** to be formed by PACS with the support of NCDC, in the blocks where FPOs have not been formed yet.
- **Micro-ATMs to Bank Mitra Co-operative Societies for providing doorstep financial services**: Dairy and Fisheries co-operative societies will be converted to Bank Mitras of DCCBs and StCBs. These Bank Mitra Co-operative Societies will be equipped with Micro-ATMs with support from NABARD to enable **'Door-step Financial Services'** which will enhance their ease of doing business, transparency, and financial inclusion. A pilot project with 1,723 Micro-ATMs has been commenced in Panchmahal and Banaskantha districts of Gujarat.
- In a bid to provide market linkage and processing facilities to fishermen, the Department of Fisheries, Government of India has allocated the work of converting 1000 existing fisheries co-operative societies into **Fish Farmer Producer Organisations (FFPOs)** with an approved outlay of ` 225.50 crore.
- **Umbrella Organisation for Urban Co-operative Banks** (**UCB**): RBI has given approval to the National Federation of Urban Co-operative Banks and Credit Societies Ltd. (**NAFCUB**) for the formation of an Umbrella Organisation for the UCB sector, which is envisaged to provide necessary IT infrastructure and operational support to around 1,500 UCBs.
- Government has taken several new initiatives for the **revival of Co-operative Sugar Mills** like New loan scheme of ` 10,000 crores, preference to Co-operative Sugar Mills for the procurement of Ethanol by GoI under the Ethanol Blending Programme (EBP).
- **Co-operatives have been allowed to register as 'buyer' on GeM portal**, enabling them to procure goods and services from over 67 lakh vendors in the GeM portal to facilitate better purchases with greater transparency.
- **National Council for Co-operative Training (NCCT)** has conducted 3,287 training programmes and provided training to 2,01,507 participants in FY 2022–23 for **promotion of awareness through training.**
- PACS to perform Operations & Maintenance (O&M) of rural piped water supply schemes (PWS): On the initiative of the Ministry of Cooperation, the Ministry of Jal Shakti designated PACS as eligible agencies to perform Operations & Maintenance (O&M) of PWS in rural areas, leveraging PACS's extensive reach in these areas. According to data from States and UTs, 16 States and UTs have identified and chosen 1,833 PACS to offer O&M services at the Panchayat/Village level.
- Ministry of Cooperation has decided to set up **National Co-operative University** for providing training, consultancy related to co-operative sector, sustainable supply of trained manpower to fulfil research and development objectives.
- A national level committee has been formed to formulate the new **National Co-operative Policy** for enabling a vibrant ecosystem to realise the vision of '*Sahakar-se-Samriddhi*'.

INSTITUTIONS RELATED TO CO-OPERATIVE SECTOR IN INDIA

National Co-operative Development Corporation (NCDC)

It is a statutory corporation (established by an Act of Parliament in 1963) under the administrative control of **Ministry of Cooperation**.

The functions of NCDC are planning, promoting and financing programmes for production, processing, marketing, storage, export and import of agricultural produce, food stuffs, certain other notified commodities, e.g. fertilisers, insecticides, agricultural machinery, lac, soap, kerosene oil, textile, rubber, etc., supply of consumer goods and collection, processing, marketing, storage and export of minor forest produce through co-operatives, besides income generating stream of activities such as poultry, dairy, fishery, sericulture, handloom, etc.

Having its **head office in New Delhi**, NCDC also operates across the country through 18 Regional/State Directorates.

Central Registrar of Co-operative Societies (CRCS)

The Office of Central Registrar of Co-operative Societies (CRCS) **deals with incorporation, regulation and winding up of co-operative societies**, with objects not confined to one State, to facilitate the voluntary formation and democratic functioning of co-operatives as people's institutions based on self-help and mutual aid, and to enable them to promote their economic and social betterment, and to provide functional autonomy, as per co-operative principles and legislative framework enshrined under Multi State Co-operative Societies (MSCS) Act, 2002. The CRCS is appointed under Article 243ZH(f) of the Constitution and Section 4 of the MSCS Act, 2002.

BONUS KNOWLEDGE

INTERNATIONAL COOPERATIVE ALLIANCE

International Cooperative Alliance (ICA), the apex body representing co-operatives which are estimated to be around 3 million worldwide, is providing **a global voice and forum** for knowledge, expertise and co-ordinated action for and about co-operatives. It was founded in **1895**, making it one of the oldest non-governmental organisations and one of the largest ones measured by the number of people represented – **1 billion co-operative members on the planet**.

More than 305 organisations from 103 countries are members of the International Cooperative Alliance.

The ICA's members are international and national co-operative organisations from all sectors of the economy, namely agriculture, banking, consumer, fisheries, health, housing, insurance, and industry & services.

did you KNOW?

INTERNATIONAL YEAR OF CO-OPERATIVES

United Nations General Assembly has proclaimed **2025** as the International Year of Co-operatives with the theme, "*Cooperatives Build a Better World*,". Previously, 2012 was declared as the First International Year of Co-operatives by United Nations General Assembly.

SUMMARY

- A co-operative has been defined by the International Co-operative Alliance (ICA) as 'an autonomous association of persons united voluntarily to meet their common economic, social, and cultural needs and aspirations through a jointly-owned and democratically-controlled enterprise.'
- **Robert Owen** (1771–1859), a British Industrialist and Philanthropist, the pioneer of the co-operative movement, envisaged modern concept of co-operation.
- The first significant step in co-operative movement in India, was the enactment of Co-operative Credit Societies Act in 1904. The main purpose was to arrange for institutional credit to the farmers for agricultural activities.
- **97th Constitution (Amendment) Act, 2011** granted constitutional status to the Co-operative Societies.
- **Part IXB** of the Constitution contains provisions for incorporation, regulation and winding up of co-operative societies and for democratic functioning of co-operative societies (Articles 243-ZH to 243-ZT). It was inserted by the Constitution (Ninety-seventh Amendment) Act, 2011.
- **Right to form co-operative societies** was included as a Fundamental Right by insertion of the words '**co-operative societies**' in **Article 19(1)(c)** in Part III of the Constitution.
- **Article 43B** was inserted in Part IV of the Constitution as Directive Principle of State Policy for promotion of co-operative societies.
- Co-operative Societies come under **State List of 7th Schedule of the Constitution**.
- Co-operative Societies can be single state society or multi state co-operative societies.
- **Multi State Co-operative Societies** allow membership from multiple states, and they are thus registered under the Multi State Co-operative Societies Act, 2002.
- In 2021, a dedicated ministry in Government of India was created for the realisation of vision
- '**Cooperation to Prosperity' (Sahakar-se-Samriddhi**).
- The vision of co-operative in India is based on the **7 universally accepted Co-operative Principles**, which are – Open and Voluntary Membership, Democratic Member Control, Member Economic Participation, Autonomy and Independence, Education, Training, and Information, Cooperation Among Co-operatives and Concern for Community.
- Based on the nature of activities, co-operatives can be broadly classified into two categories – **Financial Co-operatives** and **Non-financial co-operatives.**
- Different types of co-operative credit institutions in India can be broadly classified into two categories – Agricultural credit institutions and Non-agricultural credit institutions.
- Agricultural credit institutions can be categorised into **short-term and long-term agricultural credit institutions**.
- The short-term agricultural credit institutions, catering to the needs of short-term agricultural loans, have **three-tier federal structure** – State Central Co-operative Bank at the state level, District Central Co-operative Bank and Primary Agricultural Co-operative Societies.
- **Primary Agricultural Credit Societies** (PACS) are the grassroot level wings of the three-tier short-term co-operative credit structure. PACS, a village-level institution, deals directly with the rural (agricultural) borrowers, give them loans and collect repayment of loans given and also undertake distribution and marketing functions.

UPSC CSE PREVIOUS YEARS' PRELIMINARY EXAMINATION QUESTIONS

☞ NO QUESTIONS ASKED
2024, 2023, 2022, 2021, 2020, 2019, 2018, 2017, 2016, 2015, 2014, 2013

UPSC CSE PREVIOUS YEARS' MAIN EXAMINATION QUESTIONS

1. 'In the villages itself no form of credit organisation will be suitable except the co-operative society.' – *All India Rural Credit Survey*.
   Discuss this statement in the background of agricultural finance in India. What constraints and challenges do financial institutions supplying agricultural finance face? How can technology be used to better reach and serve rural clients? **[2014]**

☞ NO QUESTIONS ASKED
2024, 2023, 2022, 2021, 2020, 2019, 2018, 2017, 2016, 2015, 2013

CHAPTER

15

AGRICULTURE AND ALLIED SECTORS IN INDIA

CHAPTER OUTLINE

- Role of Agriculture in Indian Economy
- Current Scenario of Indian Agriculture and Allied Sectors
- Foodgrain Production in India
- Green Revolution
- Horticulture Sector
- Mission for Integrated Development of Horticulture
- Seeds
- Major Reforms undertaken in Seeds Sector
- Fertilisers
- Soil Reclamation
- Cropping Pattern
- Types of Cropping Pattern in India
- Factors Influencing Cropping Pattern
- Crop Diversification
- Contract Farming
- Draft Model Contract Farming Act, 2018
- Sahakar Mitra
- Agricultural Finance
- Sources of Agriculture Finance
- Role of NABARD
- Government Initiatives so far to Promote Agricultural Credit
- FDI in Agriculture
- Agricultural Marketing
- Model APMC Act, 2003
- Integrated Scheme for Agricultural Marketing
- Agricultural Subsidy
- Agriculture Insurance
- Restructured Weather-Based Crop Insurance Scheme (RWBCIS)
- Biotech-KISAN Programme
- Animal Rearing
- Persisting Challenges in Agriculture Sector
- Doubling of Farmers' Income Report
- E-Technology in Production and Marketing of Agricultural Produce
- Major Reforms needed under Second Green Revolution
- Climate Smart Agriculture (CSA)
- Major Technology Mission Initiatives in Agriculture
- Mechanism for Marketing of Minor Forest Produce (MFP) through a Minimum Support Price (MSP) Scheme
- Farm Laws Repealed in 2021
- Situation Assessment Survey
- Sweet Revolution
- Ethanol Blended with Petrol (EBP) Programme
- Natural Farming

ROLE OF AGRICULTURE IN INDIAN ECONOMY

- Agriculture is the largest unorganised sector of Indian Economy and it has the highest share in employment generation and livelihood creation.

- Agriculture is kept at the centre of agenda of the planning process because it helps to reduce poverty and malnutrition and improves long-term food security.
- It stimulates additional activity in the form of labour income, job creation, etc.
- It improves purchasing power, which further enhances aggregate demand.
- It helps improve India's foreign currency reserves through export of agricultural and allied products like tea, sugar, rice, fish, etc.
- **Components/sub-sectors of agriculture and allied sectors include:**

1. Crops
2. Livestock
3. Forestry and logging
4. Fishing and aquaculture

CURRENT SCENARIO OF INDIAN AGRICULTURE AND ALLIED SECTORS

- In 2025–26, ₹1,37,757 crore has been allocated to the Ministry of Agriculture and Farmers Welfare (Agriculture and Farmers Welfare: ₹1,27,290 crore and Agricultural Research and Education: 10,466 crore).
- In FY 2024–25, the agriculture credit reached to around ₹25 lakh crore, including both institutional and non-institutional credit.
- India's agriculture markets are experiencing digital revolution. The incorporation of more mandis onto the e-NAM platform demonstrates this development. The pan-India electronic National Agricultural Market (e-NAM) is a trade platform. It brings together the current State-run Agricultural Produce Marketing Committees (APMCs) mandis. As of August 2024, 1.7 crore farmers and 2.6 lakh traders were registered on the e-NAM portal.
- The Atmanirbhar Oil Seeds Abhiyan to support research and development of indigenous oilseeds such as groundnut and mustard. The strategy would prioritise research to generate high-yielding oilseed varieties, the use of modern agricultural practices, procurement processes, the establishment of strong market links, value-added efforts, and crop insurance coverage.
- In India, DAP (di-ammonium phosphate) is the most often used fertiliser after urea. After the successful implementation of Nano Urea, the Government recommends the use of Nano DAP throughout all climatic zones.
- India is the world's biggest milk producer. The dairy sector provides a living for 80 million dairy farmers and contributes significantly to the national economy. The Union Cabinet has authorised an expansion of the Animal Husbandry Infrastructure Development Fund inside the Infrastructure Development Fund (IDF). The budget invests ₹29,610.25 crore for the next three years, until 2025–26.
- The Budget recognises aquaculture's huge export potential. It intends to increase aquaculture production by 5 tonnes per hectare and quadruple exports to ₹1 lakh crore.

BONUS KNOWLEDGE

KEY TERMS USED IN AGRICULTURE

Crop

A crop is a plant or agricultural produce that is cultivated or grown on a large scale **for profit or for subsistence**. Examples of some major crops are – Foodgrains, Sugarcane, Jute and Mesta, Cotton, Oilseed, Plantation Crops.

Different types of crops in agriculture

Type of Crop	Description	Example
Foodgrain	**Foodgrain** – The small hard seed like fruits of a grass (especially a cereal plant) produced for human consumption is called Foodgrain. It includes cereals and pulses. **Cereals** – Any plant of the grass family yielding an edible grain. **Coarse Cereal** – They are small-seeded hardy crops in the dry zones or **semi-arid tropics** of Asia and Africa, indicating their high tolerance to extreme weathers **Pulses** – Pulses are annual leguminous crops yielding between 1 and 12 grains or seeds of variable size, shape and colour within a pod, used for both food and feed.	1. **Cereals** (Rice, Wheat, Nutri/ Coarse cereals) Coarse cereals are of two types – **Maize**, **Millets** [Bajra (Pearl Millet), Jowar (Sorghum Millet), Ragi (Finger Millet), Kangni (Foxtail Millet), Kodo Millet, Barri (Proso Millet), Barley, Other small millets] 2. **Pulses** (Toor, Urad, Moong, Gram, Lentils, other pulses)
Oilseed	Oil-bearing crops or oil crops or oilseeds are **seeds, fruits or mesocarp and nuts** from which edible and industrial oils are extracted.	Groundnut, Rapeseed, Mustard, Sesamum, Linseed, Castor seed, Niger seed, Safflower, Sunflower, Soyabean
Plantation Crops	Plantation crops are perennial commercial crops grown for the purpose of selling in the markets for profitability.	Tea, Coffee, Rubber, Potato
Cash crop	When the crops are **cultivated for trading** and return in **high profit**, then the crops are termed cash crops.	Jatropha (used for production of bio-fuel), Cotton, Tea, Jute, etc.
Kharif crop	Kharif crops are sown with the arrival of monsoon in different parts of the country and are **harvested** in **September–October**.	Rice, Maize, Jowar, Bajra, Jute, Groundnut, etc.
Rabi crop	Rabi crops are sown **in winter and are harvested in the spring**. The rain in winter season is harmful for rabi crops.	Wheat, Barley, Mustard, Peas, Sesame, Coriander, Onion, etc.
Zaid crop	They grow on dry lands which require no wait for monsoons and in the time period **between Rabi and Kharif crop season**, mainly from March to June.	Watermelon, Muskmelon, Bitter Gourd, Pumpkin, Cucumber, Moong dal, etc.
Industrial crop	Crops which are mainly harvested for the products used in factories or machines or used in production of industrial goods.	Buchloe, Jatropha, Switchgrass, Rubber, etc.
Ornamental crop	Ornamental crops are grown for **decorative purposes** in gardens and **landscape design projects.**	Rose, Tulip, Petunia, etc.

FOODGRAIN PRODUCTION IN INDIA

Production of important crops in two largest producing States in 2023–24

Crop	In terms of Production
Rice	Telangana, WB
Wheat	UP, Punjab
Maize	Karnataka, MP
Total Pulses	MP, Maharashtra
Total Foodgrains	UP, MP
Total Oilseeds	Rajasthan, MP
Sugarcane	UP, Maharashtra
Cotton (*in thousand bales of 170 kg each*)	Maharashtra, Gujarat
Jute and Mesta (*in thousand bales of 180 kg each.*)	WB, Bihar

Source: Ministry of Agriculture & Farmers Welfare, Government of India.

Crop-wise area under cultivation in 2023–24

Crop	Area (in Million Hectares)	Remarks
Rice	47.8	Increased over years; highest among all crops
Wheat	31.8	Increased over years
Pulses	27.5	Decreasing since last 3 years
Oilseeds	30.1	Slightly decreased from last year
Coarse Cereal	24.9	Fluctuated over the years
Sugarcane	5.8	Increased over years
Cotton	13.0	Increasing trend over years
Tea	0.62	Remained almost same over years
Coffee	0.48	Slightly increased over years

Source: Ministry of Agriculture & Farmers Welfare, Government of India, Coffee Board of India, Tea Board of India.

Rice Production in India

- India is the **second largest** producer of **rice** in the world.
- Two major rice-growing States in India are **West Bengal and Uttar Pradesh**.
- Rice grown in India is majorly classified into **basmati rice and non-basmati rice**.
- Figures relating to rice production in the recent past are given below:

Rice	2021–22	2022–23	2023–24	Remarks
Production	130.3 million tonnes	135.7 million tonnes	137.8 million tonnes	Increasing trend in last 3 years
Gross area under rice production	46.4 million hect-ares	47.7 million hect-ares	47.8 million hect-ares	Increasing trend in last 3 years
Yield per hectare	2,809 kg/hectare	2,838 kg/hectare	2,822 kg/hectare	Fluctuating trend in last 3 years

Source: Ministry of Agriculture & Farmers Welfare, Government of India

- **Major challenges** in rice production in India are as follows:
  - Rice production has high water requirements. As the population is increasing day by day, along with increasing per capita per day demand of water, rice production is going to face a serious challenge.
  - Nitrogen application rates to rice need to be reduced and it may affect production. Nitrogen use efficiency (NUE) in rice is lowest among the cereals due to ammonia volatilisation, denitrification, surface runoff, and leaching. Therefore, there is an urgent need for developing more nitrogen use – efficient varieties and rice production technologies demanding lesser water, labour, nitrogen and pesticides.
  - The same nature of **cultivation pattern** is another challenge.
  - Low soil fertility due to soil erosion resulting in loss of plant nutrients and moisture.
  - **New virulence of diseases**.

Wheat Production in India

- India is the second **largest** producer of wheat in the world.
- Two major wheat-growing States in India are Uttar Pradesh and Madhya Pradesh.
- Varieties of wheat grown in India are VL-832, VL-804, HS-365, HS-240, Shresth, Aditya, etc.
- Figures relating to wheat production in the recent past are given below:

Wheat	2021–22	2022–23	2023–24	Remarks
Production	106.8 million tonnes	110.5 million tonnes	113.2 million tonnes	Increasing trend in last 3 years
Gross area under wheat production	30.5 million hectares	31.4 million hectares	31.8 million hectares	Increasing trend in last 3 years
Yield per hectare	3,507 kg/hectare	3,521 kg/hectare	3,559 kg/hectare	Increasing trend in last 3 years

Source: Ministry of Agriculture & Farmers Welfare, Government of India

- **Major challenges** in wheat production in India are as follows:
  - Due to increasing **heat stress and water deficiency**, there is a need to develop genotypes that are either tolerant to terminal heat stress or mature early and thus escape the stress.
  - The same nature of **cultivation pattern** is another challenge.
  - Changes in **urbanisation** and migration patterns of people.
  - **New virulence of diseases** (wheat rusts and leaf blight) and insufficient vermicides.
  - **Hybrid seeds** should be made cost-effectively by decreasing the seeding rate, increasing the yield levels and altering planting technologies.
- **Major strategies** that may improve **rice and wheat** productivity in India are:
  - Propagation of location specific crop production technologies in different agro-climatic zones.
  - More use of new high-yielding varieties with promising yield potential.
  - Adoption of run-off rainwater management practices suited to the conditions of individual farmholding as well as watershed as a whole.
  - Improving soil fertility by inclusion of leguminous crops in the crop rotations or as mixed crop.
  - Promoting the integrated pest management approach for effective control of pests and diseases by emphasising the need-based application of pesticides.
  - Timely sowing, maintaining optimum plant population, timely irrigation, efficient use of fertilisers, need-based plant protection measures and timely harvesting of crop.

Pulse Production in India

- India is the **largest producer, consumer and importer** of pulses in the world.
- Three major pulses-growing States in India are **Madhya Pradesh, Maharashtra and Rajasthan**.
- Pulses account for around **24 per cent of the area under Foodgrains** (increased over years) and contribute around **8–9 per cent of the total Foodgrain** production in the country (increased over years).
- Pulses are grown in **both Kharif and Rabi seasons**. Rabi pulses contribute more than 60 per cent of the total production.
- **Major Kharif pulses** include arhar, urad and moong. **Major Rabi pulses** include gram, lentil, urad and moong.
- **Gram has the largest share** in overall pulses production among all other pulses with a share of around 40 per cent in the total production, followed by toor/arhar at around 15–20 per cent. Even in terms of area and productivity in India, gram has the highest share.
- Per capita net availability of pulse was 53.8 g/day in 2021–22 (including import), which is higher than the threshold of 52 g/day as recommended by Indian Council of Medical Research (ICMR).
- Figures relating to pulses production in the recent past are given below:

Pulses	2021–22	2022–23	2023–24	Remarks
Production	27.7 million tonnes	26 million tonnes	24.2 million tonnes	Decreasing trend in last three years
Gross area under pulses production	31 million hectares	28.9 million hectares	27.5 million hectares	Decreasing trend in last 3 years
Yield per hectare	892 kg/hectare	902 kg/hectare	881 kg/hectare	Fluctuating trend in last 3 years

Source: Ministry of Agriculture & Farmers Welfare, Government of India.

- **Major challenges** in pulse production in India are:
  - Pulses being rain-fed and protein-rich crops are more susceptible to abiotic and biotic stresses.
  - Risk-averse resource-poor farmers are unwilling to upgrade their farming with investment in modern technological tools.
  - Use of the same nature of **cultivation pattern**.
  - Insects and diseases (*pod borers, fusarium wilt, root rots and ascochyta blight in gram; pod borer, pod fly, fusarium wilt and sterility mosaic disease in toor; pod borer, aphids, cutworm, powdery mildew, rust and wilt in lentil production*).
  - Relentless quest of farmers for higher yield affects the long-term sustainability.
- **Prospective strategies** to improve pulses production and productivity:
  - Intercropping short-duration pulses (moong, urad) in sugarcane, millets, cotton, etc.
  - Advocating new cropping systems such as pigeon pea–wheat in the north, rice–lentil in the east and urad–rice in the southern part of India.

Millets Production in India

- Millet (Shree Anna) is a common term to categorise small-seeded grasses and are a Smart Food with high nutritional value, are climate resilient, and align with several UN Sustainable Development Goals (SDGs). These are also important by virtue of their mammoth potential to generate livelihood, increase farmers' income and ensure food and nutritional security all over the world.
- In India, millets are primarily a **Kharif crop** mostly grown in rainfed conditions, requiring less water and agricultural inputs than other staple crops. They are characterised by low to moderate precipitation **(200–800 mm rainfall)** requirement for their production.
- Majorly grown millets in India include Sorghum (Jowar), Pearl Millet (Bajra), Finger Millet (Ragi), Little Millet (Kutki), Foxtail Millet (Kangni), Proso Millet (Chena), Barnyard Millet (Sawa), Kodo Millet (Kodo) and other millets. Among these, three majorly grown millets in India in terms of production are **Bajra** (60%), **Jowar** (27%) and **Ragi** (11%).
- The United Nations General Assembly declared **2023** as the **International Year of Millets**.
- India's two varieties of millets namely Pearl Millet (Bajra) and Sorghum (Jowar) together contribute around 20 per cent in world production at present.
- The six major millets producing states in India are **Rajasthan**, **Uttar Pradesh, Karnataka, Maharashtra, Gujarat and Madhya Pradesh. Rajasthan** contributes around 30 per cent of the total millet production in India.
- Given the nutritional value of the millets, the Government of India notified Millets as **Nutri-cereals** in 2018.

> **Last Minute SNIPPETS**
>
> **India is the largest producer** of millets in the world. It is estimated to produce more than 12 million tonnes of millets in 2023–24. India recorded 42 per cent growth in millet production in 2023–24.

- Millets are a **Smart Food** as they are Good for Consumers, Good for the Farmer and Good for the Planet.
- Following are the **benefits of millets:**
  - Millets are nutritionally rich and superior to wheat and rice owing to their higher levels of protein with a more balanced amino acid profile.
  - **Dietary fibre content** of millets is also higher compared to some of the staple cereals.

- They also contain various **phytochemicals** which exert therapeutic properties owing to their anti-inflammatory and anti-oxidative properties.
- They have substantially higher amounts of minerals like calcium, potassium, magnesium, iron, manganese, zinc and B complex vitamins.
- They are **gluten-free** and have a low glycemic index.
- Millets are **Climate Resilient** and are the backbone for dry land agriculture. They are hardy, resilient crops that have a low carbon and water footprint, can withstand high temperatures, grow on poor soils with little or no external inputs and are thus termed as the **'miracle grains'** or **'crops of the future'**. In times of climate change, they are the most secure crops for small farmers as they are the hardiest, most resilient and climate adaptable crops in harsh, hot and drought environments.

➤ Millet production is **ecologically sustainable** and not primarily dependent on the use of chemical fertilisers. The use of pesticides is also not mandated in most of the cases.

➤ Government Interventions in recent years to promote Millet sector –

- During **International Year of Millets (IYM)-2023**, the goal was on **increasing production** and productivity, consumption, exports, value chain strengthening, branding, and raising awareness about health advantages, among other things.
- The Indian government has organised a number of events to create a people's movement to promote Indian millets, recipes, and value-added goods throughout the world. Millets were promoted during India's G20 presidency, including a **millet culinary carnival**, international trade events, a chef's conference, an exhibition of Farmers Producer Organisations (FPOs), road shows, kisan melas, chef training for paramilitary forces, and the ASEAN India Millet Festival in Indonesia and Delhi, among other things.
- The **Indian Institute of Millet Research (IIMR) in Hyderabad** also trains farmers, women farmers, homemakers, students, and young entrepreneurs in the production of value-added millet food items, daily recipes, and other activities, as well as assisting them in establishing their own businesses. The institution has also created value-added technologies such as 'Ready to Eat' and 'Ready to Cook' for millet foods, millet food branding under the '**Eatrite**' label, awareness campaigns, agri-enterprise incubators, and technology business incubators, among others.
- The Ministry of Women and Child Development has also **included millets in its Poshan Abhiyan**. Furthermore, the Ministry of Food and Public Distribution has updated its instructions to promote millet procurement through the Targeted Public Distribution System (TPDS), Integrated Child Development Services (ICDS), and Mid-Day Meal.

Last Minute SNIPPETS

The *Ministry of Food Processing Industries (MoFPI)* has authorised the **Production Linked Incentive Scheme for Food Processing Industry for Millet-based Products** (PLISMBP) for implementation from 2022–23 to 2026–27 at a cost of ₹800 crores.

GREEN REVOLUTION

➤ The father of Green Revolution is **Dr. Norman E. Borlaug (American)**. **M. S. Swaminathan (1925–2023)** is known as the father of **Indian Green Revolution**. Professor M. S. Swaminathan received the coveted Bharat Ratna award in 2024, and the Indian Agricultural Research Institute hosted a special celebration in his honour. The term 'Green Revolution' was first used by **William Gaud**.

- Political Father of Green Revolution – **Chidambaram Subramaniam**.
- Father of Wheat Revolution – **Dilbagh Singh Athwal**.

Objectives of Green Revolution

The primary objectives of Green revolution are listed below:

- To alleviate India's food issue during the Second Five-Year Plan.
- To modernise agricultural practices in rural communities. This will result in the modernisation of rural and industrial development, infrastructure, raw materials, and so on.
- To offer employment for rural and industrial workers.
- To create robust plants that can endure harsh weather and illnesses.

Characteristics of Green Revolution

- **Multiple cropping** – Two or more crops were harvested during the year along with continued expansion of farming areas.
- Packaged inputs, i.e. **HYV** seeds, fertilisers and pesticides were provided in areas where water supply was assured.
- However, Green Revolution was restricted to only five crops – **wheat, rice, maize, jowar** and **bajra**.
- **Institutional credit** increased to bring more and more farmers, including small and marginal farmers within the institutional credit fold, extended by commercial banks, co-operative banks, etc., at nominal interest rates.

Impact of Green Revolution

Positive Impacts	Negative Impacts
• Manifold **increase in agricultural production and productivity**. • **Food production rates** tripled as compared to increase in land conversion increase by 10%. • **Increased employment opportunities** due to establishment of forward and backward linkages. • Rural roads were largely built and electrification started at a good pace. • Higher and consistent production and supply help to curtail food inflation.	• **Salination** enhanced due to continuous exploitation of groundwater. • Increased **toxic levels** due to increased use of pesticides and chemical fertiliser. • Skewed development caused **inter-regional disparities**. • Pesticide resistance of insects increased and **depleted soil nutrients**. • Inappropriate application and handling of pesticides started causing **health issues**. • Transformed a large number of tenants and sharecroppers into **agricultural labourers**.

Repercussions of Green Revolution

- Revolutionary rise in productivity was restricted to limited number of **Foodgrains** only. There has been no rise in production in **pulses and commercial crops**.
- Revolution did not spread uniformly in all the regions. Only few States like **Punjab**, **Haryana**, **Maharashtra** and **Tamil Nadu** were benefited.

➤ Seeds produced under HYV technology were too **expensive** to the reach of small and marginal farmers.

➤ The **economic division gap** between rich and poor farmers substantially rose over time, and it became a serious challenge for the Indian rural economy.

All Revolutions at a Glance

Name of Revolution	Period	Revolutions Related to	Father/Mother of Revolutions
Black Revolution		**Petroleum production**	
Blue Revolution	1985 (during 7th FYP)	**Fish production**	Dr. Arun Krishnan and Dr. Hiralal Chaudhuri
Brown Revolution	–	**Leather, cocoa**	
Golden Fibre Revolution	1990	**Jute production**	
Golden Revolution	1991–2003	Overall **horticulture, honey, fruit production**	Nirpakh Tutej
Green Revolution	1966–67	**Agriculture production**	M. S. Swaminathan
Grey Revolution	1960–70	**Fertilisers**	
Pink Revolution	1996	**Pharmaceutical, onion and prawns**	Durgesh Patel
Evergreen Revolution	2017–22	Overall **agricultural production growth**	M. S. Swaminathan
Round Revolution	1965–2005	**Potato production**	
Silver Fibre Revolution	2000	**Cotton production**	
Silver Revolution	1969–78	**Egg production**	Indira Gandhi
White Revolution or Operation Flood	1970–96	**Dairy, milk production**	Dr. Verghese Kurien
Yellow Revolution	1986–90	**Oilseed production**	Sam Pitroda
Saffron Energy Revolution		For promotion and better utilisation of **solar energy**	
Red Revolution	1996	**Meat and poultry**	Vishal Tewari
Protein Revolution	2014–20	**High agricultural production**	PM Narendra Modi and Arun Jaitley

HORTICULTURE SECTOR

➤ Horticulture sector includes a wide range of crops. It includes fruit crops, vegetable crops, flowers, ornamental crops, medicinal and aromatic crops, spices, coconut, cashew, cocoa, plantation crops, etc. It even includes areas such as bee-keeping, mushroom, bamboo, etc.

- **Department of Agriculture, Co-operation & Farmers Welfare (DAC&FW)** under Ministry of Agriculture & Farmers Welfare is the **nodal department** for fostering the development of the horticulture sector in India.
- Since 2012–13, the production of horticulture crops has **outpaced** productions of Foodgrains.
- Horticulture in India contributes around 33 per cent of agricultural GDP.
- To ensure nutritional security through the natural food system and to face the climate change, the Department of Agricultural Research & Education **(DARE)** has developed 35 special trait varieties including **biofortified and stress tolerant varieties** of field and horticulture crops during 2021–22, taking the tally of biofortified varieties to 87. The **contribution of vegetables** remains the highest (over 58%) among horticulture crop productions.
- The overall horticulture production for 2023–24 is estimated to be 354.74 million tonnes. As per the latest data, horticulture production is highest in Uttar Pradesh, followed by Madhya Pradesh.
- **Tamil Nadu** leads the **flower production**, followed by Andhra Pradesh.
- To augment horticulture sector holistically, GoI launched a centrally sponsored scheme named **'Mission for Integrated Development of Horticulture (MIDH)' in 2014–15**. It subsumed under it the earlier existing National Horticulture Mission (launched in 2005–06).
- **Horticulture production**

Total Horticulture	2022–23	2023–24
Area (in Million Ha)	28.44	28.98
Production (in Million Tonne)	355.48	354.74

Mission for Integrated Development of Horticulture

- All States and UTs are covered under MIDH scheme of GoI.
- It has a fund-sharing pattern of **60:40** (i.e. 60% by centre and 40% by the States). For north-eastern and hilly States, the fund-sharing pattern is 90:10. For UTs, GoI contributes 100 per cent.
- MIDH has **subsumed all ongoing horticulture-related missions/schemes** of GoI which include – National Horticulture Mission; National Horticulture Board; Coconut Development Board; and Central Institute of Horticulture, Nagaland.
- The **major objectives of MIDH** include:
    1. Holistic growth of horticultural sector through regionally different strategies.
    2. Encourage farmers to form farmers' groups such as FIGs/FPOs and Farmer Producer Companies (FPCs) in order to achieve economies of scale and scope, branding, etc., thereby leading to increased productivity, production and profit in this sector.
    3. To promote and develop technologies with modern scientific knowledge.
    4. To create opportunities of employment generation for both skilled and unskilled persons, especially unemployed youth.
- **Strategies involved under MIDH:**
    1. *End-to-end holistic approach* starting from production, post-harvest management, processing and up to marketing.
    2. *Promote R&D technologies* in production, post-harvest management and processing of crops.
    3. Promote *crop diversification* from traditional crops to plantation crops, orchards, etc.
    4. Promote *partnership, convergence and synergy* among various stakeholders for overall development of the sector.

5. Promote *capacity building* and HR development at all levels of production process.

➤ **Sub-schemes or components under MIDH:**

1. National Horticulture Mission
2. National Horticulture Mission for North-East and Himalayan States
3. National Horticulture Board
4. Coconut Development Board
5. Central Institute of Horticulture, Nagaland

➤ **Major interventions under MIDH till now:**

1. Financial assistance to set up nurseries, tissue culture units for production of quality seeds and planting material.
2. Financial assistance for area expansion to develop new orchards for fruits, vegetables and flowers.
3. Financial assistance for rejuvenation of unproductive old orchards.
4. Promotion of protected cultivation (poly house, green house, etc.).
5. Creation of post-harvest management and marketing infrastructure.
6. Promotion of Integrated Nutrient Management (INM) and Integrated Pest Management (IPM) measures.

BONUS KNOWLEDGE

HORTNET – A project to achieve e-governance in MIDH through transparency in all processes of workflow through online application filing, processing, online payment to beneficiaries through direct benefit transfer, etc.

➤ **Agencies related to promotion of horticulture sector:**

Name	Location
National Horticulture Board (NHB)	Gurugram
Directorate of Cashew and Cocoa Development (DCCD)	Kochi
National Bee Board	New Delhi
Coconut Development Board	Kochi
Central Institute of Horticulture	Medziphema, Nagaland
Directorate of Arecanut & Spices Development	Kozhikode

➤ **Present challenges in the horticulture sector:**

1. Horticulture sector does not have any Minimum Support Price (MSP) strategy by the government as in the case of Foodgrains.
2. Lack of adequate and quality cold chain storage and transport networks.
3. Limited availability of inputs in terms of machinery and equipment.
4. Limited availability of market intelligence, mainly in terms of exports facility.

SEEDS

- The efficiency of other agricultural inputs like fertilisers is dependent on seed.
- Developed variety of seeds augment agriculture production and productivity.
- Out of the total operational holding in India, around only 10 per cent use **certified seeds** and only 10 per cent use **hybrid seeds**.
- **Seed Replacement Ratio** – It is a measure of how much of the total cropped area was sown with certified seeds in comparison to farm-saved seeds. A better seed replacement rate shows a better utilisation of the certified/quality seeds.
- India has over 4 per cent share in the global seed market with a market size of around US$ 6 billion based on 2022 data.
- **100 per cent FDI under automatic route** is now allowed by GoI in development and production of seeds.
- The share of the public sector in seed production in the country reduced from 42.72 per cent in 2017–18 to 35.54 per cent in 2020–21, while the share of the private sector grew from 57.28 per cent to 64.46 per cent during the same period, highlighting the rising role of private companies in India's seed sector.
- Since 2008, India is a member of **OECD Seed Scheme** which relates to seed certification.
- Major organisations related to seed sector are:
  - **National Seeds Corporation** (founded in 1963) – It is a Miniratna-I company wholly owned by GoI. It undertakes production of nearly 600 varieties of certified seeds.
  - National Seed Research and Training Centre, Varanasi
  - State Seed Certification Agencies
  - State Seed Corporations

Major Reforms Undertaken in Seeds Sector

1. **National Mission for Seeds** was launched in **2012** to ensure availability of high-quality certified seeds at reasonable price to farmers.
2. Another centrally sponsored scheme was launched before that in 2005–06 named 'Development and Strengthening of Infrastructure Facilities for Production and Distribution of Quality Seeds'.

The scheme is ongoing and its **objectives include** – production and multiplication of high-yielding certified/quality seeds of all crops in sufficient quantities in order to make them available even in the remotest part of India.

The components of the scheme include:

- **Transport subsidy** on movement of seeds to north-eastern and hilly areas (for all seeds except potato).
- Establishment and maintenance of Seed Bank for availability of seeds even at the time of natural calamities.
- **Regulation of quality control** of seeds as per the provisions of **Seeds Act, 1966** and strengthening central and State quality control organisations.
- **Seed Village Programme** – (i) to upgrade the quality of farmer-saved seed through training on use of modern technologies, (ii) financial assistance for distribution of foundation/certified

seeds at 50 per cent cost of the seeds and (iii) financial assistance to encourage farmers to develop seed storage capacity of appropriate quality.

- Promotion of *hybrid rice seed production* by granting financial subsidy.

Present Challenges in Seeds Sector

- Lack of awareness about quality of seeds among cultivators.
- Availability of inappropriate quality of seeds.
- Monopoly of some private companies in seed production which charge high prices.
- Lack of clarity about Genetically Modified (GM) crops and GM seeds.
- Untimely supply of seeds and that too in inadequate quantity.
- Requirement of amendments in the Seeds Act, 1966, which deals with legal framework for seed certification.

EXAM ESSENTIAL

BIOFORTIFICATION

Biofortification is the process of improving the nutritional value of food crops using traditional breeding, genetic engineering, or agronomic approaches. Biofortified seeds are bred varieties that attempt to boost nutritional content without negatively impacting soil and water ecology.

Ecological Impact of Biofortified Seeds:

Since 2014, 142 biofortified varieties including 124 field crops (Rice - 10; Wheat - 43; Maize - 20, Pearl millet - 11, Small millets - 13, Linseed - 1, Lentil - 2, Chickpea - 2, Mungbean - 1, Fieldpea - 1, Urdbean - 1, Mustard - 8, Soybean - 7, Sesame - 1, Groundnut -3) and 18 horticultural crops (Sweet potato - 5, Amaranthus - 3, Greater Yam - 2, Potato - 2 and 1 each of Cauliflower, Okra, Grapes, Banana, Guava and Pomegranate) have been developed under the aegis of the Indian Council of Agricultural Research (ICAR).

All biofortified cultivars have the same or higher yield as conventional types of the respective crops. These biofortified cultivars are less expensive to produce than existing market varieties since there is no yield penalty or additional expense associated with cultivation.

The National Food Security Mission (NFSM) provides assistance to farmers through State/Union Territory for interventions such as cluster demonstrations on improved package of practices, cropping system demonstrations, seed production, distribution of High Yielding Varieties (HYVs)/hybrids, cropping system-based trainings, and so on. The Mission also assisted the ICAR, State Agricultural Universities, and Krishi Vigyan Kendras in technological backstopping and technology transfer to farmers, all under the supervision of Subject Matter Specialists/Scientists. Under NFSM, states/ICAR may organise demonstrations of cutting-edge crop production technologies, cluster frontline demonstrations, and frontline demonstrations of biofortified varieties. States are also urged to develop and distribute biofortified seeds.

BONUS KNOWLEDGE

SEEDS ACT, 1966

- It provides legal framework for *seed certification* and ensures availability of quality seeds to cultivators.
- The Act covers seeds of food crops, oil crops, cotton seeds, seeds of cattle fodder and all types of vegetative propagating material.

- Under this Act, **Seeds Rules were notified in 1968** and the systematic seeds certification started in India in 1969.
- *Central Seed Committee* was established under the Act.
- The Act also has provisions for establishment of seed certification agencies in States, State seed testing labs along with establishment of 'Central Seed Laboratory' by the central government.
- As per the Act, there is also a restriction on import and export of seeds of notified varieties. For reference, **import of seeds and planting materials** is governed by New Policy on Seed Development, 1988 and there are varied forms of restrictions on their imports on a case-by-case basis.

In an effort to bring amendment in the old existing Seeds Act, 1966, **Seeds Bill was introduced in 2004**, but it did not materialise into bringing amendments in the existing Act due to several shortcomings. Recently, the present government has finalised a **Draft Seeds Bill, 2019**.

DRAFT SEEDS BILL, 2019

- It proposes to replace the Seeds Act, 1966 and regulate the quality of seeds sold.
- As per draft Bill, **all varieties of seeds for sale** have to be registered.
- The seeds are required to meet certain prescribed **minimum standards**.
- In order to bring greater accountability of seeds companies, the Bill proposes that **transgenic varieties of seeds** can be registered only after the applicant has obtained clearance under the Environment (Protection) Act, 1986.
- In addition, the **label of a seed container** has to indicate specified information.
- The Bill authorises the Central government **to re-constitute the Central Seed Committee**.
- The Bill exempts farmers from the requirement of compulsory registration. Farmers are allowed to sow, exchange or sell their farm seeds and planting material.
- Farmers do not have to conform to the prescribed minimum standards of germination, physical purity and genetic purity (as required by registered seeds). However, farmers cannot sell any seed under a brand name without registration.
- The Bill requires license/registration of fruit nurseries.
- The Bill **empowers the government to fix prices** of select varieties of seeds in the case of emergency situations.

Genetically Modified (GM) Crops

EXAM ESSENTIAL

- According to WHO, **Genetically Modified Organisms (GMO)** are the **plants, animals or microorganisms** in which the hereditary material (DNA) is altered in a manner that does not happen normally by mating or potentially regular recombination. It is also known as modern biotechnology/gene technology.
- When genetic modification of a plant is performed, foreign gene **(transgene)** or gene of some other organism is **artificially inserted** in the plant's own genes. This is gene modification. After this genetic modification, the plant may become **pesticide resistant**, for example.
- A gene can also be altered through chemical radiation, spontaneous alteration and traditional processing.
- **Norman Borlaug** supported producing GMs crop in order to eradicate hunger from the world.
- In India, the clearance for large-scale field trials and commercial release of a particular GM crop is given by the Genetic Engineering Appraisal Committee **(GEAC)** which functions as a statutory

body [under The Environment (Protection) Act, 1986] and under the **Ministry of Environment, Forests & Climate Change**. NOC from State governments is mandatory for field trials. Food Safety and Standards Act, 2006 prohibits import, manufacture, use or sale of GM food without FSSAI's approval.

- Initially, due to probable bio-safety and health concerns, **Bt cotton** was the only GM crop allowed in India (in the year 2002). **Bt cotton is only transgenic crop which is commercially cultivated in India.**
- In 2016, **GM mustard or Dhara Mustard Hybrid-11 (DMH-11)** was cleared by GEAC for field trail. **Thereafter in 2022**, GEAC **gave clearance** for the environmental release of DMH-11 and its parental lines for its seed production and testing as per existing ICAR guidelines, under conditions imposed by the GEAC. However, the same has been challenged in Supreme Court by the opponents. Largest GM Mustard producer in the world is Canada. Critics argue that the genetically engineered **barnase/barstar system** provides an efficient and robust alternative method for hybrid seed production **in mustard** and it has been successfully deployed in countries like Canada, Australia and America for many decades. GoI is taking efforts to introduce it in India.
- It is for reference that GEAC recommended the commercial release of **Bt brinjal in 2007 but it was blocked by the government in 2010**.
- As per the provisions of Environment Protection Act 1986, growing GM crops that are not approved by the government can lead up to **5 years' imprisonment or a fine up to ₹1 lakh or both**.
- In the world, the **United States has the largest area under GM crop cultivation** followed by Brazil, Argentina and China. **India is ranked fourth** in this regard. However, unlike India, the United States grows a variety of GM crops which include soyabean, maize, cotton, canola, etc.
- The **Biotechnology Regulatory Authority Bill**, which envisages creating a regulatory body for uses of biotechnology products including GM organisms, is pending in the Parliament since 2008.

Advantages of GM Crops	Disadvantages of GM Crops
➤ Higher crop yields ensures food security. ➤ Reduced farm costs and increased farm profit. ➤ GM crops can withstand weather fluctuations and extremes and decrease the use of pesticides and herbicides. ➤ Maturation time is relatively lower. ➤ After introduction of Bt cotton, it has transitioned India into a cotton-exporting country.	➤ Can contaminate other fields through cross-pollination. ➤ There is a danger of allergens entering into the food chain. ➤ They may increase resilient super-bugs that could destroy entire croplands. ➤ It could be a threat to the domestic and wild varieties of crops. If GM crops cross-breed with wild relatives, the foreign transgenes could 'contaminate' the natural ecosystem.

FERTILISERS

- A fertiliser is a natural or synthetic chemical-based substance that is applied to soil or plant tissues to supply one or more nutrient to enhance plant growth and fertility.
- Nutrients can be of two types: macro-nutrients and micro-nutrients. The six **macro-nutrients** are **nitrogen, phosphorus, potassium, calcium, magnesium** and **sulphur**, and the eight **micro-nutrients** are **copper, zinc, iron, manganese, boron, chlorine, molybdenum** and **nickel**.

- Indian soils are generally deficient in **nitrogen (N), phosphorus (P)** and **potassium (K)**; hence the usage of fertilisers is widely prevalent in India. These three N, P & K are also known as primary macro-nutrients.
- The development of this sector is administered by the **Department of Fertilisers** under the Ministry of Chemicals and Fertilisers whose objective is to ensure availability of fertilisers at affordable prices for maximising agricultural production. Department also administers 9 fertiliser Public Sector Undertakings (PSUs).
- Present status of fertiliser production and consumption in India:
  - In India, mainly three variants of fertilisers are produced at present – urea, diammonium phosphate (DAP) and complex fertilisers.
  - **Urea** (for nitrogen) is the most produced (86%), most consumed (74%) and most imported (74%) among all fertilisers in India.
  - In the case of phosphatic fertilisers, 56.5 per cent indigenous capacity has been developed to meet domestic requirements. However, raw materials and intermediaries required for production of phosphatic fertilisers are imported.
  - **For potash**, entire requirement is met **through imports**.

Last Minute SNIPPETS

At present, there are 36 urea-manufacturing units in the country with installed annual capacity of around 284.95 LMT including both Natural Gas-based (using domestic gas/LNG/CBM) as well as Naphtha-based. Out of these, majority are Natural Gas-based urea manufacturing units.

- **Government Initiatives so far:**
  - **Retention Pricing Scheme (RPS)** was introduced in 1977, initially for nitrogenous fertilisers. However, it was later extended even for phosphatic and potash fertilisers. Under this scheme, subsidy was provided by the government in terms of difference between retention price (cost of production + 12% post-tax return on net worth) and the statutory notified sale price. However, RPS was replaced by NPS in 2003.
  - **New Pricing Scheme (NPS)-I** in 2003, where the subsidy was determined on the basis of **group averaging of retention prices** of urea units. The farm gate price of urea was fixed by the government and the **difference between the farm gate price and the unit's cost of production/tonne** was reimbursed as subsidy by the government.

    NPS-I was followed by NPS-II (2004 to 2006) and then NPS-III (2006–14). Modified NPS-III continued from 2014 to 2015.

    However, there are certain limitations in the above product-based subsidy regime in terms of market distortions, illegal exports, rising prices of input materials, etc. Consequently, the government launched another Nutrient Based Subsidy Policy in 2010. At present, the **NPS-III and Modified NPS-III also continues alongside**.
  - **Nutrient-Based Subsidy (NBS) Policy** was launched in 2010, where an **amount of subsidy** for a fertiliser is fixed (on annual basis) based on its nutrient content in terms of micro- or macro-nutrient. At present, **21 grades of P&K fertilisers** are covered under the NBS policy.

    Major among those 21 include DAP (18-46-0), muriate of potash **(MOP)**, monoammonium phosphate (**MAP**, 11-52-0), triple superphosphate (**TSP**, 0-46-0), 12 grades of **complex fertilisers** and ammonium sulphate (**AS** – caprolactam grade by GSFC and FACT) and single superphosphate **(SSP)**.

The objective of this scheme is to foster balanced use of the fertilisers for improving soil health and also reduce the government outgo on fertiliser support. Union Cabinet approved Nutrient Based Subsidy (NBS) rates for KHARIF Season, 2024 (from 01.04.2024 to 30.09.2024) on Phosphatic and Potassic (P&K) fertilisers and the inclusion of three additional fertiliser grades under the NBS scheme.

However, the scheme has **certain limitations** – urea is not covered; there is delay in subsidy payments by the government, etc.

- **Neem-Coated Urea Policy (in 2015)**
  - As per this, it is *mandatory* to coat 100 per cent domestic/imported urea with neem oil. This helps in curbing the diversion of urea to non-agricultural sectors and also to improve crop yield.
  - Around 2.5 lakhs tonnes of neem oil is produced every year in India which is more or less sufficient to coat all the urea produced and imported.
  - Extra premium to the extent of 5 per cent of the existing MRP of urea can be charged by the companies selling Neem Coated Urea.
  - **Benefits of** Neem Coated Urea: .
    (a) Improvement in soil health.
    (b) Reduction in costs with respect to plant protection chemicals.
    (c) Reduction in pest and disease attack resulting in an increase in the yield of paddy, sugarcane, maize, soybean and tur/red gram.
    (d) Diversion of subsidised urea for non-agricultural purposes/industrial use has reduced after the introduction of the mandatory policy of production and distribution of only Neem-Coated Urea.
- **New Urea Policy (NUP)** launched in 2015 to promote indigenous production of urea.
  - **Objectives:**
    (a) Maximising indigenous urea production
    (b) Promoting energy efficiency in urea production
    (c) Rationalising subsidy burden on the government
  - NUP-2015 was initially made effective from 1 June 2015 up to 31 March 2019 but was extended in 2019 until further orders.
  - This subsidy scheme is applicable **only for gas-based urea units**.
  - For production up to 100 per cent re-assessed capacity (RAC), the gas-based urea units are entitled to get subsidy in the form of the total cost of production of urea, which includes fixed cost and variable cost.

***For Urea**, there are the following 4 ongoing policies through which subsidy is being paid to urea units:*

1. New Pricing Scheme – III
2. Modified New Pricing Scheme – III
3. New Urea Policy 2015 – for 25 gas-based urea units.
4. Another 2015 notification – for 3 naphtha-based urea units.

***For P & K**, subsidy is presently being provided through **Nutrient Based Subsidy Policy**, 2010.*

- **Direct Benefit Transfer (DBT) system for fertiliser subsidy payments (introduced in 2016)**
  - 100 per cent sponsorship on different compost grades are offered straightforwardly to the manure organisations dependent on genuine deals made by retailers to the recipients.
  - Point-of-sale (PoS) devices installed at each retailer shop to sell subsidised fertilisers to buyers and the beneficiaries (*identification through photo id*).
  - The farmers/beneficiaries will continue to receive urea at statutory subsidised prices and P&K fertilisers at subsidised prices in the market.
  - By linking the actual sales to subsidy payments, it facilitates a more transparent and faster tracking of funds along the value chain, i.e. from manufacturers to beneficiaries.
  - Diversion of fertilisers is expected to be minimised.
- **e-Urvarak** – It is a fertilisers dashboard launched to provide real-time information about the position of supply/availability/requirement of various fertilisers at national, State and district levels.

BONUS KNOWLEDGE

INTEGRATED PEST MANAGEMENT (IPM)

Food and Agriculture Organization (FAO) defines **IPM** as 'all available pest control techniques and subsequent integration of appropriate measures that discourage the development of pest populations and keep pesticides and other interventions to levels that are economically justified and reduce or minimise the risks to human health and the environment'.

EXAM ESSENTIAL

SOIL HEALTH CARD SCHEME

- Launched by the Ministry of Agriculture and Farmers Welfare in **2015**, Soil Health Card (SHC) is given to all farmers to provide each of them with information on **soil nutrient status** of their land holding.
- It is being implemented by the State governments through collection of soil sample, its test, generation and distribution of soil health card to the farmer (*agriculture being State subject*).
- For soil nutrient status, **details on 12 parameters** are mentioned in the card given to farmer:
  a. **3 macro-nutrients** namely N, P, K;
  b. **1 Secondary-nutrient** namely S.
  c. **5 Micro-nutrients** namely; Zn, Fe, Cu, Mn, B.
  d. **3 Physical parameters** namely and pH, EC, OC.
- Based on the status of above 12 parameters, the report advices him/her on the dosage of fertilisers and also the needed soil amendments to maintain soil health in the long run.
- The SHC is made available to a farmer **once in a cycle of 3 years** (not every year), in order to indicate the status of soil health of a farmer's holding for that particular period.
- **Progress till now** – In Cycle 1 (2015 to 2017), 10.74 crore SHCs were distributed and in Cycle-II (2017–21), 11.97 crore SHCs were distributed to farmers across the country.

PM-PRANAAM

"*PM Programme for Restoration, Awareness Generation, Nourishment, and Amelioration of Mother-Earth* (PM-PRANAM)" was launched by GoI in 2023. The initiative, under the ambit of Ministry of Chemicals and

Fertilisers, aims to complement the efforts initiated by States/UTs to save the health of Mother Earth by **promoting sustainable and balanced use of fertilisers, adopting alternate fertilisers, promoting organic and natural farming, etc.**

All States/UTs are covered under the PM-PRANAM. Under the said scheme, **50 per cent of the fertiliser subsidy saved by a State/UT** in a particular financial year by way of reduction in consumption of chemical fertilisers (Urea, DAP, NPK, MOP) compared to previous 3 years' average consumption, **will be passed on to that State/UT as Grant**.

Soil Reclamation

Soil Reclamation is the process of reclaiming the soil's quality like lost fertility, minerals, nutrients and moisture to make it fit for intensive use again. The reclamation of soil, its nutrients and fertility is done with an objective to increase further land use and enhance agricultural activities like cropping and irrigation.

Pedogenesis (soil development, evolution, formation and soil genesis) is the process of soil formation as regulated by the effects of place, environment and history.

CROPPING PATTERN

Cropping pattern means the portion of area under different crops at a point of time, changes in this distribution over a period of time and factors determining this change in distribution.

Alternatively, it indicates **temporal** and/or **spatial arrangement** of crops in a particular area. Temporal arrangement indicates yearly sequence of growing different crops. Spatial arrangement indicates arrangement of crops on a piece of land in various patterns (say alternative rows) at a time.

Important Facts about Cropping Pattern in India

- In 1950–51, total area under **cereals** was around 80 per cent of the total area under Foodgrains. In 2022–23, it has **reduced** to 78 per cent. *Reasons for such fall: commercialisation of agriculture, better price realisation in case of non-cereals*, etc.
- In 1950–51, total area under **pulses** was 20 per cent of the total area under Foodgrains. In 2022–23, it has **increased** to 22.01 per cent.
- In 1950–51, total area under **rice** was around 32 per cent of the total area under Foodgrains. In 2022–23, it has **increased** to around 36.08 per cent (*thereby indicating rice is grown on more than one-third of the total area under Foodgrains*). *Reasons for such rise are – special rice production programmes by the government, technological interventions, etc.*
- In 1950–51, total area under **wheat** was around 10 per cent of the total area under Foodgrains. In 2022–23, it has **increased** to around 24.05 per cent. *Reasons for such rise – technological breakthrough, price support and market infrastructure.*
- Case of **coarse cereals** is, however, **disappointing**. Area under **jowar, bajra** and **maize** has fallen from around 29 per cent in 1950–51 to around 17.85 per cent in 2022–23 of the total area under Foodgrains. *Reasons for such drastic decrease are – location specificity, susceptibility to pests and diseases, low rate of profit, restricted demand mainly by poorer sections, competition from superior cereal crops such as wheat and rice, etc.*

- Area under **oilseeds increased** from around 11 million hectares in 1950–51 to around 30 million hectares in 2022–23. *Reason is – technology mission on oilseeds during the 1980s.*
- Among commercial crops, area under **sugarcane, cotton** and **jute** has **increased**.

Types of Cropping Patterns in India

1. Mono-Cropping or Single Cropping

It refers to growing only one crop on a particular land year after year. For example, only **Rabi crops** grow in dry land.

2. Multiple Cropping or Poly-Cropping

In this system, two or more than two crops are grown annually on the same piece of land using high inputs, without affecting basic fertility of the soil. For example, banana + marigold + berseem. Multiple cropping may be of **four types**: *mixed cropping, intercropping, sequence cropping* and *relay cropping*.

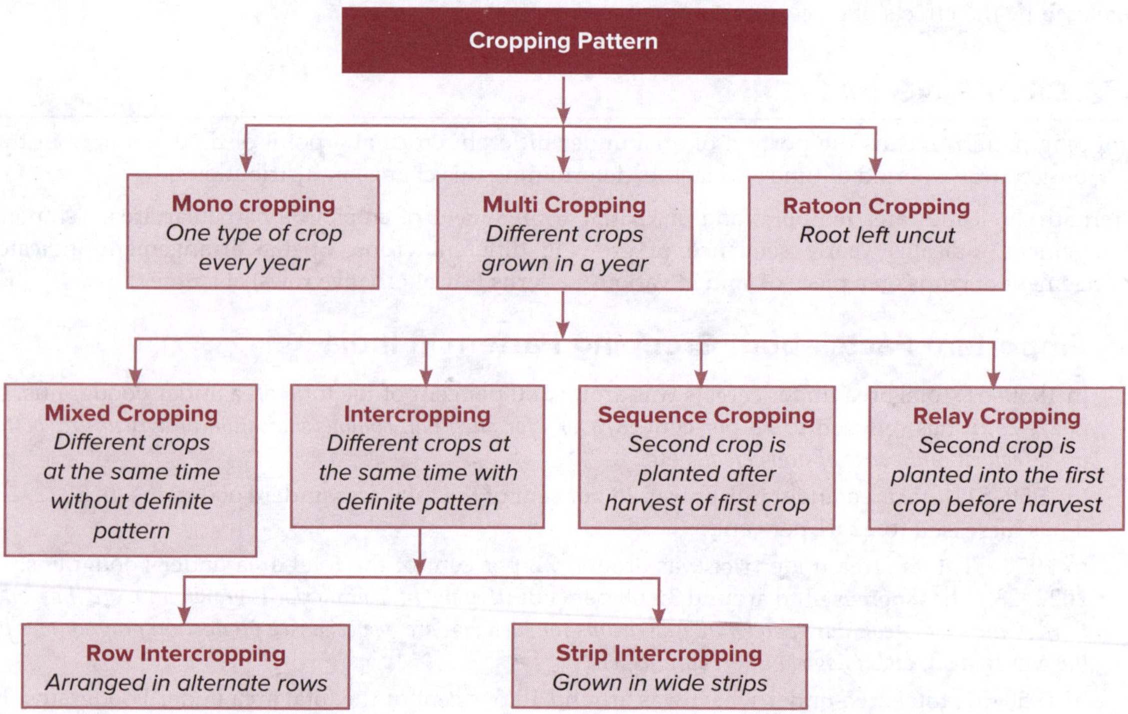

(a) **Mixed Cropping**: Growing of two or more crops **simultaneously** on the same field **without** a definite row arrangement. This practice is more common in dry areas and is done mainly for subsistence. For example, sorghum, pearl millet and cowpea are cultivated together many times.

(b) **Intercropping**: Growing of two or more crops **simultaneously** on the same field **with a definite row pattern**. Here the resources are utilised efficiently and productivity is optimum. For example, cotton is initially a slow-growing crop but groundnut is short duration and fast-growing crop. So, these two are companion crops.

Advantages of intercropping include – suppression of weeds, limiting outbreak and incidence of crop pests due to increased biodiversity, yield stability even in the case of failure of one crop, etc.

(c) **Sequence Cropping**: In this type of cropping, plants are grown two or more times in a sequence on the same land in the same year. The succeeding crop is planted after the preceding crop has been harvested. For example, rice + potato + groundnut.

(d) **Relay Cropping**: Here the seeds of another crop are sown before the previous crops are harvested in that field. For example, Cotton and Mustard.

Features:

i. Minimum plough is needed and the primary cost of cultivation is less.

ii. Weed infestation is less.

iii. Residual fertiliser of previous crops is used for succeeding crops.

3. Ratoon Cropping

Under this method, the root or the lower part of the crop is **left uncut** at the time of harvest. The crop regrows out of the root. Benefit of this cropping pattern includes decreased cost of inputs and of preparing the field. However, the productivity decreases after every cycle. Examples include sugarcane, banana, pineapple, etc.

Jhum/Shifting Cultivation

Jhum cultivation (also known as the **slash-and-burn agriculture**) is the process of growing crops by first clearing the land having trees and vegetation and burning them thereafter. The **burnt soil contains potash** which increases the nutrient content of the soil. In India, it is predominantly practiced in the north-eastern States. The local names of shifting cultivation around the world are as follows. →

Name of Shifting Cultivation	Region
Ray	Vietnam
Tavi	Madagascar
Masole	Congo (Central Africa)
Fang	Equatorial African Countries
Logan	Western Africa
Comile	Mexico
Milpa	Yucatan and Guatemala
Milya	Mexico and Central America
Konuko	Venezuela

BONUS KNOWLEDGE

MIXED FARMING

In this type of farming, crop production is combined with the **rearing of livestock**. It provides a balance and productive system of farming. Here a certain part of the gross income must be contributed by livestock activity. It also establishes a complementary relationship between crop and livestock enterprises. Crop production, rising livestock, poultry, fisheries, bee keeping, etc. go hand in hand.

VERTICAL FARMING

In vertical farming, **crops are grown indoors**, under artificial conditions of light and temperature. It aims at higher productivity in smaller spaces. It uses soil-less methods such as hydroponics, aquaponics and aeroponics. Vertical farming uses significantly less water and pesticides than traditional agricultural methods.

KHAZAN FARMING SYSTEM

The low-lying floodplains of **Goa** host an estuarine agricultural system called Khazan farming. This system is a carefully designed topo-hydro-engineered agro-aquacultural ecosystem mainly based on the **regulation of salinity and tides**.

ZERO-BUDGET NATURAL FARMING

Zero-budget natural farming (ZBNF) is a method of **chemical-free agriculture** drawing from traditional Indian practices. It was originally promoted by Maharashtrian agriculturist Subhash Palekar, who developed it in the mid-1990s as an alternative to the Green Revolution methods driven by chemical fertilisers and pesticides. Natural farming systems require **less water and are climate friendly**. It is being promoted by Central Government through **Bharatiya Prakritik Krishi Paddhati (BPKP) Programme**. The scheme promotes on-farm biomass recycling with major stress on biomass mulching, use of on-farm cow dung-urine formulations, periodic soil aeration and exclusion of all synthetic chemical inputs. At present, Andhra Pradesh and Madhya Pradesh tops regarding area coverage under BPKP.

ORGANIC FARMING

EXAM ESSENTIAL

Organic farming is a method of crop and livestock production **without** using pesticides, fertilisers, antibiotics and growth hormones.

Importance

- Can grow multiple crops in the same place and ensures optimum utilisation of natural resources.
- Improves the soil physical properties such as good aeration, easy root penetration, etc.
- Reduces human and animal health hazards by reducing the level of residues in the product.
- Prevents water pollution with the use of organic fertilisers.
- Ecological services like predation, pollination and habitats are improved.
- Organic agriculture reduces the use of non-renewable energy sources by using organic fertilisers and reducing the consumption of agrochemicals.

GoI promotes organic farming under **2 dedicated schemes**:

1. Mission Organic Value Chain Development for North Eastern Region **(MOVCDNER)**
2. Paramparagat Krishi Vikas Yojana **(PKVY)**

For certification of produce as organic, the FSSAI has notified Food Safety & Standards (Organic Foods) Regulation, 2017 which requires organic food to comply with the provisions of **any one of the following 2 certification systems**:

1. National Programme for Organic Production **(NPOP)** being implemented by *Agricultural and Processed Food Products Export Development Authority* **(APEDA)** as per the guidelines of Ministry of Commerce & Industry.
2. Participatory Guarantee System for India **(PGS-India)** under *Ministry of Agriculture & Farmer's Welfare*.

Sikkim implemented organic practices in around 75,000 hectares of agricultural land as per the guidelines of NPOP and became **India's first fully organic State** in 2015. It also received the UN Food and Agriculture Organization's *Future Policy Gold Award* in 2018 for becoming the **world's first 100 per cent organic State**.

Factors Influencing Cropping Pattern

- **Agro-ecological factors** such as extent of rainfall, climate and soil conditions.
  Areas in States like West Bengal with sufficient rainfall and waterlogging are suitable for rice cultivation. For semi-arid areas like Rajasthan, jowar and bajra are the basic crops grown.
- **Infrastructure** such as irrigation, electricity, transport and marketing organisations, availability of other inputs like seeds, fertilisers, and pesticides, etc.
- **Economic factors such as** size of the land holdings, prices of agricultural commodities, income of the farmers, etc. *For instance, farmers with small land holdings give priority to food crops in order to meet their subsistence rather than going for cash crops. Cash crops are the choice of large farmers with substantial land holdings.*
- **Socio-economic factors** such as food habits, education, age of farming population, etc.
- **Institutional and government policy measures** like farm loans, MSP, subsidies, free electricity, crop-wise target fixed by the government such as for oilseeds, millets, etc., in order to achieve a specified rate of agricultural growth.
- **Technological factors** such as HYV seeds, scientific irrigation facilities suitable for some specific crops, easy availability of modern agricultural equipment at subsidised rates, etc.

Role of Subsidies in Cropping Pattern

Subsidies include: **Minimum Support Price (MSP)**, **power subsidy**, **higher farm credit**, etc.

- Subsidies work as an **incentive to the farmers** for the production of crops even in the dry areas.
- Rice and wheat aside, in recent years, cash crops sugarcane and cotton too have taken a larger share of the crop land due to better price incentives. However, States like **Maharashtra** and **Telangana**, where sowing of sugarcane and cotton using water from borewells prevails, have seen an adverse impact on the water table.

Crop Diversification

It refers to addition of new crops in the existing agricultural farm. Major potential benefits of crop diversification include improved soil health, enhanced productivity and thereby profitability in cultivation, lower risk of loss in case of failure of one particular crop, etc.

Hence lies the need to focus more on diversifying towards high-value crops and horticulture crops.

Index of Crop Diversification

It is computed to examine whether there have been major changes in the cropping patterns. The **index value** ranges between **0 and 1** and higher the value, greater the diversification.

Data analysis on Index of Crop Diversification was published in the Economic Survey 2017–18.

Index of Crop Diversification *(few illustrations)*

States	1994–95	2010–11	2014–15	Remarks
Chhattisgarh	NA	0.503	0.491	Decreased overtime
Haryana	0.83	0.788	0.774	Decreased overtime
Himachal Pradesh	0.74	0.741	0.754	Slightly increased overtime
Jharkhand	NA	0.537	0.578	Increased overtime
Karnataka	0.92	0.937	0.938	Increased overtime and **highest in India**
Odisha	0.74	0.38	0.34	Drastically decreased overtime and is **lowest in India**
Punjab	0.71	0.664	0.658	Decreased overtime
West Bengal	0.55	0.663	0.654	Increased overtime
All India	**0.905**	**0.907**	**0.899**	**Decreased overtime**

Source: Economic Survey 2017–18.

Note: Information on Index of Crop Diversification was not released in the later Economic Surveys.

As per that, there is a **declining inter-temporal behaviour** in crop diversification for States like **Chhattisgarh, Haryana, Odisha, Punjab**, etc., which is evident in the above table. One of the **factors for such decline** in **diversification is subsidy**.

Telangana tops among the States with the highest level of crop diversification.

Protected Special Agriculture Zone

When a region is declared as a Protected Special Agriculture Zone, that region will not be granted permission for any new projects like those related to hydrocarbons. Only agri-based industries would be given permission to be built.

Tamil Nadu declared Cauvery Delta as Protected Special Agriculture Zone.

CONTRACT FARMING

It is an agreement between the farmers and the processing and/or marketing firms for the production and supply of agricultural products at pre-determined prices. The arrangement involves the purchaser in providing a degree of production support through the supply of inputs and the provision of technical advice. In return, farmer agrees to provide certain quantity of specific agricultural product.

Features of Contract Farming

- **Access to New and Reliable Markets** – By providing market guarantees to the farmers.
- **Economics of Scale** – Agriculture on a large scale is generally more cost-effective.
- **Ensuring Quality Standards** – Constant quality control helps in better usage of pesticides.

- **Modern Technologies** – Sponsors considering their direct economic interest prefer to introduce new technologies in order to improve productivity and quality and upgrade the agricultural produce for markets that demand high quality standards.
- **Information** – All relevant technical information is provided to the contracted farmers to improve productivity.
- **Price Volatility** – Generally prices are specified under contract farming, which saves the farmers from price volatility in the market.
- **Sharing of Risk** – Sponsors along with farmers share the risk of production failure due to poor weather, disease, etc.

Challenges

- Sponsors delay in providing promised inputs like seeds or they give seeds that are of low quality.
- In reality, sometimes farmers aren't given a written contract at all and that creates power asymmetries.
- Quality is determined by the sponsors and they can manipulate to bring down prices to be paid to farmer.

Existing Regulatory Structure

- In India, contract farming is regulated under the Indian Contract Act, 1872. The Act has many general provisions that are relevant to contract farming, including the formation of contracts, obligations of parties and consequences in the case of breach of contract.
- In addition, contract farming requires registration with the APMC mandis (Agricultural Produce Marketing Committee) in few States.
- Issues related to effective implementation of contract farming are:
  a. Provision of stockholding limits on produce under contract farming.
  b. Poor publicity of contract farming among the farmers about its benefits.
  c. Market fees and other levies are charged by APMCs in many States for contract framing when no services such as market facilities and infrastructure are rendered by them.
- Therefore, to overcome some of the above-mentioned issues, the Ministry of Agriculture and Farmers Welfare has come out with a draft Model Contract Farming Act, 2018.

Draft Model Contract Farming Act, 2018

The draft Model Act seeks to create a regulatory and policy framework for contract farming.

Important provisions of the Draft Model Act include:

1. Contract farming will be outside the ambit of the State APMCs. This implies that buyers need not pay market fee and commission charges to these APMCs to undertake contract farming.
2. A State-level **Contract Farming (Promotion and Facilitation) Authority** to ensure implementation of the Draft Model Act.
3. Sale and purchase of contracted produce is out of the ambit of regulation of the respective State/ UT Agricultural Marketing Act.

4. Every agreement should be registered with a **District Registering and Agreement Recording Committee**, which will be set up consisting of officials from departments such as agriculture, animal husbandry, marketing, and rural development. *(Such a committee can be set up at the district, taluka or block levels.)*
5. Well **defined dispute resolution procedure** has been laid down.
6. **Limits of stockholding** of agricultural produce will not be applicable on produce purchased under contract farming.
7. **State legislatures can enact a law** on contract farming as contracts fall under the Concurrent List of the Constitution.
8. The producer (say, farmer) can get support from the buyer for improving production through inputs (such as technology, pre-harvest and post-harvest infrastructure) as per the agreement. However, the **buyer cannot raise a permanent structure** on the producer's land. Rights or title ownership of the producer's land cannot be transferred to the buyer.

Agricultural Reforms: Farm Laws 2020

The Central Government introduced 3 new Acts related to the farming, popularly known as farm laws in 2020 to introduce agricultural reforms in India, specially related to agricultural marketing. **These three Acts were**:

1. **The Farmers (Empowerment and Protection) Agreement on Price Assurance and Farm Services Act, 2020**
2. **The Farmers' Produce Trade and Commerce (Promotion and Facilitation) Act, 2020**
3. **The Essential Commodities (Amendment) Act, 2020**

1. The Farmers (Empowerment and Protection) Agreement of Price Assurance and Farm Services Act, 2020

- The Act envisaged a system of contract farming, by providing a framework of contract farming agreement between a farmer (producer) and a sponsor (purchaser) and could even include a farm service provider (as third party).
- The Act had provisions of setting up a registration authority for electronic registry of such farming agreements.
- A farming agreement may be linked with insurance or credit instrument under any scheme of the Central Government or the State Government or any financial service provider to ensure risk mitigation and flow of credit to farmer or Sponsor or both.
- The Act provided for **minimum period of farming agreement** to be one crop season or one production cycle of livestock. Maximum period was 5 years.
- It aimed to facilitate **remunerative price discovery** for the farmers to ensure higher returns.
- Also, it provided for a mechanism of **quicker resolution of disputes** between the private players, businesses and corporates on one hand and the farmers on the other, by **prescribing the time limit** for each level of the dispute resolution process, i.e. the Conciliation Board, Sub Divisional Magistrate and Appellate Authority.
- It had a provision of penalty for contravening the agreement. Along with this, the Act had provisions to **protect the farmers against the possibility of taking action against the farmers' land** for recovery of dues.

2. The Farmers' Produce Trade and Commerce (Promotion and Facilitation) Act, 2020

- The Act creates a system of sale and purchase of agricultural commodities outside the Agricultural Produce and Marketing Committee (APMC) mandis and also promotes electronic trading of agricultural produce.
- It attempts to remove barriers to inter-state trade of agricultural products and to encourage the integration of markets for seamless supply and meeting the demand across the territory of the country.

3. The Essential Commodities (Amendment) Act, 2020

- **Six commodities *viz.* cereals, pulses, onion, potatoes, edible oils and oilseeds** were delisted from the list of essential commodities through this Act. However, there were provisions for **exception in the cases of war, famine, natural calamity or extraordinary price rise**.
- It predicted the deregulation of the storage of these commodities and **removing the stock-holding limits**, which was imposed to curb the hoardings and black marketing of the essential commodities.

The above three farm Acts were opposed by the various stakeholders – Farmers, Traders and State Governments on account of various reasons.

In view of the protests by a group of farmers and opposition to the farm laws across the country, the government decided to repeal these three farm laws and **passed The Farm Laws Repeal Bill, 2021**, in order to take everyone together on the path of inclusive growth and development.

BONUS KNOWLEDGE

CO-OPERATIVE FARMING

Under co-operative farming, farmers pool their land, livestock and other implements. The entire farm is managed as a single unit and management is elected by all the members. Every member earns a share of the total production with their land contribution and labor performed.

Advantages:

1. Co-operative farming solves the problem of sub-division and fragmentation of holdings.
2. Co-operative farm has more men–material–money resources to increase irrigation system potential and land productivity. Members could not have been able to do it individually on their small farm.

Farmer Producer Organisation (FPO)

It is an agricultural co-operative with a great number of small farmers working as a co-operative.

Farmer Producer Company (FPC)

It is a hybrid between co-operative societies and private limited companies.

New National Co-operative Policy

In order to strengthen the 'Co-operative Movement' in the country, deepening its reach to the grassroots and promoting Co-operative-based economic development, a new National Cooperation Policy is being formulated. Co-operative society is a state subject in the seventh Schedule of the constitution. In addition, Cooperation Ministry has prepared the Multi State Co-operative Societies (Amendment) Bill 2022 in order to amend the previous Multi State Co-operative Societies Act, 2002.

- Maharashtra has the highest number of such societies (567 approx.), followed by Uttar Pradesh (147 approx.) and New Delhi (133 approx.).

Sahakar Mitra

- This new scheme was launched **in 2020** by the *Ministry of Agriculture and Farmers Welfare*.
- This Scheme on Internship Programme (SIP) provides **for young professionals to work as a paid intern**.
- The scheme is an initiative of the National Co-operative Development Corporation **(NCDC)**.
- Professional graduates in disciplines such as agriculture and allied areas, IT etc. are eligible for internship. Professionals who are pursuing or have completed their MBA degrees in agri-business, co-operation, finance, international trade, forestry, rural development, project management, etc. are also eligible to work as intern.
- The said internship is for **4 months**.

EXAM ESSENTIAL

MECHANISATION OF AGRICULTURE

In order to increase agricultural productivity, mechanisation of agriculture is an essential input to the concept of modern agriculture.

As the area under cultivation is shrinking along with reducing availability of water resources and labour force, agricultural productivity can be improved through mechanisation of production and post-harvesting operations.

Mechanisation can be done at four levels of agricultural production process:

1. During seedbed preparation.
2. During sowing/planting/transplanting.
3. During weeding and interculture and plant protection.
4. During harvesting and threshing.

Benefits of farm mechanisation

- Effective use and savings in inputs such as water, labour, energy and fertilisers.
- Timely farm operations with quicker rotation of crops.
- Increase in crop productivity and production.
- Increase in the income of farmers.

In order to enhance the thrust on farm mechanisation, a **sub-mission on agricultural mechanisation** was launched by the government in **2014–15** under which State governments are given assistance to impart training and demonstrate agricultural machineries and provide financial assistance to farmers for procurement of agricultural machineries and for setting up **custom hiring centres**.

Reasons for Low Rate of Mechanisation in India

A study by NABARD made an effort to find out the reasons. Reasons found for low rate of mechanisation were:

- Economies of operations could not be effectively achieved due to small holdings by the majority of farmers.
- Inadequate access to power required for using agricultural machineries.
- High credit cost and complicated procedures of loan disbursement.
- Uninsured markets.
- Low awareness among farmers about the benefits of farm mechanisation.

AGRICULTURAL FINANCE

In India, most of the farmers are small or marginal with inadequate savings. Thus, sufficient and timely credit to farmers assumes an important place considering the requirement to finance inputs like **fertilisers, pesticides** and the long period for crop yield starting from sowing seeds, harvesting crop and sale of agricultural produce.

Sources of Agriculture Finance

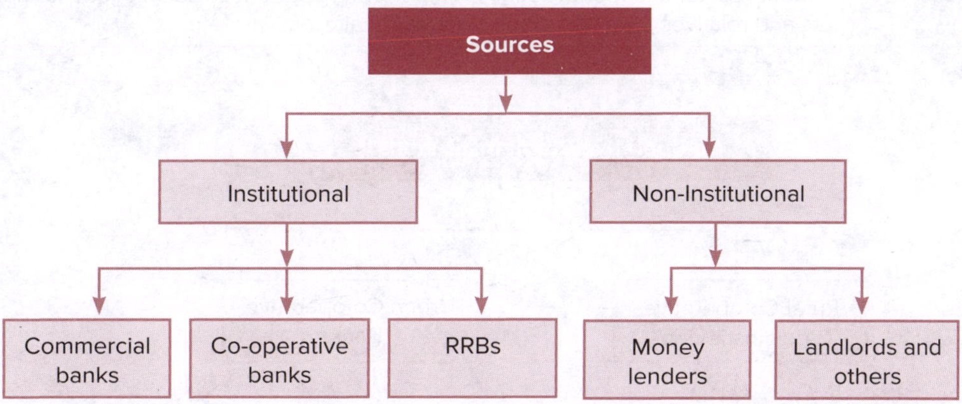

Agricultural finance can be categorised into the following:

On the Basis of Time

Type of Finance	Duration of loan	Source	Purpose
Short-term loan	Up to 15 months	Money lenders, traders, and co-operative societies	Fertilisers, pesticides, seeds, labour wages, etc.
Medium-term loan	From 15 months up to 5 years	Money lenders, co-operative societies and commercial banks	Repair and maintenance of wells, procurement of agricultural implements, etc.
Long-term loan	Beyond 5 years	Primary Co-operative Agriculture and Rural Development Banks	To bring long-term structural changes in the cultivation strategy

On the Basis of Purpose

Type of Loan	Source	Purpose
Productive	Money lenders, co-operative societies and all banks	To improve the agricultural production of agriculture like fertilisers, pesticides, seeds, labour wages, tube well repairing, digging, etc.
Consumption	Informal sector like money lenders and relatives	For subsistence and taking care of basic needs of the family.
Unproductive	Informal sector like money lenders and relatives	To perform important social obligations like marriage, rituals, festivals, etc.

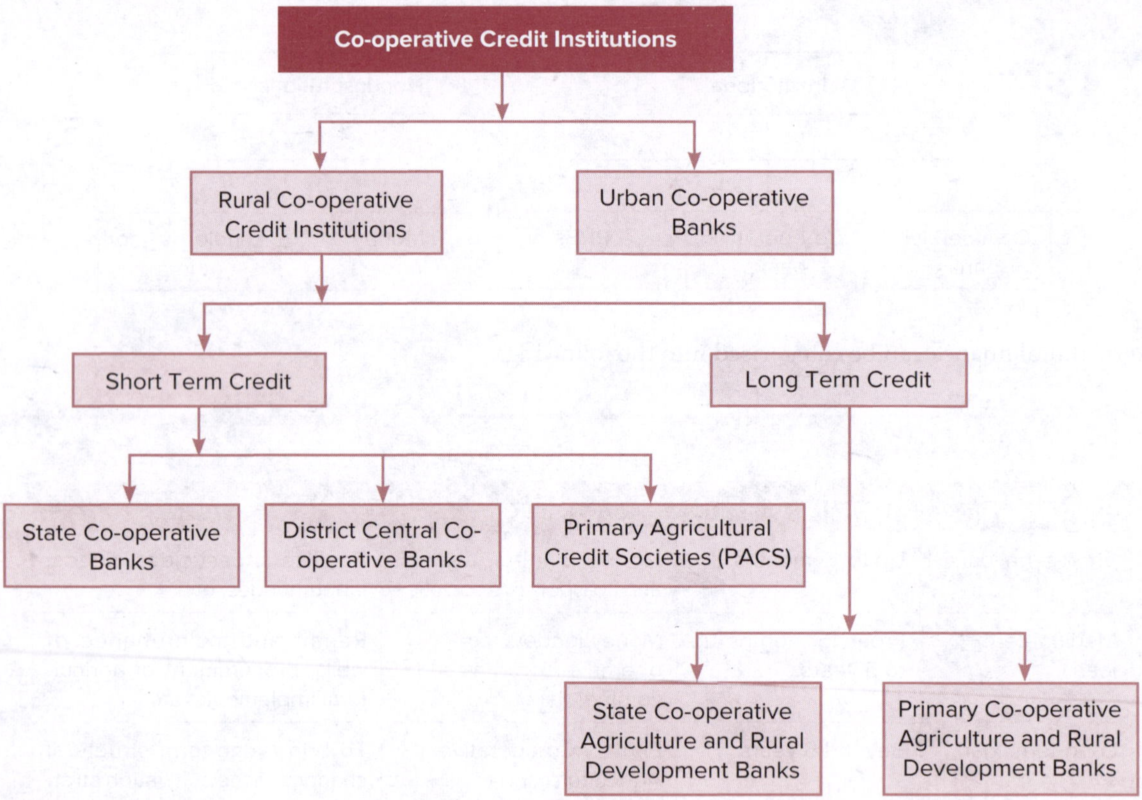

ROLE OF NABARD

- It serves as an **apex finance agency** for the institutions providing investment and production credit for promoting various developmental activities in rural areas.
- It provides **refinance to lending institutions** in rural areas. This is available to **State Co-operative Agriculture and Rural Development Banks (SCARDBs), SCBs, RRBs, Commercial Banks** and other financial institutions approved by RBI.

- It is involved in **promoting institutional development and in evaluating and monitoring projects refinanced** by it.
- **It coordinates rural financing activities** of institutions engaged in developmental works at the field level.
- It acts as a **supervisor (not regulator) for** RRBs.
- It extends **assistance to the government**, RBI and other organisations in matters relating to rural development.
- It provides **training and research facilities** for banks, co-operatives and other organisations who work towards rural development.
- It also facilitates the State governments in **reaching their targets of providing assistance** to eligible institutions in agriculture and rural development.

Status of Agricultural Finance

Agricultural Loan From	1950–51 (%)	2001–02 (%)	2021–22 (%)	Remarks
Institutional Agencies	10	61	**75**	*Financing by institutional agencies has increased considerably overtime with the help of focussed government interventions.*
Non-institutional Agencies	90	39	**25**	
Total	**100**	**100**	**100**	

Source: Economic Survey 2024–25.

Among institutional agencies, agricultural loan disbursement by **Scheduled Commercial Banks** is the highest.

Government Initiatives so far to Promote Agricultural Credit

- **No Frill Account**: 'No frill' bank account is made available with minimum or nil balance for basic banking.
- **Promoting Microfinance Institutions (MFIs)**: MFI works as a vehicle to provide microcredit or small loans to the poor without any collateral. NABARD plays an important role in this by providing re-finance at low interest rates.
- **Kisan Credit Card (KCC)**: It was designed by NABARD and introduced in 1998 to facilitate short-term formal credit to farmers. Each farmer is provided with KCC and passbook to receive cash credit facilities.
  - KCC is to be implemented by **Commercial Banks, RRBs, and Cooperatives in India as per the Government's guidelines**.
  - Eligible beneficiaries include:
    i. All Farmers – Individuals/Joint borrowers who are owner cultivators
    ii. Tenant Farmers, Oral Lessees and Share Croppers
    iii. SHGs or Joint Liability Groups of Farmers including tenant farmers, share croppers etc.
  - Beneficiaries of fishery and animal husbandry can also possess KCC. **Age limit is 18 to 75 years**.
  - Validity period of KCC is **5 years**.
  - Collateral security is waived for KCC limit up to ₹1.60 lakh.

- Notified crops/notified areas are covered under **crop insurance** for all KCC loans. KCC also provides for **personal accident insurance** which a farmer may opt for. Under it, coverage up to ₹50,000 in the case of accidental death and ₹25,000 in the case of disability due to accident is provided.
- **Purposes/Objectives of KCC include:**
  a. To meet the short term credit requirements for cultivation of crops.
  b. Post harvest expenses.
  c. Produce Marketing loan.
  d. Consumption requirements of farmer household.
  e. Working capital for maintenance of farm assets and activities allied to agriculture, like dairy animals, inland fishery etc.
  f. Investment credit requirement for agriculture and allied activities like pump sets, sprayers, dairy animals etc.

Note: The aggregate of components 'a' to 'e' above will form the short term credit limit portion and the aggregate of components under 'f' will form the long term credit limit portion.

- At present, there are **over 7.1 crore active KCCs** in the country.

➤ **Interest Subvention Scheme**: Under this, farmers can avail concessional crop loan up to ₹3 lakh at 7 per cent rate of interest. In the case of timely repayment, the interest rate gets further reduced to 4 per cent per annum. The aim of this scheme is to make the credit available at an affordable rate.

Government Initiatives towards Digital Agriculture

➤ **Unified Farmer Service Platform (UFSP)**: It is a platform consisting of core infrastructure data applications and tools that enable various public and private IT systems in the agriculture ecosystem across the country.

➤ **National e-Governance Plan in Agriculture (NeGPA)**: It is a centrally sponsored scheme which was launched in 2010–11 in 7 pilot states, later extended to all other states and 2 union territories. It aims to achieve rapid development in India through the use of Information and Communication Technology (ICT) for timely access to agriculture-related information to the farmers.

➤ **Digital Agriculture Mission**: Technologies like artificial intelligence, blockchain remote sensing, drones, robots, and GIS Technology will be used. This has been initiated for 2021–25.

➤ **AgriStack**: It is a collection of technology based interventions in agriculture to create a unified platform for farmers in order to provide them end-to-end services across the agriculture food value chain.

Challenges in Agricultural Credit Sector

Despite impressive growth in the institutional agricultural credit flow, there exists several issues and challenges:

1. **Credit Reach** – As per the NABARD's Financial Inclusion Survey Report (**NAFIS**) report **2021–22**, **76 per cent of the credit requirement** was met **from institutional sources** and 24 per cent from non-institutional sources. Further, in the absence of a proper legal framework and lack of records

relating to their agricultural activity, tenant farmers/sharecroppers/oral lessees/landless labourers face difficulty in accessing institutional credit.

2. **Share of Credit to Allied Activities** i.e., livestock, forestry and fisheries is sub-optimal in availing agricultural credit.
3. **Regional Disparity in Agricultural Credit** – Some of the States are getting much higher share, as high as 10 per cent of total agricultural credit compared to other states getting as low as 0.5 per cent.
4. **Loan Waiver by State Governments** – Loan waivers announced by state governments have affected the credit culture in the country with many borrowers withholding repayment, in anticipation of a loan waiver. This adversely affects the credit history of borrowers and their future prospects of availing fresh loan for agricultural purposes.

EXAM ESSENTIAL

AGRICULTURE INFRASTRUCTURE FUND

- It is a **Central Sector Scheme** (CSS) announced by GoI in 2020.
- The fund/scheme provides a **medium to long-term** loan financing facility to boost investment in the infrastructure related to mainly **post-harvest** and **community farming**.
- **Interest subvention** of 3 per cent on loans up to a limit of ₹2 crore and maximum for 7 years is being provided under the scheme.
- **Credit guarantee coverage** is provided for a loan up to a limit of ₹2 crore.
- Overall **₹1 lakh crore** is being provided by banks and financial institutions as loans to PACS, marketing co-operative societies, FPOs, SHG farmers, joint liability groups, multi-purpose co-operative societies, agricultural entrepreneurs, start-ups, aggregation infrastructure providers and even to the Central/State agency or local body sponsored PPP projects.
- Duration of the scheme is **10 years** (2020–21 to 2029–30).

FDI IN AGRICULTURE

Foreign direct investment can be made in India under the following two routes:

1. **Automatic Route**: Foreign investment is allowed under the automatic route **without prior approval** of the government or RBI, in all activities/sectors as specified in the FEMA Regulations.
2. **Government Route**: Foreign investment in activities not covered under the automatic route requires prior approval of the government.

Area	FDI Limit (%)	Entry Route
Floriculture, horticulture, development of seeds, animal husbandry, pisciculture, aquaculture and five plantation crops – **coffee, rubber, cardamom, palm oil tree and olive oil tree**	100	Automatic
Cultivation of **vegetables and mushrooms** and services related to agro and allied sectors	100	Automatic
Tea cultivation and processing	100	Government

AGRICULTURAL MARKETING

There are two types of agricultural markets:

- **Unregulated Markets**: There is no set of rules and regulations to conduct a business. These markets suffer from defects in functioning. For example, **Rural Haat**.
- **Regulated Markets**: Rules and regulations of business are controlled by statutory market organisations in this case. Here market charges are standardised and fixed and the practices are regulated by **Agricultural Produce Market Committee (APMC)**.

Model APMC Act, 2003

Objectives

- To provide for development of efficient marketing system.
- To promote agri-processing and agricultural exports.
- To build an effective infrastructure for the marketing of agricultural products.

Features

- It deals with selling products directly and not through regulated markets.
- There is a provision related to the establishment of **'State Agricultural Produce Marketing Standards Bureau'** for grading, standardisation and quality certification.
- It promotes public–private partnership in the 'management and development' of agricultural markets for post-harvest handling, cold storage, pre-cooling facilities, pack houses, etc.
- It advocates contract farming. It also provides for a dispute resolution mechanism.
- It publishes arrival data and rates of agricultural produce brought into the market area for sale.
- Establishment of special markets for specific agricultural commodities (for instance, perishable items).
- New market establishment by farmers for their agriculture produce and registration of market functionaries instead of licencing.
- Requires a single levy of market fee on the sale of notified agricultural commodities in any market area.

Challenges in APMC Act, 2003

- The Act retains provision of buyers paying APMC charges even when the produce is sold directly outside the APMC area.
- E-auction for agricultural produce for all mandis would bring transparency and better participation.
- Fragmentation of state into multiple market areas, each administered by the separate APMC.
- Multiple levy of mandi fees, requirement for multiple license for trading in different APMCs.
- No specific charges for storage service for horticulture produce, storing like other produce causes damage to horticulture produce which are highly perishable.
- Till now, **around 22 States** have adopted it (*agriculture being a state subject*).

BONUS KNOWLEDGE

THE STATE/UT AGRICULTURAL PRODUCE AND LIVESTOCK MARKETING (PROMOTION AND FACILITATION) ACT, 2017

- In order to make model APMC Act, 2003 more comprehensive and farmer friendly, GoI formulated and released this model Act, popularly called model APLM Act in 2017.
- The essence of this is to provide complete freedom to the cultivators and livestock rearers to sell their produce, livestock and its product to the buyers and through the marketing channel of their choice offering a better bid.
- Apart from the above, the model legal framework emphasises on attracting investment from the private sector in developing post-harvest and marketing infrastructure.
- It also provides for the declaration of the **whole State as one unified market**, warehouses/silos/cold storages as market sub-yards, rationalisation of market fee and commission charges.
- **Contract farming** has now been taken out from APMC domain which was previously existing in the 2003 Act.
- The model 2017 Act mandates APLMC to take measures **to prevent sale/purchase** of produce **below Minimum Support Price (MSP)**.
- The model 2017 Act also provides for payment to farmer-seller (in APLM market or direct purchase) on the same day.
- Arunachal Pradesh, Uttar Pradesh and Chhattisgarh have adopted the model APLM Act, 2017.

Integrated Scheme for Agricultural Marketing

Launched in 2014 by GoI, the **Integrated Scheme for Agricultural Marketing** presently consists of **six sub-schemes**:

1. Agricultural Marketing Infrastructure **(AMI)**.
2. Marketing Research and Information Network **(MRIN)**.
3. Strengthening of Agmark Grading Facilities **(SAGF)**.
4. Training, Research and Consultancy through Choudhary Charan Singh National Institute of Agricultural Marketing **(NIAM)**.
5. Agri-business Development through Venture Capital Assistance **(VCA)** and Project Development Facility.
6. National Agriculture Market **(e-NAM)**

did you KNOW? **Agridex** – The National Commodity and Derivatives Exchange **(NCDEX)** launched the country's first agricultural futures trading index – 'Agridex' – in **2020**. It comprises **10 liquid commodities** traded on NCDEX. These 10 commodities include *soyabean, chana, coriander, cottonseed oilcake, guar gum, guar seed, mustard seed, refined soy oil, castor seed and jeera*. The index represents various agricultural commodities of both Kharif and Rabi seasons, with price references throughout the year.

EXAM ESSENTIAL

DIFFERENT STANDARDS OF CERTIFICATION

Bureau of Indian Standards (BIS)

Bureau of Indian Standards (BIS) is the National Standards Body of India established under **The BIS Act, 2016**, and working under the Ministry of Consumer Affairs, Food and Public Distribution. The new 2016 Act is an amended version of BIS Act, 1986. **Functions of BIS include**:

1. **Formulation of Standards** of various industrial products (grouped in 14 sectors like chemical, food and agriculture, IT, petroleum and related products, transport engineering, etc.)
2. **Product Certification Scheme** for ensuring compliance to Indian standards. Presence of BIS standard mark **(popularly known as ISI mark)** on a product indicates conformity to the relevant Indian standard. BIS certification scheme is voluntary in nature. However, for some products, it is mandatory.

   There is also a separate certification scheme to certify goods manufactured outside India.
3. **Hallmarking** – Under this, jewellers are granted certificate of registration through Assaying & Hallmark centres to sell hallmarked gold and silver jewellery.

AGMARK

It is a certification mark for **agricultural products** in India, assuring that they confirm by a set of standards approved by the **Directorate of Marketing and Inspection**, an attached Office of the Department of Agriculture, Cooperation and Farmers Welfare under the Ministry of Agriculture & Farmers Welfare. The AGMARK Head Office is at Faridabad (Haryana). It is legally enforced in India by the Agricultural Produce Act of 1937. The present AGMARK standards cover quality guidelines for **224 different commodities** spanning from variety of **pulses, cereals, essential oils, vegetable oils, fruits & vegetables** and semi-processed products like **vermicelli**.

FPO Mark

The FPO mark is a certification mark mandatory on all **processed fruit products** sold in India such as packaged **fruit beverages, fruit-jams, crushes & squashes, pickles, dehydrated fruit products and fruit extracts**, following the Food Safety and Standards Act of 2006. The FPO mark guarantees that the product was manufactured in a **hygienic 'food-safe' environment**, thus ensuring that the product is fit for consumption. The FPO mark is provided by the *Ministry of Food Processing and Industries*.

AGRICULTURAL SUBSIDY

It is the **financial support** paid to farmers to increase their income with less input expenditure. Agricultural subsidies play a **vital role in the growth** of the agriculture sector in India.

Types of Subsidy

1. **Direct Subsidy** – Here the benefit is directly given to the farmers (in the form of cash). For example, food subsidy.
2. **Indirect Subsidy** – Subsidies reach to the farmers indirectly, not in cash. For example, subsidising companies to provide cheap fertilisers, etc.

Subsidy in Different Sectors by the Government

- **Subsidy on Farm Equipments** – This benefit encourages farmers to buy more farm equipment for farming.
- **Availability of fertilisers to farmers at lower price** – It may also be in the form of lifting tariff on import of fertilisers.
- **Subsidies for R&D** – For production of high-quality **seeds**.
- **Subsidies on Infrastructure.**
- **Subsidy in Power Sector** – An incentive to run pumping sets, tube wells, etc. Government charges lower rate.
- **Subsidy in Irrigation Sector** – Government provides facilities through construction of canals, dams and tube wells, so that all fields come under irrigation facility.
- **Employment Subsidy** – To provide more job opportunities in the business and reduce unemployment in the country.
- To comfortably face international competition, subsidy is also provided in the **export sector**. It makes farmers more competitive against foreign goods. However, there are certain restrictions imposed as per Agreement on Agriculture (AoA) of World Trade Organization (WTO).
- **Subsidised Credit Facility** – Mainly three types of finance prevail in agriculture sector – short-term, medium-term and long-term finance.
  - **Long-term finance/loan for 5–20 years** for purposes such as constructing sinking well, land levelling, fencing and permanent improvements on land, purchase of big machinery like tractor, etc.
  - **Medium-term finance** mostly includes finance for **farm equipment and small machineries**, e.g. thrasher and other equipment.
  - **Short-term finance** mainly involves crop finance. Duration of this finance is 1–2 years and rate of interest charged is quite low, i.e., 2 per cent to 4 per cent.

Points against providing Agriculture Subsidy

- Subsidies **benefit big farmers more** as compared to the small farmers.
- **Imbalanced fertilisation practice** (*use of some fertilisers to a great extent due to prevailing subsidy*) has aggravated the problem of nutrient deficiencies in the soil. It has deteriorated the fertility and productivity of the soil.
- Subsidised power from State government results in inappropriate use of water.
- **Presence of corruption** may not let full benefits of subsidy to reach to the end users, i.e. farmers.

If the above bottlenecks are tackled effectively, subsidy can be a real boon for the equitable development of the agricultural sector.

EXAM ESSENTIAL

MINIMUM SUPPORT PRICE

- It is the price at which government purchases crops from the farmers. If there is a bumper harvest, then the fall in the price cannot go below the MSP. It acts as a guarantee price to **protect farmers from distress sale**. MSP was first announced for wheat in 1966–67.

Like MSP, there is another concept called **Fair and Remunerative Price (FRP)**. MSP is the price paid by government to farmers for procurement, whereas FRP is the price fixed by government but is paid by mill owners. **FRP is fixed by government only for sugarcane**. It is because owing to its weight-losing properties, sugarcane must reach mills within a stipulated time. Thus, government procurement is not a viable solution for sugarcane.

- **Objectives of MSP** include:
  1. Providing economic safety to farmers in terms of stable remunerative price.
  2. Increasing food production and ensure food security.
  3. Influencing the cropping pattern for overall growth of agriculture economy.
- MSP is usually fixed and announced by the government at the beginning of the sowing season on the basis of the recommendations of Commission for Agricultural Costs and Prices **(CACP)**.
- While recommending MSP, CACP considers **determinants such** as – *demand and supply, cost of production, price trends in market, inter-crop price parity, a minimum of 50 per cent margin over cost of production, etc.*
- Thus, MSP announced is **1.5 times the cost of production** of the crop.
- At present, government announces **MSP for 22 mandated crops** and **FRP for sugarcane**.
- In addition to it, MSP for **Toria** and **De-Husked Coconut** is fixed on the basis of MSPs of rapeseed/mustard and copra, respectively.

22 Mandated MSP Crops

Kharif – 14 Crops	Rabi – 6 Crops	Other – 2 Crops
Paddy, jowar, bajra, maize, ragi, arhar (tur), moong, urad, cotton, groundnut, sunflower seed, soyabean, sesamum, niger seed	Wheat, barley, gram, masur (lentil), rapeseed & mustard, safflower	Copra and jute

PM-AASHA – To address the gaps in MSP Scheme, *Pradhan Mantri Annadata Aay SanraksHan Abhiyan* (PM-AASHA) was launched in **2018** to ensure remunerative prices to farmers of **pulses, oilseeds and copra**. This umbrella scheme has **three components** or sub-schemes:

1. **Price Support Scheme (PSS)** – Under it, physical procurement of **pulses, oilseeds and copra** is done by Central Nodal Agencies with proactive role of State Governments. In addition to NAFED, Food Corporation of India (FCI) also undertakes PSS operations.

2. **Price Deficiency Payment Scheme (PDPS)** – PDPS is applicable for all **oilseeds** (groundnut, soyabean, sunflower, sesamum, niger seed, rapeseed/mustard, safflower and toria). Difference between announced MSP and the modal price/selling price is made to re-registered farmers selling their produce in the notified market through auction. **The difference amount is paid directly into registered bank account** of the farmer. This scheme does not involve any physical procurement of crops.

3. **Pilot of Private Procurement and Stockist Scheme (PPPS)** – Under this sub-scheme, the participation of private sector stockists in the procurement process of **oilseeds** is being piloted in select districts. In those select districts, PPPS substitutes PSS/PDPS.

AGRICULTURE INSURANCE

- Agricultural insurance protects farmers against agricultural losses. Crop insurance was introduced in India in **1985**. Thereafter, many changes in policy/schemes as per requirements were done. Related government schemes were:
  1985 – Comprehensive Crop Insurance Scheme
  1999 – National Agricultural Insurance Scheme (NAIS)
  2007 – Weather-Based Crop Insurance Scheme (WCIS)
  2010 – Modified National Agricultural Insurance Scheme (MNAIS)
- However, above schemes suffered from a number of **drawbacks**:
  - Only 23 per cent insurance coverage of the gross cropped Area of our country.
  - Risk was not covered for all calamities.
  - Cap on premium rate resulting in lower claims received by farmers.
  - Premium for commercial and horticulture crops could be as high as 25 per cent depending on the risk factor involved.
  - Inadequate use of technologies.
  - Delay in payment of claims.
- With an objective to overcome above-mentioned drawbacks, a new crop insurance scheme was launched in **2016**. It was **Pradhan Mantri Fasal Bima Yojana (PMFBY)**.

EXAM ESSENTIAL

PRADHAN MANTRI FASAL BIMA YOJANA (PMFBY)

- PMFBY has **replaced the existing two schemes** – National Agricultural Insurance Scheme (NAIS) and Modified NAIS (MNAIS).
- It is based on the principle of **One Nation–One Scheme** and is being implemented by the **Ministry of Agriculture & Farmers Welfare**.
- It provides comprehensive coverage of risks from pre-sowing to post-harvest losses against **natural non-preventable risks** such as drought, dry spells, flood, pests and diseases, natural fire, lightening, storm, cyclone, typhoon, tempest, hurricane and tornado. **Localised calamities** such as hailstorms, unseasonal rains, landslides and inundation are **also covered** under PMFBY.
- **Target of PMFBY** is to increase the insurance coverage **from 23 per cent to 50 per cent** of the Gross Cropped Area (GCA) of our country.
- The scheme is being implemented on **'Area Approach basis'**, i.e. defined areas. **Defined area** (i.e. unit area of insurance) is **Village/Village Panchayat** level for major crops and for minor crops, defined area is above the level of Village/Village Panchayat.
- PMFBY **covers all Food and Oilseeds Crops and Annual Commercial/Horticultural Crops** for which past yield data is available and for which the requisite number of Crop Cutting Experiments (CCEs) are being conducted under the General Crop Estimation Survey (GCES).
- **Amount of premium paid by farmers** under PMFBY – **2 per cent** of sum insured or actuarial rate (whichever is less) for all kharif oilseed and food crops; **1.5 per cent** for all Rabi oilseed and food crops; **5 per cent** for commercial/horticulture crops.
- The balance premium is **shared equally by** the Central and State Governments (90:10 for NE States).

- PMFBY is **voluntary for States** (i.e. States are not mandated to adopt PMFBY).
- **Direct Benefit Transfer (DBT)** under PMFBY was introduced in 2017 to help farmers receive claims directly in their bank account, thus making **registration to Aadhaar mandatory**.
- **National Crop Insurance Portal** has been launched to provide web-based interface among stakeholders.
- In 2018, the operational guidelines of PMFBY **were revised** by GoI. Some important revisions were:
  - (a) 12 per cent interest rate per annum to be paid by insurance companies to farmers in the case of delay in settlement of claims beyond 10 days of the cut-off date.
  - (b) 12 per cent interest rate by State governments for delay in the release of State share.
  - (c) Increased time for change of crop name for insurance.
  - (d) Time for intimation of loss due to localised calamities and post-harvest losses increased from 48 hours to 72 hours.
- **Benefits of PMFBY include** – lower premium rates, quicker settlement of claims due to use of modern technologies, even post-harvest coverage, more calamities covered, farmer to receive claims against full sum insured, etc.
- **Limitations of PMFBY include** – low coverage, delay by some State governments in the release of their part of premium resulting in delay in claim payments by insurance companies, coverage against wild animal attacks only on pilot basis, etc.
- **Performance of PMFBY till now** – Target for 2016–17 and 2017–18 was 30 per cent coverage of GCA. However, it could not be achieved for reasons such as announcement of debt waiver scheme by Maharashtra and Uttar Pradesh in 2017–18. Rajasthan and Madhya Pradesh also announced debt waiver in 2018–19. However, in 2018–19, 30 per cent of GCA was insured.
- **In 2020**, the following important revisions in PMFBY have been made by GoI:
  - (a) There will now be a **restriction/capping on premium subsidy** – i.e. 30 per cent for unirrigated areas and 25 per cent for irrigated areas. Previously, there was no upper limit on government subsidy.
  - (b) Enrolment under PMFBY has now been made **voluntary for all farmers**. Previously, it was mandatory for loanee farmers.
  - (c) **States/UTs to have flexibility** to choose additional risk covers. Previously, they were mandatory.

Restructured Weather-Based Crop Insurance Scheme (RWBCIS)

- As a revamped form of WBCIS, the RWBCIS was launched in **2016** by the **Ministry of Agriculture & Farmers Welfare**.
- WBCIS intended to provide insurance protection to the cultivator against **adverse weather incidence** (*perils of rainfall, temperature, wind speed, humidity and hailstorm*).
- Major food crops, oilseeds and commercial/horticulture crops are covered under RWBCIS.
- Risk period covered is from sowing to maturity of a crop.
- The scheme uses weather parameters as **proxy** for crop yields in compensating cultivators for deemed crop losses.
- The scheme is being implemented on **'Area Approach basis'**.
- All farmers **(including sharecroppers and tenant farmers)** growing **notified crops** are eligible for coverage under RWBCIS.

- As per 2020 revision, RWBCIS has been made **voluntary for all farmers** (*previously, it was mandatory for loanee farmers*).
- **Amount of premium paid by farmers** under RWBCIS: **2 per cent** of sum insured or actuarial rate (whichever is less) for all Kharif oilseed and food crops; **1.5 per cent** for all Rabi oilseed and food crops; 5 per cent for commercial/horticulture crops.
- Compensation in terms of claims will arise only in the case of adverse weather incidence. Adverse weather incidence is equivalent to the deviation between **'Trigger Weather'** and **'Actual Weather'** data recorded at a 'reference weather station'.

Krishi Megh

Krishi Megh is the data recovery centre of ICAR. It has been built to mitigate the risk and enhance the quality, availability and accessibility of e-governance, research, extension and education in the field of agriculture in India. It is equipped with the latest technologies like **artificial intelligence** and **deep learning software** for building and deploying deep learning-based applications through image analysis, disease identification in livestock, etc. This will enable providing real-time data to the researchers.

Biotech-KISAN Programme

Biotech-KISAN programme is a farmer-centric scheme for farmers, developed by and with farmers under the Department of Biotechnology, Ministry of Science and Technology.

It is a pan-India program, following a hub-and-spoke model and stimulates entrepreneurship and innovation in farmers and empowers women farmers.

The programme links available science and technology to the farm by first understanding the problem of the local farmer and then providing scientific solutions to those problems.

ANIMAL REARING

Among domesticated animals, livestock and poultry is an integral part of rural India and income generated through them is an important secondary source for a large number of rural households.

Livestock includes *cattle, buffalo, mithun, yak, sheep, goat, pig, horse, pony, mule, donkey and camel*. Livestock sector is an important subsector of agriculture in the Indian economy. It grew at a **CAGR of 13.36 per cent** from 2014–15 to 2021–22.

The contribution of livestock in total agriculture and allied sector GVA (at constant prices) has increased from 24.32 per cent (2014–15) to 30.23 per cent (2022–23). Livestock sector contributed 5.50 per cent of total GVA in 2022–23.

Development of livestock sector has led to improvement in per capita availability of milk, eggs and meat.

Significance of Livestock

- It provides milk, meat and eggs which act as an important source of nourishment for the households.
- It is an important asset and safety net for the poor and also provides a subsidiary income.
- Animal waste such as dung is a great source of nutrients to improve soil fertility and crop yield.
- Other benefits include use of skin for leather, bulls for ploughing fields, etc.

EXAM ESSENTIAL

20th LIVESTOCK CENSUS

- Livestock Census covers all domesticated animals in **rural and urban areas** and **is a quinquennial** (every 5 years) exercise. The objective of such census is to gather information on various aspects such as species, breed, age, sex and ownership. This is done for facilitating proper planning, formulation, implementation, and monitoring of programmes meant to improve the livestock sector.
- First such Livestock Census was conducted in 1919. The 2019 Census was the 20th such census.
- The 20th Census figures were released by the *Ministry of Fisheries, Animal Husbandry and Dairying* in 2019.
- Breed-wise number of animals and birds were counted in this census.
- Among the livestock population, species included: cattle, buffalo, mithun, yak, sheep, goat, pig, horse, pony, mule, donkey and camel. Besides livestock, poultry birds, dogs, rabbits and elephants possessed by households were also counted under this census.
- For the first time, livestock data were collected online.
- The total livestock population increased from 512 million in 2012 to **535.78 million** in 2019 (showing an **increase of 4.6 per cent** over Livestock Census 2012).
- Among the total livestock population, **35.94 per cent is cattle, 27.80 per cent is goat, 20.45 per cent is buffaloes, 13.87 per cent is sheep and 1.69 per cent is pigs**. Mithun, yaks, horses, ponies, mules, donkeys and camels taken together contribute **0.23 per cent** of the total livestock.

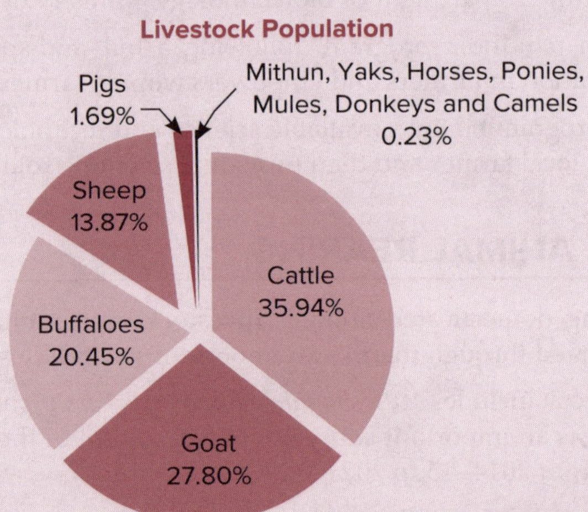

- As compared to previous census, the **percentage share of sheep and goat population has increased** whereas the percentage share of cattle, buffalo and pig has marginally declined.
- **Bovine population** (cattle, buffalo, mithun and yak) has shown an increase of 1 per cent over the previous census.
- **Cattle population** has shown an increase of 0.8 per cent over the previous census. However, female cattle population has increased greatly by 18 per cent.
- The **exotic/crossbreed** cattle population is around **one-third** of the **indigenous** cattle population.
- **Indigenous** cattle population has **declined** but at a lower pace as compared to the previous census. On the other hand, **exotic/crossbreed** cattle population has increased at a great pace.
- The **total poultry** registered an increase of 17 per cent, whereas **commercial poultry** has increased by 4.5 per cent over the previous census.
- The 21st **Livestock Census** was conducted from **September to December 2024** (*findings not yet published*). **It covered 16 species and 219 breeds**. For the first time, **data on pastoralists**, their contribution to the livestock sector, their socio-economic condition and livestock holding, has been captured separately in 21st Livestock Census.

EXAM ESSENTIAL

NATIONAL LIVESTOCK MISSION

It is an initiative of the *Ministry of Agriculture and Farmers Welfare* which commenced from 2014–15.

Objectives are:

- Sustainable development of the livestock sector.
- To ensure quantitative and qualitative improvement in livestock production systems and capacity building of all stakeholders.
- To provide State governments with the flexibility in formulating and executing scheme as per local needs.

National Livestock Mission is organised into the following four sub-missions:

1. **Sub-mission on Livestock Development** – Overall development of livestock species includes poultry, other than cattle and buffalo. Risk management and insurance as a component includes cattle, buffalo and even major & minor livestock.
2. **Sub-mission on Pig Development in North-Eastern Region** – Bringing in research and development organisations for holistic development of pigs in the North-Eastern region.
3. **Sub-mission on Fodder and Feed Development** – to increase both production and productivity of fodder and feed with the help of technological interventions in arable and non-arable areas.
4. **Sub-mission on Skill Development, Technology Transfer and Extension** – It links stakeholders to bring and adopt new technologies and practices. In other words, it provides a platform to develop and adopt technologies including frontline field demonstrations in collaboration with farmers, researchers and extension workers.

SWEET REVOLUTION

- **National Beekeeping and Honey Mission (NBHM)** aims for the overall promotion and development of scientific beekeeping in the country to achieve the goal of '**Sweet Revolution**'
- The mission was announced as part of the **Atma Nirbhar Bharat** Scheme
- The Scheme is being implemented through **National Bee Board (NBB)**
- Allocation of ₹500 crore for the National Beekeeping & Honey Mission (NBHM) for three years (2020–21 to 2022–23), and was extended through 2025 with ₹370 crores remaining, due to the importance of beekeeping as part of the Integrated Farming System in the country

Objective of NBHM

- Promote the holistic growth of beekeeping industry for income and employment generation for farm and non-farm households
- Enhance the agriculture/horticulture production
- Developing infrastructural facilities
- Including setting up of **Integrated Beekeeping Development Centres** (IBDCs)
- Honey testing labs, bee disease diagnostic labs, custom hiring centres, Api-therapy centres, nucleus stock, bee breeders, etc
- Empowerment of women through beekeeping

Besides, the scheme also aims to create awareness about the scientific beekeeping under Mini Mission-I, post-harvest management of beekeeping, beehive products, including collection, processing, storage, marketing, value addition, etc. under Mini Mission-II and Research and Technology generation in beekeeping under Mini Mission-III.

Khadi and Village Industries Commission (KVIC) has launched the innovative 'Mobile Honey Processing Van' to support farmers and beekeepers.

RED REVOLUTION

It denotes specialisation, mechanisation and standardisation of the **meat (especially buffalo) and poultry processing sector**. Now India is projected as the **second-largest beef-exporting country** (after **Brazil**) in the world. According to FAOSTAT production data (2019), **India ranks 5th** in meat production in the world.

Initiatives taken by the government in this regard:

- Establishing the first **meat and poultry food-testing laboratory** in Delhi as a one-stop solution.
- **One hundred per cent FDI** has been permitted.
- Incentives being provided to encourage **R&D in food processing**, process development and improved packaging.

Challenges:

- Meat consumption per capita is only 6 grams per day and will have to be improved to 50 grams a day.
- India accounts for only around 2 per cent of the global market, even though India has the **highest livestock population**.

BLUE REVOLUTION

The main motto of this revolution is to ensure **economic prosperity to the fishermen**. The father of this revolution were **Dr. Arun Krishnan and Dr. Hiralal Chaudhuri**.

Objectives

- To fully tap the total fish potential and triple both the production and export earnings by 2020.
- To bring in new technologies and processes and to transform fisheries sector as the modern industry like **bio flock farming**.

Recent Initiatives taken by the Government

- **Integrated Development and Management of Fisheries** was the restructured plan scheme on Blue Revolution, with total central outlay of ₹3,000 crore for implementation during the period 2015–20.
- It focused on **development and management of fisheries, covering inland fisheries, aquaculture, and marine fisheries including deep sea fishing, mariculture** and all activities undertaken by the **National Fisheries Development Board (NFDB)**.
- In the 2019–20 Budget, GoI declared a new focussed scheme **'Pradhan Mantri Matsya Sampada Yojana' (PMMSY)** to establish robust fisheries management framework and to address critical gaps in strengthening value chain, infrastructure, modernisation, production and productivity along with post-harvest management and quality control. PMMSY is aimed at bringing Blue Revolution through sustainable and responsible development of fisheries sector in India , with an investment of ₹20,050 crore for period of five years from 2020–21 to 2024–25. During 2021–22, PMMSY has supported

31.89 lakh farmers from 22 States and 07 UTs under insurance coverage and an additional 6.77 lakh farmers have been covered for livelihood and nutritional support during the lean/ban period. In the Union Budget 2020–21, the concept of **Sagar Mitras** was introduced.

- **Fisheries and Aquaculture Infrastructure Development Fund** (FIDF) has been set up with a total fund size of ₹7,522.48 crore, for providing concessional finance.
- **Kisan Credit Card (KCC)** facility has also been extended to fishers and fish farmers to help them meet their working capital and short-term credit needs.

Present Trend in Fish Production:

- As per **recent reports**, India is the **third-largest fish-producing country** in the world and accounts for around 8 per cent of the global production.
- The fish production in India reached an all-time high of 18.4 million metric tonnes during 2022-23.
- At present with 8 per cent of worldwide fish output, India ranks third in fish production, second in aquaculture, first in shrimp production, and fourth in seafood exports.
- The fisheries sector has been recognised as a '**Sunrise Sector**' and has demonstrated an outstanding double-digit average annual growth of 10.87 per cent since 2014–15.
- Out of the total fish production in India, Inland fish production is much higher than marine fish production.
- **Andhra Pradesh** has the highest inland fish production and also overall fish production as per latest available data of 2017–18. **Gujarat** had the highest marine fish production in 2017–18. 22 million metric tonnes of fish production was targeted by GOI in 2024–25.
- **In the Union Budget 2021–22**, in order to further promote the fisheries sector, five major fishing harbours – Kochi, Chennai, Visakhapatnam, Paradip and Petuaghat – were proposed to be developed as hubs of economic activity.
- To promote seaweed cultivation, a **Multipurpose Seaweed Park** at **Tamil Nadu** was also announced **in Union Budget 2021–22.**
- **In Union Budget 2023–24**, a new sub-scheme named **Pradhan Mantri Matsya Kisan Samridhi Sah-Yojana (PM-MKSSY)** has been introduced. It is a Central Sector Sub-scheme under PMMSY with targeted investment of ₹6,000 crore with the **following objectives**:
  - To enhance further the earnings and incomes of fishermen, fish vendors and micro & small enterprises engaged in fisheries sector.
  - Focused intervention to bring about formalisation of the fisheries sector and this includes digital inclusion, facilitating access to institutional finance for capital investment and working capital, incentives to bring about system and institutions to reduce risk in aquaculture and fisheries, incentivising micro enterprises operating in fisheries and aquaculture sector to work on value-chain efficiencies, and incentivising micro and small enterprises to establish supply chains for delivery of safe fish products to consumers, thereby expanding the domestic market and incentives for creation and maintenance of jobs for women in the sector.
  - Under PM-MKSSY, the **National Fisheries Digital Platform (NFDP)** was launched, successfully mobilising and registering fish producers, workers, vendors, and processors.
  - **Fisheries and Aquaculture Infrastructure Development Fund (FIDF)** was introduced to provide financial support for developing infrastructure in both marine and inland fisheries.

Challenges Ahead in Fisheries Sector:

- **Non-availability of quality seeds and fish food**, silted ponds and **lack of awareness** among fishermen.
- **Inadequate extension staff** for fisheries and **training** for fishermen.
- **Inadequate management of the outbreak of major disease**. Common fish diseases include dropsy, fin rot, cloud eye, swim bladder, gas bubble disease, EUS, etc.
- Limited availability of network with field and laboratory facilities.
- **Lack** of **reliable updated data** and resource-specific fishing vessels.

WHITE REVOLUTION OR OPERATION FLOOD

- **Initially** under First Five-Year Plan, **Key Village Scheme** was launched to improve the quality of cattle.
- **National Dairy Development Board (NDDB)** was set up under Second FYP to support, plan and organise dairy development through co-operatives.
- **Thereafter, Intensive Cattle Development** was launched during Third FYP.
- However, **in 1970**, a comprehensive programme was launched which was termed as Operation Flood or White Revolution. It continued till the 1990s.
- The whole idea of Operation Flood revolved around **village milk producer's co-operatives** which procures milk from its members and provides inputs and services along with making modern technology available.
- The Father of White Revolution was **Dr. Verghese Kurien**.

Objectives of Operation Flood:

- Increase milk production and productivity
- Improve rural income
- Assure availability of milk at reasonable prices to the consumers

Operation Flood in Different Phases

Phase I (1970–80)	Phase II (1981–85)	Phase III (1985–96)
18 premier milk sheds were connected to the consumers of four metros, viz. **Mumbai, Delhi, Chennai and Kolkata**, thereby increasing producers' share in milk market.	The milk sheds increased from 18 to 136. Outlets for milk expanded to 290 in urban markets. By the end of 1985, 43,000 village co-operatives were formed covering **42.5 lakh milk** producers.	➤ Dairy co-operatives increased to 72,000. ➤ Milk sheds increased to 173 and women members and Women's Dairy Co-operative Societies increased significantly. ➤ R&D in animal health and nutrition was focussed upon. ➤ Innovations like vaccine for **Theileriosis, bypass protein feed** and **urea-molasses mineral blocks** were made, thereby enhancing productivity.

Overall Achievements in Dairy Sector:

- Dairy sector has grown by around 6 per cent annually in last 4 years (as compared to global growth of around 2%).
- **India is ranked first** in milk production, contributing around **25% of the global milk production**.
- Milk production in India is growing at the Compound Annual Growth Rate **(CAGR) of 5.62%** over the past 10 years. On the other hand, world milk production has grown by 1.5% during 2023 in-comparison to the year 2022 (*Food Outlook June' 2024*).
- The **per capita availability** of milk is **471 grams** per day in India during 2023–24 as against the world average of 329 grams per day in 2023 (*Food Outlook June'2024*).
- **Amul Model** is regarded as the best model for dairying by small and marginal farmers. For the past one and a half decade, India is the leading producer of milk in the world.

- However, **per animal milk productivity** in India is still lower (1,806 kg/year) as compared to the world average (2,310 kg/year), and India accounts **only for around 0.01 per cent** of the global dairy **export market**.

Persisting Challenges in the Dairy Sector:

- Productivity per animal is not satisfactory.
- Livestock diseases.
- Growing pressure on fodder and feed resources with degrading and shrinking grazing areas.
- Growth in innovations and technology developments in dairy productions is far from satisfactory.
- With rising opportunity costs, the activities of grazing, feeding, cleaning and milking buffalo, daily, have become less enticing and lucrative to the rural workforce.
- It is still a secondary source of income as dairy farming is still subsidiary occupation which is affecting productivity per animal.
- Milk adulteration.
- Low level of exports of milk.

Major Initiatives by the Government:

Rashtriya Gokul Mission (*to develop and conserve indigenous breeds of bovines/cows*):

- Launched in 2014.
- Objectives: development and conservation of **indigenous breeds**, increase milk production and productivity, etc.

Indigenous breeds of cows include Gir, Sahiwal, Rathi, Tharparker, Haryana, Kankrej, Red Sindhi, Deoni, etc. **Indigenous breeds of Buffaloes** inlcude Murrah, Mehsana, Jafrabadi, Nili Ravi, Banni and Pandharpuri.

- Strategies involved to achieve the objective:
  1. Breed improvement programme for genetic cattle.
  2. To arrange quality artificial insemination (AI) service at farmer's doorstep.
  3. E-Market portal to connect breeders and farmers **(e-pashuhaat)**. By increasing disease-free cattle.
  4. Establishment of **Gokul Grams** to develop indigenous breeds.
  5. To establish two National Kamdhenu Breeding Centres to develop and conserve indigenous breeds.
  6. **Kamdhenu awards** and **Gopal Ratna Awards** for encouraging farmers/breeder societies to rear indigenous breeds of bovines.

Kamdhenu Award: For best managed indigenous herd by institutions/trusts/NGOs/ gaushalas, etc.

Gopal Ratna Award: For farmers maintaining best herd of indigenous breeds and practicing best management practices.

did you KNOW? Every year, since 2001, **1 June** is observed as **World Milk Day** by the *Food and Agriculture Organisation (FAO)* of the United Nations to acknowledge the importance of milk as a global food and to celebrate the dairy sector. In India, the birthday of Dr. Verghese Kurien, on **26 November**, is observed as **National Milk Day**.

EXAM ESSENTIAL

GOVERNMENT INTERVENTION TO IMPROVE LIVESTOCK HEALTH

National Animal Disease Control Programme (NADCP) – Launched in **2019**, the target of NADCP is to have complete control over Foot and Mouth Disease **(FMD)** and **Brucellosis** in livestock (cattle, buffalo, pig, sheep & goat) **by 2025** and its eventual eradication **by 2030**. This will lead to increased domestic production of milk and ultimately to increased exports of livestock products. **Brucellosis** is a **reproductive disease of cattle and buffaloes** caused by bacterium Brucella abortus.

Foot and Mouth Disease (FMD) is a highly **contagious viral vesicular disease** of cloven-hoofed animals such as cattle, buffaloes, sheep, goats and pigs etc. FMD leads to reduction in milk yield, decreased growth rate, infertility, reduced working capacity in bullocks, and trade embargo in the international market.

Objectives of NADCP include – vaccination of > 500 million livestock against FMD and 36 million female bovine calves annually against Brucellosis. GoI has resolved to vaccinate **100 per cent** cattle, buffalo, sheep, goat and pig population for **FMD** and 100 per cent bovine female calves of 4-8 months of age for **Brucellosis by 2025**.

The programme is being implemented by the ***Ministry of Fisheries, Animal Husbandry & Dairying* with 100 per cent funding by GoI**.

BONUS KNOWLEDGE

AGREEMENT ON AGRICULTURE

The Agreement on Agriculture (AoA) is an **international treaty of the WTO**. It was negotiated during the *Uruguay Round of* the General Agreement on Tariffs and Trade and entered into force with the establishment of the WTO in 1995.

Basic objective of AoA is to reform the principles of, and disciplines on, agricultural policy and also reduce the **distortions** in agricultural trade caused by agricultural protectionism and domestic support or subsidy provided by governments.

AoA has three pillars:

1. Domestic support or subsidy
2. Market access
3. Export subsidy commitment

More details given in Chapter 27 (International Economic Institutions).

Ethanol Blended with Petrol (EBP) Programme

The Government has now set the target of **20 per cent ethanol blending with petrol** to be achieved **by 2025**. Currently, 8.5 per cent of ethanol is blended with petrol in India.

With a view to achieve the target, the Government has allowed production of ethanol from different feed stocks, *viz.* B-Hy & C-Hy molasses, cane juice, sugar syrup, sugar and damaged Foodgrains including surplus FCI rice, maize, etc., by the distilleries either attached with sugar mills or standalone. Financial assistance in the form of interest subvention is also provided to eligible distilleries for augmentation of ethanol production capacity in the country.

PERSISTING CHALLENGES IN AGRICULTURE SECTOR

1. **Land Degradation**: Massive use of chemicals such as pesticides and fertilisers reduces the fertility for judicious application of fertilisers. Use of bio-chemicals as manures and composts must be popularised to restore the **quality of the soil**.
2. **Per Capita Land Holding**: Most holdings are small and uneconomic, so advantages of large-scale farming are not possible now; as a result farmers don't get maximum produce. Due to growth of population and breakdown of joint family system, agricultural lands are being subdivided into smaller and smaller plots. Subdivision leads to **fragmentation of holdings**.
3. **Neglect of Crop Rotation**: Farmers usually cultivate same type of crop year after year; the land loses its fertility. Farmers are reluctant **to adopt new practice** (like crop rotation, mixed cropping) instead of continuing the practices followed by their predecessors.
4. **The Use of Poor-Quality Seeds**: The main cereals are still grown mainly with unimproved seeds. Farmers need to be motivated more to cultivate with **seeds of advance varieties**.
5. **The Indebtedness of the Farmers**: Credit availability to the farmers is one of the major challenges. Indian farmers are perennial debtors; due to crop failure or low price of crops, once they fall into debt, they can never come out of it. They pass on their debt to their successors. There should be a well-structured mechanism for **proper loan availability** to farmers. This can get a boost through 100 per cent financial inclusion.
6. **Inadequate Irrigated Facility**: A huge amount of remains uncultivated for lack of irrigation facility; there is a need for **more and more minor irrigation projects** to bring the whole cultivable areas under irrigated condition.
7. **Labour Problem**: Urbanisation, migration to cities and rising wages of MGNREGS create scarcity of agricultural labours. Whereas in some areas, there is problem of surplus labour or disguised unemployment; this pushes the wage rate below the subsistence level.
8. **Poor Infrastructural Facilities**: Connecting the producing centres with urban areas is of immense need. Due to lack of better communication facilities, farmers depend on middlemen for the disposal of his produce at cheap prices. Therefore, **rural infrastructural facilities** like roads, cold storage and marketing facilities must also be revamped.
9. **Fluctuation is common in agricultural prices**: There is need for **stabilisation of value of agricultural commodities**. Although Agricultural Price Commission (now Agricultural Costs and Prices Commission) has taken up price policies like MSP, PP (Procurement Prices), etc., but all those are not enough. More policies for stabilisation of the prices of agricultural commodities needs to be undertaken.

Doubling of Farmers' Income Report

GoI in 2016 constituted an Inter-Ministerial Expert Committee (headed by **Dr. Ashok Dalwai**) to examine the issues relating to 'Doubling of Farmers' Income' (DFI) and recommend strategies to achieve the same.

The committee submitted its report in 2018 which contained the strategy for doubling of farmers' income by the year 2022.

The DFI strategy as recommended by the committee focused on **following seven sources of income growth**:

1. Improvement in crop productivity.
2. Improvement in livestock productivity.
3. Resource-use efficiency or savings in the cost of production.
4. Increase in the cropping intensity.
5. Diversification towards high-value crops.
6. Improvement in real prices received by farmers.
7. Shift from farm to non-farm occupations.

Major recommendations by the committee are enumerated below:

- NITI Aayog's **Model Land Leasing Act must be adopted by all the States/UTs** in a time-bound manner. It will bring the futile land into much needed use for operational efficiency.
- Apart from food and nutrition security, agriculture should also be **mandated to generate resources as raw materials** to feed and support industrial enterprises. Such incorporation will provide greater elasticity to the markets now circumscribed by consumption as food and fodder.
- Public **investment in agriculture must be raised to 4 per cent of the GDP**, which is currently only 2.76 per cent.
- **Modern machinery** such as laser land leveller, direct seeded rice, zero tillage, raised bed plantation and ridge plantation allow highly efficient farming.
- The **insurance sector** should design a simple natural catastrophe product with affordable premium and simple claim payment methodology.
- **Micro-irrigation systems** (MI) is one of the possible ways to improve water use efficiency; the States with penetration of MI systems and improved adoption of micro-irrigation systems have almost 40 to 50 per cent savings in energy and fertiliser consumption.
- There is need to promote use of **environment-friendly automated farm machinery tools** suited to small-scale operations. The Custom Hiring Centres (CHCs) can be set up to promote use of high-tech machinery for the mechanisation of small and marginal farm holding.
- To adopt a production strategy characterised by: From **'at any cost' to 'minimal cost'**; from **'any how approach' to 'sustainable approach'**; from **'supply-push' to 'demand-pull'** production system.
- All policies and strategies must adopt **'fork to farm' approach**, reversing the 'farm to fork' approach now accepted generally.

After acceptance of the DFI Committee recommendations, the GoI has constituted an 'Empowered Body' to review and monitor the progress. Thereafter, various interventions and schemes have been launched by government for the benefit of farmers, as have been emphasised in various sections of this chapter.

MAJOR REFORMS NEEDED UNDER SECOND GREEN REVOLUTION

- Increasing productivity by increasing the **research and development** in agricultural science and biotechnology.
- Affordable and appropriate **technologies for enhancing energy and water efficiency in order** to promote sustainable agriculture.
- Promote **rainbow revolution** and accelerate agriculture growth to ensure food and nutritional security along with price stability.

- Introduction of **new seeds** which can survive flooding, tolerate drought, extreme heat and salinity.
- Address climate change through techniques like **'precision agriculture'**. For example, land levelling through *laser leveller technology* can be highly useful in conservation of irrigation water.
- To give thrust on **'Conservation Agriculture'**. FAO defined conservation agriculture as a concept for resource-saving agricultural crop production along with acceptable profits and sustained production levels through conserving the environment. **Three broad principles** need to be given thrust under it – *practicing minimum soil disturbance through soil tillage; managing top soil to create permanent organic soil cover; crop rotations.*

Climate Smart Agriculture (CSA)

It is an approach to manage agricultural activities with the dynamics of the climate change and mitigating the effects of climate change on productivity. The concept of CSA was introduced by FAO in 2010.

Aims of CSA include:

1. Sustainably increasing productivity
2. Adapting to climate change
3. Reducing greenhouse gas emissions

Elements of CSA include:

1. Management of farms, crops, livestock, aquaculture
2. Ecosystem and landscape management to conserve ecosystem
3. Management of climate risks/impacts and take mitigation actions
4. Changes in the wider food system

Some best CSA practices include:

- To promote conservation agriculture and sustainable mechanisation
- To diversify through agro-forestry, intercropping or other diversification strategies
- To identify and utilise improved seed varieties that are adapted to climate change (e.g. drought resistant, heat tolerant and flood tolerant)
- To expand irrigation as appropriate based on water availability
- To improve fertiliser application practices to increase fertiliser-use efficiency
- To use fertilisers that are less carbon intensive
- To divert animal waste for reuse (e.g. organic fertiliser, biogas production)
- To improve water-use efficiency

In Puri district of Odisha, rice- and pulse-growing farmers are using climate smart methods of production to increase the productivity and mitigating the effects of climate change.

> **did you KNOW?**
>
> **Torrefaction** – The pollution from stubble burning in winter is a major factor for the sharp decline in air quality. India is testing Swedish technology – torrefaction that can convert rice stubble into 'bio-coal'. The government has funded a pilot project at the National Agri-Food Biotechnology Institute in Mohali (Punjab) with a Swedish company to evaluate the feasibility of the technology.

E-TECHNOLOGY IN PRODUCTION AND MARKETING OF AGRICULTURAL PRODUCE

E-technology is widely believed to comprise the Internet and associated information technologies.

- It was implemented as early as 2007, when the National Policy for Farmers was developed with an emphasis on ICTs.
- It offers numerous benefits to farmers in both production and marketing of agricultural produce in the following ways –
  - **Access to information:** E-technology enables farmers to obtain critical agricultural information such as weather predictions, market pricing, pest management strategies, and best agricultural practices. Farmers may use this information to make educated decisions regarding crop selection, planting time, harvesting, and marketing methods.
  - **Precision:** It enables farmers to apply precision agriculture tools such as sensors, GPS technology, and drones. These instruments enable farmers to monitor crop health, soil moisture levels, and nutrient content, resulting in better resource utilisation and production.
  - **Agricultural machinery:** E-technology platforms may also help farmers find providers of agricultural gear. This can help farmers rent or buy the machinery they need to increase their output.
  - **Spatial data management:** A Geographic Information System (GIS) may be used to manage and analyse spatial data on crop yield and agronomic aspects.
    Example: The ISRO's portal Bhuvan integrates GIS, satellite data, and weather information to analyse agricultural losses, map impacted regions, and expedite insurance claims to provide prompt farmer payments.
  - **Access to Credit:** Firms (banks and non-banks) engaged in financing via agricultural and rural loans can provide customised products and lower loan risk.
    Example: SBI Yono Krishi app addresses farmers' financial, input, and advising needs.
  - **Supply Chain Management:** E-technology improves supply chain management by allowing for real-time tracking of agricultural output from farm to market. Example: e-Choupal.

Major Technology Mission Initiatives in Agriculture

In the recent past, various technology-driven interventions have been undertaken towards agricultural development. Some major interventions include:

- **National e-Governance Plan in Agriculture (NeGP-A)** – A centrally sponsored scheme, NeGP-A has been adopted for development of agriculture through ICT such as Internet, Kiosks, Krishi Vigyan Kendra's, Kisan Call Centres (KCC), Common Service Centres (CSCs), etc.
- **Kisan SMS Portal** – SMS Portal for Farmers for circulation of relevant information such as giving topical and seasonal advisories and providing services through SMSs in local languages.
- **Crop Insurance Mobile App** – It is used to calculate the insurance premium for notified crops based on area, coverage amount and loan amount specific to the farmer.
- **National Agriculture Market (e-NAM)** – It is a pan-India electronic trading portal which links the existing APMC mandis to build a unified national market for agricultural commodities.
- **Seednet** – It provides information on quality seeds. The users can track information on quality control, seed replacement rate, seed multiplication ratio, breeder seeds, certified seeds, etc. Details can also be harnessed regarding seed varieties, seed bank, seed testing labs, seed dealers, test laboratories, certification agencies, etc. through the portal.

- **Green-Ag Project to reduce emissions from agriculture** – It aims to bring at least 104,070 ha of farms under sustainable land and water management and ensure 49 million carbon dioxide equivalent sequestered or reduced through sustainable land use and agricultural practices.

  Project is being implemented in 5 States – Mizoram, Rajasthan, Madhya Pradesh, Odisha and Uttarakhand.

  It is funded by the **Global Environment Facility (GEF)**, while the Department of Agriculture, Cooperation, and Farmers Welfare is the national executing agency.

  Other organisations involved in its implementation are FAO and the Union Ministry of Environment, Forest and Climate Change (MoEF&CC).
- **e-Choupal** – The **e-Choupal initiative of ITC Ltd.** provides farming information and also enables elimination of middlemen. It **also provides access to storage services** and agricultural equipment to the rural farmers. The e-Choupal network has connected 6,500 centres synchronising the efforts of 40,000 villages.
- **Use of AI:** India's Ministry of Agriculture and Farmers Welfare has used Artificial Intelligence (AI) approaches to handle numerous agricultural difficulties and assist farmers. Some of the initiatives are listed below:
  - **'Kisan e-Mitra'** is an AI-powered chatbot that helps farmers with questions concerning the PM Kisan Samman Nidhi plan. This system supports various languages and is being developed to assist also in other government programmes.
  - **National Pest Surveillance System** to combat the loss of product due to climate change. This technology uses artificial intelligence and machine learning to detect crop concerns, allowing for timely action and better harvests.
  - AI-powered analytics employing field images for crop health evaluation and monitoring using satellite, meteorological, and soil moisture information for rice and wheat crops.

SUMMARY

- **Agriculture** – Largest unorganised sector of India – highest share in employment and livelihood creation – important sector for poverty alleviation, employment generation and inclusive growth with multiplier effect – improve India's foreign currency reserves through export of agricultural and allied products like tea, sugar, rice, fish, etc.
- **Kharif Crop** – Sown with the arrival of monsoon – harvested in September–October – rice, maize, jowar, bajra, jute, groundnut, etc.
- **Rabi Crop** – Sown in winter and harvested in the spring – wheat, barley, mustard, peas, sesame, coriander, onion, etc.
- **Zaid Crop** – Summer season crop – grow on dry lands which do not have to wait for monsoon – time period is between Rabi and Kharif crop season, mainly from March to June – watermelon, muskmelon, bitter gourd, pumpkin, cucumber, moong dal, etc.
- **Green Revolution** – Father of Indian Green Revolution is M. S. Swaminathan – initiated in endowed areas and areas with adequate production potential in terms of assured water and infrastructural facilities – High-Yielding Varieties Programme relating to High-Yielding Variety (HYV) seeds was introduced for five crops – wheat, rice, maize, jowar and bajra.
- **Mission for Integrated Development of Horticulture (MIDH)** – Promotes and develops technologies with modern scientific knowledge – all States and UTs are covered – fund-sharing pattern is 60:40 – for north-eastern and hilly States, the fund sharing pattern is 90:10. For UTs, GoI contributes 100 per cent.

- **Genetically Modified Crops** – Foreign gene (transgene) or gene of some other organism is artificially inserted in the plant's own genes – clearance for GM crop is given by the Genetic Engineering Appraisal Committee (GEAC) which functions as a statutory body under the Ministry of Environment, Forests & Climate Change – examples are Bt Cotton, GM Mustard or Dhara Mustard Hybrid-11 (DMH-11).
- **Soil Health Card Scheme** – Soil Health Card (SHC) is given to all farmers to provide each of them with information on soil nutrient status of his/her land holding – nutrient status is given on three macro-nutrients, namely N, P, K; one secondary nutrient, namely S; five micro-nutrients, namely Zn, Fe, Cu, Mn, B' and three physical parameters namely pH, EC, OC.
- **Contract Farming** – An agreement between the farmers and the processing and/or marketing firms for the production and supply of agricultural products at pre-determined prices.
- **Co-operative Farming** – Farmers pool their land, livestock and other implements. The entire farm is managed as a single unit and management is elected by all the members.
- **Kisan Credit Card (KCC)** – Designed by NABARD and introduced in 1998 to facilitate short-term formal credit to farmers – each farmer is provided with KCC and pass book to receive cash credit facilities.
- **Climate Smart Agriculture (CSA)** – An approach to manage agricultural activities with the dynamics of the climate change and mitigating the effects of climate change on productivity – concept of CSA was introduced by Food and Agriculture Organization (FAO) in 2010.

UPSC CSE PREVIOUS YEARS' PRELIMINARY EXAMINATION QUESTIONS

1. Consider the following statements: **[2023]**

1. The Government of India provides Minimum Support Price for Niger (Guizotia abyssinica) seeds.
2. Niger is cultivated as a Kharif crop.
3. Some tribal people in India use Niger seed oil for cooking.

How many of the above statements are correct?

(a) Only one (b) Only two
(c) All three (d) None

2. In the context of India's preparation for Climate-smart Agriculture, consider the following statements: **[2021]**

1. The 'Climate-Smart Village' approach in India is a part of a project led by the Climate Change, Agriculture and Food Security (CCAFS), an international research programme.
2. The project of CCAFS is carried out under Consultative Group on International Agricultural Research (CGIAR) headquartered in France.
3. The International Crops Research Institute for the Semi-Arid Tropics (ICRISAT) in India is one of the CGIAR's research centres.

Which of the statements given above are correct?

(a) 1 and 2 only (b) 2 and 3 only
(c) 1 and 3 only (d) 1, 2 and 3

3. How is permaculture farming different from conventional chemical farming? **[2021]**

1. Permaculture farming discourages monocultural practices but in conventional chemical farming, monoculture practices are predominant.
2. Conventional chemical farming can cause an increase in soil salinity but the occurrence of such phenomenon is not observed in permaculture farming.
3. Conventional chemical farming is easily possible in semi-arid regions but permaculture farming is not so easily possible in such regions.

4. Practice of mulching is very important in permaculture farming but not necessarily so in conventional chemical farming.

Select the correct answer using the codes given below:

(a) 1 and 3 (b) 1, 2 and 4
(c) 4 only (d) 2 and 3

4. Among the following, which one is the least water-efficient crop? **[2021]**

(a) Sugarcane (b) Sunflower
(c) Pearl Millet (d) Red gram

5. Under the Kisan Credit Card scheme, short-term credit support is given to farmers for which of the following purposes? **[2020]**

1. Working capital for maintenance of farm assets
2. Purchase of combine harvesters, tractors and mini trucks
3. Consumption requirements of farm households
4. Post-harvest expenses
5. Construction of family house and setting up of village cold storage facility

Select the correct answer using the code given below:

(a) 1, 2 and 5 only
(b) 1, 3 and 4 only
(c) 2, 3, 4 and 5 only
(d) 1, 2, 3, 4 and 5

6. In India, which of the following can be considered as public investment in agriculture? **[2020]**

1. Fixing minimum support price for agriculture produce of all crops
2. Computerisation of Primary Agriculture Credit Societies
3. Social capital development
4. Free electricity supply of farmers
5. Waiver of agriculture loans by the banking system
6. Setting up of cold storage facilities by the governments

Select the correct answer using the code given below:

(a) 1, 2 and 5 only
(b) 1, 3, 4 and 5 only
(c) 2, 3 and 6 only
(d) 1, 2, 3, 4, 5 and 6

7. Which of the following factors/policies were affecting the price of rice in India in the recent past? **[2020]**

1. Minimum Support Price
2. Government's trading
3. Government's stockpiling
4. Consumer subsidies

Select the correct answer using the code given below:

(a) 1, 2 and 4 only
(b) 1, 3 and 4 only
(c) 2 and 3 only
(d) 1, 2, 3 and 4

8. Consider the following statements: **[2020]**

1. In the case of all cereals, pulses and oil-seeds, the procurement at Minimum Support Price (MSP) is unlimited in any State/UT of India.
2. In the case of cereals and pulses, the MSP is fixed in any State/UT at a level to which the market price will never rise.

Which of the statements given above is/are correct?

(a) 1 only (b) 2 only
(c) Both 1 and 2 (d) Neither 1 nor 2

9. With reference to chemical fertilisers in India, consider the following statements: **[2020]**

1. At present, the retail price of chemical fertilisers is market-driven and not administered by the government.
2. Ammonia, which is an input of urea, is produced from natural gas.
3. Sulphur, which is a raw material for phosphoric acid fertiliser, is a by-product of oil refineries.

Which of the statements given above is/are correct?

(a) 1 only (b) 2 and 3 only
(c) 2 only (d) 1, 2 and 3

10. With reference to pulse production in India, consider the following sentences: **[2020]**

1. Black gram (urad) can be cultivated as both kharif and rabi crop.
2. Green gram (moong) alone accounts for nearly half of pulse production.
3. In the last three decades, while the production of kharif pulses has increased, the production of rabi pulses has decreased.

Which of the statements given above is/are correct?

(a) 1 only (b) 2 and 3 only
(c) 2 only (d) 1, 2 and 3

11. 'The crop is subtropical in nature. A hard frost is injurious to it. It requires at least 210 frost-free days and 50 to 100 centimetres of rainfall for its growth. A light well-drained soil capable of retaining moisture is ideally suited for the cultivation of the crop'. Which one of the following is the crop? **[2020]**

(a) Cotton (b) Jute
(c) Sugarcane (d) Tea

12. What is/are the advantage/advantages of zero tillage in agriculture?

1. Sowing of what is possible without burning the residue of the previous crop.
2. Without the need for nursery of rice saplings, direct planting of paddy seeds in the wet soil is possible.
3. Carbon sequestration in the soil is possible.

Select the correct answer using the code given below:

(a) 1 and 2 only (b) 2 and 3 only
(c) 3 only (d) 1, 2 and 3

13. In the context of India, which of the following is/are considered to be practice(s) of eco-friendly agriculture? **[2020]**

1. Crop diversification
2. Legume intensification
3. Tensiometer use
4. Vertical farming

Select the correct answer using the code given below:

(a) 1, 2 and 3 only
(b) 3 only
(c) 4 only
(d) 1, 2, 3 and 4

14. The economic cost of Foodgrains to the Food Corporation of India is Minimum Support Price and bonus (if any) paid to the farmers plus **[2019]**

(a) Transportation cost only
(b) Interest cost only
(c) Procurement incidentals and distribution cost
(d) Procurement incidentals and charges for go downs

15. With reference to the cultivation of kharif crops in India in the last 5 years, consider the following statements: **[2019]**

1. Area under rice cultivation is the highest.
2. Area under the cultivation of jowar is more than that of oilseeds.
3. Area of cotton cultivation is more than that of sugarcane.
4. Area under sugarcane cultivation has steadily decreased.

Which of the statements given above are correct?

(a) 1 and 3 only (b) 2, 3 and 4 only
(c) 2 and 4 only (d) 1, 2, 3 and 4

16. Among the agricultural commodities imported by India, which one of the following accounts for the highest imports in terms of value in the last 5 years? **[2019]**

(a) Spices (b) Fresh fruits
(c) Pulses (d) Vegetable oils

17. As per the NSSO 70th round 'Situation Assessment Survey of Agricultural Households', consider the following statements: **[2018]**

1. Rajasthan has the highest percentage share of agricultural households among its rural households.
2. Out of the total agricultural households in the country, a little over 60 per cent belong to OBCs.
3. In Kerala, a little over 60 per cent of agricultural households reported to have received maximum income from sources other than agricultural activities.

Which of the statements given above is/are correct?

(a) 2 and 3 only (b) 2 only
(c) 1 and 3 only (d) 1, 2 and 3

18. With reference to the circumstances in Indian agriculture, the concept of **'Conservation Agriculture'** assumes significance. Which of the following falls under the Conservation Agriculture? **[2018]**

1. Avoiding the monoculture practices
2. Adopting minimum tillage
3. Avoiding the cultivation of plantation crops
4. Using crop residues to cover soil surface
5. Adopting spatial and temporal crop sequencing/crop rotations

Select the correct answer using the code given below:

(a) 1, 3 and 4 only
(b) 2, 3, 4 and 5 only
(c) 2, 4 and 5 only
(d) 1, 2, 3 and 5 only

19. With reference to the Genetically Modified mustard (GM mustard) developed in India, consider the following statements: **[2018]**

1. GM mustard has the genes of a soil bacterium that give the plant the property of pest-resistance to a wide variety of pests.
2. GM mustard has the genes that allow the plant cross-pollination and hybridisation.
3. GM mustard has been developed jointly by the IARI and Punjab Agricultural University.

Which of the statements given above is/are correct?

(a) 1 and 3 only (b) 2 only
(c) 2 and 3 only (d) 1, 2 and 3

20. With reference to agricultural soils, consider the following statements: **[2018]**

1. A high content of organic matter in soil drastically reduces its water holding capacity.
2. Soils do not play any role in the sulphur cycle.
3. Irrigation over a period of time can contribute to the salinisation of some agricultural lands.

Which of the statements given above is/are correct?

(a) 1 and 2 only (b) 3 only
(c) 1 and 3 only (d) 1, 2 and 3

21. Consider the following: **[2018]**

1. Areca nut 2. Barley
3. Coffee 4. Finger millet
5. Groundnut 6. Sesamum
7. Turmeric

The Cabinet Committee on Economic Affairs has announced the minimum support price for which of the above?

(a) 1, 2, 3 and 7 only
(b) 2, 4, 5 and 6 only
(c) 1, 3, 4, 5 and 6 only
(d) 1, 2, 3, 4, 5, 6 and 7

22. With reference to organic farming in India, consider the following statements: **[2018]**

1. 'The National Programme for Organic Production' (NPOP) is operated under the guidelines and directions of the Union Ministry of Rural Development.
2. 'The Agricultural and Processed Food Products Export Development Authority' (APEDA) functions as the Secretariat for the implementation of NPOP.
3. Sikkim has become India's first fully organic State.

Which of the statements given above is/are correct?

(a) 1 and 2 only (b) 2 and 3 only
(c) 3 only (d) 1, 2 and 3

23. Consider the following statements: **[2017]**

The nation-wide **'Soil Health Card Scheme'** aims at

1. expanding the cultivable area under irrigation.
2. enabling the banks to assess the quantum of loans to be granted to farmers on the basis of soil quality.
3. checking the overuse of fertilisers in farmlands.

Which of the above statements is/are correct?

(a) 1 and 2 only (b) 3 only
(c) 2 and 3 only (d) 1, 2 and 3

24. What is/are the advantage/advantages of implementing the 'National Agriculture Market' (NAM) scheme? **[2017]**

1. It is a pan-India electronic trading portal for agricultural commodities.
2. It provides the farmers access to nationwide market, with prices commensurate with the quality of their produce.

Select the correct answer using the code given below:

(a) 1 only (b) 2 only
(c) Both 1 and 2 (d) Neither 1 nor 2

25. Which of the following has/have occurred in India after its liberalisation of economic policies in 1991? **[2017]**

1. Share of agriculture in GDP increased enormously.
2. Share of India's exports in world trade increased.
3. FDI inflows increased.
4. India's foreign exchange reserves increased enormously.

Select the correct answer using the codes given below:

(a) 1 and 4 only (b) 2, 3 and 4 only
(c) 2 and 3 only (d) 1, 2, 3 and 4

26. Consider the following statements: **[2017]**

1. The Standard Mark of Bureau of Indian Standards (BIS) is mandatory for automotive tyres and tubes.

2. AGMARK is a quality Certification Mark issued by the Food and Agriculture Organization (FAO).

Which of the statements given above is/are correct?

(a) 1 only (b) 2 only
(c) Both 1 and 2 (d) Neither 1 nor 2

27. Why does the Government of India promote the use of 'neem-coated urea' in agriculture? **[2016]**

(a) Release of Neem oil in the soil increases nitrogen fixation by the soil microorganisms.
(b) Neem coating slows down the rate of dissolution of urea in the soil.
(c) Nitrous oxide, which is a green-house gas, is not at all released into atmosphere by crop fields.
(d) It is a combination of a weedicide and a fertiliser for particular crops.

28. With reference to 'Pradhan Mantri Fasal Bima Yojana' consider the following statements: **[2016]**

1. Under this scheme, farmers will have to pay a uniform premium of 2 per cent for any crop they cultivate in any season of the year.
2. This scheme covers post-harvest losses arising out of cyclones and unseasonal rains.

Which of the statements given above is/are correct?

(a) 1 only (b) 2 only
(c) Both 1 and 2 (d) Neither 1 nor 2

29. In the context of food and nutritional security of India, enhancing the 'Seed Replacement Rates' of various crops helps in achieving the food production targets of the future. But what is/are the constraint/constraints in its wider/greater implementation? **[2014]**

1. There is no National Seeds Policy in place.
2. There is no participation of private sector seed companies in the supply of quality seeds of vegetables and planting materials of horticultural crops.
3. There is a demand–supply gap regarding quality seeds in case of low value and high volume crops.

Select the correct answer using the code given below:

(a) 1 and 2 (b) 3 only
(c) 2 and 3 (d) None of these

30. Among the following States, which one has the most suitable climatic conditions for the cultivation of a large variety of orchids with minimum cost of production, and can develop an export-oriented industry in this field? **[2011]**

(a) Andhra Pradesh
(b) Arunachal Pradesh
(c) Madhya Pradesh
(d) Uttar Pradesh

☞ NO QUESTIONS ASKED
2024, 2022, 2015, 2013, 2012

ANSWER KEY

1. (c)	2. (d)	3. (b)	4. (a)	5. (b)
6. (c)	7. (d)	8. (d)	9. (b)	10. (a)
11. (a)	12. (d)	13. (d)	14. (c)	15. (a)
16. (d)	17. (c)	18. (c)	19. (b)	20. (b)
21. (b)	22. (b)	23. (b)	24. (c)	25. (b)
26. (a)	27. (b)	28. (b)	29. (b)	30. (b)

UPSC CSE PREVIOUS YEARS' MAIN EXAMINATION QUESTIONS

1. Explain the role of millets for ensuring health and nutritional security in India. (Answer in 150 words) **[2024]**

2. How does e-Technology help farmers in production and marketing of agricultural produce? **[2023]**

3. Explain the changes in cropping pattern in India in the context of changes in consumption pattern and marketing conditions. **[2023]**

4. What are the main bottlenecks in upstream and downstream process of marketing of agriculture products in India? **[2022]**

5. What is Integrated Farming system? How is it helpful to small and marginal farmers in India? **[2022]**

6. What are the present challenges before crop diversification? How do emerging technologies provide an opportunity for crop diversification? **[2021]**
7. What are the main constraints in transport and marketing of agricultural produce in India? **[2020]**
8. What are the major factors responsible for making rice-wheat system a success? In spite of this success how has this system become bane in India? **[2020]**
9. How far is **Integrated Farming System** (IFS) helpful in sustaining agricultural production? **[2019]**
10. What do you mean by **Minimum Support Price** (MSP)? How will MSP rescue the farmers from the low income trap? **[2018]**
11. Assess the role of **National Horticulture Mission** (NHM) in boosting the production, productivity and income of horticulture farms. How far has it succeeded in increasing the income of farmers? **[2018]**
12. How has the emphasis on certain crops brought about changes in **cropping patterns** in recent past? Elaborate the emphasis on millets production and consumption. **[2018]**
13. Explain the various **types of revolutions** took place in Agriculture after independence in India. How these revolutions have helped in poverty alleviation and food security in India? (150 words) **[2017]**
14. What are the major reasons for **declining rice and wheat yield** in cropping system? How **crop diversification** is helpful to stabilise the yield of the crops in the system? (250 words) **[2017]**
15. How do **subsidies** affect the cropping pattern, crop diversity and economy of farmers? What is the significance of **crop insurance, minimum support price and food processing** for small and marginal farmers? (250 words) **[2017]**
16. Given the vulnerability of Indian agriculture to vagaries of nature, discuss the need of **crop insurance** and bring out the salient features of the **Pradhan Mantri Fasal Bima Yojana** (PMFBY). **[2016]**
17. **Livestock rearing** has a big potential for providing non-farm employment and income in rural areas. Discuss suggesting suitable measures to promote this sector in India. **[2015]**
18. How can the **'Digital India'** programme help framers to improve farm productivity and income? What steps has the Government taken in this regard? **[2015]**
19. There is a point of view that **APMC's** set-up under the State Acts has not only impeded the development of agriculture but also has been cause of **food inflation** in India. Critically examine. **[2014]**
20. In the villages itself no form of credit organisation will be suitable except the **co-operative society** – All India Rural Credit Survey. **[2014]**
21. Discuss this statement in the background of agriculture finance in India. What constraints and challenges do financial institutions supplying agricultural finance face? How can **technology** be used to better reach and serve rural clients? **[2014]**
22. What are the different types of **agriculture subsidies** given to farmers at the national and at State levels? Critically analyse the agricultural subsidy regime with reference to the distortions created by it. **[2013]**
23. India needs to strengthen the measures to promote **Pink Revolution** in food industry for ensuring better nutrition and health. Critically elucidate the statement. **[2013]**

CHAPTER 16

FOOD SECURITY AND FOOD MANAGEMENT

CHAPTER OUTLINE

- Food Security
- SDG 2: Zero Hunger
- Food Management
- Public Distribution System
- Revamped Public Distribution System (RPDS)
- Targeted Public Distribution System (TPDS)
- Right to Food
- Food Corporation of India (FCI)
- High Level Committee on restructuring of FCI
- National Food Security Act, 2013
- Role During Pandemic
- Limitations of the present TPDS System under NFSA, 2013
- Recent Reforms to improve Public Distribution System
- National Food Security Mission
- Reports related to Food Security
- World Food Programme
- Codex Alimentarius
- Ensuring Rights of Consumers
- The Consumer Protection Act, 2019
- Farm Waste
- How Farm Waste becomes a Threat
- Steps to be followed as Precautionary Measures
- Challenges to Food Security

"Food security exists when all people, at all times, have physical and economic access to sufficient, safe and nutritious food that meets their dietary needs and food preferences for an active and healthy life" **(World Food Summit, 1996)**

FOOD SECURITY

The concepts of food security have evolved in the last thirty years to reflect changes in official policy thinking. The term originated in the mid-1970s, when the World Food Conference (1974) defined food security in terms of food supply-assuring the availability and price stability of basic foodstuffs at the international and national level.

Afterwards, the policy making around food security has traversed a long way till the widely accepted **World Food Summit (1996)** definition which reinforced the multidimensional nature of food security and included **food access, availability, food use and stability**.

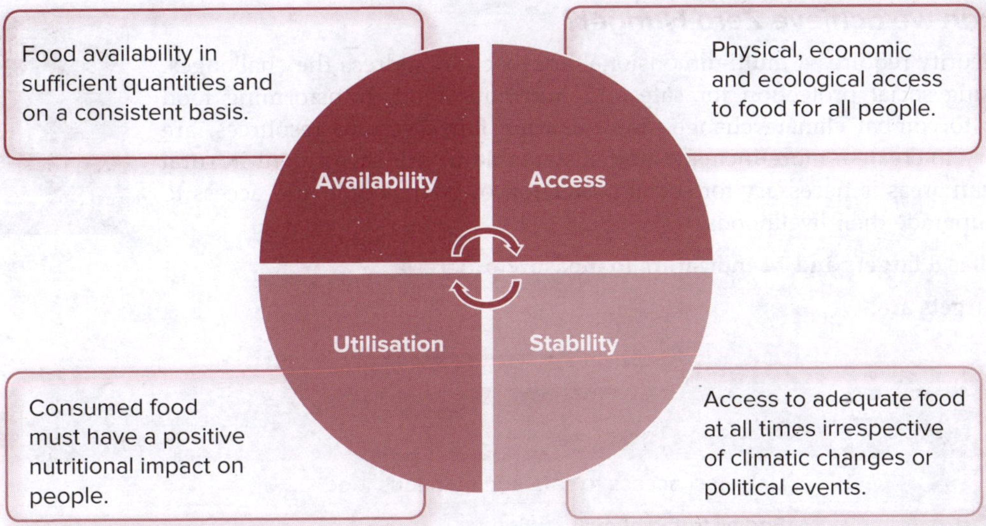

According to the Food and Agriculture Organization (FAO), food security exists when all people, at all times, have physical, social and economic access to sufficient, safe and nutritious food which meets their dietary needs and food preferences for an active and healthy life.

In other words, food security is nothing but the availability of foodstuff, in the long run, to the entire population in terms of quantity and quality and the people having purchasing power to acquire it.

To ensure the food security of our country, a major step in this regard, was taken by the Central Government in 2013, through the introduction of the **National Food Security Act, 2013 (NFSA)**. (*Discussed later in this chapter*)

SDG 2: Zero Hunger

Sustainable Development Goal 2 (SDG 2015–2030): *'End hunger, achieve food security and improved nutrition and promote sustainable agriculture.'*

The 2nd Goal out of 17 goals of Sustainable Development Goals (SDG) established by the United Nations (2015) aims to achieve 'zero hunger'. SDG 2 highlights the complex inter-linkages between food security, nutrition, rural transformation and sustainable agriculture.

Goal 2 is about making a world free of hunger by 2030. The question of hunger and food insecurity has been raised alarmingly since 2015. The trend aggravated due to a combination of several factors like pandemic, climate change, war and conflict, poverty and deepening inequalities, etc.

According to UN, "by 2022, approximately 735 million people – or 9.2 per cent of the world's population – found themselves in a state of chronic hunger – a staggering rise compared to 2019. This data underscores the severity of the situation, revealing a growing crisis."

It has been estimated that about 2.4 billion people faced moderate to severe food insecurity in 2022. This number escalated by 391 million people compared to 2019.

It has been predicted that more than 600 million people will be facing hunger in 2030 across the globe. It spotlighted the colossal challenge to achieve the zero-hunger target.

How can we achieve Zero Hunger?

Food security requires a multi-dimensional approach to address the challenges. Prioritising social protection for safe and nutritious food, transforming food systems to combat climate change, and ensuring fair access to resources, are necessary to create a more inclusive and sustainable world. Investment in rural and urban areas is necessary for social protection of poor people and access to food to upgrade their livelihoods.

SDG 2 has 8 targets and 14 indicators to measure progress.

These targets are:

	Target No.	Targets
Outcome targets	1	Universal access to safe and nutritious food
	2	End all forms of malnutrition
	3	Double the productivity and incomes of small-scale food producers
	4	Sustainable food production systems and resilient agricultural practices
	5	Maintain the genetic diversity in food production
Means of achieving targets	6	Invest in rural infrastructure, agricultural research, technology and gene banks
	7	Prevent agricultural trade restrictions, market distortions and export subsidies
	8	Ensure stable food commodity markets and timely access to information

FOOD MANAGEMENT

India runs one of the largest food management programmes in the world through a systematic implementation of food security network. India's food management programme includes food procurement, allocation, storage and the issue of food subsidy along with the various Government measures for effective food and nutritional security.

Three issues are mainly dealt by the Government under food management policy:

1. ***Procurement*** of food grains from farmers at remunerative prices.
2. ***Distribution*** of foodgrains to consumers, particularly the vulnerable sections of society at affordable prices under the National Food Security Act (NFSA), 2013 and other welfare schemes of the Government.
3. ***Maintenance of buffer stock*** to ensure food security and price stability.

The backbone of food management is the **Public Distribution System (PDS) which ensures the** distribution of foodgrains to the proper beneficiaries. Food Corporation of India **(FCI)** is the nodal agency which undertakes procurement and storage of foodgrains.

Procurement of foodgrains at Minimum Support Prices (MSP) from farmers

Storage at FCI Godowns and issue to respective States

Distribution to beneficiaries by the States at Central Issue Price under Targeted Public Distribution System (TPDS)

Food Management in India through PDS

Public Distribution System (PDS)

- The PDS was first introduced in India on 14 January 1945, during the Second World War. Thereafter, FCI launched PDS in **1965**. It is operated under the joint responsibility of the **Central and State Governments**.
- PDS seeks to provide to the beneficiaries, **two cereals** (rice and wheat) and **four essential commodities** (sugar, edible oil, soft coke and kerosene oil). The State Governments may add other essential commodities like pulses, salt, ordinary clothes, school textbooks, etc.
- These items are provided to the beneficiaries through **Fair Price Shops** (FPSs) or popularly, **ration shops**.
- **Responsibility for storage, transportation and bulk allocation of foodgrains** to the States and procurement through FCI is managed by the **Central Government** and **distribution of the same to beneficiaries and supervision of FPSs** are managed by the **State Governments**.
- Operational responsibility of **identification** of the **Below Poverty Line (BPL)** households, **issue of ration cards**, etc., lies with the State Governments.

Revamped Public Distribution System (RPDS)

It was launched in **1992** with an objective to **streamline and strengthen the PDS** and to improve its reach in far-flung, hilly, remote and inaccessible areas in order to benefit the poorer sections living there.

Targeted Public Distribution System (TPDS)

- To address the failures in PDS, the Central Government launched **TPDS in 1997** with a **focus on poor in all areas**, making this scheme a pro-poor scheme.
- The scheme divided the entire population into two categories – **Below Poverty Line (BPL)** and **Above Poverty Line (APL)**.
- Later in 2001, another category **Antyodaya Anna Yojana (AAY)** for 'poorest of the poor' was added to fix issue prices accordingly for **BPL population** whose income is **below ₹15,000 per annum**. Initially, per BPL household quantity of foodgrains supplied was 10 kg; later from April 2002, it was increased to 35 kg per household per month.

- The Central Issue Prices (CIPs) for APL were fixed at 100 per cent of the economic cost; for BPL at 50 per cent of the economic cost.
- Because of the high cost for APL, many did not buy from PDS, and it resulted in high build-up costs of excess foodgrains stored in FCI godowns. Subsequently, BPL and APL prices were reduced and fixed as mentioned below:

Category	Wheat (₹/kg)	Rice (₹/kg)
APL	6.1	8.3
BPL	4.15	5.65
AAY	2	3

RIGHT TO FOOD

The concept of Right to Food was first recognised in the UN Declaration of Human Rights in 1948. In 1996, the formal adoption of the Right to Adequate Food in World Food Summit marked a milestone achievement towards ethical and human rights dimension of food security.

National Food Security Act, 2013

Right to food has been legally recognised by India, through the implementation of NFSA, 2013 and it extends to the whole of India.

- It marks a **paradigm shift in the approach to food security from welfare to rights-based approach.** It includes:
  1. Targeted Public Distribution System **(TPDS)**.
  2. Mid-Day Meal **(MDM)** Scheme, launched in 1995 as a centrally sponsored scheme.
  3. **Integrated Child Development Services (ICDS) Scheme**, launched in 1975 as a centrally sponsored scheme.
- Under NFSA, **75 per cent of the rural population** and **50 per cent of the urban population receive subsidised foodgrains** through TPDS. It ensures supply of **subsidised foodgrains to the bottom 67 per cent of the population as per 2011 census**.
- Presently, NFSA provides coverage to over 81.35 crore persons as per Census 2011, i.e., **two-third of the population** receives highly subsidised foodgrains under NFSA. The Act provides coverage to the people under the following two categories:
  1. **Antyodaya Anna Yojana (AAY) Households** – with monthly entitlement of **35 kg foodgrains per AAY household per month**.
  2. **Priority Households** – with monthly entitlement of **5 kg per person per month** for eligible households under 'priority' category.
- Beneficiaries under the Act are entitled for subsidised foodgrains at **₹1/₹2/₹3 per kg** for **nutri-cereals/wheat/rice**, respectively.
- The identification of the beneficiaries in this case is done by the States/UTs, and it is a continuous process, which involves **exclusion of ineligible/fake/duplicate ration cards** and also **exclusion on account of death**, migration, etc. and **inclusion on account of birth and also that of genuine left-out households**.

- The Act also provides to implement **DBT** of subsidy in the form of transferring cash directly into the bank account of beneficiaries instead of giving them foodgrains, etc. at subsidised prices through ration shops.
- Till now, **in three UTs, namely, Chandigarh, Puducherry and the urban areas of Dadra and Nagar Haveli**, the NFSA is being implemented in cash transfer mode.
- The Government has released the first-ever State Ranking Index for the NFSA based on three pillars to evaluate the implementation of the National Food Security Act (NFSA), 2013, and Targeted Public Distribution System (TPDS) operations across the States and Union Territories. The third pillar focuses on nutrition initiatives of the department. Odisha has got the first rank in the State Ranking Index (score of 0.836).
- NFSA also seeks to provide food and nutritional security in human life cycle, through a widespread network of **ICDS centres** and also through schools, under the **Mid-Day Meal (MDM) Scheme**.
- A criticism of the National Food Security Act is that the beneficiaries are based on the 2011 census. The number of people likely to be affected by food security has increased since then and may have remained uncovered till date.
- For the effective and uniform implementation of NFSA 2013, the centre introduced **Pradhan Mantri Garib Kalyan Anna Yojana (PM-GKAY)**, a new integrated food security programme that was implemented from 2020 (details given later).
- PM-GKAY subsumed the two subsidy schemes of Department of Food and Public Distribution (a) Food Subsidy to Food Corporation of India (FCI) (b) Food Subsidy for decentralised procurement states dealing with procurement, allocation and delivery of free foodgrains to the states under NFSA.

Food Corporation of India (FCI)

HQ	It is a public sector enterprise headquartered in **Delhi**.
Established	FCI was established in **1965** under the Food Corporations Act, 1964 as a main agency for the execution of food policies of the Central Government.
Objectives	➤ Effective price support operations for safeguarding the interests of the farmers. ➤ Distribution of foodgrains throughout the country under PDS. ➤ Maintaining satisfactory level of operational and buffer stock of foodgrains to ensure National Food Security.
Functions	➤ Procurement, storage, movement, distribution and sale of foodgrains on behalf of the central Government. ➤ FCI procures foodgrains at **support prices** and supplies them at **issue prices**. It is sole repository of foodgrains for PDS, and it also maintains the **buffer stock** and **strategic reserves** as per **Foodgrain Stocking Norms, 2015**.
Economic cost of foodgrains to FCI	Economic Cost includes: ➤ **Procurement Price** (MSP) ➤ **Procurement Cost** (incidental & statutory charges, labour & transport charges, charges paid to State Government for storage & interest) ➤ **Distribution Cost** (freight, handling charges, losses during transport & storage, etc.)

BONUS KNOWLEDGE

FOODGRAIN STOCKING NORMS, 2015

The Central Government revised Buffer Norms in 2015 and changed its nomenclature to Foodgrain Stocking Norms. Foodgrains here include **Rice and Wheat only**. The targets of the revised norms are the following:

1. To meet the prescribed minimum stocking norms for food security.
2. To ensure monthly release of foodgrain (wheat & rice) for supply through the TPDS/other welfare schemes.
3. To meet the emergency situations arising out of unexpected crop failure, natural disasters, etc.
4. To use and supply foodgrains for market intervention to moderate their open market prices.

To meet the above targets, the foodgrain stock which is to be kept in the central pool by FCI, is classified into two categories:

1. **Operational Stock or Buffer Stock** (i.e. stock earmarked for TPDS + stock for other welfare schemes + food security stock). Operational stock is fixed by the Central Government at the beginning of each quarter.
2. **Strategic Reserves** (2 million tonnes of rice and 3 million tonnes of wheat). These 5 million tonnes of strategic reserves has to be maintained by FCI at the beginning of every quarter.

In case, the stock of foodgrains is more than the revised figures of Operational stock + Strategic Reserves in the beginning of the quarter, the excess stock is to be offloaded in the market through open sale or through exports.

Importance of Buffer Stocks for Stabilising Agricultural Prices

- Buffer stocks help in keeping up price stability. Grains are released in the market when prices rise, and procured during surplus to check price crash.
- Buffer stocks prevent market manipulation, hoarding and black marketing by unscrupulous traders.
- Food security is ensured by continuous supply of food grains during natural calamity, pandemics, etc.
- Buffer stocks mitigate the impact of seasonal fluctuations of agricultural production, and ensure steady market supply between harvests.

Challenges associated with the Storage of Buffer Stock

- Wastages due to inadequate storage infrastructure in India.
- Maintaining large buffer stocks is associated with high storage costs.
- Storage facilities are not distributed proportionately across different states, higher transportation costs and other logistical challenges are also involved.
- More than necessary procurement without timely distribution often results in overstocking, rotting of grains.
- Unscientific and outdated method of storage.

Measures to support Foodgrain Storage Infrastructure

- To upgrade the storage infrastructure for foodgrains and enhance the storage capacity in India, steel silos are constructed in PPP.
- To enhance foodgrain storage in hilly and remote areas, the use of Flospan, a type of Mobile Storage Unit (MSU), in collaboration with the World Food Programme (WFP) is being explored.
- To modernise government grain warehouses, GoI has partnered with WFP and IGMRI to pilot 'Smart Warehouse'. These warehouses utilise sensors to monitor temperature, humidity, airflow, etc. and provide real-time data to enhance storage and reduce losses.

BONUS KNOWLEDGE

High Level Committee on Restructuring of FCI

The High-Level Committee (HLC) on the restructuring of the Food Corporation of India (FCI) was established in 2014 by the Ministry of Consumer Affairs, Food and Public Distribution (MoCAF), Government of India. **Shri Shanta Kumar** served as the **Chairman** of the Committee, which submitted its report in 2015 on the restructuring of FCI.

Important Recommendations

On procurement related issues

- The committee recommended FCI to hand over all procurement operations of wheat, paddy and rice to the states that have enough experience in this regard and sufficient infrastructure for procurement.
- Levy on rice millers should be abolished.

On PDS and NFSA related issues

- GoI should postpone the implementation of NFSA in those states that have not done end to end computerisation and have not set up vigilance committees to check pilferage from PDS.
- Reduction of the number of beneficiaries under NFSA from the current 67% to 40%.

On stocking and movement related issues

- FCI should outsource its stocking operations to different agencies like Central Warehousing Corporation, State Warehousing Corporation, Private Sector under Private Entrepreneur Guarantee (PEG) scheme, etc.

On Buffer Stocking Operations and Liquidation Policy

- A transparent liquidation policy is needed which should automatically come into operation when FCI is faced with surplus stocks.

On direct subsidy to farmers

- Farmers should be given direct cash subsidy (of about ₹7000/ha) and then deregulating the fertiliser sector.

Limitations of the Present TPDS System under NFSA, 2013

- With NFSA, the **burden of subsidy** has increased to the Government.
- **Improper targeting**, i.e., there still lies issues with the proper identification of appropriate beneficiaries. Consequently, a large section of people who would have received the benefit of TPDS, have been excluded.

- **Leakages and diversion** of the foodgrains, kerosene oil, etc. by the distributors and FPS owners in many cases before they reach the poor beneficiaries. This figure of leakage may be as high as 40 per cent.
- **Delayed and irregular arrival of foodgrains** in FPSs due to an improper and casual approach in distribution in many cases.
- **Errors in the digital ration cards** given to the poor beneficiaries by mistakenly considering them under APL category. As a result, they are not able to get subsidised foodgrains.
- **Ghost Cardholders still remain** – The advantage of this phenomenon is very much enjoyed by FPS owners to perform leakages. However, with the efforts of Government, numbers of such cards have been drastically reduced.

Recent Reforms to improve Public Distribution System

1. **'One Nation, One Ration Card' or Integrated Management of Public Distribution System (IM-PDS)** – Launched in **2018** in all States/UTs, the objective of IM-PDS Scheme is to have **nation-wide portability** of ration card holders under NFS Act, 2013. Through this, migratory ration card holders can lift their entitled foodgrains **from any FPS in India**. This can be enjoyed by using the same ration card issued by their home State/UT but after biometric authentication.
2. **Automation of FPS** – In order to bring efficiency in allocation and distribution of foodgrains through tracking the sale of foodgrains to actual card holders on a real-time basis.

   So far, more than 88 per cent of FPSs in India have been automated through the installation of **ePoS (electronic point of sale) devices**, thereby ensuring end-to-end computerisation.
3. **Digitisation of Ration Cards** and their **Aadhaar seeding** to enable distribution of foodgrains to beneficiaries after biometric authentication.
4. **DBT Scheme** – It is a scheme for direct cash transfer of food subsidy to the bank account of the beneficiaries. Using subsidy amount, the beneficiaries can buy foodgrains directly from the market at a market price. It is optional for States/UTs to implement this DBT Scheme. So far, three **UTs** (Chandigarh, Puducherry and Dadra and Nagar Haveli) in India are implementing this DBT Scheme for cash transfer of food subsidy to beneficiaries directly to their bank accounts.
5. **Use of GPS technology** – To track the movement of trucks carrying foodgrains from the State depots to FPSs.
6. The Government has started distributing **fortified rice** under **Integrated Child Development Scheme** and **PM Poshan** schemes across the country from 2021–22 to fight the malnutrition and micronutrient deficiencies among pregnant women, lactating mothers, children, etc.
7. GoI is committed to achieve **100 per cent e-KYC** compliance nationwide.
8. Beneficiaries can authenticate their **Aadhaar biometrics at any Fair Price Shop.**
9. For post-harvest lending to farmers, Credit Guarantee Scheme for electronic-negotiable warehouse receipt (e-NWR)-based Pledge Financing (CGS-NPF) has been approved.

EXAM ESSENTIAL

PRADHAN MANTRI GARIB KALYAN ANNA YOJANA (PM-GKAY)

Pradhan Mantri Garib Kalyan Anna Yojana (**PM-GKAY**) is a part of Atmanirbhar Bharat for supplying **free food grains to migrants and poor**.

The scheme started during Covid-19 pandemic and has been operational since 2020. Under this scheme, the centre provides 5 kg of free food grains per month to the poor. This is in addition to the subsidised (₹2–3 per kg) ration provided under the National Food Security Act (NFSA) to families covered under the Public Distribution System (PDS). The food grain and the amount may be variable.

Benefits of the Scheme:

- PM-GKAY provides 5 kg of food grain to each family holding a ration card free of cost and the 5 kg of subsidised food grain already offered through the Public Distribution System (PDS).
- Wheat has been allocated to 6 States/UTs – Punjab, Haryana, Rajasthan, Chandigarh, Delhi, and Gujarat, and rice has been provided to the remaining States/UTs.

Eligibility to avail benefits under the Scheme:

- Families belonging to Antyodaya Anna Yojana (AAY) and Priority Households (PHH) categories are eligible for PM-GKAY. PHH are to be identified by State Governments/Union Territory Administrations as per criteria evolved by them. AAY families are to be identified by States/UTs as per the criteria prescribed by the Central Government.
- Households headed by widows or terminally ill persons or disabled persons or persons aged 60 years or more with no assured means of subsistence or societal support.
- All primitive tribal households.
- Landless agriculture labourers, marginal farmers, rural artisans/craftsmen such as potters, tanners, weavers, blacksmiths, carpenters, slum dwellers, and persons earning their livelihood on daily basis in the informal sector like porters, coolies, rickshaw pullers, hand cart pullers, fruit and flower sellers, snake charmers, rag pickers, cobblers, destitutes and other similar categories in both rural and urban areas.
- All eligible Below Poverty Line families of HIV positive persons.

The Union Cabinet approved **to continue to provide free food grains** to about 81.35 crore beneficiaries under the PM-GKAY **for a period of 05 years with effect from 1 January, 2024**.

National Food Security Mission

National Food Security Mission (NFSM) was launched as a Centrally Sponsored Scheme in 2007.

The objective was to increase the production of rice, wheat and pulses through area expansion and productivity enhancement; restoring soil fertility and productivity; creating employment opportunities; and enhancing farm level economy.

Coarse cereals were included from 2014–15 under NFSM.

Target of **additional production under NFSM:**

During 12th Five Year Plan		Beyond the 12th Plan	
	Additional Production Targets		New Additional Production Targets
Rice	10 million tonnes	Rice	5 million tonnes
Wheat	8 million tonnes	Wheat	3 million tonnes
Pulses	4 million tonnes	Pulses	3 million tonnes

During 12th Five Year Plan		Beyond the 12th Plan	
	Additional Production Targets		New Additional Production Targets
Coarse cereals	3 million tonnes	Nutri-cum-coarse cereals	2 million tonnes
Total	**25 million tonnes of foodgrains**	**Total**	**13 million tonnes of foodgrains**

At present NFSM comprises of the sub-components viz., **NFSM-Rice, NFSM-Wheat, NFSM-Pulses, NFSM-Coarse Cereals, NFSM-Nutri-Cereals and NFSM-Commercial Crops**. Currently, NFSM is being implemented in identified districts of 28 States and 2 Union Territories (UTs) *viz*. Jammu & Kashmir (J&K) and Ladakh in the country.

In 2021, **National Mission on Edible Oils – Oil Palm (NMEO-OP)** was launched to augment the availability of edible oil in the country by harnessing area expansion and through price incentives. This has been the first instance of price assurance to the oil palm farmers from the Government for the Fresh Fruit Bunches (FFBs). This is known as the Viability Price (VP) and is to protect the farmers from the fluctuations of the international crude palm oil (CPO) prices.

Outcome of the Scheme

NFSM has resulted in an increase of total foodgrains production. The productivity of foodgrains which was 2028 kg/ha in 2014–15, has increased.

Especially noteworthy is the production of pulses, which has increased tremendously.

REPORTS RELATED TO FOOD SECURITY

State of Food Security and Nutrition in the World Report

- It is published annually since 2017, with the joint efforts of:
  1. FAO
  2. International Fund for Agricultural Development
  3. United Nations Children's Fund
  4. World Food Programme
  5. WHO
- The report provides estimates on **food insecurity, hunger and malnutrition** at the global and regional levels.
- The objective behind this report is **to achieve food security, improve nutrition levels and also end hunger as per the SDG Goal 2 agenda**.

State of Food Security and Nutrition in the World 2024 (SOFI 2024) Report

- Proportion of the population unable to afford a healthy diet in India (2022) – 55.6 per cent
- Number of people unable to afford a healthy diet in India (2022) – 788.2 million
- About 13 per cent of the population of India suffers from chronic undernourishment.
- Prevalence of Wasting in Children (<5 Years) in 2022 – 18.7 per cent
- Prevalence of Anaemia in Women (15–49 Years) in 2019 – 53 per cent

Key Findings Related to India (in millions)

Earlier	Indicator	Later
2004–06 (246.5)	Number of Undernourished People	2021–23 (194.6)
2014–16 (N.R.)	Number of Severely Food-Insecure People	2021–23 (N.R.)
2014–16 (N.R.)	Number of Moderately or Severely Food-Insecure People	2021–23 (N.R.)
	Number of Children (<5 years) Affected by Wasting	2022 (21.9)
2012 (52.5)	Number of Children (<5 years) who are Stunted	2022 (36.1)
2012 (2.8)	Number of Children (<5 years) who are Overweight	2022 (3.2)
2012 (33.6)	Number of Children (<5 years) who are Obese	2022 (71.4)
2012 (171.5)	Number of Women (15–49 years) affected by Anaemia	2019 (187.3)
2012 (5.9)	Number of Infants (0–5 months) exclusively Breastfed	2022 (7.2)
2012 (7.7)	Number of Babies with Low Birthweight	2020 (6.3)

[N.R. = Not Reported]

EXAM ESSENTIAL

GLOBAL HUNGER INDEX (GHI)

GHI is a tool to measure hunger at global, regional and national levels. It reflects the progresses made or setbacks faced by countries in tackling the grave issue of hunger.

The Index is published **annually** by **Concern Worldwide and Welthungerhilfe** jointly.

The composite score under GHI to rank countries is based on **4 indicators**:

1. **Rates of undernourishment** (i.e. insufficient calorie intake due to inadequate food supply).
2. **Child Stunting** (low height as compared to the age; for children under 5 years of age).
3. **Child Wasting** (low weight when compared to height; for children under 5 years of age).
4. **Child Mortality** (deaths under the age of 5 years reflecting inadequate nutrition and unhealthy environment).

- India ranked 105th (out of 127 countries) in the 2024 GHI report, against 111th in the report of 2023.
- India's 2024 GHI score is 27.3. It is considered 'serious' as per the GHI Severity of Hunger Scale.

WORLD FOOD PROGRAMME

The **World Food Programme (WFP)** is the leading humanitarian organisation saving lives and changing lives, **delivering food assistance in emergencies** and **working with communities to improve nutrition and build resilience.**

WFP was awarded the Nobel Peace Prize in 2020 for its efforts to **combat hunger**, for its contribution to bettering conditions for peace in conflict affected areas and for acting as a driving force in **efforts to prevent the use of hunger as a weapon of war** and conflict

BONUS KNOWLEDGE

FOOD AND AGRICULTURE ORGANIZATION (FAO)

FAO is a **specialised agency of the United Nations** that leads international efforts to defeat hunger.

Headquarters: Rome, Italy

Established: 16 October 1945 (**World Food Day** is celebrated on **16 October**)

Objective: To achieve the food security for all and make sure that people have regular access to enough high-quality food to lead active, healthy lives.

World Food Summit: In 1996, FAO organised the World Food Summit. The Summit concluded with the signing of the **Rome Declaration**, which established the goal of reducing the number of people who suffer from hunger to half by the year 2015.

FAO Food Price Index (FFPI) is a measure of the monthly change in international prices of a basket of food commodities.

Codex Alimentarius

The Codex Alimentarius Commission (CAC) is an international food standards body established jointly by the **Food and Agriculture Organization (FAO)** and the **World Health Organization (WHO)** in 1963 with the objective of **protecting consumer's health and ensuring fair practices** in food trade.

The Agreement on Application of Sanitary and Phytosanitary Measures (SPS) of the World Trade Organization (WTO) recognises Codex standards, guidelines and recommendations as reference standards for international trade and trade dispute settlements.

India became the member of Codex Alimentarius **in 1964**.

International Grains Council (IGC)

The International Grains Council (IGC) is an intergovernmental organisation that aims to foster international cooperation in grains trade. IGC promotes 'expansion, openness and fairness in the grains sector'. It also stimulates grain market stability for world food security. The IGC monitors and reports on the global markets for wheat, maize (corn), rice, and other coarse grains like barley, sorghum, and oats. Its main functions include collecting and disseminating information on grain production, consumption, stocks, trade, and prices, as well as analysing and forecasting market trends.

- India is a signatory to the International Grains Agreement (IGA) 1995 and Grain Trade Convention (GTC) 1995, and it is effective from 1st July 1995.

- IGC was established in 1949 as the International Wheat Council. The present name was adopted in 1995. Headquarters of IGC: **London**.
- Its membership comprises 11 producing members **(including India)** and 18 importing members.

did you KNOW?

SAARC FOOD BANK

South Asian Association for Regional Cooperation (SAARC) countries have signed the Agreement to set up the SAARC Food Bank in pursuance of the decision taken in the 14th SAARC Summit held in New Delhi in 2007. The Food Bank aims to provide food security to the people of the region. SAARC Food Bank has a reserve of foodgrains to be maintained by each member states. The reserve consists of either wheat or rice, or a combination of both as assessed share of the country.

ENSURING RIGHTS OF CONSUMERS

Ensuring rights of consumers is the responsibility of the Department of Consumer Affairs (DCA) under the *Ministry of Consumer Affairs, Food and Public Distribution*.

In this regard, DCA deals with the following major Acts:

- Implementation of **Consumer Protection Act**, 1986.
- Implementation of **Bureau of Indian Standards Act**, 2016.
- Implementation of **Standards of Weights and Measures** – The Legal Metrology Act, 2009.
- Implementation of **the Essential Commodities (Amendment) Act, 2020**.
- Implementation of **the Prevention of Black Marketing and Maintenance of Supplies of Essential Commodities Act, 1980**.

Among above legislations, the reforms have been undertaken by the Government in recent years to bring improvements, especially in the legislative aspect of protecting consumers. Accordingly, much suitable **Consumer Protection Act**, 2019, has been enacted.

The Consumer Protection Act, 2019

The new Act **has replaced** the three-decade-old **Consumer Protection Act, 1986**. The old Act now stands repealed. It is a law which protects the interests of the consumers.

Under the Act, a **consumer is defined as** 'a person who avails the services and buys any goods for self-use. If the person buys/avails it for resale/commercial purpose, then he/she is not considered as consumer. This definition covers all types of transactions (online + offline) now'.

The **Act now covers** 'all goods and services (including telecom and housing construction) and all modes of transaction. However, free and personal services continue to be excluded from the ambit of the new Act'.

The Act enshrines following **six rights of consumers**:

1. **Right to be informed** (i.e. to have information about the quantity, quality, purity, potency, price and standard of the goods and services)
2. **Right to safety** (i.e. to be protected from hazardous goods and services, unfair and restrictive trade practices)
3. **Right to choose** (i.e. to have a variety of goods and services at competitive prices)

4. **Right to be heard**
5. **Right to seek redressal**
6. **Right to consumer education**

Major Changes incorporated in the 2019 Act

1. The new Act **now covers e-commerce** transactions, which was not there **earlier**.
2. Under the new Act, the money spent by a consumer on buying the product till that time (say after discount) will determine the value of the case **instead of** the previous practice of taking total value (say MRP) of the product/services.
3. **Product Liability**: The Act now makes manufacturers/service providers **liable for giving compensation** to the consumer in case their product causes loss/injury to the consumer due to 'defective product or deficiency in service'. **Earlier**, the consumer was compensated only with the product cost. Moreover, the **product liability** is extended to even service providers and sellers now.
4. **Definition of unfair trade practices** has also been broadened to include 'sharing of personal information by consumer in confidence, unless disclosed in accordance with any law'.
5. **There is an enhancement in pecuniary jurisdiction** of district and state-level Consumer Disputes Redressal Commission **(CDRCs)**. For district level, it has been increased from ₹20 lakh to ₹1 crore. While state-level CDRCs will hear complaints when the value of goods or service is up to ₹10 crore.
6. The Act now allows consumers to file their **complaint electronically from anywhere**. **Earlier**, they were required to file complaint in the area where seller or service provider is located. This is an apt amendment considering large increase in e-commerce transactions.
7. Now, the Act provides for establishment of a **central regulator with the name Central Consumer Protection Authority (CCPA).** CCPA will deal with issues such as violation of consumer rights, unfair trade practices, misleading advertisements and even faulty and fake products and it may also impose penalties. **Earlier**, there was no separate regulator.
8. **Penalties** have also been strengthened – up to 3 years of imprisonment or fine (₹25,000–₹1 lakh) or both. **Earlier**, it was 1 month to 3 years of imprisonment or fine (₹2,000–₹10,000) or both.
9. The new Act also provides for **'mediation'** as an alternate dispute resolution mechanism. It did not exist in the earlier Act.

FARM WASTE

It is a mixture of animal faeces, urine and milk, pesticides and other chemicals. Other common waste materials found on farms include: plastic wrap, plastic chemical containers, feed bags, fertiliser bags, paper and cardboard, machinery, motors, rubber, piping and fittings, timber, concrete, engine and hydraulic oil, dead livestock and animal medicines.

How Farm Waste becomes a Threat

- **Pesticides, ammonia, fertilisers, oils, etc.** when mixed with drinking water can have serious health threat.
- Presence of toxic chemicals reduces **the soil fertility, reduces produce quality** and results in ecological imbalance. Overall **agricultural yield** may also get affected in the long run. High levels

of **nitrogen and phosphorus released from** fertilisers, manure and animal waste in surface waters (ponds, lakes, rivers, etc.) **deplete dissolved oxygen**, thereby affecting the aquatic life.

- Other chemical compounds such as heavy metals and ammonia can also potentially **harm aquatic life and kill fish**.
- The chemicals are sprayed on farmland using sprayers, through which droplets are produced which can remain in air and may be carried away by wind. This is termed as **spray drift.**
- **Stagnant solid wastes** provide a medium for **flies to breed** through which diseases easily get transmitted to humans and other animals.
- Factory-farmed animals are given **antibiotics** in their food to prevent infection. Animal wastes contain bacteria. As only a certain portion of antibiotics is digested by farm animals, their secreted waste may also contain antibiotics. Thus, there lies a possibility for development of **antibiotic-resistant bacteria**, which may later pass to humans when water gets contaminated with the farm waste.

Steps to be followed as Precautionary Measures

- Farm wastes like fencing wire, parts of vehicles and corrugated iron should not be left out and instead be **collected or recycled**.
- Products made from **asbestos** should **not be reused or recycled**. These wastes must be handled appropriately and disposed of safely.
- **Tree and plant waste** can be left in place for natural habitation or use as firewood.
- **Biodegradable wastes** may be dumped separately in a pit for making manures.
- Burning a tree, plant and stubble is another management practice where impacts may be controlled. At the time of **burning** them, the fact of **wind direction** is to be kept in mind.
- Precaution must be taken to ensure that the manure from farms is treated, so that it **does not reach waterways and pollute them**.
- **Educating landowners, farmers**, etc. needs to be done more intensely.
- More **incentives, subsidies** should be in place by Government to effectively tackle farm waste that has to be provided.

Thus, an effective policy by the Government to tackle farm waste is the need of the hour.

CHALLENGES TO FOOD SECURITY

1. Farmers struggle to transport and store their goods due to lack of suitable infrastructure. This leads to excessive waste and poor profitability for farmers.
2. Climate change-related severe weather events have resulted in crop failures and food shortages. Floods, droughts, and heatwaves are becoming more frequent and severe, reducing food output and raising food costs.
3. Poor agricultural practices such as overcultivation, excessive pesticide usage, and inappropriate irrigation techniques have resulted in decreasing soil fertility and crop yields.

The need is to develop policy responses and adaptation of strategies based on research in agriculture to overcome the effects of climate change through climate smart agriculture, proper monitoring of public distribution program, improved storage capacities, handling water allocation for agriculture, land use patterns, food trade, post-harvest food processing etc., to ensure long term stability of food prices and food safety.

SUMMARY

- **Food Security** – According to Food and Agriculture Organization (FAO), food security exists when all people, at all times, have physical, social and economic access to sufficient, safe and nutritious food which meets their dietary needs and food preferences for an active and healthy life.
- **SDG 2: Zero Hunger** – Sustainable Development Goal 2: 'End hunger, achieve food security and improved nutrition and promote sustainable agriculture.'
- **Food Management** – The main elements of the Government's food management policy are procurement, storage and movement of foodgrains, public distribution and maintenance of buffer stocks.
- **Public Distribution System** – The PDS was first introduced in India on 14 January, 1945, during the Second World War. Thereafter, FCI launched PDS in 1965. It is operated under the joint responsibility of the Central and State Governments.
- **National Food Security Act, 2013** – Right to food has been legally recognised by India, through the implementation of NFSA, 2013 and it extends to the whole of India.
- **National Food Security Mission** – National Food Security Mission (NFSM) was launched as a Centrally Sponsored Scheme in 2007 to increase the production of rice, wheat and pulses through area expansion and productivity enhancement; restoring soil fertility and productivity; creating employment opportunities; and enhancing farm level economy.
- **World Food Programme** – World Food Programme (WFP) is the leading humanitarian organisation saving lives and changing lives, delivering food assistance in emergencies and working with communities to improve nutrition and build resilience.
- **Codex Alimentarius** – Codex Alimentarius Commission (CAC) is an international food standards body established jointly by the Food and Agriculture Organization (FAO) and the World Health Organization (WHO) in 1963 with the objective of protecting consumer's health and ensuring fair practices in food trade.
- **Farm Waste** – It is a mixture of animal faeces, urine and milk, pesticides and other chemicals. Other common waste materials found on farms are plastic wrap, plastic chemical containers, feed bags, fertiliser bags, paper and cardboard, machinery, etc.

UPSC CSE PREVIOUS YEARS' PRELIMINARY EXAMINATION QUESTIONS

1. Consider the following statements: **[2024]**

1. India is a member of the International Grains Council.
2. A country needs to be a member of the International Grains Council for exporting or importing rice and wheat.

Which of the statements given above is/are correct?

(a) 1 only (b) 2 only
(c) Both 1 and 2 (d) Neither 1 nor 2

2. The economic cost of foodgrains to the Food Corporation of India is Minimum Support Price and bonus (if any) paid to the farmers plus **[2019]**

(a) Transportation cost only
(b) Interest cost only
(c) Procurement incidentals and distribution cost
(d) Procurement incidentals and charges for godowns

3. With reference to the provisions made under the National Food Security Act, 2013, consider the following statements: **[2018]**
   1. The families coming under the category of 'below poverty line' (BPL) only are eligible to receive subsidised foodgrains.
   2. The eldest woman in a household, of age 18 years or above, shall be the head of the household for the purpose of issuance of a ration card.
   3. Pregnant women and lactating mothers are entitled to a 'take-home ration' of 1,600 calories per day during pregnancy and for 6 months thereafter.

   Which of the statements given above is/are correct?
   (a) 1 and 2 only (b) 2 only
   (c) 1 and 3 only (d) 3 only

☞ NO QUESTIONS ASKED
2023, 2022, 2021, 2020, 2017, 2016, 2015, 2014, 2013

ANSWER KEY

1. (a) 2. (c) 3. (b)

UPSC CSE PREVIOUS YEARS' MAIN EXAMINATION QUESTIONS

1. Elucidate the importance of buffer stocks for stabilizing agricultural prices in India. What are the challenges associated with the storage of buffer stock? Discuss. **[2024]**
2. What are the major challenges of Public Distribution System (PDS) in India? How can it be made effective and transparent? (Answer in 150 words) **[2022]**
3. What are the salient features of the National Food Security Act, 2013? How has the Food Security Bill helped in eliminating hunger and malnutrition in India? (Answer in 250 words) **[2021]**
4. What are the reformative steps taken by the Government to make **foodgrain distribution system** more effective? **[2019]**
5. **Food Security Bill** is expected to eliminate hunger and malnutrition in India. Critically discuss various apprehensions in its effective implementation along with the concerns it has generated in WTO. **[2013]**

☞ NO QUESTIONS ASKED
2023, 2020, 2018, 2017, 2016, 2015, 2014

CHAPTER

17

LAND REFORMS IN INDIA

CHAPTER OUTLINE

- Historical Perspective of Land Reforms
- Land Revenue Systems in British India
- Zamindari System (Permanent Settlement)
- Ryotwari System
- Mahalwari System
- Needs and Objectives of Land Reforms
- Land Reform Measures Post-Independence
- Abolition of Intermediaries
- Tenancy Reforms
- Reorganisation of Agriculture
- Critical Evaluation of Land Reforms
- Factors Responsible for the Success of Land Reforms
- Recent Government Policies/Acts related to Land Reforms
- Right to Fair Compensation and Transparency in Land Acquisition, Rehabilitation and Resettlement Act, 2013
- Right to Fair Compensation and Transparency in Land Acquisition, Rehabilitation and Resettlement (Amendment) Bill, 2015
- Model Agricultural Land Leasing Act, 2016
- Land Pooling Policy
- National Land Records Modernisation Programme
- Digital India Land Records Modernisation Programme (DILRMP)

Land reforms refer to such institutional measures which deal with **alteration of the existing patterns** of ownership, tenancy and proper management of land.

It can also be defined as the **redistribution of the rights of ownership** or use of land among the large landowners and cultivators who have very limited or no landholdings.

Moreover, it broadly deals with policies related to regulation of rent, cooperative organisations, agricultural education, etc.

BONUS KNOWLEDGE

Agrarian Reforms – **Compared to land reforms**, it is a **broader term** that **includes land reforms** along with education and training of farmers, access to markets, facilitating credit facilities for better production and marketing which helps to improve the livelihood of farmers.

HISTORICAL PERSPECTIVE OF LAND REFORMS

Throughout Indian history, numerous instances illustrate the prevalence of collective land ownership.

For the kings and emperors, land revenue was one of the major sources of revenue. Land was divided into **jagirs**. These jagirs were allotted to **jagirdars**. And they further used to split the land and allocate them to **zamindars**. Zamindars used to distribute that land to peasants for cultivation, and in return they used to collect tax/revenue from them.

During the colonial era, lands of communities and tribals were seized by zamindars and the British. Subsequently, they **introduced different systems** of tax collection through land.

LAND REVENUE SYSTEMS IN BRITISH INDIA

Three major systems were introduced:

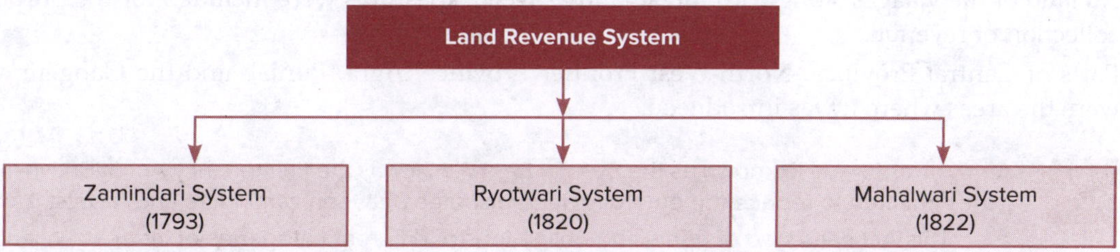

I. Zamindari System (Permanent Settlement)

- In 1793, through the **Permanent Settlement Act**, the Zamindari System was planned by **John Shore** and was introduced by **Lord Cornwallis**.
- Under this system, **zamindars were recognised as owners** of the land and they enjoyed rights to collect rent from peasants.
- The collected amount was divided into 11 parts of which **10/11 part** belonged to the East India Company and **1/11 part** was of the zamindar.
- Thus, zamindars, in order to increase their share, used to exploit helpless peasants.

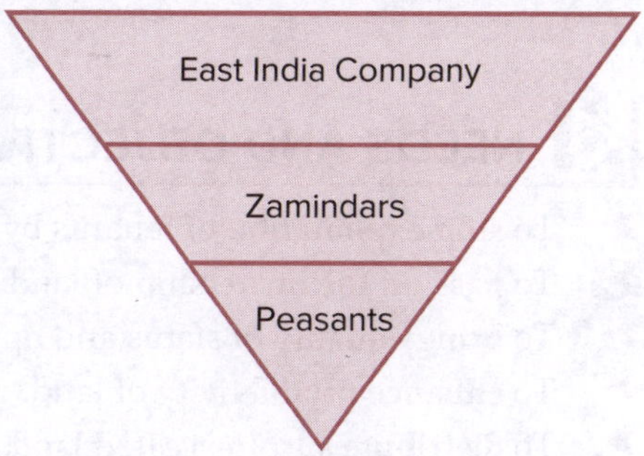

- This Zamindari System existed in the provinces of **Bengal, Bihar, Odisha, Banaras, parts of the Central Province and northern districts of the Madras Presidency**.

II. Ryotwari System

- In 1820, Sir Thomas Munro and Captain Alexander Reed introduced the **Ryotwari System**.
- **Scientific Rent theory of Ricardo** was the fundamental basis of Ryotwari System.
- This system had many features of the revenue system of Mughals in which the **revenue was directly collected by the British from the peasants** (also called Raiyats).

- Under the Ryotwari System, rate of revenue imposed was **50 per cent for dry lands** and **60 per cent for irrigated lands**.
- Revenue was fixed for **not more than 30 years** and on the basis of quality of soil and the nature of the crop.
- It was introduced in Madras, Bombay, some parts of Assam and Coorg province of British India.

III. Mahalwari System

- **In 1822, Holt Mackenzie** introduced the Mahalwari System.
- Under the Mahalwari System, land was divided into mahals, and the landlords and the village communities were jointly responsible for payment of revenue. One or more villages comprised each Mahal.
- Ownership rights on land vested with the peasant. However, revenue was collected by the village community.
- All land of the villages along with forest land as well as pastures were included for the purpose of collection of revenue.
- Parts of Central Province, North-West Frontier Province, Agra, Punjab and the Gangetic valley were the areas where it was introduced.

did you KNOW?

Act X of 1859 – Also known as the **Bengal Rent Act**, it was the first tenancy Act of British India. It was enacted to reduce the emerging land disputes between zamindars and raiyats.

- This Act consisted of rights and obligations of different categories of interests in land.
- The **main objectives** of the Act were:
  - (a) To protect and give privileges to the tenants with **occupancy rights**.
  - (b) To **restrict the powers of landlords** to increase rent.

NEEDS AND OBJECTIVES OF LAND REFORMS

- To **stop exploitation** of tenants by landlords.
- To **pass on the ownership** of land from landlords to peasants.
- To **bring equality** of status and opportunity to all sections of the rural population.
- To **enhance productivity** of land.
- To **distribute surplus vested land** among the rural poor.

Pre-independence reforms aimed to accomplish two goals:

1. To streamline land income collection.
2. To create rural aristocracy that supported British authority.

EXAM ESSENTIAL

Tebhaga Movement – This movement was launched in **1946–47** by sharecroppers of **Bengal** against the oppressive **jotedars**. **Jotedars** were rich peasants and controlled huge tracts of land in rural areas. They even controlled the local markets and money lending activities. In this movement, sharecroppers were encouraged by the **All-India Kisan Sabha (peasant wing of CPI)** and they demanded to implement the recommendations of the **Floud Commission**, which state that share croppers should retain two-thirds of the total crop.

Bhoodan Movement (land gift movement) – As the condition of landless peasants was not improving, **Acharya Vinoba Bhave** launched **Bhoodan Movement** in **1951**, at Pochampally, in Andhra Pradesh (now **Telangana**), which aimed to gift **one acre land** to each landless peasant. It was assumed that 50 million peasants were landless in 1951. By May 1955, the movement received only 3.75 million acres of land from the landowners for the distribution and soon the movement slowed down. Bhoodan Movement is also known as **Bloodless Revolution**.

Gramdan Movement – Started in **1952** and led by **Acharya Vinoba Bhave**, it was different from the Bhoodan Movement in the sense that here the received land became the property of a village association rather than an individual peasant. In this movement, a particular village was designated as Gramdan when at least 75 per cent of its residents with 51 per cent of the land signified their approval in writing for Gramdan. Magroth in Haripur, Uttar Pradesh, was the first village incorporated in Gramdan.

Since independence, India's land policy has gone through four significant phases:

The First and the Longest Phase (1950–1972) It was highlighted by land reforms, which consisted of three major initiatives: the removal of intermediaries, tenancy reform, and land redistribution through land ceilings. The elimination of intermediaries was largely successful, but tenancy reform and land ceilings were not.

The Second Phase (1972–1985) It intended to develop previously uncultivated area.

The Third Phase (1985–1995) This phase witnessed the execution of the Watershed Development, Drought Prone Area Programme (DPAP), and Desert-Area Development Programmes (DADP). The Federal Government established the Wasteland Development Agency to handle wasteland and degraded land.

The Fourth and Most Recent Phase (from 1995 onwards) It centred on disagreements over the necessity to retain land laws and efforts to reform.

LAND REFORM MEASURES POST-INDEPENDENCE

A Committee led by **J. C. Kumarappa (1949)** was formed to study the land problem. The Kumarappa Committee's report included extensive agricultural reform measures. Kumarappa Committee's report recommended some measures for comprehensive agrarian reform.

Raj Krishna categorised land reform initiatives into four categories:

1. **Liberating:** The liberating measures sought to liberate the true tillers of the soil from the landlord's tyranny. This was achieved by providing the tenant land ownership or occupancy rights. Rent fixing was carried out in a few states, including West Bengal's **Operation Barga**, where the tenancy was documented.
2. **Distributive:** The distributive measures were meant to do this by delivering actual resources to the poor, as mandated by the Indian Constitution, particularly those who needed land for productive purposes. This was done by transferring land ownership from significant landowners to landless people, particularly those from socially disadvantaged backgrounds.
3. **Organisational:** They were established in the mid-1960s with the goal of selecting and executing a certain type of agricultural production practice via use of progressive technology. These three strategies, when combined, impose strain on land resources, highlighting the need for developmental change.

4. **Developmental:** These reforms addressed additional issues related to land policy that influenced the overall growth of the agricultural sector.

Under land reforms, three broad measures were taken:

Land Reform Measures

- Abolition of Intermediaries
- Tenancy Reforms
- Reorganisation of Agriculture

> **did you KNOW?** As per the Seventh Schedule of the Indian Constitution, Land is a **State subject** and is under State list. As a result, only state legislatures have the authority to draft and implement land-reform measures. Nonetheless, because of its constitutional responsibility for social and economic planning, the central government had a considerable advisory and financial role in land policy (shared with the states). Shortly after gaining independence, the Indian government formed the National Planning Commission to carry out social and economic planning functions.
>
> However, 'acquisition and requisitioning of property' is in the **Concurrent list.**

I. Abolition of Intermediaries

- A total **57 per cent** of land area was under the zamindari system at the time of independence, and for collection of revenue, **zamindars or landlords played the role of intermediaries** between the peasants and the British Government.

↓

- Abolition of these intermediaries was a necessary step to save peasants from exploitation in terms of collection of huge revenue.

↓

- Parliament enacted 1st Amendment, 1951, inserting Article 31B which created 9th Schedule. This included Acts which regulated compensation to Zamindars. This Article is immune to constitutional challenges.

↓

- By 1956, many States passed their own **Zamindari Abolition Acts** (land being State subject). Through this reform measure, exploitative systems of land revenue like **Zamindari, Mahalwari, and Ryotwari** were abolished.

↓

- **Common lands** including forests, mines, minerals, rivers, etc. **were vested or taken over by the State Government**; **home farmlands** and lands under personal cultivation were left with intermediaries with a ceiling limit and the lessees of home farms were continued as tenants under them.
- Thus, after abolition, there became **two main categories** of holders – owners holding directly from the State and tenants who hold land from owners.
- For re-distributing land to peasants, land was acquired from intermediaries, and it involved payment of huge compensation to intermediaries by the State Government.
- In this process, **173 million acre** of land was acquired by the Government and around **2.5 crore farmers** were brought into direct relationship with the State.
- However, in spite of abolition of these intermediaries, poor cultivators continued to be exploited in different ways because of following reasons:
  a. The intermediaries were allowed to retain their home farms for **personal cultivation**.

b. The word **personal cultivation** was loosely defined and included personal supervision by zamindar or even by members of his family. Thus, they started evicting the sharecroppers.
c. In the Zamindari Abolition Acts, no protection from this eviction was provided to the sharecroppers.

BONUS KNOWLEDGE

Status after enforcement – Abolition of intermediaries declined the exploitation and oppression of tenants. However, evictions were taking place. To tackle this, the Kerala government, in 1959, declared eviction of sharecroppers by landlords as illegal. In 1978, **Operation Barga** (*discussed later*) was launched in West Bengal in favour of Bargadars (sharecroppers) to protect them from this eviction.

EXAM ESSENTIAL

Golaknath *vs.* State of Punjab Case: In 1967, Supreme court ruled in this case that the Zamindari Abolition Act contradicts with the provisions of Article 31 'Right to Property' of the Constitution of India. Thus, **in 1978**, through 44th Amendment Act, Parliament repealed Article 31 and removed the 'Right to Property' from being a Fundamental Right and it became a Legal Right.

II. Tenancy Reforms

- Tenancy was classified into three categories – **Occupancy Tenancy, Tenancy at Will and Subtenant**. Among these three, **occupancy tenants enjoyed permanent rights** like the owners, and they did not have the fear of eviction by the landlords. But **tenants at will and subtenants were at the mercy of the landlords**. Therefore, to protect their rights and to avoid exploitation by the landlords, special laws had to be enacted.
- Tenancy Reforms included three sub-measures:
  a. **Regulation of Rent** – A fixed and reasonable rent to be paid by tenants to landowners. Also, the payable rent should not exceed 1/5th to 1/4th of the gross production of land.
  b. **Security of Tenure** – This step was for assurance to cultivators about their future income. But the impact of the law was not so effective because the law permitted voluntary surrender of tenancies. Informal and oral tenancies were also still prevalent in many parts of the country.
  c. **Ownership Rights of Tenants** – It was for landless tenants to get ownership rights through transfer of title of land they plough. However, in some States, there were no legal provisions for the ownership rights in the tenancy laws. But, in States like West Bengal, Operation Barga played a crucial role in helping the tenants.

BONUS KNOWLEDGE

Tenant – A tenant occupies or possesses land through any type of claim, right or title and he pays a periodic rent. A tenant can be contractual or statutory.

Sub-tenant – Leases property from a tenant.

Occupancy tenancy – They enjoy permanent and heritable rights, security of tenure and could also claim compensation from the landlords for any improvements on land.

Tenancy at will – Tenure is fixed without any lease or written agreement and this can be terminated either by tenant or by landlord at any time.

Status after enforcement – Through **Operation Barga in West Bengal**, around 14 lakh sharecroppers were recorded by the Government. States like Kerala and Karnataka also achieved greater success as compared to other states. But the overall position of the peasants throughout the country remained unsatisfactory after tenancy reforms.

III. Reorganisation of Agriculture

It was required to enhance **agricultural production**. It included:

Reorganisation of Agriculture
- Ceiling on Agricultural Landholdings
- Consolidation of Landholdings
- Cooperative Farming

a. Ceiling on Agricultural Landholdings

Ceiling on Agricultural Landholdings indicates a **statutory absolute limit** on the amount of land an individual **can hold or own**. This ceiling has two aspects:

(i) **Ceiling on future acquisitions** and

(ii) **Ceiling on existing holdings**

The 1st Five Year Plan (FYP) focused only on (i), whereas it was only through the 2nd FYP that ceilings were recommended for (ii), i.e. existing holdings.

Land ceiling **to apply to**	Both future acquisition as well as existing land holdings
Level of land ceiling	To be based on size of **'Family Holding'** and not individual holding (as per the 1st FYP)
Exemptions from land ceiling to	Following class of farms: 1. Tea, coffee and rubber plantations 2. Compact area orchards 3. Farms for cattle breeding, dairy, wool raising, etc. 4. Sugarcane farms of sugar factories 5. Compact block farms with heavy investment and permanent structures
Steps **to prevent malafide transfers** (which were happening to avoid acquisition by the Government)	As per the 2nd FYP, land transferred by landlords was to be added to land retained by landlords to ascertain ceiling limit.

Amount of compensation to be given for land acquired using ceiling laws	2nd **FYP** recommended that States should lay down their own policy based on their existing circumstances.
Re-distribution of acquired land	During re-distribution by State Government, priority to be given to displaced tenants, farmers with uneconomic holdings and landless cultivators.

However, land being State subject, success of this land ceiling measure varied in its result. States adopting **Family Holding** to define ceiling limit were more successful in preventing **malafide transfers** than States using **individual holding**.

Marginal Holdings	Small Holdings	Semi-medium	Medium Holdings	Large Holdings
≤1 hectare	1–2 hectares	2–4 hectares	4–10 hectares	>10 hectares

b. Consolidation of Landholdings

Fragmentation of landholding is still a major bottleneck to reap the benefits of large-scale farming. A comparative status of fragmentation is depicted below:

Year	No. of Marginal Holdings	No. of Small Holdings	No. of Semi-Medium Holdings	No. of Medium Holdings	No. of Large Holdings	Total
1970–71	51%	19%	15%	11%	4%	100
2018–19	70.4%	17.70%	8.6%	2.80%	0.4%	100

This large amount of marginal land holdings was an issue but the increase in **fragmented holdings** due to reasons such as further sub-division of inherited land among new generations, pressure of increasing population and decline in joint family system has further aggravated the problem. **Fragmentation resulted in wastage of land, difficulties in adopting modernisation, disguised unemployment and low productivity.**

Thus, there is a need to find a solution.

Process of consolidation is seen as **a solution to reduce fragmentation of landholdings**. Through it, **one consolidated parcel of land is given to the farmer which is equal to the total of all** scattered plots of land under his possession.

In other words, **Consolidation** is termed as a process of planned **re-arrangement and re-adjustment of land parcels and their ownership** to form larger landholdings for the benefit of the agrarian economy.

Through legislation by States, **standard area** was fixed as the basis of consolidation. However, as per available data, only around 46 per cent of total cultivated land has been consolidated. This step of consolidation of landholdings got succeeded only in the states of Haryana, Punjab and Uttar Pradesh. However, it failed in other parts of the country because only 15 states passed laws for consolidation. The small farmers were reluctant to adopt this process as it indirectly helped the rich and influential get more fertile land through the **'major area rule'** of these state legislations.

As per the available 2015–16 estimates – Marginal and Small holdings account for as large as 47.3 per cent of the total area of cultivable land.

Average size of landholding = 0.913 hectare (as per 2018–19 data) (i.e. **decreased** over the years)

c. Cooperative Farming

To reap the benefits of economies of scale, cooperative farming provides an alternative to consolidation. **Even after focusing on it in the first three FYPs**, only 8,160 cooperative farming societies were formed by 1979, comprising just 0.38 per cent of total cultivable land.

Farmers could not be motivated for cooperative farming in spite of various incentives and subsidies given to cooperative farms by Government. Report of **Gadgil Committee on cooperative farming stated** that only $1/3^{rd}$ of these formed societies attained their goals and requirements.

As per the latest available 2018–19 data, still **88.10 per cent of the holdings are below 2 hectares (marginal and small)**, and there is a lot to be done to promote cooperative farming.

Reasons for failure of Cooperative Farming

1. Societies were mainly formed by large farmers to receive certain benefits from the Government and not by small and marginal farmers.
2. Societies lacked professional and management skills.
3. Corrupt practices by some members.
4. This failure of cooperative farming also discouraged other interested peasants.

BONUS KNOWLEDGE

SUCCESSFUL LAND REFORM MEASURES IN SOME STATES

West Bengal:

Operation Barga was launched in **1979**, in West Bengal, and was a land reform measure undertaken by the then State government for recording of bargadars (sharecroppers) to protect them against illegal eviction by landlords. Operation Barga recorded the names of approximately 1.5 million bargadars and it has been regarded as one of the most successful land reform programmes in India.

Jammu and Kashmir:

Land reforms in Jammu and Kashmir began in 1931, under the leadership of **Sheikh Abdullah**. Then, in the 1944 Naya Kashmir (New Kashmir) resolution, land reform was an integral part. The resolution promised abolition of landlordism, land to the tiller and cooperative association of tillers to regulate production and sale of crops and agricultural goods.

The **Big Landed Estates Abolition Act, 1950** provided excellent results for the landless.

In 1963, the Government set up a Land Commission to find out the various shortcomings which had crept in the land tenure pattern. The recommendations of this Commission formed the basis of J&K Agrarian Reforms Act 1972 which was further amended as the J&K Agrarian Reforms Act, 1976. Jammu and Kashmir State Land (Vesting of Ownership to Occupants) Act, 2001 (Roshni Act) envisaged the transfer of ownership rights of State land to its occupants, subject to the payment of a cost, as determined by the government.

Uttar Pradesh:

Uttar Pradesh passed the **Zamindari Abolition and Land Reforms Act in 1950**.

The UP Imposition of Land Ceiling Act was passed in 1960 that prescribed the ceiling limit of 40 acres. The land distribution programme had a positive impact on the economic and social status of the allottees and it brought qualitative change in their life and contributed to better health and education of children.

UP Government amended its Land Ceiling Act in 1973. It brought down the ceiling limit and removed many of the exemptions given in the earlier Act. According to the amended Act, ceiling was fixed at 7.3 hectare of irrigated land for a family of five.

Kerala:

In post-independent Kerala, large-scale alienation of tribal lands took place due to the immigration of people to the hill areas.

The **Kerala Land Reforms Act 1963** brought 'land to the tiller' policy which gave full ownership to the tenants in respect of the land in their possession.

The Kerala Scheduled Tribes (Restriction on Transfer and Restoration of Alienated Lands) Act, 1975 was enacted to ameliorate the plight of the tribals.

Tamil Nadu:

The Tamil Nadu **Land Reforms (Fixation of Ceiling on Land) Act, 1961 (Tamil Nadu Act 58/61)** was passed to eliminate disparities in agricultural land ownership and concentration among particular groups, as well as to divide such land among the landless poor. It is the first state to pass Contract Farming Act, as per the central guidelines.

CRITICAL EVALUATION OF VARIOUS LAND REFORMS

Land reforms were introduced not only for the improvement of the agricultural production but also to improve the socio-economic and socio-political conditions of the country. It also served as a tool for social justice. The **benefits of land reforms** were as follows:

1. After abolition of intermediaries, almost 20 million tenants were brought into **direct relationship with the Governments**. However, it also led to eviction of large number of tenants by landlords due to loopholes in legislations.
2. **Increased investments** were made by peasants (after becoming owners), thereby helping to improve land productivity.
3. In scattered instances, consolidation of landholdings helped in **increased productivity** through economies of scale.

   However, land reforms did not have any significant influence in the overall increase in productivity. The possible reasons include:
   - The reforms were not properly implemented.
   - The actual rents of agricultural land were still high.
   - Cooperative farming was not much promoted.
4. **Impact on social justice** – It is true that the land reform measures have been implemented at a slow pace, but it played a significant role in the field of social justice. By providing security of tenure and fixing the maximum limit of rent, small farmers got the social security for their future. Apart from that, **feudalism** in India had more or less been abolished.

did you KNOW?

How land ceiling policy on landholding can be considered as an effective reform under economic criteria?

Land ceiling policy on landholding shows how much land an individual or family can hold. Its purpose is to limit land concentration in the hands of a few. Such policies can improve economic efficiency by breaking large amount of land into smaller plots which results in increased agricultural output through more intensive cultivation and improved access to land for marginalised farmers. Land ceiling policies help in eliminating poverty, ensure equitable distribution of land resources, increase social welfare, and economic growth in agrarian economies like India. Land ceiling policies can be considered as a helpful economic reform for promoting efficiency in land use.

Factors Responsible for the Success of Land Reforms

- **Political will** of the Government indicative through enactment of various legislations and constitutional amendments.
- **Awareness among the peasants** about the land issues and possible reform measures.

Some of the reasons for the failure of the first phase of land reforms were:

1. The word **'personal cultivation' was not properly defined** under law, and it resulted in large-scale **eviction** of poor peasants or sharecroppers by landlords. However, West Bengal became a role model in this regard by initiating **Operation Barga** and helping sharecroppers enjoy their cultivation and other rights over the piece of land.
2. In many States, **'individual holding'** was used as a basis for identifying the ceiling limit as compared to 'family holding'. Taking advantage of this and to escape ceiling laws, zamindars started transferring their land to their own family members.
3. As per ceiling laws, **large areas of land could be retained by intermediaries/landlords for personal cultivation**. As a result, only their form changed from landlords to absentee landlords.
4. A considerable number of **tenancies were oral and informal**, so the tenants who were cultivating such land were unable to prove their position. Even in some States, the sharecroppers were not granted the status of tenants though they were cultivating a considerable part of land.
5. **Voluntary surrender of the land** was another loophole among the framed laws. Tenants were threatened and beaten up by Zamindars to surrender their land. After the recommendations of 4th FYP, voluntary surrender was regulated by some States and a law was made that landowners will not be allowed to possess the surrendered land.
6. Poor maintenance of land records by the Government was another reason for failure.

BONUS KNOWLEDGE

NEW ECONOMIC POLICY OF 1991 AND LAND REFORMS

After the introduction of Liberalisation, Privatisation and Globalisation policies by the Government and new economic reforms, land leasing and land ceiling policies were required to be more liberal. State governments even proposed for the relaxation of ceiling and tenancy laws and to encourage capitalistic or contract farming for revitalising the land market.

However, with the experiences of countries like Japan and Korea where land reforms proved helpful in faster and sustainable development of agricultural market, it was argued that land reforms should precede the new economic reforms for rapid and sustainable development without creating much pain to the rural population.

RECENT GOVERNMENT POLICIES/ACTS RELATED TO LAND REFORMS

Right to Fair Compensation and Transparency in Land Acquisition, Rehabilitation and Resettlement Act, 2013

- Being enacted in 2013, it came into force in 2014. Before this, land acquisition was governed under the **Land Acquisition Act of 1894**.
- Basic objectives of this Act were farmers' welfare and prosperity and also to provide them rational compensation.
- This Act aimed for strategic and effective development of land along with its proper utilisation.
- For strategic and defence purposes including the Central Forces and State Police Forces or for any work related to national security, government can acquire land for safeguarding the public purpose.
- The Government can also acquire land for residential purposes of landless and poor people or for those who are affected by any natural calamities and also for any scheme undertaken by the Government for the welfare of the country.
- Under this Act, the land can be acquired by the private bodies for Public–Private Partnership (PPP) projects but the ownership of the land will continue to be with the Government.
- To regulate the procedure of acquisition, Union Government also notified and made **rules** regarding right to fair compensation and transparency in land acquisition, rehabilitation and for resettlement.

Main Provisions of the 2013 Act

- **Consent**: Prior informed consent of **80 per cent** of affected families **for private projects** and **70 per cent for PPP** is required. However, Government projects do not require consent.
- **Social Impact Assessment (SIA)**: It is **mandatory except** in case of national security or emergency situations. This is to be done by involving local authorities like Gram Sabha, Municipality, etc.
- **Food Security**: The Act in general does not allow acquisition of **multi-cropped land**.
- **Compensation**: A compensation of **4 times** of the market value in rural areas and **2 times** of the market value in urban areas needs to be provided.
- A **Land Acquisition, Rehabilitation and Resettlement Authority** with the powers of Civil Court to be established under the Act to adjudicate on the related issues.
- **Land left unused** after acquisition for 5 years shall be returned to the previous owners.
- Under the rehabilitation and resettlement clause, it also includes **employment** to one member of the affected family.

Right to Fair Compensation and Transparency in Land Acquisition, Rehabilitation and Resettlement (Amendment) Bill, 2015 (Land Bill)

- It seeks **to amend Land Acquisition, Rehabilitation and Resettlement (LARR) Act 2013.**
- This Bill classifies the use of land by the Government in five categories – **defence, rural infrastructure, affordable housing, industrial corridors and infrastructure projects including PPP projects.**
- **The Bill seeks to exempt above five categories from the provisions of LARR Act 2013.**

- Exemptions to above five categories also include **relief from SIA.**
- The requirement of the **consent of 80 per cent of the landowners for private projects** and 70 per cent of the landowners for PPP projects has been **exempted** in the Bill.
- The Bill brings provisions for the compensation, rehabilitation and resettlement under **other related Acts** like National Highway Act and Railways Act in consonance with LARR Act.
- Acquisition of land for private companies under LARR Act 2013 is changed to **private entities**, which include private companies along with corporations and non-profit organisations.
- Opposed to 2013 Act, **even multi-cropped land can be acquired** for the above-mentioned five categories.
- The 2013 Act mandated return of unused land after 5 years; however, this provision is proposed to be amended to return of unused land after 5 years or the time period specified at the time of setting up of the project, whichever is later.

Present Status of the 2015 Land Bill

The Right to Fair Compensation and Transparency in Land Acquisition, Rehabilitation and Resettlement (Amendment) Bill, 2015 was introduced in the Lok Sabha on 24 February 2015, and it was passed by Lok Sabha on 10 March 2015. The Bill is **pending with the Rajya Sabha.**

Criticisms of the 2015 Land Bill

Critics say that

- Fertile, irrigated, **multi-cropped land** should be acquired **as a last resort measure only.**
- For a bottom-up and participatory approach, **SIAs should ideally be mandatory** in every case except rare cases affecting national interest.
- The **definition of projects** falling within the five exempted categories **should be clarified** to avoid misuse of the amendment.
- **Flexibility** should be provided to affected families on the **kind of compensation** that is required by them.
- Unused land (except in exceptional circumstances) **should be returned** to the original owners after 5 years.
- **Agricultural productivity and fragmentation** is a huge issue that is neglected under the Bill. An umbrella Act should be designed to enable modernisation of agriculture to increase yields.

The Government should adopt a **National Land Use Policy**, which will look at the scientific acquisition of non-cultivable land and its development; protect the interest of farmers and keep in mind the food production goals and economic goals of the country.

MODEL AGRICULTURAL LAND LEASING ACT, 2016

The Model Land Leasing Act, 2016 has been **prepared by NITI Aayog** on the basis of the recommendations of **T. Haque Committee**. It serves as a guide for the States and UTs to draft their own piece of leasing legislation on the basis of the model law, keeping in view the local requirements.

After the model law was released by NITI Aayog, Madhya Pradesh has enacted separate land leasing law and Uttar Pradesh and Uttarakhand have modified their existing land leasing laws.

Need of the Act

- Under existing State laws, there are prohibitions and restrictions with respect to agricultural land leasing (such as in the laws of Manipur, Bihar, Kerala, etc.).
- Existing laws force the land owners and lessee cultivators to have informal agreements which lead to the lessee cultivators being deprived of the benefits which are normally due to them. And also without any security of tenure.
- Without land leasing being legal, many land owners do not want to lease out their lands to other farmers as they fear that tenant-cultivator will not vacate the land after the agreed period and they would lose the title of the land.
- It is seen that the prices of agricultural lands are going up and, therefore, landless small and marginal farmers cannot afford to purchase lands.

Objectives of the Act

- To permit and facilitate leasing of agricultural land.
- To improve **agricultural efficiency and equity**, access to land by the landless and semi-landless poor, occupational diversity and for accelerated rural growth and transformation.
- To provide **recognition to farmers** cultivating agricultural land on lease. It gives them access to loans through formal credit institutions, insurance, disaster relief, etc. while protecting fully the land rights of the owners.
- To ensure that lease farming is not used to exploit tenant farmers.
- To **reduce informal tenancy** practices.
- To **consolidate operational** holding.

Key Features of the Act

- Land leasing is legalised to promote agricultural efficiency, equity and power reduction.
- Needs and interests of landlord as well as lease holder have been taken care of.
- The landlord can legally lease the land for agriculture and allied activities. In this act, it has been taken care that in any circumstances, the leased holders' claim on land will not be valid.
- Lease holder (tenant) can take loans, insurance, disaster relief and other support services.
- The act allows automatic resumption of land after the completion of agreed lease period.
- The act emphasises to incentivise tenants to make investment in land improvement.
- The provision of **'Special Land Tribunal'** has been made in the Civil Court for faster resolution of dispute.

Concerns

- It allows lease contracts between the parties for an **indefinite period**; this clause may be used by the powerful vested interests to forcefully occupy the land.
- It provides for lessor to reclaim the land in case of any damage to the 'soil health'. Soil health is not clearly defined and may give rise to disputes.
- It creates uncertainty and distrust if the lessor seeks to sell or gift out the land.

BONUS KNOWLEDGE

Cadastral data defines the geographic extent of the past, current and future rights and interests in real property and the spatial information needed to describe that geographic extent. These rights and interests are contained in land record documents. Ideally, the cadastral records should **reflect the ground reality**.

Land titling is a form of land reform in which private individuals and families are given formal property rights for land which they have previously occupied informally or used on the basis of customary land tenure.

Land Pooling Policy: A Transformative Initiative for Urbanisation in India

A major paradigm change in urban development is represented by the sustainable urbanisation and land pooling policies, which involve public-private partnerships for land assembly and are viewed as essential drivers of economic growth in India. Under the policy, land is pooled and is developed by private landowners. The owners can pool land parcels of any size for development. Norms and guidelines are prescribed. Each sector will have a 60:40 ratio, 60 per cent of the land to be developed by the land owners and 40 per cent of the land to be used for various city level infrastructure requirements like roads, water, sewerage, etc. in partnership with the private sector.

NATIONAL LAND RECORDS MODERNISATION PROGRAMME

EXAM ESSENTIAL

Digitisation of Land Records

The present system of preparing and maintaining land records is largely influenced from the Mughal period and it improvised a bit during the British rule.

Successive FYPs emphasised on proper maintenance of land records as the basis for good administration and aimed at social justice through better implementation of rural development programmes.

According to the Seventh Five Year Plan, "Land records form the base for all land reform measures and, therefore, regular periodic updating of land records is essential in all states. This will necessarily have to include a scientific survey of unmeasured land and recoding of rights of tenants and share-croppers which have remained unrecorded up till now".

Need for Digitisation

- Land records do not often represent the ground realities relating to ownership and possession.
- It has an impact on the implementation of welfare policies of government.
- There is increased duration and costs of litigation in case of property disputes. Therefore, a clear title to a property is required.
- Proper maintenance of land records is necessary for success of land reform policies.

- It will make transactions faster and transparent.
- The process of mutation/transfer and updating of land records has been slow in many States.
- Land records were maintained on paper or cloth. They are often in a very poor shape.
- Under the Smart Cities and AMRUT scheme, cities are trying to raise their own revenue through property taxes. Thus, providing clear land titles is necessary.
- Also, digitisation may enable faster land acquisition.

Challenges with Digitisation

- For the last 10 years, **data entry** with regard to land boundaries or title information at various levels is **still incomplete**.
- **Cross-verification** is required to avoid inconsistencies with ground realities.
- Use of old physical maps for its digitisation has **risk of physical damage** of the old records.
- Land ownership is established through **multiple documents maintained by different departments**, making it cumbersome to access them. For example, sale deeds are stored in the registration department, maps are stored in the survey department and property tax receipts are with the revenue department.
- Many States in the country have **not yet digitised** the basic survey documents, sketches, maps, etc.
- Due to the lack of maintenance of streamlined land records, there have been **litigations, scams and property disputes** over land ownership.

DIGITAL INDIA LAND RECORDS MODERNISATION PROGRAMME (DILRMP)

EXAM ESSENTIAL

- Centrally Sponsored Schemes viz. Computerisation of Land Records (CLR) and Strengthening of Revenue Administration and Updating of Land Records (SRA&ULR) were merged into a modified Scheme named Digital India Land Records Modernisation Programme (DILRMP) which was launched in **2008**. It is a **Central Sector scheme with 100 per cent funding** by the Government of India.
- It seeks to improve the quality and accessibility of land records in the country and move towards **guaranteed titles**.
- **National Informatics Centre (NIC)** is responsible for the installation and maintenance of hardware and software. NIC is also responsible for training to the officials and technical support.
- The major components of the programme are as follows:
  - i. Computerisation of all land records including mutations/transfers.
  - ii. Digitisation of cadastral maps and integration of textual and spatial data.
  - iii. Survey/re-survey and updation of all survey and settlement records including creation of original cadastral records wherever necessary.
  - iv. Computerisation of registration and its integration with the land records maintenance system.
  - v. Development of core Geospatial Information System (GIS).
  - vi. Aadhaar linking with land records on a voluntary basis.

Benefits of DILRMP

- **Real-time land ownership records** can be made available.
- Free accessibility to the records will reduce corruption and harassment.
- Abolition of stamp papers and payment of stamp duty and registration fees through banks, etc. will also reduce interface with the registration machinery.
- The **time** for obtaining **Record of Rights (ROR)** etc. will be drastically reduced.
- The **single-window service** or the web-enabled 'anytime-anywhere' access will save the time and effort in obtaining RoRs, etc.
- Automated **mutations** will significantly reduce the scope of fraudulent property deals.
- **Conclusive titling** will also significantly reduce litigation.
- These records will be **tamper-proof.**

Achievements of DILRMP

According to PIB (October 2024)

- Around 95 per cent of land records have been computerised they covered over 6.26 lakh villages.
- **Digitisation of cadastral maps** reached 68.02 per cent.
- 87 per cent of Sub-Registrar Offices (SROs) have been integrated with land records.
- DILRMP has been **extended until 2025–26**. New features like **Aadhaar-based integration** with land records and **computerisation of revenue courts** have been added.

Innovative Initiatives under DILRMP

i. **National Generic Document Registration System:** One nation one software for uniform registration.

ii. **Integrated Land Management Information System (ILMIS):** Digital land records database and management.

iii. **Unique Land Parcel Identification Number (ULPIN):** The ULPIN or "Bhu-Aadhar" provides 14-digit alpha numeric unique identification number for easy tracking of ownership of the land.

iv. **Bhoomi Samman Certification (Platinum Grading Certificate Scheme for States/UTs):** The target has been set for saturation of **06** basic components of the programme which are Computerisation of Record of Rights (RoRs); Digitisation of Cadastral Maps/FMBs; Linkage of RoR with Cadastral maps; Computerisation of Registration; Integration of Registration (SRO) with Land Records (Revenue Office); Modern Record Room.

Based on the achievement of the above six targets, this certification is provided.

> **Last Minute SNIPPETS**
>
> As of 2023, 161 districts in 14 States have achieved Bhoomi Samman Certificates (Platinum Grading) for completing 99 per cent and above of work under its six components.

v. **e-Court Integration:** Linking land records with e-Courts intends to provide authentic land information to the judiciary, faster case resolution, etc.

vi. **Transliteration of Land Records:** In order to address the problem of linguistic barriers in land governance, DoLR, with the technical support of Centre for Development of Advanced Computing

(C-DAC) Pune, has undertaken an initiative to transliterate the Records of Rights available in local language to **any of the 22 Schedule VIII languages** of the Constitution.

vii. **NAtional geospatial Knowledge-based land Survey of urban HAbitations (NAKSHA)**: A pilot programme launched by Department of Land Resources under MoRD, under the DILRMP, for the creation of Land Records **in Urban Areas** in selected cities, to ensure accurate and reliable documentation of land ownership, enhance urban planning, and reduce land-related disputes. The **Survey of India** is the technical partner for NAKSHA programme.

SUMMARY

- **Land Reforms** – Institutional measures which deal with alteration of the existing patterns of ownership, tenancy and proper management of land.
- **Agrarian Reforms** – Includes land reforms along with education and training of farmers, access to markets, facilitating credit facilities for better production and marketing which helps to improve the livelihood of farmers.
- **Raiyat/Ryot** – Under Ryotwari system, a ryot is someone who has the **right over land for the purpose of its cultivation** either personally or through members of the family, hired servants or partners.
- **Intermediaries** – Intermediaries were **rent collectors** such as Zamindars, Talukdars, Jagirs, Inams, etc.
- **Absentee landlords** – Absentee landlords were the owners of land (like zamindars) who **had no local connection** or who did not reside within the local vicinity of land owned by them.
- **Zamindari System** – Introduced in 1793 by Lord Cornwallis and planned by Sir John Shore – also known as Permanent Settlement Act – zamindars were recognised as owners – collected amount was divided into 11 parts of which 10/11 part belonged to the East India Company and 1/11 part was for the zamindar – existed in the provinces of Bengal, Bihar, Odisha, Banaras, parts of the Central Province and northern districts of the Madras Presidency.
- **Ryotwari System** – Introduced in 1820 by Sir Thomas Munro and Captain Alexander Reed – based on Scientific Rent theory of Ricardo – revenue was directly collected by the British from the peasants – introduced in Madras, Bombay, some parts of Assam and Coorg province of British India.
- **Mahalwari System** – Introduced in 1822 by Holt Mackenzie – land was divided into mahals, and the landlords and the village communities were jointly responsible for payment of revenue. One or more villages comprised each Mahal – Central Province, Northwest Frontier Province, Agra, Punjab and the Gangetic valley.
- **Tebhaga Movement** – 1946–47 – by bargadars (sharecroppers) of Bengal against the oppressive jotedars.
- **Pre-Independence Land Reforms** – To streamline land income collection-to create rural aristocracy that supported British authority.
- **Post-Independence Land Reforms** – Abolition of Intermediaries – Tenancy Reforms – Reorganisation of Agriculture (Ceiling on Agricultural Landholdings, Consolidation of Landholdings and Cooperative Farming).
- **Bhoodan Movement (land gift movement)** – 1951 – Acharya Vinoba Bhave – to gift 01 acre land to each landless peasant.
- **Gramdan Movement** – 1952 – Acharya Vinoba Bhave – different from the Bhoodan Movement – the received land become the property of a village association rather than an individual peasant.

- **Operation Barga** – 1979 – In West Bengal – to protect the rights of the bargadars (sharecroppers) against illegal eviction.
- **Right to Fair Compensation and Transparency in Land Acquisition, Rehabilitation and Resettlement Act, 2013** – Enacted in 2013 and came into force in 2014 – before this, land acquisition was governed under the Land Acquisition Act, 1894.
- **Model Land Leasing Act 2016** – Prepared by NITI Aayog – on the basis of the recommendations of
- **T. Haque Committee** – serves as a guide for the States and UTs to draft their own piece of leasing legislation on the basis of the model law.
- **Centrally Sponsored Schemes** – Computerisation of Land Records (CLR) and Strengthening of Revenue Administration and Updating of Land Records (SRA&ULR) were merged into a modified Scheme named Digital India Land Records Modernisation Programme (DILRMP) -launched in **2008**.

UPSC CSE PREVIOUS YEARS' PRELIMINARY EXAMINATION QUESTIONS

1. With reference to the Digital India Land Records Modernisation Programme, consider the following statements: **[2024]**

1. To implement the scheme, the Central Government provides 100% funding.
2. Under the Scheme, Cadastral Maps are digitised.
3. An initiative has been undertaken to transliterate the Records of Rights from local language to any of the languages recognised by the Constitution of India.

Which of the statements given above are correct?

(a) 1 and 2 only (b) 2 and 3 only
(c) 1 and 3 only (d) 1, 2 and 3

2. With reference to land reforms in independent India, which one of the following statements is correct? **[2019]**

(a) The ceiling laws were aimed at family holdings and not individual holdings.
(b) The major aim of land reforms was providing agricultural land to all the landless.
(c) It resulted in cultivation of cash crops as a predominant form of cultivation.
(d) Land reforms permitted no exemptions to the ceiling limits.

☞ NO QUESTIONS ASKED
2023, 2022, 2021, 2020, 2018, 2017, 2016, 2015, 2014, 2013

ANSWER KEY

1. (d) 2. (b)

UPSC CSE PREVIOUS YEARS' MAIN EXAMINATION QUESTIONS

1. What were the factors responsible for the successful implementation of land reforms in some parts of the country? Elaborate. **[2024]**

2. State the objectives and measures of **land reforms** in India. Discuss how **land ceiling policy on landholding** can be considered as an effective reform under economic criteria. **[2023]**

3. How did **land reforms** in some parts of the country help to improve the **socio-economic conditions** of **marginal and small farmers**? **[2021]**

4. Discuss the **role of land reforms** in agricultural development. Identify the **factors that were responsible for the success** of land reforms in India. **[2016]**

5. In view of the **declining average size of landholdings** in India which has made agriculture non-viable for a majority of farmers, should contract farming and land leasing be promoted in agriculture? Critically evaluate the pros and cons. **[2015]**
6. The Right to **Fair Compensation and Transparency in Land Acquisition, Rehabilitation and Resettlement Act, 2013** has come into effect from 1 January 2014. What are the key issues which would get addressed with the Act in place? What implications would it have on industrialisation and agriculture in India? **[2014]**
7. Establish the **relationship between land reforms, agricultural productivity and elimination of poverty** in the Indian economy. Discuss the **difficulties in designing and implementation** of agriculture-friendly land reforms in India. **[2013]**

☞ NO QUESTIONS ASKED
2022, 2020, 2019, 2018, 2017

CHAPTER

18

IRRIGATION IN INDIA

CHAPTER OUTLINE

Irrigation is defined as the **artificial way of supplying water** to the agricultural land in an appropriate volume, where natural supply of water is scarce or insufficient. Irrigation also includes **draining away of surplus water** from the fields. To enhance agricultural productivity and to expand the agricultural sector, surplus availability of water is crucial. Therefore, expansion of irrigation is the key strategy for the development of agricultural sector. Irrigation in India has its evidence since the **Harappan Civilisation**. The landscapes in Southern and Central parts of India are found covered with age-old tanks and wells. Some of them were probably built even before the beginning of the Christian era. In the medieval period, construction of canals took place rapidly. In the fourteenth century, **Firoz Shah Tughlaq** built the most extensive **canal irrigation system** around the Indo-Gangetic doab, which to a great extent benefitted the cultivation in the northern parts of India. In the nineteenth–twentieth centuries, the contribution of **Sir M. Visvesvaraya** was immense in the field of irrigation and water engineering. An engineer by profession, he designed **automatic sluice gates** and introduced block water irrigation system and automatic weir floodgates in the Bombay Presidency. He was the chief architect in the construction of the Krishna Raja Sagar Dam (located in Mandya district of Karnataka) in the beginning of the twentieth century. He is also remembered for introduction of an efficient way of filtering water through **Collector Wells**. **Sir Arthur Thomas Cotton**, a British irrigation engineer, is regarded as the pioneer of irrigation works in South India. **Kanuri Lakshmana Rao**, popularly known as **K. L. Rao**, designer of Nagarjunasagar and Bhakra Nangal Dams, is known as the **Father of Irrigation**. He had also mooted the idea of **interlinking of rivers** by connecting the Ganga River with the Cauvery River. Subsequently, in 1977, the Bombay-based consultant engineer **Dinshaw Dastur** proposed the **Garland Canal Scheme** around the Himalayan, Central and Peninsular India. The first Irrigation Commission after independence was set up in 1972 by the Indian government.

EXAM ESSENTIAL

KEY TERMS RELATED TO IRRIGATION

- **Culturable Command Area** (CCA) – The area which can be irrigated from a scheme and is fit for cultivation.
- **Irrigated Area (IA)** – The area is assumed to be irrigated for cultivation through sources such as Canals (Government and Private), Tanks, Tube wells, other wells and even some other sources such as micro-irrigation, etc. It is divided into two categories:
  1. **Net Irrigated Area (NIA)** – It is the area irrigated through any source once in a year for a particular crop.
  2. **Gross Irrigated Area (GIA)** – It is the total area under crops irrigated once or more than once in a year. It is counted as the number of times the area is cropped and irrigated in a year.

***Note:* Agricultural year – 1 July to 30 June**

- **Irrigation Potential Created (IPC)** – It is the total area which **can be irrigated** under a scheme on its full utilisation.
- **Irrigation Potential Utilised (IPU)** – It is the total area which is **actually irrigated** under a particular scheme.
- **Irrigation Potential Gap** – The difference between IPC and IPU is the area of land that has the potential to be irrigated but not covered due to different reasons. This is known as the Irrigation Potential Gap. Factors contributing to the gap include delays in environmental clearances for irrigation projects, problems in acquiring land, inefficiencies in water management infrastructure, etc.
- **Net Sown Area** – This represents the total area sown with crops and orchards. Area sown more than once in the same year is counted only once.
- **Gross Cropped Area (GCA)** – It is the total area sown once as well as more than once in a particular year. When the crop is sown on a piece of land twice, the area is counted twice under GCA.
- **Cropping Intensity** – It is the ratio of Gross Cropped Area to the Net Sown Area.
- **Water-Use Efficiency (WUE)** – It is the ratio between **effective water use** and **actual water withdrawal**. It helps to understand the effective use of water. In the agricultural sector in India, WUE is quite low **(around 38 per cent)** presently, whereas in developed countries, WUE is around 50–60 per cent due to the effective use of micro-irrigation.
- **Allelopathy** – It is a biological phenomenon by which an organism produces one or more bio-chemicals that influence the germination, growth, survival and reproduction of other organisms. These bio-chemicals are known as **allelochemicals** and can have beneficial **(positive allelopathy)** or detrimental **(negative allelopathy)** effects on the target organisms and the community.

Crops with High Water Requirement

Crop	Water Requirement (mm)
Rice	450–700
Sugarcane	1500–2500
Banana	1200–2200
Cotton	700–1300
Tomato	400–800
Maize	500–800
Wheat	450–650

NECESSITY OF IRRIGATION IN INDIA

- **Uncertainty of Monsoon** – Our country has faced several droughts, which affected millions of people and resulted in starvation and epidemics. In August 2023, the rainfall deficit in India was around 36 per cent. About 30 per cent of India's land area experienced different degrees of drought. Areas under 'severe', 'extreme' and 'exceptional' dry conditions were about 11.5 per cent.
- Way back in the year 1987, the whole of Eastern and Northwestern India was affected by drought and as per the relevant reports, around 300 million farmers were affected.
- **Water Holding Capacity of Soils** – Different types of soils have different capacity to retain moisture. For instance, sandy soil needs frequent irrigation than clayey soil. Laterite and Red soils have less moisture retaining capacity, and without proper irrigation, cultivation is not possible there.
- **To increase the productivity** of the **crops** and for **using High-Yielding Variety (HYV) seeds**, abundant supply of water is needed.
- **Diverse Climate** – India has a variety of climate and weather conditions. Some places experience extreme hot weather, while others experience extreme cold temperature. Places like Rajasthan, Gujarat, interior parts of the Deccan Plateau, etc. receive less than 75 cm of rainwater every year. Thus, proper cultivation in these places can be done only with the help of irrigation.
- **Rabi Crops** – Rabi crops like wheat and pulses are grown in dry and winter season. Water for their cultivation is provided through irrigation.
- **Multiple Cropping** – In multiple cropping systems, regular supply of water is needed, and this can be made possible through irrigation.
- Irrigation **can bring more land under cultivation**. As per the records, around 13.83 million hectares of land is classified as cultivable wasteland. Provision of irrigation can be helpful in making these lands cultivable. **Rajasthan** has the largest area of cultivable wasteland.
- Irrigation also **reduces the instability in the production** level. It can prevent reduction in output level during both drought and flood.
- Irrigation also has some indirect benefits through **increased agricultural production**. It increases the employment potential through irrigated lands. It also helps in developing other areas such as water transportation, income of Government, stability to the farmers' income, etc.

PREVALENT IRRIGATION SYSTEMS IN INDIA

Systems of irrigation refer to the process of storing and regulating water resources. In India, irrigation is practised mainly through tube wells, other wells, canals, tanks and multipurpose projects. Thus, we classify them into three:

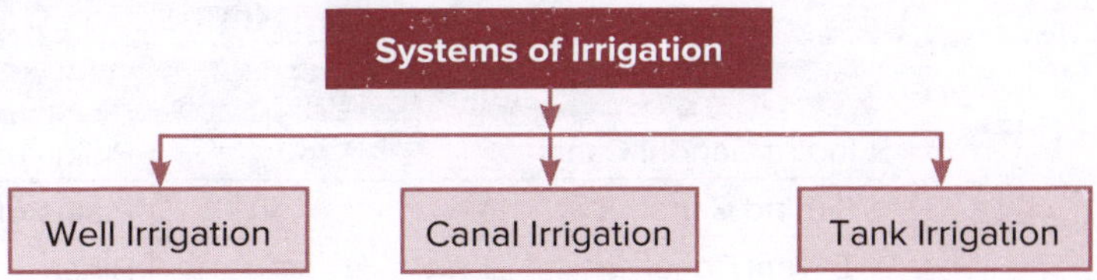

1. Well Irrigation

- It is the **most popular method** of irrigation in India. Under this system, underground water is tapped for both drinking and irrigation purposes. For the implementation of this system, a trench is dug for getting perennial supply of water. **Saline water is not preferred** for well irrigation.
- This system is popular in the **regions with plenty of ground water**. However, **peninsular part** of India is **not suitable** for well irrigation due to its rocky structure, uneven surface, and lack of underground water.
- Well irrigation can be of **two types**:
  1. Tube well irrigation
  2. Dug well irrigation
- Benefits of well irrigation include simple and the cheapest source available for poor farmers, can be used whenever required, etc.
- It is a reliable source of water during drought periods when surface water dries up.
- The main drawback of well irrigation is that it cannot be used in the areas of brackish groundwater.

2. Canal Irrigation

- Canal irrigation is the **second most popular** irrigation system in India after well irrigation.
- This system can be easily extended to those areas which are drained by perennial rivers. However, nowadays canals also reach the dry places where perennial rivers are not present.
- Canal irrigation is helpful to those areas **where moisture retaining capacity of the soil is weak**.
- Canal irrigation is administered and controlled by River Valley Projects. Thus, it **serves a dual purpose** – it provides irrigation facilities and also controls flood. Many River Valley Projects are multipurpose projects and are utilised for power generation.
- Canal irrigation can be classified into two categories:
  - i. **Inundation Canals** – These canals are built **to drain out the flood water during rainy season**. These canals do not have any weir (or low head dam) to regulate the flow of water. The irrigation through inundation canals is seasonal and depends on rainfall. **In winter or dry season, these canals are of no use**. These are mainly found in **Sutlej–Ganga valley and Brahmaputra valley**. However, attempts are being made to convert them into perennial canals by joining them with River Valley Projects or Multipurpose Projects.

BONUS KNOWLEDGE

Important Inundation Canals in India

Canals	States Irrigated
Indira Gandhi Canal	Plains of Haryana, Punjab, and Rajasthan
Sirhind Canal	Plains of Haryana and Punjab
Triveni Canal	Bihar
Sarda Canal	Uttar Pradesh
Eden Canal	West Bengal
Tilpara Canal	Jharkhand and West Bengal
Mutha Canal	Maharashtra
Sampad Sagar Canal	Andhra Pradesh
Anicut Canal	Tamil Nadu
Buckingham Canal	Andhra Pradesh and Tamil Nadu

ii. **Perennial Canals** – These canals maintain the flow of water **throughout the year**. Flow of water in this type of canals is regulated **by weir and sluice gates**. These canals draw water either from the reservoir or from the river valley projects. Perennial canals are mostly found in Punjab, Uttar Pradesh and Tamil Nadu.

- In terms of NIA under **Canal Irrigation**, **Uttar Pradesh** is at the top followed by **Rajasthan**.
- Through Canal Irrigation, sediments are brought down by river water, which get deposited on the agricultural fields and add to the fertility of the soil.
- One of the drawbacks of Canal Irrigation is that because of excessive flow of water, capillary action brings salt to the surface, which makes large areas unfit for agriculture. A large number of areas in Maharashtra, U.P., Punjab and Haryana have faced this problem. This is also known as problem of '**Reh**'.

3. Tank Irrigation

- Tanks are the reservoir of a specific size depending on the availability of water and the requirements.
- It is a **traditional way of storing water** from rainfall, streams, rivers, etc. This stored water is mainly used for irrigation.
- In different areas, fishing is carried on in tanks, thus increasing the income of the farmer.
- In **Deccan Plateau and Southern region of India**, tank irrigation is used to a large extent. In these parts of the country, the supply of water is mostly dependent on seasonal rainfall. Also, due to stony and uneven surfaces, it is difficult to excavate well or canal, thus tank irrigation is a popular system of irrigation in the regions of Deccan Plateau and Southern parts of our country.
- In terms of NIA under **Tank Irrigation**, **Andhra Pradesh (around 29 per cent)** is at the top followed by **Tamil Nadu (around 23 per cent)**.
- However, the system of tank irrigation suffers from certain **drawbacks**:

   i. Because of large expanse of shallow water tank, the evaporation takes place rapidly and results in loss of water resource.

ii. It does not ensure perennial supply of water for irrigation.
iii. It occupies a huge area of cultivable land.

EXAM ESSENTIAL

- Around **49 per cent of the Net Sown Area** in India is properly irrigated (Net Irrigated Area) and remaining around 51 per cent of the cultivable land depends on the mercy of rainwater.
- Net Irrigated Area (NIA) **has gradually increased** over the years (as per latest available data of 2018, NIA is 69.4 million hectare)

Net Irrigated Area under various systems of Irrigation

Type	Percentage of NIA under it (2001–02)	Percentage of NIA under it (2022–23)	Remarks
Canal irrigation	27%	22.85%	Decreased
Tank irrigation	4%	2.85%	Decreased
Tube well irrigation	41%	49.34% **(highest)**	**Increased**
Dug well irrigation	21%	13.46%	Decreased
Other sources of irrigation	7%	11.5%	Increased
Total	**100%**	**100%**	

Top 5 Irrigated States in terms of percentage of Net Irrigated Areas (2018–19)

State	Arable land (in '000' ha)	% of Net Irrigated Area
Punjab	4,233	97%
Haryana	3,817	86%
Uttar Pradesh	18,775	77%
Madhya Pradesh	17,121	66%
West Bengal	5,615	55%

Crop-Wise Gross Irrigated Area *(as per 2014–15 figures)*

Crop	As a % of Gross Irrigated Area under Food Grains
Rice	**41% *(2nd highest)***
Jowar	1%
Bajra	1.1%
Maize	3.6%
Ragi	0.2%
Wheat	**46.1% *(highest)***
Barley	0.9%
Total Cereals and Millets	**93.4%**
Pulses	**6.6%**
Total Foodgrain	**100%**

Source: Statistical Year Book India 2018, Economic Survey 2024–25

6th CENSUS OF MINOR IRRIGATION SCHEMES

- The 6th Census of Minor Irrigation (MI) Schemes was launched by the Ministry of Jal Shakti with the **reference year 2017–18**. The report was published in 2023.
- According to the report, **23.14 million MI schemes** have been recorded nationwide, of which **21.93 million (94.8%)** are surface water (SW) schemes and **1.21 million (5.2%)** are ground water (GW) schemes.

Leading States in number of Ground Water schemes	Leading States in number of Surface Water schemes	Leading States in total number of schemes
• Uttar Pradesh • Maharashtra • Madhya Pradesh	• Maharashtra • Karnataka • Telangana	• Uttar Pradesh • Maharashtra • Madhya Pradesh

Source: Ministry of Jal Shakti, PIB, 6th Census Report

Percentage Distribution of MI schemes by type: During 6th MI census, dugwell schemes have major share followed by shallow tubewells which is also depicted from the pie-chart given below.

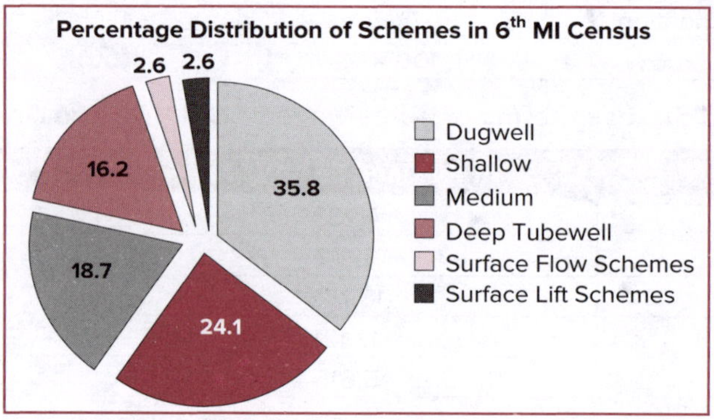

Source: 6th Census of Minor Irrigation Schemes

Leading States in Number of MI Schemes by Type

Dugwell	Shallow Tubewell	Medium Tubewell	Deep Tubewell	Surface Flow	Surface Lift
• Maharashtra • Tamil Nadu • Madhya Pradesh	• Uttar Pradesh • Madhya Pradesh • Gujarat	• Karnataka • Telangana • Bihar	• Punjab • Andhra Pradesh • Rajasthan	• Maharashtra • Karnataka • Jharkhand	• Maharashtra • Odisha • Karnataka

Source: 6th Census of Minor Irrigation Schemes

- **Dugwell** comprises highest share in the total number of MI schemes, followed by shallow tube well, medium tube well and deep tube well.
- **Uttar Pradesh** is the leading state in the number of MI schemes, followed by Maharashtra, Madhya Pradesh, and Tamil Nadu.
- There has been an increase of about **1.42 million** in MI schemes.

- The GW and SW schemes have increased by **6.9 per cent** and **1.2 per cent**, respectively.
- IPC of MI schemes has declined by 0.76 per cent. Shallow tube-well scheme has the maximum share in IPC during 6th census.
- IPU has increased about **6.1 per cent**. Shallow tube-well scheme possesses the maximum share in IPU.
- Ratio of IPU to IPC has increased from **79.7 per cent in 5th MI census to 85.1 per cent in 6th MI census**.

> **Last Minute SNIPPETS**
>
> The 7th Minor Irrigation Census is being held in 2025.

Percentage distribution of MI schemes according to lifting devices

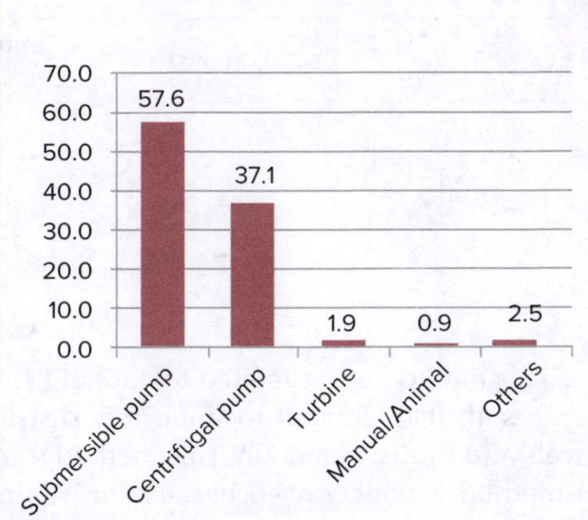

Percentage distribution of MI schemes according to source of energy

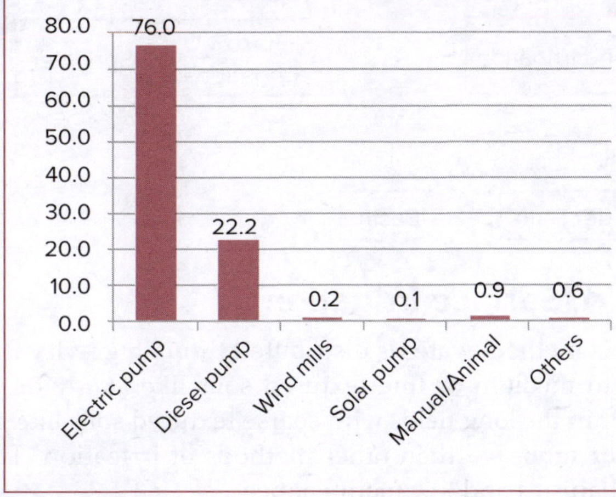

RAINFALL AND IRRIGATION SYSTEM

- Precipitation plays a significant role in the global water cycle. It is the primary source for freshwater replenishment, crucial for ecosystems and human activities. The consequences of climate change on rainfall patterns are profound. They impact agricultural practices which rely upon consistent weather conditions.
- The volatility in agricultural growth has significantly diminished over time on account of targeted interventions in India. According to the Economic Survey 2024–25, about 55 per cent of the net sown area receives irrigation. Hence, the agriculture sector remains highly vulnerable to weather variability.
- The aftermath of erratic monsoon patterns is highly pronounced for marginal and small-scale farmers. They represent about 85 per cent of India's agricultural holdings. These farmers cultivate on plots about less than 2 hectares in size. They are highly vulnerable to the repercussions of climate variability.

METHODS OF IRRIGATION

After getting water for cultivation from different sources and different systems, supply of water to the roots of the plants depends on various factors like **the level of ground, type of soil, type of crops and the availability of water**.

Based on these factors there are various methods of irrigation.

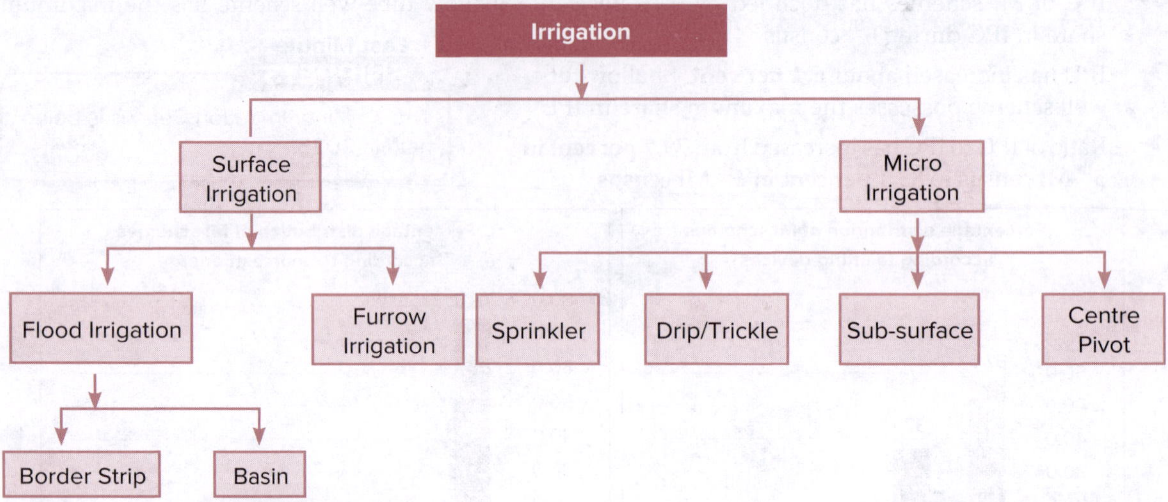

1. Surface Irrigation

In this method, water is distributed **through gravity flow**. This method is best suited to **flat land slopes** and to medium or fine textured soils like **loamy or clayey** soil. It is difficult to uniformly distribute water in the long fields with coarse textured soils like gravels and sands. Generally, this method is **more labour intensive** than other methods of irrigation. This method is **widely used** because of its simple mechanisms and low maintenance.

(i) Flood Irrigation

It involves opening a water channel in a plot/field so that water flow freely in all directions and cover the whole surface of the land. It is an **inefficient method** because only around 20 per cent of the water flown is actually used by plants.

(a) Border Strip Method In this method, crop field is divided into number of strips of width 10–15 m and of length around 90–400 m. In between the strips, embankments are made which are filled with irrigated water. Eventually, the soil absorbs water, and plants get the required amount of water from the soil.

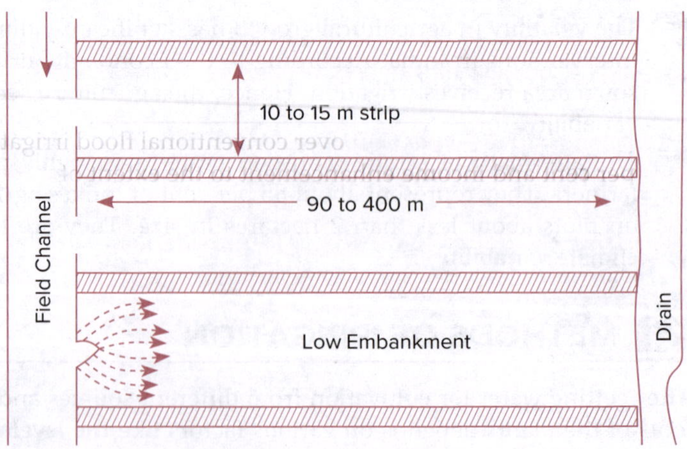

Border Strip method

(b) Basin Method Field is divided into basins of area measuring **10–100 square metre** or even **more**. Small irrigation channels are made between two adjacent basins. These small basins are filled with water to make the soil saturated. This method of irrigation is **suitable for rice cultivation**. In this method, wastage of water and soil erosion can be reduced. But due to the formation of borders between the basins in the field, **wastage of land is involved** in this method.

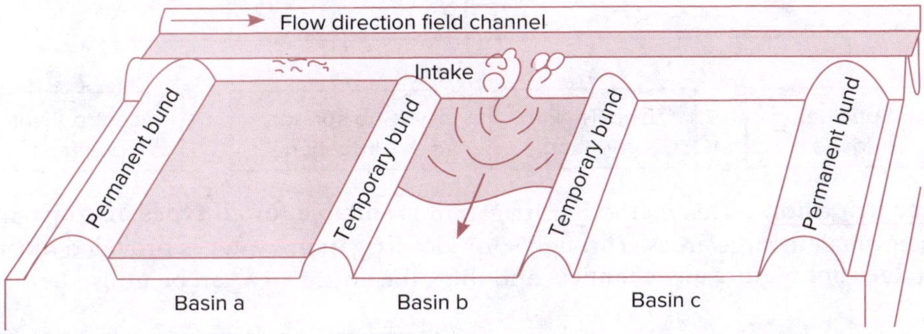

Basin method

(ii) Furrow Irrigation

Under this method, **trenches or furrows are dug** in between the rows of crops in a field. This is one of the oldest methods of irrigation and **works well for row crops** such as vegetables like beans, tomato, potato, etc. This method requires less investment and involves simple technique. Thus, it is very attractive in developing economies where highly mechanised systems are not available.

Furrow Irrigation

2. Micro-Irrigation

- It involves application of water at low volume and at frequent intervals under low pressure in the zone of plant roots.
- Unlike flood irrigation where water is lost in conveyance, micro-irrigation not only leads to **water saving** but also aids in **soil health management** and **prevents water logging**.
- As per Doubling Farmers Income (DFI) Committee Report, 2018, micro-irrigation delivers **water savings up to 40 per cent** over conventional flood irrigation, crop enhancement to the extent of 47 per cent and income enhancement to the extent of **approximately 48 per cent**.
- A dedicated **Micro-Irrigation Fund** with a corpus of **₹5,000 crore** has been set up with **NABARD**. Using this fund, NABARD is to provide loans to State Governments to undertake special and innovative projects in micro-irrigation.

Types of Micro-Irrigation

Micro-Irrigation

- Sprinkler Irrigation
- Drip/Trickle Irrigation
- Sub-surface Irrigation
- Centre-Pivot Irrigation

(a) Sprinkler Irrigation This method of irrigation is **suitable for all types of crops** and it can be extended from small to large areas. Through sprinkler irrigation, water is provided **like a rainfall** to the crops. It **does not require any channels** and thus, the entire area can be utilised.

Advantages

1. Suitable for varying sizes of land – both large and small plots.
2. Better able to direct water **flow to specific areas** of a property, avoiding water loss.
3. Ability to administer fertilisers and chemical treatments through the system.

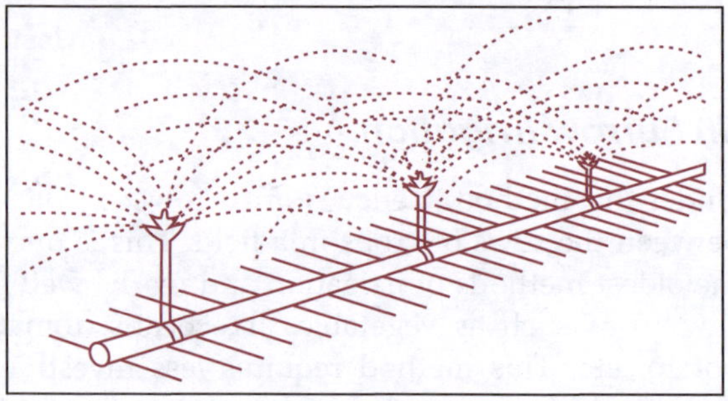

Sprinkler Irrigation

Disadvantages

1. The **initial cost** is rather **very high**.
2. Any cost of power to provide pressure must be added to the irrigation charges.
3. Wind interferes with the distribution pattern, reducing spread or increasing application rate near lateral pipe.

(b) Drip/Trickle Irrigation It is adaptable to all types of farmable slopes and **is suitable to most of the soils**. It is a technique in which water is supplied into special drip pipes which are attached with emitters having a specific spacing. Through the emitters, water is **directly supplied near the roots of the plants** with a special slow release device.

Advantages

1. Reduces water loss due to evaporation and deep drainage
2. Prevents fungal disease by minimising water contact
3. **Discourages weed growth** because water is delivered only where it is needed
4. Can eliminate many diseases which spread through drained out irrigation water having harmful chemicals like fertilisers and pesticides
5. Increases water-use efficiency

Drip Irrigation

Disadvantages:

1. Sensitivity to clogging

2. Moisture distribution issue
3. **Salinity hazards**

(c) Sub-surface Irrigation In this method, a **network of polyethylene pipes** are fixed under the ground surface to prevent run-off and to provide **water directly in the root zone** of the plants. This system is appropriate especially for **arid and windy locations**. However, this system is **costly** and **needs expert design and maintenance**.

(d) Centre-Pivot Irrigation Under centre-pivot irrigation, a **self-propelled system** in which a single pipeline supported by a row of mobile towers, is suspended 2–4 m above ground. Water is pumped into the central pipe and as the **towers rotate slowly** around the pivot point, a **large circular area is irrigated**. Benefit of such method includes uniformity of applied water, energy conservation, less risk of nutrient loss, etc.

However, this method is not suitable for rectangular/square-shaped agricultural fields. Moreover, it involves high capital cost and requires some form of energy source (electric or diesel) to operate.

Strengths of Micro-Irrigation

- Irrigation of **additional area** with same amount of water (saving of irrigation water from 20 to 48 per cent)
- Efficient deployment of other inputs such as energy, fertiliser, labour (**energy saving** – 10 to 17 per cent; **labour cost saving** – 30 to 40 per cent; fertiliser saving – 11 to 19 per cent)
- Increase in **crop productivity** (20 to 38 per cent)
- **Better quality of produce** leading to higher realisation of sale price, thereby increasing the income of farmer.
- Water-deficient land, **cultivable waste land**, etc. are being brought under cultivation due to use of micro-irrigation.

Issues/Challenges

- Need to improve the efficiency of the entire process of micro-irrigation.
- Convergence of micro-irrigation methods with water harvesting storage structures (ponds, tanks, check dams, injection wells, etc.) and related afforestation to recharge aquifers.

Last Minute SNIPPETS

As per the **Economic Survey 2024–25**, *even though there is an increase in area under micro-irrigation in India (8 per cent of irrigated area), the pace is still slow as compared to the USA (68.6 per cent) and China (13.7 per cent).*

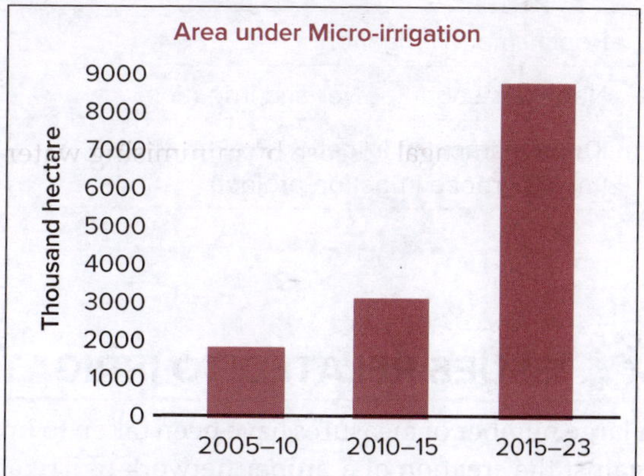

Note: Area under PDMC and other central sponsored schemes

Source: Ministry of Agriculture and Farmers Welfare, [Economic Survey 2024–25]

MINOR, MEDIUM AND MAJOR IRRIGATION PROJECTS IN INDIA

Irrigation projects in India are broadly classified as minor, medium and major projects.

- If the **Culturable Command Area** (CCA) is **less than 2,000 ha**, then it is classified as **minor irrigation project**. It comprises dug wells, tube wells, storage tanks, etc.
- If the CCA is between **2,000 and 10,000 ha**, then it is classified as **medium irrigation project**.
- If the CCA is **more than 10,000 ha**, then it is classified as **major irrigation project**.

Both medium and major projects comprise canals, bunds, dams, etc.

Some of the **major irrigation projects in India** are listed below:

EXAM ESSENTIAL

Major Irrigation Projects in India

Project	River	States
DVC (power, irrigation, flood control)	Damodar	Jharkhand and West Bengal
Gandak Project (power and irrigation)	Gandak	Bihar, Uttar Pradesh and Nepal
Kosi Project (power, irrigation, flood control)	Kosi	Bihar and Nepal
Farakka (power, irrigation, navigation)	Ganga	West Bengal
Chambal Project (power and irrigation)	Chambal	Madhya Pradesh and Rajasthan
Durgapur Barrage (irrigation and navigation)	Damodar	West Bengal and Jharkhand
Ramganga (power and irrigation)	Ramganga	Uttarakhand
Matatila Project (power and irrigation)	Betwa	Uttar Pradesh and Madhya Pradesh
Hirakud (power and irrigation)	Mahanadi	Odisha
Tungabhadra (power and irrigation)	Tungabhadra	Karnataka and Andhra Pradesh
Kakrapar (irrigation)	Tapi	Gujarat
Ukai (power and irrigation)	Tapi	Gujarat
Poochampad (irrigation)	Godavari	Andhra Pradesh
Nagarjunasagar (power and irrigation)	Krishna	Andhra Pradesh and Telangana
Kaleshwaram Lift Irrigation Project or KLIP (multi-purpose irrigation project)	Godavari	Telangana

ISSUES RELATED TO IRRIGATION IN INDIA

A large number of measures have been taken to improve irrigation. However, there are various challenges against the creation of a proper network of irrigation in India. Some are discussed below:

1. Delay in Completion of Projects

Since first Five Year Plan, we have been focussing on proliferation of irrigation projects. But delay in completion of these projects remains a major challenge. There have been delays in acquisition of land, constructing field channels, land levelling, etc.

2. Under-utilisation of Irrigation Facilities

Gap between Irrigation Potential Created (IPC) and Irrigation Potential Utilised (IPU) indicates the created irrigation facilities are not properly utilised.

3. Inter-State Water Disputes

Irrigation being a State subject, differences in opinions and priorities of various States is one of the reasons for the delay in implementation of irrigation projects.

4. Decline in Water Table

In recent period, it has been observed that the water table is declining steadily in several parts of the country. It is the result of over-exploitation of ground water and insufficient recharge through rainwater. This results in difficulties in storing water for irrigation. Thus, there is a need for convergence of irrigation methods with the creation of water harvesting structures.

Other irrigation related issues include cost of irrigation increasing with the time, problem of salinity and water logging, increasing water-borne and water associated diseases.

BONUS KNOWLEDGE

CENTRAL GROUND WATER BOARD (CGWB)

It is the National Apex Agency for ground water management and established in **1970** under the **Ministry of Water Resources**. Central Ground Water Board is a multi-disciplinary scientific organisation. The Board also takes up special studies on various aspects of ground water sector such as ground water depletion, sea water ingress, ground water contamination, etc. The **National Aquifer Mapping and Management program (NAQUIM)** is being implemented by the Central Ground Water Board (CGWB).

CENTRAL GROUND WATER AUTHORITY (CGWA)

It was set-up in **1997** under the **Environment (Protection) Act, 1986** to regulate and control the development and management of ground water resources in the country. It regulates and controls the management and development of ground water in the country and issues necessary regulatory directions for the purpose.

NATIONAL WATER INFORMATICS CENTRE (NWIC)

Under the Ministry of Jal Shakti, Department of Water Resources, RD & GR, the government set up the National Water Informatics Centre **(NWIC) in 2018**. NWIC intends to provide a standardised national GIS format and scalable web-enabled information system.

CENTRAL WATER COMMISSION (CWC)

CWC was formerly known as the Central Waterways, Irrigation, and Navigation Commission (CWINC). It was set up in **1945** by the Government on the recommendation of **Dr. B.R. Ambedkar**, Member (Labour) of the Viceroy's Executive Council. It is India's leading technical institution for water resources under the Union Ministry of Water Resources, River Development, and Ganga Rejuvenation.

NATIONAL WATER DEVELOPMENT AGENCY (NWDA)

The agency was set up in **1982** as Autonomous Society under the **Societies Registration Act, 1860**. It aims to conduct the water balance and other researches on a scientific and realistic basis for the productive utilisation of water resources.

RECENT GOVERNMENT INITIATIVES IN IRRIGATION

EXAM ESSENTIAL

Pradhan Mantri Krishi Sinchai Yojana (PMKSY)

- It was launched during 2015–16, by subsuming/amalgamating former three schemes of the Central Government, which were
  i. **Accelerated Irrigation Benefit Programme** of Ministry of Jal Shakti (Department of Water Resources, RD & GR)
  ii. **Integrated Watershed Management** of Ministry of Rural Development
  iii. **Farm Water Management** of National Mission on Sustainable Agriculture of Department of Agriculture and Cooperation
- PMKSY was launched under the Ministry of Agriculture and Farmers' Welfare. **But in 2016, the Ministry of Jal Shakti** was made the **nodal ministry** for PMKSY.
- **Motto of PMKSY** – *Har Khet Ko Paani* (HKKP).
- It had an indicative outlay of **₹50,000 crore** over five financial years (2015–16 to 2019–20).
- **Principal Components of PMKSY include:**
  1. **Accelerated Irrigation Benefits Programme (AIBP)** – It was launched in 1996–97 and has been combined with PMKSY. AIBP is presently implemented by the **Ministry of Jal Shakti** (Dept of Water Resources, RD & GR).
     It focuses on **extending loan assistance** to the States for faster completion of ongoing major and medium irrigation projects.
     The **main objective** of this scheme is **to restart** the stopped river valley projects (both major and medium) mainly due to financial constraints.
  2. **Har Khet Ko Paani (HKKP)** – This component aims at increasing the access of water and **extending the coverage of irrigation**. Focus is on ground water development, lift irrigation, diversion of water from water-plenty areas to water-scarce areas, repair, renovation and restoration of traditional water bodies, etc. It is being implemented by the **Ministry of Jal Shakti** (Dept of Water Resources, RD & GR).
  3. **Per Drop More Crop (Micro-irrigation)** – It focuses on increasing **water use efficiency** by enhancing the adoption of **micro-irrigation** and various other water saving technologies. It also focuses on promoting crop diversification and ensuring crop water budgeting. Pattern of financial assistance/subsidy to farmers for micro-irrigation scheme is **55 per cent for small and marginal farmers** and **45 per cent for other farmers**. This fund is met by the Centre and States in the ratio 60:40 (for Northeastern and Himalayan States, Centre–State sharing pattern is 90:10 and for UTs – 100 per cent by Central Government). It is being implemented by the **Ministry of Agriculture and Farmers' Welfare**.

4. **Watershed Development** – It is being implemented by the **Department of Land Resources** (under Ministry of Rural Development), and focus of this component is to undertake rainwater conservation, construction of farm pond, water harvesting structure, small check dams, soil and moisture conservation, etc.

Neeranchal National Watershed Project (NNWP)

- It was launched by the Government of India in 2016 with **50 per cent financial assistance from International Development Association (IDA) arm of World Bank**.
- **Objective of NNWP was to** support the Integrated Watershed Management Programme (IWMP) for the improvement and conservation of water resources.
- The NNWP **supported PMKSY** in hydrology and water management, agricultural production systems, capacity building, etc.
- **Wastelands have been targeted** under NNWP.
- **Four Components of NNWP include** – Central Institution and Capacity Building, National Innovation Support, Support to IWMP and Project Management and Coordination.
- Nodal Ministry of NNWP – **Ministry of Rural Development**.
- Though being implemented in all States, NNWP **focused more on nine States** – Gujarat, Rajasthan, Madhya Pradesh, Chhattisgarh, Telangana, Odisha, Andhra Pradesh, Jharkhand and Maharashtra.

Atal Bhujal Yojana

- The Atal Bhujal Yojana (ABHY), launched in **2019**, is a **Central Sector Scheme** worth ₹6,000 crore for sustainable management of ground water with community participation. It has started from 2020–21 for 5 years.
- It envisages people's participation through the formation of **'Water User Associations'**, water budgeting, preparation and implementation of Gram-panchayat-wise water security plans, etc.
- It is being implemented by the **Ministry of Jal Shakti**.
- The scheme is being funded by the **Government of India and the World Bank** on **50:50 basis**.
- It is mainly focused on seven water stressed States i.e. Gujarat, Haryana, Karnataka, Madhya Pradesh, Maharashtra, Rajasthan and Uttar Pradesh.

National Hydrology Project

- It started in **2016** as a **Central Sector Scheme** under the **Ministry of Jal Shakti** and is **supported by the World Bank**.
- The NHP will help in gathering hydro-meteorological data which will be stored and analysed on a real-time basis and can be seamlessly accessed by any user at the State/District/Village level. The project has envisaged to cover the entire country.
- **Four components of NHP**:
  1. In situ Hydromet Monitoring System and Hydromet Data Acquisition System
  2. Setting up of National Water Informatics Centre (NWIC)
  3. Water Resources Operation and Management System
  4. Water Resources Institutions and Capacity Building

➤ **Benefits of NHP:**

1. Data storage, exchange, analysis and dissemination through **National Water Informatics Centre**.
2. Lead time in **flood forecast** from 1 day to at least 3 days.
3. Mapping of flood inundation areas for use by the disaster management authorities.
4. Assessment of surface and ground water resources in a river basin for better planning and allocation for PMKSY and other schemes of Govt. of India.

BONUS KNOWLEDGE

FIRST WATER BODIES CENSUS

The Ministry of Jal Shakti has conducted the first water body census in conjunction with the sixth minor irrigation census **(reference year 2017–18)** across the country (except for Daman and Diu, Dadra & Nagar Haveli, and Lakshadweep).

Key Findings

➤ Out of the enumerated 24,24,540 water bodies, 59.5% (14,42,993) are ponds, 15.7% (3,81,805) are tanks, 12.1% (2,92,280) are reservoirs whereas the remaining 12.7% (3,07,462) are water conservation schemes/check dams/percolation tanks (9.3%), lakes (0.9%) and other water bodies (2.5%).

Top five States in number of water bodies:

West Bengal	30.8% (7,47,480)
Uttar Pradesh	10.1% (2,45,087)
Andhra Pradesh	7.9% (1,90,777)
Odisha	7.5% (1,81,837)
Assam	7.1% (1,72,492)

5 leading States with maximum number of ponds, tanks, lakes, reservoirs and Water conservation schemes/percolation tanks/check dams

Ponds	Tanks	Lakes	Reservoirs	Water Conservation Schemes / Check Dams
West Bengal	Andhra Pradesh	Tamil Nadu	West Bengal	Maharashtra
Uttar Pradesh	Odisha	Bihar	Jharkhand	Andhra Pradesh
Assam	Himachal Pradesh	Karnataka	Bihar	Gujarat
Odisha	Tamil Nadu	West Bengal	Odisha	Telangana
Jharkhand	Gujarat	Odisha	Andhra Pradesh	Jharkhand

Desertification and Land Degradation Atlas

- **India** is a **signatory** to the **United Nations Convention on Combating Desertification (UNCCD)** and is committed to combat desertification and land degradation and even intends to achieve neutral status of land degradation by 2030.
- The Atlas presents state-wise desertification and land degradation status maps depicting land use, process of degradation and severity level.

BONUS KNOWLEDGE

NATIONAL AQUIFER MAPPING AND MANAGEMENT PROGRAMME (NAQUIM)

The programme envisages mapping of aquifers (water bearing formations), characterisation and development of Aquifer Management Plans for facilitating sustainable management of Ground Water Resources. The Implementing agency is **Central Ground Water Board** (CGWB). **NAQUIM** was initiated in 2012, as a part of the 'Ground Water Management and Regulation' scheme.

THE BULDHANA PATTERN

It is a **water conservation framework** practiced in **Buldhana district of Maharashtra's Vidarbha region**, which is drought prone. In this pattern, construction activities are synchronised with water conservation like desiltation and water body deepening for construction of highways and railways. The NITI Aayog had prepared draft guidelines based on this pattern for water conservation.

ROOT ZONE MOISTURE

The **water and moisture in the soil at a depth of 39 inches** is called root zone moisture. In draught prone areas, the aquifers rely on surface moisture to percolate through soil and rocks. When there are no rains and surface moisture, the root zone moisture might vanish absolutely. The soil becomes unfit for cultivation.

Root Zone Irrigation is the only solution to soils that have lost root zone moisture. Root zone irrigation is more effective than the surface drip irrigation. Root zone irrigation is **used in cultivation of grapes**.

BHUVAN APP

- Developed **by ISRO** and launched in **2009**, it allows exploring 2D/3D representation of Earth's Surface. It is specifically tailored to view India with high resolution and includes thematic maps on disasters, crop areas, water bodies, irrigation projects, land cover, etc.
- Irrigation-related assets created under Per Drop More Crop scheme of PMKSY are **geo-tagged**. The App is enabled to provide **information** on **WUE** of various micro-irrigation projects. The App is in four local languages – English, Hindi, Tamil and Telugu.

INDIA-EU WATER PARTNERSHIP (IEWP)

The India-EU Water Partnership (IEWP) is an outcome of the 'Joint Declaration on Water' which was adopted by India and the EU in 2016 during the 13th EU-India Summit in Brussels. It intends to increase cooperation on water issues, including 'Clean Ganga' programme of the Government of India.

SUMMARY

- **Irrigation** – Artificial way of supplying water to the agricultural land in an appropriate volume – to increase agricultural productivity and to expand agricultural sector.
- **Culturable Command Area (CCA)** – Area which can be irrigated from a scheme and is fit for cultivation.
- **Net Sown Area** – Total area sown with crops and orchards – area sown more than once in the same year is counted only once.
- **Gross Cropped Area (GCA)** – Total area sown once as well as more than once in a particular year – when the crop is sown on a piece of land twice, the area is counted twice under GCA.
- **Irrigation Potential Created (IPC)** – It refers to the total area of land that is potentially irrigable through various irrigation projects and initiatives.
- **Irrigation Potential Utilized (IPU)** – It refers to the actual area of land that is irrigated by the irrigation infrastructure.
- **Systems of irrigation** – Well irrigation (most popular method in India) – tank irrigation – canal irrigation.
- **Micro-Irrigation** – Application of water at low volume and at frequent intervals under low pressure in the zone of plant roots helps in water saving, soil heath management, prevents water logging – types are sprinkler, drip/trickle, sub-surface and centre pivot.
- **Watershed Development** – Under Department of Land Resources (under Ministry of Rural Development) – focus of this component is to undertake rainwater conservation, construction of farm pond, water harvesting structure, small check dams, soil and moisture conservation, etc.
- **National Water Development Agency** – Set up in 1982 as Autonomous Society under the Societies Registration Act, 1860.
- **Bhuvan App** – By ISRO – in 2009 – exploring 2D/3D representation of Earth's Surface – tailored to view India with high resolution and includes thematic maps on crop areas, water bodies, irrigation projects, land cover, etc.
- **National Hydrology Project** – Introduced in 2016 – Central Sector Scheme – under the Ministry of Jal Shakti – supported by World Bank.
- **Atal Bhujal Yojana** – Introduced in 2019 – under the Ministry of Jal Shakti – Central Sector Scheme – for sustainable management of groundwater with community participation – funded by GOI and World Bank on 50:50 basis.

UPSC CSE PREVIOUS YEARS' PRELIMINARY EXAMINATION QUESTIONS

1. Consider the following statements: **[2023]**

1. India has more arable area than China.
2. The proportion of irrigated area is more in India as compared to China.
3. The average productivity per hectare in Indian agriculture is higher than that in China.

How many of the above statements are correct?

(a) Only one (b) Only two
(c) All three (d) None

2. Which one of the following has been constituted under the Environment (Protection) Act, 1986? **[2022]**

(a) Central Water Commission
(b) Central Ground Water Board
(c) Central Ground Water Authority
(d) National Water Development Agency

3. Consider the following statements: **[2020]**

1. 36 per cent of India's districts are classified as 'overexploited' or 'critical' by the Central

Ground Water Authority (CGWA).

2. CGWA was formed under the Environment (Protection) Act.
3. India has the largest area under ground water irrigation in the world.

Which of the statements given above is/are correct?

(a) 1 only (b) 2 and 3 only
(c) 2 only (d) 1 and 3 only

4. Which of the following is/are the advantage/ advantages of practising drip irrigation? **[2016]**

1. Reduction in weed
2. Reduction in soil salinity
3. Reduction in soil erosion

Select the correct answer using the codes given below:

(a) 1 and 2 only
(b) 3 only
(c) 1 and 3 only
(d) None of the above is an advantage of practising drip irrigation

5. With reference to micro-irrigation, which of the following statements is/are correct? **[2011]**

1. Fertiliser/nutrient loss can be reduced.
2. It is the only means of irrigation in dry land farming.
3. In some areas of farming, receding of ground water table can be checked.

Select the correct answer using the codes given below:

(a) 1 only (b) 2 and 3 only
(c) 1 and 3 only (d) 1, 2 and 3

☞ NO QUESTIONS ASKED
2024, 2021, 2020, 2019, 2018, 2017, 2015, 2014, 2013, 2012

ANSWER KEY

1. (b) 2. (c) 3. (b) 4. (c) 5. (c)

UPSC CSE PREVIOUS YEARS' MAIN EXAMINATION QUESTIONS

1. What are the major challenges faced by the Indian irrigation system in recent times? State the measures taken by the government for efficient irrigation management. **[2024]**

2. How and to what extent would micro-irrigation help in solving India's water crisis? **[2021]**

3. Suggest measures to improve water storage and irrigation system to make its judicious use under depleting scenario. **[2020]**

4. Elaborate the impact of **National Watershed Project** in increasing agricultural production from water-stressed areas. **[2019]**

5. How has India benefited from the contributions of **Sir M. Visvesvaraya** and Dr **M.S. Swaminathan** in the fields of water engineering and agricultural science, respectively? **[2019]**

6. What is **WUE**? Describe the **role of micro-irrigation** in increasing the WUE. **[2016]**

7. What is **Allelopathy**? Discuss its role in major cropping systems of irrigated agriculture. **[2016]**

☞ NO QUESTIONS ASKED
2023, 2022, 2018, 2017, 2015, 2014, 2013, 2012

CHAPTER

19

INDIAN INDUSTRY

CHAPTER OUTLINE

- Current Trend in Industrial Sector
- Evolution of Industrial Policies Prior to 1991
- New Industrial Policy 1991
- Public Sector Undertakings
- Policy of Navratnas
- Policy of Miniratnas
- Policy of Maharatnas
- Financial Autonomy to Maharatna CPSEs
- Performance of CPSEs
- Tools to measure performance of Industries
- Index of Industrial Production (IIP)
- Index of Eight Core Industries
- Annual Survey of Industries
- Purchasing Managers' Index
- Industrial Sickness
- Remedial measures undertaken in the past
- Board of Industrial and Financial Reconstruction
- The Companies (Amendment) Act, 2019
- National Company Law Tribunal
- Corporate Social Responsibility (CSR)
- Various Sectors of Manufacturing Industry
- National Investment and Manufacturing Zone
- Special Economic Zones (SEZs) in India
- Ease of Doing Business Report
- Make in India
- Start-up India
- Stand-up India
- Champion Sectors in India
- Industry 4.0 and India

Indian economy is divided into three major sectors, i.e. the primary sector (agriculture), secondary sector (manufacturing and industry) and tertiary sector (services).

The Industrial sector usually collects raw materials from the primary sector and then produces consumer goods, capital goods, etc. Industrial sector is the second major contributor of GDP in the economy among the three sectors. Therefore, the government gives a good amount of focus on the development of industrial sector.

CURRENT TREND IN INDUSTRIAL SECTOR

➤ After independence, industrial sector initially showed a rising trend towards its contribution/share in GDP. However, with the rapidly increasing share of service sector, the share of industry in overall GDP started showing a **fluctuating trend** in recent years. The Economic Survey 2024–25 estimates that the industrial sector's contribution to the GVA is 27.6 per cent for the fiscal year 2024–25.

➤ **Major sectoral classification** under industrial sector:

1. Mining and quarrying
2. Manufacturing
3. Electricity, gas, water supply and other utility services
4. Construction

did you KNOW? In 2020, **Mizoram** became the first state in India to grant industry status to **sports.**

Among above four, **manufacturing sector** has the major contribution towards GDP.

EVOLUTION OF INDUSTRIAL POLICIES PRIOR TO 1991

Name of the Policy	Features
Industrial Policy Resolution of 1948 (IPR-1948)	• A system of mixed economy was introduced. • Stressed on protecting cottage and small-scale industries by giving them priority status. • Fair wages and social security for harmonious industrial resolutions. • Focused on the development of roads, railways, electricity and irrigation. • Industries were classified into four broad categories: i. Industries with exclusive central government's monopoly: arms and ammunition, atomic energy and rail transport. ii. Mixed sector (both under government and private sectors) (basic/key industries): Six industries – coal, iron and steel, aircraft manufacturing, ship building, mineral oil, and telegraph and telephone. iii. Controlled private sector: Government controlled these industries indirectly. These 18 industries included chemicals, sugar, automobiles, cotton and woollen textiles, cement, paper, salt, fertiliser, tractor, electricity, etc. iv. Industries under private sector: Industries not included in the above three categories were included under this category.
Industrial Policy Resolution of 1956 (IPR-1956)	• Based on the P.C. Mahalanobis model. This model was also considered as the 'Economic Constitution of India' or the 'Bible of State Capitalism'. • Emphasis was on **heavy industries** and industrial development in the **backward regions**. • Promotion of technical and managerial skills for industrial growth and establishment of ITIs. • The four-fold classification of industries under IPR-1948 was changed now to a three-fold classification: i. Schedule A (strictly under central government) – 17 industries. ii. Schedule B (open to both private and public sectors) – 12 industries. iii. Schedule C (open to private sector but subject to licensing and regulation) – all other industries.
Industrial Policy Statement of 1969	• **Monopolies and Restrictive Trade Practices (MRTP) Act, 1969** was introduced on the recommendation of **Dutt Committee**. • Due to its inherent limitations, MRTP Act was later abolished and was replaced by the Competition Act, 2002.

Name of the Policy	Features
Industrial Policy Statement of 1973	• Six core industries were identified – iron and steel, cement, coal, crude oil, oil refinery and electricity. • Public–private partnership (PPP) was given emphasis and called the joint sector in which a partnership between State and Central governments and private sector was allowed. • Foreign Exchange Regulation Act (FERA), 1973 was enacted.
Industrial Policy Statement of 1977	• Introduced by Janata Government in 1977, by changing the 20-year-old industrial policy of 1956 and focused on small-scale and tiny industries. • Close interaction between industrial and agricultural sectors. • Highest priority was accorded to power generation and transmission sector. • Emphasis was given to village industries, resurrection of khadi and village industries, etc.
Industrial Policy Statement of 1980	• Importance was given to **public sector** for reasons of its **greater reliability, requirement of large investments and longer gestation period** of the projects. • Relaxation from licensing to a large number of industries. • Competition in the domestic market, technological upgradation, and modernisation. • Promotion of export-based industry and foreign investment.

BONUS KNOWLEDGE

THE INDUSTRIES (DEVELOPMENT & REGULATION) ACT, 1951

The Industries (Development and Regulation) Act of 1951 empowered government to regulate the pattern of industrial development through licensing. This was the advent of **'license raj'** in India. Through this Act, government put **three major controls: licensing**, allocation of **raw materials** to undertakings based on sanctioned output and **control over the prices**.

The major features of most of the pre-1991 policies were:

1. **Protection to local industries**
2. **Promotion of import substitution policy**
3. **Control over Indian industries** through licensing regime and stricter regulations
4. **Restrictions on foreign capital** under FERA, 1973
5. Encouragement to small-scale and cottage industries and establishment of public sector industries

EXAM ESSENTIAL

NEW INDUSTRIAL POLICY (NIP), 1991

This policy aimed to correct the distortions and weaknesses of the industrial structure of the country that had developed in four decades. Before this policy, emphasis was on regulation. The new policy shifted emphasis from regulation to development.

This policy focused on bringing in major reforms in the following areas:

- **Industrial De-licensing** – One of the most important features of NIP 1991 was abolition of compulsory industrial licensing for all industries **except 18**. This step immensely facilitated the smooth setting up of industries by the private sector.

Presently, only 6 industries compulsorily require industrial licensing:

1. Distillation and brewing of alcoholic drinks
2. Cigars and cigarettes of tobacco and manufactured tobacco substitutes
3. Electronic aerospace and defence equipment of all types
4. Industrial explosives including matchboxes, gun powder, etc.
5. Specific hazardous chemicals such as hydrocyanic acid, phosgene, Isocyanates, etc.
6. Drugs and Pharmaceuticals

- **De-reservation of Public Sector** – The policy drastically reduced the number of industries reserved for public sector. The number of industries reserved for public sector was reduced from 17 (as per 1956 policy) to only 8, viz., arms and ammunition; atomic energy; coal; mineral oils; mining of iron ore, manganese ore, gold, chrome ore, gypsum, sulfur and diamond; mining of copper, lead, zinc, tin, molybdenum and wolfram; atomic minerals; railway transport.

Presently, only 2 sectors are reserved for the public sector:

1. **Atomic Energy** *(Production, separation or enrichment of special fissionable materials and substances and operation of the facilities)*
2. **Railway Operations** *(**other than** construction, operation and maintenance of the following – suburban corridor projects through PPP; high-speed train project; dedicated freight lines; rolling stock including train sets, locomotives/coaches manufacturing and maintenance facilities; railway electrification; signalling systems; freight terminals; passenger terminals; Mass Rapid Transport Systems; etc.)*

- **Foreign Investment** was promoted, in both direct and indirect forms. The Foreign Investment Promotion Board (FIPB) was also established to promote FDI.
- **Foreign Technology Agreement** allowed industries with automatic approvals (within specified parameters) for undertaking technology agreements with foreign counterparts.
- **Amendments in MRTP Act** so that firms with assets above a certain specified limit were no longer required to get prior approval from the government to invest in de-licenced industries.
- **Dilution of Protections** earlier provided to Small-Scale Industries (SSIs) in order to promote their competitiveness.
- It also focussed on closure of sick public sector enterprises to increase efficiency of the public sector and revival of the weak units.

After 1991, Industrial reforms through LPG (*Liberalisation, Privatisation and Globalisation*) were undertaken (*LPG strategy is discussed in the 'Economic Planning' chapter*).

PUBLIC SECTOR UNDERTAKINGS

The companies **owned by the Union Government of India (GoI),** or one of the many states or territorial governments, or both are called Public Sector Undertakings (PSUs).

A company's stock needs to be majority owned **(≥51%)** by the government in order to be called a PSU.

PSUs may be classified into:

1. **Central Public Sector Enterprises (CPSEs)**
2. **Public Sector Banks (PSBs)**
3. **State-Level Public Enterprises (SLPEs)**

For a CPSE, the direct holding of the central government or other CPSEs in a particular CPSE is 51 per cent or more. They are administered by the *Ministry of Heavy Industries and Public Enterprises.* **CPSEs are operating in 4 sectors –** agriculture, mining and exploration, manufacturing and services.

In order to provide greater financial autonomy to CPSEs, they have been further classified into:

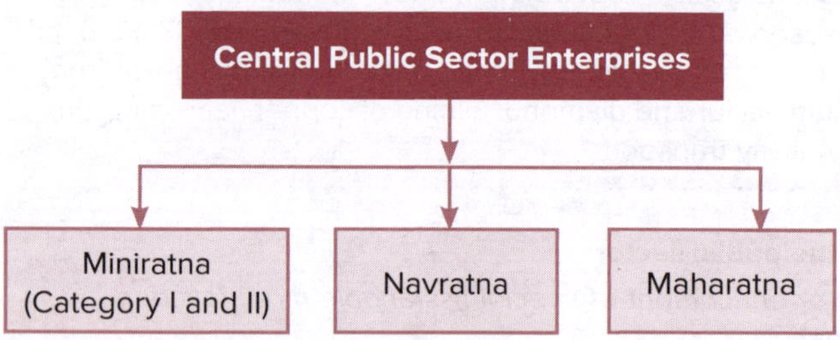

> **did you KNOW?**
> Miniratna, Navaratna, and Maharatna **are awarded by the** ***Department of Public Enterprises*** **under the** ***Ministry of Heavy Enterprises and Public Enterprises.***

Maharatna is the topmost category among the above three.

Policy of Miniratnas

The government created a category called Miniratna. The Miniratnas are divided into two categories: I and II.

Category-I Miniratna

These CPSEs should have made profits in the last 3 years continuously, earned a pre-tax profit of ₹30 crore or more in at least one of these 3 years and should have a positive net worth.

They have the financial autonomy to incur capital expenditure without government approval up to **₹300 crore** or equal to their net worth, whichever is lower.

Category-II Miniratna

These should have made profits in the last 3 years continuously and should have a positive net worth.

They have the financial autonomy to incur capital expenditure without government approval up to **₹150 crore** or up to 50 per cent of their net worth, whichever is lower.

> **Last Minute SNIPPETS**
> **As of 12 March 2025,** there are **61 Category-I Miniratna CPSEs** and **12 Category-II Miniratna CPSEs** in India.

Both the categories of Miniratnas can also enter into joint ventures and form subsidiaries in India, but under some specified restrictions.

Policy of Navratnas

These are the CPSEs that are identified as most prestigious by GoI in 1997 and given the title of *Navratnas*, allowing them greater financial autonomy to compete in the global market.

Criteria for granting Navratna Status to a CPSE

- The CPSE must have 'Miniratna Category-I' status along with Schedule 'A' listing.
- It should have at least three 'excellent' or 'very good' memorandum of understandings (MoUs) in last 5 years.
- It must obtain a composite score of 60 (out of 100) based on its performance during last 3 years. The score is based on **6 parameters,** which include:
  1. Net profit to net worth (Maximum: 25)
  2. Manpower cost to cost of production or services (Maximum: 15)
  3. Gross margin as a percentage of capital employed (Maximum: 15)
  4. Gross profit as a percentage of turnover (Maximum: 15)
  5. Earnings per share (Maximum: 10)
  6. Inter-sectorial comparison based on net profit to net worth (Maximum: 20)
- The CPSE should have four independent directors on its board.

Last Minute SNIPPETS

As of 12 March 2025, the following **26 CPSEs** have achieved the **Navratna Status:**

1. Bharat Electronics Ltd. (BEL)
2. Container Corporation of India Ltd. (CCIL)
3. Engineers India Ltd. (EIL)
4. Mahanagar Telephone Nigam Ltd. (MTNL)
5. National Aluminium Company Ltd. (NALCO)
6. NBCC (India) Ltd.
7. NMDC Ltd.
8. NLC India Ltd.
9. Rashtriya Ispat Nigam Ltd.
10. Shipping Corporation of India Ltd.
11. Rail Vikas Nigam Ltd.
12. ONGC Videsh Ltd.
13. Rashtriya Chemicals & Fertilizers Ltd.
14. IRCON International Ltd.
15. RITES Ltd.
16. National Fertilizers Limited.
17. Central Warehousing Corporation.
18. Housing & Urban Development Corporation Limited.
19. Indian Renewable Energy Development Agency Limited.
20. Mazagon Dock Shipbuilders Limited.
21. Railtel Corporation of India Limited.
22. Solar Energy Corporation of India (SECI) Ltd.
23. NHPC Limited.
24. SJVN Limited.
25. Indian Railway Catering and Tourism Corporation (IRCTC).
26. Indian Railway Finance Corporation (IRFC).

Financial Autonomy to Navratna CPSEs

Navratna status empowers CPSE to invest up to 15 per cent of its net worth in a single project but limited to an absolute ceiling of **₹1,000 crore** without government's approval. Overall ceiling on such investment in all projects put together to not exceed 30 per cent of the net worth of that CPSE.

Policy of Maharatnas

Among the three, Maharatna is the **most recent category** introduced by GoI in 2010.

Criteria for granting Maharatna Status to a CPSE

CPSEs fulfilling the following criteria are eligible to be considered for grant of Maharatna status:

- Having **Navratna** status.
- Listed in Indian stock exchange with minimum prescribed public shareholding as per SEBI regulations.
- *Average annual turnover* of more than ₹25,000 crore, during the last 3 years.
- *Average annual net worth* of more than ₹15,000 crore, during the last 3 years.
- *Average annual net profit* after tax of more than ₹5,000 crore, during the last 3 years.
- The company should have *significant global presence* or international operations.

Financial Autonomy to Maharatna CPSEs

Maharatna status empowers that CPSE to invest up to 15 per cent of its net worth in a single project but limited to an absolute ceiling of ₹5,000 crore without government's approval as against ₹1,000 crore limit for Navratnas. Overall ceiling on such investment in all projects put together should not exceed 30 per cent of the net worth of that CPSE.

Last Minute SNIPPETS

As of 12th March 2025, the following **14 CPSEs** have been awarded the covered **Maharatna status:**

1. Bharat Heavy Electricals Ltd. (BHEL)
2. Bharat Petroleum Corporation Ltd. (BPCL)
3. Coal India Ltd.
4. GAIL (India) Ltd.
5. Hindustan Petroleum Corporation Ltd. (HPCL)
6. Indian Oil Corporation Ltd. (IOCL)
7. NTPC Ltd.
8. Oil & Natural Gas Corporation (ONGC) Ltd.
9. Power Grid Corporation of India Ltd.
10. Steel Authority of India Ltd. (SAIL)
11. Power Finance Corporation (PFC)
12. Rural Electrification Corporation Limited (RECL)
13. Oil India Limited (OIL)
14. Hindustan Aeronautics Limited (HAL)

Among above 14, **Hindustan Aeronautics Limited (HAL)** is the most recent one to be awarded Maharatna status in 2024.

Performance of CPSEs

The performance of PSUs must be judged not only by their earnings in the form of profits but by the total additions they make to the flow of goods and services in the economy.

- In 2024, the Department of Public Enterprises (DPE) has demonstrated a commitment to promote economic development and efficiency in a variety of crucial sectors.
- The DPE has focused on monitoring Capital Expenditure (CAPEX) inside Central Public Sector Enterprises (CPSEs), embracing digital transformation by creating an online MoU Dashboard for CPSE Performance Assessment, and guaranteeing procurement upgrades under the DPE's control.
- In line with the government's assistance measures for Micro and Small Enterprises (MSEs), CPSEs have shown a strong commitment to inclusive procurement.

TOOLS TO MEASURE PERFORMANCE OF INDUSTRIES

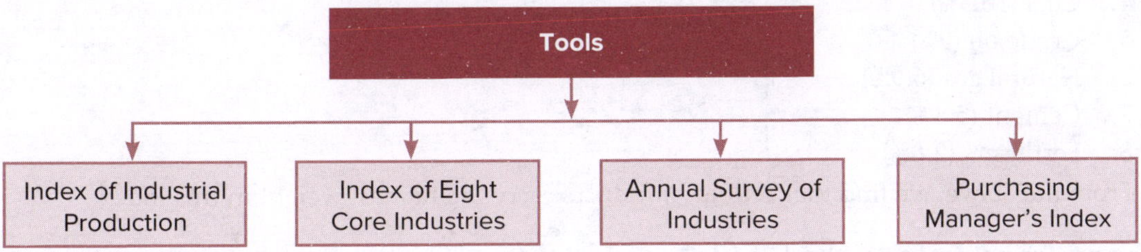

Index of Industrial Production (IIP)

- The **Central Statistics Office (CSO; now NSO)** under the *Ministry of Statistics and Programme Implementation* compiles and publishes the Index of Industrial Production (IIP) **every month.**
- IIP is a statistical measure of industrial performance.
- It measures the short-term changes in the volume of production of a basket of industrial products during a given period with respect to that in a chosen base period. Currently, the base year used is **2011–12**.
- IIP is compiled on the basis of data collected from **14 ministries.**
- While computing IIP, **weights attached** to the three sub-sectors are:

  1. For Mining Sector – **14.4 per cent weight**
  2. For Manufacturing Sector – **77.6 per cent weight**
  3. For Electricity Sector – **8 per cent weight**

  } Total = 100 per cent

- Thus, we find that the **manufacturing sector carries the highest weight** while computing IIP in the case of sectoral-based classification. In terms of use-based classification, *primary goods* carry the highest weight in measurement of IIP.

BONUS KNOWLEDGE

Quick Estimates of Index of Industrial Production and Use-based Index for the Month of November 2024 (Base Year 2011–12 = 100):

1. Quick Estimates of Index of Industrial Production (IIP) are provided on the 12th of every month (or the preceding working day if the 12th is a holiday).
2. The IIP growth rate for the month of November 2024 was 5.2%.
3. Growth rates of Mining, Manufacturing and Electricity sectors are 1.9%, 5.8% and 4.4%, respectively.

Source: Ministry of Statistics and Programme Implementation

Index of Eight Core Industries

➤ This measures the performance of eight core industries.

➤ These eight core industries **comprise 40.27 per cent of the weight in IIP.**

➤ It is considered as the barometer of the monthly industrial performance.

➤ The **eight core industries** and their assigned weights in this index are:

1. Refinery products (28%)
2. Electricity (19.9%)
3. Steel (17.9%)
4. Coal (10.3%)
5. Crude oil (9%)
6. Natural gas (6.9%)
7. Cement (5.4%)
8. Fertilisers (2.6%)

} Total = 100 per cent

From the above, we find that **refinery products** carry the highest weight in this index.

Present Trend in Index of Eight Core Industries

Industries	Growth Rate of Cumulative Index (Apr–Dec 2024) over Corresponding Period of Previous Year
Coal	+6.2%
Crude Oil	–2.1%
Natural Gas	+0.7%
Petroleum Refining Products	+2.7%
Fertilisers	+1.6%
Steel	+5.8%
Cement	+3.3%
Electricity	+5.3%

BONUS KNOWLEDGE

Capacity Utilisation (CU)

It is another economic indicator to assess demand and investment prospects of the economy. CU rates are largely able to track the pace of the manufacturing activities in the economy. The growth rate of the IIP-manufacturing index and capacity utilisation provides a snapshot of the demand conditions for India's manufacturing sector.

RBI's Business Expectation Index (BEI): This index gives a glimpse of the demand conditions in the manufacturing sector by combining parameters, which include overall business situation, production, order books, inventory of raw material and finished goods, profit margin, employment, exports and capacity utilisation.

Annual Survey of Industries

- It is the principal source of industrial statistics related to **organised manufacturing sector** in the entire country.
- Annual Survey of Industries (ASI) is **published annually by CSO** (now **NSO**), which works under the *Ministry of Statistics and Programme Implementation*.
- Information during ASI is collected as per provisions of the **Collection of Statistics Act, 2008.**
- **ASI covers:**
  1. **All the factories registered** under Sec 2(m)(i) and 2(m)(ii) of the Factories Act, 1948 (i.e. those factories employing 10 or more workers using power and those employing 20 or more without using power).
  2. Units with 100 or more employees (registered under any of the other seven Acts but under Factories Act).
  3. Registered bidi and cigar-manufacturing establishments and all electricity undertakings (not registered with Central Electricity Authority).
- **ASI does not cover:** Defence establishments, oil storage and distribution depots, departmental units such as railway workshops, government mints, sanitary, water supply, gas storage, etc.
- Data related to *unorganised manufacturing sector* is compiled by NSO every 5 years.
- Some of the **important indicators generated by ASI are:** Number of factories, production, employment, wages, invested capital, capital formation, input/output and value added on annual basis.
- It takes almost 2 years to publish the ASI report of any particular financial year.
- **Major findings as per the latest ASI 2022–23:**
  1. The report shows that the **Gross Value Added (GVA) grew by 7.3 per cent** in current prices in the year 2022–23 over 2021–22.
  2. Industries like manufacture of Basic Metal, Coke and Refined Petroleum Products, Food Products, Chemical and Chemical products and Motor vehicles were the main drivers of this growth in 2022–23. These industries, taken together, contributed about 58 per cent of the total output of the sector.
  3. **Maharashtra ranked first** in terms of GVA in 2022–23, followed by Gujarat, Tamil Nadu, Karnataka and Uttar Pradesh. The top five states, taken together, contributed more than 54 per cent of the total manufacturing GVA of India in 2022–23.
  4. These top five states, taken together, have contributed about 55 per cent of the total manufacturing employment in the year 2022–23.

BONUS KNOWLEDGE

PURCHASING MANAGERS' INDEX (PMI)

- PMI in India is published by the **Japanese firm Nikkei** but compiled by IHT Markit.
- It is an indicator of the economic health of the manufacturing and services sector.
- **Two separate PMIs** are published – **Manufacturing PMI** and **Services PMI**.
- PMI reflects the economic indicators derived from monthly surveys of **private sector companies**. The data for the index is collected through a survey of 400 purchasing managers.
- The PMI is based on **five major indicators**: *new orders, inventory levels, production, supplier deliveries and the employment environment.*

INDUSTRIAL SICKNESS

As per the provisions of the Companies Act, 2013 – '*Where on demand by the secured creditors of a company representing 50 per cent or more of its outstanding debt, the company has failed to pay that debt within 30 days of the service of demand notice, then any secured creditor may approach National Company Law Tribunal (NCLT) for declaring that company as* ***sick company****.*'

Causes of Industrial Sickness

External Causes	Internal Causes
• Power cuts • Erratic supply of inputs or raw materials • Recession in market leading to demand and credit restraints • Sudden changes in the government policies • Tough competition from foreign players in case of some industries	• Faults at the planning and construction stage such as wrong choice of location, inadequate market analysis, etc. • Purchase of inappropriate/obsolete/defective plant and machinery • Burden of unpaid debt • Entrepreneurial incompetence • Acute labour problems such as strikes, lock-outs, high attrition, etc.

Remedial Measures undertaken in the Past

- **Grant of concessions/loans by commercial banks** to sick industrial units in the form of additional working capital, recovery of interest at reduced rates, suitable moratorium on payment of interest, etc.
- Establishment of **Industrial Investment Bank of India (IIBI)** (*initially in 1971 with a different name*) to function as the development bank in order to facilitate revival of sick industrial companies. It was closed down by government in 2012.
- **Nationalisation** of the sick unit through **taking over of management** (if required) by the government.
- Grant of **income tax benefits to healthy units** in case they take over sick units through amalgamation.
- **Grant of margin money to the sick units** by government in order to enable them to obtain necessary funds from the banks/financial institutions.
- Measures for **early detection of sick units** so that timely intervention could be made by government.
- Setting up of **Board of Industrial and Financial Reconstruction (BIFR) in 1987** to determine the preventive, ameliorative, remedial and other measures required to be undertaken in respect of sick industrial companies.

EXAM ESSENTIAL

BOARD OF INDUSTRIAL AND FINANCIAL RECONSTRUCTION

(established in 1987 and dissolved in 2016)

- BIFR was set up under the provisions of Sick Industrial Companies (Special Provisions) Act, 1985. (in short **SICA**)
- As per revised norms, industrial companies whose net worth had been eroded by 50 per cent or more, were required to make a reference to BIFR.

- In 1991, public sector undertakings (PSUs) were also brought under the purview of BIFR.
- If the sickness was confirmed, BIFR was asked to determine the course of action to be followed with regard to that company. This course of action is as follows:
  - Allowing the company on its own, that is, as per the scheme already initiated by the banks/ institution to make its net worth positive within a reasonable period;
  - Having a scheme prepared through the operating agency in respect of the company;
  - Deciding on the winding up of the company.
- However, **BIFR was subject to lot of criticisms** such as considerable delays in disposing a case, preference of BIFR for rehabilitation over winding up, etc.
- **Thus, in 2016, SICA was repealed** and **BIFR was also dissolved**. All pending references/ inquiries/ appeals to BIFR were terminated.
- However, an option has been provided that such terminated appeals/references could be referred to the National Company Law Tribunal **(NCLT)** and National Company Law Appellate Tribunal **(NCLAT)** as per the provisions of Insolvency and Bankruptcy Code (*no fees is required if referred within a prescribed time limit*).

BONUS KNOWLEDGE

NATIONAL MANUFACTURING POLICY, 2011

It was announced in 2011, to enhance the share of manufacturing in GDP to 25 per cent within 2022, and create 10 crore jobs. In this regard, National Investment and Manufacturing Zones (NIMZs) are envisaged as the hub of the state-of-the-art infrastructures for such industries. 14 such NIMZs were identified throughout the country except Delhi-Mumbai Industrial Corridor.

Objectives

1. Increase manufacturing sector growth to 12–14 per cent over the medium term to make it the engine of growth for the economy. The 2 to 4 per cent differential over the medium-term growth rate of the overall economy will enable manufacturing to contribute **at least 25 per cent** of the National GDP by 2022.
2. Increase the rate of job creation in manufacturing to create 100 million additional jobs by 2022.
3. Creation of appropriate skill sets among the rural migrant and urban poor to make growth inclusive.
4. Increase domestic value addition and technological 'depth' in manufacturing.
5. Enhance global competitiveness of Indian manufacturing through appropriate policy support.
6. Ensure sustainability of growth, particularly with regard to the environment including energy efficiency, optimal utilisation of natural resources and restoration of damaged/degraded ecosystems.

THE COMPANIES (AMENDMENT) ACT, 2019

The Companies (Amendment) Act is the law covering incorporation, functioning and dissolution of companies in India. The Act came into force across India in 2013, after a large number of amendments in the previous act of 1956.

In 2019, it was again amended and has been renamed as **the Companies (Amendment) Act, 2019.**

Major amendments incorporated in the 2013 Act were:

- No minimum paid-up capital required now, i.e. requirement of paid-up capital for companies of ₹1 lakh removed.

- No requirement for commencement of business certificate.
- The requirement for **common seal** has now been made **optional** and the directors' signature is acceptable in lieu of the common seal of the company.
- It has introduced **stringent penalty** for directors of companies that invite or accept or renew deposits contravening to the Companies (Amendment) Act, 2013.
- It has declared that companies having **losses or negative reserves cannot declare dividends.**
- **Loans or guarantees** can be provided by the holding company to the **subsidiary company.**
- Providing a 'material' limit for reporting of frauds to the central government.

Major amendments incorporated in the 2019 Act were:

- In addition to enabling the **redemption of preference shares** out of profits and fresh issue of shares, amendment allowed a company to redeem preference shares **even out of capital.**
- Issue of **appointment of auditors** and their remuneration must **be tabled at the Annual General Meeting** of the public company for shareholders' approval. Previously, the Act was silent in this regard.
- **Judicial Management Mechanism** has been introduced through which company, its directors or a creditor can now apply in the High Court to place the management of the company in the hands of a qualified insolvency practitioner known as a judicial manager.

Benefits of Incorporated Amendments

- The Amendment Act is an incremental and natural step towards liberalising and rationalising some of the aspects of the Companies Act.
- It also removes some drafting ambiguities plaguing the Companies Act.
- It has also sought to align the provisions of the Companies Act with other statutes, like securities laws and the regulations of the RBI. To that extent, it is a welcome step.

BONUS KNOWLEDGE

NATIONAL COMPANY LAW TRIBUNAL (NCLT)

- It is a **quasi-judicial body** in India that sees over issues relating to **Indian companies**. The tribunal was established under the Companies Act, 2013 and was constituted in 2016 by GoI.
- It **replaced** Company Law Board and BIFR.
- It has powers under the Companies Act, 2013 to adjudicate proceedings:
  1. Initiated before **Company Law Board** under the earlier Companies Act, 1956.
  2. Pending before **BIFR** under SICA, 1985.
  3. Pending before the appellate authority for industrial and financial reconstruction.
  4. Related to **oppression and mismanagement of a company**, **winding up** of company, etc.
- It is also the adjudicating authority for **insolvency resolution process** of companies and limited liability partnerships under the **Insolvency and Bankruptcy Code, 2016**.
- Decisions of NCLT may be appealed to NCLAT and further to Supreme Court.
- NCLT has 16 benches across India. [Each bench has **one judicial member** (retired/serving High Court judge) and **one technical member** from Indian Corporate Law Service.]

CORPORATE SOCIAL RESPONSIBILITY (CSR)

EXAM ESSENTIAL

- It is a management concept whereby companies integrate the social and environmental concerns in the business operation and interaction with their stakeholders.
- In simple terms, Corporate Social Responsibility (CSR) spending by a company is a way of giving back to the society in which it is doing business and making a profit for its shareholders.
- The CSR concept in India is governed by Section 135 of the Companies Act, 2013, Schedule VII of the same Act and Companies (CSR Policy) Rules, 2014.
- The activities undertaken in pursuance of the CSR policy must be relatable to Schedule VII of the Companies Act, 2013.
- The amount spent by a company towards CSR **cannot be claimed as business expenditure.** No specific tax exemptions have been extended to CSR expenditure.
- Companies having **net worth** of ₹500 crore or more or **turnover** of ₹1,000 crore or more or **net profit** of ₹5 crore or more in any financial year have **to spend atleast 2 per cent of the average net profit of last 3 years** in every financial year.
- If a company spends more than 2 per cent, then the excess amount can be set off against the mandatory 2 per cent CSR expenditure in succeeding three financial years, subject to compliance of certain conditions.
- Even foreign companies having its branch in India are required to abide by CSR norms.
- **Activities which may be undertaken** for spending CSR amount include:

  Eradicating extreme hunger and poverty; Promotion of education; Promoting gender equality and empowering women; Reducing child mortality and improving maternal health; Combating human immunodeficiency virus, acquired immune deficiency syndrome, malaria and other diseases; Ensuring environmental sustainability; Employment-enhancing vocational skills; Social business projects; Contribution to Swachh Bharat Kosh, Clean Ganga Fund, Prime Minister's National Relief Fund (PMNRF), Prime Minister's Citizen Assistance and Relief in Emergency Situations Fund (PM CARES Fund) or any fund set up by the central government and notified by Ministry of Corporate Affairs for socio-economic development.
- However, the following activities are **specifically excluded** from being considered as eligible CSR activity:
  a. Activities undertaken **in pursuance of normal course of business** of the company.
  b. **Activities undertaken outside India**, except for training of Indian sports personnel representing any State or Union Territory at the national level or India at the international level.
  c. Contribution of any amount, directly or indirectly, **to any political party**.
  d. **Activities benefitting employees** of the company as defined in Section 2(k) of the Code on Wages, 2019.
  e. **Sponsorship activities** for deriving marketing benefits for products/services.
  f. Activities for fulfilling statutory obligations under any law in force in India.

Challenges to CSR

- Difficulties come up in most cases of shared value and social business projects because in those cases, the boundary between pure business activities and CSR activities is often obscured.

➤ Complication regarding implication of CSR activities on whether company will be eligible for tax breaks on certain CSR spending or not depends considerably on the discretion of tax authorities.

VARIOUS SECTORS OF MANUFACTURING INDUSTRY

A. Steel

India has become the second largest consumer of finished steel. India's steel sector experiences remarkable expansion, emerging as the second biggest worldwide producer, after China. Domestic finished steel output is at 89.711 million tonnes, representing a 14.3 per cent gain. The Production Linked Incentive Scheme has boosted steel industry investments, with 27 companies signing MoUs for 57 projects totalling ₹29,530 crore. CPSEs of Ministry of Steel achieved a record CAPEX in FY 2022–23, and maintained momentum in FY 2023–24.

Challenges of the Sector

1. Steel sector is very much capital intensive.
2. Supply chain management must be augmented to supplement the dominant railways with the waterways for cheaper alternative.
3. Various taxes and duties must be streamlined with the global scenarios to improve the competitiveness.
4. Improving the supply of coking coals as India is not self-sufficient in coking coals.
5. Per capita consumption of finished steel was 77.2 kg during 2021–22.

National Steel Policy, 2017

National Steel Policy, 2017, envisages to enhance domestic steel consumption, ensure high-quality steel production, and create self-sufficiency in steel production. The objectives were:

1. Improvements in quality and cost efficiency.
2. Ensuring the availability of coking coal, iron ore.
3. Enhancing domestic demand.
4. Announcement of PLI scheme for speciality steel or value-added steel.

B. Electronics Manufacturing

India aspires to be one of the manufacturing hubs of electronic products in the global landscape. Specially, recent chip shortages marked the utmost necessity of self-sufficiency in electronics manufacturing for strategic reasons also.

Challenges for the Sector

1. Cheap imports from China are getting packaged rather than unique manufacturing.
2. Lack of microchip making foundries in the country.
3. Trade-related issues with large corporations like Apple.

Recent Initiatives

1. DLI (Design Linked Incentives) schemes announced for microchip and display panel productions.
2. Electronic components and semiconductors manufacturing promotion scheme (SPECS).
3. Modified Electronics manufacturing Clusters.
4. National Policy on Electronics 2019 to make India global electronics manufacturing hub ($400 billion turnover by 2025).

C. Textile Sector

India is the **second largest manufacturer of fibre** in the world after China. It contributes around 2.3 per cent of the GDP of the country.

Challenges of the Sector

1. Lack of skill upgradation as per current trends.
2. Labour regulation is not adequate.
3. Lack of value addition opportunities and finished products.

Last Minute SNIPPETS

- PM inaugurated **Bharat Tex 2024** in New Delhi, which is an excellent platform to highlight India's exceptional capabilities in the textile industry.
- **Kasturi Cotton** is a significant step towards establishing India's own identity.
- **Five Fs** – Farm to Fiber, Fiber to Factory, Factory to Fashion, Fashion to Foreign will strengthen India's textile sector.
- **PM-Mega Integrated Textiles Region and Apparel Park (MITRA)** – 7 such mega parks to be promoted to strengthen the end-to-end textiles solutions for the entire value chain with projected turnover and employment generation of 1.9 lakh crore and 2.5 lakh, respectively.

D. Pharmaceuticals

Though the bulk of raw materials is imported from China, India is self-sufficient in pharmaceuticals. Indian pharmaceutical sector is the world's third biggest by volume, with a current market size of around US$ 50 billion. The sector has the potential to expand to US$ 120–130 billion over the next decade, with one of the primary drivers being the industry's development into the innovation arena.

Challenges of the Sector

1. Inadequate R&D facility in the country.
2. Dependence on China for the API (Active Pharmaceutical Ingredients).
3. IPR issues related to copyrights of the drugs.

Reforms Undertaken

1. National Policy on Research and Development and Innovation in Pharma-MedTech Sector in India and Scheme for **Promotion of Research and Innovation in Pharma MedTech Sector (PRIP)** has been launched.
2. PLI scheme for manufacturing of APIs.
3. PLI scheme for healthcare device manufacturing.

BONUS KNOWLEDGE

NATIONAL INVESTMENT AND MANUFACTURING ZONE (NIMZ)

NIMZs are one of the most important instruments of **National Manufacturing Policy, 2011.**

NIMZs are envisaged as large areas of developed land with the requisite eco-system for promoting world class manufacturing activity. It is to be developed as an Integrated Industrial Township with the state-of-the-art infrastructure and land use on the basis of zoning; lean and energy efficient technology; necessary social infrastructure; and skill development facilities to provide a protective environment to persons transiting from the primary sector to the secondary and tertiary sector.

NIMZs are different from SEZs in terms of size, level of infrastructure planning, governance structures related to regulatory procedures and exit policies.

Features of the proposed NIMZs are as follows:

- The State government to provide suitable land of **5,000 ha**.
- **At least 30 per cent of the total area** to be utilised for location of manufacturing units.
- **Special-purpose vehicle** to be constituted to discharge the affairs of the NIMZ.
- The central government to provide financial support not exceeding 20 per cent of project cost. The central government to improve/provide external physical infrastructure linkages to NIMZ including railroad, airport and telecommunication in a time-bound manner.

So far, four NIMZs have been accorded final approval – first at **Prakasam** (Andhra Pradesh), second at **Sangareddy** (Telangana) third at **Kalinganagar** (Odisha) and fourth at Hyderabad Pharma City NIMZ in Rangareddy District of Telangana. Moreover, eight investment regions along the Delhi–Mumbai Industrial Corridor (DMIC) project have also been declared as NIMZs.

Special Economic Zones (SEZs) in India

- SEZ is a **duty-free enclave** and is deemed to be foreign territory for the purposes of trade operations. SEZ is a geographical region that has economic laws different from a country's typical economic laws.
- The **first SEZ Policy** in India was announced in **2000.** It was intended to enhance foreign investment and to provide an internationally competitive environment for exports.
- The **SEZ Act was passed in 2005.** Its objective was to generate additional economic activity, to promote investment from domestic and foreign sources, to develop infrastructure facilities, etc.
- In 2018, the GoI constituted a committee (headed by **Baba Kalyani**) to frame the SEZ Policy of India. The **key recommendations** of the SEZ Policy Review Committee are:
  1. To shift framework from export growth to broad-based employment and economic growth.
  2. To formulate separate rules and procedures for manufacturing and service SEZs.
  3. To shift from supply-driven to demand-driven approach to improve efficiency of investment based on certain industries and current level of existing inventory in the region.
  4. To enable framework for ease of doing business.
  5. To enhance competitiveness by enabling ecosystem development by funding high-speed multi-modal connectivity, business services and utility infrastructure.

> **did you KNOW?** As of March 2025, 276 SEZs are operational in India employing more than 2.8 million people.

EASE OF DOING BUSINESS REPORT

- It was a yearly ranking which aimed to provide a basis for understanding and improving the **regulatory environment** for businesses around the world by analysing and comparing the business regulations and the protection of property rights across **190 economies** and over time.
- **World Bank Group** used to publish *Doing Business Report* since 2003. In 2021, World Bank Group management **decided to discontinue** the *Doing Business Report*.
- The **details of 10 indicators** (based on the life cycle of a business) used to compute Ease of Doing Business Index were:
  1. Starting a business – *India's ranking improved*
  2. Dealing with construction permits – *India's ranking improved*
  3. Getting electricity – *India's ranking improved*
  4. Registering property – *India's ranking improved*
  5. Getting credit
  6. Protecting minority investors
  7. Paying taxes – *India's ranking improved*
  8. Trading across borders – *India's ranking improved*
  9. Enforcing contracts
  10. Resolving insolvency – *India's ranking improved*
- These **improvements were mainly due to** the following initiatives taken by the Indian Government:
  - **Starting a Business:** Minimum capital requirement for public and private company eliminated, incorporation fee reduced to zero for companies with authorised capital up to ₹15 lakh, etc.
  - **Dealing with Construction Permits:** Online single-window system introduced at some places, risk-based classification of buildings introduced for fast tracking of the building plan approval, inspection and grant of occupancy-cum-completion certificate.
  - **Getting Electricity:** At some places, procedures for internal wiring inspection eliminated, service line charges capped to ₹25,000 in electrified areas for low-tension loads up to 150 kW.
  - **Getting Credit:** Secured creditors to be paid first during business liquidation.
  - **Paying Taxes:** Introduction of GST, corporate income tax reduced from 30 per cent to 25 per cent for companies with a turnover up to ₹250 crore, etc.
  - **Trading Across Borders:** Electronic sealing of import containers, electronic submission of supporting documents with digital signatures, enhancement of risk-based inspections for both imports and exports, whereby only about 5 per cent of goods are physically inspected, **e-Sanchit** implemented to allow traders to submit all supporting documents electronically with digital signatures.
  - **Enforcing Contracts:** *National Judicial Data Grid* introduced to generate case measurement report on local courts, The Commercial Courts Act, 2015 amended to reduce the pecuniary jurisdiction of commercial courts from ₹1 crore to ₹3 lakh in order to ensure speedier disposal of commercial disputes and reduce pendency.
  - **Resolving Insolvency:** Insolvency and Bankruptcy Code, 2016 adopted, professional institutions established to handle restructuring and insolvency proceedings, time-bound resolution process.

MAKE IN INDIA

Launched in 2014, it is an initiative to invite both foreign and domestic investors to invest in India. It is based on four pillars to boost entrepreneurship in India:

1. **New Processes:** It recognises ease of doing business as the single most important factor to promote entrepreneurship.
2. **New Infrastructure:** Government intends to develop industrial corridors and smart cities, create world-class infrastructure with the state-of-the-art technology and high-speed communication.
3. **New Sectors**: It has identified 25 sectors in manufacturing, infrastructure and service activities, and detailed information is being shared through interactive Web portals and professionally developed brochures.
4. **New Mindset:** To partner with industries in the economic development, government to act as a facilitator and not a regulator.

Important Measures Taken So Far

- The **India Aspiration Fund** has been set up under Small Industries Development Bank of India **(SIDBI)** for venture capital financing of new setups and for expanding existing units in the MSME sector.
- **SIDBI's Make in India Soft Loan Fund for Micro Small and Medium Enterprises (SMILE) scheme** has been launched to offer quasi-equity and term-based short-term loans to Indian SMEs with less stringent rules and regulations and a special focus on 22 thrust sectors of Make in India.
- Further, a **Micro Units Development and Refinance Agency (MUDRA) bank** has been set up to provide development and refinance to commercial banks/NBFCs/cooperative banks for loans to micro units. It would follow a *credit plus approach* by also providing financial literacy and addressing the skill/information gaps.

Challenges

- Market expansion to accommodate new players is limited or absent.
- Low labour cost and labour discipline is a big issue in India.
- Analysis of employment creation data in Make in India sectors indicates that the thrust sectors are not necessarily the most employment elastic ones.

EXAM ESSENTIAL

eBIZ PROJECT

The *Department of Industrial Policy and Promotion* **(DIPP)** has been pursuing an e-government project called eBiz. The main purpose of the project is to create a **one-stop-shop** of convenient and efficient services to the investors, businesses and industries.

The **key features** of eBiz are:

- Creation of a business-friendly environment.
- A service-oriented approach to investors, industries and businesses.
- Catering to all the requirements of businesses for G2B services through their life cycle.

START-UP INDIA

It is a flagship initiative of GoI since 2016, intended:

- To build a strong eco-system for nurturing innovative and start-ups in the country.
- To have sustainable growth.
- To generate large-scale employment opportunities.
- To empower start-ups to grow through innovation and design.

It envisaged establishment of **Funds for Startups** (FFS), corpus for which is ₹10,000 crore to be managed by **SIDBI.**

Important Measures Taken So Far

- Start-up Hub – to address the queries of various start-ups and assist them.
- Mobile app and portal – to provide functionalities such as making application for obtaining real-time start-up recognition certificate, SEBI registered funds, notifications issued by various departments, etc.
- Scheme for Startup IPR Protection **(SIPP)** for facilitating fast-tracking filing of patents, trademarks and designs by start-ups.
- Relaxed norms in public procurement of the start-ups.
- Building innovation centres and setting up research parks.

Challenges

- Constrained funding environment.
- High level of risks involved in such innovative projects.
- Long and time-taking government procedures.

BONUS KNOWLEDGE

Startup India Seed Fund: launched in 2021, the Government is implementing the Startup India Seed Fund Scheme (SISFS) to provide financial assistance to Startups through approved Incubators.

Under the SISFS, ₹945 crore was approved for a period of 4 years starting from 2021–22.

STAND-UP INDIA

- Launched in **2016,** the Stand-up India portal provides a digital platform based on three pillars to support enterprises promotion for **SC, ST and women entrepreneurs.**
- The portal also provides crucial links to central and state SC/ST corporations and industrial associations.
- It provides for handholding support to borrowers both at the pre-loan stage and during operations.
- The loan under the scheme is appropriately secured and backed up by credit guarantee through a scheme for which the *Department of Financial Services* is the settler.
- SIDBI facilitates bank loans repayable **up to 7 years** and between **₹10 lakh and ₹100 lakh** for Greenfield enterprises.

- With the access to bank accounts and technological education, Stand-up India is aimed to facilitate financial and social inclusion in the society.

National Productivity Council (NPC)

- NPC is a national-level organisation set up in 1958 to promote productivity culture in India.
- The NPC comes under the *Department for Promotion of Industry and Internal Trade (DPIIT), Ministry of Commerce & Industry*.
- It is an autonomous, multipartite, non-profit organisation and has been registered as a Society under the Societies Registration Act XXI of 1860.
- NPC is a constituent of the Tokyo-based Asian Productivity Organisation (APO), an inter-governmental body, of which the GoI is a founder member.

Industry 4.0 and India

The advent of the fourth industrial revolution or industry 4.0 has begun. The transformation includes new technologies such as cloud computing, IoT, machine learning, and artificial intelligence (AI) into manufacturing processes, leading to efficiencies across the value chain.

- While the adoption of these technologies in the Indian manufacturing sector is underway, large-scale adoption is yet to happen.
- The push towards self-reliance in semiconductor technology and production will help India.
- A few initiatives by the government include the SAMARTH (Smart Advanced Manufacturing and Rapid Transformation Hubs) Udyog Bharat 4.0 under the Ministry of Heavy Industries and Public Enterprises, which aims to encourage technological solutions to Indian manufacturing industry.
- Another initiative is the establishment of the Centre for Fourth Industrial Revolution in India in 2018, which looks to develop policy frameworks for emerging technologies.

EXAM ESSENTIAL

CHAMPION SECTORS IN INDIA

- **In 2020**, GoI identified champion sectors in both manufacturing and services sectors (**total 27**), for promoting their development and achieving their potential.
- The sectors have been identified for renewed focus under the **Make in India version 2.0**.
- **Department of Industrial Policy and Promotion (DIPP)**, the nodal department for 'Make in India', spearheads the initiative for the **Champion Sectors in Manufacturing** and **Department of Commerce** coordinates the initiative for the **Champion Sectors in Services**.
- **Champion Sectors in Manufacturing (total 15) include:**

1. Aerospace and Defence
2. Automotive & Auto Components
3. Pharmaceuticals and Medical Devices
4. Bio-Technology
5. Capital Goods
6. Textiles and Apparels
7. Chemicals and Petro-Chemicals
8. Electronics System Design and Manufacturing (ESDM)
9. Leather & Footwear
10. Food Processing
11. Gems and Jewellery
12. Shipping
13. Railways
14. Construction
15. New and Renewable Energy

- **Champion Sectors in Services (total 12) include:**
  1. IT & ITeS
  2. Tourism and Hospitality Services
  3. Medical Value Travel
  4. Transport and Logistics Services
  5. Accounting and Finance Services
  6. Audio Visual Services
  7. Legal Services
  8. Communication Services
  9. Construction and Related Engineering Services
  10. Environmental Services
  11. Financial Services
  12. Education Services
- A dedicated fund of ₹5000 crore has been proposed to be established to support initiatives for sectoral Action Plans of the Champion Sectors.
- This initiative aimed to raise the share of India's services sector in global services exports.

SUMMARY

- **Sectoral classification of Industries** – Mining and quarrying – manufacturing – electricity, gas, water supply and other utility services – construction.
- **Industrial Policy Resolution of 1956** – Based on P.C. Mahalanobis model – considered as the 'Economic Constitution of India' or the 'Bible of State Capitalism'.
- **New Industrial Policy, 1991** – Aimed to correct the distortions and weaknesses of the industrial structure of the country that had developed in four decades – Industrial De-licencing – De-reservation of Public Sector – Foreign Investment – Foreign Technology Agreement.
- **CPSEs are classified into** – Maharatnas – Navratnas – Miniratnas I and II.
- **Index of Industrial Production (IIP)** – Statistical measure of industrial performance – by MoS&PI – released every month.
- **Index of Eight Core Industries** – Comprise 40.27 per cent of the weight in IIP – barometer of monthly industrial performance – eight core industries including Refinery products, Electricity, Steel, Coal, Crude oil, Natural gas, Cement and Fertilisers.
- **Annual Survey of Industries (ASI)** – Related to organised manufacturing sector – published annually by CSO (now NSO).
- **Purchasing Managers' Index (PMI)** – Published by Japanese firm Nikkei but compiled by Markit Economics – indicator of the manufacturing and services sector – two separate PMIs are published – Manufacturing PMI and Services PMI.
- **National Company Law Tribunal (NCLT)** – Quasi-judicial body that sees over issues relating to Indian companies – established under the Companies Act, 2013 – constituted in 2016 by GoI – replaced Company Law Board and BIFR.
- **Corporate Social Responsibility** – Companies integrate the social and environmental concerns in the business operation and interaction with their stakeholders – way of giving back to the society in which it is doing business and making a profit for its shareholders.
- **Special Economic Zone** – Duty-free enclave and is deemed to be foreign territory for the purposes of trade operations – to enhance foreign investment and to provide an internationally competitive environment for exports.
- **Stand-Up India** – Portal that provides a digital platform based on three pillars to support enterprises to promote SC, ST and women entrepreneurs – loan under the scheme is appropriately secured and backed up by credit guarantee through a scheme for which the *Department of Financial Services* is the settler.

UPSC CSE PREVIOUS YEARS' PRELIMINARY EXAMINATION QUESTIONS

1. With reference to Corporate Social Responsibility (CSR) rules in India, consider the following statements: **[2024]**
   1. CSR rules specify that expenditures that benefit the company directly or the employees will not be considered as CSR activities.
   2. CSR rules do not specify minimum spending on CSR activities.

   Which of the statements given above is/are correct?
   (a) 1 only (b) 2 only
   (c) Both 1 and 2 (d) Neither 1 nor 2

2. Consider the following statements: **[2019]**
   As per the **Industrial Employment (Standing Orders) Central (Amendment) Rules, 2018**
   1. If rules for fixed-term employment are implemented, it becomes easier for the firms/companies to lay off workers.
   2. No notice of termination of employment shall be necessary in the case of temporary workman.

   Which of the statements given above is/are correct?
   (a) 1 only (b) 2 only
   (c) Both 1 and 2 (d) Neither 1 nor 2

3. With reference to **Quality Council of India (QCI)**, consider the following statements: **[2017]**
   1. QCI was set up jointly by the Government of India and the Indian Industry.
   2. Chairman of QCI is appointed by the Prime Minister on the recommendations of the industry to the Government.

   Which of the above statements is/are correct?
   (a) 1 only (b) 2 only
   (c) Both 1 and 2 (d) Neither 1 nor 2

4. Recently, India's first NIMZ was proposed to set up in **[2016]**
   (a) Andhra Pradesh
   (b) Gujarat
   (c) Maharashtra
   (d) Uttar Pradesh

5. With reference to 'Stand-up India Scheme' which of the following statements is/are correct? **[2016]**
   1. Its purpose is to promote entrepreneurship among SC/ST and women entrepreneurs.
   2. It provides for refinance through SIDBI.

   Select the correct answer using the code given below:
   (a) 1 only (b) 2 only
   (c) Both 1 and 2 (d) Neither 1 nor 2

6. Which one among the following industries is the maximum consumer of water in India? **[2013]**
   (a) Engineering (b) Paper and Pulp
   (c) Textiles (d) Thermal Power

7. What is/are the recent policy initiative(s) of Government of India to promote the growth of manufacturing sector? **[2012]**
   1. Setting up of National Investment and Manufacturing Zones.
   2. Providing the benefits of 'Single Window Clearance'.
   3. Establishing the Technology Acquisition and Development Fund.

   Select the correct answer using codes given below:
   (a) 1 only (b) 2 and 3 only
   (c) 1 and 3 only (d) 1, 2 and 3

8. In India, in the overall Index of Industrial Production, the Index of Eight Core Industries have a combined weight of 37.90 per cent. Which of the following are among those Eight Core Industries? **[2012]**
   1. Cement
   2. Fertilisers
   3. Natural Gas
   4. Refinery Products
   5. Textiles

   Select the correct answer using the codes given below:
   (a) 1 and 5 only
   (b) 2, 3 and 4 only
   (c) 1, 2, 3 and 4 only
   (d) 1, 2, 3, 4 and 5

9. Despite having large reserves of coal, why does India import millions of tonnes of coal? **[2012]**
   1. It is the policy of India to save its own coal reserves for future, and import it from other countries for the present use.
   2. Most of the power plants in India are coal-based and they are not able to get sufficient supplies of coal from within the country.

3. Steel companies need large quantity of coking coal which has to be imported.

Which of the statements given above is/are correct?

(a) 1 only (b) 2 and 3 only
(c) 1 and 3 only (d) 1, 2 and 3

10. Why is the Government of India disinvesting its equity in the central public sector enterprises (CPSEs)? **[2011]**

1. The government intends to use the revenue earned from the disinvestment mainly to pay back the external debt.
2. The government no longer intends to retain the management control of the CPSEs.

Which are the correct statements given above is/are correct?

(a) 1 only (b) 2 only
(c) Both 1 and 2 (d) Neither 1 nor 2

☞ NO QUESTIONS ASKED
2023, 2022, 2021, 2020, 2018, 2015, 2014

ANSWER KEY

1. (a)	2. (c)	3. (c)	4. (a)	5. (c)
6. (d)	7. (d)	8. (c)	9. (b)	10. (d)

UPSC CSE PREVIOUS YEARS' MAIN EXAMINATION QUESTIONS

1. 'Industrial growth rate has lagged behind in the overall growth of GDP in the post-reform period'. Give reasons. How far the recent changes in Industrial Policy are capable of increasing the industrial growth rate? **[2017]**

2. 'Success of **"Make in India"** programme depends on the success of **"Skill India"** programme and radical labour reforms'. Discuss with logical arguments. **[2015]**

☞ NO QUESTIONS ASKED
2024, 2023, 2022, 2021, 2020, 2019, 2018, 2016, 2014, 2013

CHAPTER

20

MSME SECTOR

CHAPTER OUTLINE

- Introduction to MSME: The Vibrant Sector of Indian Economy
- MSME Sector: Structure in India
- Role/Importance of MSMEs in Indian Economy
- Challenges to MSME Sector
- Recent Government Initiatives for Promotion of MSME Sector
- MSMEs: Engines of Growth for New India
- International Good Practices

INTRODUCTION TO MSME: THE VIBRANT SECTOR OF INDIAN ECONOMY

The Micro, Small & Medium Enterprises (MSME) sector has emerged as a highly vibrant and dynamic sector of the Indian economy, fostering entrepreneurship and generating self-employment opportunities at comparatively lower capital costs, next only to agriculture.

Last Minute SNIPPETS

The Union Budget 2025–26 introduced a series of measures aimed at strengthening the MSME sector by enhancing credit access, supporting first-time entrepreneurs, and promoting labour-intensive industries. To help MSMEs scale operations and access better resources, the investment and turnover limits for classification have been increased by **2.5 times and 2 times**, respectively. This is expected to improve efficiency, technological adoption, and employment generation.

Category	Old Capital Limit	Old Turnover Limit	New Capital Limit	New Turnover Limit
Micro	Upto ₹1 crore	Upto ₹5 crore	Upto ₹2.5 crore	Upto ₹10 crore
Small	Upto ₹10 crore	Upto ₹50 crore	Upto ₹25 crore	Upto ₹100 crore
Medium	Upto ₹50 crore	Upto ₹250 crore	Upto ₹125 crore	Upto ₹500 crore

MSME SECTOR: STRUCTURE IN INDIA

The **Ministry of MSME** is the nodal ministry, which promotes the growth and development of the sector, including Khadi, Village and Coir industries, by implementing various schemes/programmes towards credit support, technological assistance, infrastructure development, skill development and training, enhancing competitiveness and market assistance.

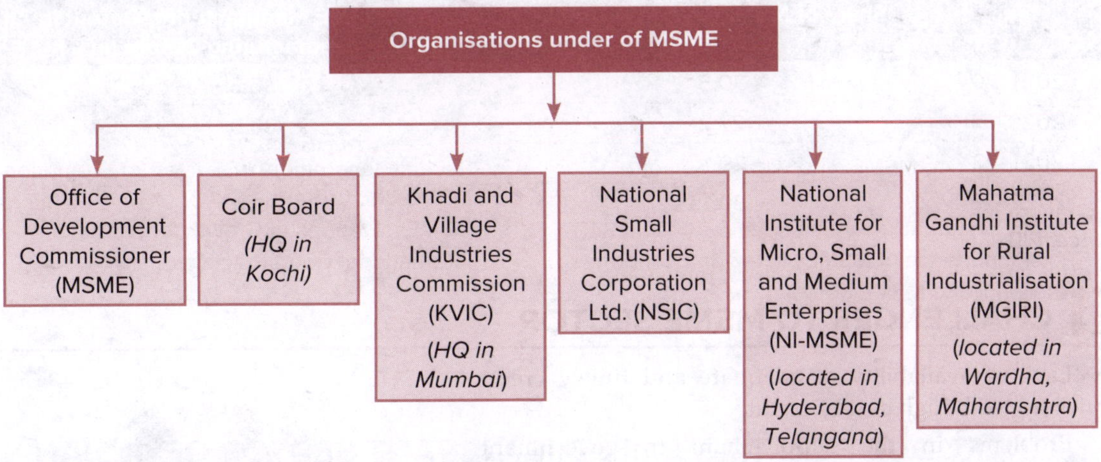

ROLE/IMPORTANCE OF MSMEs IN INDIAN ECONOMY

- MSMEs have been contributing significantly to the widening of **entrepreneurial endeavours** through business innovation in different sectors.
- MSMEs are expanding their domain across sectors of the economy, producing a **diverse range of products and services** to meet the demands of domestic as well as global markets.
- MSMEs in India are playing a crucial role by **providing large employment opportunities** at comparatively lower capital cost than large industries.
- MSMEs bolster the **industrialisation of rural and backward areas** as well as reduce regional imbalances, assuring more equitable distribution of national income and wealth.

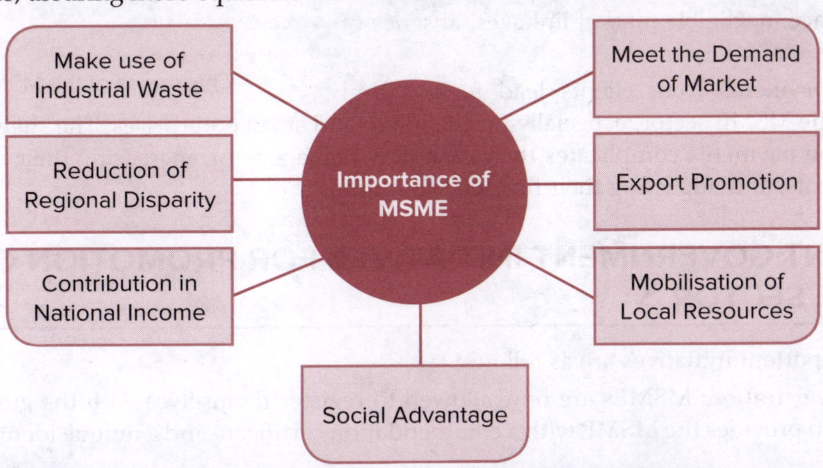

did you KNOW? In 2023–24, MSME-related products accounted for 45.73 per cent of India's total exports, reinforcing their role in positioning the country as a global manufacturing hub.

According to the data from the Ministry of Statistics and Programme Implementation, the proportion of MSME Gross Value Added (GVA) in India's total GDP and the share of MSME Manufacturing Output in India's total Manufacturing Output (in percentage points) are:

Year	Share of MSME GVA in All India GDP (in %)	Share of MSME Manufacturing Output in All India Manufacturing Output (in %)
2019–20	30.5	36.6
2020–21	27.2	36.9
2021–22	29.1	36.2
2022–23	30.1	35.4

Source: PIB

CHALLENGES TO MSME SECTOR

- Lack of availability of adequate and timely credit along with high cost of credit.
- Problems in the supply-chain to government departments and agencies.
- Problems of storage, designing, packaging and product display.
- Lack of access to global markets.
- Inadequate infrastructure facilities including power, water, road, etc.
- Multiplicity of labour laws and complicated procedures associated with compliance of such laws.
- MSMEs face legacy issues such as information asymmetry, non-registration of firms, inadequate and untimely credit, delayed receivables, technological obsolescence, negligible market linkages, absence of exit policy, etc.
- Delayed payments from clients lead to a critical issue for the MSME sector, especially for the micro and small enterprises. The sheer magnitude of the delayed payments complicates their cash flow management, increasing their working capital requirements, and impacting their financial condition.

Challenges of the MSME sector

RECENT GOVERNMENT INITIATIVES FOR PROMOTION OF MSME SECTOR

Some of the important initiatives are as follows:

1. **Udyam Registration:** MSMEs are now allowed to register themselves with the government. This registration provides the MSME with a commendation certificate and a unique identity number. As

of February 4, 2025, the Udyam Portal boasts an impressive total of 5,93,38,604 registered MSMEs, with the vast majority classified as micro-enterprises. Beyond their economic contributions, these MSMEs have generated substantial employment opportunities, providing jobs to over 25.18 crore individuals.

Benefits of Udyam registration:

- Help in availing the benefits of Schemes of Ministry of MSMEs such as Credit Guarantee Scheme, Public Procurement Policy, additional edge in Government Tenders & Protection again.
- With Udyam registration, the MSME also becomes eligible for priority sector lending from Banks.
- MSMEs may register themselves on GeM (Government e Portal) and on TReDS Platform (the invoices of receivables are traded on this platform).

2. **PM Vishwakarma:** A new scheme, known as 'PM Vishwakarma', intends to improve the quality and reach of artists and craftspeople's goods and services, as well as to guarantee that the 'Vishwakarmas' are incorporated into local and global value chains. The *Ministry of MSME* introduced the Scheme on September 17, 2023.

   PM Vishwakarma is fully funded by the Government of India with an initial outlay of ₹13,000 crore for 2023–24 to 2027–28. Since its launch, the PM Vishwakarma scheme has achieved significant milestones, with over 2.65 crore applications submitted and 27.13 lakh applications successfully registered.

   Benefits of PM Vishwakarma

   - The scheme will provide comprehensive end-to-end support to the Vishwakarmas, i.e. artists and artisans, allowing them to advance up the value chain in their respective fields.
   - It will result in a fundamental transformation in how crartists and artisans practice their jobs, improving their socio-economic standing and quality of life.

3. **Scheme of Fund for Regeneration of Traditional Industries (SFURTI):** It was established to organise the traditional industries and artisans into clusters.

   Since 2014–15, SFURTI has approved the formation of 513 clusters and 376 clusters have successfully become functional. A total grant of ₹1,336 crore has been extended to support these clusters. Sustainable employment opportunities have been generated for around 2,20,800 artisans in 376 functional clusters (as on December 15, 2024).

   Benefits of SFURTI:

   - The scheme supports the establishment of collective manufacturing enterprise of artisans, to increase their production, making them produce value-added products and enhancing marketability of products.

4. **A Scheme for Promoting Innovation, Rural Industry & Entrepreneurship (ASPIRE):** Till date, a total of 109 Livelihood Business Incubators (LBIs) were approved by ASPIRE, out of which 79 are functional. Total beneficiaries skilled are 1,09,984 and beneficiaries suitably employed are 31,725. In addition, the LBI incubation programmes resulted in the establishment of 722 micro-enterprises.

5. **Access to Technology:** A robust ICT platform, CHAMPIONS, has been launched by the Ministry of MSME. MSME Champions Scheme has been formulated with three components, namely,

   I. MSME-Sustainable (ZED),
   II. MSME-Competitive (LEAN) and
   III. MSME-Innovative (Incubation, Design, IPR).

MSME Innovative Scheme and MSME Sustainable (ZED) Certification Scheme were launched in 2022.

Benefits: MSME Sustainable (ZED) Certification Scheme aims to provide a roadmap to global competitiveness for the MSMEs of India. This scheme is an extensive drive to enable and facilitate MSMEs adopt **Zero Defect Zero Effect (ZED)** practices and motivate and incentivise them for ZED Certification while also encouraging them to become MSME Champions. **Through the journey of ZED Certification, MSMEs can reduce wastages substantially, increase productivity, enhance environmental consciousness, save energy, optimally use natural resources, expand their markets, etc.**

6. **RAMP Scheme:** Raising and Accelerating MSME Performance (RAMP) scheme, launched in 2022, aims at strengthening institutions and governance at the Centre and State, improving Centre-State linkages and partnerships and improving access of MSMEs to market and credit, technology upgradation and addressing the issues of delayed payments and greening of MSMEs. It is a World Bank supported Central sector scheme with an objective to scale up the implementation capacity and coverage of MSMEs with impact enhancement of existing MSME schemes over the five-year period 2022–23 to 2026–27. RAMP launched three sub-schemes:
   (i) MSE-GIFT (MSE Green Investment and Financing for Transformation),
   (ii) MSE-SPICE (MSE Scheme for Promotion of Investment in Circular Economy),
   (iii) MSE Scheme on Online Dispute Resolution for Delayed Payments.
7. Collateral-free loans up to ₹500 lakh (w.e.f. 01.04.23) are available to MSEs with guarantee coverage of up to 85 per cent for various loan categories through the Credit Guarantee Fund Trust for Micro and Small Enterprises (CGTMSE) under the **Credit Guarantee Scheme.**

MSMEs: ENGINES OF GROWTH FOR NEW INDIA

A resilient and healthy MSME sector is essential for achieving the goal of a self-reliant India.

With the implementation of the new policy initiatives, the MSME sector is expected to act as a catalyst for development of **'New India'**. MSME is showing the potential to be the new engine of growth for new India with focus on the following aspects:

Ease of Doing Business	Using better access to efficient factors of production through industry-friendly labour reforms, proper land acquisition policy, free access to capital, vibrant entrepreneurship culture, modern technology, enabling infrastructure, and simplified tax policy.
Export of Services	In the services sector, MSMEs may be re-oriented to enhance export of services by capitalising on the revised definition of MSME.
Leveraging PLI Scheme	Capitalising the Productivity Linked Incentive (PLI) Scheme with a total outlay of ₹1.97 lakh crore to boost 13 industry sectors with a view to harnessing Make in India.

Promoting Start-ups	MSMEs with innovative ideas may be bolstered with right incentives mainly due to burgeoning domestic market, massive funding opportunities, and evolving technology.

Policy support in the above-mentioned areas will make MSMEs the engines of growth for 'New India'. Along with that, some international best practices can be implemented.

International Best Practices

Turkey has introduced **'TURQUALITY'**, a state-sponsored scale-up programme meant for MSMEs to transform themselves into global players.

Another such initiative is **'Growth Driver Programme'** of Business Development Bank of Canada to provide multi-disciplinary support system in terms of enterprise growth and job creation in MSMEs.

SUMMARY

- New **definition of MSMEs** – Through Cabinet Committee on Economic Affairs (CCEA) – based on capital limits and turnover limits – same for both manufacturing and service sector units.
- The **Ministry of MSME** – Nodal ministry which promotes the growth of the sector; including Khadi, Village and Coir industries.
- **Significance of MSME Sector** – Widening of entrepreneurial endeavours, producing diverse range of products and services to meet domestic and global demands, providing major employment opportunities at comparatively lower capital cost than large industries and industrialisation of rural and backward areas
- **Challenges of MSME Sector** – Lack of availability of adequate and timely credit along with high cost of credit, high Non-performing assets (NPAs) of MSME loans, problems in the supply-chain to government departments, problems of storage, designing, packaging and product display, lack of access to global markets, inadequate infrastructure facilities including power, water, road, etc., multiplicity of labour laws and complexity of compliance with such laws.
- **MSME Champions Scheme** – Formulated with three components – I. 'MSME-Sustainable' (ZED), II. 'MSME-Competitive' (LEAN) and III. 'MSME-Innovative' (Incubation, Design, IPR).
- **MSME Sustainable (ZED) Certification Scheme** – Aims to facilitate adoption of Zero Defect Zero Effect (ZED) practices and thereby provide a roadmap to global competitiveness for Indian MSMEs.
- **Capacity Building of First-Time MSME Exporters (CBFTE) programme** – Launched to encourage MSMEs to provide high quality goods and services globally.
- Ministry of MSME recognised three platforms of **Trade Receivables Discounting System (TReDS)** viz. Invoicemart, M1Xchange and RXIL which will enable the MSME sector to get access to credit against invoices at a discounted rate to meet payment challenges.

UPSC CSE PREVIOUS YEARS' PRELIMINARY EXAMINATION QUESTIONS

1. Consider the following statements with reference to India: **[2023]**

1. According to the 'Micro, Small and Medium Enterprises Development (MSMED) Act, 2006', the 'medium enterprises' are those with investments in plant and machinery between ₹15 crore and ₹25 crore.
2. All bank loans to the Micro, Small and Medium Enterprises qualify under the priority sector.

Which of the statements given above is/are correct?

(a) 1 only (b) 2 only
(c) Both 1 and 2 (d) Neither 1 nor 2

☞ NO QUESTIONS ASKED
2024, 2022, 2021, 2020, 2019, 2018, 2017, 2016, 2015, 2014, 2013

ANSWER KEY

1. (b)

UPSC CSE PREVIOUS YEARS' MAIN EXAMINATION QUESTIONS

1. Faster Economic Growth requires increased share of the manufacturing sector in GDP, particularly of MSMEs. Comment on the present policies of the Government in this regard. (150 words) **[2023]**

☞ NO QUESTIONS ASKED
2024, 2022, 2021, 2020, 2019, 2018, 2017, 2016, 2015, 2014, 2013

CHAPTER

21

FOOD PROCESSING INDUSTRY IN INDIA

CHAPTER OUTLINE

- Processes and Stages of Food Processing
- Present Status of Food Processing in India
- Benefits Provided by Food Processing Industries
- Major Challenges Still Faced by Food Processing Industries
- Major Government Initiatives to Promote FPI
- PM Formalisation of Micro Food Processing Enterprises Scheme
- Production Linked Incentive Scheme for the Food Processing Industry (PLISFPI)
- Pradhan Mantri Kisan Sampada Yojana (PMKSY)
- Operation Greens Scheme
- Mega Food Park Scheme
- Modernisation of Abattoirs
- National Mission on Food Processing
- Scheme of Cold Chain, Value Addition and Preservation Infrastructure
- Agri-Export Zones
- Other Government Interventions in Recent Past
- Supply Chain Management under Food Processing Sector (Cold Chain, Super Market)
- Role of e-Commerce in Promoting FPI

Food processing is the set of methods and techniques used to transform raw ingredients into food or fresh food into other food products for consumption by humans or animals either in the home or by the food processing industry.

This **process of transformation of every food product from the cultivation of the crop to the consumption of the product,** includes *sorting, grading, packaging, branding,* etc which increases shelf life and utility.

The reasons to process food are as follows:

- **To convert** the raw agricultural and the animal husbandry roduce into edible products;
- **To preserve** the food items;
- **To extend** its availability and provide accessibility to consumers; and
- **To add value** to the products.

In the food processing sector, **India's rank is sixth** in terms of exports, production and consumption.

EXAM ESSENTIAL

WHY FOOD PROCESSING SECTOR IS IMPORTANT?

A well-developed food processing sector with higher level of processing helps in the reduction of wastage, adds value, promotes crop diversification, ensures better return to the farmers, promotes employment as well as increases export earnings. This sector is also capable of addressing critical issues of food security, food inflation and providing wholesome, nutritious food to the masses.

The **Ministry of Food Processing Industries (MoFPI)** under Government of India, which was set up in the year **1988**, is the nodal ministry for regulation and administration of food processing sector in India.

The Food Processing Industry (FPI) is considered a **sunrise sector** that has gained prominence in recent years. The following industries **come under the ambit of the Ministry of Food Processing Industries (FPIs), Government of India (GoI)**:

a. Industries relating to processing and refrigeration of certain **milk products, poultry and eggs, meat and meat products**;

b. Processing of **fish,** establishment and servicing of development council for fish processing industry; technical assistance and advice to fish processing industry;

c. **Fruit and vegetable** processing industry;

d. **Food grains milling** industry;

e. Industries relating to **bread**, oil seeds, meals (edible), breakfast foods, **biscuits, confectionery** (including cocoa processing and chocolate making), malt extract, protein isolate, high-protein food, weaning food and extruded food products;

f. **Beer** including non-alcoholic beer;

g. **Alcoholic drinks** from non-molasses base;

h. **Aerated water** and **soft drinks**.

BONUS KNOWLEDGE

AGRICULTURAL AND PROCESSED FOOD PRODUCTS EXPORT DEVELOPMENT AUTHORITY (APEDA)

- This was established **in 1986** to replace the Processed Food Export Promotion Council (PFEPC).
- APEDA functions under the **Ministry of Commerce & Industry**.
- The authority is responsible for providing financial assistance, conducting surveys, studies, subsidy schemes, etc., for the **export** of processed food from India.

PROCESSES AND STAGES OF FOOD PROCESSING

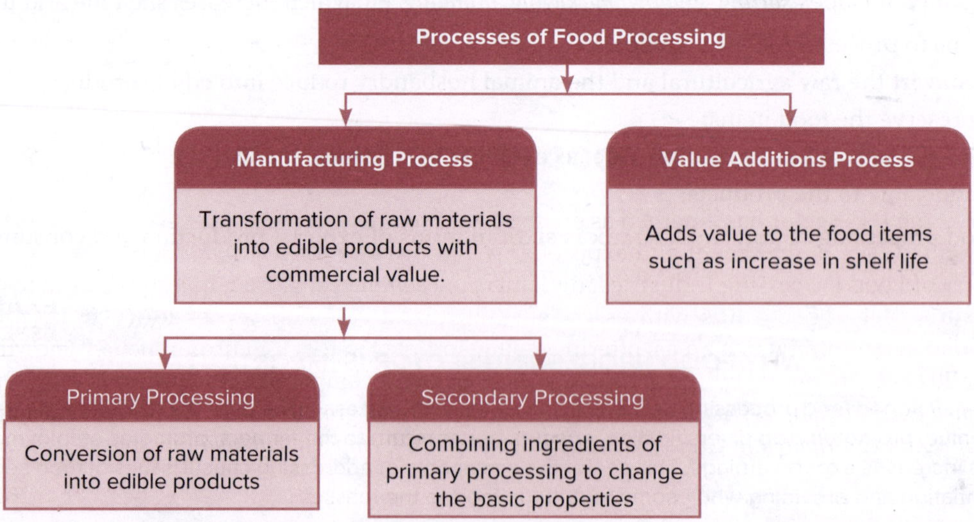

The different **stages of food processing** are as follows:

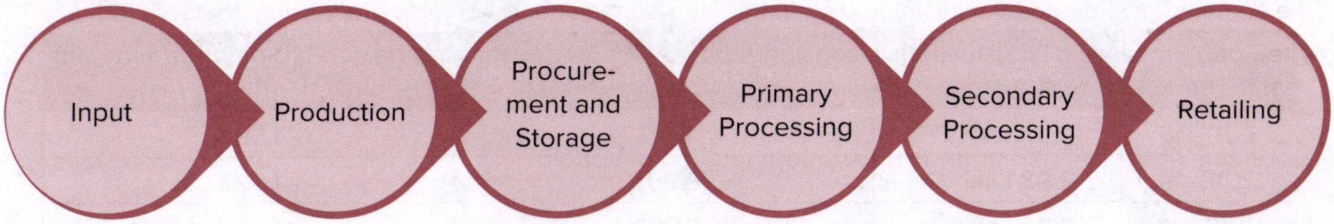

Supply Chain in Food Processing Sector

Primary Processing

It is the process of conversion of raw agricultural produce and animal husbandry produce into an edible product which is fit for consumption. This **involves cleaning, grading, sorting, packing**, etc.

Secondary Processing

This is the process of **combining ingredients** with the food produced through primary processing. This method also **changes the basic properties** of raw food materials, for example, **baking cake**.

did you KNOW? The commercial production of commonly known processed food is called Tertiary Food Processing. These are ready to eat foods, like re-heated meals served by the airlines.

BONUS KNOWLEDGE

FOOD IRRADIATION

Food irradiation is a technology that involves the application of ionising radiation to food items to enhance their safety and extend their shelf life. This process effectively reduces or eliminates harmful microorganisms and insects, making the food safer for consumption. By using **Cobalt-60** radiation, the method ensures that no harmful radioactivity or toxic radioactive residues are introduced into the food.

PRESENT STATUS OF FOOD PROCESSING IN INDIA

Food Processing (FP) sector has emerged as an important segment of the Indian economy in terms of its contribution to GDP, employment and exports. It is a priority under the Make in India initiative, with the Ministry of Food Processing Industries implementing schemes to attract investment and to develop infrastructure. Mega Food Parks with essential utilities and common processing facilities are being established in agriculturally rich areas, offering a plug-and-play model for entrepreneurs. The Ministry's budget for 2024–25 increased by approximately 30.19 per cent compared to the previous year. *The sector has performed exceptionally well with an impressive average annual growth rate of 7.3 per cent from 2015–22. It has significantly contributed to Gross Domestic Product (GDP), employment, and investment.*

Food Processing industry is highly labour intensive and has large number of factories.

Year	GVA of FPI	Rate of Growth in GVA of FPI	Percentage Share in All-India GVA
2017–18	1.91 Lakh Cr	6.7%	1.58%
2018–19	2.08 Lakh Cr	8.90%	1.62%
2019–20	2.24 Lakh Cr	7.69%	1.69%
2020–21	2.37 Lakh Cr	9.97%	1.88%
2022–23	1.92 Lakh Cr	7.3%	–

Source: Ministry of Statistics and Programme Implementation

Steps Taken to boost Exports of Processed Food

(i) **'Agriculture Export Policy'** has been introduced.

(ii) **Products Specific Export Promotion Forums** have been set up by APEDA.

(iii) APEDA has formed Export Promotion Forums (EPFs) for the products – Grapes, Onions, Mango, Banana, Pomegranate, Floriculture, Rice, Dairy Products and Nutri cereals.

(iv) A **Farmer Connect Portal** has been set up to provide a platform for farmers, Farmer Producer Organizations (FPOs) and cooperatives for interactions with exporters.

(v) **District as Export Hubs (DEH)** scheme has been implemented, using **ODOP (One District One Product)** approach.

BONUS KNOWLEDGE

FSSAI: It stands for the Food Safety and Standards Authority of India. This Authority was created in **2008** under **Food Safety and Standards Act, 2006.** Presently, FSSAI functions under the **Ministry of Health & Family Welfare** as an **autonomous body.** The main aim of this authority is to regulate and monitor the quality of the food business in India and to ensure the safety of food consumed within the country.

Benefits provided by Food Processing Industries

- Better choice of products to the consumers.
- Helps in reducing food inflation by lowering wastage of perishable products.
- Small-scale FPIs at rural level helps in reducing rural–urban migration through better employment opportunities.
- FPIs also incentivise farmers to go for crop diversification leading to larger profits.
- There is an increased export earnings with the presence of larger FPIs.

Major Challenges Still faced by Food Processing Industries

Uncontrollable Challenges

1. Fragmentation of land holdings.

2. Climatic variations and dependence on seasons along with low-capacity utilisation of raw materials of agricultural and animal husbandry.

Controllable Challenges

1. **Poor Supply Chain Linkages** – India is lacking in primary processing, proper storage and distribution facilities. India has a long and fragmented supply chain in agriculture market. This results in high wastage and high cost of food stuffs.
2. **Poor Quality Standards** – We have **less availability of laboratories** for food processing. There is a huge gap in the availability of **skilled man power** and **certification agencies** for food processing leading to low labour productivity.
3. **Supply Chain Infrastructure Gap** – Infrastructure related to the **export** of agri-products is grossly inadequate, especially **at seaports and airports**. Due to this, around 30 per cent of the produce gets spoiled.
4. **Poor marketability** of processed products.
5. **Low access to credit** and subsidised financing.
6. Provisions of the **Food Safety and Standards Act, 2006** which replaced the *Prevention of Food Adulteration Act, 1954*, are not being effectively complied by the related stakeholders.

MAJOR GOVERNMENT INITIATIVES TO PROMOTE FPI

EXAM ESSENTIAL

Several policy initiatives have been taken from time to time by the Government to promote the growth of the food processing sector in the country. Some of these are:

I. Pradhan Mantri-Formalisation of Micro Food Processing Enterprises (PM-FME) Scheme

The Government of India launched the Centrally Sponsored Scheme (CSS), under the ambit of the *Ministry of Food Processing Industries* in 2020, to modernise and enhance the competitiveness of the existing individual food processing microenterprises and ensure their transition to formal sector.

- The scheme has the fund sharing pattern between Centre and States as 60:40.
- This scheme is aimed at promoting 'vocal for local' in the sector, under the Atmanirbhar Bharat Abhiyan and adopts **One District One Product (ODOP)** approach.
- The ODOP product selected is either a **perishable agri-produce, cereal-based product** or a food product widely produced, **Minor Forest Produce** or **traditional food products** in a district and their allied sectors. An illustrative list of such products includes mango, potato, litchi, tomato, tapioca, kinnu, bhujia, petha, papad, pickle, millet-based products, fisheries, poultry, meat, as well as animal feed, among others. Besides, certain other traditional and innovative products including waste to wealth products could be supported under the Scheme. For example, honey, minor forest products in tribal areas, traditional Indian herbal edible items like turmeric, amla, haldi, etc.
- **Financial assistance** offered to the enterprises under PMFME Scheme **are as under:**
  (i) *Support to Individual / Group Category Micro Enterprises:* Credit-linked capital subsidy @35 per cent of the eligible project cost, maximum ceiling ₹10 lakh per unit;

(ii) ***Support to SHGs for seed capital:*** Seed capital @ ₹40,000/- per member of SHG engaged in food processing for working capital and purchase of small tools subject to a maximum of ₹4 lakh per SHG Federation.

(iii) ***Support for Common Infrastructure:*** Credit-linked capital subsidy @35 per cent subject to a maximum of ₹3 crore to support FPOs, SHGs, Cooperatives and any Government agency for setting up of common infrastructure. The common infrastructure will also be available for other units and public to utilise on hiring basis for substantial part of the capacity.

(iv) ***Branding and Marketing Support:*** Grant upto 50 per cent for Branding and Marketing to groups of FPOs/ SHGs/ Cooperatives or an SPV of micro food processing enterprises.

(v) ***Capacity Building:*** The scheme envisages training for Entrepreneurship Development Skilling (EDP+) programme modified to meet the requirement of food processing industry and product specific skilling.

II. Production Linked Incentive Scheme for the Food Processing Industry (PLISFPI)

- As part of the Atmanirbhar Bharat Abhiyan, the Government launched a **Central Sector Scheme (CSS),** namely **Production Linked Incentive Scheme for Food Processing Industry** which is to be implemented for a period of six years **from 2021–22 to 2026–27**.
- This scheme aims to **support creation of global food manufacturing champions** and **Indian brands of food products in the international markets,** to increase employment opportunities of off-farm jobs and to ensure remunerative prices of farm produce and higher income to farmers.
- Under the PLISFPI, the **Government provides financial incentives** to promote Indian food brands **abroad**, supporting branding and marketing activities for Indian-branded consumer food products **in global markets**. Beneficiaries are reimbursed 50 per cent of their expenditure on branding and marketing abroad, capped at 3 per cent of their annual food product sales or ₹50 crore per year, whichever is lower. Applicants are required to spend a minimum of ₹5 crore over five years to qualify.
- By mandating the **use of domestically grown agricultural products** (excluding additives, flavours, and edible oils) in the manufacturing process, the scheme has substantially increased local raw material procurement, benefiting underdeveloped and rural areas while supporting farmers' incomes.

III. Pradhan Mantri Kisan SAMPADA Yojana (PMKSY)

In 2016, the **Ministry of Food Processing Industries** launched the **SAMPADA** Yojana (Scheme for Agro-Marine Processing and Development of Agro-Processing Clusters). In 2017, the SAMPADA Yojana was renamed as Pradhan Mantri Kisan SAMPADA Yojana (PMKSY) and has incorporated ongoing schemes along with some other schemes, which aims to benefit around 20 lakh farmers.

PM Kisan **SAMPADA** Yojana is a comprehensive package, which will result in creation of modern infrastructure with efficient supply chain management from farm gate to retail outlet. As a whole, the revamped scheme is a comprehensive package, which comprises of the following **eight** components:

1. Mega Food Parks
2. Integrated Cold Chain and Value Addition Infrastructure
3. Creation/Expansion of Food Processing/Preservation Capacities

4. Infrastructure for Agro-processing Clusters
5. Creation of Backward and Forward Linkages
6. Food Safety and Quality Assurance Infrastructure
7. Human Resources and Institutions
8. Operation Greens

PMKSY aims to supplement agriculture, modernise processing and decrease the agri-waste. It is also helpful in providing better prices to farmers and creating good employment opportunities.

As of February, 2025, MoFPI has sanctioned 1608 projects including 41 Mega food Parks, 394 Cold Chain projects, 75 Agro-processing Clusters projects, 536 Food Processing Units, 61 Creation of Backward & Forward Linkages and 44 Operation Greens projects under corresponding component schemes of PMKSY across the country.

IV. Operation Greens Scheme

- **'Operation Greens'** under Pradhan Mantri Kisan SAMPADA Yojana was announced as a new central sector scheme on the line of 'Operation Flood' in the Union Budget 2018–19, for the integrated development of **Tomatoes, Onions, Potatoes (TOPS)**.
- The objectives were to enhance the value realisation of TOP farmers, i.e. price fixation to ensure farmers are given the right price for their produce; reduction in post-harvest losses; price stabilisation for producer and consumers and increase in food processing capacities and value addition, etc.
- The scheme aims to promote Farmer Producer Organizations (FPOs), agri-logistics, processing facilities and value addition, etc., in identified production clusters.
- The Scheme has two-pronged strategies:
  (i) Short-term Price Stabilisation Measures
  (ii) Long-term Integrated Value Chain Development Projects
- In the Union Budget 2021–22, to enhance the scope of long-term strategy Value Chain Development Projects Scheme has been expanded under Operation Greens from Tomato, Onion and Potato **(TOP)** crops to **(22) Twenty-Two Perishable products** in order to boost value addition in agriculture and allied products and their exports.
- 22 perishable crops identified includes **10 fruits, 11 vegetables and one marine, i.e. shrimp**.

V. Mega Food Park Scheme (MFPS) under PMKSY

- Regional horticultural crops are dominantly grown in particular areas. Generally, there is a cluster of similar farmers, traders, factories, etc., present in these areas who deal with the same type of agro-products. This scheme envisages providing world-class infrastructure facilities to strengthen those clusters. Thus, Mega Food Park scheme is based on **cluster approach.**
- The aim of this MFP scheme is to establish a 'direct linkage from farm to processing and then to consumer markets'.

- This scheme aims to maximise the value addition, minimise the wastages and enhance farmers' income by providing a proper mechanism and link to bring the farmers, traders, factories, etc., together.
- Mega Food Parks work on a **Hub and Spoke Model** under which,
  1. **Collection Centres (CCs)** collect the agricultural raw materials from the individual farmers, Farmer Groups' and Self-Help Groups (SHGs), for initial processing.
  2. These CCs then handover the raw materials to the **Primary Processing Centres (PPCs),** which have proper storage and transportation facilities. Several CCs work under one PPC.
  3. Further, these materials are transported to the **Central Processing Centre (CPC),** which is a place with a number of processing units owned by different business houses for final processing of these raw materials. CPCs have specialised cold storage facilities along with modern scientific units for processing the food.

The model of a Mega Food Park is depicted below:

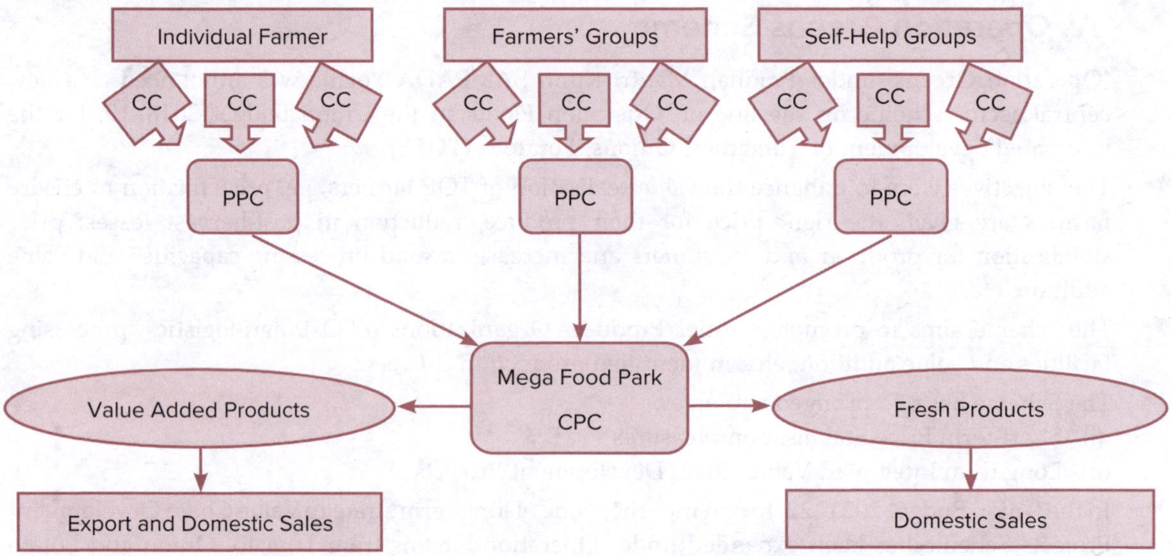

- A **Special Purpose Vehicle (SPV)** is created to set up a Mega Food Park. SPV is a limited company, set up with money from farmers' associations, private players, financial institutions, state-level agencies, etc. Thereafter, the Government gives them grant to cover a part of the project cost.
- The MFP scheme envisages a one-time capital grant of 50 per cent of the project cost (excluding land cost) subject to a **maximum of ₹50 crores.**

Benefits of MFPS

1. New employment opportunities in rural areas to reduce the rural–urban migration.
2. Efficient supply chain management from farm gate to the retail outlet.
3. MFP accommodates 30–40 FPIs. Use of common facilities like borewell, overhead tank, water treatment plant, sorting, grading, packing, etc. helps reduce the individual operational costs.
4. Food entrepreneurs can establish backward linkages (with farmers) and forward linkage (with retailers), thus leading to a compact supply chain and ultimately more profits.

5. Farmers can utilise the cold storages, ripening chambers and warehouses, thereby making less wastage and reduced distress sales.
6. Each fully operational MFP provides direct/indirect employment to about 5000 persons.

Thus, MFP ensures a win–win situation for all the stakeholders in FPI, provided the challenges are effectively handled through prompt and suitable facilitation by the Government.

did you KNOW?

As of March 2025, 24 Mega Food Parks are operational in our country. Srini Mega Food Park at Chittoor in Andhra Pradesh was established as the first mega food park in the country.

The MFP scheme has been discontinued by the Government with effect from 1 April 2021 with provision for committed liabilities for ongoing projects only.

VI. Modernisation of Abattoirs

Abattoir is a facility, where the animals are slaughtered to provide food for humans. They are in general, owned/licensed by the municipal bodies. Challenges faced by the existing abattoirs are as follows:

- Lack of modern equipment and facilities;
- Poor sanitation facilities for scientific slaughtering;
- Poor waste management and pollution control;
- Low-quality and hygiene levels, which may lead to contamination of meat and meat products.

A scheme for establishing new abattoirs and modernising existing abattoirs was launched under the **11th Five Year Plan.** It is implemented by involving local bodies/Public Sector Undertakings/Cooperatives, etc. Objectives of the scheme included:

1. Use of scientific and hygienic procedure
2. Modern technology for waste management and pollution control
3. More humane treatment with animals and minimising their transportation
4. Chilling facility to prevent microbial activity in meat
5. Better forward linkage facility for finished meat and meat products

This scheme aimed to facilitate some scientific and less painful methods of slaughtering. It has been implemented under **Public–Private Partnership (PPP)** mode.

VII. National Mission on Food Processing

National Mission on Food Processing is a **Centrally Sponsored Scheme (CSS)** launched in **2012.** It envisaged improving the outreach in terms of planning, supervision and monitoring of food processing schemes.

VIII. Scheme of Cold Chain, Value Addition and Preservation Infrastructure

This scheme aimed to establish a strong cold chain facility and linking farm gate to the consumer for agricultural, horticultural, animal husbandry and fishery products.

- Losses and wastages could be reduced with the help of efficient cold storage, transportation and minimal processing.
- The scheme has mainly four components:
  i. Processing Centre – To facilitate weighing, sorting, grading, packing and cold storage in both controlled atmosphere and modified atmosphere at the farm level.
  ii. Availability of **mobile pre-cooling vans** and reefer trucks.
  iii. Availability of distribution hubs with facilities like Variable Humidity Chambers, use of **Cleaning-in-Place (CIP)** process, fog treatment, blast freezing, etc.
  iv. Availability of irradiation facility there.

IX. Agri-Export Zones

- Agri-Export Zones (AEZs) were introduced in 2001 with the **Agricultural and Processed Food Products Export Development Authority (APEDA)** as its nodal agency.
- An AEZ is a specific geographic region in a country, demarcated for setting up agriculture-based processing industries, mainly for export.
- It works on a cluster approach to identify the potential products. It adopts an end-to-end approach to integrate the entire process right from the production stage to the market.
- Financial assistance is given by the Government for training, extension, R&D, quality upgradation, marketing, etc. Concession on custom duty is also provided on the import of capital machinery.
- As of March 2025, there are 60 AEZs in India (Maharashtra has the highest number of AEZs at present, i.e., 8 AEZs).
- **Benefits of having an AEZ:**
  a. Improvement in product quality and packaging.
  b. Better price for agricultural produce to the farmers.
  c. Increased employment opportunities in rural areas.
  d. Enhanced competitive capability of products by forming backward and forward linkages, promoting value addition and cost optimisation.

To promote exports from AEZ, both the Central as well as State Governments provide a variety of financial assistance to agri-export agencies.

X. Other Government Interventions in Recent Past

- In a bid to enhance food safety and quality, the Ministry of Food Processing Industries (MOFPI) will financially support the establishment of 100 new **NABL (National Accreditation Board for Testing and Calibration Laboratories)** food testing across India in the financial year 2025–26.
- All the processed food items have been **exempted from licensing** under the Industries (Development and Regulation) Act, 1951.
- **100 per cent FDI** has been permitted through *automatic route* for food processing sector subject to sectoral regulations.
- **100 per cent FDI** under Government *approval route*, for trading including through **e-commerce,** in respect of food products manufactured or produced in India.
- **Lower GST** for raw and processed products; nearly 80 per cent food products are covered in the lower tax slab of **5 and 12 per cent.**

- Provision of profit linked **tax holiday** and investment linked deduction under Income Tax Act, 1961.
- **Nivesh Bandhu portal** has been launched for disseminating information on the State specific resource potential, policy support and fiscal incentives offered to investors in food processing sector.
- As a measure towards improving **ease of doing food business,** the Food Safety and Standards Authority of India (FSSAI) has shifted from product-by-product approval to an ingredient and additive based approval process.

BONUS KNOWLEDGE

Organisations under the Ministry of FPI

Name of the Organisation	Location
National Institute of Food Technology Entrepreneurship and Management (NIFTEM)	Kundli, Haryana
Indian Institute of Food Processing Technology (IIFPT)	Thanjavur, Tamil Nadu
Indian Grape Processing Board (IGPB)	Pune, Maharashtra
National Meat and Poultry Processing Board (NMPPB)	New Delhi

did you KNOW?

National Institute of Food Technology Entrepreneurship and Management (NIFTEM) Act, 2021 was passed by Parliament in the year 2021 to declare NIFTEM and IIFPT as **Institutions of National Importance (INI)**.

SUPPLY CHAIN MANAGEMENT UNDER FOOD PROCESSING SECTOR

It has the following major components among several others:

I. Cold Chain II. Supermarket

I. Cold Chain

It is a temperature-controlled supply chain.

It involves a series of distribution activities which uninterruptedly maintain a temperature in order to protect the temperature-sensitive cargo *(from manufacture to the point of consumption)*.

The cold chain has **three main components:** transport, storage equipment and efficient management procedures. All three elements must combine to ensure safe transport and better storage.

The **Integrated Cold Chain Project** can be set up by Partnership/Proprietorship firms, Companies, Cooperatives, Corporations, SHGs, Farmer Producer Organisations. Under this scheme, the following facilities are created:

- Minimal processing centre at the farm gate level having facilities like weighing, sorting, grading, pre-cooling, cold storage and normal storage facilities;

- Mobile pre-cooling vans and reefer trucks;
- Distribution hubs having facilities such as multi-purpose cold stores, variable humidity stores, blast freezing, etc.

In the market, there exist two types of supply chain market: General and Supermarket

General: [Producers → Wholesalers → Retailers → Consumers]

- In this case, **non-linear supply chain** works.
- Data analysis is not done, and there is every possibility of stocking of materials for a long time which may increase storage cost and may also result in mismatch between demand and supply.

Supermarket: [Producers → Supermarket → Consumers]

II. Supermarket

Features of a Supermarket

- It provides consumers with many services at a **single point.**
- The supermarket store is divided into many departments having different types of items.
- Data analysis is done; test of consumers is identified. Storing at the supermarkets is done as per latest demand of the consumers. As a result, there is less stock and different items are not kept for a long time, thereby **decreasing the cost for storage.**
- **Better margin** is usually offered; thus more consumers are attracted.
- It is based on the principle of **linear supply chain.**
- Examples of supermarkets include *Reliance Fresh, Spencer's, Saravana Stores*, etc.

Factors that have led to the growth of Supermarkets:

1. Rise in the number of **middle-class** households.
2. Entry of **more women into the workforce** with a consequent incentive to seek for easy-to-prepare foods.
3. Rise in the use of **refrigerators,** making it possible to shop weekly instead of daily.
4. Rise in **car ownership,** facilitating journeys to distant stores and purchasing large quantities of goods.

Advantages of Supermarket

1. It provides a perfect **platform to customers to compare** the same product from different companies and take the best purchase decision.
2. **Average operating cost** in case of a supermarket is comparatively less than other retail formats.
3. Customers in many instances get a **good discount on purchases** as the supermarkets go for bulk purchase.
4. Concept of supermarket helps **reduce the role of intermediaries,** thereby helping in price reduction. Manufacturers can easily skip wholesalers and more quickly replenish retailers with stock.
5. **Detailed and computerised bill** given by supermarkets reduces the chance of discrepancy in billing.

Challenges faced by Supermarkets

1. Supermarkets in India still have a **low sales volume** as compared to developed countries.

2. Fierce **competition from unorganised retail shops** as they account for more than 90 per cent of the retail trade in India.
3. **High fixed recurring expenditure** in terms of huge rent and remuneration to a large number of employees involved.

ROLE OF E-COMMERCE IN PROMOTING FPI

It refers to buying or selling of products **via electronic means** (i.e. electronic commerce). It has many **advantages:**

- The consumer experiences the convenience of having goods **home-delivered.**
- As there is **no need of physical store,** it lowers the cost in terms of maintenance and rent of shop.
- It eliminates geographical limitations, gaining new customers with search engine visibility.
- It is easier for consumers to **compare prices** because of several shopping search engines and e-commerce websites.
- There is no need to handle currency notes or cash.
- The owner of the website gets a feedback. He can use this feedback to improve the services and make them better.

On the other hand, **limitations of e-commerce include the following:**

- Some goods cannot be sold online.
- Prior to the item getting delivered, a buyer **cannot touch or test it.**
- Consumers run the **risk of identity fraud** and other hazards as their personal details are captured by e-commerce businesses.
- **Good for Consumers, Bad for Businesses:** Undoubtedly e-commerce is an advantage to shoppers and consumers. However, at the same time, it increases difficulty for businesses. The consumer experiences the convenience of having goods home-delivered, but the logistics involved with delivering each individual item adds substantial strain to the e-commerce business operation, which sometimes becomes terrible in terms of managing logistics.

BONUS KNOWLEDGE

POST-HARVEST FOOD LOSS

Post-harvest infrastructure and processing facilities are necessary to boost the overall development of the food processing sector including reduction in post-harvest losses. MoFPI has estimated post-harvest losses in various agriculture commodities through various studies based on primary surveys. Studies commissioned by the MoFPI through (i) Indian Council of Agricultural Research-Central Institute of Post-Harvest Engineering and Technology (ICAR-CIPHET) titled 'Assessment of Quantitative Harvest and Post Harvest Losses of Major Crops and commodities in India'; and (ii) NABARD Consultancy Service Pvt. Ltd. (NABCONS) titled *'Study to Determine Post-Harvest Losses of Agri Produce in India'*.

SUMMARY

- **Food Processing** – Process of transformation of food which includes sorting, grading, packaging, branding, etc. – India's rank is 6th in terms of exports, production and consumption in FPI.
- **APEDA** – Agricultural and Processed Food Products Export Development Authority – established in 1986 – under Ministry of Commerce & Industry – provides financial assistance, conducts surveys, studies, subsidy schemes, etc., for the export of processed food from India.
- **Food Irradiation** – Applying ionising radiation (Cobalt-60) to the food items which improves the safety and extends their shelf life – eliminates micro-organisms and insects – however, cannot destroy the already present pesticides and toxins in food.
- **Mega Food Park Scheme** – To provide world-class infrastructure facilities in establishing Mega Food Parks – based on cluster approach – works on Hub and Spoke Model – aims to establish a direct linkage from farm to processing and then to consumer markets.
- **FSSAI** – Food Safety and Standards Authority of India – created in 2008 under Food Safety and Standards Act, 2006 – under the Ministry of Health & Family Welfare – aims to regulate and monitor the quality of food business in India and to ensure food safety.
- **National Mission on Food Processing** – Launched in 2012 – Centrally Sponsored Scheme – aim is to improve the outreach in terms of planning, supervision and monitoring of food processing sector schemes.
- **Agri-Export Zones (AEZs)** – Introduced in 2001 – nodal agency APEDA – specific geographic region demarcated for setting up agriculture-based processing industries mainly for export – 60 AEZs at present.
- **Pradhan Mantri Kisan SAMPADA Yojana (PMKSY)** – Umbrella scheme – launched in 2017– 08 sub-components – under Ministry of Food Processing and Industries – aims to supplement agriculture, modernise processing and decrease the agri-waste.
- **Scheme for Formalisation of Micro Food Processing Enterprises** – Launched in 2020 – aims to modernise and enhance competitiveness of existing individual micro-enterprises and ensure their transition to formal sector – 60:40 Centre–State fund sharing.

UPSC CSE PREVIOUS YEARS' PRELIMINARY EXAMINATION QUESTIONS

1. Consider the following statements: **[2018]**

1. The Food Safety and Standards Act, 2006 replaced the Prevention of Food Adulteration Act, 1954.
2. The Food Safety and Standards Authority of India (FSSAI) is under the charge of Director General of Health Services in the Union Ministry of Health and Family Welfare.

Which of the statements given above is/are correct?

(a) 1 only
(b) 2 only
(c) Both 1 and 2
(d) Neither 1 nor 2

☞ NO QUESTIONS ASKED
2024, 2023, 2022, 2021, 2020, 2019, 2017, 2016, 2015, 2014, 2013

ANSWER KEY

1. (a)

UPSC CSE PREVIOUS YEARS' MAIN EXAMINATION QUESTIONS

1. Elaborate the scope and significance of the food processing industry in India. (Answer in 150 words) **[2022]**
2. What are the challenges and opportunities of food processing sector in the country? How can income of the farmers be substantially increased by encouraging food processing? **[2020]**
3. Elaborate the **policy taken** by the Government of India to meet the challenges of the food processing sector. **[2019]**
4. Examine the **role of supermarkets** in supply chain management of fruits, vegetables and food items. How do they eliminate number of intermediaries? **[2018]**
5. What are the reasons for poor acceptance of **cost-effective small processing unit**? How will the **food processing unit** be helpful to uplift the socio-economic status of poor farmers? **[2017]**
6. What are the **impediments in marketing and supply chain management** in developing **FPI** in India? Can **e-commerce** help in overcoming these bottlenecks? **[2015]**

☞ NO QUESTIONS ASKED
2024, 2023, 2021, 2016, 2014, 2013

CHAPTER

22

SERVICE SECTOR

CHAPTER OUTLINE

- Tourism Sector
- Medical Tourism
- Eco-tourism
- Eco-tourism Vs Sustainable Tourism
- National Strategy for Sustainable Tourism
- Information Technology and Business Process Management Services
- India BPO Promotion Scheme
- Software as a Service (SaaS)
- Communication Sector
- E-commerce Sector
- Port and Shipping Services
- Space Sector
- Real Estate Sector

The emergence of services as the most dynamic sector in the Indian economy is considered as a revolution. Service sector, in India, grew more slowly than industry between the decades of 1951 and 1990. The growth of services picked up in the 1980s and accelerated in the 1990s, when the average growth rate was 7.5 per cent per annum, compared to industry and agriculture, which grew, on an average, by 5.8 per cent and 3.1 per cent, respectively.

The Services Sector is concerned with **offering intangible services** to consumers. It includes:

1. Trade, hotel, transport, storage, communication and services related to broadcasting.
2. Financial, insurance, real estate and professional services.
3. Public administration, defence and other services.

In fact, India's story of rapid growth and poverty reduction led by services has shown that industrialisation is not the only route to rapid economic development.

Importance of Service Sector

1. **Major part of Gross Value Added** – Services Sector accounts for more than 50 per cent of the GVA.
2. **Major contribution in State's economy** – In around 12 States, this sector contributes more than 50 per cent of the total Gross State Value Added.
3. **Providing Quality Employment** – It also provides employment to approximately 30 per cent of the workforce.
4. **Less efforts are required by Government** for welfare measures.
5. **FDI Inflows** – Services Sector brings more than 50 per cent of the total FDI inflows.

6. **Exports** – Around 40 per cent of the total exports of India are owed to service sector of the country.
7. Most of the start-ups in India belong to Services Sector.

As per NITI Aayog, India's service sector is strategised in the following **four ways,** each, with its own policy recommendations, helping in transforming the Indian economy:

- **Defend** – Sustaining the global presence and enhancing market growth. Focus areas are computer and information services and professional, scientific and business services.
- **Accelerate** – Stimulating all the sectors to outpace global growth. Focus areas are transport, trade and repair, education and financial services.
- **Transform** – Boosting productivity, innovation and global reach. Focus areas are travel, health and personal, cultural and recreational services.
- **Untapped** – Increasing market share and ensuring efficiency and sustainability. Focus areas are insurance and pension services, audio-visual and related services, telecommunication and postal and courier services.

Demand Elasticity of Services in India

Demand elasticity refers to the change in quantity demanded in response to a change in price.

- If the demand elasticity value is **greater than 1**, it indicates a significant change in quantity demanded relative to price changes.
- If the value is **less than 1** (inelastic demand), the quantity demanded changes only slightly with price fluctuations.
- If the value is **equal to 1**, demand elasticity is unitary, meaning quantity demanded changes at the same rate as price.

Key Insight

- **Lower demand elasticity** is observed in industries where demand is saturated. In highly saturated and oligopolistic markets, automation tends to displace labour rather than augment it.
- **Higher demand elasticity** suggests unmet market needs. In such sectors, automation enhances productivity and boosts employment, as new technologies drive demand expansion.
- **Policy implication:** Employment growth is more likely in sectors with high demand elasticity, where technology adoption leads to increased productivity and job creation.

The chart below illustrates demand elasticity across India's service sectors and its implications.

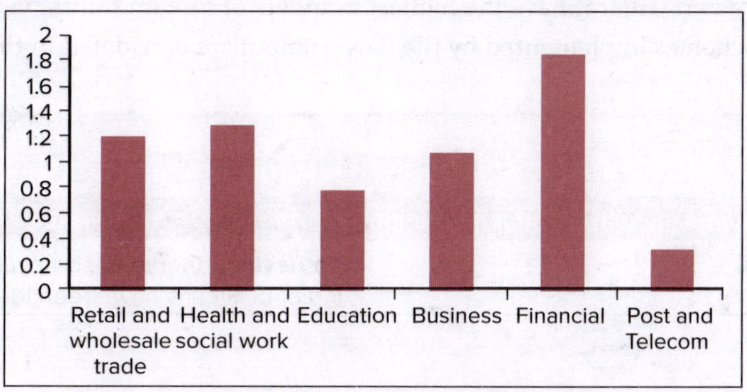

The high demand elasticity in financial, health and social work, retail and wholesale trade services could indicate that these sectors are yet to reach a stage of market saturation. Thus, productivity enhancement may result in employment generation for such areas.

Reports also substantiate that information technology (IT) improvements tend to raise employment in finance, retail and wholesale industries.

The services for the education sector reflected an inelastic demand (0.77) which may imply that productivity enhancements through automation can lead to a decline in teacher employment. However, the high degree of regulation and essential nature of this service are likely to act as buffers which will ensure productivity improvements not at the expense of teacher employment.

TOURISM SECTOR

- International Tourist Arrivals (ITAs) in India have reached 18.89 million in 2023, surpassing the previous peak of 17.91 million in 2019 and exceeding pre-pandemic levels, registering a growth of 5.47 per cent over 2019.
- India ranks 39th in the World Economic Forum's Travel and Tourism Development Index (TTDI) 2024.
- The growth in the foreign exchange earnings has also consequently declined.
- According to PIB, 'The Government of India has a vision of US$ 56 billion forex, creating around 140 million jobs in tourism sector by 2030 through inclusive growth and particularly focusing on cruise tourism, eco-tourism and adventure tourism.'
- As per the **Economic Survey 2024–25,** Deployment of Gross Bank Credit in tourism, hotels and restaurants is – 0.79 lakh crore (as of November 2024).
- As per the **India Tourism Statistics 2024** (an annual publication by Ministry of Tourism), India ranks first in tourists arrival within the Asia and Pacific region with a share of 15.36 per cent of International Tourists Arrivals (ITAs). Globally, India stands at 17th position with a share of 1.47 per cent of ITAs. India stands at 14th position in the world in terms of International Tourism Receipts (ITRs) with a global share of 1.86 per cent.
- **Tourism Trends:**
    - During 2023, the **top five source markets** for Foreign Tourist Arrivals (FTAs) in India were Bangladesh, the United States, the United Kingdom, Australia and Canada.
    - Most **domestic** tourists visit **Uttar Pradesh and Tamil Nadu** (2023).
    - **Maharashtra and Gujarat** have the highest numbers of **foreign tourist visits.**
- Major tourism schemes implemented by the Government are elucidated in the table below:

EXAM ESSENTIAL

Schemes under Tourism Sector

Name of the Scheme	Year of Implementation	Purpose
Swadesh Darshan Scheme	2014–15	To develop theme-based circuits for tourism in India. 13 circuits have been identified.

Name of the Scheme	Year of Implementation	Purpose
Swadesh Darshan 2.0	2015	To develop sustainable and responsible destinations in India following a tourist – and destination – centric approach.
PRASAD (Pilgrimage Rejuvenation and Spiritual Augmentation Drive)	2014–15	Development and beautification of the pilgrimage destinations.
E-Visa Scheme	2014–15	To promote tourism in five categories – Tourism, Business, Medical, Conference and Medical Attention.
RCS UDAN3	2019–20	This **Regional Connectivity Scheme** (RCS-UDAN) launched by the Ministry of Civil Aviation, has the purpose to facilitate/stimulate regional air connectivity by making it affordable.
SAATHI	2020–21	**System for Assessment, Awareness, and Training for Hospitality Industry** (SAATHI) was launched in association with the **Quality Council of India** to restrict any further transmission of the virus while providing accommodation and other services post-lockdown due to Covid-19 pandemic
Bharat Gaurav Scheme	2021–22	• **An Indian Railways initiative** to promote **theme-based tourist circuit trains** on the lines of Ramayana Express. • These trains can be run **either by private or State-owned operators**. • Service providers can be an individual, company, society, **trust, joint venture or consortium.**
NIDHI	2021–22	Purpose is to register accommodation units in the country in the Ministry's portal **National Integrated Database of Hospitality Industry** (NIDHI) so that the comprehensive national database can help in creating policies and strategies for the promotion and development of tourism at various destinations.
LGSCATSS	2021–22	Under **Loan Guarantee Scheme for Covid Affected Tourism Service Sector** (LGSCATSS), administered through the National Credit Guarantee Trustee Company (NCGTC), working capital/personal loans are provided to households that were impacted due to the Covid-19 pandemic to discharge liabilities and restart businesses.

BONUS KNOWLEDGE

NATIONAL TOURISM POLICY

The aims of this Policy are improving the conditions for tourism development in the country, supporting tourism industries, strengthening tourism support functions and developing tourism sub sectors.

The Key Strategic Objectives of the Policy are:

i. To enhance the contribution of tourism in the Indian economy by increasing the expenditure made on tourism and making India a year-round tourist destination,
ii. To create jobs and entrepreneurial opportunities in tourism sector,
iii. To enhance the competitiveness of tourism sector and attract private sector investment,
iv. To preserve and enhance the cultural and natural resources of the country, and
v. To ensure sustainable, responsible and inclusive development of tourism in the country.

The policy provides for a **National Tourism Advisory Council (NTAC)** chaired by the Union Minister for Tourism and comprising all the Tourism Ministers of the States, representatives of the relevant Line Ministries and Industry stakeholders to provide overall vision, guidance and direction to the development of tourism sector in the country.

Medical Tourism

India is considered a preferred destination for cardiology, orthopaedics, transplant and ophthalmology in curative care. It also enjoys high credibility in wellness and prevention and alternative medicine.

A rare combination of advanced facilities, skilled doctors and low cost of treatment has made India a popular hub of medical tourism, attracting many foreign patients every year.

- The Government plans to bring out a policy to promote India as a key destination for medical tourism.
- The proposed policy aims to promote integrated treatment with allopathy and AYUSH (Ayurveda, Yoga, Unani, Siddha and Homoeopathy) streams.
- The Union Commerce Ministry, in cooperation with ministries of tourism and health, has already launched a portal, indiahealthcaretourism.com, in three languages – Arabic, Russian and French – to provide comprehensive information to medical travellers.
- Currently, Indian medical tourism industry is pegged at around $3 billion. Globally, the medical tourism market is estimated at around $40-60 billion.
- India has ranked 10 out of the top 46 countries in the world in the Medical Tourism Index FY21, released by the Medical Tourism Association.

Eco-tourism

It involves responsible travel to natural areas that conserve the environment, sustains the well-being of the local people, and involves interpretation and education. Following are some of its benefits:

- Eco-tourism can bring about economic, socio-cultural and environmental benefits for the Government, private sector and local communities if well implemented.
- Revenue from tourist visits helps create job opportunities for locals, which in turn leads to more diversified income for them.

➤ Eco-tourism can also support environmental conservation and management if properly carried out.

Eco-tourism *vs* Sustainable Tourism

Eco-tourism	Sustainable Tourism
According to The International Eco-tourism Society (TIES), eco-tourism is 'responsible travel to natural places that improves the well-being of local people and conserves the environment.'	The World Tourism Organisation defines sustainable tourism as 'tourism that takes full account of its current and future economic, social and environmental impacts, addressing the needs of visitors, the industry, the environment and host communities.'
Eco-tourism is a subset of tourism primarily focused on natural regions.	**Sustainable tourism** is not a specific sort of tourism; rather, it is an aim for promoting **to travel responsibly**, among all types of tourists.
Eco-tourism is mainly concerned with ecological conservation and educating travellers about local habitats and natural surroundings.	2030 Agenda for Sustainable Development Goals (SDG) aims to devise and implement policies to promote sustainable tourism that creates jobs and promotes local culture and products.

National Strategy for Sustainable Tourism

National Strategy for Sustainable Tourism and the Responsible Traveller Campaign has been launched by the Ministry of Tourism in 2022 in partnership with the United Environment Programme (UNEP) and Responsible Tourism Society of India (RTSOI).

The objective of this is to increase the economic, social, and environmental benefits by building a low-carbon, inclusive and resilient tourism sector in India.

7 strategic pillars identified by this policy for the development of sustainable tourism are as follows:

1. **Promoting Environmental Sustainability**
2. **Protecting Biodiversity**
3. **Promoting Economic Sustainability**
4. **Promoting Socio-Cultural Sustainability**
5. **Scheme for Certification of Sustainable Tourism**
6. **IEC and Capacity Building**
7. **Governance**

This policy provides for setting up a National Resource Centre as a source of capacity and expertise at the national level for sustainable tourism, adventure tourism, eco-tourism and National Board on Sustainable Tourism under Secretary (Tourism).

Issues and Challenges in Tourism Sector

1. Poor Infrastructure – Accessibility (Transportation), hotels, etc.
2. Cleanliness and proper maintenance of tourist places.
3. Safety and security including women's safety.
4. Lack of availability of sufficient number of persons with adequate soft skills.

INFORMATION TECHNOLOGY AND BUSINESS PROCESS MANAGEMENT SERVICES

- The most visible and well-known dimension of the acceleration of growth in the service sector has been in the software and IT-enabled services.
- India is recognised as a global hub for IT services and has emerged as the world's 3rd largest start-up ecosystem, having 100 + unicorns. The IT services in India has propelled the growth of the service sector as part of the GDP and also bolstered the export of modern services in the era of post-economic reforms of 1991.
- The four sub-sectors of Information Technology and Business Process Management (IT-BPM) sector are as follows:
  1. IT services (51.1 per cent)
  2. Software product and Engineering Services (20.8 per cent).
  3. Business Process Management (19.8 per cent)
  4. Hardware (8.3 per cent)
- According to the Ministry of Commerce and Industry, India has emerged as the **third largest ecosystem for startups** with more than **1.59 lakh startups** recognised by the Department for Promotion of Industry and Internal Trade (DPIIT) as of January 15, 2025.
- From 2016 to October 31, 2024, recognised startups have reportedly created over **16.6 lakh direct jobs**, significantly contributing to employment generation.
- About 48 per cent of the startups in India are from Tier-II and Tier-III cities.

Last Minute SNIPPETS

According to the Economic Survey 2024–25, the industry has estimated revenues of USD 254 billion, marking a 3.8 per cent YoY growth in FY24 (excluding e-commerce).

Measures taken by Indian Government for IT-BPM Sector

1. Relaxation of Other Service Provider (OSP) Regulations
   - The relaxations are as follows:
     - Clear Definition of OSP: The applicability of new guidelines is limited to the entities that provide 'Voice based BPO Services' to its customers. Voice Based BPO Services are defined to mean call centre services.
     - Removal of registration requirements for OSP centres in India.
     - Removal of requirement of bank guarantee for any facility or dispensation.
     - Removal of distinction between the domestic and international OSPs.
     - Work from home and remote locations is allowed to agents.
     - Inter-connectivity between two or more OSP centres of same or unrelated company is allowed.
     - Infrastructure sharing among OSPs is allowed.
   - According to the NASSCOM study, these reforms are bringing positive changes in the sector.
2. **India BPO Promotion Scheme**
   - The Scheme was launched in 2014, under the Ministry of IT and Electronics.
   - It aims to incentivise the BPO/IT-ITeS operations sector in the country.
   - The Software Technology Park of India (STPI), an autonomous society of Ministry of Electronics and Information Technology (MeitY), is the nodal implementing agency of the scheme.

- Government had launched North-East BPO Promotion Scheme (NEBPS) in 2015, under Digital India Programme, to incentivise setting up of BPO/ITeS Operations in North-East Region (NER), and create employment opportunities for the youth and growth of IT/ITeS Industry.

3. In order to drive innovation and technology adoption in this sector, various policies such as **Start-up India, National Software Products Policy** and **removal of issues related to Angel Tax** have been introduced.

E-commerce Sector

Electronic commerce (e-commerce) is a system of business where companies and individuals buy and sell goods and services over the internet. e-commerce operates in different types of market segments and can be conducted over computers, tablets, smartphones, and other smart devices.

e-commerce operates in several market segments including business-to-business, business-to-consumer, consumer-to-consumer, and consumer-to-business.

Categories of different e-commerce business models are as follows:

1. Business-to-Business (B2B)
2. Business-to-Consumer (B2C)
3. Consumer-to-Consumer (C2C)
4. Consumer-to-Business (C2B)
5. Business-to-Government (B2G)
6. Government-to-Business (G2B)
7. Government-to-Citizen (G2C)

e-commerce business is based on 2 types of models – (a) **Inventory-based model** and (b) **Marketplace model**.

(a) **Inventory-based model:** In this model, e-commerce marketplaces store inventory from different brands, merchants, and sellers and sell the products directly to the consumers.

(b) **Marketplace model:** In this business model, e-commerce marketplaces provide a common platform to multiple sellers where they can display and sell their products while connecting with potential customers.

- A new Chapter has been introduced within the Foreign Trade Policy (FTP), 2023 that aims to promote e-commerce exports by bringing such exporters under the ambit of various export promotion schemes of the Government.

Features of e-commerce sector in India

- With over 800 million users (being the 2nd largest internet market in the world), India is the fastest growing e-commerce market in the world.
- According to the Global Payments Report by Worldpay FIS, India's e-commerce market is projected to post impressive gains and grow at 18 per cent annually through 2025.
- Coverage area wise, close to 100 per cent of pin codes in India have experiences e-commerce adoption.
- e-commerce market in India is projected to grow at 18 per cent rate annually by 2025.

FDI in e-commerce

(a) 100 per cent FDI is allowed under automatic route in B2B transactions of e-commerce and in marketplace model of e-commerce, but FDI is not permitted in the inventory-based model.

(b) 100 per cent FDI is allowed under Government approval route for e-commerce transactions by Food Retail Companies, subject to the condition that the products retailed are manufactured and/or produced in India.

Government Initiatives to boost e-commerce in India

- **National e-commerce Policy:** Government is working on the national e-commerce policy which envisages to establish a regulatory framework to improve ease of doing business in the sector. A draft version of the e-commerce policy was released in 2019.
- **Consumer Protection (e-commerce) Rules, 2020:** Consumer Protection (e-commerce) Rules, 2020 have been notified under the Consumer Protection Act, 2019, which define an e-commerce entity as any person who owns, operates or manages digital or electronic facility or platform for electronic commerce, but does not include a seller offering his goods or services for sale on a marketplace e-commerce entity.
- These rules stipulate that no e-commerce entity shall adopt any unfair trade practice, whether in course of business on its platform or otherwise.
- **Parliamentary Committee Report:** The Standing Committee on Commerce (Chaired by Mr. V.V. Reddy) presented a report on 'Promotion and Regulation of e-commerce in India' in 2022. [Details in the box]

BONUS KNOWLEDGE

REPORT OF THE PARLIAMENTARY STANDING COMMITTEE ON PROMOTION AND REGULATION OF E-COMMERCE IN INDIA

The Committee tabled its report in 2022.

Some Key observations and recommendations of the Committee are as follows:

- Addressing the anti-competitive practices in the e-commerce marketplace, viz. lack of platform neutrality, deep discounting, misuse of data, etc.
- Introducing necessary amendments to the Competition Act, 2002 for determining the abuse of dominant position to prevent adverse effect on the competition in digital market.
- Place certain obligations on e-commerce entities such as appointment of chief compliance officer and nodal contact person along with setting up a grievance redressal mechanism on the entity's website.
- Mandatory registration of e-commerce entities with DPIIT.
- A framework in the National E-Commerce Policy to be developed to address these issues for both foreign and domestic funded marketplaces.
- As per international practices, digital companies of a certain size need targeted regulation which are to be designated as gatekeeper entities. As per the recommendation of the Committee, a threshold should be set for qualifying entities as gatekeepers in Indian market.

- **Government e-Marketplace (GeM):** Government e-Marketplace (GeM) is an online platform (launched in 2016) for the procurement of goods and services by all the central government ministries and departments. It leverages technology to enhance transparency, efficiency and speed in public procurement. It is equipped with the tools of e-bidding, reverse e-auction and demand aggregation to facilitate the government users and help achieve them the best value of their money.
- **Open Network for Digital Commerce (ONDC):** It is an open network protocol for e-commerce in India, an initiative patronised by DPIIT, Ministry of Commerce and Industry. It envisages to

change the market from an operator-driven ecosystem to a facilitator-driven network. [Details in the box]

EXAM ESSENTIAL

OPEN NETWORK FOR DIGITAL COMMERCE (ONDC)

- **Open Network for Digital Commerce (ONDC)** is an initiative of the Department of Promotion of Industry and Internal Trade (DPIIT), Ministry of Commerce aiming at promoting open networks for all aspects of exchange of goods and services over digital or electronic networks .The mission of ONDC is to democratise digital commerce.
- ONDC is based on **open-sourced methodology**, using open specifications and **open network protocols** independent of any specific platform.
- The ONDC are a bunch of open protocols for exchange of goods and services, similar to hypertext transfer protocol (HTTP) for information exchange over internet, SMP for exchange of emails and UPI for payments.
- Thus, ONDC goes beyond the current platform-centric digital commerce model where the buyer and the seller are bound to use the same platform or application to be digitally visible and do a business transaction.
- ONDC protocols would standardise operations like cataloguing, inventory management, order management and order fulfilment. Thus, small businesses would be able to use any ONDC compatible applications instead of being governed by specific platform-centric policies.
- ONDC is expected to make e-Commerce more inclusive and accessible for consumers. Consumers can potentially discover any seller, product, or service by using any compatible application or platform, thus increasing freedom of choice for consumers.

Software as a Service (SaaS)

SaaS is a software distribution model in which a cloud provider hosts applications and makes them available to end users over the internet. It is also known as **On-Demand Software** because the users can use this software without installing them in local devices.

In cloud computing, there are several types of cloud services, viz. infrastructure, platforms, and software applications.

1. **Infrastructure as a Service (IaaS):** In this category, digital infrastructure (servers, network resources, etc.) for organising business activities, creating applications, data storage, etc. is provided over cloud services.
2. **Software as a Service (SaaS):** In this category a full stack of software applications are offered as a service to the end users or customers who can access and use. SaaS solutions are scalable and ready-to-use applications, which are developed and maintained by the cloud service provider.
3. **Platform as a Service (PaaS):** Here, hardware and software resources are offered as services over cloud for developing, testing, delivering, and managing cloud applications. There are different types like middleware, development tools, and cloud databases within the PaaS offerings.

Examples of SaaS – Services provided by Google Workspace, Salesforce, Zoom, Netflix, Microsoft 365, etc.

SaaS applications are popular because of the advantages of reduction in cost due to low maintenance, scalability of applications, and multidevice support. Some of the concerns of such services are security and integrity of user data, utility of applications in the absence of internet, and latency in data transmission over internet.

Last Minute SNIPPETS

- In the global scenario, India is the **3rd largest SaaS ecosystem** after the USA and China.
- India presently has 21 SaaS unicorns as compared to one in 2018.
- A report titled **'India: The Next Global SaaS Capital'** has been developed by Confederation of Indian Industry (CII) and EY in 2022. As per this report, the Indian SaaS market is expected to reach \$20–25 billion by 2025 from \$4–7 billion in 2020.

Communication Sector

The communication service is defined as the transmission of messages, particularly sending and receiving information. Development of satellite communication and mobile technologies gives prominence to this sector.

Telecommunication Sector

- India is the **world's second-largest** telecommunications market. China is the largest market.
- Total subscriber base in the country stood at 1203.69 million as of May 2024. The wireless market segment accounted for 97.20 per cent of the total subscriber base.
- Rural subscribers comprised 45.60 per cent of the total telephone subscribers.
- India is also the **second largest country** in terms of **internet subscribers** after China. Globally, India is the fastest growing App market.
- **FDI cap** in the telecom sector has been increased to **100 per cent** from 74 per cent. FDI inflow in the telecom sector stood at US\$ 39.32 billion between April 2000 and March 2024.

GatiShakti Sanchar Portal

Department of Telecommunication launched **'GatiShakti Sanchar Portal'** Portal for Centralised Right of Way (RoW) approvals. This will streamline the process of Right of Way (RoW) applications and permissions across the country.

BONUS KNOWLEDGE

What is RoW – RoW is a legal right for online application and permissions to Telecom Service Providers (TSPs). The procedure of laying down underground infrastructure (optical fibre) and overground infrastructure (mobile towers) is regulated by **Indian Telegraph RoW rules (2016)**.

- The portal has been developed to implement the vision of the National Broadband Mission to provide broadband infrastructure as a core utility to every citizen, governance and services on demand and, in particular, digital empowerment of the citizens of our country.
- The portal enables applicants form various Telecom Service providers (TSPs) as well as Infrastructure providers (IPs) **to apply at a common single portal** for Right of Way permissions to lay down Optical Fibre Cable and for erecting mobile towers, to State/UT Governments and local bodies.

- With streamlining the process of RoW permissions along with faster approvals, it facilitates easy rollout of 5G services, in which a Base Transceiver Station (BTS) is installed at very short intervals.
- For effective monitoring of RoW applications across the country, the portal hosts a dashboard showing State and District wise pendency status.
- The portal has been developed by **MP State Electronics Development Corporation** on behalf of DoT and is an example of the nation's 'AatmaNirbhar' movement and a milestone towards improving **Ease of Doing Business,** contributing actively to transform our country into a digitally empowered society and knowledge economy.

Challenges faced by the Telecommunication Sector

a. **High debt** in telecom sector due to large investment incurred for 5G deployment – As per ICRA **(Investment Information and Credit Rating Agency),** the total debt of the industry is around ₹6.5 lakh crore as on March 31, 2024.

b. In the years between 2021 and 2024, the telecom industry has embraced new networks, services such as 5G, increasingly competitive broadband markets, and a decentralised broadband infrastructure. These new networks, services, and applications require more proactive measures to mitigate cybersecurity risk.

c. **Intellectual property theft,** information, and cyber security threat.

d. Need to **migrate** from legacy networks to more modern infrastructure.

e. Require expansion of the coverage of 5G networks in suburban and rural regions to bridge the digital divide between urban and rural areas.

PORT AND SHIPPING SERVICES

- India has **13 major ports** as of February 2025 out of which Paradip, Chennai, Vishakhapatnam, Kandla (now Deendayal Port) and Jawaharlal Nehru Port Trust (JNPT) are the ports with highest cargo capacities.
- The efficiency in this sector is often indicated by the **TAT* (Turnaround Time)** of ships.

> **did you KNOW?** In 2020, the Union Cabinet approved for setting up the 13th major port at Vadhavan (Maharashtra).

- 567 projects have been identified under Sagarmala Programme for Holistic Development of Coastal Districts with an estimated cost of ₹59,000 crore.
- Coastal shipping traffic has grown from 74.9 MMTA in 2014 to 133 MMTPA in 2022.
- The Ministry has clear and robust pipeline of 81 projects of more than ₹42,400 crore to be awarded on PPP till FY25.
- Jawaharlal Nehru Port became the first **100 per cent Landlord Major Port**.
- Average container turnaround time in major ports of India has reduced from 48.1 hrs in FY24 to 30.4 hrs in FY25 (April–November).

***Note:** The **time** that is taken between the arrival of a vessel/ship and its departure is referred to as the **Turnaround Time (TAT).** The vessel **Turnaround Time** is used to measure the efficiency of port operations. Lower the TAT, the better it is.

SPACE SECTOR

- At present, India accounts for only about 2 per cent of the space economy, much behind the major players – USA and China. However, with recent initiatives and private sector participation, the Indian space economy has the potential to be worth US$ 44 billion within 2033 from the value of US$ 8.4 billion in 2023 with the implementation of Indian Space Policy, 2023 which envisages to capture 8 per cent of the global space market. The **three key focus areas** of Indian space programme are:
  1. Satellite communication.
  2. Earth observation.
  3. Satellite-aided navigation which includes GAGAN and NavIC*.

***Note:**

(1) GAGAN is a satellite-based augmentation system and stands for GPS-aided GEO augmented navigation which is a joint project between ISRO and the Airports Authority of India.

(2) NavIC is an autonomous regional satellite navigation system that provid**es accurate real-time** positioning and timing services.

- The two major trends of space programmes globally are space exploration and being used for national security purposes.
- **Private investments** are being attracted to deliver space-related goods and services. The major areas for these investments are:
  - Production of Polar Satellite Launch Vehicle (PSLV).
  - Satellite integration and assembly.
  - Production of composite materials.
  - Production of solid, liquid, cryogenic and semi-cryogenic propellants.
  - Production of electronic packages, avionics and satellite testing.

Recent Initiatives in the Space Sector

1. Indian Space Association (ISpA)

- It was launched in 2021.
- ISpA is a premier industry association of Space and Satellite companies.
- It was launched to undertake policy advocacy and engage with all the stakeholders in the Indian Space domain, including the Government and its agencies.
- ISpA to help in making India self-reliant, technologically advanced and a leading player in the space arena.

2. Indian Space Promotion and Authorisation Centre (IN-SPACe)

- IN-SPACe was approved in 2020, to provide a level playing field for private companies to use Indian space infrastructure.

3. New Space India Limited (NSIL)

- It has been set up in 2019, as a wholly owned Government of India undertaking, under the administrative control of the Department of Space (DOS).
- It is formed to 'own' the operational launch vehicles and space assets of ISRO.

- In the present demand-driven model, NSIL shall act as an aggregator of user requirements and obtain commitments. For example, Tata Sky signed MoU with NSIL for utilising the capacity on board of the upcoming communication satellite GSAT-24, to be built by ISRO and launched by Arianespace.
- Thus, NSIL is the commercial arm of ISRO with a primary responsibility of **enabling Indian industries to take up high technology space related activities.** It is also responsible for the promotion and commercial exploitation of the products and services emanating from the Indian space programme.

4. Antrix Corporation Limited (ACL)

- It was incorporated in 1992, as a Marketing arm of ISRO for promotion and commercial exploitation of space products, technical consultancy services and transfer of technologies developed by ISRO.

How NSIL differs from Antrix Corporation?

- Antrix handles ISRO's commercial deals with foreign customers and provides them end to end products, whereas, NSIL deals with capacity building of local industries for space manufacturing.

5. Regulatory Reforms

- Through SpaceCom and SpaceRS policies, traditional Satellite Communication and Remote Sensing Sectors have been further liberalised. This has enabled the entrepreneurs/industries to take up end-to-end activities in these domains.
- At present, FDI in space sector is allowed under Government route for satellite establishment and operations.

REAL ESTATE SECTOR

Real estate is the land along with any permanent improvements attached to the land, whether natural or man-made including water, trees, minerals, buildings, homes, fences and bridges. Real estate is a form of real property. It differs from personal property, which are things not permanently attached to the land, such as vehicles, boats, jewellery, furniture and farm equipment.

Real estate sector contributes approx. 7–8 per cent of GDP of India at present. As per a report titled **'India Real Estate: Vision 2047',** jointly prepared by Knight Frank and National Real Estate Development Council (NAREDCO), the real estate sector is expected to expand to $5.8 trillion by 2047, contributing 15.5 per cent to the GDP.

As per the JLL's 2024 Global Real Estate Transparency Index, India's real estate market transparency is positioned at 31st place in the list of 89 countries. Composite transparency score of India has been 2.4 in 2024.

> **did you KNOW?** The real estate sector in India is the second-largest business generator after agriculture, with more than 230 affiliated businesses. This sector is also very crucial to ensure 'housing for all'.

Real Estate (Regulation and Development) Act, 2016

The Act provides for State Governments to establish regulatory authority and with the following mandate:

- Register and maintain a database of real estate projects; publish it on its website for public viewing Protection of interest of promoters, buyers and real estate agents
- Development of sustainable and affordable housing
- Render advice to the Government and ensure compliance with its regulations and the Act
- Establishment of Real Estate Appellate Tribunal – Decisions of RERAs can be appealed in these tribunals
- Mandatory Registration: All projects with plot size of minimum 500 sq.mt or eight apartments need to be registered with Regulatory Authorities
- Deposits: Depositing 70 per cent of the funds collected from buyers in a separate escrow bank account for construction of that project only
- Liability: Developer's liability to repair structural defects for five years
- Penal interest in case of default: Both promoter and buyer are liable to pay an equal rate of interest in case of any default from either side
- Cap on Advance Payments: A promoter cannot accept more than 10 per cent of the cost of the plot, apartment or building as an advance payment or an application fee from a person without first entering into an agreement for sale
- Defines Carpet Area as net usable floor area of flat. Buyers will be charged for the carpet area and not the super built-up area
- Punishment: Imprisonment of up to three years for developers and up to one year in case of agents and buyers for violation of orders of Appellate Tribunals and Regulatory Authorities

BONUS KNOWLEDGE

NATIONAL REAL ESTATE DEVELOPMENT COUNCIL

National Real Estate Development Council (NAREDCO) was established as an autonomous self-regulatory body in 1998 under the aegis of the *Ministry of Housing and Urban Affairs.*

It was formed with the mandate to induce transparency and ethics in the real estate business and transform the unorganised Indian real estate sector into a mature and globally competitive business sector.

SERVICES PURCHASING MANAGERS INDEX (PMI)

India's services sector activity is gauged by PMI services. In recent years, PMI services witnessed a setback due to restrictions imposed to tackle the Covid-19 pandemic, outbreak of the Russia-Ukraine conflict, etc. The indicator expanded to 58.5 in December 2022 and reached the value of 59.0 In February 2025.

FOREIGN DIRECT INVESTMENT (FDI) IN SERVICES

As per the World Investment Report 2024 of UNCTAD, India is the fifteenth largest recipient of Foreign Direct Investment (FDI) in the top 20 host countries in 2023. 'In FY24, India's FDI inflows was US$ 70.95 billion in which the service sector was the highest recipient. *(Economic Survey 2024–25)*

ACCOUNT AGGREGATOR NETWORK

India has unveiled the Account Aggregator (AA) network; it is a financial data-sharing system that intends to revolutionise investing and credit, giving millions of consumers greater access and control over their financial records. It could expand the potential pool of customers for lenders and fintech companies.

Account Aggregator (AA) is a type of RBI regulated entity (with an NBFC-AA license). It helps an individual digitally access and share information from one financial institution he has an account with to any other regulated financial institution in the AA network. Data cannot be shared without the consent of the individual. This is the first step towards bringing open banking in India.

SUMMARY

- **Service sector –** Contributes around 53 per cent of the GVA. Service sector in India grew more slowly than industry between the decades of 1951 and 1990. The growth of services picked up in the 1980s and accelerated in the 1990s.
- **Aam Aadmi Bima Yojana –** Social Security Scheme for rural landless households under which the head of the family or one earning member in the family is covered.
- **Pradhan Mantri Jeevan Jyoti Bima Yojana** (PMJJBY) – For people between 18 and 50 years of age having bank accounts.
- **World Tourism Index** – Published by World Economic Forum.
- **Medical tourism** – Aims to promote integrated treatment with allopathy and AYUSH (Ayurveda, Yoga and Naturopathy, Unani, Siddha and Homoeopathy) streams – medical tourism industry is pegged at $3 billion.
- **Eco-tourism** – Responsible travel to natural areas that conserve the environment, sustain the well-being of the local people, and involve interpretation and education – supports conservation and environmental management.
- **Sustainable Tourism –** It takes full account of its current and future economic, social and environmental impacts, addressing the needs of visitors, the industry, the environment and host communities.
- **National strategy for sustainable tourism and the responsible traveller campaign –** It has been launched by the Ministry of Tourism in 2022. It has identified 7 strategic pillars for the development of sustainable tourism.
- **Swadesh Darshan Scheme –** To develop theme-based circuits for tourism in India.
- **Swadesh Darshan 2.0 –** It is now being implemented with the objective of developing sustainable and responsible destinations in India.
- **PRASAD –** Pilgrimage Rejuvenation and Spiritual Augmentation Drive – development and beautification of the pilgrimage destinations.
- **Sub-sectors of IT-BPM sector –** IT Services, Business Process Management, Hardware, Software Products & Engineering Services.
- **Electronic commerce (e-commerce) –** It is a system of business where companies and individuals buy and sell goods and services over the internet.
- **Open Network for Digital Commerce (ONDC) –** It is an initiative of the Department of Promotion of Industry and Internal Trade (DPIIT), Ministry of Commerce & Industry, aiming at promoting open networks for exchange of goods and services over digital or electronic networks. The mission of ONDC is to democratise digital commerce.
- **Indian Space Association (ISpA) –** Is a premier industry association of Space and Satellite companies, which aspires to be the collective voice of the Indian Space Industry.
- **Software Technology Parks of India (STPI) –** An autonomous society under MeitY.
- **National Real Estate Development Council (NAREDCO) –** Established in 1998 – an autonomous self-regulatory body under the aegis of the Ministry of Housing and Urban Affairs.

UPSC CSE PREVIOUS YEARS' PRELIMINARY EXAMINATION QUESTIONS

☞ NO QUESTIONS ASKED

2024, 2023, 2022, 2021, 2020, 2019, 2018, 2017, 2016, 2015, 2014, 2013

UPSC CSE PREVIOUS YEARS' MAIN EXAMINATION QUESTIONS

1. Normally countries shift from agriculture to industry and then later to services, but India shifted directly from agriculture to services. What are the **reasons for the huge growth of services** vis-à-vis industry in the country? Can India become a developed country without strong Industrial base? **[2014]**

☞ NO QUESTIONS ASKED

2024, 2023, 2022, 2021, 2020, 2019, 2018, 2017, 2016, 2015, 2013

CHAPTER 23

INSURANCE SECTOR IN INDIA

CHAPTER OUTLINE

- What is Insurance
- Insurance Sector in India
- Insurance Reforms
- Present Status of Insurance Sector
- Significance of IRDAI in transforming the Insurance Sector
- Domestic Systemically Important Insurers
- Recent Reforms in Insurance Sector
- Agriculture Insurance Company of India Limited
- Deposit Insurance and Credit Guarantee Corporation (DICGC)
- Performance Review and Regulation of Insurance Sector: Report by Standing Committee on Finance
- Insurance Schemes backed by the Government
- Micro insurance
- Challenges and Possibilities in the Insurance Sector

The insurance industry is a key driver in the Indian economy, serving the dual purpose of financial security and economic growth. It serves as a crucial risk management mechanism that protects individuals and enterprises from unexpected losses. Through the provision of a security net, insurance helps promote stability and bolsters entrepreneurship, allowing enterprises to flourish even under adverse circumstances.

WHAT IS INSURANCE

Insurance is a **contract, represented by a policy**, in which a policyholder receives **financial protection or reimbursement against losses** from an insurance company. The company pools clients' risks to make payments more affordable for the insured.

Depending on the type of risks covered, insurance can be of different types.

There are two main types of insurance, namely:

- **Life insurance**: Life insurance is a type of insurance coverage that pays out a certain amount of money to the insured or their designated beneficiaries on occurrence of a certain event such as death of the individual who is insured.
- **General (nonlife) insurance**: General insurance is a type of insurance policy that **provides protection** against losses and damages **not** covered by life insurance, **including** crops, automobile and other types of insurance.

Apart from Life insurance, most common forms of insurance are related to health, homes and automobiles.

The three components of any insurance type are – the premium, the policy limit, and the deductible.

Insurance Intermediaries

- Insurance intermediaries serve as a **bridge** between consumers (seeking to buy insurance policies) and insurance companies (seeking to sell those policies).
- An Insurance Intermediary means **individual agents, corporate agents** including banks and brokers – they intermediate between the customer and the insurance company. Insurance Intermediary also includes **Surveyors** and **Third-Party Administrators** but these intermediaries are not involved in the procurement of business.
- Surveyors assess losses on behalf of the insurance companies. Third -Party Administrators provide services related to health insurance for insurance companies.
- Insurance brokers are licensed by the IRDA and governed by the Insurance Regulatory and Development Authority (Insurance Brokers) Regulations, 2002.
- **Individual insurance agents** and **corporate agents** are also licensed by the IRDA and governed by the Insurance Regulatory and Development Authority (licensing of Individual Insurance Agents) Regulations, 2000 and the Insurance Regulatory and Development Authority (Licensing of Corporate Agents) Regulations, 2002, respectively.
- These Regulations lay down the Code of Conduct for the respective intermediaries.

INSURANCE SECTOR IN INDIA

History and Background of Insurance Sector

In Pre-Independence Period

Evolution of the Insurance Industry in India

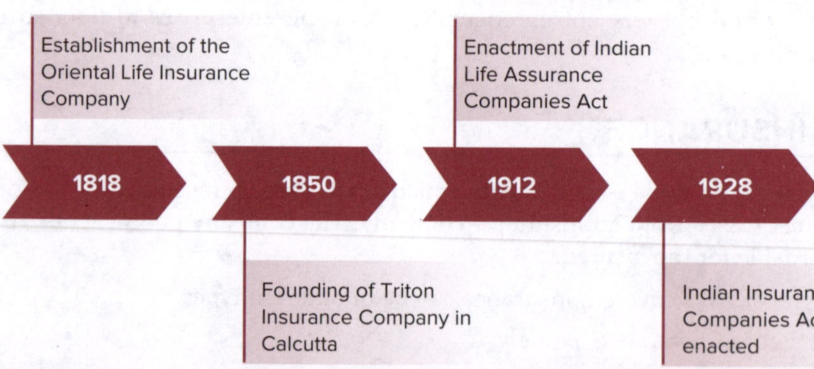

Year	Event
1818	Life Insurance business started in India with the establishment of **the Oriental Life Insurance Company.**
1850	General Insurance in India has its roots in the establishment of **Triton Insurance Company in Calcutta.**

1912	**Indian Life Assurance Companies Act** was enacted to regulate the insurance sector.
1928	The **Indian Insurance Companies Act** was enacted to enable the Government to collect important statistical information about both life and non-life businesses.

In Post-Independence Period

- To check unfair trade practices, **Life Insurance was nationalised in 1956, and Life Insurance Company (LIC) was founded** by merging 245 insurance companies and provident societies.
- LIC was established with **two basic objectives:**
  - To encourage people for life insurance in order to have greater security.
  - To mobilise savings of the people in the form of premiums for insurance.
- Nationalisation of General Insurance was, however, done from 1 January, 1973 by passing **General Insurance Business (Nationalisation) Act, 1972.**
- Through this Act, the Government nationalised 107 private sector companies (55 Indian Insurance Companies and 52 Foreign Insurance Companies).
- General Insurance Corporation (GIC) was incorporated under the Companies Act. However, in 2000, **GIC became the reassurance company** and is now known as **'GIC Re'**.
- After the operations of merging and consolidating, GIC was reorganised with four subsidiary companies:
  - National Insurance Company Limited
  - New India Assurance Company Limited
  - Oriental Insurance Company Limited
  - United India Company Limited

BONUS KNOWLEDGE

IMPORTANT CONCEPTS

- **Insurance versus Assurance:**
  - Insurance guarantees financial coverage against **short- term uncertain event**, an event which might not necessarily happen.
  - Whereas, Assurance guarantees financial coverage against loss or damage caused due to **an event that is sure to happen**.
  - Under insurance, claim payment is made only after the happening of an anticipated event. If the event does not happen, then no amount is paid as claim.
  - Whereas, in Assurance, claim payment is made either **at the happening of any uncertain event or at the time of the maturity of such policy benefits**.
- **Insurance Density** – It is calculated as the ratio of premium to total population (Total Insurance Premium/Total population).
- **Insurance Penetration** – It is measured as the Total Insurance Premium as a percentage of GDP.
- **Bank assurance** – It is a partnership between a bank and an insurance company, whereby the insurance company is allowed to sell its products to the bank's clients.
- **Micro-insurance** – It is specifically designed for the protection of low-income people, with affordable insurance products to help them cope with and recover from financial losses as this section of society is more prone to many risks which ultimately leads to incapacity to face such uncertain situations.

Importance of Insurance Sector in Economy

Some important aspects of Insurance sector are as follows:

Financial Security and Protection

Insurance is a monetary protection for the individual and family.

Medical insurance, especially life insurance and property insurance, reduces the financial impact of health crises by reducing the out of pocket expenditure of families and individuals. By managing the risks, insurance not only saves livelihoods but enables individuals to concentrate on productivity and self-improvement.

Contribution to Economic Growth

The insurance industry is a substantial contributor to the GDP of India. Premiums received by the insurance industry tend to be put into infrastructure investment, stock market, and other economic activities that promote growth and development. Also, Insurance sector generates employment in significant numbers.

Mobilisation of Savings

Insurance policies usually serve as savings tools. Endowment policies, pension plans, and unit-linked insurance plans (ULIPs) make people save money regularly, inculcating the habit of savings. These savings are invested in long-term investments, accruing benefits to the policyholders as well as the economy in general.

Promotion of Social Welfare

State-sponsored insurance programmes, for example, Pradhan Mantra Suraksha Bima Yojana and Ayushman Bharat, are designed to extend low-cost coverage to economically weaker segments of society. These programmes increase access to health care and financial security, lessening inequality and advancing social welfare.

Promotion of Innovation and Risk-Taking

Insurance allows companies and entrepreneurs to take informed risks by reducing possible losses. This encourages innovation, as people and businesses are more inclined to venture into new things and technologies without the fear of economic destruction.

INSURANCE REFORMS

In 1993, Government set up the **Malhotra Committee** to suggest reforms in the insurance sector. The recommendations were as follows:

- **Allowing private sector** in the insurance sector – Private sector was then allowed in the insurance sector. This led to the establishment of more than 50 insurance companies in India.
- Establishment of regulatory authority for insurance sector – thus **Insurance Regulatory Development Authority of India (IRDAI)** was constituted in 1999.
- Bringing down the Government's share in insurance companies to 50 per cent.
- Estranging GIC from its four subsidiaries – GIC has **withdrawn its holding** from four subsidiary companies and they are now fully owned by the Government of India.

- Decentralisation of LIC and to be converted into a company which is to be registered under the Companies Act.
- **Entry of foreign investment** but only through collaboration with Indian companies – thus, FDI in the insurance sector is increased to 74 per cent (earlier 49 per cent) and it is 100 per cent for insurance intermediaries under automatic route.

PRESENT STATUS OF INSURANCE SECTOR

- As per the Annual Report of **IRDAI 2023–24**, the insurance sector in India comprises a total of **59 insurers,** 1 re-insurer, 2 specialised insurers, and 12 Foreign Reinsurance Branches (FRB) (*as on March 31, 2024*). Among **59 insurers,** there are **26 life insurers, 25 general insurers, and 8 stand-alone health insurers.** 1 Life insurer and 2 stand-alone health insurers have been newly registered in 2023–24.

Distribution of Insurance Companies by Type

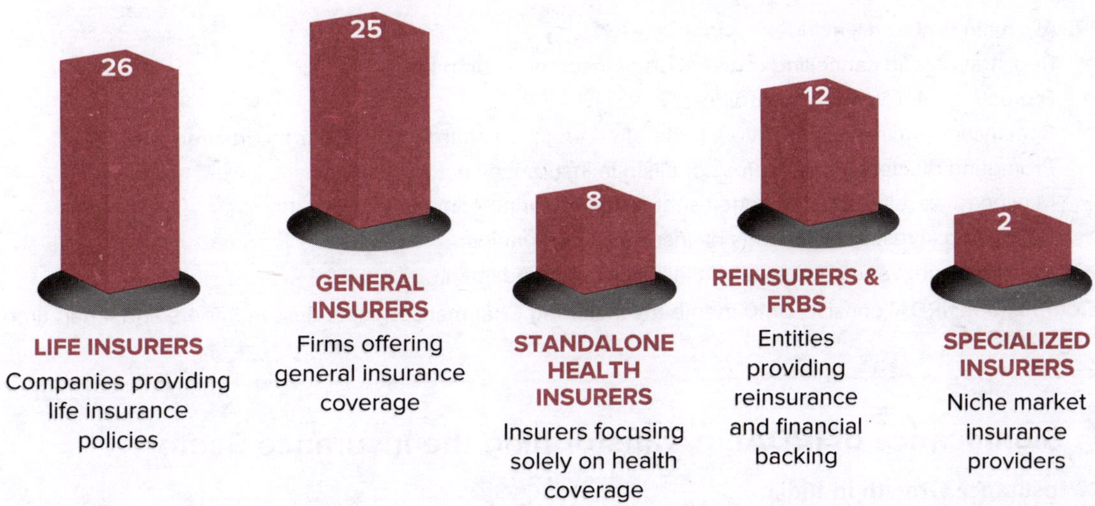

- Together with banking services, insurance services add about **7 per cent** to the country's GDP.
- **In 2023–24, India's insurance penetration was at 3.7 per cent as compared to 4 per cent in 2022–23.** The insurance penetration for Life Insurance industry marginally declined from 3 per cent in the previous year to 2.8 per cent during 2023–24. The penetration with respect to Non-Life Insurance Industry remained same at 1 per cent during 2023–24 as in 2022–23. (*Source: IRDAI Annual report 2023–24*)
- According to ***Swiss Re Sigma World Insurance Report*, India's insurance market is currently at number 10** in the world. India is going to be the fastest growing market of the G20 over the next five years.
- **Life insurance density** in India increased from US$ 9.1 in 2001–02 to US$ 70 in 2023–24. Non-life insurance density increased from US$ 2.4 to US$ 25 in the same time period. **Insurance density** in India increased from USD 92 in FY23 to USD 95 in FY24.

- According to the **Economic Survey 2024–25**, India's total insurance premium grew by 7.7 per cent in FY24, reaching ₹11.2 lakh crore. (*India's insurance market continued its upward trajectory, with total insurance premiums growing by 7.7 per cent in FY24, reaching ₹11.2 lakh crore.*)
- **Insurance penetration** in India declined slightly from 4 per cent in FY23 to 3.7 per cent in FY24. Life insurance penetration dropped from 3 per cent in FY23 to 2.8 per cent in FY24. Non-life insurance penetration remained stable at 1 per cent.

Overall, the insurance sector is very important for economic development, as it not only helps in strengthening the risk-taking ability, but also provides long-term funds for infrastructure development.

BONUS KNOWLEDGE

INSURANCE REGULATORY AND DEVELOPMENT AUTHORITY OF INDIA (IRDAI)

The IRDAI (headquartered in **Hyderabad**) was incorporated as a **statutory body** (through IRDAI Act, 1999) in **2000**, with a duty to **protect the interests of the policyholders** and ensure orderly growth of the insurance in our country.

IRDAI's main **functions** include:

- Registration and cancelling registration of insurance companies;
- Protecting interest of policy holders;
- Specifying required qualification, code of conduct, standards, etc. related to insurance sector;
- Promoting efficiency and professionalism in insurance sector;
- Making rules related to insurance sector and ensuring compliance with them;
- Regulating investment of funds by insurance companies;
- Consumer grievance redressal via Insurance Ombudsman.

Composition: IRDAI consists of 10 members, including Chairman, 5 whole time members and 4 part time members.

Significance of IRDAI in transforming the Insurance Sector

- **Insurance Growth in India**:
  1. **Insurance penetration** (percentage of insurance premium to GDP) at **3.7 per cent** in **2023–24** compared to 2.71 per cent in 2001–02.
  2. **Insurance Density** (ratio of insurance premium to population) at **$95 in 2023–24** compared to **$11.5** in 2001–02.

did you KNOW?

'Insurance for All' by 2047: IRDAI has committed to ensure every citizen has an appropriate life, health and property insurance cover by 2047.

Insurance Penetration and Density

Insurance penetration and density are two metrics often used to assess the level of development of the insurance sector in a country.

While **insurance penetration** is measured as the percentage of insurance premiums to GDP, **insurance density** is calculated as the ratio of premium to population (per capita premium).

Insurance Penetration – India vs World (percentage)

Regions	Life Insurance		Non-Life Insurance		Total (Life + Non-Life)	
	2022	2023	2022	2023	2022	2023
India	3	2.8	1	1	4	3.7
World	2.8	2.9	4	4.2	6.8	7

Insurance Density – India vs World (USD)

Regions	Life Insurance		Non-Life Insurance		Total (Life + Non-Life)	
	2022	2023	2022	2023	2022	2023
India	70	70	22	25	92	95
World	354	361	499	528	853	889

Domestic Systemically Important Insurers (D-SIIs)

Insurance Regulatory and Development Authority of India (IRDAI) identified the following insurance companies as **Domestic Systemically Important Insurers (D-SIIs):**

1. Life Insurance Corporation of India,
2. General Insurance Corporation of India, and
3. New India Assurance Company

About Domestic Systemically Important Insurers (D-SIIs)

- Domestic Systemically Important Insurers (D-SIIs) refer to insurers of such size, market importance, and domestic and global interconnectedness, whose distress or failure would cause a significant dislocation in the domestic financial system. Therefore, the continued functioning of D-SIIs is critical for the uninterrupted availability of insurance services to the national economy.
- D-SIIs are perceived as insurers that are **'too big or too important to fail' (TBTF)**. This perception and perceived expectation of government support may amplify risk-taking, reduce market discipline, create competitive distortions, and increase the possibility of distress in the future. These considerations require that **D-SIIs be subjected to additional regulatory measures** to deal with systemic risks and moral hazard issues.

Recent Reforms in Insurance Sector

1. FDI in Insurance Sector

- The FDI limit for the insurance sector has been **proposed to be raised from 74 to 100 per cent in Union Budget 2025–26.** This enhanced limit will be available for those companies which invest the entire premium in India.

2. Parliamentary Standing Committee Report on Insurance Sector

- The Standing Committee on Finance has submitted its report on '*Performance Review and Regulation of Insurance Sector*' in 2024 with major recommendations for Insurance sector.

3. Insurance (Amendment) Bill, 2021

- The Bill amends the Insurance Act, 1938. It seeks to increase the maximum FDI allowed in an Indian insurance company from 49 per cent to 74 per cent and removes restrictions on ownership and control.

- As per the Bill, majority of directors on the board and key management persons will have to be resident Indians.
- Further, the Bill specifies that at least half of the directors have to be independent directors.

4. General Insurance Business (Nationalisation) Amendment Act, 2021

- It amended the **General Insurance Business (Nationalisation) Act, 1972.**
- It **removed** the mandatory requirement of the Central Government holding not less than 51 per cent of the equity capital in a specified insurer.
- This Amendment seeks to accomplish the following: pushing for higher private participation in public sector insurance companies, raising the level of insurance penetration and thereby social protection; securing the interests of policyholders in a better manner; and contributing to faster growth of the Indian economy.
- **Power to Central Government** – To notify the terms and conditions of the service of employees of the specified insurers.

5. IRDAI (Trade Credit Insurance) Guidelines, 2021

- IRDAI released revised guidelines for General Insurance Companies (GICs). The recommendations are primarily **focused on credit insurance products for MSMEs with customised coverage.**
- The guidelines are applicable to all insurers transacting general insurance business registered under the **Insurance Act, 1938 excluding Export Credit Guarantee Corporation.**
  - They cover:
    - Sellers and suppliers of goods and services.
    - Factoring companies as defined in Factoring Regulation Act, 2011.
    - Banks and financial institutions.
- A trade credit insurance policy for banks, financial institutions and factoring companies should cover the loss on bills and invoices purchased or discounted owing to non-receipt of payment from a buyer due to commercial or political risks.
- **Benefits:** They facilitate GICs
  - to help businesses manage country risk;
  - open up access to new markets;
  - to manage non-payment risk associated with trade financing portfolios; and
  - to offer trade credit insurance with customised covers to improve businesses for SMEs and MSMEs, considering the evolving insurance risk needs of these sectors.
- A Committee of IRDAI on Micro-insurance (**Mirai Chatterjee Committee**) has suggested several micro-insurance models, viz. for coping up with the risks of death of the breadwinner of poor families, treatment of serious illnesses, reconstruction of destroyed houses, etc.

Agriculture Insurance Company of India Limited

- It is a public sector insurance company dedicated to the agricultural sector to serve the needs of farmers and to insure their crops for sustainable agriculture regime.
- Agriculture Insurance Company of India Limited (AICIL) began its business in 2003, and it looks after the National Agriculture Insurance Scheme of 1999.
- Since 2016, AICIL also began to supervise **Pradhan Mantri Fasal Bima Yojana** (PMFBY). Major parts of the shares of AICIL are owned by **NABARD (30 per cent)** and **GIC (35 per cent).**

Deposit Insurance and Credit Guarantee Corporation (DICGC)

- Deposit Insurance and Credit Guarantee Corporation (DICGC) was introduced in 1978 after the merger of Deposit Insurance Corporation and Credit Guarantee Corporation.
- Its **aim is to protect depositors** and to ensure financial stability so that the confidence on banking system can be enhanced.
- DICGC insures **all bank deposits,** such as saving, fixed, current, recurring deposit for up to the limit of **₹500,000 of each depositor in a bank (called Deposit Insurance).**

Performance Review and Regulation of Insurance Sector: Report by Standing Committee on Finance

The Standing Committee on Finance (Under the Chairmanship of Mr. Jayant Sinha) submitted its report on '**Performance Review and Regulation of Insurance Sector**' in 2024. Some of the observations and recommendations of this report are as follows:

- **Composite license for insurance business:** The Insurance Act, 1938 and the regulations of the IRDAI do not allow composite licensing to provide life, general, or health insurance under one entity. The Committee recommended introducing a provision for composite licensing of insurance companies which can reduce costs and compliances of insurers. It will also enable customers to access all-in-one insurance from a single insurance provider.
- **Health Insurance:** As per this report, a section of population in the country is one medical bill away from slipping into poverty. It has been observed that insurance products with affordable premiums and cashless settlement would encourage more people to opt for health insurance. The report recommended that the Ayushman Bharat scheme can be expanded by allowing people who are not covered by the scheme, to opt for it on a payment basis.
- **Missing Middle:** A significant portion of the population **lacks adequate health insurance coverage**, who have been identified as the Missing Middle.
- **Reduction in GST:** The report has recommended to reduce the current 18 per cent GST rate on health and term insurance products.
- **Micro Insurance:** The report has recommended that new microinsurance products need to be developed and provided at affordable rates. It recommended to reduce the minimum capital requirement of ₹100 crore to encourage small and niche insurance providers.

INSURANCE SCHEMES BACKED BY THE GOVERNMENT

Ayushman Bharat – Pradhan Mantri Jan Arogya Yojana

- It is a Government-run health insurance programme for households across the nation.
- Under the scheme, health insurance coverage of **up to ₹5 lakh per annum per household**, is provided to over 12 crores poor and vulnerable families for treatment in the secondary and tertiary hospitals, including in the private health facilities. The selection of a beneficiary under the scheme is based upon the deprivation and occupational criteria as per Socio Economic Caste Census (SECC).
- PM-JAY was earlier known as the National Health Protection Scheme (NHPS) before being rechristened. It subsumed the then existing Rashtriya Swasthya Bima Yojana (RSBY) which had

been launched in 2008. The coverage mentioned under PM-JAY, therefore, also includes families that were covered in RSBY but are not present in the SECC 2011 database. PM-JAY is fully funded by the Government and cost of implementation is shared **@ 60:40** between the Central and State Governments. For North-Eastern States and three Himalayan States (viz. Jammu and Kashmir, Himachal Pradesh and Uttarakhand), the ratio is 90:10.

Aam Aadmi Bima Yojana

- The Aam Aadmi Bima Yojana is a Social Security Scheme for **rural landless households** under which the head of the family or one earning member in the family of such households are covered. The premium of **₹200 per person per annum is shared equally** by the Central Government and the State Government. Thus, the insured person has to pay **no premium**.
- The member to be covered should be aged between **18 and 59 years**.
- The benefits under this scheme are as follows:
  - on **natural death** – ₹30,000
  - on **death due to accident or permanent total disability** due to accident (loss of two eyes or two limbs) – ₹75,000
  - on partial permanent disability due to accident (loss of one eye or one limb) – ₹37,500
- A fund called 'Aam Aadmi Bima Yojana Premium Fund' is established by the Central Government to pay the contribution by the Central Government.
- The scheme is implemented by the **Ministry of Labour & Employment.**

Pradhan Mantri Jeevan Jyoti Bima Yojana

- Pradhan Mantri Jeevan Jyoti Bima Yojana (PMJJBY) is a Government-backed **life insurance scheme** in India, launched in 2015.
- Before its launch, only 20 per cent of India's population had any kind of insurance. This scheme aimed to increase the number.
- PMJJBY is available to people between **18 and 50 years of age having bank accounts.** It has an **annual premium of ₹436** to be paid by the beneficiary. The scheme is for one year cover, and is renewable from year to year.
- The amount will be automatically debited from the account. In the case of death due to any cause, the payment to the nominee will be **₹2 lakh.**
- The scheme is implemented by the Department of Financial Services under the **Ministry of Finance.**

Pradhan Mantri Suraksha Bima Yojana

- It is a Government-backed **accident insurance scheme.**
- It was launched by GOI in 2015.
- It is available to people between **18 and 70 years of age** having bank accounts.
- It has an annual premium of **₹20** per member.
- In case of accidental death or full disability, the payment to the nominee is **₹2 lakh** and in case of partial disability, **₹1 lakh**.
- No maturity benefit or surrender benefit is available with this scheme.
- The scheme is for one year cover, and is renewable from year to year.
- This scheme is also implemented by the Department of Financial Services under the **Ministry of Finance.**

MICRO INSURANCE

Micro insurance is specifically intended for the protection of low-income people, with affordable insurance products to help them cope with and recover from financial losses. The need of insurance for underprivileged section cannot be avoided as this section of society is more prone to many risks which ultimately leads to incapacity to face such uncertain situations. Hence, the role that micro insurance plays thus becomes inevitable.

It is one of the tools associated with the process of financial inclusion. Microinsurance falls under the broader category called 'inclusive insurance'

- Various efforts have been made in the past to address the distribution challenge in micro insurance. The concept of '**micro insurance agent**' introduced in 2005 was aimed at attracting more intermediaries to this space and leverage upon the connect enjoyed by grassroots organisations like cooperatives and SHGs with a large section of the low-income segment.
- **IRDAI (Micro Insurance) Regulations, 2015** define the eligibility criteria, product features, distribution channels, and reporting requirements for microinsurance.
- As per the Regulations, **the sum assured under an Insurance product offering Life or pension or Health benefits shall not exceed ₹2,00,000**.

The major challenges in micro insurance distribution are:

- Small ticket size coupled with high transaction and service delivery costs.
- Absence of a business model that can attract good intermediaries.
- Capacity building of intermediaries.
- Lack of basic awareness and knowledge on how insurance works.

Challenges and Possibilities in the Insurance Sector

Challenges	Possibilities
• Low insurance penetration and insurance density. • Recent rise in insurance frauds which are mainly fraudulent claims, misrepresentations by committing identity theft, etc. • Poor credibility in the sector. • Complicated process of claims in India which often result in customer dissatisfaction and lack of trust in the insurance industry. • Lack of innovative products especially in non-life insurance. • Dominance of public sector. • Huge rural-urban and rich-poor divide. Rural under-penetration and lack of awareness. • Capital starved insurance companies. • Evolving risks such as climate change, geopolitical uncertainty, and increasing life expectancy.	• India's insurance sector is projected to grow at 11.1% over the next five years (2024–28), making it the fastest-growing among G20 nations. • Exploring ideas like micro-insurance, bancassurance, etc. for greater rich. • Taking help of banking correspondents, small finance banks, payments banks, etc. • Pro-active role of IRDAI – not only limited to supervision. • Simple and transparent 'Terms and Conditions'. • Checking fraudulent practices – to improve credibility in the sector. • Technological upgradation and launch of new insurance products.

SUMMARY

- **Life Insurance** – Provides a payout upon the death of the insured or after a specified policy term.
- **General (Non-Life) Insurance** – Covers risks such as health, property, automobiles, crops, and more.
- **Insurance Intermediaries** – Serve as agents between consumers and insurance companies; include individual agents, corporate agents, brokers, surveyors (for loss assessment), and third-party administrators (especially in health insurance).
- **Insurance Density** – The per capita ratio of premium, reflecting the extent of insurance usage.
- **Insurance Penetration** – The percentage of GDP that the total insurance premiums represent.
- **Pre-Independence** – Life insurance began in 1818 with the Oriental Life Insurance Company.
- **Nationalisation of life insurance** – in 1956 – led to the formation of LIC.
- **General insurance** – was nationalised in 1972 – later reorganised into several entities (GIC and its subsidiaries).
- **Establishment of the Insurance Regulatory and Development Authority of India (IRDAI)** – in 2000.
- **Micro insurance** – Designed for low-income groups – offers affordable protection to help them recover from financial losses – supports financial inclusion but also faces challenges such as high transaction costs and lower awareness.

UPSC CSE PREVIOUS YEARS' PRELIMINARY EXAMINATION QUESTIONS

☞ NO QUESTIONS ASKED
2024, 2023, 2022, 2021, 2020, 2019, 2018, 2017, 2016, 2015, 2014, 2013

UPSC CSE PREVIOUS YEARS' MAIN EXAMINATION QUESTIONS

☞ NO QUESTIONS ASKED
2024, 2023, 2022, 2021, 2020, 2019, 2018, 2017, 2016, 2015, 2014, 2013

CHAPTER

24

INFRASTRUCTURE

CHAPTER OUTLINE

- Contribution of Infrastructure to Economic Development
- Infrastructural Development as a *Sine Qua Non* of Economic Development
- Funding of Infrastructure and Various Models
- Present Challenges in Infrastructure Sector
- Recent Government Interventions
- PM Gati Shakti Initiative
- National Infrastructure Pipeline
- National Monetisation Pipeline
- National Investment and Infrastructure Fund
- National Logistics Policy
- Sector-wise Performance and Government Interventions
- Energy Sector
- Performances of Major Sub-Sectors under Energy
- Coal
- Crude Oil
- Natural Gas
- Transport Sector
- Road Transport
- Railway Transport
- Civil Aviation
- Water Transport
- Pipelines
- Telecom Sector
- Smart City Mission

Infrastructure refers to basic physical systems of a region or nation which facilitate socio-economic development and promote the production activities in the economy.

Prominent features of infrastructure include:

- Physical infrastructure services have an element of **public good** in them.
- Infrastructure does possess **externalities**; that is, the benefit arrived out of the infrastructure services exceeds the cost involved in its generation.
- **Public sector domination** can be found in the infrastructural development sector. However, Public–Private Partnership (PPP) projects are being promoted with the initiatives of the government.

> **did you KNOW?** As per the **World Economic Forum**, worldwide investment in infrastructure is expected to be US$ 79 trillion by 2040.

Classification of Infrastructure

Economic Infrastructure	Social Infrastructure
It refers to all the facilities like **power, transport and communication** which act as a support system to the economic growth process.	It refers to the central components of societal change like **schools, colleges, hospitals, parks,** etc., to uplift the Human Development Index of the country. It mainly focuses on human resource development.
It is also known as *hard infrastructure.*	It is also called *soft infrastructure.*
It requires heavy capital investment.	Capital investment requirement is comparatively less.
Their Complementary Nature: Sources of energy, better means of transport and communication, which come under economic infrastructure, are quite necessary for economic growth. However, this economic growth would be of no use if the population of the country is illiterate and unhealthy. Thus, a comprehensive focus on both of them is the key to a country's all-round economic development.	

Critical Infrastructure: Critical infrastructure encompasses the essential systems, facilities, and assets crucial for the operation of society and the economy. These infrastructures are indispensable due to the potential impact on public safety, security, health, and economic stability if they are disrupted. They comprise interconnected and interdependent physical as well as virtual components.

Critical infrastructures include energy (power plants, grids), transportation (airports, highways), water supply (treatment plants, reservoirs), communication (internet, telecom), financial services (banks, stock exchanges), emergency services (hospitals, police), government facilities, food/agriculture, cybersecurity, and manufacturing. Disruption to these systems can impact public safety, health, and economic stability.

Contribution of Infrastructure to Economic Development

The presence of infrastructure leads to:

1. Enhancement of productivity in all the three sectors – Agriculture, Industry and Services.
2. Development of backward regions and removal of regional imbalances.
3. Social transformation by enhancing opportunities for marginalised sections.
4. Employment generation through increased investment and capital formation.
5. Providing urban amenities in rural areas.
6. Faster and inclusive development.
7. National security like work done by Border Road Organisation in border areas.

Infrastructural Development as a *Sine Qua Non* of Economic Development

Development of infrastructure is certainly a *sine qua non* of economic development. For example, the major elements of economic development including establishment and development of various industries are directly dependent upon the infrastructural development of the country. Such infrastructural development includes development of power and electricity, transport and communication, better technologies related to R&D and space etc. Furthermore, the development of emerging service sector of India is directly linked with efficiency of huge population of this country. Thus, development of soft infrastructure which includes better financial system, education system, health care system, good governance, law enforcement and emergency services is of foremost importance.

Thus, if adequate attention is not given to the development of infrastructure, it will act as a hindrance to the economic development of the nation.

FUNDING OF INFRASTRUCTURE AND VARIOUS MODELS

Funding of infrastructure is done through heavy investments. The various models of investment are:

- **Public Investment Model**: In such a model, the government invests from its resources.
- **Private Investment Model**: Investment coming through private companies and institutions come under private investment; it includes both domestic and foreign investment.
- **Public–Private Partnership (PPP) Model**: This model aims at implementing the government programmes in partnership with the private sector. Through this model the private sector gets the chance to design and operate on the public sector programme and projects of the country.

  There are various variants of PPP model.

In recent years, the government has provided an increased impetus for infrastructure development and investment through the enhancement of capital expenditure. The capex outlay has been expanded to ₹11.21 lakh crore in FY 2025–26.

The Central Government has radically increased Capital Expenditure in the last five years.

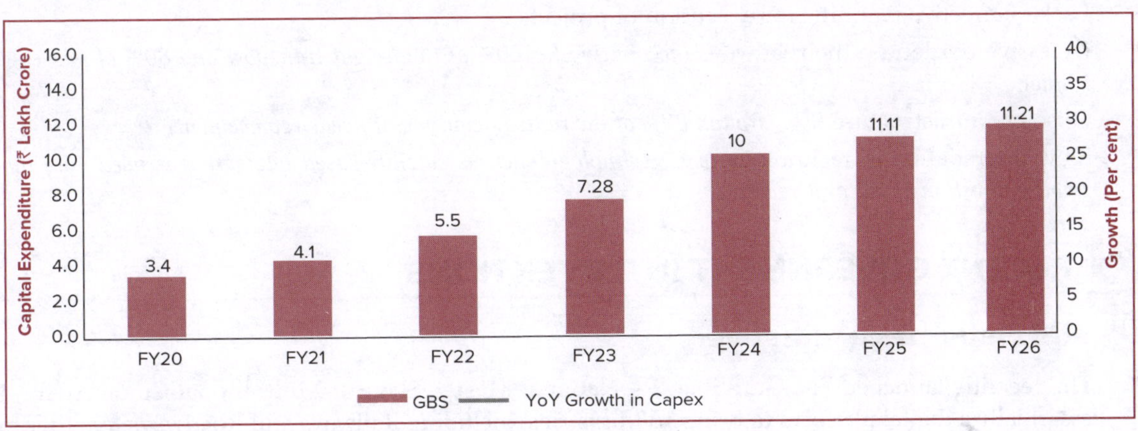

Source: Economic Survey 2024–25 and Interim Union Budget 2025–25

BONUS KNOWLEDGE

IS THERE A NEED FOR PRIVATISATION AND COMMERCIALISATION OF INFRASTRUCTURE?

Yes, there is a need for privatisation and commercialisation of infrastructure in India. Reasons being:

- **Huge Investment Needs** – it is difficult for government to meet all the investment needs on its own, especially in a developing country like India.
- **Managerial Issues in Public Sector** – public sector lacks efficiency in terms of HR functioning which results in delay in project completion and even cost escalation of infrastructure projects many times.
- **Dynamic Changes in the Technological Environment** – It is one of the major challenges faced by the government as technological development is mandated for the economic growth and development of the country. At present, most of the giant tech organisations are controlled and owned by private entities and they work hand in hand with government for the development of the country.
- **Globalisation** – availability of funds through a click of a button is a key factor in attracting foreign investment.
- **New dynamics in world capital market** – as a result of which, the **private sector has access** to the kind of resources needed for infrastructure.

PRESENT CHALLENGES IN INFRASTRUCTURE SECTOR

- Poor functioning of the PPP investment models (*especially in the power and telecom projects*) in terms of Time overrun and Cost overrun. **Time overrun** in projects refers to delays beyond the planned completion date, often caused by poor planning, scope changes, resource shortages, or external factors. This can lead to missed deadlines, delayed benefits, and increased costs. **Cost overrun** refers to project expenses exceeding the budget due to inaccurate estimates, scope changes, or unforeseen risks. Both overruns negatively impact stakeholder satisfaction, project finances, resource allocation, and organisational reputation.
- Land and forest clearance issues in terms of delays, etc.
- Lack of funds in the balance sheet of the private infrastructure companies.
- Lack of effective planning for execution of projects.
- Excessive burden on the roadways (*accounting for 60% of the freight transport and 80% of passenger traffic*).
- Obsolete infrastructure (*e.g., around 80% of the railway equipment needs replacement*).
- Slow upgradation of technology (*e.g., technology such as satellite-based navigation is used only by a small proportion of motor drivers*).

RECENT GOVERNMENT INTERVENTIONS

PM Gati-Shakti Initiative

- The recently launched **PM Gati-Shakti – National Master Plan for Multi-modal Connectivity**, is essentially a digital platform to bring 16 Ministries, including Railways and Roadways together for integrated planning and coordinated implementation of infrastructure connectivity projects.

- The multi-modal connectivity will provide integrated and seamless connectivity for the movement of people, goods and services from one mode of transport to another.
- It will facilitate the last mile connectivity of infrastructure and will also reduce the travel time for people.

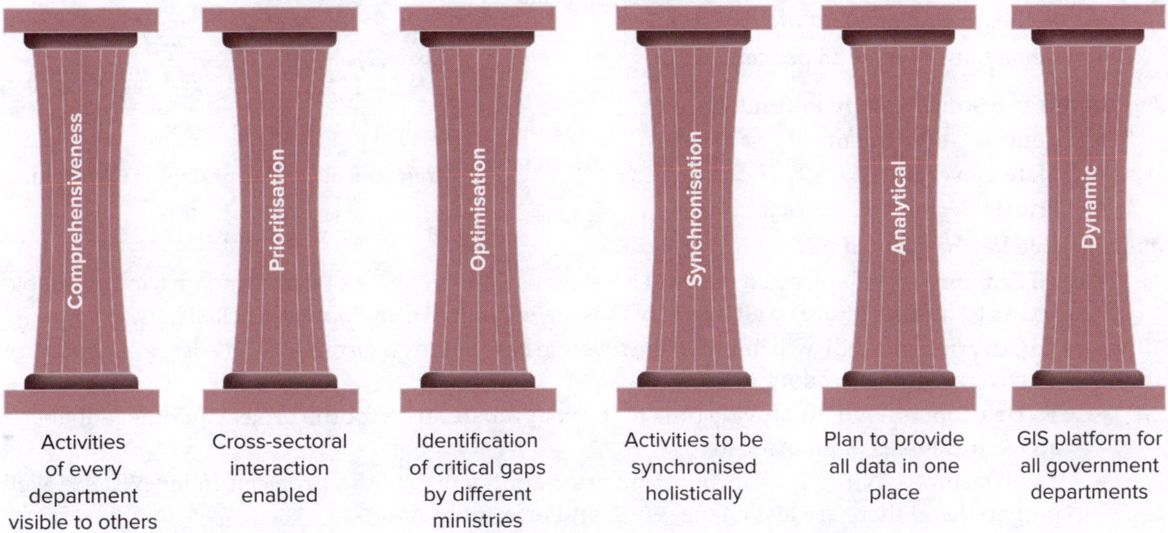

Six Pillars of PM Gati Shakti

- It will incorporate the infrastructure schemes of various Ministries and State Governments like Bharatmala, Sagarmala, inland waterways, dry/land ports, UDAN etc.
- Economic Zones like textile clusters, pharmaceutical clusters, defence corridors, electronic parks, industrial corridors, fishing clusters, agri zones will be covered to improve the connectivity and make Indian businesses more competitive.
- It will also leverage the technology extensively, including spatial planning tools with ISRO (Indian Space Research Organisation) imagery developed by **BiSAG-N (Bhaskaracharya National Institute for Space Applications and Geoinformatics)**.

National Infrastructure Pipeline (NIP)

- National Infrastructure Pipeline (NIP) has been declared in **2019** by the Government of India (GoI).
- NIP is a **group of infrastructure projects**, which are to be executed over 5 years, in order to achieve GDP of US$ 5 trillion.
- **Both economic and social infrastructure** projects are targeted under NIP and it will also try to attract the domestic and foreign investment in infrastructure.

- This projected capital expenditure is to be allocated in the following manner:
    - Energy sector – 24 per cent of NIP
    - Roads – 19 per cent of NIP
    - Urban sector – 16 per cent of NIP
    - Railways – 13 per cent of NIP
    - Remaining others – 28 per cent of NIP

  Total = 100%

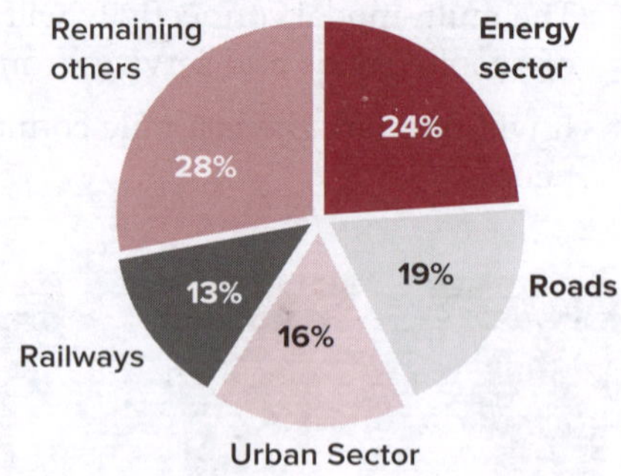

Projected allocation of Capital Expenditure

- In this investment, **share in funding to be**:
    - **Central Government** – *39 per cent*
    - **State Government** – *40 per cent*
    - **Private Sector** – *21 per cent*
- **Possible key benefits of NIP:**
    - **To Economy** – Well-planned NIP will create jobs, improve ease of living and provide equitable access to infrastructure to all, thereby making economic growth more inclusive.
    - **To Government** – NIP will improve the revenue base of the government and ensure expenditure by government in productive areas.
    - **To Developers** – NIP to provide time for better preparedness for the project bidding, enhanced access to sources of finance, etc.
    - **To Investors** – NIP will help boost investor confidence as the projects under NIP are well prepared and there are less chances of Non-Performing Assets.

Present Status of NIP

- NIP now consists of over 9,000 projects across 54 sub-sectors and covers economic and social infrastructure projects. As per India Investment Grid data, NIP currently has 9666 projects, with a total investment of more than ₹111 lakh crore under different stages of implementation.
- NIP is hosted by the **Invest India Grid (IIG)** platform and provides opportunities for States/UTs and Ministries to collate all major infrastructure projects at a single location.
- **Project Monitoring Group (PMG)** is an institutional mechanism put in place by the government for the resolution of issues related to large-scale projects and also involved in the fast-tracking of approvals/clearances for projects with an anticipated investment of ₹500 crore and above.

Last Minute SNIPPETS

As of April 2024, the transportation sector contributed 58% out of the total capital outlay under NIP, followed by the energy sector at 24%, and the water and sanitation sector at 12% and the rest 5% by other sectors such as social infrastructure and communication.

National Monetisation Pipeline (NMP)

- The National Monetisation Pipeline (NMP) has been launched by the Government of India. Over a four-year period, (2022–25), the NMP anticipates a total monetisation potential of ₹6 lakh crore through the Central Government's core assets. It is based on the principle of '**asset creation through monetisation**'.
- The framework for core asset monetisation has three key imperatives:
    i. Monetisation of 'Rights' not 'Ownership'.

ii. Brownfield de-risked assets.
iii. Structured partnership under defined contractual framework with strict performance standards.

- It **intends to increase the value of brownfield assets** by involving:
  - The private sector, transferring revenue rights rather than ownership of the projects to them and using the funds to build infrastructure across the country.
- Roads, railways and power sector assets will comprise over 66 per cent of the total estimated value of the assets to be monetised, with the remaining upcoming sectors including telecom, mining, aviation, ports, natural gas and petroleum product pipelines, warehouses and stadiums.
- **Significance:**
  - Resource mobilisation
  - Fiscal prudence
  - Mobilising private capital
  - Resource efficiency, i.e., utilising underutilised/unutilised public assets
  - Investment avenues
  - Promoting public-private partnership

Last Minute SNIPPETS

As per the Economic Survey 2024–25, during the period of FY22 to FY24, transactions of ₹3.86 lakh crore (against the target of ₹4.30 lakh crore) were completed in terms of accruals or private investments. For FY25, the aggregate monetisation target is set at ₹1.91 lakh crore.

- **Challenges:**
  - Lack of identifiable revenue streams in various infrastructure assets
  - Difficulty in attracting investors
  - Lack of independent sectoral regulators
  - Structural problems, such as legal uncertainty and the absence of a deep bond market
  - The distribution of government assets to private investors is frequently influenced by political factors, which can lead to corruption
  - Low level of capacity utilisation in gas and petroleum pipeline networks

National Investment and Infrastructure Fund (NIIF)

- National Investment and Infrastructure Fund (NIIF) was created in **2015**, to attract investment from both domestic and international sources.
- It is **India's first-ever sovereign wealth fund** with initial corpus of ₹40,000 crore.
- NIIF is an investor-owned fund manager, anchored by the GoI in collaboration with global and domestic institutional investors, and is used as an alternative source of fund **for long-term capital investment** in infrastructure development projects.
- NIIF is registered with SEBI as an Alternative Investment Fund (AIF) and has been set up as a trust under the *Indian Trust Act*. It is **not** an organ of NITI Aayog.
- Headquarters of NIIF are in **Mumbai**.
- The **objective of NIIF** is to enhance the impact on economic growth **through infrastructure development** in commercially viable projects (both greenfield and brownfield) and also including the stalled projects.
- The **Indian government has a 49 per cent stake in NIIF**, with the remaining 51 per cent being held by private sector.

- NIIF has developed into an internationally credible and commercially viable investment platform which is backed by several highly respected global and domestic investors who have invested alongside the Government of India in NIIF Funds.
- Presently, NIIF manages over US$ 4 billion of capital commitments across **three types of funds,** these funds are registered as Alternative Investment Fund (AIF) with SEBI, **namely**:
  1. **Master Fund** – Deals with investment in operating assets in core infrastructure sectors such as roads, ports, airports, power, etc.
  2. **Fund of Funds** – Deals with investment through third-party fund managers.
  3. **Strategic Opportunities Fund** – Registered as an Alternative Investment Fund II under SEBI in India. The objective is to invest largely in equity and equity-linked instruments.
- In March 2020, Asian Development Bank **(ADB)** committed to invest **US$ 100 million** equivalent into the Fund of Funds component of NIIF. In February 2021, New Development Bank committed US$ 100 million to NIIF Fund of Funds.
- Earlier in 2018, Asian Infrastructure Investment Bank **(AIIB)** had also committed **US$ 200 million** for NIIF.
- NIIF's first bilateral fund – '**India Japan Fund**' with contribution from Government of India has been proposed through an MoU between National Investment and Infrastructure Fund Limited (NIIFL) and Japan Bank for International Development (JBIC) in 2022.

BONUS KNOWLEDGE

SOVEREIGN WEALTH FUND (SWF)

It is an investment fund **owned by a government**, typically using funds derived **from a country's surplus reserves**. These reserves can originate from various sources such as state-owned natural resource revenues, trade surpluses, budget surpluses, foreign currency operations, privatisations, or governmental transfer payments.

Each sovereign wealth fund may **have specific objectives and purposes**. Some serve as venture capital for private sector investments, aiming to stimulate economic growth and diversification.

The top five largest SWFs, by assets as of February 2025, include:

1. Norway Government Pension Fund Global
2. China Investment Corporation
3. SAFE Investment Company
4. Abu Dhabi Investment Authority
5. Kuwait Investment Authority

National Logistics Policy (NLP)

- NLP was launched in 2022, by the Government of India to reduce the cost of logistics.
- Logistics costs in India have been in the range of 14–18 per cent of GDP against the global benchmark of 8 per cent. It aims to reduce the logistics cost to a single digit as soon as possible.
- Some components to increase the efficiency in logistics:
  (a) Streamlining processes,
  (b) Regulatory framework,
  (c) Skill development, and
  (d) Mainstreaming logistics

- The vision of the NLP is 'to develop a technologically enabled, integrated, cost-efficient, resilient, sustainable and trusted logistics ecosystem in the country for accelerated and inclusive growth.'
- Targets of NLP:
  - (a) Reducing the cost of logistics in India to be comparable to global benchmarks by 2030.
  - (b) Improving the Logistics Performance Index ranking – endeavour is to be among the top 25 countries by 2030.
  - (c) Creating a data-driven decision support mechanism for an efficient logistics ecosystem.
- To achieve the declared targets, a **Comprehensive Logistics Action Plan (CLAP)** as part of the NLP was launched covering eight action areas including:
  - (i) Integrated Digital Logistics Systems;
  - (ii) Standardisation of Physical Assets and Benchmarking of Service Quality Standards;
  - (iii) Logistics Human Resource Development and Capacity Building;
  - (iv) State engagement;
  - (v) EXIM Logistics;
  - (vi) Services Improvement Framework;
  - (vii) Sectoral Plans for Efficient Logistics (SPEL); and
  - (viii) Facilitation of Development of Logistics Parks.
- The four important features for the implementation of NLP are as follows:
  - **Integration of Digital System (IDS):** Integration of different systems of seven departments (like road transport, railways, aviation, commerce ministries and foreign trade).
  - **Unified Logistics Interface Platform (ULIP):** For shorter and smoother cargo movement and enabling the exchange of information confidentially on a real-time basis.
  - **Ease of Logistics (ELOG):** To enable and ensure the ease of logistics business through transparency and accessibility.
  - **System Improvement Group (SIG):** To monitor all logistics-related projects regularly.

Strengthening Multimodal and Integrated Logistics Ecosystem (SMILE)

- The Strengthening Multimodal and Integrated Logistics Ecosystem (SMILE) is a programmatic **policy-based loan (PBL)**, which comprises two subprogrammes, that aims to support government in undertaking wide-ranging reforms in the logistics sector in India to expand India's manufacturing sector and improve the supply chain facilities.
- There are four key pillars of this programme:
  - Strengthening institutional frameworks
  - Standardising warehousing
  - Improving trade logistics
  - Promoting smart, low-emission systems

BONUS KNOWLEDGE

LEADS REPORT 2024

It is the 5th edition of the annual LEADS exercise, and offers **insights into the enhancement of logistics performance** at the State and Union Territory (UT) levels. It underscores an improved overall stakeholder perception and the impact of various reforms implemented across States and UTs. This report signifies a positive trend in States' performance across key pillars: **Logistics Infrastructure, Logistics Services, and Operating and Regulatory Environment**, thereby empowering State and UT Governments with region-specific insights for informed decision-making and comprehensive growth strategies.

Highlights of Performance from LEADS 2024

Coastal Group:

- Achievers: Gujarat, Karnataka, Maharashtra, Odisha, Tamil Nadu
- Fast Movers: Andhra Pradesh, Goa
- Aspirers: Kerala, West Bengal

Landlocked Group:

- Achievers: Haryana, Telangana, Uttar Pradesh, Uttarakhand
- Fast Movers: Bihar, Himachal Pradesh, Madhya Pradesh, Punjab, Rajasthan
- Aspirers: Bihar, Chhattisgarh, Jharkhand

North-East Group:

- Achievers: Assam, Arunachal Pradesh
- Fast Movers: Meghalaya, Mizoram, Nagaland, Sikkim, Tripura
- Aspirers: Manipur

Union Territories:

- Achievers: Chandigarh, Delhi
- Fast Movers: Dadra and Nagar Haveli and Daman and Diu, Jammu and Kashmir, Lakshadweep, Puducherry
- Aspirers: Andaman and Nicobar Islands, Ladakh

GLOBAL INFRASTRUCTURE FACILITY

Launched by World Bank in 2014, (and is now a G20 initiative) the Global Infrastructure Facility (GIF) is a global, open platform that facilitates the preparation and structuring of complex infrastructure **PPPs** to enable mobilisation of private sector and institutional investor capital. The GIF platform coordinates and integrates the efforts of Multilateral Development Banks (MDBs), private sector investors and governments interested in infrastructure investment in *Emerging Markets and Developing Economies* **(EMDEs)**. The **core principles** of GIF are:

1. Providing public goods
2. Mobilising the private sector
3. Achieving value for money
4. Promoting sustainability and inclusiveness
5. Complementing individual partner efforts by supplementing existing resources

GIF supports governments in design, preparation, structuring, transaction implementation activities, etc. in bringing the well-structured and bankable infrastructure projects to the market.

In the case of India, three GIF-supported projects have been taken up till now:

1. Solar PPP Program for development of solar parks under the *Ministry of New and Renewable Energy.*
2. Rajasthan State Highways Development Project.
3. Viability Assessment for Developing Long-term Financing Mechanisms for National Highways in India.

GLOBAL INFRASTRUCTURE OUTLOOK

- Global Infrastructure Outlook (GIO) is a report which forecasts the infrastructure investment needs and gaps across **56 countries** (including India) and across **seven sectors** till the year **2040**.
- *The seven sectors dealt by GIO are – road, rail, airports, ports, telecom, energy and water.*
- GIO is developed by the organisation *Global Infrastructure Hub* along with *Oxford Economics*.
- It is a **G20 initiative**.
- It is a country-based report.
- As per the GIO report dealing with forecasts till 2040:
  - Current global infrastructure investment trend – $79 trillion.
  - Infrastructure investment needed – $94 trillion.
  - Thus, global **infrastructure investment gap** ($94 trillion – $79 trillion) = **$15 trillion**.
  - **Electricity and roads** are the two most important sectors – together they account for more than two-thirds of global investment needs.
  - The infrastructure investment gap, i.e., the extent to which estimated investment need is greater than investment expected as per current trends, is **10** per cent **in Asia**.
  - **China** accounts for **almost 30** per cent **of the global infrastructure** investment.
  - **India is the second-largest infrastructure market in Asia** after China.
  - It is estimated that for India (for the period 2016–2040):
    - Current infrastructure investment **trend = $3.9 trillion**
    - Infrastructure investment **needs = $4.4 trillion**
    - Thus, **infrastructure investment gap for India** = $0.5 trillion
  - The rate of investment in **ports** is extremely low in India.
  - The need for investment in *railways* and *telecom* is much higher than the current trends in India.
  - The need for infrastructure investment in *electricity* is much higher in India than the rest of Asia.

SECTOR-WISE PERFORMANCE AND GOVERNMENT INTERVENTIONS

Energy Sector

- It comes under **economic infrastructure**.
- Indian energy sector has observed a rapid development in recent times.
- As per World Energy Outlook 2024 of International Energy Agency (IEA), India has now become an importer of modern clean energy technologies by scaling up solar and wind power generation capacity. India is expected to meet the 2030 target of half (50%) of its electricity capacity coming from non-fossil fuel. India has targeted 20,750 circuit kilometres of Intra-state Green Energy Corridor electricity transmission lines completed or planned to be completed by 2026. Over the past five years, nearly 60 per cent of new generation capacity has been from solar PV. Demand for electricity for running household air-conditioners in India is estimated to expand nine times from

present by 2050. India has been ranked third largest primary energy consumer in the world after the United States and China.

- The sources of energy production in India are primarily coal, crude oil, renewable energy and natural gas (January 2025).

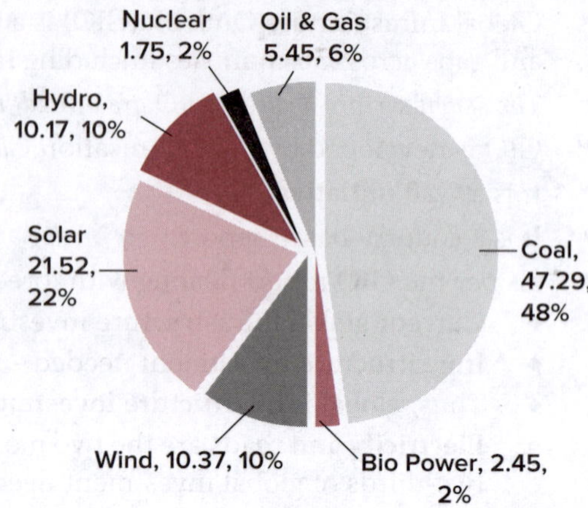

- The **Energy Strategy** or *Draft National Energy Policy (NEP) 2040* of the government aims to make India 'Energy Ready' by 2040. The objectives of the draft NEP are:
    - *Access to energy at affordable prices.*
    - *Improved security and independence.*
    - *Greater sustainability and economic growth.*
    - *Shift to less energy-intensive mode of transport.*
    - *To move towards renewable sources of energy.*
    - *Exploration of hydroelectric power (to meet peak demand).*
    - *Development and usage of energy-efficient technology.*
    - *Substitution of natural gas for oil products.*

Sources of Energy

Commercial Sources	Non-commercial Sources
• Coal, petroleum products, natural gas and electricity are major sources.	• Firewood, animal waste and agricultural waste are major sources.
• Largely used for industrial and commercial purposes.	• Mainly used for domestic and consumption purposes.
• They have a command price.	• These generally do not have a command price.
• There is both national and international market for such goods.	• There are local markets for such goods.

PERFORMANCES OF MAJOR SUB-SECTORS UNDER ENERGY

Coal

- India is the second-largest producer and consumer of coal after China.
- Coal accounts for around 55 per cent of the country's energy needs.
- Despite the push for renewables, as per the Draft National Energy Policy of NITI Aayog, the demand for coal is expected to remain in the range of 1.3–1.5 billion tonnes by 2030.

Last Minute SNIPPETS

The total coal production of India in the year 2023–24 was 997.826 Million Tonne (MT) in comparison to 893.191 MT in the year 2022–23 with a growth of about 11.71%.

- Under 'Atmanirbhar Bharat' initiative, domestic raw Coking Coal production is likely to reach 140 million tonnes by 2030.
- Consumers of coal are mainly – thermal power stations, steel plants, cement factories, railways, fertiliser factories and brick kilns.
- The coal sector **faces challenges such as**:
  - Inadequate mining technology
  - High cost of mining and exploration
  - Environmental degradation due to mining
  - Lower backward and forward linkages
  - Low grade coal
  - High sulphur content
  - Lack of coking coal, etc.
- **Government interventions in the recent past:**
  - **Coal India Limited (CIL)** was set up in 1975 with the aim to boost coal production. It is now one of the Maharatna PSUs owned by GoI. The company contributes around 82 per cent to the total coal production in India.
  - **The Coal Mines Act, 2015**, came into place to bring more transparency in the allocation of coal mines.
  - Opening up of coal mining for private sector may be the most ambitious coal sector reform. This may bring efficiency and competition in coal production, attract investments and best-in-class technology, and may help create more jobs in the coal sector.
  - **Coal-Based Ultra Mega Power Projects (UMPPs)** with a capacity of 4,000 MW or above have been launched by GoI in association with Central Electricity Authority (CEA) and Power Finance Corporation Ltd. The UMPPs are awarded to developers based on competitive bidding.

    Out of the total 15 UMPPs planned till now, **4 UMPPs** have been awarded and **2 are already functional** (Mundra UMPP, Gujarat, and Sasan UMPP, Madhya Pradesh).
  - **The Coal Mitra Web Portal** was launched in 2016, to bring flexibility in the utilisation of domestic coal by transferring it from high-cost areas to cost-efficient generating stations.
  - **Scheme for Harnessing and Allocating Koyala Transparently in India (SHAKTI)** – The scheme introduced in 2017 by the *Ministry of Coal* deals with auction and allocation of long-term coal linkages in a transparent manner for such power sector consumers.
  - India has committed in its Nationally Determined Contribution (NDC) to achieve an additional carbon sink of 2.5 billion to 3.0 billion tonnes through increased forest and tree cover by 2030.

BONUS KNOWLEDGE

CAPTIVE AND NON-CAPTIVE MINES

Captive Mines: Captive mines refer to mining operations that are **owned and operated by specific companies or entities**. The coal or minerals extracted from these mines are **intended exclusively for the use of the owning company** and cannot be sold or transferred to other entities. The concept of captive mining was particularly prevalent among industries like electricity generation, where companies would own and operate mines to secure a dedicated supply of raw materials for their operations.

Non-Captive Mines: Non-Captive mines, on the other hand, are mining operations where the extracted coal or minerals can be used for the **owner's consumption as well as sold** to other entities in the market. This means that the products from non-captive mines are not restricted to internal consumption but can be traded and sold externally based on market demand and supply dynamics.

Regulatory Framework: Under the Mines and Minerals (Development and Regulation) Act, 1957, the central government had the authority to reserve certain mines for specific end-uses, designating them as captive mines. This designation was aimed at ensuring a stable supply of critical raw materials for specific industries and sectors.

Amendment and Removal of Distinction: The Mines and Minerals (Development and Regulation) Amendment Bill, 2021, brought significant changes to this regulatory framework **by removing the distinction** between captive and non-captive mines. This amendment means that previously captive mines, are now allowed to sell their output in the open market, expanding their market reach beyond internal consumption. This change opens up opportunities for mining companies to optimise their operations and potentially increase revenue streams by tapping into broader market demand.

Crude Oil

- Crude oil production has seen a continuous decline since 2014–15. This decline has been found both in onshore and offshore production.
- **Reasons for such decline** include: *natural decline in ageing and mature fields with no major discoveries.*
- **India** is the world's **third-largest crude oil importer**, having a strategic storage capacity of 5.33 million tonnes (at Vishakhapatnam, Mangalore and Pudur) and 6 million tonnes (at Pudur and Chandikhole) is under construction.
- At the current rate of production, existing reserves will last for **only around two decades**.
- India is dependent on imports to meet around 88 per cent of its crude oil requirements; almost 50 per cent of the export earnings are used to pay oil import bills.
- **Government interventions in the recent past:**
  - **Private sector has been allowed** to participate in crude oil exploration and production.
  - Administered Pricing Mechanism **(APM)** has been dismantled.
  - Domestic companies have been allowed **to acquire international oil reserves**.
  - The **New Exploration and Licensing Policy (NELP), 1997** has been replaced by the **Hydrocarbon Exploration and Licensing Policy (HELP), 2016.** HELP has introduced a single licence for exploration and production of conventional as well as non-conventional hydrocarbon resources.
  - **Hydrocarbon Vision 2030 for Northeast** aims to double oil and gas production by 2030, hereby providing clean fuel, fast tracking of project completion and creating employment opportunities and promoting cooperation with neighbouring countries.
  - **Pratyaksh Hanstantrit Labh (PAHAL) was modified and re-introduced** in 2015. It was initially introduced in 2013. It aims at rationalising the subsidies to LPG customers in a systematic manner. PAHAL has entered the *Guinness Book of World Records,* being the largest direct benefit transfer scheme.

BONUS KNOWLEDGE

SUSTAINABLE ALTERNATIVE TOWARDS AFFORDABLE TRANSPORTATION (SATAT)

SATAT initiative, launched in 2018, envisages setting up of 5,000 Compressed Biogas (CBG) plants for the production of 15 Million Metric Tonne (MMT) per annum of CBG by 2023–24. As of October 2022, Oil and Gas Marketing Companies participating in SATAT have issued 3,694 Letters of Intent (LoI) to entrepreneurs for the procurement of CBG produced by them. Further, 38 CBG/biogas plants with installed capacity around 225 MT per annum have been commissioned by LoI holders.

LAKSHYA BHARAT PORTAL

The '**Lakshya Bharat Portal**' launched in 2021, **requires all oil and gas organisations** to upload details of various items procured by them including the future requirements.

The portal is planned to mature into a central information pool for sourcing of capital goods and MRO (Maintenance, Repair and Overhaul) of items of the oil and gas companies which in turn is expected to provide clear demand projections to enable the manufacturers to enhance their capacity and scope.

This portal, which is accessible to all stakeholders is an important step towards Atmanirbhar Bharat.

Natural Gas

- Major reserves of natural gas are found in Maharashtra (Mumbai), Gujarat, Tripura, Andhra Pradesh, Tamil Nadu and Rajasthan.
- The production of natural gas is dominated by PSUs, with its share increasing over time. Presently, share of government PSUs in natural gas production is more than 80 per cent.
- **Thus, to promote private sector participation**, the following measures have been taken by the government:
  - Simplified fiscal and contractual terms.
  - Bidding of exploration blocks under Category II and III sedimentary basins without any production or revenue sharing to government.
  - Early monetisation of discoveries by extending fiscal incentives.
  - Incentivising gas production including marketing and pricing freedom.
  - Induction of latest technology and capital.
  - More functional freedom to national oil companies for collaboration.
- **National Gas Grid** – Under it, government envisages to develop **33,764 km** natural gas pipelines across the country. Aim of National Gas Grid is to connect gas sources to major demand centres and ensure availability of gas to consumers in various sectors. **Petroleum and Natural Gas Regulatory Board (PNGRB)** has been recognised as the authority to grant authorisation to the entities for the development of City Gas Distribution (CGD) network.

Last Minute SNIPPETS

As of December 2024, the share of natural gas in energy basket of India is 7 per cent. The Government has set a target to raise the share of natural gas in energy mix to 15% by 2030. There has been large increase in natural gas production from 28.7 billion cubic meters (BCM) in 2020–21 to 36.43 BCM in 2023–24.

BONUS KNOWLEDGE

CITY GAS DISTRIBUTION NETWORK (CGD)

Petroleum and Natural Gas Regulatory Board (PNGRB) has authorised 232 geographical areas (GAs) for development of CGD network across the country covering more than 400 districts in 27 States/UTs, which covers around 71 per cent of India's population and 53 per cent of the area. As of July 2022, over 95 lakh PNG connections are there in the country whereas around 4,500 CNG stations are commissioned in India. Government of India envisages to commission 8,000 CNG stations in total in next two years.

Northeast Gas Grid: The 1,656 km long North East Gas Grid will connect eight North-Eastern States. This project is approved by Government to Indradhanush Gas Grid Limited (IGGL) with Viability Gap Funding (VGF)/Capital Grant at 60 per cent.

PETROLEUM AND NATURAL GAS REGULATORY BOARD

PNGRB is a statutory regulatory body of GoI set up in 2006, constituted under the Petroleum and Natural Gas Regulatory Board Act, 2006, under the Ministry of Petroleum and Natural Gas. PNGRB regulates the refining, processing, storage, transportation, distribution, marketing and sale of **petroleum, petroleum products and natural gas** (excluding production of crude oil and natural gas) so as to ensure uninterrupted and adequate supply of petroleum, petroleum products and natural gas in all parts of the country.

PETROLEUM PLANNING AND ANALYSIS CELL

Petroleum Planning and Analysis Cell (PPAC), attached to the Ministry of Petroleum and Natural Gas, was established in 2002. PPAC assists the government in the **administration of subsidy** on PDS Kerosene and domestic LPG and freight subsidy for far-flung areas, maintains information data bank and communication system to deal with emergencies and unforeseen situations, analyses the trends in the international oil market and domestic prices, and forecasts and evaluates the trends of import and export of petroleum.

The expenditure of PPAC is funded by **Oil Industry Development Board (OIDB)**. The cell is located in New Delhi.

TRANSPORT SECTOR

This sector has the following arms:

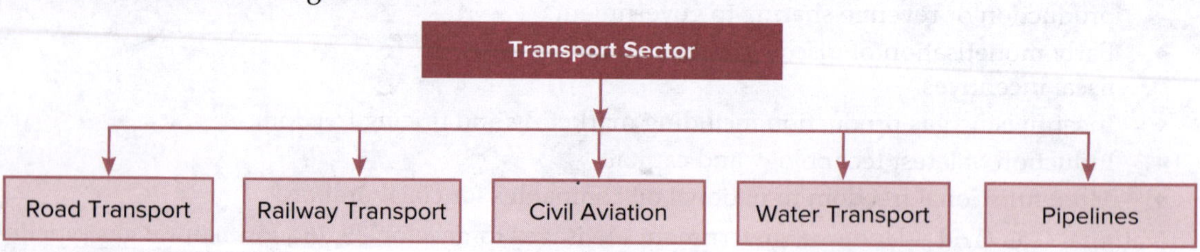

Road Transport

- Road Transport accounts for **87 per cent of the passenger traffic** and **60 per cent of the freight traffic** movement in the country.

- India has a road network of around 66.71 lakh km (second largest in the world after the United States) out of which National Highways span a total length of **1.46 lakh km**.
- In terms of **road density** [*i.e. length of road (in kilometre) per km^2 area – approximately 1.94 km/sq km*], India ranks higher than major countries like the United States, the United Kingdom and China.
- Type of roads prevailing in India are: ⟶

Type	Share in Total Road Network (approx. %)
Rural Roads	70
Urban Roads	9
Project Roads	6
Other PWD Roads	10
State Highways	3
National Highways	2
Total	**100**

- **National Highways** – managed by the *Ministry of Road Transport and Highways.* Expressways are part of National Highways.
- **State Highways** – financed and managed by State Governments through state Public Works Departments.
- **Maharashtra** has the largest length of both National Highways and State Highways among States/UTs, followed by Karnataka, Gujarat, Rajasthan and Andhra Pradesh.

Government Measures Undertaken to Improve Road Transport

- **National Highways Development Project (NHDP)** – Started in 1998, it is a project under National Highways Authority of India to upgrade, rehabilitate and widen major highways in India to a higher standard and enhance the coverage of national highways including Golden Quadrilateral. The government planned to end the NHDP in 2018 and subsume ongoing projects under a larger Bharatmala Pariyojana.
- **Bharatmala Pariyojana** – Launched in 2017–18, it focuses on enhanced effectiveness of already built infrastructure, multi-modal integration, bridging infrastructure gaps for seamless movement and integrating National and Economic Corridors. There are six key parts of the programme with target to develop 34,800 km (including 10,000 km residual NHDP stretches) of road:
  1. Economic Corridors (9,000 km)
  2. Inter-corridor and Feeder routes (6,000 km)
  3. National Corridor Efficiency Improvement (5,000 km)
  4. Border and International connectivity roads (2,000 km)
  5. Coastal and Port connectivity roads (2,000 km)
  6. Green-field Expressways (800 km).
- **Gram Sadak Yojana** – The primary objective of the PMGSY is to provide connectivity, by way of an all-weather road with necessary culverts and cross-drainage structures, which is operable throughout the year, to eligible unconnected habitations in rural areas. World Bank (2019) in an evaluation of the scheme, found that PMGSY roads had a positive impact on human capital formation in rural India.
- **Setu Bharatam** – Launched in 2016, the scheme aimed to make all national highways free of railway crossings by 2019. The scheme involved a plan for replacement of level crossings on national highways by railway over bridges (ROBs)/road under bridges (RUBs).
- **Chardham Mahamarg Vikas Pariyojna** – Launched in 2016, the project aims to develop 889 km of national highway (with minimum width of 10 m) at an approximate cost of ₹12,000 crore for easy

access to the four prominent Dhams, namely, Gangotri, Yamunotri, Kedarnath and Badrinath, situated in Uttarakhand.

- 'Special Accelerated Road Development Programme' for north-eastern region.
- **Logistics Efficiency Enhancement Programme (LEEP)** – With an aim to boost multimodal transport in India by setting up multimodal logistics parks.

BONUS KNOWLEDGE

MULTI MODAL LOGISTICS PARK

Multi Modal Logistics Parks (MMLPs) are being developed at strategic locations in the country to bring down the logistic costs and boost the national economy by reducing imports and increasing exports.

A Multi-Modal Logistics Park (MMLP) is a facility with **inter-modal freight-handling establishment, comprising warehouses, dedicated cold chain facilities, freight or container terminals and bulk cargo terminals.** It facilitates merchandise movement via road, rail, waterway and air.

The Ministry of Road Transport & Highways is the nodal ministry to develop **35 Multi Model Logistics Parks (MMLP)** under Bharatmala Pariyojana scheme as hub and spoke model across the country.

- **Parvatmala Scheme** – National Ropeways Development Programme – 'Parvatmala' was announced in the Union Budget for 2022–23 to improve connectivity in hilly areas.
  - The scheme is taken up on PPP (Public Private Partnership) mode. It is a preferred ecologically sustainable alternative in place of conventional roads in difficult hilly areas.
  - The scheme is being started in regions like Uttarakhand, Himachal Pradesh, Manipur, Jammu & Kashmir and the other North-Eastern states.

EXAM ESSENTIAL

MOTOR VEHICLES (AMENDMENT) ACT, 2019

This act amended the Motor Vehicles Act of 1988.

Key Features/Amendments:

- The Amended Act has **increased the amount of penalties** for various types of traffic-related offences. Penalty regarding motor vehicles is to be increased by 10 per cent every year. This may act as a deterrent against traffic violations.
- **New penalties have been introduced** such as for oversized vehicles, not providing way to emergency vehicles, offences by juveniles, etc.
- The Act increases the **minimum compensation for hit-and-run cases** as follows: (i) in case of death, from ₹25,000 to ₹2,00,000, and (ii) in case of grievous injury, from ₹12,500 to ₹50,000.
- The New Bill allows the central government to **order for recall of defected motor vehicles** which may harm the environment, or the driver, or other road users.
- **National Road Safety Board** to be created by the central government to advise the central and state governments on all aspects of road safety and traffic management.
- The Act provides for a scheme for **cashless treatment** of road accident victims **during golden hour**.
- The Act requires the central government to constitute a **Motor Vehicle Accident Fund**, to provide compulsory insurance cover to all road users in India.

Railway Transport

- Indian Railways is the **fourth-largest network** in the world under single management.
- Indian Railways achieved 1.47 billion tonnes freight loading till February 2025 (for FY 2024–25).
- As per the *Economic Survey* ***2024–25***, the capital expenditure on infrastructure in railways is projected to be ₹2.52 lakh crore in FY25.
- **Research Designs and Standards Organisation (RDSO)** is the R&D wing of Indian Railways.

Major Government Measures undertaken to improve Rail Infrastructure

- **Dedicated Freight Corridor (DFC)** – Funding for four DFCs was approved in 2018.
  - East–West DFC, 2,000 km long from Kolkata to Mumbai
  - North–South DFC, 2,173 km long from Delhi to Chennai
  - East Coast DFC, 1,100 km long from Kharagpur to Vijayawada
  - South–West DFC, 890 km long from Chennai to Goa
- **Rail Development Authority** – Set up in 2017 to make recommendations to the Ministry regarding:
  - Pricing of services commensurate with costs.
  - Suggest measures for enhancement of non-fare revenue.
  - Protection of consumer interests, by ensuring quality of service and cost optimisation.
- **Adarsh Station Scheme** – Under this scheme, modernisation/upgradation of 1,253 railway stations have been taken up.
- **Mission 41k** – Launched in **2017**, it **aims to save** ₹41,000 crore in the next decade in the railways energy costs through following measures:
  1. Moving 90 per cent of traffic to electric traction over diesel from present 50 per cent.
  2. 100 per cent electrification of Railways network by December 2023.
  3. By procuring electricity at cheaper rates through open market, instead of sourcing it through DISCOMs.
  4. Exploring new technologies to bring down electric consumption.
  5. The railways have already set a target of generating 1,000 MW of solar power and 200 MW of wind energy.
- **Bullet Train Project** – Being implemented by the *National High Speed Rail Corporation Limited*, **Mumbai–Ahmedabad High Speed Rail Corridor** (under implementation) will be India's first high-speed rail line. The project is expected to be completed by 2023. The corridor will use Japan Railways' Shinkansen E5 Series as its rolling stock.
- **National Rail Plan (NRP)** – In **December 2020**, the GoI came up with the NRP, which is a **long-term strategic plan** aimed for **infrastructural capacity enhancement** along with strategies to increase modal share of the railways by 2030. NRP intends to map the entire transport infrastructure of the country on a common platform and increase the modal share of rail in freight from the current level of 27 per cent to 45 per cent.
- **Kavach** – As a part of Atmanirbhar Bharat, 2,000 km of network will be brought under Kavach. 'Kavach' is an **Anti-Collision Device** (ACD) network. It is a Made-in-India technology that is designed to help Indian Railways achieve the **goal of 'zero accidents'**.
- **Vande Bharat Express** – They are **self-propelled 'engineless' train sets** with an operational efficiency of 160 kmph. Their fast acceleration and deceleration results in reduced train travel

time. Some Passenger-friendly features include European-style seats, diffused LED lighting, GPS-based infotainment systems, modular bio-toilets, fully sealed gangways for dust-free environment, centrally controlled entry/exit doors with sliding footsteps, divyang friendly toilet and automatic sliding cabin doors. As of March 2025, 136 Vande Bharat trains are running in service over Indian Railways.

- **Amrit Bharat Express:** The Amrit Bharat Express is a high-speed express train service operated by Indian Railways. It offers a cost-effective, non-air-conditioned sleeper cum unreserved service, connecting cities that are over 800 km apart or have travel times exceeding ten hours with existing services. The train comprises two locomotives, one at each end, and 22 coaches, capable of operating at speeds ranging from 110 to 130 km/h (68–81 mph). Commercial operations of this train commenced on January 1, 2024.
- **One Station One Product Scheme**: It was announced in the Union Budget 2022–23. This Scheme aims to provide opportunities for enhanced livelihood through skill development to local artisans, potters, weavers/handloom weavers, craftsmen, etc., through provision of sale outlets at railway stations across the country. This Scheme has been implemented at 535 stations with 572 outlets.
- **Amrit Bharat Station Scheme**: It has been launched for the development of railway stations on Indian Railways. As of February 2025, the scheme envisages to take up 1,309 stations for upgradation/modernisation over Indian Railways.
- **Major Economic Railway Corridor Programmes:** As declared in the Interim Budget 2024–25, three major economic railway corridor programmes have been identified under PM Gati Shakti for implementation. These are **(i) energy, mineral and cement corridors; (ii) port connectivity corridors and (iii) high traffic density corridors**. These projects will not only enable multi model connectivity but also improve logistics efficiency and reduce cost.

Civil Aviation

- **In terms of domestic market** for civil aviation, India is the **third largest** in the world after USA and China.
- In terms of domestic passenger traffic, India witnessed a double-digit Compound Annual Growth Rate (CAGR) of 14.5 per cent from 2014–15 to 2023–24.
- Major reason for the boom in civil aviation sector can be attributed to India's growing economy along with its growing purchasing power and the growing middle class.
- However, there are persisting **challenges in civil aviation sector**:
  - **Unstable balance sheets** of carriers – most airlines failed to register profits over multiple years period.
  - **Inappropriate regulation in airfares** – sometimes they are either too high or too low.
  - **Acute shortage of workforce** – in terms of pilot, cabin crew, air traffic controllers, ground staff, etc.
  - **Lack of proper training infrastructure** – in terms of training academies, instructor and equipment.
  - **Mismanagement of airport development projects** – with overlapping or insufficient catchment areas.
  - **High cost** of Aviation Turbine Fuel (*ATF costs around 40% of the total operation cost*).

- Major government initiatives, so far, in the civil aviation sector:
  - **National Civil Aviation Policy, 2016**
    - Its mission is to **provide safe, secure, affordable and sustainable air travel** for passengers and air transportation of cargo with access to various parts of India and the world.
    - **Enhance regional connectivity** through fiscal support and infrastructure development.
    - It also aims at increasing tourism, employment and a balanced regional growth.
    - **Existing 5/20 rule*** has been revised to 0/20 rule under this policy.

BONUS KNOWLEDGE

***5/20 RULE (*scrapped by GoI in 2016*)**

As per 5/20 rule, Indian carriers were required to complete at least 5 years in domestic operations **and** also to have at least 20 aircrafts in the fleet or 20 per cent of their fleet (whichever is higher) in domestic operations before the airline was permitted to fly on international routes.

However, the same has been revoked under **National Civil Aviation Policy 2016**. The government has relaxed this rule to 0/20; i.e., now carriers need deployment of only 20 aircrafts in domestic operations to be able to fly internationally.

  - **UDAN** – It is a Regional Connectivity Scheme and is a part of National Civil Aviation Policy, 2016.
    - The scheme aims to **develop regional connectivity**.
    - It aims to start operations on unconnected routes.
    - It aims to connect unserved and underserved airports, thereby giving a boost to tourism. As of February 2025, 88 unserved and underserved airports (including 13 heliports and 2 water aerodromes) have been operationalised.
    - Under the scheme, a successful bidder would have exclusive rights to operate. A number of private-sector airlines are participating in the scheme.
    - **A Regional Connectivity Fund** has been created under which the partner state will contribute 20 per cent share to the fund.
- **Krishi Udan Scheme 2.0**: It aims to ensure seamless, cost-effective, time-bound air transportation and associated logistics for all agri-produce originating especially from North-East, hilly and tribal regions of the country. So far, 58 airports are covered under this scheme.
- **Airseva 2016** is an initiative of the *Ministry of Civil Aviation* offering people a **convenient and hassle-free travel experience**.
- **Digi Yatra** involves biometric-based digital processing of passengers at airport.
- **100** per cent **FDI has been permitted for greenfield projects under the automatic route**.
- Six airports have been taken up for development under **PPP mode**. They are Ahmedabad, Guwahati, Jaipur, Lucknow, Mangalore and Thiruvananthapuram.
- As per the National Monetisation Pipeline (NMP), 25 AAI airports have been earmarked for asset monetisation over the years 2022 to 2025.
- Under Greenfield Airports Policy, 2008, government has envisaged to set up 21 Greenfield Airports. Out of these, 11 Greenfield airports viz. Durgapur, Shirdi, Kannur, Pakyong, Kalaburagi,

Orvakal (Kurnool), Sindhudurg, Kushinagar, Donyi Polo (Itanagar), Mopa and Shivamogga have been operationalised

VARIOUS AGENCIES RELATED TO CIVIL AVIATION

- **Director General of Civil Aviation** – It is a regulatory body under the *Ministry of Civil Aviation*.
- **Bureau of Civil Aviation Security** – Its responsibility is to lay down standards and measures in respect of civil flights.
- **Airport Authority of India** – It is a Public Sector Unit under the *Ministry of Civil Aviation* which is engaged in the development and building of airport infrastructure and its management.
- **Pawan Hans Helicopter Limited** – It is a *Mini Ratna-I category PSU* with the objective of providing helicopter support services for offshore exploration in the crude oil sector (to ONGC), inter-island transportation, operation in hilly and inaccessible areas, services for promotion of travel and tourism, etc.

did you KNOW?

Drone Rules, 2021

Ministry of Civil Aviation has introduced the **Drone Rules, 2021** with a focus on '*trust, self-certification, and non-intrusive monitoring*' to replace the existing Unmanned Aircraft System (UAS) Rules. Major objectives of Drone Rules are:

- Establishing a digital sky platform as a user-friendly single-window online system for streamlined approvals.
- Minimising human interface by enabling self-generated permissions on the digital platform.

Water Transport

Policies and programmes related to both inland water transport and sea transport are taken care of by the ***Ministry of Shipping***, *GoI*. Let us now discuss both the areas.

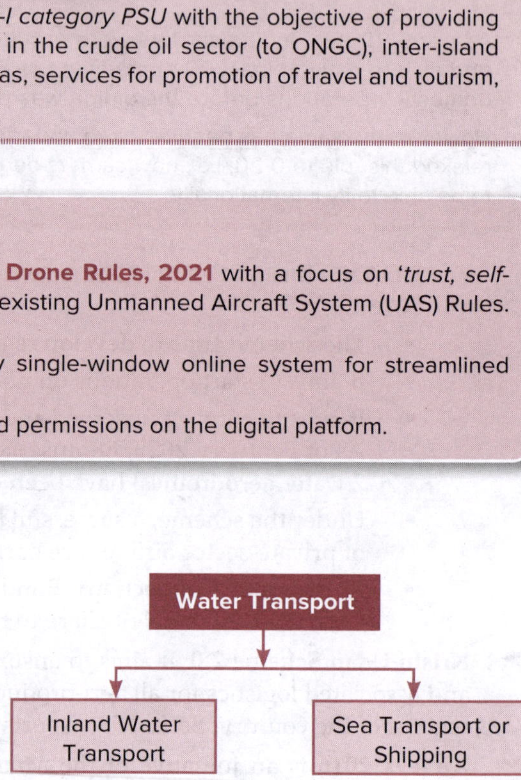

Inland Water Transport

- India has one of the **longest navigable and inland water networks.**
- Cargo transport through these inland waterways (IWs) is currently less than 1 per cent of the total cargo payment.
- **Inland Waterways Authority of India (IWAI)** is responsible for regulation related to navigation in IWs. The total navigable length of waterways in India is around 14,850 kilometres.
- Initially, there were the following five National Waterways (NWs):

NW	Details	Along River/Canal	Whether Operational?
NW 1	**Prayagraj–Haldia stretch** (1,620 km) – four states	Along Ganga–Bhagirathi–Hooghly River system	**Yes** (Vessels are plying)
NW 2	**Sadiya–Dhubri stretch** (891 km) – in Assam	Along Brahmaputra River	**Yes** (Vessels are plying)
NW 3	**Kollam–Kozhikode stretch** (205 km) – in Kerala	Of West Coast Canal along with Champakara Canal and Udyogmandal Canal	**Yes** (Vessels are plying)
NW 4	**Kakinada–Puducherry stretch** (1,095 km) covering three States/UTs	Of canals and Kaluvelly Tank, some stretches of Godavari and Krishna Rivers	Yes
NW 5	(a) **Talcher–Dhamra stretch** across many rivers/canals (b) **Geonkhali–Charbatia stretch** of Coovum Canal (c) **Harbatia–Dhamra stretch** of Matai and Mahanadi Rivers (all three in Odisha and West Bengal)	Total 623 km	Not yet
NW 6	**Bhanga-Lakhipur stretch** (121 km) – covering Manipur, Mizoram and Assam	Along Barak River	Not yet

Initiatives by the Government in the Inland Water Transport Sector

➤ In 2016, **106 more NWs** were declared as per the National Waterways Act, 2016. Thus, total NWs **now stand at 111**. Out of these 111, 13 NWs are operational at present.

- The **largest** is **NW 1**, i.e. **Prayagraj–Haldia stretch** of 1,620 km.
- The **smallest** among 111 is **NW 69**, which is a 5 km stretch along Manimuthar River in Tamil Nadu.

➤ **Jal Marg Vikas Project on NW 1** was undertaken in 2017 for capacity augmentation of navigation between Varanasi and Haldia, covering a distance of 1,380 km. Project was scheduled to complete by 2022–23 and is supported by the World Bank. However, as on February 2025, 66.01 per cent of the project is completed and 3 out of 7 milestones are yet to be completed.

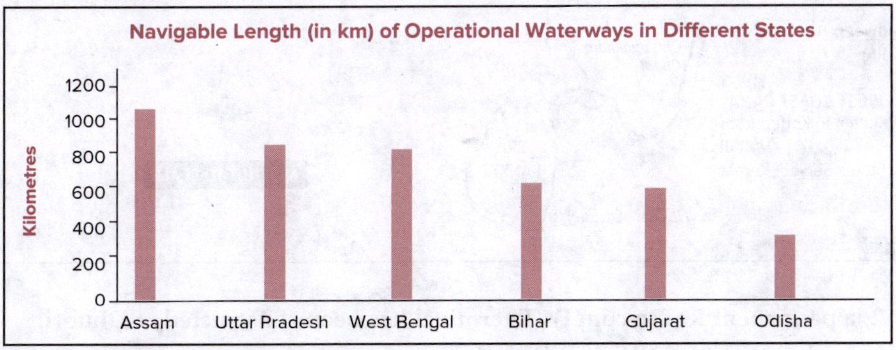

Source: Economic Survey 2024–25

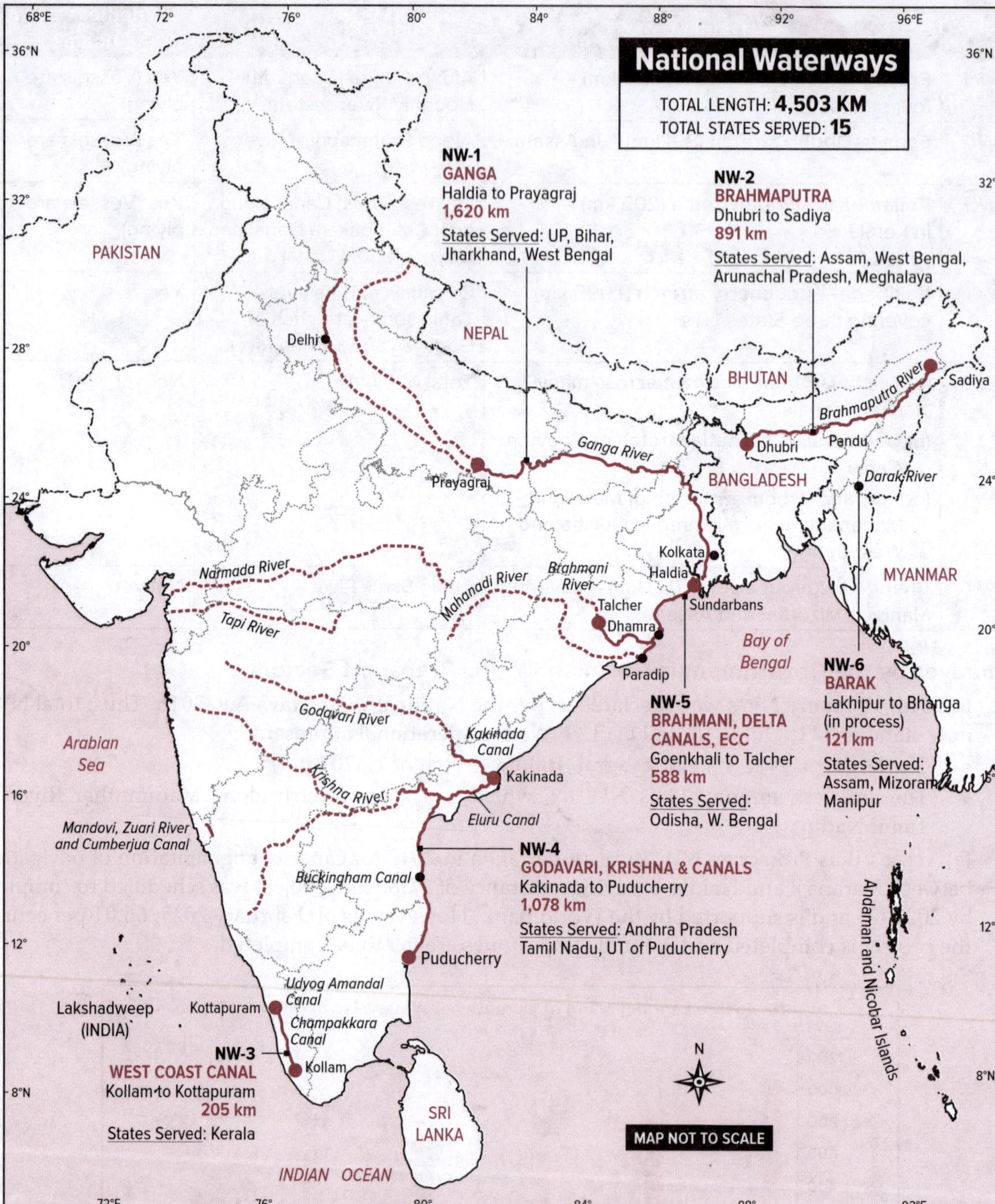

➤ **In NW 2, a permanent Ro-Ro cum IWT terminal has been constructed at Dhubri.**

➤ Dredging work in a part of NW 4 is also going on.

BONUS KNOWLEDGE

INLAND VESSELS ACT, 2021

- This Act **replaces** the century – old Inland Vessels Act, **1917**. New Act will regulate the safety, security and registration of inland vessels.
- **Key features:**
  - It provides a unified law for the whole country. Earlier there were separate laws in separate States.
  - The certificate of registration granted under the act will be valid in the entire country and there will be **no need for separate permissions from the States**.
  - There will be a **central database** for recording the details of vessels, vessel registration, crew on an electronic portal.
  - The mechanically propelled vessels will also have to be enrolled at district, taluk or panchayat or village level. The mechanically propelled vessels include ships, boats, sailing vessels, container vessels and ferries.
- The new act is **aimed at developing India's inland waterways** as a viable, thriving mode of transport, especially for cargo. The inland waterways network spans close to 15,000 km across rivers, channels, backwaters, creeks etc.

Shipping

- Almost **95 per cent** of the India's trade by volume and **70 per cent** in terms of value, are transported by sea.
- With a coastline of around 7,517 km, India has a huge scope in improvement of shipping infrastructure.
- India has **13 major ports** and around **205 notified minor and intermediate ports** handling over 90 per cent of India's export volume while 70 per cent of total export value. Initially, India had 13 major ports – Port Blair port was removed from major ports in 2010, but, **Vadhavan** (in Maharashtra) has been added as a major port in February, 2020.
- Paradip, Chennai, Vishakhapatnam, Kandla and JawaharLal Nehru Port Trust (JNPT) are the ports with highest cargo capacities.
- The **efficiency of a port** is measured through **TAT (Turnaround Time)** of ships. It is the time taken between the arrival of a vessel/ship and its departure. It has almost halved from 2010–11 to 2.25 days in 2021 (April–December). Vishakhapatnam and Mormugao ports have the highest TAT and JNPT port has the lowest. The median TAT globally is 1 day as per UNCTAD.
- **Jawaharlal Nehru Port (JNP)** has become the first major port of the country to become 100 per cent landlord port having all berths being operated on PPP model.

Infrastructural Challenges Faced by Shipping Sector

- **Capacity constraints** of Indian ports.
- Most Indian ports follow a hybrid format of the long obsolete service port model. They also suffer from the **problem of ageing**.
- Inadequate use of **modern technology** in ports, as well as **improper modernisation** is another issue.
- **Less autonomy to major port authorities** in their functioning and decision-making.

Major Government Initiatives

- **Major Port Authorities Act, 2021** has replaced the Major Port Trust Act, 1963. The new Act **provides more autonomy to the major ports** by allowing 'Board of Major Port' to fix tariff/scale for services provided and the use of port assets. Moreover, the **role of Tariff Authority for Major Ports (TAMP) is to be removed**.
- Memorandum of Understanding (MoU) was signed between India and Iran in 2015 for development of **Chabahar Port** of Iran. In 2018, GoI took over operations of two berths of the port.
- **Sagarmala Project, 2016**
  - It is flagship programme of **Ministry of Ports, Shipping and Waterways** to promote port led development in the country.
  - It is a strategic and customer-oriented initiative **to modernise ports**, that is, to transform current ports into world-class ports.
  - The aim behind this is **to reduce logistics cost of Export-Import and domestic trade with minimal infrastructure investment**.
  - Under this, **802 projects worth ₹5.4 Lakh Cr** have been identified for implementation up to 2035. These projects may be classified into:
    - Projects for port modernisation and new port development.
    - Projects for port connectivity enhancement.
    - Port-linked modernisation.
    - Coastal community development.
- **Project Unnati:** It is an exercise to prepare a *Quantitative Benchmarking Module* by covering operational, financial, HR and efficiency related parameters for **major ports** in India. Through this ongoing exercise, the key performance indicators for major ports are defined keeping into consideration the international standards.
- **Project Green Ports** has been undertaken to make ports cleaner and greener. The share of renewable energy in ports is to increase by 60 per cent. The ports have also aimed to reduce carbon emissions, per tonne of cargo handled, by 30 per cent by 2030.
- **National Maritime Development Projects is undertaken** with an aim to upgrade and modernise shipping infrastructure in India, considering global standards.
- **Port Community System** is launched which is aimed at seamlessly integrating all maritime trade-related stakeholders on a single platform.
- **e-SANCHIT** (e-Storage and computerised handling of indirect tax documents) is aimed at reducing human intervention.
- A **new Captive Policy for Port Dependent Industries** has been prepared to address the challenges of renewal of concession period, scope of expansion, and dynamic business environment.
- **Maritime India Vision 2030 (MIV2030):** Released in 2021, it is a blueprint to ensure coordinated and accelerated growth of India's maritime sector in the next decade. The objective is to develop world-class mega ports, transshipment hubs and ensure infrastructure modernisation (estimated investment ₹1,00,000–₹1,25,000 crore).
- **Maritime Amrit Kaal Vision 2047:** It is based on MIV2030 which aims to develop world-class ports and promote inland water transport, coastal shipping, and a sustainable maritime sector. It encompasses aspirations in Logistics, Infrastructure, and Shipping, supporting India's 'Blue Economy'.

- Schemes such as **Direct Port Entry and Direct Port Delivery**; **Radio Frequency Identification System (RFIS)**; and **Single Window Interface for Facilitating Trade**, are all aimed at reducing the time and cost of clearance of goods.
- **National Logistic Portal (Marine) (NLP)**: It is a one-stop platform aimed to connect all the stakeholders of the logistics community using IT, to improve efficiency and transparency by reducing costs and time delays and achieving easier, faster, and more competitive offerings of services, to promote the growth of the logistics sector; and thereby improve trade.

RECYCLING OF SHIPS ACT, 2019

This new Act restricts and prohibits the use/installation of **hazardous materials** in ship building, irrespective of whether a ship is meant for recycling or not. The existing ships on the date of implementation of the Act will have 5 years' time for compliance, whereas for new ships, such restriction is from immediate effect.

This new Act has been framed after India in 2019 acceded to the Hong Kong International Convention for the Safe and Environmentally Sound Recycling of Ships, 2009.

BONUS KNOWLEDGE

SHIPPING CORPORATION OF INDIA

- It is a government PSU, with headquarters in **Mumbai**.
- **Shipping Corporation of India (SCI)** was established in **1961**, and is presently the largest Indian shipping company.
- The main function of SCI is to manage and operate national and international lines vessels.
- SCI provides cruise liner and passenger services, bulk carrier and tanker services, and even offshore services.
- GoI gave **Navratna** status to SCI in 2008.
- However, in **November 2019**, GoI approved the **privatisation of SCI**.

GLOBAL HUB FOR GREEN SHIP

Green Tug Transition Programme (GTTP) has been launched by Indian Government in 2023 which aims to make India '**Global Hub for Green Ship**' building by 2030. India's first National Centre of Excellence in Green Port & Shipping (NCoEGPS) has been established in Gurugram, Haryana. The project starts with 'Green Hybrid Tugs', which are powered by Green Hybrid Propulsion systems, and will subsequently adopt the non-fossil fuel solutions like Methanol, Ammonia, and Hydrogen. The target has been set for the initial Green Tugs to start working in all major ports by 2025. At least, 50% of all the Tugs are likely to be converted into Green Tugs by 2030, which will considerably reduce emission as the country moves towards achieving sustainable development.

Pipelines

Pipelines are the most convenient and suitable mode of transportation for petroleum products and gases in bulk for longer distances.

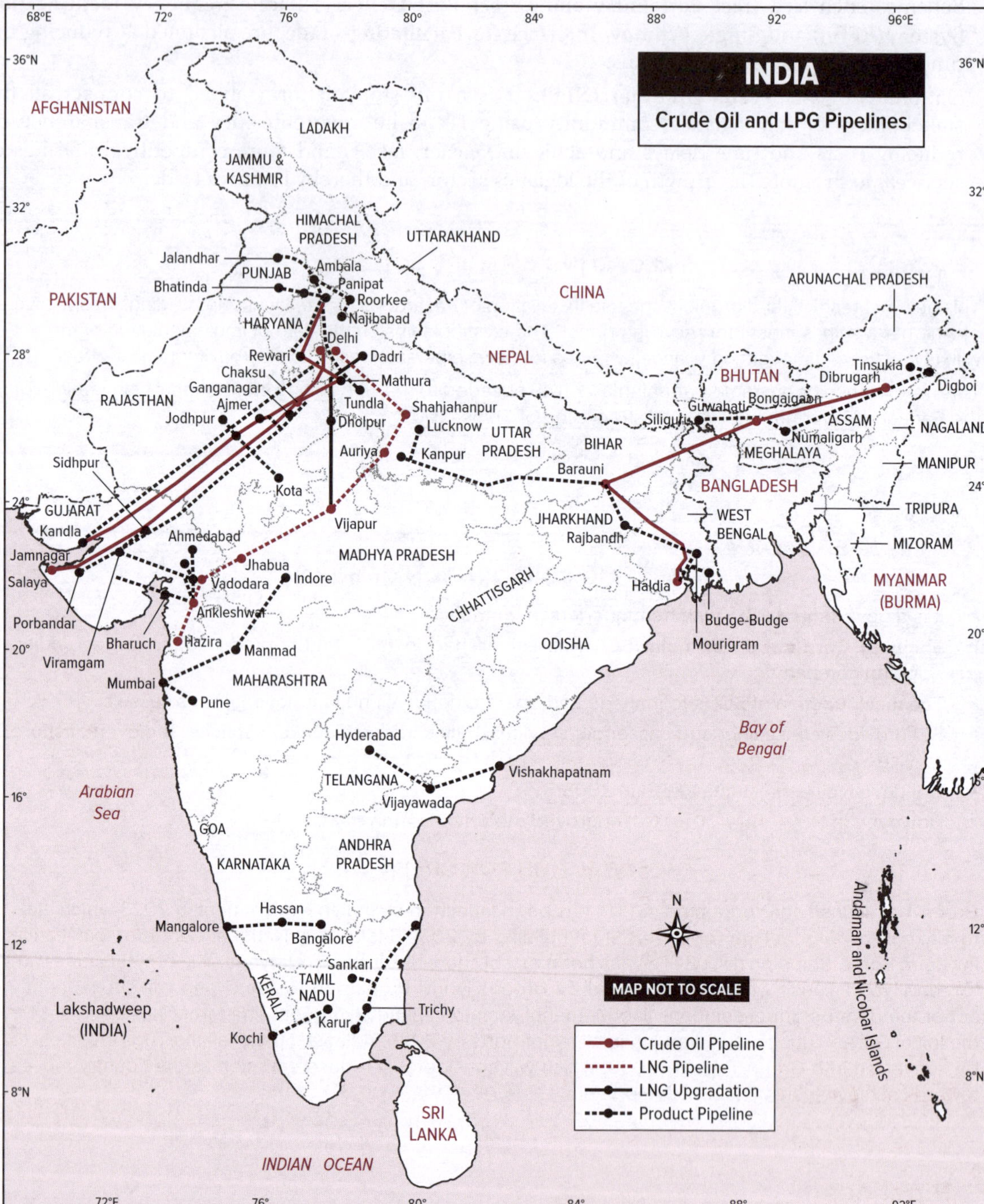

The products which can be transported through pipelines are:

- Petroleum products – Crude oil, jet fuel
- Liquid products – Water, Anhydrous Ammonia
- Gases – Natural Gas, LPG, butane
- Solid products – Coal, mineral, solid wastes

Advantages

- Pipelines require minimal energy compared to other transportation modes.
- Transit losses are minimal, reducing wastage of transported materials.
- Operating costs are significantly lower than surface transportation.
- Pipelines can traverse difficult terrains, including underwater routes.
- They are unaffected by seasonal variations or adverse weather conditions.
- Pipelines contribute to industrial development in surrounding areas.

Examples:

- Slurry pipelines from Bailadila mines to Vizag Steel Plant.
- Slurry pipelines transporting iron ore from Kudremukh mines to New Mangalore port.
- Rock phosphate concentration pipelines from Maltos mines to Debari smelter plant.

Safety and Environmental Benefits:

- Pipelines are safe, accident-free, and environmentally friendly.

Disadvantages

- Susceptible to damage during earthquakes, making leak detection challenging.
- High initial laying cost, although maintenance costs are relatively low.
- Vulnerable to security threats from terrorist activities.
- Capacity cannot be easily increased once pipelines are installed; expansion requires laying new pipelines.
- Repairing pipelines, especially detecting and fixing leaks, can be challenging.

TELECOM SECTOR

- Indian telecom network is **second largest** in the world with over 1.1 billion telephone connections (after China).
- The Telecom Sector contributes around 6.5 per cent to the country's GDP.
- FDI (equity flow) in telecommunication sector during 2023–24 (April–Sept. 2024) rose to US$670 million compared to US$282 million during 2022–23.
- India improves its ranking to 40th position (2024) from 60th position (2023) as per **Network Readiness Index (NRI) 2024** report. NRI is one of the leading global indices on the application and impact of information and communication technology (ICT) in 133 economies around the world.
- **However, there are certain challenges** faced by the telecom sector such as:
  - Substantial competition and **price cutting** by the four telecom service providers (TSPs) since 2016, thereby creating financial stress in the sector.

- As the **price of data** in our country is the lowest in the world, some operators have even filed for bankruptcy; others have merged in their quest to improve viability.
- BSNL and MTNL are also affected by this **tariff war**, and it has impacted their cash flows, resulting in mounting losses.
- Privacy and Security Issues.
- Late implementation of 5G.
- Digital Divide: Rural-Urban Divide and Male-Female Divide.

EXAM ESSENTIAL

ADJUSTED GROSS REVENUE (AGR)

- AGR is the usage and licensing fees to be paid by Telecom companies to Government as a part of the revenue sharing agreement. However, there is differing legal interpretation regarding what should be included in AGR.
- The companies thought that only revenue from telecom services is required to be paid. Whereas, the Department of Telecommunications (DoT) said that revenue from non-telecom services is also part of AGR. Supreme Court also ruled in favour of DoT. This created huge demand on Telcos.
- In such situation, to support Telecom sector, Government provided following relief measures:
  - 4 years moratorium on payment of statutory dues.
  - Allowing 100 per cent FDI through automatic route.
  - Cutting in Spectrum Usage Charges.

Major Recent Government Initiatives to improve Telecom Infrastructure

National Optical Fibre Network (NOFN)

- It was launched in 2011, to provide broadband connectivity. It was later renamed **BharatNet** in 2015.
- It is the first pillar of digital India programme being implemented in a phased manner for providing **broadband connectivity to all the 2.5 lakh Gram Panchayats (GPs)** in the country.
- The project envisages an **optimal mix of** optical fibre, radio and satellite media.
- The aim is to establish a highly scalable network infrastructure **accessible on non-discriminatory basis**, affordable broadband connectivity of 2 Mbps to 20 Mbps for all households.
- Private partners are allowed to create, upgrade, operate, maintain and utilise BharatNet. Government has approved a Viability Gap Funding support of ₹19,041 crore for the implementation of BharatNet project through **PPP Model**. It is being implemented by Bharat Broadband Network Ltd (BBNL).

Public Wi-Fi Hotspots

- Public Wi-Fi hotspots ensure last-mile delivery of broadband to users and are much easier to scale than adding new mobile towers. It bolsters connectivity inside buildings, airports, etc., and it allows for offloading from telecom networks to ease congestion.
- Wi-Fi networks offer affordable, scalable and versatile technologies that can facilitate the spread of Internet access in rural and urban areas.

did you KNOW?

PM WANI (Prime Minister Wi-Fi Access Network Interface Scheme)

It envisages setting up of public Wi-Fi networks and access points **by local Kirana and neighbourhood shops** through Public Data Offices that will not involve any licence fee or registration charges.

National Digital Communication Policy, 2018

- Objectives of the policy include:
  - Provisioning of broadband for all.
  - Creating 4 million additional jobs in the digital communication sector.
  - Enhancing the contribution of the digital communication sector to 8 per cent of India's GDP from 6.5 per cent.
  - Propelling India to the top 50 nations in the ICT Development Index of ITU.
  - Enhancing India's contribution to global value chains.
- Major strategies involved to achieve above objectives:
  - Establishing a '**National Broadband Mission (NBM)** – *Rashtriya Broadband Abhiyan*' to secure universal broadband access. Under NBM, BharatNet, GramNet, NagarNet and JanWiFi to be taken up for providing last-mile Internet connectivity. Also, **'Fibre First Initiative'** to be implemented to take the fibre to home, to enterprises and to key development institutions in urban as well as rural areas.
  - Establishment of a **National Digital Grid** – through creation of National Fibre Authority.
  - Creating a **Broadband Readiness Index for States/UTs** to attract investments and address right of way (RoW) challenges.
  - Developing a transparent, normative and fair **policy for spectrum assignments** and allocations and also strengthening and **optimising satellite communication technologies**.
  - Facilitating development of Open Access Next-Generation Networks.
    1. FDI cap in the telecom sector has been increased to 100 per cent from 74 per cent.
    2. Government has launched **PLI scheme for Large Scale Electronics Manufacturing and IT Hardware**.
    3. **Comprehensive Telecom Development Plan (CTDP) for the North-Eastern Region and Comprehensive Telecom Development Plan for Islands** to provide mobile connectivity in the uncovered villages, along National Highways and submarine fibre cable connectivity.

BONUS KNOWLEDGE

TELE-DENSITY

- It shows the number of telephones per hundred people.
- It is an important indicator of telecom penetration.
- The overall **tele-density** in India stood at **84.45 per cent** with wide differences across states. Eight license service areas – Delhi, Mumbai, Kolkata, Himachal Pradesh, Kerala, Punjab, Tamil Nadu, and Karnataka, had a tele-density of above 100 per cent. The highest and lowest range of tele-density areas are Delhi and Bihar, respectively.

Source: Economic Survey 2023–24

SMART CITY MISSION

- The aim is to develop **100 smart cities**.
- The mission is being implemented by the *Ministry of Housing and Urban Affairs.*
- Under this, the four key ingredients for a developing urban ecosystem are institutional, physical, social and economic infrastructure.
- The core infrastructure elements in a smart city would include *adequate water supply, assured electricity supply, solid waste management, efficient urban mobility and public transport, affordable housing, especially for the poor, robust IT connectivity and digitalisation, good governance, sustainable environment, safety and security of citizens and health and education.*
- The selection of the 100 cities by GoI has been done through a challenge competition.
- Participation of citizens in planning and implementation of the mission is also there to ensure sustained accountability.
- **Present status**: All 100 cities under Smart City Mission have incorporated Special Purpose Vehicles (SPVs), City Level Advisory Forums (CLAFs) and appointed Project Management Consultants (PMCs).
- **In 2020, two new indices** were launched by the *Ministry of Housing and Urban Affairs* to assess quality of life of citizens in 100 smart cities and 14 other million plus cities. Those two indices launched are:
  1. **Ease of Living Index** – to assess the ease of living of citizens across three pillars: *Quality of Life, Economic Ability and Sustainability*. For the first time, as part of the Ease of Living Index Assessment, a **Citizen Perception Survey** is being conducted.
  2. **Municipal Performance Index** – to assess the performance of municipalities based on five enablers, namely service, finance, planning, technology and governance.

SUMMARY

- **Infrastructure** – Basic physical systems of a region or nation which facilitate socio-economic development and promote the production activities in the economy – can be classified into Economic and Social Infrastructure.
- **National Investment and Infrastructure Fund (NIIF)** – Created in 2015 – to attract investment from both domestic and international sources – NIIF is registered with SEBI as an Alternative Investment Fund (AIF) and has been set up as a trust under the Indian Trust Act – headquarters at Mumbai – Indian government has 49 per cent stake in NIIF with the rest 51 per cent held by private sector.
- **PM Gati-Shakti** – National Master Plan for multi-modal connectivity is a digital platform to bring 16 Ministries together for integrated planning and coordinated implementation of infrastructure connectivity projects.
- **Global Infrastructure Facility (GIF)** – Launched by World Bank in 2014 – a global, open platform that facilitates the preparation and structuring of complex infrastructure Public Private Partnerships (PPPs) to enable mobilisation of private sector and institutional investor capital.
- **Global Infrastructure Outlook (GIO)** – Forecasts the infrastructure investment needs and gaps across 50 countries (including India) and across seven sectors till the year 2040.
- **Global Energy Transition Index** – Published annually by World Economic Forum (WEF) after comparing the energy sectors of a large number of countries.

- **National Gas Grid** – Government envisages to develop 27,000 km natural gas pipelines across the country – PNGRB has been recognised as the authority to grant authorisation to the entities for the development of City Gas Distribution (CGD) network.
- **Petroleum and Natural Gas Regulatory Board (PNGRB)** – A statutory regulatory body in India – set up in 2006 – constituted under the Petroleum and Natural Gas Regulatory Board Act, 2006.
- **International Solar Alliance** – Initiated by India in 2015 – alliance of 114 signatory countries – to work for efficient exploitation of solar energy – headquartered in Gurugram, Haryana.
- **Atal Jyoti Yojana (AJAY)** – Launched for installation of solar street lights in five States (UP, Assam, Bihar, Jharkhand and Odisha) through solar power – now has been extended to North-East States, island Union Territories, four Hilly States/UTs and also in aspirational districts of other States.
- **Logistics Performance Index** – An interactive benchmarking tool created to help countries identify the challenges and opportunities they face in their performance on trade logistics – published by World Bank.
- **Green Tug Transition Programme (GTTP)** – Launched to make India 'Global Hub for Green Ship' building by 2030.

UPSC CSE PREVIOUS YEARS' PRELIMINARY EXAMINATION QUESTIONS

1. Consider the following airports: **[2024]**

1. Donyi Polo Airport
2. Kushinagar International Airport
3. Vijayawada International Airport

In the recent past, which of the above have been constructed as Greenfield projects?

(a) 1 and 2 only (b) 2 and 3 only
(c) 1 and 3 only (d) 1, 2 and 3

2. Consider the following statements: **[2023]**

Statement-I: Interest income from the deposits in Infrastructure Investment Trusts (InvITs) distributed to their investors is exempted from tax, but the dividend is taxable.

Statement-II: InviTs are recognised as borrowers under the 'Securitisation and Reconstruction of Financial Assets and Enforcement of Security Interest Act, 2002'.

Which one of the following is correct in respect of the above statements?

(a) Both Statement-I and Statement-II are correct and Statement-II is the correct explanation for Statement-I.
(b) Both Statement-I and Statement-II are correct and Statement-II is not the correct explanation for Statement-I.
(c) Statement-I is correct but Statement-II is incorrect.
(d) Statement-I is incorrect but Statement-II is correct.

3. According to India's National Policy on Biofuels, which of the following can be used as raw materials for the production of biofuels? **[2020]**

1. Cassava
2. Damaged wheat grains
3. Groundnut seeds
4. Horse gram
5. Rotten potatoes
6. Sugar beet

Select the correct answer using the code given below:

(a) 1, 2, 5 and 6 only
(b) 1, 3, 4 and 6 only
(c) 2, 3, 4 and 5 only
(d) 1, 2, 3, 4, 5 and 6

4. Consider the following statements: **[2019]**

1. Petroleum and Natural Gas Regulatory Board (PNGRB) is the first regulatory body set up by the Government of India.
2. One of the tasks of PNGRB is to ensure competitive markets for gas.
3. Appeals against the decisions of PNGRB go before the Appellate Tribunals for Electricity.

Which of the statements given above are correct?
(a) 1 and 2 only (b) 2 and 3 only
(c) 1 and 3 only (d) 1, 2 and 3

5. With reference to **solar power** production in India, consider the following statements: **[2018]**
   1. India is the third largest in the world in the manufacture of silicon wafers used in photovoltaic units.
   2. The solar power tariffs are determined by the Solar Energy Corporation of India.

   Which of the statements given above is/are correct?
   (a) 1 only
   (b) 2 only
   (c) Both 1 and 2
   (d) Neither 1 nor 2

6. With reference to **'National Investment and Infrastructure Fund'**, which of the following statements is/are correct? **[2017]**
   1. It is an organ of NITI Aayog.
   2. It has a corpus of ₹4,00,000 crore at present.

   Select the correct answer using the code given below:
   (a) 1 only (b) 2 only
   (c) Both 1 and 2 (d) Neither 1 nor 2

7. The **Global Infrastructure Facility** is a/an: **[2017]**
   (a) ASEAN initiative to upgrade infrastructure in Asia and financed by credit from the Asian Development Bank.
   (b) World Bank collaboration that facilitates the preparation and structuring of complex infrastructure public–private partnerships (PPPs) to enable mobilisation of private sector and institutional investor capital.
   (c) Collaboration among the major banks of the world working with the OECD and focused on expanding the set of infrastructure projects that have the potential to mobilise private investment.
   (d) UNCTAD funded initiative that seeks to finance and facilitate infrastructure development in the world.

☞ NO QUESTIONS ASKED
2022, 2021, 2016, 2015, 2014, 2013

ANSWER KEY

1. (a) 2. (d) 3. (a) 4. (b) 5. (d)
6. (d) 7. (b)

UPSC CSE PREVIOUS YEARS' MAIN EXAMINATION QUESTIONS

1. What is the need for expanding the regional air connectivity in India? In this context, discuss the government's UDAN scheme and its achievements. **[2024]**
2. 'Investment in infrastructure is essential for more rapid and inclusive economic growth.' Discuss in the light of India's experience. **[2021]**
3. Access to **affordable, reliable, sustainable and modern energy** is the sine qua non to achieve Sustainable Development Goals (SDGs). Comment on the progress made in India in this regard. **[2018]**
4. What are **smart cities**? Examine their relevance for urban development in India. Will it increase rural–urban differences? Give arguments for **'smart villages'** in the light of **PURA and RURBAN** Mission. **[2016]**
5. To what factors can the recent dramatic fall in equipment costs and tariff of **solar energy** be attributed? What implications does the trend have for the **thermal power producers** and the related industry? **[2015]**
6. **National Urban Transport Policy** emphasises on 'moving people' instead of 'moving vehicles'. Discuss critically the success of the various strategies of the government in this regard. **[2014]**

☞ NO QUESTIONS ASKED
2023, 2022, 2020, 2019, 2017, 2013

CHAPTER

25

POWER AND ENERGY SECTOR OF INDIA

CHAPTER OUTLINE

- Importance of Power and Energy Sector in an Economy
- Main Sources of Energy in India
- National Solar Mission
- The National Biogas and Manure Management Programme
- Contribution of Power Sector in Economic Development
- Ministry of Power
- Power Sector DISCOMS and RDSS
- Challenges of Electricity Distribution in India
- Future of Renewable Energy in India
- International Energy Agency Electricity Report, 2024
- Rural Electrification
- Recent Achievements in Power and Energy Sector
- Government initiatives in the Power Sector
- Electricity (Amendment) Bill, 2022
- Challenges in Energy Sector
- Solutions to Forego Challenges

A major part of India lacked access to enough energy to light up their houses when it gained independence. After sunset, the only sources of light were the oil lamp and the lantern. In most of the families, all duties were accomplished by sunset. A few could afford light due to the scarcity and high cost of kerosene. An oil light placed in a window functioned as a guide for travellers or people wanting to come home. Although the classic image of a youngster studying beneath a street light can still be seen today, it is a rare occurrence. Overall, the situation has improved significantly.

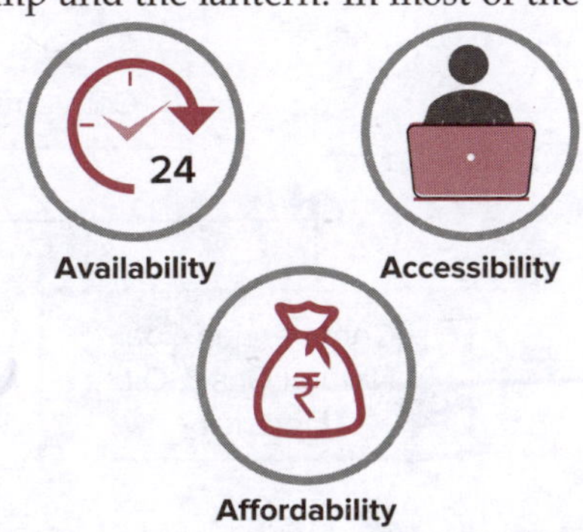

The situation improved due to improvement in three A's in energy sector, i.e. Availability, Accessibility and Affordability.

IMPORTANCE OF POWER AND ENERGY SECTOR IN AN ECONOMY

A country's economic progress and human development rely heavily on its power sector. It undoubtedly enhances the quality of life of humans as well as the biotic community in that particular area. Electricity consumption is one of the most essential indicators for determining a country's level of development.

Power is one of the most important components of infrastructure, as well as for a nation's wellbeing.

India's electricity industry is among the most diverse in the world. Conventional power generating sources include **coal, lignite, natural gas, oil, and nuclear power**. Similarly, potential non-conventional sources include **wind, solar, and agricultural and residential waste**.

The country's electricity demand has grown significantly and is anticipated to climb up further in the years to come. The whole electrical supply chain has gone through a shift as the sector's reforms progress. This chapter presents a summary of the improvements achieved in the electrical supply chain over the years, as well as new attempts to address some of the sector's significant concerns.

Massive Growth of Per Capita Electricity Consumption Since Independence

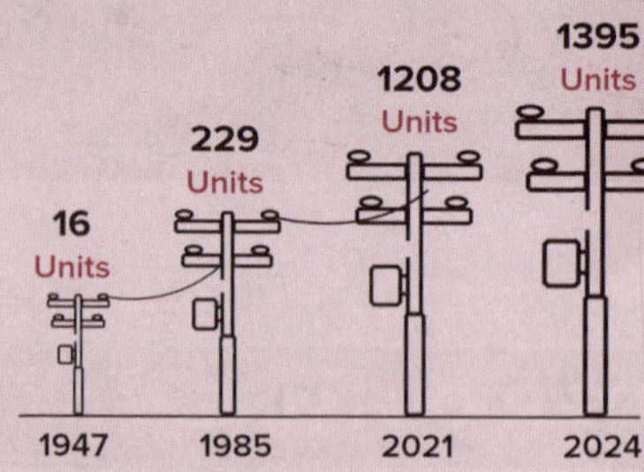

India Becoming Vibrant Power Market

- Reduced shortages
- Strengthened distribution systems
- Enhanced power availability in rural areas

MAIN SOURCES OF ENERGY IN INDIA

Natural energy sources may be divided into two categories: **Conventional** and **Non-Conventional** sources of energy.

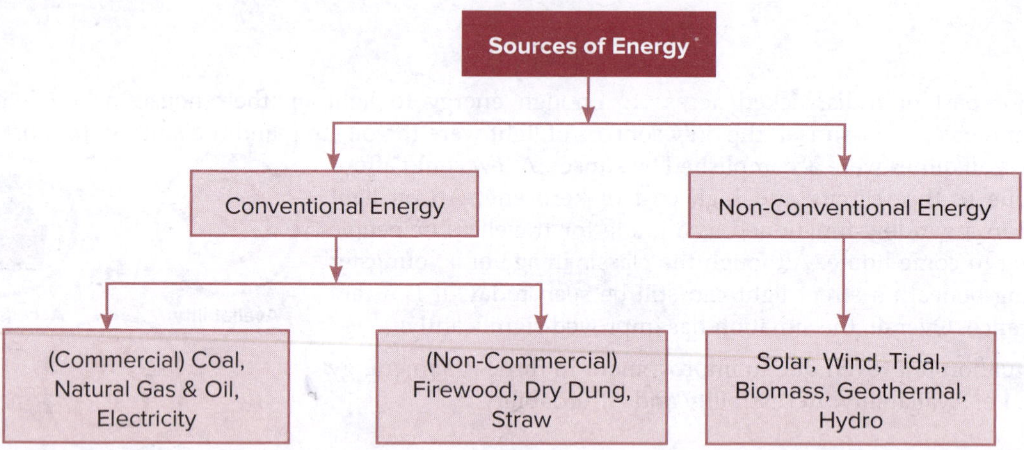

According to the **National Electricity Plan,** which was declared in 2023, the country's installed capacity for the year 2031–32 is planned to be 900,422 MW with 6,15,955 MW being carbon-free. Source details are as follows:

1. Nuclear – 19,680 MW
2. Large Hydro – 62,178 MW
3. Solar – 364,566 MW
4. Wind – 121,895 MW
5. Small Hydro – 5450 MW
6. Biomass – 15,500 MW
7. Pump Storage Power – 26,686 MW

According to the Ministry of New & Renewable Energy, the power sector has seen significant transformation in recent years. Earlier, there was a power shortage. A total of 1,93,794 MW of power producing capacity has been installed during the last nine years, providing adequate power supply. The demand has swiftly escalated. The country's energy needs have increased by 50.8 per cent since 2014. The peak demand has increased from 1,35,918 MW in 2013–14 to 2,43,271 MW in September 2023. This is almost a 79 per cent increase, and the demand has been met. The difference between energy required and energy provided is just 0.3 per cent, which is due to system limits or some **DISCOMs' lack of finances to purchase electricity**. The difference between peak demand and peak supply is about 1.4 per cent. In 2013–14, the average difference between peak demand and peak supply was 4.5 per cent, with demand at 136 GW.

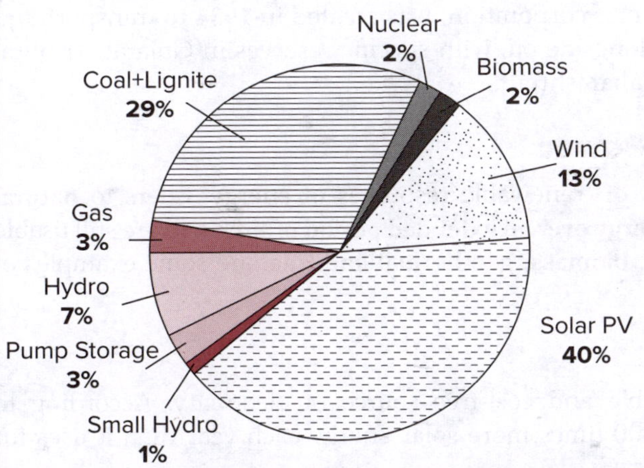

Projected Total Installed capacity: 900,422 MW

Projected All India installed capacity by 2031–32

Source: CEA's National Electricity Plan

Last Minute SNIPPETS

STATUS OF POWER SECTOR GROWTH AND INSTALLED CAPACITY

- As of November 2024, India's installed power capacity grew by **7.2%** year-on-year, reaching **456.7 GW**.
- Renewable energy accounts for 47% of the total installed capacity, with solar and wind being the dominant sources.
- Energy generation from non-fossil fuels have reached **420.8 thousand GW hours** in 2022-23, making up 22.8% of total generation.
- Renewable energy capacity increased 15.8% year-on-year, reaching **209.4 GW** by December 2024. The breakup of renewable energy resources capacity is as follows
- **Solar and Wind Power**

Solar: 97.8 GW

Wind: 48.2 GW

Hydro: 52.1 GW

Bioenergy: 11.3 GW

- India aims to achieve 50% non-fossil fuel-based energy by 2030.

Conventional Sources of Power

Coal

Coal, a key commodity, is largely used to produce thermal power. It is found within tertiary deposits and rock layers spanning two primary geological eras: **Gondwana and the Tertiary period**. In India, bituminous coal accounts for about 80 per cent of the non-coking grade coal deposits.

The Damodar Valley has India's greatest Gondwana coal deposits. They are located in the Jharkhand-Bengal coal area, which contains important coalfields such as Raniganj, Giridih, Jharia, Bokaro, and Karanpura. The largest coal field is Jharia, followed by Raniganj. Other river basins related to coal include the Mahanadi, Godavari and Sone. The most prominent coal mining sites are – Talcher and Rampur in Odisha, Singareni in Telangana, Singrauli in Madhya Pradesh, Pandur in Andhra Pradesh, Korba in Chhattisgarh, and Chanda-Wardha, Kamptee, and Bander in Maharashtra.

Meghalaya, Assam, Arunachal Pradesh and Nagaland all contain tertiary coal deposits. It is native to the Meghalayan districts of Cherrapunji, Mewlong, Darangiri, and Langrin; upper Assamese areas of Jaipur, Makum, and Nazira and Arunachal Pradesh regions of Namchik-Namphuk.

Petroleum

Crude petroleum is composed of **liquid and gaseous hydrocarbons, with varying chemical composition, colour, and specific gravity**. It is an essential fuel for all internal combustion engines in vehicles, trains, and aeroplanes. The petrochemical industry uses its byproducts to make synthetic rubber, synthetic fibre, fertiliser, medications, lubricants, wax, soap, etc. Tertiary sedimentary rocks contain crude petroleum.

Natural Gas

The **Gas Authority of India Limited,** a public sector corporation, was created in **1984** to transport and market natural gas. It is found in all oil fields alongside oil, with specific reserves in Gujarat, Tripura, Rajasthan, Andhra Pradesh, Tamil Nadu, and Maharashtra.

Non-Conventional Sources of Power

The term 'non-conventional sources of energy' or 'renewable resources of energy' refers to **natural resources that may constantly provide usable energy over an extended period of time** and are still usable even after they have been used up. **Solar, wind, biomass, geothermal and tidal** are some examples of unconventional sources of energy.

Solar Energy

Solar energy has long been the most accessible and cost-free source of electricity. According to calculations, the world receives more than 15,000 times more solar energy each year than it uses for commercial reasons.

Sun energy may be used in two ways: **solar thermal** and **solar electric (photovoltaic)**. The solar thermal route uses the sun's heat to cook meals, dry items, and generate hot water or air. Solar photovoltaic systems convert the sun's heat into energy that may be used to power motors, pumps, electric appliances, and lights in houses and other structures.

Solar thermal devices, also known as **solar collectors and receivers,** are utilised in the solar thermal route to convert solar energy into heat energy.

BONUS KNOWLEDGE

ONE SUN, ONE WORLD, ONE GRID

It was announced in COP26 held in 2021, where India and the UK agreed to bring together the International Solar Alliance and the UK's Green Grid Initiative. It not only aimed at tapping solar energy but also its accessibility across the borders. The vision behind this initiative is '*The Sun Never Sets*'.

EXAM ESSENTIAL

NATIONAL SOLAR MISSION

- The National Solar Mission, also known as the **Jawaharlal Nehru National Solar Mission (JNNSM)**, is a joint effort by the Central and State Governments of India to promote the growth of solar power throughout the country.
- The National Solar Mission, one of eight climate missions defined in the Indian government's **NAPCC (National Action Plan on Climate Change) mitigation plan**, was started in 2010 and has been revised twice.
- With an ambitious goal of **100 GW of solar photovoltaic (PV)** capacity by 2022, the mission aims to establish India as a global leader in solar energy.
- The JNNSM intends to boost India's worldwide prominence in solar energy efforts by creating a suitable regulatory framework for mass deployment.

*India's first Battery Storage and Solar Power based 'Suryagram' – **'Modhera' in Gujarat**.*

Objective

The objectives of the National Solar Mission are as follows:

- The major goal of the National Solar Mission is to position India as a leader in solar energy by establishing a suitable political environment for the fast adoption and distribution of solar technology throughout the country.
- The mission has a phased implementation strategy, which consists of three separate phases. Phase 1 includes the final year of the 11th Plan and the first year of the 12th Plan (up to 2012–2013), Phase 2 covers the next four years (2013–17), and Phase 3 covers the period 2017–22.
- Each phase includes a thorough review of progress, capability assessment, and target setting for the following stages. These evaluations are based on growing cost and technology trends, both nationally and worldwide, and are undertaken at the end of each plan as well as mid-term during the 12th and 13th plans.

EXAM ESSENTIAL

INTERNATIONAL SOLAR ALLIANCE

The International Solar Alliance (ISA) was **initiated by India** in 2015. It is an alliance of 114 signatory countries (who signed the ISA Framework Agreement) and 92 member countries (who signed and ratified the ISA Framework Agreement), most of them being sunshine countries, which lie either completely or partly between the Tropic of Cancer and the Tropic of Capricorn. The aim of ISA is to work for the efficient exploitation of solar energy. Countries that do not fall within the Tropics, can also join the alliance and enjoy all benefits as other members, with the exception of voting rights. ISA is headquartered in **Gurugram, Haryana.**

Wind Energy

Wind energy is fundamentally defined as the use of wind to create electricity. Wind's **kinetic energy is converted into electrical energy.** Because of the curvature of the planet, different sections of the atmosphere are heated to variable degrees in reaction to solar radiation entering the atmosphere.

At the poles, this warmth is both the least intense and the greatest. Because air moves from warmer to cooler climes, it creates winds, which are subsequently used to generate power by windmills and turbines.

Wind Energy Potential in India Commercially exploitable wind energy potential is estimated at over 200 gigawatts (GW). And the currently installed capacity stands at around 41 GW, representing about 20 per cent utilisation of the potential. **Challenges and reasons** for slow capacity addition could be as follows:

- Transition from feed-in tariffs to competitive bidding for tariff determination. Aggressive bidding by developers impacting profitability.
- Shift in tariff system from higher rates (₹4–5/unit) to competitive rates (₹2.5–3/unit).
- Large projects awarded to Independent Power Producers (IPPs) under bidding mechanism.

Recommendations for addressing such challenges could be:

- To repower old and inefficient turbines with advanced models.
- To formulate policies for repowering and recycling old turbines.
- To impose heavy penalties on developers backing out of projects.
- To blacklist persistent defaulters to ensure project continuity.
- To explore Offshore Wind Energy Potential, which is of about 70 GW off Gujarat and Tamil Nadu coasts.
- To promote Wind-Solar hybrid projects in order to leverage the complementary nature of solar and wind energy. Such large grid-connected projects have been encouraged under the **National Wind Solar Hybrid Policy, 2018.**

Overdue payments to wind energy developers is leading to Non-Performing Assets (NPAs). Thus, there is a need to enforce **Renewable Purchase Obligations (RPO)** across all states and also to impose penalties on defaulting entities to ensure compliance with renewable energy procurement targets.

BONUS KNOWLEDGE

NATIONAL WIND ENERGY MISSION

The National Wind Energy Mission was founded to serve as a technical hub for wind power development in India, to stimulate and accelerate the use of wind energy, and to assist the country's growing wind power sector.

*National Institute of Wind Energy (NIWE) is located in **Chennai**.*

Tidal Energy

Tidal energy is the consequence of gravitational interactions between the moon and the earth's water mass, as well as between the sun and the earth's water mass.

Tidal energy offers a significant advantage in terms of predictability. The magnitude and timing of tides may be predicted rather accurately.

The **Gulf of Khambhat** and the **Gulf of Kutch in Gujarat** are the locations in the country where tidal energy potential exists. However, the capital cost for tidal energy power plants is very high due to high civil construction and high-power purchase tariff.

BONUS KNOWLEDGE

TIDAL POWER DEVELOPMENT IN INDIA
(Standing Committee Report – 2021)

The Committee highlighted three main types of ocean energy: wave, tidal, and ocean-thermal. The theoretical potential of tidal energy is estimated at 12.5 gigawatts, while wave energy potential is around 41.3 gigawatts. However, the Committee emphasised that theoretical potential does not necessarily represent practical exploitable potential. The Committee recommended that the central government should reassess the exploitable potential of tidal, wave, and ocean energy.

Other major recommendations were:

Cost Considerations of Tidal Power Plants: Previous experiences with tidal power plants in West Bengal and Gujarat revealed high costs per megawatt (MW), leading to plant shutdowns. The West Bengal plant had a cost of ₹63.5 crore per MW, and the Gujarat plant had a cost of ₹15 crore per MW. The Committee recommended that the central government should reassess the current cost of tidal power to determine its economic viability and long-term benefits.

Setting up a Pilot Tidal Power Project: Tidal energy is not included in India's 2022 renewable energy target of 175 gigawatts, but the Ministry of New and Renewable Energy indicated that all renewable energy sources will be eligible for the 2030 target. The Committee recommended that the central government should set up a pilot tidal power project, preferably in a cost-effective location like the Gulf of Kutch.

Environmental Impact Assessment: Tidal power plants could potentially impact a large area upstream and downstream. The committee recommended that the central government should conduct an assessment to evaluate the environmental impact and ensure ecological sustainability of tidal power projects.

Research and Development Funding: Funding for research and development in the Ministry of New and Renewable Energy was significantly reduced at the revised stage between 2017 and 2020. Even the reduced funding allocation was not fully utilised during these years. The Committee recommended that the central government should maintain or increase funds for research and development, particularly for unexplored sources like tidal energy.

Biomass Energy

Biomass refers to renewable organic material derived from plants and animals, containing stored chemical energy from sunlight through photosynthesis. It can be utilised directly for heat or transformed into liquid and gaseous fuels using various processes.

Sources of Biomass for Energy Production

1. **Wood and Wood Processing Residues** such as Firewood, Wood pellets, Wood chips, Sawdust Black liquor from pulp and paper mills, etc.
2. **Agricultural Crops and Byproducts** such as Corn, Soybean, Sugar cane, Switchgrass, Woody plants, Algae, Residues from crop and food processing.
3. **Biogenic Components in Municipal Solid Wastes** such as Paper products, Cotton and wool materials, Food waste, Yard trimmings, Wood scraps, Animal Manure and Human Sewage.

These biomass sources contribute to sustainable energy production and can help reduce reliance on fossil fuels. Biomass energy can play a crucial role in the renewable energy sector by utilising organic materials to produce heat, electricity, and transportation fuels.

EXAM ESSENTIAL

NATIONAL POLICY ON BIOFUELS, 2018

The important features of this policy are:

a. Categorisation of biofuels as 'basic biofuels' (First Generation) and 'advanced biofuels' (Second and Third Generation).

b. Allowing B-molasses, sugar beet, sweet sorghum, starch-containing materials like corn, cassava, damaged food grains like wheat, broken rice and rotten potatoes, which are unfit for human consumption, for ethanol production.

c. With a thrust on Advanced Biofuels, the Policy indicates a viability gap funding scheme for 2G ethanol Bio refineries of ₹5,000 crore in 6 years, in addition to the additional tax incentives, higher purchase price as compared to 1G biofuels.

d. Government has prescribed indicative target of blending of biodiesel in diesel/direct sale of biodiesel.

e. Reduction of GST rate for procurement of biodiesel for blending programme from 12% to 5%

f. "**Pradhan Mantri JI-VAN (Jaiv Indhan – Vatavaran Anukool Fasal Awashesh Nivaran) Yojana**" 2019 has been amended in August 2024 for granting financial assistance for setting up Advanced Biofuel Projects.

g. **Target:** 20 per cent blending of ethanol in petrol and 5 per cent blending of bio-diesel in diesel by 2030.

h. Setting up of supply chain mechanisms for biodiesel production from non-edible oilseeds, used cooking oil, and short-gestation crops.

EXAM ESSENTIAL

THE NATIONAL BIOGAS AND MANURE MANAGEMENT PROGRAMME (NBMMP)

The programme aims to develop **family-style biogas plants** that will provide biogas as a source of illumination and clean cooking fuel. Slurry, a byproduct of biogas plants, is an organic bio-manure that may be used to increase crop yield while also conserving soil health. The growth of biogas technology helps to decrease environmental deterioration and prevent the emission of greenhouse gases (GHGs) into the atmosphere, such as carbon dioxide (CO_2) and methane.

Hydro Energy

The potential energy of falling water, is captured and converted into electrical energy by waterwheels.

Rivers and streams were dammed, and mills were built wherever there was enough head or elevational change. The flow of pressured water causes a turbine to spin. A power generator is coupled to the turbine.

Small Hydro Power

- Micro (Upto 100 kW)
- Mini (101 kW to 2 MW)
- Small Hydro (2 MW to 25 MW)

Geothermal Energy

Geothermal resources are hot water reservoirs that exist naturally or artificially at varying temperatures and depths under the Earth's surface.

Wells can be bored into subterranean reservoirs ranging in depth from a few feet to several miles in order to access steam and extremely hot water that can be brought to the surface for use in a variety of applications, including electricity production, direct usage, and heating and cooling.

Geyser Vs Hotsprings

Limitations of Non-conventional Energy Sources

- **Weather Dependency:** Weather has a considerable influence on non-conventional energy sources like solar and wind power, making it difficult to deliver continuous and consistent electricity.
- **Storage Insufficiency:** Non-conventional energy sources, such as solar and wind power, are typically produced in large numbers during peak hours, but it is likely that the storage solutions for this additional energy are inefficient or costly.
- **Capacity Limitations:** Non-conventional energy sources have a lower capacity than traditional energy sources such as coal and natural gas, which may limit their overall potential.
- **High Initial Expense:** Installing non-conventional energy sources may need a considerable initial investment, which may be prohibitively expensive for certain individuals or organisations.
- **Environmental Impact:** Renewable energy sources, such as large-scale hydroelectric dams that destroy habitat and uproot local inhabitants, can also have a negative impact on the environment. Biogas, although beneficial and renewable, contributes to the greenhouse impact.

Difference between Conventional and Non-conventional Sources of Energy

Conventional Sources of Energy	Non-conventional Sources of Energy
Conventional energy sources, such as coal, petroleum, and natural gas, are not renewable.	Non-conventional energy sources, such as solar and wind energy, are renewable.
These sources have been used for a long time. Example: firewood and coal.	These sources have recently emerged and are evolving day by day. Example: technology for producing power from solar panels.
The majority of these energy sources (e.g., coal and firewood) emit pollutants when used.	Solar energy, geothermal energy, and other renewable energy sources do not pollute.
They are widespread and commonly utilised sources (such as thermal power).	They are relatively new sources of energy and hence not commonly employed. Solar panels and windmills, for example, are rarely utilised.
The efficiency and production costs of conventional energy sources are low.	The efficiency and production costs of non-conventional energy sources are high.

CONTRIBUTION OF POWER SECTOR IN ECONOMIC DEVELOPMENT

Power Supply Position in India during 2023–24 and 2024–25 (upto Dec 24)

Years	Energy				Peak			
	Energy Requirement	Energy Supplied	Energy not Supplied		Peak Demand	Peak Met	Demand not Met	
	(MU)	(MU)	(MU)	(%)	(MW)	(MW)	(MW)	(%)
2023–24	16,26,132	16,22,020	4,112	0	2,43,271	2,39,931	3,340	1
2024–25 (up to December, 2024)	12,80,111	12,78,772	1,339	0	2,49,856	2,49,854		0

Source: CEA (Central Electricity Authority)

Ministry of Power

The Ministry of Power was established on July 2, 1992. Previously, it was a department (the Department of Power) inside the Ministry of Power, Coal, and Non-Conventional Energy Sources. That ministry was divided into three sections: Ministry of Power, Ministry of Coal, and Ministry of Non-Conventional Energy Sources (renamed Ministry of New and Renewable Energy in 2006).

The ministry is in charge of managing electricity production and infrastructure development, which includes generating, transmission, and distribution, as well as maintenance initiatives.

The ministry serves as a liaison between the central government, state power operations, and the private sector. The ministry also manages rural electricity programmes.

Central Public Sector Undertakings under the Ministry of Power

- National Thermal Power Corporation Limited Power Grid Corporation of India
- North Eastern Electric Power Corporation Limited
- National Hydropower Corporation
- Power Finance Corporation

Ministry of Coal

The Ministry of Coal has the responsibility of exploring India's coal and lignite deposits, as well as producing, supplying, distributing, and pricing coal through the government-owned corporations **Coal India Limited** and its subsidiaries and **Neyveli Lignite Corporation**.

The Ministry of Coal also controls the Union Government's 49 per cent equity stake in Singareni Collieries Company, a public-sector joint venture with the Telangana government.

Ministry of New and Renewable Energy

In response to the 1970s energy crisis, the **Commission for Additional Sources of Energy (CASE)** was established in 1981 by the Department of Science & Technology. The CASE was in charge of policy formulation and execution, programme development for new and renewable energy, and sector-wide coordination and intensification of R&D.

In 1982, the then-Ministry of Energy established a new agency called the **Department of Non-conventional Energy Sources (DNES)**. DNES included CASE in its umbrella.

The Ministry of Non-Conventional Energy Sources was formed in 1992. It received its present name in 2006.

POWER SECTOR DISCOMS AND RDSS (REVAMPED DISTRIBUTION SECTOR SCHEME)

The electricity industry consists of three major processes:

I. **Power generation**,

II. **Power transmission** and

III. **Power distribution**.

Distribution companies (DISCOMs) link electricity providers to households. They serve as the liaison between utilities and customers.

According to the Indian Constitution, power is a **concurrent subject**, and states are responsible for distributing and supplying power to rural and urban users. As a result, state governments own the vast majority of DISCOMs. Private DISCOMs also operate in India, although only in a few cities, such as Delhi and Mumbai.

In India's electrical supply chain, distribution plays the most crucial function, yet it could also be the weakest one. DISCOMs in India continue to confront challenges such as AT&C losses, limited investment, and metering concerns.

Challenges of Electricity Distribution in India

For many years, the majority of India's electricity distribution companies have been incurring losses every year. These cumulative losses and challenges are occurring due to the following reasons:

- **High AT&C losses:** DISCOMs' perilous financial condition is attributed to a high degree of aggregate technical and commercial (AT&C) losses, the imposition of inadequate or lower prices in comparison to the cost of electricity delivery, and insufficient subsidy assistance from state governments.
- **Poor financial health:** Power distribution companies collect payments from customers against their energy supply (bought from generators) to generate the cash flows required for the production and transmission sectors to function. Discoms are unable to pay for their energy purchases from generators on time because of the recurrent cash collection gap, which is frequently caused by customer payment delays.
- **Tariff Determination:** It is one of the most important factors influencing the health of DISCOMs. The tariff decision procedure is frequently delayed.
- **Lack of Metering:** Minimising AT&C losses is crucial for improving Discoms' operating efficiency. However, even six years after **UDAY's** inception, several tiers of the distribution chain (the feeder, the distribution transformer (DT), and the customer) are still not properly metered. As a result, it is difficult to separate and identify loss-making locations and implement corrective measures.

The **Revamped Distribution Sector Reform Scheme (RDSS)** was created to address the DISCOMs' operational problems and budgetary restrictions. The Government of India established the Revamped Distribution Sector Scheme (RDSS) with an expenditure of ₹3,03,758 crore and an expected government budgetary support (GBS) from the Central Government of ₹97,631 crore for a five-year period (FY 2021–22 to FY 2025–26). The Scheme intends to decrease aggregate technical and commercial (AT&C) losses to 12–15 per cent across India, as well as the **Average Cost of Supply (ACS)-Average Revenue Realised (ARR)** gap to zero by 2024–25.

The Scheme has **two key components:**

1. Providing financial assistance for prepaid smart metering and system metering, as well as distribution infrastructure upgrades.
2. Providing training and capacity building, as well as other enabling and supporting activities.

DISCOMs are given financial help for upgrading their distribution infrastructure, as well as for Prepaid Smart Consumer Metering and System Metering if they fulfil pre-qualifying conditions and achieve the basic minimal benchmark in reforms.

To capitalise on the different opportunities provided by the RDSS, states must emphasise the need for flexibility in prioritising investments in their action plans. This endeavour must also be supported by fulfilled pledges to speedy but thoughtful implementation.

EXAM ESSENTIAL

INTERNATIONAL ENERGY AGENCY

International Energy Agency (IEA) was set up in 1974, in response to the **1973 oil crisis, with** Headquarters in **Paris**, France. IEA collaborates with governments and industries to shape a secure and sustainable energy future for all. **Only OECD member countries** can join as IEA members. Presently, it has 31 member countries, 13 association countries, and 4 countries seeking membership (Chile, Colombia, Israel, and Costa Rica). **India joined** as an **Association country** in 2017. Funded in IEA is generally by member countries, and **voluntarily by non-member countries**, energy companies, and private donations.

Important Reports published by IEA include - World Energy Outlook, Energy Technology Perspectives (ETP), Gas Market Report, Global Electric Vehicles (EV) Outlook, etc.

IEA's Electricity Report 2025

Highlights

- **Energy Demand Growth** – Global energy demand **increased** by 4.3% in 2024.
- **China's Consumption** – China has overtaken both the US and the EU, emerging as the **highest consumer of electricity.**
- **CO_2 Emissions** – Global CO_2 emissions from electricity generation are expected to stabilise from 2025 to 2027 after a 1% rise in 2024.
- **Renewable Energy Contribution** – Renewable energy sources, including **solar, wind, and hydropower**, are anticipated to account for approximately 95% of the electricity demand growth between 2025 and 2027.

Findings on India:

- **Demand Surge** – India's electricity demand **surged by 5.8% in 2024.**
- **Thermal Power Capacity** – India's thermal power capacity is expected to **increase** to 283 GW by 2032.
- **Coal Dominance** – Coal remains the dominant energy source, comprising **74% of India's power mix in 2024.**
- **Renewable Energy Growth** – The share of renewable energy in India's power mix is projected to rise from 21% in 2024 to 27% by 2027, with **solar photovoltaic (PV) leading this expansion.**
- **Nuclear Power Expansion** – Nuclear power generation saw a **13% increase in 2024.**

RURAL ELECTRIFICATION

According to the 2011 Census, almost 80 per cent of India's population lives in rural regions, with 167.8 million homes. Of these, only 92,808,181 are electrified, while 839,133 are not. The remaining 74,179,414 homes utilise paraffin or other sources for lighting. Rural electrification is generally seen as the backbone of the rural economy.

Rural electrification encompasses five key aspects:

1. Development of rural electricity infrastructure

2. Providing household connectivity
3. Ensuring adequate electricity supply with acceptable quality
4. Providing power at affordable rates
5. Providing clean, ecologically benign, and sustainable power in an effective manner

The Government of India had launched **DeenDayal Upadhyaya Gram Jyoti Yojana (DDUGJY)** in 2014, for the rural areas with the objective of electrification of all unelectrified villages as per Census 2011; strengthening and augmentation of sub-transmission and distribution infrastructure in rural areas, including construction of HT and LT lines, metering at distribution transformers, feeders and consumers; and feeder segregation.

Similarly, **Pradhan Mantri Sahaj Bijli Har Ghar Yojana – SAUBHAGYA** was launched in 2017 for electrification of rural and urban poor households in the country. SAUBHAGYA was launched with the objective to achieve universal household electrification by providing electricity connections to all unelectrified households in rural areas and all poor households in urban areas of the country. Under the aegis of SAUBHAGYA, all households were reported electrified by the States, except few households in Left Wing Extremists (LWE) affected areas of Chhattisgarh.

RECENT ACHIEVEMENTS IN POWER AND ENERGY SECTOR

- As on 31 December, 2024, the Installed Generation Capacity of Power Sector in India is 4,62,002 MW which consists of Total fossil fuel installed capacity of 2,44,377 MW and total non-fossil fuel installed capacity of 2,17,625 MW.
- With the implementation of the Revamped Distribution Sector Scheme (RDSS), the daily average power supply has improved to 23.4 hours in FY24 in the urban areas and to 21.9 hours in the rural areas.
- Due to significant additions in generation and transmission capacities, energy shortages at the national level have reduced to a mere 0.1 per cent in FY 2024–25, a major improvement from 4.2 per cent in FY 2013–14.

Last Minute SNIPPETS

India successfully met an all-time maximum power demand of 250 GW during FY 2024–25.

Transforming the Power Sector in India

From power deficit to power surplus by addition of over **175 GW of generation capacity in the past 9 years**	**4th globally** in Renewable Energy Installed Capacity, with **43% of its total installed capacity from renewables**
2.86 crore houses connected with electricity under SAUBHAGYA	**100% village electrification** under DDUGJY
Procured price of LED bulbs decreased by almost 90% between 2014 and 2019 under UJALA	**Distribution losses of DISCOMS reduced** from 21.5% to 16.5% under RDSS

- As of January 2025, the country's non-fossil fuel energy capacity has reached 217.62 GW.
- Government of India has finalised **National Electricity Plan** from 2023 to 2032 for Central and State transmission systems to meet a peak demand of 458 GW by 2032. Under this plan, the transformation capacity will increase from 1,290 Giga Volt Ampere (GVA) to 2,342 GVA in 2032 and transmission network in the country will be expanded.

GOVERNMENT INITIATIVES IN THE POWER SECTOR

- In the Union Budget 2022–23, the government announced the issuing of **sovereign green bonds**, as well as the designation of energy storage systems, particularly grid-scale battery systems, as infrastructure.
- To promote Roof Top Solar (RTS) across the country, the *Ministry of New and Renewable Energy* has created a National Portal via which any home customer from any part of the country may apply for rooftop solar without having to wait for Discom to finalise tenders and empanel suppliers.
- **Production-Linked Incentive Scheme (Tranche II)** for **'National Programme on High-Efficiency Solar PV Modules'**.
- The **Green Energy Corridor** initiatives have been launched to ease renewable energy evacuation and reconfigure the system for future needs.
- The country's electrification is rising because of initiatives such as the **DeenDayal Upadhyaya Gram Jyoti Yojana (DDUGJY)**, the **Ujwal DISCOM Assurance Yojana (UDAY)**, and the **Integrated Power Development Scheme (IPDS)**.
- The **Pradhan Mantri Sahaj Bijli Har Ghar Yojana**, or **'Saubhagya,'** was initiated by the Government of India to attain universal home electrification.
- The **National Smart Grid Mission** was formed by the Government of India to develop and supervise the implementation of Smart Grid policies and projects in India. The NSGM also plans capacity-building programmes for distribution Sector staff in the realm of Smart Grids.
- The **Mission on Advanced and High-Impact Research (MAHIR)** was recently established to utilise emerging technologies in the power sector.
- The Government of India launched **the Revamped Distribution Sector Scheme (RDSS)** to assist DISCOMs in improving their operational efficiencies and financial sustainability by providing result-linked financial assistance to strengthen supply infrastructure based on pre-qualifying criteria and meeting basic minimum benchmarks.
- **Unnat Jyoti by Affordable LED for All (UJALA)** programme has been launched. Under the UJALA initiative, LED bulbs, LED tube lights, and energy-efficient fans are marketed to home consumers in substitution of conventional and inefficient alternatives.
- **The Street Lighting National Programme (SLNP)** was launched to replace conventional street lights with smart and energy-efficient LED street lights across India.
- Ministry of Coal has launched the **'Mine Closure Portal'**, developed by Coal India Limited in 2024, aiming to reduce accidents and improve safety practices across the industry. The objective of this portal is to improve Safety Management practices within the coal industry and to decrease accidents and incidents significantly.

> **did you KNOW?** **The National Mission for Enhanced Energy Efficiency (NMEEE)** is one of the eight missions of the National Action Plan on Climate Change (NAPCC).

ELECTRICITY (AMENDMENT) BILL, 2022

The Electricity (Amendment) Bill, 2022 was introduced in Parliament amid objections and subsequently referred to the Standing Committee for further consideration. It allows consumers to select any service provider and to grant other companies unrestricted access to power suppliers' distribution networks. The Bill amends the Electricity Act of 2003, which governs India's power industry. It establishes the Central and State Electricity Regulatory Commissions (CERC and SERCs) to oversee interstate and intrastate electricity regulation.

Provisions of the Bill

- Allows multiple Discoms in the same region. Multiple power distributors can operate in the same location.
- The regulator must decide within 90 days; otherwise, the application will be declared granted.
- It will put an end to distribution monopolies while improving corporate viability.
    1. To prevent electricity distribution businesses from charging high prices and safeguard customers.
    2. 'Mandatory' fixing of minimum as well as maximum tariff ceilings by the 'appropriate commission'.
- Promotion of **green energy.**

ENERGY TRANSITION INDEX

The **World Economic Forum (WEF)** publishes the worldwide **Energy Transition Index (ETI)** under the title **'Fostering Effective Energy Transition'** to monitor the worldwide transition to reliable, efficient, and economical renewable energy. The Index assesses 120 nations, depending on how well they have transitioned to renewable energy. It also assists governments in formulating energy transition strategies.

Last Minute SNIPPETS

India is placed at 63rd on the **World Economic Forum's Energy Transition Index 2024 rankings, improving its rank of 67th from 2023.**

Sweden has topped the index in 2024, followed by Denmark, Finland, Switzerland, and France.

Energy Transition Index, 2024

This report is published by WEF by evaluating **120 countries** on their **energy system performance and readiness for secure, sustainable, and inclusive energy systems.**

India has been improving its energy equity, security, and sustainability while 83 per cent of countries moved backwards from the last year in at least one of these three energy system performance dimensions, highlighting the difficulty in establishing a balanced transition.

The 2024 report has appreciated India's growth in the renewable energy sector where it now generates 42 per cent of its power from renewable sources and biomass, placing it as the world's fourth largest renewables market.

Since 2014, global average ETI scores have improved by 10 per cent, although only marginally during the last three years.

BONUS KNOWLEDGE

INDIAN ENERGY EXCHANGE (IEX)

- It is a **power/electricity trading platform** regulated by the Central Electricity Regulatory Commission **(CERC)**.
- It is the **first and largest** energy exchange in India providing a nationwide, automated trading platform for physical delivery of electricity, Renewable Energy Certificates and Energy Saving Certificates.
- It enables efficient price discovery and increases the accessibility and transparency of the power market in India.
- It started its operations in **2008**, and is headquartered in **Delhi**.
- IEX provides an electronic platform to the various participants in power market, comprising State Electricity Boards, Power producers, Power Traders and Open Access Consumers (both Industrial and Commercial).
- The Exchange is a publicly listed company with NSE as well as BSE.
- **Real-Time Electricity Market (RTM)** has been launched by IEX in **2020**.

BONUS KNOWLEDGE

INDIAN GAS EXCHANGE

- Indian Gas Exchange Ltd. (IGX) is India's first automated national level Gas Exchange to promote and sustain an efficient and robust **Natural Gas** market and to foster gas trading in the country. IGX started operations in **2020** as Gas Trading Platform and has been operating as the Gas Exchange since **2020**.
- IGX is a neutral and transparent marketplace where both buyers and sellers trade gas as the underlying commodity.
- IGX enables efficient and competitive discovery of gas prices and one of its most important objectives is also to maintain market integrity.
- IGX is regulated by the Petroleum and Natural Gas Regulatory Board **(PNGRB)**.

CHALLENGES IN ENERGY SECTOR

- **Security of Fuel:** Concerns regarding fuel supply and reliance on imported coal limit thermal capacity growth.
- **Transmission Losses:** High distribution-line losses in the electrical industry widen the demand-supply imbalance.
- **Financial Health of State DISCOMS:** Debt accrual as a result of populist tariffs and operational inefficiencies harms Discoms' financial health.
- **Power under-procurement:** Due to lack of fuel, budgetary constraints, and large AT&C losses, State Discoms predicted lower demand.
- **Interstate Disputes:** Disputes over river management have an impact on hydroelectric facilities and limit power transmission between states.
- **Financing Instability:** Rising loan rates cause project cost overruns and tariff increases.

- **Limited role of Private and Foreign Entrepreneurs:** The public sector practically has a monopoly in the electricity generation industry. Due to a lack of management facilities, the public sector is unable to meet the problems of electricity generation. Private and international entrepreneurs have not had an opportunity to exhibit their competence.
- **Policy Inefficiency:** Micro-level policies must be consistent with broader policies such as the Electricity Act of 2003 and the National Electricity Policy.

SOLUTIONS TO FOREGO CHALLENGES

- **Fuel Reforms:** Various aspects, such as increasing coal production by both the public and private sectors in a timely manner, increasing private sector participation in coal production, and easing regulatory frameworks, clearances, and approvals for allocation and development of coal blocks and gas infrastructure, must be addressed when formulating such reform.
- **Arriving at an Appropriate Fuel Mix:** There is an urgent need to create both conventional and non-conventional kinds of energy, and three main elements must be kept in mind while building an energy mix – **(i) The country's energy consumption pattern; (ii) fuel availability; and (iii) fuel production and import prices.** It would be advantageous to accept coal thermal as a basic component of the fuel mix over the next 20–30 years, with solar accounting for 5–8 per cent of the whole mix.
- **Balanced Regulatory Interventions:** Regulators must be aware of the sector's issues, and a policy framework must be developed and implemented to provide a win-win outcome for all stakeholders. They must take proactive measures to address the current difficulties plaguing the electricity industry.
- **Enhanced Financing Facilities for the Energy Sector:** A strong and long-term credit enhancement mechanism for funding in the energy sector must be established via enhanced engagement in the whole value chain by global funding organisations such as the **World Bank** and the **Asian Development Bank.**
- **Public-Private Partnership Model:** There is a considerable need to advocate for the widespread deployment of public-private partnership models. The private sector has played an important role in electricity generation; a more conducive environment would assist to bridge the country's energy gap.

India's power and energy sector has enormous development potential, driven by rising demand, government initiatives, and an emphasis on renewable energy. The government's commitment to sustainable energy solutions, as well as ongoing investments in the industry, will help to drive its further growth and transformation.

SUMMARY

- **Main Sources of Energy** – Conventional (coal, lignite, natural gas, oil, and nuclear power) and Non-conventional (wind, solar, agricultural and residential waste) sources.
- **Conventional Sources** – Coal (two major geological eras: Gondwana and Tertiary) – **Damodar Valley** is home to India's largest **Gondwana coal** reserves – Assam, Arunachal Pradesh, Meghalaya, and Nagaland have **tertiary coal** reserves.

- **Non-conventional Sources** – Solar energy – Sun energy may be used in two ways: **solar thermal** and **solar electric (photovoltaic)**, wind energy – wind's kinetic energy is converted into electrical energy, biomass energy – the **carbonaceous waste** generated by a range of human and natural activities is utilised to produce biomass, a renewable energy source.
- **National Solar Mission** – The National Solar Mission, also known as the **Jawaharlal Nehru National Solar Mission (JNNSM)**, is a joint effort by the Central and State Governments of India to promote the growth of solar power throughout the country.
- **Limitations of Non-conventional Energy** – Weather Dependency, Storage Insufficiency, Capacity Limitations, High Initial Expense, Environmental Impact.
- **Challenges of Electricity Distributions in India** – High AT&C losses, poor financial health, tariff determination, lack of metering, etc.
- **Electricity (Amendment) Bill, 2022** – It allows consumers to select any service provider and to grant other companies unrestricted access to power suppliers' distribution networks. It establishes the Central and **State Electricity Regulatory Commissions (CERC and SERCs)** to oversee interstate and intrastate electricity regulation.
- **Energy Transition Index, 2024** – India is placed at 63rd on the **World Economic Forum's Energy Transition Index**, making it the only large economy with rising energy transition momentum in all aspects.
- **Challenges of Energy Sector** – Security of fuel, transmission losses, poor financial health of state DISCOMS, limited role of private and foreign entrepreneurs, policy inefficiency.

UPSC CSE PREVIOUS YEARS' PRELIMINARY EXAMINATION QUESTIONS

☞ NO QUESTIONS ASKED
2024, 2023, 2022, 2021, 2020, 2019, 2018, 2017, 2016, 2015, 2014, 2013

UPSC CSE PREVIOUS YEARS' MAIN EXAMINATION QUESTIONS

1. Do you think India will meet 50 per cent of its energy needs from renewable energy by 2030? Justify your answer. How will shift of subsidies from fossil fuels to renewables help achieve the above objective? **[2022]**

☞ NO QUESTIONS ASKED
2024, 2023, 2021, 2020, 2019, 2018, 2017, 2016, 2015, 2014, 2013

CHAPTER

26

HEALTH AND EDUCATION

CHAPTER OUTLINE

Health

- Major Achievements for India in Healthcare
- Health Policies in India
- National Nutrition Policy 1993
- National Nutrition Strategy 2017
- Universal Health Coverage
- Health Insurance in India
- Rural Health Care System
- Steps Taken to Promote the Indian System of Medicines
- Investment Opportunities in India's
- Healthcare Sector, State Health Index

Education

- University Education Commission 1948
- Secondary Education Commission (1952–53)
- Kothari Commission 1964
- National Policy on Education 1968
- National Policy on Education 1986
- Sarva Shiksha Abhiyan, Mid-Day Meal Scheme
- National Curriculum Framework 2005
- Right of Children to Free and Compulsory Education Act, 2009
- National Education Policy 2020
- Rural Education Statistics

HEALTH – INTRODUCTION

Healthcare has been one of the most important social sectors in India since Independence. Providing healthcare services at affordable rates to the public has been a challenging task with a growing population and necessity of maintaining a healthy workforce. In this context, the scenario of the Indian healthcare system with recent changes implemented needs an elaborate discussion.

Major Achievements in Healthcare

- Eradication of **Smallpox** – late 1970s.
- India got the **'Polio-free certification'** from the World Health Organization in **2014. The Pulse Polio programme was** introduced in 1995.
- India achieved the goal of elimination of Leprosy as a public health problem, set by the **National Health Policy, 2002.** India was declared **'Leprosy-free' in 2005,** but the country still accounts for almost 66 per cent of the world's new Leprosy patients.

  New initiatives:
  - National Strategic Plan and Roadmap for Leprosy (2023–27).
  - National Guidelines for Antimicrobial Resistance (AMR) Surveillance in Leprosy.

- Launch of Viksit Bharat Sankalp Yatra (VBSY), Aapke Dwar Ayushman 3.0, Ayushman Sabhas, Ayushman Melas, Ayushman App.

- **Universal Immunisation Programme (UIP)** was launched in **1985.**
- The **Pre-Conception and Pre-Natal Diagnostic Techniques (Regulation and Prevention of Misuse) Act, 1994 (PCPNDT) was** enacted.
- **The Cigarettes and Other Tobacco Products Act (COTPA) 2003 was enacted.**
- **Yaws** has been eliminated from India in 2006.
- Recently, more than one crore people have been screened for Sickle Cell Disease under the National Sickle Cell Anaemia Elimination Mission.

> **did you KNOW?**
>
> **National Institute of Communicable Diseases (NICD)**
>
> The erstwhile **Malaria Institute of India (MII)** was renamed as **NICD** on 30 July 1963. The institute was established to function as a **national centre of excellence to control communicable diseases.**

Steps taken by India to reduce the prevalence and impact of Non-communicable diseases (NCDs) are as follows:

- **National Programme for Prevention and Control of Non-Communicable Diseases (NP-NCD):** It was launched under the National Health Mission (NHM) in 2010. It aims to strengthen infrastructure, human resource development, health promotion, early diagnosis, management and referral.
- **75/25 initiative:** It ensures screening and providing standard of care for 75 million individuals with hypertension and diabetes by 2025.
- **Population-Based Screening (PBS):** It is organised under the umbrella of Comprehensive Primary Health Care (CPHC) across Ayushman Bharat – Health and Wellness Centres (AB-HWC).
- Screening of common NCDs (hypertension, diabetes, oral cancer, breast cancer and cervical cancer) is done for the individuals in the age groups of 30 years and above.

Health Policies in India

Name of the Health Policy	Name of the Ministry	Key Features
National Health Policy 1983	Ministry of Health and Family Welfare	• **Health for All by the Year 2000** • Primary health care and population stabilisation • Medical and Health Education • Well-considered health insurance schemes
National Health Policy 2002	Ministry of Health and Family Welfare	• Intermediation through '**Health volunteers'** • Evenly spread speciality and super-speciality services • Time-bound and well-dispersed network of comprehensive primary health care services • Alternative Systems of Medicine in India
National Health Policy 2017	Ministry of Health and Family Welfare	• Free drugs, free diagnostics, free emergency and essential health care services in all public hospitals • By the year 2025, the under-five mortality rate to be reduced to 23 • Establishment of National Digital Health Authority (NDHA)

GOALS AND ACHIEVEMENTS

India was certified as Polio-free by the World Health Organization (WHO)	2014
A new goal is set through the National Leprosy Eradication Program (NLEP) aims to eliminate leprosy in every district	2030
A new goal is set to Eliminate HIV/AIDS (As per National Strategic Plan)	2030
To eliminate Kala Azar	2023
Eliminate Lymphatic filariasis	2027

a. Reduce the prevalence of avoidable blindness to 0.25 per cent – by 2025. National Programme for Control of blindness and Visual Impairment is implemented to achieve this goal.

b. India's MMR has reduced to 97/lakh live births in 2018–20 as compared to 130/lakh live births in 2014–16. SDG target for MMR is 70/lakh live births by 2030.

c. India's IMR has reduced from 58/1000 in 2005 to [35.2/1000 in 2019–21 (NFHS 5)] (SRS Report).

d. Increase health expenditure by Government as a percent of GDP from existing 2.1 per cent to 2.5 per cent by 2025.

NUTRITION

Nutrition and health are intricately linked for ensuring well-being of the population.

National Nutrition Policy 1993

The **National Nutrition Policy 1993** was formulated by the **Ministry of Women and Child Development, GoI,** to combat the problem of undernutrition.

Instruments of Nutrition Policy

Direct Short-Term Intervention

- To expand the nutrition intervention net through **Integrated Child Development Services (ICDS).**
- **Fortification of essential foods** – salt with iodine, iron, etc.
- Popularisation of **low-cost nutritious foods** from indigenous and locally available raw material, and to involve women in this activity.
- Control of **micro-nutrient deficiencies amongst vulnerable groups.**

Indirect Policy Instruments

The long-term strategies included:

- **Food Security:** A target of attaining **per capita availability of 215 kg/person/year of foodgrains** in order to ensure aggregate food security.
- **Improving the dietary pattern** and promotion of the production and increase the per capita availability of nutritionally rich foods.

- Policies for effecting **income transfers** to improve the entitlement package of the rural and urban poor.
- **Prevention of food adulteration** and gearing up the enforcement machinery.
- Ensuring minimum wage administration, education lit literacy, improvement of the status of women etc.

National Nutrition Strategy (NNS) 2017

National Nutrition Strategy (NNS) was published by **NITI Aayog** in 2017. An important mission under this strategy was Vision 2022.

- **Vision 2022: Kuposhan Mukt Bharat (Malnutrition-Free India).**

Objectives and Targets

- 3-point percentage/year reduction in underweight prevalence in children (0–3 years) by 2022 from NFHS-4 levels.
- 1/3rd reduction in anaemia in children, adolescents and Women of Reproductive Age (WRA).

Key Strategic Areas under NNS	Governance reform
	Convergence
	Prioritise action
	Intensification of counselling to reach the critical age group
	Innovative service delivery models
	Community based monitoring

- **Nutrition-specific interventions:**
  - i. Infant and young child care and nutrition
  - ii. Maternal care
  - iii. Nutrition and health
  - iv. Infant and young child health
  - v. Adolescent care
  - vi. Nutrition and health
  - vii. Addressing micronutrient deficiencies – including anaemia etc.

UNIVERSAL HEALTH COVERAGE

The **High-Level Expert Group (HLEG) on Universal Health Coverage (UHC)** was constituted in 2010, by the Planning Commission of India for providing easily accessible and affordable health care to all Indians. India is committed to **achieve Universal Health Care for all by 2030** which is fundamental to achieve the other Sustainable Development Goals.

Launching of **Ayushman Bharat Pradhan Mantri Jan Arogya Yojana (AB-PMJAY)** was a step towards UHC which intends to ensure that all people have access to quality health services - including prevention, promotion, treatment, rehabilitation, and palliation.

Source: High Level Expert Group Report on Universal Health Coverage for India, 2011

The PMJAY aims to provide insurance cover to the poorest 40 per cent of the population. **Over 50 crore Indians** are covered under PMJAY with a **medical insurance cover of ₹5 lakh per family per year.**

Key Challenges to Health Coverage in India

(i) Wide disparity in the quality of healthcare services in the public and private hospitals.

(ii) Traditional healers and quacks treating patients at the grass-root level in villages is a serious concern.

(iii) Non-affordability of healthcare services and low medical insurance coverage etc.

(iv) In some states, out-of-pocket expenses is significantly high, which indicates enhanced government spending is not sufficient.

(v) Critical shortage of healthcare professionals in rural areas including doctors, nurses, and allied health workers.

Rural Health Care System in India

The existing three tier system of health care infrastructure in rural India is as follows:

Primary Health Centre (PHC) It is the first contact point between the medical officer and village community. PHC is to be manned by a medical officer supported by paramedical and other staffs.

Sub Centre Most peripheral and first contact point between Primary Health Care System and Community. It is manned with at least one auxiliary nurse midwife (ANM)/female health worker and one male health worker. In order to provide complete primary healthcare services through these centres, the Ayushman Bharat programme is improving SCs and PHCs by gradually transforming them into **Health and Wellness Centers (HWCs).**

Community Health Centre (CHC) It is a 30-bedded Hospital or Referral Unit for PHCs with specialized services. CHCs are maintained under the Minimum Needs Program (MNP) or Basic Minimum Services (BMS) Program by the State Governments.

First Referral Unit (FRU) District Hospital, Sub-divisional Hospital, Community Health Centre, etc. can be declared a fully operational FRU if it provides round-the-clock services for emergency obstetric and new born care.

3-tier system of health care

Health Insurance in India

Indian healthcare system consists of more than 1.3 billion potential beneficiaries and health insurance is a growing segment of it. The health insurance industry has grown significantly after Liberalisation, Privatisation, Globalisation (LPG) reforms.

General Insurance Corporation of India is a nationalised reinsurance company under the Ministry of Finance and was incorporated in 1972 under the Companies Act, 1956. The **National Health Insurance Programme (Rashtriya Swastha Bima Yojana – RSBY)** was launched in 2007.

In 2021, NITI Aayog released a comprehensive report titled ***"Health Insurance for India's Missing Middle".***

According to the report – "At least 30 per cent of the population, or 40 crore individuals – called the **missing middle** in this report – are devoid of any financial protection for health", and "expansion of health insurance/assurance coverage is a necessary step, and a pathway in India's effort to achieve Universal Health Coverage (UHC)".

India's health sector is characterised by -

- Low Government expenditure on health,
- High **Out Of Pocket Expenditure,** and
- Low financial protection for adverse health events.

To increase health coverage, the report recommends extending PMJAY coverage to **'missing middle'.**

Government Schemes in Healthcare

EXAM ESSENTIAL

Name of the Scheme	Key Features
Ayushman Bharat	• Recommended under the **National Health Policy 2017** to achieve the vision of **Universal Health Coverage (UHC).** • It has two interlinked components – **Health and Wellness Centre (HWC)** and **Pradhan Mantri Jan Arogya Yojana (PM-JAY)** • **National Health Authority (NHA)** under the Ministry of Health and Family Welfare is the implementing agency for **Ayushman Bharat.**
Ayushman Bharat Digital Mission (ABDM)	• Launched on **27 September 2021** • The key components include – I. A **Health ID** for every citizen as their health account II. A Healthcare Professionals Registry (HPR) III. Healthcare Facilities Registries (HFR) • Ayushman Bharat Digital Mission Sandbox is a part of the Mission which acts as a framework for technology and product testing to help organisations
Janani Suraksha Yojana (JSY)	• The Yojana was launched on **12 April 2005**. • This initiative aims to reduce maternal and newborn mortality and promote institutional delivery for pregnant women from Scheduled Castes, Scheduled Tribes, and BPL households. • Eligible pregnant women, regardless of age or number of children, can get monetary support for giving birth at a government or accredited private health institution.
National Health Mission	In 2013, the Indian government merged the National Rural Health Mission and National Urban Health Mission to launch National Health Mission. It ensures • Reduction of Maternal Mortality Rate (MMR) to 100/1 lakh live births • Decrease of Infant Mortality rate (IMR) to 25/1000 live births • Lowering of Total Fertility Rate (TFR) to 2.1 • Prevention and reduction of anaemia in women aged between 15 and 49 years • Prevent and decrease mortality and morbidity from communicable, non-communicable, injuries, and new illnesses • Lower annual incidence and mortality from Tuberculosis by half • Reduce leprosy prevalence to <1/10000 people and achieve zero incidence in all areas • Annual Malaria Incidence has to be <1/1000 • Less than 1 per cent microfilaria prevalence in all districts • Kala-azar Elimination by 2015, <1 case per 10000 population in all blocks
National Digital Health Mission (NDHM)	• Launched in 2020 • Implemented by the **National Health Authority (NHA) under the Ministry of Health and Family Welfare** • **National Digital Health Blueprint (NDHB)** recommended by **J. Satyanarayana Committee (2019)** is the guiding document for the implementation of National Digital Health Mission in India.

Name of the Scheme	Key Features
Anaemia Mukt Bharat (Anaemia-Free India)	• It is a flagship initiative of the Government of India which aims to eradicate anaemia among mothers, children, and adolescents. • It was launched in 2018. • It is a life cycle approach providing preventive and curative mechanisms through a 6X6X6 strategy, including six target beneficiaries, six interventions and six institutional mechanisms for all stakeholders to implement the strategy.
eSanjeevani	• It is an innovative, indigenous, cost-effective, and integrated cloud-based telemedicine system application that enables patient-to-doctor teleconsultation to provide a continuum of care and facilitate health services to all citizens in the comfort of their homes, free of cost. • Two Verticles of this service are- I. Ayushman Bharat Health and Wellness Centres (AB-HWCs) II. eSanjeevaniOPD
Pradhan Mantri Surakshit Matritva Abhiyan (PMSMA)	• Launched in 2016, the aim of the programme is to reduce maternal and neonatal deaths. • PMSMA intends to provide comprehensive and quality antenatal care, free of cost to all pregnant women on the 9th of every month. • It guarantees a minimum package of antenatal care services to women in their $2^{nd}/3^{rd}$ trimesters of pregnancy at designated government health facilities. • The program adopts a systematic approach for engagement with private sector, motivating private practitioners to volunteer for the campaign developing strategies to generate awareness and appeal to the private sector to participate in the Abhiyan at government health facilities. • PMSMA was **extended in 2022** with name Extended-PMSMA (**E-PMSMA**), which is specifically designed to track **High-Risk Pregnancies (HRPs)** and ensure timely interventions.
Aarogya Maitri	• Launched in 2023, it is a humanitarian initiative that extends India's commitment to global health and disaster relief. • It aims to offer **essential medical supplies** to **developing countries** affected by natural disasters or humanitarian crises.

EXAM ESSENTIAL

BHISHM

Bharat Health Initiative for Sahyog Hita & Maitri (BHISHM), part of Project Aarogya Maitri, is an innovative **emergency medical aid programme**. Under it, portable '**mini cubes**' filled with essential medicines and equipment, designed for rapid deployment in various emergencies. The cube comprises 72 easily transportable components, designed for versatile delivery methods including hand-carry, bicycle, or even drone transport. In mass casualty incidents, the entire unit can be set up within 12 minutes, bridging the crucial gap between primary and definitive care during the critical 'golden hour' of emergencies.

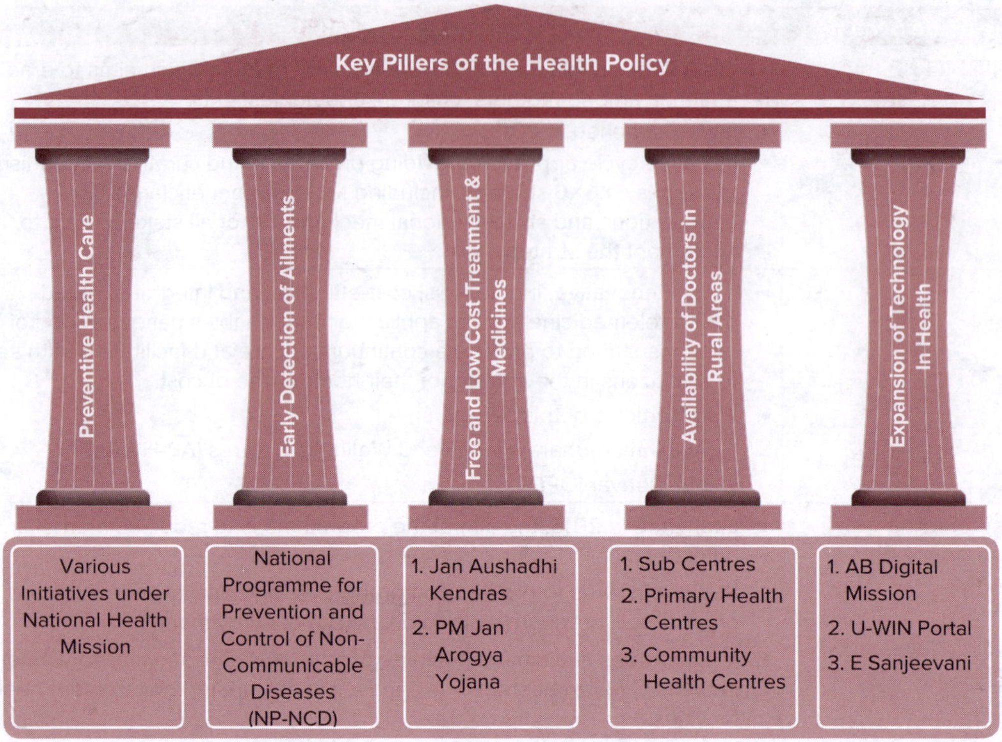

Source: Economic Survey 2024–25

BONUS KNOWLEDGE

NATIONAL DIGITAL HEALTH BLUEPRINT (NDHB)

Ministry of Health and Family Welfare has released the **National Digital Health Blueprint (NDHB)** recommended by **J. Satyanarayana Committee (2019).** This is the guiding document for implementation of National Digital Health Mission in India.

NDHB helps in providing a common platform for integration of existing disparate applications in health domain and data in public and private healthcare facilities in India.

Recommendations

- A new entity, **National Digital Health Mission (NDHM)**, is recommended to be established as a purely **government organisation** with complete functional autonomy on the lines of existing Unique Identification Authority of India (UIDAI) and Goods and Services Tax Network (GSTN).
- Establishing and managing the **core digital health data and the infrastructure** required for its seamless exchange.
- Developing a system of **Personal Health Records according to international standards in electronic format** based on citizen-consent which will be easily accessible to the citizens and to the service providers.
- Following the **best principles of cooperative federalism** while working with the States and Union Territories for the realisation of the vision.
- Promoting **Health Data Analytics** and **Medical Research**.
- Enhancing the **efficiency and effectiveness of Governance** at all levels.
- Ensuring **Quality** of healthcare.

STEPS TAKEN TO PROMOTE THE INDIAN SYSTEM OF MEDICINES

- Ministry of **AYUSH** has signed 13 MoUs to set up AYUSH Academic Chairs with foreign Universities to promote the education of Indian System of Medicines and Ayurveda.
- A scheme for Voluntary Certification of Yoga Professionals has been launched by the Ministry of AYUSH to certify the competence level of Yoga professionals.
- **Yoga Certification Board (YCB)** has been set up to bring synergy, uniformity and quality in skills and knowledge of Yoga professionals.
- Centrally Sponsored Scheme of **National AYUSH Mission (NAM)** is being implemented in the country through State and UT Governments to promote AYUSH systems.
- **'SMART'** (Scope for Mainstreaming Ayurveda Research in Teaching Professionals): The National Commission for Indian System of Medicine (NCISM) and the Central Council for Research in Ayurvedic Sciences (CCRAS), the two prominent institutions under the Ministry of Ayush, have launched 'SMART' programme aimed to boost quality research in priority healthcare research areas through Ayurveda colleges and hospitals.
- Several promotional activities like AROGYA fairs at State and National levels; multimedia campaigns etc. are undertaken by the Ministry of AYUSH.
- The Ministry of Health and Family Welfare (MoHFW) has launched an initiative to accelerate the nation's progress towards **TB eradication** by 2025.

  Components:

  i. Ni-kshay Mitra Initiative.
  ii. Ni-kshay Digital Portal.
- **Sarva Dawa Sevan or Mass Drug Administration (MDA):** The campaign was launched by Ministry of Health & Family Welfare to eliminate Lymphatic Filariasis (LF) by 2027, three years ahead of the global target.
- **WHO – Global Center for Traditional Medicine (WHO – GCTM):** This is the first centre of its kind taking shape in Jamnagar, Gujarat. During the valedictory function of World Ayurveda, three National Ayush Institutes of Eminence in Ayurveda, Unani and Homoeopathy were inaugurated –

  i. All India Institute of Ayurveda in Goa,
  ii. National Institute of Unani Medicine in Ghaziabad, and
  iii. National Institute of Homeopathy in Delhi.

NATIONAL TB ELIMINATION PROGRAMME (NTEP) 100 DAYS CAMPAIGN – DEC 2024 TO MARCH 2025

Tuberculosis (TB) is an infectious disease caused by a bacterium, Mycobacterium tuberculosis and usually spreads through respiratory droplets/ droplet nuclei in the air.

The National TB Elimination Programme (NTEP) or TB Mukt Bharat Abhiyan is a Centrally Sponsored Scheme, being implemented under the umbrella of National Health Mission (NHM) wherein free diagnostic and quality assured treatment are provided to all TB patients, along with nutritional support.

> **did you KNOW?** Since 2015, the annual TB incidence rate has declined by 18% and the mortality rate has declined 22% as of 2023. TB incidence rate has decreased from 237 cases per lakh population (in 2015) to 195 (in 2023). Similarly, TB death rate has decreased from 28 deaths per lakh population (in 2015) to 22 (in 2023).

The **100-day intensified TB-Mukt Bharat Abhiyaan**, launched in 33 States/UTs in December 2024, is an outcome of a new strategy for early TB identification and taking necessary measures.

Goals of the 100 days campaign are:

a. To increase case detection through intensified IEC campaign.

b. To reduce death among people with TB by implementing a differentiated TB care approach with nutritional support interventions.

c. To prevent occurrence of new TB cases in the community by providing TB preventive treatment to household contacts, PLHIV and vulnerable populations.

Activities under the 100 days campaign include:

1. Screening and Testing of Vulnerable Population.
2. Promptly initiation of treatment for diagnosed patients.
3. To ensure Ni-kshay Poshan Yojana benefits to all TB patients and nutrition kits for family members through Ni-kshay mitras.
4. After ruling out TB, provide TB preventive treatment for eligible high-risk individuals.

EDUCATION

Soon after Independence, it was felt that **Education for All (EFA)** was a must to achieve socio-economic progress, and education was set as a praiseworthy goal after 1947. A separate department for education was established at the centre and in all the States. Constitutional provisions also elucidated the actions to be taken by the Government and education has undergone a sea change since then.

Important Historical Developments

Important Commissions for the development of Education

Name of the Commission	Chairman	Objective	Recommendation
University Education Commission 1948	Dr. S. Radhakrishnan	To study the problems of university education	• To place education in the concurrent list • UGC should be set up to allocate funds • Rural universities should be established • Need to establish colleges for women • English should be the medium of instruction
Secondary Education Commission (1952–53)	Dr. Lakshmanaswami Mudaliar	To address the issues of school education	• A three-year national system of secondary education • Implementation of a diversified curriculum at secondary stage

Name of the Commission	Chairman	Objective	Recommendation
Kothari Commission 1964	Daulat Singh Kothari	To review the existing educational system and suggest for a betterment	• Free and compulsory education for children aged 6 to 14 years • Three language formula to be adopted • Academic freedom of teachers to pursue independent studies • Promotion of game and sports to improve physical fitness • Creation of Indian Education Service on the lines of Indian Administrative Service

Important Policies/Acts/Schemes/Agencies related to Education

National Policy on Education 1968 (based on the recommendations of Kothari Commission 1964)	• Recommended '**energetic development of Indian languages and literature**' for educational and cultural development • Three language formula and **promotion of Hindi and Sanskrit** • Special emphasis on study of English and other international languages • Development of education for agriculture and industry • Production of quality books, promotion of games and sports and adoption of 10+2+3 pattern
National Policy on Education 1986	• Emphasised to remove disparities and equalise educational opportunity for women, Scheduled Caste and the Scheduled Tribes • '**Operation Blackboard**' was launched in 1987 to provide essential facilities to the primary schools • It recommended to **initiate Open University** system, establish rural universities, and stressed on value education
Operation Digital Board (ODB) Launched by MHRD (now Ministry of Education)	Launched to provide digital and interactive boards in every classroom, on the lines of Operation Blackboard which started in 1987
Mid-Day Meal Scheme (launched in 1995)	• Launched as the National Programme of Nutritional Support to Primary Education (NP-NSPE), a centrally sponsored scheme • Re-launched in 2004 as the **Mid-Day Meal Scheme** in which one meal is guaranteed to all students in Government and Govt-aided schools and madrasahs and supported under Samagra Shiksha. It was initially started with the coverage of students only from Classes I-V, it was extended till class VIII in 2007 • According to the 'Mid-Day Meal Rules, 2015' under National Food Security Act, 2013, if Mid-Day Meal is not provided in school, the State Government shall pay food security allowance. The School Management Committee (mandated under the Right of Children to Free and Compulsory Education Act, 2009) monitors the implementation of the scheme. The Headmaster or Headmistress of the school is empowered to utilise the fund

	• Mid-day meals should provide **450 calories** and 12 grams of protein for children studying in classes I–V and **700 calories** and 20 grams of protein for children in classes VI–VIII. • In 2021, the scheme was renamed as **PM-POSHAN** (*Pradhan Mantri Poshan Shakti Nirman*) Scheme, by the **Ministry of Education**, the ministry responsible for the scheme. • The Centre and State share the cost of the Midday Meal Scheme in the ratio **60:40**.
National Curriculum Framework 2005	NCERT published fourth National Curriculum Framework 2005. It provided a guideline for syllabus, school and classroom environment, textbooks, etc. It was based on various reports of the government on education like '**Learning Without Burden**'.
Right of Children to Free and Compulsory Education Act, 2009 (RTE ACT)	• It was enacted on 4 August 2009 • It provides for free and compulsory education for children between the ages of 6 and 14 years in India under Article 21A of the Indian Constitution • It is mandatory for private schools to reserve 25 per cent of their seats for children belonging to economically weaker sections • The National Commission for the Protection of Child Rights shall examine the safeguards for violation of RTE
National Education Policy 2020	• Approved by the Central Government in 2020 and replaced the 34-year-old National Policy on Education (NPE) 1986 • Universalise the education from pre-school to secondary level with per cent Gross Enrolment Ratio (GER) by 2030 • The current 10+2 system is suggested to be replaced by **5+3+3+4 curricular structure** (corresponding ages 3–8, 8–11, 11–14, and 14–18 years) • Ensures no hard separations between arts and sciences, between curricular and extra-curricular activities, between vocational and academic streams • Setting up of a new National Assessment Centre, **PARAKH** (Performance Assessment, Review, and Analysis of Knowledge for Holistic Development) • The Centre and the States are working together to increase the public investment in Education sector to reach 6% of GDP at the earliest
National Testing Agency (NTA)	• NTA was set up by the Ministry of Education in **2017** as a premier, specialist, autonomous and self-sustained testing organisation. • It is registered as a Society under the Societies Registration Act (1860). • **The objectives of NTA** include: 1. Conduct efficient and **international Standards tests** to assess candidates' competency for admission and recruitment purposes. 2. Undertake **research on educational, professional and testing system.** 3. Identify **experts and institutions** in setting examination questions. 4. **Produce and disseminate information and research** on education and professional development standards. • In 2024, the **Radhakrishnan panel** recommended restructuring of National Testing Agency, following complaints of question paper leak in CUET-UG. The recommendations include - DigiExam on lines of DigiYatra; Restructuring of NTA to conduct higher education entrance exams only; Institutional linkage with state/district authorities; Mobile Testing Centres to facilitate candidates from rural, remote and thinly populated areas.

EXAM ESSENTIAL

PM SCHOOLS FOR RISING INDIA (PM SHRI)

The Cabinet approved this centrally sponsored scheme in 2022. These schools showcase the implementation of the National Education Policy 2020 and emerge as exemplar schools over a period of time, and also provide guidance to other schools in the neighbourhood. Under this scheme, there is a provision of setting up of more than 14500 PM SHRI Schools by enhancing the existing schools from amongst schools managed by Central government/State/UT Government/local bodies. The duration of the scheme is from 2022–23 to 2026–27; after which it shall be the responsibility of the States/UTs to continue to maintain the benchmarks achieved by these schools.

Samagra Shiksha: It is **an integrated scheme covering all classes from pre-primary to senior secondary education and it has been revamped and aligned with the recommendations of National Education Policy 2020.** The scheme intends to ensure access to quality education with an equitable and inclusive classroom environment for all children.

Samagra Shiksha is reinforcing the implementation of recommendations of NEP 2020 such as stress on Foundational Literacy and Numeracy, furnishing Holistic Progress Card (HPC), capacity building of teachers etc.

Recent Government Interventions in Education

EXAM ESSENTIAL

- **One Nation One Subscription (ONOS) Scheme:** Approved in 2024, the aim of ONOS is to provide country-wide equitable access to international high impact scholarly research articles and journal publications to students, faculty and researchers of all government-managed Higher Education Institutions and Research & Development Institutions. It is a Central Sector Scheme under the Ministry of Education with financial allocation of ₹6,000 crore for 2025–27.
- **PM-Vidyalaxmi Scheme: Launched in 2024**, it is a Central Sector scheme to provide financial assistance to meritorious students **in both public and private** higher education institutions. The scheme provides collateral free, guarantor free loans from banks and financial institutions to cover full amount of tuition fees and other expenses related to the course in higher education.

  Loan upto ₹7.5 lakh will be provided a 75 per cent credit guarantee by the Government of India. For students with upto ₹8 lakhs annual family income, 3 per cent interest subvention for loan up to ₹10 lakhs is provided. This is in addition to the full interest subvention already offered to students with up to ₹4.5 lakhs annual family income.

  Any student who gets admission in Quality Higher Education Institution (QHEIs) is eligible under the scheme. This scheme supplements Pradhan Mantri Uchchatar Shiksha Protsahan (PM-USP) Scheme.
- **National Achievement Survey (NAS) 2021:** NAS is a national level large-scale assessment conducted to obtain information about the learning achievement of students of **Classes 3, 5, 8 and 10** studying in State Govt. schools, Govt. Aided schools, Private Unaided and Central Govt. schools. NAS does not provide scores for individual student/school. It is conducted by the *Ministry of Education* to evaluate children's progress and learning competencies. About 1,18,000 schools participated in NAS 2021.

- **Vidyanjali:** This scheme of the Ministry of Education aims to strengthen schools and upgrade the quality of school education through community, private sector involvement and CSR across the country. Vidyanjali **portal connects contributors directly to the schools.** With the help of Vidyanjali, the community and volunteers directly connect with the government and government-aided schools to contribute their services and/or assets/materials/equipment through a dedicated portal.
- **Performance Grading Index (PGI):** The Performance Grading Index (PGI) has been developed by the Department of School Education and Literacy **(DoSEL)**. It aims to **evaluate the relative performance of all the States and UTs** on a uniform scale. The PGI has five domains with seventy (70) indicators, carrying a score of 1000.
- **Data Governance Quality Index (DGQI):** The **NITI Aayog** has developed DGQI platform in 2020 to assess the data preparedness of the Ministries in respect of Central Sector or Centrally Sponsored Schemes. NITI Aayog has accomplished DGQI 2.0 exercise in 2021 in which **data in respect of 3 schemes** Samagra Shiksha, Mid-Day Meal and National Means cum Merit Scholarship have been considered for the assessment.
- **Manodarpan Programme:** As a part of the *Atmanirbhar Bharat Abhiyan* (ANB), *Manodarpan* programme was conducted **by NCERT** and it is intended **to provide psycho-social support** to students, teachers and families for mental health and emotional well-being during the times of COVID-19. Under ***Manodarpan*** programme, several activities were conducted such as running of the tele-helpline, organising webinars, live interactive sessions '***Sahyog***' with practicing counsellors, etc.
- **Academic Bank of Credit:** Launched in 2021, it enables digital storage of the academic credits earned from various recognised Higher Educational Institutions (HEI) such that credits so earned can be accounted for award of degree by any given HEI.
- **New India Literacy Programme (NLIP):** This centrally sponsored scheme, which is implemented over five years from 2022–26, aims to cover a target of 5 crore learners during the five years under Foundational Literacy and Numeracy component.

  This programme has five objectives:
  i. Foundational Literacy and Numeracy
  ii. Critical Life Skills
  iii. Vocational Skills Development
  iv. Basic Education
  v. Continuing Education

Few More Information and Computer Technology (ICT) Initiatives in Education

The government takes several initiatives for bolstering the online learning infrastructure in India:

1. **SWAYAM** *(Study Webs of Active-Learning for Young Aspiring Minds)*: It is India's national **Massive Online Open Courses** (MOOC) platform, developed in 2016. It offers a large number of courses taught by instructors from various Indian universities. One aspect that sets it apart from other providers is that it allows students in India **to earn academic credit online.**
2. **Swayamprabha:** A group of 32 DTH channels providing high quality educational curriculum-based course contents covering diverse disciplines (*viz.* arts, science, commerce, engineering, technology, law, medicine, agriculture etc.) to all teachers, students and citizens across the country.

3. **National Digital Library:** Digital repository of a vast amount of academic content in different formats for all academic levels including researchers and life-long learners.
4. **Shodhganga and e-Shodh Sindh:** Digital repository platform of thesis and academic papers for research students and for larger usage of scholarly community.

BONUS KNOWLEDGE

PRERANA

The Ministry of Education launched PRERANA programme in **2024.** It is a week-long residential **Experiential Learning Programme** for selected students from class IX to XII. It aims to offer a meaningful, unique, and inspiring experience to all participants, thereby empowering them with leadership qualities. The day-wise programme schedule consists of yoga, mindfulness, and meditation sessions, followed by experiential learning, thematic sessions, and hands-on interesting learning activities. Prerana program is scheduled to run from a Vernacular School, established in 1888, in one of the oldest living cities of India, Vadnagar, district Mehsana, in Gujarat.

EXAM ESSENTIAL

ALL INDIA SURVEY ON HIGHER EDUCATION (AISHE) 2021–22

Ministry of Education has been conducting an annual web-based All India Survey on Higher Education (AISHE) since 2010–11. The survey covers all the Institutions in the country engaged in imparting higher education. Through survey, data is collected on several parameters such as teachers, student enrolment, programmes, examination results, education finance, infrastructure. Indicators of educational development such as Institution Density, Gross Enrolment Ratio, Pupil-teacher ratio, Gender Parity Index, Per Student Expenditure are also computed from the data collected. These are useful in making informed policy decisions and research for development of education sector. The **2021–22 AISHE** indicates that -

- Enrolment in higher education increased to 4.33 crore, i.e., increase of 4.58 per cent from 2020–21.
- The Female enrolment has increased to 2.07 crore from 2.01 crore in 2021–22.
- The gender parity index, or GPI, which measures the proportion of female to male GER, increased from 1 in 2017–18 to 1.01 in 2021–22.
- The top 3 States in terms of number of students enrolled: Uttar Pradesh, Maharashtra, Tamil Nadu.
- The total number of universities/university like institutions registered is 1,168, colleges 45,473 and standalone institutions 12,002.
- States with highest college density: Karnataka (66), Telangana (52), Andhra Pradesh (49).

ANNUAL STATUS OF EDUCATION REPORT (ASER) 2024

ASER is a survey of children in rural India to assess their education levels. The survey is conducted by the NGO Pratham every year, since 2005. ASER tracks **educational trends and challenges** in rural areas, evolving in **coverage, focus, and frequency**. The 2024 survey reached 649,491 children in 17,997 villages across 605 rural districts in India.

Key Findings of ASER 2024

- **Pre-primary (age group 3–5 years):**
  - States with enrolment exceeding 90 per cent in pre-primary institutions for this age – Karnataka, Gujarat, Maharashtra, Kerala, and Nagaland.
  - Anganwadi centres are the biggest provider of services in pre-primary age group in India.
- **Elementary (age group 6–14 years)**
  - States with more than a 10 percentage point increase in this proportion between 2022 and 2024 in government schools – Himachal Pradesh, Uttarakhand, Kerala, Uttar Pradesh, Haryana, Odisha, and Maharashtra.
- **Older children (age group 15–16 years)**
  - Almost 90 per cent of both girls and boys have a smartphone at home.
  - More than 80 per cent students know how to use a smartphone.
  - The proportion of schools with drinking water available increased from 74.8 per cent to 77.7 per cent.
  - The proportion of schools with books other than textbooks being used by students increased from 36.9 per cent to 51.3 per cent.

SUMMARY

- The Ministry of Health and Family Welfare adopted the first National Health Policy in 1983 till 2002.
- **NHP 2002** – Highlighted the role of Alternative System of Medicine in India.
- **National Nutrition Policy, 1993** – Was formulated by the Department of Women and Child Development (GoI).
- **Expanded Programme on Immunisation** – Launched in 1978.
- **Universal Immunisation Programme (UIP)** – Launched in 1985.
- **National Nutrition Strategy (NNS)** – Adopted by NITI Aayog in 2017.
- **Anaemia Mukt Bharat** – Launched in 2018.
- **Ayushman Bharat (PMJAY)** – A step towards Universal Health Coverage (UHC) which intends to ensure all people have access to quality health services.
- **General Insurance Corporation** – A nationalised reinsurance company under the Ministry of Finance and was incorporated in 1972 under the Companies Act, 1956.
- **Rashtriya Swastha Bima Yojana (RSBY)** – Launched in 2007.
- **Ayushman Bharat Digital Mission** – Launched in 2021 to create a seamless online platform through the provision of integration of a wide-range of data, information and infrastructure services.
- **University Education Commission** – Appointed in 1948 under the Chairmanship of Dr. S. Radhakrishnan.
- **Secondary Education Commission** – Appointed under the chairmanship of Dr. Lakshmanswami Mudaliyar in 1952.
- **National Education Commission** – Formed in 1964 under the chairmanship of **Daulat Singh Kothari**.
- **Operation Blackboard** – Launched in 1987 to provide essential facilities to the primary schools.
- **Sarva Shiksha Abhiyan (SSA)** – Launched in 2001 for elementary education.
- **Mid-Day meal scheme** – Launched in 1995 as the National Programme of Nutritional Support to Primary Education (NP-NSPE), a centrally-sponsored scheme.

- **National Curriculum Framework 2005** – Based on various reports of the government on education like *"Learning Without Burden"*.
- **National Advisory Committee** – Set up in 1993 by the MHRD, with Yash Pal as chairman, prepared a report entitled **"Learning Without Burden".**
- **Right to Education Act** – Enacted on 4 August 2009.
- **NEP 2020** – Approved by GoI in July 2020, replaced the 34-years-old National Policy on Education (NPE) 1986.
- **National Achievement Survey (NAS) 2021** – Conducted by the Ministry of Education.
- **The Performance Grading Index (PGI)** – Developed by Department of School Education and Literacy (DoSEL).
- **Manodarpan Programme** – A part of *Atmanirbhar Bharat Abhiyan*, conducted by NCERT.
- **PRASHAST (Pre Assessment Holistic Screening Tool)** – An app launched by Department of School Education and Literacy which helps in screening 21 disability conditions recognised in Rights of Persons with Disabilities (RPwD) Act.
- **NISHTHA 4.0 (ECCE)** – An online teacher training programme for Early Childhood Care and Education. It targets to train 25 lakh education personnel.

UPSC CSE PREVIOUS YEARS' PRELIMINARY EXAMINATION QUESTIONS

1. With reference to the 'Pradhan Mantri Surakshit Matritva Abhiyan', consider the following statements: **[2024]**

1. This scheme guarantees a minimum package of antenatal care services to women in their second and third trimesters of pregnancy and six months post-delivery health care service in any government health facility.
2. Under this scheme, private sector health care providers of certain specialities can volunteer to provide services at nearby government health facilities.

Which of the statements given above is/are correct?

(a) 1 only (b) 2 only
(c) Both 1 and 2 (d) Neither 1 nor 2

2. Consider the following statements in relation to Janani Suraksha Yojana: **[2023]**

1. It is a safe motherhood intervention of the State Health Departments.
2. Its objective is to reduce maternal and neonatal mortality among poor pregnant women.
3. It aims to promote institutional delivery among poor pregnant women.
4. Its objective includes providing public health facilities to sick infants up to one year of age.

How many of the statements given above are correct?

(a) Only one (b) Only two
(c) Only three (d) All four

3. Consider the following statements in the context of interventions being undertaken under Anaemia Mukt Bharat Strategy: **[2023]**

1. It provides prophylactic calcium supplementation for pre-school children, adolescents and pregnant women.
2. It runs a campaign for delayed cord clamping at the time of childbirth.
3. It provides for periodic deworming to children and adolescents.
4. It addresses non-nutritional causes of anaemia in endemic pockets with special focus on malaria, hemoglobinopathies and fluorosis.

How many of the statements given above are correct?

(a) Only one (b) Only two
(c) Only three (d) All four

4. Consider the following statements: **[2023]**

Statement-I: India's public sector health care system largely focuses on curative care with limited preventive, promotive and rehabilitative care.

Statement-II: Under India's decentralised approach to health care delivery, the States are primarily responsible for organising health services.

Which one of the following is correct in respect to the above statements?

(a) Both Statement-I and Statement-II are correct and Statement-II is the correct explanation for Statement-I.
(b) Both Statement-I and Statement-II are correct and Statement-II is not the correct explanation for Statement-I.
(c) Statement-I is correct but Statement-II is incorrect.
(d) Statement-I is incorrect but Statement-II is correct.

5. What is the aim of the programme 'Unnat Bharat Abhiyan'? **[2017]**

(a) Achieving 100 per cent literacy by promoting collaboration between voluntary organisations and government's education system and local communities.
(b) Connecting institutions of higher education with local communities to address development challenges through appropriate technologies.
(c) Strengthening India's scientific research institutions in order to make India a scientific and technological power.
(d) Developing human capital by allocating special funds for health care and education of rural and urban poor, and organising skill development programmes and vocational training for them.

6. 'SWAYAM', an initiative of the Government of India, aims at **[2016]**

(a) promoting the Self Help Groups in rural areas
(b) providing financial and technical assistance to young start-up entrepreneurs
(c) promoting the education and health of adolescent girls
(d) providing affordable and quality education to the citizens for free

☞ NO QUESTIONS ASKED
2022, 2021, 2020, 2019, 2018, 2015, 2014, 2013

ANSWER KEY

1. (b) 2. (b) 3. (c) 4. (b) 5. (b) 6. (d)

UPSC CSE PREVIOUS YEARS' MAIN EXAMINATION QUESTIONS

1. The increase in life expectancy in the country has led to newer health challenges in the community. What are those challenges and what steps need to be taken to meet them? **[2022]**

☞ NO QUESTIONS ASKED
2024, 2023, 2021, 2020, 2019, 2018, 2017, 2016, 2015, 2014, 2013

CHAPTER

27

BALANCE OF PAYMENTS

CHAPTER OUTLINE

- Balance of Payments
- Balance in Current Account
- Balance of Visibles or Balance of Trade (BOT)
- Balance of Invisibles
- Remittances
- Balance in Capital Account
- Foreign Investments
- Loans
- Banking Capital Transactions
- Net International Investment Position
- Net Errors and Omissions
- Autonomous and Accommodating Items in the BOP Account
- Foreign Exchange Reserves
- BOP Trend in India in the Pre- and Post-reform Period
- India's External Debt
- Twin Deficit Hypothesis
- J-Curve

BALANCE OF PAYMENTS (BOP)

Definition of Resident: discussed in Chapter 2

An open economy is one that communicates with other countries through several means, whereas, in a closed economy, there are no linkages with the rest of the world. Most of the modern economies are open. There are three ways to establish links with the rest of the world.

1. **Output Market:** An economy can exchange goods and services with other nations. This increases choice by allowing consumers and manufacturers to select between domestic and international items.
2. **Financial Market:** Typically, an economy may purchase/sell financial assets from/to other nations. This allows investors to select between domestic and international assets.
3. **Labour Market:** Firms may select where to put production, and employees can pick where to work. There are several immigration rules that limit the flow of workers between countries.

A nation must preserve a systematic record of these transactions. It is only then that an economy's reliance on the rest of the world and capacity to use external resources for its own development are established. We refer to this systematic record of transactions as the **Balance of Payments (BOP)**. In other words, BOP is the annual statement of accounts of monetary transactions of the **residents** of a country vis-à-vis the rest of the world. These transactions arise due to:

a. Transaction in goods (merchandise or visibles)

b. Transaction in services (invisibles)

c. Transaction in capital (loans, deposits, investments)

Autarky – *A closed economy is referred to as the state of autarky. This concept has now become obsolete.*

The BOP of a country is divided into two parts based on the nature of transactions:

I. Balance in current account

II. Balance in capital account

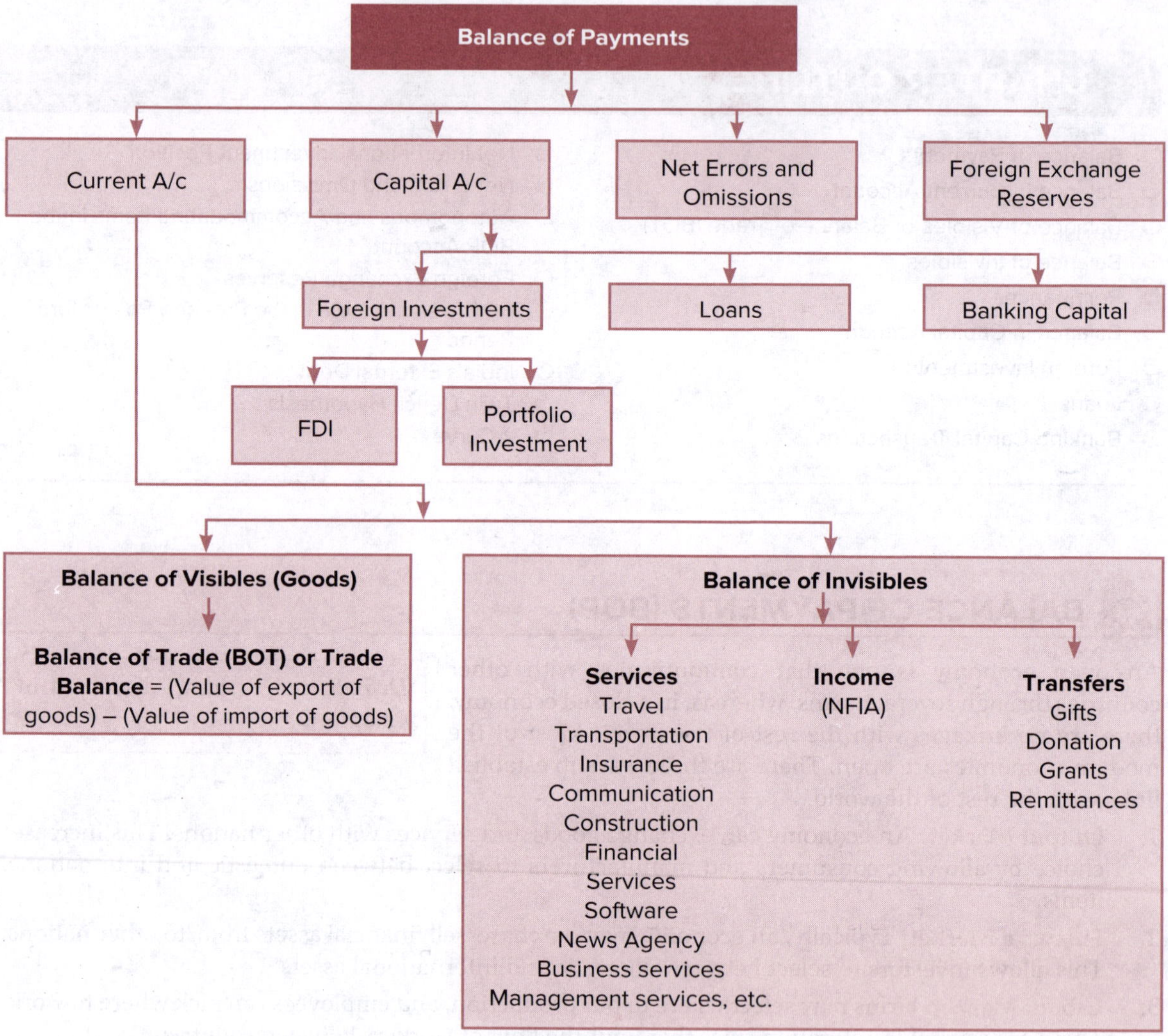

BOP involves <u>*a vertical double-entry system of accounting; i.e., for every credit,*</u> there is a debit in the books and vice versa. To explain, all inflows are credited (+ sign), and all outflows are debited (– sign) under BOP.

Thus,

Credit (Cr.) items include – exports, receivable income, transfer receipts, reduction in foreign assets, or increase in foreign liabilities.

Debit (Dr.) items include – imports, payable income, transfer payments, increase in foreign assets or decrease in foreign liabilities.

Moreover, BOP in India is compiled **on an accrual basis** (not cash basis).

BALANCE IN CURRENT ACCOUNT

It records all transactions relating to goods, services and income by residents with the rest of the world during a financial year. Current account comprises:

1. Balance of Visibles or Balance of Trade (BOT)
2. Balance of Invisibles

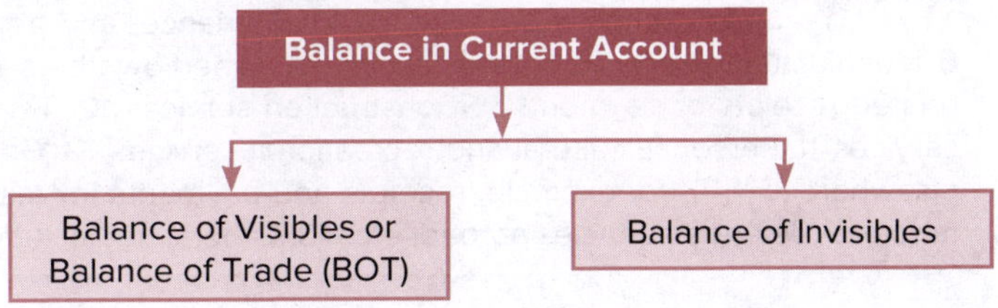

1. Balance of Visibles or Balance of Trade (BOT)

The difference between the value of imports and exports of only physical goods or visible items is called Balance of Trade.

BOT = Value of **Exports** (of goods) – Value of **Imports** (of goods)

If exports are > imports, then there occurs **trade surplus**.

If exports are < imports, then there occurs **trade deficit**.

If exports = imports, then there is **trade equilibrium**.

Note: Export and import of even capital goods like plant and machinery are included under BOT and **not** under capital account.

BONUS KNOWLEDGE

As per the International Monetary Fund (IMF) manual, the value of imports and the value of exports should be considered on a Free-On-Board (FOB) basis.

However, due to data constraints, in India, **imports are considered on CIF** amount, i.e., cost + insurance + freight

But, the value of exports is presented on FOB basis in India.

Transactions related to **non-monetary gold** are included under BOT, while monetary gold is recorded under foreign exchange reserves maintained by the RBI.

In the case of India, BOT has always been negative, i.e., trade deficit.

Balance of Trade (BOT)	Balance in Current Account
BOT includes only visible items or merchandise.	It records both visibles and invisibles.
It is a narrow concept and is a part of current account.	It is a broader concept and BOT is a part of it.

2. Balance of Invisibles

It includes the following **three broad categories** of items:

1. Services (categorised under 13 heads)
2. Transfer payments (both official and private transfers). For example, gifts and remittances.
3. Net income from and to the rest of the world (comprises compensation to employees and investment income in the form of dividend, profit and interest income)

did you KNOW? In the Indian BOP system, services are categorised under the following 13 heads. (According to the IMF manual, there should be 21 categories.) 1. Travel 2. Transportation 3. Insurance and pension services 4. Maintenance and repair services 5. Other business services 6. Manufacturing services on physical inputs owned by others 7. Financial services 8. Intellectual property–related receipts or payments 9. Construction services 10. Telecommunication, computer and information services 11. Personal, cultural and recreational services 12. Government goods and services not included elsewhere **(GNIE)** (for example, receipts and payments for maintenance of foreign embassies, diplomatic missions, defence agencies abroad, etc.) 13. Others, not included elsewhere.

In India, despite a net outflow due to interest and dividend payments, the balance of invisibles has always been positive because India is a net exporter of services and the world's largest recipient of remittances.

Therefore,

Balance of Current Account = Balance of Visibles + Balance of Invisibles

Present Status of CAD in India (*as per IMF BOP Manual 5*) (in US$ Million)

Particulars	2021–22	2022–23	2023–24
Balance of Trade (A)	–189459	–265291	–242065
Balance of Invisibles (B)	150694	198238	218778
Current Account Balance (A + B)	–38766	–67055	–23286
Current Account Deficit (as a % of GDP)	–1.23	–1.98	–0.7

Source: www.indiabudget.gov.in/economicsurvey/doc/stat/tab52.pdf

What is Current Account Deficit (CAD)?

The Current Account Deficit (CAD) measures the difference between the money received and sent out of a nation through trade in goods and services, as well as fund transfers related to domestically owned assets abroad.

What Level of CAD is Desired or Sustainable?

As per the 1993 Rangarajan Committee report, CAD of around **2 per cent of GDP** is sustainable for a developing economy like India.

Remittances

A remittance refers to money that is sent or transferred to another party. The term is derived from the word 'remit', which means to send back. Remittances can be used for any type of payment including invoices or other obligations. But the term is typically used to refer to money sent to family members back in a person's home country. During 2024, India had been the top recipient of remittances with a value of USD 129.1 billion.

Remittances are recorded in BOPs.

Role of remittances in an economy:

(a) Important for economies of small and developing countries.

(b) A way to help raise the standard of living for people abroad and help combat global poverty.

(c) In some cases, they make up a significant portion of a country's GDP.

BONUS KNOWLEDGE

LIBERALISED REMITTANCE SCHEME (LRS)

The Reserve Bank of India's Liberalised Remittance Scheme (LRS) allows resident individuals to remit a specified amount annually to another country for investment or expenditure. According to current regulations, resident individuals may remit up to USD 250,000 per financial year for any permissible current or capital account transaction, or a combination of both. While multiple remittances are allowed under LRS, the total amount cannot exceed USD 250,000 per financial year. This money can be used to pay expenses related to travelling (private or for business), medical treatment, studying, gifts and donations, maintenance of close relatives, and so on. However, the scheme is not available to corporations, partnership firms, Hindu Undivided Families (HUFs), or trusts, among others.

The remittance facility under the LRS is **not** available for the following:

i. Remittance for any purpose prohibited explicitly under Schedule I (like purchase of **lottery tickets/ sweep stakes**, **proscribed magazines**, etc.) or any item restricted under Schedule II of Foreign Exchange Management (Current Account Transactions) Rules, 2000.

ii. Remittance from India **for margins or margin calls** to overseas exchanges / overseas counterparty.

iii. Remittances **for the purchase of FCCBs** issued by Indian companies in the overseas secondary market.

iv. Remittance **for trading in foreign exchange abroad**.

v. **Capital account remittances**, directly or indirectly, **to countries identified by the Financial Action Task Force** (FATF) as "non-cooperative countries and territories" from time to time.

vi. Remittances directly or indirectly to those individuals and entities identified as posing a significant risk of committing acts of terrorism as advised separately by the Reserve Bank to the banks.

vii. Gifting by a resident to another resident in foreign currency for the credit of the latter's foreign currency account held abroad under LRS.

BALANCE IN CAPITAL ACCOUNT

It records the capital receipts and payments in the form of investments and loans flowing in and out of an economy. The components of this account are:

A. Foreign investments [includes Foreign Direct Investment (FDI) and portfolio investment]

B. Loans (external assistance, ECB and trade credit)

C. Banking capital

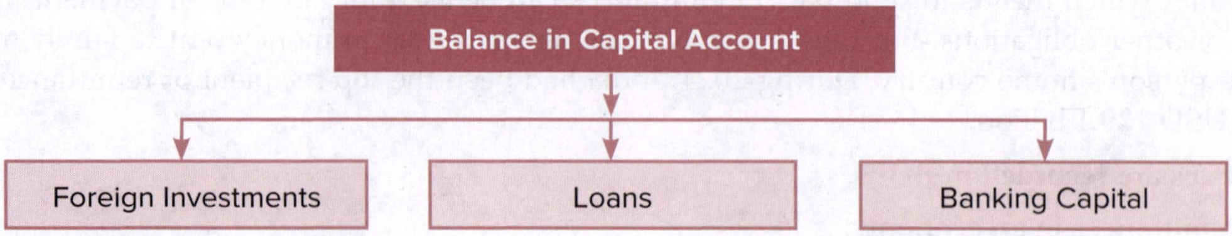

A. Foreign Investments

These are **non-debt-creating** capital transactions. They include:

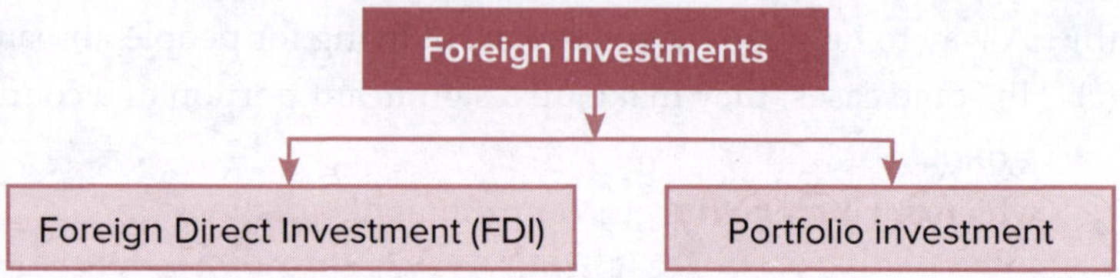

1. Foreign Direct Investment (FDI)

- It refers to the purchase of assets in the rest of the world which **allows control over the assets**, e.g., purchase of firms by Reliance in the United States.
- On the recommendation of the **Mayaram panel**, the following definition for FDI was adopted:
  - Any foreign investment **equal to or beyond (≥) 10 per cent stake in** post-issue paid-up equity capital on a fully diluted basis **in a listed company** is construed as FDI.

  Additionally, any investment in an unlisted entity, even if it constitutes only 1 or 2 per cent of the paid-up capital, is treated as FDI.
- The percentage of ownership determines whether an investment is classified as FDI or portfolio investment.
- If it is <10 per cent in a listed company, then it is termed portfolio investment.
- **Once classified as FDI, an investment remains FDI even if the stake falls below 10 per cent; it does not revert to being a Foreign Portfolio Investment (FPI).**
- **Cash is not a permissible** mode of payment for making FDI.
- **In India, only Non-Resident Indians (NRIs) and Overseas Citizens of India (OCIs) are permitted to invest in partnership or proprietorship firms on a non-repatriation basis. Foreign nationals are not allowed to invest in such entities.**

FDI may be of two types:

1. **Brownfield Investment**: In this case, the entity or a government **buys an existing plant** or company or factory in order to launch a new production activity. Since the existing units are taken over, **no new factory** is set up under brownfield investment.
2. **Greenfield Investment**: It occurs when multinational corporations enter foreign countries to **build new factories and/or stores**. This is just the opposite of brownfield investment.

Routes of FDI into India: An Indian company may receive FDI under the following two routes:

1. **Automatic Route**: Under the automatic route, FDI is **allowed without prior approval of the government or RBI** in activities/sectors as specified in the consolidated FDI policy issued by the Government of India from time to time.

2. **Government Route**: Activities not covered under the automatic route require prior approval of the government. The **Foreign Investment Promotion Board (FIPB)**, which was the responsible agency to oversee this route, was **abolished in 2017**. This abolition has enabled to attract more FDI in India by making the process simpler.

An Indian company, having received FDI either under an automatic route or under a government route, is required to comply with the provisions of the FDI policy, including reporting the FDI to RBI.

Factors which affect FDI inflows may be:

- **Rate of Inflation** – A controlled or low inflation reflects the internal economic stability of an economy which makes it suitable for attracting foreign investments. In other words, as inflation increases, the net benefit of investment decreases due to the diminishing purchasing power of the profits before they are used for consumption.
- **Rate of Real GDP Growth** – Usually the countries with higher rate of real GDP growth receive higher FDI inflows. The rapidly growing economies tend to provide larger market and demand which attribute to the greater profitability on investments. However, the relationship between FDI inflows and real GDP growth rate is bi-directional. Empirically, the larger inflow of FDI leads to a higher real GDP growth rate in an economy.
- **Trade Openness** – Components of fiscal policy and sectoral policies determine the trade openness of an economy. Thus, strict fiscal policies of government like higher tax rates might make it unprofitable for investors to invest.
- **Real Rate of Interest** – It is the inflation-adjusted interest rate. A lower interest rate tends to increase the FDI flows as it makes easier for firms to finance investment projects. Thus, a sound monetary policy also plays a significant role in garnering FDI.

Besides, economic stability, political stability, regulatory environment and infrastructure also affect the FDI inflows in an economy.

Benefits of FDI in Developing Countries

- FDI allows a significant influx of non-debt, creating capital flows which boost economic growth and improve the living standards of the country.
- FDI acts as a catalyst for modernisation and innovation through the transfer of technology and advanced production techniques. FDI can also promote competition in the domestic input market.
- Employment generation and skill development are often gained through FDI inflows which contribute to human capital development in the host country.
- FDI increases the number of new businesses and industries. The profits generated by such projects contribute to corporate tax revenues in the host country.
- FDI, being one of the driving components of global integration of capital markets, can contribute to the spread of best practices in corporate governance, accounting rules, and legal traditions in the host country.

BONUS KNOWLEDGE

SECTORS WHERE FDI IS PROHIBITED IN INDIA

FDI is prohibited in the following sectors under both the government approval and automatic route:

1. Atomic energy and railway operations
2. Lottery business (government lottery, private lottery and online lottery also prohibited)

3. Gambling and betting, including casinos, etc.
4. Chit fund business
5. Nidhi company
6. Agricultural (**except** floriculture, horticulture, development of seeds, animal husbandry, pisciculture and cultivation of vegetables, mushrooms, etc. under controlled conditions and services related to agro and allied sectors) and plantation activities (**other than** tea plantations)
7. Housing and real estate business [**except** development of townships, construction of residential/ commercial premises, roads or bridges and Real Estate Investment Trusts (REITs) under SEBI regulations]
8. Trading in Transferable Development Rights (TDRs)**
9. Manufacture of all kinds of tobacco products (like cigars, cheroots, cigarillos and cigarettes) or of tobacco substitutes.

** **Transferable Development Rights (TDRs)**

- When the state government acquires land for developing infrastructure projects like road widening, metro rail, etc. then instead of compensation, a **DRC** (Development Rights Certificate) may be **issued by the government** to the owner of land.
- This DRC allows the landowner an additional built-up area in return of the area which they have relinquished, and it enables them to develop the given area **by themselves or transfer their rights** for consideration. This is known as Transferable Development Rights (TDR).
- Through TDR, landowners get better compensation at no cost to the government.
- The developer can develop that additional area too in other geographical locations. However, TDR **cannot be transferred from a low-density area to a high-density area**.
- **Until now, only a few states** have adopted the policy of issuing TDRs (first done by Karnataka in 2005).

FDI Ranking of India

According to the World Investment Report published by the **United Nations Conference on Trade and Development (UNCTAD)**, India remains a popular location for global investors. According to the 2024 report, India ranked fourth globally in Foreign Direct Investment (FDI) for new greenfield projects in the previous year.

As per FDI Confidence Index (published by AT Kearney):

Year of FDI Confidence Index	2023	2024
Rank of India among the top 25 FDI destinations	16	18

2. Portfolio Investment

It refers to the purchase of an asset in a foreign country without gaining control over it, i.e., holding less than a 10 per cent stake in a listed company. For unlisted companies, any level of foreign investment is considered FDI.

Example of portfolio investment – Purchase of some shares of a foreign company by Reliance or even by an individual in the rest of the world. This investment instrument is more easily traded, and it does not represent a long-term interest; hence it is less permanent in nature.

Portfolio investment can be classified into two categories:

a. Foreign institutional investment **(FII)**
b. Investment through depository receipts **(ADR/GDR/IDR)**

a. Foreign Institutional Investment (FII)

- It includes investment in the securities of any other nation's company by foreign individuals and foreign institutional investors. FII is mostly made in the financial markets.
- FII is short-term in nature and is also known as **'hot money'**.
- FIIs in India are regulated by the Securities and Exchange Board of India (SEBI).
- Foreign institutional investors can buy/sell securities on Indian stock exchanges, but they **have to get registered** with SEBI.
- FIIs can invest in India's primary and secondary capital markets exclusively through the Portfolio Investment Scheme (PIS).

b. Depository Receipt

A depository receipt is a negotiable financial instrument issued by a bank, which represents a foreign company's publicly traded securities.

American Depository Receipts (ADR) – In the case of ADR, it is issued by the US banks that represent securities of a foreign company trading in the US stock market. ADRs are denominated in U.S. dollars, allowing U.S. investors to invest in non-U.S. companies. ADRs can be transferred without any stamp duty.

Global Depository Receipts (GDRs) – These are equity instruments issued in international markets. They serve the same function like ADRs, but **on a global scale** and the receipt is issued by the depository bank. In many countries, GDR represents a fixed number of shares in a foreign company. GDRs are denominated in U.S. dollars or euros and are traded on major European stock exchanges, such as the London Stock Exchange or Luxembourg Stock Exchange.

RBI publishes ADRs/GDRs as Portfolio Investment. However, **FEMA** as well as the Department for Promotion of Industry and Internal Trade **(DPIIT)** under the *Ministry of Commerce and Industry*, **treats ADR/GDR as FDI**.

Indian Depository Receipts (IDRs) – These are similar to ADRs/GDRs. These are used by foreign companies to mobilise savings from Indian capital markets. If a foreign company wants to list itself in Indian stock exchanges like NSE or BSE, it has to issue IDRs through a depository bank in India. IDR is denominated in **Rupee**. IDR is used by Indians to invest in foreign companies.

BONUS KNOWLEDGE

Participatory Notes (PNs): These are financial instruments used by investors or hedge funds **which are not registered with SEBI** to invest in Indian securities. Indian brokers who are registered with SEBI buy India-based securities or shares and then issue PNs to foreign investors. PN owner does not own the shares.

EXAM ESSENTIAL

Difference between FDI and FII

FDI	FII
FDI refers to an investment by a foreign entity in a business enterprise of another country with the intent of establishing a long-term interest.	FII is an investment made by an investor in the markets of a foreign nation.
FDI is directed at a specific enterprise, aiming to enhance its capacity, productivity, or management control. Thus, it gives investors ownership right as well as management right.	FII investments are largely directed towards the secondary market, though they may also participate in Initial Public Offerings (IPOs). It helps in increasing capital availability in general rather than enhancing the capital of a specific enterprise. This investment gives investors only ownership rights, and not management rights.
Provides the decision-making power to the firm.	Not involved in decision-making.
Investment in productive assets (whose value increases over time) like plant and machinery for a business.	Investment in financial assets like stocks, bonds, mutual funds, etc.

Present status of Foreign Investments in India (in US$ Million)

	2021–22	2022–23	2023–24
Direct Investment to India (A)	56231	42006	26469
FDI by India (B)	17644	14020	16678
Net FDI to India (A – B)	38587	27986	9790
Net Portfolio Investment (C)	–16777	–5152	44081
Total Foreign Investment Inflow (A – B + C)	**21809**	**22834**	**53872**

Source: Statistics Handbook 2023–24 by RBI

B. Loans

Loans refer to borrowings by a country's government and private sector from the international money market. They are **debt-creating capital transactions**.

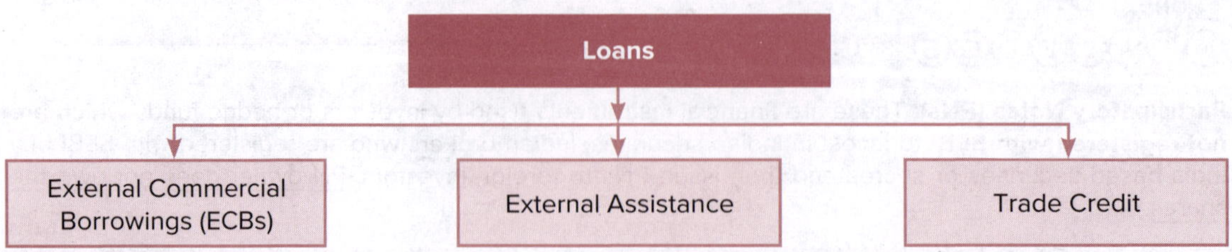

Types of Loans

1. External Commercial Borrowings (ECBs)

- ECB is a *commercial loan* raised from the international market.
- ECBs are raised at prevailing market interest rates without any concessional terms.
- **Who can raise ECB – All entities eligible to receive FDI can raise ECB** and additionally, **Port Trusts, units in SEZ, SIDBI and EXIM Bank of India** have also been allowed to raise ECB.
- ECBs generally have a minimum average maturity of three years, except in specific cases where exemptions apply.
- ECB can be borrowed in any freely convertible foreign currency.
- **ECB can be of the following types:**
  1. Loans (including bank loans).
  2. Floating/fixed rate notes/bonds/debentures (other than fully and compulsorily convertible instruments).
  3. The trade credit period is up to three years for capital goods and up to one year (or the duration of the operating cycle, whichever is shorter) for non-capital goods.
  4. Capital market instruments like Foreign Currency Convertible Bonds (FCCBs) and Foreign Currency Exchangeable Bonds (FCEBs). In India as per the present practice, **FCCBs are included in FDI only when it is converted into equity**. Otherwise, an FCCB is treated as ECB.
  5. Financial lease.
- ECB proceeds can be utilised by borrowers for all activities, **except in:**
  - Real estate
  - Investment in capital market
  - Equity investment
  - Working capital purposes except from foreign equity holder
  - General corporate purposes except from foreign equity holder
  - Repayment of Rupee loans except from foreign equity holder
  - Lending to entities for the above activities

2. External Assistance

- They are borrowings with consideration of assistance.
- It involves **lower rate of interest** and **longer maturity**. External assistance is generally given **by foreign governments, World Bank, IMF** or other international monetary institutions.

3. Trade Credit

- Trade credit is provided to an importer **by overseas suppliers, banks, financial institutions and other permitted recognised lenders**.
- It allows the importer to pay at a later date for **imports of capital/non-capital goods** permissible under the Foreign Trade Policy of GoI.
- Only a **resident of India** can take trade credit.
- Under automatic route – an amount up to **US$ 150 million per import transaction** for oil/gas refining and marketing, airline and shipping companies **and up to US$ 50 million per import transaction** for others is allowed.
- **Period of trade credit** – up to **3 years** for import of capital goods and up to 1 year or the operating cycle whichever is less for non-capital goods.

BONUS KNOWLEDGE

Debt Service Ratio: Ratio of debt service payments (Principal + Interest) of a country to that of the country's current receipts is termed as debt service ratio. The debt service ratio of India has gradually declined since 2015–16. However, **in 2023–24**, it has increased to **6.7%** from 5.3% in 2022–23 and 5.2% in 2021-22 which is primarily because of increase in debt service payments.

C. Banking Capital Transactions

It is a transaction of external financial assets and liabilities of commercial banks and other cooperative banks operating as an authorised dealer in foreign exchange. They include NRI deposits.

NRI deposits take place through 3 types of bank accounts:

1. Foreign Currency Non-Resident (Bank) Account (FCNR-B Account)

- It can be held only in the form of **term or fixed deposits** (not savings account).
- Maturity term ranges from **1 year to 5 years**.
- Only NRIs or PIOs are eligible to open FCNR-B account with a bank.
- Maintained in Pound Sterling, USD, Japanese Yen, Euro, Canadian $, Australian $ etc.

2. Non-Resident External Rupee Account (NRE Account)

- Any NRI can open an NRE account to remit funds to India through foreign banks.
- The NRE account is maintained in **Indian Rupee** and may be opened as current account, savings account or term deposits.
- The interest earned on it is tax-free.
- The amount held in this deposit, together with the interest accrued, can be repatriated.
- It is **prone to the risk** of exchange rate fluctuations.

3. Non-Resident Ordinary Rupee Account (NRO Account)

- Any person residing outside India (i.e., in a foreign country), irrespective of being Indian or not, may open and maintain an NROR account for the purpose to pay for bona fide transactions denominated in Indian Rupee or to manage the income earned in India.
- It can be maintained in the form of current, savings, recurring or even fixed deposit account.
- The NRIs may remit an amount not exceeding $1 million per financial year out of the balances held in the NRO account.
- The interest earned is taxable in this case.
- It is **not prone to the risk** of exchange rate fluctuations.

A foreign tourist visiting India can open only NRO account.

BONUS KNOWLEDGE

- **NRI** – A 'Non-resident Indian' (NRI) is a person resident outside India who is a citizen of India.
- **PIO** – A Person of Indian Origin (PIO) is a person resident outside India who is a citizen of any country other than Bangladesh or Pakistan or such other country as may be specified by the Central Government, satisfying the following conditions:
    a. Who was a citizen of India by virtue of the Constitution of India or the Citizenship Act, 1955 (57 of 1955); or
    b. Who belonged to a territory that became part of India after the 15th day of August, 1947; or
    c. Who is a child or a grandchild or a great grandchild of a citizen of India or of a person referred to in clause (a) or (b); or
    d. Who is a spouse of foreign origin of a citizen of India or spouse of foreign origin of a person referred to in clause (a) or (b) or (c)
    e. A PIO includes an 'Overseas Citizen of India' (OCI) cardholder under Section 7(A) of the Citizenship Act, 1955.

Such an OCI Card holder should also be a person resident outside India.

EXAM ESSENTIAL

NET INTERNATIONAL INVESTMENT POSITION (NIIP)

NIIP measures the gap between a nation's stock of foreign assets and foreigner's stock of that nation's assets at a specific point in time. In other words, it is the **difference between the external financial assets** and liabilities of a country. **External debt** or liabilities for its computation includes both **government debt** and **private debt**. Similarly, for external assets computation, both publicly and privately held external assets are also taken into account.

A positive NIIP value indicates that a nation is a ***creditor nation***, while a negative value indicates that it is a *debtor nation*.

According to the RBI report, India's NIIP stood at US$ –368.3 billion as of end-June 2024—an improvement since end-March 2019.

NET ERRORS AND OMISSIONS

They take into account the difficulty of recording all the wide variety of transactions that take place in the accounting period (i.e. April–March). This difficulty may arise due to the following reasons:

1. Sampling error due to the inability to enter the value of all individual transactions
2. Under-reporting and over-reporting of some transactions
3. Smuggling activities

A very small percentage of GDP is considered as net errors and omissions in the BOP account.

BONUS KNOWLEDGE

AUTONOMOUS AND ACCOMMODATING ITEMS IN THE BOP ACCOUNT

Autonomous items:

- These items refer to international economic transactions that take place due to some economic motive such as profit maximisation.
- These transactions are independent of the state of countries BOP.
- They are called '**above the line**' items.
- Example, all current account and capital account transactions.

Accommodating items:

- These items are meant to restore BOP balance or correct BOP balance.
- These items refer to transactions that occur because of other activities in the BOP, such as government financing. They are in the nature of official reserved transactions performed by the central bank (RBI).
- They are carried out by the government and the central bank in pursuit of some international economic policy objectives.
- These official reserved transactions take place when autonomous receipts are less than autonomous payments, i.e., deficit in BOP.
- Central bank finances the deficit through foreign exchange reserves, borrowing from IMF or even borrowing from other monetary authorities.
- They are called 'below the line' items.

FOREIGN EXCHANGE RESERVES

EXAM ESSENTIAL

- RBI is the custodian of foreign exchange reserves of the country and all forex transactions are routed through RBI.
- If the overall balance in BOP account is negative, this leads to decrease in official reserves and vice versa.
- India's foreign exchange reserves include:
  1. **FCAs** (Foreign Currency Assets)
  2. **Monetary gold**
  3. **SDRs** (Special Drawing Rights) (*SDRs are held in the custody of the government instead of RBI*)
  4. **Reserve Tranche Position (RTP) in the International Monetary Fund (IMF), which represents the portion of a country's quota that can be accessed without stringent IMF conditions.**

> **Last Minute SNIPPETS**
>
> As of November 2024, China has the largest amount of foreign exchange reserve, followed by Japan. In this regard, **India ranks 4th.**

- At present, **FCAs have the maximum share (around 90 per cent)** in the forex reserves of RBI, followed by gold.
- According to the Reserve Bank of India's weekly statistical supplement published on February 28, 2025, India's total foreign exchange (Forex) reserves were approximately US$ 640.56 billion in March 2024. The Foreign Currency Assets (FCA) component stood at around US$ 543.85 billion,

Gold Reserves at approximately US$ 74.58 billion, Special Drawing Rights (SDRs) with the IMF at around US$ 17.97 billion, and the Reserve Position in the IMF at approximately US$ 4.09 billion.

Reserve Tranche – It is a portion of the required quota of currency that each member country must provide to the IMF, which can be utilised for its own purposes.

BOP TREND IN INDIA IN THE PRE- AND POST-REFORM PERIOD

Period I [from 1956–57 to 1975–76]

This entire period was extremely tough for India's BOP, owing to poor growth in exports in comparison to import demand, as well as adverse external circumstances. Despite tighter import limits (via quantitative limitations) and foreign exchange laws, the current account deficit was 1.8 per cent of GDP. Foreign exchange reserves were low, often less than what was required to support three months' worth of imports. Inflows of foreign aid on extremely concessional terms covered almost the entire current account deficit (92 per cent). There was hardly any commercial deficit.

Period II [from 1976–77 to 1979–80]

These years had been very prosperous for India's BOP. India maintained a minor current account surplus (0.6 per cent of GDP on an average) and foreign exchange reserves equivalent to around seven months of imports. Export growth was strong, but the fundamental cause for the rapid improvement in the BOP was a substantial increase in net invisibles. Net invisibles rose from a mere ₹193 crore in 1974–75 to ₹2,486 crore in 1979–1980.

Period III [from 1980–81 to 1990–91]

Severe BOP crisis in India occurred due to large trade deficits. There was a decline in net receipt from visibles and a reduction in external assistance. This BOP crisis led to major economic reforms by the government.

BONUS KNOWLEDGE

INDIA'S 1991 BOP CRISIS

- The beginning of 1991 saw a major BOP crisis due to many factors like the **Gulf War** and cumulative problems of the Indian economy. India has been dependent on crude imports. When there was geopolitical disturbance due to **the Iraq crisis, India's import bill shot up due to a** sudden **increase in international crude oil prices**. It depleted India's forex reserves. International rating agencies downgraded India. This fuelled the crisis further as India's creditworthiness plunged.
- A substantial outflow of deposits held by non-resident Indians during 1990–91 added to the crisis. Reserves declined to a low of $0.9 billion in January 1991, which could have barely financed 3 weeks' worth of imports.

- India came out of this crisis with an **IMF-sponsored bail-out**. In the course of time, the Indian economy recovered, exports grew as the rupee was devalued, foreign inflows started to pick up, and India overcame the worst BOP crisis in its history.
- The rupee was devalued and aligned more closely with its market value. International investors saw this set of reforms as progress towards market orientation. Indian exporters fell encouraged as their earnings in foreign currency would fetch more Indian Rupees. Structural reforms were taken up to put the Indian economy on a competitive path.

BOP Situation in Post-Reform Period (1991–92 Onwards)

Especially since 1993–94, there has been a satisfactory trend in India's BOP situation. **Factors which have contributed to the improved BOP situation are as follows:**

- Increase in Balance of Invisibles specially due to the increase in software exports and increase in receipt of private remittances (or transfers) from abroad.
- Increase in NRI deposits under banking capital head due to the special incentives declared from time to time by RBI.
- Increase in Foreign Investment (both FDI and portfolio investment) over the years.
- Rise in Net External Commercial Borrowings over the years. But, in the period between 2014 and 2019, net ECB was negative, i.e., outflow (in net).

On the other hand, there have been factors which are **responsible for overall BOP imbalance**:

a. Increased import of goods and services due to (i) domestic price rise, (ii) cyclical fluctuations, (iii) large-scale development expenditure, (iv) population explosion, (v) change in taste and preferences of end consumers.
b. Hindrances in capital inflows due to (i) political instability and (ii) natural calamity.
c. Depreciation of domestic currency, especially when imports > exports.

Causes of BOP Deficits

a. Very low prospects of getting Concessional Aid
b. Burden of external debt
c. Declining surpluses on account of invisibles
d. Balance of trade deficits

Measures taken by the Government/RBI to overcome BOP Imbalance

a. **Credit control measures** to decrease money supply in the economy, which helps to reduce the purchasing power and thereby results in decrease in aggregate demand.
b. **Devaluation** of domestic currency (not always), which stimulates exports and reduces demand for imports.
c. **Export promotion and import control measures** such as more of export incentives and subsidies and restriction on imports through licensing, import quota, etc.
d. **Structural reforms** to put the economy on a competitive path.

Current Trend in BOP (as per IMF BOP Manual 5)

Name of the Item	2022–23 (US$ Million)	2023–24 (US$ Million)
Balance of Trade (BOT) (A)	–265291	–242065
Balance of Invisibles (B)	198236	218778
Current Account Balance (A + B)	–67055	–23287
Capital Account Balance (C)	58944	86276
Errors and Omissions (D)	–1024	712
Overall Balance (A + B + C + D)	–9135	63701

Source: 2023–24 Statistics Handbook by RBI.

INDIA'S EXTERNAL DEBT

- India's external debt data is released quarterly by the RBI.
- India's **external debt** refers to the total debt that India as a country owes to foreign creditors. The debtors, in this case, can be the **Government of India (GoI), State Governments, corporations or citizens of India**. The debt includes money owed to private **commercial banks**, **foreign Governments**, or even **IMF** and **World Bank**.
- The various components of India's external debt include:
  a. Multi-lateral debt
  b. Bilateral debt
  c. Borrowings from IMF and World Bank
  d. Trade credit
  e. External Commercial Borrowings (ECBs)
  f. NRI deposits
  g. Rupee debt
  h. Short-term debt(including short-term trade credit)
- **As per Statistical Handbook 2023–24** (*published by RBI*):

Year	2021–22	2022–23	2023–24
External Debt (US $ Billion)	**619**	**624**	**669**
External Debt (as a per cent of GDP)	19.9%	**19%**	18.9%
Debt Service Ratio	5.2	**5.3**	6.7

Short Term Debt as a percentage of Total External Debt has been around 20% in the case of India in recent years.

TWIN DEFICIT HYPOTHESIS

Economies that have **both a fiscal deficit and current account deficit** are referred to as having 'twin deficits'. As per the twin deficit hypothesis, some economists believe that a large budget deficit is correlated to a large current account deficit. For example – the United States and India have experienced both the deficits year after year. The opposite scenario featuring a fiscal surplus and current account surplus is generally viewed as much better financial position. For example – China has experienced long-term surplus and current account surplus.

J-CURVE

The J-Curve is an economic theory which states that are under certain assumptions, a country's trade balance will initially worsen after the depreciation of its currency – mainly because higher prices on imports will be greater than the reduced volume of imports.

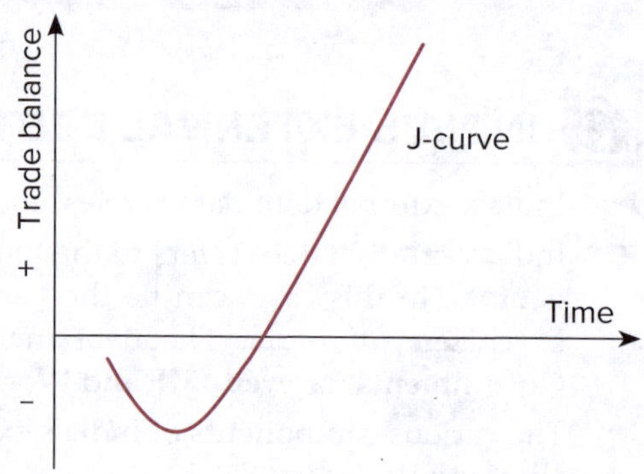

But as time progresses, export levels begin to dramatically increase, due to their more attractive prices to foreign buyers. Simultaneously, domestic consumers purchase fewer imported products due to their higher costs.

These parallel actions ultimately shift the trade balance, to present an increased surplus and smaller deficit, compared to those figures before the devaluation.

The trajectory described thus gives it the shape of an umbrella stick or J.

SUMMARY

- **Balance of Payments** – Annual statement of accounts of monetary transactions of the residents of a country vis-à-vis rest of the world – divided into two parts, namely, Balance in Current Account and Balance in Capital Account – involves a vertical double-entry system of accounting – BOP in India is compiled on an accrual basis.
- **Balance in Current Account** – Transactions relating to goods, services and income by the residents – during a financial year – summation of Balance of Visibles (Balance of Trade) + Balance of Invisibles.
- **Balance in Capital Account** – Capital Receipts and Payments – Foreign Investments (FDI and FII), Loans (External Assistance, ECB and Trade Credit) and Banking Capital.
- **FDI** – Non-debt-creating capital transaction – two types – Brownfield and Greenfield – Indian Company may receive FDI under two routes – automatic route and government route.
- **Borrowings** – Debt creating capital transactions – types include External Commercial Borrowings, External assistance and Trade Credit.
- **Net International Investment Position** – Measures the difference between the external financial assets and liabilities of a country.
- **India's forex reserves include** – FCAs, Monetary Gold, SDRs, and Reserve Tranche Position in IMF – RBI is the custodian of foreign exchange reserves.

- **Net Errors and Omissions** – Sampling error due to inability to enter the value of all individual transactions – under-reporting and over-reporting of some transactions such as smuggling activities.
- **Twin Deficit** – Fiscal deficit and current account deficit.
- **India's external debt** – Total debt that India owes to foreign creditors – includes Multi-lateral debt, Bilateral debt, Borrowings from IMF and World Bank, Trade Credit, ECBs, NRI Deposits, Rupee debts, and Short-term debts.

UPSC CSE PREVIOUS YEARS' PRELIMINARY EXAMINATION QUESTIONS

1. Consider the following: **[2021]**

1. Foreign Currency Convertible Bonds
2. Foreign Institutional Investment with certain conditions
3. Global Depository Receipts
4. Non-resident External Deposits

Which of the above can be included in Foreign Direct Investment?

(a) 1, 2 and 3 (b) 3 only
(c) 2 and 4 (d) 1 and 4

2. With reference to the international trade of India at present, which of the following statements is/are correct? **[2020]**

1. India's merchandise exports are less than its merchandise imports.
2. India's imports of iron and steel, chemicals, fertilisers and machinery have decreased in recent years.
3. India's exports of services are more than its imports of services.
4. India suffers from an overall trade/current account deficit.

Select the correct answer using the code given below:

(a) 1 and 2 only (b) 2 and 4 only
(c) 3 only (d) 1, 3 and 4 only

3. Consider the following statements: **[2019]**

1. Most of India's external debt is owned by government entities.
2. All of India's external debt is denominated in US dollars.

Which of the statements above is/are correct?

(a) 1 only
(b) 2 only
(c) Both 1 and 2
(d) Neither 1 nor 2

4. Convertibility of rupee implies **[2015]**

(a) being able to convert rupee notes into gold.
(b) allowing the value of rupee to be fixed by market forces.
(c) freely permitting the conversion of rupee to other currencies and vice versa.
(d) developing an international market for currencies in India.

5. With reference to BOP, which of the following constitute/constitutes the current account? **[2014]**

1. Balance of trade
2. Foreign assets
3. Balance of invisibles
4. Special drawing rights

Select the correct answer using the code given below.

(a) 1 only (b) 2 and 3
(c) 1 and 3 (d) 1, 2 and 4

6. Which of the following constitute capital account? **[2013]**

1. Foreign loan
2. Foreign direct investment
3. Private remittances
4. Portfolio investment

Select the correct answer using the codes given below.

(a) 1, 2 and 3 (b) 1, 2 and 4
(c) 2, 3 and 4 (d) 1, 3 and 4

7. The BOP of a country is a systematic record of **[2013]**

(a) all import and export transactions of a country during a given period of time, normally a year
(b) goods exported from a country during a year

(c) economic transaction between the government of one country and another
(d) capital movements from one country to another

8. Which of the following would include foreign direct investment in India? [2012]
   1. Subsidiaries of foreign companies in India
   2. Majority foreign equity holding in Indian companies
   3. Companies exclusively financed by foreign companies
   4. Portfolio investment

   Select the correct answer using the codes given below:
   (a) 1, 2, 3 and 4 (b) 2 and 4 only
   (c) 1 and 3 only (d) 1, 2 and 3 only

9. Both foreign direct investment (FDI) and foreign institutional investment (FII) are related to investment in a country. Which one of the following statements best represent an important difference between the two? [2011]
   (a) FII helps bring better management skills and technology, while FDI only brings in capital.
   (b) FII helps in increasing capital availability in general, while FDI only targets specific sectors.
   (c) FII flows only into the secondary market, in general while FDI targets primary market.
   (d) FII is considered to be more stable than FDI.

10. A great deal of foreign direct investment (FDI) to India comes from Mauritius than from many major and mature economies like the United Kingdom and France. Why? [2010]
   (a) India has preference for certain countries as regards receiving FDI.
   (b) India has doubled taxation avoidance agreement (DTAA) with Mauritius.
   (c) Most citizens of Mauritius have ethnic identity with India and so they feel secure to invest in India.
   (d) Impending dangers of global climate change prompt Mauritius to make huge investments in India.

☞ NO QUESTIONS ASKED
2024, 2023, 2022, 2018, 2017, 2016

ANSWER KEY

1. (a)	2. (d)	3. (d)	4. (c)	5. (c)
6. (b)	7. (a)	8. (d)	9. (b)	10. (b)

UPSC CSE PREVIOUS YEARS' MAIN EXAMINATION QUESTIONS

1. Justify the **need for FDI** for the development of the Indian economy. Why is there gap between MOUs signed and actual FDIs? Suggest remedial steps to be taken for increasing actual FDIs in India. [2016]
2. Craze for **gold** in Indians has led to a surge in import of gold in recent years and put pressure on BOP and external value of rupee. In view of this, examine the merits of the **Gold Monetisation Scheme.** [2015]
3. **FDI in the defence sector** is set to be liberalised. What influence is this expected to have on the Indian defence and economy in the short and long run? [2014]
4. (a) Discuss the impact of **FDI entry into multi-trade retail sector** on supply chain management in commodity trade pattern of the economy. [2013]
   (b) Though India allowed **FDI** in what is called **multi-brand retail** through the Joint Venture route in September 2012, the FDI, even after a year, has not picked up. Discuss the reasons. [2013]

☞ NO QUESTIONS ASKED
2024, 2023, 2022, 2021, 2020, 2019, 2018, 2017

CHAPTER

28

INDIA'S FOREIGN EXCHANGE AND FOREIGN TRADE

CHAPTER OUTLINE

FOREIGN EXCHANGE RATE SYSTEM

Exchange Rate

Exchange rate is the rate at which the domestic currency is exchanged with other international currencies (e.g. US Dollar) in the foreign exchange market. Or simply, it is the value of one currency compared to another currency. For example, if 1 US Dollar is equal to 75 Indian Rupees, then we have to pay 75 rupees to buy a good which cost 1 Dollar in USA. When the value of domestic currency falls in the international exchange market, it is termed **appreciation.** On the other hand, **depreciation** of a currency occurs when the value of domestic currency increases in the international exchange market.

Last Minute SNIPPETS

On April 24, 2025, India's exchange rate as compared to other major currencies stands as follows:

1 Pound Sterling equals	₹113.55
1 Euro equals	₹97.03
1 US Dollar equals	₹85.36
1 Chinese Yuan Renminbi equals	₹11.71
1 Japanese Yen equals	₹0.60

Factors Influencing Exchange Rates

1. **Inflation:** A country with higher inflation, typically sees depreciation in its currency.
2. **Interest Rates:** A rise in the interest rates at home, often leads to an appreciation of the domestic currency.
3. **Public Debt:** If the Government debt outpaces the economic growth, then it normally leads to depreciation.

4. **Political Stability:** Countries with greater political stability have higher valued currencies, like Switzerland. With political stability, currency appreciates.
5. **Current Account Deficit:** Countries with low current account deficits tend to have stronger currencies compared to those with high deficits.
6. **Speculation:** If there is a speculation that the value of a country's currency is going to rise, demand of that currency will increase. As a result, that currency will appreciate.

Types of Exchange Rate System

There are two types of exchange rate regime:

Types of Exchange Rate System

- Fixed (or pegged) Exchange Rate System
- Flexible (or floating) Exchange Rate System

(a) Fixed Exchange Rate As the name suggests, this rate of exchange between different currencies is **fixed by the Government**. The Government takes necessary measures to maintain the exchange rate at a desired level. The Government of a country decides the exchange rate of its domestic currency with respect to foreign currencies, and on the basis of that exchange rate, the import and export of the country take place.

Advantages of Fixed Exchange Rate System

- It ensures **stability in foreign trade** by avoiding day-to-day fluctuations.
- A fixed exchange rate implies low risk and low uncertainty that might **encourage foreigners to invest funds** into the country.
- Fixed exchange rate **eliminates the speculative activities** in international transactions. There is **no possibility of panic flight of capital** from one country to another.
- It helps to keep the **inflation low** by avoiding depreciation of the domestic currency in the international exchange market.

Disadvantages of Fixed Exchange Rate System

- It gives rise to the **problem of international liquidity.**
- It may also lead to **recession.**
- It **makes monetary policies ineffective.**
- The Government has to maintain a certain amount of foreign exchange reserve.
- International competitiveness is bypassed.

(b) Flexible (or Floating) Exchange Rate It is the rate which is determined through the **demand and supply** of different currencies in the foreign exchange market.

Under this regime, there exist two types of systems:

- **Free Float**: Under free float, rate of exchange is market determined; i.e. it is determined by the forces of demand and supply of currencies in the foreign exchange market.
- **Managed Float**: It is a **hybrid** of fixed and flexible exchange rate system. It is guided by the broad principles of careful monitoring and management of exchange rate with flexibility, while allowing

demand and supply conditions to determine exchange rate movements over a period in an orderly manner.

The Central Bank (RBI) only intervenes in the forex market to restrict the fluctuations in exchange rate **within a certain range. Exchange rate can float freely within that range.**

In India, this regime is followed.

Under Managed Float, RBI intervenes through sale and purchase of foreign currency in the international money market to restrict movement of exchange rate within a certain range. This is also known as **Dirty Float**.

Advantages of Floating (Flexible) Exchange Rate System

- **Protection from external shocks**: If the exchange rate is free to float, then it can change in response to any external shock like crude oil price rise. This reduces the negative impact of any external shock.
- **Optimum resource allocation**: Under flexible exchange rate system, resources are efficiently allocated in the area of international trade.
- **International capital movement**: Flexible exchange rate system allows movement of capital all across the world, as the member countries are not required to keep huge international reserves.
- **No requirement of a large foreign exchange reserve:** Central Banks do not require large foreign exchange reserves to defend the exchange rate as in the case of Fixed Exchange Rate.

Disadvantages of Floating (Flexible) Exchange Rate System

- It creates condition of **instability and uncertainty,** which in turn tends to reduce the volume of international trade and foreign investment.
- **Adverse effect on economic structure**: Exchange rate tends to fluctuate a lot. Fluctuating exchange rates cause changes in the price of imports and exports, which in turn destabilise the economy.
- **Inflationary effect**: This system involves greater possibility of inflationary effect of exchange depreciation on domestic price level of a country. Inflationary rise in prices leads to further depreciation of the external value of the currency.

Floating *versus* Fixed Exchange Rate

Floating Exchange Rate	Fixed Exchange Rate
Reduces the need for foreign currency reserves	Certainty of currency value gives confidence for inward investment, but there lies a higher need for forex reserves
Greater possibility of inflationary effect	Stability helps to control inflation
Insulation from any external shock, especially for export-dependent countries	The economy is exposed to external shocks
Partial automatic correction of Current Account Deficit (CAD)	Imposes responsibility on Government policies to correct CAD
More risk of speculative attack	Less chances of speculative attack

EXAM ESSENTIAL

TOBIN TAX

It is a kind of tax which is **levied on spot currency conversions, to disincentivise short term currency speculations** and is named after the economist, James Tobin.

In 1971, when the fixed exchange rates were replaced by the flexible exchange rates, there was a huge movement between the currencies that threatened to destabilise the economy.

BONUS KNOWLEDGE

WHICH EXCHANGE RATE SYSTEM SUITS AN ECONOMY BEST?

For small economies with a dominant trading partner that maintains a reasonably stable monetary policy, **fixed exchange rate system is suitable.** This has been found to be true internationally in the case of many small economies like small Caribbean islands, small Central American countries and small Pacific Island countries. Currencies of Nepal and Bhutan are also pegged to the Indian Rupee. Moreover, currencies of Africa, Namibia, Swaziland, etc. are pegged to the South African Rand.

Also, economies with huge export surplus and enormous forex reserves like China are able to follow a fixed exchange rate regime.

The other available options are free float and managed float. As free float carries the risk of sudden capital flight and speculative attacks, it can be disastrous for an economy.

Thus, a majority of countries combine features of pegged system and free float system in various degrees to follow an **intermediate exchange rate regime**. India also belongs to this category by following a managed float system.

Depreciation *versus* Devaluation and Depreciation *versus* Appreciation

Depreciation	Devaluation
It occurs when the value of domestic currency falls in the international exchange market. It **occurs automatically** through the market forces of demand and supply.	When the value of domestic currency is **deliberately reduced by the Government**, it is termed 'devaluation'.
For example, If ₹/$ increases from ₹75 per $ to ₹80 per $, it signifies depreciation.	**For example**, if the value of ₹/$ is deliberately increased by the Government from ₹75 per $ to ₹80 per $, it signifies devaluation.
It is found under **flexible exchange rate system**.	It is found under **fixed exchange rate system**.
Depreciation results in the decrease in net foreign currency outflow in the case of an import surplus country and vice versa.	Devaluation leads to excess supply of foreign currency (say $) from the international market. Therefore, the Government needs to absorb that excess supply through purchase of foreign currency, thereby giving rise to forex reserves.

Depreciation	Appreciation
When more rupee is required to buy a foreign currency (say $), it is termed 'depreciation'.	When less rupee is required to buy a foreign currency (say $), it is known as 'appreciation'.
Rupee becomes weak as compared to Dollars.	Rupee becomes strong as compared to Dollars.
Exports are likely to rise.	Exports are likely to fall.
Both Depreciation and Appreciation are phenomena under **flexible exchange rate system**.	

did you KNOW?

Less developed countries often devalue their currency because,

- Devaluation by the Government raises the demand of domestically produced goods and services and thereby exports are expected to rise.
- Rise of exports helps to raise foreign exchange flow which as a result facilitates imports of essential items.
- Devaluation also attracts private foreign investment into the economy which enables a better GDP growth.

*In **July 1991**, the Indian Government devalued the rupee by between 18 and 19 per cent to overcome the **BOP Crisis**.*

***Black Wednesday** occurred in the United Kingdom in 1992.*

***December Mistake** occurred in Mexico in 1994.*

Effects of Currency Devaluation

Gainers	Losers
Exporters	Firms who buy imported raw materials
Domestic tourist industry	Residents who holiday abroad
Workers gaining jobs in export industry	Normal consumers who buy imported goods

BONUS KNOWLEDGE

CURRENCY MANIPULATION

Currency manipulation is a policy used by the central banks or Governments of certain countries, **to artificially devaluate the value of their currencies** to leap an unfair trade advantage in global trade.

The US Department of Treasury releases the semi-annual Currency Practices Monitoring List (Currency Manipulators Watch List). There are three conditions basis which the countries are placed in the List:

1. A significant bilateral trade surplus with the US
2. A current account surplus over a 12 month period equivalent to a minimum 2 per cent of GDP
3. Continuous one-sided intervention

If any country meets two of the three conditions, that country will be placed in the watch list.

EXAM ESSENTIAL

CURRENCY WAR

When there occurs a fierce competition among countries **to cheapen their currency through devaluation** in order to gain trade advantage, it leads to Currency War. The term was coined by Brazilian Finance Minister **Guido Mantega** in 2010. Recent instances of Currency War in the last 10 years can be found between the United States and China, Japan and Eurozone, the United States and Germany, etc.

HISTORY OF EXCHANGE RATE SYSTEM IN INDIA

- **1947–71**: As India was one of the founding members of IMF, India was obligated to follow Bretton Woods system of **adjustable peg system** of exchange rate. The exchange rate was **pegged in terms of US Dollar**, which was assigned gold value at a fixed price (USD 35 per ounce of gold). India was required to maintain its market exchange rate within ±1 per cent of the defined value. The system followed was also called the **Par Value System**.
- **1971–75**: As the Bretton Wood system collapsed in 1971, with the suspension of convertibility of Dollar by the United States, the Indian rupee was then **pegged to UK's Pound Sterling** till 1975.
- **1975–92**: Instead of pegging to a single currency, the rupee was pegged to a basket of currencies and this system continued in the 1980s.
- **1992–93:** Due to major BOP crisis and consequent economic reforms, **LERMS (Liberalised Exchange Rate Management System)** was put in place which was India's initial step to enable transition towards market determined exchange rate. Under LERMS, **dual exchange rate system** was followed; i.e. 40 per cent of the export earnings were to be converted at the official exchange rate as prescribed by RBI and the remaining 60 per cent at exchange rate determined by the market forces of demand and supply. As the official exchange rate was lower than market exchange rate, this system was highly resented by exporters.
- **1993 onwards**: Dual exchange rate was replaced by the **Unified Exchange Rate System** (UERS) by allowing 100 per cent conversion (instead of 60:40) and under which **managed float** exchange rate system was adopted.

EXAM ESSENTIAL

Nominal Effective Exchange Rate (NEER) – It is a measure of the value of a currency against a weighted average of a basket of foreign currencies. The currencies are weighted according to the amount of trade with that country. NEER is not adjusted for inflation. NEER is said to appreciate when the value of domestic currency increases against a basket of different currencies in the floating exchange rate system.

Real Effective Exchange Rate (REER) – It is NEER adjusted with inflation index. REER is considered as a good measure to check international competitiveness of a currency. An increase in REER of a country indicates that the exports of the country are becoming expensive, and on the other hand its imports are becoming cheaper.

The increasing difference between NEER and REER of a country indicates that the rate of inflation in the concerned country is higher than the related countries in the compared basket of currencies.

Big Mac Index – It is used to measure the **Purchasing Power Parity (PPP)** between nations by comparing the price of McDonald's Big Mac burger.

For example, if the price of a Big Mac is $2 in the United States and it is ₹100 in India, then as per Big Mac Index, the exchange rate of rupees in terms of US Dollars is ₹50/$.

If the actual market exchange rate (₹/$) is higher than the PPP rate as per Big Mac Index, then it can be inferred that rupee is undervalued and vice versa.

However, Big Mac Index has flaws in the sense that the price of a Big Mac burger across various countries is based on the decision of McDonald's.

RESERVE ADEQUACY: FEW MONTHS OF IMPORTS RULE *VERSUS* GUIDOTTI-GREENSPAN RULE

- Traditionally, an adequate amount of forex reserve was determined in terms of reserves equivalent for few months of imports. However, with increasing importance of capital account transactions in BOP, this approach is now becoming less relevant.
- Short-term external debt among various capital account transactions has gained prominence now under BOP.
- Thus, the **ratio of short-term debt to forex reserves** has emerged as a relevant yardstick to determine reserve adequacy.
- In this regard, **Guidotti-Greenspan Rule was postulated in 1999** under which the foreign excha nge reserves of a country should cover at least 100 per cent of the short-term external debt obligations for about 1 year.

Component-wise Indian forex reserves – *explained in the previous chapter.*

Year	1991–92	End of December 2024	End of April 2025
India's Forex Reserves	$5.8 billion	$640.2 billion	$676.3 billion

Source: RBI

Last Minute SNIPPETS

- India ranks among the top 10 countries in terms of forex reserves, the first being China.
- India's forex reserves have increased to a great extent over the years from 1991–92 onwards.

BONUS KNOWLEDGE

STERILISATION AS A POLICY TOOL OF RBI

RBI has intervened excessively in recent years to prevent the rupee from appreciating too fast. This **has helped to bring in more Dollars** into the Indian economy. Moreover, with the help of slug gish imports and capital controls in recent years, we find a continuous rise in India's forex reserves.

RBI has mainly intervened through the policy of **sterilisation**.

Under sterilisation, RBI **purchases Dollars** from the market and releases Indian rupee in return – and then again sucks the excessive rupee from the economy through **sale of Government Securities (G-Secs)**. This process of sterilisation has been the RBI's important exchange rate management tool in recent years.

CONVERTIBILITY OF INDIAN RUPEE

- Convertibility means that the currency of a country can be freely converted into a foreign exchange at market-determined exchange rate.
- For example, convertibility of rupee means that those who have foreign exchange (*e.g. US Dollars and Pound Sterling*) can get them converted into rupee and vice versa at the market-determined rate of exchange.
- Convertibility is of two types: on current account and on capital account.
- Current account convertibility means ability to convert rupee into any foreign currency and vice versa for using it in current account transactions.
- Capital account convertibility implies freedom to convert local financial assets into foreign financial assets and vice versa at market-determined rates of exchange.
- **Rupee has been made fully convertible in current account** since 1994 (*as India was also obligated under Article VIII of the Articles of Agreement with IMF to avoid imposing restrictions on convertibility for current account transactions*).
- Thereafter, for suggesting a road map for **convertibility of rupee on capital account**, RBI constituted **Tarapore Committee – I and II** in 1997 and 2006, respectively.
- However, the recommendations of both Tarapore Committees are yet to be adopted. Till now, the Rupee is **partially convertible on capital account**. it means prior approval of RBI or GOI is still needed in this case.

did you KNOW?

Rupee is convertible in current account except for following four current account transactions:

1. For conversion of > $10,000 by any Indian tourist, prior approval of the RBI is required.
2. For education and treatment, any requirement in excess of $1 lakh requires prior approval of the RBI.
3. Remittances for prize money received through game shows, lottery, racing, betting, etc. are not allowed.
4. Foreign currency payment to Indian/foreign artists requires prior approval of the Ministry of Finance.

EXAM ESSENTIAL

WHAT ARE THE POTENTIAL BENEFITS AND LIMITATIONS OF FULL CONVERTIBILITY OF RUPEE?

Potential Benefits

- Convertibility helps to attract foreign investment, thereby enabling faster economic growth.
- Improved employment and business opportunities due to more foreign investment.
- Larger liquidity in financial markets.
- Progress in multiple industry sectors.

Limitations

- It exposes the economy to global vulnerabilities.
- There remains a fear of sudden capital flight which may also lead to increase in current account deficit.

Major relaxations so far under Capital Account Convertibility (CAC):

- FDI in most sectors has been allowed under automatic route and FIIs have been allowed liberally.
- ECB (External Commercial Borrowing) no longer require RBI's or GOI's approval up to a certain limit.
- Indian citizen can invest up to $2.5 lakh in foreign markets.

- Risk of speculative attacks.
- No ceiling on external debt may be disastrous.
- Contagion effect, i.e. more chances of transmission of the effect of financial crisis occurring in a particular country to the Indian economy.

As per the Tarapore Committee, there are some **pre-conditions which need to be fulfilled before going for full convertibility** of rupee:

1. Reduce fiscal deficit to 3.5 per cent of GDP.
2. Reduce public debt by setting up *consolidated sinking fund*.
3. Fix inflation target between 3 per cent and 5 per cent.
4. Strengthen the Indian financial sector.

Other than the above pre-conditions, the Committee also recommended adequate forex reserves, minimal NPAs, intervention by RBI only if REER exceeds ±5 per cent band, reduction of CAD to manageable limits, etc.

Thus, going for full convertibility of rupee may be helpful for the Indian economy to become more globally competitive. However, the decision has to be based on good preparations and not to be taken in a hurry. Some restrictions should continue even after going for the full convertibility of rupee.

BONUS KNOWLEDGE

DUTCH DISEASE

It is **a paradox** under which a good news such as discovery of oil reserves in a country may harm the country's broader economy. The term was first coined in 1977.

How it works – Say with the discovery of oil reserves, for example, there is a large influx of foreign investments in those oil reserves – leading to stronger domestic currency – this appreciation of domestic currency makes export products of manufacturing sector uncompetitive and may lead to fall in their overall exports. This phenomenon also leads to rise in imports in the economy. It was experienced in Great Britain in the 1970s. In 2014, there were reported concerns over probable Dutch Disease in Canada though it has eased down now.

INTERNATIONALISATION OF RUPEE

Indian rupee will be termed as 'internationalised' if:

- Banks, firms and residents of another country start holding it for financial security.
- It is accepted in international trade transactions.
- Non-residents are eager to invest in rupee-denominated assets, etc.

Pre-requisites of internationalisation of any currency include:

1. Sufficiency in the availability of that currency
2. Stability of that currency
3. Liquidity of that currency

Presently, **US Dollar, Euro, Pound Sterling, Yen and Renminbi** may be termed 'international currencies'. Nepal or Bhutan hold India rupee along with their own official currencies (Nepalese Rupee and Bhutanese Ngultrum, respectively) for financial security and for cross-border trade.

Potential benefits of internationalisation of domestic currency may include **savings of forex reserves in international transactions, improved foreign trade and better international capital flows.**

BONUS KNOWLEDGE

VOSTRO/NOSTRO ACCOUNTS

The term **Vostro** comes from the Latin word *yours* which means *your money is deposited at our bank*. Similarly, the term **Nostro** comes from the Latin word *ours* which means *our money is deposited at your bank*. The terms Vostro and Nostro are used to describe the same bank account.

Vostro Account is the account held **by a domestic bank in local currency for a foreign bank**. Vostro account of a country is the Nostro account of the other country in international trade. For example, suppose Bank A has no branch in Russia, but Bank B does. Now, to receive any deposit in Russia, Bank A will open a Nostro account in Bank B. To send any money to Bank A from Russia, they can deposit it in A's account in B. Then B will transfer the money to A. Recently, Russian banks opened Nostro accounts in India.

Special Rupee Vostro Accounts (SRVA) Arrangement The SRVA is an additional arrangement where it uses freely convertible currencies.

EXAM ESSENTIAL

Dollarisation is the term used when the US Dollar (or a currency of another country) is used in addition to or instead of the domestic currency of another country. It is an example of **currency substitution**. Dollarisation usually happens when a country's own currency loses its usefulness as a medium of exchange, due to hyperinflation or instability.

De-Dollarisation is a process of **reducing the Dollar's dominance** in the international market by replacing it with other currencies. In de-dollarisation, **other currencies are used except dollar for trading** oil and/or other commodities. Countries start reducing their forex reserves in dollars and take several other measures to reduce the importance of Dollar. E.g.: India-Russia Rupee-Ruble trade.

BRICS members are developing a new currency for cross-border payments. India and Malaysia have agreed to settle trade in Indian rupees, in addition to their present currencies. These are viewed as a significant step towards de-dollarisation.

Why is De-Dollarisation gaining root?

- **Weaponisation of Trade:** Sanctions and exclusion from SWIFT impose barriers to international trade. For example, sanctions were placed on Russia following the Ukraine war.
- **New Emerging Economies:** As Asia becomes an economic powerhouse, currencies such as the Indian rupee and Yuan are becoming increasingly important.
- **Diversification Benefits:** Having several foreign currency reserves reduces pressure on external industries.
- **Manipulation by the US:** The USD's dominance enables the US to influence the global financial system to its advantage, frequently at the expense of others.

CURRENCY SWAP

A bilateral currency swap is a transaction in which two parties exchange an equivalent amount of money with each other but in different currencies. The parties are essentially loaning each other money and will repay the amounts at a specified date and exchange rate. The purpose could be to hedge exposure to exchange-rate risk, to speculate on the direction of a currency or to reduce the cost of borrowing in a foreign currency.

Last Minute SNIPPETS

In 2024, RBI signed a Currency Swap Agreement with the Maldives Monetary Authority (MMA) under the SAARC Currency Swap Framework 2024–2027 and a Currency Swap Agreement between India and Japan in 2018.

RBI can use it for purposes like payment for imports, to service foreign currency loans, etc.

HARD CURRENCY *VERSUS* SOFT CURRENCY

Hard currency is a stable and reliable form of currency that is issued by the Government and widely accepted around the world. Such currency is in global demand as a store of value. Long-term stability, fiscal and economic policies of a country, strength of the economy, etc. are the relevant factors behind the emergence of a hard currency. Present examples may be *US Dollar, Pound Sterling, Japanese Yen, etc.*

Soft currency is an unstable form of currency that is less liquid, fluctuates erratically and depreciates against other currencies. Recent examples may be *Zimbabwe Dollar and Venezuelan Bolivar*.

BONUS KNOWLEDGE

INTERNATIONAL INVESTMENT POSITION (IIP)

- This report is published by IMF.
- IIP related data of India is compiled and published by RBI every quarter.
- It is based on the survey of India's foreign liabilities and assets and 13 other sources of data.
- IIP reflects:
  1. External assets of India (*includes direct investments abroad, portfolio investments, other investments abroad and foreign exchange reserves*).
  2. External liabilities of India (*includes FDIs in India, portfolio investments in India, financial derivatives and other investments from abroad*).
- Net IIP is the difference between India's total external assets and total external liabilities.
- The **Net IIP position** indicates whether a country is a net creditor or debtor nation. A positive NIIP value indicates that a nation is a creditor nation, while a negative value indicates that it is a debtor nation.
- As reported by RBI, **Net claims of Non-Residents on India** (as reflected by the net IIP) closed at USD 348.5 billion in September 2024 quarter (indicating India being net debtor). It has shown a fluctuating trend in figure in last 03 years, however, India has been a debtor nation.

FERA (1973) AND FEMA (1999)

FERA

During the initial years of the 1970s, India was facing severe foreign exchange crisis mainly due to dependence on imports of essential commodities and frequent wars against the neighbouring countries. In the background of such a scenario, the Foreign Exchange Regulation Act (FERA) was promulgated in 1973 and it came into force on 1 January 1974. This law mainly regulates certain payments, dealings in foreign exchange and securities, export and import of currencies to **conserve the foreign exchange resources** of the country and its **optimal utilisation**.

Features

1. Used to extend all over India.
2. It covered citizens of India who reside outside India and also companies or body corporate, registered or incorporated in India, whose branches and agencies are outside India.

FEMA

Foreign Exchange Management Act (FEMA) was promulgated in the year 1999, to replace the FERA, 1973. Aim of FEMA is to unite and revise the existing laws related to foreign exchange, promote foreign trade in the country and encourage foreign exchange market in India.

Features

1. FEMA broadly covers three areas – (a) Rupee convertibility, (b) Setting up of a separate Enforcement Directorate (ED) for trying out criminal offenses in foreign exchange and (c) Borrowings by the corporate sector.
2. FEMA is considered to be more liberal in allowing transactions without restrictions, and facilitated international trade.

INDIA'S FOREIGN TRADE

Foreign trade is the exchange of goods, services and capital among countries across international borders. Foreign trade has a significant effect on the share of GDP of a country.

Objectives of Foreign Trade in India

- Apart from **earning foreign exchange**, foreign trade helps in the stimulation of economic activities and **economic growth**.
- Foreign trade not only accelerates the economic growth by **expanding global market** opportunities but also makes India a globally vibrant economy.
- Foreign trade enhances the **efficiency of agriculture** in India and also **enhances technology** in various fields.

- Foreign trade helps in **improving the quality of the goods and services** produced in India, and thereby providing quality products to the consumers at better comparative prices.
- Foreign trade increases the **job opportunities** and creates **healthy relations** among the nations.

EXAM ESSENTIAL

Different Phases of India's Foreign Trade Policy

Phase I	Import Restriction and Import Substitution	1950s–1970s
Phase II	Export Promotion and Import Liberalisation	1970s–1990s
Phase III	Outward Oriented	1990s–present

Exports, Imports and Trade Balance

Year	Exports (including re-exports) (₹ crore)	Imports (₹ crore)	Trade Balance (₹ crore)	Rate of Change	
				Export	Import
				(Per cent)	
(1)	(2)	(3)	(4)	(5)	(6)
2021–22	3147021	4572775	–1425753	45.8	56.8
2022–23	3620631	5733959	–2113328	15	25.4
2023–24	2619157	4189495	–1570338	–	–
2024–25 (P)	2698637	4467342	–1768705	3.0	6.6

Source: Directorate General of Commercial Intelligence & Statistics (DGCI&S), Kolkata

Composition of India's Merchandise Foreign Trade

Category	Ranking
Sector-wise share in total exports [Apr 2024–Dec 24]	Engineering Goods > Petroleum Products > Electronic Goods > Drugs and Pharmaceuticals > Gems and Jewelleries
Sector-wise share in total imports [Apr 2024–Dec 24]	Petroleum: Crude > Gold > Coal, Coke and Briquettes etc. > Petroleum Products > Electronic Components
Exports – Country wise [2023–24 (Apr–Jan)]	USA > UAE > Netherland > China > UK
Imports – Country wise [2023–24 (Apr–Jan)]	China > Russia > UAE > USA > Saudi Arabia

Source: Ministry of Commerce and Industry

VARIOUS ECONOMIC INTEGRATIONS IN FOREIGN TRADE

Preferential Trade Area (PTA)

Under this, member countries **lower the trade barriers** among themselves **rather than eliminate** the barriers. In PTA, members are independent to create trade relations with non-member countries. This agreement gives preferential access to certain goods.

Economic Cooperation Organisation (ECO) formed in 1992, South Pacific Regional Trade and Economic Cooperation Agreement (SPARTECA) formed in 1981, etc. are examples of PTA.

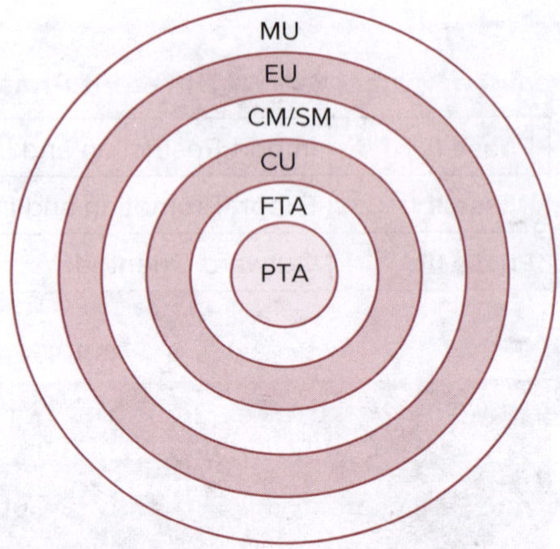

PTA = Preferential Trade Area
FTA = Free Trade Area
CU = Custom Union
CM/SM = Common Market/Single Market
EU = Economic Union
MU = Monetary Union

Free Trade Area (FTA)

It deals with **removal of trade barriers** (*both tariff and non-tariff*). It is considered as an open border relationship among regional (member) countries. Members are independent to create other trade relations with non-member countries. It is the second stage of economic integration.

Greater Arab Free Trade Area (GAFTA), ASEAN Free Trade Area (AFTA), South Asian Free Trade Area (SAFTA), etc. are examples of FTA.

BONUS KNOWLEDGE

CECA *versus* CEPA

Comprehensive Economic Cooperation Agreement (CECA) and Comprehensive Economic Partnership Agreement (CEPA) are **more comprehensive than FTAs**. The major difference between CECA and CEPA is that CECA involves only tariff reduction or elimination on listed items except the negative list and tariff rate quota (TRQ) items. Whereas, CEPA covers trade in services and investments as well. So **CEPA is broader than CECA**. India has signed CEPA with Japan, South Korea and UAE and is in talks with Canada.

- **India and Gulf Cooperating Council (GCC)** have announced the intent to pursue negotiations on the **India–GCC FTA**.
- **India–Canada CEPA negotiation has been re-launched** at the 5th India-Canada MDTI (Ministerial Dialogue on Trade and Investment) with the possibility of EPTA (Early Progress Trade Agreement).

Bilateral Trade and Investment Agreement (BTIA)

It is a kind of FTA. In 2007, India and EU began negotiations on the broad-based BTIA in Brussels, Belgium. EU wanted greater market access for automobiles, wine and spirits, financial services sector such as banking, insurance and e-commerce. EU also wanted labour, environment and Government procurements to be included. Whereas, India is demanding easier work visa and study visa norms and a data secure status, which are not being accepted by EU till now.

Regional Comprehensive Economic Partnership (RCEP)

The RCEP came into effect on 1 January, 2022. It is the world's **largest free trade zone** in terms of trade volume. Its members are ASEAN Countries, China, Japan, South Korea, Australia and New Zealand. **India has not joined yet**.

It is **aimed to** open up trade in **services** and **promote investments**. It is to help members to export a product anywhere within the bloc, without meeting separate requirements for each country.

It also covers IPRs but does not cover environmental protection and labour rights. India did not join, because of its concerns over trade deficit with China and failure of agreement to adequately liberalise services sector.

Custom Union

Under this trade agreement, members not only eliminate all trade barriers but also follow a **common policy towards non-member countries**. It is the third stage of economic integration.

Economic and Monetary Community of Central Africa (CEMAC), Gulf Cooperation Council (GCC) and East African Community (EAC) are examples of Custom Union.

Common Market/Single Market

Under such economic integration, **trade barriers are removed**; members adopt **common policies for non-member countries** and also **allow free movement of the factors of production** such as capital and labour.

ASEAN Economic Community (AEC) and GCC are examples of Common Market.

Economic Union

It is the **second-last stage of economic integration**. Economic Union has the **features of both** Custom Union and Common Market. Under this trade bloc, trade barriers are removed, and common policies are adopted for economic relations with non-member countries and freedom of movements of factors of production and goods and services. Apart from these features, under Economic Union, member countries also adopt **common economic policies**.

Central American Common Market, European Union and GCC are the examples of Economic Union.

Monetary Union (MU)

MU is the **final stage of economic integration**. It has all the features of Economic Union along with prevalence of a common currency in all member nations. Best example is **Euro Zone**.

Institutions related to Foreign Trade

- **Department of Commerce:** It is responsible for the formulation and directions for the foreign trade policy programs and also helps in establishing trade relation with other countries.
- **Board of Trade:** It maintains the trade relations and policy measures of the Government as well as takes corrective actions on behalf of the Government.

- **Commodity-Specific Organisation:** It helps in tracking the problems related to individual commodity or group of commodities in foreign trade. It also assists in promotion of export and helps in the management of import.
- **EXIM Bank of India:** Export Import bank of India was established in the year **1982** under Export Import Bank of India Act 1981. It manages the financing programmes in export and import sector and also handles overseas investment by Indian companies.

Recent Major Schemes to Promote Foreign Trade

- **Export Promotion Scheme**: To promote export and infrastructural development for the export from India, the Government launched the *Export Promotion Scheme*. It has the following two subparts:
    1. Merchandise Exports from India Scheme (MEIS)
    2. Service Exports from India Scheme (SEIS)

Note: After various export promotion schemes including Merchandise Exports from India Scheme (MEIS) were challenged in WTO, India has rolled out a new WTO-compliant scheme, namely **Remission of Duties and Taxes on Exported Products (RoDTEP)**, for all export goods with effect from 1 January 2021. Under RoDTEP, taxes and levies charged on the exported products are either exempted or remitted to exporters. The Scheme is based on the globally accepted principle that taxes and duties should not be exported. Thus, this Scheme makes our exports much more competitive in global markets.

- **Duty Exemption and Remission Scheme:** It is launched by **Ministry of Commerce and Industry**. It has two parts:
    1. **Duty Exemption Schemes** enables duty free import of inputs required for export production. It consists of Advance Authorisation Scheme and Duty-Free Import Authorisation (DFIA) Scheme.
    2. **Duty Remission Scheme** enables post export replenishment/remission of duty on inputs used in export product. It consists of Duty Entitlement Passbook (DEPB) Scheme and Duty Drawback (DBK) Scheme.
- **Export Promotion Capital Goods (EPCG) Scheme**: This scheme is related to both exports and imports. Under this scheme, capital goods are imported at zero custom duty. Only those capital goods which enhance India's export competitiveness in global market are applicable under this scheme.
- **Foreign Trade Policy (2015–20)**: The salient features of this policy are as follows:
    1. **Digitalisation** – Online procedure for all documentation, complaint registration and inter-ministerial consultations for online approval of exporting **SCOMET** items.

EXAM ESSENTIAL

SCOMET – The export of strategic items or **dual-use items** are regulated by the **Director General of Foreign Trade (DGFT)**. Dual-use items are those which can be used in both peace and war times. These items are classified as *Special Chemicals, Organisms, Materials, Equipment and Technologies (SCOMET)*. Items under SCOMET can be used for both civilian and military purposes.

2. **24×7 Customs Clearance** – This facility is available in seaports and some airports in India. It is available on certain specific imports.
3. **Movements of Consignments** – Those items whose export cannot be delayed or withheld because of some instructions from State or Central Government are called *consignments*.

4. **EPCG Authorisation** – Proper maintenance and authorisation of certificates by EPCG.
   Due to COVID-19 emergency, the GoI **extended** the Foreign Trade Policy (2015–20) till 31 March 2023.

➤ **Foreign Trade Policy (FTP) (2023):** The Union Ministry of Commerce and Industry has issued the Foreign Trade Policy 2023. FTP 2023 is based on the continuation of time-tested schemes that facilitate exports, as well as a document that is flexible and responsive to trade requirements. It is built on four pillars:

1. Incentive for Remission
2. Export promotion through collaboration: exporters, states, districts, Indian missions
3. Ease of doing business, reduced transaction costs, e-initiatives, and emerging areas of e-commerce
4. Developing districts as export hubs and simplifying SCOMET policies

Export Promotion Initiatives by FTP 2023:

- **Districts as Export Hubs:** The FTP intends to increase exports from districts by partnering with state governments and implementing the Districts as Export Hubs (DEH) project.
- **Export Promotion of Capital Goods (EPCG) Scheme:** To enable the import of capital goods for the production of high-quality goods and services, thus increasing India's manufacturing competitiveness.
- **Streamlining SCOMET Policy:** India is focusing on the 'export control' system to streamline its SCOMET policy and increase its interaction with other nations.
  Stakeholders are becoming more aware of and knowledgeable about SCOMET (Special Chemicals, Organisms, Materials, Equipment, and Technologies).
- **Facilitating E-Commerce Exports:** E-commerce exports are a promising category that requires distinct policy interventions from traditional offline trade.

➤ **Production-Linked Incentive (PLI) Scheme**: The Scheme provides incentives to companies on incremental sales for products manufactured in domestic units, which is expected to create minimum production of over US$ 500 billion in five years. Automobiles and auto components, pharmaceutical drugs, telecom and networking products, electronic/technology products, etc., are some of the sectors covered under PLI Scheme. The Scheme is expected to give a push to both domestic manufacturing capabilities and exports.

➤ **Developing District as Export Hub:** Under this Scheme, the products with export potential (including agricultural, geographical indication and toy clusters) have been identified in 739 districts across the country. District Export Promotion Committees **(DEPCs)** have been set up in each district.

➤ **Export Credit Guarantee Corporation of India Ltd. (ECGC Ltd)** provides **insurance cover to banks** against risks in export credit lending to the exporter borrowers. Government approved a capital infusion of ₹4,400 crore to ECGC Ltd. over a period of five years, i.e. from 2021–2022 to 2025–2026.

➤ **National Export Insurance Account:** Government has approved continuation of the National Export Insurance Account (NEIA) scheme and infusion of ₹1,650 crore Grant-in-Aid over 5 years. NEIA has been set up to ensure **credit risk cover** for medium and long-term exports (with high value) which are commercially viable, considering the limitations of the present insurance system in providing insurance cover to exporters.

➤ **Ubharte Sitare Fund: To promote export oriented MSMEs**, this fund of **₹250 crore** has been launched as Alternative Investment Fund (AIF). This will promote both MSME sector and exports. The fund has been set up **by EXIM Bank and SIDBI**. The Fund **covers potential companies** across various sectors such as pharma, auto components, engineering solutions, agriculture and software etc.

- **Krishi UDAN *(Ude Desh ka Aam Nagarik)* Scheme:** It was launched by the **Ministry of Civil Aviation** in 2020 to assist farmers in transporting agricultural products on international and national routes in order to improve their **value realisation. Krishi Udan 2.0** was launched in 2021, enhancing the existing provisions, mainly focusing on transporting 'perishable food products' from the hilly areas, North-Eastern States, and tribal areas.

BONUS KNOWLEDGE

INTEREST EQUALISATION SCHEME

- The Scheme has been formulated to give benefit in the interest rates being charged by the banks to the exporters – especially the MSMEs, on their pre- and post-shipment rupee export credits. From 1 October 2021 onwards, subvention rates have been reduced.
- **According to the reports**
  - India was the **7th Largest Service Exporter and 18th Largest Merchandise Exporter** in the world in 2024.
  - In 2024, India was the largest recipient of remittances (an estimated $129.1 billion) in the world (as per the World Bank).

Last Minute SNIPPETS

India's total exports (Merchandise and Services combined) for November 2024 is estimated at USD 67.79 billion, registering a positive growth of 9.59 percent vis-à-vis November 2023. Total imports (Merchandise and Services combined) for November 2024 is estimated at USD 87.63 billion, registering a positive growth of 27.47 percent vis-à-vis November 2023.

SUMMARY

- **Exchange Rate** – Rate at which the domestic currency is exchanged with other international currencies.
- **Fixed Exchange Rate** – Fixed by the Government – ensures stability in foreign trade – encourages foreigners to invest funds – eliminates the speculative activities – makes monetary policies ineffective.
- **Floating Exchange Rate** – Depends on demand and supply of different currencies – are of two types – free float and managed float – provides protection from external shocks.
- **Depreciation** – Value of domestic currency falls in the international exchange market due to market forces – more rupees is required to buy a foreign currency – exports are likely to rise – phenomenon of floating exchange rate system.
- **Devaluation** – Value of domestic currency is deliberately reduced by the Government – generally occurs in fixed exchange rate system.
- **Guidotti-Greenspan Rule** – Foreign reserves of a country should cover at least 100 per cent of the short-term external debt obligations for about 1 year.

- **Currency Swap** – Transaction in which two parties exchange an equivalent amount of money with each other but in different currencies – parties are essentially loaning each other the money and will repay the amounts at a specified date and exchange rate.
- **Hard Currency** – Stable and reliable form of currency – widely accepted around the world – US Dollar, Pound sterling, Japanese Yen, etc.
- **Soft Currency** – Unstable form of currency that is less liquid, fluctuates erratically and depreciates against other currencies – Zimbabwe Dollar and Venezuelan Bolivar.
- **Preferential Trade Area (PTA)** – First stages of economic integration – member countries lower the trade barriers among themselves rather than eliminating the barriers.
- **Free Trade Area (FTA)** – Second stage of economic integration – removal of trade barriers (*both tariff and non-tariff*).
- **Custom Union** – Third stage of economic integration – members not only eliminate all trade barriers but also follow a common policy towards non-member countries.
- **Common Market** – Fourth stage of economic integration – trade barriers are removed; members adopt common policies for non-member countries and also allow free movement of the factors of production such as capital and labour.
- **Economic Union** – Fifth stage of economic integration – features of both Custom Union and Common Market – adopt common economic policies.
- **Monetary Union** – Final stage of economic integration – features of Economic Union along with prevalence of a common currency in all member nations.

UPSC CSE PREVIOUS YEARS' PRELIMINARY EXAMINATION QUESTIONS

1. With reference to the Indian economy, consider the following statements: **[2022]**

1. An increase in Nominal Effective Exchange Rate (NEER) indicates the appreciation of rupee.
2. An increase in the Real Effective Exchange Rate (REER) indicates an improvement in trade competitiveness.
3. An increasing trend in domestic inflation relative to inflation in other countries is likely to cause an increasing divergence between NEER and REER.

Which of the above statements are correct?

(a) 1 and 2 only (b) 2 and 3 only
(c) 1 and 3 only (d) 1, 2 and 3

2. The effect of devaluation of a currency is that it necessarily **[2021]**

1. Improves the competitiveness of the domestic export in the foreign markets
2. Increases the foreign value of domestic currency
3. Improves the trade balance

Which of the above statement(s) is/are correct?

(a) 1 only (b) 1 and 2
(c) 3 only (d) 2 and 3

3. With reference to Foreign Direct Investment in India, which one of the following is considered its major characteristics? **[2020]**

(a) It is the investment through capital instruments essentially in a listed company.
(b) It is largely non-debt creating capital flow.
(c) It is the investment which involves debt-servicing.
(d) It is the investment made by foreign institutional investors in the Government Securities.

4. 'Gold Tranche' (Reserve Tranche) refers to **[2020]**

(a) A loan system of the World Bank
(b) One of the operations of a Central Bank
(c) A credit system granted by WTO to its members
(d) A credit system granted by IMF to its members

5. If another global financial crisis happens in the near future, which of the following actions/ policies are most likely to give some immunity to India? [2020]
   1. Not depending on short-term foreign borrowings
   2. Opening up to more foreign banks
   3. Maintaining full capital account convertibility

   Select the correct answer using the code given below:
   (a) 1 only (b) 1 and 2 only
   (c) 3 only (d) 1, 2 and 3
6. Consider the following statements: [2018]
   1. The quantity of imported oils is more than the domestic production of edible oils in the last five years.
   2. The Government does not impose any customs duty on all the imported edible oils as a special case.

   Which of the statements given above is/are correct?
   (a) 1 only (b) 2 only
   (c) Both 1 and 2 (d) Neither 1 nor 2
7. Consider the following statements: [2012]
   The price of any currency in the international market is decided by the
   1. World Bank
   2. Demand for good/services provided by the country concerned
   3. Stability of the Government of the concerned country
   4. Economic potential of the country in question

   Which of the statements given above are correct?
   (a) 1, 2, 3 and 4 (b) 2 and 3 only
   (c) 3 and 4 only (d) 1 and 4 only

☞ NO QUESTIONS ASKED
2024, 2023, 2019, 2017, 2016, 2015, 2014, 2013

ANSWER KEY

1. (c) 2. (a) 3. (b) 4. (d) 5. (a)
6. (a) 7. (b)

UPSC CSE PREVIOUS YEARS' MAIN EXAMINATION QUESTIONS

1. How would the recent phenomena of **protectionism** and **currency manipulations** in world trade affect macro-economic stability of India? [2018]
2. Account for the failure of manufacturing sector in achieving the goal of **labour-intensive exports**. Suggest measures for more labour-intensive rather than capital-intensive exports. [2017]
3. There is a clear acknowledgement that **SEZs** are a tool of industrial development, manufacturing and exports. Recognising this potential, the whole instrumentality of SEZs requires augmentation. Discuss the issues plaguing the success of SEZs with respect to taxation, governing laws and administration. [2015]

☞ NO QUESTIONS ASKED
2024, 2023, 2022, 2021, 2020, 2019, 2016, 2014, 2013

CHAPTER

29

INTERNATIONAL ECONOMIC INSTITUTIONS

CHAPTER OUTLINE

BRETTON WOODS INSTITUTIONS

- International economic institutions are established by the solidarity of several countries. The members of such institutions are generally the sovereign Governments.

- The twin international economic institutions – **International Monetary Fund (IMF)** and **International Bank for Reconstruction and Development (IBRD)** (of World Bank Group) – were established after the Bretton Woods conference **held in 1944 in the United States**. Hence, these two are also known as **Bretton Woods Twins**.
- Bretton Woods Conference was attended by delegates from 44 allied nations (allies of the Second World War) with a purpose to establish the international monetary and financial order after the Second World War.
- The conference is also known as **United Nations Monetary and Financial Conference**. In the conference, agreements were signed that established:
  1. **International Bank for Reconstruction and Development** – The aim was:
     - Speedy reconstruction of war-ravaged countries post–Second World War.
     - To foster economic development focusing majorly on investment to build infrastructure.
  2. **International Monetary Fund** – The aim was to promote **stability of exchange rates and financial flows**.

Note: At the conference, the proposal was also floated to establish International Trade Organization (ITO), but, it was not accepted.

INTERNATIONAL MONETARY FUND

Important Facts

- It is an autonomous organisation affiliated to UNO.
- It was established on **27 December 1945** with 30 member nations.
- **India is a founding member of the IMF** (*i.e., it joined IMF on 27 December 1945*).
- Currently, the IMF has **191 members**. The 191st member country is **Liechtenstein** (joined in **October 2024**).
- **Headquarters** of the IMF: Washington DC (United States)
- In 2021, **Gita Gopinath**, an Indian-American economist, was appointed as the first deputy managing director of the IMF, which is the organisation's number-two position. Her tenure is still ongoing.
- IMF provides **loans only to member countries**.
- IMF is **financed by all its member** countries with **each country's contribution being fixed in terms of quota** (based on relative importance of its prevailing national income and international trade with its member countries).

Last Minute SNIPPETS

- The current managing director of IMF is the Bulgarian economist **Kristalina Georgieva** (appointed for the second term since 1 October 2024 for a 5-year term).
- **The chief economist of the IMF** is **Pierre-Olivier Gourinchas** (since January 2022).

- IMF can also borrow money from other institutions.
- **During its inception, IMF** had US$ 8.8 billion fund with quota of the United States of 31 per cent. India's quota at that time was 0.5 per cent. Presently, the United States' quota is 17.43 per cent and India's quota is 2.75 per cent with 13,114.4 millions of SDR.

Objectives of IMF

- Facilitating to solve the **short-term** Balance of Payments (BOP) crisis of member countries.
- Reduction of exchange rate control.
- To facilitate balanced growth of international trade.
- To promote stable exchange rate regime.
- To promote international monetary cooperation.

Governance Structure of IMF

Board of Governors → Executive Board

Board of Governors

The **top-most decision-making body** of IMF is the Board of Governors (BoG). There is one governor and one alternate governor **from each member country** in BoG. Usually, the Finance Minister (FM) or the head of central bank of the member country is the governor in this case. (For India at IMF, normally our FM represents as governor and RBI governor as alternate governor.)

BoG of IMF enjoys many important **powers such as**, approving the quota increase of member countries, allocation of Special Drawing Rights (SDRs), admitting new member country, appointing executive directors, etc.

The BoG of IMF is **advised by two Ministerial Committees**:

1. **International Monetary and Finance Committee** (IMFC) – This body meets twice a year to discuss matters on common concerns affecting the global economy and accordingly advices BoG. Many international institutions **including World Bank** participate as **observers** in the meetings of IMFC.
2. **Development Committee** – It is a joint forum of IMF and World Bank Group which also meets twice a year. It gives advice on financial requirements for economic development in developing countries.

Executive Board

It consists of 24 Directors who usually meet several times each week.

The **Managing Director** of IMF is the head of staff and **Chairperson of the Executive Board**. They are appointed by the board for a renewable term of 5 years.

Functions of IMF

Surveillance

- It looks upon the international monetary system and monitors the economic and financial policies, thereby highlighting the possible risks to stability and advises member countries on the same.
- IMF publishes two periodic reports in this regard – **'World Economic Outlook'** and **'Global Financial Stability Report'**.

Lending

- It provides loans to member countries facing short-term BOP crisis.
- It provides **financial stability** at both domestic and global levels.

Technical Assistance

- It provides proper guidance to the member countries for strengthening their fiscal, monetary and exchange rate policies.
- It seeks to develop synergy between technical assistance and training in order to maximise their effectiveness.

EXAM ESSENTIAL

SPECIAL DRAWING RIGHTS

- IMF lends to member countries in its artificial currency unit known as Special Drawing Rights (SDRs).
- Created in 1969, SDRs are the foreign exchange reserve assets under IMF.
- SDR is not intrinsically a currency but is a unit of account maintained by IMF.
- It is neither a proper currency nor a claim on IMF.
- Its value is based on the basket of the following five major currencies:

Currency	Percentage Weights	Fixed number of Units of currency for a 5 year period, starting 1st August 2022
U.S. Dollar	43.38	0.57813
Euro	29.31	0.37379
Chinese Yuan	12.28	1.0993
Japanese Yen	7.59	13.452
Pound Sterling	7.44	0.080870

Source: imf.org

- This basket is reviewed after every 5 years.
- The value of SDRs keeps changing due to continuous fluctuations in exchange rates.
- Unlike other currencies, SDR is **not** traded in forex market.
- Criterion for inclusion of a currency in the SDR basket:
  - **Export Criterion**
    - Issuer of the currency must be an IMF member/monetary union which has IMF members, and
    - It should also be among the largest exporters of the world.
  - **Currency to be Freely Usable**
    - The currency must be widely used in international transactions for making payment and should be widely traded in principal exchange markets.
- **Growing Importance of SDR as a Global Reserve Currency** – Critics argue that there is a growing need to replace dollar by a superior sovereign currency specifically SDR. Reasons are as follows:
  - Use of US dollar may create global volatility as US economy itself is suffering from weaknesses (especially 2008 crisis onwards).
  - SDR can diversify the risk from forex holdings.

However, it is difficult to make SDR so strong that it may replace US dollar as global reserve currency because the United States enjoys the maximum voting rights (17.46 per cent) in the affairs of IMF.

IMF Quota for Member Countries

- Member countries are assigned a quota which determines their maximum contribution to the IMF's finance resources. Quotas are **denominated in SDRs.**
- Quota of a country is determined by its relative position in the global economy.
- The member country can pay up to 25 per cent of the quota in foreign currencies (i.e. US dollar, Euro, Yen, etc.). This is called **Reserve Tranche.**
- Quotas are reviewed at least after every 5 years.
- The quota system is also used to assess a member's relative position and voting rights.
- Currently, the formula to derive quota of a member country is the weighted average of:
  1. **Member country's GDP**, with assigned weight of **50 per cent**

     Here, the GDP is measured through a blend of:
     - Market exchange rates, weighing around 60 per cent
     - PPP exchange rates, weighing 40 per cent

  2. **Its economic openness**, weighing **30 per cent**
  3. **Its economic variability**, weighing **15 per cent**
  4. **International reserves**, weighing **5 per cent**
- **Role of quota** – The quota determines the member country's level of:
  1. **Subscriptions to IMF:**
     - It indicates the maximum amount of financial resources a member is supposed to deposit with IMF.
  2. **Voting Power:**
     - It determines a member's voting rights in the decision made by IMF.
     - A member's vote comprises basic votes + additional votes for each 1 lakh SDR of quota.
  3. **Access to IMF Financing:**
     - A member's access to finance in IMF is based on its quota.

Last Minute SNIPPETS

- **Present IMF Quota and Vote Share of some member countries –**

Member Country	Quota (%)	Vote Share (%)
US	17.44 (highest)	16.51 (highest)
China	6.41	6.08
UK	4.24	4.03
India	**2.76**	**2.63**

Note: In terms of quota and vote share, the largest member is the **United States,** and the smallest member is **Tuvalu.**

Types of Financing by IMF

Financing by IMF

Concessional Lending

1. Extended Credit Facility (ECF)
2. Standby Credit Facility (SCF)
3. Rapid Credit Facility (RCF)

Non-concessional Lending

1. Stand-by-Arrangement (SBA)
2. Extended Fund Facility (EFF)
3. Rapid Financing Instrument (RFI)
4. Flexible Credit Line (FCL)
5. Precautionary and Liquidity Line (PLL)

Concessional Lending

Through the **Poverty Reduction and Growth Trust (PRGT) Facility**, lending is exclusively extended to only **Low-Income Countries (LICs)**, who are its members, on concessional terms, featuring **zero interest rates**, provided through various facilities aimed at poverty reduction and economic growth.

Under PRGT, there are three concessional lending facilities provided by IMF:

1. **Extended Credit Facility (ECF):** Sustained **medium- to long-term loan** for prolonged BOP problems of LICs.
2. **Standby Credit Facility (SCF):** Loan to LICs to meet **short-term BOP** crisis and other financial adjustment needs due by domestic or external shocks.
3. **Rapid Credit Facility (RCF):** For **urgent BOP** needs of LICs.

Note: Since 2015, IMF helps **poor countries** which are hit by natural disasters, by giving them funds under **Post-Catastrophe Debt Relief Trust**.

Non-Concessional Lending

These facilities are based on **market-determined interest rate along with some surcharges** and are provided to all member countries. Its types include:

1. **Stand-by Arrangement (SBA):** For providing non-concessional loans to address short-term or potential BOP problems of member countries. It is similar to SCF, which is there for LICs. The loan under SBA is given for up to 3 years (but normally for the duration of 12–18 months).

   However, conditionalities or a set of **corrective policy actions** are bound to be followed by loanee member countries in terms of **Washington Consensus of IMF**.
2. **Extended Fund Facility (EFF):** To address **medium- and long-term BOP problems** of member countries (similar to ECF which is there for LICs).
3. **Rapid Financing Instrument (RFI)**: Loan to meet urgent BOP needs (similar to RCF which is there for LICs).
4. **Flexible Credit Line (FCL)**: Under this, funds are provided to member countries with very strong fundamentals, policies and track records of policy implementation. The purpose is **to boost market confidence** during the period of heightened risks. The duration of loan is of 1 year or 2 years. There is **no cap on access to IMF funds** under FCL.

Till now, only three member countries **(Colombia**, **Mexico** and **Poland)** have used the FCL.

5. **Precautionary and Liquidity Line (PLL)**: It is designed for member countries with sound fundamentals and policies and track record of implementation of such policies. In order to qualify for PLL, they may face moderate vulnerabilities and not necessarily meet the FCL qualification standards. The duration of loan by IMF under PCL is either 6 months or 1–2 years.

   Two member countries (Republic of North Macedonia and Morocco) have used the PLL.

Note:

- Majority of the loans provided by IMF are through SBA.
- As of February 2025, the largest ever financial assistance given by IMF to a member country is to Argentina (US$ 31 billion).
- Ukraine and Egypt are second and third, respectively, with the loan amount of US$ 11.16 billion and US$ 8.17 billion, respectively.
- **India is not an LIC as per IMF**, and thus **not eligible for concessional lending** by IMF.

BONUS KNOWLEDGE

WASHINGTON CONSENSUS

- There are a set of policies and conditions known as **IMF Conditionalities**, which is supposed to be followed by member countries taking financial assistance. The term **Washington Consensus** was first used in 1989, by English economist John Williamson.
- These Conditionalities by IMF are in addition to the collateral submitted by member countries for financial assistance.
- If the conditions are not met, the funds may be withheld by IMF.
- Some of these conditions (also known as Washington Consensus) for structural adjustment are:
  1. Devaluation of currency
  2. Higher interest rates to stabilise the currency
  3. Balancing budget and not overspending
  4. Removal of price controls and state subsidies
  5. Enhancing the rights of foreign investors vis-à-vis national laws
  6. Trade liberalisation or lifting import and export restrictions

These conditions are imposed by IMF to ensure that the loan-taking member countries are able to resolve their BOP crisis and are able to repay to IMF.

Financial Resources of IMF

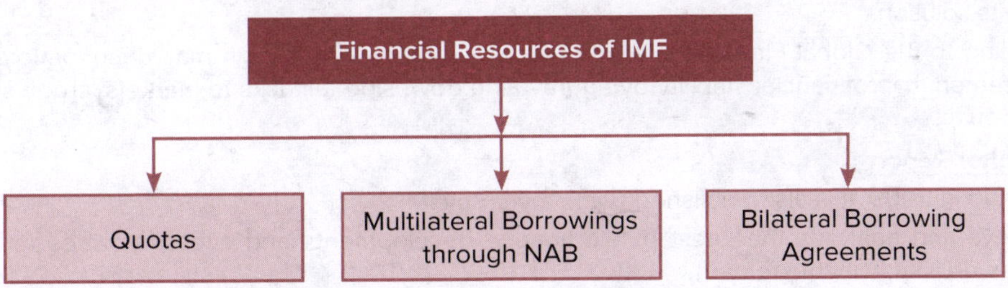

- **Quotas** – IMF's main source is the funds provided by member countries to IMF as per assigned quota.
- **Multilateral Borrowings through NAB** – It is an additional source of funding for IMF. These borrowings are made by IMF presently through NAB (till 2018 – through both GAB and NAB).

  GAB and NAB are credit arrangements between IMF and group of member countries. Institutions to provide supplementary resources to IMF, to get additional funds, required to meet exceptional situations of financial crisis.

  - **General Arrangements to Borrow (GAB)** – Existing since 1962 but lapsed in December 2017.
  - **New Arrangements to Borrow (NAB)** – NAB has 40 participant member countries with total fund size of US$ 250 billion.

  India gave US$ 12 billion loan to IMF under NAB to meet sovereign debt crisis of Europe.
- **Bilateral Borrowing Agreements** – After quotas and NAB, in order to meet financial needs of members, IMF also goes for Bilateral Borrowing Agreements (BBA). BBA also has 40 participants with total commitment of US$ 440 billion.

Note: Concessional lending and debt relief given by IMF are financed through separate contribution-based trust funds.

EXAM ESSENTIAL

MAJOR REPORTS PUBLISHED BY IMF

World Economic Outlook (WEO)

- Usually published **twice a year** by IMF (usually April and October).
- Showcases the staff economists' analysis and forecasts of global economic developments and policies **in the member countries** of IMF during the near and medium term.
- The report **also indicates the risks and uncertainty** that may threaten growth of member countries.
- **As per World Economic Outlook (January 2025),** global growth is projected at 3.3 per cent both in 2025 and 2026, which is below the historical (2000–19) average of 3.7 per cent. WEO 2025 also predicted that Global headline inflation would decline to 4.2 per cent in 2025 and to 3.5 per cent in 2026.

Global Financial Stability Report (GFSR)

- Like WEO, it is also published by IMF, **twice a year** (April and October).
- GFSR provides an **assessment of the stability of global financial markets** and emerging markets financing based on **current market conditions**.
- It **tries to figure out financial and structural imbalances** that may pose as a risk and accordingly suggests solutions.
- According to the Global Financial Stability Report (October 2024), high macroeconomic uncertainty can threaten macrofinancial stability by aggravating downside tail risks to markets, credit supply, and GDP growth.

Fiscal Monitor Report

- Launched in 2009, it is also published **twice a year** by IMF.
- It surveys and analyses the latest public finance developments and access policies to put public finances on a sustainable footing.

External Sector Report

- It is published **annually** by IMF since 2012.
- External sector reports emphasis on global external developments and provide multilaterally consistent assessments of external positions of the world's largest economy representing over 90 per cent of the global GDP.

Regional Economic Report

- It talks about recent economic development and growth prospects for various countries in a particular region.
- It also discusses the policy developments that have affected economic performance in the regions.

BONUS KNOWLEDGE

Global Housing Watch – The Global Housing Watch was launched **by IMF** in **2014**. It tracks the developments in housing markets across the globe on a quarterly basis by providing current data on **house prices** as well as metrics used to assess valuation in housing markets, such as house-price-to-rent and house-price-to-income ratios.

Financial Sector Assessment Program (FSAP) – FSAP is a joint program of **IMF and World Bank**, which was launched in **1999** during the Asian financial crisis. It provides a comprehensive analysis of a country's financial sector.

India and IMF

- India is the founding member of IMF.
- 2003 onwards, the relationship between India and IMF has transformed:
  - **Earlier**, India was a borrower. **Now**, it has emerged as a lender. India lent to IMF in 2012 to bail out Eurozone countries.
  - India is the **13th largest** IMF quota-holding member country (2.75 per cent).
  - India's **voting rights** have increased from 2.3 per cent to 2.63 per cent.
- **IMF has helped India** during two BOP crisis:
  - India borrowed under the Extended Fund Facility (EFF) in 1981.
  - India borrowed under two SBAs in 1991.
- **India has subscribed** to the IMF's **Special Data Dissemination Standard** (i.e. committed to observe Global Accounting Standards in Government finances, along with providing information on data dissemination practices.)

Recent Reforms undertaken by IMF

- More influencing power to the Developing member nations:
  - More than 6 per cent transfer of voting rights from the United States and European countries to emerging member nations.
  - Increase in voting rights of:
    - India, from 2.3 per cent to 2.63 per cent.
    - China, from 3.8 per cent to 6.08 per cent.

- Chinese Renminbi was included in the SDR basket in 2016.

Reforms demanded by some members of IMF

- Further restructuring of the voting rights, especially of emerging economies like India and China.
- Conditionalities should be paired with other reforms such as trade reforms.
- Need of more resources to the IMF.
- Selection of the IMF Chief to be done on the basis of merit.
- To end the US domination in IMF.
- IMF should also look into long-term crisis management rather than providing only short-term solutions.

Has IMF failed to achieve the objectives with which it was created?

IMF, to a large extent, has fulfilled the objectives with which it was created:

- Stability in exchange rates
  - It allowed variations in exchange rate by 1 per cent (positive and negative).
  - It has adopted a system of stability with flexibility.
- Check on multiple exchange rates
  - Countries are not allowed to have multiple exchange rates.
- Broadening of the credit structure
  - Earlier IMF would only provide loans for short-term BOP problems. Recently, it has started providing credit for fundamental BOP disequilibrium.
  - Also, IMF is now providing credit even for developmental projects.
- Growth in the long run for developing economies
  - Conditionalities imposed by IMF have proved to be beneficial for many developing member countries for their long-term growth.

However, critics argue that IMF has failed on many parameters:

Lack in Flexibility

- IMF is considered a very rigid organisation.
- It has been noted that it is incapable of adopting rapid changes.

High Interest Rates

- IMF charges very high rate of interest on the non-concessional funds lent to member nations.

Conditionalities

- For some developing economies, the conditions put by IMF at the time of giving loan did not take into account the country's circumstances, and thus, it has failed to resolve economic problems of those countries.

Failure in complete removal of exchange rate restrictions

- Some countries still practice exchange rate restrictions in some form or the other.

Other Criticisms of IMF

- 'One Size Fits All' policy under which it prescribes similar solutions to all member countries.
- Failure in prediction of the Global Recession of 2008–09, let alone its prevention.
- Veto power of the United States; i.e. the US can easily veto in any decision of IMF as it holds more than 16 per cent of the voting power and total 85 per cent votes are required to pass any major reform.

WORLD BANK GROUP

Important Facts

- The term **'World Bank'** generally refers to **IBRD and IDA** as they have the same head and management, while the term **'World Bank Group'** refers to a group of five institutions, namely
  1. International Bank for Reconstruction and Development **(IBRD)**
  2. International Development Association **(IDA)**
  3. International Finance Corporation **(IFC)**
  4. Multilateral Investment Guarantee Agency **(MIGA)**
  5. International Centre for Settlement of Investment Disputes **(ICSID)**
- Among them, **IBRD first came into existence**.
- To be a member of World Bank, a country needs **to be a member of IMF first**.
- **India is a member of four of them** (except ICSID).
- **Headquarters** of World Bank Group Institutions are located at **Washington DC (United States)**.
- Present President of World Bank – **Ajay Banga** (since June, 2023 and with a 5-year term).
- World Bank has set two goals for the world to achieve by 2030:
  1. End extreme poverty by decreasing percentage of people living on less than $1.90 a day to no more than 3 per cent.
  2. Promote shared prosperity by fostering the income growth of the bottom 40 per cent of every country.

Name	Established in	Headquarters	Members	Is India a Member?
IBRD	1945	Washington DC	**189**	Yes
IDA	1960	Washington DC	175	Yes
IFC	1956	Washington DC	186	Yes
MIGA	**1988**	Washington DC	182	Yes
ICSID	1966	Washington DC	165	**No**

International Bank for Reconstruction and Development (IBRD)

- It is the **original** World Bank Institution (i.e. the first to be established among group of five).

- IBRD was established on **27 December 1945** as per decision in the Bretton Woods Conference of 1944. IBRD started its operations from 25 June 1946.
- The **initial objective** of establishing IBRD was to assist the Second World War ravaged countries in their reconstruction. Later, the economic development of developing and poor nations became the goal.
- **India is the founding member** of IBRD.
- Currently, IBRD has **189 members** (Headquarters: Washington DC).

Functions of IBRD

- It **lends money to Government** of middle-income countries and creditworthy LICs.
- It provides **long-term loans** in large volumes, with longer maturity and low rate of interest.
- It promotes key policy and institutional reforms such as safety net or anti-corruption reforms.
- It helps preserve borrowers' financial strength (by supporting them during their financial crisis).

Relation of IBRD with India

- The shareholding of India in IBRD is 3.15 per cent (seventh largest shareholder).
- India has a voting right of 3.01 per cent.
- It supports India with an integrated package of financing, advisory services and knowledge.

International Development Association (IDA)

- IDA was established in 1960 with **India as its founding member**.
- At present, there are **175 member countries** of IDA (Headquarters: Washington DC).
- It is known as the **'Soft Lending Arm'** of World Bank.
- IDA provides **loan** on zero or very low interest rate for a longer period stretched over **30–38 years** along with 5- to 10-year grace period.
- 74 countries are currently eligible to receive IDA resources.
- As on February 2025, those countries whose relative poverty (measured in terms of per capita income) was **below $1,335** (updated annually) were eligible for assistance by IDA. IDA also provides support to those countries that are above the operational cut-off of $1,255 but lack creditworthiness which is needed to borrow from the IBRD. Some countries, such as Nigeria and Pakistan, are IDA-eligible based on per capita income levels and are also creditworthy for some IBRD borrowing. They are referred to as **'blend' countries**.
- Along with concessional loans, **IDA also provides grants** to countries at risk of debt distress. Moreover, it helps in **relieving debts** of the poor countries under initiatives such as Heavily Indebted Poor Countries **(HIPC)** and Multilateral Debt Relief Initiative **(MDRI)**.
- IDA also helps during crises and emergencies through a tool known as **'Crisis Response Window'**.
- It aims to catalyse economic growth, improve living standards and reduce inequalities and the loan is provided to address primary education, basic health facilities, clean water supply and sanitation, etc.
- IDA is funded largely through borrowings from the financial market and contributions from the Government of its richer member countries.
- **Relation of IDA with India:** IDA has supported activities that have had a considerable impact in India. They include:
  - Universalising primary education;

- Empowering rural communities through a series of rural livelihoods projects;
- Revolutionising agriculture through support to Green and White (Milk) Revolutions;
- Helping to combat Polio, Tuberculosis and HIV/AIDS.

International Finance Corporation (IFC)

- It was established in **1956** (Headquarters: Washington DC)
- Presently, it has **186** member countries (including India as founding member).
- IFC is focused exclusively on the promotion of **private sector** in developing countries.
- It provides **investments**, **technical expertise** and **advisory services** to build a sound private sector in developing economies.
- It gives **loans to private companies** rather than to Governments.
- The objective behind this is to mobilise financial resources for private enterprises, support businesses, create job opportunities and provide necessary services to the vulnerable.
- IFC facilitates the inflow of both domestic and foreign private capital.
- **Renewable energy generation, improving food security** and **infrastructure building** are the focus areas of IFC.
- IFC raises funds **by issuing bonds** in the international capital market. These include:
  - US Dollar Benchmark Bond
  - Local Currency Bonds
  - Theme Bonds (supporting a specific program, e.g. Green Bond, Social Bonds, etc.)
- **Relation of IFC with India:**
  - In 2014, IFC floated **Rupee Bond** and **Masala Bond** in the global credit market to fund Indian companies.
  - India has been the largest country in IFC's investment portfolio for several years.

Multilateral Investment Guarantee Agency (MIGA)

- It was established in **1988** (Headquarters: Washington DC).
- At present, it has **182 members** (including India).
- It has **two main functions**:
  1. Promoting **Foreign Direct Investment (FDI)** by providing **insurance to private sector foreign investors** against losses caused by non-commercial risks (political risks). Political risk includes:
     - i. Currency transfer
     - ii. Expropriation
     - iii. War and Civil Disturbance
  2. Providing **Credit Enhancement Guarantee** to cross-border private sector investors and lenders.
- **Objectives** of MIGA include:
  - To raise FDI inflows in developing countries.
  - To reduce poverty, increase standards of living and achieve higher economic growth in developing countries.
- **Relation of MIGA with India**:
  - Till now, MIGA does not have any exposure in India.
  - It is engaging with Government of India (GoI) to explore opportunities for its guaranteed products.

International Centre for Settlement of Investment Disputes (ICSID)

- It was established in **1966**.
- At present, it has **165** member countries **(India is NOT a member)**.
- It is a **dispute resolution organisation**.
- Its aim is **to settle investment-related disputes** between member countries; hence, it helps in reducing investment risks.
- Settlement of an investment dispute through ICSID is **voluntary**, but once parties agree to settle the dispute, they cannot withdraw unilaterally.

EXAM ESSENTIAL

MAJOR REPORTS PUBLISHED BY WORLD BANK

World Development Report

- It is published **annually** since 1978 by IBRD or World Bank.
- The report provides an in-depth analysis of a specific aspect of the economic development.

Key Points of World Development Report 2024

1. This report focuses upon the challenges faced by the middle-income countries to overcome middle-income trap and to move beyond a certain level of economic development.
2. The report emphasises on 3Is – Investment, Infusion of technology and Innovation, to accomplish the objectives of economic development.
3. As per the report, the major challenges faced by the middle-income countries are - aging populations, rising protectionism in advanced economies, and the need for rapid energy transition.
4. This report suggests that the transition from middle income to high income can be facilitated through the policies which encourage competition, talent development, and effective crisis management.

Doing Business Report

- It is also known as *Ease of Doing Business Report*, published annually by World Bank.
- The report is based on the studies to analyse 10 quantitative indicators as to whether **regulation** enhances/lowers down the business activity.
- Higher ranking of a country in this list means that its regulatory environment is more conducive to and favourable for undertaking businesses.
- The report mainly tries to address three questions:
  1. When does the Governments change regulation for developing private sector?
  2. What are the features of reformist Governments?
  3. What are the effects of regulatory change on economic and investment activities?
- **In the last available 2020 Doing Business Report:**
  - **Ten business indicators** of 190 economies were compared to prepare the ranking.
  - India very well improved its rank this time (from 77 to 63).
  - India improved its rank in 7 out of the 10 indicators.
  - Following an investigation that revealed 'data irregularities' in its 2018 and 2020 editions (released in 2017 and 2019, respectively) and possible 'ethical matters' involving bank staff, the World Bank announced it **would discontinue** the practice of issuing 'Doing Business Reports'.
  - It will introduce a new method for assessing the business and investment climate.

Global Economic Prospects Report

- The report examines global economic development and prospects with special focus on Emerging Market and Developing Economies **(EMDEs)**.
- It is issued by Word Bank Group **twice** a year (in January and June).
- As per the **2024 GEP Report**, the global economy is expected to grow at a rate of 2.4 per cent, the weakest in 30 years. The risk of a worldwide recession has decreased, resulting in a stronger global economic position than the previous year. However, rising geopolitical tensions may create a new near-term risks to the global economy. While the global economy is better than it was a year ago, many emerging nations' medium-term prospects have deteriorated. The factors responsible for this are slow growth, slow global trade, and tight financial conditions.

Global Findex Database

- It is a comprehensive data set on financial inclusion (how people save, borrow, make payments, manage risk, etc.).
- It was launched **by World Bank** with funding from the Bill & Melinda Gates Foundation. The database has been **published every 3 years** since 2011.

Poverty and Shared Prosperity Report

- It is a **biennial report** released **by the World Bank**. It provides consistent and accurate estimates of trends in global poverty and shared prosperity.

Transformative Carbon Asset Facility (TCAF)

It was launched by the World Bank in **2015** to provide finance innovative, results-based carbon market mechanism under Article 6 of the Paris Climate Change agreement.

IMF *Versus* World Bank

IMF	World Bank
IMF was established in 1945.	Its first wing IBRD was established in 1945.
Objectives of IMF include: • Exchange rate stability. • Resolve short-term BOP problems of member countries.	**Objective of World Bank is:** • Promotion of economic and social development in developing and poor countries.
Provides loan to Governments of the member nations (generally at market interest rate).	Provides loan to both Governments and the Private Sector of the member nations. (on concessional terms).
No associated institutes and therefore a smaller staff.	It has five associated institutes and hence a larger size of staff.
Funding of IMF comes through – quota subscription from every member, multilateral borrowings and even bilateral borrowings.	It borrows through selling bonds and notes directly to the member nations and also receives contribution from richer member countries.

NEW DEVELOPMENT BANK OR BRICS DEVELOPMENT BANK

- In 2012, **BRICS** nations proposed to set up Multilateral Development Bank.
- The need for New Development Bank (NDB) was felt because of:
    - IMF and WB were inclined more towards the developed Western countries.
    - BRICS nations have less than 15 per cent voting rights in IMF at present although they account for around half of the population of the world.

New Development Bank

Logo of New Development Bank

- NDB actually came into existence at the **2015** summit in Russia.
- Headquarters of NDB is located at **Shanghai, China**.
- **The main functions of NDB are:**
    - To support **infrastructure and sustainable development projects** (both public and private) through loans, guarantees, equity and other financial instruments.
    - To also provide technical assistance for the same.
- Lending by NDB mainly **covers areas** such as – transport, clean energy, irrigation, water management and sanitation, urban development and social infrastructure.
- **Important features of NDB:**
    - There were initially five founding member nations of NDB – **Brazil, Russia, India, China and South Africa** (i.e. BRICS nations). The membership is **also open for all UN members**. However, the collective share of BRICS nations cannot be less than 55 per cent of the voting power.
    - Under the Bank's General Strategy: 2017–2021, the NDB had planned to expand the membership gradually for its long-term development. **Thus in 2021, four (4) new members namely Bangladesh, UAE, Uruguay and Egypt, joined NDB**.
    - Present authorised capital of NDB is US$ 100 billion and subscribed capital is US$ 50 billion.
    - The bank has a **One Member, One Vote Policy** and **no Veto policy**, unlike World Bank and IMF.
    - The bank aims to have a **short processing time for loan** (i.e. designing, negotiating and approving the loan within six months).
    - The present President of NDB is **Mrs. Dilma Vana Rousseff** from Brazil (since March 2023). She succeeded **Marcos Prado Troyjo** from Brazil.
        - The tenure of the President is five years.
        - The election of the President of NDB is to be done on rotational basis.
- **India and NDB –** Some important projects approved by NDB in India are:
    - US$ 350 million loan for upgradation of around 1,500 km district roads in Madhya Pradesh.
    - US$ 345 million loan for water sector restructuring project in Rajasthan.
    - US$ 250 million investment in Solar Energy and Wind Farms for generation of almost 5,000 MW of renewable energy.
- **Achievements of NDB so far:**
    - NDB received AA+ international credit rating in 2020.
    - It issued its first green bond raising RMB 3 billion in the Chinese Bond Market.

- In 2021, the NDB issued CNY 2 billion RMB-denominated Bonds in the China Interbank Bond Market, bringing the total outstanding amount of RMB bonds issued by NDB to CNY 17 billion.
- Share of its five member countries in global GDP has increased from 27 per cent to 33 per cent between 2010 and 2018.
- It has approved more than US$ 4.6 billion loans to member countries so far, with a strong emphasis on renewable energy.
- There has been an enhanced partnership with member countries for stronger impact, through signing of a large number of MOUs.

➤ **Challenges faced by NDB** at present –

1. **China's Domination** – It is also anticipated that NDB may be used by China for its larger visions like Silk Road and Maritime Silk Road initiative.
2. **Competition with AIIB** (Asian Infrastructure Investment Bank).
3. Constant **availability of funds**.

EXAM ESSENTIAL

CONTINGENT RESERVE ARRANGEMENT

➤ It was introduced in 2015 by the BRICS countries **to overcome the BOP problems** of BRICS countries by providing **short-term liquidity support** through liquidity and precautionary instruments.

➤ The CRA along with NDB is viewed as an example of increasing South–South cooperation.

➤ For CRA, there is a total capital contribution of US$ 100 billion (highest by China: $41 billion).

➤ The **voting right of India** is equal to that of Brazil and Russia, i.e. **18.10 per cent**.

➤ China has the highest voting right of 39.95 per cent in CRA.

➤ It wants to ensure equity and inclusiveness to the availability of a backup arrangement so that the BRICS nations can go ahead with its necessary and bold policy decisions.

➤ It is expected to boost their foreign exchange reserves.

ASIAN DEVELOPMENT BANK

➤ Asian Development Bank (ADB) was established in **1966** as a Multilateral Development Bank initially with 31 member countries (including India).

➤ ADB presently has **69** member countries (latest being **Israel** – added in 2024).

➤ There are member countries **even from outside Asia** such as the United States.

➤ Headquarters – **Mandaluyong, Philippines**.

➤ Like World Bank, it has a weighted voting system, votes being distributed in proportion to members' capital subscription.

➤ **Japan holds the largest portion** of share capital, followed by the United States, China and India.

➤ Due to this, all Presidents of ADB till now belong to Japan. President has a 5-year term and may be re-elected.

➤ **Present President of ADB – Masato Kanda** (since February 2025).

➤ **Objectives of ADB:**

- To eradicate poverty from Asia and Pacific region and to help developing countries improve the quality of life.

- To bring economic stability and sustainable development.

➤ **Functions of ADB:**
- Providing loans and equity investment for economic and social advancement of the developing member countries.
- Technical assistance in planning and execution of projects.

➤ **Asian Development Outlook** is an **annual** publication by ADB.

➤ **India and ADB:**
- India is a founding member and is the fourth-largest shareholder in ADB.
- Till now, ADB has approved more than 200 sovereign loans for India in various projects such as:
  - **In Transport Sector** – South Asia Subregional Economic Cooperation and the Bihar New Ganga Bridge project.
  - **In Energy Sector** – The demand side energy efficiency investment project for energy-efficient lightning in streets and homes and water pumps.
  - **In Urban Sector** – Atal Mission for Renewable and Urban Transport, Smart City Initiative, etc.
  - **In Finance Sector** – Lending to PNB for **Solar Rooftop Investment Program**, which further facilitated the Government in achieving the target of 40 GW of solar rooftop capacity by 2022.
  - **In Agriculture and Natural Resource Sector** – Providing assistance in key areas of water use efficiency and climate resilience.
  - **Infrastructure sector** – Visakhapatnam–Chennai Industrial Corridor. Coastal Climate Resilience in Karnataka and Kerala states.

➤ Under non-sovereign aids, ADB provides **direct financial assistance** in the form of direct loans, equity investments, debt securities and trade finance.

➤ ADB has adopted a new corporate strategy for the coming decade – **Strategy 2030:**
- Highlighting the new operational priorities and approaches to respond more effectively to global and regional development challenges.
- It is also in alignment with **SDGs 2030**, the Addis Ababa Action agenda, the Paris Agreement on Climate Change, the Sendai Framework for Disaster Risk Reduction and the G20 agenda on infrastructure development.

➤ In the South Asian Region, ADB focused on rapid urbanisation, environmental deterioration and unemployment; providing better education and health services; and building climate and disaster resilience.

➤ **Challenges** – ADB faces shortage of funds. Also, domination of larger shareholders such as Japan and the United States blocks attempts to expand the share capital.

ASIAN INFRASTRUCTURE INVESTMENT BANK (AIIB)

➤ It is a **multilateral development bank** set up in 2016 to improve social and economic outcomes in **Asia**.

➤ The idea of the establishment of such bank was proposed by China to provide support and improvement in infrastructure building in the Asia-Pacific region.

- Due to the discontent in the West-dominated multilateral bodies such as IMF and World Bank, many of their members are joining AIIB.
- AIIB presently has a membership of **110 countries** including 14 prospective members. **Nauru** is the latest members of AIIB.
- There are member countries **even from outside Asia**, such as Australia, Canada, Brazil, France, Germany, UK, South Africa, etc.
- **The United States and Japan are not the members** of AIIB.
- Headquarters of AIIB – **Beijing**, China.
- Present President – **Jin Liqun** (from China).
- **Focus areas of AIIB are** – rural infrastructure and agricultural development, energy and power, environment protection, urban development, water supply and sanitation, transportation and telecommunication.
- The AIIB has accumulated capital of US$ 100 billion (of which US$ 29.78 billion is contributed by China).
- The **voting shares** are based on the **size of member countries' economy**.
- **India and AIIB:**
  - India is the **second-largest stakeholder** in AIIB after China.
  - Till now, India has been the **largest borrower** of the bank.
- **AIIB *versus* ADB:**
  - AIIB is a much new organisation as compared to ADB.
  - Japan and the United States dominate ADB, whereas China dominates AIIB. The United States and Japan are not the members of AIIB.
  - Both ADB and AIIB have AAA credit ratings.
  - Subscribed capital and assets of AIIB are much less than those of ADB.
  - Lending till now by AIIB is quite less than that by ADB.

Last Minute SNIPPETS

As of **February 2025**, AIIB has approved around 306 projects in various countries.

- **Achievements of AIIB:**
  - AIIB gained the 'Permanent Observer' status by the United Nations in 2018.
  - The energy sector holds the largest share (20 per cent) in the investment portfolio of AIIB.
  - AIIB has successfully finished the:
    - Andhra Pradesh Rural Road Project
    - Sustainable Rural Sanitation Services Program (SRSSP) in Egypt
    - Strategic Irrigation Modernisation and Urgent Rehabilitation in Indonesia
- **Criticisms:**
  - Critics argue that AIIB needs to transform its investment projects from 'Hard Infrastructure' to 'Comprehensive Infrastructure'.
  - AIIB has to shift towards a more environment-friendly approach regarding funding of projects.

EXAM ESSENTIAL

ORGANISATION FOR ECONOMIC COOPERATION AND DEVELOPMENT (OECD)

- Established in 1961, it is an organisation of **38 countries** (mainly high-income economies and having high HDI).
- Most recent one to join OECD is **Colombia, in 2020 and Costa Rica, in 2021**.
- Its members **also includes** non-European states **(such as the United States, Japan, etc.)**.
- **India is not a member** of OECD. Though, India is the member of OECD Development Centre.
- **Even China is not a member of OECD**.
- Its headquarters is located in **Paris**.
- **Secretary General is the head of OECD** (presently **Mathias Cormann** since June 2021).
- OECD is **an official UN observer**.
- **Objective of OECD** is to stimulate economic progress and world trade.
- **Frascati Manual**, which is prepared by **OECD**, is a recognised methodology for collecting research and development statistics and is an essential tool for statisticians and policy makers.
- **Programme for International Student Assessment (PISA)** is a worldwide program/study initiated **by OECD** which provides comparable data on education policy and outcomes and gives comprehensive analysis. The PISA test evaluates the applicability of knowledge that the students have learned through primary and secondary education. **In 2018**, the GoI decided to participate in PISA.
- **Service Trade Restrictiveness Index** is computed by OECD since 2014. (In 2019 index, India ranked the lowest).
- **India and OECD:**
  - India is **a member** of OECD Development Centre.
  - Since 2007, India is engaged with the Body Accession Membership.
  - Since 2017, India is participating as an associate/participant in 21 OECD bodies and **adheres to 9 OECD legal instruments** such as on corporate governance, fiscal matters, nuclear energy, etc.
  - India plays an active role in OECD's regional activities in Asia along with cooperation in international forum.
- **Importance of OECD:**
  - OECD member countries contribute around 63 per cent of the world's GDP and around 75 per cent of the world's trade.
  - OECD members possess 18 per cent of the world's population.
  - According to the **OECD Research Report**, '*The Long View: Scenarios for the World Economy to 2060*,'
    - Global real GDP growth will slow from 3.5 per cent in 2018 to 2 per cent in 2060.
    - By 2060, India, China, and Indonesia will account for nearly half of global economic output.

EUROPEAN BANK for RECONSTRUCTION and DEVELOPMENT (EBRD)

- Established in 1991, EBRD is a multilateral developmental investment bank.
- It has **75 countries** from across the globe and **2** European Union institutions (EU and European Investment Bank) as members.
- **India is the shareholder of EBRD** since 11th July 2018.
- The latest members of EBRD are Iraq, since November 2023 and Benin since April 2024.
- EBRD **supports** through funding mainly for development of **private sectors**.

- Its headquarters is located in **London**.
- **Present president of EBRD – Odile Renaud-Basso** (since July 2020).
- **The United States** is the largest shareholder in EBRD.
- **Though India has a shareholding** in EBRD, it is **not** a recipient of its finances.
- **Benefits** of EBRD membership to India:
  - Enhanced investment opportunities which will further induce employment.
  - Glowing international profile and promotion of economic interest.
  - Increased scope of cooperation through co-financing opportunities in different sectors.
  - Enhanced international markets opportunity.

BONUS KNOWLEDGE

BANK FOR INTERNATIONAL SETTLEMENTS (BIS)

The Bank for International Settlements (BIS) is an **international financial institution** which is owned by central banks. It promotes monetary and financial cooperation, and serves as a bank for central banks. The BIS pursues its work through its meetings, programmes and through the Basel Process by hosting international groups pursuing global financial stability and promoting their interaction. It also provides banking services to central banks and other international organisations. It has two representative offices in Hong Kong SAR and in Mexico City as well as innovation hub centres around the world. It serves as a bank for central banks because it provides banking services to institutions such as the European Central Bank and Federal Reserve. It was established in 1930, and the headquarters are located in Basel, Switzerland.

History of the BIS

It was founded in 1930 as a clearing house for German war reparations imposed by the Treaty of Versailles. Its original members were France, Britain, Italy, Japan, Belgium, Germany, United States and Switzerland. During the time of the Bretton Woods Agreement, BIS played a crucial role in maintaining International currency convertibility.

WORLD TRADE ORGANISATION (WTO)

Evolution of WTO

ITO (International Trade Organisation)

The initial proposition of setting up ITO to handle the trade side of international economic cooperation **was rejected** under the Bretton Woods Conference in 1944.

GATT (General Agreement on Tariffs and Trade)

- GATT was signed in 1947 with 23 founding members to establish a free and fair international trade regime among member countries for **goods**.
- The basic objectives of GATT were:
  - To promote non-discriminating trade
  - To eliminate tariff and non-tariff trade barriers
  - To remove trade disputes through consultations

- By 1993, there were 123 countries as members of GATT. The members of GATT used to control 90 per cent of the world trade.
- However, the GATT lacked:
    - Inclusion of the **trade in services** and **intellectual property rights**, and
    - Institutional structure.
- Under GATT, negotiations among member countries through **Trade Rounds** were held at irregular interval of years.
- **Total eight rounds** of negotiations were held under GATT (last one being **Uruguay Round** from 1986 to 1994).
- Uruguay Round was the longest round among the eight rounds of GATT. It continued for 8 years.
- Negotiations and consensus under Uruguay Round led to the creation of World Trade Organisation (WTO) through signing of **Marrakesh Agreement**.

BONUS KNOWLEDGE

THE MARRAKESH AGREEMENT

The Marrakesh Agreement was an agreement signed in Marrakesh, Morocco, by 123 nations on 15 April 1994, marking the end of the 8-year-long Uruguay Round and establishing the World Trade Organisation, which officially came into being on 1 January 1995.

Important Facts about WTO

- WTO was established on **1 January 1995** by replacing **GATT**.
- It is an ITO dealing with a variety of issues and with an objective to promote free and fair international trade. Its scope is much broader than GATT.
- The headquarters of WTO are in **Geneva, Switzerland**.
- WTO is headed by a **Director General** whose term is 4 years and is renewable.
- Current Director General – Ngozi Okonjo-Iweala **(since March 2021)**.
- **Membership of WTO**
    - WTO presently has **166 member states** (including **India** as a founding member).
    - The **latest members** to join WTO were **Comoros (165th)** and **Timor Leste** (166th in February 2024 during the 13th Ministerial Conference).
    - The European Union (EU) is also a member of WTO.
    - A WTO member must be a **customs territory with full autonomy** in the conduct of external commercial relations. They may not be full sovereign nations. Thus, Hong Kong and Taiwan are also WTO members.
- WTO is **not** a part of the United Nations.
- WTO follows the voting system of **'one country, one vote'** unlike IMF and World Bank.
- WTO publishes the **World Trade Report** every year.
- The highest decision-making body of WTO is the **Ministerial Conference**.
- Decisions under WTO are made through **consensus**. It is achieved through informal negotiations between small groups of members and these negotiations are often called green room negotiations (if occurring in director general's office) or **mini-ministerial** (if occurring in other countries).

India has conducted two mini-ministerials till now (in 2018 and 2019).

Last Minute SNIPPETS

As per World Trade Report 2024 -

- The average global per-capita income (inflation adjusted) has increased from USD 7050 (FY 1995) to USD 11570 (FY 2023) (increased by about 65%). While for low and middle income countries it is tripled, that is, increased from USD 1835 (FY 1995) to USD 5337 (FY 2023).
- WTO membership has helped to boost the trade amongst the members by 140% approximately.
- Trade-led economic growth in last three decades has significantly contributed to the reduction of extreme poverty in the low and middle income countries. Individuals living under extreme poverty have decreased from 40% (FY 1995) to below 11% (FY 2022), while the shares of global exports of these countries have increased from 16% to 32%.

Organisational Structure of WTO

WTO works through the following constituents:

Ministerial Conference → **General Council** (also acts as DSB and TPRB) → **Councils for Trade** (CT for Goods, CT for Services, CT for TRIPS)

1. Ministerial Conference (MC)

- MC is attended by the Ministers of Commerce and Trade of all Member States.
- The MC normally **meets once in every 2 years**.
- Till now, 13 MCs have been held. Following are the details:

Ministerial Conference	Year	Place
1st	1996	Singapore
2nd	1998	Geneva, Switzerland
3rd	1999	Seattle, USA
4th	2001	Doha, Qatar
5th	2003	Cancun, Mexico
6th	2005	Hong Kong
7th	2009	Geneva, Switzerland
8th	2011	Geneva, Switzerland
9th	2013	Bali
10th	2015	Nairobi, Kenya
11th	2017	Buenos Aires, Argentina
12th	2022	Geneva, Switzerland
13th	2024	Abu Dhabi, United Arab Emirates
14th	**2026**	**Yaounde, Cameroon** *(proposed)*

Last Minute SNIPPETS

13th MINISTERIAL CONFERENCE

The World Trade Organisation (WTO) hosted its 13th Ministerial Conference (MC13) in Abu Dhabi, UAE, between February 26 and March 2, 2024.

The meeting brought together trade ministers from across the globe to:

- Review the multilateral trading system.
- Plan for future WTO activity.
- Chart the future trajectory of the WTO.

Key Findings:

- **Dispute Settlement System:** A renewed commitment to have a fully operational system by 2024.
- **Special and Differential Treatment (S&DT):** It was decided to increase its application in developing and least developed countries (LDCs).

Outcomes:

- **Agriculture:** For the first time in more than two decades, a document has been agreed upon, indicating progress.
- **Fisheries:** A consensus is close to being established by the middle of the year.
- **E-commerce:** Unfortunately for India, the exemption from customs tariffs is extended for at least two more years.

Achievements and Challenges for future:

- India and South Africa effectively blocked China's bid to establish an investment facilitation treaty into the WTO framework.
- India should continue to advocate for policy space in sensitive sectors, notably agriculture.
- The WTO must step up its efforts to remain relevant in a divided global setting, going beyond certifying biannual meeting failures as achievements.

2. General Council (GC)

- It is attended by the **Ambassadors** (or equivalent) of the Member States in Geneva **every year**.
- GC has the authority to act on behalf of MC.
- GC also works as:
  - **Dispute Settlement Body (DSB)**
  - **Trade Policy Review Body (TPRB)**

3. Councils for Trade

It includes:

i. Council for Trade in Goods.

ii. Council for Trade in Services.

iii. Council for Trade-Related aspects of Intellectual Property Rights (TRIPS).

All these three councils report to GC.

4. Numerous Committees and Workshops

These are appointed for specific purpose, and they report to Goods Council, Services Council or IPR council and, therefore, answerable to GC.

BONUS KNOWLEDGE

WTO'S DISPUTE SETTLEMENT MECHANISM

- In case of the violation of WTO's Rules of Trade, **bilateral consultation** between the parties/member States is looked into as the first stage of settlement.
- In case it fails, then any of the party **within 60 days** may request General Council for adjudication. Here, GC acts as a DSB.
- The judgment of DSB may be challenged by the parties at the Appellate Body of WTO (**WTOAB**).
- WTOAB may uphold, modify or reverse the earlier judgement of General Council.
- However, the **order of WTOAB** is binding on both the parties.
- If the erring country does not follow the order, the other country is allowed to take retaliatory measures. However, **no such other punishment** is there if one does not follow the order.
- Thus, poor countries generally suffer as they cannot retaliate against developed nations.

Three Major Principles of WTO

1. Most Favoured Nation (treating other partners equally)

- A WTO member should not discriminate between its trading partners; i.e., it should have same trade conditions for all other WTO members.
- In other words, if a WTO member grants any favour or advantage to any of its trading partners, then the same has to be granted to all other WTO members.
- All WTO members are statutorily obliged to grant one another the MFN status.
- However, there may be some cases of exceptions:
    - **Regional Economic Integrations**: Lower or eliminated tariffs among the group members may be set, thereby discriminating against outside the group WTO members. For example, ASEAN, NAFTA, etc.
    - Special access to developing countries in the trade market (say, through lowered or zero tariffs).
    - A country can raise barriers against the products that are considered to be traded unfairly from specific countries.
    - Under security exception clause.

did you KNOW?

THE CASE OF INDIA AND PAKISTAN

The MFN status was accorded by India to Pakistan in 1996, but Pakistan is yet to accord MFN status to India.

In 2019, after the extremely unfortunate Pulwama terror attack, India withdrew the MFN status to Pakistan and hiked customs duty on all its exported goods by Pakistan to India, by 200 per cent. This was done taking national security into consideration and under 'security exception' clause of WTO.

2. National Treatment

- This principle is based on **non-discrimination between domestic products and foreign products**.
- In other words, there should be **no discrimination with imported products** in terms of import tariffs or other Government regulations.
- It implies that both the imported and domestic products should be treated equally within the national boundary, thereby providing a level playing field.
- Charging Customs Duty on an import is **not a violation** of National Treatment because the principle of National Treatment applies only when the product, service or an IPR enters the domestic market.

BONUS KNOWLEDGE

Case of Solar Panels Under National Solar Mission

Under National Solar Mission of GoI, the guidelines mandated that 30 per cent of a project must have **domestic content requirements**, so as to incentivise the growth of domestic solar cells and module manufacturing industries.

However, this was challenged by a US trade representative in the WTO as violative of 'National Treatment' principle. Government of India lost the case after the judgement passed by GC against India was upheld by WTOAB in 2016.

On the other hand, India won another major solar case against the United States in **2019** for violation of National Treatment principle by the United States. The WTO panel upheld India's claim that renewable energy subsidies and local content requirements mandated by eight American states were violating the principle of 'National Treatment'. This is a major strategic advantage for India in terms of **tit for tat** win.

3. Special and Differential (S&D) Treatment with Developing Countries

It emphasises on leniency to developing countries in terms of:

- More time for fulfilment of WTO agreements.
- Provision to increase trading opportunities through greater market access.
- Provisions such as anti-dumping, safeguards, technical barriers to trade, etc.

Generalised System of Preferences (GSP) – Under S&D provisions, a scheme called GSP prevails. The scheme at present is **available to** Least Developed Countries (LDCs) who are WTO members. GSP is a **preferential tariff system** which provides scope for **tariff reduction** for LDCs by other WTO members.

Special Products (SP) and Special Safeguard Mechanism (SSM) – Under S&D provisions, these two mechanisms have been introduced in Doha Round for **developing country members only**.

SPs are agricultural commodities of special importance to the farming communities in developing countries. Doha Round allowed for imposition of higher import tariffs on SPs.

With regard to **SSM**, the developing countries can temporarily impose higher than bound tariff rates on the import of a particular agricultural product. This is allowed if there is a sudden surge in imports of that product in the developing member country.

Major WTO Agreements

Agreement on Agriculture (AoA)

- Executed in 1995, the objective of AoA is to make policies which are feasible to the market and to reform and liberalise trade in this sector along with removing barriers to trade.
- AoA is based on three pillars:
  - **Only up to Reasonable Level of Domestic Support:**
    - Domestic support means subsidies that Government provides to the farmers in food, fertilisers, power, etc. Three types of subsidies are discussed under it:
      1. **Green Box** – It includes those subsidies, which do not distort trade and are given by Government in order to compensate them for deficiency in agricultural environment. Examples include – payments for lack of access to research, lack of training, lack of marketing information, weak rural infrastructure, etc. Green Box subsidies are **allowed** under AoA with no prescribed limit.
      2. **Blue Box** – These subsidies are tied to programmes that limit production. In other words, even if they directly link production to subsidies, they also set limits on production by way of quotas. Thus, Blue Box subsidies are less trade distorting.

         At present, there are **no limits prescribed** under AoA on spending by Government for Blue Box subsidies.
      3. **Amber Box** – Subsidies under this box are deemed to be **trade distorting** by encouraging excessive production through subsidies on fertilisers, seeds, irrigation and power.

         As per AoA, these subsidies are **subject to limits**.

         For developed countries, the subsidy limit is 5 per cent of the value of agricultural production, and for developing countries, the limit is 10 per cent.
  - **Enhance Market Access:**
    - All member countries should throw open their domestic market by reducing tariffs on imports and through conversion of non-tariff barriers into tariff barriers.
  - **Phase out Export Subsidies:**
    - For a period of 6 years, developed countries have to reduce the value by 36 per cent and the volume by 24 per cent of export subsidies.
    - Meanwhile, for a period of 10 years, developing countries have to reduce the value by 24 per cent and the volume by 10 per cent of export subsidies.
- **Impact of AoA on India**
  - Critics argue that this is an unfair limitation on India's food procurement policy by WTO through restrictions imposed under Amber Box.
  - Indian Government runs an MSP program for 22 crops which is further used to run the PDS under which low-income people are supplied food grains at much cheaper prices. Such subsidy provided by GoI falls under the Amber Box category and the WTO has put a cap on Amber Box subsidies.

- The limitation on subsidy amount is not objectionable by India, but the calculation of subsidy is very much objectionable. The **calculation of subsidy is based on the prices pertaining to 1986–88**.
- To temporarily resolve it, a **'Peace Clause'** was ratified at the Bali Ministerial Conference in **2013**.

did you KNOW?

- **As per the Peace Clause**, *'no member country would be legally barred from food security programmes for its own people, even if the subsidy breaches the limits prescribed under Amber Box'.*
- The Peace Clause has been extended indefinitely till any permanent solution is reached by WTO in this regard.

Non-Agricultural Market Access (NAMA)

- Non-Agricultural Market Access (NAMA) negotiations of the WTO are based on the Doha Ministerial Declaration of 2001. It intends to reduce tariffs on exportable goods that are not covered by the Agreement on Agriculture. Non-agricultural products include industrial goods, forestry products, manufactured goods, textiles, fuels and mining products, footwear, fish and fisheries etc.
  - **Less Than Full Reciprocity (LTFR)** is a term associated with the reduction commitments of NAMA mandates (introduced in the Uruguay Round). It is interpreted by the developing countries that they would take on lower percentage reduction commitments than the developed countries.
  - **Anti-Concentration Clause (ACC)**: It intends to ensure that developing countries do not concentrate their flexibilities under specific NAMA products.

General Agreement on Trade in Services (GATS)

- These set of regulations govern the trade in services among WTO members.
- Its objective is to liberalise trade in services.
- The GATS agreement covers four modes of delivery of services:
  - **Cross Border Supply** – which includes BPO, transportations, distance education and training, etc.
  - **Local Delivery of Services** – by foreign banks, insurance companies.
  - **Consumption Abroad** – includes services availed by tourists in foreign countries.
  - **Movement of Personnel** – for delivery of services.

Agreement on Trade-Related Aspects of Intellectual Property Rights

- It is the most comprehensive agreement on intellectual property, signed by all the WTO members.
- It contains rules governing how copyrights, patents, trademarks, geographical indications, industrial designs, etc. will be used to identify products and how it should be protected once trade in them is involved.

EXAM ESSENTIAL

INTELLECTUAL PROPERTY RIGHTS

Given to the creator of intellectual property, WTO defines it as the rights given to persons over creation of their mind. Types of Intellectual Property Rights include:

Patent

- A patent is a statutory right for an invention granted:
  - For a limited period of time
  - To the patentee by the Government
  - In exchange of full disclosure of his invention for excluding others
- Patent protection is territorial right; separate patents should be obtained for separate countries.
- There is no patent valid worldwide.
- Term of every patent in India is 20 years from the date of filing of patent application, irrespective of whether it is filled with provisional or complete specification.

Trademark

- It is also known as brand name.
- It is a visual symbol which may be a word signature, name, device, label, numerals or combination of colours.
- Used by one undertaking to distinguish its goods/services from other undertakings.
- It is protected under intellectual property rights.
- The term of a trademark is for 10 years, which can be renewed.

Copyright

- Bundle of rights given by the law to the creators of literary, dramatic, musical and artistic works and the producers of cinematograph films and sound recordings.
- It includes the rights of reproduction of the work, communication of the work to the public, adaptation of the work and translation of the work.
- The scope and duration of protection provided under copyright varies with the nature of the protected work.
- Copyrights are considered territorial rights, which mean that they do not extend beyond the territory of a specific jurisdiction.

Geographical Indication

- It originates from a definite geographical territory.
- It is used to identify agricultural, natural or manufactured goods.
- The manufactured goods should be produced or processed or prepared in that territory.
- It should have a special quality or reputation or other characteristics.
- Examples include Basmati rice, Darjeeling tea, Kanchipuram silk saree, Alphanso mango, Nagpur orange, Kolhapuri chappal, Bikaneri bhujia, Agra petha, etc.

Industrial Designs

- Covered under the Trade and Merchandise Mark Act, 1958, it provides protection to the form of outward appearance for aesthetic style of an object.
- The duration of the registration of a design is initially 10 years from the date of registration.

Trade Secrets

- It is generally a formula, a practice which is not known by the common people and can be used as an advantage over the competitors.
- Trade secrets are permanent in nature.

BONUS KNOWLEDGE

NATIONAL INTELLECTUAL PROPERTY RIGHTS POLICY

- It was released by GoI in 2016.
- It is in compliance with the WTO's agreement on TRIPS and aims to sustain entrepreneurship and boost 'Make in India' scheme.
- The policy aims to push IPRs as marketable financial assets, promote innovation and entrepreneurship, while protecting public interest.

Highlights

- Special thrust on awareness generation and effective enforcement of IPRs, besides encouragement of IP commercialisation through various incentives.
- It suggested making the Department of Industrial Policy and Promotion (DIPP) the nodal agency for all IPR issues.
- Copyright-related issues to shift under DIPP's ambit from that of the Human Resource Development (HRD) Ministry.
- Examination time for trademarks has been reduced from 13 months to 8 months, with the new target being to bring the time down to 1 month.
- Films, music and industrial drawings to be all covered by copyright.

Trade-Related Investment Measures (TRIMs)

- It is observed that certain investments distort the market and investors. TRIMs recognise the measures to overcome such issues.
- TRIMs apply only to measures that affect **trade in goods** (not services).
- All member nations are directed not to discriminate between domestic and foreign investments, particularly when the Government spending is involved.
- WTO gives list of prohibited investment measures like local content requirements, export obligation, technology transfer, etc., that violates trade.
- **India opposes TRIMs** on the basis that investment is not a trade matter, and therefore, WTO which is a trade body should not interfere in the matter of investment.

Sanitary and Phytosanitary Measures

- How can a member country ensure that food imported from other country is safe to eat? Also, how can they ensure that strict health and safety regulations are not being used by that member country as an excuse for protecting domestic producers?
- To address the above issues, a separate **agreement on food safety and animal and plant health standards** (Sanitary and Phytosanitary Measures Agreement, or SPS) prevails under WTO and it sets out the concerned basic rules.
- The SPS agreement allows member countries to set their own standards on food safety and animal and plant health. But, it also states that regulations must be scientific.
- However, member countries are more encouraged to use international standards so that they are unlikely to be challenged legally in a WTO dispute.

- The various forms in which SPS measures may be applied are:
    i. Product to come from disease-free area
    ii. Specified treatment of the product
    iii. Setting an allowable level of pesticide residue in the product
    iv. Permitted use of only certain additives in the food

BONUS KNOWLEDGE

TRADE FACILITATION AGREEMENT (TFA) of WTO

- Need of TFA – Red Tapism poses a burden for moving goods across borders. Trade facilitation in terms of simplification, modernisation and harmonisation of export and import processes has therefore emerged as an important issue for the world trading system. This led to the need of TFA.
- TFA came into force in **2017**. It is the **result of Doha Round** which occurred in 2001. Text of the TFA was **adopted by WTO members during** 2013 Bali Ministerial Conference.
- TFA contains provisions for expediting the **movement, release** and **clearance** of goods, including goods in transit.
- India has ratified the TFA.

WORLD TRADE OUTLOOK INDICATOR (WTOI)

It was introduced **by WTO** in **2016**. WTOI was designed to provide real-time information on the trajectory of world trade and its recent trend. WTOI provided a headline figure to show performance against trend on a quarterly basis. A reading of 100 indicates trade growth in line with recent trends, a reading greater than 100 suggests above-trend growth, while a reading below 100 indicates below-trend growth.

In 2019, WTOI was replaced by WTO with 2 new barometers:

1. **WTO's Goods Trade Barometer**
2. **WTO's Services Trade Barometer**

Both the above barometers provide similar real-time information.

Achievements of WTO

- Use of restrictive measures for BOP reasons has gone down significantly.
- There have been radical changes in trade, exchange and domestic reforms in the developing countries with improved investment opportunities and thus economic growth.
- Through the Trade Policy Review Mechanism, the process of continuous monitoring of trade policy development has led to the promotion of greater transparency.

Criticisms of WTO

- Many trade reforms have been incomplete in many countries.
- The majority share of the benefits of WTO has gone to the developed countries. Not all WTO members are equally integrated in the multilateral system of economic development.
- The combination of globalisation and technological changes has created growing social division against the low-skilled workers.
- The implementation-related issues have become a source of serious concern.

EXAM ESSENTIAL

INTERNATIONAL FUND FOR AGRICULTURAL DEVELOPMENT (IFAD)

- IFAD, the UN's rural development agency, was established as an international financial institution in 1977. The organisation is an outgrowth of the **1974 World Food Conference**.
- It is the only multilateral development organisation that focuses exclusively on rural economy and food security.
- It funds and supports initiatives that improve land and water management, develop rural infrastructure, educate and train farmers to use more efficient technologies, improve resilience to climate change, improve market access and more.
- It invests in rural people, empowering them to **reduce poverty, increase food security, improve nutrition and strengthen resilience**.
- The headquarters of IFAD is situated in **Rome, Italy**.
- IFAD has **177 Member** States comprising developing, middle and high-income countries from all regions.
- **India is a founder member** and a key contributor to IFAD.
- The current President of the IFAD is **Alvaro Lario**.

Objectives of IFAD include:

- To increase the productive capacity of poor people.
- To increase benefits for them from market participation.
- To strengthen the environmental sustainability and climate resilience of economic activities.

IFAD and India:

- IFAD has been active in India since 1979.
- It focuses on improving the access of the rural poor to technological development in agriculture, financial services, natural resources and value chains.
- It also works to share information and lessons about food security and poverty.
- IFAD's focus areas in India are reducing rural poverty, agriculture evolution of tribes, empowering women, etc.

OTHER INTERNATIONAL ECONOMIC ORGANISATIONS

G3

- It was a free trade agreement signed between three countries, namely, **Mexico, Colombia** and **Venezuela**.
- The agreement was signed for 10 years from 1995 to 2005.
- It covered areas such as:
  - Intellectual Property Rights
  - Public sector investment
  - Easing of trade restrictions
  - Reducing 10 per cent tariff over a period of 10 years

- The agreement didn't last long, as there was no active participation on the part of Venezuela.
- But it resulted in strengthening of trade between Mexico and Colombia.

G7

- Formed in 1975, G7 consists of highly industrialised countries.
- The group comprises 7 countries as its members – **United States, Canada, Germany, Britain, France, Italy** and **Japan**.
- Russia joined as its member in 1997, after which G7 became G8.
- However, in 2014, Russia was ejected of G8 membership. Thus, G8 again transformed into G7.
- In 2020, the then US President showed his keenness to expand G7 to G11 by including **India, Russia, South Korea** and **Australia** as its members.

G20

- It was established in **1999**, to bring together systematically important **industrialised and developing economies** to discuss key issues in the global economy.
- **India is a member** of G20.
- It includes the **finance ministers and central bank governors** of 19 countries and EU.
- Together the member countries represent around 90 per cent of the global GDP, 80 per cent of world trade as well as two-third of the world's population.
- It has helped tackle the financial and economic crisis of 2008 and strengthen international cooperation among member nations.
- The **IMF works closely with the G20** on issues related to global economic growth and financial stability.
- G20 has **no permanent staff** of its own and the **chairmanship rotates annually** between nations divided in regional group.
- India has contributed to G20 on many issues such as:
  - Financial sector regulatory reforms.
  - Climate change.
  - Economic Growth and fiscal consolidation.

G20 Common Framework

- In order **to deal with protracted liquidity problems and insolvency**, G20 Common Framework program has been introduced. It is also intended to support the implementation of IMF reform program.
- This framework aims to deal with the issue of unsustainable debts faced by various countries (specifically low-income countries).
- It is supported by both traditional creditors (Paris Club – such as France and USA) and new creditors like India, Turkey and China.
- It is the Common Framework for Debt Treatments beyond the Debt Service Suspension Initiative (DSSI).
- Recently, Chad has requested debt restructuring under the framework.

Last Minute SNIPPETS

G20 SUMMIT 2024

- The Summit was hosted **by Brazil** at Rio de Janeiro in November 2024. The summit was attended by the leaders of 19 member countries along with European Union and African Union. The Rio Declaration of 2024 G20 Summit was focused on cooperation in taxation process amongst the member countries, climate change, hunger eradication, gender equality and global governance reforms.
- In the context of climate change, by 2050, the pollutants related to greenhouse gas emissions will no longer be used by G20 member countries. The group also committed to promote public and private investments in nature-based solutions.
- For fighting hunger and poverty, the group has launched the **Global Alliance Against Hunger and Poverty**. This alliance is backed by 82 countries, 2 continental blocs, 24 international organisations, 9 financial institutions and 31 philanthropic and non-governmental organisations. The primary focus of the alliance is to provide immediate help to the countries with severe situation ensuring "*no one is left behind*".

G33

- It is a forum of **developing countries** formed during the WTO's Cancun Ministerial Conference in 2003, to protect developing countries' interests in agricultural trade negotiations.
- The G33 Group is also known as the 'Friends of Special Products in Agriculture'.
- It has a total of **48 members** (dominated by India) which are **net agri-products importing developing countries**.
- Its members comprise developing countries like Indonesia and India **with defensive farm interest that involves protecting farmers from imports**.
- Its demands were:
  - Limitation on the level of market opening of agri-imports of developing countries
  - Creation of special product exemption
  - Special safeguard mechanism which would allow tariff increases against import surges
- These demands by them advocated for the creation of Special Products and Special Safeguard Mechanisms by WTO under AoA.
- In 2017, some more demands have been raised by G33:
  - **Subsidy given under MSP program** so that farmers should not be considered as trade distorting subsidies.
  - There should be a change in the calculation method of subsidies which does not take into account true effect of inflation as it is based on market prices prevailing in 1986–88.

Organisation of Petroleum Exporting Countries (OPEC)

- It is a permanent inter-Governmental organisation created at the Baghdad Conference in **1960**.
- Headquarters is in **Vienna**, Austria.
- Presently, OPEC has **12 members** – Iran, Iraq, Kuwait, Saudi Arabia, Venezuela, Libya, UAE, Algeria, Nigeria, Gabon, Equatorial Guinea and Congo.

- Last member to join is **Congo in 2018**.
- **Angola has withdrawn** its membership from OPEC (effective from 1st January 2024).
- **Objectives** of OPEC include:
  - Coordination and unification of petroleum policies among member countries.
  - To secure fair and stable prices for petroleum producers.
  - To have an efficient economic and regular supply of petroleum to consumer nations.
  - To have a fair return on capital to those investing in the industry.

> **did you KNOW?** **World Oil Outlook (WOO)** – It is the publication of OPEC. It highlights the possible future challenges and opportunities of the global oil industry and stirs up cooperation and transparency among the stakeholders.

Organisation of Arab Petroleum Exporting Countries (OAPEC)

- OAPEC was **founded in 1968** with the signing of an agreement in Beirut on 9 January 1968 among Kuwait, Libya (then known as the Kingdom of Libya) and Saudi Arabia.
- OAPEC is dedicated to the growth and prosperity of the global oil industry through close and productive partnerships between its members.
- The organisation carries out its functions and responsibilities through four organs, namely – The Council of Ministers, The Executive Bureau, General Secretariat and The Judicial Board.
- Eleven member countries of OAPEC include **Algeria**, **Bahrain**, **Egypt**, **Iraq**, **Kuwait**, **Libya**, **Qatar**, **Saudi Arabia**, **Syria**, **United Arab Emirates** and **Tunisia**.
- Secretary General of OAPEC is **Jamal Essa Al Loughani**.
- **Objectives of OAPEC include:**
  - Ensure adequate arrangements for the coordination of its members' petroleum economic policies;
  - Ensure appropriate arrangements for the harmonisation of the legal systems applicable in the Member States to the extent necessary for the Organisation to conduct its activities;
  - Encourage members to share information and knowledge and to offer training and employment opportunities to citizens of the Member States where such opportunities exist;
  - Encourage cooperation among members in finding solutions to problems in the petroleum industry;
  - Utilise member resources and common opportunities in setting up joint projects in various stages of the petroleum industry.

World Economic Forum (WEF)

- World Economic Forum is an international organisation for **public–private cooperation**.
- It was established in **1971** as a not-for-profit foundation **(NGO)**.
- It is headquartered in **Geneva, Switzerland**.
- It provides an interactive platform to the world's foremost CEOs of private companies, heads of state, ministers and policy-makers, experts and academicians, international organisations, youth, technology innovators and representatives of the civil society. They discuss to bring long-term positive change.

- For this, a conference is held by WEF at Davos every year (in January).
- **Three key focus areas** of WEF are – mastering fourth industrial revolution, solving the problems of Global Commons and addressing global security issues.
- World's **1,000 leading companies are the members** of WEF.
- **Major Annual Reports published by WEF** include:
  1. Global Competitiveness Report
  2. Global Information Technology Report
  3. Global Gender Gap Report
  4. Global Travel and Tourism Report
  5. Global Risks Report
  6. Global Enabling Trade Report

did you KNOW?

Davos Manifesto – Initially launched in 1973, the WEF launched the **new** Davos Manifesto in **2020**. It is a set of ethical principles that guides companies in the era of the Fourth Industrial Revolution. It states that companies should pay their fair share of taxes, have zero tolerance towards corruption, uphold human rights and strive for competitive level-playing field.

Closing the Skills Gap Task Force – It was launched by the *Union Ministry of Skill Development and Entrepreneurship, GoI*, in collaboration with the WEF in 2018. It aims to reshape the education and address the current skill gap.

World Food Programme (WFP)

- The World Food Programme (WFP) is the foremost humanitarian organisation, saving and improving lives by providing emergency food aid and working with communities to enhance nutrition and resilience.
- It was **founded in 1961** by the **Food and Agriculture Organisation (FAO) and United Nations General Assembly (UNGA)**.
- Its headquarters is situated in **Rome, Italy**.
- The organisation and its activities are guided by Sustainable Development Goal 2, which aims **to end hunger by 2030**, improve food security and nutrition, and promote sustainable agriculture.
- It works in more than 120 countries, providing food aid in emergencies and working with communities to improve nutrition and resilience.
- It has been operating in India since **1963**.
- It won the **Nobel Peace Prize in 2020**.
- The report published by WFP is a **Global Food Crisis Report** that describes the extent of acute hunger in the world.

WFP and India

WFP has been working in India since 1963, facilitating not just food distribution but also providing technical assistance. Through these efforts, India successfully attained self-sufficiency in cereal production. Focus areas of WFP are:

- Making the targeted public distribution system more efficient and transparent.
- Fortification of government-supplied food to increase nutritional value.

- Food insecurity mapping and monitoring.
- Improve nutrition for persons at high risk of malnutrition, particularly mothers, children, and teenage girls, by 2025.

ASEAN

- It is the Association of South-East Asian Nations (ASEAN).
- It was established in **1967** in Bangkok by Indonesia, Malaysia, Philippines, Singapore and Thailand. It is headquatered in **Jakarta**, Indonesia.
- Currently, it has **10 member States** and **2 observer States**.
- India is **neither** a member **nor** an observer.
- Its aim is to accelerate economic growth, social progress and cultural development along with promotion of peace and stability in the region.
- **Regional Comprehensive Economic Partnership (RCEP)** is a **free trade agreement** in the Asia-Pacific region between the 10 member States of ASEAN and 5 of ASEAN's FTA partners – Australia, China, Japan, New Zealand and South Korea. India, which is also ASEAN's FTA partner, withdrew from RCEP in 2019.
- **Dr. Kao Kim Hourn** is the current and the 15th Secretary-General of ASEAN, since 2023.
- India is a
  - Sectoral partner of ASEAN since 1992
  - Dialogue partner of ASEAN since 1996
  - Summit-level partner of ASEAN since 2002
  - Strategic partner of ASEAN since 2012

East Asia Summit (EAS)

- It was established in **2005**, for strategic dialogue and cooperation on the key political security and economic challenges facing the Indo-Pacific region.
- It is a forum of **18 countries** of the Asia-Pacific region **(including India)**.
- Priority areas of EAS include the following **six** – Environment and Energy, Education, Finance, Global Health Issues and Pandemic Diseases, Natural Disaster Management and ASEAN Connectivity. India endorses regional collaboration in all six priority areas.
- The 18th East Asia Summit was held in Jakarta, Indonesia in 2023.
- The 19th Summit will be held in 2024 in Vientiane, Laos.

Asia-Pacific Economic Cooperation (APEC)

- It is a regional economic forum of 21 countries on the Pacific Rim. It was established in 1989 and aims to promote inclusive growth, greater prosperity and free trade in the Asia-Pacific region.
- It is headquartered in Singapore.
- Members include Australia, Brunei Darussalam, Canada, Chile, People's Republic of China, Vietnam, Hong Kong, China, Indonesia, Japan, Republic of Korea, Malaysia, Mexico, New Zealand, Papua New Guinea, Peru, Philippines, Russia, Singapore, Chinese Taipei, Thailand and United States of America.

Asia-Pacific Trade Agreement (APTA)

- It was formerly known as the Bangkok Agreement.
- APTA intends to promote economic development of its members and adopt mutually beneficial trade liberalisation practices for regional trade expansion and economic cooperation. It was signed in 1975.
- Members: Bangladesh, China, **India**, Republic of Korea, Lao PDR, Sri Lanka and Mongolia.

South Asia Subregional Economic Cooperation (SASEC)

- The South Asia Growth Quadrangle (SAGQ) was formed in **1996** by Bangladesh, Bhutan, India and Nepal (BBIN) to accelerate sustainable economic development and to enhance cross-border connectivity. Then it led to the creation of SASEC program with the assistance of ADB in 2001.
- Members of SASEC include Bangladesh, Bhutan, **India**, Maldives, Myanmar, Nepal and Sri Lanka.
- SASEC promotes cross-border connectivity, prosperity, economic opportunities and a better quality of life among the member nations.

Eurasian Economic Union (EAEU)

The EAEU was established by the Treaty on the Eurasian Economic Union (2014). The EAEU promotes free movement of goods, services, capital, etc. It provides common policies in transport, industry and agriculture, energy, etc. within the Union and fosters competitiveness and cooperation between the member states.

Its member states include Republic of Armenia, the Republic of Belarus, the Republic of Kazakhstan, the Kyrgyz Republic and the Russian Federation.

Bay of Bengal Initiative for Multi-Sectoral Technical and Economic Cooperation (BIMSTEC)

- BIMSTEC is an economic bloc, formed in June 1997, as a result of the Bangkok Declaration.
- The headquarters of BIMSTEC is situated in **Dhaka, Bangladesh**.
- Initially on June 6, 1997 BIMSTEC was established with four member countries, namely **Bangladesh, India, Sri Lanka, and Thailand**.
- **Nepal** joined BIMSTEC as an observer state in 1998, and became a full-fledged member together with Bhutan in February 2004.
- Members are along the Bay of Bengal coastline and adjoining regions, creating a cohesive regional community. Five of the seven members are from South Asia. The countries include Bangladesh, Bhutan, India, Nepal, and Sri Lanka, with the remaining two from Southeast Asia. They are Myanmar and Thailand.
- Objectives of BIMSTEC are as follows:
  - Promoting fast economic growth in the subregion.
  - Fostering equality and collaboration among stakeholders.
  - Encouraging cooperation and mutual assistance among member nations on shared goals.
  - Encourages mutual aid in education, research, and technology, among other areas.

Better Than Cash Alliance

- It is based in the **United Nations**. The Better Than Cash Alliance is a partnership of Governments, international organisations and companies that promote the transition from cash to responsible digital payment.
- **India joined Better Than Cash Alliance in 2015.**
- A joint peer learning exchange on fintech solutions for responsible digital payments at the last mile was organised by India and UN-based Better Than Cash Alliance **in 2020**.

World Customs Organisation (WCO)

- The WCO was established in **1952** as the Customs Co-operation Council (CCC). WCO aims to enhance the efficiency and effectiveness of customs administrations.
- Its headquarters is located at **Brussels, Belgium**.
- Different customs instruments of WCO are – The International Convention on the Harmonised Commodity Description and Coding System (HS Convention, adopted in 1983), the Arusha Declaration on Customs Integrity (adopted in 1993), the SAFE Framework of Standards to Secure and Facilitate Global Trade (adopted in 2005), etc.
- **Authorised Economic Operator (AEO)** is a programme under the WCO SAFE Framework of Standards to secure and facilitate Global Trade.
- WCO publishes **Illicit Trade Report**.
- Harmonised System (or 'HS') is a six-digit identification code and a multipurpose international product nomenclature, developed by the WCO.

International Energy Agency (IEA)

- The IEA was established during the 1973–74 oil crisis to ensure the supply and security of oil.
- To join the *IEA, a country must be a member of the OECD*. **India** became an association country of IEA in 2017.
- The headquarters of IEA is located in **Paris, France**.
- IEA publishes various reports such as Key World Energy Statistics (KWES), Global Energy Review, World Energy Outlook, Global Electric Vehicle Outlook, the Future of Rail Report, etc.
- India and the International Energy Agency (IEA) signed a Strategic Partnership Agreement to strengthen their cooperation in global energy security, stability and sustainability.
- The IEA invited **India**, the world's **third-largest energy consumer**, to join as a full-time member in 2021.

World Energy Outlook

World Energy Outlook is an energy report of the International Energy Agency (IEA).

Last Minute
SNIPPETS

FINDINGS OF WORLD ENERGY OUTLOOK 2024

The 2024 World Energy Outlook (WEO) includes analysis over several sensitivity cases on key factors affecting oil, gas and electricity demand in the Stated Policies Scenario (STEPS).

- The growth rate of electricity demand is much faster than overall energy demands. Focus on electricity generation through renewable sources has led to meet the increasing energy demand.
- The 2024 WEO emphasises that clean energy meets virtually all growth in energy demand in aggregate in the STEPS between 2023 and 2035.
- The report also indicated that the clean energy investment in emerging and developing economies (outside China) stuck at 15% of the global share although these economies account for almost one-third of global GDP and home to two-thirds of the global population.

IEA Technology Collaboration Programme on Bioenergy (IEA Bioenergy TCP) – IEA Bioenergy TCP is an international platform which aims to improve cooperation and information exchange between national programmes in bioenergy research and development of different countries. **India joined the IEA Bioenergy TCP as a member in 2019**. It facilitates the market introduction of advanced bio-fuels and reduce emissions and crude imports.

SUMMARY

- **Bretton Woods Conference** – Held in 1944 in the US – attended by delegates from 44 allied nations – to establish the international monetary and financial order after the Second World War – also known as United Nations Monetary and Financial Conference – conference resulted in establishment of IBRD and IMF.
- **International Monetary Fund** – Autonomous organisation affiliated to UNO – established on 27 Dec 1945 – headquarters at Washington, DC – each country's contribution fixed in terms of quota – facilitates to solve the short-term BOP crisis of member countries – publishes two periodic reports – World Economic Outlook and Global Financial Stability Report.
- **Special Drawing Rights (SDR)** – Created in 1969 – artificial currency unit used by IMF to lend to its members – SDR is not traded in forex market.
- **World Bank** – Generally refers to IBRD and IDA as they have the same head and management, while the term 'World Bank Group' refers to a group of five institutions, namely, International Bank for Reconstruction and Development (IBRD), International Development Association (IDA), International Finance Corporation (IFC), Multilateral Investment Guarantee Agency (MIGA) and International Centre for Settlement of Investment Disputes (ICSID) – to be a member of World Bank, a country needs to be a member of IMF first – India is a member of four of them (except ICSID) – headquarters of all five are at Washington, DC.
- **Organisation of Arab Petroleum Exporting Countries (OAPEC)** – Was **founded in 1968** with the signing of an agreement in Beirut on 9 January 1968 among Kuwait, Libya and Saudi Arabia.
- **New Development Bank (BRICS Development Bank)** – Came into existence at the 2015 Summit in Russia – headquarters at Shanghai, China – supports infrastructure and sustainable development projects – has One Member, One Vote Policy.

- **World Food Programme (WFP)** – Is the foremost humanitarian organisation, saving and improving lives by providing emergency food aid and working with communities to enhance nutrition and resilience. It was **founded in 1961** by the **Food and Agriculture Organization (FAO) and United Nations General Assembly (UNGA)**.
- **Asian Development Bank (ADB)** – In 1966 – as a Multilateral Development Bank – has 69 member countries including India (latest being Israel – added in 2024) – headquarters at Manila, Philippines.
- **International Fund for Agricultural Development (IFAD)** – Established as an international financial institution in 1977. The organisation is an outgrowth of the **1974 World Food Conference.**
- **Asian Infrastructure Investment Bank (AIIB)** – In 2016 – to improve social and economic outcomes in Asia – has membership of 110 nations (including India) – headquarters at Beijing, China.
- **Bay of Bengal Initiative for Multi-Sectoral Technical and Economic Cooperation (BIMSTEC)** – An economic bloc, which was formed in June 1997, as a result of the Bangkok Declaration. The headquarters of BIMSTEC is situated in **Dhaka, Bangladesh**.
- **World Trade Organization (WTO)** – Established on 1 Jan 1995 by replacing GATT – headquarters at Geneva, Switzerland – has 166 member states (including India as founding member) – follows the voting system of 'one country, one vote'.
- **World Economic Forum** – Established in 1971 as a not-for-profit foundation – headquartered at Geneva, Switzerland – provides an interactive platform to the world's foremost CEOs of private companies, heads of State, Ministers and policy-makers, experts and academics, international organisations, youth, technology innovators and representatives of civil society.

UPSC CSE PREVIOUS YEARS' PRELIMINARY EXAMINATION QUESTIONS

1. Consider the following statements about G20: **[2023]**

1. The G20 group was originally established as a platform for the Finance Ministers and Central Bank Governors to discuss the international economic and financial issues.
2. Digital public infrastructure is one of India's G20 priorities.

Which of the statements given above is/are correct?

(a) 1 only (b) 2 only
(c) Both 1 and 2 (d) Neither 1 nor 2

2. With reference to the 'G20 Common Framework', consider the following statements: **[2022]**

1. It is an initiative endorsed by the G20 together with the Paris Club.
2. It is an initiative to support low income countries with unsustainable debt.

Which of the statements given above is/are correct?

(a) 1 only (b) 2 only
(c) Both 1 and 2 (d) Neither 1 nor 2

3. '**Rapid Financing Instrument**' and '**Rapid Credit Facility**' are related to the provisions of lending by which of the following? **[2022]**

(a) Asian Development Bank
(b) International Monetary Fund
(c) United Nations Environment Programme Finance Initiative
(d) World Bank

4. Consider the following statements: **[2022]**

1. Asian Infrastructure Investment Bank
2. Missile Technology Control Regime
3. Shanghai Cooperation Organisation

India is a member of which of the above?

(a) 1 and 2 only (b) 3 only
(c) 2 and 3 only (d) 1, 2 and 3

5. In which one of the following groups are all the four countries members of G20? **[2020]**

(a) Argentina, Mexico, South Africa and Turkey

(b) Australia, Canada, Malaysia and New Zealand
(c) Brazil, Saudi Arabia and Vietnam
(d) Indonesia, Japan, Singapore and South Korea

6. With reference to **Trade-Related Investment Measures (TRIMS)**, which of the following statements is/are correct? **[2020]**

1. Quantitative restrictions on imports by foreign investors are prohibited.
2. They apply to investment measures related to trade in both goods and services.
3. They are not concerned with the regulation of foreign investment.

Select the correct answer using the code given below:

(a) 1 and 2 only (b) 2 only
(c) 1 and 3 only (d) 1, 2 and 3

7. With reference to **Asian Infrastructure Investment Bank (AIIB)**, consider the following statements: **[2019]**

1. AIIB has more than 80 member nations.
2. India is the largest shareholder in AIIB.
3. AIIB does not have any members from outside Asia.

Which of the statement(s) given above is/are correct?

(a) 1 only (b) 2 and 3 only
(c) 1 and 3 only (d) 1, 2 and 3

8. The **Global Competitiveness Report** is published by the **[2019]**

(a) International Monetary Fund
(b) United Nations Conference on Trade and Development
(c) World Economic Forum
(d) World Bank

9. Consider the following statements: **[2017]**

1. India has ratified the **Trade Facilitation Agreement (TFA)** of WTO.
2. TFA is a part of WTO's Bali Ministerial Package of 2013.
3. TFA came into force in January 2016.

Which of the statements given above is/are correct?

(a) 1 and 2 only (b) 1 and 3 only
(c) 2 and 3 only (d) 1, 2 and 3

10. With reference to the **'National Intellectual Property Rights Policy'**, consider the following statements: **[2017]**

1. It reiterates India's commitment to the Doha Development Agenda and the TRIPS Agreement.
2. Department of Industrial Policy and Promotion is the nodal agency for regulating intellectual property rights in India.

Which of the above statements is/are correct?

(a) 1 only (b) 2 only
(c) Both 1 and 2 (d) Neither 1 nor 2

11. India's ranking in the **'Ease of Doing Business Index'** is sometimes seen in the news. Which of the following has declared that ranking? **[2016]**

(a) Organisation for Economic Cooperation and Development (OECD)
(b) World Economic Forum
(c) World Bank
(d) World Trade Organization (WTO)

12. **'Global Financial Stability Report'** is prepared by the: **[2016]**

(a) European Central Bank
(b) International Monetary Fund
(c) International Bank for Reconstruction and Development
(d) Organisation for Economic Cooperation and Development

13. The term **'Regional Comprehensive Economic Partnership'** often appears in the news in the context of the affairs of a group of countries known as: **[2016]**

(a) G20 (b) ASEAN
(c) SCO (d) SAARC

14. In the context of which of the following do you sometimes find the terms **amber box, blue box** and **green box** in the news? **[2016]**

(a) WTO affairs
(b) SAARC affairs
(c) UNFCCC affairs
(d) India-EU negotiations on FTA

15. With reference to the International Monetary and Financial Committee **(IMFC)**, consider the following statements: **[2016]**

1. IMFC discusses matters of concern affecting the global economy, and advises the International Monetary Fund (IMF) on the direction of its work.
2. The World Bank participates as observer in IMFC's meetings.

Which of the statements given above is/are correct?

(a) 1 only (b) 2 only
(c) Both 1 and 2 (d) Neither 1 nor 2

16. India is a member of which among the following? **[2015]**

1. Asia-Pacific Economic Cooperation (APEC)
2. Association of South-East Asian Nations (ASEAN)
3. East Asia Summit.

Select the correct answer using the code given below.

(a) 1 and 2 only (b) 3 only
(c) 1, 2 and 3 (d) India is a member of none of them

17. Which one of the following issues **'Global Economic Prospects'** report periodically? **[2015]**

(a) The Asian Development Bank
(b) The European Bank of Reconstruction and Development
(c) The US Federal Reserve Bank
(d) The World Bank

18. Which of the following organisations brings out the publication **'World Economic Outlook'**? **[2014]**

(a) The International Monetary Fund
(b) The United Nations Development Programme
(c) The World Economic Forum
(d) The World Bank

☞ NO QUESTIONS ASKED
2024, 2021, 2018, 2013

ANSWER KEY

1. (c)	2. (c)	3. (b)	4. (d)	5. (a)
6. (c)	7. (a)	8. (c)	9. (a)	10. (c)
11. (c)	12. (b)	13. (b)	14. (a)	15. (c)
16. (b)	17. (d)	18. (a)		

UPSC CSE PREVIOUS YEARS' MAIN EXAMINATION QUESTIONS

☞ NO QUESTIONS ASKED
2024, 2023, 2022, 2021, 2020, 2019, 2018, 2017, 2016, 2015, 2014, 2013

CHAPTER

30

POPULATION AND DEMOGRAPHIC DIVIDEND

CHAPTER OUTLINE

- Theories of Population
- Malthusian Theory
- Zero Population Growth Theory
- The Optimum Theory of Population
- Stages of Demographic Transition
- India's Population: Trend in Size, Growth Pattern, Birth and Death Rates
- Causes of Rapid Growth in Population in India
- Population *versus* Economic Development in India
- Measures to check Population Explosion
- Family Planning Programme
- Population Policies undertaken by Government
- Evaluation of Government Policies
- Missing Women in Sex Composition
- Causes of Low Female–Male Ratio
- Demographic Dividend
- Benefits of Demographic Dividend
- 'Squandering' Demographic Dividend
- Challenges related to Demographic Dividend
- Tackling Skill Deficit through Human Capital

THEORIES OF POPULATION

Economics and population growth are intricately linked. One of the several ways to economic growth through the population is labour. Large population in a country indicates a larger workforce and easier access to labour. More labour leads to more production which fosters economic growth of a country.

There are a number of theories of population. The objective of studying economics is to determine the optimal allocation of the available resources, and the demand of resources at a point of time depends on the size of the population. There are several theories of population, the four most prominent amongst which are:

- Malthusian theory of population growth
- Zero population growth theory
- The Optimum theory of population
- The theory of demographic transition

Malthusian Theory

The 18th century British philosopher and economist, **Thomas Malthus** proposed that the populations would continue expanding until growth is stopped or reversed by a disease, famine, war or calamity. These will act like natural checks for population growth. According to him, the food supply lacks pace, compared to the population growth and hence the **food shortage is inevitable**. The growth of the food supply and other resources is linear; it lessens the standards of living and eventually population decline. This event is known as the **Malthusian catastrophe**. Thomas Malthus proposed his hypothesis in **An Essay on the Principle of Population in 1798**.

Zero Population Growth Theory

Professor Emeritus Paul R. Ehrlich of Stanford University claimed that the overall environment (not just food, as claimed by Malthus) controls the population.

As per the theory, the privileged class will try to exploit the limited resources available and there will be a scarcity of necessary items for life. To counter that, he suggested that Zero Population Growth (ZPG) should be achieved in a manner that the rate of birth and death and inward and outward migration should match, so that the total population should remain constant.

This theory is often criticised on the ground that it is the restatement of Malthusian Theory in the 20th century.

The Optimum Theory of Population

This theory is defined by a condition where individuals are getting the highest possible per capita income, considering the available resources and given level of technology. This theory was put forward by **Edwin Cannan** in 1924.

The Optimum Theory of Population studies the relationship between **population size and the production of wealth.** Optimum Population refers to a state where the size of the population is neither greater nor lower than the socially desirable level. In other words, Optimum Population is that which gives the maximum income per head.

Features of the Theory

1. At a given level of technology, it balances the population with the available resources.

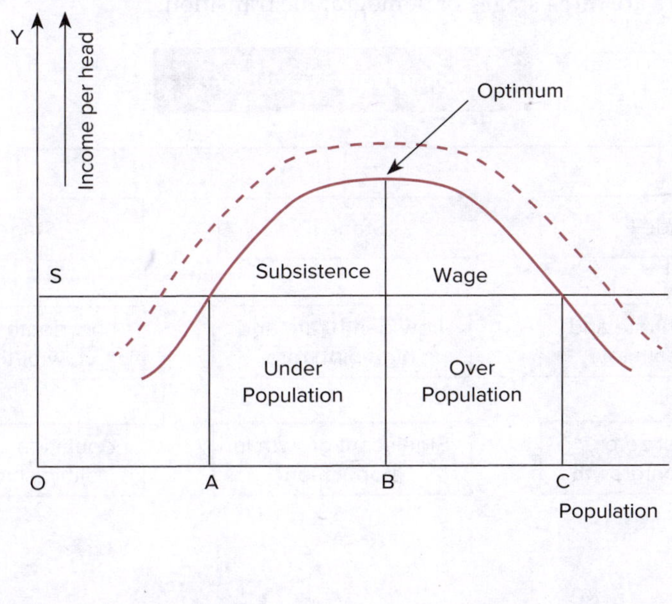

2. Optimum population is a dynamic population that changes with the changing quantity and quality of a country's available resources.
3. An optimum population ensures or secures a maximum return per head.
4. An optimum population is the population that produces full employment.
5. The management or control of economy that has optimum population is very easy.
6. Optimum population also ensures the highest standard of living in a country.

Theory of Demographic Transition

Warren Thompson proposed this theory. The theory of demographic transition suggests that population growth is linked to overall levels of economic development and that every society follows a typical pattern of development-related population growth. **There are three stages of demographic transition** in any society.

Before discussing demographic dividend, let us first understand the stages of demographic transition which impacts the growth rate of population in a country.

STAGES OF DEMOGRAPHIC TRANSITION

EXAM ESSENTIAL

- Stages of demographic transition throw light on **changes in birth rate and death rate** and therefore make it easier to understand the growth rate of population.
- This also helps in understanding the relationship between the population and economic development.
- According to *E. G. Dolan*, '**Demographic transition refers to a population cycle** that begins with a fall in the death rate, continues with a phase of rapid population growth and concludes with a decline in birth rate'.
- In particular, there are **three stages** of demographic transition.

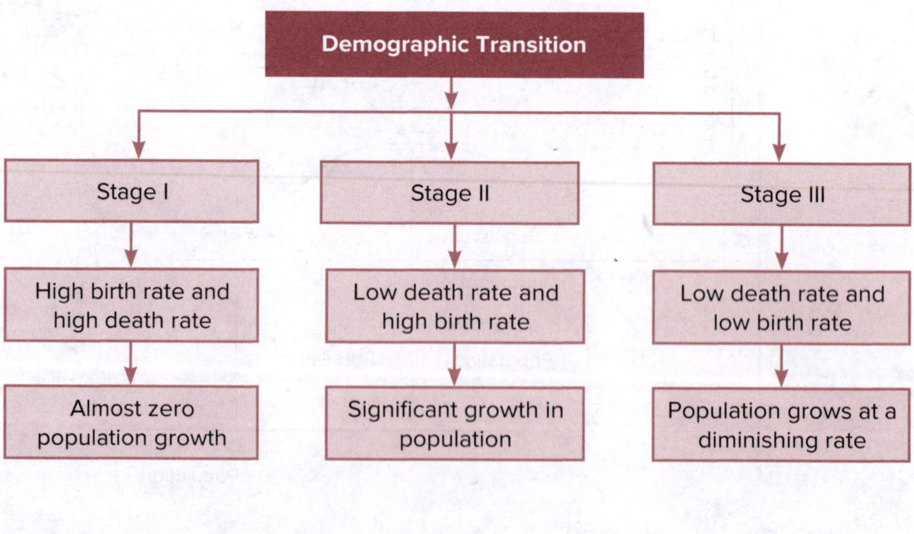

Stage I

- Stage I of demographic transition indicates **high birth rate and high death rate**. Both birth rate and death rate remain approximately equal over time, and thus a static equilibrium with almost **zero population growth** prevails.
- **High Death Rate** – Lack of medical facilities, low availability of food and lack of quality education are the main causes of high death rate.
- **High Birth Rate** – Low level of education, poverty and low participation of women in economic growth are some major causes of high birth rate.
- This stage of demographic transition is prevalent **mostly in underdeveloped economies**. For example, in an agrarian economy, children at an early age contribute to production, and in such economies children are traditionally considered as the security for their parents in their old age. Consequently, high birth rate is prevalent in such an economy.
- Moreover, per capita income in agrarian economies is low which leads to low standard of living. Therefore, a good number of people live on an inadequate diet with awful housing facilities. Additionally, poor health facilities lead to high death rate.
- Some economies in Africa and South America are still going through this stage. **India crossed this stage in the 1920s**.

Stage II

- This stage of demographic transition shows a **low death rate and a high birth rate**. Thus, Stage II is characterised by **significant growth in population**.
- **Low Death Rate** – Due to improvement in the living standards and medical facilities, expansion of education and efforts of the Government in fighting with endemics like cholera, plague, etc.
- **High Birth Rate** – This occurs because a large section of population at this stage is dependent upon agriculture, and children contribute in the production. Apart from this, people follow large family norm and the status of women is also comparatively lower.
- This stage of demographic transition is prevalent in those economies where a large section of population is living in poverty. Some **economies in Asia and South America** are still going through this stage. **India is believed to be in the later phase of this stage**.
- The proportion of children and youth are higher in such economies. Thus, in future, these economies may get **substantial demographic dividend**.

Stage III

- This stage is characterised by **low death rate and low birth rate**. Consequently, **population grows at a diminishing rate**.
- **Low Death Rate** – Expansion of medical facilities, availability of basic requirements, improvement in the living standards, expansion of education, etc. are some of the reasons for lower rate of mortality.
- **Low Birth Rate** – Due to the expansion of industries, people are inclined towards small family norms. Also, the participation of women in economic activities improves their status, and improvement in education, etc. leads to low birth rate.

- **Economies of Western Europe and North America** and some economies of Asia like **Japan**, etc. are in the third stage of demographic transition.
- Nations at this stage **suffer from ageing of population** as the proportion of elderly people is relatively higher due to low birth rate and low death rate.

The graph on the right shows the relation between the stages and growth in population: →

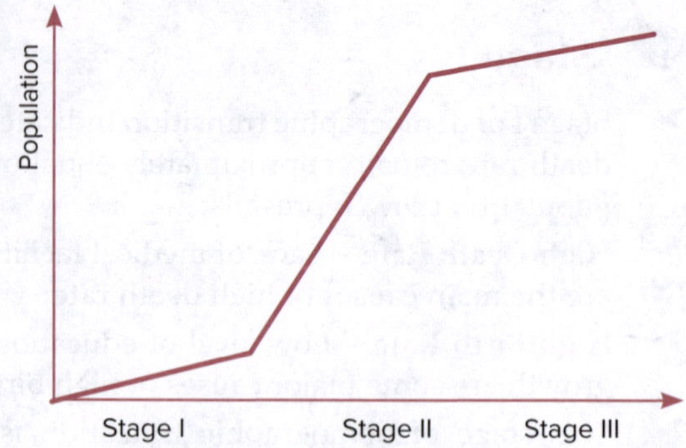

INDIA'S POPULATION: TREND IN SIZE, GROWTH PATTERN, BIRTH AND DEATH RATES

- With just 2.4 per cent of total land area of the planet, India accommodates around 17.7 per cent of the world's total population.
- India's population is **more than the combined population of** the United States, Brazil, Bangladesh, Japan and Indonesia.
- Following is the census report for growth of population in India since independence. This data also clearly shows that **India is in the later phase of Stage II** of demographic transition.

Year	Birth Rate per 1000 Persons	Death Rate per 1000 Persons
1951	39.9	27.4
1961	41.7	22.8
1971	36.9	14.9
1981	33.9	12.5
1991	29.5	9.8
2001	25.4	8.4
2011	21.8	7.1

Year	Population (crore)	Density (per sq. km)
1951	36.11	117
1961	43.92	142
1971	54.82	177
1981	68.33	216
1991	84.64	267
2001	102.87	325
2011	121.09	382

Last Minute SNIPPETS

As per the PIB, India (1.4 billion) remains one of the most populous countries of the world. By 2036, the population of India is expected to reach about 152.2 crore. Slight improvement is anticipated in female percentage of 48.8 per cent as compared to 48.5 per cent in 2011. The proportion of individuals under 15 years is projected to decrease from 2011 to 2036. This is due to declining fertility. The proportion of the population aged 60 years and above is predicted to significantly increase during this period.

Causes of Rapid Growth in Population in India

- Generally, there are three possibilities for increase in the population of a country, which are – **high birth rate, low death rate and immigration**.
- In case of our country, high birth rate and low death rate are prevalent for increase in population.

Causes of High Birth Rate	Causes of Low Death Rate
Around 54.6 per cent of the population in India is dependent on agriculture. And mostly, primitive methods are used for agricultural production in India; thus, having more children fulfils the labour demand with less expenditure on labour. This provides the rationale behind having bigger family. (*As per Annual Report, 2020–2021, Department of Agriculture*)	Eradication of deadly diseases like small pox and rinderpest and control over the epidemics caused by malaria, tuberculosis, etc. have contributed to lowering the death rate.
Poverty is another factor which leads to high birth rate. It has been observed that the poor population considers children as asset for their old age. And also, more members will bring more earnings as they depend on their own labour.	Improved supply of drinking water and spread of improved sanitation and hygiene along with relevant awareness programs by the Government have helped Indians to stay protected from various diseases.
Social factors like lower age of marriage, religious superstitions, lack of education, lower status of women, etc. are some of the reasons for high birth rate in India.	Expansion of medical facilities and the establishment of Integrated Child Development Services (ICDS) centres in rural areas have also helped.

However, as compared to the post-Independence figures, the birth rate has lowered. Reasons may be:

- **Expansion of education** (through schemes like Sarva Shiksha Abhiyan) results in making rational thoughts and **family planning**. Consequently, people prefer to have less number of children and envisage providing them a better education facility.
- Spread of **awareness programs** like Kanyashree, Beti Bachao Beti Padhao, etc. has helped in reduction of child marriage. **Stringent legal provisions** for sex selection in terms of Pre-Conception and Pre-Natal Diagnostic Techniques (PC & PNDT) Act etc. have also helped in reduction of sex selection and girl child mortality.

BONUS KNOWLEDGE

POPULATION PYRAMID (AGE – SEX PYRAMID)

- It is a graphical representation of distribution of various age groups in a given population of a country or region. Since this distribution in graph takes the **shape of a pyramid**, it is called as population pyramid.
- Conventionally, males are represented in the left and females are in the right.
- On the ***x*-axis**, **population size** is shown. And **age group** is represented on the ***y*-axis.**
- There are **three types of population pyramid:**
  i. **Stationary** – If percentage of population is constant over time i.e. Birth rate is equal to death rate.
  ii. **Expansive** – If it is wider at younger age groups. It happens when birth rate is higher and life expectancy is lower.
  iii. **Constructive** – Pyramid is narrowed at the bottom. Here percentage of older population is relatively higher. This occurs with lower death rate, lower birth rate and longer life expectancy.

India's population pyramid is as follows:

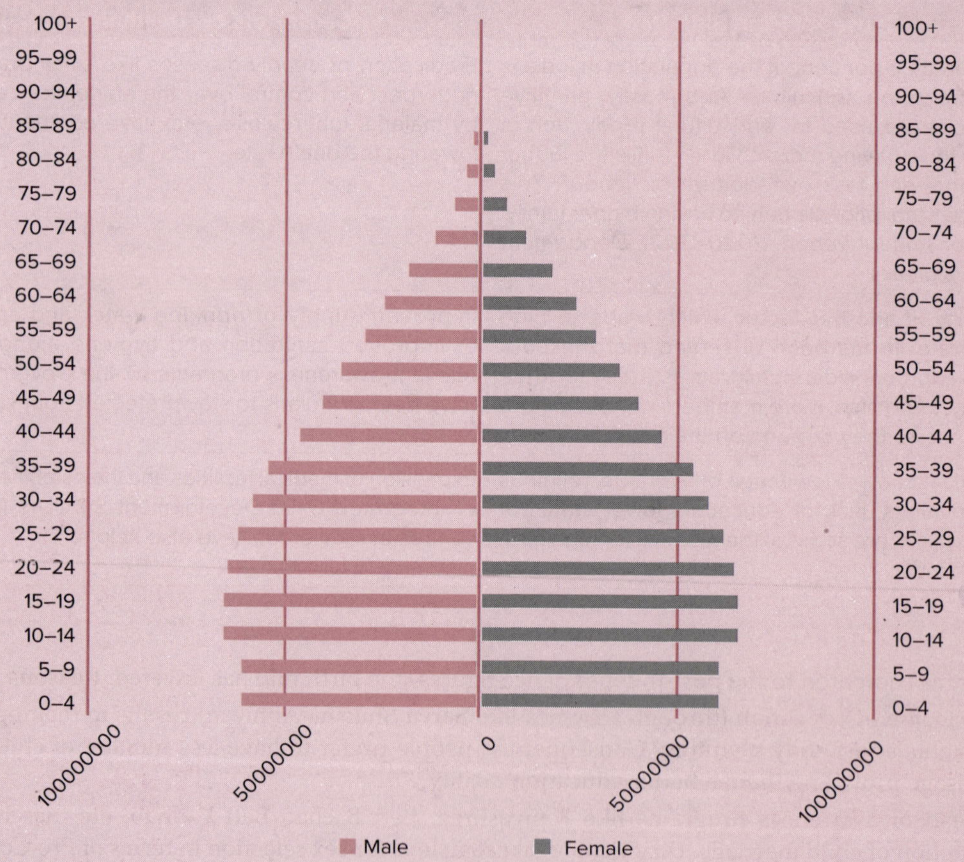

POPULATION *VERSUS* ECONOMIC DEVELOPMENT IN INDIA

Although India has a population of around 144 crore, but the **total dependency ratio is just 48.66** (much lower than world's dependency ratio of 54.55). This indicates the high potential of India for its economic growth as more than 50 per cent of its total population is capable of participating in the economic growth.

However, our country faces **major problems** regarding economic development. Some of them are discussed below:

i. *Population Density* – According to the data available with the United Nations (2021), population density of India is estimated as **468.7 persons per sq. km** (it was 382 persons per sq. km in 2011). Because of this rapid growth of population, **per capita cultivable land is decreasing**. Consequently, there is **tremendous pressure on agricultural productivity**. Such condition is unfavourable for economic growth.

ii. *Strain on Resources* – With growing population, resources available in the country are not sufficient to fulfil the growing demand of people. Thus, **capital accumulation has become quite difficult**.

iii. *Unemployment* – Unemployment is believed to be the **by-product of population growth**. Due to the unavailability of resources, a large section of population has **skill deficit**. Consequently, unemployment is increasing and this leads to other problems like poverty, crime, corruption, etc.

iv. *Environmental Damage* – Rapid growth of population and consequent demand for more resources with rampant unplanned development impact the environment severely.

MEASURES TO CHECK POPULATION EXPLOSION

Nevertheless, population of a country is an asset for its economy if the maximum section of it belongs to the age group of 15 to 64 years **(working age group)** – and also, if most of them are employed and free from poverty. Unfortunately, in India, a large section of population is either jobless or is employed in such a way that they are vulnerable to displacement.

Such scenario leads to other social problems like poverty, child labour, inadequate education, low access to health facilities and so on.

Thus, to address such situation, measures are broadly classified into three categories:

Economic Measures

i. *Expansion of Industries* – It has been observed that the employees in industrial sector prefer a small family size as compared to the persons indulged in agricultural sector. In industrial sector, employees have to face frequent transfers and have to maintain a living standard. Thus, they plan to restrict their family size. Hence, expansion of industrial sector can be helpful to restrict the population to some extent.

ii. **Opportunities of Employment** – For those people who could not fulfil their basic amenities, children are believed to be an asset for them and their support for old age. Once they get employed and get aware of the difficulties of getting a job, they restrict their family size and maintain proper standard of living with the endeavour to provide better education to their children.

iii. *Reduction of Income Inequality* – Equal distribution of resources can help provide basic amenities and thus it can change the attitude of people towards increasing the family size. Also, awareness towards quality education and proper living standards flourishes when they get stable source of income.

Social Measures

i. ***Expansion of Education*** – Educated people envisage to provide quality and higher education to their children. Therefore, they prefer small size and they get inclined towards better family planning.

ii. ***Improving Status of Women*** – Status of women in every society matters a lot in controlling population.

Family Planning Programme

Significance of family planning can be easily understood through the **example of China**. China's One Child Policy had reduced the birth rate to 12 per 1,000, though the policy has been abolished by China in 2015 due to having too many old people and too few young people.

According to United Nations Population Fund **(UNFPA) report 2012**, only 55 per cent of married Indian **women at the age of childbearing, used contraception,** whereas in Sri Lanka it was 68 per cent and in China it was 85 per cent.

Thus, family planning has a key role in regulating the rate of population growth. Following may be some **methods under family planning programme:**

i. **Public Information Programme** – This programme endeavours to raise consciousness among the people about the importance of family planning. Government uses media in the form of newspapers, television, radio to spread awareness, etc. For example – *Bula Di* drive in West Bengal.

ii. **Incentives** – The system of providing incentives to those who accept small family norms and also to those people who **opt for sterilisation**. Since, family planning is voluntary in India and people are less informed about the benefits of small family norms, available Government schemes are not getting sound success in this regard.

iii. **Family Planning Centre** – Family Planning Centre in India is an integral part of clinical centres established in rural areas like ICDS. These centres distribute contraceptives and incentives and spread awareness about the significance of family planning and small family size.

Population Policies undertaken by Government

According to economists, intervention of Government in family planning could be helpful in utilising the population for growth of the economy, and it can also reduce the burden of poverty and other co-related problems.

Pre-Independence Committees on Family Planning

Name	Year	Recommendations
Radha Kamal Committee	1940	Creating awareness about the cheap and safe methods of birth control, increasing the age of marriage, expansion of birth control clinics, discouraging polygamy, etc.
Bhore Committee	1943	Recommended that for controlling the growth rate of population, ***'deliberate limitation of family'*** approach is needed.

Since independence, Government of India and some State Governments took various initiatives and framed various policies related to population control. Some are discussed below:

Family Planning in the 1950s (Clinical approach)

In the 1950s, Government organisations were specifically concentrating in expansion of clinical services in both rural and urban areas. In this approach both aspects – population control and clinical facilities – were emphasised.

However, this clinical approach could not achieve desired results. In the Census of 1961, it has been observed that the growth rate of population was higher than expected.

Family Planning in the 1960s (Extension approach and experimentations)

In 1966, a separate department was established called the **Department of Family Planning** under the *Ministry of Health, Family Planning and Urban Development.*

Mass media was also used for the promotion of family planning and for controlled growth of population. During the late 1960s, this programme became target oriented and more funds were allocated. However, the results were unsatisfactory.

Family Planning in the 1970s (Camp approach)

In this decade, Government endeavoured to continue the family planning in an integrated way in addition to maternity health care, child health care, nutrition services, etc.

Apart from these steps, the **National Population Policy, 1976** was also implemented. Some of the key features of this policy were:

i. Financial incentives on birth control.

ii. The **minimum age of marriage** for both girls and boys had been increased to **18** and **21** years, respectively.

iii. Improvement in the literacy levels among females through both formal and informal methods of education.

iv. Popularisation of family welfare programmes and about the benefits of family planning through all means of media.

v. Expansion of quality education.

> **did you KNOW?** **During the period of Emergency**, the Central Government allowed few States to make rules for **compulsory sterilisation**; thus in some places, forced sterilisation programme was initiated. However, in 1977, the new Government ruled out such coercive policies of the previous Government.

Family Planning in the 1980s (Cafeteria approach)

Through the experiences of last three decades, policy makers were assured that only family planning is not sufficient to control the population growth. Rather it is a by-product of economic growth or improvement in economic condition.

Thus, the **Working Group on Population Policy** set up under the aegis of Planning Commission had recommended for long-term goals for reduction in reproductive rates.

It was envisaged to bring down the *crude birth rate* (number of live births per 1,000) to 29.1 per 1,000 by the end of this decade. Although the goal was too ambitious, however, by 1991, the crude birth rate was little higher than 29.9 per 1,000.

Family Planning in the 1990s (Target free approach)

By 1997, crude birth rate was brought down to 26 per 1,000 and additionally, the LPG policy had provided tremendous scope for economic development which contributed in qualitative improvements in the standard of living among people.

In the year 2000, Government came up with **National Population Policy, 2000**. Some of its features were:

i. **Reduction of maternal mortality rate** to less than 100 per 1 lakh crude births.
ii. Reduction of **infant mortality rate** to less than 30 per 1,000.
iii. Access to the vaccines of all preventable diseases and universal **immunisation** of children.
iv. Encouragement and promotion of **delayed marriages**.
v. Promotion of **small family norms** and its direct effects on total fertility rate.
vi. Inclusion of other **social sector programmes** related to family planning and welfare of the citizens.
vii. Establishment of **National Commission on Population** to provide overall guidance for population stabilisation (chaired by Prime Minister). Presently, the Commission functions under the ***Ministry of Health and Family Welfare***.
viii. Classification of objectives as short-term, medium-term and long-term goals. For example:
   (a) **Immediate objective was** to improve the **reproductive health and child care**.
   (b) **Medium-term goal** was to keep the **Total Fertility Rate (TFR) at 2.1 children per woman** (Replacement level).
   (c) **Long-term objective** was **population stabilisation by 2045**.

Evaluation of Government Policies

Unequivocally, Government had framed various policies and schemes for population control and family planning. However, family planning without expansion of quality education could not give desired results. Apart from this, some more probable limitations of the previous policies are discussed below:

i. *Aggrandisement of the use of contraceptives* – Since independence, endeavours of population control were mostly based on clinical approach, spread of family planning through different media and motivating people to opt for sterilisation. Comparatively, some States in southern India like Tamil Nadu, Kerala and Goa had reduced the birth rates from 35 to 15 per 1,000. The reason behind such achievement was their focus to increase literacy rates (specifically the female one).
ii. *Coercive methods for population control* – During emergency, forceful sterilisation had hurt the dignity of people. Such methods of population control could not provide any satisfactory result. In 1975, the crude birth rate was 37.4 and it just reduced to 36 by 1980. This indicates the limited achievement of such policies of Government to improve the living standard and reduce population growth.
iii. *Adoption of policies in compliance to Indian Society* – The policies (both clinical approach and extension approach) for population control in India were adopted from Western countries.

Basically, Indian people belong to different strata, various ideologies, beliefs and cultures. Being such a diverse country we could have implemented such policies which are compliant to our society and a national consensus must have been evolved before adopting such approaches.

EXAM ESSENTIAL

THE POPULATION REGULATION BILL, 2019

The Population Regulation Bill was proposed in July 2019 as a private member bill. This Bill calls for two children policy in India. Some of the features of this Bill are discussed below:

i. **Government employees** should provide an undertaking according to which he/she will not procreate more than two children.

ii. The Bill provides for **benefits to Central Government and central public sector enterprises (PSE) employees** on adopting two living children norm through sterilisation operation himself or of the spouse. These benefits include:

   (a) *One additional increment during entire service.*
   (b) *Subsidy towards purchase of plot/house from Housing Board/Development Authority.*
   (c) *Loan on nominal rates from banks/financial institutions for constructing/purchasing a house.*
   (d) *Rebate on income tax.*
   (e) *Subsidy on travel by road, rail or air.*
   (f) *Rebate on electricity charges, water charges, house tax, vehicle registration, telephone bill, etc.*
   (g) *Paternity leave of 12 weeks.*
   (h) *2 per cent increase in employer's contribution under pension scheme.*
   (i) *Free healthcare facility and insurance coverage.*
   (j) *Free healthcare facility to single child till he/she attains 25 years age.*
   (k) *Preference to single child for admission in educational institutions.*
   (l) *Free education up to graduation level and scholarship beyond graduation level for a single girl child.*

iii. Having more than two living children shall make them ineligible to avail above incentives. And they will have **reduction in subsidies** on loan and interest rates on saving instruments, higher than normal rates for availing loans from any financial institutions or even **reduced benefits of Public Distribution System (PDS)**.

iv. However, those Government employees who already have more than two children before the commencement of this Act **shall be exempted**.

v. Citizens with more than two children (living) **should not be qualified for being chosen as MP, MLA or member** of any local self-Government. However, this restriction shall not apply to citizens who have more than two children before the commencement of the Act.

Is legislation on population regulation really required in the current scenario?

Yes	However, critics argue that
According to a report, **by 2027**, India will probably become the **most populous country** in the world.	The Total Fertility Rate (TFR) of India is declining. Moreover, the TFR at replacement level was targeted as 2.1 and according to National Family Health Survey data, **current TFR is 2.0** (just above the targeted value). The TFR cannot be revived once it declines. (*As per latest NFHS 2019–21 survey*)
Proportion of marriageable age group is higher and hence population will continue to grow.	Critics argue that by restricting the number of children, India **may not have enough educated young population** to continue its technological revolution in future.

Yes	However, critics argue that
11 northern and eastern States/UTs of India contribute 42% of the population.	We **may also face a negative population growth** as at present some Western countries are facing this concern. Moreover, the tax rate will eventually increase as less young people will be there and they may receive lesser returns in their old age.
Literacy rate of India is still 74.04 per cent and it is already discussed that how literacy directly affects the population growth.	Some human rights activists also argue that such move of Government **may result in discrimination against woman** since their birth. Restriction on having more children can lead couples to opt for **sex selective abortions due to 'son meta preference'**.
Nearly 70 million people in India are living in poverty. And population is also one of the factors of increasing poverty.	We may also face problems similar to China's One Child Policy which resulted in **gender imbalance** and **high dependency ratio** in future.

BONUS KNOWLEDGE

Replacement Level Fertility: It is the **(Total Fertility Rate) TFR** at which a population exactly replaces itself from one generation to the next, without migration. Replacement level fertility rate is approximately 2.1 children per woman for most countries. As per the latest NFHS survey 2019–21, the TFR has been decreased to 2.0. In Sikkim it is 1.1, which is the lowest in the country. In Goa it is 1.3, and in West Bengal it is 1.6.

Total Fertility Rate (TFR) in an economy is the average number of live births a woman would have by the end of her child-bearing age.

MISSING WOMEN IN SEX COMPOSITION

EXAM ESSENTIAL

The term *missing women* in sex composition refers to shortfall of women population as compared to the desired women population in a country. Generally, it is measured through female–male ratio (FMR).

This phenomenon is prominent in Asian economies, regions of Middle-East and North African countries. The trend of FMR in India is shown in the table.

Year	FMR
1951	0.946
1961	0.941
1971	0.930
1981	0.934
1991	0.927
2001	0.933
2011	0.940

According to NFHS 5 (2019–21), current FMR is 1.020

It should be noted that some southern States in India are performing extremely well in overcoming the problem of low FMR. Rather Kerala's FMR is 1.084 as per 2011 census.

However, **BIMARU** *(Bihar, Madhya Pradesh, Rajasthan and Uttar Pradesh)* States along with some other State having higher economic growth such as Punjab and Haryana have lower sex ratio than the all-India sex ratio.

Causes of Low Female–Male Ratio

i. **Nutrition and health deprivations** against women and female child.

ii. **Inadequate access to quality education** for women which reduces their confidence in making decisions during sex selected births.

iii. Failure of administration in full-fledged implementation of the strict rules against **female foeticide** even after the promulgation of PC & PNDT Act, 2004.

iv. Around 58 per cent of the total population is based on **agriculture**. Thus, a male child in family is thought to be helpful in increasing the production.

v. Since the proportion of poor is higher in our country and they consider male child as an **asset for their old age**, there is lesser eagerness for accepting the girl child.

vi. Rules against **dowry system** are insignificant to abandon such traditions. This puts a burden on parents of female child, which prevents them from bringing up a girl child.

Child Sex Ratio (CSR)

- It is defined as the number of girls per 1,000 boys in the age group of **0–6 years**. In India there was a sharp decline in the child sex ratio between 2001 and 2011. In 2001, it was 927 and by 2011, it declined to 919. This is a **great cause of concern**.
- Due to this, it has been estimated that around 38.82 lakh women below 60 are missing worldwide. In that, around 8.56 lakh belong to India only.
- However, in maintaining the CSR, southern States of India have repeatedly performed well, specifically Karnataka and Kerala.

Measures to Overcome

- To improve FMR and CSR, Government has introduced various initiatives and launched a wide range of policies through the last seven decades.
- They include establishment of ICDS centres and also reservation of seats for women in legislative bodies.
- In many States, Government provides financial assistance to girl child once they complete their schooling. Moreover, various scholarship programmes are run by Government where only girls can avail such assistance, for example, Kanyashree scheme in West Bengal.
- Other GoI schemes for women include *Beti Bachao Beti Padhao*, One Stop Centre scheme, Swadhar Greh scheme, *Rashtriya Mahila Kosh*, etc.

DEMOGRAPHIC DIVIDEND

EXAM ESSENTIAL

Also known as demographic bonus or demographic window, it is the rise in the rate of economic growth due to a rising share of working age (15–64 years) population.

Benefits of Demographic Dividend

- Savings and investments across the country increase, which automatically generates capital resources. The higher the demographic dividend, larger the surplus available for investment for a country, which results in wealth accumulation.
- Lowering taxes may also be one of the benefits when demographic window of a country increases because the proportion of working age also increases.
- Government will be able to invest more in productive activities and reduce its expenditure in subsidies and social services.
- Expansion of education and investment in health services are the direct effects of increasing demographic bonus.

'Squandering' Demographic Dividend

The World Bank projected a robust economic growth for South Asia, including India, in its South Asia regional update, *Jobs for Resilience (2024)*, but it warned that the region is unable to utilise its demographic dividend. The momentum of job creation in that region fell short of the growth in the working-age population.

India's robust economic expansion retains the region's output growth, which is stronger than that of other emerging market economies. But the potential of demographic dividend is largely unspent. The employment growth of that region was beneath the average growth in its working-age population during the 2000–23 period.

The fragile employment trends in that region were concentrated primarily in non-agricultural sectors and economic climate, which had stifled the growth of businesses. Skill development, participation of women in the workforce, access to finance, openness to trade and improving education can address the issue. India and its neighbours must generate sufficient jobs to sustain young population.

Challenges related to Demographic Dividend

- The share of **population above 60 years** is continuously rising. It was 8.4 per cent in 2020 (*as per SRS Statistical report 2020*) as against 7.5 per cent in 2001.
- **Channelising the current labour force** is a challenging task as India's working-age population is projected to grow by approximately 9.7 million in 2021–31 and may further decline to 4.2 million by 2031–41.
- **Skill deficit** of Indians leads to increasing rate of unemployment and creating a worse situation where the growing workforce is unskilled and unemployable with increasing demands of the society. Thus, training the growing workforce with earning skills and making them employable is another challenge for India.
- **Ageing population** in India is going to be another concern in its economic growth. In 2011 census, it was estimated that 104 million people in India were over 60 years of age. By 2050, around

20 per cent of the population will be above 60 years of age. Therefore, in the coming two decades, a demographic burden is awaiting the Indian economy.

Dependency Ratio: Dependency ratio is defined as the ratio of dependent population to working population, i.e.

Dependency Ratio = Dependent Population (Population in the age group 0–14 and 60 and above) ÷ Working Population (15–59 years)

In 2021, as per World Bank report, India's dependency ratio stood around 48. It was 79.3 in 1970.

This decrease in dependency ratio is a good indicator.

Measures to Overcome above Challenges

The peak of the demographic dividend in India is fast approaching but the positive impact is still not visible. To overcome the **problems related to skill deficit, ageing population, unemployment etc., the** Government has adopted several measures. Some are discussed below:

i. Schemes like *Deen Dayal Upadhyaya Grameen Kaushalya Yojana, Pradhan Mantri Kaushal Vikas Yojana, National Apprenticeship Promotion Scheme, Scheme for Higher Education Youth in Apprenticeship and Skills (SHREYAS) etc.*, are some skill development programs launched by Government. They are directed towards rejuvenating the youth population in finding jobs and increasing their participation in economic growth.

ii. To generate employment in rural areas, the Government has an ongoing scheme called **MGNREGA**.

iii. More and more use of **PPP models** is also a step in this direction to aptly use demographic dividend.

iv. To address the problems related to an ageing population, Government may **increase the age of retirement** and expansion of **quality health services** to utilise such workforce leading to a positive impact on economic development.

v. **Expansion of education** and making higher education accessible to a large fraction of the population can generate a profitable diaspora and can reduce the concerns related to unemployment.

TACKLING SKILL DEFICIT THROUGH HUMAN CAPITAL

Human capital refers to increasing the knowledge, skill levels and capacities of the people of the country. It is termed as an **intangible asset** that plays a great role in the economic growth and development of a nation.

Hence, there is a need to transform the working age population into human capital in order to reap the benefits of demographic dividend in India.

General education improves knowledge of the people while skill training enhances their employability and equips them to tackle the requirements of labour market.

Persisting skill deficit among the working age is one of the important factors for **dropping rates of employability**. **Skill mismatch** is another reason.

BONUS KNOWLEDGE

- **United Nations Population Fund (UNFPA) –** The agency was set up in 1969 as the United Nations Fund for Population Activities. The aim of UNFPA is to safeguard sexual and reproductive rights for all, especially women and young people.
- The International Conference on Population and Development (**ICPD**) was organised in Cairo in 1994. It emphasised upon women's empowerment and autonomy as the basis for sustainable social progress.
- **World Population Day** is celebrated annually on **July 11** to focus on the significance of population issues.

SUMMARY

- **Three Stages of Demographic Transition** – High Birth and High Death Rate (stage I) – High Birth and Low Death Rate (stage II) – Low Birth and Low Death Rate (stage III) –India is in later phase of stage II.
- **Population Pyramid** – Graphical representation of distribution of various age groups in a given population of a country or region – three types: stationary (percentage of population is constant over time); expansive (birth rate is higher and life expectancy is lower); and constructive (percentage of older population is relatively higher).
- **Measures to check population explosion** – Economic measures, social measures, family planning programme, etc.
- **Causes of Low Female–Male Ratio** – Nutrition and health deprivations – inadequate access to quality education – female foeticide, etc.
- **Child Sex Ratio** – Number of girls per 1000 boys in the age group of 0–6 years.
- **Demographic Dividend** – Rise in economic growth due to rising share of working age (15–64 years) population.
- **Challenges to obtain desired Demographic Dividend** – Decline in labour force participation rate – increasing unemployment – skill deficit – ageing population, etc.
- **Measures to overcome these challenges** – Reduce skill deficiency – generate employment through job creation schemes like MGNREGA – Expansion of quality healthcare services and education.
- **Human capital** refers to increasing knowledge, skill levels and capacities of the people of a country. It is an **intangible asset** that plays a great role in the economic growth and development of a nation.

UPSC CSE PREVIOUS YEARS' PRELIMINARY EXAMINATION QUESTIONS

1. The total fertility rate in an economy is defined as: **[2024]**
   (a) the number of children born per 1000 People in the Population in a year.
   (b) the number of children born to couple in their lifetime in a given population.
   (c) the birth rate minus death rate.
   (d) the average number of live births a woman would have by the end of her child-bearing age.

2. **Human capital** formation as a concept is better explained in terms of a process which enables: **[2018]**
   1. Individuals of a country to accumulate more capital.
   2. Increasing the knowledge, skill levels and capacities of the people of the country.
   3. Accumulation of tangible wealth.
   4. Accumulation of intangible wealth.

Which of the statements given above is/are correct?

(a) 1 and 2 (b) 2 only
(c) 2 and 4 (d) 1, 3 and 4

3. To obtain full benefits of demographic dividend, what should India do? **[2013]**

(a) Promoting skill development
(b) Introducing more Social security schemes
(c) Reducing infant mortality rate
(d) Privatisation of higher education

☞ NO QUESTIONS ASKED
2023, 2022, 2021, 2020, 2019, 2017, 2016, 2015, 2014

ANSWER KEY

1. (d) 2. (c) 3. (a)

UPSC CSE PREVIOUS YEARS' MAIN EXAMINATION QUESTIONS

1. Comment on the challenges for inclusive growth which include **careless and useless manpower** in Indian context. Suggest measure to be taken for facing these challenges **[2016]**

2. 'While we flaunt India's **Demographic Dividend**, we ignore the **dropping rates of employability**.' What are we missing while doing so? What will the jobs that India desperately needs come from? Explain. **[2014]**

☞ NO QUESTIONS ASKED
2024, 2023, 2022, 2021, 2020, 2019, 2018, 2017, 2015, 2013

CHAPTER

31

SKILL DEVELOPMENT

CHAPTER OUTLINE

- Skill Development – Indian Perspective
- Skill Development and Inclusive Growth
- Ministry of Skill Development and Entrepreneurship (MSDE)
- National Skill Development Corporation (NSDC)
- National Skill Development Agency
- National Skill Development Fund
- Timeline of Skill Development Initiatives in India
- Policy Initiatives
- National Policy for Skill Development and Entrepreneurship 2015
- National Skill Development Mission
- List of Skill Development Schemes
- Digital Skilling – Training for Future Skills
- Skill Development Integrated with School Education
- Challenges to Skill Development in India
- International Collaboration for Skill Development

SKILL DEVELOPMENT – INDIAN PERSPECTIVE

India has a unique demographic advantage with more than 50 per cent of the population in the working age group. But, this advantage can be harnessed only when human capital is improved.

Human capital refers to increasing the knowledge, skill levels and capacity of the people of the country. It is an intangible asset that plays a great role in the economic growth and development of a nation. Hence, there is a need to transform the working population into human capital to harness the perceived benefits of **demographic dividend** in India.

- According to **Human Development Report (HDR) 2020**, India's skilled labour force is 21.2 per cent. The size of India's formally skilled workforce was only 2 per cent in 2014 (*as per the Labour Bureau Report 2014*).
- According to the 2015 Report on National Policy on Skill Development and Entrepreneurship, only 4.7 per cent of India's total workforce had received formal skill training, compared to 52 per cent in the United States, 80 per cent in Japan, and 96 per cent in South Korea.
- A National Skill Development Corporation (NSDC) skill gap study conducted between 2010 and 2014 revealed an additional net incremental requirement of 10.97 crores of skilled manpower in 24 key sectors by 2022.

Last Minute SNIPPETS

According to Periodic Labour Force Survey **(PLFS) 2023–24**, around 75 per cent of Indians between 15–59 age group, did not receive vocational and technical training. The remaining had received training in a variety of formal and informal settings.

Thus, there is a huge gap in the Indian education system between academic knowledge and skills acquired by the youth through traditional education. Skill development and employment are the best means to bridge this gap and mobilise the youth energy to bolster the socio-economic growth of the country.

SKILL DEVELOPMENT AND INCLUSIVE GROWTH

- Skilled human resource at all levels is essential for inclusive growth. Skill development for inclusive growth is, therefore, an imperative to ensure that young people from different backgrounds participate in the development story.
- Skill development cannot be perceived in isolation. It should be an integral process of connecting the skill training with education and employment at the same time.
- The government agencies and system cannot accomplish this task alone. Private sector, NGOs, and educational institutions with experience in skill training, need to be involved in the process of skilling.
- All sections need to be given equal importance. Along with the youth, other marginalised sections of society, viz. women, tribals, etc. need customised training programmes to suit their diverse and specific needs.

LINKAGES BETWEEN EDUCATION, SKILL AND EMPLOYMENT

- Education is the foundation for skill development and employment generation. It fosters personal development, nurtures creativity of individuals and provides the ability to acquire and apply knowledge.
- Vocational education can bridge the skill gap in workforce. It provides the practical training the industry requires, and links education with job readiness. The National Education Policy (NEP) 2020 places strong emphasis on vocational education and its integration with general education, aiming to make it a mainstream part of the education system. It will help students in achieving different skills to meet the requirements of the industries and to upgrade the quality of education.
- Investment in skills and education is crucial for competitive workforce in a rapidly evolving global economy. The Union Cabinet has approved the continuation and restructuring of the Central Sector Scheme '**Skill India Programme** (SIP)' till 2026. The overlay outlay is about ₹8,800 crore from the period 2022–23 to 2025–26.

> **did you KNOW?** The United Nations General Assembly declared **15 July** as the World Youth Skills Day in **2014**.

MINISTRY OF SKILL DEVELOPMENT AND ENTREPRENEURSHIP (MSDE)

- The Ministry of Skill Development and Entrepreneurship was formed as the nodal Ministry of Government of India in 2014, to coordinate all skill development efforts across the country.
- The Ministry is responsible for the coordination of all skill development efforts across the country, removal of disconnect between demand and supply of skilled manpower, building the vocational

and technical training framework, skill upgradation, building of new skills and innovative thinking not only for existing jobs but also jobs that are to be created.

- The Ministry aims to skill on a large scale with speed and high standards in order to achieve its vision of a **'Skilled India'**.
- It is aided in these initiatives by its **functional arms** – Directorate General of Training (**DGT**), National Council for Vocational Education and Training (**NCVET**), National Skill Development Corporation (**NSDC**), National Skill Development Fund (**NSDF**) and 37 Sector Skill Councils (**SSCs**) as well as 33 National Skill Training Institutes (**NSTIs/NSTI(w)**), about 15,000 Industrial Training Institutes (**ITIs**) under DGT and 187 training partners registered with NSDC.
- **Vision Statement 2025** of MSDE is – *'Unlock human capital to trigger a productivity dividend and bring aspirational employment and entrepreneurship pathways to all'*.

NATIONAL SKILL DEVELOPMENT CORPORATION (NSDC)

- National Skill Development Corporation (NSDC) was established as a not-for-profit public limited company in **2009** under **Public Private Partnership (PPP) model**. The Government of India through MSDE holds 49 per cent of the share capital of NSDC, while the private sector has the balance 51 per cent of the share capital.
- NSDC aims to promote skill development by supporting creation of vocational institutions and provides funding to build scalable and profitable vocational training initiatives. Its mandate is also to enable support system which focuses on quality assurance, information systems and train the trainer academies either directly or through partnerships.
- NSDC acts as a catalyst in skill development by providing funding to enterprises, companies and organisations that provide skill training.

NATIONAL SKILL DEVELOPMENT AGENCY (NSDA)

- National Skill Development Agency (**NSDA**) was set up as an **autonomous body** in 2013 under MSDE for resolving the inter-ministerial and inter-departmental issues and eliminating duplicates of efforts of the Centre.
- The **National Skills Qualifications Framework (NSQF)** is anchored in NSDA and is implemented through the National Skill Qualification Committee (NSQC). A permanent secretariat for NSQC is set up in NSDA.
- In 2019, NSDA was subsumed in the **National Council for Vocational Education and Training (NCVET)**. NCVET now acts as an overarching skills regulator.

NATIONAL SKILL DEVELOPMENT FUND

- The Government of India set up the National Skill Development Fund in **2009** to raise fund for skill development in both the Government and Non-Governmental sectors.
- A public Trust formed by the Government of India is the **custodian of the fund**.

TIMELINE OF SKILL DEVELOPMENT INITIATIVES IN INDIA

1969	1	First Industrial Training Institute
2008	2	National Skill Development Corporation Established
2009	3	First National Policy on Skill Development
2013	4	National Skills Qualification Framework and NSDA Established
2014	5	Ministry of Skill Development and Entrepreneurship Established
2015	6	National Policy on Skill Development and Entrepreneurship
2015	7	National Skill Development Mission

POLICY INITIATIVES

National Policy for Skill Development and Entrepreneurship, 2015

- Recognising the need for skill development in India, the first National Policy on Skill Development was formulated by the Ministry of Labour and Employment in **2009**.
- Considering the paradigm shift in skilling and entrepreneurship ecosystem in the country and harnessing the experience gained through implementation of various skill development programmes, the policy was revised and the second **National Policy for Skill Development and Entrepreneurship**, 2015, was notified on 15 July 2015.
- The primary objective of this policy is to meet the challenge of skilling at scale with **speed, standard (quality)** and **sustainability**.
- It aims to provide an umbrella framework for all skilling activities being carried out within the country, to align them to common standards and link skilling with demand centres.
- The policy also seeks to coordinate and strengthen factors essential for the growth of entrepreneurship across the country.

- To achieve the declared vision, the **National Policy for Skill Development and Entrepreneurship, 2015** has **4 thrust areas**:
    1. Addressing key obstacles to skilling; including low aspirational value, lack of integration with formal education, lack of focus on outcomes, low quality of training infrastructure and trainers, etc.
    2. To align supply and demand for skills by bridging existing skill gaps, promoting industry engagement, operationalising a quality assurance framework, leveraging technology and promoting greater opportunities for apprenticeship training.
    3. Equity is a focus of the policy, which targets skilling opportunities for socially/geographically marginalised and disadvantaged groups.
    4. Skill development and entrepreneurship programmes for women.
- In the entrepreneurship domain, the policy seeks to connect entrepreneurs to mentors, incubators and credit markets, foster innovation and entrepreneurial culture, improve ease of doing business and promote a focus on social entrepreneurship.

National Skill Development Mission

- The National Skill Development Mission was announced in the Union Budget 2015–16 and was officially launched in 2015 on the occasion of **World Youth Skills Day**.
- The mission has been developed to create convergence across sectors and States and expedite the skill training activities.
- The mission has a three-tiered, high-powered decision-making structure:
- Governing Council of National Skill Development Mission is chaired by the Prime Minister and provides overall guidance and policy direction.
- The Steering Committee, chaired by Minister in Charge of Skill Development, reviews the mission's activities in line with the directions set by the Governing Council.
- The Mission Directorate, with Secretary, Skill Development as Mission Director, is in Charge to ensure implementation, coordination and convergence of skilling activities across Central Ministries/Departments and State Governments.
- Following institutions function under the overall guidance of the mission:
    - **National Skill Development Agency (NSDA)**,
    - **National Skill Development Corporation (NSDC)**, and
    - **Directorate General of Training (DGT):** The DGT advises on training policies, trains instructors, provides technical support, runs women-centric training institutes apart from maintaining the skill training structures of Advanced Training Institutes (ATIs), Regional Vocational Training Institutes (RVTIs) and other such institutes.

LIST OF SKILL DEVELOPMENT SCHEMES

EXAM ESSENTIAL

Skill development related schemes can be classified into two categories. One set of schemes is implemented by MSDE and the other is implemented by various other ministries at different points of time.

Schemes Implemented by MSDE

Skill India Programme

The Skill India Programme was launched by the government in **2015** to provide a job-ready and skilled workforce by equipping it with employable skills. The objective of the mission was to skill people and enhance their employability by training them in skill sets of their choice.

The vision of Skill India Mission is to create an ecosystem conducive to an empowered economy with a job ready skilled workforce:

i. By skilling on a large scale with speed and quality,

ii. By complying with industry recognised standards and

iii. To promote a culture of innovation-based entrepreneurship.

This will generate wealth and employment along with ensuring sustainable livelihoods for all citizens in the country.

Skill India offers courses across 40 sectors in the country which are aligned to the standards recognised by both the industry and the government under the **National Skill Qualification Framework**.

Pradhan Mantri Kaushal Vikas Yojana 4.0 (PMKVY 4.0), the Pradhan Mantri National Apprenticeship Promotion Scheme (PM-NAPS), and the Jan Shikshan Sansthan (JSS) Scheme are the three key components under the composite Central Sector Scheme of 'Skill India Programme'.

These initiatives aim to provide structured skill development, on-the-job training, and community-based learning, ensuring that both urban and rural populations, including marginalised communities, have access to high-quality vocational education.

Last Minute SNIPPETS

The GOI has approved the continuation and restructuring of 'Skill India Programme (SIP)' **till 2026** with an overlay outlay of ₹8,800 crore from the period 2022–23 to 2025–26.

Pradhan Mantri Kaushal Vikas Yojana 4.0 (PMKVY 4.0)

- Launched initially in 2015, PMKVY is the flagship skill development programme of MSDE.
- It has the overall objective to help Indian youth take up industry-relevant free skill training to get better livelihoods.
- PMKVY has three training components :
  A. **Short Term Training** (STT)
  B. **Recognition of Prior Learning** (RPL).
  C. **Special Projects (SP)**

- Pradhan Mantri Kaushal Kendras (PMKKs) set up at the district level are envisaged as state-of-the-art, visible and aspirational model training centres.
- Between 2015 and 2022, three versions of the scheme have been implemented with varied approach and strategy. The next phase of PMKVY, i.e., **PMKVY 4.0** under the umbrella scheme of the '**Skill India Programme**' is being implemented between **FY 2022 and 2026.**

A. Short-Term Training (STT)

- NSQF aligned courses, ranging between **300 and 600 hours**, are provided under STT. Courses of higher duration based on industry/sectoral demand are also offered. Training is delivered through accredited and affiliated training centres. On-Job Training (OJT) is an inherent component under STT as mandated by NCVET, and the duration of OJT depends on the job role.
- The target group under STT includes candidates **(15–45 years age)** looking for fresh skilling, re-skill/upskill, out-of-education candidates, school/college dropouts or unemployed youth of Indian nationality.
- Any organisation, legally established as a society, trust, proprietorship, Company/Limited Liability Partnership (LLP) / Government Institute/ Organisation, etc., can be a training provider under the STT scheme. Short-Term Training (STT) is to be permitted by Skill Hubs (Colleges, Schools, and Government Institutions), PMKKs and selected Training Centres (TCs), including ITIs.

B. Recognition of Prior Learning (RPL)

In 2015, the Skill India Mission was launched and under its flagship scheme, PMKVY, **Recognition of Prior Learning (RPL)** programme was launched with a focus on re-skilling and up-skilling in prominent trades. Target group includes **candidates (18–59 years age) with prior learning experience** or skills and willing to get assessed and certified. Interested candidates will have to undergo coursework for certification at a higher level based on assessment. The scheme is about recognition of existing skills after a **12 to 80 hours orientation cum bridge course** by provision of PMKVY certificate to candidates.

There are three major objectives of RPL:

- To align the competencies of the unorganised workforce of the country with the standardised National Skill Qualification Framework (NSQF).
- To enhance the opportunities for employment and provide alternative means for higher education.
- To provide opportunities for reducing inequalities.

The data of certified beneficiaries is made available to industries through **ASEEM (Aatmanirbhar Skilled Employee Employer Mapping)** portal and the application. The platform provides skilled workforce to industries as per market demand.

Benefits of RPL

- With RPL certification, people have noted an increase in income levels. Under PMKVY, more than 63 per cent beneficiaries have obtained a relatively higher position at their workplace.
- The International Labour Organisation (ILO) has also accepted that employment opportunities have increased with RPL.

C. Special Projects (SP)

Special project is a component of PMKVY wherein **short/fresh term trainings** are provided to candidates in NSQC approved job roles. Special projects are different from short-term training component of PMKVY by virtue of it being a project/need based with more flexibility in terms of compliances which are hard to be met for successful training of target beneficiaries in remote areas.

BONUS KNOWLEDGE

PRADHAN MANTRI KAUSHAL KENDRA (PMKK)

To further the **Skill India Mission**, MSDE has initiated the establishment of state-of-the-art, visible and aspirational **model training centres in every district of India**. These model training centres are referred to as Pradhan Mantri Kaushal Kendra (PMKK).

Under this project, the **private training partners, selected through RFP**, can avail a **secured loan of up to ₹70 lakhs** per PMKK at a subsidised interest rate to procure and set up labs, training-relevant machinery, training aids, etc.

PMKK centres are to be given a dedicated training mandate for three years under PMKVY Scheme, till the time the scheme exists.

PM National Apprenticeship Promotion Scheme (PM-NAPS)

- This scheme is for promoting **apprenticeship training** and increasing the engagement of apprentices **by providing financial support to industrial establishments** undertaking apprenticeship programme under The Apprentices Act, 1961.
- To support both apprentices and establishments in India, **25 per cent of the stipend, up to ₹1,500 per month per apprentice**, is provided through Direct Benefit Transfer (DBT) during the training period, by the Central Government. The scheme is designed for individuals aged **14 to 35 years**, ensuring inclusive access to skill development opportunities across various demographics.
- PM-NAPS encourages apprenticeship opportunities in prevailing manufacturing, including emerging fields such as AI, robotics, blockchain, green energy, and Industry 4.0 technologies.

Jan Shikshan Sansthan (JSS)

- This scheme, presently under MSDE, is implemented **through the NGOs** with **100 per cent** grants from the Government of India.
- The objective is to impart skill training to **non-literates, neo-literates, persons with rudimentary level of education, and school dropouts up to 12th class** in the age group of **15–45 years** in rural areas and urban slums.
- The priority groups are women, SCs, STs, OBC and minorities in the rural areas and urban low-income areas.
- The JSS, formerly known as **Shramik Vidyapeeth**, has been functioning in the country since **1967.**
- The annual coverage of the beneficiaries under JSS is around 4 lakh, out of which **85 per cent are women.**

EXAM ESSENTIAL

NATIONAL SKILLS QUALIFICATIONS FRAMEWORK (NSQF)

It is a **competency-based framework** that organises all qualifications according to a series of levels of knowledge, skills and aptitude. These levels, graded from 1 to 10, are defined in terms of learning outcomes which the learner must possess. The learner can acquire the certification for competency needed at any level through **formal, non-formal or informal learning**.

NSQF in India was notified on 27 December 2013. NSQF is under the Ministry of Skill Development & Entrepreneurship (MSDE). It is mandatory for all training/educational programmes/courses to be NSQF-compliant.

Industrial Training Institutes (ITIs)/Craftsmen Training Scheme (CTS)

- The Craftsmen Training Scheme (CTS) was introduced by the Government in **1950** to ensure a steady flow of skilled workers in different trades for the domestic industry, by providing vocational training through **Government and Private Industrial Training Institutes (ITIs)**.
- Presently, 15034+ Industrial Training Institutes (ITIs) are operational across the country.
- It provides long-term training on various Engineering/Non-Engineering/Divyang courses of duration ranging from **6 months to 2 years**.
- The Ministry of Skill Development and Entrepreneurship **(MSDE)** is implementing the Craftsmen Training Scheme (CTS). However, the ITIs are under the administrative and financial control of the State Governments under the scheme.

Craft Instructor Training Scheme

- To provide comprehensive training in skills and training methodology to the instructor trainees to make them conversant with the methodology of teaching and techniques of transferring hands-on skills, to further train skilled manpower for the industry.
- Under this scheme, the **eligible candidates are those who possess NTC/ NAC/Diploma/Degree qualifications**.

Skill Acquisition and Knowledge Awareness for Livelihood Promotion (SANKALP)

- It is a programme of the MSDE with loan assistance from the World Bank.
- It aims to improve short-term skill training qualitatively and quantitatively through strengthening institutions, bring in better market connectivity and inclusion of marginalised sections of the society.
- It also aims to decentralise skilling initiatives and align skill development programmes with local demand and aspirations of the youth.
- The scheme was launched in **2018**.
- Under the National Component and State Components of SANKALP, 64 and 700 projects, respectively, have been taken up in the area of Skill and Entrepreneurship development and strengthening of monitoring.

AVSAR Project: It certifies women from Self-Help Groups (SHGs) and transgenders in vocational courses under the SANKALP programme.

> did you KNOW?
>
> **INDIAN INSTITUTE OF SKILLS (IIS)**
>
> The GoI, in **2018**, approved the setting up of **three** Indian Institute of Skills at Mumbai, Ahmedabad and Kanpur **under PPP Mode**. IIS are being set up as State-of-the-art skill institutions considering the best practices from internationally renowned Skill Institutions. Among three, the Mumbai and Ahmedabad Institutes have been established by The Tata Education and Development Trust as a PPP partner.

Some Other Initiatives

i. **Skill Management and Accreditation of Training Centres (SMART)** is a single window IT initiative by MSDE, to facilitate the accreditation, affiliation and continuous monitoring of the **Training Centres** (TCs) for providing training for NSQF-aligned job roles in the skill ecosystem.

It has now been migrated to the unified portal known as **Skill India Portal.** In Skill India Portal, any entity can create a training centre and apply for its affiliation and accreditation after registering itself as a '**Training Provider**'.

ii. **Skills Strengthening for Industrial Value Enhancement (STRIVE) by MSDE,** is a World Bank-assisted Government of India project with the objective of improving the relevance and efficiency of skills training provided through **Industrial Training Institutes (ITIs)** and apprenticeships.

The main objective is to achieve improved performance of ITI, improved teaching and learning and improved and broadened apprenticeship training.

iii. **The Skill Loan Scheme by MSDE,** is designed to provide institutional credit to individuals for skill development courses aligned to National Occupations Standards and leading to a certificate/diploma/degree by training institutes as per NSQF.

iv. **Nai Roshni** – a **Leadership Development Programme** for Minority Women by the **Ministry of Minority Affairs,** is a Central Sector Scheme for training women belonging to minority communities in the age group of **18 to 65 years**. It includes various 5-6 days training modules like Leadership of women, Educational Programmes, Health and Hygiene, Financial Literacy, Life Skills, Legal Rights of Women, Digital Literacy, etc. It has now been merged as a component of **Pradhan Mantri Virasat Ka Samvardhan** (**PM VIKAS**) scheme w.e.f. FY 2022–23, aiming to improve livelihoods of minorities, particularly artisan communities, through skill development, education and leadership training, to support their entrepreneurship interventions. **No training centres are set up by the Ministry** under this scheme. The selected Programme Implementing Agencies (PIAs) are required to implement the project directly through their organisational set-up in the locality/ village/ area in which training is conducted.

v. **Deen Dayal Upadhyaya – Grameen Kaushalya Yojana (DDU-GKY)**

- DDU-GKY was launched in 2014. The scheme aims to **transform rural poor youth into an economically independent and globally relevant workforce** by providing demand led skill training at no cost to the rural poor, with the youth in the age group of **15–35 years** in focus.
- DDU-GKY is a part of the **National Rural Livelihood Mission (NRLM),** tasked with the dual objectives of adding diversity to the incomes of rural poor families and cater to the career aspirations of rural youth.

vi. **Rural Self Employment and Training Institutes (RSETIs)**

➤ **The scheme was launched in 2009 by Ministry of Rural Development** to impart residential free training and post training follow up with credit linkage to promote entrepreneurship among the rural youth. RSETIs are **Bank** lead institutions.

EXAM ESSENTIAL

PM VISHWAKARMA

- The **Ministry of Micro, Small & Medium Enterprises (MSME)** launched the Central Sector Scheme 'PM Vishwakarma' in 2023, **to support traditional artisans and craftspeople** of rural and urban areas. PM Vishwakarma Yojana is **fully funded by the Central Government**
- Key features of the scheme:
  - **Recognition:** Beneficiaries receive PM Vishwakarma Certificate & ID Card, enabling access to all scheme benefits.
  - **Skill Upgradation:**

    Basic Training (40 hours over 5–7 days, ₹500/day stipend): Covers skill enhancement, modern tool usage, digital transactions, and marketing.

Advanced Training (15 days, ₹500/day stipend): Focuses on entrepreneurship, modern technology, and business expansion.

- **Toolkit Incentive:** Up to ₹15,000 provided via e-RUPI/e-vouchers for modern tool procurement, improving productivity and product quality.
- **Credit Support:** Collateral-free loans are provided @ ₹1 lakh (1st tranche) and @ ₹2 lakh (2nd tranche) in the form of 'Enterprise Development Loans' with interest subvention to promote business growth.
- **Digital Empowerment:** Beneficiaries to receive ₹1 per digital transaction, up to 100 transactions per month, credited directly to their accounts for each digital payout or receipt.

➤ The applicant **must be above 18 years of age** and must be an artisan or craftsperson working with hands and tools in one of the **18 family-based traditional trades** *(such as Carpenter, Blacksmith, Locksmith, Goldsmith, Potter, Sculptor, Stone breaker, Cobbler, Mason, Basket Weaver, Doll & Toy Maker, Barber, etc.)* in the unorganised sector on a self-employment basis.

DIGITAL SKILLING – TRAINING FOR FUTURE SKILLS

➤ In an effort to assess the need for digital skills training in India, a report titled *'Building Digital Skills for the Changing Workforce'* has been prepared by **AlphaBeta and commissioned by Amazon Web Services (AWS)**. According to the report, about **27.3 million workers** representing 7 per cent of India's workforce will need digital skills training in the coming years.

➤ Digital skills are broadly defined as the skills needed to '**use digital devices, communication applications, and networks to access and manage information**,' from basic online searching and emailing to specialist programming and development.

➤ Digital skill is not equal to education in the classic **STEM** (Science, technology, engineering and mathematics) disciplines.

➤ **Skill India Digital (SID):** SID is an innovative digital platform associated with Skills and Jobs, promoting robust framework of India Stack Global and securing top-notch security and scalability. The platform provides discovery and proposals through advanced AI/ML technology to single out suitable skill sets and digital job exchange.

SKILL DEVELOPMENT INTEGRATED WITH SCHOOL EDUCATION

➤ The **National Education Policy (NEP) 2020** envisages curriculum integration of essential subjects and skills in all schools and higher education institutions in a phased manner to provide necessary vocational skills for a variety of occupations along with awareness about the benefits of vocational education.

➤ The Department of School Education and Literacy (under Ministry of Education) is implementing the scheme of vocationalisation of school education under the umbrella of '**Samagra Shiksha**' – an integrated scheme for school education, a centrally sponsored scheme. The scheme aims at integrating vocational education with general academic education in all schools, enhancing employability and entrepreneurial abilities of the students, providing exposure to work environment; and generating awareness among students about various career options so as to enable them to make choice in accordance with their aptitude, competence and aspirations.

- **Skill Hubs** are nodal skill centres identified to provide skill development and vocational training opportunities to target population segments from class 6th to 8th (introduction to world-of-work through orientation, industry visits, bag-less days), 9th to 12th (aimed at exposing students to skill development avenues), school dropouts and out-of-education (aimed for academic credit, mainstreaming back to education and or apprenticeship and employment linkages).

CHALLENGES TO SKILL DEVELOPMENT IN INDIA

- Insufficient training capacity – the training not being sufficient to ensure a job after completion of training and causing low employability rate.
- Mismatch in skill demand and training available in different sectors and regions.
- Underdeveloped infrastructure of training centres.
- Lack of entrepreneurship skills among trained people, which leads to less than expected job creation after completion of training.
- Low industry interface of the training institutes impacts the placement of trainees.
- Low student mobilisation and enrolment in skill institutes like ITIs and polytechnics compared to their enrolment capacity. This is due to low awareness level among youths about the skill development programmes.
- Lower public perception about vocational training compared to formal education in India.

BONUS KNOWLEDGE

INTERNATIONAL COLLABORATION FOR SKILL DEVELOPMENT

- With an aim to make India a **Skill Capital of the World** and improve mobility of skilled manpower, the National Skill Development Corporation (NSDC) International has been set up, which aims to create a network of institutions across India. This network of institutions will be called **Skill India International (SII) Network**. It shall be created through the empanelment of state-of-the-art government and private institutions.
- MSDE has also signed MoUs with 11 countries, viz. Australia, Belarus, China, Denmark, France, Germany, Japan, Qatar, Switzerland, UAE, and the United Kingdom in the field of skill development and vocational education training.
- NSDC has signed 18 B2B MoUs with countries like Australia, Canada, Germany, Japan, Malaysia, Kingdom of Saudi Arabia, UAE, etc.
- NSDC and the International Labour Organisation (ILO) have announced strategic partnership 'to advance skill development and lifelong learning in India and globally'. This collaboration intends to equip individuals across the world with essential competencies and qualifications and enhance employability and sustainable economic growth.

SUMMARY

- **Human Capital** – An intangible asset involving knowledge, skill levels and capacity of the people of a country.
- **Ministry of Skill Development and Entrepreneurship** – Was formed as the nodal Ministry of Government of India in 2014, to coordinate all skill development efforts across the country.

- **Vision Statement 2025 of MSDE** – 'Unlock human capital to trigger a productivity dividend and bring aspirational employment and entrepreneurship pathways to all'.
- **National Skill Development Corporation (NSDC)** – Established as a not-for-profit public limited company in 2009 under Public Private Partnership (PPP) model. Government holds 49 per cent share and Private Sector holds 51 per cent share.
- **National Skill Development Agency (NSDA)** – Set up as an autonomous body in 2013 for resolving the inter-ministerial and inter-departmental issues and eliminating duplicates of efforts of the Centre. In 2019, NSDA was subsumed in the **National Council for Vocational Education and Training (NCVET)**.
- The first National Policy on Skill Development was launched by the Ministry of Labour and Employment in 2009. The policy was revised as **National Policy for Skill Development and Entrepreneurship, 2015**.
- **National Skill Development Mission** – Launched on 15 July 2015, on the occasion of World Youth Skills Day.

UPSC CSE PREVIOUS YEARS' PRELIMINARY EXAMINATION QUESTIONS

1. With reference to Pradhan Mantri Kaushal Vikas Yojana, consider the following statements: **[2018]**

1. It is the flagship scheme of the Ministry of Labour and Employment.
2. It, among other things, will also impart training in soft skills, entrepreneurship, and financial and digital literacy.
3. It aims to align the competencies of the unregulated workforce of the country to the National Skill Qualification Framework.

Which of the statement(s) given above is/are correct?

(a) 1 and 3 only (b) 2 only
(c) 2 and 3 only (d) 1, 2 and 3

2. With reference to 'National Skills Qualification Framework (NSQF)', which of the statement(s) given below is/are correct? **[2017]**

1. Under NSQF, a learner can acquire the certification for competency only through formal learning.
2. An outcome expected from the implementation of NSQF is the mobility between vocational and general education.

Select the correct answer using the code given below:

(a) 1 only (b) 2 only
(c) Both 1 and 2 (d) Neither 1 nor 2

3. 'Recognition of Prior Learning Scheme' is sometimes mentioned in the news with reference to **[2017]**

(a) Certifying the skills acquired by construction workers through traditional channels.
(b) Enrolling the persons in universities for distance learning programmes.
(c) Reserving some skilled jobs to rural and urban poor in some public sector undertakings.
(d) Certifying the skills acquired by trainees under the National Skill Development Programme.

☞ NO QUESTIONS ASKED
2024, 2023, 2022, 2021, 2020, 2019, 2016, 2015, 2014, 2013

ANSWER KEY

1. (c) 2. (b) 3. (d)

UPSC CSE PREVIOUS YEARS' MAIN EXAMINATION QUESTIONS

1. Skill development programmes have succeeded in increasing human resources supply to various sectors. In the context of the statement analyse the linkages between education, skill and employment. **[2023]**
2. 'Demographic Dividend in India will remain only theoretical unless our manpower becomes more educated, aware, skilled and creative.' What measures have been taken by the government to enhance the capacity of our population to be more productive and employable? **[2016]**

☞ NO QUESTIONS ASKED
2024, 2022, 2021, 2020, 2019, 2018, 2017, 2015, 2014, 2013

CHAPTER

32

INDIA'S GIG ECONOMY

CHAPTER OUTLINE

- Emergence of Gig Economy in India
- Gig vs Platform Economy
- Social implications of the gig economy as a new economic paradigm
- Gig economy from the business perspective
- Gig economy from workers' perspective
- Potential of India's Gig Economy
- Size of Gig Economy in India
- Different Collar Jobs
- Challenges associated with the Gig Sector
- Gig economy as empowerment of women in India
- Labour Code for the Gig Economy
- How could the conditions of gig workers be improved

Gig economy is a system in which people are involved in temporary and flexible work through online platforms. They work on project-by-project basis rather than being regular employees of a company. This basically means that they perform short-term 'gigs' for various clients through digital marketplaces. Examples include freelance designers who offer design services through online platforms, food delivery riders on apps like Swiggy, Zomato, rideshare drivers (Uber, Ola, Rapido), home service providers (Urban Company), and content creators.

According to the Code on Social Security, 2020 (India), ***"A gig worker is a person who performs work or participates in work arrangements and earns from such activities, outside of the traditional employer-employee relationship."***

The gig economy can be traced back in the earliest stages of human history. Prior to the Industrial Revolution, the majority of work was labour-intensive, where farmers, craftsmen and artisans used to work on individual projects. In these early economies, where people exchanged labour and skills for goods and services, the idea of gig labour was essential.

EMERGENCE OF GIG ECONOMY IN INDIA

India's startup ecosystem has been expanding quickly.

As recruiting full-time employees for startups results in significant fixed cost, contractual freelancers are employed for non-core tasks.

To strengthen their tech platforms, startups are also considering hiring freelancers with skilled technology (per project basis) in fields including engineering, product, data science, and machine learning.

After the pandemic, MNCs are implementing flexible recruiting practices, particularly for specialised projects, to lower operating costs. The gig culture in India is greatly influenced by this tendency.

Key Area	Details
1. Expanding Startup Ecosystem	• Startups growing rapidly • Hiring freelancers for non-core tasks • Helps avoid high fixed employee costs
2. Tech Talent Demand	• Increased use of project-based hiring • Skilled freelancers in Engineering, Product, Data Science, ML • Supports tech platforms
3. MNCs & Post-Pandemic Shift	• MNCs adopting flexi-hiring post-COVID • Useful for niche & short-term roles • Aims to cut operational costs • Drives gia culture growth

did you KNOW? In 2020, the Global Gig Economy Index highlighted India's growth in the freelance market, ranking it among the top 10 countries, with a notable increase in freelancers from 11 per cent to 52 per cent between 2018 and 2019.

KEY FEATURES OF A GIG ECONOMY

- **Short-Term and flexible contracts** – Workers work in temporary and flexible jobs instead of looking for a full-time job.
- **Freelance and Independent Work** - Gig workers are usually self-employed or independent contractors.
- **Digital Platforms** – They are connected through different online platforms and portals.
- **Pay-Per-Task or payment on hourly basis**- Workers are paid per task or payment is given on hourly basis. No specific salary is given.
- **Decentralised Workforce** – Workers are allowed to work from home or anywhere outside the office. Employers may choose the most talented individuals for a project without being restricted by geographical location. Employees are no longer required to sit at a particular location.
- **Technology-Driven** – Work is performed and facilitated with the use of apps and digital tools for communication, payment, and job management.
- **Diverse Work Types** – Gig economy includes different types of industries such as transport, delivery, and other creative work.
  - **Global Opportunities** – Workers have access to a global workforce and can seek jobs or clients anywhere in the world.
  - **Demand-Driven** – The availability of work is dependent on consumer demand and overall market.
  - **Self-Promotion** – Freelance workers need to promote themselves and use social media to get clients.

Gig workers can be categorised as **platform** and **non-platform** workers. Platform workers depend on online software apps or digital platforms like Uber, Ola, Zomato, and they have flexible jobs outside traditional employer-employee relationships. Non-platform gig workers, on the other hand, do not utilise online platforms or apps to find or perform work. They can work either full-time or part-time and are usually casual wage earners.

The gig economy is sometimes referred to as the **'freelance economy'** or the **'on-demand economy'**. These terms are frequently used interchangeably to refer to the same idea of flexible work schedules made possible via online resources.

GIG *vs* PLATFORM ECONOMY

The platform economy and gig economy are closely related but they have some differences. The gig economy mainly represents the labour market where independent workers are involved in short-term or freelance work.

On the other hand, the platform economy describes a system in which digital platforms are used for connecting buyers and sellers, service providers and workers. The platform economy consists of not only gig work but also some other types of work.

A Comparative Study

Aspect	Gig Economy	Platform Economy
Focus	Short-term, freelance work	Digital platforms enabling all types of exchange
Workers	Independent/freelancers	Can include workers, businesses, and consumers
Example	Freelance designer	Amazon, Airbnb, Upwork, Zomato
Scope	Subset of platform economy	Broader system for digital transactions

SOCIAL IMPLICATIONS OF THE GIG ECONOMY AS A NEW ECONOMIC PARADIGM IN INDIA

India's gig economy is changing the socio-economic condition of the country very fast. It is bringing more opportunities and challenges day by day. It has brought about a paradigm shift in the nature of employment, where flexible, short-term contracts are given importance over the long-term jobs and the permanent employment. Individuals get greater freedom from this, specially in cities, and it provides avenues for disadvantaged classes of people, including women and youth, to enter the workforce. But it also gives rise to powerful social consequences. The dependence of Gig economy does not ensure a timely and stable source of income. In this case, the income is unpredictable and it triggers socio-economic inequality as several workers experience tenuous earnings without adequate access to social benefits such as healthcare and retirement plans. Apart from these, it creates fear and insecurity among workers, most especially low-paid and informal wage earners. Gig economy also has the effect of undermining institutionalised community life since workers also lack stable communities and social networks. Although it provides the opportunities for flexibility and work-life balance, particularly among women, it also widens gender pay differentials and increases informal work practices. Psychological implications of irregular compensation, loneliness, and job instability also persist here.

GIG ECONOMY FROM DIFFERENT PERSPECTIVES

From the Business Perspective

- **Cost-effective:** It is much convenient and cost- effective from the business perspective. By hiring off-site workers, companies can avoid the costs such as maintaining workspaces in physical forms and large offices. They also save considerable amount of money on employee benefits, retirement plans, and paid sick leaves since independent contractors are not entitled to these benefits.
- **No Middleman:** Such a set-up provides a direct contact between companies and freelancers which eliminates the need for intermediaries in the hiring process.
- **Unique Opportunity:** It has unique work culture that attracts individuals who want to earn extra amount of income. The flexibility provided by gig work can impact employee motivation, leading to increased productivity.

From a Worker's Perspective

- **Independence:** In such a set-up, workers have the choice to work from any location, whether it is a home office for writing articles, content creation from anywhere in the world or driving for Uber, Ola, etc.
- **Flexibility:** Gig workers have the flexibility to select their own working hours. Tasks may have timelines but they have the flexibility to decide when to complete and how to complete the task in a proper way.
- **Income:** It provides an opportunity for individuals to earn extra income, which makes it an appealing option for those looking for boosting their income.

WHO WORKS IN THE GIG ECONOMY?

The main reason for working in the gig economy is generating additional income and having sufficient work flexibility. The following individuals can work in a gig economy.

- **Free agents:** These individuals choose independent work by choice as their primary source of income.
- **Casual wage earners:** They engage in independent work by their own will to increase their income from other sources.
- **Reluctant workers:** Those who primarily rely on independent work for their livelihood.
- **Financially weak:** Due to financial constraints, some people engage in supplemental independent work.

BONUS KNOWLEDGE

According to a report by Boston Consulting Group, **India's gig workforce comprises 15 million workers** employed across industries such as software, shared services and professional services.

Potential of India's Gig Economy

An estimated **56 per cent of new jobs** in India are created by gig economy companies for both white-collar and blue-collar workers.

Although the gig economy is common in India's blue-collar sectors, there is also a growing need for gig workers in white-collar sectors, including software developers, web designers, content writers, consultants for specific projects, and salespersons.

The gig economy has the potential to contribute 1.25 per cent to India's GDP in the long run and support upto 90 million employment in non-farm sectors.

Last Minute SNIPPETS

The gig economy will play a significant role in closing the gap between unemployment and income as India works towards its declared objective of being a USD 5 trillion economy by 2025.

SIZE OF GIG ECONOMY IN INDIA

According to a NITI Aayog's report on *"India's Booming Gig and Platform Economy"*, approximately 47 per cent of the gig workforce is currently in medium-skilled employment, 22 per cent is in high-skilled jobs, and 31 per cent is in low-skilled jobs.

According to a research conducted by the **Boston Consulting Group (BCG)**, the gig economy is more popular in developing nations (5–12%) than in developed nations (1%–4%).

The majority of these professions fall into lower-paying categories, including microtasking, ridesharing, delivery, care, and wellness.

By 2029–2030, the Indian gig economy is predicted to grow to 2.35 crore workers.

BONUS KNOWLEDGE

DIFFERENT COLLAR JOBS

- **Blue-Collar Worker:** A blue-collar worker is a person engaged in manual labour and is paid on an hourly basis.
- **White-Collar Worker:** A salaried professional, usually refers to management and general office staff.
- **Gold-Collar Worker:** It describes highly knowledgeable individuals who are extremely valuable to the company. For instance, physicians, lawyers, research scientists, etc.
- **Grey-Collar Worker:** The term 'grey-collar worker' describes the majority of employed individuals who are neither white nor blue-collar.

  Although the term 'grey-collar' refers to people who continue to work after they reach retirement age. For instance, security guards, medical personnel.
- **Green-Collar Worker:** A person who works in the environmental areas of the economy is known as a green-collar worker.

  Example: Persons employed in Greenpeace, the World Wide Fund for Nature, solar panels, and other alternative energy sources.
- **Pink-Collar Worker:** Employment in a job that is traditionally considered to be women's work and is often low-paid.
- **Red-Collar Worker:** Government workers of all types.
- **Open-Collar Worker:** An employee who works remotely, particularly online.

CHALLENGES ASSOCIATED WITH THE GIG SECTOR

- **Unregulated Nature:** Since the gig economy is so unregulated, workers have minimal benefits and limited job security.

  Few argue that India's gig economy, which excludes workers from social security, insurance, and other benefits, is a continuation of the country's long-standing, uncontrolled informal labour sector.
- **Need for Skills:** A worker must possess sufficient skills. A person's bargaining power will inevitably be restricted unless they are exceptionally talented.

  While companies often spend money on staff training, gig economy workers will need to pay for their own skill upgrades.
- **Demand-Supply Mismatch:** The gap between supply and demand will increase over time, lowering wages, as there are already far more prospective online independent workers than jobs.

EXAM ESSENTIAL

GIG ECONOMY AS EMPOWERMENT OF WOMEN

- **Work and family balance:** Women may balance their traditional roles as homemakers and caregivers with their jobs due to gig employment's flexible scheduling and part-time work.

  Women in rural areas now have the chance to make money by selling their goods online because of the expansion of websites like Amazon and Flipkart.
- **Flexibility to enter and exit:** Cultural and societal standards in India make it difficult for many women to find work. Women can work on-demand in the gig economy, which lets them enter and exit the workforce whenever they choose.
- **New job opportunities:** Women in tier- 2 and tier- 3 cities now have new job options where they do not have to travel far by virtue of technology and gig work. Women now have more options to work in industries where contacts are handled via phone calls and apps due to the rise in the usage of digital technology and the growing acceptance of working virtually for sales and distribution positions.
- **Financial independence:** Gig work allows women the ability to make decisions, earn additional money, and gain confidence, all of which are critical elements of women's empowerment.
- **More satisfying occupations:** Women now have access to higher-paying, more skilled positions like marketing, design, and consulting owing to the gig economy. These jobs can be more profitable than traditional employment options with a gender wage gap.

CONCERNS OF GIG WORK FOR WOMEN

- **Existing Issues in the Labor Market**:
  - The gig economy presents substantial obstacles to female participation since it reinforces the labour market's pre-existing issues, including the digital divide, gender pay disparity, biased algorithms, and gender stereotypes. As a result, it is critical to identify and resolve these innate structural problems in the digital ecosystem.
  - One major obstacle to women's participation in gig work is the gender gap in digital access. Only 21% of Indian women use mobile internet, according to the GSMA Mobile Gender Gap Report 2020. This results in unequal access to digital technologies that are required to participate in the platform economy.

    Despite the lack of a thorough database on gig workers in the nation, it has been noted that platforms show occupational segregation based on gender stereotypes.

Men perform more transportation and delivery work than women, who mostly work in structured domestic and caregiver roles, as well as beauty and wellness services.

- **Wage Disparity:** Gig economy is a sector where wage gaps appear. According to pre-pandemic reports, the salary gap between men and women gig workers in India was between 8% and 10%. In reality, research indicates that women undervalue themselves and take on lower-paying employment as a result of learned inequality, which increases the already-present wage gap in the gig economy.
- **Biasness against Women:**
  - The platforms' 'on-demand' work schedules and reward systems frequently discriminate against women.
  - Women frequently miss out on the benefits of peak hours, when demand and salaries are high, due to their involvement in childcare and household responsibilities.

LABOUR CODE FOR GIG ECONOMY

- The **Code on Wages, 2019**, which applies to both organised and unorganised sectors, including gig workers, stipulates a universal minimum pay and floor wage.
- Gig workers are acknowledged as a new occupational category in the **Code on Social Security, 2020**.

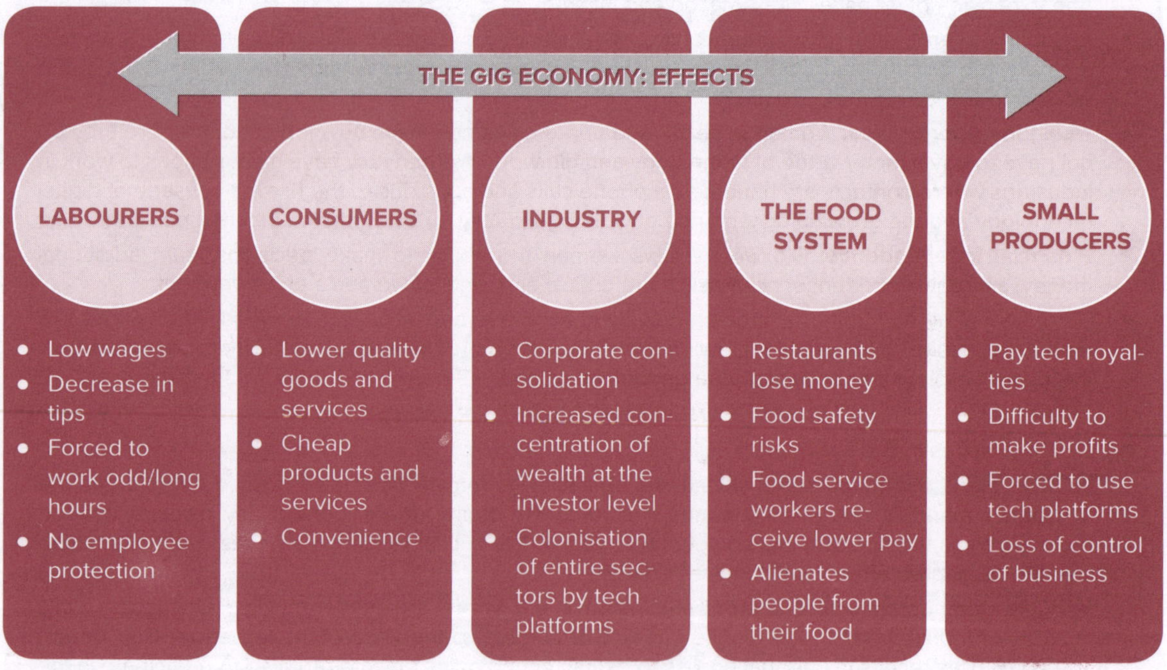

Issues in the Security Code

- Platform workers are now eligible for benefits such as maternity benefits, life and disability coverage, old age protection, provident fund, employment injury benefits, etc. under the Code on Social Security, 2020. However, eligibility does not imply that benefits will be provided. Additionally, none of the provisions secure these benefits, which means that the Central government may occasionally create welfare programmes that address these aspects of personal and professional security, but they are not guaranteed.
- According to the Code, workers, platform aggregators, and the central government all have responsibility for providing fundamental welfare measures. However, it makes no mention of which stakeholder is in charge of providing what amount of benefit.

HOW COULD THE CONDITIONS OF GIG WORKERS BE IMPROVED?

- **By providing Fiscal advantages:** According to NITI Aayog's report, *'India's Booming Gig and Platform Economy,'* companies that offer livelihood prospects and have a significant female workforce, may be eligible for fiscal advantages like tax rebates or startup grants.
- **By providing Retirement Benefits:** The same report also suggested that businesses should implement policies that provide retirement or old age plans and benefits, as well as additional insurance coverage for unforeseen circumstances. As a "critical step in providing assured minimum earnings and social security from income loss in the wake of uncertainty or irregularity in work," businesses should think about offering income assistance to employees. In addition to health coverage, it recommends providing paid sick leave to employees.

Last Minute SNIPPETS

The Rajasthan Platform Based Gig Workers (Registration and Welfare) Act, 2023

The Rajasthan State Assembly recently passed the *Rajasthan Platform-Based Gig Workers (Registration and Welfare) Act, 2023.* This legislation mandates the establishment of a dedicated board to oversee the registration and welfare of gig workers, aiming to address their vulnerabilities and support collective negotiation and bargaining.

The board will also serve as an independent grievance redressal mechanism. Furthermore, the Act provides for the creation of a social security fund, financed through a fee levied on each transaction conducted via gig platforms.

- **Empowerment of the Gig Workers:** By creating an umbrella union that gives them collective negotiating power, gig workers must be empowered. They will have a stronger position compared to the platforms owing to the formal recognition and information symmetry.
- **Mandatory Coverage to Platform Workers:** Although the labour code's recognition of gig workers has raised hopes, the parameters of their social security are not well defined, and there are no established regulatory bodies. Therefore, platform workers must be provided with required coverage under centrally sponsored programmes. Since women gig workers are often more vulnerable in the platform economy, this can be facilitated through by the aggregators.

- **Need to Build the Right Physical and Social Infrastructure:** The appropriate social and physical infrastructure must be established to encourage women to participate in gig labour.

Developing public care infrastructure and promoting societal norms that encourage men to perform unpaid care and household duties equally can help women transition into gig work.

INDIA'S INITIATIVES FOR THE GIG WORKERS

- **Code on Social Security, 2020:** This Act envisages extending social security benefits to gig workers and acknowledges them as a distinct category.

  It has been criticised, meanwhile, for not having universal coverage, legal requirements, or gig worker accountability systems.
- **e-Shram Portal:**
  - Pradhan Mantri Shram Yogi Maandhan Yojana
  - Pradhan Mantri Jeevan Jyoti Bima Yojana (PMJJBY)

State-Level Initiatives

- Rajasthan Platform-Based Gig Workers (Registration and Welfare) Act, 2023
- **Karnataka's Bill on Gig Workers:** The bill mandates formal registration, grievance mechanisms, and transparent contracts. It might have issues such as the classification of gig workers as independent contractors, which excludes them from key labour protections.

Thus, to sum up, Gig economy offers a new way to work flexibly and make money through various online platforms. The demand for location-independent work, shifting career goals, and different pay structures have all contributed to its growth. All of these elements have contributed to the gig economy's expansion and rise in popularity in India.

However, there are still a lot of issues such as inadequate benefits and the potential for worker exploitation. India must create appropriate legislation to protect the interests of workers and organisations.

SUMMARY

- **Gig economy** – refers to short-term, flexible, and task-based jobs enabled by digital platforms.
- **Gig workers** – individuals who earn outside the traditional employer-employee framework (as per Code on Social Security, 2020).
- Gig economy characterised by – flexibility, tech dependence, on-demand services, and global outreach.
- Gig workers – classified into platform (app-driven) and non-platform (offline/casual) workers.
- Gig work includes – various categories like blue-collar (manual), white-collar (professional), and pink-collar (female-oriented).
- **Challenges** – lack of regulations, job insecurity, low pay, and absence of benefits.
- **For women, gig work offers** – flexibility, safer working conditions, and financial independence.
- **Challenges for women** – wage gaps, tech barriers, and gender-based discrimination.

UPSC CSE PREVIOUS YEARS' PRELIMINARY EXAMINATION QUESTIONS

☞ NO QUESTIONS ASKED
2024, 2023, 2022, 2021, 2020, 2019, 2018, 2017, 2016, 2015, 2014, 2013

UPSC CSE PREVIOUS YEARS' MAIN EXAMINATION QUESTIONS

1. Examine the role of 'Gig Economy' in the process of empowerment of women in India. **[2021]**

☞ NO QUESTIONS ASKED
2024, 2023, 2022, 2020, 2019, 2018, 2017, 2016, 2015, 2014, 2013

CHAPTER

33

CARE ECONOMY AND GENDER TRANSFORMATIVE APPROACH IN INDIA

CHAPTER OUTLINE

- Care Economy
- Care Diamond
- Differences between Care Economy and Monetised Economy
- The Purple Economy
- Gender and Work
- Issues with For-Profit Care Services
- International Instruments towards Gender Equality
- Unpaid Care Work and Gender Inequalities
- Care Jobs and the Future of Work
- Trend in Gender Gap in the Provision of Unpaid Care Work
- Fostering Women-led Development in India
- Rise in Female Labour Force Participation Rate (FLFPR) in India
- Government Schemes for the Welfare of Senior Citizens in India

CARE ECONOMY

The care economy refers to the paid and unpaid care work provided by people as a part of human welfare, survival and reproducing the labour force. It is the foundation of all human development. The care economy contributes towards the emotional and spiritual needs of people significantly. Care works are fundamental pillars of social protection system. **Care work** encompasses activities such as feeding a baby, nursing, cooking, cleaning, etc. It also includes a wide range of sectors like education, health, etc.

CARE DIAMOND

Care Diamond includes four prime institutional stakeholders in society in which the care work of society can be distributed. They are – **the State, markets, households, and communities**.

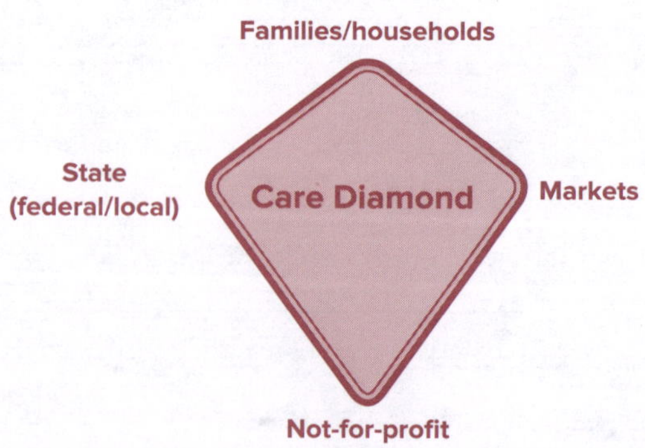

Women and girls within the household sector perform the larger part of care work. The unequal distributions of care responsibilities implicate women rights and demand equality across livelihood, income, well-being, public participation, etc. Redistribution of care work across different stakeholders is the need of the hour for gender equity and fostering human rights.

DIFFERENCES BETWEEN CARE ECONOMY AND MONETISED ECONOMY

Care Economy	Monetised Economy
It includes **unpaid or underpaid care-activities**, domestic work, etc.	It refers to the **formal paid work** in different sectors.
Values are not measured in monetary terms, **not accounted in GDP**.	Values are directly measured in terms of money, mostly **accounted in GDP**.
Historically associated with **women and produces** gender disparities.	More gender-inclusive, more women are now participating in formal workforce.
Creates a supportive environment in the family, pivotal for societal well-being.	Drives economic growth and creates jobs.

Care Economy

- **Unpaid Care Works**
  Care of old and sick persons, Care of persons with disabilities, Domestic work, Community care, Childcare
- **Paid Care Works**
  Health, Formal Education, Personal care, Paid Domestic help, Income, etc.

THE PURPLE ECONOMY

The purple economy is another name of care economy. It has obtained the name from the colour adopted by many feminist movements. The purple economy recognises the urgency and importance of care works, women empowerment, gender equality, gender-just transitions, autonomy of women to the functioning of the economies, wellbeing and sustainability of societies.

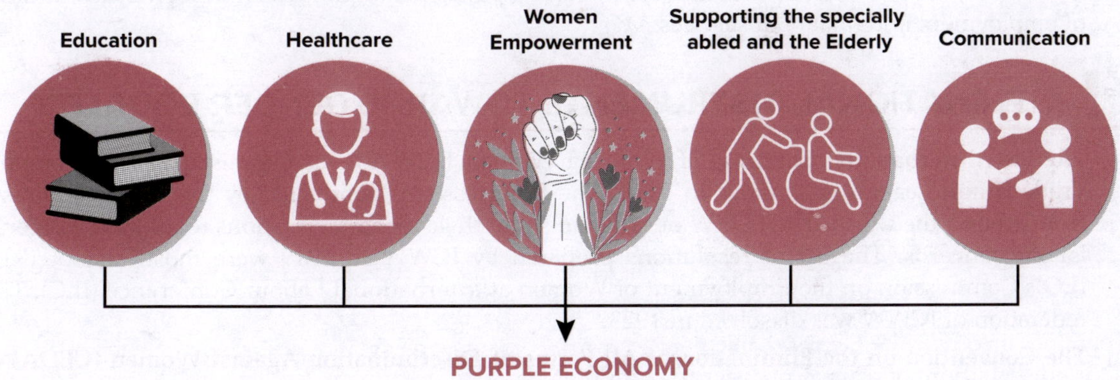

did you KNOW?

According to United Nations, *'By 2030, the number of care recipients is predicted to reach 2.3 billion, driven by an additional 0.1 billion older persons and an additional 0.1 billion children aged 6 to 14 years. Women perform 76.2 per cent of the total amount of unpaid care work, 3.2 times more than men.'*

GENDER AND WORK

Women have always been an integral part of the informal cash economy in developing countries. In India, the custom has traditionally existed in the communities that the women used to be in charge of the household economy by taking up the responsibilities of the household works. The role of women is also growing in formal production in the secondary and tertiary sectors and other specialised workplaces.

Within the domestic sphere, work performed by women is characterised by the following:

- Enabling environment for men and children like – cooking, washing, childcare, etc. and looking after sick and old members.
- Tasks performed by women at home are unrecognised.
- The household tasks are unproductive as they don't fetch income.

There has been an extremely negative approach towards the employment and formal labour of women. The subsistence and childcare work are completely unpaid and financially unaccounted. Apparently, the enormous amount of labour that takes place in the informal sector by women remains completely invisible.

ISSUES WITH FOR-PROFIT CARE SERVICES

- Difficulties arise in assessing the care quality services provided by the for-profit organisations; it is often income driven.
- High competition involved among the for-profit providers; it tends to increase the cost but not the quality of services.
- Care is highly labour-intensive; training infrastructure is not up to the mark and there is unavailability of skilled staff.
- Sometimes, the providers reduce the cost by cutting payments to staff which worsen the conditions of employment and quality of services.

INTERNATIONAL INSTRUMENTS TOWARDS GENDER EQUALITY

- **The First International Congress of Working Women (ICWW)** was organised by the Women's Trade Union League of America in **1919**. The Congress was conducted by the labour feminists from around the world. The ICWW outlined to share their recommendations to address women's labour concerns. The list of resolutions prepared by ICWW in 1919 were mostly adapted by ILO's Commission on the Employment of Women at International Labour Conference (ILC). The federation of ICWW was dissolved in 1923.
- **The Convention on the Elimination of All Forms of Discrimination Against Women (CEDAW)** was signed by the governments in **1979**, and it came into force in **1981**. At present, CEDAW has

189 state parties. It is often regarded as the **international bill of rights for women.** CEDAW is the first significant legally binding instrument, taking a comprehensive approach towards prohibiting discrimination against women.

- **The Beijing Declaration and Platform for Action** – was signed by 189 governments in **1995**. It was the first international legal instrument to incorporate a detailed action plan towards gender equality. The action plan formulated strategies to ensure equality and foster human rights for women. It addressed the issues of poverty, education, violence against women, economy, decision-making, etc.
- **MDG3** (Millennium Development Goal 3) focused on the gender equality. It was adopted in the Millennium Summit of the United Nations in **2000**. According to the **MDG MONITOR**, *'There was only one target under millennium development goal 3: to eliminate gender disparity in primary and secondary education by 2005, and in all levels of education by 2015.'* **The crucial achievements of MDG3 included** increase in the number of girls in school, reduction of the proportion of women in vulnerable employment, increase in the representation of women in parliament, etc.

  As per the **MDG MONITOR,** 'In Southern Asia, the number of girls enrolled in primary school was 74 for every 100 boys in 1990. By 2015, there were 103 girls enrolled for every 100 boys.'
- **SDG5** (Sustainable Development Goal 5) succeeded MDG3 in 2015. It has a broader perspective towards promoting gender equality. According to the UN, *'Gender equality is not only a fundamental human right, but a necessary foundation for a peaceful, prosperous and sustainable world. There has been progress over the last decades, but the world is not on track to achieve gender equality by 2030.'*
- **UN Women**, an institute of UN which, works for the promotion and global champion of gender equality and the empowerment of women. UN Women was set up by integrating the UN Development Fund for Women and other entities. It became operational in 2011.
- **Women Deliver 2023 Conference (WD2023):** The conference took place in Kigali, Rwanda in 2023, and the theme was Space, Solidarity and Solutions. The conference committed to advocate inclusive and sustainable solutions for gender equality. A global report was presented by UN Women and UNDP at the WD2023 which highlighted a comprehensive picture of progress for gender development. The report proposed the Women's Empowerment Index (**WEI**) and the Global Gender Parity Index (**GGPI**). According to the report, *'Less than 1 per cent of women and girls live in countries with both high levels of women's empowerment and high gender parity, while more than 90 per cent of the world's female population – 3.1 billion women and girls – live in countries characterised by a large women's empowerment deficit and a large gender gap.'*

Both paid and unpaid care works are important pillars of humanity, compassion and social justice. They are crucial for our societies. They are pivotal to survive and thrive and drive economic growth. According to ILO, women and girls perform **more than three-quarters** of the total amount of unpaid care work across the world. Two-thirds of care workers are accomplished by women. Demographic and socio-economic transformations are enhancing the demand for care workers.

There are deficits for decent working environment for care workers. As per the ILO,

- In 2015, 2.1 billion people had the dire need of care, among whom 1.9 billion were children under the age of 15, and 0.2 billion were older persons.
- By 2030, the number might increase by 200 million, including 100 million older persons.

Currently, about 110–190 million people with disabilities urgently need assistance throughout their lives. But working conditions of care workers are poor. Current deficits in care work and its quality and unsustainable working environment will produce severe global care crises. It can further aggravate gender inequalities in the world of work. The policy environment should put forward to address the issues of care work, policy should be oriented towards determining and upgrading the level of employment, improving working conditions, pay and status of care workers, etc. Migration policies need to be engineered to yield positive outcomes.

As per the ILO, *the representativeness of care workers' organisations and the coverage of social dialogue mechanisms can play a crucial* role.

The additional care would require adequate care policies to address the extra demand for paid care work.

UNPAID CARE WORK AND GENDER INEQUALITIES

"Women perform 76.2 per cent of the total amount of unpaid care work, 3.2 times more time than men."

–ILO

Though unrecognised and invisible, unpaid care work makes substantial contribution to families and societal well-being. As per the time-use survey data in 64 countries (representing 66.9 per cent of the world's working-age population), about 16.4 billion hours are spent in unpaid care work every day, which would amount to **9 per cent of global GDP**. It is identical to US$11 trillion (purchasing power parity 2011). The majority of unpaid care work includes household work (81.8 per cent), followed by direct personal care (13.0 per cent) and volunteer work (5.2 per cent). (ILO)

Attitudes and viewpoint of the society towards the gender division of paid work and unpaid care work are switching and they are significantly positive towards women's paid work.

As per the ILO, about 70 per cent of women and 66 per cent of men prefer that women be in paid work and 647 million persons of working age are outside the labour force on account of family responsibilities.

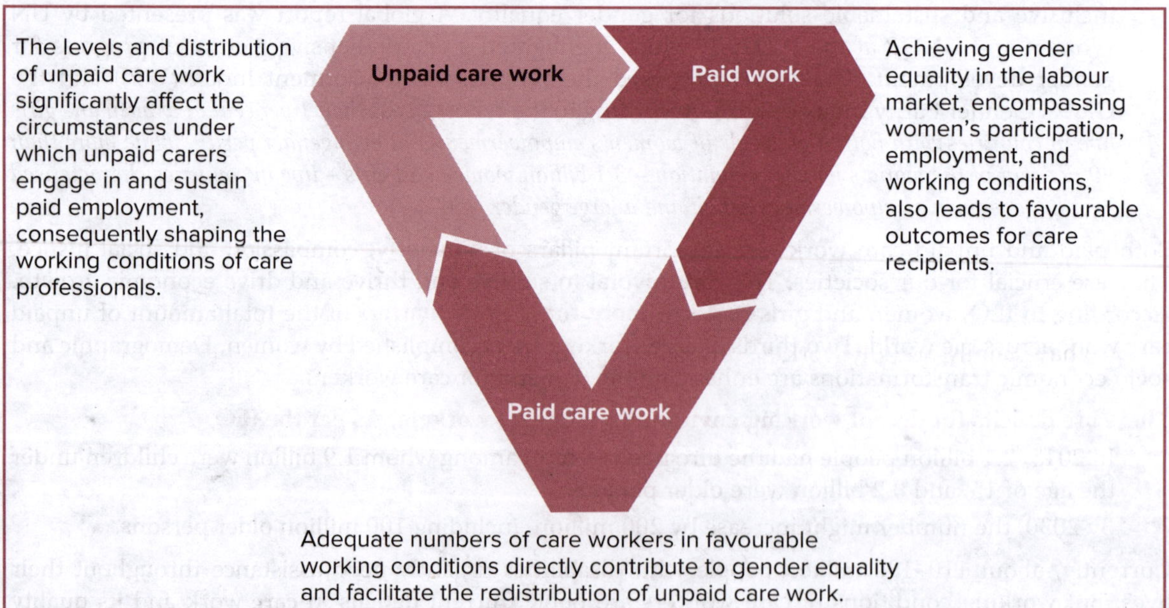

The unpaid care work-paid work-unpaid care work cycle

CARE JOBS AND THE FUTURE OF WORK

As per the report **'Care Work and Care Jobs for the Future of Work' of ILO, if we invest in the care economy for achieving the SDGs, it can create about 475 million jobs by 2030**.

Good-quality care employment contributes to gender equality. It also promotes benefits for care recipients and care workers.

Investment in Care Jobs

Global calls are needed for urgent action to address looming global care crisis. According to ILO – a **'high road' to care work** can generate about 475 million jobs by 2030.

- The care deficit require total public and private expenditures on care service provision of US$18.4 trillion. It is about 18.3 per cent of total projected GDP of the 45 countries in 2030.
- This job creation potential will be galvanised by additional 66 million jobs in health and social work, 54 million jobs in education compared with 2015 levels. The additional 120 million jobs in the care sectors will give rise to 149 million indirect jobs.

> *'A high road to care work means recognising, reducing and redistributing unpaid care work and achieving decent work for care workers, including domestic and migrant workers.'*
>
> *–ILO*

The 5R Framework for Decent Care Work of ILO to attain high road to care work and gender equality: Recognise, Reduce, Redistribute, Reward, Representation

- **Recognise:** Account for the value of unpaid care works.
- **Reduce:** Lessen the all-inclusive time spent on unpaid care works by sustainable policy and support infrastructure.
- **Redistribute:** the unpaid and unrecognised care works done by women.
- **Reward:** Promoting decent work for care workers.
- **Representation:** of the marginalised care providers, social dialogue and collective bargaining.

Suggested Policy Interventions in Care Jobs

a. To enhance investment in quality care services, policies and care-supportive infrastructure, gender friendly technologies.

b. To upgrade the labour market policies holding up the reintegration of unpaid care providers into labour force.

c. To have family-friendly working arrangements for all workers.

d. To ensure the right to universal access to quality care services.

e. Gender-responsive social protection systems, publicly funded leave policies for women and men, etc.

f. To regulate the decent terms and conditions of employment.

g. To ensure equal pay for work of equal value for all care providers.

h. To provide safe, stimulating work environment.

i. To plan and implement policy measures to protect migrant care workers.

j. To ensure women's effective participation in decision making.
k. To provide equal opportunities to women for leadership in political, economic life.
l. To promote freedom of association for care providers.
m. To advocate social dialogue of collective bargaining in care sectors.

Measures to transform Care Economy into Monetised Economy

- **Recognition of** the economic value of unaccountable and unpaid care work and **Equal Pay for Equal Work**. Promotion of opportunities to get involved in the formal labour force through skill development.
- Implementation of policies like Work From Home (WFH) culture, subsidised healthcare, etc. to support women in the twin roles as workers and caregivers.
- **Fostering Women's Entrepreneurship** in sectors associated with care services.
- **Elderly and Healthcare Services:** Creating job opportunities in the healthcare sector, including nursing, geriatric care, and other health-related services. Setting up affordable and high-quality childcare services and healthcare services for the seniors.

TREND IN GENDER GAP IN THE PROVISION OF UNPAID CARE WORK

As per the **ILO survey** and analysing **Time-Use Data** –

- The gender difference in time spent has slightly narrowed and women pursue to provide the majority of unpaid care work in those countries where time-use data is available.
- Gender difference limits women's potential to enhance their hours in paid, formal work.
- There is a marginal increase in women's employment rates of only **2.8 percentage points globally from 1997 to 2012**.
- The gender gap in unpaid care work decreased slightly from **1 hour and 49 minutes in 1997** to 1 hour and 42 minutes in 2012.
- In 2012, women performed about 32.5 per cent of total paid work in the 23 countries for which data is available.
- Overall, women contributed to **47.9 per cent** of total work in 2012, compared with **46.9 per cent in 1997**.

FOSTERING WOMEN-LED DEVELOPMENT IN INDIA

The Women's Reservation Bill [Nari Shakti Vandan Adhiniyam (NSVA)] in 2023, along with the year of India's G20 Presidency, spotlighted '**women-led development**' as one of the foremost priorities. Increasing importance towards women's workforce participation is noticeable globally. Professor **Claudia Goldin** has been awarded the Nobel Prize in Economic Sciences (2023) for her contribution to key drivers of gender differences in the labour market. For women-led development to be substantiated, we have to bring about the prerequisites of equal opportunity and improve the quality of life of women.

Women-led SHGs are crucial for economic, social, and political empowerment of women at the village level. The Deendayal Antyodaya Yojana-National Rural Livelihood Mission (DAY-NRLM) is the SHG programme of GoI. It covers about nine crore women through 83 lakh SHGs. GoI has targeted to create

2 crore **'Lakhpati Didis'**. They are women with annual earnings of ₹1 lakh and more through **skilling** SHG members.

Female participation has been quite satisfactory due to capital formation through **Startup India**, Skill India Mission and other initiatives of GoI.

Rise in Female Labour Force Participation Rate (FLFPR) in India

In India, FLFPR has been rising in recent years. According to the Economic Survey 2024–25, FLFPR has risen from 23.3 per cent in 2017–18 to 41.7 per cent in 2023–24. This rise is driven by the growing participation of rural women in workforce. The enhancement in FLFPR is the prime driver of the overall improvement in the labour market indicators.

FLFPR has increased across different states. In 2017–18, 20 states/UTs had FLFPR of less than 20 per cent. This number went down to 3 in 2023–24. Now, most states (21) in India have a FLFPR in the range of 30–40 per cent. In seven states/UTs, FLFPR stands at greater than 40 per cent in 2023–24. Sikkim has the maximum FLFPR of 56.9 per cent.

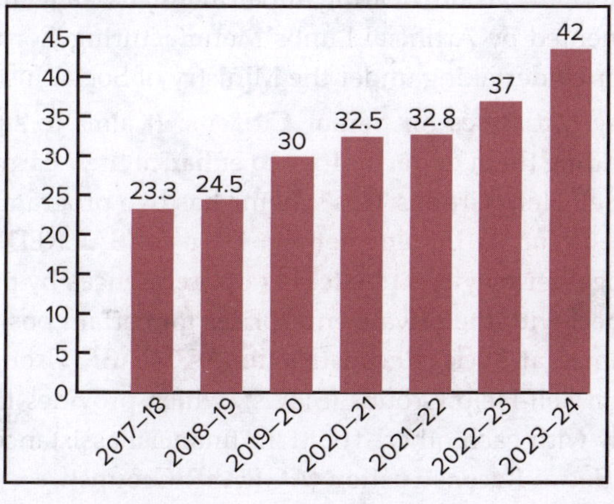

Female Labour Force Participation Rate (rural+urban), usual status, 15 years and above
Source: PLFS

The increase in the rural FLFPR is the main driver of the rise in overall FLFPR in India. Women have been the key beneficiaries of various initiatives by GoI and different states to foster entrepreneurship. As of October 2024, about 73,151 startups with at least one woman director were recognised under the Startup India Initiative. World Bank study also highlighted that furthering women-owned, growth-oriented enterprises can boost FLFPR and economic growth significantly in rural India. Harnessing the power of women entrepreneurs is crucial for India's economic future and development.

GOVERNMENT SCHEMES FOR THE WELFARE OF SENIOR CITIZENS IN INDIA

The population of senior citizens is approximately 10.38 crore (as per 2011 census), amounting to **8.6 per cent** of the total population in the country. **National Policy on Older Persons, 1999 emphasises on**

State support to ensure financial and food security, health care, shelter, etc. The umbrella scheme of **Atal Vayo Abhyuday Yojana**, under the **Ministry of Social Justice and Empowerment,** has the vision to create a society where senior citizens live a healthy, happy, empowered, dignified and self-reliant life alongwith strong social and inter-generational bonding. This Scheme has following sub-schemes:

1. **Integrated Programme for Senior Citizens (IPSrC):** Grants-in-aid are given for running and maintenance of Senior Citizens Homes/Continuous Care Homes, Mobile Medicare Units etc. to the Implementing Agencies (IAs) such as Registered Societies/Panchayati Raj Institutions (PRIs)/ Local bodies; Non-Governmental/Voluntary Organizations.
2. **State Action Plan for Senior Citizens (SAPSrC):** Each State/UT is expected to frame their own State Action Plans for the welfare of senior citizens. Department of Social Justice and Empowerment releases funds to the States/UTs for formulation and implementation of their State Action Plans.
3. **Rashtriya Vayoshri Yojana (RVY):** This Central Sector Scheme (CSS) is funded from Senior Citizens' Welfare Fund and under it, **aids and assistive living devices are provided to senior citizens** belonging to BPL category or those who earn less than ₹15000/- per month and suffer from age related disabilities such as low vision, hearing impairment, loss of teeth and loco-motor disabilities. The Scheme is implemented by Artificial Limbs Manufacturing Corporation of India **(ALIMCO)** which is a Public Sector Undertaking under the Ministry of Social Justice and Empowerment.
4. **Livelihood and Skilling Initiatives for Senior Citizens:** It aims to supplement the efforts of the senior citizens by providing them **opportunities to enhance their earning** and sense of self-respect through formation of Self Help Groups This scheme has two programmes:
   i. **Senior Able Citizens for Re-Employment in Dignity (SACRED) portal** – The portal allows bringing people together by **virtual matching of preferences** by providing the Senior Citizens a platform to connect with the private enterprises for certain positions.
   ii. **Action Groups Aimed at Social Reconstruction (AGRASR Groups):** The Senior Citizens are encouraged to form Self-Help Groups (SHGs), which provides them a platform to share the time constructively with each other. To attain financial assistance, **SHGs** function as **'Action Groups Aimed at Social Reconstruction (AGRASR Groups)'.**
5. **Promoting Silver Economy:** Innovative Start-ups are identified and encouraged for developing products, processes and services for the welfare of the elderly under this initiative. The selected start-ups/start-up ideas can be provided equity support of up to ₹1 crore per project while ensuring that the total Government equity in the start-up should not exceed 49 per cent. For this, the **SAGE portal** has been launched in 2021.
6. **Channelizing CSR funds for Elderly care:** Under Schedule VII of Section 135 of the Companies Act, setting up old age homes, day care centres and such facilities for Senior Citizens are now approved items for CSR funding.
7. **National Helpline for Senior Citizen (14567):** To address the grievance of the elders.
8. **Vayo Shreshtha Samman:** National Award for Senior Citizens 'Vayo shreshtha Samman' are conferred to eminent and outstanding institutions or organizations and individuals from different categories, on **1st October (International Day for Older Persons)** every year by the Hon'ble President of India.

SUMMARY

- **Care Economy** – Paid and unpaid care work provided by people.
- **Care Diamond** – Four prime institutional stakeholders in society – the State, Markets, Households and Communities. Among them, the care work of society can be distributed.
- **Purple Economy** – Also referred to as the care economy, obtained the name from the colour adopted by many feminist movements.
- **Silver Economy** – All those economic activities, products and services designed to meet the needs of people over 50.
- **The First International Congress of Working Women** (**ICWW**) – Organised by the Women's Trade Union League of America in 1919.
- **Convention on the Elimination of all forms of Discrimination Against Women (CEDAW)** – Signed by the governments in 1979 and it came into force in 1981.
- **Beijing Declaration and Platform for Action** – Signed by 189 governments in **1995.**
- **The 5R Framework for Decent Care Work of ILO to attain high road to care work and gender equality** – Recognise, Reduce, Redistribute, Reward, Representation.

UPSC CSE PREVIOUS YEARS' PRELIMINARY EXAMINATION QUESTIONS

☞ NO QUESTIONS ASKED
2024, 2023, 2022, 2021, 2020, 2019, 2018, 2017, 2016, 2015, 2014, 2013

UPSC CSE PREVIOUS YEARS' MAIN EXAMINATION QUESTIONS

1. Distinguish between 'care economy' and 'monetised economy'. How can care economy be brought into monetised economy through women empowerment? **[2023]**

☞ NO QUESTIONS ASKED
2024, 2022, 2021, 2020, 2019, 2018, 2017, 2016, 2015, 2014, 2013

CHAPTER

34

INVESTMENT MODELS

CHAPTER OUTLINE

- Relationship between Investments and GDP
- Relationship between Savings and Investments
- Factors affecting Investments
- Classification of Models of Investment
- Induced Investment
- Autonomous Investment
- Public-Private Partnership (PPP) Model
- Salient Features of PPP
- Advantages of the PPP Model
- Disadvantages of the PPP Model
- Present Challenges with respect to PPP in Infrastructure Projects
- Suggested Reforms under the PPP Approach
- Airports and PPP
- PPP Opportunities in Railways
- Swiss Challenge Method
- Economic Planning and use of Investment Models therein
- Harrod–Domar Model (HDM)
- Lewis Model of Economic Development
- Solow–Swan Model
- Feldman–Mahalanobis Model
- Rao–Manmohan Model

- Investment is a process in which **money is exchanged for a better return or profit-yielding asset**. It can also be said that Investment is capital formation, a gross or net addition to capital stock which can boost the economy with surplus returns or profit.
- Therefore, **investment is highly appreciated for the economic growth and development** of a nation. Investments also help to reduce poverty, unemployment, malnutrition, etc.
- Both Government and Private sectors invest in an Economy. Investments from private sector not only reduces the burden of government financially but also generates employment opportunities and shares the accountability of the process of nation building.
- Based on regulatory framework and contribution of both private and public sector, various models of investments have been defined so far. Such investment models are discussed later in this chapter.

RELATIONSHIP BETWEEN INVESTMENTS AND GDP

GDP of a country can be defined as the sum of consumption expenditure, Government spending, net exports and the investments. Thus, mathematically GDP can be expressed as:

$$GDP = C + G + I + NX$$

where

C = Consumption expenditure

G = Government expenditure

NX = Net Exports = Exports (X) – Imports (M)

I = Gross Investments.

Also, from the above expression, we get,

$$I = GDP - (C + G + NX)$$

RELATIONSHIP BETWEEN SAVINGS AND INVESTMENTS

- Investment comprises of **private** (corporate and household) investment and **public** investment.
- Domestic investments are generally financed through domestic savings – either through private (corporate and household) savings or through public savings. **External savings (foreign pension funds, etc.) can also be used to fund domestic investments. However, it can increase the Current Account Deficit (CAD).**
- Economic growth is largely driven by the level of savings and the rate of investment.
- It should be noted that if interest on savings accounts increases then the rate of investment usually declines. Thus, monetary policy of a country significantly affects the rate of investment.
- The fiscal policy of government including the rates of taxes and slabs of taxes also drive the rate of investment in an economy.

FACTORS AFFECTING INVESTMENTS

Investment in any sector depends on two basic factors:

(i) *Income* – Higher is the income, more will be the investment.

(ii) *Rate of Interest in Banks* – Higher is the rate of interest, lesser will be the investment.

Other factors which affect the investment in a country are **tax rate, inflation, possible rate of return on capital investment, availability of the factors of production** like cheaper land and labour, proper transportation and communication, energy availability, etc. and above all the policies of the Government.

CLASSIFICATION OF MODELS OF INVESTMENT

On the basis of the sources of investments, investment models are classified as:

- **Domestic Investment Model** – When the source of the investment is from within the country, such an investment is known as domestic investment model.
- **Public Investment Model** – When the Government itself invests in some project in order to get better returns and particularly to reduce poverty and enhance employment, such an investment model comes under the **public investment model**.
- **Private Investment Model** – When a private player invests in a project for good returns, then the investment model is considered as **private investment model**. Private investment model can be both domestic and foreign.

TYPES OF INVESTMENT

REAL	Investment made in new plant and equipment
AUTONOMOUS	Does not change with the changes in income level
INDUCED	Changes with the change in income level
FINANCIAL	Investment for financial instruments such as shares, bonds, securities
PLANNED	Investment made with a plan and for specific objectives
UNPLANNED	Instrument made without planning
GROSS	Total amount of money spent for the creation of new capital
NET	Gross Investment – Capital Consumption

Autonomous Investment	Induced Investment
Investment which is independent of income and profit	Investment which is for earning profit
Generally done in Government Sector	Generally done in Private Sector
Autonomous investment curve is parallel to the horizontal axis because it is not affected by the change in income level	Induced investment curve is upward rising because investment rises with rise in income

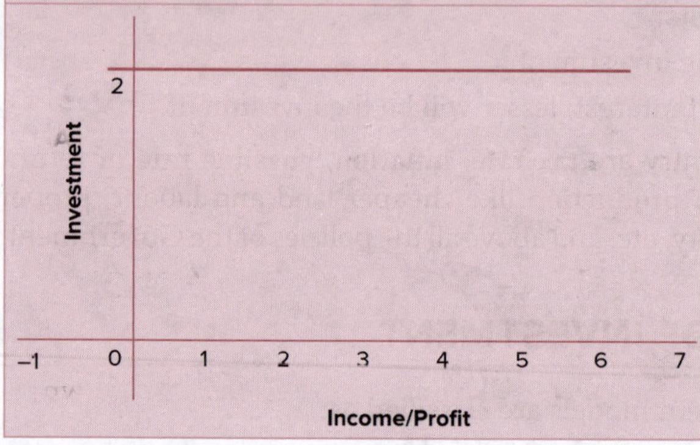

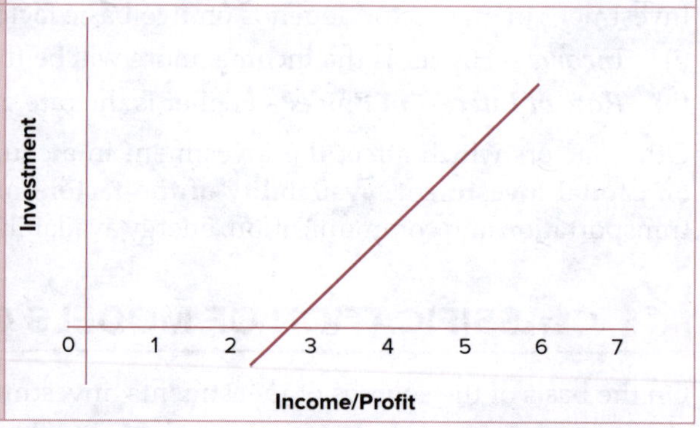

EXAM ESSENTIAL

INVESTMENT MULTIPLIER

- Investment multiplier (IM) indicates that any public or private investment has positive impact not only on the prescribed project but also on many other dimensions of an economy. For example – If investment is done for a particular project, then it not only improves the infrastructure of a country but also increases the income of workers, suppliers and various industries related to that project.
- **A higher investment multiplier indicates that creation and distribution of wealth in that economy is efficient.**

- Generally, investment multiplier is dependent on **Marginal Propensity to Consume (MPC) and Marginal Propensity to Save (MPS)**.

  where, MPC = (Change in Spending)/(Change in Income)

  MPS = (Change in Saving)/(Change in Income)

The value of MPC and MPS always lies between 0 and 1

In a closed economy, MPS + MPC = 1

$$\text{Investment Multiplier} = \frac{1}{1 - \text{MPC}}$$

In other words, as **multiplier** shows the effect of change in total national investment on the amount of total national income, it equals the ratio of the change in total income to the change in investment.

The larger is the investment multiplier, the more efficient it is at creating and distributing wealth throughout an economy. An investment multiplier measures the financial impact of a public or private project. Since resources are limited, **sectors/projects with higher investment multiplier is generally chosen** to maximise the output or return.

For example, **investments in electricity sector and physical infrastructure such as roads, railways, etc. have a positive multiplier effect**, and they boost the economic growth, employment and income.

Incremental Capital Output Ratio (ICOR) – It explains the relationship between the level of investment in an economy and the resultant increase in GDP. In other words, it can also be said that it is the additional capital required to increase one unit of output.

ICOR = (Annual Investment)/(Annual Increase in GDP)

ICOR is also used to measure the level of production efficiency of an economy. For example – if ICOR of a country is ₹100, that means an investment of ₹100 is required to increase the annual GDP of ₹1. Thus, **higher ICOR is not preferred as it indicates that the economy's own production is inefficient**.

PUBLIC-PRIVATE PARTNERSHIP (PPP) MODEL

EXAM ESSENTIAL

When the **Government and the private players join hand together to finance a project**, such a model is considered as a Public-Private Partnership (PPP) model.

Salient Features of PPP

1. Under PPP, **a legal relationship** is defined between the Government or a Government-owned entity and a private sector entity **for a specified period**.
2. PPP also has **well-defined allocation of risk** between the private and public entities, but the **ownership remains with the public sector** in most of the cases.
3. Policies and projects under PPP are **regulated by the** ***Department of Economic Affairs, Ministry of Finance***.
4. There are **various models of PPP**, each having its own merits and demerits.

PPP models of investments are based on the negotiations between the public and private entities. **These models can be classified on the basis of following two aspects**:

PPP

- **Based on Investment Share**
  - Management Contracts
  - Turnkey
  - Lease
  - Concession Agreement
  - Private Finance Initiative
  - Private Ownership
- **Based on Operational Type**
  - BOT
  - BOO
  - BOLT
  - BROT
  - LDO
  - EPC
  - HAM

Let us first discuss the models based on investment share:

- **Management Contracts** – Private sector skills are used for service design and delivery, operational management, labour management and equipment procurement. However, the **public sector retains the ownership** of the project. Usually, the contract period is short, typically varying from **2 to 5 years**.
- **Turnkey** – A private contractor is selected through a bidding process. The private contractor designs and builds a facility for a fixed fee, rate or total cost, which is one of the key criteria in selecting the winning bid. This method is also known as **design-build**.
- **Lease** – The leaseholder is responsible for **operating and maintaining the infrastructure** facility (that already exists) and services, but generally the operator is not required to make any large investment.
- **Concession Agreement** – Government grants **specific rights to a private company** to build and operate a facility **for a fixed period**. The Government can retain the ultimate ownership of the facility. The concessionaire pays to the Government for the concession rights and the Government may also pay the concessionaire. The agreement provides for meeting certain specific conditions.

The Government undertakes this kind of PPP projects for capital formations. NITI Aayog is considering a project in this model for the operation and maintenance of passenger ropeways.

- **Private Finance Initiative (PFI)** – The **private company handles the upfront costs** instead of the Government. The project is then leased to the public, and the **Government authority makes annual payments** to the private company. At the end of the contract period, the project may or may not be transferred to the public sector. The annuity model for **financing of national highways** in India is an example of PFI model.
- **Private Ownership** – The private sector remains responsible for design, construction and operation of an infrastructure facility, and in some cases, the public sector may give up the right of ownership of assets to the private sector.

Let us now discuss PPP models based on the operational type:

- **Build Operate Transfer (BOT)** – **Build Operate Transfer** is a simple and conventional PPP model. Under this model, a **private player is responsible to design, build, operate and transfer the facility to the public sector** after an agreed period of time. Here the word 'operate' indicates that the private partner will operate the project for the contracted period and then it will be transferred back to the public sector. The private partner has the responsibility to finance, construct and maintain the project. **In return, they are allowed to collect the revenue** from the users of the facility. The projects of PPP under the National Highway Authority of India (**NHAI**) are the major examples of the BOT model. It **reduces the responsibility of the Government** to maintain the project. The present issue with the BOT model is that most of the private sector infrastructural entities have huge debts and are now unable to get loans or capital to invest in the projects. Thereby, investments have declined in highways. Thus, **as an alternative to BOT, the Hybrid Annuity Model** was brought in to counter the failure of BOT model in recent times.

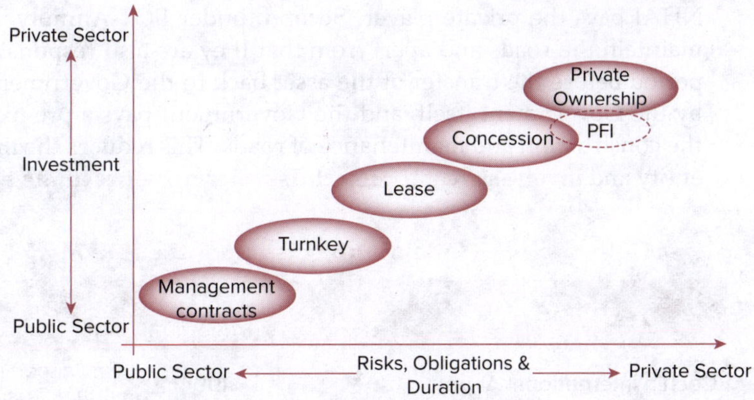

Basic features of PPP models

- **Build Own Operate (BOO)** – **Build Own Operate** model is a variant of the BOT model but the **ownership rests with the private partner**. Under BOO, there are mutual agreements between the public and private sector partners about the purchase of goods and services under the model.
- **Build Operate Lease Transfer (BOLT)** – Under **Build Operate Lease Transfer** model, the **Government provides a concession to the private partner to build the project and lease the project to the Government**. In return, the Government will pay the lease charges for a specific lease period and then on the completion of this period, the project is transferred to the Government.
- **Build Rehabilitate Operate Transfer (BROT)** – It is a variant of the BOT arrangement. Under the BROT arrangement, a private developer builds an add-on to an existing facility or completes a partially built facility and rehabilitates existing assets, then operates and maintains the facility at its own risk for the contract period. BROT is a popular form of PPP in the **water sector**. Recently, Assam has opted is model for one of its projects.
- **Lease Develop Operate (LDO)** – **Lease Develop Operate model** allows the **Government or the public sector to retain the ownership of the project** which is developed and operated by the private partner. Government receives payments from the private player based on the lease agreement. The most appropriate example under this model is the **facilities at airport**.
- **Engineering, Procurement and Construction (EPC)** – **Engineering, Procurement and Construction** is one of the oldest types of contracting agreement in the construction industry. Under EPC, the **companies are responsible for the designing, construction, execution and delivery of the project**. Companies that deliver EPC projects are also known as EPC contractors. The asset is transferred to the Government after it is made. In this model, **funds have to be invested by the Government**. Due to limited fiscal space of the Government, the BOT model was preferred in the 1990s and 2000s. However, **in recent years, several projects have been awarded by the NHAI on EPC basis** due to financial incapacity of the private sector.
- **Hybrid Annuity Model (HAM)** – **Hybrid Annuity Model** is the combination of EPC and BOT models. **This model combines 40 per cent EPC and 60 per cent BOT-Annuity**. It was basically introduced **for road infrastructure projects**. NHAI has awarded around 30 projects under the HAM model. This model **works in two phases**; first under EPC model, roads are laid and for this

NHAI pays the private player. Second, under BOT-Annuity, private partners build, operate and maintain the roads and apart from that they are also responsible for toll collection for a specified period before the transfer of the asset back to the Government. But the toll revenue risk is taken by the Government itself, and the Government pays a pre-fixed annuity to the private sector for the construction and maintenance of roads. This reduces the financial burden on the private sector entity and **involves greater project risk sharing between the two**.

Major Projects under the PPP Model in India

Projects	Year of Agreement	Remarks
Cochin International Airport	1994	First airport in India developed under the PPP model
Jawaharlal Nehru Port (Maharashtra)	1999	Developed under the BOT model
Kakinada Deepwater Port (Andhra Pradesh)	1999	Developed under the BOT model
Golden Quadrilateral	2001	It is a National Highway network connecting four major metro cities in India – Delhi (North), Kolkata (East), Mumbai (West) and Chennai (South). Delhi to Kolkata – NH19 Delhi to Mumbai – NH48 Mumbai to Chennai – NH48 Chennai to Kolkata – NH16
Gangavaram Port (Andhra Pradesh)	2002	Developed under the BOOT model
Mumbai–Pune Expressway (Maharash-tra)	2004	Developed under the BOT model
Mumbai Metro (Maharashtra)	2007	Developed under the BOOT model
Hyderabad Metro (Andhra Pradesh)	2010	Developed under the BOT model
Ahmedabad, Lucknow, Mangalore Airport	2020	Being developed under the Concession model
Bangalore Airport Extension (Karnataka)	2020	Being developed under the BOT model

Advantages of the PPP Model

- **Efficiency of the private sector entity in planning and execution** is generally better than that of the traditional public sector enterprises.
- **Expertise and skills** of private enterprises often bring in international experience and high-end technology.
- Since the funds are generally invested by a private player, the **funding requirement of creating new physical infrastructure for Government is lowered**.
- **Users pay the charges** for the created infrastructure and **not the taxpayers**.
- Infrastructure development takes place at a **greater speed** and in an efficient manner.

- **Project risks are shared** between the Government and the private sector.

Disadvantages of the PPP Model

- While PPP in physical infrastructure may be suitable, it **may not be suitable and feasible for delivery of social infrastructure** such as education and health as they do not have profit implications.
- **Control of Government is reduced** over such service providers.
- **User charges** under PPP are often high, making the services inaccessible to vulnerable sections of the society.
- **Aggressive bidding** makes proper completion of the projects difficult.
- There still lie pertinent issues **with respect to the audit** of PPP arrangements.
- There are often **feasibility issues** in various such PPP projects.

Present Challenges with respect to PPP in Infrastructure Projects

EXAM ESSENTIAL

- **Slowdown in economy** led to pessimistic business sentiments and high interest rates. As a result, lending to the highways sector got restricted.
- The financial challenges worsened due to **aggressive traffic projections** to access funds and achieve financial closure.
- Lack of efficient project preparation activities. **DPR (Detailed Project Report) is not prepared efficiently**, leading to costs overruns later.
- Delay in land acquisition.
- Delay in obtaining approvals and clearances (multiple clearances at the Centre, State and local levels).
- Overleveraged balance sheet of developers.
- **Absence of dedicated PPP policy** or regulation at the national level.
- Huge **dependency on commercial banks** for PPP financing.
- **Aggressive bidding** is one of the major reasons for delays or cancellation of PPP projects as banks are becoming more and more cautious in funding such projects. It also causes low participation from genuine bidders.
- Due to the long-term nature of PPP contracts, uncertain market conditions, lack of capacity at both Government and private player levels, etc., **disputes are bound to arise** during the life cycle of PPP projects.
- With regard to airports, **land acquisition** for a greenfield airport has become difficult despite the top-level push. Suggested Reforms under the PPP Approach
- Generally, at present, long-term project risks are being totally borne by the private sector. **Balanced risk-sharing** between the Government and private party (concessionaire) is needed. This can be done by **proper and transparent mechanism for viability gap funding.**
- **Avoiding a *one-size-fits-all approach***: restructuring PPP contracts based on requirements for each project.
- Robust dispute resolution mechanism.
- **Proper exit norms.**

- Delay in environmental clearances, etc. need to be reduced. Ideally, **'Plug and Play' model should be adopted** wherein clearances are taken before the projects are awarded to the private player/concessionaire. It helps in reducing time and cost overruns.
- **Adequate availability of funds** for the private sector: private sector participants should have access to long-term credit, especially credit from international markets. Also, financing costs of the projects should be lowered for ensuring financial viability.
- Ensuring **fair and optimum user charges**.
- **Re-negotiation** of contracts should be done **only in selected cases**. It is often seen that private sector players indulge in aggressive bidding to get the contract and then seek to re-negotiate contracts by demanding more resources (*by projecting lower revenue realisation or unseen rise in costs*).
- Strengthening the **regulatory regime** through independent regulators.
- **Faster land acquisition** is required (*for example, the case of UDAN scheme related to regional air connectivity*).

BONUS KNOWLEDGE

KELKAR COMMITTEE ON PPP

The **Committee on Revisiting and Revitalising the PPP model of Infrastructure Development** (Chaired by Dr Vijay Kelkar) submitted its report to the Finance Ministry in **2015**. The key recommendations were:

- **To amend the Prevention of Corruption Act, 1988,** and other conduct rules. It punishes even genuine errors in decision-making. There is a need to protect bureaucrats for decisions made with bona fide intention.
- Inequitable allocation of risk in PPPs should be reduced. ***One-size-fits-all* approach should be avoided.** Sector- and project-specific contexts should be kept in mind.
- Presently, PPP projects have a **long gestation period** of over 20–30 years. A private entity is at a disadvantage when there are changes in the economic or policy environment which are beyond its control.
- A **quick dispute resolution mechanism** for PPP projects is required.
- PPP should **focus more on service delivery** rather than fiscal savings.
- There should be a **national PPP policy or law**.
- **Capacity building** is needed for regulators and other stakeholders.
- Establishment of Infrastructure PPP Project Review Committee **(IPRC)** and Infrastructure PPP Adjudicatory Tribunal **(IPAT)**.
- Kelkar Committee also recommended for **implementation of GST**.

Airports and PPP

India has become the **third largest aviation market** in the world and is also one of the fastest growing markets in the world. Large **increase in the number of passengers** is putting a strain on the existing major airports, and also there has been demand for accessible and affordable regional air connectivity for which the **UDAN scheme** has been launched by the Government.

PPP in aviation sector brings **expertise, funding, better managerial practices and international experience**.

Due to funding constraints of the Government and the Airports Authority of India (AAI), PPP route has been adopted to modernise the airports.

Several airports in India have already been **developed** in the PPP mode, namely **New Delhi, Mumbai, Bengaluru, Kochi, and Hyderabad.** AAI has leased out six of its airports at Lucknow, Ahmedabad, Mangaluru, Jaipur, Guwahati, and Thiruvananthapuram for better operations, management, and development of these airports under PPP mode.

Several other greenfield airports are also in the pipeline.

However, challenges for airport development through PPP are:

- The biggest challenge is undoubtedly **land acquisition**. Airports require vast area/patch of land, and its acquisition has been difficult due to protests and demand for compensation.
- Funding constraints.
- Clearances from **the state Govern**ment.
- Poor planning and cost overruns.
- **Pressure on AAI** to manage large number of airports
- Viability issues, especially with regard to smaller airports.
- Policy and regulatory uncertainties.
- Reluctance of airlines to operate in smaller aircrafts.

PPP Opportunities in Railways

Indian railways operate the **fourth largest railways network** in the world. Being the lifeline of the nation, the Indian railways require a huge amount of investments for operations and modernisations. Recently, Indian railways have invited investments in PPP model not only for the capital requirements but also the private sector domain expertise.

Objectives

1. Supplementing Government investment in rail infrastructure projects by private capital flows.
2. Involving the States in creation/development of rail infrastructure for the common public good.
3. Timely creation of rail transport capacity to avoid supply-demand mismatch.
4. Ensuring availability of transport needs consistent with the expected GDP growth.

PPP Models related to Railways

1. **Non-Government Railway Model:** First and last mile connectivity projects at either end of the rail transportation chain providing connectivity to ports, mines, logistics parks or industries.
2. **Special Purpose Vehicle (SPV) Model:** Applicable for sanctioned bankable new line and Gauge Conversion projects having clearly identifiable stakeholders either as user of the line or of the utilities such as ports, mines, exporters, plants and the State Governments.
3. **Railway Projects on BOT awarded through Competitive Bidding:** Applicable to the sanctioned Railway projects where it is not possible to identify a stakeholder or strategic investor who can take a lead in making investment in the project line. The projects under this model will generally be long rail corridors carrying traffic generated from various streams.
4. **Connectivities funded by users, but to be used as multi-user lines:** The project developer will develop, construct and maintain the line as per IR standards. IR shall operate the line, collect the freight and pay 50 per cent of the apportioned earning computed.
5. **Capacity Augmentation (Doubling/Thirdline/Fourth line, etc.) with funding provided by customers:** This model addresses doubling/multiple line projects where some customers are

beneficiaries of the capacity addition and may be interested in funding the project for expeditious completion/commissioning.

Swiss Challenge Method of PPP

The Swiss challenge method is a process of awarding project contracts to private players. Any person with credentials can submit a development proposal. The government then puts the details of the project out in the public and invites proposals from others interested in executing it. On receipt of these bids, the original contractor gets an opportunity to match the best bid. If it can match, then it gets the contract; if not, the most suitable bidder after it gets the chance.

This method is used in India by different states including Karnataka, Andhra Pradesh, Rajasthan, Gujarat, etc. for IT, ports, power, health, roads and housing projects.

The following diagram shows how a Swiss Challenge Method works:

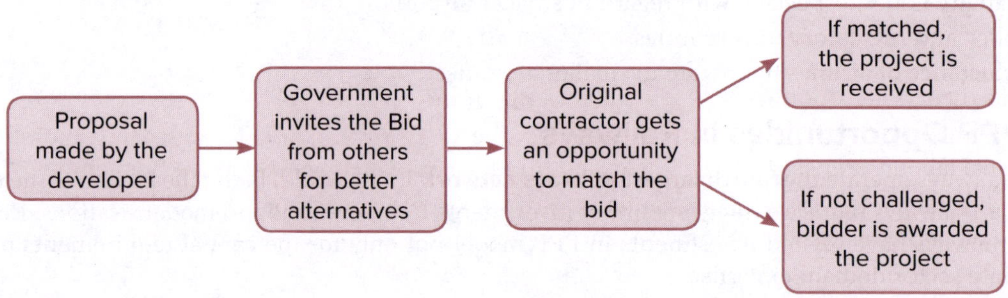

BONUS KNOWLEDGE

VIABILITY GAP FUNDING (VGF) SCHEME

The VGF scheme was **launched in 2004** to support **infrastructure projects** covered under PPPs. VGF means a grant to support projects that are not economically viable. In December 2020, the *Cabinet Committee on Economic Affairs* has approved the updated VGF scheme to support PPPs in social infrastructure along with extending the existing scheme to continue support to core sector infrastructure.

The revamped VGF scheme has two sub-schemes with a total outlay of ₹8,100 crore.

Sub-scheme 1 supports social sector projects such as wastewater treatment, water supply, solid waste management, health and education sectors, etc.

Sub-scheme 2 supports demonstration or pilot projects in the health and education sector.

The aim of the updated VGF scheme is to promote PPPs in social and economic infrastructure and to ensure their proper operation and maintenance. It will make the economically and socially essential projects commercially viable.

ECONOMIC PLANNING AND USE OF INVESTMENT MODELS THEREIN

Harrod–Domar Model (HDM)

- It was independently developed **by Ray F. Harrod 1939 and Eusey Domar in 1946**. According to this, there are three kinds of growth rate:

1. **Warranted growth rate** is the growth rate under which all savings are absorbed into investment.
2. **Actual growth rate** is the real increase in the GDP of economy.
3. **Natural growth rate** is the rate required to maintain full employment.

- This model explains the economic growth of a country and states that the **growth depends on the quantity of labour force and capital**. It suggests that **more investments result in capital accumulation which leads to economic growth**.
- **According to HDM, the growth rate is influenced by two main factors:**
  1. **Rate of investment.**
  2. **Productivity of investments**, i.e., **capital output ratio**, which is the ratio between capital and output. For instance, if to get an output of ₹5, capital of ₹20 is required, then the capital output ratio will be 4. A **lower** *capital output ratio is always better* for an economy as it indicates that investment is more efficient, resulting in higher economic growth rate.

As per HDM, **Rate of Economic Growth = Rate of Investment/Capital Output Ratio**

Lewis Model of Economic Development

- This theory of economic development is based on the **use of unlimited supply of labour**.
- The unlimited supply of labour is available due to (i) subsistence wages of agricultural labour, casual labour, domestic servants, etc. and (ii) the continuous increase in the population.
- In this model, Lewis states that capitalists attract surplus labour from the above-mentioned sectors at a bit higher wages than the subsistence wage – for economic development and to enhance profit.
- Lewis explained this method of development in terms of **inter-sectoral relationship in a dual economy** of capitalists and subsistence sector.
- In India, the Lewis model was **used for industrial development by former prime minister Jawaharlal Nehru**.
- **Agricultural sector** of India has huge number of surplus labourers, and if these surplus labourers are taken away, then the net output of agricultural sector will not be affected. These surplus labourers are attracted at a bit higher wages for industrial development and growth of the country.

Solow–Swan Model

It is an **extension to the HDM**. It relates to **long-run** economic growth with the population growth, capital accumulation, increase in productivity and technological progress.

Feldman–Mahalanobis Model

It is one type of neo-Marxian economic model developed independently by Grigory Feldman in 1928 and Prasanta Chandra Mahalanobis in 1953. This model suggests that **to reach a high standard of consumption, investment is essentially required to increase the capacity for the production of capital goods**. This model also **focuses on rapid industrialisation** and advocates for **huge imports** through foreign loans. The model was adopted by the Government of India actively during the **2nd Five Year Plan** (1956–61).

Rao-Manmohan Model

This model, named after Prime Minister P.V. Narasimha Rao and then Finance Minister Dr. Manmohan Singh, is widely associated with the economic liberalisation of the Indian economy in 1991.

Key features of this model are:

- **Economic liberalisation:** It entails lowering government regulation of the economy, eliminating licensing restrictions, and promoting private sector involvement.
- **Structural Reforms:** Changing industrial, financial, and trade policies to increase productivity and competitiveness.
- **Global Integration:** Using trade liberalisation to integrate India into the world economy and promote FDI.

BONUS KNOWLEDGE

Blended Finance

According to OECD (Organization for Economic Cooperation and Development), 'Blended finance is the strategic use of development finance for the mobilisation of **additional finance towards sustainable development in developing countries**'.

Blended finance entices commercial capital towards the projects that contribute to a sustainable development and provide financial returns to the investors. This is an innovative approach to augment the total amount of resources in developing countries, complementing their own investments and fill their SDG financing gap.

Plug and Play Model

Government promotes innovative 'plug and play infrastructure' approach to attract investment. In Plug and Play concept, **Government supervises the prerequisites for a business**-like electricity, water supply, road connectivity, etc.; regulatory clearances are put in place, then the project is awarded to the private firms through an auction; firms do not need to manage the basic needs to set up a business. The 'plug and play' scheme had first gained its ground in the Union Budget 2015–16.

Take-out Financing

Take-out financing intends to provide finance **for longer duration projects** and acquire infrastructure loans given by the Commercial Banks from their book by specially created infrastructure lending institutions to prevent any asset-liability mismatch. **Infrastructure Development Finance Corporation** was set up to put aside a corpus from the Union Budget to promote infrastructure funding. India Infrastructure Finance Company was also set up to refinance infrastructure loans of Commercial Banks.

SUMMARY

- **Investment** – Exchange of money for better return or profit-yielding assets – highly appreciated for the economic growth and development of a nation.
- **Gross Investment** = GDP – (Consumption + Government Expenditure + Net Exports)
- **Factors affecting investments** – Tax rate – inflation – possible rate of returns on capital investment – availability of factors of production.
- **Induced Investment** – Varies in accordance with the income and profit – increase in income and profit implies increase in induced investment.
- **Autonomous Investment** – Independent of factors like income and profit – mostly associated with social welfare – occurs due to increase in population, development of new technology, etc.

- **Investment Multiplier (IM)** – Has positive impact not only on the prescribed project but also on many other dimensions of economy – higher IM indicates efficient creation and distribution of wealth in that economy.
- **Incremental Capital Output Ratio (ICOR)** – Ratio of annual investment to annual increase in GDP – measures the level of production efficiency of an economy.
- **Public–Private Partnership Model** – Legal relationship is defined between the Government or a Government-owned entity and a private sector entity for a specified period – regulated by the Department of Economic Affairs, Ministry of Finance – well-defined allocation of risk between the private and public entity.
- **Feldman–Mahalanobis Model** – Neo-Marxian model – to reach a high standard of consumption, investment is essentially required to increase the capacity for the production of capital goods – focuses on heavy industrialisation – adopted in second five-year plan in India.
- **Rao–Manmohan Model** – Associated with economic liberalisation, structural reforms and global integration.

UPSC CSE PREVIOUS YEARS' PRELIMINARY EXAMINATION QUESTIONS

☞ NO QUESTIONS ASKED
2024, 2023, 2022, 2021, 2020, 2019, 2018, 2017, 2016, 2015, 2014, 2013

UPSC CSE PREVIOUS YEARS' MAIN EXAMINATION QUESTIONS

1. Why is Public Private Partnership (PPP) required in infrastructural projects? Examine the role of PPP model in the redevelopment of Railway Stations in India. **[2022]**
2. Explain the meaning of investment in an economy in terms of capital formation. Discuss the factors to be considered while designing a concession agreement between a public entity and a private entity. **[2020]**
3. Among several factors for India's potential growth, **savings rate** is the most effective one. Do you agree? What are the **other factors available for growth potential**? **[2017]**
4. Examine the development of airports in India through joint ventures under the **Public–Private Partnership model**. What are the **challenges faced by the authorities** in this regard? **[2017]**
5. Justify the **need for FDI** for the development of the Indian economy. Why there is a **gap between MOUs signed and actual FDIs**? Suggest **remedial steps** to be taken for increasing actual FDIs in India. **[2016]**
6. Explain how **Private–Public Partnership arrangements** in long gestation infrastructure projects can transfer unsustainable liabilities to the future. What arrangements need to be put in place to ensure that **successive generations' capacities are not compromised**? **[2014]**
7. Adoption of **PPP model for infrastructure development** of the country has not been free from criticism. Critically discuss the **pros and cons** of the model. **[2013]**

☞ NO QUESTIONS ASKED
2024, 2023, 2021, 2019, 2018, 2015

CHAPTER

35

SUSTAINABLE DEVELOPMENT AND CLIMATE CHANGE

CHAPTER OUTLINE

- The Club of Rome and Limits to Growth
- Brundtland Commission and Our Common Future
- The Earth Summit
- Millennium Summit and the United Nations Millennium Declaration
- Millennium Development Goals
- Rio+20
- Sustainable Development Solutions Network (SDSN)
- Sustainable Development Goals
- SDG India Index
- Sustainable Climate Finance
- Global Climate Risk Index and India
- Climate Change Performance Index (CCPI)
- Climate Change Action Plan (CCAP)
- Concept of Inter-generational and Intra-generational Equity of Sustainable Development
- Recent Concepts in News

The **green economy** can be defined as an economy that aims for sustainable development by **reducing environmental risks and ecological scarcities**. It is a macroeconomic approach which aims to generate employment and income by investing in such economic activities, assets and infrastructure that reduce carbon emission and pollution and enhance energy efficiency. It is socially inclusive, protects environment and prevents the loss of biodiversity.

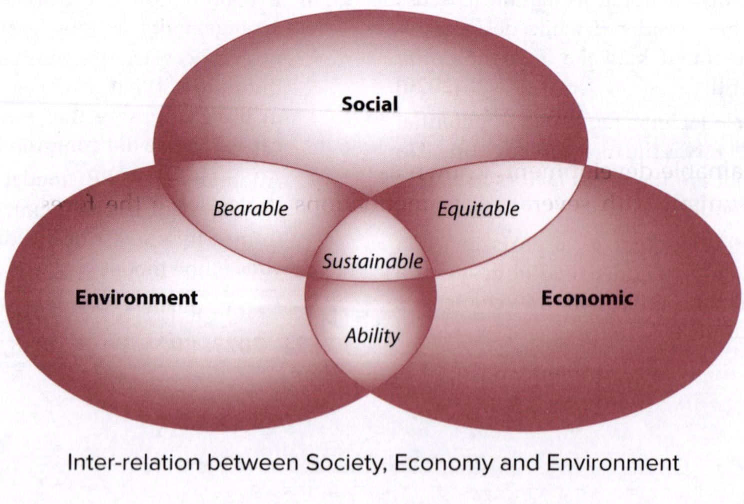

Inter-relation between Society, Economy and Environment

THE CLUB OF ROME AND LIMITS TO GROWTH

The Club of Rome was founded in **1968** in Rome, Italy. It addresses the multiple crises and humanity and planet facing challenges, and seeks comprehensive solutions. The Club consists of around **100 members** of notable economists, scientists, business leaders, politicians, etc. The key areas of impact like climate-planetary emergency, reclaiming and reframing economics, youth leadership, etc. are prioritised by the Club.

The **Club's seminal report, The Limits to Growth,** was published in **1972**. It marched for the global sustainability movement and alerted the world to the consequences of the human activities and the health of our planet. The report highlighted the nature and limits to growth of economy with limited resources, technology and limits to growth, the state of global equilibrium, etc.

BRUNDTLAND COMMISSION AND OUR COMMON FUTURE

The Brundtland Commission, also known as the **World Commission on Environment and Development** (WCED), was created to help the nations towards the goal of sustainable development. It operated from 1983 to 1987 and published the Brundtland report – *Our Common Future* – in **1987**. The report defined sustainable development as the **'development which meets the needs of current generations without compromising the ability of future generations to meet their own needs'**.

BONUS KNOWLEDGE

THE EARTH CHARTER

The concept of the Earth charter was postulated in 1987 by **Maurice Strong and Mikhail Gorbachev** (members of Club of Rome) to guide the Sustainable Development. The EC is an ethical foundation for actions, it intends to build a more just, sustainable and peaceful global society in the 21st century.

THE EARTH SUMMIT

The delegates from 178 nations met in **Rio De Janeiro**, in **June 1992**, for the largest UN conference – 'The United Nations Conference on Environment and Development **(UNCED)**' also known as **'The Earth Summit'**. The summit was intended to put sustainable development at the forefront and to frame common action plan to stop environmental degradation. An action plan was framed in this summit with regard to sustainable development, known as **'Agenda 21'**. A **non-legally binding** document was presented in this summit with several recommendations to conserve the forestry known as **'Forest Principles'**.

- **Outcome documents of the Earth Summit**: Rio Declaration on Environment and Development, Agenda 21, Forest Principles.
- **Important legally binding agreements that were signed**: Convention on Biological Diversity (CBD), UN Framework Convention on Climate Change (UNFCCC), United Nations Convention to Combat Desertification (UNCCD).

MILLENNIUM SUMMIT AND THE UNITED NATIONS MILLENNIUM DECLARATION

The Millennium Summit was held **in 2000**, at the United Nations' headquarters in New York City. It was aimed to analyse the role of the United Nations in the 21st century. The United Nations Millennium Declaration was ratified by world leaders to eradicate poverty, hunger, disease, illiteracy, environmental degradation and discrimination against women.

Millennium Development Goals (MDGs)

The United Nations Millennium Development Goals (MDGs) are the **eight goals** set by the 189 UN Member States in September 2000 after the UN Millennium Declaration. It set out time-bound goals with a deadline of **2015**. Such eight MDGs were:

1. Eradicate extreme poverty and hunger
2. Achieve universal primary education
3. Promote gender equality and empower women
4. Reduce child mortality
5. Improve maternal health
6. Combat HIV/AIDS, Malaria and other diseases
7. Ensure environmental sustainability
8. Develop a global partnership for development

The final MDG Report found that the 15-year effort has produced the **most successful anti-poverty movement** in history:

1. Since 1990, the number of people living in extreme poverty has declined by more than half.
2. The proportion of undernourished people in the developing regions has fallen by almost half.
3. The primary school enrolment rate in the developing regions has reached 91 per cent, and many more girls are now in school compared to 15 years ago.

RIO+20

The *United Nations Conference on Sustainable Development* **(UNCSD or Rio+20)** was held in Rio de Janeiro, Brazil, in **2012**. Rio+20 re-energised the political commitment to sustainable development and its dimensions on economic growth, social improvement and environmental protection. Rio+20 **focused on the Green economy** in the context of sustainable development and poverty eradication and to develop an institutional framework for sustainable development. The United Nations High-level Political Forum on Sustainable Development **(HLPF)** was established in 2013 and mandated in 2012 by the outcome document of Rio+20 – **'The Future We Want'**.

SUSTAINABLE DEVELOPMENT SOLUTIONS NETWORK (SDSN)

The UN Sustainable Development Solutions Network (SDSN) was set up **in 2012**. SDSN mobilises scientific and technological expertise and promotes practical solutions for sustainable development. It supports the implementation of the Sustainable Development Goals (SDGs) and the Paris Climate Agreement. The **World Happiness Report** is published by the SDSN.

Sustainable Development Goals

After MDGs, the **Sustainable Development Goals (SDGs) were adopted** by all United Nations Member States **in 2015**, to end poverty, protect the planet and ensure that all people enjoy peace and prosperity by 2030. The **17 SDGs** are integrated – that is, they recognise that action in one area will affect outcomes in others, and that development must balance social, economic and environmental sustainability.

SDGs also recognised the need of localised modifications of the goals to be more effective in respective countries.

Last Minute SNIPPETS

In India, **NITI Aayog is monitoring the progress of SDGs** in the country. In 2018, **Haryana** became the **first state** in India to have its annual budget focused on the attainment of SDGs.

India has secured 109th rank with overall score of 64.0 in the Sustainable Development Report 2024.

SUSTAINABLE DEVELOPMENT GOALS

Source: Deni Nandar Sukanwar/Shutterstock

BONUS KNOWLEDGE

SPILLOVER RANKINGS

Different countries' actions have positive or negative impacts on other countries' abilities to carry through the SDGs.

The Spillover Index assesses such spillovers along 3 dimensions:

(i) environmental and social impacts embodied into trade,

(ii) economy and finance, and

(iii) security.

A higher spillover score indicates a country causes more positive and fewer negative spillover effects.

Spillover score of India was 95.74 in the Sustainable Development Report 2024.

EXAM ESSENTIAL

Green Climate Fund (GCF) – At COP 16 held in Cancun (in 2010), the Green Climate Fund (GCF) was established within the framework of the **UNFCCC**. The Fund is governed by the GCF Board. GCF is intended to mobilise a flow of climate finance to invest in low-emission and climate-resilient development.

Global Environment Facility (GEF) – The Global Environment Facility (GEF) was set up on the eve of the **1992 Earth Summit**. Through strategic investments, the GEF works to tackle the planet's most pressing environmental problems. The **GEF Small Grants Programme** provides financial support to civil society and community initiatives in different countries.

Clean Development Mechanism (CDM) – The Clean Development Mechanism is defined in **Article 12** of the **Kyoto Protocol**. A country with an emission-reduction commitment under the Kyoto Protocol (Annex B Party) is allowed to implement an emission-reduction project in developing countries. Such projects can generate tradable **Certified Emission Reduction (CER) credits**, each credit is equivalent to **one tonne of CO_2** and it can be counted towards meeting Kyoto targets.

Adaptation Fund (AF) – The Adaptation Fund (AF) was established **in 2001** under the **Kyoto Protocol** of the UNFCCC, it was set up at CoP 7 in Marrakech, Morocco. It aims to finance projects in developing countries to adapt to climate change.

The Fund is financed by Governments and private donors, and from a 2 per cent share of proceeds of Certified Emission Reductions (CERs) issued under the Clean Development Mechanism (CDM) projects. The Fund is supervised and managed by the Adaptation Fund Board (AFB).

Ministry of Environment, Forest and Climate Change, GoI, is the **National Designated Authority (NDA)** for Adaptation Fund. **NABARD** was accredited as **National Implementing Entity (NIE)** for Adaptation Fund in 2012.

The National Adaptation Fund for Climate Change **(NAFCC)** was set up to promote adaptation activities in the States and Union Territories of India.

The Ministry of Environment, Forest and Climate Change marked the Hazard Line for the mainland coast of India under the Integrated Coastal Zone Management (ICZM) project. The Coastal Regulation Zone Notification 2019 was notified to protect the ecology of coastal stretches and marine areas to foster sustainable development.

SDG India Index

NITI Aayog released SDG India Index and Dashboard **from 2019**. India is the first country in the world to develop a Government-led, sub-national measure of progress on SDGs. The *SDG India Index* was developed in collaboration with the **Ministry of Statistics and Programme Implementation (MoSPI), United Nations in India, and Global Green Growth Institute**.

Last Minute SNIPPETS

SDG India Index 2023–24

- Overall SDG score for the country is 71 for 2023–24, improving from 66 in 2020–21 and 57 in 2018 (Baseline report).
- Significant progress is achieved in Goals 1 (No Poverty), 8 (Decent Work and Economic Growth), 13 (Climate Action) and 15 (Life on Land).
- Goal 13 (Climate Action) records highest increase in score from 54 in 2020–21 to 67 in 2023–24, followed by Goal 1 (No Poverty) from 60 to 72.
- Between 2018 and 2023–24, fastest moving States were Uttar Pradesh (increase in score by 25), followed by J&K (21), Uttarakhand (19), and Sikkim (18).

BONUS KNOWLEDGE

DECARBONISING TRANSPORT PROJECT

'Decarbonising Transport in Emerging Economics' was launched by **NITI Aayog** along with the **International Transport Forum** of OECD. The project allows India to implement its climate ambitions into action by providing an analytical assistant to point out the climate actions and by making policies based on data analysis.

NITI Aayog and World Resources Institute (WRI) India, jointly launched the '**Forum for Decarbonising Transport**'. It is a part of the NDC-Transport Initiative for Asia (NDC-TIA) project.

Indian Carbon Market (ICM) can help India to achieve the NDC goal of reduction of Emissions Intensity of the GDP by 45 per cent by 2030 compared to the 2005 levels.

SUSTAINABLE CLIMATE FINANCE

Climate finance is a term which refers to **financial resources for climate change mitigation, adaptation** or **resiliency**.

As per UNFCCC, *Climate Finance refers to finance that aims at reducing emissions, and enhancing sinks of greenhouse gases* and aims at reducing vulnerability of, and maintaining and increasing the resilience of, human and *ecological systems* to negative climate change impacts.

The related finance can come from private and public sources. It can be channelled by various intermediaries such as multilateral development banks or other development agencies. Those agencies are particularly important for the transfer of public resources from developed to developing countries in light of UN Climate Convention obligations that developed countries have.

There are two main sub-categories of climate finance, based on objectives:

1. **Mitigation** finance – that aims to reduce global carbon emissions.
2. **Adaptation** finance – that aims to respond to the consequences of climate change.

Globally, there is a **much greater focus on mitigation,** accounting for over 90 per cent of spending on climate. Renewable energy is an important growth area for mitigation investment and has growing policy support. Climate Finance can come from private and public sources. Financial Instruments such as green bonds, carbon offsetting, and payment for ecosystem services are some promoted solutions.

However, there are many challenges with climate finance. Firstly, there are **difficulties with measuring and tracking financial flows**. Secondly, there are also **questions around equitable financial support** to developing countries for cutting emissions and adapting to impacts. It is also **difficult to provide suitable incentives** for investments from the private sector.

The **UNFCCC, the Kyoto Protocol and the Paris Agreement** necessitated financial assistance from countries which have more financial resources to the more vulnerable countries.

Last Minute SNIPPETS

New Collective Quantified Goal (NCQG) on Climate Finance

At COP29, the countries agreed on a NCQG on climate finance, **aiming to triple climate finance for developing countries** to USD 300 billion annually **by 2035**, with developed countries taking the lead. The NCQG is a new global climate finance target. This finance is crucial for developing countries to adopt low-carbon technologies, protect themselves from climate threats, and achieve sustainable development.

This builds on the previous commitment to mobilise $100 billion per year by 2020, which was met in 2022.

Economic Survey 2020–21 highlighted the importance of **sustainable financing** to meet the Government's development priorities. It also mentioned few steps undertaken in this regard:

- **National Voluntary Guidelines for Responsible Financing**: It was finalised in 2015. These are financial sector-specific guidelines that combine and adapt international and national best practices.
- RBI included **lending** to **social infrastructure** and **small renewable energy projects** within the **priority sector targets**.
- **'Voluntary Guidelines on Corporate Social Responsibility'** were issued in 2009, to mainstream the concept of business responsibility.
- **A Committee** was constituted to review and update the **Business Responsibility Reporting** (BRR) formats for listed as well as unlisted companies.
- *Union Budget 2019–20* proposed the creation of a **Social Stock Exchange** under the regulatory ambit of SEBI for listing social enterprises and voluntary organisations.
- India has launched green indices such as S&P BSE CARBONEX (in 2012), MSCI ESG India (in 2013), S&P BSE 100 ESG Index (in 2017), etc. to allow passive and retail investors to invest in 'green' companies.
- The **RBI** has set up a new unit – **'Sustainable Finance Group' (SFG)** in 2021, within its Department of Regulation, to address the Climate change-related financial risks.
- **RBI** joined the Central Banks and Supervisors **Network for Greening the Financial System (NGFS)** in 2021. RBI published a *'Statement of Commitment to Support Greening India's Financial System – NGFS'* in 2021.
- **RBI** is a member of a Task Force on **Climate-related Financial Risks**, which was set up by the Basel Committee on Banking Supervision and the International Platform on Sustainable Finance.
- The **External Commercial Borrowings (ECBs)** norms of RBI have been liberalised and has enabled the Indian renewable energy companies and other firms to tap the ECB route to raise finance through green bonds and sustainable bonds.

did you KNOW?

The availability of adequate and affordable finance remains a serious impediment in India's climate actions. India has ratcheted up its efforts to mobilise private capital through sovereign green bonds to meet climate action goals.

- **Green Bonds** are financial instruments to generate proceeds for investment in climate-suitable and environmentally sustainable projects.

- **According to SEBI's data** on green debt securities, 15 Indian corporates issued green bonds of value ₹4,539 crore during the period of 2017 to 2022. (*Economic Survey 2022–23*)
- **The Union Budget 2022–23** has also announced the issue of Sovereign Green Bonds to reduce the carbon intensity of the economy.
- The Sovereign Green Bonds framework of India has been issued and designed to comply with the recommendations of the **International Capital Market Association (ICMA) Green Bond Principles (2021)**.
- The RBI published its **'Statement of Commitment to Support Greening India's Financial System' – Network for Greening the Financial System (NGFS) in 2021**.
- New sustainability reporting requirements have been issued by **SEBI, under the Business Responsibility and Sustainability Report (BRSR)**. The BRSR was made mandatory for the top 1000 listed entities (by market capitalisation) from 2022–23.
- **According to the IFC** – "**Blended Finance** for Climate Investments in India maintains that catalytic capital will be critical for investments in private sector climate projects in India."
- **'Greenium', or Green Premium,** is the pricing benefits based on the argument that investors are willing to pay extra or accept lower production in exchange for sustainable footprint. It refers to the additional cost of choosing sustainable technology.

- **India's initiatives at the international stage:**
  1. **International Solar Alliance (ISA)** has launched a **'World Solar Bank'** and **'One Sun One World One Grid Initiative'** – of global importance to bring about solar energy revolution globally. The proposed World Solar Bank would provide dedicated financing window for solar energy projects across the members of ISA.
  2. **Coalition for Disaster Resilient Infrastructure (CDRI)** was launched in **2019** at the **UN Climate Action Summit**. CDRI functions as an inclusive multi-stakeholder platform led and managed by national Governments, where knowledge is generated and exchanged on different aspects of disaster resilience infrastructure. The CDRI is co-chaired by **India and the United Kingdom**.
  3. In 2019, **International Platform on Sustainable Finance** was launched by the **European Union** together with the authorities of Argentina, Canada, Chile, China, India, Kenya and Morocco on the margins of the International Monetary Fund/World Bank annual meeting in Washington DC. **India joined in 2019** to increase the mobilisation of private capital towards environmentally sustainable investments.

Global Climate Risk Index and India

Global Climate Risk Index is published by German Watch, an Environment Think Tank. The purpose of this Index is to point out the climate-related adverse impacts on countries.

India has ranked 6th in the Climate Risk Index (CRI) 2025.

Climate Change Performance Index (CCPI)

CCPI aims to enhance transparency in international climate politics and enables **comparison of climate protection efforts** and progress made by individual countries. The index is released by Germanwatch.

The criteria for comparison includes **four categories**, with 14 indicators: GHG Emissions (40% of the overall score), Renewable Energy (20%), Energy Use (20%), and Climate Policy (20%). **India has ranked 10th in CCPI 2025.**

EXAM ESSENTIAL

KIGALI AMENDMENT

- The Kigali Amendment to the Montreal Protocol is an international, **legally binding** agreement entered into force in 2019 **to cut the production and use of hydrofluorocarbons (HFCs)**.
- Initially, the amendment was ratified by 65 countries. As of October, 2024, 164 states, including the European Union and India, have ratified the Kigali Amendment.
- **HFCs** are used as replacements of hydrochlorofluorocarbons **(HCFCs)** and chlorofluorocarbons **(CFCs)**, but they are powerful greenhouse gases with significant global warming potential.
- The Amendment aims a massive reduction in the use of HFCs, which is widely used as refrigerant substitutes for ozone-depleting substances that have been phased out under the Montreal Protocol.
- India has successfully achieved **the complete phase-out of hydrochlorofluorocarbon (HCFC)-141 b** – a chemical used mainly as a blowing agent in the production of rigid polyurethane (PU) foams. It is one of the most potent ozone-depleting chemicals after CFCs.

Intended Nationally Determined Contributions (INDC) are the climate pledges and intended reductions in greenhouse gas (GHG) emissions of countries under the UNFCCC. All countries that signed the UNFCCC were asked to declare their INDCs at the UN's 2013 climate negotiations in Warsaw (CoP 19). The INDC will become the first Nationally Determined Contribution (NDC) when a country ratifies the Paris agreement. India, with 4.1 per cent of the world's GHG emissions, became the 62nd country to ratify the Paris climate accord in 2016. **Greenco Rating System** is developed by Confederation of Indian Industry (CII) and it has been acknowledged in India's Intended Nationally Determined Contribution (INDC) document, submitted to UNFCCC in 2015.

BONUS KNOWLEDGE

NATIONALLY DETERMINED CONTRIBUTION (NDC)

An NDC is a set of long-term goals to cut carbon emissions and adapt to climate impacts that every country signatory to the Paris Agreement has to provide, and update every five years.

In 2022, the GOI approved India's updated Nationally Determined Contribution (NDC), to be submitted to the United Nations Framework Convention on Climate Change (UNFCCC) for the period up to 2030, comprising eight goals, as under:

1. To put forward and further propagate a healthy and sustainable way of living based on traditions and values of conservation and moderation, including through a mass movement for 'LIFE'– 'Lifestyle for Environment' as a key to combating climate change.
2. To adopt a climate friendly and a cleaner path than the one followed hitherto by others at corresponding level of economic development.
3. To reduce Emissions Intensity of its GDP by 45 per cent by 2030, from 2005 level.
4. To achieve about 50 per cent cumulative electric power installed capacity from non-fossil fuel-based energy resources by 2030, with the help of transfer of technology and low-cost international finance including from Green Climate Fund (GCF).
5. To create an additional carbon sink of 2.5 to 3 billion tonnes of CO_2 equivalent through additional forest and tree cover by 2030.

6. To better adapt to climate change by enhancing investments in development programmes in sectors vulnerable to climate change, particularly agriculture, water resources, Himalayan region, coastal regions, health and disaster management.
7. To mobilise domestic, new and additional funds from developed countries to implement the above mitigation and adaptation actions in view of the resource required and the resource gap.
8. To build capacities, create domestic framework and international architecture for quick diffusion of cutting edge climate technology in India and for joint collaborative R&D for such future technologies.

EXAM ESSENTIAL

KATOWICE CLIMATE PACKAGE

The Katowice Climate Package, a compilation of Paris Rulebook documents, was adopted at the 24th session of the UNFCCC climate change conference held in 2018 in Katowice, Poland. The key takeaways of Katowice package are the guidance on Nationally Determined Contributions (NDCs).

GLASGOW CLIMATE PACT

It is an agreement reached at the 2021 United Nations Climate Change Conference (COP26) of all countries that were parties to the Paris Agreement of 2015.

The Pact is planning **to reduce unabated coal usage**. According to the Glasgow Climate Pact, the use of unabated coal should be "phased down" for Coal in India, China and other coal reliant countries and abolition of fossil fuel subsidies. (*The pledge "phase out" was changed to "phase down", though India didn't replace 'phase out of coal with 'phase down' at COP 26*). The "Glasgow Climate Pact" also emphasises on adaptation, mitigation, finance, technology transfer, loss and damage etc.

CONCEPT OF INTER-GENERATIONAL AND INTRA-GENERATIONAL EQUITY OF SUSTAINABLE DEVELOPMENT

The principle of inter-generational equity refers to equity between generations. It includes duty of present generation towards future generations to preserve environment and natural resources, so that all future generations shall have an equal opportunity to enjoy nature.

The concept of Sustainable development also stipulates that the human societies must meet their needs without compromising the ability of future generations. The Brundtland Commission emphasised on the conservation of our planet and to protect future generation. The present generation should promote development that preserves the regenerative capacity of natural ecological system. To achieve sustainable development, we should limit the population within the carrying capacity of the planet, input efficient technologies and the green energy must be promoted.

The concept of intra-generational equity of sustainable development refers to equity between people of same generation. It deals with judicious distribution of resources.

To achieve intra-generational equity, notion of inclusive development, social and environmental justice must be promoted.

According to Rio Principle 6, 'The special situation and needs of developing countries, particularly the least developed and those most environmentally vulnerable, shall be given special priority. International actions in the field of environment and development should also address the interests and needs of all countries.'

The principle of ***Common but Differentiated Responsibilities*** was formalised in **Earth Summit 1992**. According to this principle all States are responsible for addressing the issues of global environmental degradation but they are not equally responsible, recognising the wide disparities in levels of economic development between different States.

The seminal report, 'Our Common Future', was published in 1987 which defined the term 'sustainable development'. Then, greater emphasis was given on the concept of intra-generational equity and the principle of CBDR was also included in several international environmental agreements.

The National Electric Mobility Mission Plan (NEMMP) 2020 is a National Mission document which provides the vision and the roadmap for the faster adoption of electric vehicles and their manufacturing in the country. This plan has been designed to enhance national fuel security and to provide affordable and environmentally friendly transportation.

Electric Vehicles (EVs) can drastically reduce carbon emissions:

- EVs are more energy efficient and can reduce greenhouse gas emission. Maintenance cost will also be lowered.
- They will lessen dependency on fossil fuels, gasoline products and expand the energy baskets.
- The transition from internal combustion engines to EV will cut down carbon dioxide emissions acutely and many other pollutants.

Low-Carbon Economy

A low-carbon economy refers to an economy that causes a minimal output of GHG emissions into the atmosphere, particularly carbon dioxide. In this economy, carbon trading is an effective component. Under the Kyoto Protocol climate agreement, carbon credits are utilised in market-oriented system of carbon trading. It permits countries and companies to sell their carbon credits for money.

Methanol Economy

Methanol is a low-carbon, hydrogen carrier fuel. It is produced from high ash coal, agricultural residue, CO_2 from thermal power plants, etc. Methanol Economy program is initiated **by NITI Aayog**. It is aimed to reduce import of crude oil and reduce GHG emissions. It also intends to convert coal reserves and municipal solid waste into methanol and set up Methanol Production Plants.

Blending of 15 per cent methanol in gasoline can result in at least 15 per cent reduction in import of gasoline/crude. It will reduce GHG emissions by 20 per cent in terms of particulate matter, NO*x* and SO*x*.

According to NITI Aayog, Methanol Economy will result in minimum 15 per cent of reduction in fuel bill, additionally, ₹6000 crore can be saved annually by blending of 20 per cent DME (di-methyl ether – a derivative of methanol) in LPG.

India is on track to decouple its economic growth from GHG emissions. As per the second Biennial Update Report (BUR) submitted to UNFCCC in 2018, India's emission intensity of GDP reduced by 21 per cent in 2014 over the level of 2005. To certify the use of cleaner automobile fuel, India has switched from BS-IV to BS-VI emission norms on 1 April, 2020.

India's first indigenously designed **High Ash Coal Gasification Based Methanol Production** Plant at BHEL R&D Centre, Hyderabad began working.

BONUS KNOWLEDGE

NATIONAL GREEN HYDROGEN MISSION (NGHM)

The NGHM was launched in **2023** with a vision to make India an energy-independent nation, and to de-carbonise critical sectors. The Mission is aimed facilitate demand creation, production, utilisation and export of Green Hydrogen and mobilisation of over ₹8 lakh crore investment by 2030.

Salient Features

- To create green hydrogen production capacity of at least 5 MMT per annum.
- Cumulative reduction in fossil fuel imports over ₹1 lakh crore and creation of over 6 lakh jobs.
- Renewable energy capacity addition of about 125 GW and abatement of nearly 50 MMT of annual GHG emissions.

Likely Outcomes by 2030

- Financial incentive targeting domestic manufacturing of electrolysers and production of Green Hydrogen.
- Regions capable of supporting large scale production and/or utilisation of Hydrogen to be developed as Green Hydrogen Hubs.

Aimed Interventions

- Development of an enabling policy framework to support establishment of Green Hydrogen ecosystem.
- Robust Standards and Regulations framework.
- Public-private partnership framework for R&D.
- Skill development programme Policy Framework.

Recent Initiatives

- GAIL launched project of blending Hydrogen in City Gas Distribution grid.
- 2 per cent by volume of hydrogen is blended in CNG network, 5 per cent by volume of hydrogen is blended in PNG network at City Gas Station of Avantika Gas Limited (AGL), Indore.
- Hydrogen-based Fuel-Cell Electric Vehicle (FCEV) Buses were launched in Leh by NTPC.

Source: Ministry of New and Renewable Energy

EXAM ESSENTIAL

EMISSIONS GAP REPORT

United Nations Environment Programme's (**UNEP's**) Emissions Gap Report provides a yearly review of the difference between where GHG emissions are predicted to be in 2030 and where they should be, to avoid the worst impacts of climate change.

According to the Emission Gap Report 2024:

- Cutting off greenhouse gases by 42% is needed by 2030 and 57% by 2035 to get on track for 1.5°C pathway.
- A failure to increase ambition in these new NDCs and start delivering immediately would put the world on a temperature increase of 2.6–3.1°C over the course of this century.

ADAPTATION GAP REPORT

- The report is annually published by United Nations Environment Programme (**UNEP**). It assesses the planning, progress, financing and implementation of adaptation actions.

As per the 2024 report:

- The progress in adaptation financing is not enough to bridge the gap between needs and flows, which may lag in adaptation planning and implementation targets.
- International public adaptation finance flows to the developing countries enhanced from US$22 billion in 2021 to US$28 billion in 2022.

Other reports published by UNEP:

Global Resources Outlook, Global Chemicals Outlook, Global Waste Management Outlook, Global Environmental Outlook, etc.

Emission Trading

Emission trading, which is set out in **Article 17 of the Kyoto Protocol**, allows countries to sell the excess capacity of emissions – 'permitted to them but not used' – to the countries that have already crossed their targets.

Gujarat unveiled India's first **emissions trading scheme** to slash air pollution. It allows industries to buy and sell permits to stay below the cap, emissions trading programme is aimed to cut particulate air pollution and facilitate sustainable economic growth.

To reduce the carbon emissions, China has issued first **tradable forest carbon credit stamps** to utilise the market mechanisms.

BONUS KNOWLEDGE

SEA LEVEL RISE

- Fifth Assessment Report (AR5) of Intergovernmental Panel of IPCC indicated that global mean sea level rose by 190 mm over the period 1901–2010.
- In IPCC report of 2019, it was projected about 0.6 to 1.1 m global sea level rise by 2100.
- Sea level rise has been a major threat for India and other coastal nations.
- Sea level rise has the potential cascading impacts which may lead to losses of coastal ecosystems and services. It may lead to devastating coastal flood, groundwater salinisation, destruction of coastal infrastructure, climate refugee crisis and many other severe harmful implications.

EXAM ESSENTIAL

GREEN GDP

Green GDP is the index of the economic growth of a specific nation which takes into consideration the environmental consequences of the economic growth. To calculate Green GDP, from the final goods and services produced, the cost of natural consumption (i.e. **resource depletion**, **environmental degradation**, etc.) is subtracted. It is a measure of how a country is prepared for sustainable economic development. Centre is initiating the measurement of green GDP of the States.

However, it is **quite difficult to estimate Green GDP** as there are serious challenges in quantifying the amount of depletion in resources or of environmental degradation.

Green Tax – The *Ministry of Road Transport and Highways* has approved a proposal to levy a 'Green Tax' on old vehicles which are polluting the environment.

- Transport vehicles older than 8 years could be charged Green Tax at the time of renewal of fitness certificate, at the rate of 10 per cent to 25 per cent of road tax.
- Personal vehicles to be charged Green Tax at the time of renewal of Registration Certification after 15 years.
- Public transport vehicles, such as city buses, to be charged lower Green tax.
- Higher Green tax (50% of Road Tax) for vehicles being registered in highly polluted cities.

Green Tax will dissuade people from using vehicles which damage the environment and motivate to switch to newer, less polluting vehicles. Green tax is intended to reduce the pollution level, and make the polluter pay for pollution.

Gross Environment Product (GEP) – By implementing the concept and calculation of the GEP we shall understand the impact of anthropological pressure on our ecosystem and natural resources – air, water, soil, forests. This will enable us to make policies which will allow sustainable development. **Uttarakhand is the first State to measure GEP.**

GREEN CREDIT PROGRAMME (GCP)

Green Credit Initiative was launched by India at COP 28. It is included under the Lifestyle for Environment or LIFE movement. The Green Credit Rules, 2023, were notified in 2023 under the Environment Protection Act, 1986. The mechanism intends to foster voluntary environmental positive actions and issuance of green credits. The initiative is independent of the carbon credit under Carbon Credit Trading Scheme 2023.

KEY CONCEPTS IN NEWS

Flex Fuel Vehicles (FFV)

The Automobile Manufacturers in India have been advised to start manufacturing Flex Fuel Vehicles (FFV) and Flex Fuel Strong Hybrid Electric Vehicles (FFV-SHEV) complying with BS-6 Norms to reduce India's import of petroleum and it also intends to provide direct benefits to farmers. The Production Linked Incentive (PLI) scheme has also included automobile and auto components of flex fuel engines to accelerate the introduction of Flex Fuel vehicles. **Flex-fuel** engines can run on **gasoline and doped petrol with different levels of ethanol blends**.

Climate Action and Finance Mobilisation Dialogue (CAFMD)

India and US have launched the Climate Action and Finance Mobilisation Dialogue (CAFMD). The dialogue will strengthen the India-US bilateral cooperation on climate and environment. It also intends to demonstrate, how the world can align climate action with resilient and inclusive economic development. The dialogue has been launched under the India-US Climate and Clean Energy Agenda, 2030 Partnership.

Carbon Watch

Chandigarh became the first State/UT in India to launch Carbon Watch mobile application to assess the carbon footprint of an individual.

Renewable Energy Certificate (REC)

It is a market-based mechanism that helps the states to meet their regulatory requirements or Renewable Purchase Obligations (RPOs) and promote the development of renewable energy. 1 REC is as equivalent to 1 MWh. RECs are traded on **two power exchanges in India – Indian Energy Exchange (IEX)** and **Power Exchange of India (PXIL)**. The price of RECs depends on **market demand** and remain between the **'floor price' (minimum)** and **'forbearance price' (maximum),** fixed by the **Central Electricity Regulatory Commission (CERC).** Recently, Government has approved the amendments in REC mechanism.

Common Carbon Metric (CCM)

The Common Carbon Metric (CCM) has been developed by UNEP's Sustainable Buildings and Climate Initiative. It intends to set up a uniform system to define the climate impact of buildings through a compatible protocol to help architects, designers, the construction industry etc.

The Climate Equity Monitor

It is an online dashboard and intends to assess the performance of Annex-I Parties under the UNFCCC. The performance of the Non Annex-I Parties (developing countries) will be also supplied for comparison. The website has been conceptualised by several researchers from India, including the Climate Change Group at the M.S. Swaminathan Research Foundation (MSSRF), Chennai.

Invasive Species Specialist Group (ISSG)

A global network of scientific and policy experts on invasive species, it has been organised under the Species Survival Commission (SSC) of the IUCN.

Ozone Cell

India became a part of the Vienna Convention and the Montreal Protocol in 1991 and 1992, respectively. The Ministry of Environment, Forest and Climate Change set up an Ozone Cell as a National Ozone Unit (NOU). It intends to provide necessary services for effective implementation of the Montreal Protocol and phasing out of Ozone Depleting Substances (ODSs) in India.

The Lifestyle for Environment (LiFE)

The India-led global mass movement was announced in 2021. It intends to promote individual and community action to conserve the environment. The Green Credit Programme (GCP) and Ecomark scheme are included under the LiFE Movement to produce market-based incentives for environment-positive actions.

The Global Methane Pledge (GMP)

It is a framework to support nations for taking action to cut down methane emissions by 30 per cent from 2020 levels by 2030. This could reduce about 0.2°C of warming by 2050. The GMP was launched at the COP26 in 2021 by Climate and Clean Air Coalition (CCAC) partners United States and European Commission.

Sustainable Aviation Fuel (SAF)

Sustainable Aviation Fuel (SAF) is an alternative fuel produced from non-petroleum feedstocks. SAF cuts down emissions from air transportation. SAF can be blended with traditional jet fuel at different levels with limits between 10 per cent and 50 per cent. The international aviation industry has set the target to reach net zero carbon by 2050.

Benefits

- If SAF is blended with conventional fuel, it can be used in existing infrastructure.
- SAF can reduce greenhouse gas emissions significantly.

Production

SAF can be made from non-petroleum-based renewable feedstocks like agricultural waste, municipal solid waste, woody biomass, industrial waste, etc.

WaterCredit

- WaterCredit is a **microfinance tool** to work in the water and sanitation sector. WaterCredit is a global initiative launched by Water.org, a non-profit organisation.
- Water.org launched WaterCredit in India in 2004.
- WaterCredit intends to provide small loans to poor people who require access to affordable financing for household water.

SUMMARY

- **Earth Summit** – Delegates from 178 nations met in Rio de Janeiro – in 1992 – United Nations Conference on Environment and Development (UNCED) – an action plan was framed called Agenda 21 – non-legally binding document 'Forest Principles' was also represented.
- **United Nations Conference on Sustainable Development (UNCSD or Rio+20)** – Held in Rio de Janeiro, Brazil – in June 2012 – focused on the Green economy in the context of sustainable development and poverty eradication and to develop an institutional framework for sustainable development.
- **Millennium Development Goals (MDGs)** – Eight goals – set by 189 UN member states – in 2000 – after the UN Millennium Declaration.
- **Sustainable Development Goals (SDGs)** – Replaced MDGs – adopted by all United Nations Member States in 2015 to end poverty, protect the planet and ensure that all people enjoy peace and prosperity by 2030.
- **SDG India Index** – Released by NITI Aayog – in collaboration with the Ministry of Statistics and Programme Implementation (MoSPI), United Nations in India and Global Green Growth Institute.
- **Climate Finance –** Local, national or transnational financing to support mitigation and adaptation actions to address climate change.
- **Decarbonising Transport in Emerging Economics** – Launched by NITI Aayog along with the International Transport Forum of OECD.

- **Global Climate Risk Index** – Published by German Watch, an Environment think tank – to point out the climate-related adverse impacts on countries.
- **Kigali Amendment – 2019** – An international, legally binding agreement – to cut the production and use of hydrofluorocarbons (HFCs).
- **National Hydrogen Energy Mission** – Announced in Union Budget 2021–22 – focuses on generation of hydrogen from green power resources – crucial to decarbonise heavy industries and clean electric mobility.
- **Emissions Gap Report** – Published by UNEP, provides a yearly review of the difference between where greenhouse emissions are predicted to be in 2030 and where they should be to avoid the worst impacts of climate change – Over the last decade, the top four emitters – China, USA, EU27+UK and India.
- **Climate Equity Monitor** – An online dashboard, intends to assess the performance of Annex-I Parties under the UNFCCC.
- **Green GDP** – Takes into consideration the environmental consequences of the economic growth.
- **Green Tax** – Ministry of Road Transport and Highways has approved to levy Green Tax on old vehicles – to dissuade people from using vehicles which damage the environment and to motivate to switch to newer, less polluting vehicles.
- **Sustainable Aviation Fuel (SAF)** – An alternative fuel produced from non-petroleum feedstocks.

UPSC CSE PREVIOUS YEARS' PRELIMINARY EXAMINATION QUESTIONS

1. Consider the following materials: **[2024]**

1. Agricultural residues
2. Corn grain
3. Wastewater treatment sludge
4. Wood mill waste

Which of the above can be used as feedstock for producing Sustainable Aviation Fuel?

(a) 1 and 2 only (b) 3 and 4 only
(c) 1, 2, 3 and 4 (d) 1, 3 and 4 only

2. 'Invasive Species Specialist Group' (that develops Global Invasive Species Database) belongs to which one of the following organisations? **[2023]**

(a) The International Union for Conservation of Nature
(b) The United Nations Environment Programme
(c) The United Nations World Commission for Environment and Development
(d) The World Wide Fund for Nature

3. Which one of the following best describes the term "greenwashing"? **[2022]**

(a) Conveying a false impression that a company's products are eco-friendly and environmentally sound
(b) Non-inclusion of ecological/environmental costs in the Annual Financial Statements of a country
(c) Ignoring the disastrous ecological consequences while undertaking infrastructure development
(d) Making mandatory provisions for environmental costs in a government project/programme

4. With reference to WaterCredit, consider the following statements: **[2021]**

1. It puts microfinance tools to work in the water and sanitation sector.
2. It is a global initiative launched under the aegis of the World Health Organization and the World Bank.
3. It aims to enable the poor people to meet their water needs without depending on subsidies.

Which of the statements given above are correct?

(a) 1 and 2 only (b) 2 and 3 only
(c) 1 and 3 only (d) 1, 2 and 3

5. The 'Common Carbon Metric', supported by UNEP, has been developed for **[2021]**
   (a) assessing the carbon footprint of building operations around the world.
   (b) enabling commercial farming entities around the world to enter carbon emission trading.
   (c) enabling Governments to assess the overall carbon footprint caused by their countries.
   (d) assessing the overall carbon foot-print caused by the use of fossil fuels by the world in a unit time.
6. Consider the following statements: **[2016]**
   1. The Sustainable Development Goals were first proposed in 1972 by a global think tank called the 'Club of Rome'.
   2. The Sustainable Development Goals have to be achieved by 2030.

   Which of the statements given above is/are correct?
   (a) 1 only (b) 2 only
   (c) Both 1 and 2 (d) Neither 1 nor 2
7. The term 'Intended Nationally Determined Contributions' is sometimes seen in the news in the context of **[2016]**
   (a) pledges made by the European countries to rehabilitate refugees from the war-affected Middle East.
   (b) plan of action outlined by the countries of the world to combat climate change.
   (c) capital contributed by the member countries in the establishment of Asian Infrastructure Investment Bank.
   (d) plan of action outlined by the countries of the world regarding Sustainable Development Goals.
8. What is Rio+20 Conference often mentioned in the news? **[2015]**
   (a) It is the United Nations Conference on Sustainable Development.
   (b) It is a Ministerial Meeting of the World Trade Organization.
   (c) It is a Conference of the Inter-Governmental Panel on Climate Change.
   (d) It is a Conference of the Member Countries of the Convention on Biological Diversity.

☞ NO QUESTIONS ASKED
2020, 2019, 2018, 2017, 2014, 2013

ANSWER KEY

1. (c)	2. (a)	3. (a)	4. (c)	5. (a)
6. (b)	7. (b)	8. (a)		

UPSC CSE PREVIOUS YEARS' MAIN EXAMINATION QUESTIONS

1. The adoption of electric vehicles is rapidly growing worldwide. How do electric vehicles contribute to reducing carbon emissions and what are the key benefits they offer compared to traditional combustion engine vehicles? **[2023]**
2. The Intergovernmental Panel on Climate Change (IPCC) has predicted a global sea level rise of about one metre by AD 2100. What would be its impact in India and the other countries in the Indian Ocean region? **[2023]**
3. Do you think India will meet 50 per cent of its energy needs from renewable energy by 2030? Justify your answer. How will the shift of subsidies from fossil fuels to renewables help achieve the above objective? Explain. **[2022]**
4. Explain intra-generational and inter-generational issues of equity from the perspective of inclusive growth and sustainable development. **[2020]**
5. Define the concept of carrying capacity of an ecosystem as relevant to an environment. Explain how understanding this concept is vital while planning for sustainable development of a region. **[2019]**
6. 'Access to affordable, reliable, sustainable and modern energy is a *sine qua non* to achieve Sustainable Development Goals (SDGs)'. Comment on the progress made in India in this regard. **[2018]**
7. Should the pursuit of carbon credits and clean development mechanisms set up under UNFCCC be maintained even though there has been a massive slide in the value of a carbon credit? Discuss with respect to India's energy needs for economic growth. **[2014]**

☞ NO QUESTIONS ASKED
2024, 2021, 2017, 2016, 2015, 2013